D1567213

Prehispanic Settlement Patterns

in the Lower Santa Valley Peru

SMITHSONIAN SERIES IN ARCHAEOLOGICAL INQUIRY

Robert McC. Adams and Bruce D. Smith, *Series Editors*

The Smithsonian Series in Archaeological Inquiry presents original case studies that address important general research problems and demonstrate the values of particular theoretical and/or methodological approaches. Titles include well-focused, edited collections as well as works by individual authors. The series is open to all subject areas, geographical regions, and theoretical modes.

OTHER BOOKS IN THE SERIES:

The Archaeology of Western Iran
Settlement and Society from Prehistory to the Islamic Conquest
Edited by Frank Hole
0-87474-526-8 Hardcover

Status and Health in Prehistory
A Case Study of the Moundville Chiefdom
Mary Lucas Powell
0-87474-756-2 Hardcover

Stylistic Boundaries among Mobile Hunter-Foragers
C. Garth Sampson
0-87474-838-0 Hardcover

Prehispanic Settlement Patterns in the Lower Santa Valley Peru

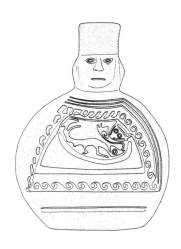

A Regional Perspective

on the Origins

and Development of

Complex North Coast Society

David J. Wilson

SMITHSONIAN INSTITUTION PRESS

WASHINGTON, D.C.   LONDON

Library of Congress Cataloging-in-Publication Data

Wilson, David J. (David John), 1941–
Prehispanic settlement patterns in the lower Santa Valley, Peru.
(Smithsonian series in archaeological inquiry)
Bibliography: p.
Includes index.
1. Indians of South America—Peru—Santa River Valley—An-
tiquities. 2. Santa River Valley (Peru)—Antiquities. 3. Land set-
tlement patterns, Prehistoric—Peru—Santa River Valley. 4.
Peru—Antiquities.
I. Title. II. Series
F3429.1.S37W55 1988   985   87-62622
ISBN 0-87474-984-0

British Library Cataloguing-in-Publication Data is available.

Al pueblo del Valle de Santa—
pasado y presente

Contents

Preface ix

List of Illustrations xv

CHAPTER 1

Introduction 1

METHODOLOGICAL BACKGROUND 1

Virú Valley Project
Recent Settlement Pattern Studies
Recent Studies on the Peruvian Coast

THEORETICAL BACKGROUND 5

Origins of Societal Complexity on the Coast
General Considerations

OVERVIEW OF THE SANTA VALLEY PROJECT 6

Choice of Research Location
Previous Research in the Region
Brief Outline of Substantive Results
Outline of the Research Timetable

PLAN OF PRESENTATION 15

CHAPTER 2

The Socioenvironmental Setting 17

THE NATURAL ENVIRONMENT 18

Present-day Setting: Land and Sea
Geological Changes Over Time
Reconstruction of the Paleoenvironment
Geomorphology and Prehispanic Site Preservation
Delineation of Regional Survey Boundaries
Definition of Subregional Environmental Sectors

THE CULTURAL ENVIRONMENT 34

Modern Occupation of the Survey Region
Modern Occupation and Prehispanic Site Preservati
Traditional Subsistence Agriculture in the Region
Reconstruction of the Prehispanic Agricultural Syst
Spanish Documentary Sources on Santa Valley

CHAPTER 3

Research Methods and Chronology 55

PREFIELD RESEARCH 56

FIELD METHODS 57

Regional Survey
Laboratory Mapping and Analysis

POSTFIELD ANALYTICAL AND ORGANIZATIONAL PROCEDURES 64

Assessing Prehispanic Chronology
Prehispanic Sites and Structures
Locational Analysis

CHAPTER 4

The Sequence of Prehispanic Site Types and Settlement Patterns 89

LAS SALINAS PERIOD (CERRO PRIETO/ PRECERAMIC) 90

Inland and Coastal Windbreak Sites
Coastal Midden Sites
Settlement and Demographic Patterns
Inferences About Subsistence
Interregional Comparisons

CAYHUAMARCA PERIOD (GUAÑAPE/EARLY HORIZON) 100

Habitation Sites
Defensive Sites
Ceremonial-Civic Sites
Cemetery Site
Settlement and Demographic Patterns
Ceramic Distributions
Inferences About Subsistence
Interregional Comparisons

VINZOS PERIOD (PUERTO MOORIN/BEGINNING EARLY INTERMEDIATE PERIOD, OR EIP) 140

Habitation Sites
Defensive Sites
Ceremonial-Civic Sites
Cemetery Site
Settlement and Demographic Patterns

Ceramic Distributions
Inferences About Subsistence
Interregional Comparisons

EARLY SUCHIMANCILLO PERIOD (EARLY-MIDDLE GALLINAZO/EARLY EIP) 151

Habitation Sites
Defensive Sites
Ceremonial-Civic Sites
Cemetery Sites
Other Remains: Desert Ground Drawings
Other Remains: Corral Features
Settlement and Demographic Patterns
Ceramic Distributions
Inferences About Subsistence
Interregional Comparisons

LATE SUCHIMANCILLO PERIOD (LATE GALLINAZO/MIDDLE EIP) 177

Habitation Sites
Defensive Sites
Ceremonial-Civic Sites
Cemetery Sites
Other Remains: Corral Features
Other Remains: Subterranean Gallery
Settlement and Demographic Patterns
Ceramic Distributions
Inferences About Subsistence
Interregional Comparisons

GUADALUPITO PERIOD (HUANCACO/LATE EIP) 198

Habitation Sites
Other Ceremonial-Civic Sites/Structures
Cemetery Sites
Other Remains: Guadalupito Roads and Canals
Settlement and Demographic Patterns
Ceramic Distributions
Inferences About Subsistence
Interregional Comparisons

EARLY TANGUCHE PERIOD (TOMAVAL/EARLY MIDDLE HORIZON) 224

Habitation Sites: Main Valley and Coast
Ceremonial-Civic Sites: Main Valley
Road-Settlement Network of Santa-Chao Desert

Great Wall System
Cemetery Sites
Other Remains: Canal-Field System, Corrals,
 Petroglyphs
Settlement and Demographic Patterns
Ceramic Distributions
Inferences About Subsistence
Interregional Comparisons

LATE TANGUCHE PERIOD (TOMAVAL/LATE
 MIDDLE HORIZON)   261

Habitation Sites
Defensive Sites
Cemetery Sites
Other Remains: Use of Santa-Chao Network
Settlement and Demographic Patterns
Ceramic Distributions
Inferences About Subsistence
Interregional Comparisons

EARLY TAMBO REAL PERIOD (LA PLATA/LATE
 INTERMEDIATE)   272

Habitation Sites
Defensive Sites
Cemetery Sites
Settlement and Demographic Patterns
Ceramic Distributions
Inferences About Subsistence
Interregional Comparisons

LATE TAMBO REAL PERIOD (ESTERO/LATE
 HORIZON)   281

Habitation Sites
Cemetery Sites
Other Remains: The Road Network
Settlement and Demographic Patterns
Ceramic Distributions
Inferences About Subsistence
Interregional Comparisons

CHAPTER 5

The Origins and Development of
Complex North Coast Society:
A Regional Perspective   295

THE RISE OF CHIEFDOM SOCIETIES IN THE
 EARLY PERIODS (PRE-1800 B.C. TO A.D.
 400)   296

The Evolution of Site Types
Distributional Patterns of Population and Settlement
Warfare and Subsistence
Population, Subsistence, and Warfare
Analysis of Cluster-Level Ceramic Assemblages
A Multivariate Developmental Model

THE RISE OF THE FIRST MULTIVALLEY STATES
 (CA. A.D. 400–900)   332

Overall Nature and Extent
Santa as a Province of the Moche State
Santa as a Province of the Black-White-Red State

THE BEGINNING OF REGIONAL DEMOGRAPHIC
 DECLINE (CA. A.D. 900–1350)   345

Overall Nature
The Evidence from Santa Valley

THE FINAL PERIOD: CHIMÚ-INCA HEGEMONY
 (CA. A.D. 1350–1532)   349

Overall Nature and Extent
Santa as a Province of the Chimú State

CHAPTER 6

Conclusions   353

Bibliography   359

Appendices   365

I ARTIFACT DESCRIPTIONS   365
II TABULAR PRESENTATION OF CITADEL,
 SETTLEMENT, AND CERAMIC
 DATA   535

Preface

This report is based on a systematic and comprehensive regional settlement pattern survey carried out in the Lower Santa Valley, North Coast of Peru over a 14-month period from May, 1979 to July, 1980. Primary funding for the Santa Valley Project was provided by a National Science Foundation predoctoral grant (BNS 7816226), which included support for air travel to and from Peru, per diem expenses for Peruvian field assistants, purchase of airphotos, laboratory rental, and vehicle rental and maintenance. Additional funds covering per diems for American field assistants and other project expenses were provided in a grant from the Wenner-Gren Foundation for Anthropological Research. Per diem expenses for my family and me were covered by a grant from the HEW Fulbright-Hays Overseas Doctoral Research Program, and a grant from the Center for Field Research provided funding for three small teams of Earthwatch volunteers who worked with us over a period of several months at the beginning of the fieldwork in Santa. The combined financial support from the four grants was $24,176—a modest sum perhaps by present-day standards in overseas scientific research, but nonetheless one that allowed us to achieve all of the project objectives as outlined in the grant proposals as well as to extend survey coverage over an area roughly two times larger than had originally been planned.

The overall work of carrying out the Santa Valley research—including planning the project, obtaining funds, prefield research, fieldwork, data analysis, mapping, preparation of illustrations, and writing up the principal results—has occupied a period of over eight years, beginning in early 1977 and extending on nearly continuously to the completion of the final draft of this report in early 1986. A number of colleagues have given vital help and encouragement during this period, especially in the initial stages of project planning and prefield ceramic studies. To mention them by name for their contributions is as much an acknowledgment of the multipersonal support that any project, however small, must have to achieve success as it is a recording of the preliminary investigative steps upon which such a project is based.

Among the individuals (and institutions) in the U.S. to whom a debt of gratitude is owed, I especially thank: Donald Collier, Michael Moseley, and Robert Feldman (Field Museum of Natural History), for prefield orientation and for graciously permitting detailed study and photography on various occasions of ceramic type collections from Virú, Casma, and Santa Valleys; Donald Thompson and Denise Carlevato (University of Wisconsin), for information on Casma Valley ceramic diagnostics; Jeffrey Parsons and Richard Ford (University of Michigan Museum of Anthropology), for permitting study of a small Virú Valley type collection; Thomas and Shelia Pozorski (Carnegie Museum of Natural History), for orientation and the loan of a jeep during my prefield trip to the North Coast in 1977; Craig Morris, Delfin Zúñiga, and the late Junius Bird (American Museum of Natural History), for permitting study of Santa and Virú Valley ceramic collections, aerial photographs taken by the 1932 Shippee-Johnson Peruvian Expedition, as well as the late James Ford's field notes, sketches, and ceramic seriation chart from his one-week 1946 survey of sites in Santa Valley; Richard Keatinge and Phyllis Martin (Columbia University), for telling me about HEW Fulbright-Hays funding and encouraging me to apply for it; the late Clifford Evans, Jr. (Smithsonian Institution), for detailed communications on aspects of the 1946 Virú Valley project and on Virú ceramics housed at the Smithsonian; Donald Proulx and Richard Daggett (University of Massachusetts), for showing me an extensive series of slides of Nepeña Valley ceramic types and for continually sending detailed communications related to their most recent research there; Geoffrey Conrad (Harvard Peabody Museum), for permitting photography of a number of Moche and Chimú ceramic vessels; Michael Coe and Joan Cohen (Yale Peabody Museum), for permitting study and photography of selected Virú Valley ceramic types from collections made by Wendell Bennett in the 1940s; Douglas Sharon (San Diego Museum of Man), for detailed information on Santa Valley fortresses and the Great Wall, based on his and Gene Savoy's 1962 aerial and ground surveys; Christopher Donnan (UCLA Museum of Cultural History), for information that supplemented his 1973 report on Moche culture and funerary practices in Santa Valley; the late Gary Vescelius (U.S. Virgin Islands Office of Archaeological Services), for communications on survey work carried out in the Suchimán area of Santa Valley in 1964 by him, Gene Savoy, Douglas Sharon, Hernan Amat, and Hermilio Rosas; and Daniel Sandweiss (Cornell University), for identification of some of the shellfish species we collected along Bahías de Chimbote and Samanco.

The research in Peru was conducted under the auspices of the Universidad Nacional Mayor de San Marcos, with a permit issued by the Instituto Nacional de Cultura. I am indebted to the officials of both institutions for their interest in and support of the Santa Valley Project. To my colleague and friend Ramiro Matos Mendieta, Director of the Laboratorio Arqueológico of San Marcos University, I owe an especially profound debt of gratitude. Dr. Matos provided us with expert guidance and assistance at all stages of the research, and facilitated our dealings with the proper authorities at the national and departmental levels. Other Peruvian colleagues whose help and advice benefitted the project include Mercedes Cárdenas, Federico Kauffmann Doig, Francisco Iriarte, Lorenzo Samaniego, and Jorge Silva. I must also express appreciation to the staffs of the Instituto Georgráfico Militar (IGM), the Oficina Nacional de Evaluación de Recursos Naturales (ONERN), and the Servicio Aerofotográfico Nacional (SAN). Archaeologists who have had occasion to use the services of these agencies will attest to the courtesy and professionalism of the staffs, as well as to the excellent quality of their maps and airphotos—both indispensable tools in conducting systematic research at the regional level.

In Santa, we were received with warm hospitality into the home of Don Victor Llacas and his wife, Doña Isabel, and were made to feel a part of their family and the community. Local authorities were at all times cooperative in facilitating our research, as were the people of Santa Valley. During our 14-month stay, several archaeological projects were running concurrently in adjacent regions, and I wish especially to thank Steven Wegner (University of California at Berkeley), for allowing us to view ceramic types from his excavations at Balcón de Judás site in Huaráz, Callejón de Huaylas; and Donald Proulx, who accompanied us to a number of the more outstanding Nepeña Valley sites and provided valuable information on major ceramic diagnostics collected during his 1979 fieldwork there.

The Santa Valley Project was first and foremost a team effort, with a number of individuals from Peru, Argentina, and the U.S. working with us for varying periods of time ranging from several weeks to over six months. To the extent that project goals were achieved and additional light has been thrown on critical processes of prehispanic cultural development in the North Coast area, then the members of the teams who assisted me must share equally in that success; they include Benigno Araico, Stephen Benjamin, Manuel Chávez, Kate Cleland, Connie Cochran, Kenneth Fain, Hernán González, María Mercedes Herrera, Douglas Lambert, Christopher Libby, Victor Llacas Díaz, Ethan Mascoop, Julia Middleton, Fidelia Notman, Mark Notman, Manuel Roncal Díaz, Victor Manuel Roncal, Brian Rosencrantz, Allan Schollenberger, Diana Wilson, Glen Wilson, Joan Zoffnass, and Paul Zoffnass.

For their teaching, encouragement, and help with all stages of the Santa Valley reserach, I am deeply indebted to the members of my doctoral committee at the University of Michigan Museum of Anthropology. Kent V. Flannery, Chair of the committee, is responsible for initially encouraging me to study Peruvian North Coast archaeology. His publications on the rise of sociocultural complexity, and those on the application of systematic methods in archaeological research and analysis, have strongly influenced my approach to the study of prehispanic regional settlement patterns. Most importantly, the unique combination of intellectual rigor, lucid writing, humor, and dedication to the development of the scientific approach in archaeology that Kent Flannery imparts to students and associates alike is at once an encouragement and a challenge to put forth one's own best efforts in every phase of carrying out a research project. Jeffrey R. Parsons provided me the opportunity to participate in several seasons of settlement pattern surveys in the Valley of Mexico, and to work as his research assistant as the data from this research were prepared for publication. Much of the methodological approach employed in the Santa Valley research as well as the methods of data presentation are the direct outgrowth of this invaluable experience. Jeff Parsons has taken a keen interest in all phases of the Santa Valley work, and I have profited from numerous discussions with him as the research proceeded toward completion of this report. I am also indebted to him for making available his vehicle to us during the fieldwork; without it we would have achieved substantially less areal coverage. Henry T. Wright has contributed significantly both to the development of the project as well as to the methodological and theoretical approaches taken in conducting the research. He has constantly encouraged my interest in the North Coast, and, in publications on his Near Eastern work and state origins, has profoundly influenced my thinking about the role of hypothesis testing in attempting to relate research methods and data to theories of sociocultural evolution. John Eadie, of the Department of History, served as the fourth member of the committee. A leading scholar on Roman remains in Jordan and elsewhere in the Mediterranean area, Dr. Eadie has provided an especially useful comparative perspective on possible interpretations of Santa Valley remains dating to the periods of maximum sociocultural complexity.

Along with Professors Flannery, Parsons, and Wright, Richard I. Ford of the Museum of Anthropology provided invaluable suggestions that strengthened my initial grant proposal to NSF. I also thank Roberto Frisancho of the Department of Anthropology for his encouragement and for providing a recommendation during the process of obtaining research funds.

To my wife, Diana Finch Wilson, and sons, Jonathan and Christopher, I extend my love and thanks for their constant support during the long period required to carry out the research. My wife has contributed in numerous ways to the success of the project at every stage of its development, not the least of which were in providing critical evaluation of the accompanying text and in becoming the financial mainstay of the family during the early stages of preparation of the report.

The preparation of the initial set of drafts of this report was aided substantially by the constructive comments of Professors Flannery, Parsons, and Wright. I also owe a great debt of gratitude to an anonymous reviewer and to Daniel Goodwin of Smithsonian Institution Press, both of whom provided many helpful criticisms and suggestions for streamlining this presentation of the Santa Valley Project results. Michelle Smith, of Smithsonian Press, deserves much of the credit for the final form this book has taken—including placement of all non-artifact illustrations in the body of the text itself. Considering that the dissertation is 1581 pages long (with a relatively scant 433 pages of text, one hastens to add, in addition to some 1000 pages of site descriptions, ceramic descriptions, and illustrations), it clearly was necessary to bring the final manuscript down to an "economical" size. Many hard decisions have thus had to be made, in consultation with the editorial staff at Smithsonian Press, to achieve this goal—including the removal of nearly 100 illustrations (mostly of minor sites and other less centrally important data) as well as the 480 single-spaced pages of detailed site descriptions that accompany the dissertation. The reader interested in having access to these data will therefore probably wish to obtain a copy of the dissertation (Wilson 1985) from University Microfilms International. In this regard, it must be noted that anyone who compares the reproductions of the project illustrations in this book with those done by UMI will find that the techniques of reproduction used by UMI for dealing with line drawings frequently produce inferior photocopies—a substantial disappointment to me after having spent nearly a year preparing the illustrations that accompany the dissertation. For that reason alone, I am very grateful for the superb quality that Smithsonian Institution Press has achieved in the drawings reproduced here.

All of the illustrations accompanying the dissertation (a total of 376) and this report (280) were drawn by the author, and, with the exception of Figs. 185, 186, and 187, all are a direct result of the work carried out during the 1979–80 Santa Valley Project. In both the dissertation and this (now much changed) report, I have attempted to facilitate comprehension and interpretation of the numerous prehispanic structural remains mapped during the project through consistent use of a combination of plan, elevation, profile, and perspective views. The inspiration for doing this must be credited to the influence of at least three major works among the more outstanding studies that have recorded the often remarkably well preserved archaeological remains of the Central Andes. In chronological order, they include *Peru: Incidents of Travel and Exploration in the Land of the Incas,* by E. George Squier (1877); *Prehistoric Settlement Patterns in the Virú Valley, Peru,* by Gordon R. Willey (1953); and *Inca Architecture,* by Graziano Gasparini and Jeff Parsons for suggestions on presenting the settlement data in map form.

With regard to the ceramic illustrations, I have attempted as much as possible to employ graphic techniques similar to those used in Bennett (1950), Collier (1955), and Strong and Evans (1952). The reasons for doing this are several: First, in contrast to many later publications on Peruvian archaeology, the Virú Valley researchers appear to have been strongly oriented (as I have attempted to be) toward as complete a visual and written description of ceramic diagnostics as possible. Second, Virú and Santa share similar ceramic types at various times in the sequence, and similar graphic techniques should facilitate comparison of the ceramic assemblages from both valleys. Third, for scientific as well as aesthetic reasons, I have thought it important to emphasize the ceramics as much as the settlement patterns and large-scale plan views of specific structural remains—in keeping with the overall objective of presenting an integrated and systematic picture of prehispanic societal development in the Lower Santa Valley region.

David J. Wilson
Dallas, 1987

Illustrations

CHART

1. Prehispanic periods of the Lower Santa Valley region and
   related sequences 9

FIGURES

1. Map of the north Peruvian coast and highlands 2
2. Lower Santa Valley survey area and adjacent coastal
   valleys 3
3. Major environmental features of the Lower Santa Valley
   region 22
4. Survey sectors of the 1979–80 Santa Valley Project 33
5. Topographic cross-sections in the Upper, Middle, and
   Lower Valley sectors 35
6. Modern settlements, roads, and river crossings 36
7. Key to ancient canal maps in Figs. 8–13 43
8. Principal ancient canals of the Upper Valley 44
9. Principal ancient canals of the Middle and Lower Valley
   45
10. Detail map of ancient canals and associated archaeological
    sites in the area north of Vinzos 46
11. Principal ancient canals of the Lower Valley 47
12. Detail map of ancient canals, serpentine field systems, and
    sites in the southern area of Pampa Las Salinas 48
13. Detail map of ancient canals, serpentine field systems, and
    sites in the northern area of Pampa Las Salinas 49
14. Map showing Servicio Aerofotográfico Nacional (SAN)
    airphoto and Instituto Geográfico Militar (IGM)
    topographic map coverage of the survey region 50
15. Map showing location of the 1020 discrete archaeological
    sites in the Lower Santa Valley survey region 83
16. Key to settlement pattern maps 92
17. Location key to settlement pattern maps of Las Salinas
    Period, Figs. 18–21 93
18. Settlement pattern map of Las Salinas Period: Upper Valley
    sector 94
19. Settlement pattern map of Las Salinas Period: Upper and
    Middle Valley sectors 95

20. Settlement pattern map of Las Salinas Period: Coast
    sector—south 96
21. Settlement pattern map of Las Salinas Period: Coast
    sector—north 97
22. Location key to settlement pattern maps of Cayhuamarca
    Period, Figs. 23–24 101
23. Settlement pattern map of Cayhuamarca Period: Upper
    Valley sector 102
24. Settlement pattern map of Cayhuamarca Period: Middle
    Valley, Lower Valley, and Coast sectors 103
25. Plan and profile views of Structures 120 and 121 105
26. Plan and profile views of Structures 115, 116, and 117, a
    possible elite residential unit at SVP-CAY-4 106
27. Plan view of the southern part of an early habitation
    site 107
28. Plan and profile views of Structure 119 citadel 111
29. Plan and profile views of Structure 107, a citadel site with
    combined habitation, ceremonial-civic, and defensive
    functions 112
30. Plan and profile views of Structure 1 citadel 113
31. Wall details of selected Cayhuamarca Period citadel
    structures 114
32. Plan and profile views of Structure 6 citadel 115
33. Plan view of Structure 27 citadel 116
34. Plan view and perspective detail of Structure 28 citadel
    117
35. Plan, profile, and detail views of Structure 33 citadel . . 118
36. Plan, profile, and detail views of Structure 41 citadel . . 119
37. Plan and profile views of Structure 34 citadel 120
38. Perspective view of Structure 34 citadel 121
39. Plan view of Structure 35 citadel 122
40. Plan and profile views of Structure 45 citadel 123
41. Perspective view of Structure 45 citadel and nearby
    Cayhuamarca Period sites 124
42. Plan view of Structure 49 citadel 125
43. Plan view of Structure 52 citadel 126
44. Perspective view of Structure 52 citadel 126
45. Plan and detail views of Structure 55 citadel 127
46. Plan and detail views of Structure 71 citadel 127
47. Plan and profile views of Structure 72 citadel 128

48. Plan and profile views of Structure 90 citadel 128
49. Plan and profile views of Structure 95 citadel 129
50. Plan and profile views of SVP-CAY-5 ceremonial-civic
    site 131
51. Perspective view of the main structures at SVP-CAY-5 and
    nearby sites 132
52. Plan and profile views of Structure 108 ceremonial-civic
    site 132
53. Plan and profile views of Structure 37 huaca 133
54. Plan view of SVP-CAY-29 ceremonial-civic site 134
55. Plan and profile views of Structure 70 platform 135
56. Plan, profile, and detail views of Structure 97 huaca ... 136
57. Location key to settlement pattern maps of Vinzos Period,
    Figs. 58–60 141
58. Settlement pattern map of Vinzos Period: Upper Valley
    sector 142
59. Settlement pattern map of Vinzos Period: Upper Valley,
    Middle Valley, and Santa-Chao Desert sectors 143
60. Settlement pattern map of Vinzos Period: Middle and
    Lower Valley sectors 144
61. Plan view of the northwestern sector of SVP-VIN-9/SVP-
    ESUCH-11 146
62. Plan and profile views of Huaca Yolanda Complex 147
63. Location key to settlement pattern maps of Early
    Suchimancillo Period, Figs. 64, 65, and 66 152
64. Settlement pattern map of Early Suchimancillo Period:
    Upper Valley sector 153
65. Settlement pattern map of Early Suchimancillo Period:
    Middle Valley sector 154
66. Settlement pattern map of Early Suchimancillo Period:
    Lower Valley sector 155
67. Plan view of the upper eastern sector of SVP-ESUCH-1
    habitation site 156
68. Plan and detail views of the west-central sector of SVP-
    ESUCH-1/SVP-LSUCH-9 habitation site 157
69. Plan view of adjacent habitation sites dating to
    Suchimancillo (northern sector) and Early Tanguche
    (southern sector) 158
70. Plan view of Structure 5, a possible elite residential unit at
    SVP-ESUCH-19/SVP-LSUCH-45 159
71. Plan view of Huaca Santa Complex, a large site with
    combined habitation, ceremonial-civic, and defensive
    functions dating to Early Suchimancillo and later periods
    161
72. Plan and detail views of Structure 7 citadel 163
73. Plan and profile views of Structure 39 citadel 164
74. Plan and detail views of Structure 56 citadel 165
75. Plan and profile views of minor defensive works at SVP-
    ESUCH-17 site 166
76. Plan and profile views of minor defensive works at SVP-
    ESUCH-82 site 167
77. Three views of Structure 51 huaca 168
78. Three views of Structure 11 huaca, with a detail view of
    intrusive adobes dating probably to Guadalupito Period
    169
79. Plan view of the Feature J group of desert ground drawings
    at SVP-ESUCH-112 172
80. Plan view of the Feature K group of desert ground drawings
    at SVP-ESUCH-112 173
81. Plan view of the Feature L group of desert ground drawings
    at SVP-ESUCH-112 173
82. Plan view of Structure 110, a probable llama corral with
    associated Suchimancillo Period habitation structures
    174
83. Location key to settlement pattern maps of Late
    Suchimancillo Period, Figs. 84–87 178

84. Settlement pattern map of Late Suchimancillo Period:
    Upper Valley sector 179
85. Settlement pattern map of Late Suchimancillo Period:
    Upper and Middle Valley sectors 180
86. Settlement pattern map of Late Suchimancillo Period:
    Middle Valley sector 181
87. Settlement pattern map of Late Suchimancillo Period:
    Lower Valley sector 182
88. Plan and detail views of Structure 91 and associated
    buildings at SVP-LSUCH-121 site 184
89. Three views of Structure 102, a probable ceremonial-civic
    building at SVP-LSUCH-153. Note general similarity to
    Structure 91/SVP-LSUCH-121 185
90. Plan and profile views of Structure 38 citadel 186
91. Three views of Structure 57/SVP-LSUCH-116 188
92. Plan and profile views of Structure 40 huaca 190
93. Plan and profile views of huaca structures at
    SVP-LSUCH-84 191
94. Three views of Structure 96 huaca 192
95. Plan view of Structure 114, a probable llama corral at SVP-
    LSUCH-15 habitation site 194
96. Plan, section, and elevation views of Feature Y
    subterranean gallery at SVP-LSUCH-20 195
97. Location key to settlement pattern maps of Guadalupito
    Period, Figs. 98, 99, and 102 199
98. Settlement pattern map of Guadalupito Period: Upper and
    Middle Valley sectors 200
99. Settlement pattern map of Guadalupito Period: Middle and
    Lower Valley sectors 201
100. Detail map of Guadalupito Period habitation and cemetery
    sites in the vicinity of SVP-GUAD-93/El Castillo site
    202
101. Detail map of Guadalupito Period habitation and cemetery
    sites in and around SVP-GUAD-111, the probable
    regional center of the Moche state in the Lower Santa
    Valley 203
102. Settlement pattern map of Guadalupito Period: Lower
    Valley and Coast sectors 204
103. Detail map of Guadalupito Period sites on the desert
    margin to the northeast of the modern settlement of
    Santa 205
104. Plan and perspective views of Structure 86 at SVP-
    GUAD-91 208
105. Plan view of the large adobe-walled enclosure and
    associated remains at SVP-GUAD-135 209
106. Plan and profile views of Structures 87 and 88 at SVP-
    GUAD-93/El Castillo site 210
107. Elevation detail of polychrome club-and-shield mural
    located on the lower northern face of Structure 88 at
    SVP-GUAD-93/El Castillo site 211
108. Plan view of Pampa de los Incas Complex 213
109. Plan and profile views of Structures 19 and 20 at SVP-
    GUAD-111/Pampa de los Incas Complex. See Fig. 108
    for relative locations of the two huacas 214
110. Plan and profile views of Structure 22 habitation terraces,
    located in the northeastern sector of Pampa de los Incas
    215
111. Plan and profile views of Structure 43, a ceremonial-civic
    site with intrusive later burials 216
112. Plan and profile views of Structure 81, a large huaca
    platform with Guadalupito occupation and intrusive
    burials dating to Early Tanguche 217
113. Plan and profile views of the principal structural remains at
    SVP-GUAD-132/Huaca China site 218
114. Location key to settlement pattern maps of Early Tanguche
    Period, Figs. 115, 116, 118, 119, 120, 121, and 122 .. 225

115. Settlement pattern map of Early Tanguche Period: Upper Valley and Santa-Chao Desert sectors 226
116. Settlement pattern map of Early Tanguche Period: Upper Valley, Middle Valley, and Santa-Chao Desert sectors 227
117. Detail map of ancient roads and associated Early Tanguche habitation sites in the central Quebrada Palo Redondo area 228
118. Settlement pattern map of Early Tanguche Period: Middle Valley, Lower Valley, and Santa-Chao Desert sectors 229
119. Settlement pattern map of Early Tanguche Period: Lower Valley and Coast sectors 230
120. Settlement pattern map of Early Tanguche Period: Coast sector—south 231
121. Settlement pattern map of Early Tanguche Period: Santa-Chao Desert sector—northwest 232
122. Settlement pattern map of Early Tanguche Period: Santa-Chao Desert sector—northeast 233
123. Plan and detail views of Structure 129, an agglutinated habitation unit with occupation dating to Early Tanguche Period 235
124. Plan view of two large terraced habitation sites, with occupation dating to Early Tanguche and later periods 236
125. Plan view of an Early Tanguche Period roadside village, showing ancient rock-lined roads, canals, field lines, dwellings, and a possible corral 237
126. Plan and profile views of Structures 111 and 112 at SVP-ETAN-1 local center 239
127. Plan view of Structure 36 and associated remains at SVP-ETAN-7 local center 240
128. Plan view of Structure 48 and associated remains at SVP-ETAN-22 local center 241
129. Plan view of the principal structural remains at SVP-ETAN-56 local center 242
130. Plan and profile views of Structures 99 and 100 at SVP-ETAN-100 local center 242
131. Plan view of Huaca Jedionda Complex, the probable regional center of Early Tanguche Period 243
132. Detail map of Early Tanguche roads and associated habitation sites on Pampa Santa Elvira. See Fig. 118 for location 245
133. Detail plan view of rock-lined roads and associated habitation structures at SVP-ETAN-242. See Fig. 132 for location 246
134. Detail map of ancient rock-lined roads and associated Early Tanguche Period sites on Pampa de los Pancitos . . . 247
135. Plan and perspective views of Feature AA at SVP-ETAN-320, a probable ceremonial-civic site. See Fig. 134 for location 249
136. Plan views of Features AB and AC at SVP-ETAN-320 250
137. Map of the Great Wall system of the Lower Santa Valley 252
138. Detail drawings of selected sections of the Great Wall, at Locations 1, 2, 4, 7, 9, and 10 (see Fig. 137) 253
139. Petroglyphs dating probably to Early Tanguche Period (A-C: SVP-ETAN-336; D-L: SVP-ETAN-15) 257
140. Petroglyphs dating probably to Early Tanguche and earlier periods (A-B: SVP-ESUCH-19/SVP-LSUCH-45; C: SVP-CAY-17/SVP-VIN-16; D: near SVP-ETAN-100; E: near SVP-ETAN-435; F: near SVP-ETAN-414) 258
141. Location key to settlement pattern maps of Late Tanguche Period, Figs. 142–144 262

142. Settlement pattern map of Late Tanguche Period: Upper and Middle Valley sectors 263
143. Settlement pattern map of Late Tanguche Period: Middle Valley and Santa-Chao Desert sectors 264
144. Settlement pattern map of Late Tanguche Period: Lower Valley and Coast sectors 265
145. Plan view of SVP-LTAN-23 habitation site, located on a small shelf high above the north side of the river in the Middle Valley 267
146. Plan and profile views of a large terraced habitation site, with occupation dating to Late Tanguche and Early Tambo Real Periods 268
147. Plan view of the large terraced habitation site of SVP-LTAN-40 269
148. Location key to settlement pattern maps of Early Tambo Real Period, Figs. 149–151 273
149. Settlement pattern map of Early Tambo Real Period: Upper and Middle Valley sectors 274
150. Settlement pattern map of Early Tambo Real Period: Middle and Lower Valley sectors 275
151. Settlement pattern map of Early Tambo Real Period: Lower Valley and Coast sectors 276
152. Plan and profile views of Structure 101, a probable single-family dwelling of Early Tambo Real Period 277
153. Location key to settlement pattern maps of Late Tambo Real Period, Figs. 154–156 282
154. Settlement pattern map of Late Tambo Real Period: Upper and Middle Valley sectors 283
155. Settlement pattern map of Late Tambo Real Period: Middle Valley, Lower Valley, and Coast sectors 284
156. Settlement pattern map of Late Tambo Real Period: Santa-Chao Desert sector 285
157. Plan and profile views of Structure 44 enclosure at SVP-LTR-3 habitation site 287
158. Plan and perspective details of Structure 89, a large tapia-walled enclosure at SVP-LTR-30 habitation site 288
159. Plan and detail views of Huaca El Gallinazo, a multicomponent prehispanic habitation and cemetery site with Colonial Period occupation in the northeast sector 289
160. Plan view of the principal structural remains at Alto Perú Complex, the probable regional center of Late Tambo Real Period. A modern pueblo joven has covered almost all of the prehispanic site, with the exception of Areas C and D 291
161. Population profile for the prehispanic periods of the Lower Santa Valley survey area, pre-1800 B.C. to A.D. 1532 296
162. Site population size histograms for the early periods of the Lower Santa Valley sequence: Las Salinas through Guadalupito 297
163. Site population size histograms for the late periods of the Lower Santa Valley sequence: Early Tanguche through Late Tambo Real 298
164. Settlement pattern of Las Salinas Period 299
165. Demographic pattern of Las Salinas Period 300
166. Settlement pattern of Cayhuamarca Period 301
167. Demographic pattern of Cayhuamarca Period 302
168. Settlement pattern of Vinzos Period 303
169. Demographic pattern of Vinzos Period 304
170. Settlement pattern of Early Suchimancillo Period 305
171. Demographic pattern of Early Suchimancillo Period . . . 306
172. Settlement pattern of Late Suchimancillo Period 307
173. Demographic pattern of Late Suchimancillo Period 308
174. Settlement pattern of Guadalupito Period 309
175. Demographic pattern of Guadalupito Period 310

176. Settlement pattern of Early Tanguche Period 311
177. Demographic pattern of Early Tanguche Period 312
178. Settlement pattern of Late Tanguche Period 313
179. Demographic pattern of Late Tanguche Period 314
180. Settlement pattern of Early Tambo Real Period 315
181. Demographic pattern of Early Tambo Real Period 316
182. Settlement pattern of Late Tambo Real Period 317
183. Demographic pattern of Late Tambo Real Period 318
184. A multivariate developmental model for the early pre-state
      periods of the Lower Santa Valley sequence 331
185. Scene from a Moche pottery vessel of Trujillo provenience,
      showing a battle between warriors of two distinct cultural
      backgrounds. The victorious warriors—shown on the left
      in the lower panel, and on the right in the upper panel—
      presumably are members of the Moche army. Redrawn
      from Kutscher (1954:21) 339
186. Scene from a pottery vessel of Chimbote provenience,
      showing warriors of the Moche army leading naked and
      bleeding prisoners across the intervalley desert. Redrawn
      from Kutscher (1954:24) 340
187. Scenes from two Moche pottery vessels. The top scene
      shows naked prisoners from a defeated army approaching
      a ruler seated atop a huaca structure. The bottom scene
      shows a llama caravan approaching a ruler with what
      may be tribute from a conquered coastal valley (top:
      redrawn from Donnan 1978:35; bottom: redrawn from
      Sawyer 1968:47) 341
188. Map showing collection proveniences of Las Salinas Period
      (Cerro Prieto/Preceramic) 367
189. Las Salinas Period artifacts, including flake scrapers and
      probable grinding stones (Note: collection provenience
      numbers are shown adjacent to the lower edge or side of
      each artifact in these and all other drawings in Figs. 189–
      280 368
190. Map showing collection proveniences of Cayhuamarca
      Period (Guañape/Early Horizon) 370
191. Cayhuamarca Period ceramics: Bowls 1a, 1b, 2, 3, 4,
      and 5 371
192. Cayhuamarca Period ceramics: Bowls 6a and 6b 374
193. Cayhuamarca Period ceramics: Jars 1, 2a, 2b, 3a,
      and 3b 376
194. Cayhuamarca Period ceramics and lithics: Jar 4,
      miscellaneous sherds (a–e), and stone artifacts (f–g)
      379
195. Map showing collection proveniences of Vinzos Period
      (Puerto Moorin/Beginning EIP) 381
196. Vinzos Period ceramics: Bowls 1, 2, 3, 4a, and 4b 382
197. Vinzos Period ceramics: Jars 1, 2a, 2b, and 2c 384
198. Vinzos Period ceramics: Jars 3a, 3b, and 3c 387
199. Vinzos Period ceramics: Jars 4a, 4b, 5a, 5b, and 5c . . . 389
200. Vinzos Period ceramics: Jar 6, and miscellaneous
      sherds 391
201. Map showing collection proveniences of Early Suchimancillo
      Period (Early-Middle Gallinazo/Early EIP) 394
202. Early Suchimancillo Period ceramics: Bowls 1a, 1b, 2a, 2b,
      and 3 395
203. Early Suchimancillo Period ceramics: Bowls 4, 5, 6a, 6b,
      and 7 398
204. Early Suchimancillo Period ceramics: Jars 1, 2, 3,
      and 4a 401
205. Early Suchimancillo Period ceramics: Jars 4b, 5, 6, 7,
      and 8a 403
206. Early Suchimancillo Period ceramics: Jars 8b, 8c, 8d,
      8e, 9, and 10 406
207. Early Suchimancillo Period ceramics: miscellaneous
      decorated sherds 409
208. Early Suchimancillo Period ceramics: miscellaneous
      sherds 411
209. Map showing collection proveniences of Late Suchimancillo
      Period (Late Gallinazo/Middle EIP) 414
210. Early-Late Suchimancillo jar 415
211. Late Suchimancillo Period ceramics: Bowls 1, 2, 3, 4,
      5, and 6 417
212. Late Suchimancillo Period ceramics: Bowl 7 419
213. Late Suchimancillo Period ceramics: Jars 1a, 1b, 1c, 2a, 2b,
      and 2c 421
214. Late Suchimancillo Period ceramics: Jars 3a, 3b, 3c,
      4a, and 4b 425
215. Late Suchimancillo Period ceramics: Jars 5a, 5b, 5c, 5d,
      5e, and 5f 427
216. Late Suchimancillo Period ceramics: Jars 6, 7, 8, 9,
      10, and 11 431
217. Late Suchimancillo Period ceramics: Jar 12, and related
      miscellaneous bowls and jars (a–e) 433
218. Late Suchimancillo Period ceramics: Broad Band White-on-
      Red jars 435
219. Late Suchimancillo Period ceramics and shells:
      miscellaneous sherds (a–j), and Spondylus (k–l) 437
220. Late Suchimancillo Period ceramics: human effigy jars and
      figurines 439
221. Late Suchimancillo Period ceramics: human
      effigy jars 440
222. Late Suchimancillo Period ceramics: human
      effigy jars 441
223. Late Suchimancillo Period ceramics: miscellaneous
      sherds 442
224. Map showing collection proveniences of Guadalupito Period
      (Huancaco/Late EIP) 444
225. Guadalupito Period ceramics: Bowls 1 and 2; Jars 1
      and 2a 445
226. Guadalupito Period ceramics: Jars 2b, 3a, and 3b 447
227. Guadalupito Period ceramics: flaring bowls 449
228. Guadalupito Period ceramics: sherds from Red-on-White
      flaring bowls 450
229. Guadalupito Period ceramics: miscellaneous decorated
      sherds 451
230. Guadalupito Period ceramics: human effigy neck jars
      (a–f, i, j), figurines (g–h), and molds (k–l) 453
231. Guadalupito Period ceramics: miscellaneous sherds 454
232. Guadalupito Period ceramics: side and end views of a
      Moche style jar depicting warriors 455
233. Guadalupito Period ceramics: miscellaneous whole
      vessels 457
234. Guadalupito Period ceramics: miscellaneous sherds, and
      diagnostics of Moche Phases III–V 458
235. Map showing collection proveniences of Early Tanguche
      Period (Tomaval/Early Middle Horizon) 460
236. Early Tanguche Period ceramics: Bowls 1 and 2; Jars
      1a, 1b, 2a, 2b, 2c, and 2d 461
237. Early Tanguche Period ceramics: Jars 3, 4a, 4b, and 5; and
      selected grayware bowls and jars 465
238. Early Tanguche Period ceramics: miscellaneous decorated
      and plainware jars 467
239. Early Tanguche Period ceramics: miscellaneous plainware
      and decorated jars, and a Black-and-White/Redware fish
      effigy jar 468
240. Early Tanguche Period ceramics: miscellaneous decorated
      jars, and a polychrome tripod bowl 469
241. Early Tanguche Period ceramics: painted and pressmolded
      annular-base bowls, including fragments of bases with
      maker's mark 471
242. Early Tanguche Period ceramics: schematic wedges showing

Black-and-White/Redware design motifs on the interior
of annular-base bowls 472

243. Early Tanguche Period ceramics: Red/White-slipped jars
(a–d), and Black-and-White/Redware jars (e–g) . . . 474

244. Early Tanguche Period ceramics: side and end views of two
Black-and-White/Redware jars 475

245. Early Tanguche Period ceramics: Black-and-
White/Redware jars 476

246. Early Tanguche Period ceramics: Black-and-
White/Redware jars 477

247. Early Tanguche Period ceramics: human effigy neck jar
fragments 479

248. Early Tanguche Period ceramics: human effigy neck
vessels 480

249. Early Tanguche Period ceramics: three views of a White-on-
Redware effigy jar with feline hair 481

250. Early Tanguche Period ceramics: human effigy neck jar and
a double spout-and-bridge vessel 482

251. Early Tanguche Period ceramics: fragments of musical
instruments (a–b), figurines depicting musicians (d–g),
and figurines of warriors (h–n). (Note: a fragment of
marine shell is depicted in c, above) 483

252. Early Tanguche Period ceramics: Black-and-
White/Redware female figurines 484

253. Early Tanguche Period ceramics: miscellaneous items,
including animal effigies, a spindle whorl, and a partly
hollow tube of unknown function 485

254. Early Tanguche Period ceramics: two views of an animal
effigy jar 486

255. Early Tanguche Period ceramics: miscellaneous
pressmolded and appliquéd motifs 487

256. Early Tanguche Period ceramics: examples of decorated
sherds of probable exotic origin. See ceramic descriptions
in Appendix I for suggested places of origin 488

257. Map showing collection proveniences of Late Tanguche
Period (Tomaval/Late Middle Horizon) 491

258. Late Tanguche Period ceramics: Bowls 1 and 2; Jars 1, 2a,
2b, and 3 492

259. Late Tanguche Period ceramics: Jars 4a, 4b, redware
drawings, and profiles of selected grayware sherds . . 495

260. Late Tanguche Period ceramics: selected whole jars with
incised and raised circle-and-dot design 497

261. Late Tanguche Period ceramics: schematic rectangles
showing raised-incised and raised circle-and-dot design
motifs 498

262. Late Tanguche Period ceramics: selected jars with incised
and pressmolded design motifs 500

263. Late Tanguche Period ceramics: selected jars with
pressmolded decoration 501

264. Map showing collection proveniences of Early Tambo Real
Period (La Plata/Late Intermediate) 503

265. Early Tambo Real Period ceramics: Grayware Bowls 1, 2,
and 3; Grayware Jars 1, 2, 3a, and 3b 504

266. Early Tambo Real Period ceramics: Grayware Jars
4a, 4b, 4c, 5, and detail drawings 507

267. Early Tambo Real Period ceramics: selected grayware
jars 509

268. Early Tambo Real Period ceramics: miscellaneous grayware
sherds 510

269. Early Tambo Real Period ceramics: pressmolded grayware
spout-and-handle jars with appliquéd, modeled, and
stippled decoration 511

270. Early Tambo Real Period ceramics: selected redware and
grayware jars 512

271. Early Tambo Real Period ceramics: Redware Bowls 1, 2,
and 3; Redware Jars 1, 2, 3, 4a, 4b, and 4c 514

272. Early Tambo Real Period ceramics: details of selected
redware sherds 517

273. Map showing collection proveniences of Late Tambo Real
Period (Estero/Late Horizon) 519

274. Late Tambo Real Period ceramics: Grayware Bowls 1, 2, 3,
and 4; Grayware Jar 1 520

275. Late Tambo Real Period ceramics: Grayware Jars 2a, 2b,
2c, and 2d 522

276. Late Tambo Real Period ceramics: Grayware Jars 3a, 3b,
3c, and 3d 525

277. Late Tambo Real Period ceramics: Grayware Jar 4, and
detailed drawings of Grayware Bowls 2 and 4 527

278. Late Tambo Real Period ceramics: miscellaneous
grayware 528

279. Late Tambo Real Period ceramics: Redware Bowls 1 and 2;
Redware Jars 1, 2, 3a, 3b, 4, and 5 530

280. Late Tambo Real Period ceramics: miscellaneous redware,
grayware, and blackware 533

PLATES

1. Gemini satellite view of Lower Santa Valley and adjacent
coastal and sierra regions, looking toward the northeast.
Coastal sector of Santa stands out clearly in left center of
photograph, and to the east can be seen the Santa-
Tablachaca confluence, the Cañón del Pato, and the
upper reaches of the river between the Cordillera Negra
and the snow-capped Cordillera Blanca. Chao and Virú
Valleys are visible to the north of Santa, as are Nepeña
and Casma to the south, with wide stretches of coastal
desert lying in between 7

2. Structure 33, a major citadel with occupation dating to
Cayhuamarca and later periods, looking toward the west.
See Fig. 35 for plan and detail drawings 11

3. Huaca mound of SVP-ESUCH-50/Structure 47 rises out of
cultivated fields near Quebrada del Panteón. See Fig. 64
for location (for plan view, see Fig. 116 in Wilson 1985)
. . . . 11

4. Aerial view of SVP-GUAD-111/Structure 19, a site with
probable administrative and elite residential functions
that formed the core of Pampa de los Incas Complex, the
major population center of Guadalupito/Moche Period.
For drawings, see Figs. 101, 108, and 109 12

5. Ridgetop wall of Pampa Blanca area, the uppermost part of
the Great Wall system on the north desert margin of the
Lower Santa Valley. For location of this section, see Fig.
116 (wall lies immediately to southeast of SVP-ETAN-28;
see also Loc. 9, in Figs. 137 and 138) 12

6. Section of ancient rock-lined road near SVP-ETAN-417, in
the Santa-Chao Desert (see Fig. 116) 13

7. Serpentine field system and adjacent Las Salinas canal,
located in the desert north of the Santa Valley mouth
(see Fig. 12) 14

8. View upriver in the narrow desert canyon just below the
Santa-Tablachaca confluence. Although uninhabited
today, this area was densely occupied in Suchimancillo
times and all available pockets of irrigable land (e.g.,
center—left) were under cultivation 19

9. Huaca Corral area, looking downriver in the middle part of
the Coast sector. Houses and fields in foreground lie on
land that has been reclaimed following a change in the
river's course in recent decades 20

10. Mouth of Lower Santa River, looking south at point where
the Panamerican highway crosses the valley 20

11. Traditional wattle-and-daub, or *quincha*, structures lie on the desert near cultivated fields of Huaca Corral area 37

12. Well-preserved dwelling dating to Cayhuamarca/Early Horizon Period (ca. 1000–350 B.C.), with Structure 28/SVP-CAY-19 (Fig. 34) visible to the south across quebrada in background. Low rock walls probably provided stability to a superstructure built of organic materials. Note that this dwelling sits on what is essentially the same surface as when site was occupied 38

13. Whole vessels, sherds, metal fragments, and human skulls left by huaqueros on surface of the looted, intrusive cemetery at SVP-ESUCH-47/SVP-LSUCH-79, a ridgetop fortress on north side of river in the Middle Valley sector (Fig. 85) 39

14. Crossing the *oroya* cable seat at Tablones 58

15. View to southeast of Structure 109 and associated windbreaks at SVP-VIN-9/SVP-ESUCH-11. See Fig. 58 for site location and Fig. 61 for plan view 60

16. Aerial view of Huaca Yolanda Complex, located on the north desert margin in the Middle Valley (see Fig. 62) 73

17. High aerial view of Structure 28/SVP-CAY-19, located on Pampa de Cayhuamarca 2.5 km to the southeast of the valley floor. See Fig. 23 for location of site and Fig. 34 for plan view 76

18. View to north of SVP-ETAN-7 site, one of the excellently preserved local centers of Early Tanguche Period. See Fig. 115 for site location and Fig. 127 for plan view ... 79

 Introduction

The 1979–80 Santa Valley Project was carried out with the basic initial objective of investigating the relative roles of irrigation agriculture, population growth, and warfare in the origins and development of complex prehispanic society in a single, strategically located coastal Peruvian valley. Using systematic procedures of regional settlement pattern survey and site mapping pioneered during the 1946 Virú Valley Project, and later improvements in method developed primarily in Mesoamerica, a comprehensive study of extant surface remains was made over the entire area comprising the coastal and inland sectors of the Lower Santa Valley, the mouth of Quebrada de Lacramarca, and the Santa-Chao desert to the north.

My purpose in this report is to outline in detail the principal results of the research, with a primary emphasis on presentation of the data gathered during the fieldwork as well as the implications of these data for understanding major prehispanic societal developments at the local and regional levels in this area of the Peruvian North Coast (Fig. 1). The second major emphasis is a detailed presentation of methods used in gathering, organizing, and analyzing the Santa Valley data, with a view toward contributing to the development of archaeological data retrieval at the local and regional levels in the coastal Peruvian setting. The third, and final, emphasis is the presentation of a series of arguments showing the relevance of the Santa Valley data both in understanding critical developments in the North Coast sequence and in constructing cross-cultural, generalizing theories of the origins and development of complex irrigation-based society.

At the same time, underlying arguments are made for

the critical need to take a systematic and comprehensive approach to such studies, and for the detailed and complete presentation of both methods and principal results. Indeed, given recent advances in settlement pattern methods in other nuclear areas of the world, as well as the rapid destruction of prehispanic sites as population and agriculture expand in many coastal valleys, it can be argued that no other approach to regional studies of the coastal Peruvian archaeological record can easily be justified.

METHODOLOGICAL BACKGROUND

Virú Valley Project

As mentioned above, the pioneering study of the regional patterning of prehistoric settlement was conducted as part of the coordinated anthropological and geographical study carried out by members of the 1946 Virú Valley Project (cf. Ford and Willey 1949; Willey 1953). To provide background for the discussion of more recent developments in settlement pattern studies, it is thus appropriate briefly to review key aspects of the methods used in the survey of the Virú Valley (Fig. 2). Perhaps the single most important innovation of the Virú survey was the use of 1:10,000-scale aerial photographs to facilitate field orientation and direct plotting of the sites encountered by the survey team. Among other things this enhanced the ability of the team to assess accurately the nature, extent, and relative location of prehispanic sites in the region. Nevertheless, no systematic criteria were used in assessing what constituted a site, although in

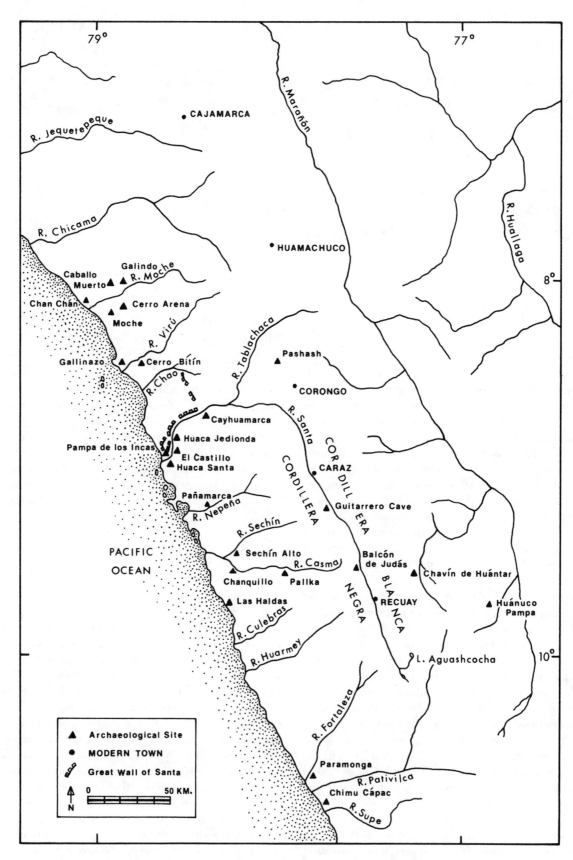

79°

R. Jequetepeque

• CAJAMARCA

R. Marañón

R. Chicama

R. Huallaga

• HUAMACHUCO

8°

Caballo
Muerto ▲ Galindo ▲ R. Moche
Chan Chán ▲   ▲ Cerro Arena
            ▲
           Moche

R. Virú

77°

Gallinazo ▲ ▲ Cerro Bitín
              R. Chao

R. Tablachaca

▲ Pashash

• CORONGO

▲ Cayhuamarca

R. Santa

Pampa de los Incas ▲ Huaca Jedionda

▲ El Castillo
▲ Huaca Santa

CORDILLERA   CARAZ

C
O
R
D
I
L
L
E
R
A

▲ Pañamarca
   R. Nepeña

▲ Guitarrero Cave

R. Sechín

PACIFIC

OCEAN

▲ Sechín Alto
            R. Casma
Chanquillo ▲ ▲ Pallka

▲ Balcón
   de Judás

B
L
A
N
C
A

▲ Chavín de Huántar

▲ Las Haldas

R. Culebras

• RECUAY

▲ Huánuco
   Pampa

N
E
G
R
A

R. Huarmey

? L. Aguashcocha

10°

R. Fortaleza

▲ Archaeological Site

• MODERN TOWN

Great Wall of Santa

▲ Paramonga

R. Pativilca

0   50 KM.

▲ Chimu Cápac

N

R. Supe

Fig. 1. Map of the north Peruvian coast and highlands.

2

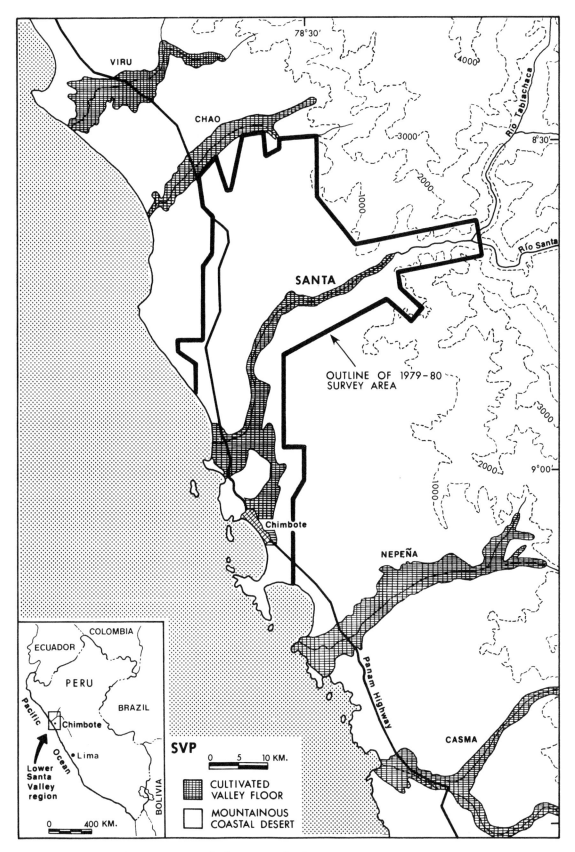

Fig. 2. Lower Santa Valley survey area and adjacent coastal valleys.

3

some cases the extent of well preserved architectural remains or midden debris was used to estimate the area covered by prehispanic occupation.

Sites themselves were classified according to a four-fold functional scheme—including living sites, community-ceremonial structures, fortified strongholds, and cemeteries (Willey 1953:7). Moseley and Mackey (1972:67–68) have criticized the use of this scheme since, in their view, the four categories carry broad behavioral connotations but lack specificity. Since there is little or no real functional input with respect to the "social factors" operating behind the categories, the result according to Moseley and Mackey is "more a chronicle of population growth and movement within the valley than a functional or processual study." This criticism of the Virú survey is to a certain extent justified, but the view taken here is that a strong case can be made for the overriding value of settlement pattern data in making empirically-based inferences about site function and sociocultural development. However, to achieve reasonable success such a functionally and processually oriented approach must rest, among other things, on (1) explicit definition of the criteria used in establishing different categories of site size and function; (2) careful examination of period-to-period changes in the numbers, size, internal configuration, and overall location of sites and other remains; and (3) attention to how these changes correlate with such critical factors as subsistence focus, the development of canal systems, population growth and decline, warfare, and levels of sociocultural complexity.

The sampling techniques used in the Virú Valley survey are somewhat more open to criticism. In the first place, the survey was not exhaustive—i.e., one aimed at recovering data on all sites located throughout the valley. Indeed, from later analysis of the airphotos Willey estimated that only 25% of all prehispanic sites in Virú were found and mapped during the survey. Second, although sites ideally were to be selected at random for inclusion in the survey, the sample was in fact highly skewed toward larger sites with clearly visible remains and sites in the upper valley where little natural vegetation is present. The survey therefore tended in reality to exclude smaller sites with little or no surface architecture, as well as lower valley sites in areas of thicker vegetation. Nevertheless, all sectors of Virú were inspected and an attempt was made to obtain a roughly representative sample of all site types.

In sum, despite its pioneering nature the Virú settlement pattern survey represents a major advance in archaeological research in that it was the first attempt to retrieve data on an entire prehistoric regional cultural system (Parsons 1972:128). For the first time, hypotheses could be proposed about the development of cultural complexity as reflected in changing settlement configurations. Coupled with the excavations carried out by other members of the Virú project, the surface survey outlined a picture of increasing population size and cultural complexity through the period of apparent incorporation of the valley into interregional state systems such as Moche, in addition to an eventual decline in population numbers toward the end of the prehispanic sequence.

Recent Settlement Pattern Studies

During the three decades since publication of the results of the Virú Valley survey, increasingly comprehensive and sophisticated studies of regional settlement patterns have been conducted in other nuclear areas of the world where pristine irrigation-based states arose—most notably in Mesopotamia, on the Diyala and Deh Luran Plains (Adams 1962, 1965, 1970, 1981; Adams and Nissen 1972; Johnson 1973; Wright and Johnson 1975); and Mesoamerica, in the Valley of Mexico, the Valley of Oaxaca, and the lowland Maya area (Ashmore 1981; Blanton 1972; Blanton et al. 1982; Bullard 1960; Parsons 1968, 1971, 1974; Parsons et al. 1982; Sanders 1960, 1965; Sanders et al. 1979; Willey et al. 1965).

Among the outstanding advances in regional survey methods has been the work of Sanders and Parsons, and their associates, over more than a decade of research in the Valley of Mexico. A major focus of their research objectives has been an attempt to specify certain key parameters that bear on the nature and patterning of settlements (cf. Parsons 1974). These include (1) delineation of the natural boundaries of the region, (2) definition of the spatial distribution of prehispanic occupation, (3) determination of the contemporaneity of occupational remains, and (4) determination of the function of occupational loci. Perhaps the most important aspect of the Valley of Mexico research has been the attempt to obtain a nearly 100% sample of sites over a large area of prehispanic occupation. This reduces to a minimum the possibility of excluding sites that are crucial for understanding both functional relationships among settlements in a given period, as well as developments at the local and regional levels throughout the sequence.

The Valley of Mexico survey methods have been developed in the context of a region where intensive agriculture and frequent plowing are practiced. Although this has resulted in the destruction of architectural remains on many sites, from an archaeological standpoint it has had the positive effect of limiting natural vegetation and continually bringing prehispanic occupational debris up to the ground surface. Since soil cover in many places is less than 1 m deep and has been subjected to severe erosion brought about by timber clearing, sheep grazing, and plowing, surface collections of potsherds may contain material from a number of different periods. Thus, once an area has been surveyed and map tracings have been prepared from field airphotos on which the

4

extent and density of surface debris have been recorded, it is possible to obtain a reasonably accurate picture of changing site configurations and regional settlement patterns throughout the sequence.

In order to make inferences about changes in demographic patterns through time, Sanders and Parsons have equated a series of relative sherd densities with a range of population densities derived from modern ethnographic data on traditional agricultural communities of the Central Mexican Highlands. Using the population density figures thus obtained, in addition to measurements from the map tracings of the areal extent of prehispanic occupational debris, it is possible to estimate the population size of sites of each period (but see Tolstoy and Fish 1975). However, these population figures are not taken as the actual numbers of people living in the region during a given period; rather, the consistent application of the method to sites over a wide area and throughout the sequence is intended to give a relative, but empirically based, idea of changes in demography over a long period of time.

Combining these demographic data with detailed plans showing the nature and extent of architectural remains on better-preserved sites, the Valley of Mexico researchers are now able to outline critical sociocultural developments for the period between 1000 B.C. and A.D. 1520 in all areas not covered by dense modern occupation. Throughout the earlier part of this period, a steady process of population growth can be traced, in addition to major shifts in settlement size and location apparently brought about as the Teotihuacán state emerged in the centuries immediately before and after the beginning of the Christian era. Significant new hypotheses have been advanced to account for the rise and fall of Teotihuacán as well as the processes leading to the late prehispanic Aztec florescence (cf. Sanders et al. 1979; Parsons 1974; Parsons et al. 1982; see also Blanton et al. 1982).

Recent Studies on the Peruvian Coast

Considering the clear advantages of the innovative approach to the study of a prehistoric regional system taken by members of the Virú Valley Project, as well as more recent developments in survey methods such as those outlined for Valley of Mexico, surprisingly little research of comparable spatial and temporal scope has been undertaken on the coast of Peru since 1946. A review of the literature indicates that, prior to the 1979–80 Santa Valley survey, several settlement pattern studies had been carried out either in a small area of a valley (Bankes 1972; Earle 1972; Moseley 1975c; Patterson 1971; Patterson and Lanning 1964; Rowe 1963b; Thompson 1962a, 1962b, 1964) or in most of the lower and middle sectors (Dillehey 1976; Donnan 1973; Proulx 1968, 1973).

However, all of these studies either dealt with a limited sample of sites in a coastal valley region or were confined

to an examination of settlements in only one prehispanic period. For example, Earle's Lurín Valley study was limited to the presentation of data for the inland sector of the lower valley during the Early Intermediate Period (ca. 400 B.C. to A.D. 700). And Donnan's study, while covering much of the lower and middle sectors of Santa Valley, was confined almost entirely to an examination of cemeteries dating to the period of Moche occupation during the later part of the Early Intermediate. Indeed, among the studies cited above, only that of Proulx in Nepeña Valley (Fig. 2) approaches the scope of the settlement pattern research in Virú. But it is fair to say that, while it appears to have been more systematic in terms of overall regional coverage and site retrieval than the Virú survey, Proulx's Nepeña study is noncomprehensive— i.e., it does not consistently provide data on the size, density of occupational debris, and density of structural remains for many of the habitation and other site types included in the survey (e.g., see Proulx 1968:19–24).

From the lack of comprehensive and systematic regional settlement pattern coverage for any of the nearly 100 coastal Peruvian valleys, it clearly follows that none of the survey research conducted during the period from 1946–1979 provided us with anything approaching adequate regional estimates of either population numbers in a single period or demographic trends throughout a sequence. Nor were we provided with reliable data on either changes in the size, internal complexity, and function of sites or on major shifts in settlement patterns throughout a region over time. Yet one of the underlying contentions of this study—and a principal rationale for carrying out the Santa Valley research—is that some researchers investigating the origins and development of complex prehispanic societies on the Peruvian coast have seemed to be proceeding as if these critically lacking data were either already known or of little importance for their arguments.

THEORETICAL BACKGROUND

Origins of Societal Complexity on the Coast

To provide a brief introductory framework for theoretical issues that are discussed later in light of the Santa Valley data, it is useful to review some of the arguments that have been made about the origins and development of complex prehispanic coastal Peruvian societies. A few of these arguments are of a general nature in that they are intended to demonstrate how existing coastal archaeological data can be used to support cross-cultural theories of the rise of sociocultural complexity and the state. One example of this generalist use of existing data is Cohen's (1971, 1977) argument that population pressure on the Central Coast was the principal causal force leading to the establishment of sedentary fishing villages and, eventually, to the development of an agricultural subsistence system. Another is Carneiro's (1961, 1970) argument that, following the introduction of agriculture, population pressure within the classic circumscribed environmental setting of the coast led to intervillage conflict and aggrandizement and, eventually, to the rise of state society at the regional level.

However, most of the arguments about the origins and development of prehispanic societal complexity on the coast have focused more specifically on such problems as: (1) which of the two main subsistence systems—maritime or agricultural—was more directly antecedent or causal in providing the major source of food, population growth, and organizational complexity in the rise of stratified society; (2) the sociopolitical nature of such cultural phenomena as Chavín, Recuay, Gallinazo, Moche, Wari, Chimú, and the Inca; and (3) whether these cultures represent periods when North Coast valleys were (a) uniformly and profoundly influenced by a widespread religious cult (i.e., Chavín), (b) incorporated into local multivalley states (i.e., Gallinazo, Moche, Chimú) or coast-sierra states (i.e., Chavín, Recuay), or (c) part of large pan-Central Andean empires (i.e., Wari, Inca). For example, there is fairly wide agreement among coastal researchers and other archaeologists that both Moche and Chimú represent expansionist multivalley state societies that were centered in the Moche Valley (e.g., Benson 1972; Conrad 1978; Donnan 1973; Fagan 1985; Keatinge 1982; Moseley 1982; Price 1971; Proulx 1973; Rowe 1948; Strong and Evans 1952; Wenke 1984; Willey 1953). On the other hand, Central Andean archaeologists appear to be split into opposing camps when discussing the extent of the Wari state of the Middle Horizon Period (ca. A.D. 700 to 1100). Some North Coast-centered researchers have argued that Wari did not extend its control over the North Coast (e.g., Mackey 1982), while some Ayacucho-centered researchers have argued that it did (e.g., Isbell and Schreiber 1978; Lumbreras 1974).

General Considerations

The problem with both the general and specific arguments outlined above is not primarily one of whether they are correct; rather, it is one of assuming that arguments about such processes as population pressure and the incorporation of coastal valleys into interregional conquest states could be at all supported or understood in the absence of comprehensive regional settlement data. But while an emphasis on data from a more limited spatial and temporal focus is clearly inadequate to the task of describing and explaining these processes, neither is it practical or necessary to attempt to study in a single project an entire multivalley system. Furthermore, if one assumes that the appearance of societal complexity can be equated broadly with the rise of nonegalitarian society, and that such a society can in turn be equated with the establishment of a network based on increasing intersite interaction and dependency, then the problem at once becomes one requiring a local and regional focus. Thus in taking a comprehensive perspective on an entire region—and assuming adequate representation of sites of all periods—one at once has the possibility of looking both at local developments leading toward regional sociocultural complexity, and at changes brought about at the regional level as a coastal valley became a functioning part of larger multivalley polities.

Several fundamental assumptions underlie this approach to the study of the origins and development of societal complexity. The first is that nonegalitarian societies—i.e., chiefdoms and states—can be defined in the broadest sense as hierarchically organized networks of settlements that extend their influence or control over increasingly large geographic areas. Second, it follows from this that changes in the internal nature, size, and overall configuration of both local and regional settlement groupings result from critical aspects of the developmental processes giving rise to these societies. Third, from the first and second assumptions, it follows that studying multivalley state formation from a provincial perspective is a useful and strategically sound research tactic. Taken as a whole, these assumptions imply not only that many coastal valleys may provide a suitable focus for research oriented toward investigating the rise of societal complexity, but also that it may be as useful to study interregional state formation from the perspective of a strategically selected provincial valley (e.g., Santa) as it is to focus on the area of presumed core developments (e.g., Moche). It should be emphasized that such a perspective is not entirely new to Central Andean archaeological research—at least with respect to the highlands. Two projects have been carried out in the Andean sierra—the first by John Murra, Craig Morris, and Donald Thompson in the Huánuco area, and the second by Ramiro Matos, Jeffrey Parsons, Timothy Earle and their associates in the Junín-Tarma-Jauja area—which have demonstrated the utility of a systematic regional approach in studying Inca state organization at the provincial level (cf. D'Altroy and Earle 1985; Earle et al. 1980; Morris 1972, 1976; Morris and Thompson 1985; Parsons and Matos Mendieta 1978).

OVERVIEW OF THE SANTA VALLEY PROJECT

Choice of Research Location

In light of the preceding discussion of general methodological and theoretical issues, the Lower Santa Valley for a number of reasons provides an ideal focus for research aimed at investigating the relative roles of irrigation agriculture, population growth, and warfare in the

Plate 1. Gemini satellite view of Lower Santa Valley and adjacent coastal and sierra regions

rise of complex prehispanic coastal society. First of all, the Lower Santa region presents a classic example of environmental circumscription—i.e., an area containing a limited amount of irrigable land flanked by wide stretches of higher desert wasteland (Fig. 2). The Pacific Ocean lies to the west, and steep arid slopes of the western flank of the Central Andean cordillera rise to elevations of over 4000 m to the east. Below the confluence of the Santa and Tablachaca Rivers—at the point where the canyon of the Santa begins gradually to widen—the valley floor is flanked by rugged mountains and open sandy pampas of the coastal desert, which extend some 30 km north to Chao Valley and 45 km south to Nepeña. As with other nearby valleys, the cultivable land providing the main focus of prehispanic sociocultural development thus forms a narrow, sharply defined oasis cutting

down across the barren coastal desert to the ocean (see Plate 1). And with the possibility of precise quantification of such critical parameters as irrigable land and water supply, the Lower Santa Valley closely approximates an ideal environmental microcosm for studies of long-term cultural adaptation in the prehistoric setting.

Second, Santa is one of the few rivers on the Peruvian littoral that extends deeply up into the Andean cordillera, and its huge sierra catchment basin supplies more than enough water for irrigation agriculture throughout the year. Indeed, even with the use of increasing amounts of land for cultivation of such water-hungry plants as rice and sugar cane, at present only about 7% of the total annual discharge of the river is required for agriculture. With an average annual air temperature of 21° C and a benign temperate climate

7

year-round, as many as two or three crops per year are possible (Grobman et al. 1961:29; ONERN 1972b:384 ff.; Robinson 1971:136). It is therefore probable that Santa Valley had the potential to produce relatively larger annual harvests in prehispanic times than other nearby valleys of comparable size limited by a seasonal water supply. From this it follows that the prehispanic demographic potential of Santa was at least on a par with, if not greater than, that of such valleys as Virú, Chao, and Nepeña (cf. ONERN 1972b, 1973). As argued later, this relatively high potential has important implications, both for (1) the strategic position of Santa relative to other nearby valleys that formed part of the succession of interregional states in the North Coast sequence, and for (2) the attractiveness of Santa as a focus of raiding and conquest throughout the agricultural period.

Third, enough antecedent archaeological work had been carried out in the Lower Santa region to have established the presence of ceramic types considered to be diagnostic of the major periods from Early Horizon through Late Horizon Period (ca. 1000 B.C. to A.D. 1532) in adjacent valleys with (then) better-known sequences. In addition, the antecedent research in Santa had established the presence of a wide range of prehispanic settlement types and other remains, which included habitation sites, larger sites with associated public architecture, hilltop fortresses, pyramidal mounds, cemeteries, canals, field systems, as well as extensive sections of walls.

Finally, the primary survey area of roughly 400 km² encompassed within the main Lower Santa Valley—including the lower 70 km of the Santa River and adjacent desert margins that constitute its entire coastal sector—is small enough to allow a survey team composed at any one time of no more than three to six persons to cover systematically the entire region in a single modestly funded project.

Previous Research in the Region

Among early researchers whose work focused primarily on cemeteries and funerary ceramics were: G. A. Dorsey (fieldwork in 1892; collection of whole vessels mostly of Moche date, now housed at Field Museum), Rafael Larco Hoyle (fieldwork in 1934; Recuay vessels from the Tablones area of Santa), and William Clothier (fieldwork in 1943; Recuay and Middle Horizon vessels from the Vinzos area). More recently, in 1966–67 Christopher Donnan (1973) carried out extensive work of a similar nature in the lower and middle parts of the valley, finding a total of 78 cemeteries as well as seven small habitation sites dating to the period of Moche occupation.

The first work to focus principally on nonfunerary aspects of prehispanic occupation in Santa was a series of pioneering photographic flights carried out in 1931 by the Shippee-Johnson Peruvian Expedition (cf. Shippee 1932, 1933). During the flights, members of the expedition discovered an extensive series of over 40 hilltop fortresses located for the most part on the south desert margin of the valley, and what appeared to be an essentially continuous "Great Wall" running from a point near the coastline well up the valley along the north desert margin. Prior to the Santa Valley Project, limited additional studies of these remains were conducted by a number of other researchers—including Cornelius Roosevelt and Julio C. Tello, in 1934 (cf. Roosevelt 1935); James A. Ford, in 1946 (unpublished notes at American Museum); Paul Kosok, in 1949 (cf. Kosok 1965:187–194); Gene Savoy and Douglas Sharon, in 1962 (cf. Savoy 1970:28–35); Gary Vescelius and his associates, in 1964; and Mercedes Cárdenas, in 1976–77 (cf. Cárdenas Martín 1977, 1978).

In addition to the studies of specific types of remains such as the funerary ceramics, fortresses, and walls mentioned above, limited site surveys were carried out by several researchers in the years between 1946 and 1979. In 1946, following completion of his research in Virú, James Ford conducted a brief but reasonably extensive survey in the middle and lower parts of Santa, locating 58 sites from which he made surface collections that are now housed at the American Museum of Natural History. In 1949, during his landmark study of ancient coastal irrigation systems, Paul Kosok located and mapped some 40 sites. Additional surveys were carried out in the late 1950s and early 1960s by Hans Horkheimer (e.g., see Horkheimer 1965:27–29) and by Gary Vescelius (personal communication, 1978). In the years before 1979, the most extensive survey of the region was that carried out by Mercedes Cárdenas, of the Pontífica Universidad Católica del Perú, as part of a larger interregional project aimed primarily at obtaining a chronological picture of the use of maritime resources in prehistoric times. During their research in the Santa-Lacramarca area, members of the project located a total of 187 sites dating to most of the major periods from Preceramic through Late Horizon. As with previous projects in the region, however, data on individual sites were essentially restricted to a listing of presumed period of occupation and general state of preservation, with sites of all periods studied shown as numbers on a single, small-scale map.

Brief Outline of Substantive Results

During the course of our 1979–80 fieldwork in the Lower Santa Valley region, systematic and comprehensive survey was extended over an area of more than 750 km² (Fig. 2). Within this region, we mapped and collected data on a total of 1020 discrete archaeological sites (Note: the number is 1246, counting each period of occupation at multicomponent sites; by way of comparison, 315 discrete sites and 496 total occupations were located during the Virú Valley Project; cf. Willey 1953:423–448). These include habitation, fortress, ceremonial-civic, and cemetery sites dating to one or more of ten prehispanic periods extending from the Preceramic through the Late Horizon, over a time period from pre-1800 B.C. to A.D. 1532. Among a number of other remains located and mapped during the survey were canals, serpentine field systems, rock-lined roads, the Great Wall system of Santa, as well as petroglyphs, murals, and an extensive series of large ground drawings placed on the sides of hills out away from the main valley floor.

Period chronology and numbers of sites. The prehispanic chronological sequence presented here for the Lower Santa region (see Chart 1) is based on (1) intensive study in the U.S. of major type collections from Santa, Virú, Nepeña, Casma, and other regions; (2) reference to the reasonably extensive literature on ceramics of these regions; and (3) analysis of the 382 surface collections made throughout most of the survey area during our fieldwork. Using names of local places associated with concentrations of sites of each of the ten periods, the following chronology has been constructed (number of sites and Virú Valley/Central Andean period equivalents for each Santa Valley period are indicated in parentheses): *Las Salinas* (36 sites; Cerro Prieto/Preceramic); *Cayhuamarca* (54 sites; Guañape/Early Horizon); *Vinzos* (45 sites; Puerto Moorin/Beginning Early Intermediate Period, or EIP); *Early Suchimancillo* (130 sites; Early-Middle Gallinazo/Early EIP); *Late Suchimancillo* (153 sites; Late Gallinazo/Middle EIP); *Guadalupito* (205 sites; Huancaco/Late EIP); *Early Tanguche* (440 sites; Tomaval/Early Middle Horizon); *Late Tanguche* (56 sites; Tomaval/Late Middle Horizon); *Early Tambo Real* (49 sites; La Plata/Late Intermediate); and *Late Tambo Real* (78 sites; Estero/Late Horizon).

In order to facilitate the later discussion of major developmental junctures in the sequence, the ten Santa Valley periods have been placed in three main temporal groupings: early, middle, and late. The *early periods* are considered to be those which precede the time of probable state formation, and include Las Salinas, Cayhuamarca, Vinzos, Early Suchimancillo, and Late Suchimancillo. The *middle periods* are those during which Santa Valley appears to have become a province of two successive multivalley states, and include Guadalupito and Early Tanguche. The *late periods* are those during which the Santa region appears to have been a part of smaller, shifting spheres of interaction, culminating with its incorporation into the Chimú and Inca states. These periods include Late Tanguche, Early Tambo Real, and Late Tambo Real.

Based on the analysis of paste, surface treatment, decorative motifs, as well as discrete and continuous attributes of vessel form, a total of 197 major ceramic types has been identified for the nine ceramic periods from

CHART 1

PREHISPANIC PERIODS OF THE LOWER SANTA VALLEY REGION AND RELATED SEQUENCES

Estimated Absolute Chronology	SANTA VALLEY PERIOD	Virú Valley Period	Central Andean Period
1532			
1350	LATE TAMBO REAL	Estero	Late Horizon
	EARLY TAMBO REAL	La Plata	Late Intermediate
1150	LATE TANGUCHE		
900		Tomaval	Middle Horizon
	EARLY TANGUCHE		
650			
	GUADALUPITO	Huancaco	
400	LATE SUCHIMANCILLO	L	
200		Gallinazo M	Early Intermediate
	EARLY SUCHIMANCILLO	E	
A.D. / B.C.		L	
	VINZOS	Puerto Moorin	
350		E	
		L	
	CAYHUAMARCA	Guañape	
		M	Early Horizon
1000			
	(?)	E	Initial Period
1800 -			
	LAS SALINAS	Cerro Prieto	Preceramic

Cayhuamarca through Late Tambo Real. Support for the chronological position of each of these nine periods is provided by a systematic review of the literature on ceramic diagnostics of adjacent regions (see Appendix I). This procedure has also made it possible to relate 185 out of the 197 Santa Valley types—or 95%—to specific temporal diagnostics of these nearby regions. Fully 130 out of the 197 types have close or essentially identical counterparts in Virú Valley, which is by far the greatest number of types shared between Santa and any other adjacent region (it is also at least in part a reflection of the exhaustive description and illustration of ceramic types by members of the Virú Valley Project). Other regions or sites sharing substantial numbers of temporally diagnostic ceramic types with Santa at various times in the sequence include the following: Moche Valley (19 types), Pashash site (20 types), Callejón de Huaylas (10 types), Nepeña Valley (16 types), and Casma Valley (16 types).

Structure, site, and regional maps. Among the maps prepared during the project were approximately 180 large-scale plan views showing architectural details of individual structures—including nearly all major fortresses, all large pyramidal and platform mounds, all

9

probable local and regional administrative centers, and substantial numbers of habitation structures, minor fortresses, minor platform mounds, and corrals. An additional 70 plan views were made that show the location and configuration of all or most of the structural remains at sites of various types—including habitation, ceremonial-civic, and defensive sites. It was therefore possible to obtain an essentially complete sample of extant structures presumably built by corporate labor groups, as well as a reasonably representative sample of habitation sites of all types and sizes.

Another set of over 65 maps at varying scales has been prepared to show the location and patterning of all sites in each of the ten prehispanic periods of the Lower Santa Valley. Included among the maps for each period are (1) a single regional-level map at 1:400,000 scale indicating the location and principal function of all sites; and (2) a set of local-level topographic maps at 1:100,000 scale showing the same settlement data in greater detail against a background of 100-m contour intervals. Since the latter group of settlement pattern maps is still not at sufficiently large scale to show the actual outline of all occupations (i.e., many of the smaller sites would be *lost* from view at 1:100,000 scale), a final set of 20 drawings was prepared to show the outline of each of the 1246 sites at the same scale—generally between 1:10,000 and 1:20,000—it was mapped on the airphoto during the fieldwork (cf. Wilson 1985).

Description and chronology of the principal remains. As part of the overview of the 1979–80 research, in this section brief introductory descriptions and dating are provided for the principal prehispanic remains of the Lower Santa region. In order of presentation, these remains include hilltop fortresses, ceremonial-civic structures and sites, major population centers, the Great Wall system, the network of rock-lined roads, and canals and field systems.

As mentioned earlier, the presence of a large number of spectacularly located *fortress sites* in the Lower Santa region has been known since the Shippee-Johnson flights of 1931. However, prior to our research almost none of these sites had been located accurately on regional maps nor had detailed plans been made of them—with the single exception of a (unpublished) plane-table plan view of a citadel site in the Cayhuamarca area, prepared in 1964 by Gary Vescelius and his associates (Vescelius, personal communication, 1978). During our fieldwork, a total of 62 defensive structures was found throughout the survey region (e.g., Plate 2). In addition to mapping the location and size of these sites on the airphotos, detailed transit-stadia and Brunton-tape plan views were made of 29 major citadels as well as of a number of minor defensive sites. Judging from associated ceramic diagnostics and architectural features, over 90% of the defensive structures—or some 57 out of 62—date to the early part

of the ceramic sequence, predating the time of probable state formation.

As in the case of the fortresses, limited study and mapping of *ceremonial-civic sites* had been done prior to our research (e.g., Donnan 1973), but very little was known about the overall nature and scope of these remains. During the course of the project, we located and mapped in detail a total of 43 sites that are presumed to have a primarily religious and/or public function (e.g., Plate 3). Slightly over half of these sites—or 23 out of 43—have associated ceramic and architectural diagnostics dating to the pre-state ceramic periods. Of the remaining 20 sites, fully 18 date to Guadalupito and Early Tanguche, the two principal periods of multivalley state formation.

Some of the *major population centers* (e.g., Plate 4) were known from the work of previous projects, although data were limited principally to the brief written descriptions and accompanying series of oblique and aerial photographs published in Kosok (1965:185–194)—including such sites as Huaca Jedionda ("Buena Vista"), Pampa de los Incas Complex ("Santa Clara"), Alto Perú Complex, Huaca Santa Complex, and Huaca Yolanda. Out of the total of 903 habitation sites mapped during our fieldwork, only a relative handful of 14 sites was found to have population sizes estimated at greater than 2000 persons. From one to three occupations ranging in size between 2000 and 6000 persons were found for each of the seven periods from Vinzos through Early Tambo Real, thus excluding only the earliest two periods (Las Salinas and Cayhuamarca) and the last period (Late Tambo Real).

During the research, we also located and mapped on the large-scale field airphotos all extant remains of the *Great Wall system* (e.g., Plate 5). The system extends in four major sections along the lower 40 km of the north desert margin of Santa, with two additional long sections that extend out across the desert between Santa and Chao Valleys, adjacent to steep slopes of the western Andean cordillera. With a total length of slightly over 70 km, the Great Wall system is miniscule compared to its (justly more renowned) counterpart in China. Nonetheless, its total estimated volume of 207,000 m^3 makes it one of the more significant engineering feats of an extensive nature in the Central Andes. The consistent association of the six wall sections with sites and roads of Early Tanguche suggests that the system dates to this time period.

The *road-settlement network* of the Santa-Chao desert is itself one of the more interesting products of prehispanic engineering studied during our fieldwork. Yet, astonishingly, nowhere in the archaeological literature does one find specific mention of the complex system of roads and nearly 200 associated sites which extends along at least four principal routes across the desert from Santa to Chao (e.g., see Kosok 1965; von Hagen 1955; Note: von Hagen must have traveled along the main central route

Plate 2. Structure 33, a major citadel with occupation dating to Cayhuamarca and later periods

Plate 3. Huaca mound of SVP-ESUCH-50/Structure 47 rises out of cultivated fields near Quebrada del Panteón

11

Plate 4. Aerial view of SVP-GUAD-111/Structure 19, a site with probable administrative and elite residential functions that formed the core of Pampa de los Incas Complex

Plate 5. Ridgetop wall of Pampa Blanca area, the uppermost part of the Great Wall system on the north desert margin of the Lower Santa Valley

12

Plate 6. Section of ancient rock-lined road near SVP-ETAN- 417, in the Santa-Chao Desert

leading out of Quebrada Cenicero, but passes it off as being of Inca date and does not mention any of the associated sites; Kosok must have driven right down the middle of this same road on a visit to Hacienda Tanguche in the early 1940s, but mentions neither the road nor the sites located alongside it). Ranging in width between 4 and 20 m, the roads are defined principally by lines of desert rocks placed along their edges (e.g., Plate 6) and by an almost continuous scatter of prehispanic sherds. Numerous Early Tanguche occupations lie adjacent to almost every section of the four main routes, indicating that the probable date of construction of the network is Early Middle Horizon Period.

The final category of major prehispanic remains consists of *canals and field systems*. Well preserved sections of ancient canals were found throughout the valley, both on the desert margins adjacent to the main valley floor between Chuquicara and the ocean as well as in Pampa Las Salinas area to the north of the valley mouth (e.g., Plate 7). Although the total length of extant prehispanic canals does not exceed 45 km, the reconstruction presented in this report of some 10 major canals indicates that length to be nearer 160 km. Judging from the overall location of sites in the system of each period, however, it is likely that the maximum length of all (desert margin)

canals in use at any one time did not exceed 130 km. The latest sites found associated with the early upvalley irrigation system date to Late Suchimancillo Period, but, judging from the size and complexity of the Cayhuamarca settlement system associated with the upvalley canals, it is highly probable that irrigation agriculture began at least by Early Horizon times (ca. 1000 to 350 B.C.).

Subsistence and demographic trends. Based on the fragments of prehispanic canals as well as maps (ONERN 1972b) which show the location and extent of traditional modern contour canals, it is possible to reconstruct with reasonable accuracy the maximum hectarage of prehispanic cultivation in the various sectors of the valley. Combining this reconstruction with the settlement data on the overall location of sites in each period, it is also possible to estimate the maximum hectarage of land under cultivation at each point in the sequence. As argued later, these data have critical implications for discussions of such processes as (1) the general development of irrigation agriculture in the pre-state and state periods, (2) the changing relationship between estimated population and the carrying capacity of the land under cultivation, and (3) the changing role of maritime subsistence in sociocultural development. In addition, the

13

Plate 7. Serpentine field system and adjacent Las Salinas canal, located in the desert north of the Santa Valley mouth

data on subsistence-settlement patterns provide the basis for arguments about the possible socioecononmic role of Santa Valley in the multivalley state systems of Guadalupito, Early Tanguche, and Late Tambo Real Periods.

One of the principal methodological results of our research in the Lower Santa region has been the development of a systematic approach to estimating the population size of coastal Peruvian sites. Taking into account the generally excellent preservation of structural remains on habitation sites of all periods in the sequence, the method is based primarily on field estimates of site size and relative densities of structural remains, as well as on analysis of the detailed site maps. By applying this method to the comprehensive data retrieved on habitation sites throughout the survey area, it is possible to make estimates of the total population potential of each period and outline the demographic development of the Lower Santa region throughout the sequence.

Outline of the Research Timetable

The Santa Valley research has been carried out in essentially three stages extending between 1977 and 1985:

The first stage began in May, 1977 with a brief recon-

naissance trip to the North Coast to look over Santa and adjacent valleys, primarily to investigate the feasibility of systematic regional survey methods in the area. The next 24 months—during which I was teaching in the Department of Anthropology at the University of Michigan-Flint—were devoted to planning the project, obtaining funds, and making a number of visits for intensive study of North Coast ceramic collections to various places including the Field, American, and Yale Peabody Museums.

The second stage of research—consisting of the fieldwork in Santa Valley—began in May, 1979 and extended over a period of 14 months through June, 1980. During this time, approximately one month was spent in Lima obtaining permits, conferring with colleagues and officials of the Instituto Nacional de Cultura, and purchasing airphotos and topographic maps. The actual fieldwork in Santa occupied a period of 12 months—with nine months devoted to field survey, mapping of sites and structures, collection of surface ceramics, and preparation of large-scale map tracings from the field airphotos. Another three months were spent in the field laboratory at Santa carrying out intensive ceramic analysis, which included preparation of a complete set of full-scale drawings of the 382 collections made during the

14

survey. The remaining month in Peru was used to visit sites in the neighboring valleys of Moche, Virú, Chao, Nepeña, and Casma, as well as sites in the Callejón de Huaylas area and elsewhere in the adjacent sierra.

The final stage of the research consisted of working up the field data for the doctoral dissertation and eventual publication, and was carried out full-time in the U.S. over a period of 48 months, between January, 1981 and January, 1985. An additional three months in early 1986 were devoted to making a number of necessary revisions (some of them substantial; cf. Wilson 1985), in order to prepare the thesis text for publication.

PLAN OF PRESENTATION

As is made clear in the preceding introductory sections, this report consists of a full presentation of the main data collected during the 1979–80 Santa Valley Project. An alternative to complete coverage would have been to focus more briefly and specifically on only one part of the sequence, presenting all relevant data and their attendant implications—e.g., on the early periods from Cayhuamarca through Late Suchimancillo, with an examination of the relative roles of agriculture, population dynamics, and warfare in the origins of sociocultural complexity. However, the rationale for the essentially complete approach taken here is that each of the major time periods—early, middle, and late—takes on its primary significance when viewed comparatively in light of the data from the other periods. The presentation of the full range of data collected on the ten prehispanic periods in the Lower Santa sequence therefore places each one in the broadest possible evolutionary perspective, including changes and continuities from period-to-period and from early-to-middle-to-late in the sequence. It may be argued that this kind of approach is one of the most powerful aspects of a comprehensive regional perspective in contributing to our understanding of the development of societal complexity.

By the same token, the approach taken in selecting the graphic materials prepared during the project has been to include a fully representative (and nearly complete) range of the site and structure maps made in the field, as well as a complete presentation of drawings of the principal ceramic types. Because of a fortunate combination of adequate funding, personnel, and time, as noted earlier we were able to include all major structural remains in the region in the mapping effort, rather than having to prejudge which among all remains might prove to be exemplary or properly representative. Likewise, enough time was available to me in the field and later in the U.S. to ensure that an adequately representative set of drawings of the artifact collections could be presented here. In this manner, comparative studies of structural, site, and ceramic remains in Santa and other areas can draw on the full range of variation in types, sizes, and configurations. Put simply, since it impossible to predict which among all structural remains or ceramic types may prove to have critical future utility in ultimately throwing light on either Santa or some other region, it is considered better to include them all.

The organization of the data and arguments presented is as follows:

Chapter II outlines major aspects of the natural and cultural environments, drawing on data from both ancient and modern contexts to establish the physical, biological, and prehispanic cultural settings for human occupation and societal adaptation in the Lower Santa region. In addition, this chapter deals with the related topics of prehispanic site preservation, delineation of regional survey boundaries, definition of subregional survey sectors, and methods used in reconstructing the nature and extent of the prehispanic subsistence system at various points in the sequence.

Chapter III, on research methods and chronology, begins with a detailed discussion of the approach to regional survey and mapping used in the Santa Valley research. This section is of particular importance since it not only outlines the pioneering use in the coastal Peruvian setting of systematic regional survey methods developed for the most part elsewhere in the world, but also discusses how these methods were adapted to take into account conditions of excellent site preservation that are perhaps equalled elsewhere only in the Nile Valley of Egypt. The second half of this chapter outlines the methods used in assessing prehispanic chronology, the nature of structures and sites, regional settlement patterns, regional ceramic distributions, agricultural carrying capacity, and levels of sociocultural integration.

Chapter IV consists of a summary presentation in chronological, period-by-period order of the full range of data collected during the 1979–80 research on (1) structures and sites of different types, (2) the overall regional patterning of these remains, and (3) the main characteristics of regional subsistence and demography. The presentation of data for each period ends with a brief comparative discussion of structures and site types, as well as the patterning of settlements and other remains, in the better-known valleys immediately to the north and south of Santa (i.e., Virú and Nepeña).

In Chapter V, the archaeological and environmental data presented in earlier chapters are combined in a synthetic framework within which the principal arguments about the origins and development of complex society in the Santa area of the North Coast are put forth. Like Chapter IV, this chapter proceeds in chronological manner from early to late in the sequence, but establishes a more general perspective by focusing on four principal developmental stages in the regional sequence—including (1) the rise of chiefdom society in the early period, (2) the rise of multivalley states in the middle period, (3) regional demographic decline in the first part of the late period, and (4) Chimú-Inca hegemony during the last part of the sequence.

Chapter VI briefly presents the main conclusions of the Santa Valley research. It includes a discussion of the overall nature of North Coast sociocultural evolution as viewed from the perspective of a single, strategically located valley, as well as comments on the importance of methodological approach in constructing theories of the origins and rise of societal complexity.

Most of the principal data collected during the Santa Valley Project are presented in the two appendices that accompany this report: Appendix I presents detailed illustrations as well as accompanying descriptive and locational data for the major artifact types—principally ceramics—resulting from the analysis of the collections made during the fieldwork. Appendix II consists of three tabular presentations (Tables 25, 26, 27), whose length is such that their inclusion in the text itself would have substantially disrupted its sense and flow (Tables 1–24 are all much shorter in length and are included in the text). Table 25 summarizes the principal data on the 20 citadel structures dating to Cayhuamarca Period, Table 26 presents in summary form the main locational and descriptive data on each of the 1246 sites in the survey region, and Table 27 presents similar data on each of the 382 artifact collections. As noted in the preface, due to cost considerations it was not possible to include in this report the 480 pages of single-spaced site descriptions that accompany the dissertation (see Appendix B, in Wilson 1985). It is worth emphasizing again that the reader interested in specific details about the 1246 occupations encountered during the Santa Valley Project may thus find it of some utility to obtain a copy of the dissertation from University Microfilms.

It should be noted in passing here that the format of the ceramic descriptions of Appendix I incorporates numerous aspects of formats used by researchers in the 1946 Virú Valley Project (cf. Collier 1955; Strong and Evans 1952) and in the recent Valley of Mexico work (cf. Parsons 1971; Parsons et al. 1982). At the same time, ideas resulting from the analysis of the Santa Valley ceramic data have also been incorporated in the descriptions of this appendix. Perhaps the most innovative feature in this regard is that complete data on provenience and numbers of sherds are given for each one of the 197 ceramic types described; thus, essentially the full number of sherds collected from the surface of sites in the Santa region is accounted for in terms of type and precise geographical provenience.

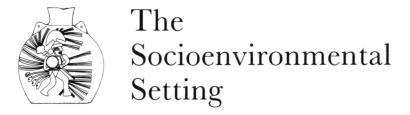 The
Socioenvironmental
Setting

As with most other areas of the Peruvian littoral, the North Coast area between Supe and Chicama Valleys presents a setting of remarkable and, indeed, dramatic contrasts within which prehispanic human adaptation and sociocultural development were played out. Due to the unique and well-known juxtaposition of colder up-welling marine waters and warmer land, the prevailing southwesterly tropical air masses condense and lose their moisture-carrying capacity as they sweep across the Peru Coastal Current, only to heat up again as the resulting fog strikes the littoral. Thus, although between the months of May and October the coast is often drenched in thick fog, appreciable amounts of rainfall occur only a few times a century. Broken at infrequent intervals by the narrow river valley oases which run out of the western cordillera to the ocean (Fig. 1), the land presents a scene of nearly absolute desert characterized by large rock-covered pampas, windswept barkhan dunes, and rugged coastal outliers of the main cordillera.

Occasional clumps of vegetation dot the desert surface, and include: achupaya (*Tillandsia*), an epiphytic plant which clings to the dunes and draws moisture from the periodic fogs blown inland off the Pacific; and algar-robo (*Prosopis juliflora*), a xerophytic tree which derives its moisture from deeper subsurface waters in the bottoms of *quebradas*, or dry washes. Essentially, however, the land between the valleys is devoid of vegetation and is for most practical purposes of little economic value to the inhabitants of the littoral. Thus the desert in pre-hispanic times was, as it is now, primarily a place to be crossed in getting from one valley oasis to the next—and is not (except in special circumstances to be discussed later) an important focus of human activity.

In distinct contrast to the generally unproductive na-

ture of the coastal desert, the waters of the adjacent Pacific are among the most biologically productive in the world, and from the time of the earliest human occupation have provided an important focus of subsistence activities (cf. Parsons 1970; Moseley 1975c; Osborn 1977). Nevertheless, as I have argued elsewhere (Wilson 1981), the maritime environment is subject to lengthy, aperiodic downturns in productivity brought about by the incursion of warmer tropical waters and the cessation of nutrient upwelling during the phenomenon known as "El Niño". Both the archaeological data on settlement patterns, site complexity, and limited fishing technology of pre-agricultural coastal dwellers as well as the demographic data on modern subsistence fishing villages support the argument that the primary basis for prehispanic societal development in this area (and probably elsewhere on the coast as well) was not the relatively limited waters of the ocean. Rather, as the data from such coastal regions as Virú, Santa, Nepeña, Casma, and Ancón-Chillón clearly show, the main subsistence support for significant early population growth and the development of sociocultural complexity was the practice of irrigation agriculture on the flatter alluvial deposits adjacent to the rivers which cut down across the barren littoral.

This chapter outlines principal features of the terrestrial and maritime environments of the Lower Santa region, as well as related data on aspects of cultural adaptation within this setting. Indeed, use of the term *socioenvironmental* (cf. Flannery 1972) in the chapter heading is intended to emphasize that cultural evolution can be viewed profitably as a two-part process—i.e., one that includes not only the main features of the overall natural environment (e.g., location and extent of irrigable land, dynamics of river flow), but also critical aspects of so-

Table 1. Average Yearly and Monthly Water Discharge in Millions of Cubic Meters for Selected North Coast Rivers in the Lower Santa Valley Area[a]

River	Average Yearly Discharge	Average Monthly Discharge[b]											
		Jan	Feb	Mar	Apr	May	Jun	Jul	Aug	Sep	Oct	Nov	Dec
Jequetepeque	945.1	77.2	155.0	284.7	215.2	66.1	29.3	16.2	10.2	8.6	21.0	31.7	29.8
Chicama	783.3	68.6	122.7	236.1	185.1	61.2	26.6	17.5	11.7	8.8	13.0	16.3	15.7
Moche	320.8	47.1	50.8	97.4	77.5	20.3	5.1	2.0	1.0	0.9	5.9	7.4	5.2
Virú	105.4	14.4	27.0	37.9	27.0	9.8	1.5	0.7	0.3	0.1	2.5	3.9	1.3
Santa	4593.9	510.4	720.7	943.3	690.0	334.5	209.9	155.1	138.1	135.8	187.2	240.1	328.8
Nepeña	74.7	6.9	17.5	28.1	17.1	3.5	1.8	1.6	1.3	0.9	1.0	0.9	1.1
Casma	172.4	28.7	36.4	57.4	42.7	5.4	0.3	0.1	0.1	0.1	1.1	4.0	5.2

[a]Based on figures for the years 1948-1957 reported in Robinson (1964:166-169).

[b]Periods with monthly discharge figures representing moderate or severe water deficits (i.e., less than 20×10^6 m^3 of flow) for irrigation agriculture are shown with dashed underlining (cf. ONERN 1972b: 327; 1973:213; Reparaz 1956:34-35).

ciocultural adaptation within that setting (e.g., coastal agricultural practices). The first section, on the natural environment, begins with a description of the main geological and biological features of the region, as well as a discussion of what changes can be discerned in these features over the 3000+ years of the prehispanic sequence. This leads to a brief examination of the probable nature of the pre-agricultural paleoenvironment of the Lower Santa Valley. The effect of geomorphological processes on prehispanic site preservation is then discussed, specifically in relation to the nature of our sample of sites and other remains. The section on natural environment ends with a discussion of the approach taken in delineating the regional survey boundaries and in defining subregional environmental sectors.

The second section, on the cultural environment, begins with a description of relevant aspects of modern occupation in the survey region—including the nature and location of modern towns and roads, regional demography, changes in overall settlement patterns from prehispanic to recent times, and the implications of traditional house types for reconstructing the nature of ancient dwellings. Following this, the effect of modern occupation on prehispanic site preservation is discussed, thereby rounding out the examination of the effects of both natural and cultural processes on the sample of sites. The discussion continues with the presentation of data on traditional agriculture in the Santa region, followed by a reconstruction based on the 1979–80 research of the prehispanic agricultural subsistence system. The section on cultural environment ends with a brief discussion of ethnohistoric data related to the Lower Santa region.

THE NATURAL ENVIRONMENT

Present-day Setting: Land and Sea

Santa Valley: sierra sector. The Santa River rises in Laguna Aguashcocha (Fig. 1), at an elevation of over 4000 m above sea level in the frigid, grassy *puna* to the south of the Callejón de Huaylas. From this point it runs for 230 km in the Andean sierra before breaking through the western flank of the cordillera in its final 70-km descent to the ocean. The principal geological feature of the highland sector is the narrow valley of the Callejón itself, which starts roughly at Cátac, some 45 km downstream from the source, and extends for a distance of over 100 km to Caráz, located at an elevation of 2285 m. Between Cátac and Caráz, the Callejón de Huaylas is flanked on the east by the higher snowcapped Cordillera Blanca, which captures the bulk of the precipitation brought by the prevailing easterlies out of the Amazon lowlands, and on the west by the lower snowless Cordillera Negra. The river descends on a relatively gentle 1% gradient through the Callejón, flanked by extensive settlements and field systems cultivated by rainfall agriculture. The subsistence-settlement system of this area is located primarily in the *quechua* ecological zone between elevations of 2300 and 4000 m above sea level. This entire highland sector of the Santa—including the upper reaches in the puna and the lower reaches in the Callejón—serves as a giant catchment basin for the river which extends over an area of some 10,200 km² (ONERN 1972b:273). In sharp contrast, other rivers in this part of the North Coast either penetrate only a short distance into the sierra (e.g., Moche, Virú, and Chao) or have headwaters on the dry upper western slopes of the Cordillera Negra (e.g., Nepeña and Casma). Thus, as shown in Table 1, none of these nearby rivers to the north and south even approaches the volume of discharge of the Santa River.

Downstream from the Callejón, in the short 30-km distance between the small towns of Caráz and Huallanca, the Santa drops below the zone of abundant annual rainfall and descends on a steep 3% gradient through the spectacular desert gorge of the Cañón del Pato. It is worth noting that the precipitous and essentially impassable nature of this deep gorge forms a barrier that, prior to the construction of the modern road, would have effectively cut off riverine communication between the highland and coastal areas of the Santa Valley—thus making

Plate 8. View upriver in the narrow desert canyon just below the Santa-Tablachaca confluence

them in effect two distinct environmental microcosms connected only tenuously by the river itself. Indeed, as argued later, it is probable that prehispanic contacts between people of the two areas mostly occurred via relatively easier and more direct access routes that run directly over the intervening Cordillera Negra.

In the final part of the sierra sector, the river descends on a relatively gentle 1.5% gradient over a distance of 55 km between Huallanca and Chuquicara, a small settlement located in the uppermost reaches of our survey region. Throughout this distance, the river is flanked almost continuously by very steep desertic slopes of the cordillera, and modern and prehispanic settlement is confined to a few pockets of wider land and less steep mountain slopes. Most of the latter extend up into the quechua zone of annual rainfall in the 10-km distance between the settlements of Huallanca and Yuracmarca (i.e., at a point some 45 km farther upriver beyond the uppermost part of the survey region).

Santa Valley: coastal sector. The upper part of the survey region begins 2 km above Chuquicara and the confluence of the Santa and Tablachaca Rivers, precisely at the point where the canyon begins gradually to open up (and thus permit human occupation and agriculture)

as it approaches the coast. In its first 230 km the river has descended 3500 m in elevation, from over 4000 m to just 500 m above sea level, and has entered the *pre-montane* desert ecological zone, which extends between the ocean and roughly 500–600 m above sea level (ONERN 1972b). It is here that the first tiny pockets of irrigable land begin to occur, following the essentially uninhabitable canyon of the Santa lying immediately upstream (Plate 8). Here also, one finds the beginning of an essentially continuous distribution of prehispanic sites extending along both sides of the river in its final 70-km descent to the sea. Although the narrow valley floor in this upper part of the survey area is well within the pre-montane desert zone, canyon slopes to the north, east, and southeast extend very steeply up above 3000 m elevation into the quechua zone over a relatively short distance of 25 km (see Fig. 2). Thus, although the Cañón del Pato cuts off easy access via the river to the Callejón de Huaylas, other highland areas with modern (and presumably prehispanic) settlements focused on rainfall agriculture lie within a distance that probably could have been walked in a single day's journey.

It is not until a point some 15 km farther downriver from the Santa-Tablachaca confluence that the valley bottom begins to widen appreciably beyond its narrow

Plate 9. Huaca Corral area, looking downriver in the middle part of the Coast sector

Plate 10. Mouth of Lower Santa River, looking south at point where Panamerican highway crosses the valley

20

sierra configuration of 50–100 m. Over the next 30 km, as the river enters the middle part of the coastal sector, the valley floor expands gradually in width—ranging from 500 m in the upper reaches to about 2 km in the lower area (Plate 9). The active floodplain of the river also broadens considerably in this area, reaching a maximum width of nearly 800 m at several points. The main advantage of this increased width for human inhabitants of the area is that the total volume of river flow—which over a year's time averages a massive 140 m³/second (ONERN 1972b:288)—is spread out thinly enough among several channels to permit the Santa to be crossed by wading on foot. But this generally can be done only during the months from May-October—i.e., at a time corresponding to the dry season in the sierra. Even then, however, the Santa discharges such tremendous quantities of water that attempting to wade across it is a risky proposition at best (as we found out during one such attempt).

From the 16th- and 17th-century Spanish documentary sources, we know that the inhabitants of Santa and other coastal valleys used small rafts constructed of gourd floats placed in nets to get across deeper sections of the river. Travelers and cargo were placed on these rafts, and several persons would swim ahead pulling them by ropes while one or two more swam behind and pushed (Cobo 1964 [1653], II:266). But crossing the Santa even by means of the relatively secure rafts apparently was a harrowing experience for the Spanish newcomers, and some who tried to get across by swimming on their own were drowned in the attempt (Cieza de León 1969 [1553]:325). Although gourd rafts and other types of watercraft (e.g., inflated sea lion skins) have not been found in prehispanic contexts, it is probable they were used to cross the Santa and other coastal rivers from the time of the earliest human occupation.

In the final 17 km of its descent to the ocean, the river drops on a nearly level .6% gradient. Although the width of the active floodplain is about the same as in the middle sector, the valley floor widens substantially here—ranging from over 2 km wide in the upper reaches to about 8 km wide along the beaches (Plate 10). As shown in Fig. 3, the lower sector of the valley is connected to the mouth of Quebrada de Lacramarca via a 5-km section of valley floor that slopes very gently down to the latter area. Because of this feature, the Santa Valley in a sense may be considered as having two mouths, or outlets, to the Pacific—at least in terms of topography. Indeed, although there is no presently apparent sign that the river discharged via the Lacramarca mouth during the past several thousand years, this may well have been the case at some point in recent geological times (i.e., during the Pleistocene). In any case, no geological impediment stands in the way of bringing water from Santa to Lacramarca via simple contour canals, and this was done

during at least one period in the prehispanic sequence, as it is today.

Throughout most of the coastal sector, the active floodplain of the river has cut fairly deeply into the valley floor, with depths ranging from over 10 m in the uppermost part of the survey area to less than 3 m in the lower part. Although the Santa carries large volumes of water throughout the year, a comparison of two complete sets of airphotos taken some 25 years apart (in 1943 and 1969) indicates that in most sections the river does not meander noticeably over the short term. The principal exception to this pattern occurs at the juncture between the middle and lower parts of the valley, where the valley narrows down to a width of less than 1 km along a stretch of some 4 km (see Fig. 3). The floodplain occupies roughly half of the valley floor in this area and is not deeply downcut, probably due to the presence of a massive block of underlying granite (see ONERN 1972b, Mapa No. 2: Geográfico Minero). In 1943, the Santa ran immediately adjacent to cliffs along most of the west edge of the narrows, and, as is clear from the airphoto taken in that year, cultivated land was confined almost entirely to the east side of the river. By 1969, and continuing on until our research in 1979–80, the river occupied the middle of the narrows, and much more land had become available to the west of the river. At the same time, less land is presently available for cultivation along the east edge.

The short-term meandering of the river in this area has at least two implications for analysis of prehispanic subsistence-settlement systems. First, in a sector where the river meanders back and forth across the valley floor, the location and size of settlements seem at least in part to be dependent upon the availability of farmland. Thus, while only one or two houses appear in the 1943 airphoto along the west edge of the narrows, there are now as many as ten houses located on formerly active floodplain in and around the small settlement of Huaca Corral. Roughly the same number of houses (ca. five) appears to have been present on the east side of the river between 1943 and the present. Second, it is clear from the comparison of the airphoto sets that river width in any given sector remains constant over time. Thus, in carrying out measurements of the amount of land under cultivation it can be safely assumed that total hectarage remains roughly constant over time, irrespective of the precise location of the river. At the same time, it is clear that farmers in Santa are able quickly to reclaim and cultivate land that has recently been part of the active floodplain.

Out on the valley floor away from the river, the principal geological features consist of scattered rocky hills and low stabilized sand dunes. These features are found primarily in the lower part of the valley—specifically in the area to the north of Cerro Tambo Real, a desert range which separates the mouths of Santa and Lacramarca.

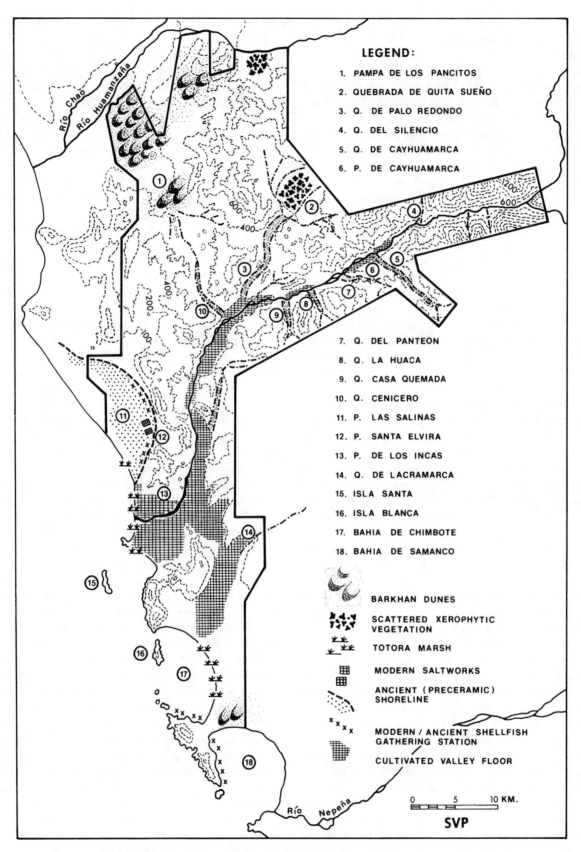

LEGEND:

1. PAMPA DE LOS PANCITOS
2. QUEBRADA DE QUITA SUEÑO
3. Q. DE PALO REDONDO
4. Q. DEL SILENCIO
5. Q. DE CAYHUAMARCA
6. P. DE CAYHUAMARCA
7. Q. DEL PANTEON
8. Q. LA HUACA
9. Q. CASA QUEMADA
10. Q. CENICERO
11. P. LAS SALINAS
12. P. SANTA ELVIRA
13. P. DE LOS INCAS
14. Q. DE LACRAMARCA
15. ISLA SANTA
16. ISLA BLANCA
17. BAHIA DE CHIMBOTE
18. BAHIA DE SAMANCO

BARKHAN DUNES
SCATTERED XEROPHYTIC VEGETATION
TOTORA MARSH
MODERN SALTWORKS
ANCIENT (PRECERAMIC) SHORELINE
MODERN / ANCIENT SHELLFISH GATHERING STATION
CULTIVATED VALLEY FLOOR

0   5   10 KM.

SVP

Fig. 3. Major environmental features of the Lower Santa Valley region.

22

None of the hills and dunes is large enough to show up on the smaller-scale 1:400,000 and 1:100,000 maps included in this report, but all are clearly visible on the large-scale airphotos at 1:15,000. The most prominent of the hills is El Castillo, which rises nearly 100 m above surrounding fields and commands a view of the entire lower part of the valley. El Castillo hill takes its name from a large Guadalupito Period pyramidal structure sitting on its summit, and is located near the desert margin just to the north of the connecting arm between Santa and Lacramarca (see Figs. 99, 100). Farther downvalley, in the area immediately to the west of Cerro Tambo Real, lies Huaca China, another hill with impressive architectural remains dating to Guadalupito times (see Fig. 113). The final one of the more prominent hills is situated adjacent to the north side of the Panamerican bridge (see Fig. 6). The modern settlement of Pueblo Joven San Ignacio occupies the northwest edge of this hill, while extensive prehispanic remains dating to Late Suchimancillo, Early Tanguche, and Early Tambo Real Periods occupy its summit and eastern side.

Most of the dunes found in the midst of the valley floor lie in the area to the north of Cerro Tambo Real. Nearly all of them rise some 2–6 m above surrounding fields, and are therefore high enough to have survived encroachment at the hands of farmers seeking additional land to place under cultivation. Their long-term stability is attested to by the fact that prehispanic remains were found on every one of ten major dunes, most of which are covered with occupational remains that date to Late Tambo Real Period. By far the largest of the ten dunes is the one occupied by the Late Tambo Real site of Alto Perú, which covers an area of nearly 20 ha (see Fig. 160; see also Kosok 1965, p. 192, Fig. 13). A modern settlement—also known as Alto Perú—now occupies most of the site.

The maritime environment.   Included within the survey region is a long section of Pacific coastline which extends for a distance of 50 km, from Bahía de Samanco to a point some 10 km north of the river outlet. In the northern area, most of the land adjacent to the shoreline is occupied by thick totora (*Scirpus* sp.) marshes which extend at least 100 m inland from the ocean. These marshes would have had substantial value in prehispanic times as a source of reeds for constructing *caballitos*, the small one-person crafts used for fishing offshore waters at least as early as the Moche Period (cf. Benson 1972:72–73). As shown in Fig. 3, scattered areas of totora marsh are also present along the shoreline to the south of the river mouth, as well as along the east edge of Bahía de Chimbote. But most of the southern side of the Santa Valley mouth is occupied by gently sloping sandy beaches and adjacent higher dunes, the latter extending inland an average of 200 m from the ocean. Judging from our field observations in these areas, the sublittoral zone

adjacent to the beaches appears to drop fairly steeply off to the west.

Aside from the beaches and totora marshes, the other two principal microenvironments along the ocean include: (1) the area of steep cliffs along Cerro de Chimbote, located between the mouths of Santa and Lacramarca; and (2) the protected inland side of the large peninsula which juts out from the coastline in the far southern sector. The low cliffs at the base of the steep western slopes of Cerro de Chimbote run for a distance of 6 km, and are frequented by line fishermen from Santa and Lacramarca who approach the area using a narrow trail that provides the only easy access. Since we found a number of sites dating back as far as the Preceramic on slopes adjacent to the trail, it is probable that this route has been in existence since the earliest human occupation of the region—i.e., over a period of more than 3700 years. It is also of interest to note that some of the prehispanic sites in this area date to the ceramic periods following the time when caballito rafts are depicted on Moche pottery. Thus, even during later periods when inhabitants of the region were clearly able to get out in the ocean to engage in net fishing, the presence of sites along the Cerro de Chimbote cliffs suggests that line fishing from shore also played a part in subsistence activities.

A similar area of cliffs and adjacent deep water runs for 10 km along the western edge of the peninsula separating Bahías de Chimbote and Samanco, in the far southern sector. However, nearly all of the cliffs in this area rise steeply out of the ocean to heights of over 100 m and were therefore obviously unsuitable for line fishing. On the other hand, the shoreline areas along the eastern edge of the peninsula, to the north and south of the narrow sandy strip of land which connects to the mainland, not only are the focus of intensive maritime gathering activities at present but appear to have been so during at least one of the prehispanic periods as well. During the survey of this part of the peninsula, a total of 30 prehispanic sites was found on gentler slopes overlooking the calm waters of Bahías de Chimbote and Samanco. Judging from associated ceramics, almost all of these sites date to Early Tanguche Period (see Fig. 120). Among the associated shellfish remains found on the surface are the following (species name, where known, is given in parentheses): almeja (*Semele* sp.); caracol grande; caracol negro (*Tegula atra*); carretero, or puñete; choro (*Aulacomya ater*); concha abanico (*Argopecten* sp.); marisco (*Fissurella* sp.); navajuela (*Tagelus* sp.); and señorita (*Crepipatella* sp.). Remains of marine crustaceans also were found, including crabs of the type called cangrejo peludo.

Our informants for the Spanish name identification of these marine species from archaeological contexts were several young divers who, along with several dozen others from the Chimbote area, make their living searching for the same species in the shallow waters at the edge of the bays. They not only were able to identify unhesitatingly each species by its Spanish name, but provided information on where each is found. According to them, sublittoral waters at the edge of the bay are divided by local divers into two zones on the basis of depth: *no profundo* (shallow, or less than 3 m) and *profundo* (deep, or greater than 3 m). Nearly all of the above species are found in the shallower inshore waters extending out from the shoreline some 25–50 m, depending on the slope of the sublittoral area. Two species (navajuela and caracol grande) were identified as coming from deeper waters farther offshore, while a third (almeja) appears to be found primarily in waters of intermediate depth. One additional note of interest is that we saw little evidence in this area of marucha (*Donax* sp.), which is almost the only species of shellfish found at presumably contemporaneous sites in the western part of the road-settlement network of the Santa-Chao desert (see Figs. 118, 121).

Desert mountains, quebradas, and pampas. As Fig. 3 makes clear, most of the length of the valley floor between the Santa-Tablachaca confluence and the ocean is flanked by generally rugged desert mountains. These mountains extend nearly continuously along both sides of the valley, providing a natural barrier to outside entry that rises to heights of over 3000 m in the upper sector and 200 m in the lower sector. Downriver from the steep canyon walls of the uppermost sector, however, the terrain becomes more varied—with lower rolling hills and intervening pampas located adjacent to the cultivated valley floor. Aside from the narrow gently sloping coastal plain that lies adjacent to the ocean, the principal routes of travel in and out of the main valley area consist of a number of quebradas which, over countless millenia, have cut narrow passages down through the mountains along both edges of the valley.

On the north desert margin, the two principal dry washes of this nature are Quebrada Cenicero and Quebrada Palo Redondo (Fig. 3). *Quebrada Cenicero*, the narrower and more steeply ascending of the two extends up to the northwest to a low pass that communicates with Pampa de los Pancitos and the broad inland plain leading to the middle and lower sectors of Chao Valley. *Quebrada Palo Redondo*, the broader of the two, extends gently up to the northeast from the valley floor. Its upper northern branches lead toward a higher pass that provides access to the uppermost sector of Chao, while its upper northeastern branches lead up toward the main western slopes of the cordillera. Indeed, these latter branches penetrate far enough into the sierra that they occasionally bring flash floods down over the boulder-strewn surface of the quebrada, coating the central channel with a thin layer of red silt. Because of this, subsurface water is high enough in the upper part of the quebrada to support a thick stand of algarrobo trees

which extends over several square kilometers. The water table is too low to reach by hand-dug wells, however, and water for the family that lives here making a living by cutting wood and producing charcoal has to be trucked in via a rough dirt road across Pampa de los Pancitos from the Chao Valley (see Fig. 6). The members of this family are the only present human occupants of the entire desert area between Santa and Chao Valleys.

A relatively greater number of quebradas penetrates the south desert margin, primarily in the upvalley area opposite Quebrada Palo Redondo. Proceeding down from the uppermost one, they include *Quebrada de Cayhuamarca, Quebrada del Panteón, Quebrada La Huaca, Quebrada Casa Quemada*, and *Quebrada de Vinzos* (see Fig. 3; Note: Vinzos is shown unlabeled on the map; it extends up to the north from the upper northeastern corner of the lower valley sector). Of all these washes, only Quebrada de Cayhuamarca extends well up into the mountains. In its upper reaches, the quebrada is contained within a narrow, steepsided canyon that runs up onto the main flank of the cordillera. From this point on, a series of trails and settlements leads across the Cordillera Negra to the Callejón de Huaylas. As argued later, Quebrada de Cayhuamarca is one of the most likely routes of prehispanic communication between the Lower Santa region and the Callejón—especially during Late Suchimancillo Period, when intensive coast-sierra contacts appear to have taken place. It may also have served as a route of access connecting the upper sectors of Santa with those of Lacramarca.

Most of the desert lying between Santa and Chao Valleys consists of coastal outliers of the main Andean chain, with mountains ranging in elevation between 500 and 1500 m above sea level. Due to the rugged nature of the terrain as well as the general lack of flora and fauna, signs of ancient and modern human occupation are here confined entirely to the few intervening quebradas and pampas that provide principal routes of travel between the two valleys and points beyond. The primary area of flatter terrain in the Santa-Chao desert is *Pampa de los Pancitos*. As shown in Fig. 3, this pampa forms a natural strategic point where several of the quebradas leading in and out of Santa Valley converge. One of these—Quebrada Cenicero—has been discussed above. Another quebrada system leads down to the southeast toward Quebrada Palo Redondo from Pampa de los Pancitos, via a low desert pass. A final route to Santa Valley from Pancitos leads due south across Coscomba Pass, and thence down onto the narrow coastal plain. Two additional routes lead north toward Chao Valley from Pampa de los Pancitos. The first one heads toward the northwest, crossing a large gently sloping pampa whose entire northern end is covered by lines of barkhan dunes. Fed by the prevailing southwesterlies and sand blown inland off the beaches, these dunes probably have been a feature of this part of the desert since before the earliest human occupation of the region. The second main route of travel to the north from the Pampa de los Pancitos "hub" leads toward the middle sector of Chao Valley along the upper eastern edge of the lines of barkhan dunes.

It is of interest to note that extensive remains of pre-hispanic rock-lined roads and associated settlements are found along every one of the natural routes of travel between Santa and Chao Valleys mentioned above. On the other hand, the only modern route of travel crossing the desert from Santa to Chao is the Panamerican highway, which lies along the far western edge of the survey region.

The final area of the Santa-Chao desert where large areas of flat, open terrain provided major routes of pre-hispanic intervalley travel is *Pampa Las Salinas*, which extends over a huge expanse of 80 km² immediately to the north of the cultivated mouth of Santa Valley. As discussed in the next section, the greater part of this pampa appears to have been formed over the last 3500 years during a series of well-demarcated episodes of tectonic uplifting. Of principal interest at this point, however, is the indication that this area and adjacent *Pampa Santa Elvira* were major centers of prehispanic communication routes and commerce—as evidenced by the complex local network of roads, sites, canals, serpentine field systems, walls, and the presence of a large salt-works. This last consists of two contiguous areas where a relatively thin layer of soil has been dug away in modern times (and almost certainly earlier) to expose heavily salt-laden subsurface waters. A network of modern dikes has been constructed in each of these areas, forming a series of evaporative ponds in which the salt is produced. Since several large Early Tanguche sites were found associated with the saltworks (e.g., see SVP-ETAN-249 site description, in Wilson 1985), it seems probable that salt production in this area dates back at least as early as the Middle Horizon Period.

Several other smaller pampas are found within the survey region, all of them located immediately adjacent to the north and south sides of the main valley floor, and all serving as important foci of prehispanic occupation during one or more periods. Proceeding downvalley from the uppermost one, they include Pampa de Cayhuamarca, Pampa Blanca, Pampa de Vinzos, and Pampa de los Incas (Fig. 3). *Pampa de Cayhuamarca* lies on the south desert margin of the upvalley sector, 2.5 km to the southeast of the cultivated valley floor and 250 m in elevation above it. A high ridge lies between the pampa and the valley floor, and access involves following circuitous routes via Quebrada de Cayhuamarca and Quebrada del Panteón, which flank it respectively on the northeast and southwest. Pampa de Cayhuamarca is therefore in a naturally very defensible position, and was the focus of an extensive group of habitation and citadel sites during the pre-Guadalupito ceramic periods (e.g., see sites SVP-

CAY-17 through SVP-CAY-20, in Fig. 23; see also Fig. 40, in Wilson 1985).

Pampa Blanca lies some 7 km farther downvalley, on the north desert margin opposite the mouths of Quebradas del Panteón and La Huaca. In addition to being the focus of a major prehispanic canal and field system, this pampa contains a large Guadalupito mound and was heavily occupied in Early Tanguche Period as well. *Pampa de Vinzos* lies 11 km farther downvalley from Pampa Blanca, on the south desert margin some 100 m in elevation above the cultivated valley floor. This pampa was the focus of occupation during several periods—including Early Suchimancillo, Late Suchimancillo, and Guadalupito. *Pampa de los Incas* is located near the mouth of the valley, on the north desert margin, and covers a large expanse of over 2 km². It formed the single major focus of occupation during Guadalupito Period, and was occupied by scattered habitation and cemetery sites throughout the remainder of the sequence.

Geological Changes Over Time

Some of the data indicating changes in the appearance of the physical environment have been discussed in the preceding section, specifically with regard to the evidence of limited meandering of the river over the short term. In this section several other geomorphological processes that have brought about both localized and widespread changes in the environment will be discussed. These include tectonic uplifting, earthquakes, major floods, dune movement, and riverine deposition of alluvium on the valley floor. With the exception of alluvial deposition, all are processes whose effects we were able to document with reasonable certainty during the course of the research. Although, as argued later, most of the processes have probably had little effect on site preservation over the past 3700+ years, it is nevertheless important for understanding the physical context within which sociocultural adaptation has occurred briefly to establish their nature and extent.

Coastal uplifting. Probably the most dramatic evidence of geomorphological change is the tectonic uplifting that has taken place in Pampa Las Salinas. During the survey of this area, we discovered a total of at least five major ancient shorelines that run in a north-south direction across the present coastal plain, between the ocean and a point some 5 km inland. All of these shorelines show up very distinctly on the 1:16,000-scale airphotos used to conduct the work here. As indicated in Fig. 3, the highest and oldest of the shorelines begins near the present beach, 3.5 km to the north of the river mouth. From this point, it heads inland in a northeast direction and then, following the 25-m contour line along gentler slopes at the base of the coastal range, turns out again toward the present coastline. The entire ancient shoreline is demarcated by a white belt of shellfish fragments that extends in a line 50–100 m wide around the former sublittoral area adjacent to the ancient beach. At various points above the ancient beach, we found a series of 15 small sites of probable Preceramic date (e.g., see Fig. 21). This indicates that the first major episode of uplifting (which led to the formation of Shoreline No. 2) occurred at some time following the establishment of a maritime subsistence-settlement focus in the area.

The other four ancient shorelines converge on the oldest one at roughly the same point in the far southern part of Pampa Las Salinas (see Fig. 12). Beginning about 1 km inland from the present beach, all of them lie more or less parallel to the coastline in a closely spaced grouping, separated one from the other by intervals of 300 to 900 m. The overall grouping itself is located approximately midway between the present coastline and the most ancient shoreline. With regard to physical appearance, each one of the shorelines is delineated on its inland side by a narrow, rocky ridge that rises several meters above the adjacent plain. Aside from several small rock features of possible cultural origin, no indication was found of prehispanic occupation on or adjacent to Shorelines 2, 3, 4, and 5.

Earthquakes. Considering the proximity of the active subduction zone of the Nazca Plate and the resulting movement this brings about on the adjacent landmass at the western edge of the South American continent, it is not surprising that the area in and around Santa is one of frequent earthquake activity. For example, minor tremors occurred a number of times during our stay in Santa Valley. The most recent major quake, or *sismo*, of May 31, 1970, had its epicenter in the ocean off Casma Valley. It not only brought down most adobe structures in Santa but caused some structural damage to rock-walled citadels dating back to Cayhuamarca Period. Indeed, an aerial photograph taken in 1931 by Shippee-Johnson of one of these citadels shows it to be in essentially pristine condition. The citadel was still in good enough condition nearly 50 years later to allow us to prepare a transit-stadia plan (see Fig. 34), but it had fallen down considerably compared to its earlier state. It therefore seems probable that its present deteriorated condition is due in large part to the sismo of 1970. Most importantly, these data imply that such megaquakes have occurred very infrequently in the past several thousand years. This assertion appears to be borne out by the fact that we found little evidence anywhere in the survey region of major changes in the physical environment brought about by landslides or slippage of rocks on steeper slopes.

Flooding. In addition to causing extensive damage to structures in the coastal area, the sismo of 1970 brought down a huge chunk of snow and ice off Huascarán peak in the Cordillera Blanca. The resulting mass swept down a steep canyon bringing huge boulders and other debris with it, and, near the bottom, leapt over the 200-m high bank of the canyon and buried the town of Yungay along with most of its 18,000 inhabitants. Reaching the narrow bottom of the Callejón below Yungay, the slide temporarily blocked the flow of the Santa River and caused a massive buildup of water. Shortly thereafter, the water broke through the slide and swept down the Cañón del Pato and on through the coastal sector of the valley to the sea. The results of this flood are still visible in the uppermost part of the coastal sector, where deep solidified remnants of silt and debris cling to cliffs adjacent to the river in some areas. Several local residents of Santa also informed us that extensive flooding occurred alongside the river in the lower part of the valley, with consequent destruction of fields and farm buildings.

During the rare years of major El Niño occurrences (e.g., 1891, 1925, 1941, and 1982), much more widespread and destructive conditions of flooding are present on the North Coast. For example, during the 1925 occurrence, some 395 mm of rainfall were recorded in Moche Valley during the month of March alone (Murphy 1926:44), with intermittently heavy rains occurring for a period of over two months between February and April. Given the general lack of vegetation on the desert, the flash flooding caused by such infrequent heavy rains usually has disastrous effects on canals, roads, bridges, and habitation structures lying in or near normally dry quebradas. However, while the occurrence of major El Niño conditions is certain to have disrupted prehispanic North Coast agricultural systems, such events are unlikely to have constituted a major limiting factor with respect to the population size of valleys in the area. Instead, as argued in Chapter V, such factors as water supply and the amount of irrigable land are more likely to have set critical limits on demographic potential than the relatively infrequent, short-term disruptions brought about by El Niño-induced flooding. Nevertheless, as I have argued elsewhere (Wilson 1981), one must make a distinction with regard to the effects of El Niño between (1) the relatively minor, reparable damage to agricultural systems; and (2) the severe, year-long decline in biological productivity of marine waters. This latter effect of major El Niño occurrences clearly would have constituted a critical limiting factor for primarily maritime subsistence-settlement systems of the late Preceramic (for an example of a failure to appreciate these clear distinctions and their demographic implications, see Quilter and Stocker 1983).

Eolian sand. As mentioned earlier, much of the northwestern corner of the survey region is characterized by deposits of windblown sand that travel across open areas of the desert in the form of barkhan dunes. Although the principal area where such dunes form is located some 3 km out to the northwest of Pampa de los Pancitos, scattered barkhans also lie across the Pancitos area itself (e.g., see Fig. 134). Whether scattered widely or grouped more closely together, all of the barkhans encountered in the survey region consist of discrete dunes surrounded by areas of relatively sand-free, rock-covered desert. Because of this characteristic, as well as the fact that barkhans travel nondestructively as a function of the movement of individual grains of sand falling forward down their leeward slipface (Shelton 1966:198), archaeological features are not damaged by their passage and can be traced easily among even the more closely spaced dunes.

In addition to the barkhans, another type of sand deposit found in the area of Pampa de los Pancitos consists of long dunes of triangular shape with knife-edged crests. These dunes form on the leeward side of smaller hills rising above the pampa, and are characterized by a long tapered point that is shaped by the southwesterly winds blowing over and around the sides of the hills (see Fig. 134). Like the barkhans, they are found in association with some of the prehispanic remains of Pampa de los Pancitos area. However, unlike the barkhans, they are essentially immobile and undoubtedly have existed on the same spot since a time substantially prior to any human occupation of the region.

Alluvial deposition. Compared to tectonic uplifting, earthquakes, flooding, and eolian sand, the deposition of canal-borne silt on the valley floor is probably the most subtle process of change that has occurred in the survey region. We were able to find only a few places where thick deposits of alluvium could be viewed in profile, but it is likely that alluvial deposition has been gradually building up the valley floor since the beginning of irrigation agriculture. In other words, this process is most likely due to the cultural practice of irrigation, and not to the natural buildup that occurs during massive floods such as the one brought about by the 1970 earthquake. If one were to imagine that silt-bearing canal systems had never been constructed on the desert margins and the valley floor, then it is likely that a distinctly different valley floor would have to be postulated compared to the one seen at present. Indeed, as discussed later, alluvial deposition is the process most likely to have had an effect on site preservation—at least in the lower sector of the valley.

Reconstruction of the Paleoenvironment

As the preceding discussion of tectonic uplifting and alluvial deposition implies, the earliest inhabitants of the region lived in an environment that was markedly different in some respects from that of the present. It is also clear that the valley floor and the shallow inshore waters

of the Pacific—which were the two principal foci of prehispanic subsistence activities—must themselves be viewed as dynamic aspects of the overall socioenvironmental setting. In other words, both must be viewed as changing in response to geological as well as cultural forces, and thereby posing novel adaptive problems over time.

Coastal area. With respect to the maritime environment, the evidence provided by the series of ancient shorelines indicates that the coastline north of the river has changed substantially in configuration since the beginning of human occupation in the area. From the standpoint of human adaptive systems, however, the more important aspect of the changing coastline is the *absence* of marine middens along all but the oldest of the shorelines. This implies that uplifting may have reduced significantly the productivity of the shellfish beds that thrived in the shallow sublittoral waters of Las Salinas Period. Thus, although the abundance of maritime sites along protected waters of Bahías de Chimbote and Samanco indicates that another marine microenvironment of equal or greater productivity was available, it cannot be ruled out that the process of coastal uplifting was one of the factors leading to changes in overall subsistence-settlement focus. In any case, as we shall see in discussing the Cayhuamarca and Vinzos Periods, the subsistence-settlement system of the early ceramic periods was substantially different from that of Las Salinas Period.

Valley floor area. With respect to the terrestrial environment, certain characteristics of the present setting as well as the nature of traditional agriculture suggest hypotheses about how the valley floor looked prior to the start of irrigation agriculture. First of all, as mentioned earlier, fully 93% of the runoff carried out of the sierra by the river makes it to the ocean—in spite of the practice of intensive agriculture in nearly every possible location on the floor of the valley. Thus, unlike most other nearby rivers whose much more limited water supply is entirely used up for irrigation prior to reaching the sea, the Santa undoubtedly has continued a pattern of downcutting in the river bed throughout the time since the introduction of irrigation agriculture. The Santa is therefore probably somewhat more entrenched than other nearby rivers.

Second, like other nearby valleys, the main valley floor during this long period probably has been in an aggrading state brought about by the transport of silt-laden waters onto the fields via the canal systems, as mentioned above. Since the general practice in valleys like Santa is to construct fields in a series of level, linchet-like terraces descending step by step downvalley and in toward the river away from the main canals on the desert margin, the present setting is clearly much different in appearance from the pre-agricultural environment. Although one can only speculate on its general morphology, it seems likely that the valley floor at this early point in time sloped gently downvalley and in toward the river in most sectors.

Finally, judging from the thick *matorral* scrub vegetation that presently thrives on the higher water table in a thin strip along the edges of the active floodplain (e.g., see Fig. 9), it is probable that a significantly larger portion of the pre-agricultural valley floor was covered by such vegetation (roughly estimated to have covered 60 km²). However, given a gently sloping valley floor and a correspondingly much deeper water table out away from the river—especially in the wider middle and lower parts of the valley—it is likely that riverine plants would give way to scattered xerophytic vegetation within a kilometer or so of the river. Finally, judging from the very thinly scattered vegetation of the unirrigated upper reaches of Quebrada de Lacramarca, it is likely that xerophytic plants eventually would thin out altogether within a distance of two or three kilometers away from the river.

Given this scenario, then, it is probable that the fringes of the pre-agricultural valley floor were characterized by very sparse vegetation, especially on the lower valley floor. This would also have been the case in the lower part of Lacramarca, where only the central portion of the quebrada has a water table high enough to support thicker stands of xerophytic vegetation. In sum, as opposed to the present appearance of the valley floor—which, from the steeper desert margins inward to the river, is nearly everywhere covered by cultivated fields and associated plants thriving on the universally high water table—the pre-agricultural environment would have been characterized by much less extensive vegetation. Proceeding in toward the river in the middle and lower sectors, one would have encountered in sequential order the following microenvironments: (1) the steeper, barren slopes of the main desert margin; (2) a transitional zone of thinly distributed xerophytic vegetation several kilometers in width, interspersed with large patches of essentially barren valley floor; and (3) a zone of thicker riverine matorral vegetation within a kilometer or so of the river.

It may also be suggested that the relatively larger size of the riverine matorral zone compared to that present today would have provided an attractive niche for various fauna—possibly including deer, as well as foxes, birds, and lizards. In sharp contrast, the practice of agriculture has now reduced this niche to almost nothing, and nowhere adjacent to the river did we see any animals other than lizards and, very occasionally, foxes. Nevertheless, given the relatively small area covered by riverine matorral even in the pre-agricultural environment, it is unlikely that the fauna and flora of this area ever supported a population in excess of several hundreds of persons (e.g., the population estimate for the inland sector of the valley during Las Salinas Period is slightly over 400 persons).

Geomorphology and Prehispanic Site Preservation

The physical environment of the Santa region obviously has been subject to various kinds of changes over time. However, it appears likely that none of these changes has had widespread cataclysmic effects anywhere in the survey area; rather, the data indicate that the appearance of the physical environment has changed in generally slow, incremental fashion over the 37+ centuries of human occupation. Thus, while major geological forces have been exerted continually on the coastal area as a function of the ongoing tectonic processes that characterize the western edge of the continent, *we found no evidence of changes that can be described as catastrophic*. In other words, there is no evidence in the Lower Santa region that major chunks of land have fallen out to sea or onto the valley floor to be washed away by the river, leaving what one researcher in the area to the north of Santa has called "white holes"—thereby characterizing a purported process that somehow parallels in earthly terms a well-known (and substantially less theoretical) astrophysical phenomenon of opposite hue.

Indeed, one of the major conclusions to be drawn from the results of our research in Santa is that, in looking at the period-to-period development of the regional subsistence-settlement system, there is an essentially continuous and orderly succession of changes that parallels rather closely in sociocultural terms the gradual changes that have been described as characterizing geomorphological processes. While this has important implications that will be discussed later, here it is important to point out that this fundamental characteristic of the archaeological record of the Lower Santa region in and of itself provides substantial support for the arguments made about the noncatastrophic, gradual nature of geological change in the area.

In the following discussion of prehispanic site preservation, the terrestrial environment is divided into two basic areas: (1) the irrigable valley floor; and (2) the desert margins, including all noncultivable land in the survey region.

Irrigable valley floor. As mentioned earlier, it is probable that significant alluvial deposition has occurred in almost all parts of the cultivated valley floor. If it is assumed that any sites were located on the valley floor itself—especially earlier ones with insubstantial architecture—then it is likely they would have been buried gradually by alluvium carried in by the irrigation canals over the hundreds of years following their abandonment. However, given the fact that we found no deeper cuts in the valley floor where alluvial strata could be examined for signs of cultural debris, the only present means of

Table 2. Estimated Hectares of Prehispanic Irrigable Land in the Lower Santa Valley[a]

Sector	Subsector	Estimated Ha of Irrigated Land in 1944	Additional Ha of Irrigated Prehispanic Land	Total Ha of Irrigated Prehispanic Land	Sector Subtotal
Upper Valley	Tablones to Chuquicara	73.2	77.0	150.2	470.3
	Pampa Blanca to Tablones	205.5	114.6	320.1	
Middle Valley	Vinzos-Tanguche	1133.2	148.7	1281.9	1431.3
	Huaca Corral-La Toma	149.4	0.0	149.4	
Lower Valley	Rinconada-Santa-Cambio Puente	6179.1	232.9	6412.0	9405.8
	Lacramarca mouth	2748.7	0.0	2748.7	
	Las Salinas desert	0.0	245.1	245.1	
	Total Ha:	10,489.1	818.3	11,307.4	

[a]Estimates are based on planimeter measurements made from tracings of SAN airphotos at 1:10,000 and 1:20,000 scales.

testing for such sites would be to carry out extensive core sampling in the cultivated area of the valley. In any case, during intensive survey of almost all cultivated parts of the valley not covered by thick cane fields or flooded rice paddies, we found no sites on the floor itself in the up-valley sectors and only two sites on the floor in the lower sector.

Interestingly, these two lower valley sites (which date to Guadalupito Period) consist of sherd scatters extending over cultivated fields in the area to the southwest of the modern settlement of Santa (see SVP-GUAD-168, 169; in Fig. 102). Although the presence of sites in this area does not necessarily imply that alluvial deposition has not been a general, ongoing phenomenon on the main valley floor, it does at least imply that this has been less than a universal process. Moreover, although coring would be necessary to attempt a resolution of the problem, it is possible to construct a reasonable scenario whereby it appears unlikely that significant numbers of sites ever were located on the cultivable valley floor.

In the first place, from the settlement pattern data it is clear that the upper and middle sectors were the primary focus of the subsistence-settlement system throughout the early periods from Cayhuamarca through Late Suchimancillo. However, as shown in Fig. 3 (and Table 2), the size of the irrigable valley floor in these sectors is relatively limited. Thus, given the presence of suitable locations for sites on the adjacent desert margins in virtually every part of this area, it is unlikely on general grounds that the valley floor ever was used for anything other than farming. Indeed, as discussed in Chapter V, the analysis of maize-based carrying capacity supports this argument in demonstrating that most, if not all, of the available supply of land in the upvalley area had to be farmed on a multicrop basis from the start of irrigation agriculture in Cayhuamarca Period.

This argument does not at first glance appear to hold up as well for the lower sector of the valley, where the population of any given period probably never approached anything near the potential of the land to support it (see Chapter V). Nevertheless, as in the case of the upvalley sectors, prehispanic sites dating to all ceramic periods from Early Suchimancillo on are distributed nearly continuously along both sides of the valley (see Fig. 15), and many of these sites are of very substantial size. Thus, in contrast to the modern period when larger settlements are located principally out on the valley floor, it appears that the location of preference in prehispanic times was generally the desert margins. A variation on this postulated pattern occurs during Late Tambo Real Period, when there are not only large numbers of sites on the south desert margin but also, as mentioned earlier, on nearly all of the low hills and dunes that rise in the midst of the valley floor. But the fact that so many of these hills and dunes are occupied seems further to underscore the argument that people preferred not to locate settlements on irrigable land. Moreover, it may also be the case that the thicker matorral vegetation occupying the area within a kilometer or two of the river was never cleared away at any time in the prehispanic sequence—either because of technological difficulties or because population levels never rose high enough to make its use necessary for agriculture. If this is so, then it is possible that cleared land was at nearly as much of a premium in the lower valley as it was in the upper and middle valley.

Desert margins. Assessing the nature of prehispanic site preservation in the nonirrigable areas away from the valley floor is much less problematical than in the cultivated areas affected by alluvial deposition. Instead of dealing with what might have occurred, one is able to deal with the actual remains of the hundreds of sites found throughout the survey area—as well as with their local and regional patterning—in assessing the processes of change and preservation throughout the sequence. As implied earlier, the single most important factor bringing about long-term preservation of prehispanic sites on the desert margins and elsewhere away from the valley floor is the fact that significant amounts of rainfall occur only a few times a century. Thus, as in other extremely arid areas of the world such as the Nile Valley, one finds remarkable preservation of organic materials on the surface—even at sites dating back some 3700 years to the Preceramic Period. For example, at SVP-SAL-23, a site located along the oldest Las Salinas shoreline (see Fig. 12), we found excellently preserved fragments of cotton netting associated with lithics, shellfish remains, and whale vertebrae in a context that is clearly preceramic in date.

Elsewhere in the survey area, on the surface of several single-component Early Suchimancillo sites (e.g., SVP-ESUCH-87), we found well preserved fragments of maize cobs dating back roughly to the beginning of the Christian era. Indeed, the same sort of preservation is characteristic of most rock-walled structures in areas that have been left untouched by either subsequent periods of prehispanic occupation or the later, Colonial and modern inhabitants of the region. For example, in the habitation sector of SVP-CAY-4 (see Fig. 26), a site dating back to Early Horizon times in the uppermost part of the main valley area, we found walls essentially intact and standing to their original height of ca. 50 cm. Aside from the finding of organic materials on a few Las Salinas Period sites, however, the earliest general preservation of organic remains in the sequence dates roughly to the time just after B.C./A.D.—i.e., to Early Suchimancillo Period.

The critical point illustrated by this kind of preservation is that one can find mappable remains of structures dating back over 3700 years B.P., as well as substantial amounts of organic materials dating back nearly 2000 years. And all of these remains appear to be on the same desert surface as that occupied by the prehispanic inhabitants. Thus, *in carrying out archaeological research in valleys such as Santa, by careful attention to mapping and collection of surface debris one can retrieve substantially intact and complete data without resorting to excavation.* This is not meant to imply, however, that excavation is not of potentially significant utility in carrying out research in coastal valleys; rather, it points to the fact that, as in the case of Near Eastern *tells*, the formation of archaeological strata in the extremely arid environment of the littoral occurs almost entirely as a function of successive occupations and the resulting buildup of cultural debris.

For example, at some sites we found evidence in pits dug by the *huaquero* grave robbers of cultural strata and organic debris extending down at least 3 m below the surface (e.g., see SVP-ESUCH-126/Huaca Santa and SVP-ETAN-147/Huaca Jedionda site descriptions, in Wilson 1985). However, the buildup of deeper cultural debris appears to have occurred only in limited sectors of these sites—generally restricted to the slopes along their lower edges. Thus, for example, at Huaca Santa it was possible by means of an extensive set of ceramic collections made on the surface throughout the site to ascertain the presence and roughly estimate the areal extent of temporal diagnostics dating to five periods—including Early Suchimancillo, Late Suchimancillo, Late Tanguche, Early Tambo Real, and Late Tambo Real (a sixth, minor component is represented by limited numbers of Guadalupito burials). In general, wherever deeper midden debris was found associated with sites in the survey region, it was still possible through intensive surface survey to find between three and six components—often dating back to the earliest periods in the ceramic sequence. Cultural stratification therefore appears to have been a phenomenon restricted to limited areas of sites, and does not appear to have obliterated most of the earlier occupations at multicomponent sites.

Returning to the geological changes—including uplifting, earthquakes, flooding, and dune movement—that have occurred throughout the sequence, it is appropriate to examine very briefly their specific effects on site preservation. Although tectonic uplifting undoubtedly has brought about a gradual rise in elevation throughout the coastal land surface, it is most evident in the restricted area of Pampa Las Salinas. Yet, while massive forces clearly have been at work here to cause a general rise in elevation of some 10–25 m, prehispanic remains dating to the preceramic and later periods have not been affected in any visible way by the uplifting process. And, as mentioned earlier, while earthquake damage is present in the form of partially fallen walls at some citadel sites in the upvalley sector, nowhere did we find evidence of massive earth movements or landslides covering up areas where prehispanic sites might have been located. Indeed, confirmation of the general preservability of sites throughout both desert margins—even including sites at the base of steeper upvalley slopes—is evident from the essentially continuous distribution of sites of all periods (see Fig. 15).

Damage resulting from flooding, such as that which occurred during the sismo of 1970, appears to have been confined narrowly to the areas immediately adjacent to the river in the upper parts of the main valley. On the other hand, flash flooding in quebradas of the Santa-Chao desert (probably during major El Niño events) has destroyed minor portions of the extensive network of roads which crisscrosses this area (e.g., see Fig. 117). However, the settlement pattern here seems to have been one of confining site locations to the higher ground above quebradas, away from the danger of flooding. Since quebradas constitute a minor percentage of the total desert landscape where the road-settlement network is located, it is a relatively simple matter to reconstruct the portions of roads that have been washed away by occasional floods over the centuries since their construction.

With regard to the barkhan dunes of the far northwestern corner of the Santa-Chao desert, it is possible that a few very small sites have been covered by sand. Because of the discrete nature of dune formation, however, we were able to detect and map with little difficulty the ancient routes of travel by following the continuous, light scatters of sherds that mark them in this area. Interestingly, a number of ancient sites consisting of scattered low, rock-walled structures were found immediately alongside the main lines of barkhan dunes. Assuming continuity of the conditions maintaining their formation, it is therefore likely that the barkhan lines are in the same position today as they were in prehispanic times, and that no sites ever were located in the midst of the dunes themselves.

To sum up this section, if the arguments based on the assessment of data on major geological and agricultural processes affecting site preservation are reasonably correct, then our sample of 1246 occupations essentially approximates a complete one (the effects of modern occupation on site preservation are discussed later, in the section on cultural setting). At the very least, there appears to be no localized sector in the nonirrigated, desertic parts of the survey region where sites of any of the nine ceramic periods have been completely destroyed or covered over. At the same time, while we shall probably never know with certainty whether anything other than a handful of prehispanic sites was located on the cultivable valley floor during one or more periods in the sequence, it seems likely that few sites would have been placed on the critically important irrigable parts of the floor—especially considering the fact that nearly universal use could be (and was) made of nonirrigable site locations on the floor itself as well as throughout the adjacent desert margins.

Delineation of Regional Survey Boundaries

As originally outlined in the grant proposals for the Santa Valley Project, the boundaries of the survey region were to encompass an area of 365 km²—including the lower 50 km of the coastal sector of the river, from Tablones to the ocean, as well as the desert margins within about 2 km on each side of the valley floor. This modest areal coverage therefore would have excluded prehispanic sites of the far southern coastal sector, the mouth of Lacramarca, Pampa Las Salinas, most of the Santa-Chao desert, and the uppermost canyon between Tablones and Chuquicara. As it turned out, however, a fortunate combination of funding, personnel, and time allowed the inclusion of the entire 70 km of the coastal

sector of the river and systematic coverage of an area of over 750 km² (see Fig. 3).

The effective southern (or southeastern) boundary of the research region was extended an average of 4 km out from the valley floor, to the point where the terrain of the south desert margin becomes too steep for locating settlements. The central section of this southern boundary is essentially on the topographic divide between Santa Valley and the upper reaches of Quebrada de Lacramarca. The uppermost section runs up against very steep slopes of the western cordillera, while the lowermost section extends out some 4 km beyond the east edge of Lacramarca and includes all of Bahía de Chimbote and the large peninsula to the south.

The boundaries of the survey region to the north of the river were defined both by the extent of the ancient road-settlement network occupying the main part of the Santa-Chao desert and by the limits of Preceramic Period occupation along the oldest shoreline of Pampa Las Salinas area. The western boundary of the survey here runs roughly along the inland flank of a narrow range of coastal hills, thus excluding only the narrow coastal plain which extends some 20 km up to the mouth of Chao Valley. The northeastern boundary of the survey in the Santa-Chao desert runs roughly along the lower flank of the main cordillera between the two valleys, and then turns inland along very steep Andean slopes toward the Santa-Tablachaca confluence. The far northern boundary of the survey projects out in three broad strips to the edge of Chao, and was delineated so as to include all sites and roads running between Santa and Chao as well as all flatter terrain where prehispanic remains potentially could have been located.

The overall survey region, as so defined, includes (1) all sites associated in any way with the entire irrigable valley floor watered by the coastal sector of the Santa River; (2) all maritime sites located within reasonably easy traveling distance of the water and other resources available on the main valley floors of Santa and Lacramarca; and (3) all sites and roads of the inland part of the Santa-Chao desert. Considering the nearly complete nature of the sample of prehispanic remains, it may thus be argued that the Santa Valley data offer a unique picture of sociocultural adaptation and development within an entire coastal valley microcosm throughout the prehispanic sequence (for discussions of the problem of defining meaningful ecosystem boundaries at the community, or regional, level, see Clapham 1973:15–16, 120–121; Miller 1978:770 ff.; Odum 1971:146 ff.).

Definition of Subregional Environmental Sectors

For comparative purposes, such as understanding relative differences in total hectares of irrigable land and period-to-period changes in settlement and population, the length of the valley has been divided into Upper,

Middle, and Lower Valley sectors, with additional divisions of the survey region including the Coast and Santa-Chao Desert sectors (Fig. 4). As should be clear from the preceding discussion, it is difficult to discuss different parts of the region without making reference to at least these five sectors—although until this point they have been left undefined in any precise way. While the establishment of the five subregional sectors therefore results in part from the need to divide the region into manageable units for discussing period-to-period patterns and trends, an examination of the settlement maps showing the evolution of the subsistence-settlement system throughout the sequence supports the argument that these sectors are also meaningful environmental units in an ecological sense.

The *Upper Valley* sector is defined as the area of the valley floor and adjacent desert margins between the Santa-Tablachaca confluence and Quebrada La Huaca. This sector is roughly 30 km in length, and, as shown in Table 2, contains an estimated total of 470 ha of irrigable land—including both the area of modern cultivation (280 ha) and the area adjacent to prehispanic canals (190 ha). Also included in this sector is the lower part of Quebrada de Cayhuamarca, which, along with adjacent desert slopes, was surveyed to a point some 10 km up from the river to the southeast.

The *Middle Valley* sector is defined as the area of the valley floor and adjacent desert margins between Quebrada La Huaca and the point some 20 km downriver where the valley floor narrows down sharply before opening up to the coastal delta. This sector contains an estimated total of 1430 ha of irrigable land. It should be noted here that the precise location of the dividing line between the Upper and Middle Valley sectors is to some extent arbitrary, with Quebrada La Huaca providing a convenient named location for placement of the line. However, two key aspects of the environmental context suggest that La Huaca is the best choice for the division between the two sectors. First, it is just upvalley above this quebrada where the narrow canyon of the Santa begins to open up as the river breaks through the confines of the main cordillera massif. Second, it is also here where the shorter modern canals of the Tablones and Suchimancillo areas leave off and longer canals leading on downvalley toward the Tanguche and Vinzos areas begin (see Fig. 6 for location of these modern settlements). Indeed, it follows that this breakoff point between canal systems was probably also characteristic of the prehispanic period—with shorter systems in the Upper Valley and relatively longer systems in the Middle Valley sector.

The *Lower Valley* sector includes the valley floor and adjacent desert margins of the lower 15 km of Santa Valley, as well as Pampa Las Salinas and the mouth of Quebrada de Lacramarca. These last two areas were cultivated during one or more periods in the prehispanic

sequence by canals taken off the Santa River, and are therefore logically considered as part of the same overall agricultural sector immediately inland from the ocean. This sector contains an estimated total of 9405 ha of land suitable for prehispanic cultivation, judging both from the location of traditional contour canals as well as from ancient canals found throughout. Also included in this sector are the two principal groups of desert mountains which flank the mouth of Santa Valley—including Cerro Gallinazo and Cerro Las Salinas, on the north, and Cerro Tambo Real and Cerro de la Caja, on the south.

The *Coast* sector is defined as including all prehispanic sites within 1 km of the ocean. As shown in Fig. 3, although a minimal amount of irrigable land and sunken fields are both associated with this sector at the mouth of Santa Valley itself, everywhere else the land adjacent to the modern (and ancient) shoreline consists either of barren desert or thick totora marshes. As mentioned earlier, the length of coastline included within the survey region is roughly 50 km, and probably includes all maritime sites that were focused on Santa and Lacramarca for water and other subsistence needs.

Finally, the *Santa-Chao Desert* sector encompasses the remaining northern part of the survey region, covering some 350 km² of the 750 km² included within the research area. Since the procedure followed in delineating the western, northern, and eastern boundaries of this sector has been discussed above, here it remains only to discuss that followed in defining its southern limits that border on the Middle Valley and the lowermost part of the Upper Valley sector. In reality, the question of the precise location of the southern boundary of Santa-Chao is a moot one, except for Early Tanguche Period when sites run out in an essentially continuous distribution extending clear to Chao Valley (e.g., see Fig. 176). In the area where the boundary runs fairly close to the Middle Valley floor, sites were defined as part of Santa-Chao if they lay along ancient roads out to the northwest beyond the area irrigated by prehispanic canals. In contrast, the southern limits of Santa-Chao in the upvalley area are defined somewhat more arbitrarily by a break in the distribution of Early Tanguche sites—i.e., the boundary here separates groups of sites essentially focused on the upper reaches of Quebrada Palo Redondo from those located closer to the valley floor.

It is useful to return briefly to the assertion that the five subregional sectors are not only a convenient heuristic device, but also represent meaningful environmental units that correspond closely to the overall distribution of sites in the settlement system of each period. For example, the Cayhuamarca Period system can be characterized as focused nearly exclusively on the Upper and Middle Valley sectors (see Fig. 166). The same is true of the Vinzos Period system, with the exception of eight sites in the Quebrada Palo Redondo area of Santa-Chao (see Fig. 168). Both Early and Late Suchimancillo are peri-

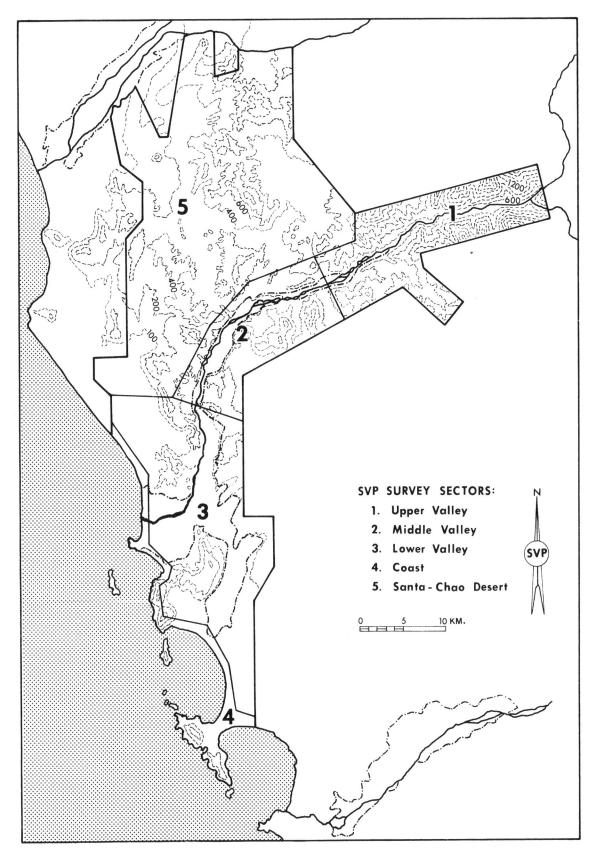

Fig. 4. Survey sectors of the 1979–80 Santa Valley Project.

ods when the subsistence-settlement system is focused on all three of the main valley sectors (see Figs. 170, 172). In contrast, the Guadalupito Period system is essentially a Middle and Lower Valley phenomenon (see Fig. 174). Similar characterizations can be made about the four remaining periods in the sequence, although the system of Early Tanguche Period represents something of an exception in that it extends only partly into the Upper Valley and is rather unevenly distributed in the Lower Valley (see Fig. 176).

Fig. 5 summarizes in a series of five topographic cross-sections some of the principal features of the valley floor and adjacent desert margins that have been discussed in the section on the natural environment. The five cross-sections are aligned roughly at right angles to the river, and elevations above sea level are shown at the customary scale of two times that of horizontal distances. Beginning with the uppermost one, their locations as measured in distance downvalley from the Santa-Tablachaca confluence are 3, 20, 40, 58, and 62 km, respectively. As the cross-sections show, steeper slopes of the cordillera enclose the narrow valley floor throughout the Upper Valley, giving way to progressively lower coastal outliers of the Andes in the Middle and Lower Valley sectors. Likewise, the width of the cultivated valley floor becomes increasingly greater as a function of distance down from the Santa-Tablachaca confluence (it will be noted that no valley floor is indicated in the uppermost cross-section, at 3 km down from the confluence, where only scattered small pockets of irrigable land are found).

THE CULTURAL ENVIRONMENT

Modern Occupation of the Survey Region

According to recent census data published in ONERN (1972b:15–17), the overall population size of the survey region is approximately 225,000 persons. Some 200,000 people live in the large industrial and fishing port town of Chimbote, located along the ocean at the mouth of Quebrada de Lacramarca, while the remaining 25,000 are distributed in much smaller towns and hamlets throughout the rest of the main valley area (Fig. 6). Beyond indicating the population breakdown between Chimbote and its regional hinterland, the census data unfortunately do not show the demographic distribution among the settlements that constitute present town and rural society in the region. Therefore this brief overview of modern settlement patterns relies on locational data taken from recent ONERN and IGM maps (see Fig. 14), as well as on subjective assessments made during our fieldwork. Nevertheless, a number of interesting patterns emerge from a consideration of the locational data and our own observations, some of which point to substantial differences between prehispanic and modern times.

Probably the single most important factor in understanding the present distribution of settlements is the location of the major roads that cross the region, of which there are essentially only two. The more important of these is the Panamerican highway, a paved two-lane road that runs along the far western edge of the survey area. The other route is a rough, narrow dirt road that runs upvalley from Santa to the Callejón de Huaylas via Huallanca and the Cañón del Pato. Farther upvalley, beyond the small settlement of Rinconada, the road runs onto the desert margin and for the most part remains there as it follows the route taken by the old Chimbote-Huallanca railway line before the 1970 earthquake. As Fig. 6 shows, nearly all settlements in the survey region are located directly along either the Panamerican or the coast-sierra routes, with the exception of Tanguche, Huaca Corral, and Puerto Santa. This points to the likelihood that a critical factor in modern settlement location is accessibility to the major transportation routes providing links with the main centers of Chimbote and Santa (population ca. 7000), as well as with centers outside the region.

If our estimate of a total of 1000–1500 persons living in the Upper and Middle Valley sectors is roughly correct, then it is clear that even excluding Chimbote the demographic center of gravity is located in the Lower Valley sector. Interestingly, although only 4–6% of the population of Santa Valley proper lives in the Upper and Middle Valley, a substantially greater relative percentage of cultivated land is present in these two sectors. Thus, judging from planimeter estimates made on the 1943–44 set of airphotos, 15% of the total land cultivated by traditional contour canals—or 1560 out of 10,490 ha—is located in the upvalley sectors. A possible reason for this demographic skewing relative to the distribution of cultivated land is that a number of people in the Lower Valley make their living from pursuits other than agriculture—i.e., as shopkeepers, teachers, fishermen, workers in canneries and fish meal plants, and taxi drivers. The distribution of agriculturalists may therefore be roughly commensurate with the distribution of cultivated land. In any event, it is of interest to note that under the reforms instituted by the recent military government, which held the reins of power in Peru from 1968–1980, cultivated land in various sectors of the valley has come under the control of local cooperatives made up of people who reside locally.

As mentioned, the 1970 population estimate for Chimbote was 200,000 persons, which is some 20 times greater than the estimate for 1940. With increasing emphasis on the fishing industry and recent construction of a large steel plant, the population of the city undoubtedly has grown to a point nearer 300,000 since the last census was made. With its boomtown economy, Chimbote has become a powerfully attractive focus of migration from outside the region—not only from other coastal valleys but

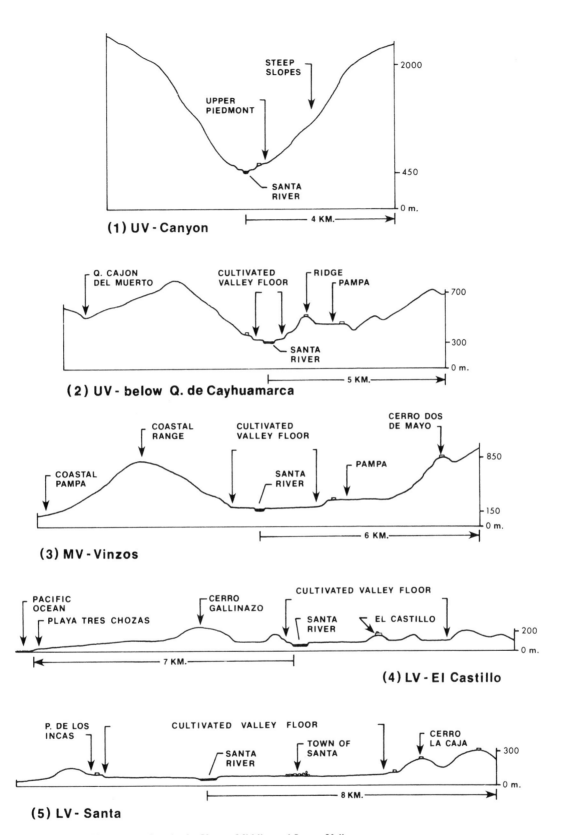

(1) UV - Canyon

STEEP SLOPES

UPPER PIEDMONT

SANTA RIVER

2000

450

0 m.

4 KM.

(2) UV - below Q. de Cayhuamarca

Q. CAJON DEL MUERTO

CULTIVATED VALLEY FLOOR

RIDGE

PAMPA

SANTA RIVER

700

300

0 m.

5 KM.

(3) MV - Vinzos

COASTAL RANGE

CULTIVATED VALLEY FLOOR

CERRO DOS DE MAYO

COASTAL PAMPA

SANTA RIVER

PAMPA

850

150

0 m.

6 KM.

(4) LV - El Castillo

PACIFIC OCEAN

PLAYA TRES CHOZAS

CERRO GALLINAZO

CULTIVATED VALLEY FLOOR

SANTA RIVER

EL CASTILLO

200

0 m.

7 KM.

(5) LV - Santa

P. DE LOS INCAS

CULTIVATED VALLEY FLOOR

SANTA RIVER

TOWN OF SANTA

CERRO LA CAJA

300

0 m.

8 KM.

Fig. 5. Topographic cross-sections in the Upper, Middle, and Lower Valley sectors.

35

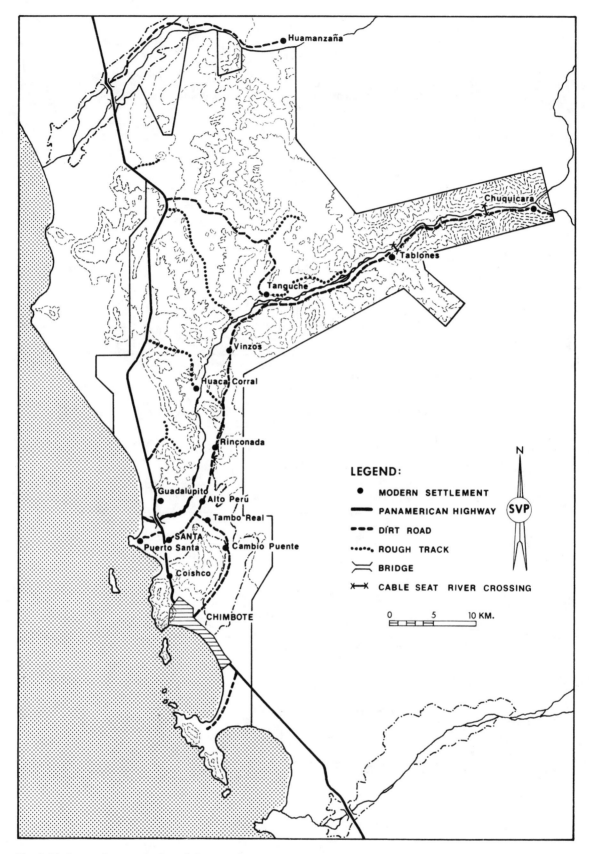

Fig. 6. Modern settlements, roads, and river crossings.

Legend:

LEGEND:
- ● MODERN SETTLEMENT
- — PANAMERICAN HIGHWAY
- – – DIRT ROAD
- ••••• ROUGH TRACK
- ⟩⟨ BRIDGE
- ✕—✕ CABLE SEAT RIVER CROSSING

0   5   10 KM.

Settlements: Huamanzaña, Chuquicara, Tablones, Tanguche, Vinzos, Huaca Corral, Rinconada, Guadalupito, Alto Perú, Tambo Real, SANTA, Puerto Santa, Cambio Puente, Coishco, CHIMBOTE

Plate 11. Traditional wattle-and-daub, or *quincha*, structures lie on the desert near cultivated fields of Huaca Corral area

probably from the adjacent sierra as well, judging from the occasional Quechua speakers we encountered during the fieldwork. Most of the residents of Chimbote make their living from nonagricultural pursuits, although many who live on the northeastern edge of town subsist by farming sections of the irrigated floor of Lacramarca. No data are available on how much of the food supply comes from the agricultural production of the Santa-Lacramarca area, but it is probable that large amounts of the food that supports the regional population are grown locally.

Most recent migrants to the region live in adobe and thatch dwellings on the outskirts of Chimbote, or in several *pueblos jóvenes* (young towns) that have sprung up on low hills and dunes rising above the floor of the valley. The largest of these are Coishco, Alto Perú, and San Ignacio (this last one located just to the northwest of the Panamerican bridge). Following the conversion of haciendas to collectively owned agricultural cooperatives in the period after 1968, small population centers have also grown up around the hacienda sites themselves. The fact that such settlements as Guadalupito, Tambo Real, Rinconada, Vinzos, Tanguche, and Suchimán (this last one located at the mouth of Quebrada del Panteón) all began

as haciendas is indicated by the designation "Hda." (Hacienda) on maps made prior to 1968.

Traditional house types. The main types of traditional dwellings at recent settlements and elsewhere in the valley consist of (1) adobe-brick houses, and (2) wattle-and-daub thatched houses known as *quinchas* (Plate 11). Both of these dwelling types are usually characterized by rectangular layouts measuring a minimum of 4 × 3 m in area, with walls about 2 m high. Both have at least one doorway, but only the adobe type was observed to have windows. Since rainfall almost never occurs in appreciable quantities, both house types normally have flat thatched roofs supported by light wooden beams, over which a thin layer of mud plaster is often laid down. Aside from the materials used in construction, the principal difference between adobe and quincha dwellings is that walls of the latter type are often inserted 10–20 cm into the ground to provide stability to the structure. The quincha walls themselves consist of individual vertical canes (*caña brava*) placed side by side around the perimeter, with additional stability provided by several horizontally-positioned canes woven into the vertical uprights and by narrow vertical posts at the corners. As described

37

Plate 12. Well-preserved dwelling dating to Cayhuamarca/Early Horizon Period (ca. 1000–350 B.C.)

by Gillin (1947) for Moche Valley, quincha houses whose walls have not been inserted into the ground usually have a low footing of mud built up around the edges of the structure to keep the walls firmly in place.

This last feature is of particular interest with regard to the nature and function of the low rock walls (ca. 50 cm) which characterize most habitation structures of a number of periods in the prehispanic sequence of Santa, especially the pre-Guadalupito and Tanguche Periods (e.g., Plate 12). It appears likely that such walls served the same stabilizing purpose as the low mud footing around modern quincha dwellings. Although adobe and quincha dwellings are both found in prehispanic contexts in Santa, the latter type is by far the more common of the two—including (1) a variant with inserted cane walls (low stubs about 10 cm high are usually all that now remain of the walls), and (2) a variant that appears to have had non-inserted cane walls (all that remains of these dwellings is the low, rock-walled footing). As one would logically expect, the presence/absence of rock-walled footings around prehispanic quincha dwellings appears in part to have been a function of the nature of the ground surface—i.e., rock walls are often absent in areas of very

sandy, loose soil (e.g., the dunes of the Lower Valley) and present where the ground surface is less sandy (e.g., on the desert out away from the valley floor). However, rock-walled footings often characterize quincha dwellings even in areas of very loose soil. Indeed, as argued in Chapter V, it is possible that the preferential focus on one or the other variant of quincha dwelling was more a function of either regional cultural norms or external influences than strictly the result of adaptation to the type of ground surface that prevailed.

In any case, a possible reason for the preferential focus on what in some ways appears to be a less sturdy dwelling (i.e., compared to the much more solid adobe-brick type of construction) is suggested by the damage caused by the sismo of 1970. Many adobe structures in the town of Santa, for example, collapsed during the severe tremors that accompanied the quake, and a number of people caught inside were either badly injured or killed by falling walls. On the other hand, as far as we could ascertain, no one living in quincha houses was injured at all. Since earthquakes are reasonably frequent in the area, it may well be that the quincha dwelling type is partly an adaptation to such events, although their essentially

Plate 13. Whole vessels, sherds, metal fragments, and human skulls left by huaqueros on surface of the looted, intrusive cemetery at SVP-ESUCH-47/SVP-LSUCH-79

open, well-ventilated nature also suggests they are a highly efficient adaptation to the temperate, rainless environment.

Modern Occupation and Prehispanic Site Preservation

Judging from our research, there appear to be four principal modern activities affecting the preservation of archaeological sites in the survey region. Listed in descending order with respect to the severity of their effects on prehispanic remains, these include (1) huaquero grave robbing, (2) encroachment by modern settlements, (3) encroachment by agricultural activities, and (4) road construction.

Huaqueros. As most persons who have visited or worked on the coast of Peru are aware, the desert margins of valleys appear to have been gone over thoroughly by local people digging for *huacos*, or ancient pottery ves-

sels, to sell to collectors. The unfortunate result of this activity, of course, is that large numbers of prehispanic cemetery sites have been substantially if not entirely destroyed—with small craters and burial materials strewn everywhere about the desert surface. From a scientific viewpoint, the damage to human remains and grave contents means that data of potentially great value to physical anthropologists and archaeologists are completely fragmented and ripped out of context. The single "fortunate" aspect of this devastation, however, is that the huaqueros are much less concerned about taking care to remove all pottery vessels intact than with quickly exposing the graves.

Thus at nearly every one of the 446 prehispanic cemeteries located during our fieldwork we encountered large numbers of potsherds from both utilitarian and fancy burial wares scattered about the surface. Indeed, in a number of cemeteries vessels of both types were found intact or nearly intact, apparently left there because the huaqueros considered them to have no monetary value. Because of the nature of the remains found and collected, we were therefore able to establish consistent associations between utilitarian pottery and the better-known and temporally diagnostic decorated pottery, thereby making it possible to date habitation sites where only the former pottery types were found. In addition, the finding of whole or nearly whole vessels in cemeteries has made it possible to illustrate a substantial body of data from *known* proveniences on ceramic forms and decoration for all periods from Early Suchimancillo Period on (e.g., see Plate 13).

Encroachment by modern settlements. Neither the growth of settlements nor the founding of new ones appears to have caused anywhere near the destruction brought about by huaquero activities. This seems due in large part to the fundamental shift in settlement location between prehispanic and modern times. Hamlets and towns are now located at the edge of the valley floor or, as mentioned earlier, in the midst of it along the roads, rather than primarily on the desert margins. Nevertheless, both our fieldwork and the comparison of airphoto sets taken several decades apart indicate that limited damage to several sites and outright disappearance of a few have occurred with recent growth of settlements or the establishment of new ones. The principal places where severe destruction has occurred are the settlements of Chimbote, Coishco, and Alto Perú. However, it must also be stressed that these three settlements constitute a very small portion of the overall survey area, and therefore have not affected our sample in anything other than a minor way.

With its expansion in recent years, Chimbote appears to be the principal source of damage and disappearance of archaeological remains. However, this destruction has been restricted essentially to the northwest sector of the town, judging both from our work in the field and from detailed examination of airphotos taken during the time when the population of Chimbote was around 10–15,000 persons. Moreover, most of the affected remains are confined to steeper desert slopes to the east above a large area of sunken fields that is still partially visible in this sector. Kosok (1965:188) mentions having observed "irrigation canals, pyramids, and other sites" in this area during his trip to the region in the 1940s. During our fieldwork we located one large, very poorly preserved pyramidal mound here (see SVP-GUAD-202 site description, in Wilson 1985), and were able to trace out the principal ancient canal that runs around the desert margin (see Fig. 11). At least one probable habitation site of small size (ca. 2–3 ha) was observed on the airphoto, but it is now completely covered by houses of Barrio San Pedro. Judging from the dating of most other remains in the area, this site probably dates to Guadalupito Period.

There are a couple of other places in the survey area

where the establishment of modern settlements has brought about similar destruction of prehispanic sites. The first of these places can be seen in an oblique aerial photograph included in Kosok (1965, Fig. 3, p. 188), where what appear to be the remains of a large, heavily looted cemetery are located in a narrow quebrada at the edge of Cerro de Chimbote peninsula. The large pueblo joven of Coishco now extends completely over the site, and has destroyed every trace of prehispanic remains. The second place is the recently established pueblo joven of Alto Perú, which has destroyed nearly all of the remains of SVP-LTR-47 site that show up so excellently in another of the oblique aerial photographs included in Kosok (1965, Fig. 13, p. 192). Nevertheless, in this case we were able to use an enlargement of an earlier vertical airphoto to map the site in detail (see Fig. 160), and were able to date it securely from several collections of the surface sherds that still cover most of the site area.

Encroachment by modern agriculture. Very little destruction of prehispanic sites appears to have occurred as a result of recent agricultural activities. As mentioned earlier, most sites are located either on the nonirrigable slopes of the desert margins or on hills and dunes rising out of the valley floor. However, we did encounter the remains of one small habitation site (SVP-LTR-51) that originally was located on a very low dune near the site of SVP-LTR-47/Alto Perú. During the weeks immediately preceding our survey of this area, the dune had been leveled to expand the size of surrounding cultivated fields, although scattered prehispanic debris including diagnostic sherds still lay about the surface over an area of .5 ha. The only other area where modern cultivation poses a significant danger to prehispanic sites lies 3 km to the SSW of SVP-LTR-51, along the so-called "Río Seco" desert margin due east of Santa. Most of the sites of this area—including a number of Late Tambo Real occupations (see SVP-LTR-59 through SVP-LTR-64, in Fig. 155) and at least one Guadalupito site (see SVP-GUAD-162, in Fig. 103)—have been partially or completely placed under cultivation. Interestingly enough, this has been achieved by recent migrants to the Santa region who have renovated sections of prehispanic canals that, in the 1943–44 SAN airphoto, lay out on the desert several hundred meters to the east of the valley floor.

Road construction. Limited damage to prehispanic remains has also occurred as a result of the construction of roads and highways in the survey region, but this sort of destruction generally has been very minor. For example, the modern dirt road which follows the old railway bed upvalley along the desert margin has crossed the lowermost edge of some sites (e.g., see Fig. 146), or has come close to major structural remains without damaging them (e.g., see Figs. 36, 96). In addition, minor damage has occurred to otherwise excellently preserved sites and roads of Early Tanguche Period in the Pampa de los Pancitos area, where the recently constructed dirt road to Tanguche runs off to the east from the Panamerican highway and cuts across the northern sector of SVP-ETAN-321 (see Fig. 134). In general, the Panamerican highway itself runs several hundred meters out to the west of the ancient road-settlement system, and only minor damage has been sustained by prehispanic remains in this part of the Santa-Chao Desert.

Traditional Subsistence Agriculture in the Region

With the significant exceptions of Holmberg's (1950, 1952) study of the village of Virú and Gillin's (1947) study of Moche, the literature on agricultural subsistence practices in coastal valleys is relatively scanty. Even the massively detailed studies carried out under the auspices of the National Office of Natural Resource Evaluation (ONERN 1972a, 1972b) are limited essentially to description of such material aspects of the agricultural system as canal networks, soil types, and land use patterns. However, taken in conjunction with the studies of traditional villages such as Moche and Virú, these data provide a good basis for outlining selected major characteristics of community-level subsistence patterns. Indeed, the data on traditional subsistence agriculture are of critical importance in reconstructing the nature of the prehispanic system and in providing a meaningful context for the analysis of maize-based carrying capacity.

As implied earlier, the principal difference between Santa and all other nearby valleys is the amount of water from sierra runoff that is available for irrigation; as shown in Table 1, the Santa stands apart from nearby rivers in having a much greater average yearly discharge. Although the total amount of available irrigable land is an equally critical factor in assessing comparative demographic potential, at this point it is sufficient to note that the unique abundance and year-round flow of water suggest that some differences must also exist with regard to agriculturally-oriented cultural practices between Santa and adjacent valleys. For example, the Virú River differs from the Santa in having not only a substantially reduced average yearly discharge of water (105×10^6 m^3 vs. 4590×10^6 m^3), but also a highly irregular and unpredictable flow from year to year, even during the months of maximum seasonal discharge. Thus, as Holmberg points out, water in Virú is often insufficient to irrigate all fields, and crop yields are correspondingly diminished. Because of this, a substantial body of ritual and religious practices has grown up around the water supply—with an inadequate supply in any given year explained as the result of a community failure to carry out religious fiestas properly (Holmberg 1950:118–119). Moreover, water in Virú traditionally was controlled by officials of the state or by locally appointed commissioners who supervised its distribution throughout the canal net-

work by means of minor officials called *mitayos* (Holmberg 1950:373). In this manner, the community was able to maintain rigorous control over water usage, with each landholder allowed only enough water to grow one crop per year.

No data are available on traditional irrigation-related religious practices for Santa, but, with fully 43 times the flow of the Virú River and only 7% of water ever used for agriculture, it is unlikely that such practices would focus on the supply of water. By the same token, it is equally unlikely that the organized system of water distribution characteristic of valleys with limited water supply would ever have been necessary in Santa, where water is freely available on a year-round basis. On the other hand, communally-organized activities related to the cleaning of irrigation canals in Virú are probably characteristic of traditional communities in Santa as well. Prior to the 1940s, when collective practices began to give way to more individualistic concepts of canal cleaning and maintenance, the agricultural year in Virú started with the *fiesta de la acequia* (festival of the irrigation canal). This fiesta was a community activity accompanied by religious observances, during which the men of the village worked together to clear and repair the main canal for the arrival of the first water in late December or early January. Similarly, labor in the fields was carried out until recently by means of communal work groups called *mingas* (Holmberg 1950). When a farmer needed work done in his fields, he would invite his neighbors to help, and, following completion of the work would treat them to a feast and drinking party. Having provided him with needed labor, the neighbors in turn had created a reciprocal obligation for obtaining his help in their fields at some future date.

Both communal canal cleaning and the minga are institutions with a time depth extending back into the prehispanic period in the Central Andes (e.g., see Rowe 1963:210–212), and it is likely that such practices were generally characteristic of the agricultural subsistence system of valleys such as Santa. Again, aside from the comparatively small amount of irrigable land in Santa, the principal difference between it and other valleys is that an ample supply of water runs year-round in the irrigation canals. But the main canals have to be maintained on a continual basis, and this requires stopping water flow from time to time in order to clean and repair them. In addition, during the months of maximum flow in the river, water occasionally breaks through a weakened section of canal bank and floods the area below. When this happens, the men of the village nearest the break cooperate to restore the canal to working order. For example, during our fieldwork a massive break occurred in the main canal above Rinconada—largely due to the inattention at the canal intake some kilometers upriver of the nighttime *vigilante* (who, fearing justifiable retribution, quickly departed the area). As a result of the break, a large area of cultivated fields and most of the settlement were flooded with water and silt, destroying several hectares of crops and severely damaging houses and personal possessions. Cleanup and repair of the canal required work by groups of men from the Rinconada agricultural cooperative over a period of several weeks following the washout.

The modern canal network. Because of the inclusion of detailed large-scale maps in the studies made by ONERN (1972b; see also 1972a, 1973), it is possible to outline precisely the main features of the modern canal network of Santa, as well as compare it to those of adjacent valleys. Eight of the nine principal irrigation canals in Santa are simple, unlined earthen ditches that follow natural contours at the base of desert hills adjacent to the cultivated valley floor. Although a few minor cuts have been made through low intervening piedmont spurs, and short aqueduct fills are sometimes employed to cross quebrada mouths, in general these *canales rústicos* require little engineering skill beyond that necessary to contain the water and maintain an even, gentle gradient. With widths ranging between 1–5 m and depths of 1 m or less, their average water-carrying capacity is generally below 5 m³/second, but in spite of this they supply enough water to irrigate a total of 9700 ha—or over 90% of the land in the Upper, Middle, and Lower Valley sectors.

The recent construction in the 1960s of the Canal de Derivación between Quebrada La Huaca and the mouth of Lacramarca has allowed the addition of over 4000 ha of formerly nonirrigable desert pampa to the agricultural system—primarily in the area to the northeast of Tambo Real and along the east desert margin of Lacramarca. This expansion of the traditional system was achieved by blasting some 19 tunnels through the rocky hills of the desert margin to maintain maximum head, and by constructing a wide concrete-lined ditch with a water-carrying capacity of 13 m³/second (ONERN 1972b:368 ff.). In relation to our survey, the principal effect of the extension of the irrigated area of the region was to move the east desert margin of Lacramarca 1–2 km farther out to the east beyond that shown in Fig. 3. However, the position of the old, or traditional, desert margin is still clear from a narrow strip of sandy ground and associated prehispanic sites, and we thus had little difficulty finding and mapping all archaeological remains in this area (see Fig. 102).

The location of intakes (*tomas*) and the length of traditional canals in Santa and adjacent valleys obviously are a function of a number of environmental factors—including the nature of the hilly desert margin, the configuration of the valley floor, the amount of available irrigable land, and the overall gradient of the riverbed. Ideally, assuming the configuration of a given coastal valley were a perfect V-shaped delta and the river ran down its center, one might expect canals to take on the appearance of a series of nested Vs—with canals running off symmetrically from the same points on each side of the river. To a certain extent canals in the lowermost part of coastal valleys do take on this appearance (e.g., see Mapa No. 8, for Virú, in ONERN 1973). However, as the detailed maps of Santa Valley make clear, all of the above-mentioned environmental factors are quite variable throughout the main valley area, and canals are taken off wherever possible and in accordance with the irrigation requirements of land located farther downriver.

Moreover, in viewing the maps of the Santa, Virú, and Nepeña networks, it is at once clear that canals are positioned throughout most of these valleys in intricate patterns that imply strong interdependency, if not cooperation, among farmers of various local areas. Thus, even though in Santa the Upper and Middle Valley sectors together form a single, interconnected network that stands essentially apart from the Lower Valley, the intakes for the main canals of this last sector are located in the lowermost part of the Middle Valley. Farmers of the Lower Valley are therefore dependent upon the good offices of those in the Middle Valley in ensuring the continued integrity of the canal intakes so that water will reach their fields.

As we shall see later, the essential regional interdependency evidenced by the actual configurations of traditional canal networks in valleys such as Santa, Nepeña, and Virú has critical implications for the nature of relations among the various local prehispanic population/settlement groupings. Since these implications are discussed in detail in Chapter V, here it is sufficient to underscore the probability that peaceful within-valley relations probably characterized local groups of agriculturalists from the start of irrigation farming in Early Horizon times. In addition, it seems clear from the nature of modern traditional canal networks that they would be exceedingly vulnerable to outside disruption. In other words, raiders from other regions potentially could have cut off the water supply—either at undefended intake points or anywhere else along the canals where local farmers had not taken defensive measures. Nonetheless, as we shall argue later, there are good reasons why outside raiders might not have aimed their attacks at this part of the agricultural system.

Modern subsistence crops. In his study of traditional agriculture in the village of Virú, Holmberg (1950) reports that over 80% of the land was planted in maize (*Zea mays* L.). Even as recently as the 1960s, before the advent of extensive cash cropping of rice and sugar cane, as much as 70% of the land in Virú was devoted to maize farming (ONERN 1973:182). In keeping with traditional practices dating back to prehispanic times in the Central Andes and elsewhere in native America, such cultigens as crookneck squash (*Curcurbita moschata*), gourds

(*Lagenaria siceraria*), and beans (*Phaseolus vulgaris*) are often planted along with maize in the same field. Other modern crops with a history of cultivation extending back essentially throughout the ceramic part of the prehispanic sequence (cf. Towle 1952; Lanning 1967) include yuca (*Manihot* sp.), camote (*Ipomoea* L.), ají (*Capsicum* L.), palta (*Persea americana*), lúcuma (*Lucuma bifera*), peanuts (*Arachis hypogaea* L.), pallar (*Canavalia* spp.), and cotton (*Gossypium* spp.).

Nevertheless, of all crops planted by traditional coastal agriculturalists, it is maize alone that appears to be the object of special attention. There are good reasons for this. First, maize has high nutritional value when consumed together with beans, since as is well known these two plants contain complementary sets of amino acids that provide a complete protein which supplants any critical need for meat (cf. Heiser 1973:116). Second, maize is especially valuable because it can easily be dried and stored for future use. For example, in Virú maize is stored for up to two years without insect damage in pits dug in the desert sands around the village (Holmberg 1950). Its special place in the subsistence system of Virú is further attested to by the fact that, like the limited water supply, it forms an important focus of religious and ritual activity. For example, it is believed that maize must be planted and harvested during the full moon, or else it will become subject to insect damage.

Unlike Virú, where the restricted water supply limits the number of crops per year to one, in Santa Valley the ample year-round flow of water allows farmers to obtain at least two and, sometimes, as many as three crops of maize and other cultigens per year (ONERN 1972b:229). Indeed, because of the mild climate with temperatures averaging 20° C throughout the year, all along the coast farmers generally are able to obtain anywhere from two to four crops of maize per year, depending on the water supply and control of insects (Grobman et al. 1961:29). Because of this, coastal maize yields are generally higher than elsewhere in Peru—with averages ranging between 2500 and 4000 kilograms per hectare (kg/ha) of dry grain. Maize yields in Santa fall squarely within this range, averaging between 2600 and 3800 kg/ha of dry grain per year (ONERN 1972b:237). Small quantities of nitrogen-rich fertilizer are used by some farmers to replenish the soil, but as Gillin (1947) notes for the village of Moche—where traditional agriculturalists do not use fertilizer—it is likely that nitrogen supplies are adequately restored by planting beans and lentils in the maize fields.

Reconstruction of the Prehispanic Agricultural System

Having outlined selected aspects of traditional subsistence agriculture, it is appropriate at this point to present the data on the prehispanic agricultural system gathered during our research. As mentioned earlier, dur-

ing the course of the survey all fragments of ancient canals and areas of ancient field systems were mapped on the large-scale airphotos. In addition, when the remains of cultigens were noted on the surface of sites, names of plant species were recorded either directly on the airphotos or in the fieldnotes. Utilizing these data and those on traditional modern agriculture, it is possible to outline the main aspects of prehispanic subsistence agriculture in the Lower Santa region. When these data are combined with the settlement pattern data (as is done in Chapters IV and V), it is also possible to outline in some detail the principal developmental features of the subsistence system.

Ancient canals and field systems. Fragments of probable ancient canals were found along the desert margin on both sides of the river throughout the Upper, Middle, and Lower Valley (see Figs. 7–13). Aside from their fragmentary nature and the windblown sand and silt that partially fill them, there are three criteria that aid in assessing these canals as prehispanic in date. First of all, in areas where modern canals presently run the ancient irrigation ditches are invariably located several meters higher in elevation. For example, the modern ca-

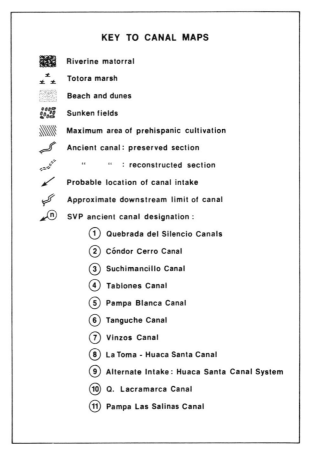

Fig. 7. Key to ancient canal maps in Figs. 8–13.

43

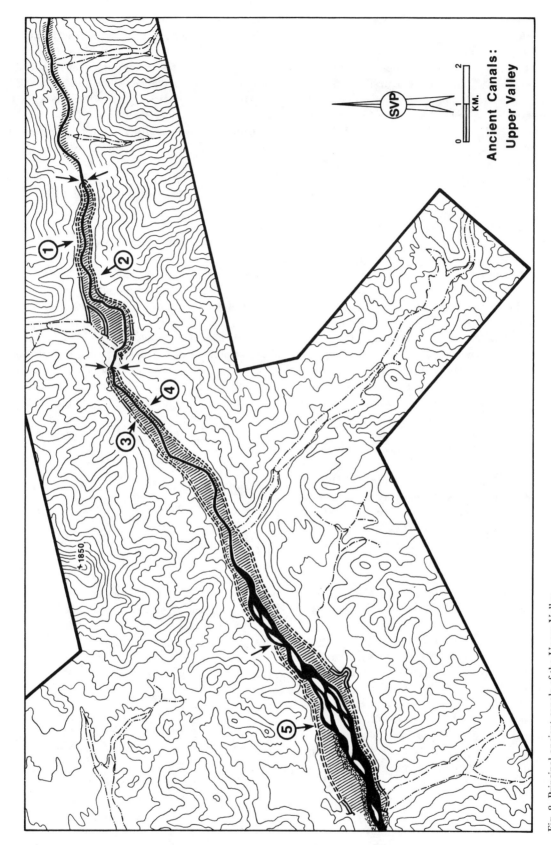

Fig. 8. Principal ancient canals of the Upper Valley.

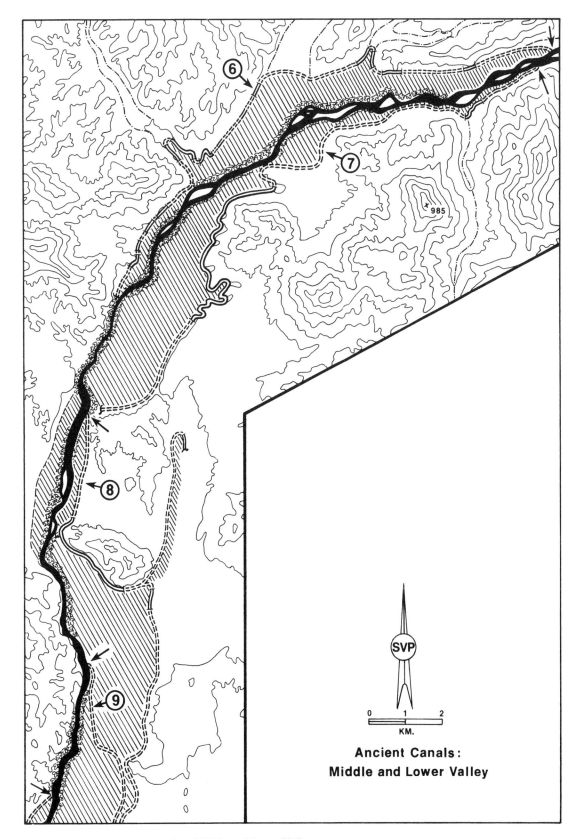

Fig. 9. Principal ancient canals of the Middle and Lower Valley.

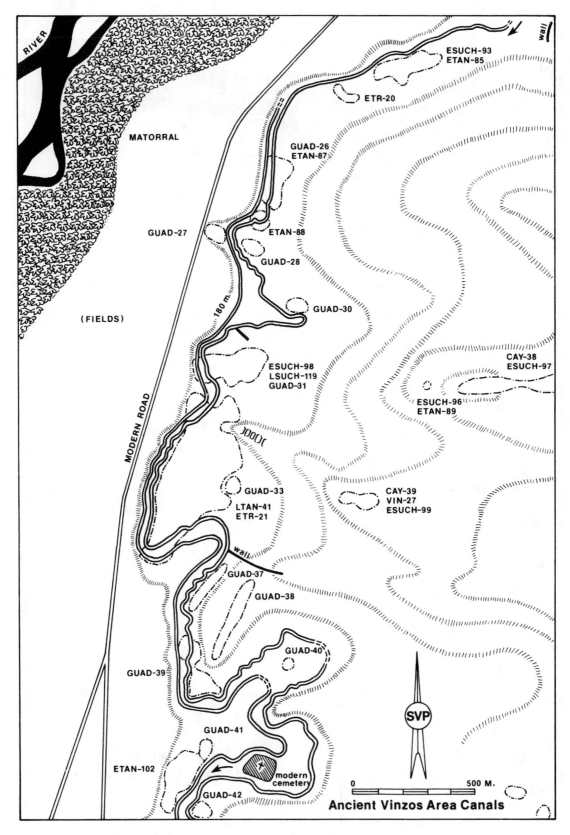

RIVER

MATORRAL

(FIELDS)

MODERN ROAD

180 m.

100 m.

wall

ESUCH-93
ETAN-85

ETR-20

GUAD-26
ETAN-87

GUAD-27

ETAN-88

GUAD-28

GUAD-30

ESUCH-98
LSUCH-119
GUAD-31

CAY-38
ESUCH-97

ESUCH-96
ETAN-89

GUAD-33

LTAN-41
ETR-21

CAY-39
VIN-27
ESUCH-99

wall

GUAD-37

GUAD-38

GUAD-40

GUAD-39

GUAD-41

SVP

ETAN-102

modern
cemetery

GUAD-42

0   500 M.

Ancient Vinzos Area Canals

Fig. 10. Detail map of ancient canals and associated archaeological sites in the area north of Vinzos.

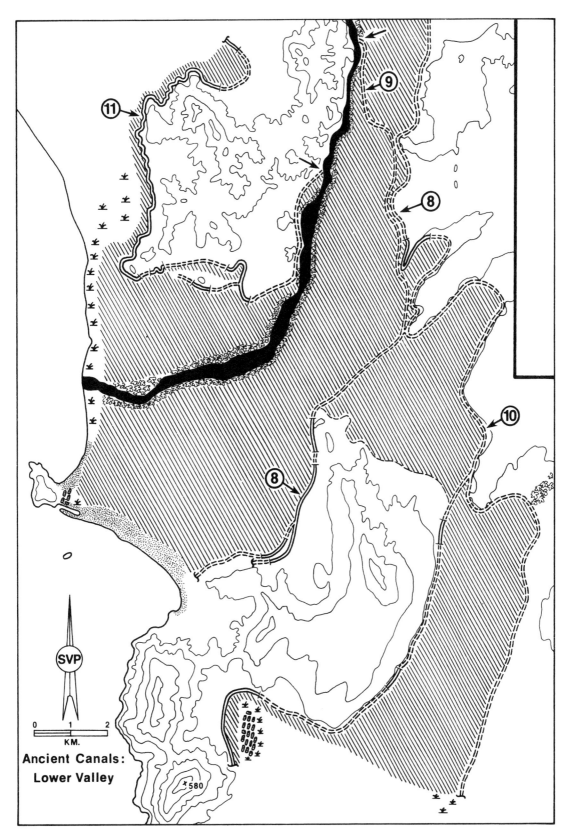

Fig. 11. Principal ancient canals of the Lower Valley.

47

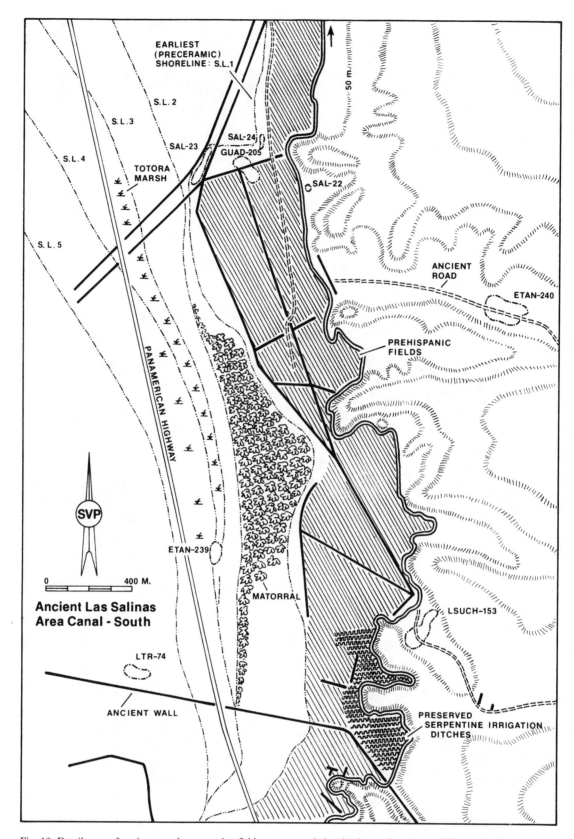

Fig. 12. Detail map of ancient canals, serpentine field systems, and sites in the southern area of Pampa Las Salinas.

48

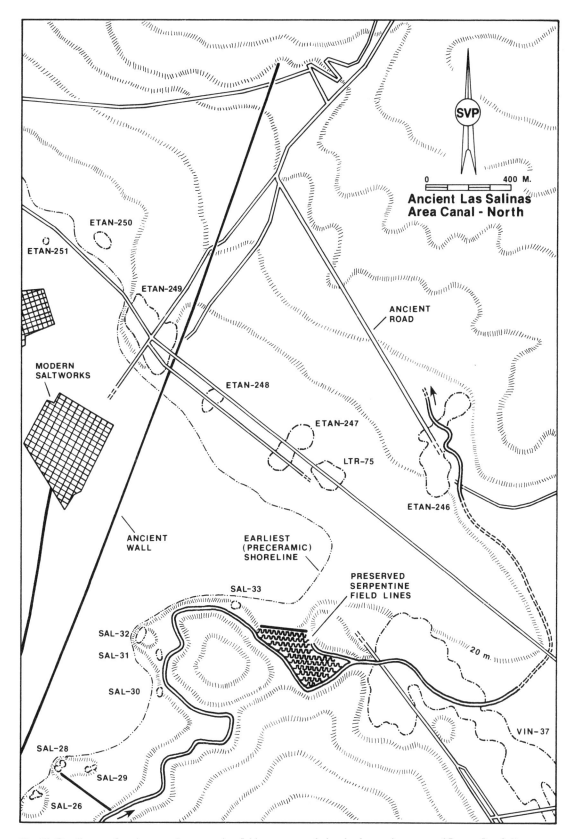

Fig. 13. Detail map of ancient canals, serpentine field systems, and sites in the northern area of Pampa Las Salinas.

nal in the Vinzos area runs at or slightly below the 180-m contour level, downslope to the west of the two probable ancient canals located here. Whether or not this indicates that prehispanic canals generally were longer than more recent ones, it is clear from our research that the area irrigated by traditional contour canals in modern times (10,490 ha) is some 817 ha less than that of the prehispanic period (11,307 ha).

Second, in almost all areas of the valley numerous prehispanic sites were found in close association with the fragments of canals shown on the maps (e.g., see Figs. 10, 12, 13). Third, in at least two areas of the valley the remains of excellently preserved serpentine canal systems were found adjacent to the fragmentary remains of the main ditches (e.g., see Plate 7). These include the Quebrada del Silencio Canals in the Upper Valley (Fig. 8), and Pampa Las Salinas Canal in the Lower Valley (Figs. 11–13). Both systems are located in areas where irrigation agriculture does not appear to have been practiced since the prehispanic period, judging both from the deteriorated state of the systems in some places and from the absence of any settlements of more recent times.

Although some of the ancient canal sections run for a number of kilometers along the desert margin, nowhere did we find prehispanic canals that are completely intact. The reconstruction of the 11 main canals shown in Figs. 8, 9, and 11 must therefore be considered as a tentative one. Nevertheless, with the exception of the nearly intact Quebrada del Silencio and Pampa Las Salinas Canals, the proposed reconstruction shown on the maps is based on the length of the comparably-sized modern ditches that lie below them, as well as on the location of modern intake points. In addition, the location of sites along the desert margin in each of the ceramic periods not only provides some confirmation of the overall length of the reconstructed canals, but is probably also an indication of changes in these lengths as a result of period-to-period changes in settlement location and local population size.

Brief descriptions of the 11 ancient canals—including reconstructed length in kilometers, proposed dating based on associated sites, and other descriptive data of interest—are as follows (the numerical designation of each canal is the same as that used in Figs. 7, 8, 9, and 11):

(1) *Quebrada del Silencio* (Fig. 8): length ca. 4 km; Cayhuamarca through Late Suchimancillo, and Early Tanguche Periods; narrow canal averaging 1 m wide and .5 m deep; excellently preserved because of remote location.

(2) *Cóndor Cerro* (Fig. 8): length ca. 5 km; Cayhuamarca through Late Suchimancillo, and Late Tanguche Periods; narrow canal with only two poorly preserved fragments remaining; elevation is ca. 30–50 m above the deeply incised riverbed in a narrow area of the Upper Valley.

(3) *Suchimancillo* (Fig. 8): length ca. 8 km; Cayhuamar-ca through Late Tanguche Periods; narrow canal with one preserved section in its upper reaches.

(4) *Tablones* (Fig. 8): length ca. 15 km; Cayhuamarca through Late Suchimancillo Periods; narrow canal with three well preserved sections throughout its length.

(5) *Pampa Blanca* (Fig. 8): length ca. 5 km; Early Suchimancillo through Late Tambo Real Periods; narrow canal with an excellently preserved section in its lower reaches; associated with very well preserved agricultural and habitation terracing which extends over an area of nearly 50 ha.

(6) *Tanguche* (Fig. 9): length ca. 20 km; Vinzos through Late Tambo Real Periods; narrow canal with at least 11 excellently preserved sections throughout its length; the longest remaining section is located in the mouth of Quebrada Palo Redondo.

(7) *Vinzos* (Figs. 9, 10): length ca. 20 km; Cayhuamarca through Late Tambo Real Periods; as shown in Fig. 10, this canal system actually consists of two adjacent ditches, with the higher and longer one dating probably to a later period; both canals are relatively wide, with an inverted trapezoidal cross-section measuring 1.5 m wide at the top, 1 m at the bottom, and .5 m deep; the upper canal was built on very steep desert slopes, with extensive quantities of adobe used to build up the outer edge to heights of as much as 8–10 m along the hillside (see Kosok 1965, Fig. 17, p. 193).

(8) *La Toma-Huaca Santa* (Figs. 9, 11): length ca. 26 km; the Lower Valley section of this long canal dates from Early Suchimancillo through Late Tambo Real Periods; the best preserved remaining fragment lies along the southern edge of Cerro Huaca Jedionda, in the upper reaches of the Lower Valley sector (Fig. 9); recent agricultural activity has partially destroyed the central sections of the fragments near Huaca Santa (Fig. 11).

(9) *Alternate Intake: Huaca Santa System* (Fig. 11): length ca. 8 km; the existence of this canal in prehispanic times is conjectural (because it is would have crossed the area now covered by modern cultivation), but is based on the presence of a modern canal located in the same place.

(10) *Quebrada Lacramarca* (Fig. 11): length ca. 35 km, measuring from the point near Tambo Real where the canal takes off from La Toma-Huaca Santa Canal; Guadalupito Period; narrow canal, with excellently preserved sections along the west edge of Lacramarca and along hills northwest of sunken fields in Chimbote area (this latter area is now contained within the property of SiderPerú steel mill); the existence of a canal along the east side of Lacramarca is conjectural, but highly probable, given the location of Guadalupito Period settlements all along here (see Fig. 102).

(11) *Pampa Las Salinas* (Figs. 11–13): length ca. 15 km; upper reaches in Pampa de los Incas area (see Fig. 108) date from Early Suchimancillo through Late Tambo Real Periods, while lower reaches in Las Salinas area

date to Early Tanguche and possibly Guadalupito; wide canal with inverted trapezoidal cross-section measuring 1.5 m wide at the top, 1 m at the bottom, and .5 m deep; as shown in Figs. 12 and 13, this canal is associated with excellently preserved serpentine field systems at two major points in Las Salinas area (see discussion below; see also Kosok 1965, Fig. 8, p. 190, for a clear aerial shot of the same area shown in Fig. 12).

The two principal kinds of preserved field systems found in the region include (1) fields with serpentine furrows and (2) sunken fields. As mentioned above, the best preserved serpentine fields are located along Pampa Las Salinas Canal. Due to time constraints, it was not possible to map these systems in detail, although their main characteristics and overall extent (245 ha) are clear from the detailed examination and photography we carried out in the field. All along the main canal, smaller secondary canals run down several meters in elevation to the area of ancient cultivation. These secondary ditches are ca. 25–50 cm wide and usually head straight downslope, with rock lining used on the bottom and sides to prevent erosion. Upon reaching the fields, narrow tertiary canals at the upslope end were used to feed water to the serpentine channels extending throughout each plot. In a number of places, one notes furrows extending up from the flat plain right onto the steeper slopes that lie below the main canal itself. This indicates that it was probably necessary to take maximum advantage of all available irrigable land in this area; indeed, it also implies that the land located out to the west and north—in the area of the ancient Las Salinas shorelines and the modern saltworks—was too salt-laden to be utilized (Note: for canal systems with very similar configurations in the Moche and Pisco Valleys, see Zegarra 1978, Láminas 3 and 6). Serpentine ditches of Pampa de los Incas area show up well in a photograph taken in 1934 by Cornelius Roosevelt (1935, Fig. 11, p. 29), but recent activity in the area has all but obliterated them.

The second kind of system consists of sunken fields. These were found in only two areas of the survey region, including the mouth of Santa Valley near Puerto Santa and the mouth of Quebrada de Lacramarca to the northeast of Chimbote (Fig. 11). Both sets of fields cover relatively minor areas compared to the total estimated area of prehispanic cultivation—with the Puerto Santa group extending over about 30 ha (see SVP-ETR-42 site description, in Wilson 1985) and the Chimbote group extending over at least 100 ha. Since both areas are presently used for cultivation of totora reeds, and part of the Chimbote group has been destroyed by the SiderPerú steel mill, it is difficult to ascertain whether they are of prehispanic origin. Nevertheless, the close association of sites of Guadalupito Period (Chimbote group) and Early Tambo Real Period (Puerto Santa group) suggests that such a date is likely.

Estimating the area of prehispanic cultivation. As implied in Figs. 8, 9, and 11, estimating the total area of potential prehispanic cultivation was a relatively straightforward procedure involving the measurement of all irrigable land that lies below the level of the ancient desert margin canal systems of the valley. These measurements (and all other areal calculations in the analysis) were carried out using a compensating polar planimeter on tracings made from the large-scale SAN airphotos used for the fieldwork, and the results are summarized in Table 2. Since the cultivable land encompassed within the ancient canal system includes virtually all areas watered by traditional contour canals, the major part of the estimate—or some 10,490 out of 11,307 ha—was defined in terms of the area covered by fields in the year the airphotos were made (1943–44; see Fig. 14). But, as mentioned in the section on paleoenvironment, it is possible that riverine matorral vegetation of the prehispanic period extended over a wider strip on each side of the Santa than that indicated for the Lower Valley sector in Fig. 11. Therefore the estimate of 10,490 ha based on 1943–44 land usage may be somewhat high. This is a moot point, however, since there is no time in the prehispanic sequence when population numbers appear to have reached anything approaching levels that would have required use of all land in the Lower Valley sector (see Chapter V).

As mentioned earlier, it is interesting to note that at various times in the sequence cultivation was practiced on an additional area totaling some 817 ha, none of which seems to have been used since prehispanic times. For example, modern cultivation in the Upper Valley does not extend more than 1.5 km upriver beyond Tablones. Yet, judging from excellently preserved ancient canals and field systems as well as from the presence of small pockets of irrigable matorral land adjacent to the river, an additional total area of 77 ha was cultivated on both sides of the Santa in the remaining 16-km distance between Tablones and Chuquicara. As shown in Table 2, in general the extent of prehispanic agriculture was greater than that of recent times in nearly every area of the Upper, Middle, and Lower Valley sectors. With regard to the Lower Valley, however, it must be emphasized that this argument refers mainly to the *outer* edges of cultivation, on or near the desert margin, and not to the inner edges along the river where a substantial area of land now under cultivation may have been covered with thick matorral in prehispanic times.

In any case, taking into consideration the full areal extent of the settlement system of each of the nine ceramic periods, the amount of land encompassed at any given point in the sequence averaged about 4750 ha, with total hectares in use estimated as having ranged between 1900 ha (Cayhuamarca and Vinzos Periods) and 8800 ha (Guadalupito Period). Furthermore, as discussed later,

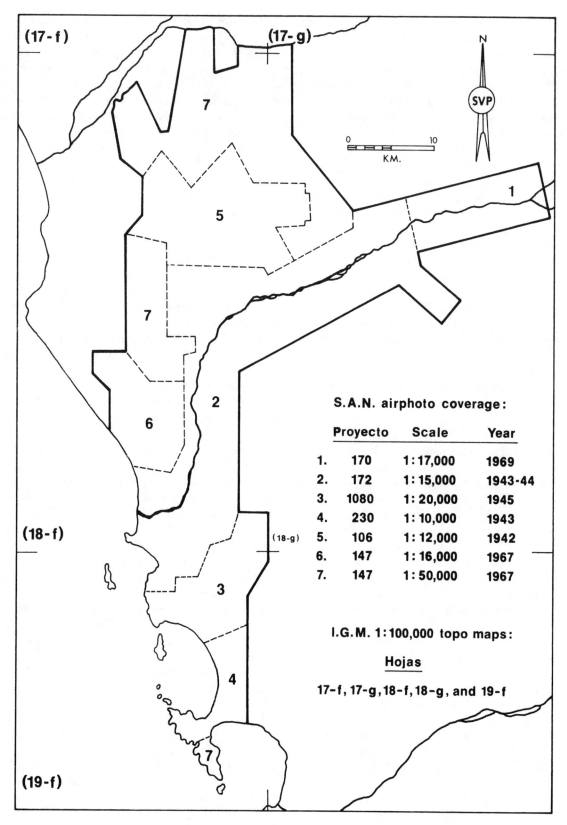

(17-f)　　　　　　(17-g)

7

5

7

2

6

S.A.N. airphoto coverage:

	Proyecto	Scale	Year
1.	170	1:17,000	1969
2.	172	1:15,000	1943-44
3.	1080	1:20,000	1945
4.	230	1:10,000	1943
5.	106	1:12,000	1942
6.	147	1:16,000	1967
7.	147	1:50,000	1967

I.G.M. 1:100,000 topo maps:

Hojas

17-f, 17-g, 18-f, 18-g, and 19-f

(18-f)　　　　　　(18-g)

3

4

7

(19-f)

Fig. 14. Map showing Servicio Aerofotográfico Nacional (SAN) airphoto and Instituto Geográfico Militar (IGM) topographic map coverage of the survey region.

when one considers the population estimates of each period in relation to three variables—including hectares of land, maize-based carrying capacity, and the possible number of crops per year—it can be shown that the amount of land encompassed by the system of each period was sufficient to support at least the estimated (maximum) population.

Data on cultigens. The two kinds of data on prehispanic cultigens gathered during our research include preserved remains of the plants themselves and depictions of plants on pottery vessels. Although the preservation of organic surface remains (including preceramic textiles and cotton netting) is generally excellent in Santa, actual remains of cultigens were found on the surface of only a relatively limited number of sites. Moreover, these remains are confined for the most part to large (easily visible) dessicated fragments of a very restricted number of plants—including maize cobs, pacae, and cotton fibers.

Maize cobs constitute by far the most numerous remains noted on the surface. This is probably because they are very durable, are easily spotted in the surface occupational debris, and are too heavy to be blown away by the strong winds that often occur during the afternoon. In any case, while pacae and cotton were noted on the surface of only a few sites, maize cobs were found at a total of 16 sites. Many of these sites are multicomponent, and thus it is difficult to pinpoint precisely the dates of any of the organic surface remains. However, maize was consistently found in single-component contexts dating back to Early Suchimancillo, Late Suchimancillo, and Guadalupito Periods (e.g., see SVP-ESUCH-87, SVP-LSUCH-105, and SVP-GUAD-97 site descriptions, in Wilson 1985).

Interestingly enough, as in the case of actual plant species noted on the surface of sites, the number of types of cultigens depicted in pottery is quite limited—including primarily maize, as well as warty/crookneck squash and peanuts. But many more sites of the various periods had such depictions on the associated pottery than had actual preserved plant remains on the surface. In light of the importance of maize in the traditional subsistence and ritual systems, it is perhaps not surprising to note that it is by far the most commonly depicted plant. Indeed, its earliest appearance in ceramic form (i.e., Early Suchimancillo Period) exactly parallels that of the actual remains found. From Early Suchimancillo on to the end of the prehispanic sequence, depictions of maize are found in the assemblage of all periods except Late Tanguche (Note: for depictions of maize, see Figs. 231, 272, 277, 278c, 280; for squash, see Figs. 240a, 267-upper left; for peanuts, see Figs. 229b, 246-lower left).

However, in spite of the apparent time depth of maize and other cultigens based strictly on ceramic representations, it is important to note that plant effigies do not appear at all in the pottery assemblages of Cayhuamarca and Vinzos Periods (nor, indeed, do human effigies, with the exception of a single example in the Vinzos assemblage). The absence of plant depictions thus does not necessarily imply that maize and other cultigens were not present in the subsistence system from Cayhuamarca/Early Horizon times on; rather, it implies only that such effigies were not yet a part of ceramic assemblages. Since surface plant remains are uniformly absent on the surface of single-component Cayhuamarca and Vinzos sites (and rare on Suchimancillo sites), it seems likely that this is due more to conditions of preservation than to whether or not they were part of the subsistence system. From excavations in the nearby valleys of Chicama (Bird 1948) and Moche (Pozorski 1979), it is clear that maize, beans, squash and other cultigens were present in the North Coast area at least by Early Horizon times, and there is little reason to believe that such productive crops would not have reached Santa by this time as well. Moreover, as argued in Chapter V, there is probably no other way that the large populations of Cayhuamarca and Vinzos Periods could have sustained themselves (estimates are ca. 6000 and 7900 persons, respectively).

Spanish Documentary Sources on Santa Valley

Almost no data are available on the Lower Santa region from the 16th- and 17th-century documentary sources, aside from detailed commentary by Pedro de Cieza de León based on his trip across the valley in the late 1540s (cf. Cieza de León 1969 [1553]:325–326). Although Santa is mentioned in a number of documents—including Cobo (1964 [1653]); Córdova (1965 [1586]); and Vázquez de Espinosa (1969 [ca. 1630])—for the most part commentary is limited to the large volume of water in the river and to descriptions of the small Spanish settlement of Santa María de la Parrilla (now Santa) founded in the 1550s. Even Cieza's comments on the region are relatively brief compared to other areas he visited in the Central Andes. However, they do provide a fascinating glimpse not only of the physical appearance of the valley as it looked to a keenly observant traveler in the years just after the Spanish conquest, but of reputed Late Horizon historical events that had occurred as Santa was incorporated into the Inca state.

As he had been in crossing other nearby valleys to the north, Cieza was struck by the sharp contrast between the large number of prehispanic remains he noted everywhere in the valley and the very small number of remaining native inhabitants (some 400, by his estimate). According to Cieza, still extant native oral traditions about Santa indicated that it had been "very heavily populated, and there were great warriors and native lords there". Indeed, the people of Santa seem to have been able to hold off the initial onslaught of the Inca army for a time during its conquest of North Coast valleys. Nevertheless, the subjugation of Santa was carried out—in the end apparently more by diplomacy than by brute force. According to Cieza, the Incas "ordered great lodgings and many storehouses erected there, for this valley is one of the largest, and broader and longer than any we have seen so far" (it may be noted here that Cieza's enthusiasm seems to have gotten the better of him in his comparison of the size of Santa to valleys to the north; in previous days, he had crossed such valleys as Jequetepeque, Chicama, and Moche which are larger by far than Santa). Cieza also refers to the great numbers of graves he saw throughout the desert margins of the valley, as well as the extensive remains of irrigation canals and overgrown fields dating to the prehispanic time period.

Although reference to other Spanish documentary sources is made in later chapters, here it is useful briefly to comment on several aspects of Cieza's observations in relation to our research. First, it is interesting to note his reference to numerous prehispanic graves in the valley. Since these graves by definition are visible only when they have been dug up, it is clear that a significant proportion of the many thousands of looted burials ones sees today are the result of prehispanic activity. Thus, whatever the earlier reasons for digging up the burials of one's ancestors, such an activity obviously has substantial time depth in Santa Valley. Second, Cieza's observations on canals and field systems provide additional confirmation of the preconquest origin of the features we encountered, beyond what appears to be their clear association with sites and ceramics dating to the prehispanic period. Third, in spite of the assertion of the ethnohistorical sources that prior to the Inca conquest Santa had been made a part of the Chimú state, it is interesting to note that the local population still was able to put up a vigorous, sustained defense against the advancing Inca army. This implies not only a measure of valley-wide political organization in the face of an outside military threat, but also a fair degree of local autonomy in relation to the Chimú state.

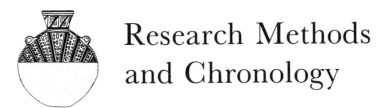

Research Methods and Chronology

As discussed in the preceding chapter, the Lower Santa region like most coastal Peruvian valleys offers a nearly ideal setting for the recovery of data on archaeological remains dating throughout the sequence of prehispanic occupation. In an essentially rainless environment with little or no vegetation to obscure these remains and with serious recent disturbance limited primarily to ancient cemetery areas, it is thus possible to retrieve efficiently and accurately a great quantity and variety of data. And, as argued in Chapter I, the recent development in the Near East and Mesoamerica of more systematic and comprehensive methods of carrying out studies of ancient settlement patterns has provided a powerful approach to understanding the origins and development of sociocultural complexity in such a setting. In addition, however, the unique conditions of architectural preservation, as well as the lack of significant surface disturbance at most noncemetery sites, require some adaptation of these methods in order to assess adequately the archaeological record of a coastal valley.

This chapter outlines the methods and organizational procedures employed in carrying out the Santa Valley research, and, at appropriate points, discusses how the methodological approach taken represents either adaptations of approaches used elsewhere or innovations that take into account unique aspects of coastal archaeology. Though no rationale need be given for presenting a detailed accounting of methods used in pursuing a scientific investigation, it is important nonetheless explicitly to underscore the critical relationship between the methods used and the potential of a given body of data for adequately testing or constructing theories of sociocultural evolution. In presenting such an accounting one is not only allowing adequate appraisal of the nature of the

data, but constructing part of the logical groundwork necessary for drawing reasonably robust conclusions. In this regard, it may be argued that one of the outstanding characteristics of leading settlement pattern research—from the pioneering Virú Valley Project to such recent studies as the Valley of Mexico survey—is the explicit and full presentation of research methods used. The discussion of this chapter, then, follows the lead of these earlier studies in attempting to achieve as briefly as possible a similarly complete presentation of methodological approach.

The first section, on prefield research, discusses the brief reconnaissance trip taken to the North Coast in 1977, and the studies carried out at various U.S. museums of ceramic type collections from Santa and adjacent valleys. The second section, on field methods, begins by outlining the approach taken in carrying out regional survey. Included here are discussions of the types of airphotos and topographic maps used, field logistics, survey techniques, artifact collection procedures, structure and site mapping procedures, and field notes. The field methods section concludes with a discussion of laboratory procedures followed in preparing regional map tracings and recording data on ceramic collections. The final section, on postfield analytical and organizational procedures, begins by discussing the methods used in assessing prehispanic chronology—including general approach, the identification of principal regional ceramic diagnostics, period nomenclature, the problem of period length, and identification of nonceramic temporal diagnostics. Following this, the methods employed in analyzing and organizing data on prehispanic structures and sites are outlined—including preparation of illustrations, assessing basic site function, categories of occupational density, categories of site size and function, assessing multicomponent occupations, and assigning final site numbers. The final section concludes with discussions of the approach taken in carrying out locational analysis—including regional settlement patterns, delineation of subregional settlement clusters/groupings, demographic trends, ceramic distributions, maize-based carrying capacity, and assessing levels of sociocultural complexity.

In May, 1977, a short reconnaissance trip was made to the North Coast in order to examine several valleys for the feasibility of conducting regional settlement pattern research. Although almost any valley in the 640 km-long area between Chillón and Lambayeque would have been of potential interest, the search was narrowed from the start to the area between Moche and Casma Valleys (see Fig. 1). For several decades this area has been the focus of the most intensive archaeological research of any section of the Peruvian coast, and ceramic chronology (including utilitarian as well as decorated pottery) is generally much better known than other areas. Among the valleys briefly visited were Virú, Chao, Santa, Nepeña, and Casma. Since regionally-oriented research already had been carried out in Virú and Nepeña, it was decided to exclude both valleys from consideration. Although neither valley had been the focus of the kind of systematic and comprehensive survey described in this report, the data from both were complete enough that resurveying them at best would merely have duplicated the efforts of previous researchers—with little hope of offering additional data of importance on most major sites. On the other hand, a visit to Chao confirmed the probability that it was relatively too small and of minor demographic potential to provide an interesting and challenging focus of research—in spite of the presence of a few important sites, including Las Salinas de Chao, Cerro de la Cruz, and Cerro Huasaquito. Casma Valley, while little studied on a systematic regional basis, seemed rather too large an undertaking in a project of potentially limited funding—in spite of the presence of a number of interesting defensive, ceremonial-civic, and habitation sites, including Cerro Sechín, Chanquillo, Sechín Alto, Mojeque, Pallka, Manchán, and El Purgatorio.

In contrast, as discussed in Chapter I, Santa had several distinct advantages, including a relatively medium-sized coastal sector and limited, but extensive, previous research indicating the presence of major interregional ceramic diagnostics and large numbers of sites dating throughout the prehispanic coastal sequence. Of equal importance was the fact that Santa is strategically located, both with respect to major north Central Andean cultural developments (i.e., Gallinazo, Recuay, Moche, Wari/Black-White-Red, and Chimú) as well as to the then better-known ceramic sequences of Moche, Virú, Nepeña, and Casma. All of this suggested that a comprehensive survey could be carried out throughout most, if not all, of the Lower Santa region with relatively modest funding and personnel, and that there existed a reasonable possibility of establishing a chronological sequence to date sites on the basis of associated ceramic debris.

The working hypothesis during the beginning stages of the research was that we could *bracket* our initial understanding of the Lower Santa Valley sequence, within the broader context of a detailed prior knowledge of the better known sequences of adjacent valleys to the north and south. As in a number of coastal valleys where only studies of a limited nature have been carried out, previous research in Santa had focused more on decorated wares than on utilitarian wares. Since the latter are usually of critical importance in assessing the chronology of habitation sites, it was therefore considered essential that we study type collections made by coastal researchers who had focused on both decorated *and* utilitarian wares in their attempts to assess chronology. From the publications on the 1946 Virú research, it was clear that both kinds of wares had been taken systematically into account in establishing chronology as well as in dating sites in that valley (cf. Bennett 1950; Collier 1955; Ford 1949; Ford and Willey 1949; Strong and Evans 1952; Willey 1953). Thus, under the assumption that intensive study of the Virú type collections available in the U.S. would give us a better grasp of the relationship between both kinds of wares at the outset of the Santa research, visits were made to the principal museums where these collections are housed—including the Field, American, and Yale Peabody Museums.

Since the Field Museum was the most accessible of these institutions in terms of travel time, and the Virú collections there are nearly complete, through the kind assistance of its curatorial staff I was able to make a number of visits along with several prospective field assistants for detailed study and photography. During these visits, we were also given permission to study a ceramic type collection from Casma Valley that Donald Collier and Donald Thompson had made during their fieldwork there in the 1960s (cf. Collier 1960; Thompson 1962). This allowed us to gain some appreciation of ceramic continuities and differences between Virú and Casma throughout much of the prehispanic sequence. Finally, we studied and photographed a collection of whole vessels primarily of Moche and Early Middle Horizon dates, made by G. A. Dorsey in 1892 at Hacienda Suchimán in the Upper Valley sector of Santa.

The few Virú Valley ceramic types not present in the Field Museum collections were located and studied during later visits to the American and Yale Peabody Museums. At the American Museum, it was also possible to study a large collection of sherds made by James A. Ford in 1946, during a one-week survey of 58 sites throughout Santa Valley. This provided substantial verification that Virú and Santa shared major ceramic types (including Guañape Red Plain, Huacapongo Polished Plain, Castillo Plain, Valle Plain, Virú Plain, and Tomaval Plain) during most of the sequence. In addition, Craig Morris and the late Junius Bird granted me permission to study Ford's field notes from his Santa survey, as well as a seriation chart analyzing his collections from there. This proved to be most valuable since, of 15 ceramic types identified in his notes and analysis of the 15,000-sherd collection, 11 types were similar enough to those he had studied in preceding months of study in Virú Valley to be given Virú type names. Finally, brief visits were also made to: University of Massachusetts, where Donald Proulx kindly reviewed with me an extensive series of slides of major Nepeña Valley ceramic types, including sherds and whole vessels; and Harvard Peabody Museum, where Geoffrey Conrad gave me permission to photograph a number of Moche and Chimú whole vessels.

During the course of the prefield ceramic study, we were thus able to achieve the initial objective of intensively studying the ceramics of valleys immediately to the north and south of Santa, as well as collections from Santa Valley itself. At the same time, we had confirmation from examining Ford's unpublished data on Santa ceramics that the study of sequences from adjacent valleys was a preparatory procedure of substantial value. For comparative purposes and to facilitate the use of this knowledge in the field, a large reference catalog was compiled that contained (1) color photographs and photocopies of published descriptions of every one of the Virú Valley ceramic types; (2) photographs of the principal Santa Valley types collected by Ford, and identified by him with Virú Valley type names; and (3) photographs and data on major types from Casma, Nepeña, and Moche Valleys. In addition, two of my principal field assistants had acquired extensive knowledge of Virú and Casma ceramic diagnostics through their visits to the Field Museum, thereby preparing them adequately to aid in the identification of surface sherds from the start of fieldwork.

FIELD METHODS

Regional Survey

Airphotos and topographic maps. All regional and local maps of the Lower Santa region presented in this study are based on (1) a series of 1:100,000-scale topographic charts, obtained at the Instituto Geográfico Militar (IGM); and (2) a series of matte-finish airphoto sets at scales ranging between 1:10,000 and 1:50,000,

obtained at the Servicio Aerofotográfico Nacional (SAN). In addition, as discussed later, several of the larger site complexes in the survey area were mapped in detail using SAN airphoto enlargements at scales ranging between 1:3000 and 1:7000. As indicated in Fig. 14, throughout most of the region we were able to carry out fieldwork and general settlement mapping using airphotos that ranged between 1:10,000 and 1:20,000 scale.

Thus, in terms of the total number of settlements located during the project, fully 950 out of 1020 discrete archaeological sites (or 93%) were mapped at scales that permitted precise assessment of sizes ranging from as small as .1 ha to as large as 70 ha. Only 70 sites (or 7%) were included in the smaller-scale 1:50,000 coverage used in the northern, eastern, and western parts of the Santa-Chao sector. Here, however, we were still able accurately to assess site sizes—which range generally between .25 and 2 ha, except for the 55-ha site of Cerro Huasaquito (SVP-ETAN–404)—partly on the basis of the field airphotos themselves, but also by site-to-site house counts made in the field as the survey progressed. Although individual structures were not visible on the 1:50,000-scale airphoto sets, ancient rock-lined roads, trails, and sites could be distinguished clearly on the airphotos in most other areas. For example, in the central part of Pampa de los Pancitos—where the remains of sites and roads are particularly complex—the 1:12,000-scale airphoto coverage clearly showed not only the variable widths of the roads but also every one of the individual structures on most sites (e.g., see Fig. 134, a map traced directly from the field airphotos).

Since the scale of the seven airphoto sets used in the project varies from series to series, the area in square kilometers covered by the airphotos of individual sets also varies according to scale. For example, the airphotos of the 1:15,000-scale SAN 172 series cover a 24-km² area measuring 6 km (E-W) × 4 km (N-S), while those of the 1:50,000-scale SAN 147 series cover a 100-km² area measuring 10 km on a side. The actual physical size of the airphoto sets also varied, with dimensions ranging between 50 × 50 cm and 20 × 20 cm. All were therefore of a size that allowed them to be carried along easily in the field for use in orienting the survey team and recording archaeological remains.

Field logistics. As is apparent from the regional maps (e.g., see Fig. 6), the large area covered by the Santa Valley survey presented a certain number of logistical challenges. For example, a distance of some 85 km (50 mi) lies between the southernmost part of the survey region, along Bahía de Samanco, and the northernmost part, along the south desert margin of Chao. Fortunately, however, a two-wheel drive pickup truck was available for use during most of the period of the fieldwork, and the system of modern roads and rough tracks allowed us to gain access to nearly every part of the study

Plate 14. Crossing the *oroya* cable seat at Tablones

area with a minimum of difficulty. As Fig. 6 shows, access to the south desert margin of Santa Valley presented no problems at all since the coast-sierra dirt road runs all along the edge of the valley between the Panamerican highway and the uppermost part of the survey. By the same token, access was gained to the north desert margin of the Middle and Lower Valley sectors via the highway to the north of the valley, using three dirt roads and rough tracks that run back down to the southeast toward the river.

Relatively greater problems of access were encountered in two principal areas of the survey region. The first of these is the north desert margin of the Upper Valley sector. Although in 1979–80 it was possible to drive several kilometers upvalley from Tanguche as far as Pampa Blanca, the lack of a road in the remaining 25-km distance between there and the Santa-Tablachaca confluence made surveying the area via this access route extremely difficult, in terms of both travel time and field logistics. Fortunately, however, there were two places in the Upper Valley where we could get across the river from the south desert margin by means of one-person seats slung from steel cables (*oroyas*). Since the cable seats lie only 3–5 m above the torrent, and at least one of the crossings is some 60 m (200 ft) wide, simply getting

across the river to the north side was a reasonably eye-opening way to begin the day's survey (Plate 14). Once across, it was necessary to walk downriver or upriver as far as 10 km to carry out survey—i.e., equivalent to about two hours travel time one-way over generally rough terrain. Counting the two-hour roundtrip from Santa on the road, it was therefore often necessary to work 14-hour days in order to get in six to eight hours of actual field survey and mapping.

The other area that presented logistical difficulties was the eastern edge of the Santa-Chao sector. A dirt track runs part of the distance up Quebrada Palo Redondo off the main Tanguche road, providing the principal means of access to this area (Fig. 6). However, surveying and mapping the ancient road-settlement network that runs across this 29-km stretch of desert involved roundtrip hikes of up to 20 km (see Fig. 114). Everywhere else in the survey region, however, we had little difficulty in getting the vehicle to within three or four kilometers of most areas under study. When necessary, boulders were placed in the rear end of the pickup to gain traction for negotiating steep grades (e.g., on the Huaca Corral track), and we found that most of the off-road areas of Pampa de los Pancitos could be crossed with the vehicle by staying on hard-packed sand (two long boards were carried to extricate the vehicle from occasional traps of softer sand).

A total of 150 days was spent out in the field, away from our laboratory and residence in Santa. Although this time can be translated to meaningful research terms in various ways, one means of accounting for the days of actual fieldwork is to express them in terms of the number of sites studied per day. Thus, given 1020 discrete sites and subtracting roughly 25 days spent making detailed plan views of more complex structures and sites, we were able to study an average of about eight sites per day. With an average eight-hour survey day, this works out to one site studied per hour of fieldwork. Actually, however, the complexity of a number of sites required substantially more time than this (e.g., Pampa de los Incas Complex), while many less complex ones required less (e.g., those of the Santa-Chao sector).

In general, the chronology of survey coverage of the various sectors proceeded from the Upper Valley down through the Middle Valley, from the Lower Valley southward to the Bahía de Samanco area, and, finally, to the Santa-Chao Desert. However, because of several factors—including an extended period of two months in the midst of fieldwork when the vehicle was in use elsewhere in Peru—it was necessary to break off several times from this general schedule and focus on areas around the town of Santa that could be reached on foot or by local taxi. Thus most of the Lower Valley sector was finished before we had yet reached the uppermost part of the survey area, around Chuquicara, and the north desert margin of the Middle Valley, near Huaca Corral. Complete coverage of all sectors was eventually achieved, of course, and the only real effect of this complicated scheduling of areal coverage was that, as we ended the work in the region, collection numbers and site numbers reflected the sequence of work—and not a neat, geographically-ordered sequence of numbering.

Survey methods. Although a total of 23 persons assisted the principal investigator at one point or another during the research, participation was scheduled so that we consistently had a single survey team composed of three to five persons throughout most of the fieldwork. Field survey generally was carried out by focusing on the area encompassed within an individual airphoto, and we then proceeded with systematic coverage until all archaeological remains on that airphoto had been studied. However, because of logistical difficulties involved in continually crossing the river or in using the roundabout Tanguche access route, in the upvalley area we generally surveyed the south side of the river on several adjacent airphotos before crossing the Santa to complete coverage of the opposite side. Depending on the size of the area covered by the airphoto and the complexity of remains, a minimum of one week normally was required to complete the survey of the area it encompassed. However,

when a number of complex structural remains and sites were found closely spaced in a given area covered by the airphoto (e.g., pre-Guadalupito remains in the area centered on Quebrada de Cayhuamarca), the preparation of detailed plan views often required 5–10 additional days of work.

The survey procedure itself was adapted from that developed by Jeffrey Parsons in settlement pattern research in the Valley of Mexico (cf. Parsons 1971:16–20; Parsons et al. 1982:63–68). In this procedure, a centrally-positioned person carries the airphoto taped to a lightweight plywood board, and members of the survey team are spaced at intervals of 15–50 m on either side depending on the complexity and density of the archaeological remains encountered. The team moves methodically in a line across the terrain, with each person calling out every 25–50 m or so, depending on the scale of the airphoto, the nature of all remains encountered—including varying densities and periods of associated ceramic diagnostics. As survey proceeds, these data are recorded with a sharp 3H pencil directly on the airphoto, and, given a reasonable degree of care in handling it, this produces an indelible record that can be used in the field laboratory for preparing map tracings. As applied to the Santa Valley, this general approach to regional survey worked quite well in practice. However, other aspects of the methods developed in Valley of Mexico—such as those used in estimating population on the basis of sherd densities—were modified to take into consideration the relatively much better preservation of structural remains that characterizes the coast of Peru.

In order to place these modifications in perspective, it is useful to describe briefly the approach developed by Parsons. In Valley of Mexico, where many centuries of extensive plowing and erosion due to overgrazing have taken place, all traces of sites often have been destroyed except for a scatter of surface sherds and rock rubble. Thus, as mentioned in Chapter I, estimates of the population size of a given site are based not only on the areal extent of these remains but also on their density. Specific numerical densities of sherds are equated with specific density "labels" that are used to communicate subjective visual estimates to the person with the airphoto. These labels run along an explicit continuum (cf. Parsons 1974:84–87) that is expressed in terms of sherds per square meter—from "nada" (no sherds), through "very light", "light", "light-to-moderate", "moderate", and "heavy" (sherds almost or actually stacked up on one another). In turn, the subjective visual estimates of sherd densities have been equated arbitrarily with a continuum of population densities that, given the conditions of site preservation, allow a reasonable means of assessing relative changes in regional population numbers throughout the sequence.

In a limited way, this method of assessing the density of occupational debris also was used during the Santa

Plate 15. View to southeast of Structure 109 and associated windbreaks at SVP-VIN-9/SVP-ESUCH-11

Valley survey. However, it quickly became apparent that the preservation of habitation structures of all periods throughout the region was generally excellent, and that we would therefore achieve greater accuracy by estimating population on the basis of densities of structural remains (e.g., see Plate 15). In the case of smaller, less complex sites it was possible to count individual structures as survey proceeded across them. Moreover, since structures are often visible on the airphotos between 1:10,000 and 1:15,000 scale, even in the case of larger, more complex sites it was possible to count individual habitation structures directly on the airphotos. As discussed later in this chapter (in the section on categories of occupational density) a four-fold continuum was devised during postfield analysis of airphotos, field notes, and site plans to translate densities of habitation structures per hectare to population densities. Nevertheless, during the period of fieldwork we generally also continued to use Valley of Mexico-type sherd density calls in conjunction with the periods represented on a site, simply as a means of recording the variable amounts of occupational debris.

In terms of the nature of regional coverage and our sample of sites within the boundaries of the survey area,

no presumptions were made about where sites might and might not be located in surveying the Upper, Middle, and Lower Valley, and Coast sectors. Thus, as we proceeded from area to area within these sectors the survey team covered every part of the ground surface where it was feasible for the prehispanic people of the valley to locate sites—including the valley floor, adjacent desert margins, ridges, higher mountaintops, and pampas. Although, as implied above, it generally was possible to ascertain the presence of a site in any given area by examining the airphoto, this was not always the case. For example, some of the less complex hilltop citadels of Cayhuamarca Period do not show up on the SAN 172 series airphotos (in spite of their large scale), nor are these citadels visible in the field when one views the hilltops from down on the valley floor. I mention this simply to make the point that the only way to find many sites in the rugged inland coastal setting is to climb up onto the hills of the desert margin and examine every area carefully.

The single exception to this essentially 100% coverage of the survey region was the Santa-Chao Desert sector, where the ancient road-settlement network is distinctly visible on the airphotos (e.g., see the tracing from the field airphoto in Fig. 134) and is confined to quebrada margins, open pampas, and mountain passes. All other parts of the barren area between Santa and Chao Valleys are occupied by steep desert mountains, and, although the airphotos were examined carefully for any possible remains, it was therefore unnecessary to cover this rugged intervening terrain.

Artifact collection procedures. In terms of overall regional strategy, among the primary objectives of the research were not only to date sites on the basis of associated ceramics but also to obtain collections from sites throughout the area of occupation during each of the major periods. As should be clear from a comparison of the collection provenience map for any given period with the settlement pattern map of that period (e.g., compare Fig. 190 to Fig. 22, for Cayhuamarca Period), in general we were able to achieve satisfactorily widespread collection coverage. However, since the rule in making collections obviously is to find a reasonable sample of sherd diagnostics (e.g., five or more) to collect on sites of a given area, in a few places we found ourselves restricted by the general paucity of such remains. The principal area of this nature is the Santa-Chao Desert. Although at nearly all of the 200 sites of this sector we were able to find at least one or two good Early Tanguche Period sherd diagnostics (e.g., Black-White-Red ware) to date associated habitation structures, almost nowhere were sherds available in large enough numbers to warrant making collections—with the principal exception of SVP-ETAN–321 site (see Fig. 121; and Coll. 382, in Table 27). Thus, although our control over site chronology in this sector appears to be good, we were not able to amass a local ceramic assemblage to compare Santa-Chao to other sectors of the survey region.

Since we were covering a large survey area, and fully 80% of the sites encountered had not been studied by previous researchers, the Santa Valley research was in some respects of an exploratory nature. The strategy of sherd collection at individual sites could not therefore include a random sampling design, since such designs are based usually on a prior knowledge of the exact configuration of a site. In contrast, in nearly all cases we were collecting a site at the same time as we were determining its configuration (see discussion under laboratory procedures, below, for methods of assessing site boundaries). In general, then, we followed methods used in Valley of Mexico under a similar set of conditions. For example, at large sites where sherd debris was extensive and distributed in relatively dense quantities, we attempted to make ceramic collections in as many sectors as possible in places where it appeared subjectively that a representative sample could be obtained. All diagnostics were then collected, including rim sherds and decorated fragments, as well as undecorated body sherds in

cases where diagnostic forms or paste types were noted (e.g., annular-base bowls or kaolin ware).

Nevertheless, due to the general absence of significant surface disturbance at most noncemetery sites in the survey area (as opposed to Valley of Mexico, where frequent plowing tends to bring sherds to the surface), ceramic diagnostics often were rather scarce. In these cases, it was necessary to make collections over the entire area of the site, including all surface diagnostics that could be found. This was especially the situation encountered at sites dating to the earlier, pre-Guadalupito ceramic periods. Still, the number of sherds in each of the 382 collections averaged only 35, with a range from about 10 to as many as 200 sherds per collection (see Column 2, in Table 27).

Since our primary objectives in making collections were to date the sites on the basis of associated remains, and, ultimately, to compare assemblages on an area-to-area and period-to-period basis, the great majority of artifacts collected consisted of ceramic vessels and sherds. In this regard, it is of interest to note that nearly 100 whole or nearly whole pottery vessels were found on the surface of sites during the survey. Most are from looted cemeteries where they had been left by huaqueros—apparently, as mentioned in the preceding chapter, because they were broken or were considered to have little value on the antiquities market. Aside from the ceramics constituting the bulk of the collections, a very few nonceramic artifacts also were collected—including wood and bone implements, marine shells, and lithics. Interestingly enough, in spite of intensive examination of the surface of all sites, we found only one projectile point during the survey (see Fig. 194g). Artifacts of copper, such as shawl pins (*tupus*), occasionally were noted on the surface of looted cemeteries, but were always found in fragmentary condition and not collected.

Each artifact collection was placed in one or more bags made of sturdy cotton cloth called *tocuyo*, especially prepared for the project by a seamstress in Santa. The smaller, 25 × 25-cm size of these bags was determined by the need to fit several of them into the backpack carried by each member of the survey team. At the time the collection was made, each bag was labeled with indelible ink from a felt tip marker pen. Using Collection 382 as an example, the bag label included the project designation, the collection number, and the airphoto number as follows:

SVP
Coll. 382
106–41

If more than one bag was required to contain the collection, then each bag was also marked "Bag 1 of 3," "Bag 2 of 3," and so on. Where collections were taken from a specific area in relation to a structure that had been assigned a project number, then this information was noted on the bags as well, below the airphoto number. For example, the collection (in a single bag) from the interior of Structure 1 was labeled as follows:

SVP
Coll. 4
E69N284
Struc. 1 (int.)

Structure and site mapping procedures. In addition to the smaller-scale regional maps of sites and other archaeological remains prepared with the SAN airphoto sets, a series of nearly 180 detailed structure and site plans was prepared with transit-stadia and Brunton-tape during the course of the fieldwork. Depending on the area covered by the structure or site being mapped, these plan views were drawn on 50 × 50-cm (20 × 20") or 28 × 22-cm (8 1/2 × 11") gridded engineering paper at scales ranging between 1:100 and 1:400. For example, the plans of nearly all Cayhuamarca Period citadels were made at scales ranging between 1:200 and 1:400 on 50 × 50-cm paper. With regard to mapping instruments, we generally used the transit and stadia rod in making plans of more complex structures containing a large number of rooms and walls, since this allowed a more efficient mapping effort and more accurate results. However, since this procedure involved hand-carrying a heavy transit (David White Model 8200) and a wooden tripod, in addition to other necessary gear, transit-stadia mapping generally was restricted to sites that could be reached within one hour's hike from where the vehicle was parked.

Many of the more remote fortresses located at elevations as high as 700 m (2295 ft) above the valley floor therefore had to be mapped with Brunton compass and metric tape. Although this method is not generally speaking as accurate as using transit-stadia, we found that with Brunton-tape we usually could achieve accuracy of less than 1–2 m error of closure (cf. Davis, Foote, and Kelley 1966:204) in mapping complex citadels that ran for 100 m, or more, along a hilltop. Considering the alternatives of either taking substantially more time to lug the heavy transit gear for several hours up steep slopes or, worse yet, not mapping the structure at all, this small amount of imprecision was considered of minor importance; indeed, it usually was possible to eliminate error of closure altogether by remapping sections of a given structure.

A minimum of three to four persons was required to carry out the mapping procedures, depending upon which of the two instrument sets was used. In the case of the transit procedure, one person was situated on the transit, another on the stadia (a collapsible Chicago-style metric rod), while a third prepared the plan. The plan itself was prepared by taping the gridded paper to a rigid

plywood board, and using a ruled straight edge, steel dividers, French curves, a 360° protractor, and a sharp 4H pencil. In the Brunton procedure, one person used the compass, two others managed the 30-m metric tape (sometimes a difficult task in the strong afternoon winds), and a fourth prepared the plan. None of the site and structure plans took more than two day's work to prepare, and most took one day or less. Using these mapping procedures, we were able to make detailed plan views of nearly every structure of interest found in the survey region—including essentially all citadels, most minor fortresses, all major huacas, most minor huacas, every smaller site of probable public or administrative function, and a large number of habitation structures and sites.

It is appropriate to mention in passing here that the methods outlined above were considered to be substantially more accurate and rewarding in terms of the architectural data retrieved than relying on airphoto enlargements to make structure plans. Since almost no enlargement is ever of a precision adequate enough to show the exact position and nature of such specific details as corners, doorways, or passageways, it usually is necessary to check out every one of these features in the field. And since most enlargements become too blurred to use as they approach the 1:100 and 1:400 scales mentioned above, maps made with them are usually much more limited in details shown—because the enlargements usually must be kept at 1:1000-scale or smaller to avoid complete blurriness. Thus, when one weighs the little amount of time and effort saved in using enlargements against the relatively much greater detail one is able to show on large-scale instrument maps, the latter become decidedly more attractive. Perhaps more importantly, since funding for archaeological projects is always limited and one rarely can get back to every complex structure studied during a regional project, it seems clear that the least one can do is take the time to record accurately the data at hand.

Nevertheless, we encountered a few larger site complexes that, while clearly requiring some sort of mapping effort beyond the smaller-scale airphoto outline, were simply too large to map in a reasonably short time. In these cases, given the time constraints and the need to cover a large survey region, the use of very large-scale airphotos was a reasonable compromise solution. Included among the sites mapped using this procedure are: Huaca Santa Complex (Fig. 71), Pampa de los Incas Complex (Figs. 101, 108), SVP-ETAN–44/etc. (Fig. 124), Huaca Jedionda Complex (Fig. 131), SVP-LTAN–15/etc. (Fig. 146), SVP-LTAN–40 (Fig. 147), and SVP-LTR–47/Alto Perú Complex (Fig. 160). The Late Tanguche site of SVP-LTAN–40 provides a good example of why using an airphoto enlargement was the better way to map it. This site is located on the steep north desert margin of the Middle Valley sector, just below the mouth of Quebrada Cenicero. With high-density terracing covering a very large area of 14.2 ha and terraces running continuously from a point near the river upslope to a point some 200 m (656 ft) higher in elevation (Fig. 147), mapping this site with instruments clearly would have taken many days.

As with the collections, prehispanic structures were assigned numbers according to the order in which they were surveyed and mapped, and these numbers have been retained as permanent designations for both the dissertation and this report. It should be noted that the great majority of structures (and sites) in the region are unnamed. This is primarily because most are located on the arid desert margin or on remote hilltops out away from the valley floor, and modern inhabitants of Santa Valley rarely if ever have reason to pass anywhere near most of them.

Field notes. In addition to recording data on the airphotos and in the form of structure and site plans, a detailed set of written notes was made during each day of the fieldwork. These notes included observations on: (1) each collection (specific nature of the provenience, initial impressions of the dating, density of surface sherds, and size of the collection area), (2) nonceramic occupational debris (e.g., types and average sizes of adobe bricks, lithics, textile fragments, charcoal, cultigens, and marine shells), (3) each structure for which a plan was made (nature and condition of the architecture, and nature of associated ceramics and other debris), (4) specific prehispanic remains designated as "features" (e.g., desert ground drawings and petroglyphs), and (5) specific geographical points designated as "locations," usually places of interest along more extensive types of prehispanic features (e.g., a section along the Great Wall system).

Laboratory Mapping and Analysis

Regional map tracings. Following the completion of systematic survey throughout the area covered by a given airphoto, a large sheet of Albanene tracing paper was placed over the airphoto and all archaeological remains as well as relevant modern and natural features were recorded. With contiguous groupings of two to four airphotos placed on each of these map tracings, this procedure resulted in a highly readable and accurate picture of all prehispanic remains over large areas of each survey sector. It also provided a large-scale base map from which data could be retrieved on the location, size, and configuration of sites and other remains. As mentioned earlier, although the areal extent of sites often was clear from the well-preserved remains of rock-walled structures, we also noted on the airphotos the extent and chronology of associated occupational debris. Once the extent of these remains was noted on the map tracings, it

was a relatively easy procedure not only to determine the boundaries of a site but to assess changes in size over time at multicomponent sites.

As described up to this point, our map tracing procedure was similar to that used in the Valley of Mexico. However, due to the comparatively incipient nature of our research on the North Coast, the initial designation of site chronology on the tracings differed from Valley of Mexico procedures. Since the beginning of survey research in the late 1960s in the latter area, the main ceramic diagnostics (utilitarian and decorated) associated with each of the prehispanic periods have been well known. It has thus been possible in making field map tracings to outline the sites of each period with a different colored pencil. This is a relatively simple and straightforward procedure with several distinct advantages, including: (1) allowing the observer immediately to distinguish the occupations of various periods shown on the tracings; (2) making it possible to assign separate, sequential sets of field numbers to the occupations of each period as fieldwork proceeds; and (3) permitting the accurate representation of the often variable extent of occupational periods represented on multicomponent sites.

In contrast, although we had reasonably good knowledge of many ceramic diagnostics as we began the Santa Valley research, it was considered more prudent to use a single color to outline sites and other remains of all periods—at least in the initial stages of mapping. This did not disallow later application of the Valley of Mexico procedures, since the areal extent of the occupation of different periods was marked directly on the airphoto and map tracing for each site; rather, it merely forestalled such procedures until intensive analysis of the ceramic collections had been completed at the end of the fieldwork. Thus all archaeological remains—including sites, walls, roads, field systems, and canals—were outlined in orange pencil on the original set of field map tracings. All modern features—including towns, roads, and individual farm houses—were outlined in yellow; agricultural features and matorral vegetation were marked in green; and the ocean, river, and modern canals were marked in blue.

Analysis of ceramic collections. Most of the sherds and whole vessels collected during the fieldwork were covered with a thin layer of dirt or silt, and it was therefore necessary to wash them for storage and analysis in the field laboratory in Santa. Once a collection had been cleaned and dried, the sherds were marked in ink with the number of the collection and placed back in the labeled cloth bag for storage. Following the completion of survey, the final three months in Santa were devoted to an intensive, three-stage analysis of the collections.

During the previous months of work in the field, a reasonably good understanding had been achieved of the major ceramic types characteristic of the various periods in the sequence, and the first stage of analysis involved making full-scale drawings of the types present in each of the 382 collections. Using a diameter calculator board and a Formagage for precise assessment of rim sherd and vessel configuration, nearly 130 separate 50 × 50-cm gridded sheets were filled with drawings of rim profiles and decorated sherds, as well as accompanying descriptive and quantitative data on rim diameter, temper, firing, paste color, and presumed dating. At the same time, drawings of sherds in multicomponent collections were arranged in tentative groupings and labeled by period. Finally, one or more full-scale drawings were made of each of the whole vessels collected during the research. In this manner, some 8000 separate drawings of ceramic diagnostics were prepared, representing nearly 67% of the 12,000 total diagnostic sherds collected. Most importantly, since ceramic collections could not be taken back to the U.S. for additional detailed study, an essentially complete visual and descriptive record had been obtained to use as an aid in carrying out postfield analysis.

In contrast to the sequential order (from 1–382) followed in preparing the drawings, during the second stage of the field analysis the collections were studied in period-by-period groupings—proceeding in chronological order from the earliest to the latest of the ceramic periods. In this way, a close comparative examination could be made of all collections of presumed Cayhuamarca date, for example, in order to check for any inconsistencies in the preceding stage of analysis. This not only functioned as a double-check procedure, but also was an efficient way to gain a better understanding of changes in ceramic assemblages from period to period in the sequence. Finally, at the end of the second stage any refinements in dating were marked on the collection drawings, and the degree of confidence in the results was rated according to a four-part validity scale characterizing the components of each collection (i.e., excellent, good, fair, and poor; see Table 27; see also Willey 1953:423–448 for a similar procedure).

In the third stage of field ceramic analysis, the collections were again reviewed in numerical order from 1–382, and a detailed set of notes was made in a separate set of field books to accompany the data in the collection drawings. Following this, a number of representative sherd types and whole vessels were selected for closeup black-and-white and color slide photography to aid in later interpretation of the period assemblages.

POSTFIELD ANALYTICAL
AND ORGANIZATIONAL PROCEDURES

Assessing Prehispanic Chronology

General approach. As discussed in the preceding sections, we began the research with a background of inten-

sive prefield study of all available ceramic type collections from Santa and valleys to the north and south, as well as of the published literature on ceramics of these valleys and the adjacent sierra (major publications on the ceramics of Santa, Moche, Virú, Nepeña, Casma, and the adjacent sierra areas of Pashash and the Callejón de Huaylas include: Bennett 1939, 1944, 1950; Benson 1972; Clothier 1943; Collier 1955, 1960; Donnan 1973, 1976, 1978; Donnan and Mackey 1978; Ford 1949; Ford and Willey 1949; Grieder 1978; Kroeber 1925a, 1925b, 1926, 1930; Kutscher 1954; Larco Hoyle 1944, 1945, 1948, 1963a, 1963b; Lynch 1980; Proulx 1968, 1973; Strong and Evans 1952; Tello 1956; Willey 1953). This background provided a basis for understanding the Lower Santa sequence in terms of both interregional ceramic similarities as well as the differences between the Santa assemblage and those of adjacent regions. Given the collection of ceramics from sites throughout the main valley area, it also was possible to approach the goal of understanding regional developments from period to period on the basis of a large number of single-component collections. At the same time, the extensive regionwide coverage of the collections raised the possibility that analysis of similarities and differences could be carried out on a between-sector basis, at the regional level, with the objective of elucidating within-valley sociocultural relations.

Finally, given the procedures followed in making ceramic collections, as well as the three-stage analysis at the end of the fieldwork, it appeared likely that substantial progress could be made toward understanding period-by-period associations between utilitarian/plainware ceramics and decorated wares. As argued earlier, achieving an understanding of these associations is especially critical for dating habitation sites characterized primarily or entirely by utilitarian/undecorated surface ceramics, and, of course, ultimately in attempts to assess demographic trends throughout the prehispanic sequence. In some contrast to our own objective of achieving such an understanding, the general approach of many researchers on the coast of Peru—clearly under the strong influence of attempts to seriate gravelots on the basis of decorated funerary wares (e.g., see Rowe 1961)—has been to ignore utilitarian ceramics altogether. For example, Proulx (1968:12) has argued that "plainware has little value for distinguishing chronological positions. . . ." On the other hand, under the assumption that one does not usually accomplish what one does not set out to achieve, our approach to this issue was to treat it as an empirical question—i.e., a fundamental objective of the research was to test the proposition that specific plainware types cannot be related to specific decorated temporal diagnostics.

While it is clear that more work will have to be done in terms of stratigraphic and chronological control, the general thrust of the Santa Valley research—as exemplified by the ceramic descriptions and illustrations of Appendix I, and discussed in some detail below—is that a clear relationship does indeed exist between specific utilitarian and decorated form types in each one of the major periods of the ceramic sequence. Both types of wares can therefore be considered as equally sensitive time markers. At the same time, it cannot be overemphasized that, to the extent the goal of demonstrating this relationship has been achieved, it could not have been done without the work of previous researchers in Santa, as well as Nepeña, Casma, Virú, and Moche.

Preparation of ceramic drawings and descriptions. Turning now to more specific procedures of postfield ceramic analysis, I will briefly describe methods used in preparing the illustrations and descriptions included in this report before going on to outline in detail the principal ceramic diagnostics of the Lower Santa region. Using the set of ceramic illustrations prepared in the field, the procedure followed in deciding which among the 8000 individual drawings would be included here was to focus principally on the least ambiguous collections—including single-component collections for the most part, as well as multicomponent collections with clearly distinguishable diagnostics (e.g., a collection with a discontinuous mixture of early and late materials, rather than one with successive periods represented). All rim profiles and other diagnostics from these collection were then traced at full scale on gridded paper (to maintain proper orientation), representing some 1500 of the total sherds and vessels included in the field drawings.

Each of the 1500 drawings was then individually cut away from the gridded tracing sheet—with all field data including the collection number retained on each one—and laid out in period-by-period groupings. Then, proceeding from early to late in the sequence, these period groupings were divided into smaller type groupings based on differences in (1) vessel type (e.g., bowls, jars, figurines), (2) paste color (e.g., reddish-brownware, redware, kaolin, grayware), (3) discrete form attributes (e.g., flaring rim, everted rim), and (4) presence-absence and/or type of surface decoration (e.g., plainware, red stippled, Black-White-Red). In addition, certain type groupings were further divided on the basis of differences in continuous attributes within that grouping, usually because these groupings varied on this basis from area to area in the region (e.g., see differences in neck height for Vinzos Jars 5a, 5b, and 5c, in Fig. 199). Some types also were separated out on the basis of clearly overriding decorative features, such as exterior red-polished slipping, and then subdivided on the basis of discrete form attributes (e.g., see Early Suchimancillo Jar 8, in Figs. 205–206). Once the type groupings had been made, the selection of drawings to be included here was made with the objective of showing the complete range of variation in form, wall thickness, rim diameter, and decoration.

Ultimately, some 1000 sherds and vessels were included in the illustrations—representing the full range of Santa Valley types and roughly 8.3% of the total of 12,000 diagnostic sherds collected.

As should be clear, the principal goal of this part of the analysis was not to generate a new set of type names, but rather to illustrate as completely as possible the diversity of ceramic types within a period as well as period-to-period changes in assemblages. In this regard, it is relevant to note that to a certain degree the analysis was constrained by the prior establishment in the literature of type names. Thus, for example, type names such as Black-White-Red that are common in North Coast usage have generally been retained in devising type names for each Santa Valley period. Another rather more implicit constraint was the familiarity gained over many months of fieldwork with certain aspects or attributes of ceramics that seemed important as the collections were being made. Nevertheless, a far greater number of subtleties of form and decoration were noted in the postfield analysis, and these should prove to be of substantial utility in assessing collections made in future research in the area. Finally, it is worth stressing that the type groupings of Appendix I are presented as *hypotheses* about the ceramic chronology of the Lower Santa sequence—hypotheses that are not only substantiated by reference to field procedures and the literature on other areas, but clearly subject to modification as research proceeds.

Following the establishment of the principal ceramic types, the next step in the analysis involved a systematic reappraisal of the 130 drawing sheets made in the field in order to record data for each of these types on a collection-by-collection and period-by-period basis. Since the drawings and accompanying data covered essentially all of the 12,000 diagnostic sherds collected and analyzed during the fieldwork, this procedure allowed a quantitative expression of the full range of variation in numbers, overall form, paste, surface characteristics, and regional distribution for each of the nearly 200 types that constitute our collections from the Lower Santa region. These data were then summarized and analyzed statistically for each type, and used in the preparation of the ceramic descriptions of Appendix I.

The following data are included under each ceramic description: (1) *number* (total sherds, expressed both as a raw count and as a percentage of the period assemblage), (2) *general description* (overall form; rim diameter range, mean, and standard deviation; wall thickness range), (3) *paste* (grain size of temper, paste color), (4) *surface characteristics* (exterior/interior color, decoration), (5) *distribution* (general comments on sector-by-sector distribution, exact numbers of sherds for each provenience by collection and site number), (6) *chronological assessment* (comments on value of type as a time marker), and (7) *interregional comparisons* (similarities to contemporaneous types in the literature on ceramics from Moche, Virú,

Table 3. Summary of Principal Features of Ceramic Assemblages by Period in the Lower Santa Valley Sequence

Period[a]	Total Sherds in Assemblage	Percentages of Major Paste Types				Percentages of Selected Major Vessel Types				
		Reddish-Brownware	Redware	Grayware	Kaolin Ware	Bowls	Jars	Human Effigies	Animal Effigies	Maize Effigies
LTR	723	0.0	21.7	78.3	0.0	11.8	87.9	1.1	0.7	3.3
ETR	900	0.0	62.0	38.0	0.0	7.3	91.7	0.1	0.8	0.3
LTAN	620	0.0	96.8	3.2	0.0	7.0	93.0	0.2	0.7	0.0
ETAN	2283	0.0	97.9	1.9	0.2	10.5	85.0+	4.9	0.9	0.1
GUAD	1582	0.0	100.0	0.0	0.0	8.1	65.0+	4.2	0.9	0.5
LSUCH	2534	10.6	76.3	0.4	12.7	12.1	74.0	2.2	0.7	0.1
ESUCH	1665	39.0	56.3	0.3	4.4	12.9	80.0	0.5	0.3	0.1
VIN	688	93.0	6.0	1.0	0.0	11.2	86.8	0.2	0.0	0.0
CAY	1017	99.0	0.0	1.0	0.0	47.0	51.0	0.0	0.2	0.0

[a]LTR = Late Tambo Real; ETR = Early Tambo Real; LTAN = Late Tanguche; ETAN = Early Tanguche; GUAD = Guadalupito; LSUCH = Late Suchimancillo; ESUCH = Early Suchimancillo; VIN = Vinzos; CAY = Cayhuamarca.

Nepeña, Casma, Pashash, Callejón de Huaylas, and other more distant areas).

Thus, in addition to accounting for nearly every sherd collected during the fieldwork, the ceramic descriptions also relate each type insofar as possible to those of presumably contemporaneous date in nearby regions. Although some Lower Santa types were found to have no apparent counterparts in other regions, there was no period in the ceramic sequence when fewer than 84% of all types could not be related on an interregional basis. Specifically, the total number of types and the percentage of these that could be so related are as follows: Cayhuamarca (16 types, 100%), Vinzos (20 types, 100%), Early Suchimancillo (29 types, 93%), Late Suchimancillo (39 types, 87%), Guadalupito (16 types, 100%), Early Tanguche (19 types, 89%), Late Tanguche (12 types, 100%), Early Tambo Real (21 types, 90%), and Late Tambo Real (25 types, 84%). The importance of these data does not lie in specific numbers and percentages, however, since these clearly are a function of the criteria used in establishing types and of the completeness of other published regional samples; rather, it lies simply in the fact that the Lower Santa sequence can be tied securely into other regional sequences from Cayhuamarca Period on.

Other data resulting from the analysis of the ceramic collections are summarized in Table 3. These include (1) total number of sherds in each period assemblage, (2) percentages of major paste types, and (3) percentages of selected vessel types. The series of columns showing percentages of major paste types in each period assemblage are of particular interest at this point, specifically in providing additional support for the argument of a secure chronological position for each of the nine ceramic periods. These columns show an orderly period-to-period change, not only in the percentage of any given paste type but also in the percentage of each paste type in relation to others. For example, reddish-brownware is

the principal paste diagnostic of Cayhuamarca and Vinzos Periods, and continues on in smaller and smaller percentages in the assemblages of Early and Late Suchimancillo Periods. At the same time, the percentage of redware in the period assemblages increases steadily from Vinzos on through Guadalupito Period. Likewise, the percentage of redware in the assemblages from Early Tanguche on decreases as a function of the increasing amount of grayware. In contrast, kaolin ware is characteristic of only three periods in the sequence—most importantly including Early and Late Suchimancillo, when strong contacts probably existed between the Lower Santa region and Recuay peoples of the adjacent sierra. Small amounts of kaolin ware are also present in the Early Tanguche assemblage, with the appearance of limited numbers of Cajamarca III cursive-decorated kaolin tripod bowls.

Principal ceramic diagnostics. In this section the main temporal diagnostics of each of the nine ceramic periods are outlined. In addition, the diagnostics of each period are briefly discussed in relation to their counterparts in nearby regions. Most of the discussion represents a summary of the sections on chronological assessment and interregional comparisons in Appendix I, and reference to the descriptions will provide additional details as well as specific references to the literature on adjacent regions. The main criteria used in selecting principal period diagnostics include: (1) consistent appearance in probable single-component collections; (2) reasonably widespread distribution throughout the area of occupation during the period in question; and (3) a reasonably strong relationship based on similarities of paste, form, and surface treatment to temporal markers of other regions. Some types with more restricted distributions are mentioned as well, especially when they are among those considered by coastal researchers to be major interregional temporal diagnostics (e.g., unraised circle-and-dot design on shallow bowls, a diagnostic of Early Horizon Period; cf. Proulx 1973:23–25; Tello 1956).

Among the 16 reddish-brownware ceramic types of *Cayhuamarca Period* (see Figs. 190–194), there are 12 that can be designated as principal time markers. These include eight bowl types (Cayhuamarca Bowls 1a, 1b, 2, 3, 4, 5, 6a, and 6b) and four jar types (Cayhuamarca Jars 2a, 2b, 3a, and 3b). Most of the bowl types are undecorated, with two main variants consisting of (1) plain surfaces and (2) highly polished exterior and interior surfaces. The two decorated exceptions are Bowl 1b, which has unraised circle-and-dot design on the exterior; and Bowl 6b, which has pattern burnished design. Only four examples of Bowl 1b were found during the survey, however, so its utility as a time marker is limited. On the other hand, pattern burnished bowls are widely distributed and constitute 8.8% of the period assemblage. These bowls also were found in minor quantitites in one Vinzos Period context (see Vinzos Bowl 4b, in Appendix I), but are generally one of the best diagnostics of Cayhuamarca Period collections throughout the Lower Santa region. Although a very few rim and body sherds from jars were found to have exterior decoration—including zoned punctate, groups of parallel brush marks, and groups of parallel burnishing marks (e.g., see Fig. 194 a, b, c)—most of the sherds among the four principal jar diagnostics are plainware.

With regard to interregional relationships, fully 75% (9/12) of the principal Cayhuamarca bowl and jar diagnostics (Bowls 1a, 2, 4, 5, 6a, and all four jar types) can be related on the basis of form, paste, and surface treatment to Middle and Late Guañape types of Virú Valley—including Guañape Red Plain (cf. Strong and Evans 1952) and Guañape Red Polished (cf. Collier 1955). Other interregional relationships include: (1) two types (Bowl 3, Jar 2a) related to Quinú Period materials from Pashash (cf. Grieder 1978); (2) one type (Bowl 6b) related to Early Huaylas pattern burnished from Guitarrero Cave (cf. Lynch 1980); (3) three types (Bowls 1b, 2, 6b) related to Early Horizon ceramics from Nepeña Valley (cf. Proulx 1973); and (4) three types (Bowls 1b, 4, 6b) related to ceramics from Pallka, in Casma Valley (cf. Tello 1956). In spite of all these interregional similarities, however, Cayhuamarca Period seems better characterized by the differences that exist between Santa and adjacent regions. For example, almost none of the decorated Guañape types (see Guañape Incised Rib, Guañape Modeled, Ancón Fine-line Incised, Ancón Modeled, etc., in Strong and Evans 1952) is present in the contemporaneous Santa assemblage. And of the remarkable number of 68 Early Horizon design motifs from Casma Valley (cf. Tello 1956) only three or four are present in Santa. Interestingly, Donald Proulx (personal communication) reports that some 10 of the 68 Casma motifs are found in Nepeña Valley. The distribution of

Early Horizon motif types proceeding up the coast from Casma to Santa thus appears to be a clinal one, and we shall return to the implications of this in a later chapter.

Of the 20 reddish-brownware ceramic types of *Vinzos Period* (see Figs. 195–200), there are 12 that are designated as principal time markers. They include five bowl types (Vinzos Bowls 1, 2, 3, 4a, and 4b) and seven jar types (Vinzos Jars 2a, 2b, 3b, 3c, 5a, 5b, and 5c). Four of the bowl types (Bowls 1, 2, 3, and 4a) each have two main variants represented in the collections, including (1) an undecorated, or plainware, variant (40% of the sherds); and (2) bowls decorated on the interior surface and exterior walls with more or less randomly placed, parallel groups of burnishing lines (60%). The remaining bowl type (Bowl 4b) consists of White/Black-decorated vessels found in association with a small quantity of pattern burnished bowls of possible Vinzos date. Plain and burnished-decorated variants are also characteristic of each of the seven jar types, with roughly 55% of the sherds having randomly placed burnishing lines on the exterior walls and neck as well as on the rim interior.

With regard to interregional relationships, 92% (11/12) of the principal Vinzos bowl and jar diagnostics (excluding only Bowl 4b) can be related on the basis of form, paste, and surface treatment to the contemporaneous Huacapongo Polished Plain type of Puerto Moorin Period in Virú Valley (cf. Collier 1955; Strong and Evans 1952). Although all of the Virú-Santa type relationships are therefore quite pronounced, probably the most readily visible similarity when examining sherds in the field is that between Vinzos Jars 5a, 5b, and 5c (see Fig. 199)—with their diagnostic vertical necks and sharply everted, narrow rims—and Form 5 of the Huacapongo Polished Plain type (cf. Strong and Evans 1952, Fig. 37, p. 258). Other interregional relationships include: (1) two jar types (Jars 3b, 3c) related in form to Salinar Period vessels from Moche Valley, illustrated in Donnan and Mackey (1978); and (2) the pattern burnished type (Bowl 4b) found in Nepeña, Casma, and at Guitarrero Cave. Since Huacapongo Polished Plain analogs have not been reported for any of these other areas, however, it may be concluded that by far the strongest interregional ties continue to be with Virú. It should also be mentioned in passing here that the "existence" of Puerto Moorin Period was critiqued by a nonparticipant in the Virú Valley Project (cf. Bennyhoff 1952:231–249) on the basis of the analytical methods used to isolate Huacapongo Polished Plain. During the Santa Valley work we found types in unmixed contexts at over 20 sites that are similar in form, paste, and surface treatment to this general Virú Valley type. I therefore concur unreservedly with James Ford's (1952:250) response to Bennyhoff that "everyone who has worked with the [Huacapongo Polished Plain] material is convinced that this is a distinctive and easily recognizable category".

Of the 29 redware, reddish-brownware, and kaolin ce-

67

ramic types of *Early Suchimancillo Period* (see Figs. 201–208), 20 types are designated as principal time markers. They include six bowl types (Early Suchimancillo Bowls 1a, 1b, 3, 4, 5, and 6b), eleven jar types (Early Suchimancillo Jars 2, 3, 4a, 4b, 5, 7, 8a, 8b, 8c, 8d, and 8e), as well as three general ceramic types. These last include White-and-Orange/Redware, kaolin ware, and animal effigy lugs on jar body sherds. As in the preceding Vinzos Period, there are two unpainted bowl types, with variants that include (1) plainware and (2) bowls with burnished-line decoration. In contrast to Vinzos Period, however, the number of sherds decorated with burnishing lines is either sharply reduced (e.g., on the reddish-brownware variant of Bowl 1a), or burnishing lines appear on a different paste variant altogether (e.g., most sherds of Bowl 4, a vessel of uniformly oxidized redware). The remaining four bowl types have the following kinds of painted decoration: (1) interior/exterior or exterior polished red slip (Bowls 1b, 6b), (2) Black-and-White or Black/Orange-slipped White kaolin (Bowl 3; see Fig. 202 a-c), and (3) polychrome decoration on the exteriors of fully red-slipped vessels (Bowl 5). Among the 11 jar types, six are essentially plainware (Jars 2, 3, 4a, 4b, 5, and 7), although a few sherds with vague traces of polished red slipping or burnished-line decoration are present in the sample. Two paste color variants—reddish-brownware and redware—are characteristic of nearly every one of the jar types, with roughly half of the total number of sherds in each of the two categories. In contrast, Jars 8a–8e are all characterized by thick, highly polished red slipping as well as by generally very broad everted rims (see Figs. 205–206).

Interregional relations in Early Suchimancillo Period were rather clearly stronger between the Lower Santa region and the adjacent sierra than with any other region. Based on similarities of form, paste, and surface treatment, the strongest sierra contacts occurred with the nearby Pashash area—with 45% (9/20) of the Early Suchimancillo bowl and jar types (Bowls 1a, 1b, 6b; Jars 7, 8a, 8b, 8c, 8d, 8e) related to Quinú Period and Recuay Quimít phase ceramics from that site (cf. Grieder 1978). Three other Early Suchimancillo types (Bowls 4, 5, 6b) are similar to Recuay bowls illustrated in Bennett's (1944) report on excavations in the Callejón de Huaylas. In addition, one type (Bowl 3) has essentially identical counterparts at Balcón de Judás site at Huaráz, in the Callejón (Note: this similarity is based on my own assessment on two occasions of materials excavated by Steven Wegner in 1979–80). With regard to coastal relationships, five main ceramic types from Santa are closely related to Early-Middle Gallinazo Period types excavated in Virú Valley, including (1) Jar 2, which is quite similar to forms categorized under "Callejón Unclassified" by Strong and Evans (1952); (2) Jars 4a and 4b, both of which are related to vessels excavated by Bennett (1950) at V-59/Gallinazo site; (3) White-and-

Orange/Redware, which has an essentially identical counterpart in the Castillo White, Red, Orange type (cf. Bennett 1950; Strong and Evans 1952); and (4) animal effigy lugs, which are similar to those of the Castillo Modeled type (cf. Strong and Evans 1952).

Among the 39 redware, reddish-brownware, and kaolin types of *Late Suchimancillo Period* (see Figs. 209–223), 28 types are designated as principal time markers. They include five bowl types (Late Suchimancillo Bowls 2, 3, 4, 6, and 7), eighteen jar types (Late Suchimancillo Jars 1b, 1c, 2a, 2b, 2c, 3a, 3b, 3c, 4a, 4b, 5b, 5c, 5d, 5f, 6, 8, 10, and 12), as well as five general ceramic types—including jars with triangular punctate exterior rim design, Broad Band White-on-Red ceramics, kaolin ware, human effigies, and animal effigies. Three of the bowl types (Bowls 2, 3, and 4) are characterized primarily by fully oxidized undecorated redware, with additional minor quantities of other paste types. The remaining two bowl types consist of (1) small, open bowls with exterior zoned incised design (Bowl 6; see Fig. 211); and (2) small, open bowls exhibiting a variety of paste types and decorated features (Bowl 7; see Fig. 212). With the exception of Jars 1b, 6, 8, and 12, all of the Late Suchimancillo jar diagnostics listed above are primarily plain redware types, with very small percentages of other paste types— including reddish-brownware—present in the sample. The decorated jar types include: (1) small, globular kaolin jars with low, upturned rims (Jar 1b; see Fig. 213); (2) redware jars with constricted mouths and a unique exterior flange (Jar 6; see Fig. 216); (3) human effigy neck vessels (Jar 8; see Figs. 216, 221, 222); and (4) redware jars with vertical necks, sharply everted rims, and exterior reed-punched designs (Jar 12; see Fig. 217; note the similarity of rim form to Vinzos reddish-brownware Jars 5a, 5b, and 5c, and to Early Suchimancillo redware/reddish-brownware Jar 9). Turning to the general ceramic types listed above, mention should be made of the Broad Band White-on-Red type, one of the few ceramic categories designated by decorative style rather than vessel form. As Fig. 218 shows, a variety of jar forms are decorated with this type of painting, and it is interesting to note that almost all are of very friable, or crumbly, redware paste—probably indicating some problems with paste and control over the firing process (cf. Shepard 1956:91–93).

With regard to interregional relationships, 50% (14/28) of the principal Late Suchimancillo ceramic diagnostics (Bowls 1, 6; Jars 2a, 2b, 2c, 3a, 3b, 3c, 5b, 5f, 12; triangular punctate-decorated jars, human effigies, and animal effigy lugs) can be related on the basis of form, paste, and surface characteristics to several contemporaneous Late Gallinazo vessel types of Virú—including Castillo Plain, Castillo Incised, Gallinazo Broadline Incised, and Valle Plain (cf. Bennett 1950; Strong and Evans 1952). Redware animal effigy lugs (Fig. 223), found mostly on body sherds, are also clearly related in paste and form to the Castillo Modeled type illustrated in Bennett (1950, Fig. 22, p. 79) and Strong and Evans (1952, Fig. 63, p. 314). Other interregional relationships include: (1) five types (Bowls 2, 3, 4; Jars 6, 10) related to Recuay Yaiá phase ceramics from Pashash (cf. Grieder 1978); and (2) one type (Bowl 7, No. 7, under Late Suchimancillo Period in Appendix I) exhibiting similarities to ceramics from Shankaiyán site in the Callejón de Huaylas, illustrated in Bennett (1944). In addition, most of the Late Suchimancillo kaolin bowl and jar diagnostics (see especially Figs. 212; 219 b, c, f; 221 g), as well as some of the human effigies (see Fig. 221 c, e), seem clearly related to contemporaneous early Recuay types of the adjacent sierra.

Among the 16 redware ceramic types of *Guadalupito Period* (see Figs. 224–234), 10 types are designated as principal time markers. They include one bowl type (Guadalupito Bowl 2), three jar types (Guadalupito Jars 2a, 2b, and 3b), as well as six general ceramic types—including flaring funerary bowls, White-on-Red, Red-on-White, human effigies, depictions of Ai Apaec (the Moche Fanged God), and spout diagnostics. Of the main bowl and jar types, only Jar 3b (see Fig. 226) was found to be restricted to plainware. The remaining types in the sample are characterized by both plain and decorated variants, with the latter including white-slipped and White-on-Red subvariants. All of the six general ceramic types are well-known Moche Period diagnostics, and all are extensively illustrated in the literature. It should also be noted that the paste type and method of construction of Guadalupito vessels are themselves diagnostic features of the period. Thus, in contrast to the redware of other (mostly later) periods, vessels invariably are fired to a brick red color, and many vessels are moldmade judging from the characteristic finger marks on the insides of walls, where the wet clay was pressed against molds (Note: for an example of this diagnostic feature on a vessel from Taitacantín, in Virú, see Kroeber 1930, Pl. XXV-4). In addition, Guadalupito vessels are not only well fired but among the thinnest-walled ceramics of any period.

With regard to interregional relationships, all of the principal Guadalupito bowl and jar diagnostics can be related on the basis of form, paste, and surface characteristics to contemporaneous Moche ceramics of valleys from Chicama to Nepeña. For example, similarities exist between every one of the Santa types and those of Huancaco Period in Virú—including Huancaco Red and White and later Early Intermediate variants of Castillo Plain (cf. Strong and Evans 1952). It is interesting to note, however, that while there are similarities with respect to colors used in decoration (e.g., white, cream, and red) and design features (e.g., compare the Guadalupito ceramic illustrations to those in Strong and Evans 1952:326), there is also substantial variability in the number and types of specific motifs present in the

assemblages of each of the valleys. Among other things this suggests that ceramics were produced locally for the most part during this period, even though potters clearly followed Moche canons rather closely.

Of the 19 redware ceramic types of *Early Tanguche Period* (see Figs. 235–256), 15 types can be designated as principal time markers. They include nine jar types (Early Tanguche Jars 1a, 1b, 2a, 2b, 2c, 3, 4a, 4b, and 5), as well as a number of general types—including decorated annular-base bowls, Red/White-slipped, Black-and-White/Redware (Black-White-Red), human effigies, double spout-and-bridge vessels, and exotics such as Cajamarca III (cursive decoration on tripod kaolin ware bowls) and Central Coast polychrome. Four of the jar types (Jars 1a, 1b, 2c, and 4b) are characterized by undecorated redware. Decoration on most of the remaining types (Jars 2a, 2b, 3, and 4a) consists of pressmolded designs—usually including such features as zoned stippling (e.g., see Fig. 238-top) and interlocking scroll motifs (e.g., see Figs. 239-middle; 240 c), which appear on roughly 20% of the sherds in the sample. The final decorated type (Jar 5) has a distinctive elevated ridge around the shoulder of the vessel (see Fig. 237). A great variety of handles is present on most of these jar types—including horizontal strap, vertical strap, vertical notched, vertical lug, and vertical human arm-and-hand. Most of the handle types continue on into Late Tanguche Period (appearing on raised circle-and-dot, or Casma Incised, vessels), so taken by themselves are limited to indicating a general Middle Horizon time frame.

It is difficult to do full justice in limited space to the great variety of Early Tanguche decorated ceramic types described and illustrated in Appendix I. Nevertheless, it is useful to call attention to certain aspects of selected general types. Annular-base bowls—one of the best diagnostic indicators of the period—are decorated in three principal ways, including Black/Orange, Black-and-White/Redware, and red pressmolded (see Figs. 241–242). The Black-and-White/Redware style is itself another major diagnostic of the period, and appears on a variety of vessel forms—including bowls, jar, animal and human effigy jars, and figurines (see Figs. 242, 243 e-g, 244, 245, 246). Human effigy neck vessels are also excellent diagnostics of Early Tanguche, especially including double-lobe human ear handles (e.g., see Fig. 247-second row down); and figures with distinctive headgear consisting of a headband and attached straps on each side of the face, and often including hair whose ends appear to be feline heads (e.g., see Figs. 247-bottom, and 249; Note: for analogous earlier features in Central Andean art, see Rowe 1962 on Chavín "kennings"). This is also one of the few periods in the Lower Santa sequence when human females are depicted in the ceramic assemblage (e.g., see Fig. 252; the other period is Guadalupito).

With regard to interregional relationships, some 73% (11/15) of the principal Early Tanguche ceramic diagnostics (Jars 1a, 1b, 2a, 2b, 2c, 3, 4a, 4b, 5; annular-base bowls; and Black-and-White/Redware) can be related on the basis of form, paste, and surface characteristics to a number of early Tomaval vessel types of Virú Valley—including late forms of Castillo Plain (cf. Bennett 1939; Collier 1955). At least four main ceramic types of this period (annular-base bowls, Black-and-White/Redware, double spout-and-bridge vessels, and human effigy neck vessels) exhibit broader interregional relationships with contemporaneous types in valleys from Moche to Casma, and on south to Supe and the Central Coast (cf. Donnan and Mackey 1978; Kroeber 1925a, 1925b, 1930; Menzel 1977; Proulx 1968, 1973; Tello 1956).

Of the 12 redware ceramic types of *Late Tanguche Period* (see Figs. 257–263), six types are designated as principal time markers. They include one bowl type (Late Tanguche Bowl 2) and five jar types (Late Tanguche Jars 2a, 2b, 3, 4a, and 4b). The single bowl type consists of large open vessels with plain exteriors and incised cross-hatching on the interior, probably indicating use as a grater in food processing. Two variants characterize each of the jar types, including (1) undecorated jars and (2) jars decorated with raised circle-and-dot designs and adjacent rows of punctate motifs (e.g., see Figs. 260–261). As shown in Fig. 260, incised scallops are often appliquéd on the necks of Jars 4a and 4b.

Interregional ceramic relationships in Late Tanguche Period consist almost entirely of similarities between Santa and adjacent valleys to the south. Raised circle-and-dot punctate designs are the major diagnostic feature of contemporaneous late Middle Horizon vessel types in Nepeña (cf. Proulx 1973) and Casma (cf. Collier 1960), but, aside from limited finds along roads and at a few sites in the Santa-Chao Desert sector, do not appear on ceramics in valleys to the north of Santa. However, at least two types with relationships to Virú Valley appear in the Late Tanguche assemblage—including grater bowls, and large grayware vessels (see Fig. 259) that are very similar to forms of the Virú Plain grayware type (cf. Collier 1955). But it should be noted that this latter type is present in the assemblages of all of the last three periods in the Lower Santa sequence, and is therefore limited to a more general diagnostic function in assessing chronology of the late period.

Of the 21 redware and grayware ceramic types of *Early Tambo Real Period* (see Figs. 264–272), 18 types are designated as principal time markers. They include five bowl types (Early Tambo Real Grayware Bowls 1, 2, 3; and Redware Bowls 1, 2) and thirteen jar types (Early Tambo Real Grayware Jars 2, 3a, 3b, 4a, 4b, 4c, 5; and Redware Jars 1, 2, 3, 4a, 4b, 4c). All of the bowl types are plainware, although a few sherds with incised cross-hatching are present in the Redware Bowl 1 sample. Most of the jar types also are plainware, with the exception of Grayware Jar 5 and Redware Jars 2, 4a, and 4b. Decoration on these exceptional types consists of raised

circle-and-dot punctate design and incised scallops, which appear on a few sherds in the Grayware Jar 5 and Redware Jar 2/4a samples as well as on most sherds of the Redware Jar 4b type (e.g., see Fig. 272). Although the overall design motif is essentially identical to that of the preceding Late Tanguche Period, the principal distinguishing feature is that the Early Tambo Real paste contains very large (3–10 mm) black rock inclusions as temper. Indeed, this characteristic temper is also present in the paste of some other redware and grayware types of this period, especially (and not surprisingly) in the thicker-walled vessels.

Aside from the minor continuation of the raised circle-and-dot type—which also characterizes contemporaneous assemblages in valleys to the south (cf. Proulx 1973:74)—over 75% (14/28) of the principal Early Tambo Real redware/grayware bowl and jar types can be related on the basis of form, paste, and surface characteristics to contemporaneous La Plata Period types of Virú Valley. These include (1) the grayware types Queneto Polished Plain, Tomaval Plain, Virú Plain, Estero Plain, and San Juan Molded; and (2) the redware type Rubia Plain (cf. Collier 1955).

Among the 25 grayware and redware ceramic types of *Late Tambo Real Period* (see Figs. 273–280), 18 types are designated as principal time markers. They include four bowl types (Late Tambo Real Grayware Bowls 2, 4; and Redware Bowls 1, 2), twelve jar types (Late Tambo Real Grayware Jars 1, 2a, 2b, 2c, 2d, 3a, 3b, 3c, 3d, 4; and Redware Jars 1, 3b), as well as several general ceramic diagnostics. These last include various grayware/redware moldmade and effigy diagnostics (e.g., see Figs. 278 a-h, 280-top row), and Chimú and Inca diagnostics (Fig. 280). Although plainware variants are present in some of the bowl type samples, all four bowl types are primarily characterized by decorated exteriors consisting of zoned pressmolded stippling, as well as by appliquéd features which include large maize cob effigies. It should also be noted that the slightly recessed, zoned stippled panels present on some vessels is quite distinctive compared to any other period (e.g., see Redware Bowl 1, in Fig. 279). With the exception of zoned stippling on one Redware Jar 1 sherd, however, none of the principal jar diagnostics has much decoration on the exterior surface—aside from elaborate strap handles and, occasionally, deep incising on the exterior rib at the juncture of the neck and body. Nevertheless, as indicated in Fig. 278 c and e, some pressmolded and appliquéd decoration is present on body sherds of indeterminate jar type. With respect to other general ceramic diagnostics, it is also of interest to note that while Chimú and Inca time markers were not encountered together in a single context, both were found to be consistently associated with single-component Late Tambo Real Period collections. Thus, although the Chimú diagnostics undoubtedly precede the Inca ones in time, these chronological distinctions are not apparent in the overall assemblage of Late Tambo Real.

Finally, with regard to interregional relationships, virtually every one of the principal ceramic diagnostics of Late Tambo Real can be related on the basis of form, paste, and surface treatment to contemporaneous Estero Period types of Virú Valley. These include Estero Plain, Rubia Plain, and late forms of Tomaval Plain and Virú Plain (cf. Collier 1955).

Period nomenclature. Prior to the Santa Valley Project, the most complete published chronology for the region consisted of a five-period sequence corresponding to the Early Intermediate through Late Horizon Periods, and including Gallinazo, Moche, Wari, Chimú, and Inca (cf. Donnan 1973, Chart 1). With the exception of burial sites in the period of Moche occupation, however, almost nothing was known about the overall nature and extent of occupation in any of these five periods. Moreover, although Vescelius' and Ford's brief surveys had established the presence of Early Horizon ceramics at several of the fortress sites in the Upper Valley sector, these data were unpublished. The early occupation of the valley was therefore equally unknown. As outlined in the preceding sections, by carrying out prefield study of ceramic sequences of this general area of the North Coast (thereby building on the work of previous researchers), and by following systematic and comprehensive methods of data retrieval, it has been possible to construct a nine-period ceramic sequence that ties in closely to the sequences of adjacent regions. Combined with the evidence of Preceramic occupation in the region, a general ten-period sequence has resulted from our work.

Having established the outlines of such a sequence, it became clear that we were faced with the problem of assigning some sort of period nomenclature that would adequately reflect the results of the research. For several reasons, it was decided that it would be better to avoid use of the "Intermediate/Horizon" terminology, first introduced by Kroeber (1944) and later refined by Rowe (1960) on the basis of his research in the Ica area of the Peruvian South Coast. In the first place, because we had established the presence of four distinct periods of occupation in Early Intermediate Period, and two in Middle Horizon (see Chart 1), use of this nomenclature would have involved either invoking temporal adjectives (e.g., "Early Early Intermediate" at worst, or "Early EIP" at best) or such phase designations as Early Intermediate I, II, and so on. The former approach was ruled out as obviously too cumbersome, and the latter seemed rather too prosaic a way to label a sequence in which important period-to-period changes were taking place. Indeed, in this latter approach critical and often distinctive cultural developments are essentially consigned to anonymity.

In addition, while the Intermediate/Horizon is useful in communicating on a general basis about pan-Central Andean archaeology, it also carries with it the *a priori* assumptions that (1) horizon periods are ones characterized by general interregional sociocultural or political unification of some kind; and that (2) intermediate periods are ones of local, or regional, developments. The results of our research indicate that such assumptions clearly are too simplistic. For example, even considering the proximity of Chavín de Huántar site (ca. 170 km away; see Fig. 1), Early Horizon Chavín culture seems to have exerted little if any influence on Santa. By the same token, assigning such cultural names as "Recuay", "Gallinazo", "Moche", or "Chimú" also brings with it the implicit assumption of strong interregional ties, if not sociopolitical unification. Although such interregional relations may indeed characterize a given period, the view taken here is that it is up to the researcher to indicate (1) reasonable criteria for establishing their existence, and (2) which of the data are presumed to provide corroborative evidence.

The general procedure followed in assigning period nomenclature to the Lower Santa sequence was to choose local community names that are associated with one or more significant concentrations of sites of each of the ten periods. At the same time, an attempt has been made as much as possible to avoid names that might confuse the chronological position of a period. For this reason (and following a suggestion by Ramiro Matos) use of "Santa" was ruled out, since "la cultura Santa" was used by Larco Hoyle (1963b) to refer to Recuay-influenced Early Intermediate Period, while Tello (1956) used it as an alternate synonym for "Huaylas Yunga" culture of the early part of Middle Horizon Period. Rather than having to choose a distinct name for each of the ten periods, however, it was possible to pinpoint three general times—Suchimancillo, Tanguche, and Tambo Real—when two successive, ceramically and chronologically distinct periods could be assigned "Early" and "Late" designations.

In the case of Suchimancillo, both the early and late periods are characterized by small but significant percentages of Recuay-related kaolin ware, indicating a time of probably strong socioeconomic relations with groups of the adjacent sierra. Ceramic types of Early and Late Suchimancillo are also related stylistically to Early-Middle and Late Gallinazo types of Virú Valley. In the case of Tanguche, both the early and late periods are characterized by pressmolded stippled redware, as well as by a number of minor stylistic resemblances (e.g., similar handle types on pottery vessels). Finally, in the case of Tambo Real, both the early and late periods are characterized by the presence of substantial percentages of grayware and by numerous stylistic similarities. There are also similarities between subsistence-settlement systems that relate the early and late periods of Suchimancillo, Tanguche, and Tambo Real—especially in the case

71

of the first and last of these three general time periods (e.g., compare Figs. 170 and 172, and 180 and 182).

Absolute chronology and period length. As outlined in the section on temporal diagnostics, each of the nine ceramic periods in the Lower Santa sequence can be related on the basis of a preponderance of type similarities to the periods in the Virú Valley sequence, as well as to those of other nearby regional sequences. In addition, relying both on radiocarbon dates for stratigraphically excavated ceramics and on similarities between North Coast diagnostics and those of other Central Andean areas, general consensus has been achieved among coastal researchers and other archaeologists on the main chronological outlines of the North Coast sequence (e.g., see Donnan and Mackey 1978, Chart 1, p. 6; Lumbreras 1974, Fig. 11a, p. 14; Proulx 1973, Table 1, p. 6). As indicated in Chart 1 of this report, it is thus possible to make reasonably precise estimates of the absolute chronology of the ten periods in the sequence. However, while it has been possible generally to relate the Lower Santa sequence to those of other regions, the estimates of absolute chronology indicated in Chart 1 are clearly subject to refinement as research proceeds in the region.

A related question to be considered here is the relative length of the periods in the Lower Santa sequence. As Chart 1 indicates, all of the periods from Vinzos through Late Tambo Real are estimated to be of about the same length—with a range of duration between 200 and 300 years, and an average length of 250 years. In contrast, the estimated length of Cayhuamarca Period is about three times greater than that of the other ceramic periods. As discussed in the section on ceramic diagnostics, however, among the principal time markers of this period are the widespread pattern burnished and red polished bowl types. Both of these interregional temporal diagnostics are generally thought to date to the later part of Early Horizon Period. For example, Lynch (1980:230) reports that the pattern burnished sherds found at Guitarerro Cave were assigned by Gary Vescelius to the Early Huaylas style, which conventionally is dated from 700 to 400 B.C. Likewise, the red polished bowl type of Virú Valley is assigned by Collier (1955:200) to the contemporaneous Late Guañape Period. It therefore appears likely that most, if not all, Cayhuamarca sites date to the later half of the time period shown in Chart 1, and that the length of the period is not substantially greater than that of succeeding periods. The starting date of 1000 B.C. is thus somewhat early, but takes into account the few sherd diagnostics found associated with the above types that exhibit presumably earlier features such as the unraised circle-and-dot motif (cf. Proulx 1973:22–25; Tello 1956:44).

Nonceramic temporal diagnostics. In addition to the ceramic time markers, a number of other indicators of prehispanic chronology were noted during our research, including (1) adobe brick types, (2) rock and adobe wall types, and (3) a variety of specific site types. Although the utility of these indicators varies in terms of chronological precision, all are useful in placing prehispanic remains generally within the early, middle, or late periods in the sequence. But since none of the three types of remains is characterized by the quantity, variability, and widespread distribution of ceramic debris, none can be considered as sensitive as sherds in indicating specific periods. In making decisions about site dating, we therefore tended to rely more on ceramics than on other diagnostics in attempting to pinpoint precisely the period(s) of occupation—at least where surface ceramics were present. However, in the few cases where no associated sherds could be found, it was still generally possible to date structural remains on the basis of their similarity to numerous other sites where consistent associations had been noted between ceramic diagnostics and architectural features. For example, a few citadels with no associated Cayhuamarca sherds were dated to that period on the basis of strong architectural similarities to other nearby citadels (see SVP-CAY-28, 32, 36; in Figs. 40–41, 43, 46; see also Wilson 1985, Appendix B).

On the other hand, given the more general position of some nonceramic time markers in the sequence, the absence of ceramic diagnostics of a given period in a multicomponent assemblage at a large site was in several cases taken to be an indication that no occupation had occurred during that period. For example, at Huaca Yolanda Complex (see Plate 16, and Fig. 62) sherd diagnostics dating to Vinzos, Early Suchimancillo, and Late Suchimancillo were found in association with architectural remains throughout the site. Although the circular sunken court located out to the east of the main complex may well indicate a Cayhuamarca/Early Horizon occupation here, the total absence of diagnostics of that period was considered significant—especially in light of (1) the generally excellent preservation of ceramics in early multicomponent contexts elsewhere in the vicinity, and (2) the complete lack of Cayhuamarca Period sites throughout this area of the north desert margin. Nevertheless, these criteria are mentioned here not to provide an airtight case for the dating of Huaca Yolanda (excavation at a future time may turn up an earlier period of occupation), but rather to provide some indication of the overall set of factors considered in attempting to date sites of this nature.

Judging from our findings in the Lower Santa region, as well as from the literature on adjacent regions, the following six adobe types are among the better general time markers:

(1) *finger-marked conical* (see Fig. 56): this adobe type usually is considered to be an excellent Early Horizon diagnostic in the North Coast area (cf. Bennett 1939:83–86; Proulx 1973:14–18; Strong and Evans 1952:219–220;

Plate 16. Aerial view of Huaca Yolanda Complex, located on the north desert margin in the Middle Valley

Thompson 1962:206), and in Santa was used as the principal time marker in dating SVP-CAY-22, 29, and 52 (see Figs. 53, 54, and 56).

(2) *truncated-conical* (see Figs. 53, 56): this type was found associated with conical adobe bricks at SVP-CAY-52, as well as at SVP-CAY-22, and, like conical adobes, is considered to be a good Early Horizon diagnostic; finger marks were noted on the larger bricks.

(3) *loaf-shaped:* this type is found in Early Horizon contexts at Cerro Sechín, in Casma, and at Punkurí Bajo, in Nepeña (cf. Proulx 1973:18); however, in Santa Valley it was found in association with a low platform mound of probable Early Suchimancillo date (see SVP-ESUCH-122 in Wilson 1985, Appendix B; Note: rectangular adobes with maker's marks, of probable Guadalupito date, were also found on this mound).

(4) *rectangular cane-marked:* although considered by the Virú Valley researchers to be primarily a Late Gallinazo diagnostic (e.g., Strong and Evans 1952:219–220), in Santa this type is diagnostic of both Late Suchimancillo and Guadalupito Periods, but especially of the latter period (e.g., see SVP-GUAD-93 in Wilson 1985, Appendix B; and Fig. 106).

(5) *rectangular with maker's mark* (e.g., see Fig. 78): this type is considered by definition to be a Moche Period

time marker in Moche Valley itself (cf. Hastings and Moseley 1975; Moseley 1975b), and the results of our research in Santa indicate that it is probably the same there as well; it was found in only two contexts, both of them in or near Pampa de los Incas Complex (the Guadalupito Period regional center): (1) Structure 19, one of the principal pyramidal platforms in the region (see SVP-GUAD-111/Structure 19, in Fig. 109); and (2) Structure 11, located immediately to the south (Fig. 78), where bricks with maker's marks probably are intrusive from Guadalupito Period.

(6) *rectangular plain:* this adobe type is associated with various structural types at sites of nearly every period from Late Suchimancillo through Late Tambo Real, and is therefore probably the least diagnostic of all six brick types—at least when assessed by itself and not as part of a specific type of structure.

Two wall types were found to be associated with sites of specific time periods. The first consists of rock walls that stand 2–4 m high, constructed of large roughly squared rectangular boulders placed as external facing on both sides of a rock rubble core. As shown in Fig. 31, the interstices between larger boulders are filled with smaller stones which are of variable size and shape but often have the same roughly rectangular configuration.

73

This "megalithic" wall type is generally at least 2 m wide, and is characteristic only of Cayhuamarca Period citadels—at least when built in the form described here. However, it is an early variant of a more general wall type known as "double-faced rubble-filled" by some coastal researchers. This general "dfrf" type (pronounced "duffruff" by North Coast *cognoscenti*) characterizes rock-walled habitation structures of every period from Cayhuamarca on to the end of the sequence, and it is therefore not a good diagnostic time marker taken by itself. It consists specifically of smaller walls measuring about 50 cm high and 50 cm wide, and usually has cobble-sized stones used as facing on the interior and exterior sides. Neither of the two "dfrf" wall types was observed to be constructed with mud mortar—i.e., all appear to have been dry laid.

The second of the two temporally diagnostic wall types consists of those built of plain or cane-marked adobe bricks, with walls standing 2–3 m high and having a battered form of construction—i.e., to achieve stability and endurance they are generally a minimum of 1.5 m wide at the bottom and taper to less than .5 m wide at the top. Battered adobe brick walls were found to characterize some large Guadalupito Period enclosures (e.g., see Fig. 105), as well as some sections of the Great Wall system in Pampa de los Incas area (see Figs. 146–147). Indeed, considering the indication that battered adobe brick walls are generally more characteristic of Guadalupito Period, it may be the case that at least part of the Great Wall system in this area of the valley was begun prior to Early Tanguche times. It should also be noted that many sections of the Great Wall farther up-valley consist of battered rock walls, which are a later subvariant of the Guadalupito type.

The final nonceramic temporal diagnostic consists of a number of specific structures and site types. Since these are discussed in detail in Chapter IV, here it is necessary only briefly to list the main types (the period they are diagnostic of is shown in parentheses): (1) large hilltop or ridgetop citadels (Cayhuamarca through Late Suchimancillo); (2) circular sunken courts (Cayhuamarca and Vinzos, and possibly earlier, with some minor continuation in Suchimancillo as well); (3) small ridgetop fortresses, usually with associated defensive ditches and bulwarks (Suchimancillo); (4) small, shallow rock-lined tombs which are hexagonal or pentagonal in plan view (Early and Late Suchimancillo); (5) smaller adobe pyramidal or platform mounds (Cayhuamarca through Guadalupito); (6) larger adobe pyramidal or platform mounds (Guadalupito and Early Tanguche); and (7) large adobe compounds, or enclosures (with battered adobe brick walls: Guadalupito; with solid adobe, or *tapia,* walls: Late Tambo Real; Note: this latter type is not listed above as a major temporal diagnostic because of its limited distribution in the region).

General approach. Following the completion of the ceramic analysis, several steps were taken in preparation for the analysis of the settlement data. First, the set of 1:100,000-scale IGM topographic maps was used to prepare a large, 100 × 90-cm inked base map with 100-m contour intervals, including the entire Lower Santa region between Chao and Nepeña Valleys. A series of blueline and sepia-tone copies was then made from the base map for use in preparing large-scale regional settlement and ceramic distribution maps for each period in the sequence. Second, the field map tracings showing the location and extent of all archaeological remains were used to prepare a complete set of additional tracings on which the sites of each period were outlined with different colors. This was done as a preparatory step to assigning final Santa Valley Project site numbers, a procedure described briefly later in this section. Third, following the assignment of final site numbers, a set of detailed formal site reports was prepared for the 1246 occupations found in the survey region. Each report includes data on the natural environment and archaeological remains taken from the airphotos, map tracings, field notes, photographs, and IGM maps; and, where appropriate, also includes verbatim collection, structure, and feature descriptions as well as copies of plans and other drawings made on the site. Following this, the brief site descriptions included in Appendix B of the dissertation (Wilson 1985) were prepared.

Although not included in this report, it is useful to mention that the following data are included under each site description in Appendix B of the dissertation: (1) *natural setting* (elevation in meters above sea level and above surrounding lower terrain, general location and survey sector, nature of occupied and surrounding terrain, distance from valley floor or ocean); (2) *archaeological remains* (general nature of remains, areal extent of site in hectares, detailed descriptions of principal structural remains mapped or recorded in field notes, nature of surface debris, site numbers of other periods of occupation, distance to nearby sites of the same period); (3) *collections* (collection numbers, if any, and references to illustrations of each artifact from the site shown in Appendix D of the dissertation); and (4) *classification* (type of occupation either by basic function or by category of site size and function, and the population estimate). Each site description also includes references to illustrations of a nonceramic nature (site plans, structure drawings, feature drawings).

In general, the illustrations of structures and sites have been prepared so that they can be understood with little need for additional orientation or interpretation in the text. However, it is useful briefly to comment on the types of illustrations included here and the procedures followed in organizing them. Since Santa Valley Project site numbers are referred to in the presentation of the data, the first group of illustrations for each period includes the series of topographic maps at 1:100,000 scale showing the location, site number, and primary function of each occupation. For each period, these settlement maps are preceded by a 1:400,000-scale location key map, which shows the position of each one in relation to the overall survey region. In accordance with the procedure followed in assigning final site numbers to the occupations of each period (see below), the ordering of the individual settlement maps proceeds from the Upper Valley downriver to the Lower Valley, then to the far southern part of the survey region, and, finally, to the Santa-Chao Desert in the north.

In cases where the occupations of a given period and locale were grouped too closely together to show up clearly and distinctly on the 1:100,000-scale maps, it was necessary to include a map at even larger scale. These detail maps were made directly from the field tracings and show the outline of each of the sites included (e.g., see Figs. 100, 117). It will be noted that only the detail maps are of sufficiently large scale to show the actual outline of a site, as opposed to indicating the site with the functional symbols used on the 1:100,000-scale settlement maps. Since showing all 1246 occupations in such detail would have required literally dozens of maps for each period, it was necessary to show the actual site outlines in a more compact way. This was achieved by placing them on a series of site outline figures (see Wilson 1985, e.g., Figs. 195–200), which include compass orientation, scales of the airphotos used to map the sites, and symbols showing the location and function of major structures.

The main group of illustrations for each period includes plan views, profiles, perspectives, and detail drawings of the structures and sites themselves. The general rule followed in preparing each illustration was to include all graphic data we had collected during the fieldwork in as compact an arrangement as possible. Thus in many cases it was possible to include all views of a structure on the same drawing (e.g., see Fig. 91). However, in the case of relatively more complex structural remains such as Cayhuamarca citadels, it was necessary to place plan and perspective views on separate drawings (e.g., see Figs. 37–38).

A final note is in order regarding the perspective drawings: Although it would have been most advantageous to include closeup aerial oblique photographs of many structures, there are at least two principal reasons why this could not be done. First, many structures such as citadels are located on the highest hilltops of a given area, and there is no way to get above them for a perspective shot from a point nearby. Second, given the rugged terrain and unpredictable drafts of warm air rising off the

desert, the pilot who flew us over the region for aerial photography was understandably reluctant to drop down among the peaks (as we would have wished) and get close enough for really optimum shots (e.g., Plate 17). The two-point perspective drawings provide a reasonable solution to this problem, since they were prepared from an observer's station point of 40 m (130 ft) above and slightly away from the site (Note: although detailed perspective drawings were prepared for nearly every one of the 20 Cayhuamarca Period citadels, due to space restrictions most of these are not included in this report; cf. Wilson 1985, Appendix D). It should also be noted that the perspectives are schematic reconstruction views. Although they reflect precisely the plan view, as well as data collected on different wall and structure heights, in most cases specific features of rock or adobe construction are not shown, or are restricted to small sections where we took closeup photographs and prepared detail drawings.

Assessing basic site function. At the most fundamental level, sites were described in terms of the following functional categories: habitation, defensive, ceremonial-civic, and cemetery.

A *habitation function* was inferred in the majority of cases from the presence of numbers of smaller rock-walled structures on a site, often with associated occupational debris consisting of both inorganic materials (e.g., lithic debitage, grinding stones, marine shells, utilitarian/fire-blackened pottery) as well as organic materials (e.g., netting, cordage, maize cobs, reed thatching, charcoal bits, and ash). Although areas of deeper midden debris were noted along the lower edges of a number of large multi-component sites such as Huaca Santa and Huaca Jedionda (see Figs. 71, 131), associated cultural debris was found more often scattered in lighter quantities across the surface of sites, in and around the remains of habitation structures.

Types of dwellings include (with periods they are characteristic of shown in parentheses): (1) low, rock-walled windbreaks (dating to Las Salinas Period and, to a lesser degree, to Cayhuamarca and Vinzos; e.g., see Fig. 61); (2) low, rectangular rock-walled structures (dating from Cayhuamarca Period on; e.g., see Fig. 26); (3) remains of structures built entirely of reed thatching (dating as early as Guadalupito Period, but very characteristic of Early and Late Tambo Real Periods as well); and (4) rectangular structures built of adobe bricks, with walls standing 1.5–2.0 m high (primarily Late Tambo Real, with isolated examples as early as Guadalupito; e.g., see Fig. 159). As mentioned in Chapter II, none of the rock-walled habitation structures in the survey region exceeds a height of 50–100 cm, and it is likely that some sort of wattle-and-daub, or quincha, superstructure was associated with them. It is thus probable that the

Plate 17. High aerial view of Structure 28/SVP-CAY-19, located on Pampa de Cayhuamarca 2.5 km to the southeast of the valley floor

impermanent parts of dwellings either failed to preserve well or, more likely, were removed by later inhabitants of the region. For example, the wall posts depicted on pottery as early as Moche times (e.g., see Fig. 187-top) would probably have been at a premium, given the general scarcity of wood on the intensively cultivated up-valley floor.

Habitation sites in the Lower Santa region were found in a variety of configurations, most importantly including: (1) single, isolated dwellings (very rare; e.g., see Fig. 32, in Wilson 1985); (2) settlements with dispersed dwellings (e.g., see Figs. 27, 134); (3) settlements with agglutinated, or conjoined, dwellings (e.g., see Figs. 25, 68, 145); and (4) settlements on steeper slopes, with dwellings laid out in tightly packed, conjoined lines on rock-faced terraces (e.g., see Figs. 124, 131). In general, sites characterized by one or more of the four dwelling configurations are found in all of the settlement systems from Cayhuamarca on, and therefore no given one can be said to be particularly diagnostic of any part of the sequence. Indeed, a number of sites in various periods were found to be characterized by two or more of the dwelling configurations—most commonly including agglutinated structures surrounded by more dispersed dwellings. Nevertheless, it should be noted that the agglutinated type does not become common until Early Suchimancillo Period, while large terraced sites are primarily a feature of the Early Tanguche, Late Tanguche, and Early Tambo Real systems.

Two main types of sites were inferred to have had a *defensive function*, in other words, a function related to raiding and warfare. The first of these consists of citadels, or large rock-walled enclosures that generally are located on higher ridges and hilltops of rugged desert terrain as far as 2–3 km away from the cultivated valley floor (e.g., see Figs. 28–49). In addition to their defensible position, citadels are characterized by all or many of the following features: massive enclosure walls, bastions, a limited number of entrances, simple ramparts and parapets, associated dry ditches and bulwark walls, and evidence of substantial habitation. With regard to this last feature, citadels often have evidence of habitation both on the interior of the structure itself and on the exterior in the form of associated smaller dwellings. Thus in most cases their function seems clearly not to have been one of temporary refuge, but rather one of serving as a permanent locus of settlement during the periods when warfare and raiding were continually occurring. It may also be

76

noted that while a few citadels contain features that suggest a secondary ceremonial-civic function (e.g., see Structure 34, in Figs. 37–38), their primary functions seem to have been related to defense and habitation.

The second type of defensive site consists of minor fortresses. These are generally characterized by one or more smaller, rock-walled structures, and associated dry ditches and bulwarks, laid out in a line along narrow ridgetops or piedmont spurs (e.g., see Fig. 75). Minor fortresses often are present on several ridges immediately above a large habitation site lying adjacent to the irrigated valley floor, but also are found in association with smaller settlements. In any case, while associated occupational debris provides some indication of limited habitation, their primary function seems to have been to serve as part of the defensive perimeter of nearby habitation sites located in more vulnerable positions, and perhaps to serve as temporary places of refuge as well.

Judging from associated ceramic diagnostics, minor fortresses are primarily characteristic of Early and Late Suchimancillo Periods. Major citadel structures, on the other hand, are an important feature of the settlement systems of Cayhuamarca, Vinzos, Early Suchimancillo, and Late Suchimancillo. Isolated examples of minor fortresses and citadels are also found in the Late Tanguche and Early Tambo Real systems.

Several categories of sites, or parts of sites, are interpreted as having had a *ceremonial-civic function*, that is, a function related to activities of either a religious or public nature, and generally involving participation by individuals at the community-wide, if not supracommunity, level. Without specifying further what the nature of these activities was, it is at least assumed they were centered on the following four types of architectural features: (1) circular sunken courts; (2) pyramidal and platform structures, called *huacas;* (3) open plaza areas; and (4) large adobe-walled compounds containing one or more huacas or plazas. All of these features are characterized by their relatively formal layout, and a general lack of evidence that they served primarily as a focus of habitation (major exceptions to this latter aspect occur in Guadalupito and Early Tanguche Periods, as discussed in Chapter IV).

In sharp contrast to the generally remote location of defensive sites, it is of interest to note that nearly all sites and structures classed as ceremonial-civic are located in very open, nondefensible positions—either out on the valley floor (both in the midst of cultivated fields and on low hills) or on the edge of the desert margin (e.g., see Plate 3). The only exception to this pattern consists of a few probable ceremonial-civic sites of Early Tanguche date that are found immediately adjacent to rock-lined roads in the Santa-Chao Desert. In any case, all sites having a primarily ceremonial-civic function are found in relatively very accessible and visible positions throughout the survey region.

The final basic category of settlement consists of sites with a *cemetery function*. Although for general classificatory purposes burial sites can be subsumed under the broader category of ceremonial-civic sites (e.g., see Table 8), it is useful to consider them as a separate category here. They not only lack the monumental public architecture that characterizes the sites discussed above, but also have been subject to a devastation at the hands of huaquero graverobbers that sets them distinctly apart from any other type of occupation. Indeed, in contrast to every other type of site in the survey region, definition of the 446 cemeteries we found was achieved solely as the result of locating the looted, cratered areas left by the huaqueros.

Thus, although cemetery sites could be dated in every case by the usually ample remains of broken and whole funerary vessels—including both plain and fancy wares—very little else was found to be intact. Among the debris scattered about the surface, one normally finds numerous disarticulated human skeletal remains as well as mummified remains (occasionally of very small infants). Tomb architecture in nearly all cases was found to be very badly damaged, and although we attempted to salvage as much data as possible from these remains, our efforts represent very little considering the potential wealth of data had none of these sites been disturbed. Other remains noted on the surface of cemeteries include: textile fragments from clothing or funerary shrouds (usually heavily sunbleached); common household items such as fire-blackened vessels, gourds, copper tupu pins, and bone needle fragments; and items of food or trade, such as maize cobs, cotton, local marine shells, and whole or fragmentary *Spondylus* shells from warm Ecuadorian waters (cf. Murra 1975; Paulsen 1974).

Categories of occupational density. As discussed earlier, one of the primary objectives of the Santa Valley research was to retrieve data that would provide the basis for developing a method of estimating site population and, by extension, overall regional population size in each period. This objective was achieved through large-scale mapping of habitation sites of all types, as well as by marking the extent and density of dwellings for sites of all periods on the field airphotos. As outlined earlier, even at sites for which large-scale plans were not made, data on total number of habitation structures were available either from density estimates and dwelling counts recorded in the field notes or from direct counts on the airphotos. Through visual and quantitative analysis of these data, it has been possible tentatively to identify discrete habitation units at sites representing all sizes, densities, and types in the survey region.

Once the areal extent of a site had been measured using a compensating polar planimeter, it thus became possible to express occupational density in terms of the number of discrete habitation units per hectare as well as to assess the differences among sites in terms of average densities of these units. In turn, by assigning five persons to each unit, the data on densities of structural units could be translated into meaningful demographic terms. Although this is to some extent an arbitrary procedure, it is not entirely unreasonable in light of similar methods used elsewhere (e.g., Haviland 1972; Naroll 1962). Moreover, given extensive site mapping as well as generally excellent structural preservation, this method is considered to represent a better adaptation to the unique conditions characterizing the coast than one based on surface sherd densities alone. In any case, a comparison of sites resulted in the establishment of four principal categories of occupational density. Expressed in terms of persons per hectare (p/ha), these density categories are: (1) *low* (15 p/ha), (2) *low-to-moderate* (50 p/ha), (3) *moderate* (100 p/ha), and (4) *high* (250 p/ha).

With regard to methods of estimating occupational density on preceramic sites, it should be noted that the field counts of structures resulted in a separate category of 30 p/ha for Las Salinas Period (see Table 26; Note: this density figure is therefore two times that suggested for these sites at an earlier stage of the research; cf. Wilson 1983:222). However, the four principal density categories work consistently well for all nine ceramic periods—both in representing the differences in occupational density among sites of various types and locations throughout the region, and in accounting for differences in intrasite densities. For example, the low density category is characteristic of many sites in the Santa-Chao Desert sector, and of a smaller number of sites of all periods along the main valley floor as well. Since a low density site contains an average of only 15 p/ha, with intervening distances between structures averaging 50–75 m, the assessment of discrete habitation units is a securely based procedure (e.g., see Fig. 134). The low-to-moderate and moderate density categories are equally securely based, since distinct habitations can be pinpointed with reasonable certainty along with intervening areas where no evidence of occupation is present. Excluding the Santa-Chao sector, most sites fall into one or the other of these two categories (e.g., see Fig. 27 for a low-to-moderate density site; and Figs. 124 and 146 for moderate density sites).

On the other hand, the high density category is somewhat less securely based, since both in the field and on the airphotos it was difficult to distinguish where one "discrete unit" leaves off and another begins (e.g., see Fig. 147, where the units are only roughly indicated on the site plan). Nevertheless, the existence of this category reflects a very real difference between such sites as highly nucleated, terraced occupations and those in the other three categories. In terms of the total of 903 habitation sites dating to the ten periods in the sequence, only a relatively small percentage (3.8%, or 34 out of 903) appear to fall into the high density category.

Table 4. Total Estimated Hectares of Habitation for each Category of Occupational Density by Sector and Period[a]

Survey Sector	Density Category[b]	Period									
		SAL[c]	CAY	VIN	ESUCH	LSUCH	GUAD	ETAN	LTAN	ETR	LTR
Upper Valley	L	(5)	3	2	22	26	-	54	12	-	-
	L-M		35	14	119	107	8	12	10	10	-
	M		15	20	44	92	-	33	15	13	2
	H		2	1	2	17	-	1	-	-	-
Middle Valley	L	(9)	1	1	14	31	1	39	2	1	1
	L-M		5	10	29	15	10	31	18	12	2
	M		17	10	22	25	27	53	21	6	9
	H		-	2	5	15	-	13	17	-	-
Lower Valley	L	(-)	-	-	1	3	5	9	1	1	8
	L-M		3	11	75	28	24	9	3	3	51
	M		-	18	2	19	148	61	52	50	64
	H		-	-	1	-	9	22	14	-	-
Coast	L	(18)	-	-	-	-	-	1	-	2	-
	L-M		-	11	-	-	2	21	1	11	1
	M		1	-	-	-	-	19	-	3	1
	H		-	-	-	-	-	-	-	11	-
Santa-Chao	L	(-)	-	-	-	-	-	124	3	-	2
	L-M		-	-	-	-	-	76	-	-	2
	M		-	-	-	-	-	-	-	-	-
	H		-	-	-	-	-	-	-	-	-
Sub-totals	L	(32)	4	3	37	60	6	227	18	4	11
	L-M		43	46	223	150	44	149	32	36	56
	M		33	48	68	136	175	166	88	72	76
	H		2	3	8	32	9	36	31	11	-
Total Occupied Hectares		32	82	100	336	378	234	578	169	123	143

[a]Estimates are based on planimeter measurements from field airphoto tracings, and are rounded to nearest hectare.

[b]Categories of occupational density (persons/ha in parentheses): L = Low (15 p/ha); L-M = Low-to-Moderate (50 p/ha); M = Moderate (100 p/ha); H = High (250 p/ha).

[c]See Table 26 for occupational densities used in calculating population estimates for Las Salinas Period sites.

In sum, although all of these categories are subject to refinement as research proceeds in the general region, they are considered to be an adequate first approximation of differences in occupational density. The data resulting from this part of the analysis are summarized by survey sector and density category in Table 4 for each of the ten periods. In addition, as an aid in assessing period-to-period trends, subtotals for each of the occupational density categories are shown in the table, along with total (undifferentiated) hectares of habitation.

Categories of site size and function. Once the population of sites had been estimated on the basis of overall size and density of occupational remains, the data for each of the periods were analyzed by means of a series of histogram sets with varying size intervals. Visual inspection of these histogram sets was then carried out to establish categories that not only would represent adequately the breaks occurring between size groupings in each period, but that would apply reasonably well to site groupings of all periods. At the same time, the analysis of the large-scale site and structure plans indicated that a limited number of sites in each period from Early Suchimancillo on was characterized by the presence of unique public architecture or relatively formal layouts that set

Plate 18. View to north of SVP-ETAN-7 site, one of the excellently preserved local centers of Early Tanguche Period

them apart from other sites—either at the local or regional level. Considering the larger size of most of these sites and/or their greater internal complexity, it thus seemed likely that most if not all of them represent centers of supracommunity religious and sociopolitical activities.

The results of these two related analyses suggested the establishment of a series of settlement categories that would reflect differences in size as well as presumed function for all sites in the sequence. The specific category designations were selected on the basis of (1) their utility in comparing and contrasting inhabited sites in each period, as well as over time; and (2) personal preference for terms that would represent adequately the full range of settlement data collected in the region. Five categories of site size and function ultimately were established, including (1) *hamlet* (5–99 persons), (2) *small village* (100–499 persons), (3) *large village* (500–2000+ persons), (4) *local center*, and (5) *regional center*. Only three sites among the 1246 occupations of all periods were designated as regional centers, and each qualifies in its respective period as having had either the largest population of any site in the survey region or the largest and most internally diverse architectural complex, if not both. The

three regional centers include: (1) Pampa de los Incas Complex (Guadalupito Period; population estimate 3520; see Fig. 101); (2) Huaca Jedionda Complex (Early Tanguche Period; population estimate 5870; see Fig. 131); and (3) Alto Perú Complex (Late Tambo Real Period; population estimate 1650; see Fig. 160).

The estimated population of the 34 total sites in the local center category averages about 1400 persons, but ranges widely on a period-to-period basis between a minimum of 50 and a maximum of 5870 persons. As the wide range in sizes suggests, local centers of some periods did not stand out as unique on the basis of both size and architecture. This is primarily a characteristic of Early Tanguche Period, however, when the average population of these presumed centers is 310 persons, with a range between 50 and 785 persons. On the other hand, each of the Early Tanguche local centers stands out in its local area as having unique and relatively large agglutinated structures, with additional features that include possible corrals, storage areas, and elite residences (e.g., see Plate 18, and Figs. 126–130; see also Figs. 210, 213, 214, in Wilson 1985).

Intermediate in size between these smaller, architecturally unique local centers and the large regional center of Huaca Jedionda are a number of villages that are characterized by very substantial populations, but which contain no indication of anything other than non-complex, internally undifferentiated habitation areas. Assuming the correctness of singling out certain sites as centers of specialized, local sociopolitical functions that are hierarchically *supraordinate* to hamlets and villages but *subordinate* to the presumed regional center, then the Lower Santa data clearly run counter to the notion that one can indiscriminately apply the rank-size rule to make sense of all settlement systems (cf. Crumley 1976:59–70; see also Haggett, Cliff, and Frey 1977:110–113).

Assessing multicomponent sites. As mentioned in the section on field methods, the general procedure used to assess boundaries of sites involved drawing lines around the total extent of structural remains and associated occupational debris. Although this was a relatively straightforward procedure for the 825 single-component sites found in the survey region, greater complexities arose in dealing with the remaining 195 multicomponent sites—not only because of the often variable area covered by ceramic diagnostics of each period represented in the surface debris, but because of the probability that site function sometimes changed over time. The problem of assessing changing areal extent and function of occupations also varied in accordance with the total area covered by a site, since we were generally limited by the scales of the airphotos to writing field calls down at the equivalent of 50 m apart. Thus, at least on smaller sites, it often was difficult to indicate the "microchanges" in period diagnostics occurring over distances of less than 50 m. For this reason, the estimates of hectarage given for the smaller multicomponent sites in Table 26 (and Appendix B, in Wilson 1985) must be taken as approximations.

Nonetheless, the fundamental characteristic of nearly all larger multicomponent habitation sites (i.e., over 5 ha in area) was that diagnostics of various periods could be found in mixed contexts extending over large areas. Among other things, this clearly implies that it cannot be assumed that debris from other periods was removed, or cleaned away, by inhabitants of later periods. As mentioned earlier, all periods noted in assessing surface ceramics were marked on the airphoto as survey proceeded across a site. Since we were able to make collections at 84% (164 out of 195) of the multicomponent sites, it was therefore possible to achieve a good measure of control over the chronological development of the larger, more complex occupations. At the same time, it is realized that the data indicating changes in the size of sites over time may be refined at a future date through excavation.

Briefly to summarize the data on multicomponent occupations (see Table 26), the breakdown of sites by number of period components—either as assessed in the field or by analysis of ceramic collections—is as follows: two

components (131 sites), three components (49 sites), four components (9 sites), five components (3 sites), and six components (3 sites).

Final Santa Valley Project site numbers. The procedure followed in assigning final project site numbers are simple and straightforward to describe. After the period identification maps had been prepared, the sites of each period were numbered in separate sequential and geographical orderings. Beginning with the uppermost site in the main valley area of Santa, numbering proceeded from there downriver to the mouth of the valley, alternating between opposite sides of the river. Assuming that in a given period there were sites outside the Upper, Middle, and Lower Valley sectors, numbering then proceeded from the main valley mouth and coastal area of Santa southward to Quebrada de Lacramarca, on down the coast to Bahía de Samanco, thence to Pampa Las Salinas, and, finally, northward through the Santa-Chao Desert to the south margin of Chao.

As indicated by the earlier mention of selected site numbers of various periods, each project site designation consists of three parts, including (1) *SVP* (Santa Valley Project), (2) *period name abbreviation* (SAL=Las Salinas, CAY=Cayhuamarca, VIN=Vinzos, ESUCH=Early Suchimancillo, LSUCH=Late Suchimancillo, GUAD=Guadalupito, ETAN=Early Tanguche, LTAN=Late Tanguche, ETR=Early Tambo Real, LTR=Late Tambo Real), and (3) *site number* (1 to n). As will be clear to coastal researchers, the site numbering procedure used here is thus substantially different from the Peruvian Valley system used by some archaeologists in the past. In the earlier system, coastal valley sites were identified with a three-part designation consisting of (1) *PV* (Peruvian Valley), (2) *valley number* (e.g., Santa is the twenty-eighth valley proceeding from north to south along the coast), and (3) *site number*.

There are a number of problems with the Peruvian Valley system, and it is appropriate to mention them here. First of all, it does not include a period designation, and sites therefore are treated strictly as spatial entities with no indication of the temporal component(s) represented. Second, the system is based entirely on numbering sites in the chronological, day-to-day order they are found during various projects. Thus, given the erratic survey logistics and incomplete sampling of sites that have characterized most projects in the past, numbers are scattered in disarray all over a region—depending on where researchers have chosen to work and what periods or kinds of sites they have focused on. Among other things, this makes maps exasperating and, indeed, nearly impossible to read (e.g., see Proulx 1973:ix; Wallace 1971, map foldout). Third, the numbers in the Peruvian Valley system are considered as almost sacred designations—i.e., once assigned, they are supposed to apply forever to a site. This has meant that later researchers in a valley often have had to pore over usually very small-scale maps of a region (if any were published at all), pinpointing all "old" sites already numbered so that the numbering sequence for "new" sites could carry on from that point. And, once established, a chaotic numbering system only becomes more so as new sites are added. Fourth, the system does not prescribe how sites found in the intervalley desert areas are to be numbered (in the case of the 200 intervalley sites we found in Santa-Chao, one presumably would number sites in the southern half of the sector with PV 28 and those in the northern half with PV 27). Fifth, I strongly suspect that while most coastal researchers know the numbers of the valleys in their own area of research focus, most North Coast archaeologists would not immediately recognize "PV 69" as Nazca, for example (indeed, it is often difficult enough for foreign researchers to learn the sequence of 98 *names* of valleys extending from Tumbes to Tacna). Thus using these designations does not make the location of a given site immediately apparent, at least without the aid of a key to valley numbers. Sixth, and finally, the Peruvian Valley system is not accompanied by any set of criteria for what constitutes a "site". For example, it ignores the possibility that a site designated by a single number may actually represent two or more sites of distinct periods that are either immediately adjacent to each other or only slightly overlapping (and yet look "continuous" on the ground).

The system used in the Santa Valley research is not offered as a panacea for all the vagueness and difficulties associated with the Peruvian Valley system, however. For example, the first part of the Santa Valley site designation (SVP) could stand for a project carried out in Saña, Supe, Sihuas, or Sama, as well as Santa. In addition, each occupation at multicomponent sites is given a different number. (Note: nevertheless, numbers for all components are shown on every site plan, and mentioned for each occupation in Table 26 of this report and in Appendix B of the dissertation; site designations are therefore completely cross-referenced.) For example, the habitation part of Huaca Santa Complex is SVP-ESUCH-126, SVP-LSUCH-149, SVP-LTAN-53, SVP-ETR-43, and SVP-LTR-68. But these different occupations are not coextensive—i.e., they cover 70, 14, 20, 33, and 20 ha, respectively—and the Peruvian Valley system would be even more vague in subsuming them all under a single designation assigned to the overall spatial entity called "Huaca Santa" (itself an ascribed name based on local tradition and no knowledge of the occupational periods represented in differing areas along this part of the south desert margin of the Lower Valley).

Aside from avoiding most of the problems associated with the Peruvian Valley system, the one used here would seem to have at least two principal advantages. First, since a site is always identified by period, there is no vagueness about its chronology in discussing it. Sec-

ond, numbering sites according to a geographically ordered system should facilitate the understanding and efficient use of maps by other researchers. Indeed, knowing how many sites there are in a given period and where they are located generally, it is reasonably easy to find any given site number using the system followed here. For example, in Late Suchimancillo there are 153 occupations distributed throughout the Upper, Middle, and Lower Valley. One can therefore expect to find SVP-LSUCH-75 located roughly halfway downvalley between the uppermost and lowermost sites on the 1:100,000-scale settlement maps (see Figs. 83, 85).

Locational Analysis

General approach. As mentioned earlier, regional analysis of settlement patterns and ceramic distributions was carried out at the most general level by using blue-line (Ozalid) maps prepared from the 1:100,000-scale inked topographic base map. All sites for each period were placed on separate settlement maps, with the primary function of each occupation indicated by means of the symbols shown in Fig. 16. This facilitated detailed visual analysis of (1) the location and relative number of sites of all types in a single period; and (2) changes occurring from period to period in the overall location, type, and size of sites. While analytical procedures based on general visual analysis might at first glance seem pedestrian, nonetheless some of the most robust conclusions of the Santa Valley research can be drawn from such an approach. For example, as argued later, the changes in the overall subsistence-settlement system that occur from Late Suchimancillo to Guadalupito provide one of the most striking illustrations presently available in the North Coast sequence of the effect of probable conquest and subsequent imposition of state-level policy—namely, in dramatically reorganizing regional subsistence focus and sociopolitical priorities.

In addition, the analysis of period-to-period changes in settlement patterns suggested the potential value of mapping out regional distributions of ceramics for each period on a separate set of 1:100,000-scale drawings. This procedure involved showing the presence/absence of the principal pottery diagnostics for each of the site proveniences in a given period. In order to distinguish among all types, each was color coded or assigned a specific symbol. Then the overall regional distribution of types was analyzed visually by outlining intersite groupings of each of the main types. Although the maps for periods with greater numbers of types and more continuous distributions ended up taking on a somewhat "counterintuitive" appearance, this approach made it possible to assess at once the general distribution of any given ceramic type.

Unfortunately, because of their color coding and general complexity the ceramic distribution maps could not

81

be transformed for inclusion here—either to smaller-scale 1:400,000 versions or to segmented 1:100,000 versions such as was possible for the settlement pattern maps. Nevertheless, the interested reader may wish to reconstruct these maps from the data presented for each ceramic period in Appendix I, specifically by utilizing the detailed collection provenience maps and the data on numbers and distributions of each ceramic type for all collections in the period assemblage. Indeed, this is one of the principal justifications for including such detailed data in the ceramic appendix.

In conjunction with the regional settlement maps at 1:400,000 scale, a series of ten regional demographic maps was prepared at the same scale (see odd-numbered maps, in Figs. 164–183). These maps depict in graphic form the population estimates made on the basis of site size and density of structural remains, and they follow standard demographic practice in representing area-to-area differences in population size by means of black circles of varying sizes. The accompanying population size intervals vary somewhat from period to period, depending on the range of site population sizes, but in general are organized according to the following categories: 0–99, 100–499, 500–999, 1000–4999, and 5000+ persons. As should be clear from the figures, the demographic maps complement the 1:400,000 settlement pattern maps by depicting both the overall population distribution in each period as well as the location of major population concentrations.

Delineation of settlement clusters/groupings. As the settlement pattern maps make clear, almost by definition the distribution of sites in each of the ten prehispanic periods is "clustered" in the sense that occupations are located in essentially nonrandom groupings—in relation either to (1) the linear configuration of those parts of the natural environment that can be utilized for subsistence (i.e., the irrigable valley floor and the modern/ancient Pacific shoreline), or (2) the linear nature of cultural adaptations to the socioenvironmental setting (i.e., ancient canals and roads that run along the valley margins or cut across sections of the intervalley desert). In a very real sense, then, no aspect of the natural environment of a coastal valley such as Santa, or indeed cultural adaptations to it, can be viewed as fitting the classic geographic models based on the physical context of a "flat, unbounded plain" (cf. Haggett, Cliff, and Frey 1977:55 ff.; Hodder and Orton 1976:53 ff.; contrast this argument with that underlying the analysis in Conrad 1978).

From the settlement maps it is also reasonably clear that the linear settlement distributions of a number of periods are characterized by subregional clusters of sites, with gaps of 2–5+ km occurring between each of the clusters (see settlement maps in Figs. 164–183). In addition, sites in nearly all of these clusters appear to be distributed more or less continuously in relation to certain parts of the socioenvironmental setting, including (1) natural features such as hilltops suitable for defensive constructions; and (2) cultural features such as ancient canals, ceremonial-civic sites, and local or regional centers. Yet, as shown in Fig. 15, when all 1020 discrete occupations in the sequence are placed together on the same map, it becomes clear that there is no area on either desert margin of Santa Valley and the mouth of Lacramarca that was unsuitable for occupation at one point or another in the sequence (note also the discrete, but internally continuous, linear groupings of sites throughout the ancient road network of Santa-Chao). The comparison of the map showing a continuous overall distribution of sites of all periods (i.e., Fig. 15) to the maps of the settlement systems of individual periods thus suggested that the gaps between clusters in the main valley area might be of some significance.

On the other hand, a comparison of the ten site distribution maps also indicates that there are at least two periods—Guadalupito and Early Tanguche—when the regional settlement pattern is relatively more continuous than in other periods. This overall distributional continuity is more pronounced in Early Tanguche Period, specifically with respect to the Upper, Middle, and Lower Valley sectors (e.g., see Fig. 176). But such continuity is also the essential characteristic of the Guadalupito system, with the exception of a gap on the west side of the river in the upper reaches of the Lower Valley sector (see Fig. 174). Nevertheless, on the maps of the two periods it is also possible to discern local site groupings within the overall regional pattern. Since these are referred to specifically in the ceramic distribution analyses of Chapter V, here it is useful to list those noted for Guadalupito Period to provide an example; they include (1) the Upper-Middle Valley, (2) Pampa de los Incas area, (3) El Castillo area, (4) Huaca Santa area, and (5) the mouth of Quebrada de Lacramarca.

It should be emphasized that however tentative the hypothesized settlement clusters and groupings might be in terms of their ultimate sociocultural significance, dealing with subregional groups of sites was a useful procedure in the quantitative analyses of local ceramic assemblages as well as maize-based carrying capacity—irrespective of the possibility that they might reflect important processes of societal adaptation and development. Moreover, the delineation of specific clusters on the maps made it possible to assign numeric designations to each one, thus providing an additional means of referring precisely to certain groups of sites. Finally, it should be noted that the cluster outlines were drawn on the maps in conjunction with the analysis of modern and ancient canal locations throughout the main valley floor (see Figs. 7–13). Since the delineation of discrete clusters at once implies (but does not necessarily prove, as we shall see) a certain degree of subsistence autonomy, sub-

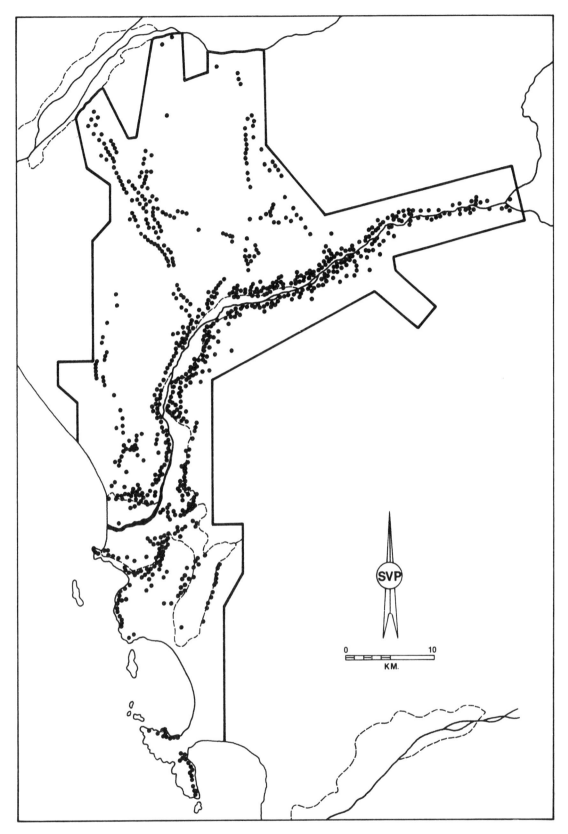

Fig. 15. Map showing location of the 1020 discrete archaeological sites in the Lower Santa Valley survey region.

83

regional cluster delineations were made not only with respect to the 2–5+ km gaps between them, but also when it appeared clear that separate canal systems could have been maintained in each local cluster.

Ceramic distributions. Following the preparation and analysis of ceramic distribution maps showing the presence/absence of types at each collection provenience, the next procedure in the analysis was based on the tabulation of the number of sherds of each type for the period components from each provenience. The data on number of sherds by type in each collection were then arranged in the form of *arrays*, or matrices, on separate sheets for each of the nine periods—with the geographically ordered collections occupying the rows of each period array and the principal types occupying the columns. As should be clear, the number of rows in each array varied according to the number of collections in which a given period component was found to be present—ranging from 30 collections for Late Tambo Real to 127 for Late Suchimancillo. Likewise, the number of columns depended on the number of principal types included in the analysis of each period assemblage—ranging from 8 in Late Tanguche to 25 in Late Suchimancillo.

The general direction taken in carrying out quantitative analysis of the nine ceramic period arrays was suggested by the findings of the visual analysis of the settlement and ceramic distribution maps, described in the preceding sections. Thus, given the reasonably clear evidence of subregional clustering in the early and late periods, it seemed appropriate to investigate the possibility that the ceramic data might throw some light on the relationship between these clusters or groupings. In addition, given the relatively low numbers of sherds found on sites (it will be recalled that the average number per collection is 35, with a range between 10 and 200 sherds), it also seemed useful to combine the data on the individual collections of each cluster and grouping into single assemblages, and then compare them—both on the basis of contiguous assemblages (i.e., each cluster/grouping assemblage against its nearest upvalley and downvalley neighbors) as well as on an overall regional basis (i.e., each cluster/grouping assemblage against all other contemporaneous ones). The basic units of the analysis were therefore contained within a *2 × n array*, with each of the two rows representing cluster/grouping assemblages and the columns representing the principal types.

Analysis of the 2 × n arrays was then carried out using the Brainerd-Robinson coefficient of agreement (cf. Doran and Hodson 1975:135) and a program written in BASIC by the author for a PET 4016 microcomputer (a "dinosaur" recently replaced by an IBM PC). As is well known, the Brainerd-Robinson statistic involves expressing as percentages the quantity of sherds for each type in collections to be compared. The percentages in one row

are then subtracted from those in the other on a column-by-column (type-by-type) basis. Finally, the absolute values of the differences are summed and the resulting overall value is subtracted from 200 (the number representing complete similarity) to provide a measure of the similarity between the assemblages being compared. The specific objectives of the analysis were to examine not only assemblage similarities between clusters/groupings in each period, but also how the similarity coefficients changed from period to period (the results are summarized in Tables 15–23, Chapter V).

Since the implications of the analysis are outlined in Chapter V, we may confine the discussion here to a brief consideration of some of the assumptions underlying the analysis. Part of the utility of comparing the cluster assemblages of the earliest, pre-state periods arises in considering some of the implications of Carneiro's (1970) "coercive theory." Specifically, if it is assumed that pre-state warfare were occurring as argued in his model on an *intra*valley, rather than *inter*valley, level, then this might be reflected in relatively lower similarity coefficients between cluster assemblages—i.e., one assumes there would be less rather than more sharing of assemblage traits. By the same token, if there were an orderly change from less similarity in the earlier periods to more similarity in the later pre-state periods, then this might support Carneiro's assumption that local settlement groups were being incorporated into the systems of ever-larger subregional conquest polities. However, as we shall see later, the results of the analysis of the early assemblages generally do not support the fundamental assumption of intravalley warfare at any point in the pre-state sequence. In addition, the analysis has implications for the nature of regional interaction in other, later periods.

Nevertheless, it must be emphasized that the results of the quantitative analysis of ceramic assemblages are offered primarily as an interesting adjunct to the results of maize-based carrying capacity analysis, which, taken in conjunction with the nature of local irrigation systems, provides a definitive counterargument to the notion that early warfare occurred on a regional rather than interregional basis.

Maize-based carrying capacity. The analysis of agricultural carrying capacity was carried out with two principal objectives in mind. First, such an analysis provides a measure of prehispanic population potential that is derived independently of the procedures used in estimating population numbers on the basis of site size and density of structural remains. In this sense, it therefore has utility in throwing light on the relationship between overall numbers of people at the regional level and the capacity of the land to sustain them. In addition to providing a basis for constructing arguments about population-land relationships, however, this aspect of the analysis also has implications for the possible nature of subsistence systems in periods when relatively smaller populations in Santa probably were part of large inter-regional conquest states. The second objective was to assess carrying capacity on a cluster-by-cluster basis, especially in the earlier, pre-state periods when it is particularly critical to get some idea of whether or not local populations could have sustained themselves independently of other groups in the valley. Thus, as we shall see in Chapter V, if it can be demonstrated that there is substantial disparity at the local level between the (smaller) amount of available land and the (larger) numbers of people occupying nearby sites—*even given a best-case estimate based on a strategy of triple-cropping*—then this has critical implications for the nature of relations not only between contiguous clusters but on a regionwide basis as well.

Although the principal assumptions and procedures underlying the analysis of agricultural carrying capacity have been outlined in detail in earlier publications on coastal Peruvian archaeology (cf. Wilson 1981, 1983), it is useful to review them here to provide a logical point of reference for the specific analytical results discussed in Chapter V. In carrying out this kind of analysis, one must be able to estimate with a reasonable degree of precision essentially five aspects of the prehispanic population-land relationship:

The first aspect involves *estimating the average caloric requirements* for all men, women, and children in an aboriginal coastal population. Using the guidelines set down by the Food and Agricultural Organization of the United Nations (cf. FAO 1954, 1957a, 1957b), these requirements can be expressed in terms of the Recommended Daily Allowance (RDA) for a preindustrial population. The suggested RDA of 1994 kilocalories (kcal) for this population is based on several reference points—including an annual ambient temperature averaging 25° C; average weights of 50 kg for men and 40 kg for women; and the assumption that the population is a "young" one—i.e., it is characterized by high birth and death rates, and is neither growing nor contracting rapidly in numbers. The suggested RDA of 1994 kcal can be adjusted for coastal Peru—where the annual ambient temperature averages 20° C—by observing the FAO guideline of a 3% increase in average kilocalories per person for every 10° below the reference temperature, resulting in a per capita RDA of 2023 kcal/person, or 738,395 kcal/person/year.

The second aspect of agricultural carrying capacity analysis involves the selection of an *index of subsistence productivity*. As outlined elsewhere (Wilson 1981:101–103), I have followed Sanders and Price (1968:92–93) in assuming that estimates of potential population density can be made on the basis of maize productivity. However, it must be emphasized that using maize as an index carries with it the assumption of a nutritionally balanced

diet that included such staples as beans and squash, a small amount of animal protein, and a host of other crops (e.g., *Capsicum*) providing necessary minerals and vitamins. It will be recalled from the discussion of Chapter II that a nutritionally adequate complex of cultigens, supplemented by secondarily important maritime resources, probably has been characteristic of coastal valleys such as Santa since at least the Early Horizon Period. In sum, although maize traditionally has been one of the two or three most important crops in prehispanic and modern times, in the approach taken here it is merely a convenient index for estimating productivity per hectare of land.

The third aspect of estimating carrying capacity therefore involves *selecting a means of translating data on archaeological remains of maize to specific production figures*. In this part of the analysis, I have used Kirkby's (1973:126) graph showing the relationship between maize cob length and average yield of dried seed in metric tons (and kilograms) per hectare. Although average cob length estimates are available from some North Coast areas for the various prehispanic periods (cf. Bird 1978; Bird and Bird 1980), they are of limited utility since they are based in part on samples that include incomplete cobs. And although we found whole cobs on the surface of a few sites in Santa (e.g., see SVP-LSUCH-127/SVP-GUAD-50/SVP-LTR-9, in Wilson 1985, Appendix B), they were from mixed contexts and too limited in number to provide an adequate sample for such estimates. Thus, as discussed in Chapter V, the cob length estimates used here (see Table 11) are taken from averages for whole cob samples collected primarily at South Coast sites (cf. Grobman et al. 1961, Table 5, p. 60). For example, assuming an average Early Horizon cob length of 7.5 cm, the estimated average single-crop production based on Kirkby's graph would be 480 kg/ha. It may be noted that this is a modest estimate compared to the modern double-cropping productivity range of 2600–3800 kg/ha (i.e., 1300–1900 kg/ha for single-cropping), discussed in Chapter II. For example, assuming a double-cropping strategy, the Early Horizon production would be 960 kg/ha, or only about 25–37% of the modern figures.

The fourth aspect of the analysis of the population-land relationship is a relatively straightforward procedure involving *translation of maize productivity figures to caloric figures*, as measured in kilocalories per kilogram (kcal/kg). This has been done using FAO estimates of the average caloric productivity of maize in grain form (3.56 kcal/gm, or roughly 3500 kcal/kg; cf. FAO 1954:10–11).

The final aspect of the carrying capacity calculations has to do with *estimating the amount of land available and the number of crops possible per year*. The regionwide estimates of available land were carried out with a planimeter, as mentioned in Chapter II, and included all land associated with the settlements of each period (see Table 11, fifth column from the left; see also Chapter II for methods used in estimating potential area of prehispanic cultivation). By the same token, the cluster estimates included only the land associated with each subregional group of sites. Finally, from the discussion of traditional subsistence cropping in Chapter II, the analysis is carried out with regard to the three basic cropping strategies (single-, double-, and triple-cropping) that characterize Santa Valley, with its abundant year-round supply of water.

In sum, it is important to emphasize that in estimating maize-based carrying capacity one is dealing with at least three major variables that change over time. These include (1) cob length, which appears to have increased very gradually throughout the sequence; (2) total hectares of land under cultivation; and (3) cropping strategy. Thus it cannot be assumed that prehispanic carrying capacity can be understood as a single, immutable figure derived on the basis of overall potentially cultivable land in a valley—without taking into account the increasing productivity of the cultigen used as an index and the total extent of settlement (and inferred land use) in each period. It must also be mentioned that in the absence of specific prehispanic data on furrow and plant spacing, the analysis assumes that such variables have remained constant from ancient to modern times (this assertion would appear to be supported in part by the apparent lack of strong differences in these variables between ancient and modern times; cf. Kus 1972; Zegarra 1978).

Assessing sociocultural complexity. A final concern in outlining the procedures of locational analysis is briefly to establish a framework for assessing sociocultural complexity at the regional level. As argued in the introductory chapter, if we assume that complex nonegalitarian societies are fundamentally characterized by hierarchically organized networks composed of numerous sites of various functions, then the problem of elucidating the origins and rise of societal complexity must be approached at the level of the local and regional patterning of settlement. In an earlier section of this chapter, it has also been argued that the preparation of maps of successive subsistence-settlement systems in a region establishes a very robust context for understanding period-to-period changes in site types and location, population size, and other archaeological features such as construction and use of canal and field systems, routes of communication, and walls. In addition, at least two other related approaches are useful in throwing light on societal evolution at the local and regional levels—including (1) the analysis of changing hierarchies of site size and function, and (2) an attempt to assess critical developmental junctures in the changing subsistence-settlement system with respect to cross-culturally valid stages of sociocultural integration.

As discussed in a preliminary article on the Lower Santa Valley research (Wilson 1983), the growth of early irrigation-based societies in nuclear areas appears to have involved not only *quantitative* change, i.e., a "proliferation of parts"; but also *qualitative* change, i.e., a "proliferation of parts *and* subparts," so that these societies became more centralized, integrated, and hierarchically organized. For purposes of the analysis and discussion carried out in later chapters, it is assumed that one good measure of the qualitative changes leading to the rise of nonegalitarian society is a more or less continuous growth in the hierarchy of site size and function. Thus it is assumed that the Lower Santa sequence qualifies as a "classic" example of the origins and rise of societal complexity if in the earlier periods there is not only (1) a general quantitative increase in numbers of sites (e.g., from 36 in Las Salinas to 440 in Early Tanguche) and estimated regional population (from ca. 1000 to 36,000 persons), but also (2) a qualitative increase in the hierarchy of site size and function (from two to as many as five tiers).

The latter qualitative change does not mean, of course, that we may automatically conclude that a chiefdom or state exists when a certain number of tiers is present in the developing hierarchy. The number of hierarchical tiers is at least in part related to the population ranges and distinguishing criteria used in defining those tiers. Thus we cannot necessarily assume anything other than that sociocultural complexity is increasing as the number of tiers increases. But even this conclusion, taken by itself, is a clear indication that we are dealing with an orderly process—i.e., that along with the quantitative changes in numbers of sites and people came a qualitative change to a higher level of complexity in the network of settlements comprising the system. And if, taken together, these changes are such that a new level of sociocultural integration appears to have been reached, then whatever we call this level (e.g., "ranked society" or "chiefdom"; "stratified society", "civilization", or "state") it is clear that we are dealing with transformations that demand definition and explanation.

The categorization of changing levels of sociocultural integration is therefore no different than distinguishing periods of chronological development (e.g., Las Salinas through Late Tambo Real, or the early, middle, and late periods), or categories of basic site function and occupational density. Clearly, to a certain extent quantitative ranges and qualitative distinguishing criteria are arbitrary (i.e., an argument can always be made that the breaks between categories should be placed higher or lower on a scale, or earlier or later in the sequence). But they are nonetheless a necessary part of the analysis of developmental changes—at least if we are not to lump all sites and the entire sequence together in one mass of data that are viewed as essentially indistinguishable. The critical point is that in making *explicit* the criteria used in establishing categories one is making clear the analytical assumptions by which the data can be assessed, understood, and cross-culturally compared. Since all of the ceramic period subsistence-settlement systems in the Lower Santa sequence appear to represent varying kinds of local, regional, or interregional nonegalitarian societies it is appropriate to conclude this chapter with brief definitions and comments on chiefdom and state societies.

Chiefdom societies are now viewed as the first to arise beyond the level of egalitarian societies, and in the Central Andes and elsewhere they appear to have occurred whenever developing subsistence systems provided a source of food that was capable of intensification and/or diverse and unpredictable enough from year to year to select for higher-order coordinative and redistributive functions. On the other hand, food procurement systems that were characterized primarily by a focus on wild food resources—and therefore incapable of substantial intensification—in general do not appear to have provided the basis for evolution beyond an egalitarian level.

It is worth noting that the latter type of food procurement system appears to characterize exactly the reputed maritime-oriented "civilizations" that some coastal researchers have argued were present on the Peruvian littoral by the late Preceramic (e.g., Moseley 1975c). It thus appears likely that a primarily maritime-oriented system with minor, secondary reliance on horticulture would have been limited to an egalitarian level (cf. Wilson 1981; see also Raymond 1981)—not only because of technological limitations (e.g., in getting out to the major offshore concentrations of pelagic marine species), but also because of unpredictable and devastating downturns in overall marine productivity (to which preceramic peoples do not appear to have adapted by developing, for example, storage facilities for dried fish). *In contrast, the early irrigation-based systems on the Peruvian coast were not only by definition capable of intensification and the development of storage techniques, but, as argued later, were characterized by features that selected for higher-order coordinative functions* (e.g., the uneven distribution of population in relation to locally available land, and the maintenance and integrity of local canal systems).

Among the specific characteristics (and archaeological correlates) of chiefdoms are the following: relatively larger populations (numbering from several thousands to several tens of thousands); control over a number of settlements encompassed within a local area or region of substantial size (measuring from several tens to as many as several hundreds of square kilometers); an incipient hierarchy of settlement size and function (e.g., three to four size levels, or tiers); "chiefly" villages or centers that are often of substantial size (numbering from many hundreds to several thousands); evidence of the rise of elite and commoner groups (as evidenced by such features as intrasite and intersite differences in dwellings); and the beginnings of corporate labor and supravillage productive activities (as manifested in smaller-scale monumental architecture, part-time craft specialization, interregional trade, and construction of major canals, field systems, and roads).

State societies appear to have developed primarily in areas characterized by arid or semiarid environments where an ample supply of water, relatively abundant amounts of irrigable land, and the introduction of a productive complex of cultigens together provided the basis for intensive agriculture and the rise of substantial populations (numbering at first in the many tens of thousands and, later, in the hundreds of thousands). The precise set of factors leading to pristine state formation in each of the nuclear areas must have differed according to the nature of the socioenvironmental setting. For example, the rise of the early Egyptian state took place in a setting characterized not only by influences from states in adjacent Mesopotamia, but also by the presence of thousands of square kilometers of land whose fertility was replenished annually by the massive silt load of the Nile (cf. Butzer 1976).

In contrast, none of the Peruvian coastal valleys is characterized both by an essentially inexhaustible water supply and huge amounts of land. Instead, these valleys may be described in a sense as a series of closely spaced "mini-Niles"—each one characterized by its relatively small size (with cultivable land ranging between 7 km², in Ocoña, and 600 km², in Piura) and a limited supply of water (with annual river discharge averaging between 30×10^6 m³, in Tacna, and 5000×10^6 m³, in Santa). Thus, as indicated in Tables 1 and 24, the majority of North Coast valleys are limited either by water supply or by the areal extent of irrigable land, if not both (Virú and Nepeña, for example, are limited by both water and land supply, while Santa is limited only by the latter). In turn, this probably set the maximum developmental potential of most individual valleys in the North Coast area at the chiefdom level. However, a few regions such as Moche Valley (and probably Casma) appear to have been characterized by a relatively favorable combination of ample cultivable land and adequate water that gave them a demographic edge over their neighbors and, ultimately, the capability of initiating the formation of multivalley conquest states.

In addition to substantially larger populations and favorable combinations of cultivable land and water supply, among the characteristics (and archaeological correlates) of early states are the following: control over a very large and often diverse area (ranging from several thousands to several tens of thousands of square kilometers); a developed hierarchy of site size and function that includes primary centers of substantial size, regional centers, local centers, and undifferentiated habitation sites (i.e., at least four to five levels, or tiers); the rise of legally constituted coercive power or authority, usually based on the creation, maintenance, and strategic deployment of a large military force (and manifested in such features as population resettlement, massive hydraulic and land reclamation projects, monumental architecture, and large-scale trading and road networks); widespread, and often uniform, distribution of major cultural traits (including diagnostic ceramic and architectural forms, as well as iconographic themes and styles); full-time craft specialization (with mass production of pottery, textiles, and other items in specified areas of higher-order sites, as well as widespread regional uniformity of form and decorative style); and social stratification (which may be reflected in various component features of the settlement system, including internal diversification of capitals and regional centers, residence based on occupational specialization, and diverse mortuary practices).

CHAPTER 4

The Sequence of Prehispanic Site Types and Settlement Patterns

The preceding two chapters have established the outlines of the socioenvironmental setting within which prehispanic developments in the Lower Santa Valley took place, as well as the research methods employed in carrying out the regional study of these developments. This chapter presents the data gathered on each of the ten periods in the Santa Valley sequence by examining, first, the nature of site types and other remains, and, second, the patterning of prehispanic settlements. The first part of the discussion of each period is thus restricted for the most part to the site and intrasite levels—focusing on site and structural types, as well as discrete but more extensive remains such as roads, trails, and walls. Following this, each period discussion deals with the settlement data—focusing on the overall patterning of sites and population (see Table 5), in addition to some of the evolutionary implications of changes in these patterns over time.

Depending on the numbers and kinds of site types assessed as dating to it, the first part of the data presentation for each period follows the same basic order: (1) *habitation sites* (including undifferentiated occupations, possible elite residences, local centers, and regional centers), (2) *defensive sites* (citadels and minor fortresses), (3) *ceremonial-civic sites* (larger complexes and huaca mounds), (4) *cemeteries,* and (5) *other remains* (including corrals, desert ground drawings, a subterranean gallery, trails, roads, walls, and petroglyphs). In the second part, specific aspects of broader regional patterns are discussed, including (6) *settlement and demographic patterns,* (7) *ceramic distributions,* and (8) *inferences about subsistence.* Finally, in order to provide some framework for the discussion in Chapter V of major interregional developments, as well as a comparative context for understanding

period-to-period developments in Santa Valley, the discussion of each period ends with a brief section on (9) *interregional comparisons* (including, whenever relevant, data on contemporaneous site types and settlement patterns in nearby regions such as Nepeña, the Callejón de Huaylas, Virú, and Moche).

With regard to interregional comparisons, it should be noted that in general the data from Virú are most heavily relied upon to provide some perspective for the Santa Valley data. This is primarily because Virú Valley is the only one of the nearby regions mentioned above where a comparably fine-grained sequence has been established, and where substantial amounts of data were retrieved on different site types of each period throughout the region (cf. Bennett 1950; Collier 1955; Ford and Willey 1949; Strong and Evans 1952; Willey 1953). For example, as indicated in Chart 1, the Virú Valley researchers established a sequence of four basic periods extending over the

Table 5. Population Estimates by Survey Sector and Period

| | Survey Sector | | | | | |
Period	Upper Valley	Middle Valley	Lower Valley	Coast	Santa-Chao	Total Population
LTR	230	970	9010	165	105	10,480
ETR	1775	1160	5175	3550	–	11,660
LTAN	2160	7215	8960	50	50	18,435
ETAN	4820	10,615	11,750	2945	5800	35,930
GUAD	395	3170	18,375	80	–	22,020
LSUCH	19,085	7395	3285	–	–	29,765
ESUCH	11,045	5055	4010	–	–	20,110
VIN	2960	2005	2350	–	540	7855
CAY	3855	1940	150	15	–	5960
SAL	170	245	–	565	–	980

ca. 1650-year time period from Early Horizon through the end of Early Intermediate (i.e., Guañape, Puerto Moorin, Gallinazo, and Huancaco). These four periods correlate quite well with the periods resulting from our own research in Santa (i.e., Cayhuamarca, Vinzos, Suchimancillo, and Guadalupito).

In contrast, researchers in Nepeña have established only two basic periods—Early Horizon and Early Intermediate—to account for developments that occurred in the long time period mentioned above (cf. Proulx 1968, 1973). Moreover, Proulx views the Recuay and Moche occupations in Nepeña as spatially discrete and essentially coeval phenomena, in contrast to our own findings in Santa that Recuay-related ceramic diagnostics are consistently—and indeed nearly universally—associated with pre-Moche Suchimancillo materials. In other words, in Santa they are contemporaneous with Suchimancillo Period, not Guadalupito, just as in Virú the Callejón-related pottery was found in Gallinazo contexts and not Huancaco ones (cf. Strong and Evans 1952:347–351). Leaving aside the problem of chronology in the valley to the south, it is nevertheless impossible to compare the Vinzos-Suchimancillo time period of Santa (and the Puerto Moorin-Gallinazo time period of Virú) to the Nepeña sequence since nothing comparable has been identified there.

Similarly, researchers in Casma Valley to date have identified only two periods of occupation in the early part of the ceramic sequence—i.e., Early Horizon and Late Formative—with nearly 700 years of the Early Intermediate Period still remaining unknown (cf. Collier 1962; Tello 1956; Thompson 1962a, 1962b, 1964). Finally, while researchers in Moche have established four early ceramic periods (Cupisnique, Salinar, Gallinazo, and Moche) that are comparable to the early part of the Virú and Santa sequences mentioned above, with the exception of a summary article by Bankes (1972) essentially no data are yet available in the literature on the settlement survey carried out over a decade ago in the lower part of the valley by the members of the Harvard Chan Chan-Moche Valley Project.

With regard to the discussion of site types, it should be noted that several larger multicomponent sites present something of a problem in determining the period under which they are to be discussed. This is especially true of sites such as Huaca Santa, for example, where overlapping and noncoextensive occupations of five different periods are spread out over the area where complex architectural remains are found. Although it is probable that many of the architectural remains at Huaca Santa date to the later periods of occupation, the most extensive surface debris dates to Early Suchimancillo (see SVP-ESUCH–126, in Fig. 71; see also SVP-ETR–43 and SVP-LTR–68 site descriptions in Wilson 1985, Appendix B). For this reason, and for the sake of convenience,

Huaca Santa Complex is discussed under the earliest period of occupation and the site plan has been included in the Early Suchimancillo section of the accompanying illustrations. Sites such as Huaca Santa are also discussed in terms of their size and relative regional importance under later periods, although as implied above it is sometimes difficult specifically to assign architectural remains to one or another period. In general, where ceramic debris of various periods and surface architecture on a site are more or less precisely coextensive, the discussion of these remains has been placed under the earliest period of occupation—with the realization that at least some of the architecture may date to later periods.

To facilitate an initial understanding of the chronological placement of the ten Santa Valley periods, the better known Virú Valley/Central Andean period equivalents are identified in parentheses in the section heading for each one.

LAS SALINAS PERIOD (CERRO PRIETO/PRECERAMIC)

Thirty six sites were identified as belonging to the preceramic period of occupation in the survey region (see Figs. 16–21; and Wilson 1985, Fig. 22, for site outlines). All of these sites are presumed to have been used primarily for habitation, and for purposes of discussion may be divided into two groups: (1) 21 inland and coastal windbreak sites (SVP-SAL-1 to 21), and (2) 15 coastal midden sites (SVP-SAL-22 to 36). It is useful at this point to provide a cautionary note regarding our dating of these sites as preceramic. In general, preceramic regional settlement data are inherently more problematical than those of the ceramic periods. This is true both with regard to (1) the difficulties involved in distinguishing between aceramic sites that date to the preceramic period of occupation and those that actually date to the ceramic time period, but, by definition, have no associated sherds; and (2) the essential impossibility of identifying preceramic occupation at sites that also were occupied in one or more of the later, ceramic periods and are covered with sherd debris.

However, for several reasons it seems likely that most, if not all, of the sites identified as belonging to Las Salinas Period are indeed preceramic in date. First of all, considering the generally excellent preservation of organic and other surface remains dating back several thousands of years in the dry coastal setting, the presence of even the relatively more fragile remains such as cotton netting in conjunction with the absence of any sherds is a possible indicator of a preceramic date—at least when these remains are found in association with coastal midden sites such as those along the oldest Las Salinas shoreline (e.g., see SVP-SAL-23 site description in Wil-

90

son 1985, Appendix B). Second, all of the sites dated as preceramic are not only of smaller size (i.e., 1 ha or less), but, outside of the area of Las Salinas shoreline, are characterized by the presence of limited numbers of windbreak dwellings. Although this structural type is found at a few sites dating to the early periods in the ceramic sequence, it appears to be a good general preceramic architectural diagnostic in the region. Third, the location of fully two-thirds of the sites along the coast at a time when the subsistence-settlement system is thought to have been primarily maritime in nature also fits into the overall preceramic pattern (e.g., see Bird 1948; Moseley 1975c; Pozorski 1979).

Inland and Coastal Windbreak Sites

Twelve of the 21 preceramic sites at which windbreak structures are found lie in the Upper and Middle Valley sectors, well inland from the ocean (Figs. 18, 19). The terrain where these sites are located varies generally as a function of distance downstream from the Santa-Tablachaca confluence—with the upper sites situated closer to the river, but separated from it by steeper slopes, while the lower sites lie out in rolling desert terrain farther away from the valley floor. The elevation of all 12 sites above the valley floor ranges from 10 to 150 m, with an average elevation of 70 m (see Table 9). In contrast, although none of these sites occupies the higher ridges and hilltops that served as locations of preference in all of the following early periods from Cayhuamarca through Late Suchimancillo, it is of interest to note that the average distance of 890 m away from the valley floor is the greatest of any period in the sequence. As we shall see later, this has implications not only for the nature of within-valley relations in this period but also points to a fundamental difference between Las Salinas Period and the other early periods which follow.

Compared to habitation sites of later periods, the size of inland sites is generally quite small, with a range between .25 and 3.5 ha. Likewise, the number of windbreaks is relatively limited, with a range between 3 and 20 discrete dwellings per site. The windbreaks themselves usually have semicircular walls of rough fieldstone which measure less than 1 m high and 2–4 m long. The open side of the structures normally faces upcanyon away from the strong southwesterly winds that blow inland off the ocean during the early part of the afternoon. Due to the relatively simple nature of these sites, we did not prepare plan views of any of them during the course of the fieldwork. However, plan views made of several windbreak sites of later periods provide a good general idea of the nature of preceramic sites (e.g., Figs. 61, 65; see also Plate 15). Nowhere on these sites did we find evidence of organic structural remains, but, considering the universally low height of the rock walls, it seems probable that some type of thatching made of reeds or branches originally was present to provide additional protection from the wind and sun.

With regard to occupational debris, it is almost easier to characterize the inland windbreak sites by what we did *not* find than by what is present. Thus, although limited amounts of lithic debitage were noted on the surface of SVP-SAL-1, no recognizably worked stone was noted anywhere else nor were organic surface remains of any kind found. In terms of the arguments made later in this report about the possible nature of the earliest warfare, it is also interesting to note that no defensive works such as walls and ditches were found in or near these or other preceramic sites in the region—in spite of the clear indication that a need (based possibly on defensive considerations) existed to live well out on the barren desert away from the watered valley floor.

Nine coastal occupations (SVP-SAL-13 to 21, in Figs. 20, 21) are included under the general category of windbreak sites, although at two of them—SVP-SAL-16 and SVP-SAL-17—only rock-faced terraces remain, and the presence of habitation structures is an inference based on scattered rock rubble. Briefly to deal first with the two exceptional sites, both are larger than most or all of the other coastal occupations (including the Las Salinas middens) and are therefore presumed to have had larger populations. Of the two, SVP-SAL-7 is the more unusual in that it has a very large size of 8.75 ha and contains extensive terracing on which no sherds are found (see Wilson 1985, Appendix B). In the absence of windbreaks, the population estimate of 260 persons is somewhat conjectural but nonetheless conservative considering the size of the site.

With the exception of SVP-SAL-21, located along the edge of a small quebrada adjacent to Bahía de Samanco, all of the remaining coastal sites south of the Santa River are situated on steep, rocky headlands overlooking the rough waters of the ocean. All are therefore located in areas that would have been suitable for line fishing. On the other hand, SVP-SAL-21 is situated in an area that is presently the focus of intensive shellfish gathering, and preceramic subsistence presumably was based on a similar focus. It should be noted, however, that all of the nine coastal sites in question contain scattered remains of shellfish, thus indicating a general reliance on this aspect of maritime subsistence in the area south of the river. Indeed, as indicated in Figs. 20 and 21, none of the occupations immediately to the south of the mouth of Santa Valley is located farther than 2.5 km from shallower ocean waters, via the narrow trail that connects them to the Santa and Lacramarca areas. As in the case of the inland sites, these occupations are generally small and contain a few scattered windbreaks ranging in number between 3 and 10 discrete structures. Likewise, no lithics of an obviously worked nature were found nor are

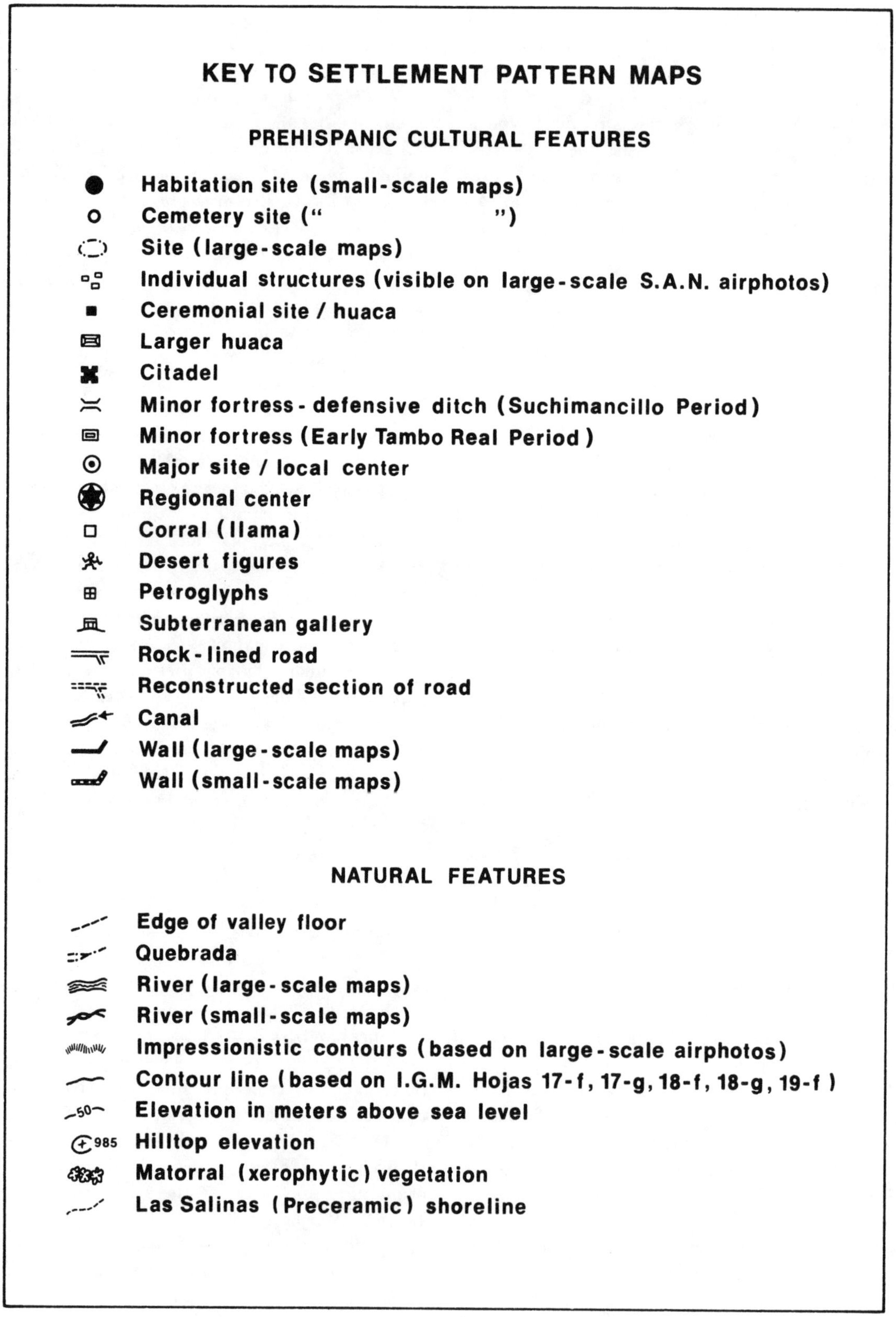

KEY TO SETTLEMENT PATTERN MAPS

PREHISPANIC CULTURAL FEATURES

●   Habitation site (small-scale maps)

○   Cemetery site ("   ")

⊂⊃   Site (large-scale maps)

⊡   Individual structures (visible on large-scale S.A.N. airphotos)

■   Ceremonial site / huaca

▣   Larger huaca

✖   Citadel

⋈   Minor fortress - defensive ditch (Suchimancillo Period)

▣   Minor fortress (Early Tambo Real Period)

⊙   Major site / local center

✪   Regional center

□   Corral (llama)

⚂   Desert figures

⊞   Petroglyphs

血   Subterranean gallery

⟚   Rock-lined road

⟚   Reconstructed section of road

⟋   Canal

⟍   Wall (large-scale maps)

⟋   Wall (small-scale maps)

NATURAL FEATURES

⟋   Edge of valley floor

⟫   Quebrada

≋   River (large-scale maps)

⟿   River (small-scale maps)

⟋⟍   Impressionistic contours (based on large-scale airphotos)

⌢   Contour line (based on I.G.M. Hojas 17-f, 17-g, 18-f, 18-g, 19-f)

⟋50⟍   Elevation in meters above sea level

⊕985   Hilltop elevation

❀❀   Matorral (xerophytic) vegetation

⟋   Las Salinas (Preceramic) shoreline

Fig. 16. Key to settlement pattern maps.

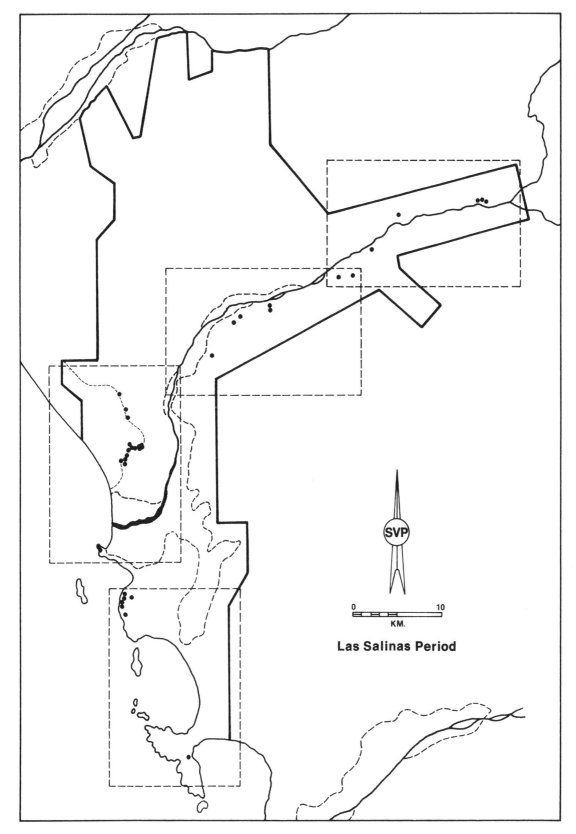

Fig. 17. Location key to settlement pattern maps of Las Salinas Period.

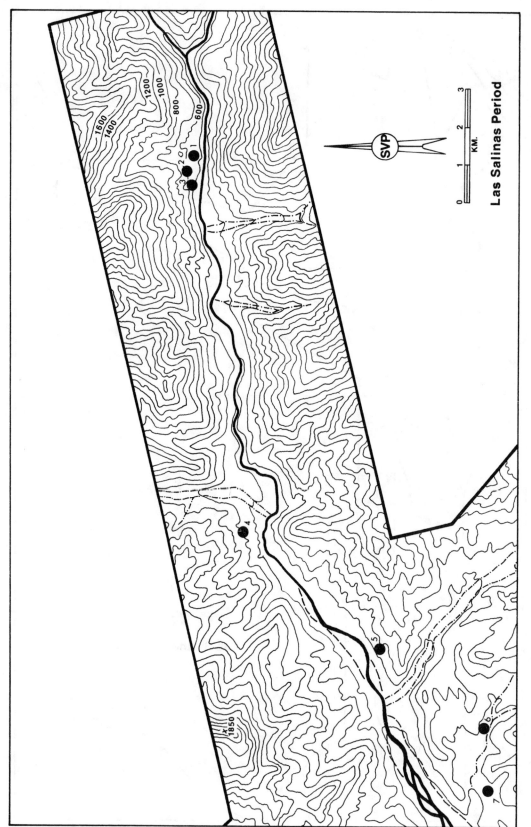

Fig. 18. Settlement pattern map of Las Salinas Period: Upper Valley sector.

94

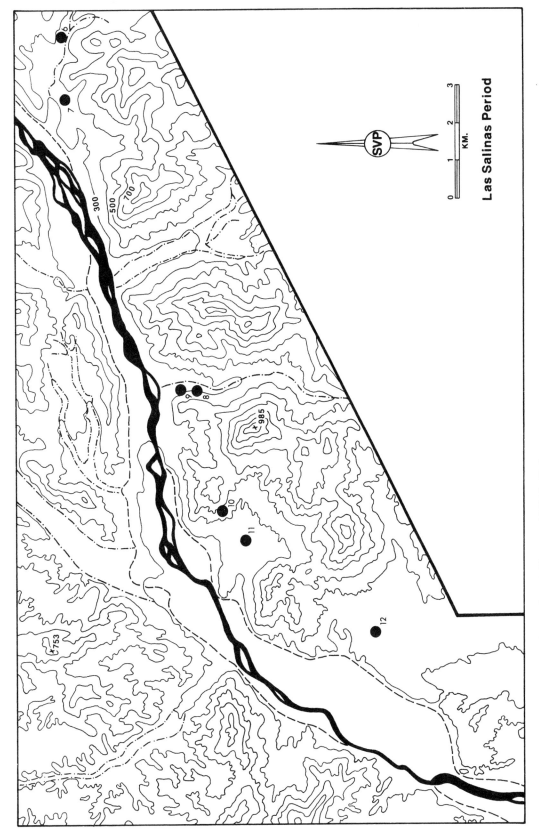

Fig. 19. Settlement pattern map of Las Salinas Period: Upper and Middle Valley sectors.

95

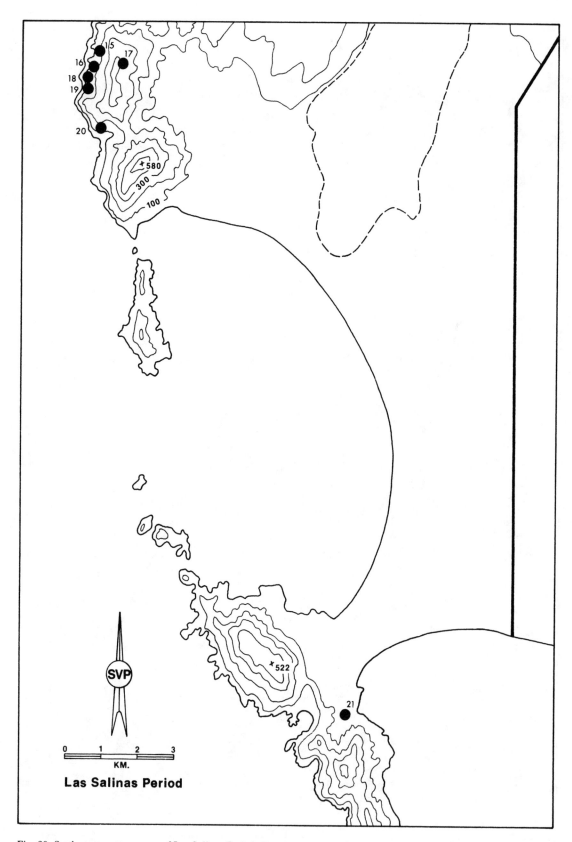

Fig. 20. Settlement pattern map of Las Salinas Period: Coast sector—south.

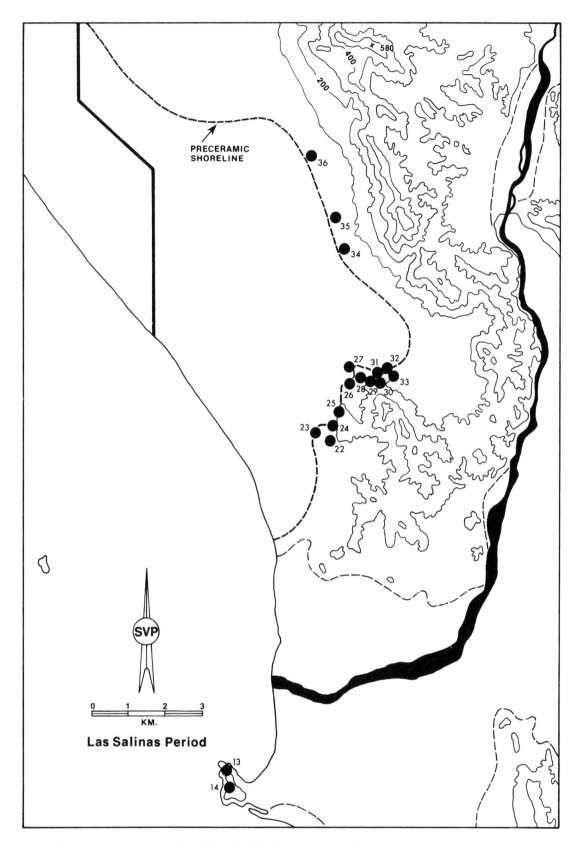

PRECERAMIC
SHORELINE

SVP

0 1 2 3
KM.

Las Salinas Period

Fig. 21. Settlement pattern map of Las Salinas Period: Coast sector—north.

97

any rock walls present that could be construed as defensive in nature.

Coastal Midden Sites

The remaining 15 sites dating to the preceramic time period (SVP-SAL–22 to 36) are located on or immediately above the most ancient Las Salinas shoreline, which runs roughly on the present 25-m contour line around the base of steeper hills lying to the north of the mouth of Santa Valley. All are characterized by relatively smaller sizes than the other sites of Las Salinas Period, as well as by the absence of any detectable architectural remains on the surface. The principal features defining these sites include discrete concentrations of shellfish debris that stand out clearly as manuports, in contrast to the continuous line of natural debris which defines the ancient beach lying two or more meters in elevation below. At every one of the 15 occupations we also found scattered lithic debris that clearly is exotic to the ancient shoreline area. Two of the occupations—SVP-SAL–23 and SVP-SAL–24—stand out, however, in having especially rich concentrations of debris. For example, the debris noted on the surface of SVP-SAL–23 includes scattered fragments of textiles and cotton netting, light densities of lithics that include flake and core tools (see Coll. 364 artifacts, in Fig. 189), heavy concentrations of shellfish remains, and several bones of marine mammals including a large whale vertebra. Similar remains were noted at SVP-SAL-24, including flat-sided stones that may have been used for grinding seeds or other vegetal materials in food processing activities (see Coll. 365 artifacts, in Fig. 189).

Thus, although the subsistence base of the Las Salinas area sites appears to be similar to that of the southern coastal occupations, it differs in having a greater variety of marine remains as well as indications of reliance on nonmaritime food sources. Judging both from this variety and the density of midden debris, it appears likely that the northern coastal sites were used for habitation as well as for food gathering activities. In the absence of any structural remains on the surface, it may be speculated either that they were built of completely perishable materials or that excavation at a future date will reveal rock walls similar to those at the windbreak sites described above. The universal absence of rock rubble of a size suitable for walls suggests that the former of these two speculations is the correct one—i.e., structures probably were built entirely of organic materials.

Settlement and Demographic Patterns

As should be clear from discussions of previous chapters as well as from a comparison of settlement and demographic maps (see Figs. 164–183), Las Salinas Period in many ways represents the time of minimum complexity

of the prehispanic subsistence-settlement system—both in terms of low population numbers and the apparent lack of any diversity in the nature of the settlements themselves. In this sense, then, a consideration of the main characteristics of the preceramic system provides some perspective on more complex developments of the following early ceramic periods. In spite of the overall lack of complexity, however, it is of interest to note that the 36 small habitation sites of this period are distributed widely throughout the main valley area and adjacent Pacific coastline at the mouth of the Santa River. Among other things, this pattern implies a broad subsistence focus on the two main microenvironments of the pre-agricultural setting—i.e., the shallow inshore water of the ocean and the matorral thickets of the riverine area.

Assuming contemporaneity of all sites, a little over 40% of the estimated population—or 415 out of 980 persons—was located in the 12 windbreak sites of the Upper and Middle Valley sectors. The remainder was located in the 24 windbreak and midden sites lying to the south along the rugged seacoast and to the north along the shallow waters of ancient Bahía Las Salinas. Sites in the upper sectors are very widely scattered throughout the 37 km-long area of occupation there, with essentially no indication of an adaptation which selected for or required any major local population concentrations. Considering the fact that sites of these two sectors are located, on the average, farther away from the watered valley floor than at any other time in the entire sequence, it seems at least possible that a need existed for defense against raiding—either from nearby sites or from outside the region.

On the other hand, the great majority of the inhabitants of Las Salinas shoreline are distributed in a closely spaced concentration of 12 sites, all of which are situated in relatively very exposed positions along or immediately above the waters of the ancient bay. This strongly suggests a context characterized by an absence of any external threat. It must be noted, however, that all of the nine sites to the south of the river are located in rugged and inaccessible terrain, suggesting a pattern similar to that of the Upper and Middle Valley.

Inferences About Subsistence

Judging from the location of sites throughout the area of Las Salinas occupation, at least two distinct kinds of subsistence orientation appear to characterize this period—including (1) a coastal maritime system, and (2) an inland riverine matorral-oriented system. Since marine shell debris characterizes many inland sites of virtually all of the ceramic periods, it is of some significance to note that no such debris was found on any of the 12 inland preceramic sites. Because of this, it seems likely that the primary subsistence focus of people in the Upper and Middle Valley was on gathering-hunting in the dense thickets of vegetation that probably extended all along the edges of the river. On the other hand, our data indicate that people of the coastal area had a somewhat broader focus that included shellfish gathering, net fishing, hunting or scavenging of large marine mammals (definitely including whales, and perhaps sea lions as well), and the stone-ground processing of vegetal materials collected/grown near the valley floor or in adjacent marshy areas (as evidenced by the presence of metates, or batanes, and manos at some sites).

Considering the sharp distinction between the systems of the Upper-Middle and Coast sectors, as well as the lack of any marine shell on the upper sites, it may be tentatively suggested that the Las Salinas settlement pattern represents two separate groups—each focused on a distinct microenvironment. Moreover, the general lack of seasonality in the marine or riverine environments, as well as the lack of parity in the population estimates of the two areas (i.e., 415 vs. 565 persons), provide additional support for the argument that we are not viewing a system characterized by a single, smaller transhumant population that alternated between the coast and inland environments in its occupation of the regional microenvironments. Indeed, it is difficult to argue that such a group of people would have inhabited such dissimilar site locations (i.e., relatively remote desert pampas and quebradas vs. highly exposed coastline) merely as a result of short-term changes in subsistence focus. Instead, it seems likely that a separate group occupied the Upper and Middle Valley sites in a context characterized by at least some threat of external or intersite attack, while the people of the Las Salinas coast were part of a local system characterized by peace rather than strife.

Whatever the precise nature of the preceramic system, however, it is of substantial interest to note that the up-valley sites of Las Salinas Period provide evidence of reasonably widespread occupation in the area that would become the main focus of settlement in the agricultural system of Cayhuamarca and Vinzos Periods. Given the lack of any surface cultigens on the 12 sites of the upper sectors, it is difficult to determine whether the preceramic sites represent in part a transitional adaptation leading to the early agricultural system. This seems to be at least a possibility, however.

Interregional Comparisons

Nepeña Valley. Five sites of probable preceramic date and two additional occupations possibly dating to this period are described by Proulx (1973:8–11) for Nepeña, and several of them appear to be quite similar to those found in the Lower Santa Valley region. Among them is PV 31–208, a small site located along the northwestern edge of the small protected bay which lies south of the valley mouth (see Fig. 2). In addition to dense refuse consisting of shellfish and other marine animal remains,

as well as charcoal, twigs, and cordage, Proulx notes that the outlines of several rectangular stone structures are visible on the surface of the site. It is also of interest to note that all of the Nepeña Valley preceramic occupations found to date (cf. Proulx 1973, Fig. 2, p. 9) appear to be located well within 1 km of the present shoreline, which may indicate that Nepeña has not been subject to the continual episodes of tectonic uplifting that have so dramatically changed the northern side of the mouth of Santa Valley.

Virú Valley. Three definite and two possible sites dating to the preceramic time period are described by the Virú Valley researchers (cf. Bird 1948; Strong and Evans:17–23; Willey 1953:38–42). Survey and test excavations at the coastal site of V-71/Huaca Prieta de Guañape, the best known of the Cerro Prieto Period occupations, indicated the presence of small conjoined rooms and several stone-lined semisubterranean habitations. Later occupations dating to the ceramic time period cover an overlying area of some 6 ha at V-71, so it is difficult to assess the size of the preceramic site. However, judging from the preceramic strata present in Test Pits 1 and 2 on the north and south-central parts of the mound, it seems likely that the Cerro Prieto Period site covered about one-third of the area of the later occupation; at ca. 2 ha, then, this site was not appreciably larger than most contemporaneous sites in Santa and Nepeña Valleys. The other two definite Cerro Prieto occupations lie along the shoreline immediately to the south of V-71, while the two possible preceramic sites lie inland in the middle part of the valley.

In sum, both Nepeña and Virú exhibit some similarities to the system of Las Salinas Period with regard to the location, size, and nature of preceramic sites. But with an apparent maximum of seven and three sites, respectively, both valleys present comparatively much less populated systems than that described for the Lower Santa region. Moreover, the only sites of reasonably definite preceramic date identified for the two valleys lie along the Pacific coastline. Thus, at least in the case of Nepeña, there is as yet no indication that sites were located in the upper and middle sectors—in a system that would have been preadaptive to the upvalley developments that take place in the Early Horizon Period agricultural system. On the other hand, the early agricultural system of Early-Middle Guañape Period in Virú is essentially focused on the coast and lower valley areas—i.e., the same area, more or less, where preceramic occupation had occurred. The evidence from both Virú and Santa thus provides at least some indication in terms of site location of systems that were preadaptive for the beginnings of irrigation agriculture. Although a more detailed comparative assessment of the three regional systems will have to await systematic and comprehensive resurvey of the valleys to the north and south, as well as excavation in selected Lower Santa and Nepeña sites, it appears likely that the relatively much larger number of sites in the Las Salinas Period system of Santa represents a larger preceramic population.

CAYHUAMARCA PERIOD (GUAÑAPE/EARLY HORIZON)

A total of 54 discrete sites was identified as belonging to the Cayhuamarca Period of occupation (Figs. 22–24; see Wilson 1985, Fig. 26, for site outlines). In contrast to the preceding period, when all sites appear to have served a single function related to habitation, the number of types in Cayhuamarca that can be distinguished on the basis of primary or sole function rises to four—including habitation sites (24 occupations), citadels (21 occupations), ceremonial-civic sites (8 occupations), and cemeteries (1 occupation).

Habitation Sites

Undifferentiated occupations. Roughly 44%—or 24 out of 54—of the occupations of Cayhuamarca Period consist of internally undifferentiated sites—i.e., occupations that appear to have had no other function than habitation. These sites are distributed more or less evenly on the steeper slopes and occasional pampas that lie alongside the valley floor throughout most of the Upper and Middle Valley sectors (see SVP-CAY-1, 2, 7, 10, 11, 14, 16, 20, 27, 30, 33, 35, 41–46, 48–51, 53, and 54, in Figs. 23, 24). Excluding the estimates for inhabited citadels discussed later, undifferentiated habitation sites range in size between .25 and 6.75 ha and in population between 20 and 625 persons—with an average size of about 2 ha and an average population estimate of 140 persons. Thus, although their average size in hectares is only about two times greater than that of Las Salinas Period sites, their estimated population size is well over five times greater than the average of 25 persons per site in the preceramic (see Table 6).

The elevation of habitation sites above the valley floor ranges between 25 and 500 m and distance away from it ranges between 25 and 2000 m—with an average elevation of 110 m above the floor and an average distance of 445 m away from it. Thus, although on the average sites are located much closer to the main source of food and water than the upvalley occupations of Las Salinas Period (average of 890 m away), they are generally located at higher elevations than in the preceding period (average of 70 m above the floor). Nonetheless, sites still are located in remote, defensible positions out on the desert terrain away from the river.

The two principal structural types found at undifferentiated habitation sites of this period include windbreaks and rectangular dwellings. Windbreaks are found at only a few sites in the system (e.g., SVP-CAY-7, in Fig. 27), but, judging from the presence of good Early Horizon ceramic diagnostics on the desert surface in and around them, the use of such structures clearly continued in Cayhuamarca times. An additional diagnostic aspect of Cayhuamarca windbreaks is that many consist of multiroom dwellings, in contrast to the single-room structures that generally characterize the preceding period. Rectangular habitations constitute by far the more common structural type on the Cayhuamarca sites in question, and, like the windbreaks, often consist of multiroom dwellings (e.g., Plate 12; see also Figs. 31, 32, in Wilson 1985). Both types of dwellings have low rock walls ranging in height between 50 and 100 cm. Likewise, both seem very likely to have had additional walling which consisted of reeds or sticks, similar to the modern quincha dwellings described in Chapter II. Although, as mentioned above, structural densities on Cayhuamarca sites are substantially greater than in Las Salinas Period, both windbreaks and rectangular dwellings generally are distributed individually at intervals of from 5–25+ m across a site. Distances between structures usually are much greater on pampa sites than on terraced sites, although densities on the latter type of site still do not approach those of later periods.

Possible elite residences. As described above, most habitation sites of Cayhuamarca Period appear to exhibit very little internal variation in the size and formality of dwellings. In other words, while the number of persons may have varied somewhat from house to house depending on individual family size, there is little indication on the 24 habitation sites discussed above of any sharp differences in dwellings that might correspond to differences in social status or position. However, there is at least one habitation site in the system—SVP-CAY-3—where structures *are* present that may correspond to such differences. Indeed, another site with possible elite residences is found nearby—in association with a citadel and a large ceremonial-civic complex (see SVP-CAY-4 and SVP-CAY-5, in Figs. 26, 28, 50, 51). Because of this, it is useful briefly to discuss both sites for purposes of description and comparison. Additional structures of a possible elite residential nature are found at a number of other citadel and ceremonial-civic sites, and are discussed in the two sections following this one.

SVP-CAY-3 lies at the edge of a large piedmont shelf immediately to the east above a narrow quebrada in the Upper Valley canyon, 4.5 km below the Santa-Tablachaca confluence (see Fig. 51). Some 50 scattered windbreak structures are found in the upper part of the site, and two comparatively more formal agglutinated structures lie in the lower central part (see Structures 120 and 121, in Fig. 25). Good Cayhuamarca sherd diagnostics were found in association with all of the structural remains, indicating that all are probably of the same

100

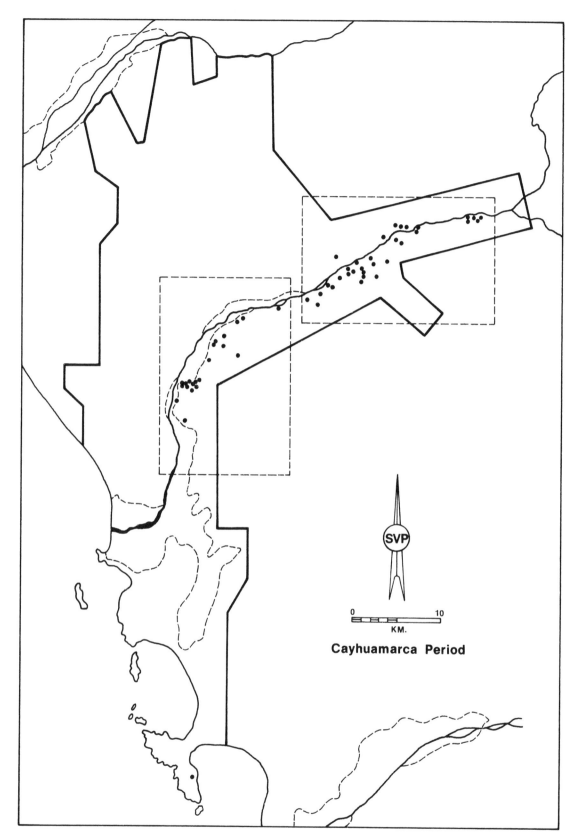

Fig. 22. Location key to settlement pattern maps of Cayhuamarca Period, Figs. 24–25.

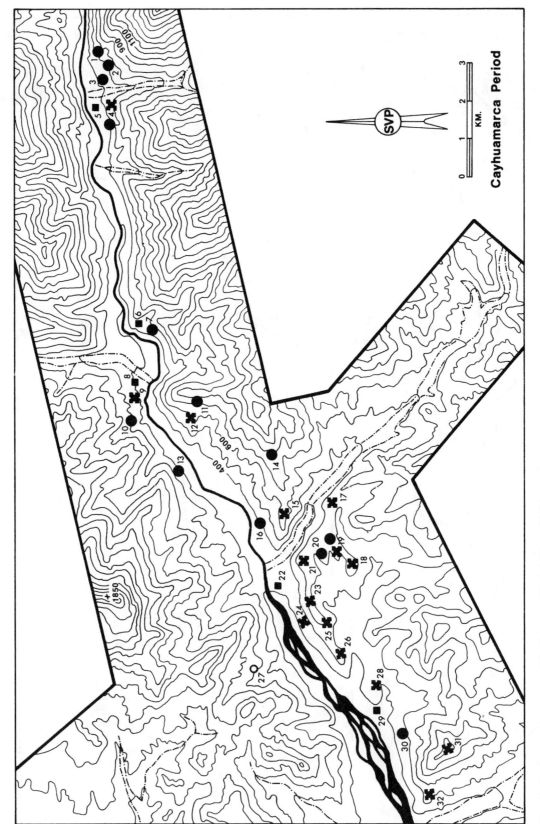

Fig. 23. Settlement pattern map of Cayhuamarca Period: Upper Valley sector.

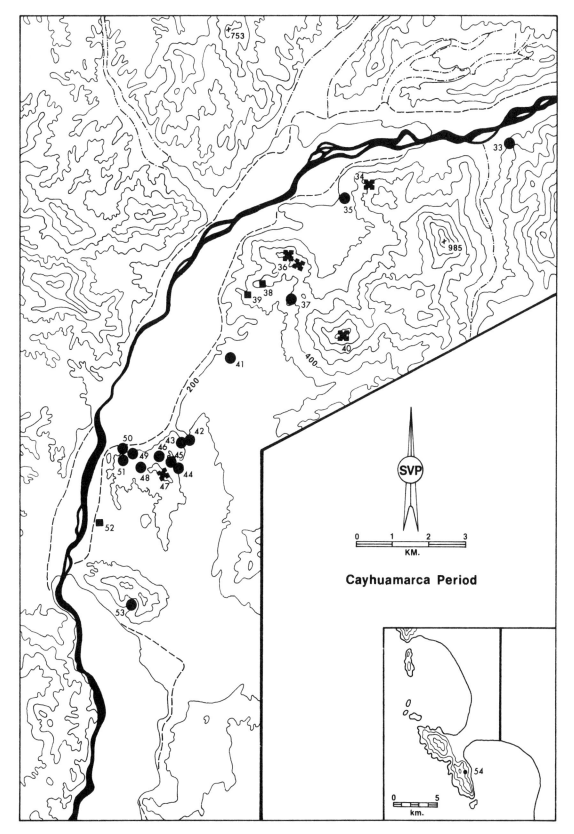

Fig. 24. Settlement pattern map of Cayhuamarca Period: Middle Valley, Lower Valley, and Coast sectors.

date. The combined population of Structures 120 and 121 is estimated at 50 persons and that of the windbreaks is estimated at 150 persons. Judging from the differences in size of rooms contained within the agglutinated structures, at least several smaller storage rooms are present in each as well as greater numbers of larger rooms used for habitation. Rock-faced terracing and associated ceramic debris in the southeast corner of Structure 120 appear to indicate an outdoor activity area. In sum, given the sharp contrast between the two kinds of dwellings on the site, it seems likely that Structures 120 and 121 represent elite residences and that the associated windbreaks represent nonelite dwellings.

The principal habitation structures at SVP-CAY-4, which lies opposite SVP-CAY-3 on the other side of the narrow quebrada, provide another example of possible elite residential units. Their elite nature is suggested in part by their association with a major citadel (Structure 119, in Fig. 28) and a large ceremonial-civic complex (SVP-CAY-5, in Figs. 50, 51), and in part because of their relatively formal layout in comparison to other habitation units on the site. One of the formal residential units on SVP-CAY-4 (Structure 118, not shown here; see Wilson 1985, Fig. 28) lies along an ancient trail about 50 m downslope to the northwest of the citadel. The others (Structures 115 and 116, in Fig. 26) lie 75 m farther down gentle slopes to the west beyond Structure 118. As with the structures at SVP-CAY-3, these units include larger rooms suitable for habitation, smaller rooms that probably were used for storage, and adjacent rock-faced terraces suitable for outdoor activity areas. An additional feature of particular interest on the site is Structure 117, located near one of the residential units (Fig. 26). It is clearly too small to have served as a burial place (indeed, structures of this type are not characteristic of burials of any period in the Lower Santa sequence), but its size and the presence of a small niche suggest the possibility that Structure 117 served as a shrine of some sort. In any case, it is unique in the survey region. Elsewhere on the habitation part of the site, structures are relatively poorly preserved but appear to have been smaller and substantially less complex than Structures 115, 116, and 118, much like the windbreaks at SVP-CAY-3.

Defensive Sites

The Cayhuamarca settlement system is characterized by a number of excellently preserved habitation sites as well as by several impressive ceremonial complexes, but perhaps the single outstanding site type of this period consists of citadel structures. Judging both from associated Early Horizon ceramic diagnostics and from a number of architectural features, a total of 21 citadels was built in Cayhuamarca Period—representing a little over 33% of the 62 discrete defensive sites found in the region. In terms of overall numbers, more defensive sites are oc-

cupied in two of the following early periods—i.e., 40 in Early Suchimancillo and 32 in Late Suchimancillo. But at no time in the sequence do these numbers exceed the importance of Cayhuamarca defensive structures, at least when expressed as a percentage of the total number of discrete occupations of the period—i.e., 21 out of 54 occupations, or nearly 40%, compared to 25% in Vinzos, 30% in Early Suchimancillo, 20% in Late Suchimancillo, 3.5% in Late Tanguche, and 8% in Early Tambo Real.

Moreover, when compared to the defensive sites of any other period, Cayhuamarca citadels stand out not only as more impressive architecturally—e.g., walls are generally more massive and site plans more complex—but also in terms of their more remote location out in the rugged desert terrain away from the valley floor in the upvalley sectors (see SVP-CAY-4, 9, 12, 15, 17–19, 21, 23–26, 28, 31, 32, 34, 36, 40, and 47, in Figs. 23–24). Although in all periods of fortress construction the choice of site location must have been related to general defensive needs as well as constrained by the nature of available terrain, on the average Cayhuamarca citadels are located farther away from the valley floor and higher above it than defensive sites in any other period. They range in distance between 50 m and 3.5 km away from the floor, with an average of about 1 km away from it. They range in elevation between 25 and 700 m (2296 ft) above the valley floor, with an average of 243 m (800 ft) above it.

One means of appreciating the relative remoteness of the citadel sites is to express their location in terms of travel time it took our survey team to reach most of them. While a very few citadels are located within a short 5-minute walk from the modern road (e.g., Structure 119/SVP-CAY-4 and Structure 41/SVP-CAY-24), most of the rest range between one and two hour's rigorous climb up from the valley floor—assuming no heavy gear is lugged along. Whatever the origin of warfare in this period, conflict clearly must have been a significant part of the adaptive context to require placing sites so far from the watered valley floor.

In addition to the summary of characteristic features listed in Table 25, nearly all of the 21 Cayhuamarca citadels are shown in large-scale plan views, and some are shown in perspective views (Figs. 28–49; for the views not included in this report, see Wilson 1985, Figs. 34, 37, 40, 42, 43, 45, 46, 49, 53, 57, 62, 64, 66, 68). As a point of orientation for the reader, it should be noted that the ordering of the citadels illustrated here has been done from upvalley down—primarily to allow a quick visual appraisal of site-to-site similarities and differences on an orderly geographic basis. Nevertheless, the following discussion is carried out in accordance with the main types (or subtypes) of citadels rather than on a geographic, site-to-site basis.

Before going on to outline some of these types, it is

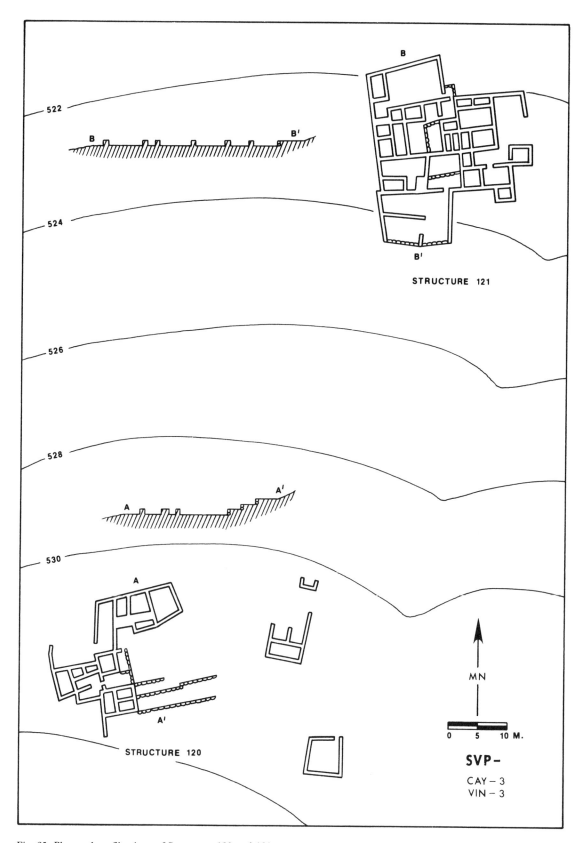

Fig. 25. Plan and profile views of Structures 120 and 121.

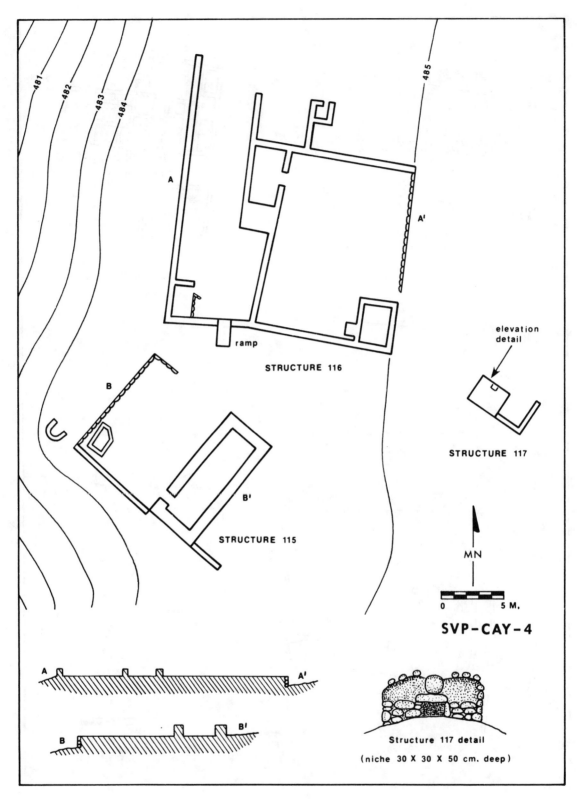

Fig. 26. Plan and profile views of Structures 115, 116, and 117, a possible elite residential unit at SVP-CAY-4.

106

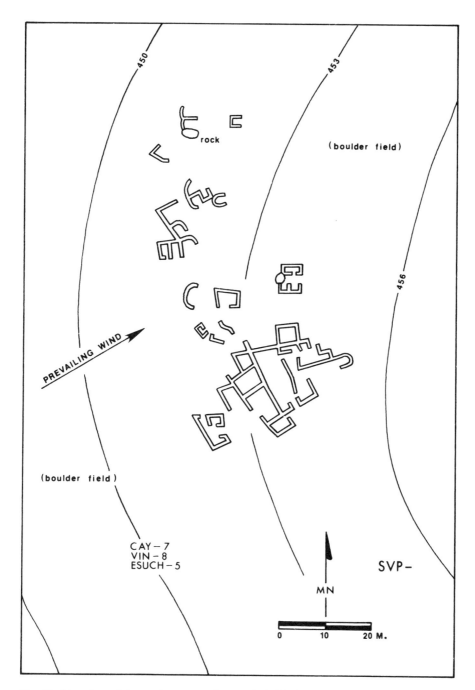

Fig. 27. Plan view of the southern part of an early habitation site with occupation dating to Cayhuamarca, Vinzos, and Early Suchimancillo Periods.

107

useful briefly to elaborate on the principal features of citadels mentioned in Chapter III—especially since the Cayhuamarca citadels are by definition the prototype of all defensive structures of the periods that follow. These features include: (1) high, remote locations above the valley floor; (2) massive rock enclosure walls which range roughly from 1–2 m thick and from 2–4 m high; (3) large bastions on the exterior corners or sides of the main enclosure wall which measure ca. 4 × 2 m in plan view and are usually of the same height as the wall itself; (4) baffled-indirect and/or narrow-direct entrances in limited numbers; (5) simple ramparts and parapets formed by higher ground surfaces on the inner sides of the main enclosure wall; (6) interior rock-walled divisions and structures, with associated occupational debris; (7) one or more dry ditches, or moats, cutting across every relatively gentle access slope or ridge that approaches the site; (8) rock bulwark walls placed adjacent to the upslope side of the ditches; and (9) exterior habitation structures, either immediately adjacent to the citadel structure or within several hundred meters of it (population estimates range between 50 and 375 persons, with an average of about 130 persons).

Nearly all of these features provide support for the argument that the citadel sites indeed were used for defense against attack by enemy raiders. For example, main enclosure walls are generally high, and either surround the entire hilltop or as much of it as necessary to provide protection. Entrances in the main walls are few, and narrow enough to be closed off (at least five citadels appear to have had no entrances at all). Likewise, the presence of bastions, ramparts, and parapets suggests the strategic need to engage the enemy in a crossfire, failing an attempt to stop an attack along the outer perimeter near the ditches. The ditches themselves—which in combination with bulwark walls often provide a very effective barrier totaling some 3 m in height—clearly attest to the primarily defensive nature of the sites where they are found. Moreover, all of these features stand in sharp contrast to those present on the sites assessed as having had a ceremonial-civic function (see below).

However, it also seems clear that beyond their primary uses for defense and habitation a number of Cayhuamarca citadels had other functions as well—probably including use as elite residences and for ceremonial-civic activities. For this reason, and to facilitate an understanding of the variety of citadels present in the system, it is convenient to divide them into subtypes on the basis of the number of functions that appear to have been served. These subtypes include (1) *single-function citadels* (i.e., defense), (2) *dual-function citadels* (defense and habitation), and (3) *multifunction citadels* (defense; habitation, including elite and nonelite; and ceremonial). Although such a division of subtypes clearly is related to assumptions based on the interpretation of extant architectural

features, as well as on the nature of the associated debris, it establishes categories that probably are more mutually exclusive than a division based on specific citadel configurations or presence/absence of features such as double enclosure walls, bastions, inner structures, or dry ditches—most of which are distributed widely, if discontinuously, throughout the system.

Single-function citadels. Based upon such criteria as the absence of occupational debris and habitation structures, only three citadels appear to have served a single function. All three of these citadels (Structures 29 and 30/SVP-CAY-18, and Structure 41/SVP-CAY-24) are located in the general vicinity of the main concentration of sites of this period, namely, in the area just downvalley to the southwest of Quebrada de Cayhuamarca. Structures 29 and 30 (cf. Wilson 1985, Fig. 43) are located adjacent to each other on a narrow ridgetop that lies immediately to the southwest above the Pampa de Cayhuamarca groups of citadels and habitation sites (see ridge to right of pampa in Fig. 5-Cross-section No. 2). No surface sherds were noted in or around either structure, and their dating is based primarily on the uniform presence of Cayhuamarca ceramic diagnostics at nearby sites exhibiting strong architectural similarities—including double enclosure walls constructed of large flat-sided boulders, with smaller rocks filling the interstices (e.g., see Fig. 31). Judging from the presence of eight other citadel sites in the immediate vicinity, the function of Structures 29 and 30 probably involved transitory use for peripheral defensive measures during times of raiding.

Structure 41 presents something of an anomaly compared to any of the other 20 citadels dating to this period (Fig. 36; for a general perspective view, see Wilson 1985, Fig. 49) . On the one hand, it exhibits several of the principal diagnostic features that appear to be restricted to Cayhuamarca defensive structures—including large bastions, a massive enclosure wall, and details of wall construction very similar to those shown in Fig. 31. On the other, it is situated in one of the least defensible positions of any Cayhuamarca citadel—i.e., on a very low piedmont shelf within a distance of 75 m of the cultivated valley floor. Moreover, the vulnerable downslope side of the structure was left open, and is only partly protected by large outcrops of rocks. Indeed, the non-defensible features suggest that this site had a ceremonial-civic function, although defensive use cannot be ruled out. It is also interesting to note the similarity between this structure and the multifunctional Structure 1/SVP-CAY-12 (Fig. 30), where a double-walled inner structure encloses an outcrop of rocks. In both cases, rock outcrops so dominate the interior of the structure that it is tempting to argue they had some sort of religious significance—similar perhaps to that of certain rock outcrops in the sierra, where they are seen as a physical manifestation of the spirits, that is, as huacas (e.g., see Cobo 1964 [1653]:145 ff.; Poma de Ayala 1978 [ca. 1567–1615]:71; see also Rowe 1963a:296).

Dual-function citadels. The greatest number of Cayhuamarca citadels—or 13 out of 21—appear to have had essentially two main functions, including use both as fortresses in the event of raiding and as habitation sites. Two principal kinds of evidence for more or less permanent occupation are present. The first consists of scattered ceramic debris representing the full range of decorated and undecorated Cayhuamarca pottery. This debris usually is found in and around all of the main structures on the site, as well as in association with lesser structural remains. These lesser remains constitute the second kind of evidence for permanent habitation, in that they consist of smaller rock-walled structures found either inside the main enclosure walls and structures or on the exterior around one or more sides of the citadel.

Dual-function citadels are found throughout most of the area of occupation, extending along a 27-km distance from just above Quebrada de Cayhuamarca down to the lower part of the Middle Valley below Vinzos. Indeed, with the exception of the two single-function citadel sites discussed above and two multifunction citadels (Structure 34/SVP-CAY-25 and Structure 52/SVP-CAY-32), all of the Cayhuamarca citadels in this part of the survey area appear to be best characterized as fortress-habitation sites (see SVP-CAY-15, 17, 19, 21, 23, 26, 28, 31, 34, 36, 40, and 47, in Figs. 23–24). The population estimate for these dual-function citadels ranges between 50 and 150 persons, with an average of about 110 persons per site.

For purposes of discussing the most salient characteristics of the 13 citadels, it is useful to divide them into two main subgroups on the basis of terrain and configuration of the site plan: (1) *citadels covering larger areas,* usually extending narrowly along a ridgetop for several hundred meters; and (2) *citadels covering smaller areas,* usually occupying a more compact ridge or hilltop. Proceeding from the uppermost one on downvalley, there are seven citadels that cover larger areas: Structures 6, 31, 33, 49, 55, 90, and 95 (for all but Structure 31, see Figs. 32, 35, 42, 45, 48, and 49, respectively; for Structure 31, see Wilson 1985, Fig. 46). Proceeding from upvalley down, the remaining six citadels that cover smaller areas are: Structures 27, 28, 35, 45, 71, and 72 (see Figs. 33, 34, 39, 40–41, 46, and 47, respectively).

Citadels covering larger areas can be distinguished generally from those in the other group on the basis of two main diagnostic features. First, the long ridges where they are located usually are defined by one or more extremely steep slopes running down away from the site. It was therefore necessary for the outer defensive wall to enclose only those parts of the site that were exposed to

attack via relatively gentler slopes. Indeed, at several citadels—including Structures 6, 33, 49, and 90—slopes along the open part of the main enclosure wall are either cliffs or so steep as to be essentially impassable. Second, in contrast to structures of the other group, citadels on these steepsided ridges are characterized by a general absence of bastions around the main outer walls. This seems likely to be due to the overall steepness of surrounding slopes—i.e., defenders already had a pronounced natural height advantage over attackers and there was apparently no need to protect the main walls further by placing the enemy in a crossfire. For example, no bastions at all are present at Structure 31 (cf. Wilson 1985, Fig. 46), where steep slopes lie to the north, east, and south of the site (a defensive ditch lies across gentler slopes of the ridge, to the west). Likewise, the steep slopes surrounding Structure 90 (Fig. 48) apparently obviated the need for any bastions. On the other hand, at least some of the few bastions present at other citadels in this group appear to have served as (protected) entrances into the upper part of the site (e.g., see Structures 33 and 95, in Figs. 35 and 49).

In contrast, nearly all of the six citadels in the second group are located on hilltops with relatively more gentle surrounding slopes. It therefore appears to have been necessary, first of all, to protect the site by completely enclosing it within the main outer wall. Aside from surrounding defensive ditches at a few of these citadels (see Structures 45, 71, and 72), no other perimetral defensive constructions are present. Second, apparently due to the nature of surrounding slopes, all of the smaller compact citadels are surrounded by massive bastions ranging in number from four to as many as eight. In at least three cases (see Structures 28, 35, and 45), bastions seem well situated to have engaged the enemy in crossfire from all sides. In the other three cases (Structures 27, 71, and 72), bastions are missing only where steeper slopes lie along one of the sides of the site.

It should be noted that the same Cayhuamarca ceramic diagnostics and features of construction are found at sites in both groups of dual-function citadels. The differences between the two groups thus do not appear to be the result of temporal distinctions. Moreover, citadels of both groups are found distributed together in the area between Quebrada de Cayhuamarca and Quebrada del Panteón. Thus the differences between the two groups do not appear to be due to cultural distinctions characterizing separate areas of the valley. In sum, it seems likely that the overall configuration of these sites, as well as the number and kinds of specific defensive features present on each one, are due primarily to the nature of the terrain.

Multifunction citadels. The final citadel subtype includes structures at five sites whose functions appear to have included not only the primary ones of defense and habitation, but also probable use as a focus of ceremonial-civic activities and/or elite residence (see SVP-CAY-4, 9, 12, 25, and 32, in Fig. 23). As with the dual-function citadels, both primary functions are suggested by the following: (1) a relatively remote and defensible location on a higher ridge or hilltop; (2) the presence of specific defensive characteristics such as massive enclosure walls, limited numbers of entrances, bastions, and dry ditches; and (3) the presence of habitation structures and occupational debris in and around the site. In turn, the secondary functions are suggested both by the presence of relatively unique architectural features in or adjacent to the citadel and by a comparison of these features to those at surrounding sites. More specifically, the assertion of an elite residential function is supported by the formal layout of habitation structures contained within the citadel itself, compared to habitation structures on the adjacent exterior or at nearby sites. The assertion of a ceremonial-civic function is supported by the presence of features that are either normally found at sites whose primary function appears to have been a public one or that are relatively unique compared to other citadels in the region.

Although the assertion of both of these secondary functions at the same citadel must be considered a tentative one, it does appear that at least four of the five citadel sites noted above can be so characterized. Proceeding downvalley from the uppermost one, they include Structures 119, 107, 1, and 34 (see Figs. 28, 29, 30, and 37–38). Briefly to discuss each of these four citadels, it will be recalled that Structure 119 lies on a ridge immediately to the southeast of several probable elite residences at SVP-CAY-4 (e.g., see Fig. 26). Cayhuamarca occupational debris was found on the interior of this citadel, in association with smaller rectangular structures that may have served a similar elite residential function. A low circular feature on the interior has the appearance of an altar or shrine. Possible elite habitation of Structure 107 is suggested by the contrast between the formal layout of the interior habitation structures and the simpler nature of dwellings found at the nearby habitation sites of SVP-CAY-10 and SVP-CAY-13. The additional use of the site for ceremonial activities is suggested by the circular sunken court located outside the main enclosure wall, to the north (Fig. 29).

The assertion of probable elite habitation at Structure 1 is supported by the strong contrast between the few formally laid out habitation structures on the interior and the relatively quite simple nature of the 75–100 windbreaks located on the exterior (see SVP-CAY-12 site description in Wilson 1985, Appendix B). An additional ceremonial-civic function at Structure 1 is suggested, as mentioned earlier, by the presence of a large double-walled inner enclosure surrounding two massive rock outcrops. Finally, the assertion of an elite residential

function at Structure 34 is supported by the difference between the formal layout of interior habitations and the simpler nature of dwellings on terraces surrounding the citadel. An additional ceremonial-civic function here is suggested by the terraced circular sunken court feature formed by the central part of the inner structure, as well as by the smaller sunken court on the northwestern side of the inner court.

The final citadel site with a possible multifunctional nature is Structure 52/SVP-CAY-32 (Figs. 43–44), which is located on a lower piedmont ridge some 150 m (492 ft) above the northwest edge of the mouth of Quebrada La Huaca. No other Cayhuamarca site is located near this citadel, except for Structure 49/SVP-CAY-31 which lies 450 m higher in elevation farther up precipitous slopes of the ridge 1.75 km to the southeast (see Figs. 23, 42). Moreover, there are no exterior habitation structures present that provide a contrast to the extensive series of formally laid out dwellings on the interior, and it is therefore difficult to ascribe an elite residential function to this structure. On the other hand, the relatively isolated nature of the large inner structure in the southeast end, as well as the well-delineated stairway leading up to it from a low rock-faced terrace, suggest possible use of this area for ceremonial-civic activities.

Ceremonial-Civic Sites

A total of eight sites dating probably to Cayhuamarca Period were found whose function appears to have been primarily or wholly related to public activities (see SVP-CAY-5, 6, 8, 22, 29, 38, 39, and 52, in Figs. 23, 24). Like the citadels, these sites are distributed throughout the main area of occupation. However, in sharp contrast to every other site type of this period all but two of the ceremonial-civic sites are located either (1) on the open, lower slopes of the desert margin adjacent to the valley floor or (2) on the floor itself in the midst of irrigated fields (the two exceptions are the ridgetop platforms at SVP-CAY-38 and SVP-CAY-39, discussed below). Five of the eight sites—including SVP-CAY-5, 6, 8, 38, and 39—were dated on the basis of both associated Cayhuamarca surface sherds found in and around the principal structural remains, as well as the presence of specific architectural features commonly considered to be diagnostic of Early Horizon Period—including finger-marked adobes, truncated-conical adobes, and circular sunken courts. No associated surface sherds could be found at the remaining sites—including SVP-CAY-22, 29, and 52—and dating here was carried out strictly on the basis of diagnostic architectural features. With regard to overall dating, it should be noted that every one of the eight sites is located closeby the main groups of Cayhuamarca habitation and citadel sites, thus providing additional corroborative evidence for the proposed Early Horizon date.

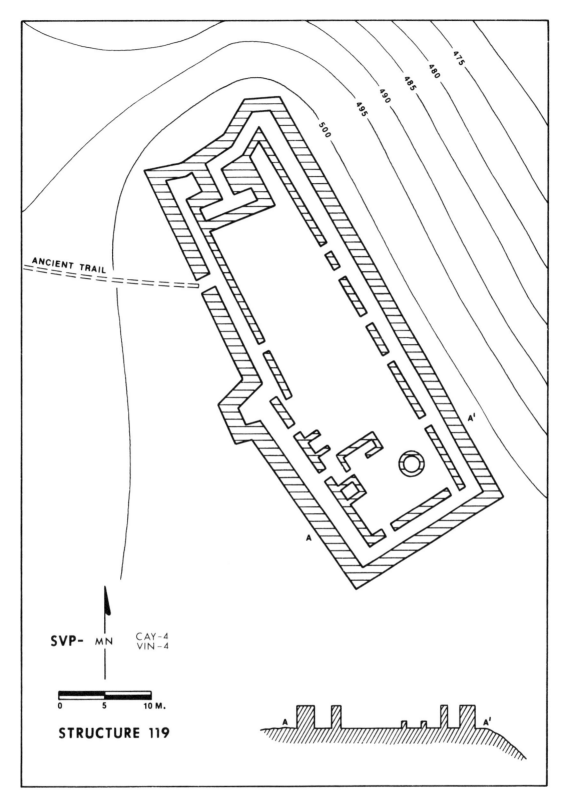

ANCIENT TRAIL

475
480
485
490
495
500

SVP- MN   CAY-4
VIN-4

0   5   10 M.

STRUCTURE 119

A   A'

Fig. 28. Plan and profile views of Structure 119 citadel.

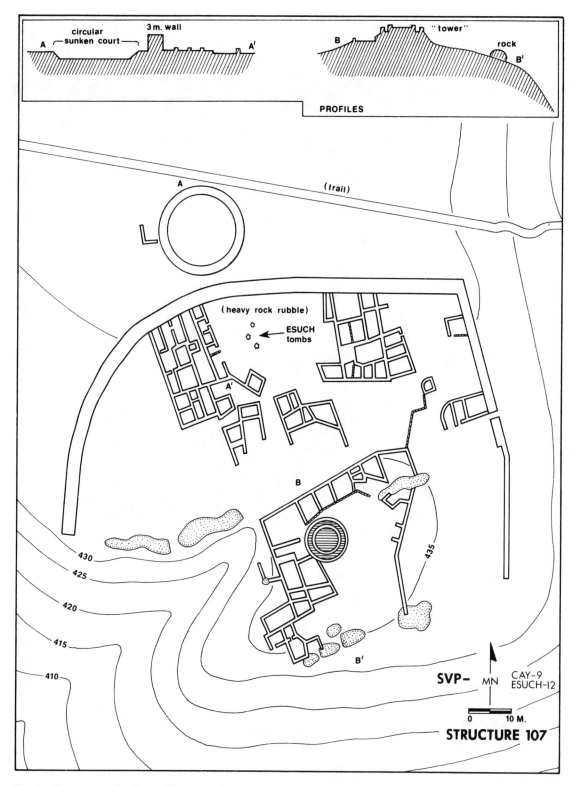

PROFILES

circular sunken court   3 m. wall   A'

"tower"   rock   B'

A   (trail)

(heavy rock rubble)

ESUCH tombs

A'

B

430
425
420
415
410

435

B'

SVP-   MN   CAY-9
ESUCH-12

0   10 M.

STRUCTURE 107

Fig. 29. Plan and profile views of Structure 107, a citadel site with combined habitation, ceremonial-civic, and defensive functions.

112

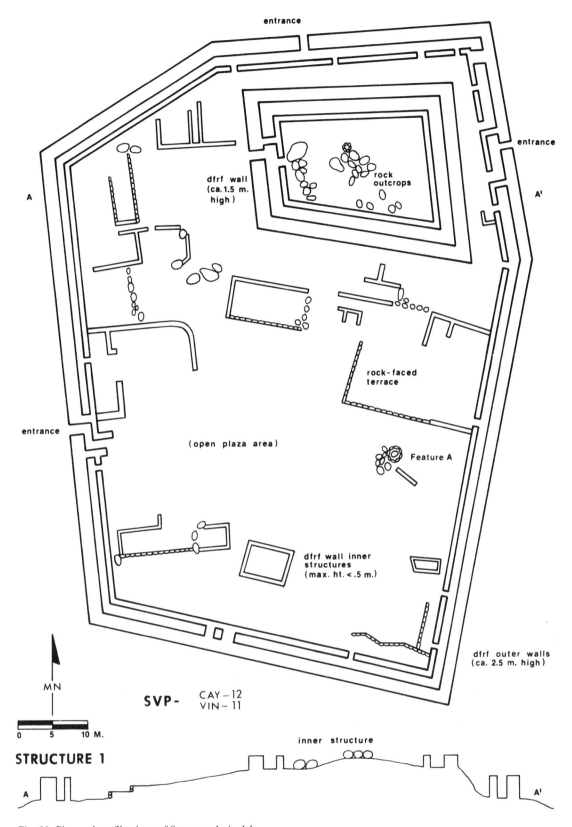

entrance

entrance

A

A'

dfrf wall
(ca. 1.5 m.
high)

rock
outcrops

rock-faced
terrace

entrance

(open plaza area)

Feature A

dfrf wall inner
structures
(max. ht. < .5 m.)

dfrf outer walls
(ca. 2.5 m. high)

MN

0   5   10 M.

SVP-   CAY – 12
VIN – 11

inner structure

STRUCTURE 1

A   A'

Fig. 30. Plan and profile views of Structure 1 citadel.

113

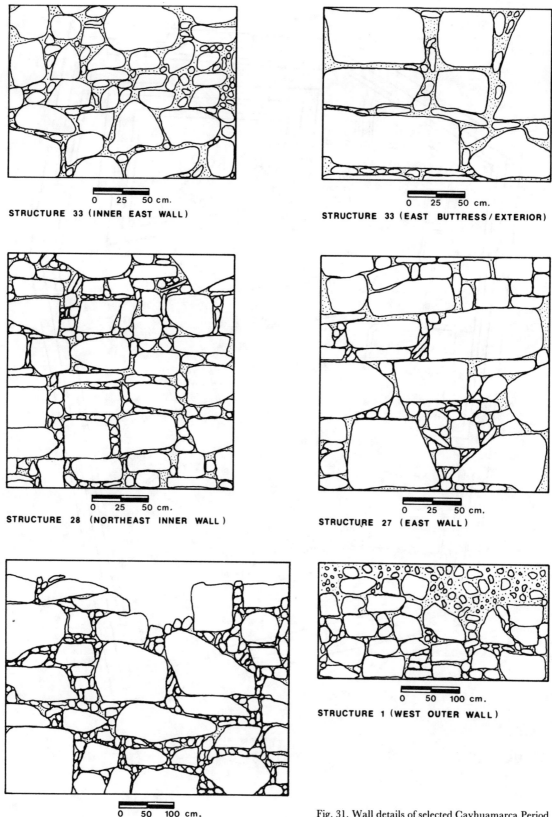

STRUCTURE 33 (INNER EAST WALL)
0   25   50 cm.

STRUCTURE 33 (EAST BUTTRESS/EXTERIOR)
0   25   50 cm.

STRUCTURE 28 (NORTHEAST INNER WALL)
0   25   50 cm.

STRUCTURE 27 (EAST WALL)
0   25   50 cm.

STRUCTURE 6 (NORTH OUTER WALL)
0   50   100 cm.

STRUCTURE 1 (WEST OUTER WALL)
0   50   100 cm.

Fig. 31. Wall details of selected Cayhuamarca Period citadel structures.

114

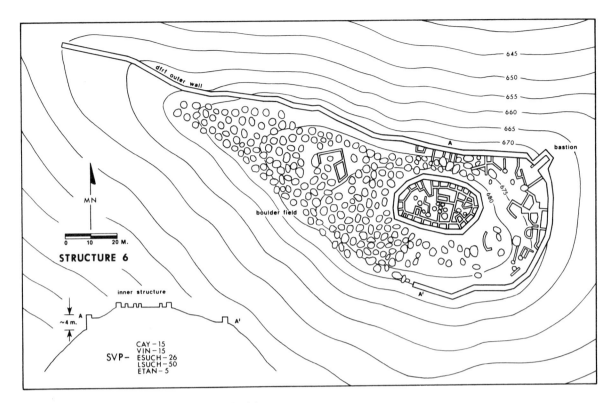

Fig. 32. Plan and profile views of Structure 6 citadel.

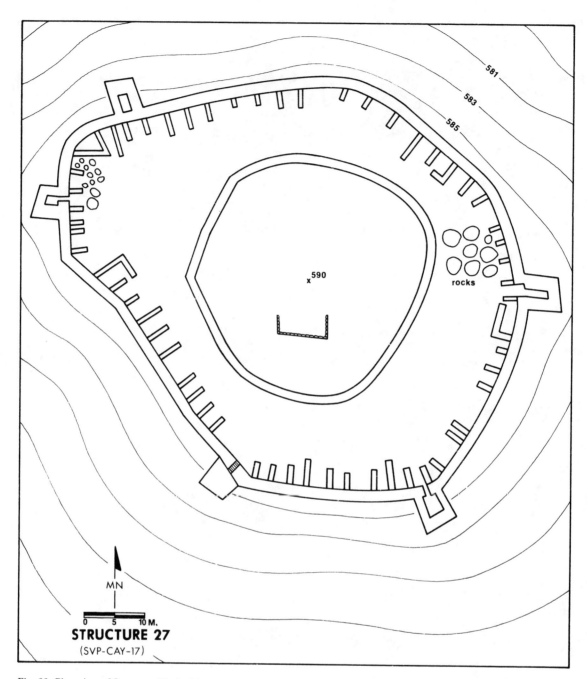

Fig. 33. Plan view of Structure 27 citadel.

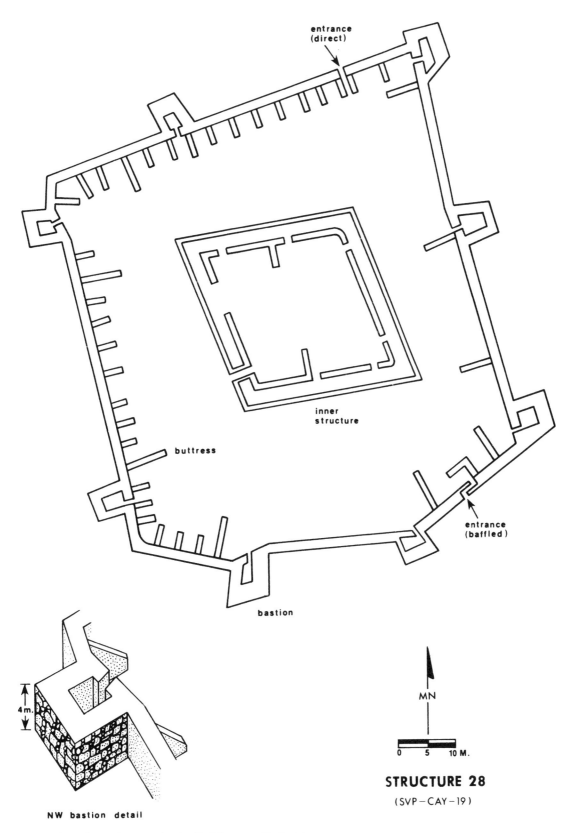

entrance
(direct)

entrance
(baffled)

inner
structure

buttress

bastion

NW bastion detail

4 m.

MN

0   5   10 M.

STRUCTURE 28
(SVP—CAY—19)

Fig. 34. Plan view and perspective detail of Structure 28 citadel.

117

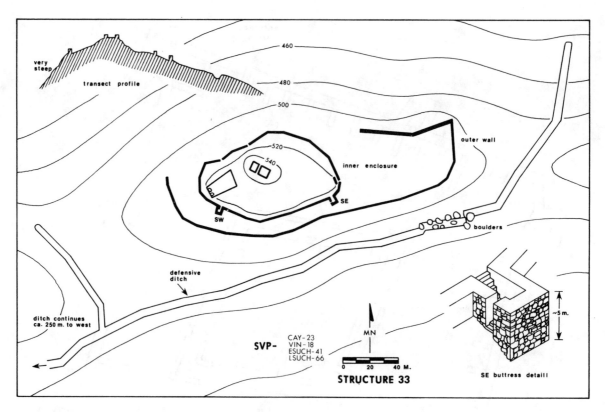

Fig. 35. Plan, profile, and detail views of Structure 33 citadel.

118

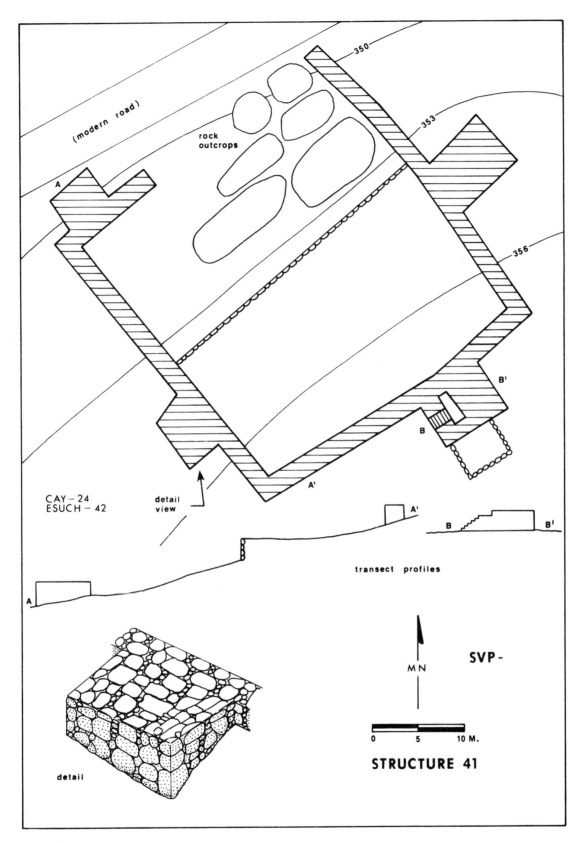

Fig. 36. Plan, profile, and detail views of Structure 41 citadel.

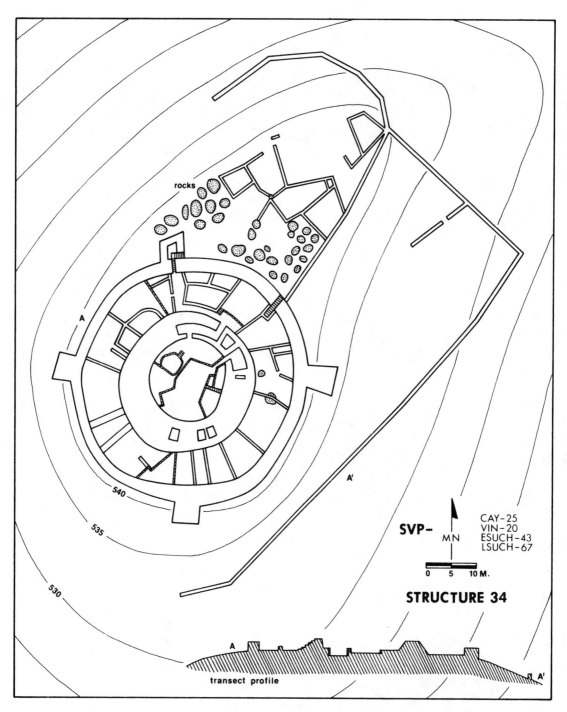

rocks

SVP-
MN

CAY-25
VIN-20
ESUCH-43
LSUCH-67

0   5   10 M.

STRUCTURE 34

540
535
530

A
A'

A
A'
transect profile

Fig. 37. Plan and profile views of Structure 34 citadel.

120

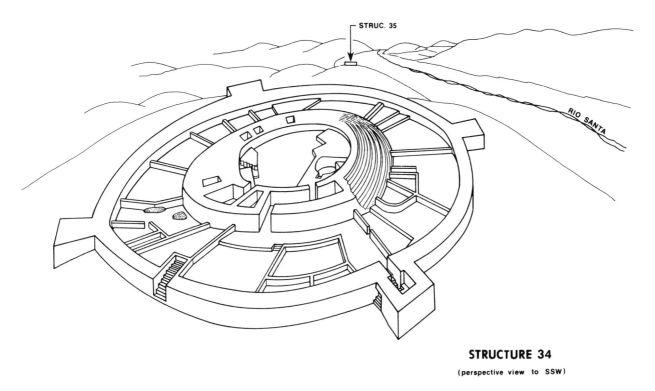

STRUC. 35

RIO SANTA

STRUCTURE 34

(perspective view to SSW)

Fig. 38. Perspective view of Structure 34 citadel.

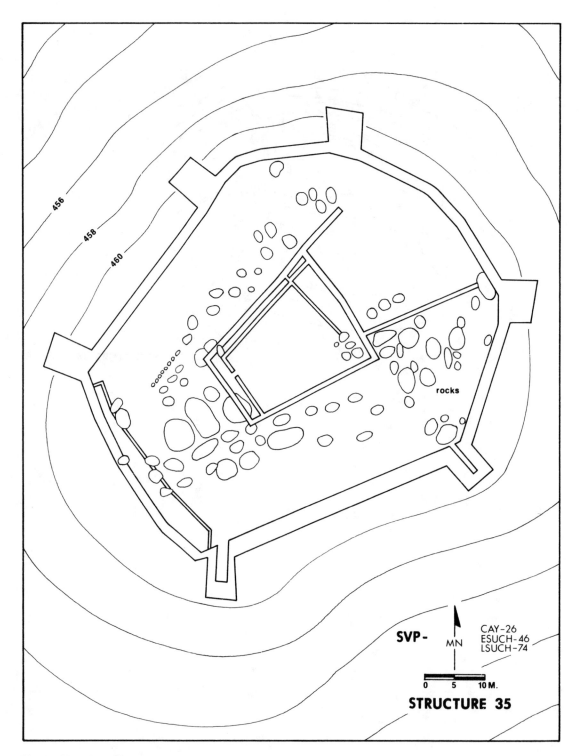

Fig. 39. Plan view of Structure 35 citadel.

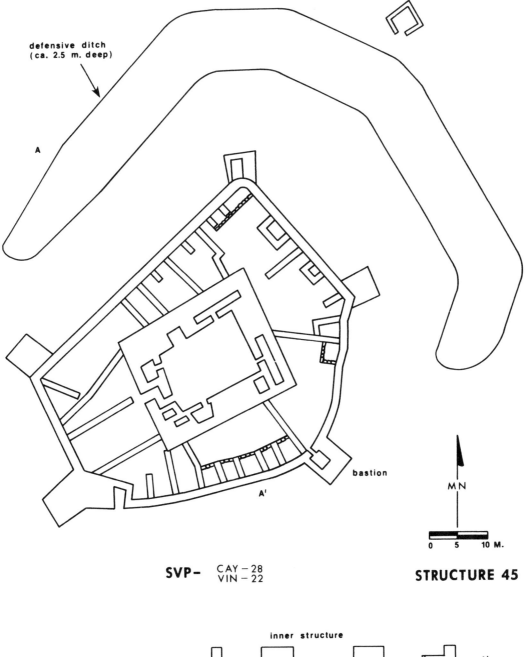

defensive ditch
(ca. 2.5 m. deep)

A

bastion

A'

SVP- CAY – 28
VIN – 22

MN

0 5 10 M.

STRUCTURE 45

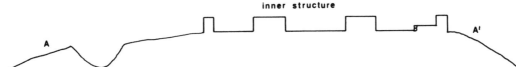

inner structure

A

B

A'

Fig. 40. Plan and profile views of Structure 45 citadel.

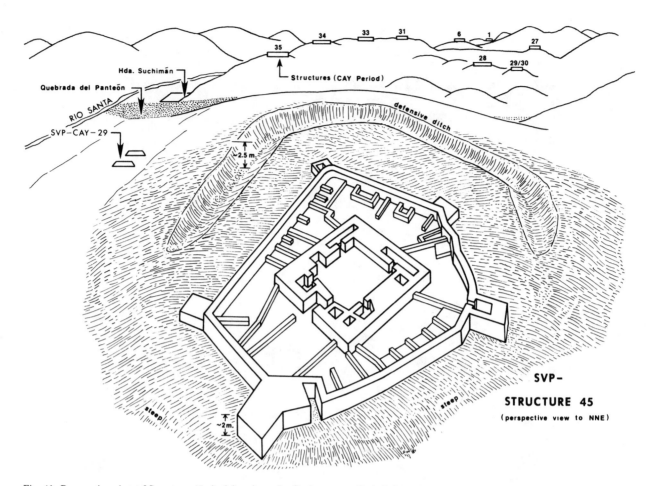

Fig. 41. Perspective view of Structure 45 citadel and nearby Cayhuamarca Period sites.

124

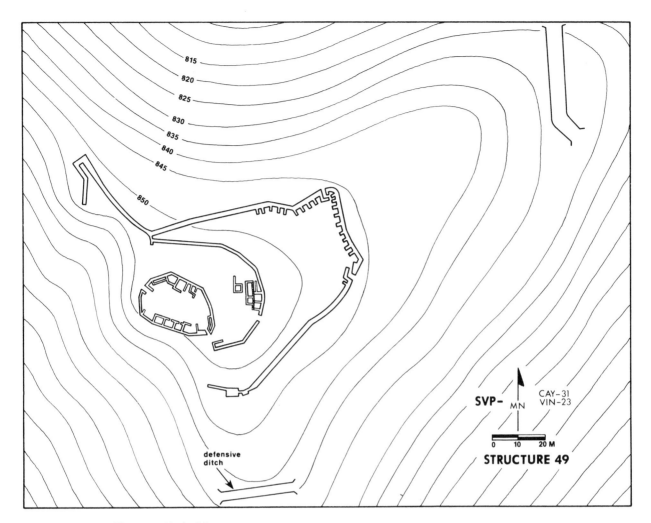

Fig. 42. Plan view of Structure 49 citadel.

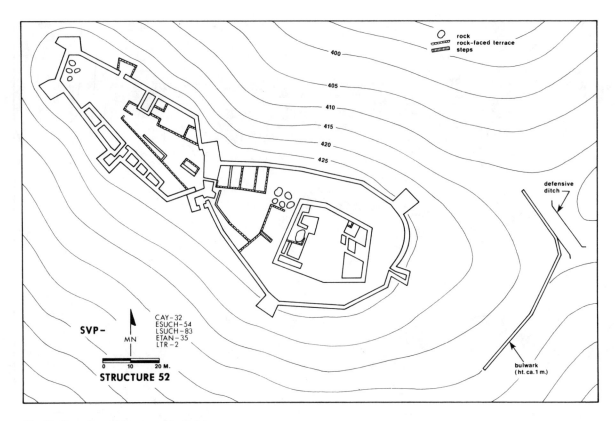

Fig. 43. Plan view of Structure 52 citadel.

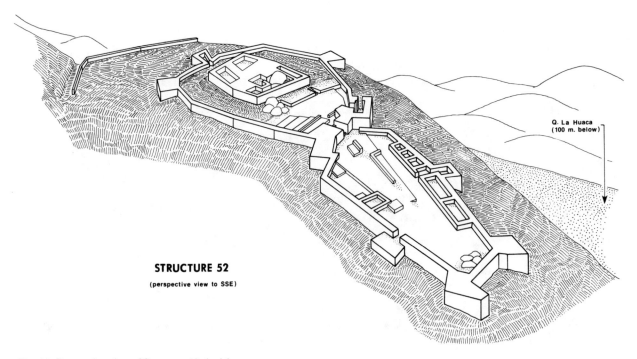

STRUCTURE 52

(perspective view to SSE)

Fig. 44. Perspective view of Structure 52 citadel.

126

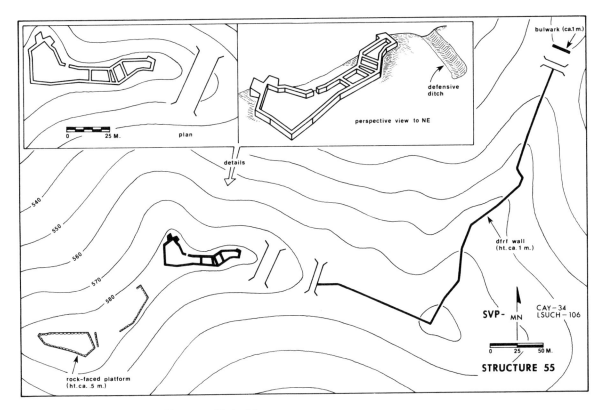

Fig. 45. Plan and detail views of Structure 55 citadel.

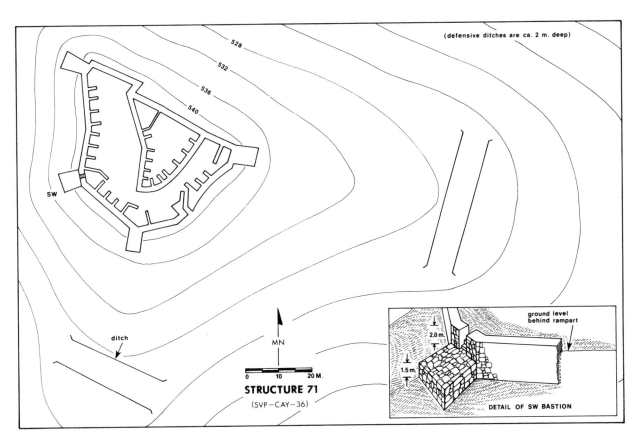

Fig. 46. Plan and detail views of Structure 71 citadel.

127

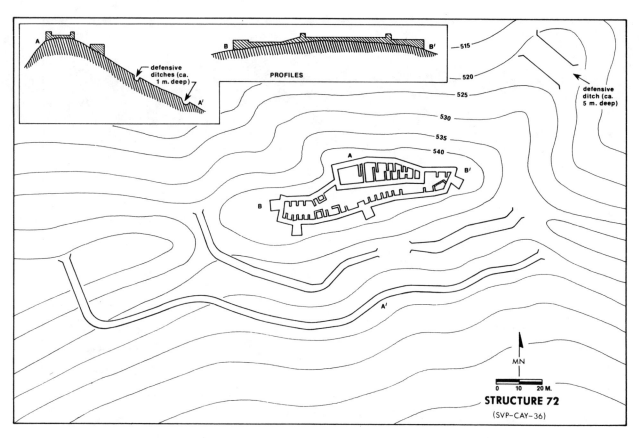

Fig. 47. Plan and profile views of Structure 72 citadel.

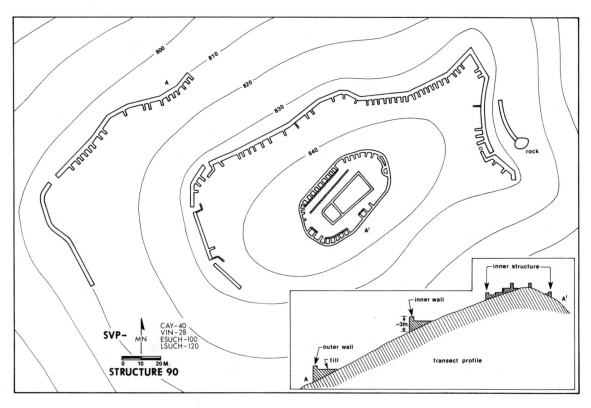

Fig. 48. Plan and profile views of Structure 90 citadel.

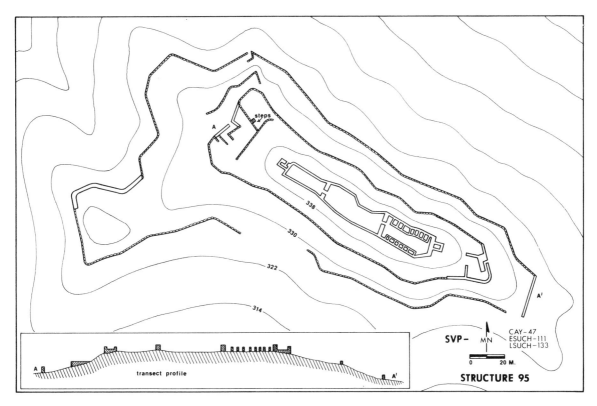

Fig. 49. Plan and profile views of Structure 95 citadel.

In order to examine briefly the main characteristics of the eight ceremonial sites, it is useful to divide them into three main subtypes that are roughly distinguishable on the basis of overall size—including (1) *smaller huacas,* (2) *medium-sized huacas,* and (3) *larger complexes.* It should be emphasized that none of these subtypes is restricted to one local place in the main valley area; thus, as mentioned earlier in the case of citadel subtypes, the distribution of specific ceremonial-civic subtypes does not appear to be related either to localized cultural traditions or to temporal differences. On the other hand, as discussed later, both of the larger complexes and two of the medium--sized sites are found associated with the main population concentrations of the period, including the upper part of the Middle Valley and all of the Upper Valley sector.

It should also be mentioned that, although ceremonial-civic sites are discussed below on the basis of the subtype they pertain to, the illustrations are organized in the same manner as those of the citadels—i.e., on an area-to-area, geographic basis from the uppermost part of the valley on down. As in the case of the citadels, this procedure should facilitate an understanding of site-to-site similarities and differences.

Smaller huacas. The smallest Cayhuamarca ceremonial-civic sites consist of structures built primarily of

conical and truncated-conical adobes, with some indication of additional construction material composed of earth and rock rubble (see Structures 37 and 97, in Figs 53 and 56). Structure 37, the larger of the two, is situated in a maize field immediately downvalley from the mouth of Quebrada de Cayhuamarca. It consists of a simple rectangular, flat-topped platform measuring 56 × 48 m in area, with sloping sides rising to a height of 5 m. Several truncated-conical adobes with finger-marked decoration running down their long axis were noted in and around the edge of a huaquero pit in the top of the platform. No Cayhuamarca sherds were found on or near the mound, however, nor are any other structural remains present.

Structure 97 is located on a rock outcrop immediately to the southeast above a modern canal, overlooking narrow cultivated fields alongside the river in the area of La Toma-Huaca Corral. It covers an area of about 16 × 9 m and stands to a maximum height of 4 m. As shown in Fig. 56, two kinds of adobe walls are present on the mound—including finger-marked conical and plain truncated-conical bricks. The southwest wall of the structure is particularly well preserved, and remains of mud plaster and an exposed end showing details of adobe construction techniques were noted here. As in the case of Structure 37, no ceramics are present on the

129

mound nor are other structural remains present in the vicinity.

Medium-sized huacas.   Four huaca structures of intermediate size are found distributed widely in the area of occupation, within the 27-km distance between Quebrada del Silencio and rugged mountains just to the northeast of the modern settlement of Vinzos. Proceeding downvalley from the uppermost one, these include Structures 113, 108, 70, and 68 (for Structures 108 and 70, see Figs. 52 and 55; for Structures 113 and 68, see Figs. 71 and 77 in Wilson 1985). Good Cayhuamarca sherd diagnostics were found on or adjacent to all of these structures, although, as shown in the plan views, sherds dating to later periods are also present in nearly every case—indicating probable continuing use in Vinzos, Early Suchimancillo, and Late Suchimancillo Periods. Among the four structures are two rock rubble mounds and two ridgetop platforms.

Structure 113 (Wilson 1985, Fig. 71), the simpler of the two rock rubble mounds, lies on a small piedmont spur immediately overlooking the deep, narrow upper canyon of the Santa, upvalley and directly to the east across the river from the large alluvial fan at the mouth of Quebrada del Silencio. Structure 108 (Fig. 52; see also Wilson 1985, Fig. 73, for a perspective view) lies across the river and downvalley from Structure 113, on gentle lower piedmont slopes overlooking the mouth of Quebrada del Silencio. As shown in the plan and perspective views, it consists of a larger platform with sloping sides which covers an area of 35 × 31 m and is capped on the northwest part of the summit by a smaller mound of similar configuration. A raised circular court with an interior bench lies on the ground surface at the northeast end of the platform, and appears to have provided the principal means of access to it. Although somewhat fallen in places, this is one of the best preserved of all ceremonial-civic sites dating to Cayhuamarca.

Structures 70 and 68 (Fig. 55; and Fig. 77 in Wilson 1985) lie 25 km downvalley from the above two structures. As shown in the illustrations, each consists of a low rock-faced platform lying on a flat, narrow ridgetop that slopes more or less gently down away from the site. Although both platforms have low perimetral walls or rock-faced terraces, neither appears to be intrinsically defensible nor is their overall configuration anything like that of the 21 Cayhuamarca citadels. Interestingly, however, both structures—which lie on adjacent ridges some 700 m apart—are located in relatively remote positions well over 700 m from the valley floor and 185 m in elevation above it (note the proximity of SVP-CAY-36 citadel site to the two platforms, in Fig. 24). Although very limited habitation is indicated by associated Cayhuamarca occupational debris and a few scattered dwellings, it seems likely that the primary function of both platforms was ceremonial-civic in nature.

Larger complexes.   In comparison to the smaller and medium-sized huaca sites, the remaining two public sites of probable Cayhuamarca date clearly qualify as major complexes (see SVP-CAY-5 and SVP-CAY-29, in Figs. 23, 50–51, 54). The two complexes cover comparatively large areas of 2 ha and 3.5 ha, respectively, and consist of groups of platform mounds, circular sunken courts, as well as various lesser structures, walls, rock-faced terraces, and plazas.

SVP-CAY-5 lies on a large, gently sloping rock-covered piedmont shelf in the remote canyon of the Upper Valley, just to the southeast of the narrow valley floor and the dirt road leading from the Santa-Chimbote area to the Callejón de Huaylas. Because of its remote location and the fact that it is almost completely hidden from the modern route of travel, this site is in a nearly pristine state of preservation, aside from minor deterioration that has occurred in the 2350+ years since its apparent abandonment in Cayhuamarca times. As shown in the plan and perspective views (Figs. 50–51), four principal features form the architectural core of the site (see A-D, in Fig. 50). A large platform mound (A) capped by what appear to be the remains of small habitation structures and/or storage areas overlooks a rectangular plaza in the southwest part of the site. On the northern edge of the plaza, lies a large circular sunken court (B) built into the hillslope at the edge of the piedmont shelf. Another platform mound (C) lies on gentle slopes 20 m to the east of the low rock-faced terrace that delimits the eastern edge of the main plaza. The remains of a single multiroom habitation structure lie on the summit of this mound, to the northwest of the sunken court. Finally, a similar platform mound (D) of smaller size lies farther out to the east, and at least 10 additional structures—most of which appear to have served as dwellings—lie scattered around the eastern and northern peripheries of the site. Very light amounts of Cayhuamarca sherds were found across most of the site area, and these low densities plus the limited number of habitation structures probably indicate a permanent population of no more than 50 persons. However, the nature of the architectural remains and the presence of limited numbers of dwellings on the principal mounds—especially including C and D—appear to support the argument that at least some of the structures were inhabited by a priestly elite.

SVP-CAY-29 complex is located on gentle piedmont slopes overlooking the narrow cultivated valley floor, immediately downvalley from Quebrada del Panteón and the small modern settlement of Suchimán (Fig. 23). Perhaps because of the proximity of the modern settlement and the use of adobe as the primary construction material, SVP-CAY-29 is in a generally much poorer state of preservation than SVP-CAY-5. However, two well preserved circular sunken courts are present as well as two well-delineated mounds. The larger of these mounds consists of an L-shaped structure with maximum dimensions of 110 × 90 m, and has a single smaller, rock-walled structure on its top. Some 70 m out to the northeast of here is a smaller S-shaped mound, with a number of partially preserved rock-walled habitation structures lying in its northwest corner. Several finger-marked, truncated-conical adobes were noted lying in and beside a huaquero pit on the summit of the mound.

As shown schematically in Fig. 54, the remainder of SVP-CAY–29 complex is taken up by a series of adobe mounds and linked-terrace areas, almost all of which are in a very poorly preserved state. The large 3.5-ha site area is well delineated by a low rock-faced terrace that runs for a distance of 240 m along the northwestern edge, and by a low adobe wall running along most of the southeastern edge. As in the case of SVP-CAY-5, it appears likely that limited (probably elite) habitation occurred here—with an estimated 50 persons living in the structures adjacent to the S-shaped mound. No Cayhuamarca sherds were found in an intensive search of the site, but the above-mentioned architectural features point reasonably clearly to an Early Horizon date. The large number of Cayhuamarca habitation and citadel sites located upvalley and downvalley from here provides additional strong support for this date, and suggest that SVP-

CAY-29 served as a major focus of ceremonial-civic activities.

Cemetery Site

Of the 446 cemetery occupations found in the survey region, only one site containing pottery of possible Cayhuamarca date was located (see SVP-CAY-27, in Fig. 23). The Cayhuamarca material consists of a single sherd from a small, heavily looted cemetery that is located in a relatively very remote position in relation to other presumably contemporaneous sites (the nearest occupation on the north desert margin lies 5.5 km upvalley from this site, at SVP-CAY-13). The sherd itself is from a polished grayware vessel—possibly a stirrup spout jar or a bottle—and is decorated with unraised circle-and-dot motif and an animal in high relief that may be either a llama or a feline (see Coll. 125 sherd, in Fig. 194 d). Although all of these features clearly fit within the general characteristics of Early Horizon wares of the northern area of the Central Peruvian Andes, all other sherds found on the surface of this small burial site are Late Suchimancillo in date. Assuming that the sherd in question is indeed from a Early Horizon vessel, it may very

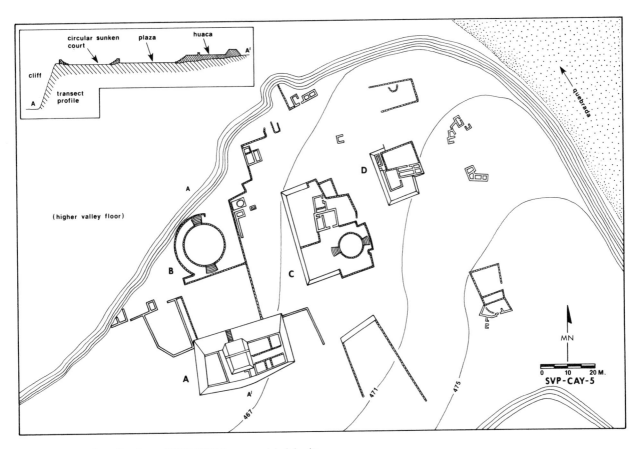

Fig. 50. Plan and profile views of SVP-CAY-5 ceremonial-civic site.

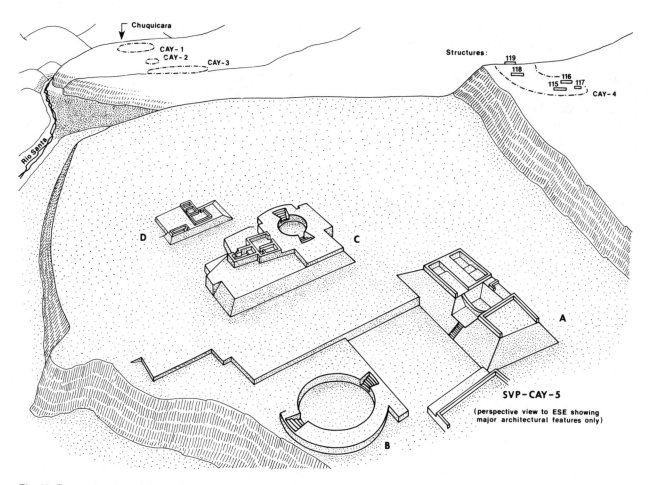

Fig. 51. Perspective view of the main structures at SVP-CAY-5 and nearby sites.

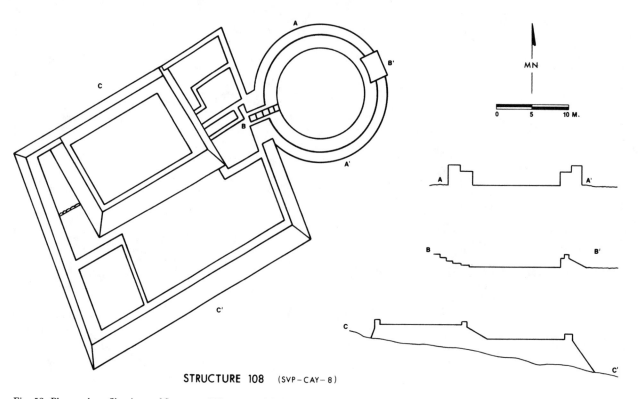

STRUCTURE 108 (SVP–CAY–8)

Fig. 52. Plan and profile views of Structure 108 ceremonial-civic site.

132

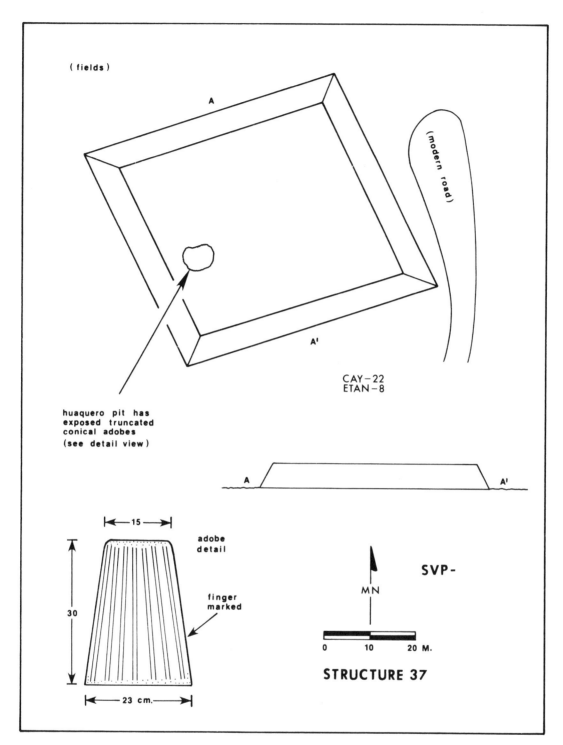

(fields)

A

(modern road)

CAY–22
ETAN–8

huaquero pit has
exposed truncated
conical adobes
(see detail view)

A'

A   A'

15

adobe
detail

finger
marked

30

23 cm.

MN

SVP–

0   10   20 M.

STRUCTURE 37

Fig. 53. Plan and profile views of Structure 37 huaca.

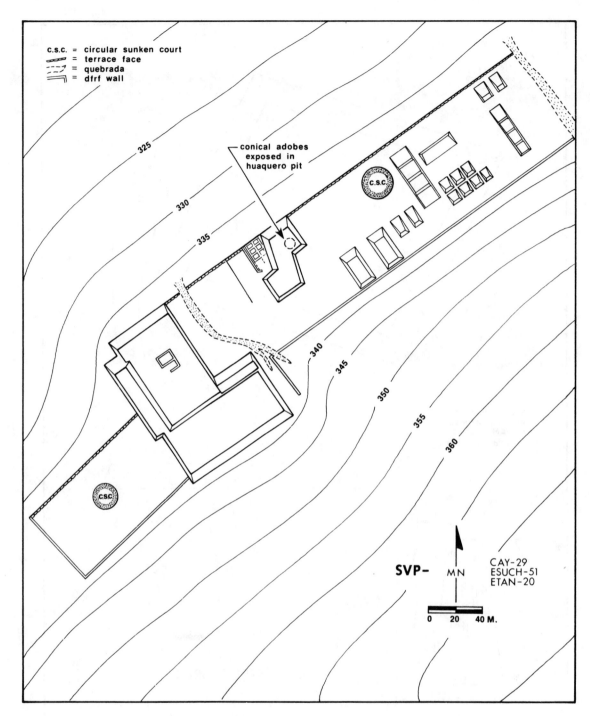

Within the figure:

c.s.c. = circular sunken court
= terrace face
= quebrada
= dfrf wall

325
330
335
340
345
350
355
360

conical adobes
exposed in
huaquero pit

C.S.C.

C.S.C.

SVP- MN

CAY-29
ESUCH-51
ETAN-20

0   20   40 M.

Fig. 54. Plan view of SVP-CAY-29 ceremonial-civic site.

134

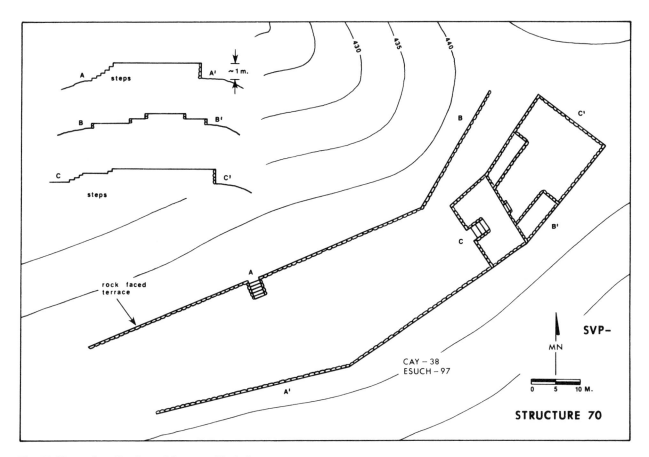

Fig. 55. Plan and profile views of Structure 70 platform.

135

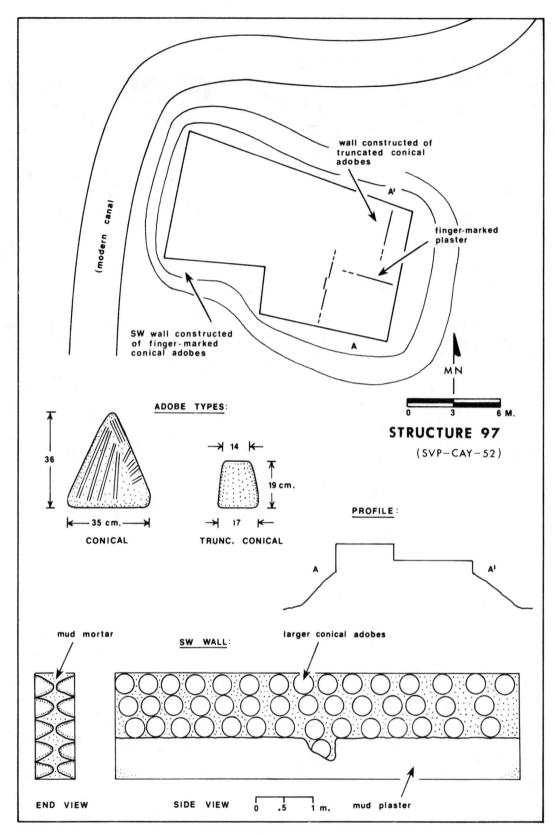

Fig. 56. Plan, profile, and detail views of Structure 97 huaca.

136

well be a curated piece—i.e., it may be either an heir-loom from Cayhuamarca times or a fragment found at a later date that subsequently was placed in a Late Suchimancillo tomb.

Settlement and Demographic Patterns

As argued later, in Chapter V, the Cayhuamarca system appears to represent the period of earliest major agricultural development in the Lower Santa region—especially taking into consideration the probability that such a large and relatively complex system could not have rested on the limited gathering-hunting base that characterizes preceramic subsistence. In any case, all but one of the 54 sites of Cayhuamarca Period are located in the Upper and Middle Valley sectors. Moreover, it is of interest to note that all but five of the 53 sites constituting the upvalley system are located on the south side of the river.

The overall location of sites in the Early Horizon system thus appears quite similar to that of the upvalley system of Las Salinas Period—with essentially all sites downvalley from Quebrada de Cayhuamarca located on or near the south desert margin, while the only part of the north margin where sites are located is in the much more inaccessible Upper Valley canyon. Given the possibility of an upvalley system adapted to external raiding in Las Salinas Period and the near certainty of such a system in Cayhuamarca times, it appears likely that the generally more rugged and steep terrain of the south margin below Quebrada de Cayhuamarca provided a more defensible setting for sites than did the terrain of the north desert margin.

Aside from similar overall site locations in the upvalley area, however, the settlement systems of Las Salinas and Cayhuamarca Periods are quite distinct—with that of the former consisting entirely of small undifferentiated habitation sites, while that of the latter consists of habitation sites, elite residences, citadels, and ceremonial-civic sites distributed more or less evenly throughout the area of occupation. Thus the Cayhuamarca system not only has much greater internal diversity than Las Salinas, but also essential homogeneity in terms of the site type components that are found in each local area. From these characteristics alone, it is possible to draw at least two principal conclusions: First, the general diversity of site types indicates a system that is substantially more complex than that of the preceramic. Second, the fact that the same group of site types is found in each local area of occupation suggests that the socioenvironmental stresses and factors affecting the system—including warfare and the establishment of irrigation agriculture—were essentially the same everywhere.

Indeed, the internal nature of the four clusters characterizing the Cayhuamarca subsistence-settlement system

suggests not only a remarkable degree of area-to-area similarity in the upvalley sectors, but the probability that each cluster of sites operated at least to some extent independently of those adjacent to it. As shown in Fig. 166, all three of the smaller settlement groups (Clusters 1, 3, and 4) contain the same three components—including a number of habitation sites, one or several citadels, and one or two ceremonial-civic sites. The distribution of sites in Cluster 2, on the other hand, is somewhat more complex. Here also, however, one notes a system characterized by what appears to be strategic placement of habitation sites near citadels, widespread distribution of citadels themselves, and strategic location of a few ceremonial sites at wider intervals in the cluster.

With regard to the nature of local intersite relations, perhaps the most important conclusion to be drawn from the relative number and distribution of site types is the unlikelihood that any part of the early agricultural system was characterized by autonomous, mutually bellicose settlements. First, assuming that the widespread distribution of fortresses is ample indication that warfare was a critical stress affecting the entire system, the relatively small number of citadels in Clusters 1, 3, and 4 as well as their central location both suggest that groups of several surrounding habitation sites were focused on the same citadel for defense. The same is probably also true for Cluster 2, although here there are many more discrete citadel sites with closely associated habitation areas than there are discrete single-function habitation sites. Second, the presence of one or two centrally located ceremonial-civic sites in Clusters 1, 3, and 4 suggests that public and/or religious activities were also carried out on a supravillage basis, perhaps having to do with aspects of both the agricultural cycle and warfare. By the same token, the widespread distribution of a few ceremonial-civic sites among the other site types of this cluster suggests a similar supracommunity focus, probably involving more localized groups of settlements within the cluster itself.

As summarized in Table 5, the overall population estimate for Cayhuamarca Period is 5960 persons—with 3855 persons in the Upper Valley, 1940 persons in the Middle Valley, 150 persons in the Lower Valley (lower part of Cluster 4), and only 15 persons at the single maritime site in the Coast sector. The population distribution with respect to Clusters 1, 2, 3, and 4 is 950, 3005, 1040, and 950 persons, respectively (see Table 12). Thus, judging from the areal extent and structural densities of inhabited sites, Clusters 1, 3, and 4 are roughly equal in size while Cluster 2 is about three times larger in estimated population numbers. This disparity between Cluster 2 and the other clusters in and of itself suggests that warfare was not being carried out between local settlement groupings in this period, although even more definitive support for the argument of attacks from outside the region is provided in Chapter V.

Ceramic Distributions

Preliminary comments. In light of the arguments made here and in the next chapter about the nature of intercluster relations, it is of particular interest to examine the distribution of the main ceramic types of Cayhuamarca and other periods throughout the area of occupation. In the present chapter, the discussion of ceramic assemblages of this and later periods is confined to the overall regional distribution based on presence/absence of each type in the collections from different sites—i.e., it is essentially a qualitative treatment of the assemblage of each period, as opposed to the quantitative analysis discussed in Chapter V.

As mentioned in the chapter on research methods, the complexity of the large-scale type distribution maps prepared for each period is such that they are not included with the (necessarily) smaller-scale illustrations showing collection proveniences that accompany the ceramic drawings of Appendix I (e.g., see Fig. 190). Indeed, in the case of several periods with many types and complex distributions, it was necessary to prepare a separate map for utilitarian types and a separate one for decorated types. In any case, it should be emphasized again that the distributions discussed here can be easily mapped out using (1) the collection provenience maps (Note: before attempting to reconstruct ceramic distributions, the interested reader might want to prepare photocopy enlargements of these maps to a scale approximating 1:100,000); and (2) the data on specific proveniences and numbers of sherds for each ceramic type (e.g., see Cayhuamarca Period in Appendix I). It should also be noted that the principal ceramic types are mentioned below without specifically identifying the illustrations in which they appear; nevertheless, reference to the figures and descriptions of Appendix I should pinpoint the distinctive characteristics of these types in relation to the rest of the period assemblage.

Cayhuamarca distributions. The most widespread ceramic type found at sites in the main area of occupation—and indeed one of the principal diagnostics of the period—is Cayhuamarca Bowl 6, both in its plain/polished form (Bowl 6a) and in its pattern burnished form (Bowl 6b). This type appears at nearly all sites between SVP-CAY-1 and SVP-CAY-53, including occupations on both sides of the river. The other two types with a widespread distribution are Cayhuamarca Bowl 4 and Jar 1, both of which appear at many sites in Clusters 1, 2, and 3. However, it is of some significance to note that the greatest diversity in terms of numbers of types is confined to Clusters 1 and 2—including additional types such as Cayhuamarca Bowl 1 and Jar 3.

Moreover, in light of similar patterns that characterize later periods in the pre-Guadalupito sequence, it is especially interesting to note that the diversity of types is strongest in the area of Cayhuamarca Cluster 2, which is centered on Quebrada de Cayhuamarca itself. As we shall see for the Suchimancillo Periods (when highland influences are particularly strong), this pattern suggests that at least some of the influences on Santa were communicated from other regions via Quebrada de Cayhuamarca—which provides a connecting route both to the sierra, as well as to the upper reaches of Quebrada de Lacramarca (and thence to Nepeña and Casma).

Inferences About Subsistence

As mentioned in an earlier chapter, the first period in which the preserved remains of cultigens such as maize appear on the surface of single-component sites is Early Suchimancillo. However, as argued later in analyzing maize-based carrying capacity, the size, extent, and complexity of the Cayhuamarca occupation argue strongly for a system based on maize and other productive crops such as beans and squash—all of which were present in Moche and other nearby valleys by Early Horizon times. In addition, although the time of construction of canals in the upvalley sectors can only be assigned conservatively to the latest of the occupations represented at associated sites (e.g., Quebrada del Silencio canals lie adjacent to Cayhuamarca, Vinzos, Early Suchimancillo, and Late Suchimancillo Period sites), the overall nature of the Cayhuamarca settlement system argues as much for a system based on intensive irrigation as it does for one based on early forms of the cultigens mentioned above.

With regard to other subsistence items, it is also of interest to mention that marine shells were noted on a number of sites of this period—including SVP-CAY-26, 36, 44, and 54—located at least as far inland as Quebrada de Cayhuamarca, 46 km upvalley from the mouth of the river. Thus, given the apparently general absence of coastal sites dating to Cayhuamarca (and considering the clearly identifiable ceramic diagnostics on maritime sites of later periods), it may be argued that access to marine resources was considered to be an important part of the food supply but did not entail the establishment of a number of pottery-using sites. In other words, maritime-oriented camps may have been located along the coast but probably were temporary in nature.

Interregional Comparisons

Nepeña Valley. Based on his most recent research on Early Horizon in Nepeña, Proulx (1985; see Map 5, p. 269) describes 18 sites that, judging from general ceramic and architectural similarities, are contemporaneous with the 54 Cayhuamarca Period sites of the Lower Santa region. Among the main categories of sites are the following: smaller and larger undifferentiated habitation sites (4 occupations), multifunctional sites with possible elite residences (3 occupations), fortresses (3 occupations), ceremonial sites consisting of one or more huaca structures (5 occupations), and cemeteries (1 occupation). Since very few large-scale plans of these sites have been prepared, and site sizes have not been estimated with precision, it is unfortunately difficult to make anything other than the most general of comparative assessments. Nevertheless, from Proulx's descriptions it does appear that Early Horizon developments in Nepeña were similar to those in Santa.

Included among these similar developments are (1) the rise of the temple mound as an important part of the early agricultural subsistence-settlement system, (2) the rise of elite residential units occupying parts of sites with relatively more complex and formal stone-walled architecture, (3) the rise of warfare, and (4) a nearly total lack of evidence for burial sites. Proulx also notes aspects of the location of site types that appear to be quite similar to the Lower Santa region. For example, all of the main temple mounds of Nepeña are located on or adjacent to the valley floor. Interestingly enough, however, almost no sign of associated habitation debris was found at these ceremonial-civic sites, and all are located in the Middle Valley sector—indicating at least two features that contrast sharply with the Lower Santa system. Most of the remaining sites in the valley are located on higher, rugged terrain lying above and somewhat away from cultivated fields in the Upper Valley.

Perhaps the most significant difference between Santa and Nepeña is the much stronger evidence in the latter region of Chavín-related influences (cf. Proulx 1973:14 ff.). Various kinds of architectural, ceramic, and iconographic evidence are present to support this argument, including (1) carefully cut and finished, massive rock-walled architecture in larger compounds and at some fortresses, similar to that found at Chavín de Huántar site in the adjacent sierra (e.g., see Kiske/PV 31–46 and Kushi-Pampa/PV 31–56, in Proulx 1973); (2) use of large carved clay feline heads in decorating temple mounds (e.g., see Punkurí Bajo/PV 31–10); and (3) the finding of classic Chavín pottery and caches of stone implements carved in the Chavín style, in temple mounds (e.g., Punkurí Bajo).

Virú Valley. For the Middle-Late Guañape time period in Virú, Willey (1953:42–61) describes 18 sites that are roughly contemporaneous with those of Cayhuamarca Period in Santa. The main categories of site types include: undifferentiated living sites (11 occupations), exposed dwellings sites with possible elite and/or public structures (2 occupations), community buildings (3 occupations), and cemeteries (2 occupations).

Most of the inhabited sites of this time period—or 11 out of 13—consist of small earth-refuse or midden occu-

pations covering an area of roughly 1 ha each, with no remains of structures showing on the surface. It is interesting to note that three of these sites were detected either by excavation (see V-171, V-272) or by appearance in the lower strata showing along the banks of the river in the middle valley (V-311). Only two sites with the exposed surface dwellings characteristic of most occupations in Santa Valley were found during the Virú survey (see V-83, V-85). Judging from the detailed plan views of these sites (cf. Willey 1953, Figs. 7–8, pp. 49–50), however, they are quite similar to the Cayhuamarca habitation sites found on gentle slopes and flat pampas—consisting of small multiroom dwellings built of double-faced rock walls and scattered at intervals of 2–20 m apart over an area of 1–3 ha. The number of houses on each of the two exposed dwelling sites was estimated at a minimum of 30, and the number of rooms at 70, probably indicating a total population not exceeding 150 persons at each site. Similar to the rock-walled dwellings of all periods in the Santa sequence, none of the Virú structures has walls exceeding a "few centimeters" in height. As in Santa, it thus appears likely that the superstructure of these dwellings consisted of perishable materials (cf. Willey 1953:51). Both V-83 and V-85 also have one or two buildings that are located somewhat away from the other dwellings, and whose relatively more formal architecture suggests they had a public and/or elite residential function.

As mentioned above, three sites were classified as having buildings whose primary function probably was related to community, or public, activities. Two of these occupations (V-85 and V-127) contain structures that are essentially similar to those found at the exposed dwelling sites. Thus, although they are located apart from nearby habitation structures and have more formal layouts, none is particularly complex in nature (e.g., see Fig. 10, p. 59, in Willey 1953). The probable public building at V-71, the third site (also known as the Temple of the Llamas), consists of a low rectangular rock-faced platform with steps leading up the east side. Two llama burials were found under the foundation along the west side of the platform, and a third one was found adjacent to the south wall (cf. Strong and Evans 1952:27–34).

In sum, a number of broad similarities exist between Virú and Santa Valleys during this period, including (1) the overall size and nature of habitation sites, (2) the presence of possible elite residential structures at some habitation sites, (3) the presence of ceremonial-civic structures, and (4) very limited numbers of detectable cemetery sites. However, at least two striking differences may be noted here in comparing the two valleys. First, there is no evidence in Virú of the construction of major citadel, or fortress, sites during the period of early agricultural development—in sharp contrast to Santa and Nepeña. Second, a comparison of Virú and Santa ceremonial-civic sites shows that those of the latter region are not only more numerous but more varied and complex as well.

Of the two best-known valleys to the south and north of the survey region, the Early Horizon settlement pattern of Nepeña is more like that of the Lower Santa area—with a diversity of occupations located entirely in the Upper and Middle sectors (cf. Proulx 1985, Map 5, p. 269). In contrast, the Middle-Late Guañape system of Virú is different from either Santa or Nepeña in two important ways, including (1) the presence of sites scattered throughout all sectors of the valley, but especially concentrated in the lower valley; and, as mentioned above, (2) the absence of fortified sites. Given the fact that fully 75% (9/12) of the principal Cayhuamarca bowl and jar types can be related on the basis of form, paste, and surface treatment to the Middle-Late Guañape assemblage of Virú, while only 25% (3/12) can be so related to Nepeña, it seems clear that the identification of stronger interregional ties must include primarily valleys to the north, and the identification of potential enemies must include valleys to the south.

VINZOS PERIOD (PUERTO MOORIN/BEGINNING EARLY INTERMEDIATE PERIOD, OR EIP)

A total of 45 discrete sites was identified as belonging to the Vinzos Period of occupation (Figs. 57–60; for site outlines see Wilson 1985, Fig. 83). As in the preceding Cayhuamarca Period, the number of site types that can be distinguished on the basis of primary or sole function is four—including habitation sites (30 occupations), citadels (11 occupations), ceremonial-civic sites (3 occupations), and cemeteries (1 occupation).

Habitation Sites

Undifferentiated occupations. In contrast to Cayhuamarca Period, when 24 out of 54 discrete sites—or roughly 44%—consist of undifferentiated nonelite occupations, the overall proportion of these sites in Vinzos Period is 30 out of 45—or 67%. As in the case of Cayhuamarca habitations, however, Vinzos habitation sites are distributed more or less evenly throughout the area of occupation (see SVP-VIN-1, 2, 3, 5, 6, 8, 10, 13, 14, 19, 21, 24, 25, and 29–45, in Figs. 58–60). Excluding the population estimates for inhabited citadel sites discussed in the following section, Vinzos habitation sites range in size between .25 and 26 ha and in population between 25 and 2050 persons—with an average size of about 2.6 ha and an average population estimate of 210 persons. These figures are thus higher in comparison to the Cayhuamarca averages of 2 ha and 140 persons per site. But it should be noted that, if the relatively very large site of SVP-VIN-37 (26 ha) is excluded from the

computations, the Vinzos averages become 1.8 ha and 147 persons per site—which is essentially the same as in the preceding period.

The elevation of undifferentiated habitation sites above the valley floor ranges between 25 and 300 m and distance away from it ranges between 25 and 2550 m—with an average elevation of 75 m above the floor and an average distance of 525 m away. Average elevation above the floor is thus lower than the 110 m of Cayhuamarca Period, although average distance away from it is somewhat greater than the 445 m of the preceding period. In general, as in Cayhuamarca and Las Salinas Periods, sites continue to be located well away from the more open (and therefore less defensible) desert margins immediately adjacent to the valley floor.

Another one of the continuities extending into Vinzos Period is the retention of the same variety of structural types that characterizes habitation sites of the earlier period. As mentioned, these include windbreaks (e.g., see Fig. 27), single-room and multiroom dwellings with rectangular or irregular-polygonal layouts (Fig. 27), and agglutinated structures (Fig. 25). And, as with Cayhuamarca Period, structural densities on sites in the upvalley sectors appear to be related primarily to the nature of the terrain—with dwellings packed closely together in lines on steeply sloping terraced sites and more widely scattered at sites located on gently sloping or flatter terrain. However, in some contrast to the low density Vinzos Period sites of Pampa Las Salinas and Quebrada Palo Redondo area (see SVP-VIN-37 through SVP-VIN-45 site descriptions in Wilson 1985, Appendix B), even main valley sites located on less rugged terrain have a relatively high degree of nucleation.

At least part of the difference between sites of the main valley area and those located on the desert out to the north is likely due to the more open nature of the terrain in the latter area. However, the open desert sites also are characterized by a more linear distribution of habitations—i.e., structures are often lined up in a single file along trails. The interpretation of these early trails is made somewhat difficult by the fact that they are crisscrossed by rock-lined roads of Early Tanguche date (e.g., see roads cutting across SVP-VIN-37, in Fig. 13, and roads to the northwest of SVP-ETAN-411, in Fig. 116). Nevertheless, it is apparent that the Vinzos trails represent the establishment of formal communication routes that linked sites of Pampa Las Salinas and Quebrada Palo Redondo to those of the main valley area. Considering the southwest-northeast orientation of the trail linking sites from SVP-VIN-39 to SVP-VIN-43, it is also possible that some communication existed between the Quebrada Palo Redondo sites and the adjacent sierra. Purported prehispanic remains shown on IGM Hojas 16-g and 17-g (see Fig. 14 for location of these map sheets) indicate that sierra occupation begins within a distance of some 35 km to the northeast of Quebrada

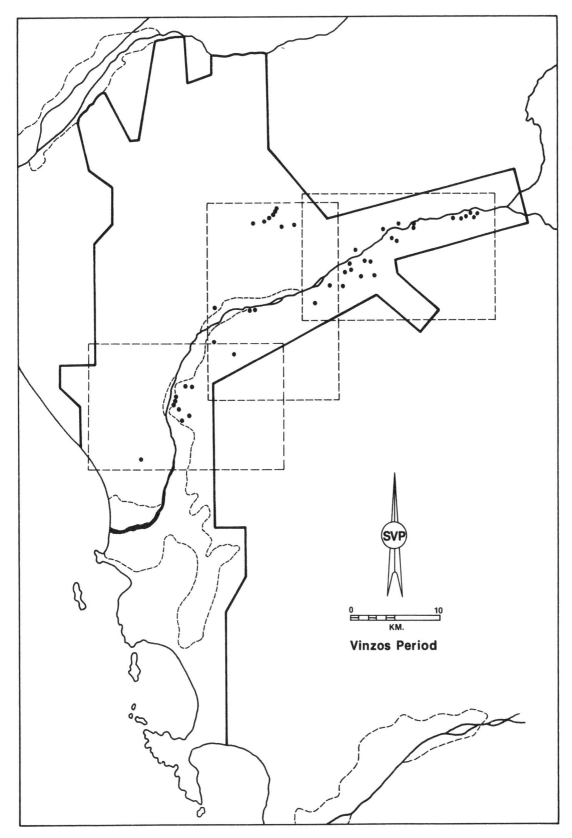

Fig. 57. Location key to settlement pattern maps of Vinzos Period, Figs. 80–82.

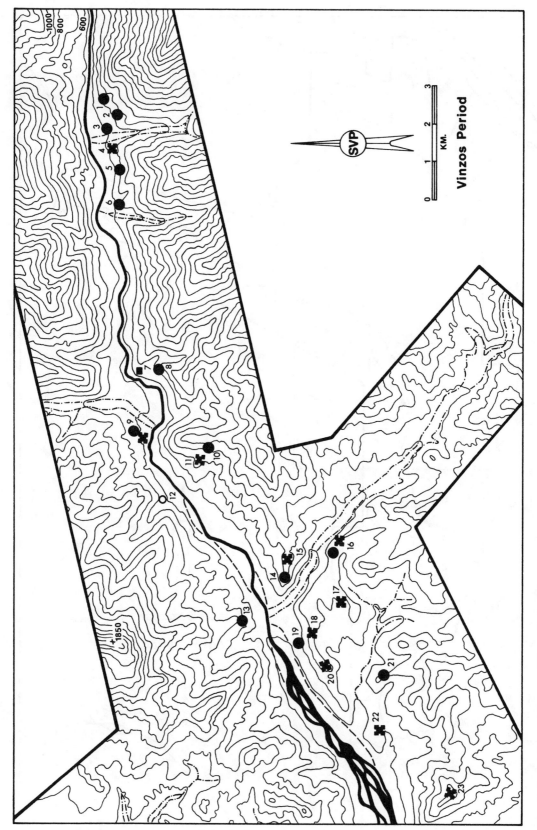

Fig. 58. Settlement pattern map of Vinzos Period: Upper Valley sector.

142

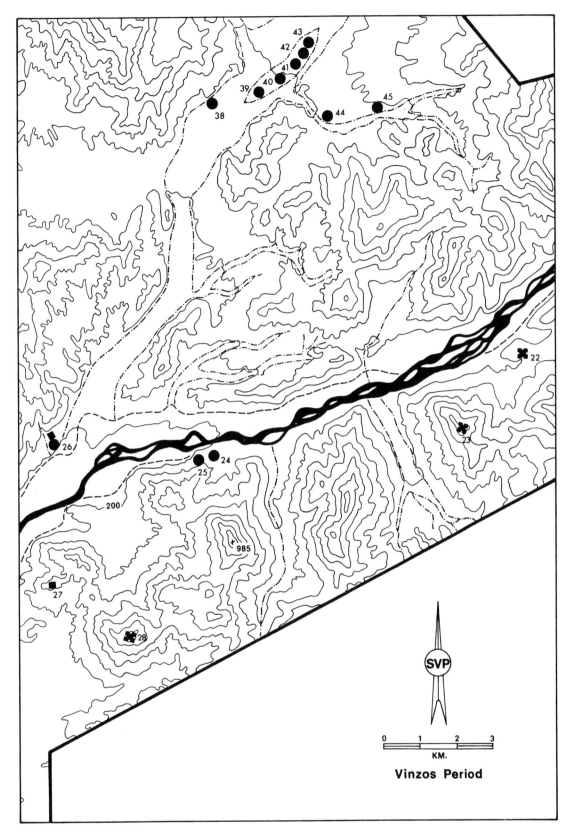

Fig. 59. Settlement pattern map of Vinzos Period: Upper Valley, Middle Valley, and Santa-Chao Desert sectors.

143

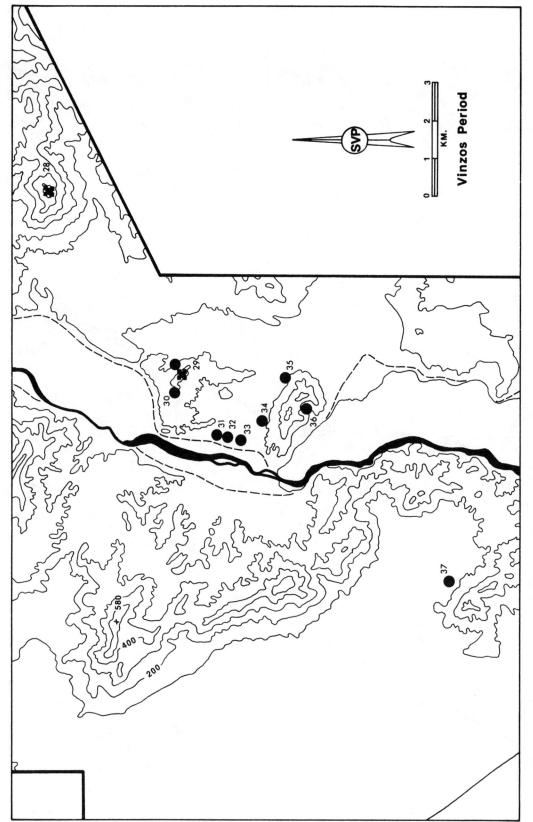

Fig. 60. Settlement pattern map of Vinzos Period: Middle and Lower Valley sectors.

Palo Redondo, in the area of Pampa de Guanacón. The IGM maps also show that the Lower Santa region is linked to the Guanacón area via trails of possible prehispanic origin.

SVP-VIN-37 is clearly the most remarkable of all nine desert sites, both in terms of its extensive 26-ha size as well as the nature of remains found on it. Because of its size and the generally indistinct nature of rock-walled habitation structures covering some parts of the site, time constraints ruled out preparation of a plan view using either field mapping equipment or an airphoto enlargement. From field examination of the nature and extent of dwellings it is nevertheless clear that SVP-VIN-37 covered an area measuring some 1500 m long, with a width varying between 100 m in the southern sector and 500 m in the northern sector. Judging from the moderate structural densities in the northern sector and low-to-moderate densities in the south, the total population is estimated at 2050 persons. This makes SVP-VIN-37 by far the largest habitation site of the three earliest periods in the sequence.

Interestingly enough, our brief but intensive survey across the site failed to turn up any sign of major differentiation of structures, nor were any remains of seashell debris noted (in spite of the fact that the ancient Las Salinas shoreline must have been located within just a kilometer or so of the site area at the time of the occupation). Moreover, although a well preserved ancient canal is present on the site (see Fig. 13), our field observations indicate that it cuts intrusively through the rock walls of the Vinzos Period dwellings—indicating that it probably dates to a later period, indeed, most likely to Early Tanguche (see SVP-VIN-37 site description in Wilson 1985, Appendix B). There is thus no indication of a focus on maritime subsistence nor any sign that a canal had been built to bring water for drinking and irrigation of fields.

Possible elite residences. As in Cayhuamarca Period, only a few sites whose function appears to have been primarily related to habitation contain structures of relatively greater size and formal layout that suggest possible use as elite residences (see SVP-VIN-3, 9, and 21, in Fig. 58). As in the preceding period, however, a number of such structures are found in direct association with citadels and ceremonial-civic sites, and these are discussed in the next two sections. Vinzos Period occupation at SVP-VIN-3 occurs in and around two large agglutinated structures that appear to have been built in the preceding Cayhuamarca Period (see Structures 120 and 121, in Fig. 25). As mentioned in the discussion of SVP-CAY-3, a group of some 50 scattered windbreaks extends up gentle slopes to the south and southeast of these structures. Since Vinzos Period sherd diagnostics appear to be confined to the agglutinated structures alone, however, there are no immediately adjacent and contemporaneous habitations to which the agglutinated

dwellings can be compared. Nevertheless, structures at the nearby sites of SVP-VIN-2, 5, and 6 are much smaller in size and less formal in appearance, suggesting that use of Structures 120 and 121 continued to involve the same elite function indicated earlier for the Cayhuamarca occupation.

In contrast, the structural remains at SVP-VIN-9—which lies above the western edge of the mouth of Quebrada del Silencio, some 8 km downriver from SVP-VIN-3—exhibit strongly contrasting and directly adjacent dwelling types that argue for the presence of an elite residential structure (see Fig. 61, and Plate 15). Interestingly, as in the case of SVP-VIN-3/SVP-CAY-3, a total of some 50 windbreak structures is present here. Judging from associated ceramic debris, however, occupation of the windbreaks is limited to Vinzos and Early Suchimancillo Periods—making this one of the latest manifestations of this dwelling type in the sequence. The same mix of occupational debris also was noted in and around the principal structure, which lies on a low rise at the upper northwestern edge of the site, overlooking the windbreaks. As shown in Fig. 61, the principal structure differs sharply from the windbreaks in having a larger, rectangular plan and interior rock walls dividing it into two smaller rooms as well as a larger outer room. Four aspects of this structure—including the size of the rooms, the associated occupational debris, the contrast with the windbreaks, and the contrast with structures at early ceremonial-civic sites in the region—all argue that its primary function was one of elite residence.

Finally, the remains at SVP-VIN-21—located on a narrow ridge high above Quebrada del Panteón, some 9.5 km farther downvalley—present contrasting structural types that again argue for a division into elite and nonelite residential areas. Most of the occupation of this site occurred on rock-faced terraces extending across the narrow rocky slope in the lower sector. Structural remains are mostly found in a poor state of preservation in this sector, although a number of smaller structures can be detected. In any case, the extent of terracing and associated occupational debris suggest that most of the estimated population of 200 persons lived here. Higher up the ridge to the east lies a larger, more formally laid out structure with an indirect entrance to two interior rooms (see Fig. 85, in Wilson 1985). The contrast between this structure and the smaller habitation structures covering the lower sector of the site argues for a possible elite function.

Defensive Sites

Judging from the presence of Vinzos diagnostics in the associated sherd debris, 12 out of the 21 Cayhuamarca citadel sites continued to be occupied in the later of the two periods (see SVP-VIN-4, 9, 11, 15–18, 20, 22, 23, 28, and 29, in Figs. 58–60). From the analysis of architec-

145

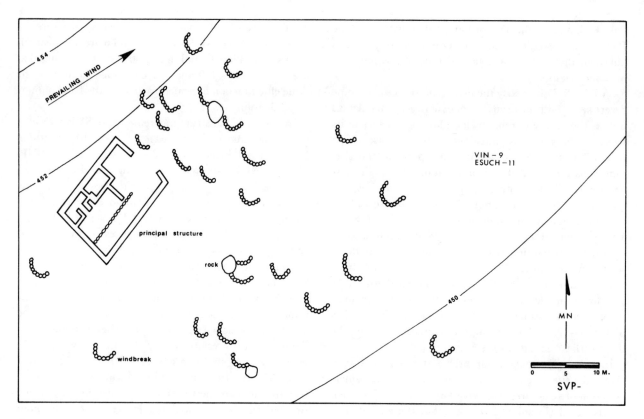

Fig. 61. Plan view of the northwestern sector of a habitation site with occupation dating to Vinzos and Early Suchimancillo Periods.

tural and ceramic temporal diagnostics at all defensive sites in the region it thus appears likely that no new fortresses were built in Vinzos Period. As discussed below in the section on settlement patterns, a comparison of the Cayhuamarca and Vinzos systems indicates that at least one of the principal reasons for this may be the essential continuity of the overall pattern of occupation in the Upper and Middle Valley sectors. Indeed, citadels continue to be the principal inhabited site type in the Upper Valley in Vinzos Period, and most Cayhuamarca fortresses of this sector appear to have been occupied (the Vinzos population estimate for all 12 citadels ranges between 5 and 150 persons, with an average of about 80 persons). Considering the generally excellent preservation of Cayhuamarca citadels over the long term, the lack of associated Vinzos sherds at the other citadel sites—all of which are physically proximate to sites of the Vinzos system—does not rule out continued use of a more transitory nature.

In any case, the citadels with associated Vinzos occupation generally include many of those located in more remote positions with respect to the valley floor. As in Cayhuamarca Period, however, occupied citadels range in distance between 50 m and 3.5 km away from the floor, with an average of 1.2 km away from it. They range in elevation between 25 and 700 m above the valley floor, with an average of 225 m above it. The average figures

away from and above the floor are thus only slightly greater than the figures of 1 km and 243 m, respectively, for Cayhuamarca Period.

Specifically with regard to the subtypes of defensive structures occupied in Vinzos Period, it is interesting to note that they include the following: (1) nearly 67%—or 8 out of 12—of the *dual-function citadels* (see Structures 6, 27, 28, 33, 45, 49, 90, and 95, in Figs. 32, 33, 34, 35, 40–41, 42, 48, and 49); and (2) 80%—or 4 out of 5—of the *multifunction citadels* (see Structures 119, 107, 1, and 34, in Figs. 28, 29, 30, and 37–38). Thus there is evidence not only of continuing use of many of the larger and smaller dual-function citadels, but of the importance of multifunction citadels as foci of probable ceremonial-civic activities and elite residence.

Ceremonial-Civic Sites

Only three sites whose function appears to have been ceremonial-civic in nature were found to have associated ceramic debris dating to Vinzos Period (see SVP-VIN-7, 26, and 27, in Figs. 58, 59), compared to eight such sites in Cayhuamarca Period. Indeed, of the three sites only SVP-VIN-26/Huaca Yolanda appears to have had its inception in Vinzos Period, with SVP-VIN-7 and SVP-VIN-27 continuing in use from Cayhuamarca times. However, as in the case of many of the Cayhuamarca

146

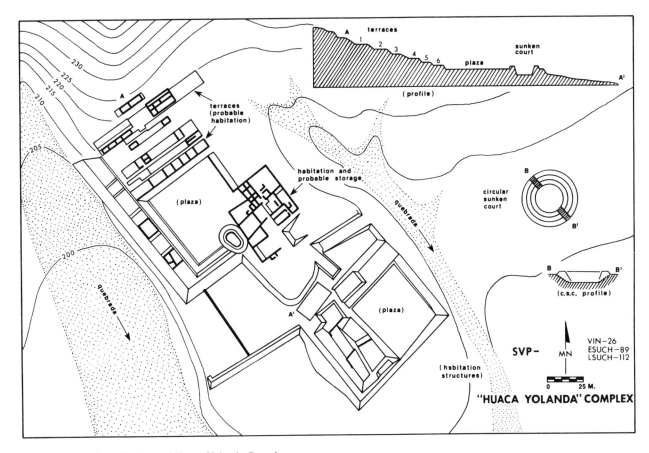

Fig. 62. Plan and profile views of Huaca Yolanda Complex.

citadels at which no Vinzos sherds appear to be present, the proximity of a number of Cayhuamarca ceremonial-civic sites to Vinzos occupations allows for the possibility that they were used on a somewhat different basis—i.e., these sites may have continued to play a role in public activities, but were no longer functioning as places of habitation and/or use of pottery vessels.

Medium-sized huacas. Both SVP-VIN-7 and SVP-VIN-27—the two Vinzos sites with Cayhuamarca occupation—consist of medium-sized huacas (see Figs. 71 and 77, in Wilson 1985), and both have been discussed under ceremonial-civic sites of the preceding period. SVP-VIN-7 is a small platform mound with sloping sides, associated rock-faced terracing, and an attached enclosure. As in the Cayhuamarca Period, occupation appears to have been confined to the immediate area of the mound itself—with significant habitation over a broader area occurring only later, in Early and Late Suchimancillo Periods. SVP-VIN-27 consists of a roughly rectangular, rock-faced platform with a partial enclosure wall.

Included among the group of medium-sized Cayhuamarca huacas that may have continued in use—but for which no definite ceramic evidence of Vinzos occupation

could be found—are SVP-CAY-8, SVP-CAY-38, and SVP-CAY-52 (see Figs. 23–24, and Figs. 52, 55, and 56, respectively).

Larger complexes. In contrast to the two medium-sized huacas with Vinzos occupation, SVP-VIN-26/Huaca Yolanda consists of one of the larger and more complex probable ceremonial-civic sites in the Lower Santa region (see Fig. 62, and Plate 16; see also Kosok, Fig. 18, p. 194). Indeed, in spite of the (diagnostically early) circular sunken court feature out to the northeast of the main complex and the fact that Vinzos Period ceramic debris is found associated with many of the main architectural features of the complex, for at least two reasons it is likely that many of the remains here date to Early and Late Suchimancillo Periods. First, ceramic diagnostics of the two later periods generally are more abundant and widespread throughout the area shown in Fig. 62. Second, and perhaps more importantly, it seems highly likely that more substantial numbers of people would have been required to build much of this complex than are indicated by the very sparse number of Vinzos sites in the immediate vicinity.

Both Early and Late Suchimancillo Periods are characterized by more abundant numbers of nearby habitation sites (see Figs. 65 and 133), and therefore by greater access to corporate labor groups to construct as well as staff and use such a site. Whatever the period or periods of principal use, it is likely that much of Huaca Yolanda Complex was begun in the period of Vinzos occupation. It may also be the case that at least limited parts of the site date to even earlier periods. Nonetheless, an intensive search of the site failed to turn up any Cayhuamarca sherd diagnostics. Thus, although the associated pottery clearly indicates the hand of Vinzos people here in spite of the absence of nearby sites with large populations, the same cannot be said for an inferred Cayhuamarca date since neither Cayhuamarca sherds nor Cayhuamarca sites are present in the immediate vicinity.

Included among the group of larger Cayhuamarca complexes that may have continued in use during Vinzos Period—but for which no definite ceramic evidence of Vinzos occupation could be found—are SVP-CAY-5 and SVP-CAY-29 (see Figs. 23, 24, and Figs. 50–51 and 54, respectively).

Cemetery Site

As in Cayhuamarca Period, only one site with a burial function was found with associated sherds dating to Vinzos Period (see SVP-VIN-12, in Fig. 58). Unlike the rather uncertain dating of the Cayhuamarca cemetery, however, this one contains what appear to be definite Vinzos ceramic diagnostics in association with scattered, looted graves consisting of simple sandy pits (no tomb architecture was noted), as well as greater quantities of Early Suchimancillo sherds. The looted graves themselves extend over a very small area of less than .1 ha, although broken pottery is strewn over a larger area of steeper slopes covering 1 ha or slightly more.

As indicated in Table 8, the first relatively substantial numbers of cemetery sites in the region do not occur until Early Suchimancillo Period (which has 27 separate cemetery occupations). In light of the fact that none of the subsequent periods in the sequence has fewer than 25 discrete cemeteries, the paucity of both Cayhuamarca and Vinzos burial sites presents something of an anomaly. Since the set of ceramic diagnostics for each period appears to be well understood—not only from our research but also from work in Virú and adjacent valleys—the lack of such sites does not appear to be an artifact of our understanding of these diagnostics. Since cemetery sites clearly must exist somewhere in the systems of Cayhuamarca and Vinzos, it is possible either (1) that burial patterns of the two periods were radically different from those of later periods (e.g., cemeteries of these periods may be located farther out in the desert near the main citadel and habitation sites, rather than on the steeper rocky slopes and in quebrada mouths adjacent to the valley floor which were used from Early Suchiman-

cillo Period on); or (2) that because huaqueros are essentially the only agents of discovery of cemeteries, patterns of looting have for some reason been confined to areas that exclude those used for Cayhuamarca and Vinzos burials.

Settlement and Demographic Patterns

As indicated by a comparison of Figs. 166 and 168, Vinzos Period in a number of ways represents a continuation of the basic pattern of settlement established in the preceding period. Thus the great majority of the 45 sites in the system is located in the Upper and Middle Valley—with all but 12 occupations situated on the south desert margin of the main valley area. Nevertheless, slightly over 55% of Vinzos sites represent new occupations. As the settlement maps make clear, these include the large occupation at SVP-VIN-37 in Pampa Las Salinas, eight settlements in the upper reaches of Quebrada Palo Redondo, and the ceremonial-civic site of SVP-VIN-26/ Huaca Yolanda.

With regard to the number and types of Vinzos settlements, it is noteworthy that habitation sites located in the more rugged and defensible terrain of the south desert margin continue to be distributed in reasonably close association with 12 of the 20 citadel structures dating to Cayhuamarca times. Given the arguments presented earlier for a threat of external attack from the south in the Cayhuamarca system, it is also of interest to note that the only Vinzos sites located in exposed positions lie on the north desert margin of the valley (see Figs. 59, 60). Thus not only does warfare apparently continue as a major socioenvironmental stress, but, assuming an external threat, it seems much more likely to have come from valleys to the south (i.e., Nepeña, Casma) than from valleys to the north (i.e., Chao, Virú).

The kinds of settlement types constituting the Vinzos system are essentially the same as in Cayhuamarca, although, as noted above, fewer ceremonial-civic sites appear to have been occupied in this period compared to the preceding one. Nevertheless, many sites of the main valley area are located near ceremonial-civic centers of Cayhuamarca Period, and it is possible that at least some of them continued in use through Vinzos Period. Taking this argument into consideration, then, one sees a system in which local settlement groups from place to place in the valley contain the same fundamental set of components characteristic of the preceding system—including habitation sites, possible elite residences, citadels, and ceremonial-civic centers. Indeed, in spite of the number of "microchanges" in site location from Cayhuamarca to Vinzos times, the main valley system is characterized by the same settlement clusters as in the preceding period—with the exception of a division of Cayhuamarca Cluster 2 into Vinzos Clusters 2 and 3 (which takes into consideration the abandonment of two or three intervening sites in the area just upvalley from Quebrada de Cayhuamarca).

As summarized in Table 5, the overall population estimate for Vinzos Period is 8755 persons, which represents a rather modest increase of ca. 1900 persons over the preceding period. The population now appears to be somewhat more evenly distributed among the various sectors—with 2060 persons in the Upper Valley, 2005 persons in the Middle Valley, 2350 persons in the Lower Valley, and 540 persons in Santa-Chao. As shown on the demographic map (Fig. 169), the population of the main valley area is somewhat less evenly distributed along the desert margin in the Upper and Middle Valley than in Cayhuamarca times. Nevertheless, the population estimates for Clusters 1, 2, 3, 4, and 5 (1180, 825, 955, and 1310 persons, respectively; see Table 12) indicate a situation of substantially more parity among all main valley settlement groups than in Cayhuamarca Period. Thus, although it may be argued that if between-cluster warfare were not occurring in Cayhuamarca times then intercluster relations in the Vinzos system probably were peaceful as well, we may temporarily forestall more definitive resolution of this problem until Chapter V.

Ceramic Distributions

Several vessel types have an extensive, essentially regionwide distribution in this period—including Vinzos Bowl 4, Jar 1, and Jar 2. Otherwise, although there are a number of excellent period diagnostics (including most importantly the Huacapongo Polished Plain types), the distribution of ceramic types is characterized by somewhat more localized groupings and a considerable amount of overlapping in the central part of the main valley system. For example, Vinzos Jar 3 is found everywhere but Cluster 4, Vinzos Jar 5 everywhere but Cluster 5, Vinzos Bowl 1 everywhere but Cluster 4 and at SVP-VIN-37, Vinzos Bowl 2 everywhere but Cluster 1, while clay panpipes are restricted to Clusters 1, 2, and 3. It is of substantial interest to note also that ceramic assemblages of sites in the area centered on Quebrada de Cayhuamarca—including those in Vinzos Clusters 2 and 3—continue to exhibit the same relatively higher numbers and diversity of types as in Cayhuamarca Cluster 2.

Inferences About Subsistence

As in the case of Cayhuamarca sites, no preserved remains of cultigens were noted on the surface of single-component Vinzos Period occupations. However, as argued in Chapter V, it seems probable that by this period the subsistence system was based primarily on intensive irrigation agriculture. The presence of eight sites in association with the large stand of algarrobos in the upper part of Quebrada Palo Redondo also suggests that some resource specialization existed—in this case focused on the harvesting of the edible (and nutritious) beans produced by these trees. Like the single family that presently inhabits this area of the desert, the Vinzos groups may also have been engaged in cutting wood for charcoal production.

Finally, it should be mentioned that marine shells were found on Vinzos Period sites located at least as far as 45 km inland—including SVP-VIN-19, 20, 29, 33, and 34. This suggests the likelihood that maritime resources continued to be an important part of the subsistence system, in spite of the absence of sites with associated Vinzos ceramic diagnostics along the coastline.

Interregional Comparisons

Virú Valley. Willey (1953:61–101) describes 83 sites for the Early-Late Puerto Moorin time period in Virú that appear to be contemporaneous with the 45 occupations of Vinzos Period. Most of these sites, or 64 out of 83, date to the earlier part of Puerto Moorin, with 11 sites dating to the later phase and 9 sites unplaced as to phase. Although it is not the main purpose of this discussion to examine specific aspects of Virú chronology, it should be noted that the distinction between the Early and Late phases of Puerto Moorin was based by Ford and other members of the Virú project (e.g., Ford 1949; Willey 1953:61) on changing percentages of Huacapongo Polished Plain in relation to gradually increasing amounts of Castillo Plain (the latter being primarily a Gallinazo-Huancaco diagnostic). This procedure stands in some contrast to the method followed in our Santa research, namely, one of pinpointing principal period-specific diagnostics by attempting to identify a number of sites where single-component collections of that hypothesized period were present.

Willey (1953:61–63) discusses in detail the problem of the puzzling decline in numbers of sites from Early to Late Puerto Moorin. Among other things, he suggests the possibility that a change in settlement pattern to the valley floor and subsequent heavy alluvial deposition brought about an *apparent* reduction in sites that in fact does not exist. On the other hand, Willey clearly was more concerned in his 1953 report that the actual reason for the apparent decline was a miscalculation in the estimated length of Late Puerto Moorin—i.e., it may have been much shorter in length than the Early phase (and thus might be expected to have many fewer occupations represented than the Early phase), or, even *more* likely, simply did not exist. Because of these problems, and the possibility that most if not all sites are indeed contemporaneous, in the brief discussion that follows Puerto Moorin sites are treated as belonging essentially to a single period. Since over 77% of the sites date to Early Puerto Moorin anyway, this procedure at most creates only minor discrepancies in numbers of each site type. With this in mind, the main categories (and numbers) of site types are as follows: living sites (ca. 60 occupations), fortresses (7 occupations), ceremonial-civic sites (ca. 12 occupations), and cemeteries (4 occupations).

As in the preceding Guañape Period, most Virú living sites—or some 45 out of 60—consist of midden accumulations and earth-refuse mounds containing associated surface sherds of Puerto Moorin date. The remaining 15 sites are similar to all of the Vinzos Period habitation sites of Santa Valley in having well preserved dwellings with low double-faced, rubble-filled rock walls. And, as in Santa, a variety of structural types is present, including (1) scattered individual dwellings with one or several rooms (e.g., see V-87, in Willey 1953, Fig. 13, p. 72), (2) agglutinated dwellings containing as many as 10–15 conjoined rooms (e.g., see V-144, in Fig. 15, p. 77), and (3) scattered windbreaks of lunate shape (e.g., see V-86, in Fig. 12, p. 71).

Willey makes no reference to any internally differentiated living sites where structures of possible elite residential function are present, although judging from the plan views at least one of the 15 exposed dwelling sites may have such remains (see V-177, in Fig. 14, p. 73). Although no areal estimates are given for the majority of sites, the extent of structural remains shown in the plan views indicates they are roughly of the same size as those in Santa. It is also of interest to note that Willey refers to a very large midden accumulation near the ocean along the north desert margin. Puerto Moorin debris here extends over an area several hundred meters wide and up to 3 km long. This site is therefore clearly in the same size category as SVP-VIN-37 in Santa, and, similarly, is the first occupation of substantial size in the sequence.

Briefly summarized, the data on the remaining site types are as follows: Puerto Moorin ceremonial-civic sites are all of a single type consisting of "solid, sloping-sided, flat-topped masses of earth, gravel, adobe, and rock" with a plan that generally is rectangular (Willey 1953:67). As outlined under the next Santa Valley period, these structures are therefore much more similar to pyramidal mounds dating to Early Suchimancillo than to the few ceremonial-civic sites with Vinzos occupation. Two hilltop redoubts and five hilltop platform sites are described by Willey as having a function probably related to defense. V-80/Bitín Fortress and V-132/Cerro del Pino, the two redoubts, appear to be generally similar to Cayhuamarca-Vinzos citadels in having a main enclosure wall and agglutinated habitation structures on the interior (see Figs. 18 and 19, in Willey 1953). Indeed, considering the presence of probable temple mounds inside each structure, the two principal Virú fortresses appear to be quite like the multifunction citadels of Santa. However, as indicated by the plan

views, neither is as complex as the Santa citadels, and such features as formal wall construction techniques, bastions, and dry ditches are lacking.

In sum, the large number of Puerto Moorin sites and the extensive occupation of all sectors of Virú suggest that this period represents a time of sociocultural complexity at least as great as (if not greater than) that of the Lower Santa region. Puerto Moorin marks the first appearance of fortified sites in Virú—including seven occupations located primarily on hills rising high above the south desert margin of the valley. Although this may indicate a threat of external attack from the south, the fact that Santa Valley shares fully 92% (11/12) of the main bowl and jar types of Vinzos Period with Virú—most especially including a very close correspondence in terms of paste, form, and surface treatment with the Huacapongo Polished Plain type—appears to rule out the possibility of conflict between the two valleys. By contrast, there is no evidence of any relationships at all between Santa and valleys to the south (at least in part, of course, because the Beginning and Early phases of Early Intermediate Period have not yet been identified in Nepeña). On the basis of presently available data, then, it appears that the threat of external attack on the Lower Santa system continued to be from the south.

Moche Valley. As mentioned earlier, almost none of the data from the surveys carried out by the Harvard Chan Chan-Moche Valley are yet available in the literature, with the notable exception of a summary article by Bankes (1972) on pre-Middle Horizon settlement patterns in the lower valley. Judging from the relative numbers rather vaguely assigned by Bankes out of a total of 30 sites to Salinar, Gallinazo, and Moche periods of occupation, it appears that the number of Salinar (Puerto Moorin/Vinzos) sites in the lower valley does not exceed five or six. Among these is the large site of Cerro Arena, which lies on a ridgetop that extends out toward the valley floor from the south desert margin, a little over 3 km to the east of Moche site.

Judging from Brennan's (1980) extensive and detailed program of study and excavations carried out in the late 1970s, Cerro Arena consists of a complex habitation site containing evidence of some 2000 nonelite domestic structures as well as several areas of elite residential structures—all of which extend over a very large area of about 2 km². From its greater size and architectural complexity, Cerro Arena is clearly more complex than any of its contemporaries in Virú and Santa. Indeed, the first Santa Valley site that even approaches Cerro Arena in size and complexity is SVP-ESUCH-126/Huaca Santa (70 ha), and the first to exceed it in this regard is the 2-km² Guadalupito/Moche Period complex of Pampa de los Incas. From the Cerro Arena data we thus have a tantalizing, if incomplete, glimpse of the relatively greater complexity that probably characterized the early settlement system in the valley that ultimately would give rise to the multivalley Moche polity.

EARLY SUCHIMANCILLO PERIOD (EARLY-MIDDLE GALLINAZO/EARLY EIP)

A total of 130 discrete sites was identified as belonging to the Early Suchimancillo Period of occupation (Figs. 63–66; for site outlines see Wilson 1985, Figs. 92–93). From the four basic site types of the preceding two periods, the number of types that can be distinguished on the basis of primary or sole function rises to five—including habitation sites (72 occupations), defensive sites (34 occupations), ceremonial-civic sites (6 occupations), cemeteries (16 occupations), and desert ground figures (5 occupations). This period also marks the rise of two major new subtypes: the local center and the minor defensive site.

Habitation Sites

Undifferentiated occupations. The overall proportion of occupations in the Early Suchimancillo settlement system with configurations characterized by undifferentiated dwellings is 69 out of the 130 discrete sites—or 53%. As in the preceding two periods, these sites have an essentially even distribution throughout the area of occupation (see SVP-ESUCH-1, 2–11, 14, 15, 17, 21–23, 25, 27, 28, 32, 35, 38, 39, 44, 45, 52, 53, 55, 56, 58–60, 62–66, 70, 71, 78, 79, 84–88, 91, 93–95, 98, 101–106, 108–110, 114–116, 121, 124, and 125, in Figs. 64–66). They range in size between .25 and 22.75 ha and in population between 5 and 1400 persons—with an average size of 2.4 ha and an average population estimate of 160 persons. The average figures therefore represent an overall increase in size in relation both to Vinzos (1.8 ha/147 persons, excluding SVP-VIN-37) and to Cayhuamarca (2 ha/140 persons). The elevation of habitation sites above the valley floor ranges between 0 and 300 m and distance away from it ranges between 0 and 1300 m—with an average elevation of 60 m above the floor and an average distance of 270 m away. Thus, while the average elevation of such sites continues to drop in modest increments relative to earlier periods, the average distance away from the valley floor is substantially less than that of the preceding periods (890 m, 445 m, and 525 m, respectively, in Las Salinas, Cayhuamarca, and Vinzos).

In terms of the variety of structural types found on habitation sites, Early Suchimancillo represents a continuation of the main kinds of rock-walled structures of earlier periods—including (1) smaller single-room and multiroom dwellings with rectangular or irregular-polygonal layouts, (2) larger agglutinated structures, and (3) windbreaks. Both the smaller multiroom and larger agglutinated dwelling types appear to have become firmly established in this period, with a continuing decline in

the use of simple lunate-shaped windbreak structures. SVP-ESUCH-1, located 3.5 km below the Santa-Tablachaca confluence on a broad piedmont shelf overlooking the narrow Upper Valley canyon (Fig. 64), provides an example not only of the kinds of structures present on sites of this period but of the excellent preservation of archaeological remains in areas that are remote from modern occupation.

SVP-ESUCH-1 contains a large number of dwellings and related features extending over an area of 12 ha. Because of time constraints, it was therefore not possible to map the site in its entirety. However, we were able to prepare detailed plan views of a large agglomeration of terraced dwellings in the upper eastern sector (Fig. 67), as well as of smaller groupings of dwellings in other sectors of the site (for the west-central sector, see Fig. 68; for the east-central and western sectors, see Wilson 1985, Figs. 95, 97). Although earlier occupational debris dating to Cayhuamarca and Vinzos is present in the upper eastern sector, it is probable that most of the remains here date to the Early Suchimancillo time of occupation. As shown in Fig. 67, this part of the site consists of very well preserved dwellings that range in size and configuration from scattered single-room and multiroom structures to large agglutinated structures containing ten or more rooms. Judging from the smaller size of a few rooms in many of the structures, it seems likely that they served a storage function. In addition, we found two discrete areas of concentrated lithic debitage on low rock-faced terraces (areas that presumably were left unroofed), as well as five places in and around dwellings where grinding stones (batanes) are present. None of these remains appears to have been disturbed since the abandonment of the site some 1700–1800 years ago, and they clearly attest to the presence of discrete activity areas that include preparation of stone tools and food processing. It is of interest to add here that broken pottery dating to Early Suchimancillo and the two earlier periods of occupation was noted everywhere in and around the structures and terraces, and the heavily patinated, rock-covered surface of surrounding slopes gave no indication that subsurface remains might be present.

Other types of habitation structures and associated features are found elsewhere on SVP-ESUCH-1, downslope to the north and west of the eastern sector. For example, the three or four discrete dwellings found in one part of the east-central sector (Wilson 1985, Fig. 95) are simpler and less nucleated than those upslope to the east. In addition, the probable storage features here consist of three different types that include (1) rock-lined pits, placed either on the interior or immediate exterior of a dwelling (see Structure 124); (2) a line of two small contiguous chambers lying atop a low rock-faced terrace, immediately upslope from a grinding stone (see Structure 125); and (3) a line of three chambers that forms the south wall of a dwelling (see Structure 126). Similar stor-

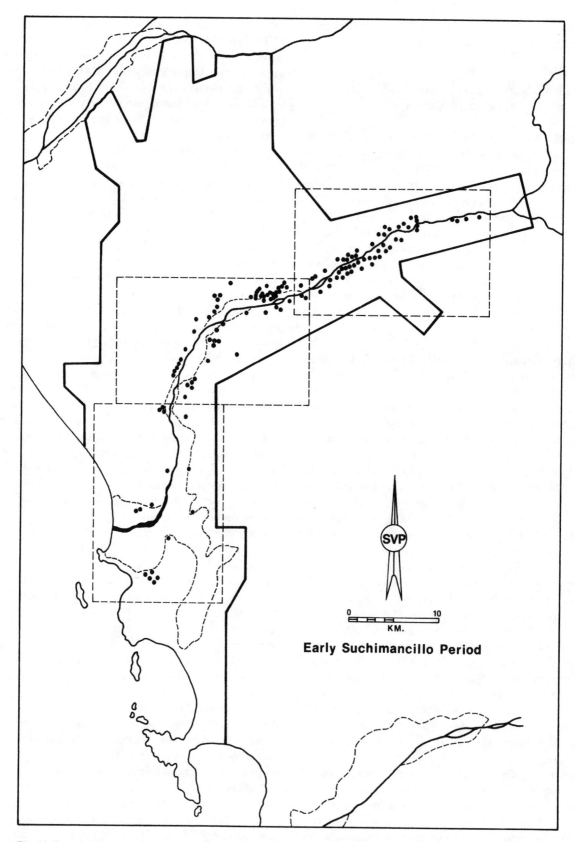

Fig. 63. Location key to settlement pattern maps of Early Suchimancillo Period, Figs. 64, 65, and 66.

SVP

0   10
KM.

Early Suchimancillo Period

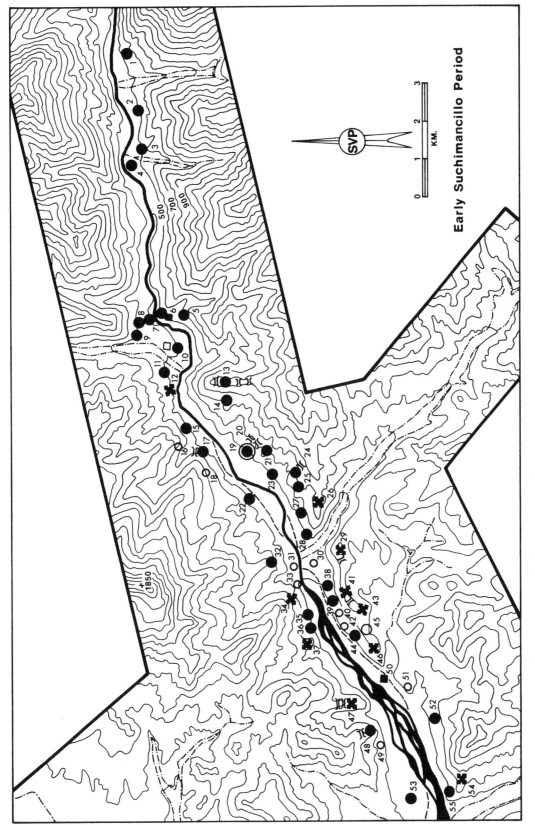

Fig. 64. Settlement pattern map of Early Suchimancillo Period: Upper Valley sector.

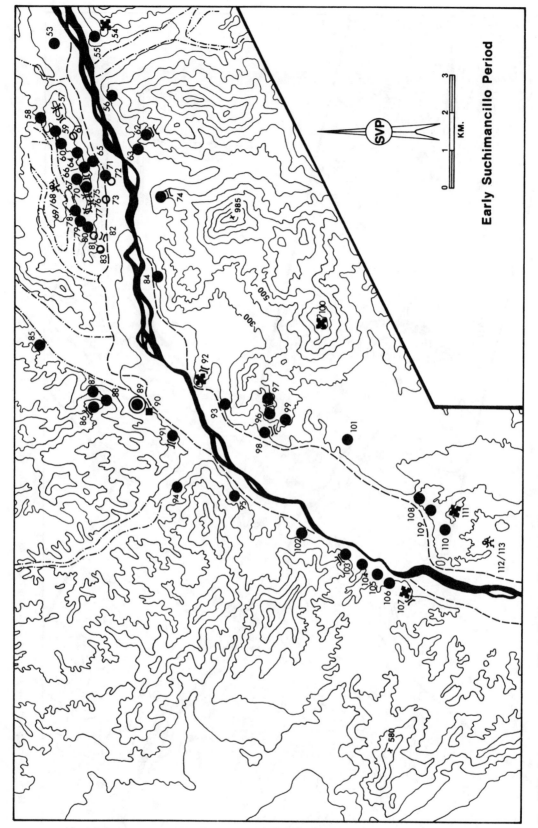

Fig. 65. Settlement pattern map of Early Suchimancillo Period: Middle Valley sector.

154

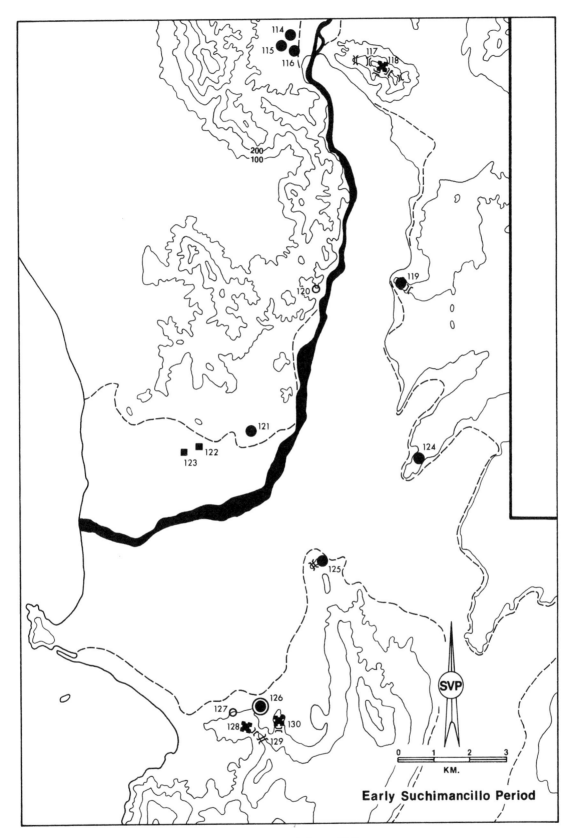

Fig. 66. Settlement pattern map of Early Suchimancillo Period: Lower Valley sector.

155

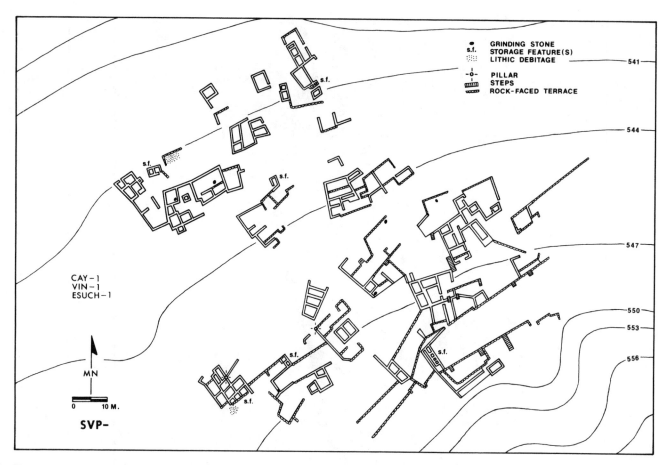

Fig. 67. Plan view of the upper eastern sector of SVP-ESUCH-1.

age features and associated grinding stones are found in an agglutinated structure in the west-central sector (Fig. 68). Finally, probable storage features found in one of the structures of the western sector include most prominently a single line of small, doorless chambers lying on edge of the bluff overlooking the narrow canyon floor (Wilson 1985, Fig. 97). These features lie downslope from a group of large rock-walled structures that probably functioned both as shelters from the prevailing upcanyon winds, and as support for quincha superstructures that were open along the east side and provided protection from the sun.

Downvalley some 7.5 km from the uppermost Early Suchimancillo occupation lies SVP-ESUCH-9, another habitation site with excellently preserved structural remains. However, as shown in Fig. 69, all of the dwellings with associated Suchimancillo occupation at this site consist of scattered single-room or multiroom windbreaks. Interestingly, a nucleated group of four or five larger multiroom structures with strikingly different layouts lies downslope to the south of the windbreaks. But the debris associated with this latter group consists entirely of (much later) Early Tanguche material. In any case, SVP-ESUCH-9/SVP-LSUCH-28 is one of the few

sites of the Suchimancillo time period at which windbreak structures constitute the primary dwelling type.

Elsewhere in the survey region, the principal structures present on habitation sites consist either of (1) dwellings similar to the isolated and agglutinated structures discussed above, in the case of sites located on flatter ground; or (2) contiguous rectangular structures laid out in lines on rock-faced terraces, in the case of sites located on steeper slopes. Thus although some aspects of habitation sites appear to have changed substantially from earlier times, use of specific dwelling types and their densities on a site appear to have continued to be mainly a function of adaptation to the variable terrain of the desert margin.

Local centers. As mentioned above, Early Suchimancillo marks the appearance of the first habitation sites that can be tentatively classified as local centers—i.e., as sites that appear to have functioned at a supraordinate hierarchical level in relation to all or most other sites in their local areas (see SVP-ESUCH-19, 89, and 126, in Figs. 64, 65, and 66). It will be recalled, however, that an incipient form of this hypothesized relationship between a few specialized sites and a number of surrounding ones

156

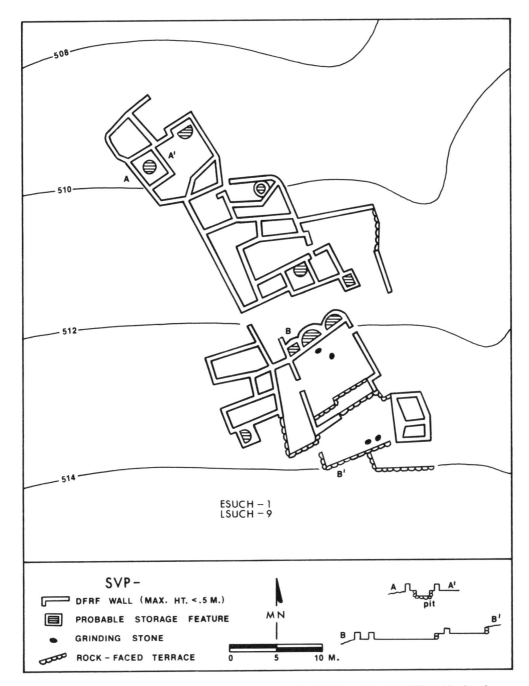

Fig. 68. Plan and detail views of the west-central sector of SVP-ESUCH-1/SVP-LSUCH-9 habitation site.

occurs as early as Cayhuamarca and Vinzos Periods—specifically with regard to centers that probably served as foci of local supracommunity activities of a public and/or religious nature. The local centers of Early Suchimancillo are characterized by similarly unique configurations and a widespread regional distribution, but several features distinguish them from the earlier ceremonial-civic centers as well—including (1) generally much larger resident populations, (2) more consistent evidence of possible elite residences, and, in some cases,

(3) the presence of ceremonial-civic features such as plazas and pyramidal mounds.

SVP-ESUCH-19, the uppermost one of the three probable local centers, lies on steeper slopes and adjacent flatter ground of the desert margin near the lower end of the Upper Valley canyon (see Fig. 64; see also Wilson 1985, Fig. 92). It extends over a large area of 62 ha, with a length of about 2 km and an average width of 500 m. The entire area of occupation is covered with scattered groups of low, rock-walled habitation struc-

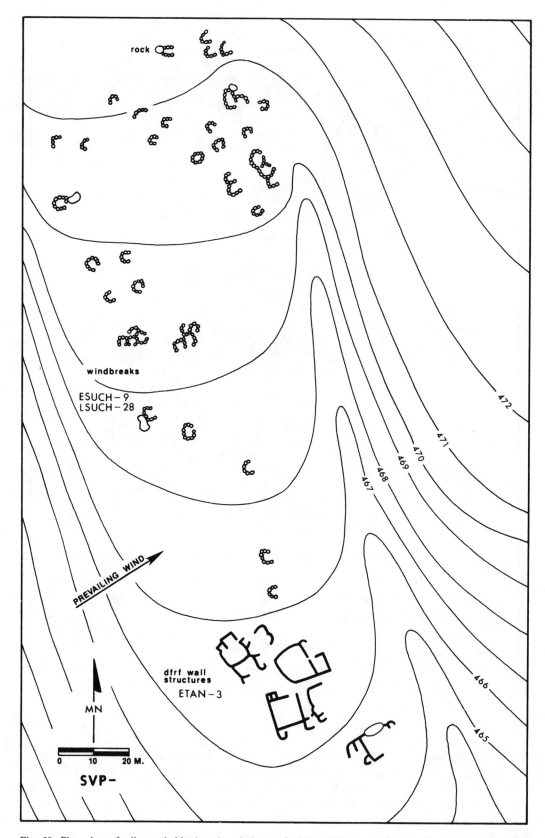

Fig. 69. Plan view of adjacent habitation sites dating to Suchimancillo (northern sector) and Early Tanguche (southern sector).

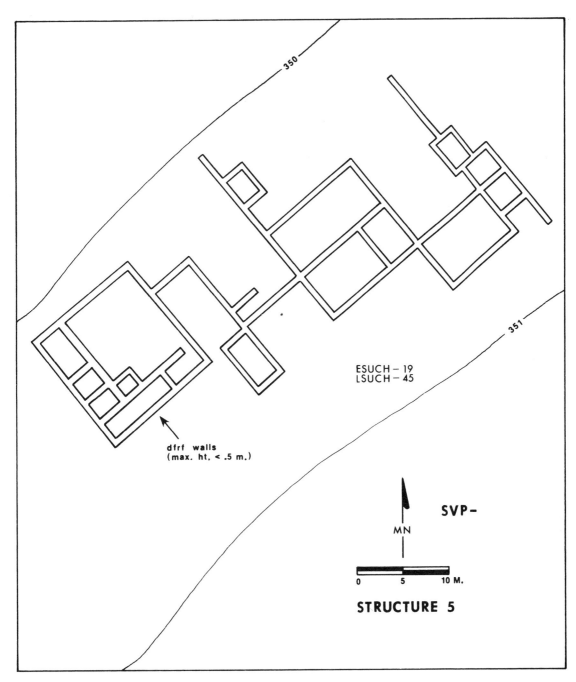

ESUCH – 19
LSUCH – 45

dfrf walls
(max. ht. < .5 m.)

SVP–

MN

0   5   10 M.

STRUCTURE 5

Fig. 70. Plan view of Structure 5, a possible elite residential unit at the large habitation site of SVP-ESUCH-19/SVP-LSUCH-45.

tures in generally low-to-moderate densities, and the population is estimated at 3100 persons. In addition to its large size, SVP-ESUCH-19 has two other features that cause it to stand out from nearby sites. First, it was defended by two small fortress sites located along the upper southeastern flank (see Wilson 1985, Fig. 92/SVP-ESUCH-19 and Fig. 108/SVP-ESUCH-20). Second, two large agglutinated structures are found on low mounded areas that rise above the flat terrain of the north-central sector of the site. Structure 5 (Fig. 70), the

better preserved of the two, has walls built of large riverine rocks with nearly all corners turning very neatly on right angles—thus providing a sharp contrast to the smaller and less formally laid out surrounding dwellings. A similar structure was noted some 200 m away from Structure 5, near the central-northwestern edge of the site, but was in too poor a state of preservation to map. Judging from the central commanding position of these structures, however, it seems likely that both served as foci of elite residence.

SVP-ESUCH-89/Huaca Yolanda lies 20 km farther downvalley from SVP-ESUCH-19, along the western edge of the cultivated mouth of Quebrada Palo Redondo, and has been briefly described under Vinzos Period ceremonial-civic sites (see Plate 16, and Figs. 62, 65). As mentioned there, the wider extent of occupational debris containing Early and Late Suchimancillo sherd diagnostics, as well as the presence of comparatively much greater numbers of surrounding Suchimancillo sites, suggest that Huaca Yolanda reached its period of maximum importance and use during the time following the Vinzos occupation. As indicated by the illustrations, this complex is one of the more outstanding sites of any period in the survey region, both in terms of its excellent preservation and its formal layout. A series of six rock-faced terraces lies in the upper sector of the site, containing numerous rock-walled habitation structures and associated Vinzos and Suchimancillo occupational debris. Immediately downslope to the southeast of the terraces lies a large plaza measuring 55 × 50 m in area and enclosed within low, narrow platforms. Additional habitation structures are located on a series of multilevel platforms along the southwest side of the plaza, and a very large agglutinated structure lies on flatter ground in the southeastern corner. Included within this latter structure are a number of rooms of a residential nature (possibly including elite habitation), as well a few smaller doorless chambers of a size suitable for storage. Finally, another smaller plaza lies downslope at the southeastern end of the site, flanked on the southwest and northwest sides by a series of rock rubble mounds. Architectural remains and associated occupational debris at SVP-ESUCH-89 extend over a total area of 6.2 ha, and the population is estimated at a relatively small 450 persons. Compared to nearby contemporaneous sites, however, Huaca Yolanda stands out clearly as having had central importance in the local subsistence-settlement system.

SVP-ESUCH-126/Huaca Santa, located near the ocean some 30 km downvalley to the south of Huaca Yolanda, appears to have been the largest of all Early Suchimancillo occupations—with diagnostic ceramics of this period found over a total area of 70 ha and a population estimated at 3500 persons (see Figs. 66, 71). Its interpretation within the context of the Early Suchimancillo settlement system is rendered somewhat difficult, however, by the presence of occupational debris dating to five later periods in the sequence. Although it is therefore likely that much of the architecture shown in the plan view dates to the later periods, a few observations can be made about the possible nature of the earliest period of occupation detected here. First of all, it is clear not only that the Early Suchimancillo site was larger than that of any succeeding periods but that all of the associated defensive works date to the Suchimancillo Period (see walls in the southeast corner of the site, in Fig. 71; and SVP-ESUCH-128, 129, and 130, in Fig. 66).

Huaca Santa site is therefore quite similar to the large site of SVP-ESUCH-19 discussed above, especially in terms of the associated defensive works. Early Suchimancillo debris is associated with a huge area of what appear to be undifferentiated habitations in the western sector of the site, as well as with larger compounds and more formal architecture covering an equally large area in the eastern sector. This latter area also includes several mounded areas that may have served as temple platforms, and seems likely to contain elite residences as well.

In sum, given the complexity of architectural remains as well as the strong suggestion of multiple functions, SVP-ESUCH-126 is likely to have had a supraordinate position in the sociopolitical hierarchy of this period. Unlike the other two local centers, however, very few Early Suchimancillo occupations are found anywhere else in the Lower Valley sector. This suggests the possibility that Huaca Santa served as a large nucleated outlying garrison for the main settlement system located in the upvalley sectors.

Defensive Sites

Citadels. As implied in the preceding discussion of the fortress works associated with local centers, Early Suchimancillo marks the appearance of the minor defensive site in the regional system. The system also continues to be characterized by a number of citadel sites containing relatively complex structural remains and larger populations. From a total of 12 occupied citadels in Vinzos Period, the number of sites of this type rises to 18—i.e., to a number that is nearly equal to the 20 citadel sites occupied in Cayhuamarca Period. Indeed, half of the 18 Early Suchimancillo citadel occupations consist of Cayhuamarca fortress sites that either continue in occupation from the Vinzos time period (7 sites), or that were reoccupied following an apparent hiatus of occupation (2 sites). Included in this group are SVP-ESUCH-12, 26, 41, 43, 46, 54, 100, and 111 (see Figs. 64, 65, 66; and Figs. 29, 32, 35, 37–38, 39, 43–44, 48, and 49, respectively); and SVP-ESUCH-29 (see Wilson 1985, Fig. 46). All of the remaining nine citadels are found at sites whose construction appears to date to the Early Suchimancillo Period. These sites include SVP-ESUCH-34, 36, 37, 47, 92, 107, 118, 128, and 130.

As exemplified in the plan views of some of the citadels built in Early Suchimancillo Period (see Figs. 72–74; see also Wilson 1985, Fig. 103), these structures generally are much more variable in configuration and less complex architecturally than the citadels of Cayhuamarca Period. Indeed, citadel remains at four of the Early Suchimancillo sites consist primarily of a single major enclosure wall or associated defensive works of other kinds that we found either too poorly preserved or too unprepossessing architecturally to warrant preparation

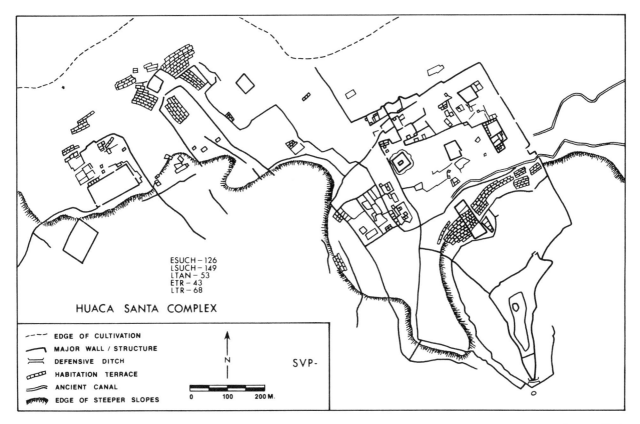

ESUCH – 126
LSUCH – 149
LTAN – 53
ETR – 43
LTR – 68

HUACA SANTA COMPLEX

---- EDGE OF CULTIVATION
⌐ MAJOR WALL / STRUCTURE
≥ DEFENSIVE DITCH
⊏⊐ HABITATION TERRACE
≥ ANCIENT CANAL
⟋⟍ EDGE OF STEEPER SLOPES

N

SVP-

0   100   200 M.

Fig. 71. Plan view of Huaca Santa Complex, a large site with combined habitation, ceremonial-civic, and defensive functions dating to Early Suchimancillo and later periods.

of a site map. Judging from associated occupational debris, however, most of the 18 citadel occupations are similar to those of preceding periods in having what appear to have been large populations of a more or less permanent nature. Estimated population numbers range between 10 and 300 persons, and the average of 110 occupants is the same as that mentioned earlier for dual-function Cayhuamarca citadels.

Moreover, as indicated on the settlement maps, Early Suchimancillo citadels have a similarly wide distribution throughout most of the occupied area of the survey region. In terms of the remoteness of sites out on the desert away from the valley floor, however, this period marks the beginning of a trend toward substantially greater proximity to the main source of food and water. Taking into consideration the location of all citadels as well as minor defensive sites, Early Suchimancillo fortresses range in distance between 25 and 3500 m away from the valley floor, with an average of 590 m (average distances in Cayhuamarca and Vinzos are 1000 m and 1200, respectively). Elevations range between 25 and 700 m above the floor, with an average of 205 m (average elevations in Cayhuamarca and Vinzos are 243 and 255 m, respectively).

Minor defensive sites. Added to the 18 citadel occupations are another 24 sites whose configuration and size suggest an important, but somewhat less prominent, function in the defensive network of the period (Note: although detailed plan views were made in the field of over 11 of the minor defensive sites, space restrictions allow only two of these drawings to be shown here, in Figs. 75 and 76; for the other nine sites see Wilson 1985, Figs. 105, 107–110, 112–115; for at least three others see Cerro Loreto ridge map in Wilson 1985, Fig. 90). As in the case of the citadels, these minor defensive sites are distributed more or less evenly throughout the settlement system, from the middle part of the Upper Valley on downriver to the coast.

Two main subgroups of sites are present in this category—including (1) 16 sites whose primary function appears to have been defensive in nature, with population estimates ranging from 0 to 110 persons and a (low) average of 20 persons per site (see SVP-ESUCH-13, 20, 24, 48, 57, 70, 74–77, 80, 82, 96, 117, 119, and 129, in Figs. 64–66); and (2) nine habitation sites at which minor defensive works are found (see SVP-ESUCH-17, 19, 62, 65, 91, 95, 98, 103, and 125, in Figs. 64–66). Population estimates for this latter group are roughly the

161

same as those of the former group, at least when the defensive works themselves are viewed as discrete entities apart from the areas devoted primarily to habitation and other nondefensive functions.

As shown schematically on the topographic settlement maps, minor defensive sites are universally found on narrow, gently sloping ridges in the midst of the steep desert terrain rising immediately above the edges of the valley floor. A number of these sites are located on the highest part of ridges lying hundreds of meters above the cultivated floor of the valley (e.g., see SVP-ESUCH-13 in Wilson 1985, Fig. 105, which lies 500 m above the floor; see also sites on Cerro Loreto ridge in Wilson 1985, Fig. 90). However, more often than not minor defensive works lie on lower ridges down near the valley floor (e.g., SVP-ESUCH-17 and SVP-ESUCH-82, in Figs. 75 and 76). With respect to their specific configuration, nearly all of the 24 minor defensive sites of Early Suchimancillo Period are characterized by ditches and associated bulwark walls built across the spine of the ridge to enhance the naturally defensible position of the fortress.

The other structural remains on these sites usually are found within the area protected by the ditches and bulwarks, and consist either of a single smaller structure or of several structures of varying size laid out in a line along the ridge. Structural remains at a few sites were found to be even more limited, consisting of one or more rock-faced terraces on which scattered occupational debris was noted. In addition, as outlined in the site descriptions (Wilson 1985, Appendix B), some sites also contain associated intrusive burials dating to Early and Late Suchimancillo, or later periods. In spite of the indication of small attendant populations at most minor defensive sites, it seems likely that they functioned primarily as places of temporary refuge and defense for modest-sized groups of people during attacks on nearby habitation sites. Indeed, the relatively much simpler configuration of structural remains in comparison to citadels of Early Suchimancillo or preceding periods argues that such defensive works had a primary function related to transitory defensive needs.

Ceremonial-Civic Sites

Aside from the probability that ceremonial-civic activities were among the major functions of SVP-ESUCH-89/Huaca Yolanda local center, such activities probably also were carried out at six other widely distributed, but substantially smaller and less complex, sites. Judging from associated surface ceramics, two of these six smaller sites were built in Cayhuamarca Period—with one reoccupied and the other continuing in use from Vinzos times (see SVP-ESUCH-97 and SVP-ESUCH-99, in Fig. 55 and in Wilson 1985, Fig. 77). As shown in the plan views, both sites consist of ridgetop platforms that have unique configurations in relation to

all other sites of any period in the survey region. Although both are located in relatively remote positions in the desert hills high to the east above Vinzos settlement, several major Early Suchimancillo habitation sites are located nearby to the north, and continuing use in this period is entirely plausible.

All four of the remaining sites consist of isolated pyramid mounds located in the midst of the valley floor (3 sites) or immediately adjacent to it (1 site)—including SVP-ESUCH-50, 90, 122, and 123 (see Figs. 64–66). SVP-ESUCH-50/Structure 47 (Plate 3; for drawings, see Wilson 1985, Fig. 116) is located in cultivated fields near the mouth of Quebrada del Panteón in the Upper Valley sector, and consists of a rock-rubble mound measuring 40 × 33 m in area and 5.7 m high. SVP-ESUCH-90/Structure 51 (Fig. 77) lies 13.5 km downvalley to the southwest, on the desert margin near the mouth of Quebrada Palo Redondo, and consists of a multilevel polygonally-shaped mound measuring 45 × 40 m in area and 5.75 m high. As shown in Fig. 65, SVP-ESUCH-90/Structure 51 lies just to the southwest of Huaca Yolanda site. SVP-ESUCH-122/Structure 11 and SVP-ESUCH--123/Structure 10 lie adjacent to each other on the cultivated valley floor, some 24 km farther downvalley from the Huaca Yolanda area (see Fig. 78 and Wilson 1985, Fig. 119). They consist of smaller mounds measuring 30 × 30 × 5 m and 35 × 30 × 2.5 m, respectively. Although some of the adobes found on Structure 11 are rectangular with maker's marks (and therefore most probably of Guadalupito/Moche date), sherd diagnostics as well as loaf-shaped bricks found elsewhere on the mound suggest that the main period of construction and use dates to Early Suchimancillo.

Cemetery Sites

As mentioned in Chapter III, the location and dating of cemetery sites is essentially a function of where and how the huaqueros have operated in their search for pottery vessels and other grave goods. Given the nearly universal looting that has occurred throughout most areas of the desert margin in the 50-km distance between Quebrada del Silencio and the ocean—both in the mouths of quebradas and on adjacent desert slopes—it is of some interest to note that Early Suchimancillo is the first period in the sequence for which a substantial number of cemeteries can be identified. As shown in Figs. 64–66, although burial sites of this period are more or less evenly distributed in relation to other site types, the principal concentration occurs in the lower part of the Upper Valley and the upper part of the Middle Valley.

A total of 27 Early Suchimancillo cemeteries was found in the survey region, and these may be categorized under two main subtypes—including (1) 16 single-function burial sites situated apart from habitation or defensive sites, generally on steeper slopes, in quebrada

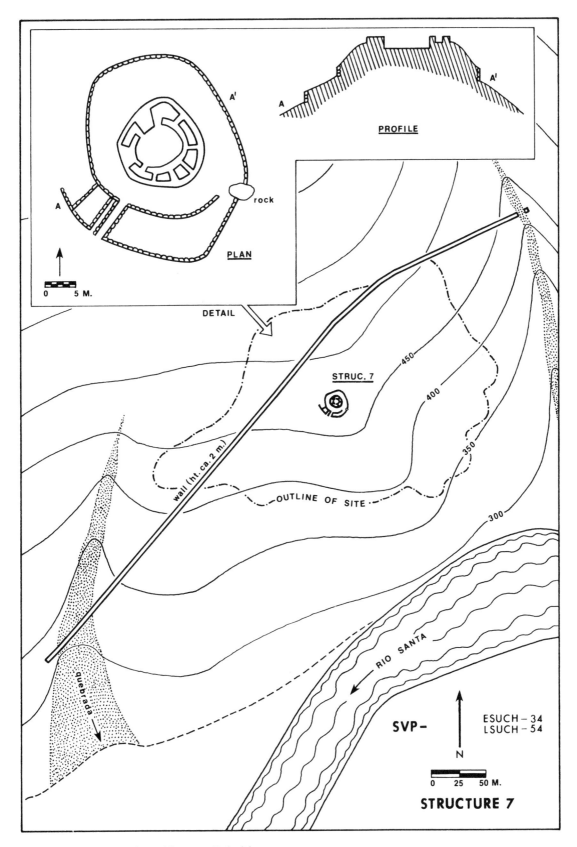

PROFILE

PLAN

0   5 M.

DETAIL

450

STRUC. 7

400

350

wall (ht. ca. 2 m.)

OUTLINE OF SITE

300

RIO SANTA

quebrada

SVP-

ESUCH - 34
LSUCH - 54

N

0   25   50 M.

STRUCTURE 7

rock

Fig. 72. Plan and detail views of Structure 7 citadel.

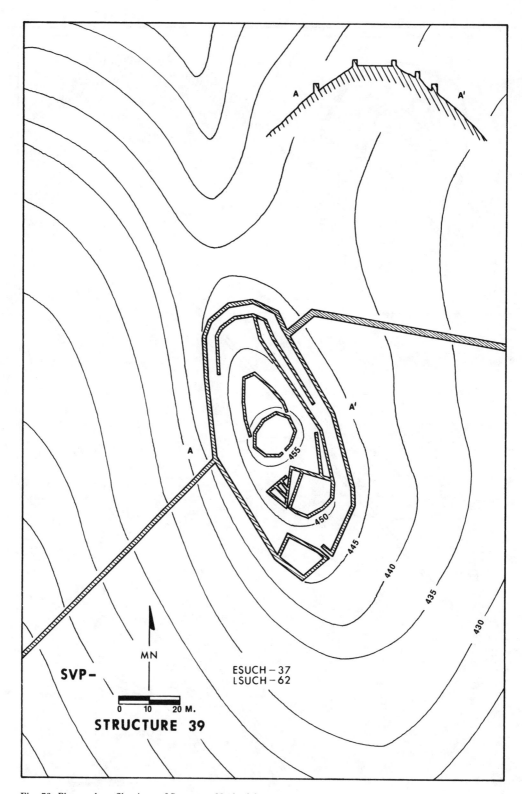

SVP–

MN

0   10   20 M.

STRUCTURE 39

ESUCH – 37
LSUCH – 62

Fig. 73. Plan and profile views of Structure 39 citadel.

164

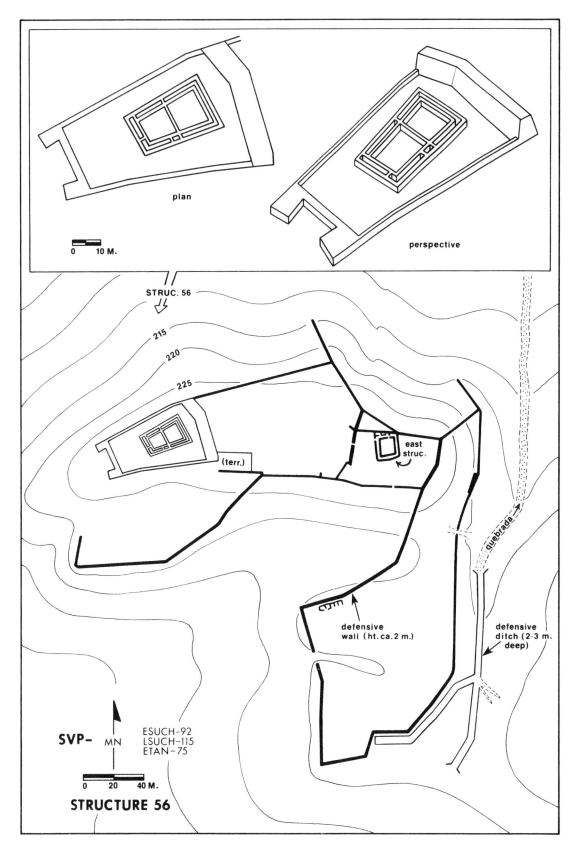

plan

perspective

0   10 M.

STRUC. 56

215
220
225

(terr.)

east
struc.

quebrada

defensive
wall (ht. ca. 2 m.)

defensive
ditch (2-3 m.
deep)

SVP-   MN   ESUCH-92
LSUCH-115
ETAN-75

0   20   40 M.

STRUCTURE 56

Fig. 74. Plan and detail views of Structure 56 citadel.

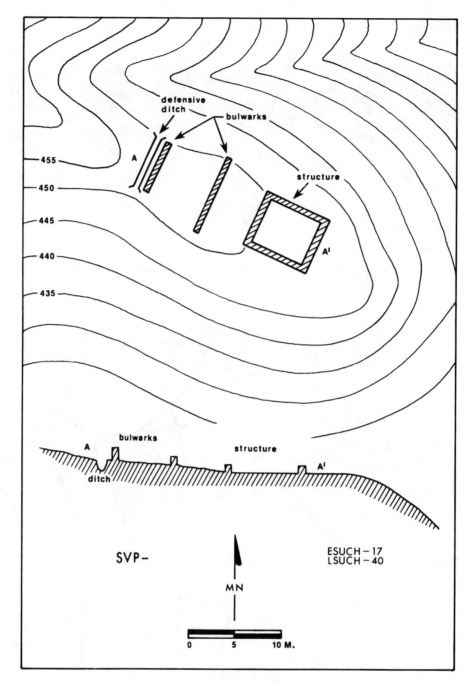

Fig. 75. Plan and profile views of defensive works at SVP-ESUCH-17 habitation site.

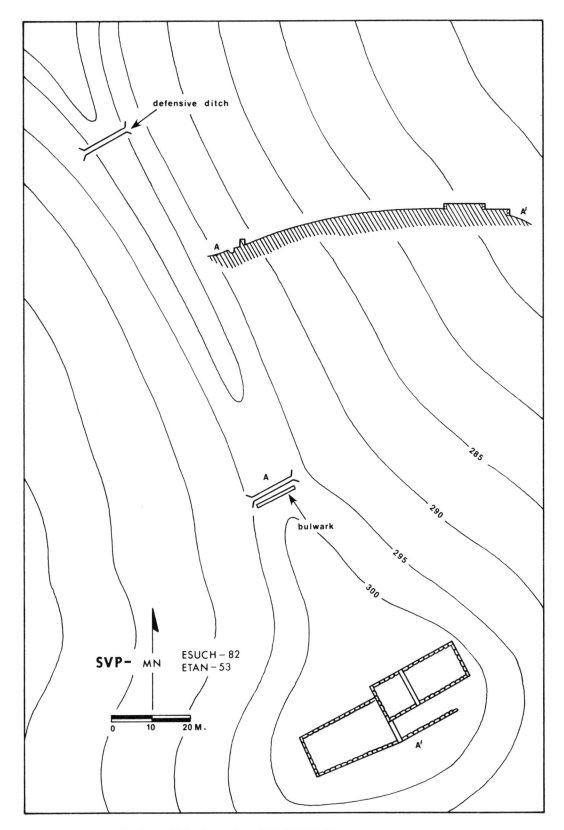

Fig. 76. Plan and profile views of defensive works at SVP-ESUCH-82.

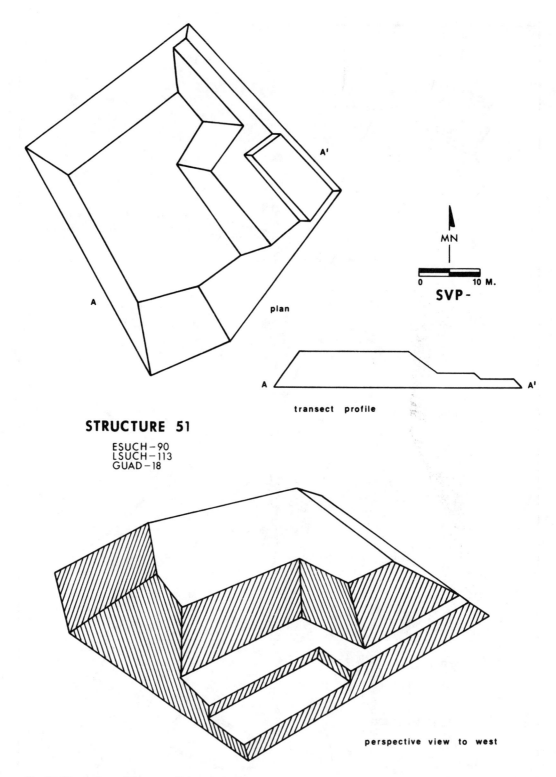

A'

MN

0   10 M.

SVP-

plan

A

A   transect profile   A'

STRUCTURE 51

ESUCH – 90
LSUCH – 113
GUAD – 18

perspective view to west

Fig. 77. Three views of Structure 51 huaca.

168

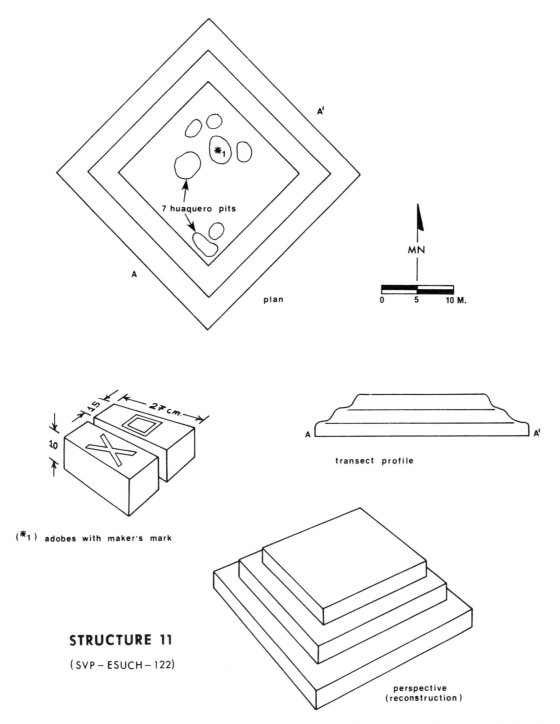

plan

MN

0 5 10 M.

A A'

transect profile

(*1) adobes with maker's mark

STRUCTURE 11

(SVP – ESUCH – 122)

perspective
(reconstruction)

Fig. 78. Three views of Structure 11 huaca, with a detail view of intrusive adobes dating probably to Guadalupito Period.

mouths, or on flatter ground immediately above the edges of quebradas (see SVP-ESUCH-16, 18, 30, 31, 33, 40, 42, 49, 51, 61, 72, 73, 81, 83, 120, and 127, in Figs. 64–66); and (2) 11 burial sites which are part of larger occupations whose primary functions included habitation and/or defense (see SVP-ESUCH-17, 19, 20, 35, 44, 45, 47, 71, 98, 119, and 128, in Figs. 64–66).

Since nearly all cemetery sites are found in a state of substantial chaos brought about by the destructive activities of the graverobbers, it often is difficult to assess the precise spatial relationship of burial grounds in relation to habitation structures at the latter group of multi-function sites. But in most cases it appears that the general practice was to locate burials in discrete areas apart from dwellings, rather than in or around them. For example, in the area of Suchimancillo settlement across the river from Tablones, burial sites generally occupy the steep rocky slopes rising above the narrow cultivated valley floor, with habitation areas occupying terraces and adjacent flatter ground at the base of these slopes. The burials themselves often were placed on narrow, rock-faced terraces, apparently constructed in an effort to stabilize the steep rocky ground.

Interestingly, Early Suchimancillo marks the appearance of small, rock-lined tombs with pentagonal or hexagonal plan views and measurements of roughly 50 cm in diameter and 50–75 cm deep. Although no complete human skeletal or mummified remains were noted in these tombs, their size clearly indicates that burials either were secondary or the body of the deceased was very tightly flexed and bound. This tomb type does not appear to have been universally present on each of the Early Suchimancillo burial sites—i.e., some burials may have been placed in simple sandy pits. However, it is found throughout most of the area of occupation. Judging from associated sherd diagnostics, tombs of this type are entirely restricted to Early and Late Suchimancillo Periods and seem quite likely to be one of the principal manifestations of cultural influences coming out of the adjacent sierra.

Other Remains: Desert Ground Drawings

Among the more intriguing archaeological remains found during our research in Santa Valley are two major groups of desert ground drawings, both of which are very similar in technique of construction to those found on the Nazca Plain over 750 km to the south. The Santa ground drawings are situated in areas covered by a thin, more or less uniform layer of heavily patinated rock which overlies the lighter sandy desert soil. One or a combination of three principal techniques were employed in constructing the figures (see Figs. 79–81; for additional ground drawings mapped during the survey see Wilson 1985, Figs. 123–128). These include (1) the formation of what might be termed "positive" figures by removal of the

dark desert pavement from the area *inside* their outline to expose the lighter sandy ground surface; (2) the formation of "negative" figures by removal of the desert pavement from the area immediately *outside* their outline; and (3) the addition of low piles or lines of rocks to the drawing, either to produce specific features (e.g., eyes, mouths) or to accentuate further the outline of the ground drawing.

The first of the two groups of drawings lies on low, gently rolling desert terrain within a kilometer to the east of the narrow valley floor of Huaca Corral-La Toma area (see SVP-ESUCH-112/113, in Fig. 65). With the exception of a few larger drawings at the southern end of the Feature L group here (see Fig. 81), most of the 30-odd figures on the site are quite faint and difficult to discern unless looked at directly from adjacent hills during an optimum time of day—i.e., when the angle of the sun is oblique enough to produce shadows and, thus, some additional definition of the figures. The principal reason for their faintness, however, is that over the centuries the lighter ground surface which provides their main definition has become nearly as darkly patinated as the surrounding desert. Indeed, we were able to find the figures on this site only on the second survey pass through the area, and several return visits at different times of the day ultimately were required in order to map and photograph properly all but the faintest ones.

The second group of ground drawings lies some 15 km upvalley to the northeast, in rugged desert terrain located along the sides of Quebrada El Silencio, a major dry wash at the northern base of Cerro Loreto ridge (see SVP-ESUCH-67/68/69, in Fig. 65; Note: Quebrada *El* Silencio is a distinct wash from the one called Quebrada *del* Silencio, which lies farther upriver in the Upper Valley canyon; see Fig. 3). The figures of this second group are even fainter than those of the first, and probably would not have been noticed had we not been prepared by our experience in finding and mapping those of the downvalley group. Indeed, it is worth noting that other drawings of this nature may well be present in the survey region, but are now simply too faint to be seen unless viewed directly under good lighting conditions.

Since all of the 35+ ground drawings we were able to locate and map are described in detail in Wilson 1985 (Appendix B), the discussion here is confined to outlining some of their more outstanding characteristics. Following this, the section closes with a brief discussion of the tentative Early Suchimancillo dating proposed for the drawings.

General description. Proceeding roughly by order of their presentation in the illustrations accompanying this report and the dissertation, it will be noted that the ground drawings found at SVP-ESUCH-112 consist of three main groups (labeled Features J, K, and L), as well as a number of smaller groups and individual figures located in various other places around the site. It is also of interest to note that the upvalley drawings of Quebrada El Silencio are very similar to the small groups found at the downvalley site, in that no more than two or three are situated together in a single place.

As shown in Fig. 79, Feature J consists of a number of very large figures, most prominently including (1) two humans (note what appears to be a spear thrower in the left hand of one of them), (2) a bird, and (3) an abstract creature (a lizard?) that has a grill-like appendage at the rear. Feature K is perhaps the most intriguing of all the Santa Valley ground drawings in that it provides evidence of the nature and importance of probable contacts with the adjacent sierra. As Fig. 80 shows, Feature K contains a group of 13 figures, including (1) a man (note the male genitalia); and (2) twelve animals that seem clearly to be Andean camelids, most probably llamas. The largest of the llamas measures slightly over 6 m high × 4 m long (ca. 20 × 13 ft), and the smallest, 55 m away at the northern end of the group, measures 1.5 m high × 1 m long. Indeed, only the northern figures—including the man and nearby llamas—could be said to approximate real-world size. It is also of interest to note the presence of bird wings and tail feathers below the two southernmost llamas, as well as the 280°-Azimuth line (roughly aligned with the path of the sun across the sky). Feature L constitutes the final main group of drawings at SVP-ESUCH-112, and, as shown in Fig. 81, includes a number of abstract figures as well as a bird and a trapezoidal face. The remainder of the drawings here consist of birds (probably condors) and abstract figures (see Figs. 123, 124, and 125 A, in Wilson 1985).

A mix of naturalistic and abstract geometric figures is likewise present at the upvalley sites of SVP-ESUCH-67/68/69. Of particular interest in this group are: (1) a lizard-like creature that seems to be the object of attention of an alligator, or cayman, with open jaws (Wilson 1985, Fig. 126 B); and (2) additional depictions of birds that appear to be owls (Fig. 127 A-top and Fig. 127 B, in Wilson 1985).

Dating. While the Early Suchimancillo date proposed for the ground drawings must be considered as tentative, it is based on three lines of evidence that together provide fairly solid evidence of the period of construction. First of all, Early Suchimancillo habitation sites constitute by far the most numerous group of occupations found in association with both the upvalley and downvalley groups of drawings (Fig. 65; see also Wilson 1985, Fig. 90). It is therefore at least conceivable that people of this time period produced the drawings. Second, judging from other evidence—including the presence of sierra-influenced or sierra-derived ceramics, tomb types, and a subterranean gallery—Early and Late Suchimancillo together constitute the time of apparent maximum contact between the Lower Santa Valley and people of the adjacent sierra. Thus the depiction in the drawings of a number of animals native to the sierra and Amazonian selva—including llamas, condors, and caymans—fits best with the suggested Suchimancillo date. Third, a small collection of sherd diagnostics dating to Early Suchimancillo Period was found on the surface of SVP-ESUCH-112 (Coll. 345), just upslope to the southeast of the line-and-partial ellipse at the southern end of Feature J (see Fig. 79).

Other Remains: Corral Features

Early Suchimancillo is the first period during which architectural features are present that appear very likely to have served as corrals, namely, as walled enclosures for animals (e.g., see Fig. 82). Only two such enclosures can be dated with reasonable certainty to Early Suchimancillo—one located alongside an ancient trail at SVP-ESUCH-10 in the Quebrada del Silencio area, and the other located some 7.5 km farther downvalley on the opposite side of the river at SVP-ESUCH-38 (see Fig. 64, and Wilson 1985, Appendix B). Both of the enclosures in question are essentially free of occupational debris on the interior, and, aside from possible storage or shelter for humans/animals represented by interior buildings at the far west end of Structure 110, seem most suited to penning animals. Since the only domesticated Andean animals that would require such penning are limited strictly to camelids (llamas, alpacas), and drawings of llama figures are a prominent feature of SVP-ESUCH-112 (see preceding section, and Fig. 80), the nature of the principal occupants of the corrals seems quite clear. (For an excellent discussion of data indicating the clear importance of llamas—both for transport and as a source of meat—in North Coast valleys from Early Horizon times on, see Shimada and Shimada 1985.)

Settlement and Demographic Patterns

Early Suchimancillo represents the first period of substantial growth of the subsistence-settlement system beyond that established during the initial stages of (probable) intensive irrigation agriculture in Cayhuamarca and Vinzos Period. From the roughly 45–50 sites occupying the Upper and Middle Valley in the preceding two periods, the number of occupations in these sectors has now grown to 118—or well over two times the number of former occupations. Sites are now distributed nearly continuously on both the north and south desert margins throughout most of the Upper and Middle Valley, and the first substantial occupation of the main Lower Valley occurs—with 12 sites located on the north and south margins of this sector, as well.

Although in many ways the Early Suchimancillo system appears to be an outgrowth of developments in preceding periods, it is noteworthy that fully 88% of the

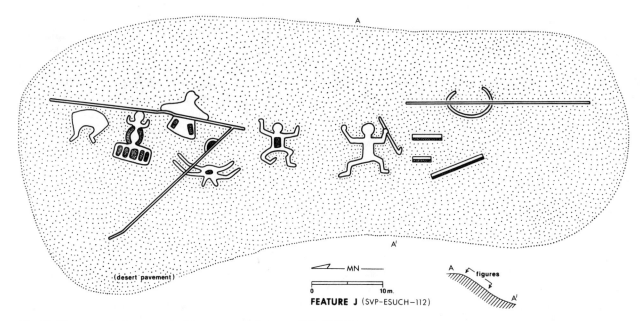

Fig. 79. Plan view of a large group of desert ground figures at SVP-ESUCH-112.

sites of this period are new occupations, reflecting not only a substantial amount of population growth but also changes in settlement location at the local level. Perhaps the principal similarity between the Early Suchimancillo and Cayhuamarca-Vinzos systems is the continuation throughout the area of occupation of a close association between habitation and defensive sites. But this period also sees the expansion of the habitation-defensive system on the south desert margin of the Upper-Middle Valley, as well as the establishment of similar systems along much of the opposite margin and on the south side of the Lower Valley sector. With a total of 42 citadels and minor defensive sites located throughout most of the area of occupation, the Early Suchimancillo settlement pattern clearly implies that warfare continued to be a major stress affecting the adaptive structure of the developing regional system.

Two aspects of this system stand out as major new developments compared to the preceding two periods. The first of these is the appearance of the earliest local centers in the region. As mentioned above, these sites stand out as larger and/or internally more complex than any of the surrounding undifferentiated habitation sites in the local system. Interestingly enough, the three hypothesized local centers of this period are very widely distributed throughout the system—with SVP-ESUCH-19 located on the south margin of the upvalley area, SVP-ESUCH-89/Huaca Yolanda located 20 km farther downvalley on the opposite margin, and SVP-ESUCH-126/Huaca Santa located 30 km on downvalley along the south side of the Lower Valley.

The second major innovative feature of the Early

Suchimancillo system is what appears to have been at least a partial shift in the locus of elite residences. Thus, from the pattern of associating isolated smaller elite residences with ceremonial-civic centers, citadels, or small habitation sites, there is a change to one of locating such residences inside local centers. Although at SVP-ESUCH-89/Huaca Yolanda there is reasonably clear evidence that elite residences are intimately associated with features of probable ceremonial-civic function (see Fig. 62), the other two sites appear to have had an essentially secular function with no evidence of associated ceremonial buildings. However, it is worth emphasizing that sites such as Huaca Yolanda and the proliferation of small pyramidal structures throughout much of the area of occupation suggest that ceremonial aspects of the system continued to play a prominent role in promoting and maintaining supravillage activities.

Demographically, the Early Suchimancillo system represents an exponential increase in regional population, with an estimated overall population size 2.5 times larger than that of the preceding period—or some 20,110 inhabitants distributed throughout the area of occupation (see Table 5, and Fig. 161). The most substantial increase in population is in the Upper Valley, where the estimated 11,045 inhabitants represent over 3.7 times the population of Vinzos Period. The estimated populations of 5055 and 4010, respectively, in the Middle and Lower Valley represent somewhat more modest increases of roughly two times the numbers found there in the preceding period. Another remarkable aspect of the Early Suchimancillo system is the change from the rough parity of estimated population size among clusters of

172

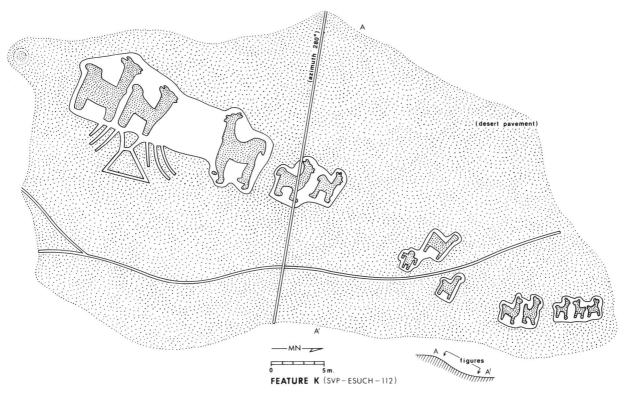

Fig. 80. Plan view of a large group of desert ground figures at SVP-ESUCH-112.

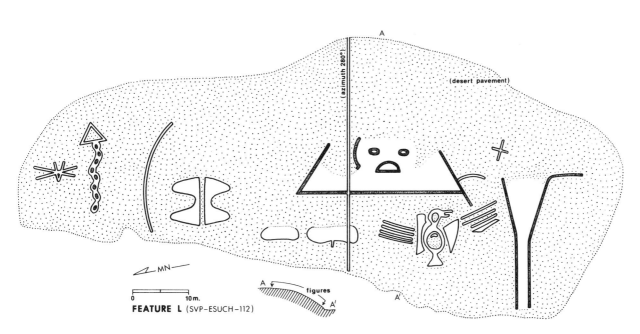

Fig. 81. Plan view of a large group of desert ground figures at SVP-ESUCH-112.

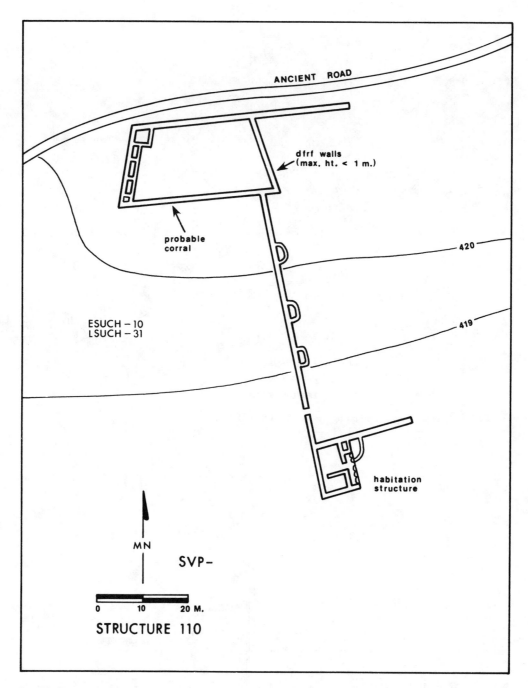

ANCIENT ROAD

dfrf walls
(max. ht. < 1 m.)

probable
corral

ESUCH – 10
LSUCH – 31

420

419

habitation
structure

MN

SVP–

0   10   20 M.

STRUCTURE 110

Fig. 82. Plan view of Structure 110, a probable llama corral with associated Suchimancillo Period habitation structures.

174

Cayhuamarca and Vinzos to a situation of sharp disparity among clusters—with Early Suchimancillo Cluster 1 having an estimated 1070 persons, Cluster 2 having 15,030 persons, and Cluster 3 having 4010 persons (see Table 12).

These demographic data, as well as the overall location and types of settlements in the system, have two principal implications for the nature of within-valley and interregional relations in this period. First, the continuous distribution of sites on both sides of Cluster 2 argues at the very least against the possibility that warfare could have been conducted among sites on the same side of the river (the possibility of across-valley warfare is dealt with below). Second, the overwhelming demographic superiority of Cluster 2 compared to other settlement clusters argues strongly against the possibility that warfare was occurring between clusters. From these arguments it may be concluded that the threat of attack was from outside the region.

Ceramic Distributions

By the time of Early Suchimancillo Period, the regional ceramic assemblage had become much more complex and diverse than in the preceding two periods. This is exemplified by the following: (1) an increase in the total number of principal time markers (i.e., from 12 in Cayhuamarca, and 12 in Vinzos, to 20 in Early Suchimancillo); (2) an increase in the number of paste types (from two in Cayhuamarca, to three in Vinzos, and to four—including kaolin—in Early Suchimancillo; see Table 3); (3) the first appearance of substantial numbers of human, animal, and maize effigies; and (4) the appearance of polychrome wares.

In addition, the regional distribution of ceramic types is substantially more complex than before. Briefly to characterize this complexity, it is possible to detect at least four major categories of ceramic distributions linking various parts of the subsistence-settlement system—including (1) types that are very widespread throughout Clusters 1, 2, and 3 (Early Suchimancillo Jars 1, 3, and 4); (2) types that are somewhat less widespread, but still found nearly everywhere in all three clusters (Early Suchimancillo Jars 6, 7; and red polished ware, including Bowls 1b, 2b, 6b, and Jars 8a–8e); (3) types that are essentially or entirely confined to the 37-km length of Cluster 2 (Early Suchimancillo Bowl 1, Jar 5); and (4) types that not only are confined to Cluster 2, but concentrated especially in the uppermost 25 km of this area (including all of the previously mentioned types, plus Castillo White-Red-Orange, numerous kaolin types, and Early Suchimancillo decorated Bowls 3, 5).

Indeed, the distribution of types in the last two categories appears to be essentially a clinal one—with greater numbers of kaolin and other decorated types in the Quebrada de Cayhuamarca-Quebrada del Silencio area, and fewer types and less diversity as one proceeds either downvalley toward Huaca Corral area or upvalley toward Cluster 1. On the other hand, there is no detectable difference at all between the north and south desert margins—with both sides of the river having a coextensive distribution of all types, and covarying in terms of the number and quantity of types as a function of increasing distance away from the Quebrada de Cayhuamarca area.

From these distributional data, one may suggest the following two conclusions: First, the evidence of strong ceramic ties between the north and south sides of the valley suggests correspondingly strong socioeconomic ties, in spite of the fact that canals by definition belonged to completely separate networks on each side of the river; and (2) the Quebrada de Cayhuamarca area appears to have continued to be a major focus of cultural diversity, perhaps indicating use of the quebrada itself (and, secondarily, the main upper canyon) as a major route of communication with other regions (e.g., 65%, or 13 out of 20, of the principal ceramic types are related to ceramics of the adjacent sierra, including Pashash and the Callejón de Huaylas).

Inferences About Subsistence

As mentioned earlier, Early Suchimancillo is the first period in the sequence for which preserved remains of maize were found on the surface of single-component sites—including SVP-ESUCH-87 (partial cobs) and SVP-ESUCH-119 (stalks and leaves). By B.C./A.D. times there is thus reasonably clear evidence of maize agriculture based probably on intensive irrigation; indeed, as argued later, there is no other way a system composed of as many as 20,110 inhabitants could have subsisted.

Maritime food products also continue to play a role in the subsistence system, with marine shells noted on SVP-ESUCH-9, 19, 38, 43, 47, 63 (*Tagelus* Sp.), 80, 86 (*Donax* Sp.), 88, 109, 114, 125, 126, and 128—i.e., essentially throughout the system from the coast to a point some 53 km inland. In contrast to later periods, however, there are as yet no detectable maritime sites located in the Coast sector—possibly indicating that such sites, if any, continued to be occupied on a very transitory basis that did not involve the use of ceramic vessels.

Interregional Comparisons

Virú Valley. For the Early-Middle Gallinazo time period in Virú, Willey (1953:101–107) reports on a total of some 41 sites that are contemporaneous with the 130

175

occupations of Early Suchimancillo Period. Of this number, 13 are dated to Early Gallinazo and 28 to Middle Gallinazo. As in the case of the distinction between the Early and Late phases of Puerto Moorin Period, the procedures used by the Virú researchers to distinguish among the three Gallinazo phases were based essentially on changing type percentages resulting from strip matching of seriation charts. Indeed, as Bennett (1950:88) notes, the analysis did not result in the identification of any sherd diagnostics that would distinguish the Early from the Middle phase of Gallinazo. On the other hand, as in the case of Suchimancillo Period Santa Valley, a number of very distinctive ceramic types are present in the Gallinazo assemblage by which the Early-Middle time period can be distinguished from the Late. Because of this, lumping Early and Middle Gallinazo together for comparison to Early Suchimancillo is a reasonable procedure. Based on the assessment of primary or sole function, the main categories (and numbers) of sites resulting from this procedure include the following: living sites (ca. 34 occupations), fortresses (3 occupations), ceremonial-civic sites (3 occupations), and cemeteries (1 occupation).

Interestingly, in his discussion of Gallinazo living sites, Willey (1953:106) notes that the scattered small-house village characteristic of the preceding Guañape and Puerto Moorin Periods does not continue into Early-Middle Gallinazo. In contrast, as noted earlier in this section, in Santa this village type continues from Cayhuamarca and Vinzos Periods on into Early and Late Suchimancillo. Indeed, it may be noted here that habitation sites with scattered dwellings are found in most, if not all, of the later periods in the Santa Valley sequence (e.g., see the Early Tanguche sites of the Santa-Chao Desert, in Fig. 134). But Early Suchimancillo/Gallinazo Santa and Virú are at least similar in that agglutinated villages are one of the principal types of habitation site in both valleys. As implied earlier, however, most of the Early Suchimancillo terraced sites form a distinctive type whose configuration seems more a function of adaptation to areas of steeper terrain than a reflection of varying sociocultural patterns. Nevertheless, the increasing popularity in both valleys of agglutinated villages in relation to sites with more scattered structures may represent some changes in sociocultural patterns—perhaps including the ascendancy of cooperative, extended family households.

Judging from Willey's discussion of Gallinazo living sites, all appear to be similar to the undifferentiated habitation subtype of Santa in that no evidence of possible elite residences is present. However, several Virú sites are characterized by a new type that Willey calls the "Semi-isolated Large House," and it is conceivable that these represent elite residential structures. The Early-Middle Gallinazo time period also marks the rise of eight living sites categorized as "Pyramid-Dwelling-Construction Complexes"—which are described as sites with combined habitation and ceremonial-civic functions. They thus seem clearly comparable to the three Early Suchimancillo Period local centers of the Lower Santa region. V-59/Gallinazo site is the best known of the complexes, with beginnings in Early Gallinazo. By the later part of Gallinazo Period, this massive complex of conjoined habitations and pyramidal platforms had extended over an area of 2–3 km² and contained an estimated population of several thousands of people. V-59 therefore appears to have been at least as large as SVP-ESUCH-126/Huaca Santa (with an estimated 3500 persons), and most probably larger.

One of the most striking contrasts between Virú and Santa during this time period is the much smaller number of fortress sites present in the Virú settlement system. The Early Suchimancillo system contains 42 sites at which defensive works constitute either a primary or secondary function, representing ca. 31% of the 130 sites of the period. In contrast, the three probable defensive sites of Early-Middle Gallinazo—including a hilltop redoubt, a hilltop platform, and a castillo-fortification complex—represent only 7% of the sample of 41 sites. As discussed further in Chapter V, the disparity in numbers of defensive sites clearly suggests a substantially more bellicose adaptive context for Santa Valley as compared to Virú.

With regard to overall settlement patterns, the Early-Middle Gallinazo subsistence-settlement system seems no more complex—and probably less so—than that of the Lower Santa region. This contrasts with the pattern of the preceding Puerto Moorin Period, when the Virú system had substantially more sites distributed over a wider area than did Vinzos Period Santa. A total of some 41 sites is scattered more or less evenly in the main sectors of Virú, with several probable local centers distributed throughout the system. Interestingly enough, as in Puerto Moorin Period, the only fortress structures are located on hills rising above the south desert margin, thus indicating a possible threat of external attack from the south. But, in contrast to Puerto Moorin/Vinzos, when 92% of the main ceramic types of Santa are similar to those of the Virú assemblage, only 25%—or 5 out of 20—principal types of Early Suchimancillo are related on the basis of form, paste, and surface treatment to those of Virú. Moreover, at least one of these types ("Callejón Unclassified") shows sierra-related influences. Assuming that the reduction in numbers of related ceramic types between Santa and Virú from Puerto Moorin/Vinzos to Early-Middle Gallinazo/Early Suchimancillo times is indicative of a corresponding lessening of socioeconomic ties, then at the same time it is equally plausible that external warfare was being conducted between Santa and valleys either to the north or south. (Of course, it will be recalled that an immediately earlier, *pre-*Moche assemblage that is contemporary with Gallinazo and Suchimancillo has yet to be identified in Nepeña.)

A total of 153 discrete sites was identified as belonging to the Late Suchimancillo Period of occupation (Figs. 83–87; for site outline maps see Wilson 1985, Figs. 135–137). As in the preceding period, the number of site types that can be distinguished on the basis of primary or sole function is five—including habitation sites (91 occupations), defensive sites (21 occupations), ceremonial-civic sites (2 occupations), cemeteries (38 occupations), and a subterranean gallery (1 occupation). The two major subtypes that appeared in the preceding period—local centers and minor defensive sites—continue to be present in the settlement system.

Habitation Sites

Undifferentiated occupations. The proportion of occupations in the Late Suchimancillo system with configurations characterized by undifferentiated dwellings is 84 out of the 153 discrete sites—or 55%—which is essentially the same as in Early Suchimancillo (53%). As before, undifferentiated habitation sites are distributed evenly throughout the area of occupation (see SVP-LSUCH-1, 2–9, 12, 14–19, 21–24, 26–31, 33–39, 47–49, 51–53, 55, 56, 58, 63, 64, 68–70, 77, 82, 84, 86–88, 90, 95, 98, 100, 104, 108–110, 114, 117, 119, 121–124, 126–132, 135, 142–148, and 153, in Figs. 84–87). These sites range in size between .1 and 23.4 ha and in population between 5 and 1875 persons—with an average size of 2.9 ha and an average population estimate of 190 persons. The trend toward generally increasing average size and population thus continues from the preceding three ceramic periods (2 ha/140 persons, 1.8 ha/147 persons, and 2.4 ha/160 persons, respectively, for Cayhuamarca, Vinzos, and Early Suchimancillo).

The elevation of habitation sites above the valley floor ranges between 0 and 200 m and distance away from it ranges between 0 and 1900 m—with an average elevation of about 50 m above the floor and an average distance of 175 m away. Thus the trend begun in Cayhuamarca of locating sites in positions that are less-and-less remote in relation to the main source of food and water continues on into Late Suchimancillo. However, as we shall see in discussing Guadalupito and later periods, habitation sites on the average still are relatively remote from the valley floor.

The variety of structural types present on habitation sites appears to have continued essentially unchanged from Early Suchimancillo times—with the main types including (1) smaller sized single-room and multiroom dwellings of rectangular or irregular-polygonal layout, (2) larger agglutinated structures, and (3) windbreaks. However, in relation to some later periods in the se-

quence—when many habitation sites are characterized by perishable structures made entirely of adobe or thatching—nearly all Late Suchimancillo sites have dwellings with rock-walled foundations. Indeed, of the 84 undifferentiated sites, only eight sites (9.5%) are characterized primarily or entirely by scattered debris and an absence of rock-walled dwellings (see site descriptions for SVP-LSUCH-95, 104, 110, 124, 127, 143, 144, and 147, in Wilson 1985, Appendix B). Otherwise, sites generally have excellently preserved rock-walled dwellings, often including both larger agglutinated as well as smaller multiroom structures on the same site.

SVP-LSUCH-9 site, located 3.5 km downriver from the Santa-Tablachaca confluence, provides a good example of the mix of structural types found on a single site (Fig. 68; see also Wilson 1985, Figs. 95, 97). With more extensive occupation dating to Early Suchimancillo Period, this site has been described in some detail under undifferentiated habitations of that period (SVP-ESUCH-1). Nevertheless, to further underscore the remarkable preservation of structures and other remains that characterizes even the earliest sites in the region, it is worth listing some of the main features of SVP-LSUCH-9/SVP-ESUCH-1: (1) intact walls standing to a height of 50–100 cm at nearly all structures; (2) the presence in many structures of two main categories of rooms, including large ones suitable for habitation and smaller ones probably used for storage; (3) additional smaller storage features consisting of rock-lined pits in the floors of dwellings or on the desert surface immediately outside; (4) open, rock-faced terraces in and around structures, indicating probable activity areas; and (5) several kinds of nonceramic artifacts—including grinding stones and lithic debitage—found *in situ*, indicating something of the nature of on-site activities.

As in preceding and later periods, the arrangement and proximity of dwellings on habitation sites seems most likely to have been a function of the terrain as well as the size of local populations—with smaller, more widely scattered structures found on sites where ample areas of gentle slopes or flat ground were available, and conjoined lines of rectangular structures and rock-faced terraces found on sites in steeper terrain. A good example of the first of these two main site configurations is SVP-LSUCH-121, located at the base of a hill on the high desert pampa to the east of the Vinzos Valley floor (see Figs. 86, 88). Structure 91, the principal architectural feature on the site, seems likely to have served primarily as a locus of public functions and is discussed in the section on ceremonial-civic sites (below). However, the remaining structures here consist of a series of five or six widely spaced dwellings that stretch out across the sandy desert surface in a line nearly 200 m long. SVP-LSUCH-153, another site with essentially the same architectural components, lies 16.5 km farther downvalley from SVP-LSUCH-121, on gentle desert slopes overlook-

177

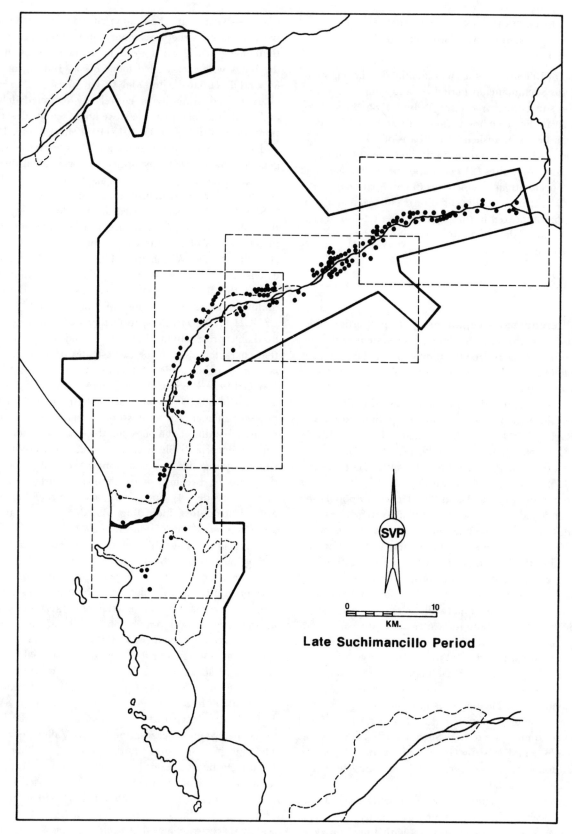

Fig. 83. Location key to settlement pattern maps of Late Suchimancillo Period, Figs. 84–87.

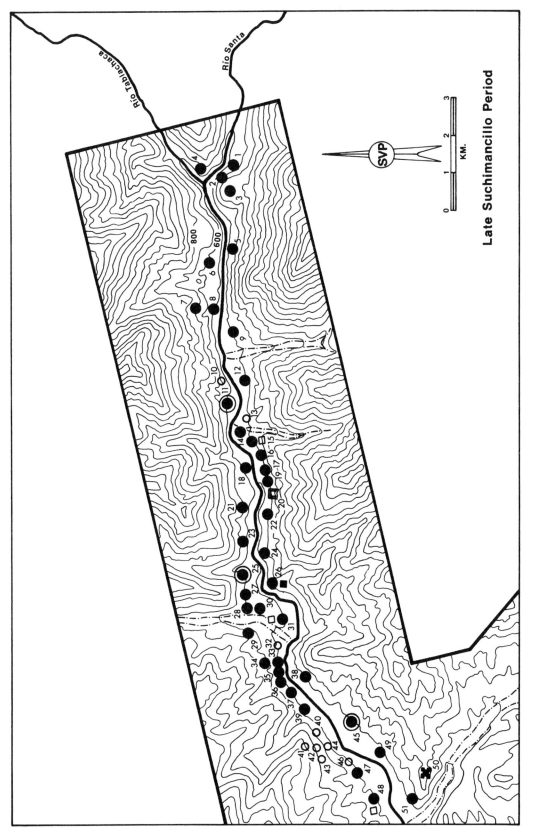

Fig. 84. Settlement pattern map of Late Suchimancillo Period: Upper Valley sector.

179

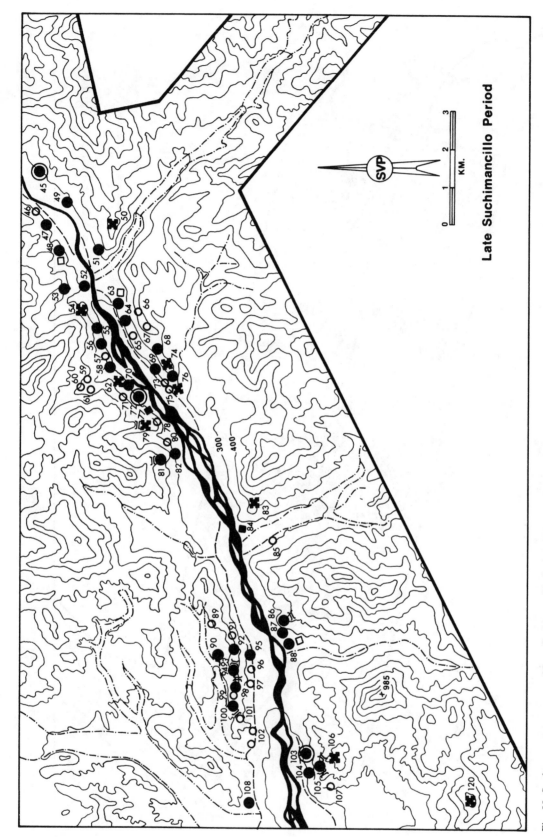

Fig. 85. Settlement pattern map of Late Suchimancillo Period: Upper and Middle Valley sectors.

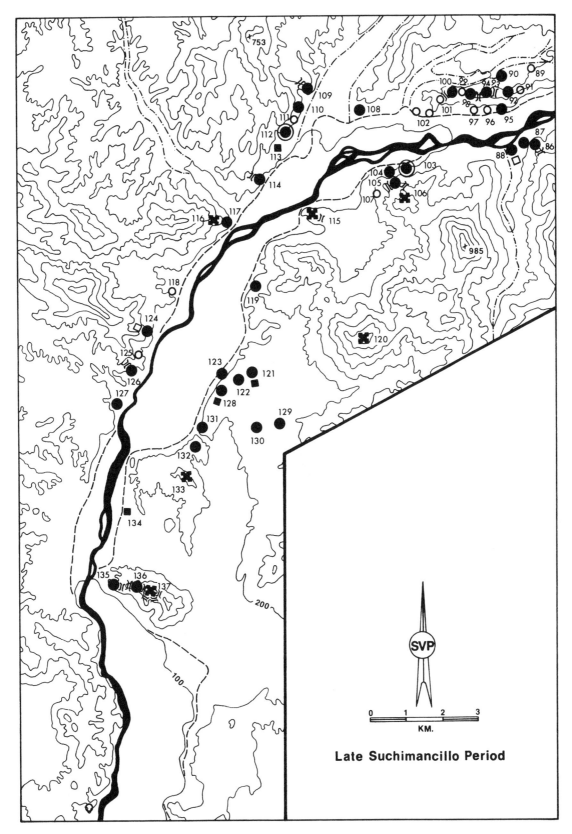

Fig. 86. Settlement pattern map of Late Suchimancillo Period: Middle Valley sector.

181

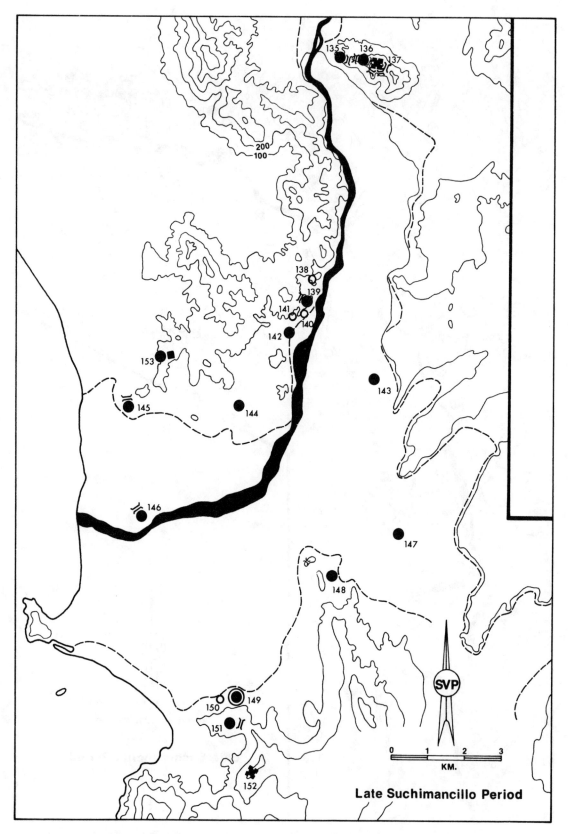

Fig. 87. Settlement pattern map of Late Suchimancillo Period: Lower Valley sector.

182

ing the coastal plain to the north of the Santa Valley mouth (see Fig. 89; see also Wilson 1985, Figs. 140–141).

Local centers. Seven sites are present in the Late Suchimancillo settlement system that on the basis of location, generally larger size, and more complex internal configuration can be classified as supraordinate to the undifferentiated habitation sites discussed above (see SVP-LSUCH-11, 25, 45, 72, 103, 112, and 149, in Figs. 84–87). As shown on the settlement maps, all but one of these sites are located in the Upper and Middle Valley where the great majority of Late Suchimancillo sites are found. However, as in all other periods, local centers are widely distributed throughout the area of occupation. They range in area from 7 to 41 ha and in estimated population size from 490 to 3100 persons, with an average area of 17 ha and an average population of 1700 persons. They are thus much larger in area and population than the other habitation sites of the period. Moreover, each is characterized by specific architectural features—including probable public buildings and elite residential units—that set them apart (and, presumably, hierarchically above) all other surrounding sites.

SVP-LSUCH-11 lies on the north side of the river in one of the more remote areas of the Upper Valley sector. However, it is connected to nearby upvalley and downvalley sites by a trail that, in areas of steeper slopes and cliffs, was literally carved out of the sides of the canyon and shored up with rock-faced terracing. The site itself is located in a pocket of gentler slopes overlooking the river, and contains a circular court feature that makes it unique among all other sites in the local area (see Wilson 1985, Appendix B, for a more detailed description).

SVP-LSUCH-25 is a similar site located nearly 5 km farther downvalley, along the Late Suchimancillo Period trail. Unfortunately, it is too large and complex to have included in our 1979–80 mapping effort. Judging from examination in the field and on the airphoto, however, it contains several large buildings that may have served as foci of elite residence and public activities.

SVP-LSUCH-45 lies 5.5 km farther downvalley, on the opposite side of the river. Judging from associated sherd diagnostics, Late Suchimancillo occupation covers 42 ha of a larger, 62-ha site dating to Early Suchimancillo. It includes associated minor defensive works as well as two large agglutinated residential structures. These latter stand out in some contrast to all other habitation structures on the site, and may therefore have served an elite residential function (e.g., see Structure 5, in Fig. 70; see also discussion of SVP-ESUCH-19, under local centers of Early Suchimancillo).

SVP-LSUCH-72 lies along the north desert margin 6.5 km downvalley from SVP-LSUCH-45. Two large terraced habitation areas covering a total area of 9.5 ha and extensive burial grounds scattered over an additional area of 11.5 ha make this site stand out in relation to

other, generally smaller and less complex occupations located nearby. In addition, SVP-LSUCH-72 has extensive minor defensive works—including long rock walls and dry ditches—that protect sections of the habitation areas of the site.

SVP-LSUCH-103 lies some 11 km farther downvalley, and consists of an intensively terraced and densely inhabited site that covers an area of 12.4 ha, extending for nearly 1 km along steeper desert slopes above the narrow valley floor directly across from Tanguche settlement. With an estimated population of 3100 persons, SVP-LSUCH-103 appears to have contained the most number of people of any site of the period. A small adobe huaca measuring 30 × 10 × 2 m lies on the lower edge of the site, in the east-central sector.

SVP-LSUCH-112/Huaca Yolanda lies across the river to the WNW of SVP-LSUCH-103, and is the sixth in the series of probable local centers (see Plate 16, and Fig. 62). As discussed in the section on Vinzos Period, Huaca Yolanda appears to have had its beginnings in the earliest part of Early Intermediate Period. However, judging from more extensive associated Early and Late Suchimancillo debris and the larger number of occupations dating to each of the two periods, the site reached its maximum use in Suchimancillo times.

SVP-LSUCH-149/Huaca Santa, located over 30 km downvalley from Huaca Yolanda, is the last in the series of local centers (see Fig. 71). Judging from field assessments and extensive surface collections here, Late Suchimancillo occupation covers an area of only 14.2 ha, or about 20% of the area estimated to have been covered by Early Suchimancillo occupation. It is difficult to assess whether this seemingly abrupt change in site size is an artifact of later, overlying occupation or whether in fact it represents a reduced population (Note: support for the argument that our assessment of Late Suchimancillo occupation is essentially correct comes from the fact that no habitation debris dating to the following Guadalupito and Early Tanguche Period was found here at all; thus, the hiatus of occupation between Late Suchimancillo and the last three periods in the sequence suggests that Huaca Santa was "temporarily" dying out by the end of Suchimancillo times). The Late Suchimancillo site contains a large enclosure that may have served as a corral (see Wilson 1985, Fig. 151). The relatively larger size of the occupation as well as extensive associated defensive works (see SVP-LSUCH-151, 152, in Fig. 87) indicate a position of probable paramount importance in the local Lower Valley settlement system.

Defensive Sites

Late Suchimancillo is the last period in the sequence when a substantial number of defensive sites appears to have played an important role in the settlement system. As summarized in Table 8, defensive works are present

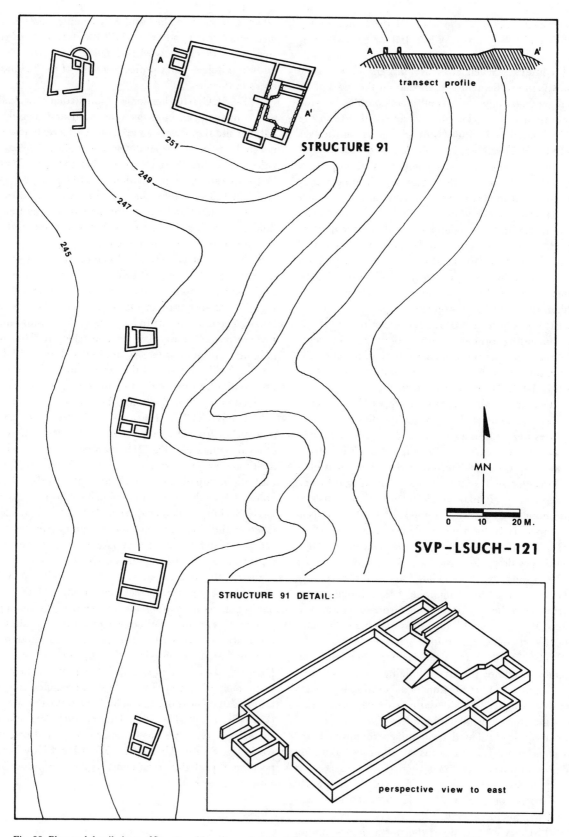

Fig. 88. Plan and detail views of Structure 91 and associated buildings at SVP-LSUCH-121, a site with public and habitation functions.

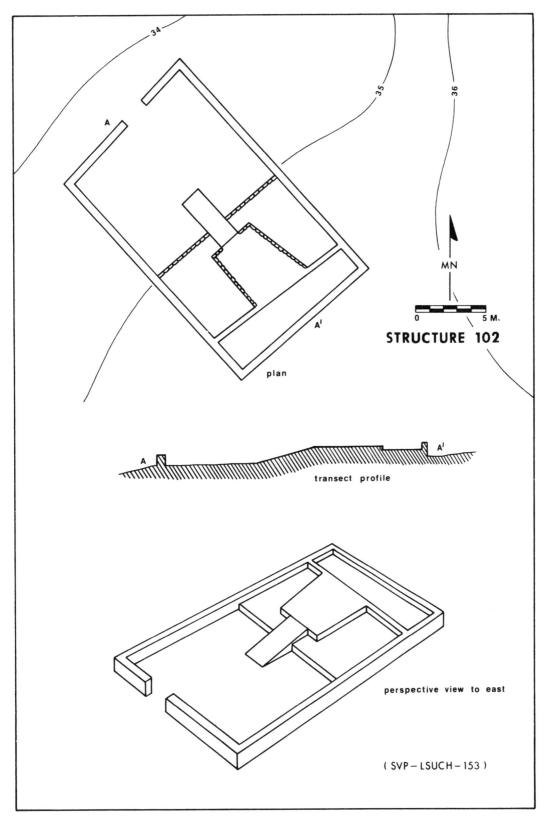

STRUCTURE 102

0   5 M.

MN

plan

transect profile

perspective view to east

(SVP – LSUCH – 153)

Fig. 89. Three views of Structure 102, a probable ceremonial-civic building at SVP-LSUCH-153. Note similarity to Structure 91.

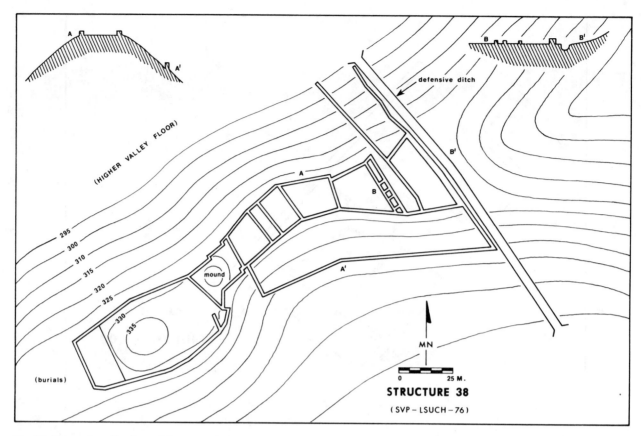

Fig. 90. Plan and profile views of Structure 38 citadel.

at a total of 32 sites—including 14 citadels as well as 18 sites with minor defensive constructions. Although this number represents a drop of 10 sites from the number apparently occupied in Early Suchimancillo, the two types of fortresses continue to be distributed throughout the area of occupation between Quebrada de Cayhuamarca and the ocean (see Figs. 84–87; see also Wilson 1985, Fig. 90, for defensive sites on Cerro Loreto ridge). With respect to average location away from the valley floor, Late Suchimancillo defensive sites are comparable to those of Early Suchimancillo in being located generally closer to the main source of food and water than Cayhuamarca and Vinzos fortresses. They range in distance between 50 and 3500 m away from the floor, with an average of 640 m away (compared to 1000 m, 1200 m, and 590 m, respectively, in Cayhuamarca, Vinzos, and Early Suchimancillo). Elevations range between 50 and 750 m above the floor, with an average of 215 m (compared to 243 m, 255 m, and 205 m, respectively, in the preceding three periods).

Citadels. Interestingly enough, judging from sherd diagnostics associated with citadel structures of the region, only three such sites appear to have been built in Late Suchimancillo Period (see SVP-LSUCH-76/Structure 38, in Fig. 90; and SVP-LSUCH-152/Structures 60 and

61 in Wilson 1985, Fig. 144). As shown in Fig. 90, Structure 38 is one of the largest citadels of any period—with rock walls enclosing an area nearly 200 m long and 20–40 m wide, and a 150 m-long defensive ditch protecting the exposed northeastern flank of the site. This citadel lies on the lower, downvalley point of Cayhuamarca-Panteón ridge, which it will be recalled is the location of four major Cayhuamarca Period citadels (e.g., see SVP-CAY-21, 23, 25, and 26, in Fig. 23). Structures 60 and 61, the other two citadels of apparent Late Suchimancillo date, lie atop adjacent peaks on Cerro Huamachacata in rugged mountainous terrain immediately to the south of Huaca Santa site (see SVP-LSUCH-149, 152, in Wilson 1985, Fig. 144). Both citadels are reasonably impressive in terms of size (dimensions are 45 × 32 m and 42 × 31 m, respectively), but each is relatively quite simple in plan compared to other citadels occupied in this and earlier periods. Indeed, a general lack of associated debris and other structural remains indicates the likelihood of only transitory occupation of the site.

Of the remaining 11 citadels containing evidence of Late Suchimancillo use: six date from Cayhuamarca Period, with additional occupation in the intervening Vinzos and/or Early Suchimancillo Periods (see SVP-LSUCH-50, 74, 83, 106, 120, and 133, in Figs. 84–86; for specific citadels, see Structures 6, 35, 52, 55, 90, and 95,

186

in Figs. 32, 39, 43–44, 45, 48, and 49, respectively); and five date from Early Suchimancillo Period (see SVP-LSUCH-54, 62, 115, 137, and 151, in Figs. 84–87; for specific citadels, see Structures 7, 39, and 56, in Figs. 72, 73, and 74). The estimates of population size for all 14 Late Suchimancillo citadel occupations range in number between 0 and 270 persons, with an average of 118 persons per site (compared to an estimated average of 110 inhabitants per site in both Early Suchimancillo and Cayhuamarca Periods).

Minor defensive sites. As in the case of Early Suchimancillo Period, minor defensive sites form an important part of the fortifications of Late Suchimancillo—with the main subgroups in this category including (1) eight sites whose primary function appears to have been defensive in nature, and whose average population estimate is 45 persons (see SVP-LSUCH-81, 92, 93, 94, 105, 116, 136, and 139, in Figs. 85–87); and (2) 10 habitation sites at which minor defensive works form an integral, but secondary, part of the overall occupation (see SVP-LSUCH-58, 72, 86, 98, 100, 109, 114, 126, 135, and 146, in Figs. 85–87).

In comparison to the citadel structures, a larger number of minor defensive works appear to have been constructed in Late Suchimancillo—with nine sites dating to this period alone and nine dating from the preceding period. Their general location remains the same as in Early Suchimancillo, with virtually all of them situated on high, narrow ridges in the rugged terrain rising within a kilometer or so of the valley floor. And as in the preceding period, minor defensive works include dry ditches and bulwark walls wherever necessary to protect against attack via relatively gentle access slopes.

In some contrast to the rock-walled defensive works of Early Suchimancillo, however, Late Suchimancillo marks the appearance of at least one adobe structure that can be interpreted as a defensive site (Structure 57/SVP-LSUCH-116, Fig. 91). Structure 57, or "Huaca El Cenicero" as it is called by the inhabitants of nearby Tanguche, lies on a narrow ridge accessible from the valley floor only by climbing very steep, rocky slopes rising over 125 m in elevation. SVP-LSUCH-81 site (Fig. 85; for site plan see Wilson 1985, Fig. 145), located 14 km upvalley, is similar to Huaca El Cenicero in having reasonably impressive architectural remains—at least in terms of their overall extent of 55 × 35 m—but little associated debris is present to indicate anything other than transitory use by people of nearby habitation sites.

Ceremonial-Civic Sites

An impressive number of structures with a primarily ceremonial-civic function was present in the Lower Santa region by the time of Late Suchimancillo Period. As in all other later periods, however, while people may well

have made use of earlier sites for public activities, one is constrained to limit hypothesized times of primary use to those periods for which concrete evidence is present—in the form of either sherd diagnostics or specific architectural features such as adobes and wall types. Using these criteria, six ceremonial-civic structures appear to have been constructed in Late Suchimancillo Period (see SVP-LSUCH-77, 84, 121, 128, 134, and 153, in Figs. 85–87). In addition, judging from associated sherds, continuing use appears to have been made of Structure 51 pyramidal mound at SVP-LSUCH-113/SVP-ESUCH-90 (see Fig. 77). In relation to the numbers of occupations given at the beginning of this section on Late Suchimancillo site types, it should be noted that only two of the seven total ceremonial-civic structures constitute discrete sites located apart from other types of occupation—namely, SVP-LSUCH-113 and SVP-LSUCH-134. In fact, all of the rest form a part of smaller habitation sites (one small village and four hamlets) whose primary function was not ceremonial-civic.

In spite of the small number of ceremonial-civic structures apparently built in this period, a wide variety of structural types is present—including (1) adobe castillos built into the side of desert hills at the edge of the valley floor (see Structures 40 and 96, in Figs. 92 and 94); (2) rock-walled enclosures with interior rubble-and-adobe platforms at one end (see Structures 91 and 102, in Figs. 88 and 89); (3) a free-standing pyramidal mound and associated platform (see Structure 53, in Fig. 93); and (4) a rock-walled, U-shaped platform (see Structure 93 in Wilson 1985, Fig. 148).

As mentioned with regard to Structure 57/Huaca El Cenicero in the preceding section, the first adobe castillos in Santa Valley appear in the Late Suchimancillo Period. In keeping with the general definition of these structures by archaeologists working in other North Coast valleys, *castillos* are distinguished from other adobe structures by their usually commanding position either on ridges and hilltops high above the valley or built into the edge of the steeper desert margin adjacent to the floor. Considering their location, the name "castillo" (castle-fortress) was probably applied to some of these structures by local inhabitants who *assumed* their function was related to defense. Nevertheless, the only castillo structure in the Lower Santa region for which such a function can be hypothesized with a reasonable degree of certainty is Huaca El Cenicero itself—and primarily because of its ridgetop location. In contrast, two other castillos in the settlement system—including Structure 40 (Fig. 92) and Structure 96 (Fig. 94)—are located adjacent to the valley floor in exposed, nondefensible positions. Furthermore, there is no evidence that either was surrounded by enclosure walls. It therefore seems highly likely that they served a public or religious function for people at nearby sites, rather than a defensive one.

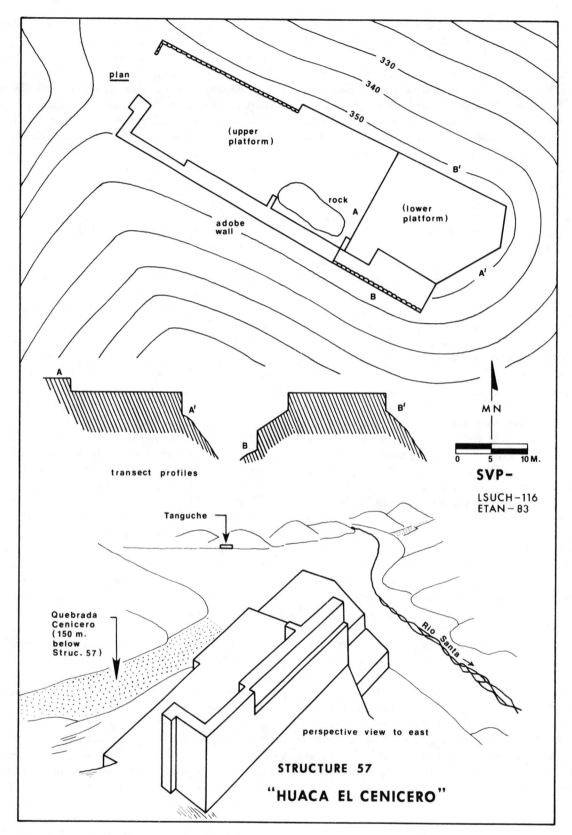

plan

330
340
350

(upper
platform)

B'

rock   A

(lower
platform)

adobe
wall

B

A'

A

A'

B'

B

transect profiles

MN

0   5   10 M.

SVP-

LSUCH-116
ETAN-83

Tanguche

Quebrada
Cenicero
(150 m.
below
Struc. 57)

Rio Santa

perspective view to east

STRUCTURE 57

"HUACA EL CENICERO"

Fig. 91. Three views of Structure 57/SVP-LSUCH-116.

The probable ceremonial-civic function of the rock-walled enclosures with interior platforms has been mentioned earlier, in the section on Late Suchimancillo habitation sites. These enclosures (see SVP-LSUCH-121 and SVP-LSUCH-153, in Figs. 88 and 89) are quite unlike nearby structures for which a habitation function is inferred—both in terms of the general absence of occupational debris and their distinct configuration. However, since this structural type is unique to Late Suchimancillo Period in the survey region, and to my knowledge has not been reported for other valleys, it is difficult to suggest what type of public function was served (Note: as we shall see later, this doubt about function may be contrasted sharply with larger Guadalupito/Moche huacas, which from associated debris and iconography of the period can be interpreted with some confidence).

Structure 53/SVP-LSUCH-84 (Fig. 93), the single free-standing pyramidal mound of apparent Late Suchimancillo date, lies on a low ridge overlooking the narrow valley floor at the mouth of Quebrada La Huaca (indeed, the name of the wash is derived from the mound). Although it is one of the largest huacas of the pre-Guadalupito time period, Structure 53 is roughly similar in overall configuration to pyramidal structures of Early Suchimancillo (e.g., see Structure 51, in Fig. 77), and continues the tradition begun as early as Cayhuamarca times of locating such structures either on the edge of the desert margin or in the midst of irrigated fields down on the valley floor.

Cemetery Sites

As in many other aspects of their subsistence-settlement systems, Late Suchimancillo and Early Suchimancillo are quite similar with respect to burial practices. Among these similarities are the presence of substantial amounts of kaolin ware in graves and the widespread use of rock-lined tombs of quadrilateral or, more often, pentagonal or hexagonal plan. These tombs are universally small in size, with a diameter averaging around 50 cm and a depth of 50–75 cm, suggesting either secondary or very tightly flexed burials. Although many cemeteries are so badly damaged that the nature of tomb architecture is difficult to ascertain, rock-lined tombs appear to have been in widespread use throughout much of the area of Late Suchimancillo occupation—specifically including some 40% of all burial sites of the period (compared to about 20% in Early Suchimancillo). The distribution of these tombs is encompassed within the 28 km-long area between Quebrada del Silencio and the upper part of the Vinzos valley floor (see the area from SVP-LSUCH-32 to SVP-LSUCH-118, in Figs. 84–86). As the settlement and demographic maps of the period show, in many ways this area may viewed as the "heart" of the Late Suchimancillo system. For example, the area of greatest

variety and concentration of kaolin and other distinctive wares of the period is roughly coextensive with this part of the Upper and Middle Valley.

Late Suchimancillo cemetery sites are not limited to the area of principal occupational density and complexity, however. As shown in Figs. 84–87, these sites extend for a distance of 60 km along the valley floor between SVP-LSUCH-10 (located 5.5 km below the Santa-Tablachaca confluence) and SVP-LSUCH-150 (located just inland from the ocean in the western part of Huaca Santa). A total of 56 Late Suchimancillo cemeteries was found in this overall area, including the following two principal categories: (1) 38 single-function burial sites, located on ridgetops, steeper rocky slopes, or in and alongside the lower reaches of quebradas (see SVP-LSUCH-10, 13, 32, 40–44, 46, 57, 59, 60, 61, 65–67, 71, 73, 75, 78–80, 85, 89, 91, 96, 97, 99, 101, 102, 107, 111, 118, 125, 138, 140, 141, and 150, in Figs. 83–87); and (2) 18 nondiscrete burial sites which are part of larger occupations whose primary functions included habitation and/or defense (see SVP-LSUCH-35, 36, 45, 51, 55, 58, 68, 72, 81, 82, 95, 105, 110, 117, 127, 135, 139, and 147, in Figs. 84–87).

Other Remains: Corral Features

As discussed in the section on Early Suchimancillo site types, the first probable corral features in the Lower Santa region coincide with what appears to be the beginning of intensive contacts with people of the adjacent sierra. As argued earlier, the suggested function of enclosing animals as well as the identity of these animals seem abundantly clear from the ground drawings of llamas found at SVP-ESUCH-112 (see Fig. 80). Indeed, the argument for further development and intensification of contacts with the sierra (and probably within-region socioeconomic relations as well) is supported by a substantial rise in numbers of these corral features—i.e., from only two such features in Early Suchimancillo Period to seven in Late Suchimancillo.

It is of some significance to note that in the intensively occupied Upper and Middle Valley sectors sites with corrals are spaced alongside ancient trails on both sides of the river at more or less regular intervals, ranging from 5–11 km apart (see SVP-LSUCH-15, 31, 48, 63, 88, and 124, in Figs. 84–86). As discussed in the next chapter, this seems to imply not only a degree of regularity in coast-sierra socioeconomic interaction but also a measure of central planning or coordination at the regional level. However, it is also important to note that the only local center with a probable corral feature is SVP-LSUCH-149/Huaca Santa (see Fig. 71; for a plan view see Wilson 1985, Fig. 151). The rest of the sites where these features are found are either hamlets or small villages. This suggests the possibility that corral sites functioned more as way stations along the major communica-

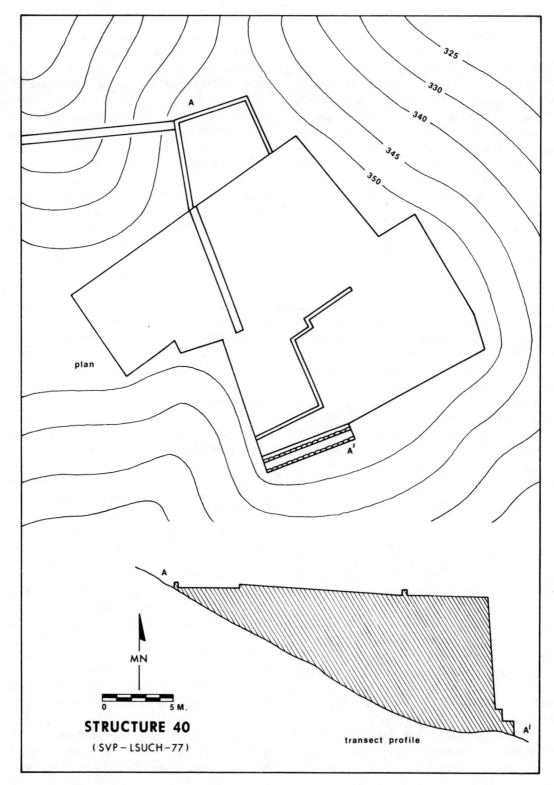

plan

A

A'

MN

0   5 M.

STRUCTURE 40

(SVP – LSUCH–77)

A

A'

transect profile

Fig. 92. Plan and profile views of Structure 40 huaca.

190

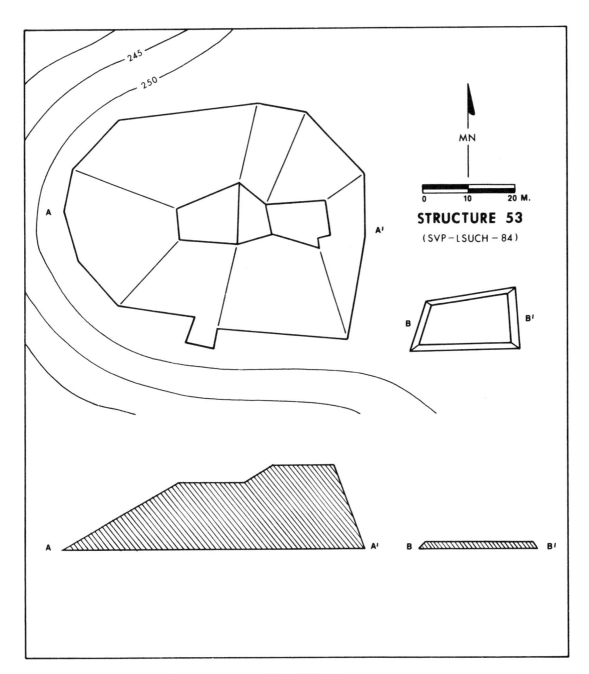

Fig. 93. Plan and profile views of huaca structures at SVP-LSUCH-84.

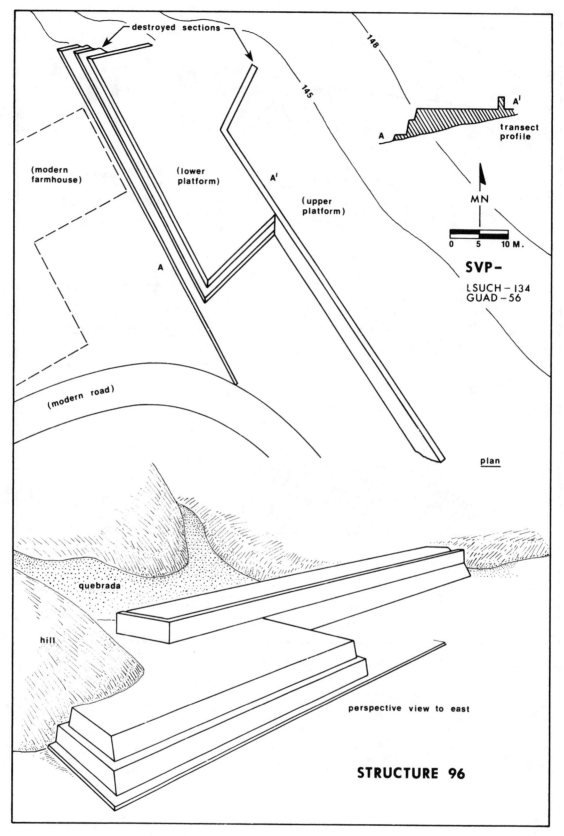

Fig. 94. Three views of Structure 96 huaca.

tion routes (i.e., similar to Inca *tambos*) on each side of the river than as foci of local redistribution of trade goods.

A good example of a probable corral is provided by Structure 114/SVP-LSUCH-15, located alongside a very well preserved section of ancient trail overlooking the south side of the Upper Valley canyon (for general location, see Fig. 84). As shown in the plan view (Fig. 95), a few smaller structures are attached to this large 39 × 34-m rock-walled enclosure (similar to Structure 110 at SVP-LSUCH-31/SVP-ESUCH-10; see Fig. 82)—indicating possible minor habitation and/or storage. However, the rest of the interior is free of structural remains and occupational debris, thus standing in contrast to other, smaller structures scattered elsewhere across the site that clearly served a habitation function (the population estimate for this site is 200 persons). The narrow upcanyon trail runs across the site, downslope 15 m to the north of Structure 114—suggesting that the corral was strategically located alongside the route followed by llama trains.

Other Remains: Subterranean Gallery

One of the more intriguing architectural features of any period in the sequence is the subterranean gallery located on the south side of the river in the central part of the narrow Upper Valley canyon (see SVP-LSUCH-20/Feature Y, in Figs. 84, 96). As shown in the detail drawings, Feature Y lies just below the ground surface at the edge of a rocky bluff overlooking the river (and the narrow modern road cut). Three kinds of evidence are present that date this feature more or less precisely to Late Suchimancillo—including (1) scattered sherd diagnostics of this period found on the boulder-covered surface of the bluff above the gallery, (2) the presence of large numbers of Late Suchimancillo sites in the immediate vicinity, and (3) a remarkable similarity to subterranean galleries of Recuay Period in the Callejón de Huaylas (cf. Bennett 1944; see also SVP-LSUCH-20 site description, in Wilson 1985).

It is rather more difficult, however, to pinpoint with any reasonable degree of certainty what the function of the gallery was—beyond suggesting the likelihood that it did not have anything to do with burial or normal habitation. For example, no associated human skeletal remains or funerary pottery were noted that would suggest use as a burial chamber. Likewise, although a wealth of well preserved Late Suchimancillo habitation remains is available for comparison throughout the area of occupation, no feature even remotely resembling this one is present anywhere else. Among various possible functions, it may be very speculatively suggested that the gallery served as a special place of priestly elite habitation—perhaps involving an oracle.

Settlement and Demographic Patterns

Just as the Vinzos system is closely analogous to Cayhuamarca in terms of overall extent, numbers, and types of settlements, so too is the Late Suchimancillo system similar to Early Suchimancillo in much the same ways. As shown in Figs. 172 and 173, the Late Suchimancillo subsistence-settlement system is characterized by a very densely settled Upper Valley sector, with additional substantial numbers of people in the Middle and Lower Valley. Except for a gap on both sides of the river in the Pampa Blanca area, sites are now distributed nearly continuously along both desert margins in the 47-km distance between the Santa-Tablachaca confluence and the lowermost part of the Middle Valley. But, whereas nearly 90% of Early Suchimancillo occupations were new sites not inhabited or used in Vinzos, only 62% of Late Suchimancillo sites are new—indicating a greater degree of conservatism in spite of the overall expansion of the system.

With regard to the nature of site types, Late Suchimancillo exhibits fundamental similarities to all of the preceding ceramic periods, especially in terms of the close association nearly everywhere in the system between defensive and habitation sites. For example, citadels and minor defensive sites are distributed throughout all of Late Suchimancillo Clusters 2 and 3. On the other hand, the only occupied fortress sites found in the uppermost area of occupation are located in the lower third of Cluster 1. Given the fact that the uppermost defensive structures commence roughly at the point where the steep narrow canyon walls of the Upper Valley begin to open up, as the river descends toward the Middle Valley, it may well be the case that the canyon itself provided a natural defensive barrier against attack (Note: in contrast to Late Suchimancillo, the presence in the Upper Valley canyon of Cayhuamarca and Vinzos citadels—including those in Cayhuamarca Cluster 1 and Vinzos Cluster 1—may be explainable by the relatively much lower population numbers characterizing the pre-Suchimancillo systems of this sector).

Considering the fact that defensive sites are located everywhere else in the system from this point on down to the coast, it appears likely that the only threat of external attack was from adjacent coastal valleys and not from out of the nearby sierra. Moreover, given the clear indication that of all periods in the sequence this is the one of strongest ties to the adjacent sierra (see discussion below), there probably would have been no need for defensive structures in the upper two-thirds part of the Upper Valley canyon.

Late Suchimancillo is the first period in which there is a close association between single-component sites and the extant remains of ancient routes of travel (specifically, trails) along the north and south desert margins.

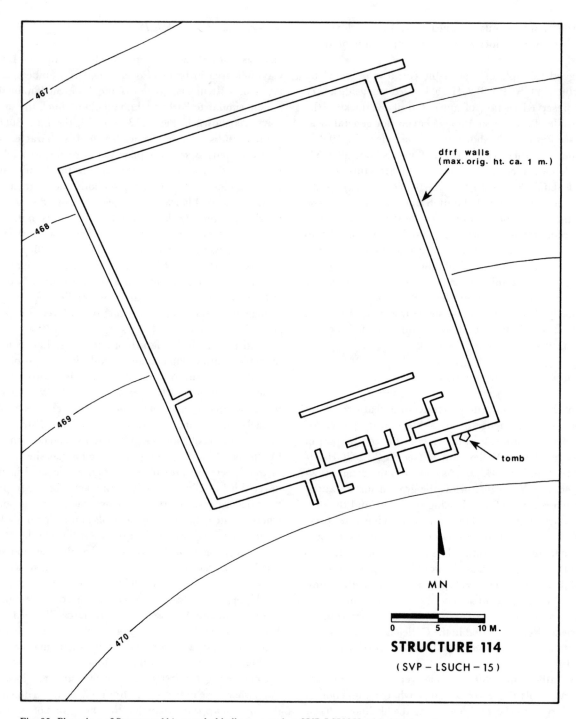

467

468

469

470

dfrf walls
(max. orig. ht. ca. 1 m.)

tomb

M N

0   5   10 M.

STRUCTURE 114

(SVP – LSUCH – 15)

Fig. 95. Plan view of Structure 114, a probable llama corral at SVP-LSUCH-15 habitation site.

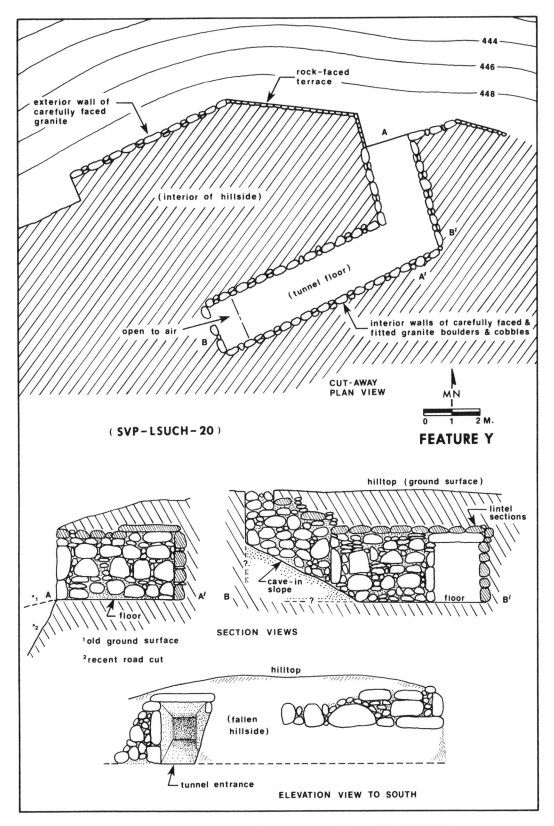

444

446

448

exterior wall of
carefully faced
granite

rock-faced
terrace

A

(interior of hillside)

B'

(tunnel floor)

A'

open to air

interior walls of carefully faced &
fitted granite boulders & cobbles

B

(SVP-LSUCH-20)

CUT-AWAY
PLAN VIEW

MN

0   1   2 M.

FEATURE Y

hilltop (ground surface)

lintel
sections

¹A

A'

cave-in
slope

floor

B'

floor

B

old ground surface

recent road cut

SECTION VIEWS

hilltop

(fallen
hillside)

tunnel entrance

ELEVATION VIEW TO SOUTH

Fig. 96. Plan, section, and elevation views of Feature Y subterranean gallery at SVP-LSUCH-20.

These routes run along the lower part of steep canyon slopes on both sides of the river in Cluster 1, in an area where all or the great majority of sites date to Late Suchimancillo. As discussed earlier in this section, a series of local centers and smaller habitation sites with probable llama corrals is distributed at short intervals of 5–11 km along these ancient routes. The local centers indicate a continuation from Early Suchimancillo times of supraordinate sites in the developing sociopolitical hierarchy. At the same time, the corral sites and trails probably indicate the formal establishment of interregional and within-valley communication routes, along which passed llama trains laden with agricultural products (e.g., maize and cotton from Santa) and ceramics (e.g., Recuay-related wares from the Callejón de Huaylas).

With regard to the distributional pattern of local centers, it may be noted that the complexity of the Late Suchimancillo system clearly appears to be an outgrowth of developments that took place in the preceding period—with only three very widely scattered local centers in Early Suchimancillo and a total of nine much more closely spaced centers in Late Suchimancillo. Given the population distribution in the three settlement clusters of Late Suchimancillo (see Fig. 173), it does not seem unexpected that these centers are distributed more or less in accordance with the number and density of settlements—with four local centers in Cluster 1, two in Cluster 2, and only one in Cluster 3. Thus, while many Late Suchimancillo cultural diagnostics are distributed throughout the system (e.g., see the following section on ceramic distributions), it appears that the complexity of the system was greatest in the area nearest to the adjacent sierra region—with which socioeconomic ties probably were much stronger than with any adjacent coastal valley.

The distribution of the nearly 30,000 people estimated to have inhabited the Late Suchimancillo system is one of the most intriguing of all periods in the sequence. It will be recalled from the chapter on the socioenvironmental setting that the distribution of irrigable land in the main valley area is as follows: 470 ha in the Upper Valley, 1430 ha in the Middle Valley, and 9405 ha in the Lower Valley (see Table 2). Yet, contrary to what one might "logically" expect, the Late Suchimancillo population is distributed in nearly exact *inverse* proportion to the distribution of irrigable land—with 19,085 persons estimated to have inhabited sites of the Upper Valley, 7395 persons in the Middle Valley, and 3285 persons in the Lower Valley.

With regard to the dating of the sites constituting the Late Suchimancillo system, it should be emphasized strongly that nothing in the settlement pattern of this period argues against the essential contemporaneity of most if not all sites. For example, the large population of the uppermost sector has ample precedent in the population size established by Early Suchimancillo times in the

area. Thus, while the Early Suchimancillo population estimate for the Upper Valley area (11,045 persons) represents over 2.5 times the Vinzos estimate (2960 persons), that of Late Suchimancillo (19,085 persons) represents an increase of only 1.7 times over Early Suchimancillo. (Note: the population distribution by cluster, rather than sector as given above, is 18,835 persons, 7645 persons, and 3285 persons, respectively, for Late Suchimancillo Clusters 1, 2, and 3). Indeed, nothing in the ceramics noted in any inhabited sector argues against the contemporaneity of Late Suchimancillo sites, with a fairly strong degree of uniformity noted from site to site.

Finally, with regard to the nature of warfare in this period, the continuous distribution of settlements in Clusters 1 and 2 strongly suggests that conflict was not occurring among sites on one or the other side of the river (see following section for arguments against across-valley warfare). Nor does between-cluster warfare seem likely, given the strong disparity in the population sizes of the three clusters. Instead, it is probable that the threat of attack continued to come from outside the region.

Ceramic Distributions

The number and diversity of diagnostic Late Suchimancillo ceramic types exhibit the same increase in complexity that characterizes other features of the developing subsistence-settlement system of the region. For example, from a total of 20 principal time markers in the preceding period, the number now rises to 28, with a distribution at least as complex as that of Early Suchimancillo if not more so. As in the case of the preceding period, it is useful to categorize the distributions of ceramic types linking settlements according to four varying degrees of areal extent. These distributional categories include (1) types that are very widespread throughout Clusters 1, 2, and 3 (Late Suchimancillo Jar 7 and various kaolin wares); (2) types that are more or less widespread, but not quite as uniformly distributed in the three settlement clusters as those in the first category (Late Suchimancillo Bowls 5, 6; Jars 4, 5b, 5e, 5f; and human effigy neck vessels); (3) types that are more restricted in distribution, including most of Cluster 2 and the lower half of Cluster 1 (Late Suchimancillo Bowl 4; Jars 2, 5a, 5c, 5d, and Jar 6/Broad Band White-on-Red); and (4) types that are primarily or wholly restricted to the uppermost part of Cluster 2 and the lower half of Cluster 1 (Late Suchimancillo Bowls 1, 2; and animal effigies).

As implied by the distributional categories, Late Suchimancillo is similar to the earlier ceramic periods in that the greatest number and diversity of types continues to be centered on the Quebrada de Cayhuamarca area. But the Late Suchimancillo pattern also differs from that of Early Suchimancillo, for example, in exhibiting a more

196

marked falloff in number and diversity of types immediately upvalley from Quebrada del Silencio. Nevertheless, the distribution from Quebrada de Cayhuamarca on *downvalley* is characterized by the same gradual reduction in number and diversity of types found in the preceding period. Among other things, the overall pattern suggests that the primary focus of internal innovation and/or contact with other regions was now even more strongly centered on Quebrada de Cayhuamarca, which has been suggested earlier as the principal communication route between people of the Lower Santa region and those of the adjacent sierra.

Two other distributional patterns are of interest to note here. First, Late Suchimancillo is the period of the greatest number of sites where whole Spondylus shells are found—including SVP-LSUCH-107, 116, and 135, all of which are located in Cluster 2. The presence of these shells appears to indicate that, in addition to maintaining strong ties with the nearby sierra, the Lower Santa region was part of more far-flung trading networks that included contact with the sources of Spondylus in warm Ecuadorian waters hundreds of kilometers to the north.

Second, as in Early Suchimancillo, the analysis of the Late Suchimancillo ceramic maps shows that the pattern of type distributions changes almost entirely as a function of increasing distance upvalley and downvalley from the lower half of Cluster 1, and not with respect to the different sides of the valley—i.e., both the north and south desert margins share the same diversity and numbers of types, and distributions on both sides covary as a function of distance away from the apparent cultural "heart" of the system. Among other things, this second pattern suggests that strong cross-river contacts continued to be maintained between groups of each desert margin, and that there is no support for an argument of across-valley conflict. Indeed, it is worth noting that strong cross-river ties are maintained today between people of Suchimancillo (north side) and Tablones (south side). These contacts apparently include kinship ties, judging from comments made to us in our preparations to use the cable-seat crossing of that area.

Inferences About Subsistence

As in the case of Early Suchimancillo Period, well preserved maize cobs are found on a few sites—including at least one single-component occupation (SVP-LSUCH-105) as well as several mixed contexts where additional ceramics dating to earlier and later periods are present (e.g., see SVP-LSUCH-103/SVP-ESUCH-84 and SVP-LSUCH-143/SVP-GUAD-93, in Wilson 1985, Appendix B). Late Suchimancillo is the latest of several periods associated with sections of the Quebrada del Silencio and Condór Cerro canal systems (see Figs. 7, 8), and intensive agriculture probably had been developed as fully as

possible in the upvalley canyon by this time period. Finally, as in the case of all preceding periods, marine shells are found on a number of sites located well inland from the ocean (e.g., see SVP-LSUCH-28, located in the Quebrada del Silencio area).

Interregional Comparisons

Virú Valley. In his tabular summary of Late Gallinazo sites in Virú, Willey (1953:177) lists a total of some 62 sites that are contemporaneous with the 153 occupations of Late Suchimancillo Period. Based on the assessment of primary or sole function, the main categories of site types include the following: living sites (54 occupations), fortresses (5 occupations), and ceremonial-civic sites (3 occupations). It should be noted that 12 of the living sites consist of Pyramid-Dwelling-Construction Complexes, which appear to be quite similar in inferred function to local centers of Santa Valley. Interestingly, in contrast to the presence of rock-walled dwellings at nearly all habitation sites of Late Suchimancillo Santa (i.e., at ca. 90%, or 83 out of 91), a much greater variety of inhabited occupations is present in Late Gallinazo Virú. These include (1) 12 habitation sites with well preserved rock-walled dwellings, most of which are located in the upper valley; (2) 25 sites of a more amorphous nature that appear to consist largely of adobe-walled buildings, and include all of the Pyramid-Dwelling-Construction Complexes; and (3) 17 sites that consist entirely of midden or earth-refuse accumulations.

By far the largest concentration of Late Gallinazo adobe-walled constructions in Virú is that centered in a 5-km² area around and to the south of V-59/Gallinazo site. Numerous adobe pyramidal mounds are located in this huge complex, in addition to extensive groups of dwellings with a characteristic "honeycomb" pattern that appears to have excluded the use of intervening passageways, corridors, or plazas. Given population estimates in a magnitude of many thousands of people for the Gallinazo Group of sites (e.g., the estimates of discrete rooms alone, based on sample excavations, run as high as 30,000; cf. Bennett 1950:68–69; Willey 1953), there appears to have been a more pronounced development of urbanism in Virú Valley than in Santa during the latest part of the pre-state sequence.

Among other distinctive aspects of the Late Gallinazo settlement system are the following: (1) the presence of only five sites with an inferred defensive function, including four large adobe castillos situated in two widely spaced groups on each side of the narrows leading from the middle to the upper valley (in contrast to 32 discrete, widely distributed defensive sites in Santa); and (2) the complete absence of discrete single-function burial sites, with cemeteries apparently restricted to habitation sites (in contrast to Santa, where both types of cemetery sites are present).

With regard to overall settlement pattern, Late Gallinazo Period appears to represent a time of significant increase in sociocultural complexity compared to the preceding Early-Middle Gallinazo system—especially considering the appearance of the large urban sprawl at V-59/Gallinazo site in lower Virú. But, judging from the fact that the total number of 62 Late Gallinazo occupations constitutes only 40% of the total number dating to Late Suchimancillo Santa, it is likely that the subsistence-settlement system of the latter valley was at least as complex as that of Virú Valley, if not more so. In any case, given the strong indication of an extensive and well developed defensive system in Santa, it is highly unlikely that a multivalley Gallinazo state including Santa and Virú ever existed. Nevertheless, the Lower Santa ceramic assemblage of this period exhibits reasonably strong similarities to that of Virú (50%, or 14 out of 28 types, are similar in form, paste, and surface treatment to those of Virú), and even stronger ties are indicated with the adjacent sierra (including nearly all kaolin types). In the apparent absence of any ties with valleys to the south and assuming that warfare was an interregional phenomenon, it is therefore probable that the threat of external attack continued as in earlier periods to be from valleys to the south.

GUADALUPITO PERIOD (HUANCACO/LATE EIP)

A total of 205 discrete sites was identified as belonging to the Guadalupito Period of occupation (Figs. 97–103; for site outline maps see Wilson 1985, Figs. 160–162). Primarily due to the clear lack of evidence that any defensive sites were built or occupied in this period, the number of site types that can be distinguished on the basis of primary or sole function drops for the first time in the sequence. Only three of the four basic types of the Late Suchimancillo system therefore continue into Guadalupito Period—including habitation sites (83 occupations), ceremonial-civic sites (6 occupations), and cemeteries (116 occupations). However, local centers continue to play a role in the settlement system of the valley, and Guadalupito marks the appearance of the first probable regional center—i.e., a very large, internally complex site that appears to have functioned as a provincial-level administrative center for a multivalley state whose capital was located elsewhere.

Habitation Sites

Undifferentiated occupations. The proportion of occupations in the Guadalupito system whose configuration appears to have been characterized by undifferentiated dwellings is 79 out of 205 discrete sites—or 39%—which represents the lowest figure of any ceramic period to this point in the sequence (the figures are 47%, 67%,

53%, and 55%, respectively, for Cayhuamarca, Vinzos, Early Suchimancillo, and Late Suchimancillo). As indicated by the numbers of occupations of each site type given above, the principal reason for this drop is the large number of cemetery sites in the system. Habitation sites, in any case, continue to be distributed more or less evenly throughout the area of occupation (see SVP-GUAD-1, 3, 8, 13, 20–22, 25, 27, 32, 39, 40, 46–48, 51, 52, 54, 56, 57, 61, 63, 65, 67, 68, 71, 72, 74, 78, 86–89, 91, 92, 94, 97, 98, 102, 104, 109, 110, 112, 113, 119, 121–124, 127, 130, 132–135, 137, 150, 161, 168, 169, 174, 176, 177–181, 184–187, 190, 195, 197–199, 201, 203, and 205, in Figs. 98–103).

These sites range in size between .25 and 13 ha and in population between 5 and 1875 persons—with an average size of 2.5 ha and an average population estimate of 212 persons. Thus, while there appears to have been a drop in average site size compared to Late Suchimancillo, the general trend toward increasing numbers of inhabitants on sites continues from the earlier periods (average sizes are 2 ha/140 persons, 1.8 ha/147 persons, 2.4 ha/160 persons, and 2.9 ha/190 persons, respectively, for Cayhuamarca, Vinzos, Early Suchimancillo, and Late Suchimancillo).

The elevation of habitation sites above the valley floor ranges between 0 and 90 m and distance away from it ranges between 0 and 1000 m—with an average elevation of 15 m above the floor and an average distance of 90 m away. Indeed, as the settlement maps indicate, in most areas sites are located immediately adjacent to the valley floor if not on low hills rising in the midst of it. As discussed later in this report, in one sense overall site location represents the culmination of the trend begun in earlier periods of positioning sites closer and closer to the valley floor. At the same time, however, Guadalupito site locations seem clearly to have resulted from the imposition of a multivalley state system on the region, as argued later.

Aside from the proximity of sites to the valley floor and the abrupt change in overall focus of the subsistence-settlement system, another noteworthy change is that related to the nature of dwellings on habitation sites. As mentioned in the preceding section, some 78 out of 84 undifferentiated Late Suchimancillo sites—or 90.5%—have rock-walled structural remains. In strong contrast, only 30 out of the 79 undifferentiated habitation sites of Guadalupito Period—or 38%—have rock-walled dwellings, with the remaining sites consisting of scattered midden debris. Moreover, there is a striking difference between the Upper and Middle Valley, on the one hand, and the Lower Valley, on the other—with 80% (20/25) of sites in the former sectors characterized by rock-walled dwellings and only about 19% (10/54) of sites in the latter sector having such remains. Thus the latter area represents a nearly exact reversal of percentages of rock-walled dwellings vs. midden scatters compared to the

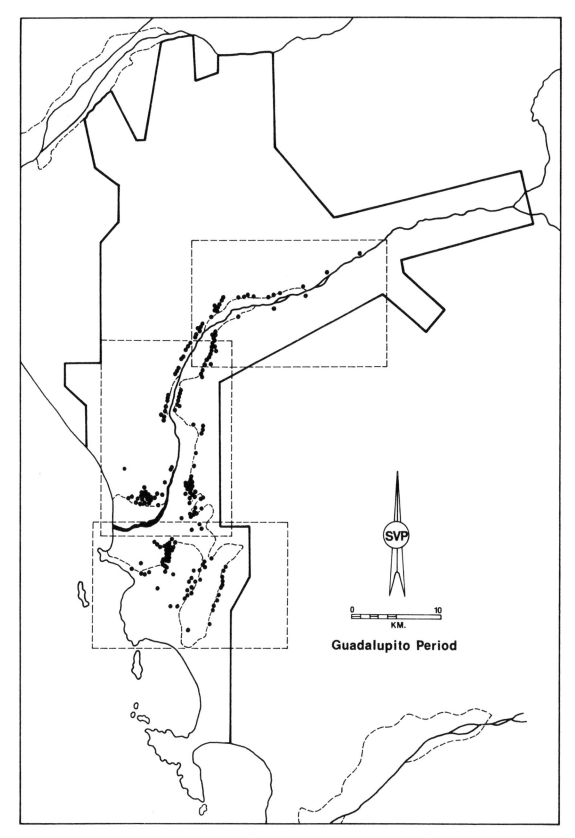

Fig. 97. Location key to settlement pattern maps of Guadalupito Period, Figs. 98, 99, and 102.

SVP

0   10
KM.

Guadalupito Period

199

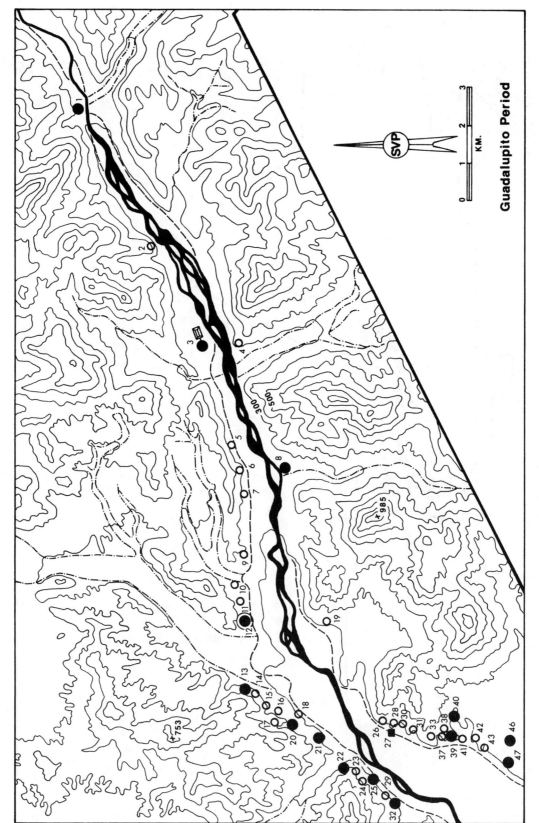

Fig. 98. Settlement pattern map of Guadalupito Period: Upper and Middle Valley sectors.

200

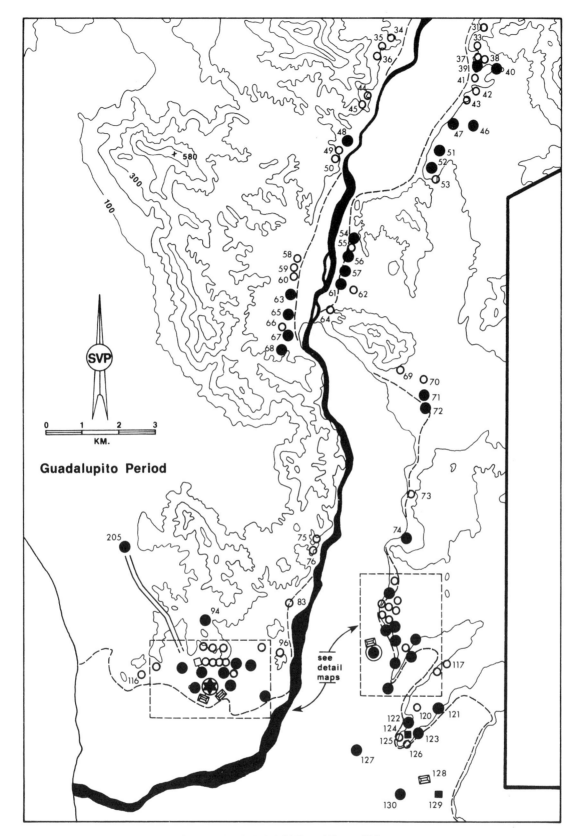

Fig. 99. Settlement pattern map of Guadalupito Period: Middle and Lower Valley sectors.

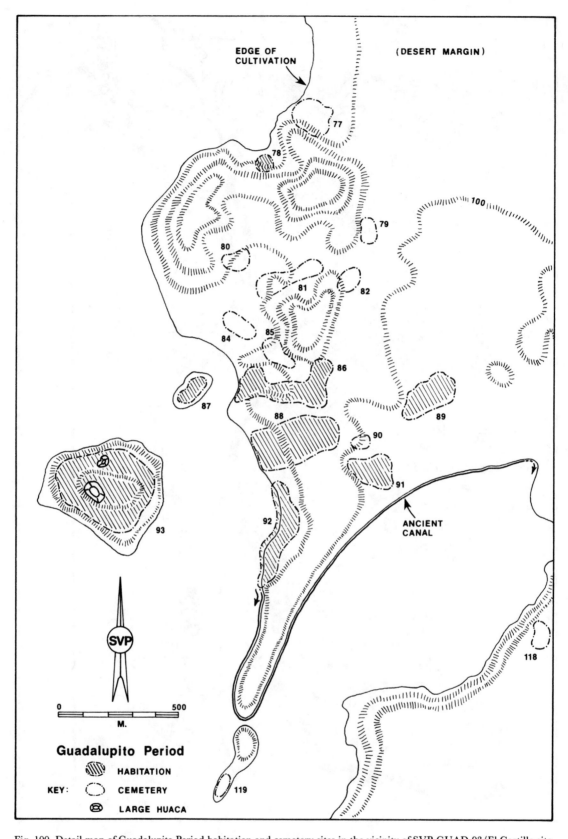

EDGE OF
CULTIVATION

(DESERT MARGIN)

77

78

100

79

80

81

82

84

85

86

87

88

89

90

91

93

92

ANCIENT
CANAL

118

0   500
M.

SVP

Guadalupito Period

HABITATION

KEY: CEMETERY

LARGE HUACA

119

Fig. 100. Detail map of Guadalupito Period habitation and cemetery sites in the vicinity of SVP-GUAD-93/El Castillo site.

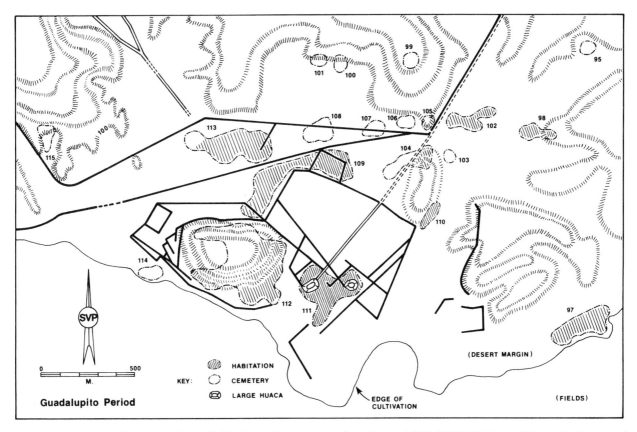

Fig. 101. Detail map of Guadalupito Period habitation and cemetery sites in and around SVP-GUAD-111, the probable regional center of the Moche state in the Lower Santa Valley. See also Figs. 171–177.

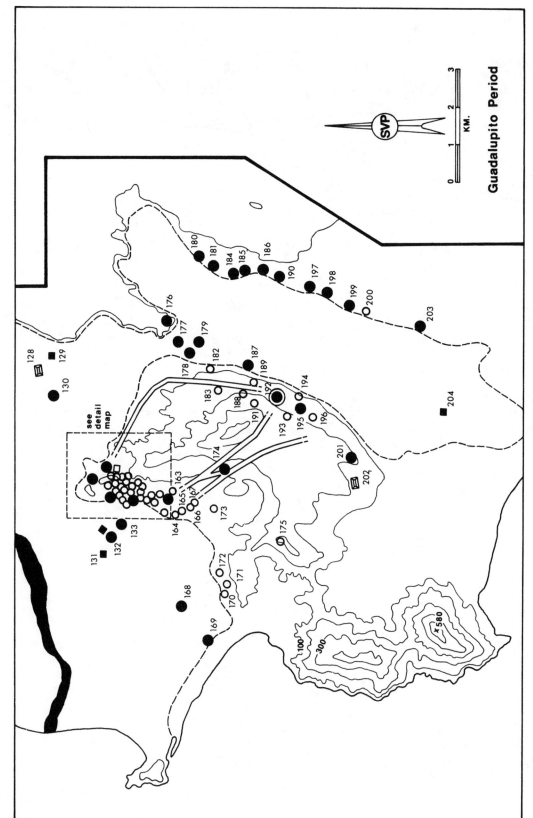

Fig. 102. Settlement pattern map of Guadalupito Period: Lower Valley and Coast sectors.

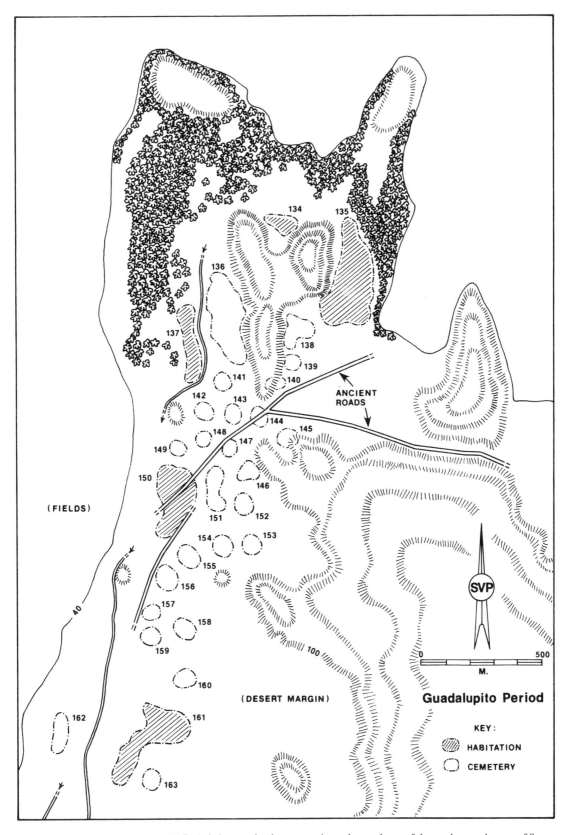

Fig. 103. Detail map of Guadalupito Period sites on the desert margin to the northeast of the modern settlement of Santa.

former area (i.e., 19% vs. 81% in the Lower Valley compared to 80% vs. 20% in the Upper-Middle Valley).

With regard to the sharp change in Lower Valley dwelling types from Late Suchimancillo to Guadalupito times, it should be noted that stones suitable for constructing a stabilizing base around quincha habitations are available more or less everywhere on the desert margins. It may therefore be suggested that a possible reason for the change from rock-walled foundations to dwellings built entirely of perishable materials was the imposition of Moche construction practices on Santa Valley—especially in the primary area of occupation in the Lower Valley (even more striking changes apparently brought about by the Moche state are discussed later).

As will be obvious from the preceding discussion of dwelling types, one of the potential problems presented by most Guadalupito sites of the Lower Valley relates to the method of calculating population based on field estimates of rock-walled structural densities. In general, however, the Lower Valley midden scatters—some of which extend over huge areas of up to 30 ha (see SVP-GUAD-192 in Wilson 1985, Appendix B)—did not present the expected problems. Habitation sites containing remains of quincha structures, as well as maize cobs, marine shells, charcoal bits, and sherds, were found to be of two main types. These include (1) sites where the debris extended essentially continuously (and often deeply) over the entire occupied area, and (2) sites where debris was found in discrete patches scattered throughout the occupied area (see Table 26, in Appendix II, for specific densities as assessed on each site). The first of these two site types was related by analogy to unterraced, rock-walled habitation sites of the main valley where structures are packed closely together—i.e., sites of moderate structural densities, with an average population estimate of 100 persons/ha. The second type was related to similar sites where structures are less densely packed—i.e., sites of low-to-moderate densities, with an average population estimate of 50 persons/ha. In addition, these relationships correlate well with densities of quincha dwellings observed on traditional modern settlements, and indeed were applied in calculating population estimates of many Lower Valley midden sites of later periods in the sequence.

In spite of the general nature of habitation structures on most undifferentiated sites, this should not be taken to imply that sites do not contain well preserved remains. A number were found to have excellently preserved adobe structural remains—including such features as large huacas, and walls that delineate roads and agricultural fields (e.g., see Pampa de los Incas Complex, in Figs. 101, 108). In addition, several sites contain large rectangular compounds built either of double-faced, rubble-filled walls or, more commonly, of adobe. At least some of these compounds are essentially free of occupational debris on the interior, and thus seem likely to have served as corrals (e.g., see Fig. 105; see also Wilson 1985, Fig. 163). But several compounds do contain extensive occupational debris on the interior, and provide the first evidence of the use of adobe-walled enclosures for habitation in the regional sequence.

Structure 86/SVP-GUAD-91, located on the desert immediately to the east of SVP-GUAD-93/El Castillo site, provides a good example of one of these inhabited adobe compounds (Figs. 100, 104). Indeed, as shown in the plan and perspective views, this compound is unique in the survey region in having a solid mass of adobe construction occupying the northeastern end. A more typical compound is exemplified by Structure 83/SVP-GUAD-121 (see Fig. 99 for site location; for a plan view of the structure see Wilson 1985, Fig. 165). This large rectangular enclosure measures roughly 115 × 90 m in area, and contains extensive but poorly preserved remains of adobe-walled structures as well as occupational debris. As in the case of other sites where compounds of this nature are present, even more extensive occupational debris covers the exterior area—in this case covering an area of nearly 6.5 ha around and to the southwest of Structure 83.

Local centers. Three Guadalupito occupations stand out in terms of their relatively larger size and/or greater internal complexity compared to the habitation sites discussed above. Proceeding from the upriver area downvalley, they include SVP-GUAD-12, SVP-GUAD-93, and SVP-GUAD-192 (see Figs. 98, 99, 100, and 102).

SVP-GUAD-12 is located in the Middle Valley sector on desert hills at the eastern side of the mouth of Quebrada Palo Redondo, just to the north above the small modern settlement of Tanguche. Compared to some sites of the Lower Valley, it covers a relatively small area of 5 ha. Nonetheless, extensive rock-faced habitation terraces on the upper slopes of the site and dense midden debris on the lower slopes support the argument of a moderate-density occupation numbering an estimated 500 persons. No other Guadalupito site in the upvalley sectors has an estimated population above 450 persons, and most do not exceed an estimated 250 persons (see SVP-GUAD-1 through SVP-GUAD-68, in Table 26). Moreover, SVP-GUAD-12 is centrally situated with regard to the overall pattern of occupation in these sectors, and lies near a major natural route in and out of the valley via Quebrada Palo Redondo. Finally, the site contains two (very poorly preserved) adobe huacas of medium size—each measuring roughly 25 × 25 × 5 m—that set it apart from all other larger sites of the Upper and Middle Valley.

SVP-GUAD-93/El Castillo site is located on a large desert hill in the east-central part of the main Lower Valley, 2 km to the east of the river (see Figs. 99, 100, 106, 107; for two additional illustrations of remains at this site see Wilson 1985, Figs. 168–169). The hill itself rises some 70 m in elevation above the surrounding cultivated valley floor, and covers a large area of 400 × 300 m. As the site drawings show, Guadalupito occupation extends over most of the hill, and the two major adobe huacas occupying the summit and lower northern slopes make SVP-GUAD-93 one of the most prominent landmarks of the Lower Valley sector. Indeed, Structure 87—the more outstanding of the two huacas and the namesake of the hill—can be seen from nearly every place in the Lower Valley between the ocean and a point 18 km inland. The site therefore clearly would have served as an impressive symbol of the presence and power of the Moche state in the region (Note: the issue of Moche statehood is taken up in Chapter V).

Structure 87 appears to be composed entirely of cane-marked adobes and has a relatively massive volume measuring 48 × 25 × 13 m. An excellently preserved walled stairway runs up the southeastern side of the pyramid (Fig. 106; see also Wilson 1985, Fig. 168, for two views of the stairway), providing access to a (now severely damaged) summit platform that extended over a maximum area of 40 × 14 m. A large plaza lies to the southeast of the main structure, and is flanked on the south by a massive adobe-faced terrace wall that extends for over 60 m along the summit of the hill and rises 6.5 m high (Fig. 106; see also Wilson 1985, Fig. 168, for a perspective view). This terrace and Structure 87 together constitute the main architectural features visible from the valley floor out to the south of El Castillo hill.

Structure 88, the other major adobe huaca on SVP-GUAD-93, is perched against the steep lower edge of the hill at a point some 70 m to the northeast of the summit and nearly 70 m lower in elevation. It is much more poorly preserved than Structure 87, but, as shown in Fig. 106, its northern end appears to have consisted of two massive adobe blocks placed adjacent to the main downslope side of the huaca—perhaps in part to prevent slippage of the structure down the steep foot of the hillside. Several adobe-walled structures and scattered occupational debris cover the southern end of the huaca, at the point where it grades into the hillside, and these remains may provide some evidence of elite habitation on the site. By far the most intriguing feature on Structure 88, however, is the evidence we found of painted murals located on the lower face of the northernmost support block. These murals consist of polychrome motifs painted over a plastered and red-painted facade. Although most are now extremely faint, the best preserved section of the murals was still visible enough in 1979–80 to record in the form of an elevation drawing (see Fig. 107). This section alone consists of four club-and-shield motifs which cover a large area measuring about 3 m long and 1 m high, and would have been easily visible not only to passersby on the valley floor below but to people living in sites along the desert margin out to the northeast.

Extensive and deep midden debris—including maize cobs, lithics, textile fragments, cordage, adobes, and remains of quincha structures—covers an area of nearly 10 ha around the northern side of El Castillo hill. The population estimate for the entire site is 1035 persons, making this one of the larger Guadalupito habitation sites of the Lower Valley. Moreover, Structures 87 and 88 are among the most impressive adobe huacas of the period, and clearly attest to the importance of this site in the ceremonial-civic activities of the local settlement system. In this regard, it may be noted that SVP-GUAD-93 seems unlikely to have served a defensive function, in spite of the remote location of Structure 87 and associated remains high up on the summit of the hill. There are no remains of defensive works around the base of the hill, nor is the wall delineating the southeastern end of the plaza high enough (at ca. 50 cm) to have prevented easy access via the gentler eastern slopes leading up to Structure 87.

SVP-GUAD-192, the last of the three sites designated as local centers, lies 10 km due south of SVP-GUAD-93/El Castillo along gentle-to-steeper sandy slopes overlooking the western side of Quebrada de Lacramarca. With a length along the hillside of 825 m and an average width of 500 m (for site outline see Wilson 1985, Fig. 162), the 29.5-ha area covered by this site makes it the largest occupation of Guadalupito Period—apart from the overall site complex constituting the probable regional center at Pampa de los Incas. SVP-GUAD-192 is typical of most Lower Valley sites in that it consists essentially of undifferentiated occupational debris. But its relatively huge size compared to surrounding Lacramarca sites, and the indication that two major Guadalupito roads converged on the site (see Fig. 102), make it a likely candidate for a local center.

Regional center. Among all the inhabited sites of Guadalupito Period, SVP-GUAD-111 and associated occupations of Pampa de los Incas area constitute the largest and most complex concentration of architecture and other remains anywhere in the region (see SVP-GUAD-98 through SVP-GUAD-114, in Figs. 101, 108–110; for additional detail views see Wilson 1985, Figs. 174–177). Covering a total area of 2 km², this site complex includes the following principal features: numerous massive adobe walls extending over a combined length of many kilometers, ancient roadways, canals, aqueducts, agricultural fields with serpentine furrows, two very large adobe huacas (Structures 19 and 20), seven smaller huacas of varying size and configuration, eight major cemetery areas, and eight habitation sites (most importantly including SVP-GUAD-111 and 112) which contained an estimated population totaling 3520 persons.

Judging from the presence of the two massive adobe pyramidal structures and the complexity of associated adobe-walled remains, SVP-GUAD-111 served as the nucleus of Pampa de los Incas Complex (see Fig. 101).

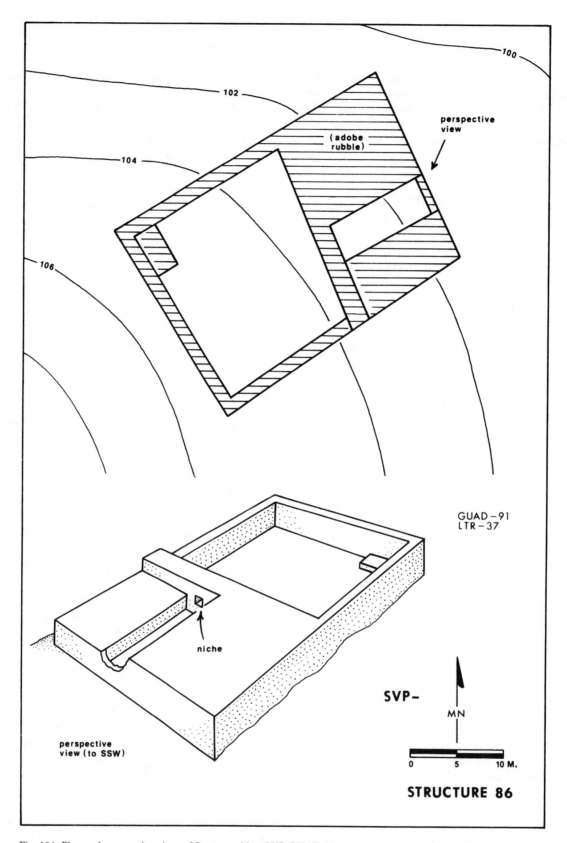

Fig. 104. Plan and perspective views of Structure 86 at SVP-GUAD-91.

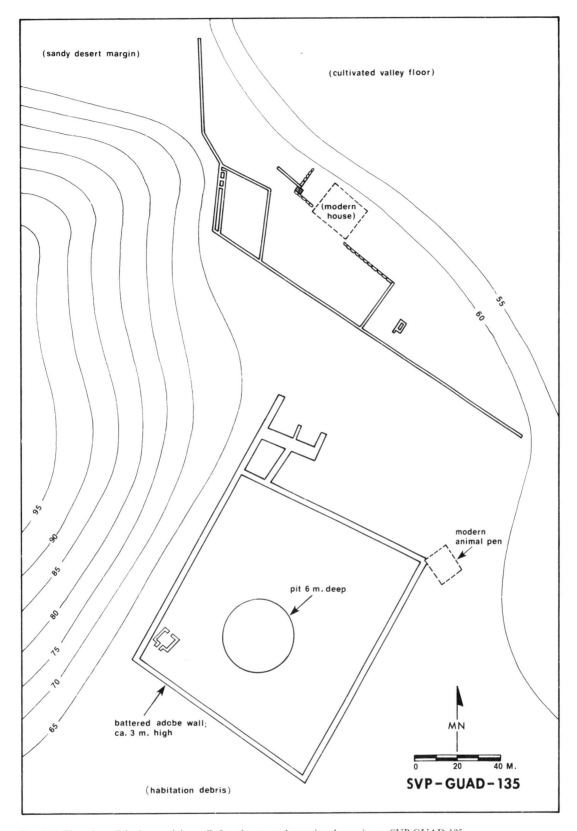

(sandy desert margin)

(cultivated valley floor)

(modern house)

55

60

modern animal pen

95

90

85

80

pit 6 m. deep

75

70

65

battered adobe wall; ca. 3 m. high

(habitation debris)

MN

0   20   40 M.

SVP-GUAD-135

Fig. 105. Plan view of the large adobe-walled enclosure and associated remains at SVP-GUAD-135.

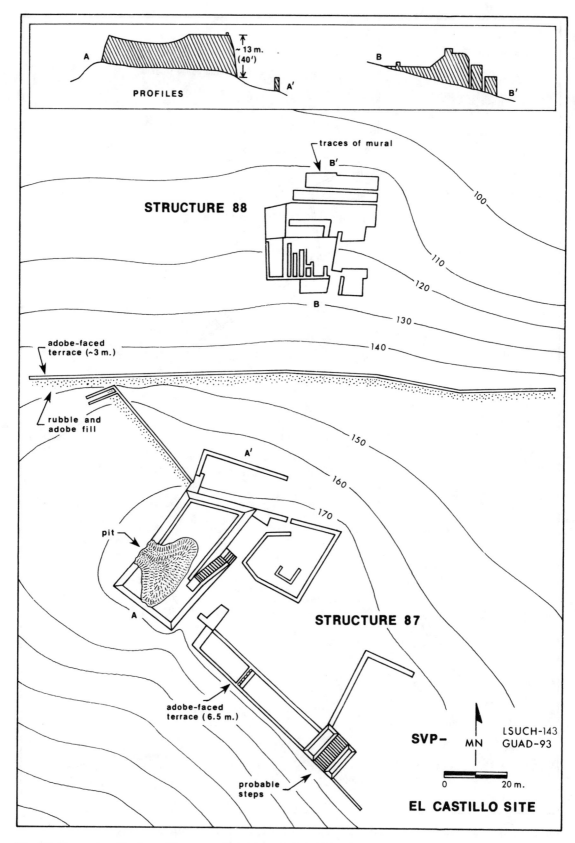

PROFILES

~ 13 m. (40')

traces of mural

STRUCTURE 88

B'

B

100

110

120

130

adobe-faced terrace (~3 m.)

140

rubble and adobe fill

A'

150

160

170

pit

STRUCTURE 87

A

adobe-faced terrace (6.5 m.)

probable steps

SVP-

MN

LSUCH-143
GUAD-93

0   20 m.

EL CASTILLO SITE

Fig. 106. Plan and profile views of Structures 87 and 88 at SVP-GUAD-93.

210

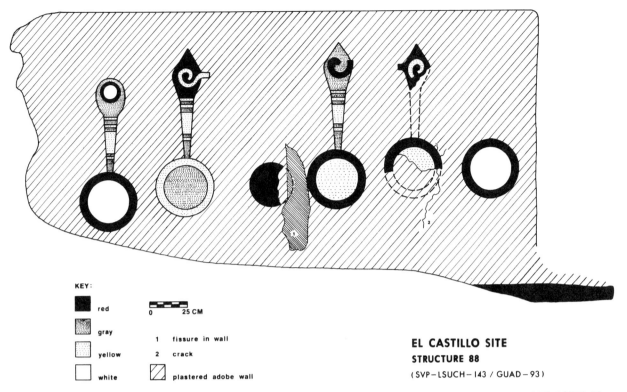

KEY:

■ red

▨ gray

□ yellow

□ white

0 ⊢━━━┥ 25 CM

1 fissure in wall

2 crack

▨ plastered adobe wall

EL CASTILLO SITE
STRUCTURE 88
(SVP – LSUCH – 143 / GUAD – 93)

Fig. 107. Elevation detail of polychrome club-and-shield mural located on the lower northern face of Structure 88 at SVP-GUAD-93.

Indeed, the position of the ancient adobe-walled road-way in relation to Structure 19 suggests that this huaca in particular served as the principal focal point of the entire complex. As the plan views show, the roadway approached the site from the desert out to the northeast, crossed over SVP-GUAD-104, and ended up against the northeastern base of Structure 19. Moreover, the nature of the huaca itself supports the argument that it func-tioned among other things as the residence of the region-al, or provincial, administrator during the time of Moche hegemony. First of all, it is the largest of any adobe huaca dating to Guadalupito Period—with dimensions of 132.5 × 110 m and a height of 16.3 m (see Plate 4, and Fig. 109-top). Second, although Structure 19 is now in a generally poor state of preservation, occupational debris is still visible on most of the platform levels comprising the sides and top of the huaca. Third, the main roadway into the site leads directly up to the highest platform via a series of well-demarcated ramps. It is also interesting to note that one of the few adobes with maker's marks detected anywhere in the region was found on the sum-mit of Structure 19—thus providing some evidence for the kind of corporate labor construction practices ad-duced by archaeologists working at Huaca del Sol, the presumed center of the Moche state (Note: among the earliest scholars to suggest this was Kroeber 1930:60–61; for the most definitive presentation of the argument, see Moseley 1975b; Hastings and Moseley 1975).

In light of the hypothesized central administrative role played by SVP-GUAD-111 and Structure 19, it is also of interest to note the evidence of pottery production found at the nearby site of SVP-GUAD-112. As shown in Fig. 101 (see also Plate 4-left center), this site occupies a substantial part of the large hill (Cerro de la Colina) which rises above the southern edge of Pampa de los Incas—and includes cemetery areas and a densely ter-raced habitation site covering an area of 7.5 ha on the eastern and southern sides of the hill. At one place in the lower east-central sector of SVP-GUAD-112, we found a number of fragments of ceramic molds containing in negative relief such Moche-style features as almond-shaped eyes and ears with lobe spools/plugs (see Fig. 230 k, l). Although there may well have been other places of moldmade pottery production in the valley during this period, this is the only site at which reasonably direct evidence of such production was found. Considering its proximity to the probable locus of regional administra-tive activities during the time of Moche state occupation, SVP-GUAD-112 appears to be a most likely candidate for a center of craft production (see Wilson 1985, Appen-dix B, for further details).

In addition to Structure 19, a number of other adobe huacas of smaller size are located elsewhere in the com-plex. The most impressive of these is Structure 20, lo-cated within the confines of SVP-GUAD-111 site about 125 m to the east of Structure 19 (see Figs. 108, 109-

211

bottom). It covers a smaller area of 92.5 × 25 m, but, with an estimated summit elevation of 18.75 m above the pampa, stands somewhat higher. Similar to Structure 19, a number of platform levels with extensive occupational debris were found on the huaca—indicating that it also served as a place of habitation, perhaps including elite residence. Other, even smaller mounds are located in the far eastern sector of Pampa de los Incas Complex (see Wilson 1985, Fig. 174), as well as in the area along the northern periphery of the complex (Wilson 1985, Figs. 175–177).

A final feature of some interest consists of an excellently preserved series of rock-faced terraces and associated rock-walled enclosure at SVP-GUAD-104 (Fig. 110). This site covers the northern tip of a low hillside in the northeastern part of the pampa, immediately to the east of the low pass where the main ancient roadway approached the regional administrative complex and Structure 19 (see Structure 22, in Fig. 108). SVP-GUAD-104 appears to have served not only for habitation and burial, similar to all other sites in the complex, but the rock-walled enclosure placed adjacent to the roadway against the hillside may have been used as a corral as well.

Other Ceremonial-Civic Sites/Structures

In addition to the adobe pyramidal platforms located at SVP-GUAD–93 and various locations in Pampa de los Incas Complex, a number of other adobe huacas of probable Guadalupito date were found in the survey region. For purposes of briefly discussing their main characteristics, it is useful to divide these structures into two principal subtypes—including (1) *larger huacas* that approach the size of the massive structures found at SVP-GUAD–93 and SVP-GUAD–111, and (2) *smaller huacas* that are similar in size to those found on the northern periphery of the regional administrative complex. Outside of the local and regional centers, the total number of sites with huacas is 10. Four of these sites appear to have had a function primarily related to habitation (see SVP-GUAD-3, 27, 124, and 132, in Figs. 98, 99, and 102), leaving the six sites categorized as primarily ceremonial-civic in nature in the opening paragraph of this section on Guadalupito Period. The latter group consists of isolated huaca structures on and around the great majority of which no indication of habitation was noted (see SVP-GUAD-114, 128, 129, 131, 202, and 204, in Figs. 101, 102). However, as discussed below, at least one of these isolated huacas (Structure 81/SVP-GUAD-128) appears to have had a substantial resident population on the summit and sides of the mound itself, similar to Structures 19 and 20 at SVP-GUAD-111.

Larger huacas. One of the four sites with larger huaca structures is situated in a relatively remote location on

Pampa Blanca in the Upper Valley sector (see SVP-GUAD-3, in Fig. 98), while the remaining three are located near major population concentrations in the Lower Valley. As shown in Fig. 111, Structure 43 mound at SVP-GUAD-3 has one of the most amorphous layouts of any huaca structure in the sequence, extending over a large area with maximum dimensions of 85 × 65 m. Its average height of slightly over 1 m also makes it by far the lowest major platform mound of Guadalupito date. The two smaller, symmetrically positioned rectangular platforms out to the northeast, and two additional 1.5-m high mounds of roughly elliptical shape on the main structure itself, lend support to the argument of a primarily ceremonial-civic function for this part of SVP-GUAD-3 site—a function which includes a small cemetery containing Moche funerary diagnostics on the southwestern part of the main structure.

Structure 81/SVP-GUAD-128, located in the midst of cultivated fields to the east of the small modern settlement of Tambo Real, is one of the most impressive huacas of any period (Fig. 112; see also perspective view in Wilson 1983, Fig. 14). As shown in the plan and perspective views, Structure 81 covers a very large area of 110 × 90 m and has a maximum height of 11 m. Indeed, among Guadalupito/Moche ceremonial-civic mounds it is second in size only to Structure 19 at SVP-GUAD-111. Constructed primarily of plain rectangular adobes placed in layers separated by reed matting, the overall asymmetric bulk of the structure stands somewhat in contrast to the formal layout of its principal summit features. These include the following: (1) a lower plaza surrounded by low plastered walls, at its northeastern end; (2) a similarly enclosed upper plaza at the southwestern end which contains two pit features; (3) a series of narrow ramps and steps connecting the two plazas; and (4) symmetrically positioned approach ramps on each side of the northeastern end of the structure. As shown in the plan drawing, the larger of the approach ramps begins at a point some 40 m away from the huaca and rises nearly 10 m in elevation, directly up to the southeastern side of the lower summit plaza. Light, but extensive, occupational debris on the summit and surrounding levels provides the basis for an estimated resident population of 180 persons.

Structure 66/Huaca China, located at SVP-GUAD-132 on the main valley floor a little over 5 km to the southwest of Structure 81 site, is another one of the impressive (if not enigmatic) archaeological monuments of Guadalupito Period (see Fig. 113). Like Structure 87/El Castillo site at SVP-GUAD-93, it is situated atop a desert hill rising in the midst of the valley floor and is therefore highly visible for several kilometers around. As shown in the plan and section views, the principal architectural remains consist of two battered (or upwardly tapered) adobe walls that run at a height of roughly 3.5 m around the contours of the hill. An adobe platform

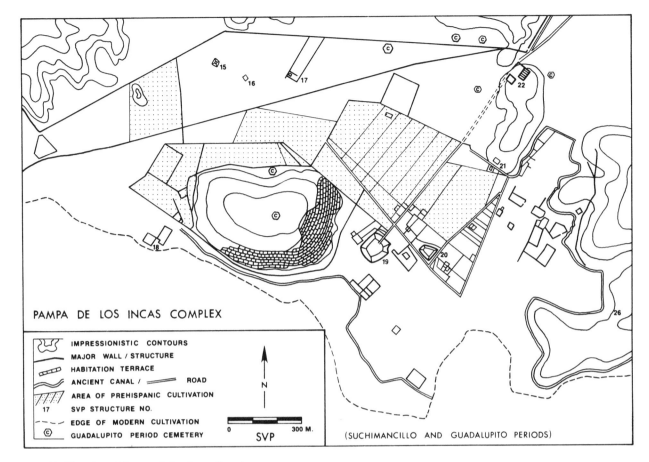

PAMPA DE LOS INCAS COMPLEX

	IMPRESSIONISTIC CONTOURS
	MAJOR WALL / STRUCTURE
	HABITATION TERRACE
	ANCIENT CANAL / ════ ROAD
17	AREA OF PREHISPANIC CULTIVATION
	SVP STRUCTURE NO.
- - -	EDGE OF MODERN CULTIVATION
ⓒ	GUADALUPITO PERIOD CEMETERY

N

0   300 M.

SVP

(SUCHIMANCILLO AND GUADALUPITO PERIODS)

Fig. 108. Plan view of Pampa de los Incas Complex.

containing a smaller U-shaped structure is found on the summit of the hill, and additional adobe-walled structures lie downslope along the lower northern wall. In general, Structure 66 bears little resemblance to the variety of structures of earlier periods classified as defensive in nature—i.e., it is not situated in a remote location, nor does it have such features as dry ditches, bastions, or a defensible interior summit structure. On the other hand, it is clearly different from all other Guadalupito structures classified as ceremonial-civic—thus leaving open the issue of the nature of its functions.

The final one of the four larger huacas is located at SVP-GUAD–202 on the outskirts of Chimbote, in the upper part of the densely populated modern barrio of San Pedro. Because of its location, it has been heavily damaged and there is little that can be said about it beyond indicating that its dimensions of 100 × 75 m suggest it was one of the major pyramidal platforms of Guadalupito Period.

Smaller huacas. Similar to the distribution of larger huaca mounds, only one of the six sites with smaller huacas was found in the upvalley area (see SVP-GUAD-27, in Fig. 98). The others are situated in the

Lower Valley sector, primarily near the main populated areas of Guadalupito Period (see SVP-GUAD-114, 124, 129, 131, and 204, in Figs. 101, 102). Proceeding from the uppermost site on downvalley, the smaller huacas include the following sites at which structural remains were well enough preserved to map in detail: (1) Structure 59/SVP-GUAD-27, which consists of a rectangular red-plastered adobe building and two adjacent mounded areas flanking an intervening plaza (see Wilson 1985, Fig. 182); and (2) Structure 85/SVP-GUAD-124, a low rectangular adobe platform with a parallelogram shape (Wilson 1985, Fig. 183). Both of these huaca sites are found on low desert ridges overlooking the cultivated valley floor. The remaining four sites all have very poorly preserved, essentially unmappable huaca structures.

Cemetery Sites

As in other aspects of the Guadalupito subsistence-settlement system, cemetery sites reflect what appears to have been an essential break with the preceding Late Suchimancillo system. It will be recalled that the majority of Suchimancillo burial sites in the main upvalley area of occupation contain small, rock-lined tombs with pen-

213

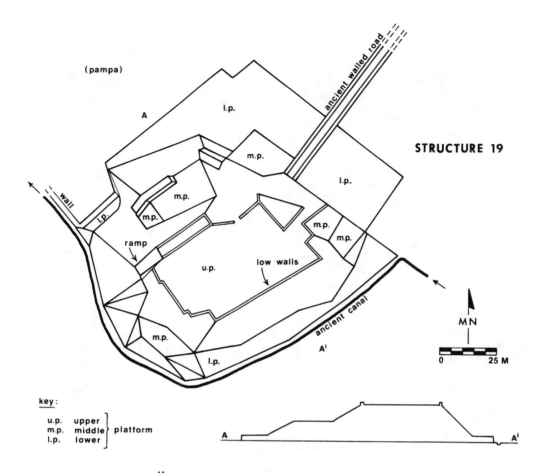

(pampa)

A

l.p.

ancient walled road

m.p.

STRUCTURE 19

l.p.

wall

l.p.

m.p.

m.p.

m.p.

m.p.

ramp

low walls

u.p.

m.p.

l.p.

ancient canal

A'

MN

0   25 M

key:

u.p.   upper ⎫
m.p.   middle ⎬ platform
l.p.   lower ⎭

A   A'

"HUACAS TEMBLADERA"
(SVP-GUAD-111)

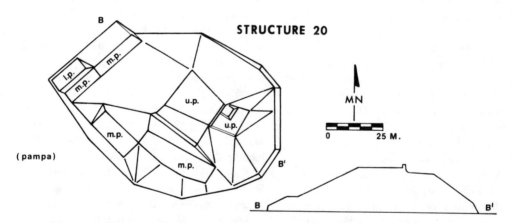

B

STRUCTURE 20

l.p.

m.p.

m.p.

u.p.

u.p.

m.p.

MN

0   25 M.

(pampa)

m.p.

B'

B   B'

Fig. 109. Plan and profile views of Structures 19 and 20 at SVP-GUAD-111/Pampa de los Incas Complex. See Fig. 108 for relative locations of the two huacas.

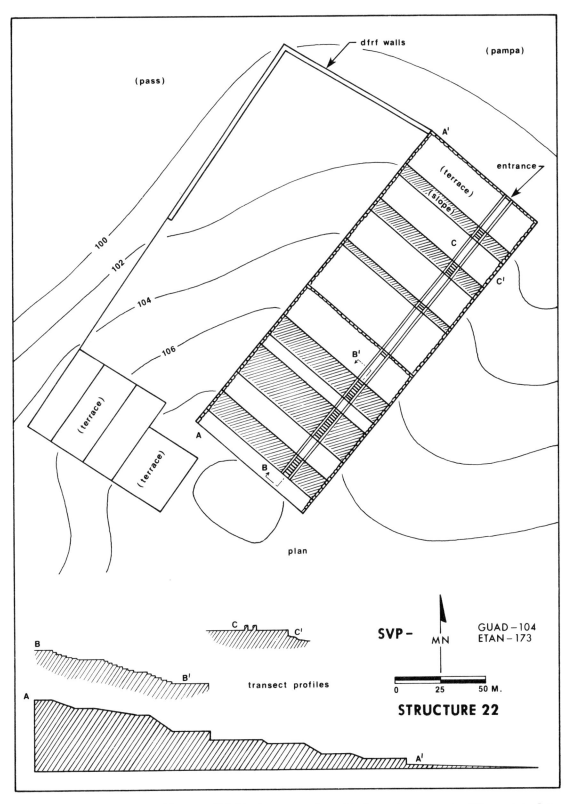

Fig. 110. Plan and profile views of Structure 22 habitation terraces, located in the northeastern sector of Pampa de los Incas Complex.

215

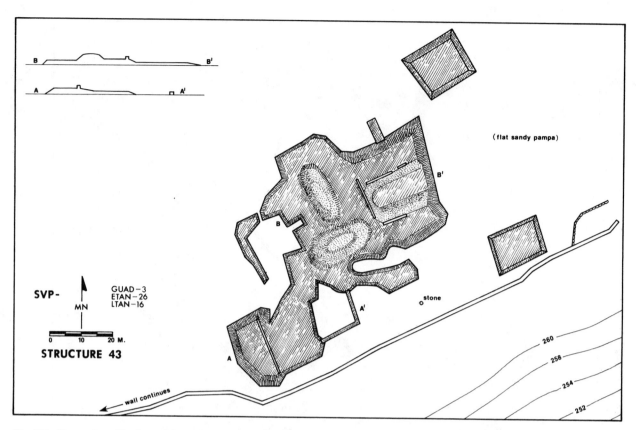

Fig. 111. Plan and profile views of Structure 43, a ceremonial-civic site with intrusive later burials.

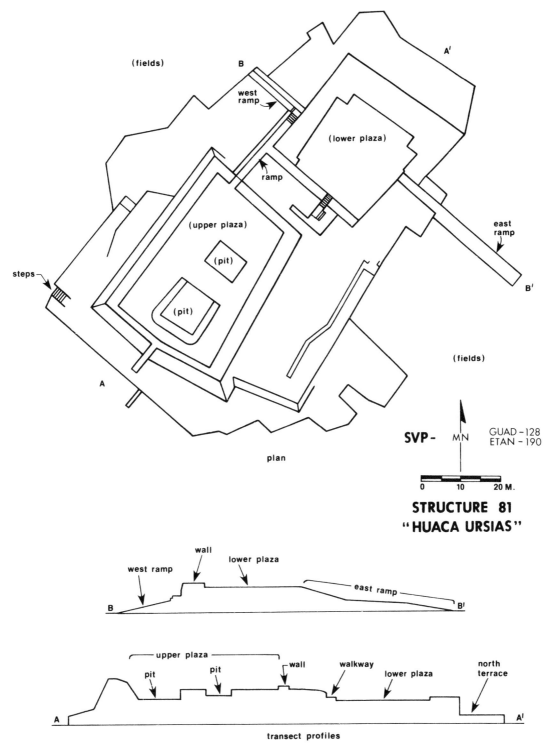

(fields)

B

west
ramp

ramp

(lower plaza)

A'

east
ramp

B'

(upper plaza)

(pit)

(pit)

steps

A

(fields)

plan

SVP-   MN   GUAD-128
             ETAN-190

0   10   20 M.

STRUCTURE 81
"HUACA URSIAS"

west ramp

wall

lower plaza

east ramp

B   B'

upper plaza

pit   pit   wall   walkway   lower plaza   north
                                                         terrace

A   A'

transect profiles

Fig. 112. Plan and profile views of Structure 81, a large huaca platform with Guadalupito Period occupation and intrusive burials dating to Early Tanguche.

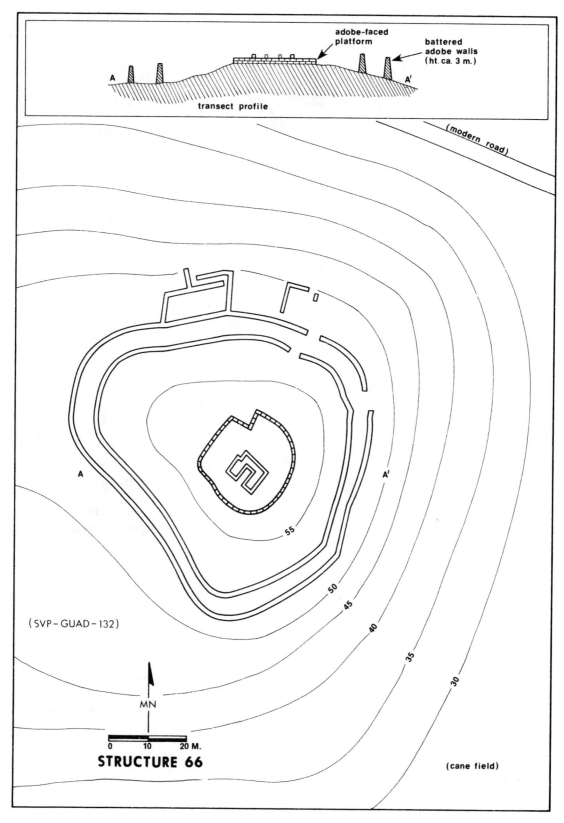

Fig. 113. Plan and profile views of the principal structural remains at SVP-GUAD-132, Huaca China site.

tagonal or hexagonal plans—suggesting a general tradition of either tightly flexed or secondary interments. In contrast, judging from what we could find of intact tomb architecture as well as from Donnan's (1973) study of Moche burial patterns in Santa, Guadalupito Period tombs generally consisted of narrow, rectangular adobe-brick constructions of a size that would accommodate burials in extended position.

Compared to any other period except Early Tanguche, a remarkable number of Guadalupito Period burial sites was found during the survey—including (1) 116 discrete cemeteries located generally near the valley floor, either in quebrada mouths or on wide stretches of gently sloping, sandy desert pampa (see SVP-GUAD-2, 4–7, 9–11, 14–19, 23, 24, 26, 28–31, 33–38, 41–45, 49, 50, 53, 55, 58–60, 62, 64, 66, 69, 70, 73, 75–77, 79–85, 90, 95, 96, 99–101, 103, 105–108, 115–118, 120, 125, 126, 136, 138–149, 151–160, 162–167, 170–173, 175, 182, 183, 188, 189, 191, 193, 194, 196, and 200, in Figs. 98–103); and (2) 31 cemeteries that are part of sites of varying sizes and functions (hamlets, small and large villages, local and regional centers) whose primary use was for habitation (see SVP-GUAD-1, 3, 13, 20–22, 25, 32, 47, 48, 54, 56, 57, 61, 63, 65, 67, 71, 72, 86, 88, 92, 97, 104, 109, 111, 112, 121, 130, 134, and 185, in Figs. 98–103).

Moche burial wares are arguably one of the outstanding ceramic funerary traditions of the North Coast area, and it may well be their fame on the world art market that gives huaqueros incentive to search out sites of this period for systematic looting. Indeed, this may be suggested as one of the main reasons for the high percentage of Guadalupito burial sites in relation to the total number of occupations of the period—i.e., 72%, or 147 out of 205 sites (the figures are 21%, 37%, 28%, 45%, 57%, and 49%, respectively, for Early Suchimancillo, Late Suchimancillo, Early Tanguche, Late Tanguche, Early Tambo Real, and Late Tambo Real; Note: percentages are based on *total* number of discrete and nondiscrete cemeteries, as shown in Table 8, compared to the total number of occupations of the period). In other words, the high percentage of burial sites in the Guadalupito system may be an artifact of strategically and economically directed activities of modern huaqueros, rather than an indication that Guadalupito/Moche people were somehow more "funerarily-oriented" than those of other periods (this leaves open, of course, the question of how the huaqueros identify the Moche burial sites in the first place).

Finally, it is of some interest to refer to the nature of the distribution of Guadalupito cemeteries (Note: only discrete cemeteries located apart from habitation sites have been shown on the settlement maps, primarily to keep the maps as uncluttered as possible). Although, as stated earlier, the present-day signs of a cemetery on the desert surface are strictly a function of where the huaqueros have chosen to carry out their looting, it is inter-

esting nevertheless to note the following patterns: (1) cemetery sites generally are evenly distributed in relation to habitation sites, but there are a few stretches of desert margin where only cemeteries can be found (e.g., see SVP-GUAD-5 through SVP-GUAD-9, in Fig. 98); and (2) there are at least three areas where an especially high concentration of cemeteries justifies calling them *necropolises*, that is, locations to which it appears the dead were brought from kilometers around. These latter areas include (a) the east desert margin of the Middle Valley sector (see Fig. 98), (b) the northern periphery of Pampa de los Incas Complex (Fig. 101), and (c) the desert margin to the east and southeast of SVP-GUAD-132/Huaca China site (Figs. 102, 103). These two main patterns of cemetery distribution seem noteworthy. While the first may indicate that a few small, related habitation sites can no longer be detected in areas where (presumably) isolated cemeteries are found, the second clearly indicates that the use of necropolises became widespread during this period. In other words, there appear to be places where one might expect to find numerous cemeteries and only a few habitations or none at all.

Other Remains: Guadalupito Roads and Corrals

Several sections of ancient roads are found within the survey region that can be dated reasonably securely to Guadalupito—primarily on the basis of associated habitation sites containing good ceramic diagnostics of the period. Interestingly, the only road sections that can be so dated are restricted entirely to the desert margins immediately to the north and south of the Lower Valley sector, within a relatively short distance of 7 km of the ocean (see Figs. 99, 102). As shown on the settlement maps, it is likely that these sections formed a local network that, in turn, was part of a single major route connecting Santa and valleys to the north and south. In sharp contrast to the generally inland location of the much more extensive and complex Early Tanguche road-settlement network, the route connecting provinces of the Moche state appears likely to have run adjacent to the ocean (if not along the beaches) much of the way. Given our data indicating a relatively noncomplex Moche road network, the important point to make here is that the appearance in Early Tanguche of the extensive and complex Santa-Chao network is all the more remarkable.

Another unique feature of the Moche Period road network is that the *presumed* route of intervalley travel out to the north of the Santa Valley mouth is not marked by sherd debris, nor is there any indication that it was delineated by the low lines of rocks that are universally characteristic of the following period. Considering the extensive Middle Horizon sherd debris found on the Early Tanguche roads, it may be tentatively concluded that the volume of intervalley trade was substantially less (or at least of a different nature) in Guadalupito times. It should also be noted that no site with associated Guadalupito/Moche sherds was found anywhere in the inland desert network of Early Tanguche Period, nor were any Moche sherds noted on the road surfaces of this network.

Briefly to deal with specific sections of Guadalupito roads, it appears likely that the major route leading north from Pampa de los Incas was the one that runs between the northern periphery of the regional administrative complex and SVP-GUAD-205, located 4 km to the northwest (see Fig. 99). The section shown on the map is excellently preserved from a point just to the north of ancient fields and walls associated with the complex. From there, it crosses a low pass and heads down to the northwest before becoming lost on the sandy coastal plain. The other well preserved section of road in this general area is the one leading out to the northeast from Structure 19/SVP-GUAD-111 (e.g., see Fig. 101). But, as implied by its absence on the settlement map of the area (Fig. 99), this section of road is relatively quite short. In any case, it is possible that it ran near SVP-GUAD-94, which is situated in a quebrada system to the north of the low desert hills that lie along the northern edge of Pampa de los Incas Complex.

Two interconnected and roughly parallel roads run from Santa to Lacramarca across the high, sandy intervening range lying to the south of SVP-GUAD-132/ Huaca China site (Fig. 102). Although it becomes lost in the sand along the northern edge of Quebrada de Lacramarca, the route running through the small roadside site of SVP-GUAD-174 appears to be oriented in a direction that leads to the mouth of Nepeña Valley. The other of the two roads crosses over the southern end of Cerro Tambo Real range toward SVP-GUAD–192, the probable local center of the Lacramarca area. A third major route between Santa and Lacramarca consists of a generally very well preserved road that heads out along the west desert margin of Lacramarca and then turns to the northwest, passing near SVP-GUAD-135.

It is of interest to note that two of the three possible corral enclosures that can be dated to this period lie adjacent to the main coastal roads discussed above. One of these corrals has been mentioned earlier, in connection with the discussion of Pampa de los Incas regional center (see Fig. 110). The other consists of the adobe-walled enclosure found at SVP-GUAD-135 habitation site (see Figs. 102, 103, and 105). As shown in Fig. 105, this enclosure covers a large area of 110 × 95 m in the northwestern part of the site. Extensive occupational debris covers an additional area of 6.3 ha around the exterior of the structure, to the northeast and southwest. The general absence of structures and associated debris on the interior of the enclosure suggests a nonhabitation function possibly related to corraling llamas. The third one of

the hypothesized corrals of this period is located at SVP-GUAD-52, on Pampa de Vinzos in the Middle Valley sector (see Wilson 1985, Fig. 163). It is worth noting that this structure bears some resemblance to corrals of Late Suchimancillo Period, both in terms of its configuration and its rock-walled construction. Assuming its function has been correctly assessed, the Pampa de Vinzos corral suggests that llamas were used to transport goods between the upper and lower parts of the valley, in addition to the coastwise traffic implied by the location of corrals along the main Guadalupito/Moche roads.

Settlement and Demographic Patterns

As indicated by a comparison of Figs. 172 and 174, Guadalupito is the first period in the Lower Santa sequence for which it can be argued that an almost revolutionary change has taken place in the subsistence-settlement system. For example, the system of each of the earlier ceramic periods appears to have had ample developmental antecedents in the period immediately preceding it—most importantly including the widespread establishment of settlements in the Upper and Middle Valley. In sharp contrast, with the exception of the apparently abrupt change from the mixed occupational focus including coast and inland sectors in Las Salinas to one focused almost entirely on the inland sectors in following periods, there is no precedent in the sequence for the nearly complete abandonment of the Upper Valley sector that characterizes the Guadalupito system.

Indeed, as argued later, given the probability that Guadalupito is the time of external conquest and multi-valley state formation, the abrupt change in focus to the Lower and Middle Valley in and of itself seems to be one of the primary indicators of an imposition of state control and policy on the Lower Santa region. Nevertheless, in spite of the revolutionary change in subsistence-settlement focus, it is also important to emphasize that certain developmental antecedents for the Guadalupito system do indeed appear to be present in the system of Late Suchimancillo Period—thereby providing a basis for the changes that occurred during the occupation of the region by the Moche state. These include most importantly: (1) the probable development of intensive canal irrigation practices in the upvalley and downvalley areas; (2) the establishment of scattered sites including minor habitations, major population centers, and defensive works in the mouth of the valley by Early and Late Suchimancillo times; and (3) a regional population numbering in the several tens of thousands that could be mobilized for the major canal and site construction projects that took place throughout the Lower Valley and much of the Middle Valley during the Guadalupito/Moche time period.

Beginning with SVP-GUAD-1, located across the river from the mouth of Quebrada de Cayhuamarca, a total of 205 sites constitutes the Guadalupito settlement system—with fully 90% of these representing occupations established for the first time in the sequence. Although the percentage of new occupations is thus quite similar to that characterizing the Early Suchimancillo system (88%), in light of the abrupt change in overall focus the Guadalupito system is radically more different from its Late Suchimancillo predecessor than is the Early Suchimancillo system from its Vinzos one.

As discussed in detail earlier in this section, the Guadalupito system also represents both (1) an evolutionary outgrowth of the trend from preceramic times on of locating sites closer and closer on the average to the less defensible edge of the valley floor; and (2) a radical break with all earlier ceramic periods in that there are no sites in the system which can be identified unequivocally as defensive constructions. With regard to the first point, it is likely that with the increase in population and sociocultural complexity over time the people of the Lower Santa region were increasingly better organized and capable of defending themselves in more exposed positions. With regard to the second point, once the regional system was incorporated into the multivalley state—clearly by *coercion*, as argued later—there appears to have been no need to locate sites in anything but exposed positions, nor was there any need to construct fortresses.

As in the preceding Suchimancillo periods, the three sites identified as probable Guadalupito local centers are very widely distributed throughout the area of occupation, in close association with the main population concentrations of the Middle and Lower Valley (see Figs. 174, 175). However, in contrast to Late Suchimancillo, Guadalupito marks the appearance of a center so large and complex that it seems very likely to have occupied a pivotal position at the top of the hierarchy of control in the entire regional system. Considering the strong Lower Valley focus of the subsistence-settlement system as well as the location of Guadalupito/Moche roads near the coastline, it is not surprising that the regional center of Pampa de los Incas appears to be strategically located on the north desert margin—very closeby the main population concentrations centered on SVP-GUAD-93/El Castillo, SVP-GUAD-132/Huaca China, and SVP-GUAD-192 (in Lacramarca). Indeed, as discussed later, the shift of the regional center in Early Tanguche Period to a different location higher up the valley provides an illuminating contrast in attempting to understand the evolutionary implications of these two successive periods of multivalley state control.

As indicated in Fig. 175, the great majority of the ca. 22,000 persons estimated to have inhabited the Guadalupito system is located in the lowermost part of the valley—with a total estimate of 18,375 persons in the Lower Valley, a much smaller estimate of 3170 persons in the Middle Valley, and only 395 persons in the Upper Valley (see Table 12). Thus the Lower Valley population is 5.6 times greater than that of the preceding period, while by contrast the Middle Valley and Upper Valley represent only 40% and 2%, respectively, of the Late Suchimancillo population in the upvalley sectors. The population distribution of Guadalupito Period therefore represents not only a complete reversal of the distribution of the preceding period, but one that for the first time in the sequence is more or less exactly in accordance with the distribution of available irrigable land.

Ceramic Distributions

Two notable changes occur in the number and regional distribution of principal ceramic time markers, both of which may be viewed as strongly paralleling the revolutionary changes that characterize the regional settlement system. First, Guadalupito is the first period in the sequence during which there is a reduction in the total number of ceramic types that can be identified as principal time markers—i.e., from 12 major time markers in Cayhuamarca, to 12 in Vinzos, 20 in Early Suchimancillo, and 28 in Late Suchimancillo, the number drops sharply to 10 in Guadalupito. Second, there is a substantial change in the nature of the regional distribution of these types compared to all four of the preceding ceramic periods. In contrast to the complex clinal distribution centered on Quebrada de Cayhuamarca that characterizes Late Suchimancillo and earlier periods, the distribution of nearly all Guadalupito types is essentially uniform throughout the region (including Guadalupito Bowl 1; Jars 1, 2a, 2b, 3a; and human effigies and flaring funerary bowls). In other words, there are very few major types that are not found nearly everywhere in the area of occupation—from sites in the uppermost area of occupation on down to the main population concentrations of the Lower Valley.

Nevertheless, Pampa de los Incas Complex is also characterized by the greatest single concentration of all types as well as the most diversity over a small area. Moreover, as discussed earlier, the only ceramic molds for mass production of pottery found anywhere in the region were noted on the surface of SVP-GUAD-112, the large terraced site lying adjacent to the probable central administrative focus of the provincial system at SVP-GUAD-111/Structure 19. Finally, it should be noted that the only ceramic type with a restricted regional distribution—Guadalupito Jar 3b—was found in the Pampa de los Incas area.

In sum, assuming the imposition of a generalized set of Moche state policies on the Lower Santa region, then one manifestation of these policies may have been the establishment of a limited and standardized set of ceramic types. However, this should not be taken to imply that ceramic types display no variability of form or decoration compared to those of previous periods; indeed, Moche funerary ceramics exhibit one of the most complex and variable decorative styles of any period in the sequence. Rather, it seems clear that provincial potters in the Moche state worked within a relatively restricted *general* set of pottery forms and decorative styles (e.g., White-on-Red, Red-on-White, stirrup spouts, flaring bowls), while at the same time there existed a good deal of minor variability from valley province to valley province with respect to such specific features as motifs and color combinations (e.g., see the comparison of Moche styles of Santa and Virú, in Appendix I).

Inferences About Subsistence

By the time of Guadalupito Period it is probable that the basic crops characteristic of the Central Andean area had all long before been introduced to the subsistence economy of the Santa region—including cotton, maize, various kinds of squashes and beans, peanuts, root crops, and a number of fruits such as pacae, lúcuma, guava, chirimoya, and avocado (cf. Lanning 1967:15; Towle 1957, 1961). In any case, specific cultigens noted on the surface of Guadalupito sites include maize (at SVP-GUAD-97, 121) and cotton (at SVP-GUAD-50). In addition, peanuts, maize, and squash are depicted on the pottery of this period (see Figs. 229 b, 231 f, and 233-top right).

As in all preceding ceramic periods, marine shells are found on the surface of sites essentially throughout the system—including sites as far inland as Pampa Blanca (SVP-GUAD-3). But except for SVP-GUAD-169, which lies within the Coast sector, Guadalupito represents a continuation of the apparent pattern dating as far back as Cayhuamarca Period of not establishing along the coast permanent pottery-using sites that specialized in maritime subsistence activities.

With regard to the overall nature of subsistence, perhaps the most striking aspect of the Guadalupito system is the indication not only of a sharp (and undoubtedly forced) change in the overall location of settlements, but the opening up of the mouth of Quebrada de Lacramarca to intensive canal agriculture. Judging from the settlement pattern of Lacramarca, coupled with the expansion of cultivated land was a policy of locating habitation sites (probably composed mostly of farmers) all along the upper edges of the canals, overlooking the floor of the quebrada. Indeed, judging from the relatively great expansion of settlement in the main Lower Valley, the entire cultivated area of Santa-Lacramarca not only served the regional population but may very well also have provided substantial amounts of tribute in the form of food and industrial products (e.g., maize and cotton) to the

Moche state—a point that is taken up again in the next chapter.

Interregional Comparisons

Nepeña Valley. Proulx (1968, 1973) reports on a total of 22 Moche sites that, judging from the nature of associated ceramics and adobe architecture, are contemporaneous with the 205 Guadalupito Period sites of the Lower Santa region. The main categories include the following: habitation sites (2 occupations), ceremonial-civic sites (1 large center, 6 isolated pyramidal mounds), and cemeteries (13 occupations).

Aside from the same high ratio of cemetery sites in relation to total occupations that has been noted earlier for Santa, perhaps the most remarkable parallel in the Moche systems of the two valleys is the similarity between the site of Pañamarca (PV 31–38) and architectural features found at SVP-GUAD-111/Structure 19 and SVP-GUAD-93/Structures 87–88 in Santa. Pañamarca lies on the north side of the river in the Lower Valley sector of Nepeña, and, judging from the plan view in Schaedel (1951:107), the principal architectural remains extend over an area of 250 × 200 m (5 ha). The main structure rises in five stages and has basal dimensions of about 50 × 36—making it much smaller in area than the majority of adobe huacas of Guadalupito Period Santa (Structures 19, 20, 81, 87, and 88 have basal dimensions of ca. 133 × 110, 93 × 25, 110 × 90, 48 × 25, and 35 × 33 m, respectively). The height of the Pañamarca structure is not given in either report, but assuming a minimum probable height of 4.5 m per stage it was at least 22.5 m tall. Thus it was somewhat higher than the tallest huacas of Guadalupito Period in Santa Valley (e.g., Structures 19 and 20 have heights of about 16 m and 19 m, respectively).

In light of our finding of polychrome murals depicting club-and-shield motifs on Structure 88 at SVP-GUAD-93/El Castillo site, those depicting militaristic and religious themes found at Pañamarca take on particular interest. One of the militaristic scenes at the Nepeña site shows a fight between two warriors—with one pulling the other's hair out by the roots (cf. Schaedel 1951:112–114; see also Bonavía 1974, p. 63, for a line drawing of this fight scene). Other individuals in the Pañamarca murals appear to represent priestly and warrior figures, both of whom are shown carrying tumi knife weapons. Finally, according to Bonavía (1974:76–77), ritual human sacrifice is depicted in another of the murals here (see Donnan 1976, Fig. 108, p. 123, for a line drawing of this scene).

Having mentioned the principal similarities between Santa and Nepeña, it should be clear from a comparison of Fig. 174 and the Moche Period map of Nepeña (Proulx 1973, Fig. 7, p. 41) that the two subsistence-settlement systems are quite distinct in terms of overall complexity and numbers of occupations. Whereas the Santa system contains 205 sites distributed throughout the Lower and Middle Valley, as well as part of the Upper Valley, the Nepeña system contains only 22 sites located for the most part along a limited area of the south margin of the Middle Valley sector. As argued by Proulx (1973), both the low number of Moche habitation sites as well as the lack of any evidence for a Moche occupation of Casma (the next valley to the south) suggest that the Nepeña system formed a minor, but nonetheless key, role as the southern boundary of the state.

Virú Valley. Willey (1953:178–234) describes a total of 106 Huancaco Period sites that are contemporaneous with the 205 occupations of Guadalupito Period. Based on the assessment of primary or sole function, the main categories of site types include the following: living sites (62 occupations), defensive sites (3 occupations), ceremonial-civic sites (18 occupations), and cemeteries (23 occupations).

Interestingly, the variety of structural types on living sites that characterized Late Gallinazo Period appears to have continued through Huancaco times—including the following three principal categories: (1) 19 sites with un-differentiated rock-walled dwellings, most of which consist of the same low, double-faced walls that are found in Santa Valley; (2) 18 sites with adobe-walled structures, including 10 undifferentiated habitation sites and at least 8 sites classified as Pyramid-Dwelling-Construction Complexes (Note: as in the case of Late Gallinazo, this site type appears to represent local centers); and (3) 25 sites consisting either of midden debris or earth-refuse mounds.

Judging from Willey's (1953:205–210) description of V-88-89/Castillo de Huancaco, this site is the principal candidate for a regional center in the period of Moche occupation. Although smaller in overall area than the 5-km² Late Gallinazo complex centered on V–59, it is described as the largest and best preserved adobe site in Virú Valley. Castillo de Huancaco is located on the northwestern tip of Cerro Compositán, a large hill which rises above the south desert margin of the lower valley. Similar to the maximum dimensions of the architectural remains at Pañamarca site in Nepeña, Castillo de Huancaco complex covers an area of 280 × 200 m (5.6 ha). And, as in the case of most major Guadalupito/Moche sites in Santa, the greater part of the complex consists of adobe-walled structures and solid adobe pyramidal platforms—including the use of both plain and cane-marked rectangular bricks. It is interesting to note that the principal structure consists of a five-stage terraced pyramid, as at Pañamarca. Although it has a slightly larger area of 54 × 42 m, its height of 7 m makes it substantially lower than the major huacas of both Santa and Nepeña. Like

the facade of Structure 88 at SVP-GUAD-93/El Castillo in Santa, however, the main structure appears to have had plastered red-painted walls.

Three adobe castillo structures of Huancaco Period—V-62/Castillo de San Juan, V-67/Huaca Santa Clara, and V-130/Huaca Huancaquito—are described by Willey (1953:224–227) as possible fortifications. Judging from his descriptions and photographs, however, these structures may well have been ceremonial-civic sites similar to the huacas at SVP-GUAD-111 and SVP-GUAD-93, in Santa. For example, Huaca Santa Clara lies on Cerro Virú, one of the two largest isolated hills rising above the valley floor (it is 300 × 300 m at the base and about 60 m high, making it very similar to El Castillo hill). In some contrast to the Santa site of El Castillo, however, the main structures on the summit consist of smaller conjoined rooms and associated adobe platforms. No exterior perimetral walls are noted in Willey's site description.

Another major similarity between Virú and Santa is the substantial number of smaller and larger adobe huacas present in the system—included both as part of habitation sites and as isolated structures scattered around the area of occupation. However, in some contrast to several of the major huacas of Santa Valley—especially including Structures 19 and 20/SVP-GUAD-111 and Structure 81/SVP-GUAD-128—almost none of the larger huacas of Virú appears to have occupational debris. The single exception to this general pattern is V-149/Huaca El Gallo site, located in the Huacapongo branch of the upper valley (cf. Willey 1953:210–213).

With a total of 106 sites of various types located throughout the valley, the Huancaco/Moche system of Virú is clearly much more complex than the Nepeña system. Nevertheless, Virú Valley does not have quite the number of massive pyramidal constructions that are found in Santa, nor does the total number of sites approach the 205 occupations of Santa (but note that the 62 habitation sites of Virú are roughly comparable in number to the 83 sites of this type found in Santa, at least when both valleys are compared to Nepeña).

In sum, a comparison of the provincial systems of the three valleys suggests that the Lower Santa region played a relatively more prominent role in the multi-valley state system than did either Nepeña or Virú. It is also interesting to note that the incorporation of Virú Valley into the Moche state does not appear to have had nearly the dramatic impact on settlement location that it did in Santa, primarily of course because the Late Gallinazo system occupied the same general area as that of the following Huancaco/Moche Period. Given these differences, as well as the much more widespread evidence of defensive constructions in pre-Moche Santa, it is likely that (1) the armies of the Moche state found the people of

Late Suchimancillo culture to be relatively more difficult to conquer, and (2) the imposition of state policies and control was a longer and more disruptive process in Santa than in either Virú or Nepeña. If this is so, then the evidence for a wider distribution of large pyramidal constructions in Santa may indicate the need for a greater effort to establish reinforcing mechanisms aimed at ensuring local-level compliance from the populace.

EARLY TANGUCHE PERIOD (TOMAVAL/EARLY MIDDLE HORIZON)

A total of 440 discrete sites was identified as belonging to the Early Tanguche Period of occupation in the Lower Santa survey region (see Figs. 114–122; for site outlines see Wilson 1985, Figs. 195–200). The number of site types that can be identified on the basis of primary or sole function is four—including habitation sites (347 occupations), ceremonial-civic sites (6 occupations), cemeteries (85 occupations), and petroglyph sites (2 occupations). As in the preceding period, the number of subtypes of habitation sites is three—including undifferentiated occupations, local centers, and a regional center. At a broader level, the fundamental type triad of habitation, ceremonial-civic, and cemetery sites established in the region at least by Early Suchimancillo continues to be characteristic of the settlement system. As in the case of many other periods, the Early Tanguche system also has its own unique set of site types and other remains—most notably including (1) the series of adobe and rock walls that constitute the Great Wall system, and (2) the extensive network of rock-lined roads and nearly 200 associated sites that crisscrosses the intervalley desert to the north.

Since the network of Santa-Chao sites and roads probably represents only a small part of a more extensive state-run intervalley socioeconomic system—and the Great Wall itself may be viewed as dividing this local network from that of Santa Valley proper—it is appropriate to deal separately with the two local systems in discussing the principal site types and subtypes of the period. This section therefore begins with a consideration of habitation and ceremonial-civic sites of the main valley and coastal sectors of Santa-Lacramarca, and then goes on to outline the main characteristics of similar remains in the road-settlement network of the desert out to the north (including Pampa Santa Elvira and Pampa Las Salinas, in the Lower Valley-north, as well as the Santa-Chao area itself). The section on Early Tanguche continues with brief discussions of cemetery sites and other remains (the canal-field system of Las Salinas area, corral enclosures, and petroglyph sites), settlement and demographic patterns, ceramic distributions, inferences about subsistence, and, finally, comparisons to nearby regions.

Habitation Sites: Main Valley and Coast

Undifferentiated occupations. The proportion of occupations in the main valley and coastal settlement system whose internal configuration appears to have been characterized by undifferentiated dwellings is 142 out of 239 sites—or 59%—which represents a substantial rise from the 39% of the preceding period. As implied by the numbers of sites of each type indicated at the beginning of this section, the principal reason for this increase appears to be the drop from Guadalupito to Early Tanguche times in the total number of discrete cemeteries relative to all occupations—i.e., from a ratio of 116 cemeteries out of 205 sites, or 57%, in Guadalupito, the ratio becomes 85 cemeteries out of 239 sites, or 36%.

As shown on the settlement maps, habitation sites are widely distributed throughout the area of occupation in the main valley sectors, and indeed constitute almost the only site type in the Coast sector (see SVP-ETAN-2, 3, 4, 10, 11, 17, 18, 21, 24, 25, 28, 29, 33, 37, 42, 43, 45, 50, 54, 55, 59–61, 63–71, 74, 80, 81, 84, 85, 90–95, 99, 101–103, 105–108, 110, 115–117, 119–122, 124, 126, 128, 130–143, 146, 149, 150, 154–156, 159, 161, 166, 168, 170, 173–177, 179, 180, 183–185, 188, 189, 191–194, 199, and 201–238, in Figs. 115–122). They range in size between .25 and 11.5 ha and in population between 5 and 2060 persons—with an average size of 1.8 ha and an average population estimate of 151 persons. It is interesting to note that while a decrease thus occurs in the average size and population estimate of undifferentiated sites compared to Guadalupito Period (with averages of 2.5 ha and 212 persons), the average population *density* on Early Tanguche sites remains essentially the same as in the preceding period (151 persons/1.8 ha = ca. 84 p/ha, compared to 70 p/ha, 81 p/ha, 67 p/ha, and 66 p/ha, respectively, in Cayhuamarca, Vinzos, Early Suchimancillo, and Late Suchimancillo).

The elevation of undifferentiated habitation sites above the cultivated valley floor ranges between 0 and 220 m and distance away from it ranges between 0 and 400 m—with an average elevation of 20 m above the floor and an average distance of 85 m away. Thus the average location of habitation sites in the Upper, Middle, and Lower Valley sectors continues to be much the same as in the preceding period, with site locations of both Early Tanguche and Guadalupito standing in sharp contrast to those of the preceding ceramic periods. Moreover, as argued in the next chapter, it is clear that the probable reason for locating sites in essentially nondefensible positions has to do with the same widespread conditions of peaceful intervalley relations that characterized the preceding Moche state.

However, as discussed later in this section, there are a number of striking differences between the (provincial) systems of Guadalupito and Early Tanguche. One of

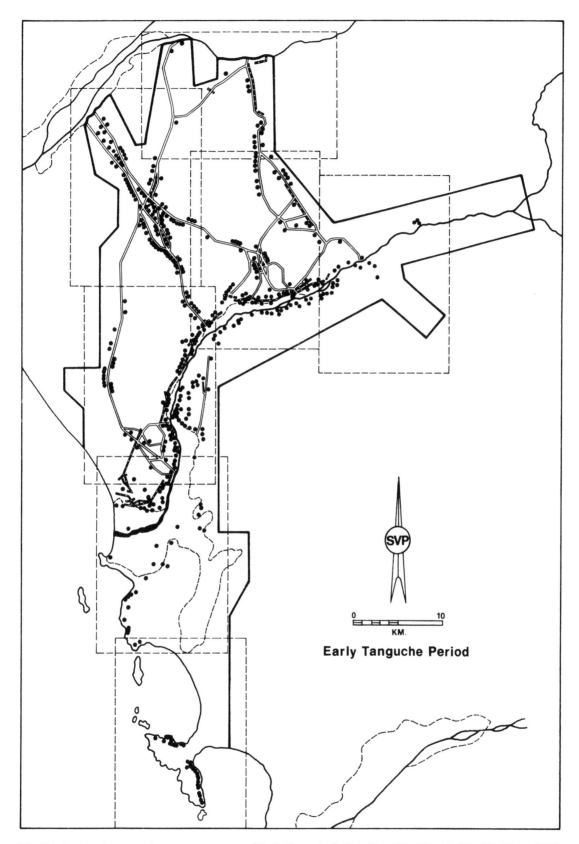

Fig. 114. Location key to settlement pattern maps of Early Tanguche Period, Figs. 115, 116, 118, 119, 120, 121, and 122.

SVP

Early Tanguche Period

0   10
KM.

225

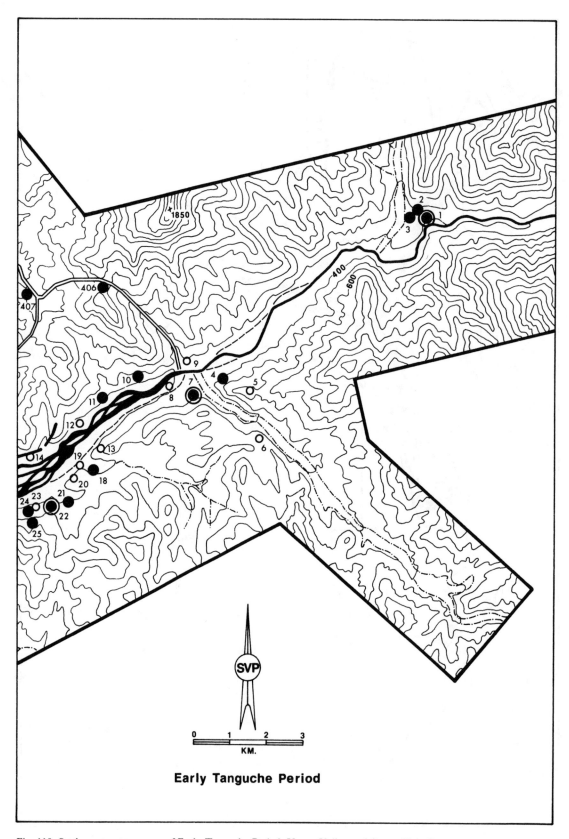

Fig. 115. Settlement pattern map of Early Tanguche Period: Upper Valley and Santa-Chao Desert sectors.

226

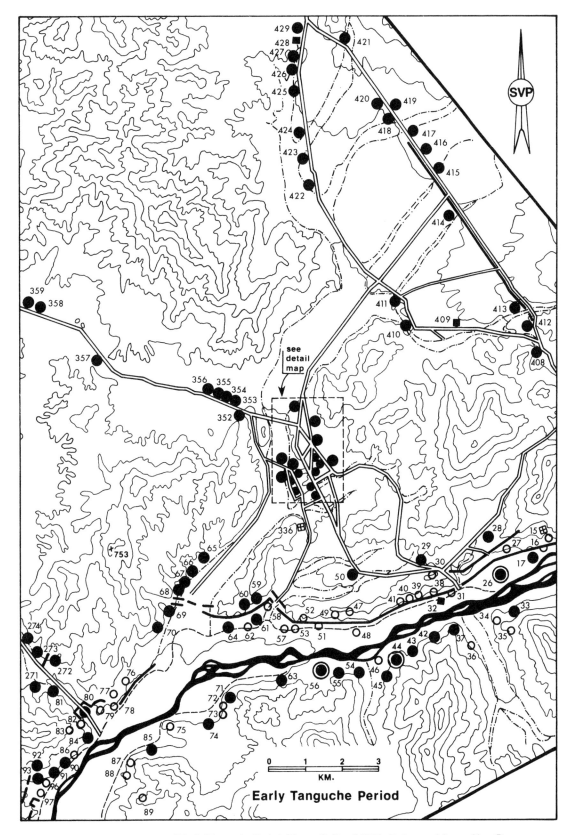

Fig. 116. Settlement pattern map of Early Tanguche Period: Upper Valley, Middle Valley, and Santa-Chao Desert sectors.

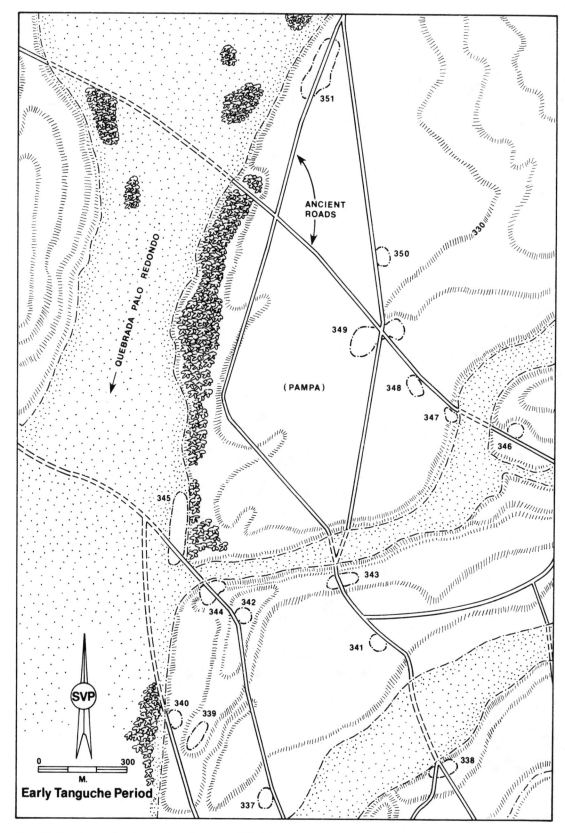

Fig. 117. Detail map of ancient roads and associated Early Tanguche habitation sites in the central Quebrada Palo Redondo area.

228

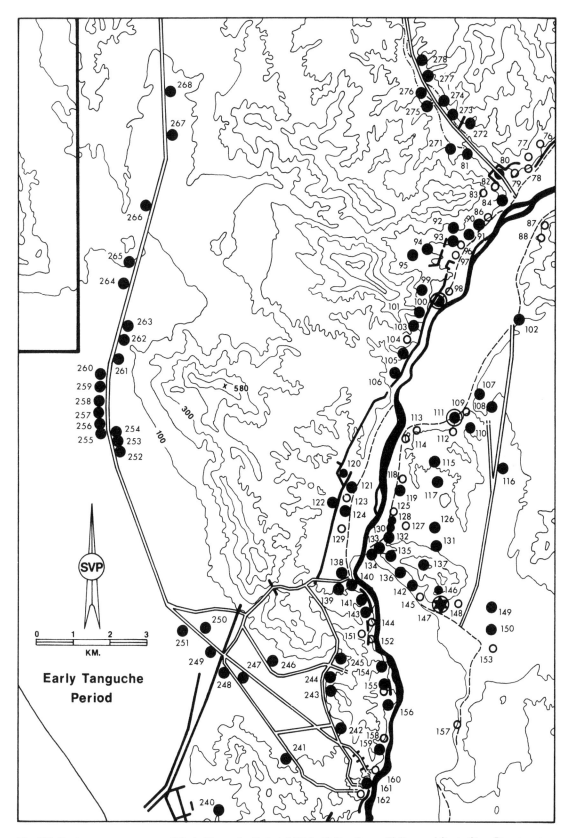

Fig. 118. Settlement pattern map of Early Tanguche Period: Middle Valley, Lower Valley, and Santa-Chao Desert sectors.

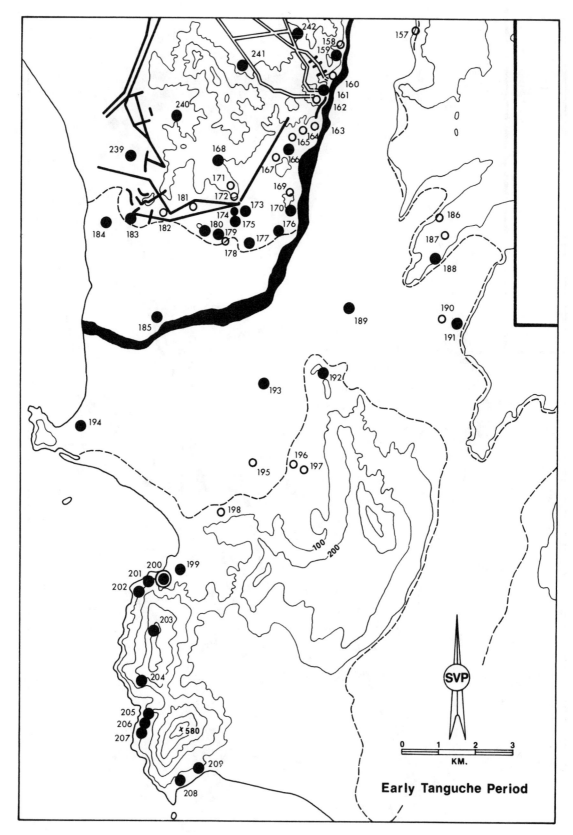

Fig. 119. Settlement pattern map of Early Tanguche Period: Lower Valley and Coast sectors.

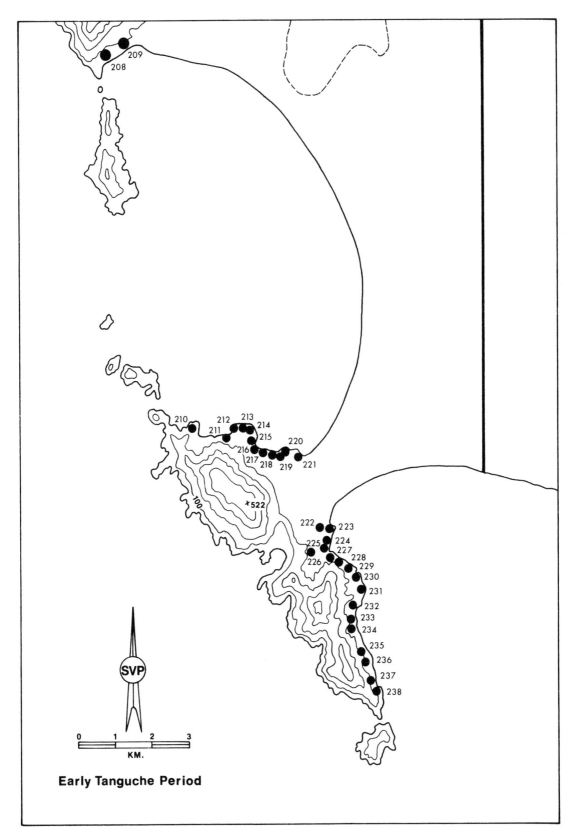

Fig. 120. Settlement pattern map of Early Tanguche Period: Coast sector—south.

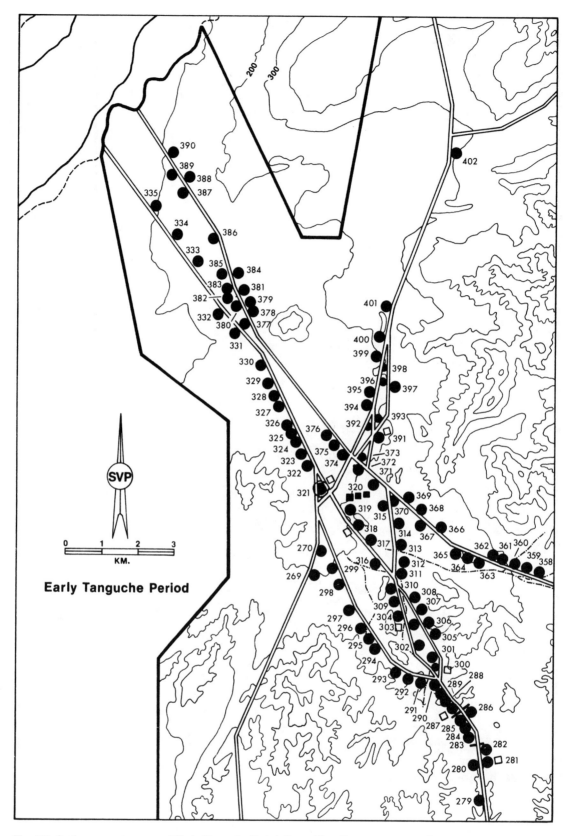

Fig. 121. Settlement pattern map of Early Tanguche Period: Santa-Chao Desert sector—northwest.

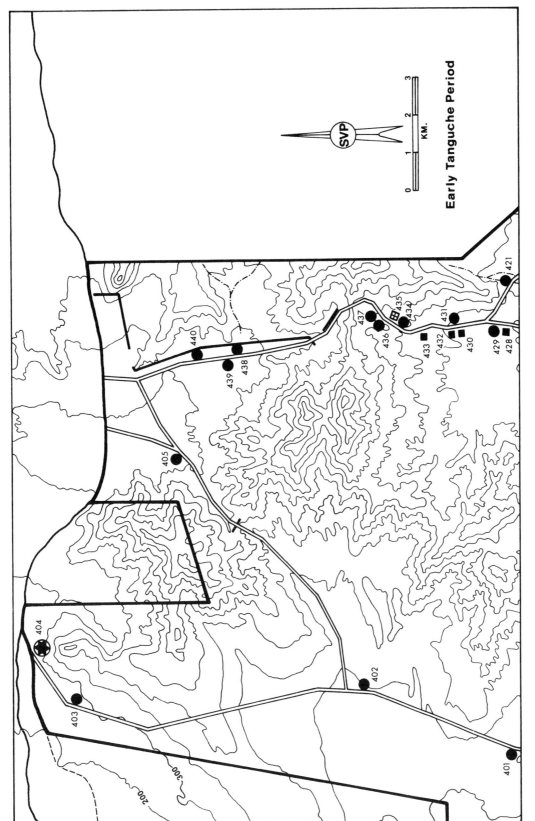

Fig. 122. Settlement pattern map of Early Tanguche Period: Santa-Chao Desert sector—northeast.

these has to do with the nature of most dwellings on habitation sites. It will be recalled that only 30 out of the 79 undifferentiated Guadalupito habitation sites—or 38%—are characterized by rock-walled dwellings, with only 20% of all sites in the Lower Valley having such structures. In strong contrast, 126 out of the 142 undifferentiated habitation sites of Early Tanguche in the main valley and coastal sectors—or 89%—have rock-walled dwellings, with specific figures of 94% in the Upper-Middle Valley and 84% in the Lower Valley-Coast sectors. This represents not only a marked change from Guadalupito Period, but a return to the constructional pattern of pre-Guadalupito periods (e.g., 91% of all Late Suchimancillo settlements have rock-walled habitation structures). Among other implications of these data, it can at least be noted here that they may throw light on general ongoing regional construction patterns as well as on the revolutionary break in these patterns represented by the Guadalupito Period system.

A further difference of some significance between the constructional patterns of Guadalupito and Early Tanguche is that while only a miniscule number of sites in the former period are placed on rock-faced terraces in areas of steeper slopes (i.e., 3 out of 79, or 4%), at least 45 out of the 142 undifferentiated habitation sites of Early Tanguche Period—or 32%—are placed on rock terraces. Again, as in the case of the dwellings themselves, this appears to mark a return to the pattern of such pre-Guadalupito periods as Late Suchimancillo, for example, when 30%—or 25 out of 84—habitation sites are characterized primarily by rock-faced terracing. In sum, one sees an essentially dichotomous pattern to this point in the sequence—with (1) generally perishable structures located primarily on gentle desert slopes, in Guadalupito; and (2) generally rock-walled structures located both on desert pampas and steeper slopes, in the Early Tanguche/pre-Guadalupito time periods.

As exemplified by Structure 129/SVP-ETAN-4 (see Fig. 123), Early Tanguche Period also marks a return to the general pre-Guadalupito pattern of making use of large, multiroom agglutinated structures for habitation, in addition to other types of dwellings. Structure 129 itself may be a Late Suchimancillo dwelling that was reoccupied in Early Tanguche. It is also of interest to note that the Late Suchimancillo site here consists of extensive rock-faced terracing and densely packed structures covering an area of 12.5 ha, with a population estimate of 1875 persons. In contrast, the Early Tanguche reoccupation in and around Structure 129 covers a more reduced and less densely occupied area of 6.75 ha, with the population estimated at 675 persons.

Two examples of Early Tanguche sites located on steeper slopes with rock-faced terracing are shown in Fig. 124. SVP-ETAN-43 and SVP-ETAN-44 cover areas of 3 ha and 7.2 ha, respectively, and lie on the desert margin immediately overlooking the present river channel in the area just upstream from Quebrada Casa Quemada, in the Middle Valley (see Figs. 3, 116). It should be noted that SVP-ETAN-43 is an example of an undifferentiated habitation site (population estimate is 300 persons), while the larger enclosures and rock-walled dwellings at SVP-ETAN-44 are typical of the remains characterizing many local centers of this period.

SVP-ETAN-116 (Fig. 125) provides an excellent example of a low-density roadside settlement—with scattered discrete habitation structures (at least 27 of which can be counted over an area of 10.4 ha), as well as a large probable corral enclosure lying in between the two rock-lined roads that cut across the site. Other features of particular interest here include field lines covering a well defined, compact area of 4 ha, and an 850 m-long remnant of a canal system. It is of interest also to point out that this site is located in a relatively remote position in the middle sector of Quebrada de Vinzos. However, as suggested by the accompanying section of rock-lined road, SVP-ETAN-116 lay along one of the main routes of travel that connected both the upper and lower valley as well as the Santa-Chao network and the Santa Valley proper.

Local centers. Among a number of outstanding site types and other remains dating to Early Tanguche is a series of nine settlements that appear likely to have served as local centers (see SVP-ETAN-1, 7, 22, 26, 44, 56, 100, 111, and 200, in Figs. 115, 116, 118, and 119; see also SVP-ETAN-321, in the section on the Santa-Chao system). Indeed, given the probability that no other period approaches the overall regional complexity of the Early Tanguche subsistence-settlement system, it seems significant that no other period except Late Suchimancillo has anywhere near this number of local centers. As argued later, this has implications not only for understanding the nature of the multivalley Black-White-Red polity of the Middle Horizon Period, but also for contrasting it with its predecessor in the region, the Moche state.

A number of internal features and locational characteristics of the nine probable local centers causes them to stand out in relation to the undifferentiated habitation sites discussed in the preceding section (Note: although all of the centers were mapped, only six of the plan views have been included here, in Figs. 124, 126–130; for the remaining three plan views see Wilson 1985, Figs. 210, 213–214). First, with regard to their internal configuration, the structures on all of these sites are larger and more formally laid out than those at surrounding sites. Second, most contain a variety of building types that suggests multiple uses—including (1) structures containing numerous larger rooms and associated occupational debris which may have served as areas of elite and/or administrative residence; (2) attached rooms or separate structures containing smaller chambers that ap-

234

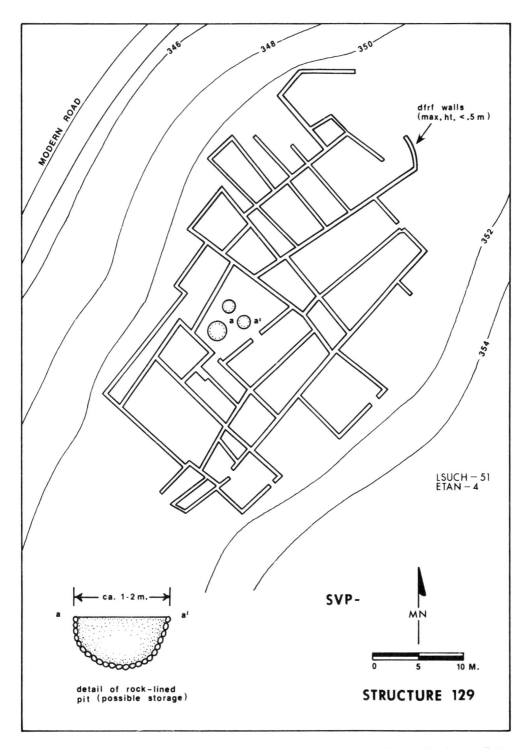

Fig. 123. Plan and detail views of Structure 129, an agglutinated habitation unit with occupation dating to Early Tanguche Period.

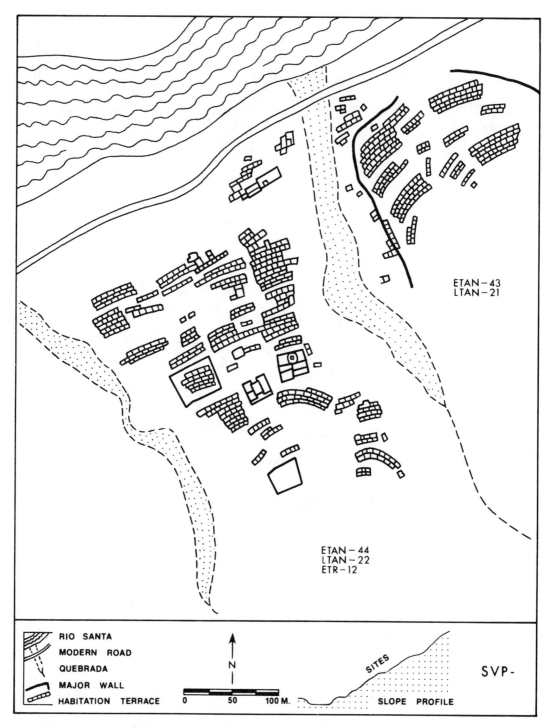

ETAN — 43
LTAN — 21

ETAN — 44
LTAN — 22
ETR — 12

RIO SANTA
MODERN ROAD
QUEBRADA
MAJOR WALL
HABITATION TERRACE

N

0   50   100 M.

SITES

SVP-

SLOPE PROFILE

Fig. 124. Plan view of two large terraced habitation sites, with occupation dating to Early Tanguche and later periods.

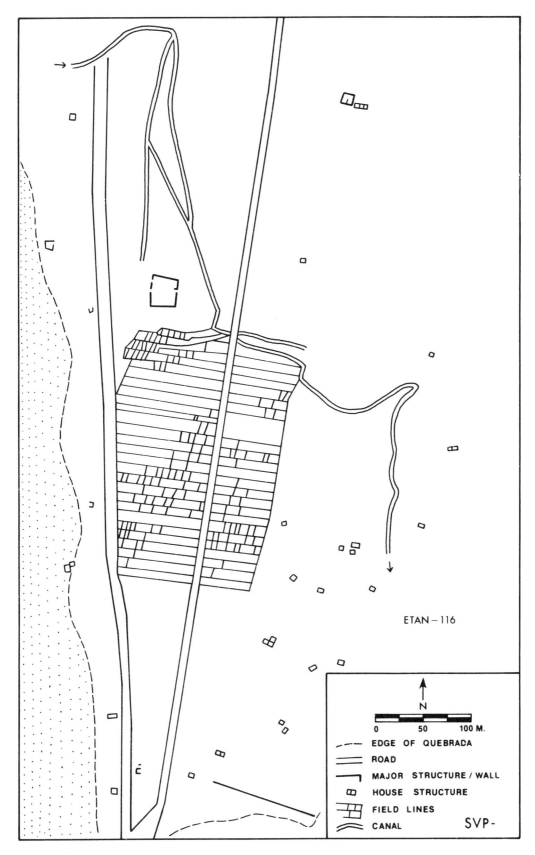

Fig. 125. Plan view of an Early Tanguche Period roadside village, showing ancient rock-lined roads, canals, field lines, habitation structures, and a possible corral.

pear suitable for use as storage areas; and (3) larger enclosures whose interiors are essentially free of dwellings and occupational debris, suggesting they were used as llama corrals. Third, a number of these sites also have structures and/or open plazas that suggest use as ceremonial-civic foci (e.g., see Figs. 127, 128, 129, and 130).

Another general aspect of the architectural remains at local centers is that many have structures with a unique (and probably diagnostic) configuration involving rooms—or, more often, principal walls enclosing conjoined groups of rooms—that are trapezoidal in shape (e.g., see Figs. 126–129). Moreover, groups of two of the larger trapezoidal shapes are placed in symmetrical relationships that include (1) back-to-back juxtaposition, with a series of connecting rooms (see Structure 111, in Fig. 126); and (2) placement of the narrower ends against each other (e.g., see western corner of Structure 36, in Fig. 127; and northeastern end of Structure 48, in Fig. 128).

Finally, with respect to specific location, these sites generally are found either on low ridges and piedmont spurs immediately overlooking the valley floor and the main routes of travel (see SVP-ETAN-1, 7, 22, 56), or on pampas and desert slopes adjacent to the floor (see SVP-ETAN-26, 44, 100, and 111). The principal factor in locating several local centers slightly above and away from the floor seems related primarily to the need to find a large expanse of flatter desert—i.e., nonagricultural—ground on which to construct the site (e.g., see SVP-ETAN-7, in Plate 18). However, none is situated more than a short walk or brief climb away from the main routes of ancient travel along the edge of the north and south desert margins. Indeed, all of the sites in question appear to be located strategically so as to be easily accessible from these routes of communication and commerce.

It should also be noted that while some of the local centers are relatively large in relation to the majority of undifferentiated habitation sites, most are of a size comparable to hamlets and small villages. Thus, while local centers clearly are distinguishable from other habitation sites in terms of their greater internal complexity, they range modestly in size from 50 to 785 persons, with only two sites (SVP-ETAN-26 and SVP-ETAN-44) having population estimates exceeding 500 persons.

Regional center. Compared to the nine local centers and 142 undifferentiated habitation sites of this period, SVP-ETAN-147/Huaca Jedionda (Fig. 131) stands out clearly as the most likely candidate for the primary center of the main valley subsistence-settlement system. In order to appreciate its uniqueness, it is useful to compare SVP-ETAN-147 to Pampa de los Incas Complex, the probable regional center of the preceding period. It will be recalled that the Guadalupito center appears to have had its nucleus in and around the two massive pyramidal structures at SVP-GUAD-111, but extends over a relatively very large area of 2 km² that includes eight habitation sites and a population estimated at 3520 persons. In contrast, SVP-ETAN-147 covers a much smaller area of only 37.4 ha and is one of the most densely occupied sites of any period, with a much larger population estimated at 5870 persons. Indeed, although it is not an integral part of a single larger complex of sites and other remains such as the Guadalupito center, SVP-ETAN-147 lies just down from SVP-ETAN-126 and SVP-ETAN-142, two other very large sites with population estimates of 2060 persons and 1800 persons, respectively. The resulting combined estimate for the principal sites of the Huaca Jedionda area is 9730 persons, or over 25% of the entire regional population estimate of Early Tanguche Period and more than 2.7 times the estimate for Pampa de los Incas Complex.

Perhaps the most comparable feature shared by the regional centers of both periods is the presence of large adobe pyramidal mounds. As shown in Fig. 131, a single massive huaca platform occupies an extensive area of 125 × 90 m in the lower central part of SVP-ETAN-147. Although now in a much deteriorated state, it seems likely that the height of this platform did not exceed 5–7 m. It therefore covers less area and stands much lower than Structure 19/SVP-GUAD-111, which has dimensions of ca. 133 × 110 × 16 m. Nevertheless, the mound at SVP-ETAN-147 is the second most massive adobe building in the Lower Santa sequence, and like Structure 19 contains extensive remains of occupational debris—perhaps indicating that it functioned as the residence of the principal regional administrator. (Note: this platform, the ramp leading up its southern side, and much of the terracing at SVP-ETAN-147 show up very well in a Shippee-Johnson aerial photograph included in Kosok 1965, Fig. 7, p. 190; for comparative purposes, see Plate 4 in this report and the aerial oblique shot of Pampa de los Incas Complex, in Fig. 11, p. 191, of Kosok's book.)

A final point of importance is that, like the local centers of this period, SVP-ETAN-147 is located very near one of the main ancient roads leading through the Lower Santa region (see Fig. 118). As the settlement maps show (see especially Fig. 176), Huaca Jedionda Complex is located approximately in the center of the regional settlement system—at least as measured along a north-south line running the 85-km distance between the south margin of Chao and the southern tip of Chimbote-Samanco peninsula (i.e., SVP-ETAN-147 is more or less equidistant between SVP-ETAN-404/Cerro Huasaquito and SVP-ETAN-238). It therefore appears to be strategically located with respect to the main central road leading across the Santa-Chao Desert to Santa, Lacramarca, and ultimately Nepeña, as well as centrally positioned with respect to the subsistence-settlement system of the main valley area.

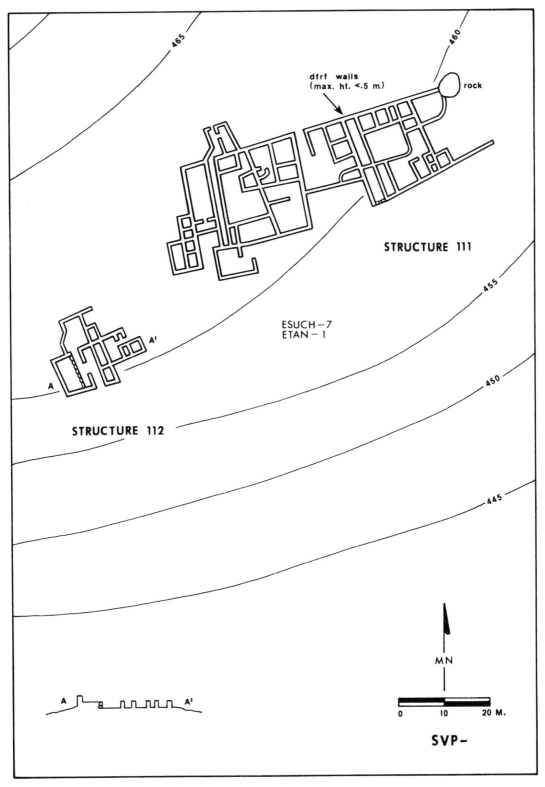

STRUCTURE 111

ESUCH-7
ETAN-1

STRUCTURE 112

dfrf walls
(max. ht. <.5 m.)

rock

MN

0   10   20 M.

SVP-

Fig. 126. Plan and profile views of Structures 111 and 112 at SVP-ETAN-1 local center.

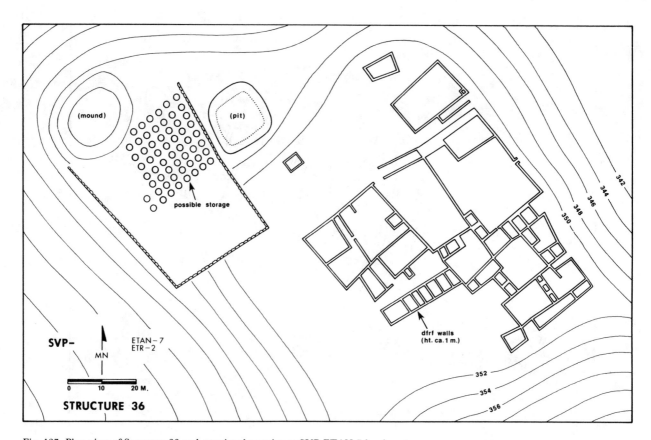

Fig. 127. Plan view of Structure 36 and associated remains at SVP-ETAN-7 local center.

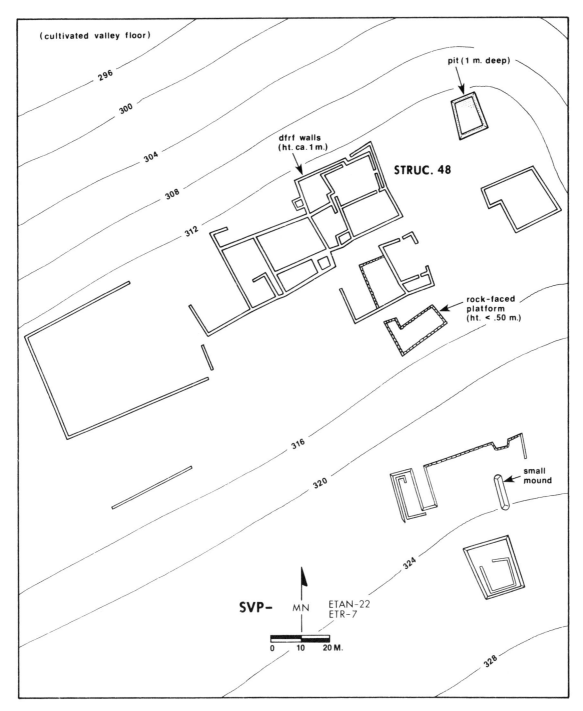

Fig. 128. Plan view of Structure 48 and associated remains at SVP-ETAN-22 local center.

241

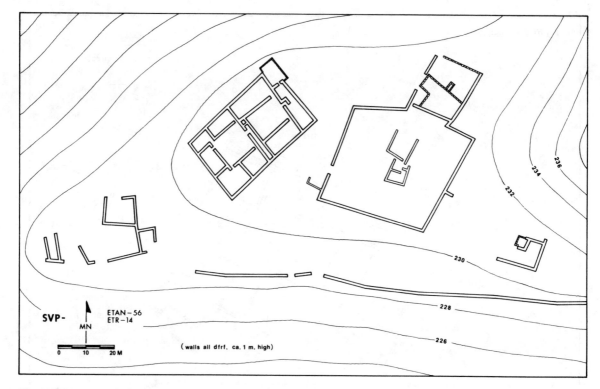

Fig. 129. Plan view of the principal structural remains at SVP-ETAN-56 local center.

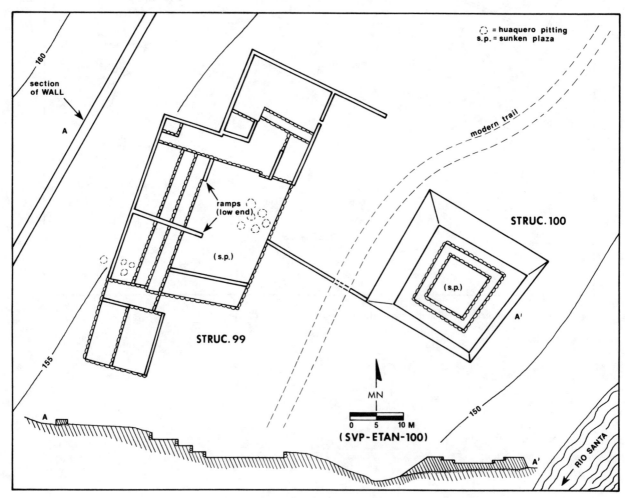

Fig. 130. Plan and profile views of Structures 99 and 100 at SVP-ETAN-100 local center.

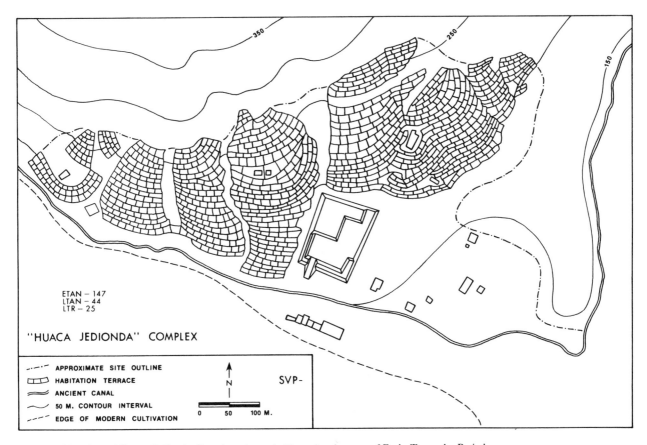

ETAN − 147
LTAN − 44
LTR − 25

"HUACA JEDIONDA" COMPLEX

```
-·-·-·  APPROXIMATE SITE OUTLINE
⊏⊐⊐   HABITATION TERRACE                    ↑
≈≈    ANCIENT CANAL                          N            SVP-
⌒⌒    50 M. CONTOUR INTERVAL
-·--  EDGE OF MODERN CULTIVATION    0   50   100 M.
```

Fig. 131. Plan view of Huaca Jedionda Complex, the probable regional center of Early Tanguche Period.

Ceremonial-Civic Sites: Main Valley

Interestingly, although several local centers and SVP-ETAN-147 itself contain remains of plazas and huaca structures whose function can be inferred to be ceremonial-civic, only two such structures are found elsewhere in the main valley and coast sectors, and both consist of relatively very minor remains (see SVP-ETAN-32 and SVP-ETAN-175, in Figs. 116 and 119). The general lack of such structures throughout this area stands in some contrast to Guadalupito and earlier periods, when substantial numbers of adobe huacas and other ceremonial-civic sites appear to have been in use.

The first of the two structures consists of a small adobe mound (not mapped) with maximum dimensions of 5 × 5 × 2 m, and is found adjacent to a major section of the Great Wall at SVP-ETAN-32. Aside from a very light scatter of Early Tanguche (and Colonial) sherds, no other remains were noted on this site. The other possible ceremonial-civic structure forms a small part of SVP-ETAN-175, a hamlet located adjacent to low desert hills in the northeastern corner of Pampa de los Incas Complex (see Structure 21, in Fig. 108). Structure 21 is one of the unique prehispanic architectural features in the survey region, consisting of a rectangular sunken, adobe-walled court measuring 12.5 × 6 m in area and 2 m deep

(for plan, profile, and perspective views see Wilson 1985, Fig. 216). The presence of a niche in the wall and a small rectangular pit in the floor, as well as the nature of the court itself, suggest a nonhabitation (possibly ceremonial) function.

Road-Settlement Network of Santa-Chao Desert

As mentioned earlier, one of the most intriguing results of the project is the discovery of over 250 km of rock-lined roads and 200 associated sites that extend in a surprisingly complex network across the barren desert separating Santa and Chao Valleys. This network follows major quebradas and pampas, and covers nearly every portion of available nonmountainous terrain (Figs. 114–119, 121–122, and 132–134; see also Figs. 12–13). This section deals briefly with each of the major components of the Santa-Chao network—including roads, habitation sites (193 occupations), the probable local center (SVP-ETAN-321), the probable regional center of Chao Valley (SVP-ETAN-404/Cerro Huasaquito site), and ceremonial-civic sites (5 occupations).

The roads. The method of construction of Early Tanguche roads in the Santa-Chao sector and elsewhere in the region was relatively simple—at least compared, for

243

example, to some sections of the Inca highway built on steeper slopes in the sierra. It involved cleaning away all or most of the desert rocks from the route of travel, and placement of a single line of cobbles and boulders along each edge of this cleared route to delineate it (e.g., see Plate 6, and Fig. 133; see also Fig. 218, in Wilson 1985). As indicated on the settlement maps, sections of many roads in the region run almost arrow-straight for distances of up to 8 km, clearly implying formal planning and engineering layout—probably using such simple, but effective, methods as placing three or more long sticks in the ground at intervals of several hundred meters, over which sightings could be made and near-straight alignments achieved. In contrast to other regional engineering projects such as the Great Wall system, the overall technical requirements of route selection, road layout, clearing, and rock alignment probably did not involve many months or years of labor—at least assuming that road construction gangs numbered in the several hundreds of persons.

Just as many road sections were laid out in straight lines, so too were the widths of many sections maintained uniformly within tolerances of 1–3 m over several kilometers. In general, however, road widths vary not only in accordance with the nature of available terrain but also from section to section along any given route. For example, the main route crossing the eastern side of Santa-Chao was built at trail width (1–2 m) in its southernmost part, where it climbs steeply up some 1000 m (3280 ft) in elevation over the mountainous terrain leading out of the valley toward the upper reaches of Quebrada Palo Redondo (see area of SVP-ETAN-406, in Fig. 115). At SVP-ETAN-413, the road expands to a fairly uniform width of 3 m and runs in a straight line for 8 km to SVP-ETAN-421. From there on to SVP-ETAN-440 and the upper Chao Valley at Huamanzaña, the road again runs at trail width through rugged mountain terrain.

On the other hand, the roads that cross the wider expanses of Pampa de los Pancitos, to the west, run at widths ranging generally between 5 and 20 m. As in the case of the eastern route, however, their individual widths vary from section to section—at least partly as a function of changing terrain. For example, the route that leads up Quebrada Cenicero from SVP-ETAN-80 toward SVP-ETAN-321 was built at a constant width of 18–20 m in most sections (see Figs. 116, 118). At SVP-ETAN-300, the rock lines along each side of the ancient road are an impressive (and somewhat mystifying) *90 m apart*. Farther to the north, as the road passes across SVP-ETAN-318 toward SVP-ETAN-321 local center, it maintains a width of 25 m (see Fig. 134). Finally, as the road heads out across the sandy flats north of SVP-ETAN-321, it runs in a straight line for 5 km with a constant width of 17 m.

Over the 1200+ years since the roads were built, sec-

tions of most of them have been destroyed or damaged either by occasional El Niño-induced flooding in quebradas (e.g., see Figs. 133, 134) or by later passersby and blowing sand (e.g., most of the section between SVP-ETAN-251 and SVP-ETAN-268, in Fig. 119). Nevertheless, even in the longer sections affected by such processes, the route of travel is demarcated by rock-walled dwellings of the habitation sites that stretch out along it as well as by a nearly continuous line of scattered potsherds. Indeed, it should be pointed out that all of the roads in the area to the west of Quebrada Palo Redondo (i.e., excluding those in the quebrada itself and points to the east) are demarcated by continuous scatters of both sherds and marine shells, with the latter consisting almost entirely of tiny wedge-shaped clams of the species *Donax*. This implies that the roads and sites of this area were focused on the transport and consumption of marine products as well as pottery. It is also worth noting that the presence of broken pottery all along the roads in every part of the desert network implies that loads were not always impervious to bad packing and subsequent damage.

Both plain and decorated wares dating to Early Tanguche Period were observed all along the roads, as well as in the associated sites themselves. As implied by the roads shown on the settlement maps of Late Tanguche, Early Tambo Real, and Late Tambo Real (see Figs. 141, 148, and 153), additional limited numbers of sherd diagnostics dating to later periods were noted along the easternmost road and the one that leads toward Pampa de los Pancitos from Quebrada Cenicero, as well as in a few isolated sites. Some parts of the network were therefore in continuing use following its construction and principal use in Early Tanguche Period. Moreover, it is likely that the initial *informal* establishment of some routes occurred as early as the first occupation of valleys in this area of the North Coast—i.e., by Las Salinas and Cayhuamarca times.

Undifferentiated habitation sites. As shown on the settlement maps, the 193 habitation sites of the Santa-Chao Desert are distributed throughout most of the road network (see SVP-ETAN-239, 240–319, 322–335, 337–403, 405–408, 410–429, 431, 434, and 436–440, in Figs. 115–119, 121, 122; for site outlines see Wilson 1985, Figs. 198–200). Several features characterize virtually every one of the desert habitation sites, no matter which of the routes in the Santa-Chao network they are located along. First, they are relatively smaller and have lower densities of structural remains than sites in the main valley and coastal sectors. Sites range in size between .1 ha and 8.5 ha and in population between 5 and 235 persons—with an average size of .9 ha and an average population estimate of 28 persons per site (in contrast, although the .25–11.5-ha range of sites in the main valley and coastal sectors is similar, their population ranges more widely

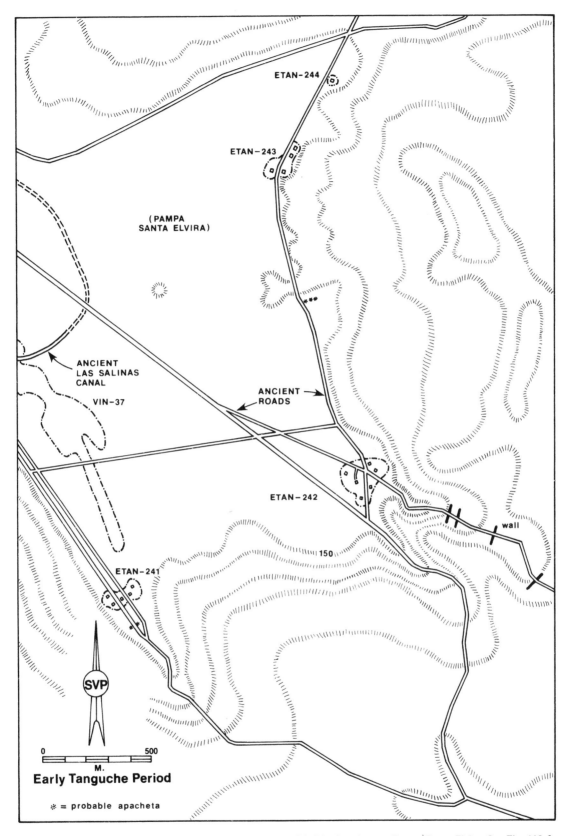

Fig. 132. Detail map of Early Tanguche roads and associated habitation sites on Pampa Santa Elvira. See Fig. 118 for location.

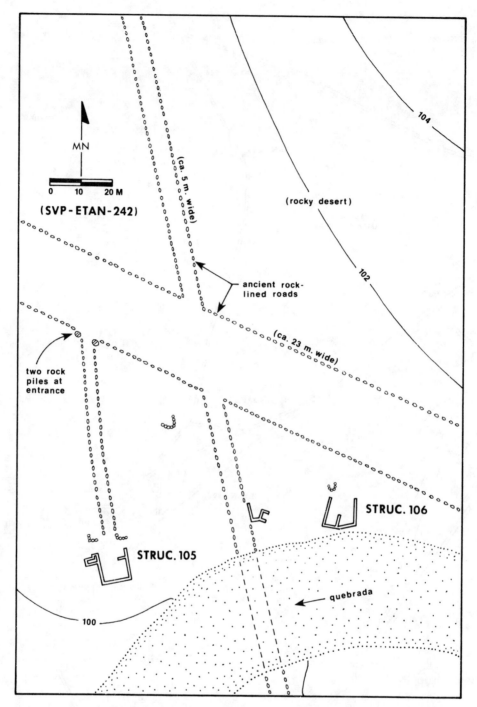

Fig. 133. Detail plan view of rock-lined roads and associated habitation structures at SVP-ETAN-242. See Fig. 132 for location.

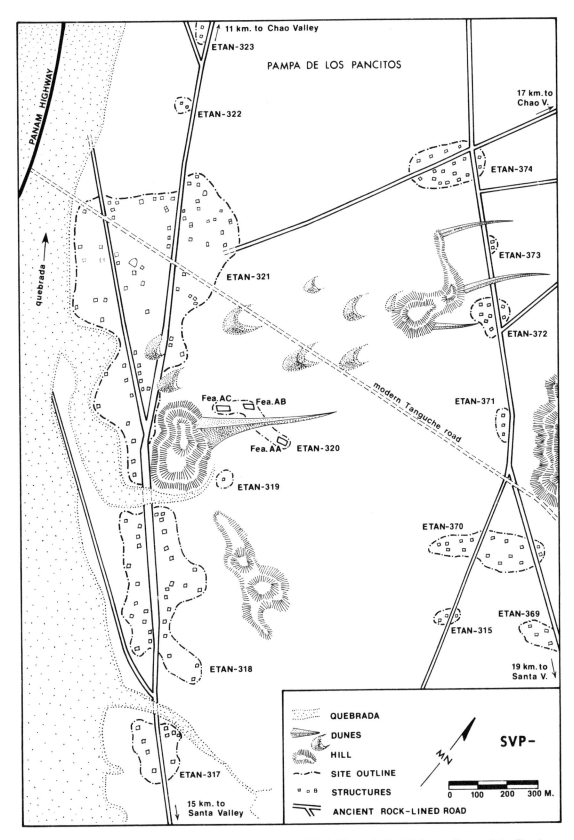

Fig. 134. Detail map of ancient rock-lined roads and associated Early Tanguche Period sites on Pampa de los Pancitos.

247

between an estimated 5 and 2060 persons, with an average of 151 persons per site). Structural densities in general range between low and low-to-moderate, as indicated graphically in the tracings made directly from field airphotos (see Figs. 132, 134). Second, every one of the desert sites has rock-walled dwellings consisting either of single-room or multiroom structures (e.g., see Fig. 133; see also Fig. 218, in Wilson 1985). Judging from the low height of the walls (50–100 cm) and the lack of associated rubble, desert dwellings had the same sort of perishable superstructure that characterizes main valley sites. Finally, all of the sites have generally very light scatters of Early Tanguche sherd diagnostics, with no deep midden deposits presently visible anywhere.

As in the case of the type of debris found on the roads, the single main distinction between habitation sites of the eastern and western parts of the network is that those of the latter area all have very light scatters of associated *Donax* shells in and around the remains of dwellings. It should also be noted that the shell concentrations are confined to the roads and sites alone—i.e., they are *not* found on the desert surface away from the structural remains themselves, and were therefore clearly brought in to be utilized in the desert sites by people traveling along the roads.

Local center. As implied earlier, SVP-ETAN-321 stands out as having formed a probable central focus for many of the sites in the Santa-Chao sector (see Fig. 134). This site lies more or less equidistant between the two valleys, at the point where the three main ancient routes of travel (and natural corridors) out of the Upper, Middle, and Lower sectors of Santa Valley converge. In addition to a clearly strategic nodal position, SVP-ETAN-321 is by far the largest site anywhere in the desert between Santa and Chao—with an area of 33 ha and a population estimated at nearly 500 persons. Moreover, field survey and analysis of the airphotos indicate the presence of perhaps as many as 8–10 large rock-walled enclosures that appear likely to have functioned as llama corrals. Although such enclosures are found at other sites in this sector (see below), only one or two per site are usually present. Finally, it should be noted that SVP-ETAN-321 lies very near the main site of probable ceremonial-civic function in the Santa-Chao Desert (see SVP-ETAN-320, discussed later), which provides additional support for the argument that this was the principal nodal point in the desert road-settlement network.

Regional center (Chao Valley). SVP-ETAN-404/ Cerro Huasaquito, a large terraced site located on steeper slopes overlooking the south desert margin of Chao, was included in the 1979–80 survey coverage primarily because it lies at the terminus of the route leading due north to Chao from SVP-ETAN-321 and Pampa de los Pancitos area. Judging from our informal inspections of other nearby sites of Chao, Cerro Huasaquito is one of the largest and most intensively terraced sites in the entire valley. The site area extends over 55 ha and contained a population provisionally estimated at some 5500 persons in the early part of Middle Horizon Period— assuming our assessment of structural densities and sherd diagnostics is reasonably correct (for an excellent vertical aerial photograph, see Kosok 1965, Fig. 12, p. 186).

Ceremonial-civic sites. A total of seven sites containing structural remains of probable ceremonial-civic function is found in the Santa-Chao sector—including (1) five sites at which these remains appear to have formed the principal or sole focus of activities (see SVP-ETAN-320, 409, 430, 432, and 433, in Figs. 116, 121, 122); and (2) two sites where habitation structures are more predominant in relation to those of presumed ceremonial-civic function (see SVP-ETAN-426 and SVP-ETAN-428, in Figs. 116 and 122). With the exception of SVP-ETAN-320, all of these sites are located directly along the main eastern route leading between the upper valley areas of Santa and Chao.

The ceremonial-civic structural type at all six sites along the eastern road consists of the following: a single U-shaped structure composed mainly of large, roughly rectangular rocks about 1 m high and placed vertically in the ground, with the open end of the building facing in a northern direction. In general, no significant occupational debris was found inside the structures—although the only sherds found in or around them are good Early Tanguche plainware and decorated diagnostics. Other than the proposed ceremonial-civic function, it is difficult to suggest what the use of these structures might have been. In any case, they are markedly unique in construction compared to the normal double-faced rubble-filled walls of most habitation structures in the region, and generally are more carefully built. It is possible that they served as roadside shrines of some sort, both for inter-valley travelers and for local inhabitants along the eastern road.

SVP-ETAN-320 is another of the more enigmatic sites found in the survey region (see Figs. 134–136). As indicated in the plan and profile views, it consists of three large, roughly rectangular cleared areas measuring 112 × 49 m, 100 × 48 m, and 98 × 51 m, respectively. The three features are therefore fairly similar to one another in overall area, especially with respect to width. It must be confessed that a first "knee-jerk" hypothesis when we found them was that they looked very much like modern soccer fields. But, of course, few if any soccer players would ever want to get up a match in the barren desert midway between Santa and Chao Valleys (even including, one suspects, the residents of Tanguche who occasionally pass by this site on the dirt road several hundred meters to the north; see Fig. 134). Indeed, the

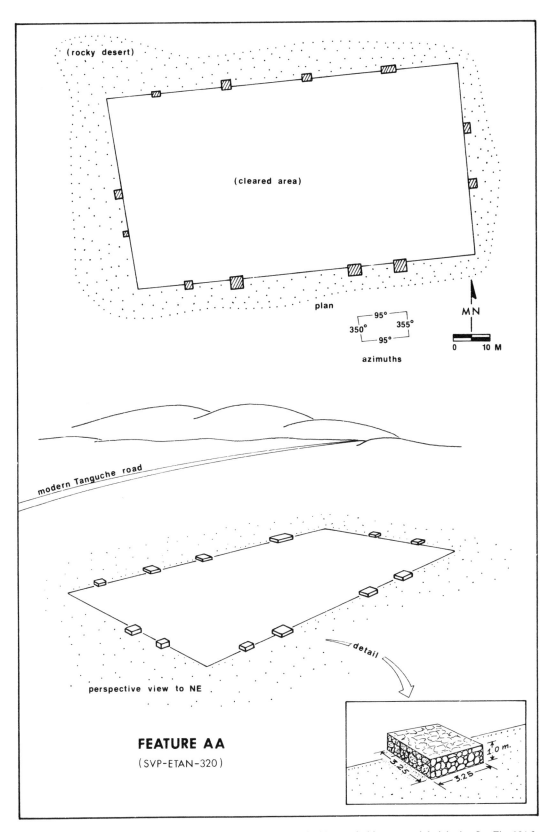

(rocky desert)

(cleared area)

plan

azimuths

95°
350°   355°
95°

MN

0   10 M

modern Tanguche road

perspective view to NE

detail

FEATURE AA

(SVP-ETAN-320)

1.0 m.
3.25
3.25

Fig. 135. Plan and perspective views of Feature AA at SVP-ETAN-320, a probable ceremonial-civic site. See Fig. 134 for location.

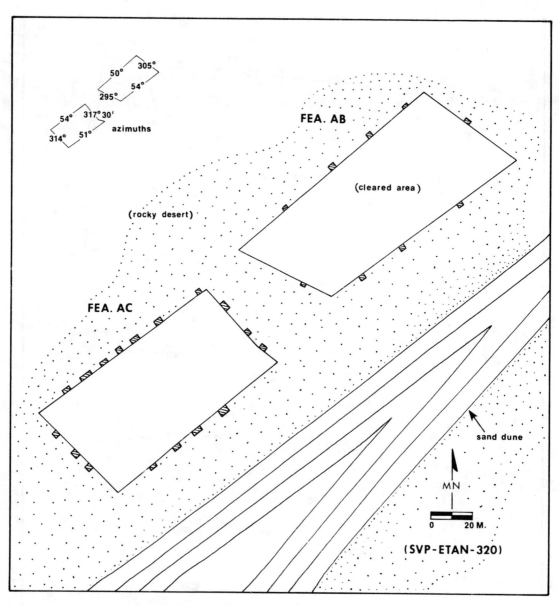

Fig. 136. Plan views of Features AB and AC at SVP-ETAN-320.

features show up on the 1:12,000-scale airphoto taken in the year 1942 (SAN Proyecto 106)—which *predates* the building of the modern road—and clearly are situated in intimate association with the extensive prehispanic remains located nearby. Additional support for the assertion of a prehispanic date is present in the form of the heavily patinated surfaces of the stones which compose the rectangular piles surrounding the edges of the cleared areas. In sum, although we found no associated sherds on or immediately around the three features, it seems clear that they are contemporaneous with the nearby network of Early Tanguche roads and sites.

It is more difficult to suggest what function these features might have had, beyond speculating that they served as plazas on which public activities were carried out (it is worth noting that no ancient roads or trails were observed to lead directly up to the edges of the features). Whatever their use, several salient aspects of Features AA, AB, and AC may be pointed out: First, each of the features is not only distinctive in shape, but at least two of them (Features AB and AC) have what appears to be an almost deliberately different and asymmetric plan (precise azimuths of each edge are shown in the drawings). Second, each of the three features has a different number of stone piles surrounding it—with 9 found at Feature AB, 12 at Feature AA, and 17 at Feature AC. Third, each of the stone piles surrounding a given cleared area is slightly distinct from the rest in terms of

250

size. Fourth, with the exception of Feature AA, the piles themselves are placed in asymmetric groupings around the edges of the cleared areas.

To my knowledge, no similar remains have been found or reported on in the literature of the North Coast area. We are thus confronted with remains whose function will probably have to be reassessed as study of the Middle Horizon road-settlement network is extended into other intervalley desert areas of the North Coast.

Great Wall System

The system of Great Walls that runs along the desert margin on the north side of Santa Valley is one of the few prehispanic monuments that had achieved some notoriety prior to our survey (e.g., see Kosok 1965; Roosevelt 1935; Savoy 1970; Shippee 1932, 1933; von Hagen 1976). It was first reported on in the literature by Robert Shippee, following his and George Johnson's aerial photographic studies in 1931. Judging primarily from their brief flights up and down the valley, Shippee argued that the wall appeared to extend continuously along the north desert margin between the ocean and the sierra town of Corongo, located some 90 km inland. Having thus been reported on as a single entity, the system quickly became known as the "Great Wall of Peru" (e.g., see Savoy 1970; von Hagen 1976), and was touted as the longest "defensive wall" in the Americas. At least part of the support for the argument of a defensive function came from the ethnohistoric documents outlining the tradition that Santa had been conquered by the Chimú during the last part of the prehispanic sequence (e.g., Cieza de León 1969 [1553]). It was thus assumed that the Great Wall system had been constructed by (immediately) pre-Chimú peoples of the region as one of the means of protecting themselves against the impending invasion. The pre-Chimú date had first been suggested by Julio C. Tello in 1934, during a brief visit to sites associated with the main wall sections of the Lower Valley (cf. Roosevelt 1935).

Our research confirms the pre-Chimú date of the wall system, and provides strong support for the argument of an Early Middle Horizon date for most if not all of its main sections. On the other hand, the results of intensive survey and analysis of regional airphotos both indicate that the Great Wall did not extend farther upvalley than the upper part of Pampa Blanca area—that is, to a point some 40 km inland from the ocean (Fig. 137). Instead, after a 5-km gap taken up by a 1000 m-high outlier of the main western flank of the Andes, the wall system runs northwest to Chao Valley in two major sections across more or less gently sloping terrain at the base of the cordillera. Moreover, as shown in Fig. 137, the wall system does not presently consist of a single continuous entity, and, judging from the complete lack of any re-

mains (e.g., rock rubble) in the main intervening gaps, never did. Instead, it extends in five major sections along the north desert margin, each of which is separated from the other by gaps that are roughly 2 km in length. Finally, our research indicates that the wall probably would not have served as an effective defensive barrier, not only because attacking forces could easily have gotten around it in the gaps but also because in no place does it appear to have exceeded an easily surmountable height of 2.5 m. Indeed, the difficulties of defending such an extensive barrier—even with an army of several thousands—would have been extremely great, primarily because it would have been next to impossible to predict which specific places a large group of attackers might focus on in an attempt to penetrate it (Note: the possible function of the wall system is discussed later in this section, and briefly again under settlement and demographic patterns).

As exemplified in the drawings made at selected, well preserved points along the Great Wall system (see Fig. 138), the nature of construction materials as well as the configuration of wall sections vary from place to place throughout the system. In general, however, walls were built in battered fashion—i.e., with a wide base and sloping sides leading up to a narrow top, to provide maximum stability. Various materials and construction techniques were employed—including solid adobes, solid rock, and a combination involving a rock base and adobe top. Although we did not dismantle any sections to examine interior construction, from observations of exposed profiles adjacent to fallen sections it appears that rock walls were not built using adobe mortar and that adobe walls themselves often were dry laid (e.g., see Location 7, in Fig. 138). The greatest variety of construction techniques and materials was noted in the main walls at Pampa de los Incas, although adobe walls nevertheless appear to predominate here. Walls elsewhere in the system are built almost entirely of rock or, in the case of those on Pampa Las Salinas, of adobe on the pampa flats and rock on the steeper slopes to the northeast (see wall adjacent to SVP-ETAN-248, in Fig. 118).

Brief descriptions of the seven main sections of the Great Wall system—including their basic reconstructed length in kilometers as well as their length counting additional immediately associated walls—are as follows:

(1) *Pampa de los Incas walls* (Figs. 119, 137; see also Figs. 101, 108): Beginning at a point within 1 km of the ocean, this wall system runs out across the northern part of Pampa de los Incas and turns to the northeast, across another narrower pampa, before ending high up on steeper desert hills to the north. It has a basic length of 6 km, and a total length of 14.8 km counting all walls in the local area.

(2) *Pampa Las Salinas-Saltworks walls* (Figs. 118, 119, 137; see also Figs. 12 and 13 for large-scale tracings from

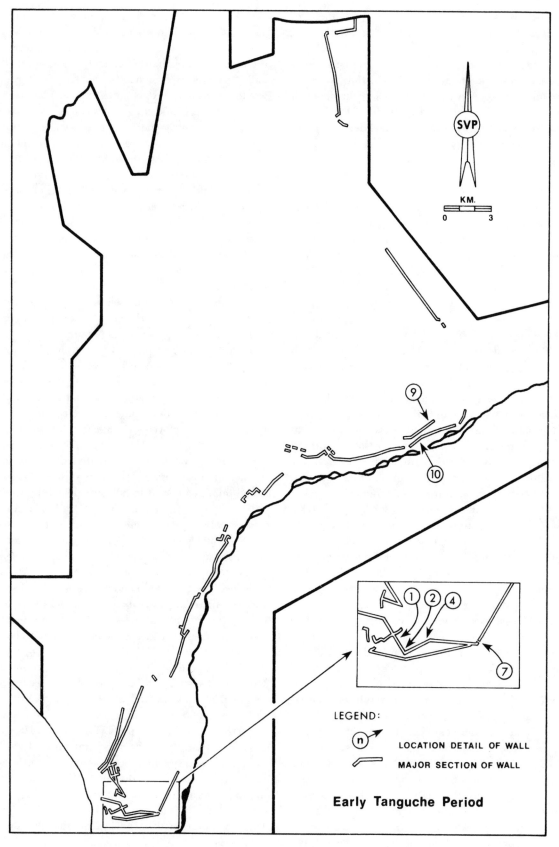

Fig. 137. Map of the Great Wall system of the Lower Santa Valley.

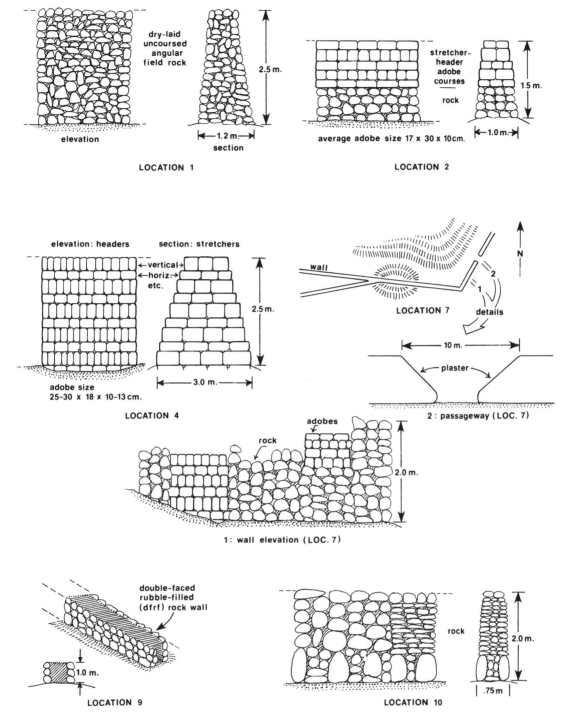

Fig. 138. Detail drawings of selected sections of the Great Wall, at Locations 1, 2, 4, 7, 9, and 10 (see Fig. 137).

253

airphotos): The system begins in the southern part of Pampa Las Salinas, just to the north of the western end of the Pampa de los Incas walls, and runs across the entire main coastal entrance to Santa Valley in Las Salinas and Pampa Santa Elvira areas. It has a basic length of 7.5 km, and a total length of 15.6 km counting all associated walls.

(3) *Huaca Corral-Cerro Blanco walls* (Figs. 118, 137): This wall system begins 2 km to the northeast of the Pampa Las Salinas walls, on the other side of a steep range of sand-covered desert hills, and runs more or less continuously on up the valley to the Cerro Blanco area (see area to southwest of SVP-ETAN-97, in Fig. 118). It has a basic length of 10.4 km, and a total length of 11.4 km counting all associated walls.

(4) *Quebrada Cenicero walls* (Figs. 118, 137): This short wall system begins 2 km farther up from the upvalley end of the Huaca Corral-Cerro Blanco wall system. It is associated with the main ancient central road coming down into the valley from SVP-ETAN-321 and Pampa de los Pancitos, and continued for 2 km on upvalley from Cenicero toward the mouth of Quebrada Palo Redondo. The total length of the system appears to have been about 2.4 km.

(5) *Tanguche-Pampa Blanca walls* (Figs. 115, 116, 137): This is the longest (essentially) continuous wall system in the region. Its downvalley end is associated with the road leading down to the Tanguche area from the Quebrada Palo Redondo road-settlement network. From there it continues on upvalley, crossing the areas where other roads came down Quebrada El Silencio and Quebrada Pampa Blanca and, finally, ends up against the main flank of the Andes. One of the more spectacular sections of this system (easily visible from across the river, on the south desert margin) is the 2 km-long wall which runs up the spine of a high ridge just to the northwest of SVP-ETAN-27 (see Plate 5, and Fig. 116). The entire system has a basic length of 12.7 km, and a total length of 16.6 km counting all major associated walls.

(6) *upper Quebrada Palo Redondo wall* (Figs. 116, 137): This wall system begins in Quebrada Cajón del Muerto ("Coffin Wash"; see SVP-ETAN–412, in Fig. 116), and runs in a straight line toward the northwest, up onto a high gently sloping piedmont plateau, before dropping back down onto the broad plain which lies at the head of Quebrada Palo Redondo. As shown in Fig. 116, the wall runs adjacent to the ancient rock-lined road, covering a total distance of 5.8 km. It may be noted that the functions of this wall may have been two-fold, including serving as an indicator of the main eastern route of travel and as a symbol of ethnic divisions between groups of the desert and adjacent Andes.

(7) *northeastern Santa-Chao/Huamanzaña walls* (Figs. 122, 137): This system begins in rugged, remote desert mountains some 8.75 km along the main ancient eastern road

to the northwest of the upper Quebrada Palo Redondo wall. It runs along the eastern edge of the road for a total distance of 7 km, ending at a point just to the southwest of the small modern settlement of Huamanzaña, in the Upper Chao Valley.

Summing the lengths of all seven local wall sections in the Great Wall system, the basic (minimum) length is 51.8 km and the total length (counting all associated walls) is 73.6 km. Given the total length of the wall system, and assuming an average cross-sectional area of 2.8125 m² for all sections (area is computed for a trapezoidal cross-section with a basal width of 1.5 m, a top width of .75 m, and a height of 2.5 m), the total volume of material in the Great Wall of Santa Valley can be calculated as follows: 73.6 km × 1000 m/km × 2.8125 m² = 207,000 m³.

As in the case of most archaeological remains of an extensive nature, the essential lack of associated sherd debris provides a challenge in attempting to pinpoint the period of construction of the Great Wall system. Nevertheless, there are at least three principal lines of evidence that argue for an Early Tanguche date of construction. First, the method of building battered walls either entirely of rock or with a rock base capped by adobes appears to be a good diagnostic of Early Tanguche. This type of wall construction is found at a number of sites with associated Early Tanguche debris (e.g., see Wilson 1985, Fig. 206). On the other hand, building walls entirely of adobe appears to be a good Guadalupito diagnostic (e.g., see SVP-GUAD-135, in Fig. 105), and it may well be the case that at least some of the major wall sections of this nature in Pampa de los Incas area were begun in the period preceding Early Tanguche.

Second, the entire system of walls is distributed in intimate association with the Early Tanguche road-settlement network. For example, a major wall section is found in each place along the north desert margin where the ancient road network approaches Santa Valley (note also the short walls lying to either side of road sections in narrow quebradas and passes of the Santa-Chao Desert, in Figs. 121, 122). Indeed, although many sections are now in a generally poor state of preservation, apparent entrances are found in at least two places along walls—precisely at the point where roads enter the valley. These include (1) the narrow, rock-lined road that approaches SVP-ETAN-26 local center, cutting through the 2 km-long wall on Pampa Blanca ridge (see Fig. 116); and (2) the main ancient route running through SVP-ETAN-249, which cuts through the wall of Pampa Las Salinas area (see Fig. 118).

Third, and perhaps most importantly, the wall system fits best within the context of the Early Tanguche settlement system. Thus, in contrast to the pre-Guadalupito periods when no system of Great Walls appears to have been present in the valley (in spite of the apparently continual threat of attack), it seems significant that a series of walls should appear at a time when the settlement system extends continuously out across the intervalley desert. In other words, the extension of the regional settlement system to include the intervalley desert areas appears to indicate not only a state of interregional peace but also the probability of intensive interregional socioeconomic ties. Within this context of unprecedented valley-to-valley settlement continuity and interaction, the wall therefore becomes necessary both as a boundary delineating regional sociocultural groupings and as a means of controlling extensive coastwise commerce.

Cemetery Sites

In keeping with the restriction of huaquero activities to areas where nearly all prehispanic and modern settlements occur, Early Tanguche cemetery sites are found principally along both sides of the desert margin throughout most of the area of occupation in the main valley sectors. But although we found no evidence of these remains in association with habitation sites of the Coast and Santa-Chao sectors, with 123 total burial sites this period is second only to Guadalupito in overall numbers of cemeteries (see Table 8).

As in many other periods, by far the larger number of cemetery sites—or 85 out of 123—consists of discrete, single-function burial grounds, most of which are located in the mouths of quebradas or along the base of steeper slopes on the desert margins (see SVP-ETAN-5, 6, 8, 9, 12–16, 19, 20, 23, 27, 30, 31, 34–36, 38–41, 46–49, 51–53, 57, 58, 62, 72, 73, 75–79, 82, 83, 86–89, 96–98, 104, 109, 112–114, 118, 123, 125, 127, 129, 144, 145, 148, 151–153, 157, 158, 160, 162–165, 167, 169, 171, 172, 178, 181, 182, 186, 187, 190, and 195–198, in Figs. 115, 116, 118, 119). The remaining 38 cemeteries occur as integral parts of habitation sites—including hamlets, small and large villages, and local and regional centers (see SVP-ETAN-17, 33, 56, 61, 64, 84, 91, 100–103, 105, 110, 121, 124, 132, 133, 136, 142, 143, 147, 154–156, 159, 161, 166, 175, 176, 180, 184, 188, 189, 192–194, 242, and 272, in Figs. 116, 118, and 119).

Another similarity with other periods is that cemeteries are generally so badly looted that it is difficult to ascertain the nature of grave architecture. However, judging from the presence of scattered adobes and rocks on the surface of many sites, as well as from the nature and size of several semi-intact tombs that were observed, it appears likely that burial patterns characteristic of Guadalupito Period continue on into Early Tanguche times—including the use of adobe bricks and field rock in building rectangular tombs of a size suitable for extended burial. But the absence of architectural remains of this kind on many looted cemeteries makes it likely

that large numbers of burials consisted simply of shallow unlined graves.

Other Remains: Canal-Field System, Corrals, Petroglyphs

Las Salinas canal-field system. Mention has been made in the chapter on socioenvironmental setting of the excellently preserved system of canals and associated serpentine furrows found in the Pampa Las Salinas area (e.g., see Plate 7). As shown schematically in Figs. 12 and 13, this system runs along the lower western edge of Cerro Las Salinas and around its northern and northeastern edges, toward the modern saltworks. At least two aspects of the system and adjacent remains are worth detailing here since they appear to indicate that, even if its upper reaches on Pampa de los Incas were built as early as Guadalupito Period, much of the system was completed and in heavy use in Early Tanguche times.

First, only a relatively narrow strip of land encompassing some 245 ha appears to have been suitable for irrigation (see Table 2). The rest of the terrain consists of the heavily salt-encrusted flats that comprise Pampa Las Salinas itself. In this regard—and considering the substantial 15-km length of the main canal and the considerable effort expended in constructing the overall system (including making at least one cut through a low intervening piedmont spur)—it may well be that its purpose was not only for irrigation but also to supply additional water to the flats for more efficient production of salt. Second, as the settlement maps show, Early Tanguche is the single period in the ceramic sequence when large numbers of sites are found in this area—including the complex road-settlement network of Pampa Santa Elvira (see Fig. 132) and four sites found adjacent to the salt-making basins (see Fig. 12). It is therefore likely that much if not all of the Las Salinas canal system dates to Early Tanguche Period and served as a source of water for drinking, irrigation, as well as possible salt production.

Corrals. Considering the evidence of strong interregional ties in this period (including pronounced intervalley ceramic similarities and the network of desert roads and settlements), it is not surprising that at least 16 probable llama corrals were noted in the regional system. Interestingly enough, five out of six corral enclosures found on the south desert margin are located either at local centers in the Upper and Middle Valley (see SVP-ETAN-7, 22, 44, and 56, in Figs. 127, 128, 124, and 129) or at SVP-ETAN-147/Huaca Jedionda, the probable regional center of the period (Fig. 131). The remaining corral feature on the south desert margin is found at SVP-ETAN-116, which lies along the ancient road that leads from SVP-ETAN-147 toward the upvalley local centers and the Santa-Chao road network (Figs. 118, 125).

Also, considering the fact that the densest distribution of sites in the desert network is along the central road in the vicinity of SVP-ETAN-321, it appears significant that seven out of the remaining 10 corral enclosures are located along this route (see SVP-ETAN-80, 281, 287, 301, 304, 318, and 321, in Figs. 118, 121). Moreover, SVP-ETAN-116 and SVP-ETAN-147/Huaca Jedionda are both situated on the same central coastwise road, although on the south side of the river—probably indicating that a major ford or some other means of crossing the river with animals existed immediately to the south of Quebrada Cenicero. In any case, given the concentration of sites and corrals along the central road, it seems likely that it served as the main route linking the Santa Valley to Santa-Chao and points farther north.

The three remaining corrals in the system are found at the following sites: (1) SVP-ETAN-26, a local center and probable nodal point of some importance in the road network (see Fig. 116); (2) SVP-ETAN-101, located 15 km father downvalley on the same side of the river as SVP-ETAN-26 and SVP-ETAN-80 (see Figs. 116, 118); and (3) SVP-ETAN-391, situated on the main road leading north from SVP-ETAN-321 toward Cerro Huasaquito site in Chao Valley (see Fig. 121).

In sum, considering the large number of probable corral enclosures found along the major roads and communication routes of the Early Tanguche settlement system, it seems likely that llamas were widely used as a means of transporting goods from place to place in the valley as well as between separate regional systems along the coast.

Petroglyphs. It is of interest to note that the great majority of petroglyph sites in the survey region appear to date to Early Tanguche, judging primarily from their location either along the roads of the Santa-Chao network or near large concentrations of sites of this period in the main valley area (see SVP-ETAN-15, 336, 435, and near SVP-ETAN-100, in Figs. 116, 118, 122). As shown in Figs. 139 and 140, individual petroglyphs range generally in size between 15 and 40 cm high—consisting primarily of (1) naturalistic depictions of humans (smiling faces are very common), and (2) animals (including birds, lizards, scorpions, and possibly dogs). A single nearly life-size depiction of a human figure (Fig. 140 F) was discovered on a narrow, flat rock near SVP-ETAN-414, a small site located along the eastern Santa-Chao road. Among the more interesting mixtures of realistic and abstract features is the depiction of a human foot with a long "middle toe", from SVP-ETAN-435 site farther north of here along the ancient eastern road.

Compared to Early Tanguche, very few petroglyphs were found that can be more or less securely dated to other periods in the sequence. Two of the three petroglyphs illustrated here are of probable Late Suchimancillo date, since they were noted on large boulders

within the local center of SVP-ESUCH-19/SVP-LSUCH-45 (see Fig. 140 A, B). The remaining petroglyph was found on a boulder located on the ridge downslope to the northwest of SVP-CAY-17/SVP-VIN-16 (Structure 27), in the Quebrada de Cayhuamarca area (see "cat-on-the-front-wheel-of-a-bicycle", in Fig. 140 C), and presumably dates to one or the other of the two earliest ceramic periods.

Settlement and Demographic Patterns

If the system of Guadalupito Period may be fairly described as representing a revolutionary break with the strongly upvalley-oriented developmental pattern of preceding periods, then so may the Early Tanguche system be described as representing nearly the same kind of break with the main valley-oriented pattern of all earlier periods including Guadalupito. Indeed, aside from its greater overall extent and internal diversity, among the main aspects of the Early Tanguche system that argue for the presence of an even more complex multivalley state system in this area of the North Coast are (1) the unprecedented appearance of a complex intervalley road-settlement network; and (2) the more or less equally intensive focus on both agricultural and maritime subsistence, as evidenced by sites located throughout most parts of the coast and main valley sectors.

Interestingly, if one takes into consideration only the 239 sites located outside the Santa-Chao network, it can be readily seen by comparing the settlement maps (Figs. 174 and 176) that Early Tanguche represents a substantial shift in the focus of main valley settlement. This shift, which is arguably as revolutionary as that which occurred from Late Suchimancillo to Guadalupito times, is exemplified by the fact that nearly all sites in the main valley appear to be new occupations (94% are new, while 6% represent continuing occupation from Guadalupito). Thus, as indicated by the demographic maps (Figs. 175 and 177), it is clear that the population "center of gravity" of Guadalupito Period is in the Lower Valley while that of Early Tanguche is in the lower part of the Middle Valley. The strong shift of settlement and population to the upvalley area appears to have been accompanied by the virtual abandonment of agricultural communities in the mouth of Quebrada de Lacramarca. Indeed, considering the long distance between here and major groups of nearby habitation sites, it is likely that the Lacramarca agricultural system itself was abandoned. Thus, whatever the reasons for the strong shift in the subsistence-settlement focus, the multivalley state system of Early Tanguche appears to have been characterized by rather sharply different priorities and policies.

It is also of interest to point out that seven of the eight main-valley sites designated as local centers are located in the Middle and Upper Valley sectors. In addition, the probable regional center of SVP-ETAN-147 lies at the

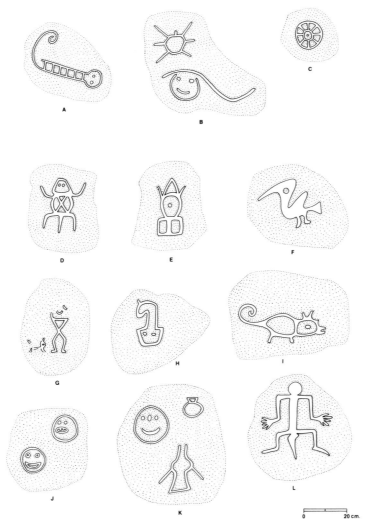

Fig. 139. Petroglyphs dating probably to Early Tanguche Period (A–C: SVP-ETAN-336; D–L: SVP-ETAN-15).

lower end of this string of seven local centers. The regional center therefore appears to have been strategically located more with respect to the overall regional network of roads and sites than to the main valley system alone. This may be one of the primary indicators that considerations regarding the location of major sites were being carried out within a larger interregional context involving intensive socioeconomic and political ties, as also appears to have been the case in the preceding Guadalupito Period (Note: the nature of the Black-White-Red state and the possible location of its capital are discussed in Chapter V).

The sharp shifts in the distribution of population from Guadalupito to Early Tanguche can be appreciated by examining sector-by-sector changes: In the Upper Valley the population rises by over 12 times, from an estimated 395 to 4820 persons; in the Middle Valley it rises by 3.3 times, from 3170 to 10,615 persons; and in the

Coast sector it rises by nearly 39 times, from 80 to 2945 persons. In contrast, in the Lower Valley sector the population estimate drops from 18,375 persons to only 11,750, or to 64% of that in Guadalupito Period.

The remaining outstanding features of Early Tanguche Period are (1) the road-settlement network of Santa-Chao; and (2) the Great Wall system, which separates sites in the main valley area from those of the desert. Both of these features have been discussed in detail above, and we may therefore confine the discussion here to a brief consideration of their more general regional implications.

Given the arid nature of the Santa-Chao desert as well as the location of roads and settlements, several points can be made with regard to the general function of the archaeological remains of this sector. First of all, it is probable that the road-settlement network was part of a much wider interregional system that extended along the

257

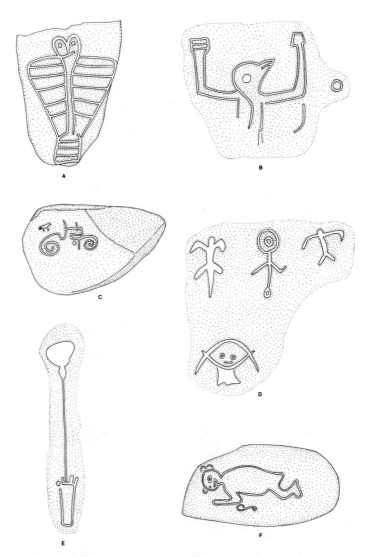

Fig. 140. Petroglyphs dating probably to Early Tanguche and earlier periods (A–B: SVP-ESUCH-19/SVP-LSUCH-45; C: SVP-CAY-17/SVP-VIN-16; D: near SVP-ETAN-100; E: near SVP-ETAN-435; F: near SVP-ETAN-414).

coast well beyond the relatively narrow confines of the survey region itself. In other words, at the very least it seems likely to have crossed the intervalley desert from Chao to Virú and on to Moche, to the north, and from Lacramarca to Nepeña and on to Casma, to the south. Second, the fact that settlements are distributed throughout most parts of the road network indicates that they probably were an essential component of the intervalley system. Third, the fact that the settlements are situated in a waterless desert and only along ancient roads indicates their inhabitants must have relied completely on Santa and/or Chao Valleys for food and water, as well as for other necessities such as pottery and materials for clothing. In other words, the desert sites existed only because the roads were there. Fourth, even though the estimated population of 5800 persons associated with the

desert sector is relatively substantial (especially considering the total lack of water), it is still only a modest fraction of the total estimated Early Tanguche population of 35,900 (i.e., 16%, or 5800/35,900; Note: the estimate of 5800 persons *excludes* sites of Pampa Las Salinas and Pampa Santa Elvira as well as SVP-ETAN-404/ Cerro Huasaquito site). Fifth, the size of the desert population and the widespread distribution of sites here both imply that goods were moving essentially continuously between Santa and Chao, and perhaps to points beyond.

The Great Wall system also has been described in detail earlier in this section, and it is necessary only to comment briefly here on the implications regarding its function. As argued earlier, since it seems clear that the wall system could not have served as an effective defensive barrier, it is unlikely that it was constructed with

258

such a purpose in mind. Instead, it is probable that the system served two or three related *non*-defensive functions. First, given the fact that this is the only period when a large group of people was occupying the intervalley area, it may be that the Great Walls of the north desert margin served as an extensive, visible barrier erected as a symbol of the social, or ethnic, divisions between groups in Santa Valley proper and the Santa-Chao Desert. Second, given the likelihood that Santa was a province in a multivalley state characterized not only by intensive interregional socioeconomic and political ties but also by a formal road-settlement network facilitating the maintenance of those ties, it is probable that the Great Walls served as symbolic barriers confining the flow of traffic and commerce to the road network itself. Finally, one must not overlook the nature of a larger state and its capacity to organize corvée labor groups for almost any activity that is deemed important to undertake. In this sense, then, the wall system may have served as a visible manifestation of the presence and controlling power of the Black-White-Red state in the region.

Ceramic Distributions

Although, as argued above, the Guadalupito and Early Tanguche subsistence-settlement systems are strikingly different in many ways, it is also the case that Early Tanguche is quite similar to Guadalupito in the uniformly widespread distribution of most principal ceramic types—including Early Tanguche Bowls 1, 2; Jars 1, 2, 3, 4; and other diagnostics of the period such as human effigy neck vessels, Black-and-White/Redware, and plain and decorated annular-base bowls.

All of these and other principal types are found at sites essentially everywhere in the main valley system, from the Lower Valley on upriver nearly 55 km inland to the uppermost settlements located along the edge of Quebrada del Silencio. Indeed, even the ceramic exotics from such far-flung regions as Cajamarca and the Central Coast are found everywhere throughout the system. Among other things, this distributional pattern clearly implies that sites in all areas were a more or less integral part of the intensive interregional commerce that characterized this period. The widespread distribution of all types also indicates that both Guadalupito and Early Tanguche stand in sharp contrast to the more uneven, clinal distribution of the four ceramic periods preceding multivalley state formation.

A final note of interest is that although the 15 principal ceramic types identified for Early Tanguche represent a substantial increase over the 10 types identified for Guadalupito, both systems still exhibit much less diversity of types than in either Early Suchimancillo (20 types) or Late Suchimancillo (28 types). It is therefore possible that Early Tanguche potters worked within the same relatively narrow set of state-imposed canons regarding vessel form and decoration that appears to characterize Guadalupito Period.

Inferences About Subsistence

In spite of the fundamental differences between the subsistence-settlement systems of Guadalupito and Early Tanguche, it is likely that the agricultural system of the latter period remained essentially the same as in the preceding period. The two systems are sharply divergent, however, with respect to the innovative focus in Early Tanguche of 40-odd sites on the maritime environment along the seacoast to the south of the Santa Valley mouth (see Fig. 120). Although at least one later period is characterized by a number of sites in positions that imply a systematic maritime focus, Early Tanguche is unique among all prehispanic periods except Las Salinas in having so many of these sites. Indeed, given the evidence elsewhere in the system for the imposition of a formal network of desert roads and settlements, it seems equally plausible that the dense, regular pattern of maritime sites along the southern bays is another example of state-imposed socioeconomic organization. In any case, it is clear from the uniformly widespread distribution of *Donax* shells throughout sites and roads of the western part of the Santa-Chao network that maritime products from the shallower inshore waters of Chimbote-Samanco were reaching many sites in the regional Early Tanguche system and perhaps points beyond.

Interregional Comparisons

Nepeña Valley. Proulx (1968, 1973) lists a total of 102 Middle Horizon sites that, judging from associated ceramics, appear to be contemporaneous with Early and Late Tanguche Periods in Santa Valley. Although he does not divide the Middle Horizon into phases equivalent to Early and Late Tanguche Periods, it is clear from his discussion of ceramic diagnostics that it is possible to detect an earlier phase characterized by the so-called "Huari Norteño A" style and a later one characterized by "Huari Norteño B". Judging from his discussion and the ceramic illustrations, it is also clear that the first of these two styles is similar in nearly every respect to the ceramics of Early Tanguche Period—including (1) a large percentage of redware in the assemblage; (2) the use of pressmolding techniques in pottery production; and (3) the presence of such decorated types as Black-White-Red, effigy neck jars, annular-base bowls, and double spout-and-bridge vessels with tapering spouts. Likewise, the Huari Norteño B style is characterized by the same consistent use of raised circle-and-dot decoration that is found in the ceramic assemblage of Late Tanguche Period in Santa.

Given Proulx's discussion of earlier and later Middle Horizon ceramics, it is possible to assess his excellently detailed descriptions of sherd diagnostics found on the 102 Middle Horizon sites of Nepeña and assign an early and/or late date to each occupation. This procedure results in an approximate count of 72 occupations for early Middle Horizon and 30 occupations for the late phase. The breakdown by category of site type for the 72 occupations that appear to be contemporaneous with the 440 Early Tanguche sites of Santa Valley is as follows: habitation sites (20 occupations), ceremonial-civic sites (5 occupations), cemeteries (44 occupations), and lookout/defensive sites (3 occupations). It is unnecessary to deal further with these site types except perhaps to note that early Middle Horizon sites of Nepeña appear to have characteristics that are quite similar to those described for Early Tanguche—including a predominance of stone architecture, a large number of terraced sites, and the use of stone walls to create internal divisions.

Of particular interest, however, is the presence in Nepeña of a road-settlement network that is similar in many respects to the one described for Santa. For example, like Santa, the Nepeña network is centered primarily on the north and south desert margins of the Middle Valley sector. Although not yet studied or mapped in detail, a single rock-lined road appears to have connected the main network of Nepeña to that of Santa via the lower part of the intervening Nepeña-Lacramarca desert, heading in the general direction of SVP-ETAN–189 (cf. Proulx 1973, Fig. 11, p. 85). In addition to the roads, Proulx (personal communication) reports that at least two major walls are located along the north desert margin of Nepeña. The longer of the two apparently begins some 3 km inland from the ocean and extends on upvalley in discrete sections for a total distance of about 15 km, running along the southern edges of Cerro Caylán and Cerro Nepeña and ending near Cerro de las Lomas. A 4-km gap separates this longer wall from a much shorter one which runs for 3 km along the southern base of Cerro San Cristóbal, in the area to the west of the large, terraced Middle Horizon site of PV 31–14. Judging from Proulx's maps of the road-settlement network and his description of the wall locations, it seems clear that the Great Walls of Nepeña exhibit the same close association with the main routes of intervalley travel that characterizes the Lower Santa region. A final note of interest is that the overall focus of the Nepena settlement system in this period is very similar to that of Santa, in that it is located primarily in the Middle and Upper Valley sectors.

Virú Valley. In his tabular summary of Tomaval Period site types, Willey (1953:296) lists approximately 115 occupations that, judging from ceramic and architectural similarities to the Santa region, are roughly contemporaneous with the 440 occupations of Early Tanguche. It must be noted, however, that this long period of time sandwiched between Early and Late Intermediate

Periods in Virú is not divided into the two distinct phases that are detectable in the Middle Horizon assemblages of Santa and Nepeña. While it is likely that at least some of the 115 Virú occupations date to late Middle Horizon, it is interesting to note that Casma Incised/raised circle-and-dot—the principal diagnostic of the late Middle Horizon in Santa, Nepeña, and Casma—does not appear in the assemblage of Virú Valley (as noted earlier, it probably does not occur north of the central Santa-Chao Desert).

In any case, the main categories of site types in Middle Horizon Virú include the following: living sites (80 occupations), defensive sites (2 occupations), ceremonial-civic sites (13 occupations), and cemeteries (20 occupations). As in the preceding Huancaco Period, compared to Santa Valley a greater variety of structural types is present on habitation sites—including (1) 43 sites with larger or smaller irregular agglutinated rock-walled dwellings, (2) 7 sites with remains of adobe-walled dwellings, and (3) 21 sites consisting entirely of midden debris or earth-refuse mounds on which completely perishable structures were in use.

Aside from the strong shared focus on dwellings characterized by low double-faced rock walls, the principal architectural similarity between Santa and Virú is the appearance of large rock-walled compounds with numerous internal divisions that include habitations, storage areas, and possible corrals. In Santa, most of these sites have been placed in the local center category, both because of the sharp distinction between their architecture and that of nearby habitation sites and because of their widespread regional distribution along major roads. In contrast, Willey classifies the Virú sites as Rectangular Enclosure Compounds. Although he does not single them out as local socioeconomic and ceremonial-civic foci, judging from their widespread distribution and complex architecture they seem quite comparable to local centers in Santa (e.g., compare V–297 and V–123—in Willey 1953, Figs. 57 and 59—to SVP-ETAN-56 and SVP-ETAN-200, in Fig. 129 and Wilson 1985, Fig. 214). Another strong architectural similarity is that between corral enclosures in Santa and what Willey calls Great Rectangular Enclosure Compounds. These are large rock-walled enclosures having dimensions of up to 130 m on a side, with no internal divisions or other signs of habitation (e.g., see V-271, in Willey 1953, Fig. 61, p. 266).

Two of the main large rectangular enclosures of Virú—V-171 and V-172—are located at some distance apart along the south side of the river in the lower valley, and may indicate the route taken by a road that connected coastal and upvalley sites. It is also worth noting that Tomaval is very likely the time of construction of the main transvalley highway in Virú. This road is similar to many sections of the Santa-Chao Desert network, not far to the south, in that it follows a straight line for a distance of some 18 km across the mouth of the valley. However, as Willey (1953:370) points out, there are surprisingly few sites (and no major centers) along this road, in spite of its probable Middle Horizon date. From this he draws the conclusion that Virú was not a major part of the intervalley socioeconomic system of this period. In this regard, it is worth adding that my informal perusal of airphotos of the Chao-Virú desert indicates that additional ancient roads linking the two valleys are located farther inland from the transvalley road, in an area not covered by the Virú survey. It is thus likely that further research in this area will turn up additional links with the intervalley network, and support the hypothesis that Virú was a more integral part of the early Middle Horizon North Coast system than implied by the nature of the transvalley highway alone.

LATE TANGUCHE PERIOD (TOMAVAL/LATE MIDDLE HORIZON)

A total of 56 discrete sites was identified as belonging to the Late Tanguche Period of occupation in the Lower Santa region (Figs. 141–144; for site outline map see Wilson 1985, Fig. 231). This obviously represents a sharp drop from the 440 sites dating to the preceding period. Moreover, in contrast to the four main site types of Early Tanguche, the number of types that can be distinguished on the basis of primary or sole function drops to three—including habitation sites (32 occupations), defensive sites (2 occupations), and cemeteries (22 occupations). As in all periods from Early Suchimancillo to the end of the sequence, undifferentiated occupations and local centers appear as the principal subtypes of habitation sites in the settlement system. With regard to the site types characteristic of other periods, it is also of interest to point out that Late Tanguche is one of only two periods in the sequence to which no ceremonial-civic structures can be assigned (the other period is Early Tambo Real). This is not to imply that sites containing larger or smaller huacas were not in use; rather, it appears probable that no sites or structures were built whose main function was ceremonial-civic. On the other hand, Late Tanguche is characterized by a minor resurgence of sites of a clearly defensive (or defensible) nature, and because of the presence of larger numbers of people they are classified as citadels.

Habitation Sites

In spite of the indications that Late Tanguche represents an abrupt break with the pattern of increasing complexity that had characterized the preceding 2700+ years of the sequence, it is worth noting at the outset of this section that several aspects of the settlement system belie any facile assertion of a complete breakdown in sociocultural complexity. For example, two of the largest

and most densely occupied terraced habitation sites of any period appear to have been constructed in Late Tanguche (see SVP-LTAN-15 and SVP-LTAN-40, in Figs. 146 and 147; see also site descriptions in Wilson 1985, Appendix B). In addition, several other large terraced habitation sites dating to Early Tanguche times continue to be occupied (see SVP-LTAN-22/SVP-ETAN-44 and SVP-LTAN-44/SVP-ETAN-147). Indeed, Late Tanguche is ranked third (after Early Tanguche and Late Suchimancillo) among the last seven periods in the sequence in overall number of probable local centers (see Table 7).

Undifferentiated occupations. The proportion of undifferentiated occupations in the Late Tanguche settlement system is 27 out of the total of 56 sites—or 48%—which represents a drop from the figure of 59% for the main valley-coastal system of the preceding period. As in all of the preceding periods, however, habitation sites are widely distributed throughout the area of occupation (see SVP-LTAN-1, 2–4, 14, 16, 18, 20, 21, 23, 26–28, 34–37, 39, 41, 45, 47–49, 51, and 54–56, in Figs. 142–144; Note: the Late Tanguche occupation at SVP-LTAN-56/SVP-ETAN-321 is of an indeterminate size estimated at "1+ ha", and thus is not indicated among the site outlines shown in Wilson 1985, Fig. 231).

These sites range in size between .25 and 15.1 ha and in population between 25 and 755 persons—with an average size of 2.5 ha and an average population estimate of 164 persons. Since these figures represent a substantial increase in average size coupled with only a very modest increase in average population—i.e., compared to the averages of 1.8 ha and 151 persons per site for the main valley-coastal habitation sites of the preceding period—the average population density on sites drops from 84 persons/ha in Early Tanguche to 66 persons/ha in Late Tanguche. It should be noted, however, that the average occupational density figure for Late Tanguche is essentially the same as the figures for both Early and Late Suchimancillo Periods, and therefore is within the general range of from 66 to 85 persons/ha characterizing all periods to this point in the ceramic sequence.

With regard to the nature of dwellings, Late Tanguche sites of the upvalley sectors are quite similar to those of Early Tanguche in that nearly all sites—or 17 out of 19—are characterized by low rock-walled dwellings. But only half of the sites in the Lower Valley have rock-walled structural remains, while the rest consist of scattered debris and remains of quincha dwellings. It should be pointed out, however, that the small number of eight sites in this sector compared to 76 occupations in Early Tanguche makes it less useful to compare the two periods here. In any case, Late Tanguche continues the long-term regional pattern—broken only in Guadalupito, to this point in the sequence—of a strong focus on rock-walled bases around the lower edges of dwellings.

261

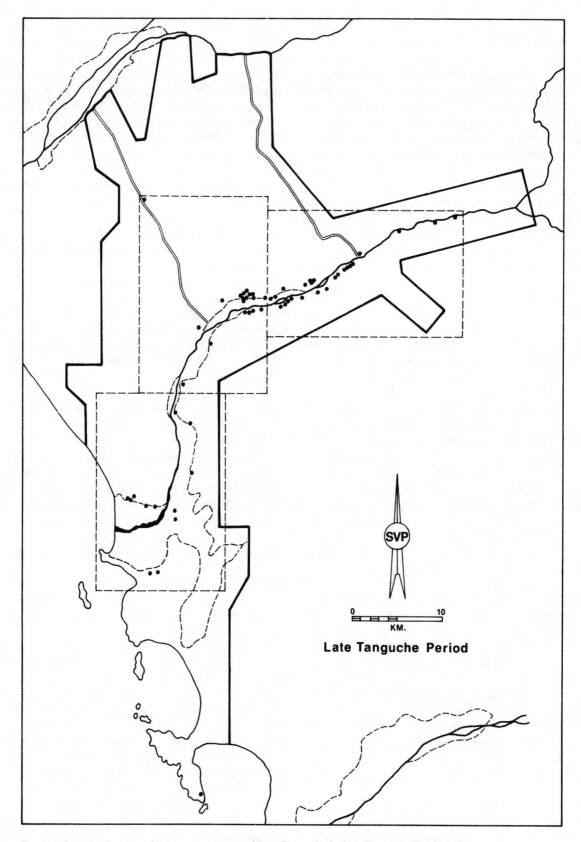

Fig. 141. Location key to settlement pattern maps of Late Tanguche Period, Figs. 142–144.

262

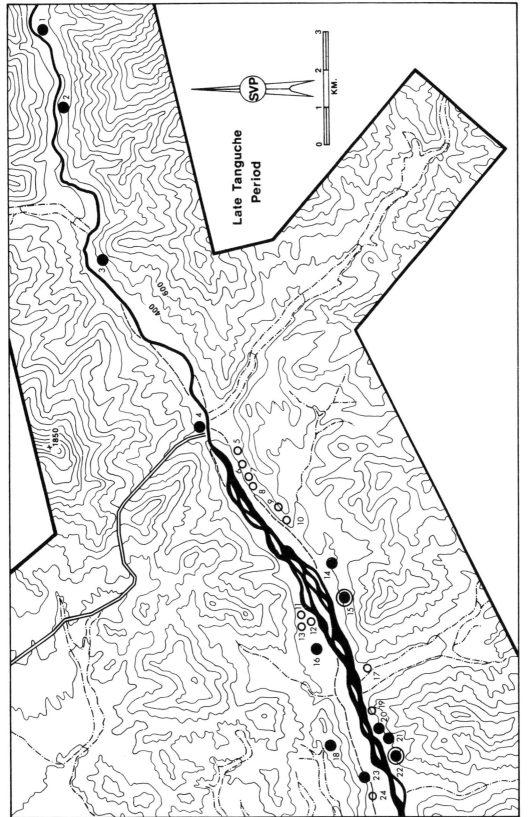

Fig. 142. Settlement pattern map of Late Tanguche Period: Upper and Middle Valley sectors.

263

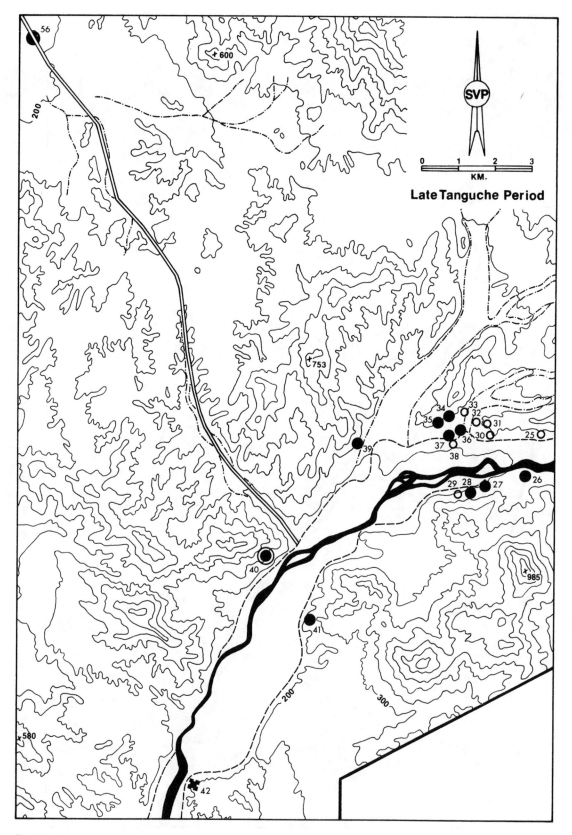

Fig. 143. Settlement pattern map of Late Tanguche Period: Middle Valley and Santa-Chao Desert sectors.

264

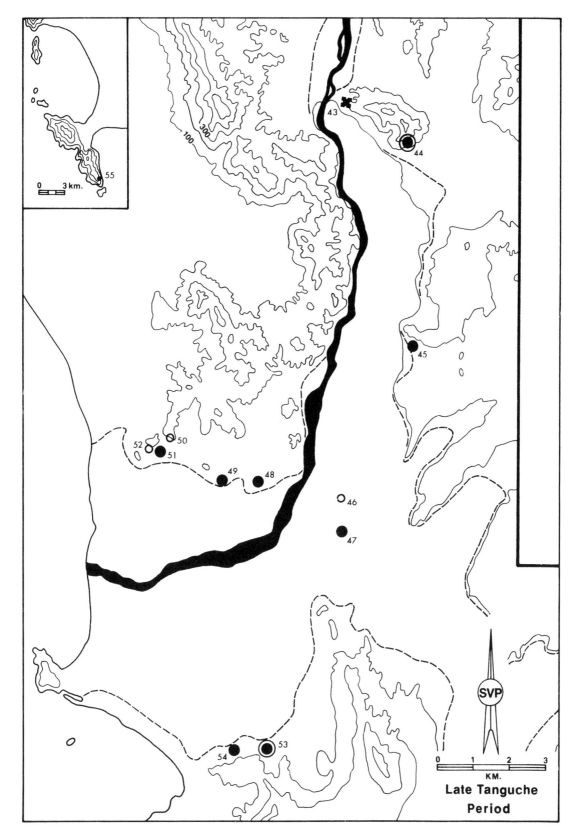

Fig. 144. Settlement pattern map of Late Tanguche Period: Lower Valley and Coast sectors.

265

The elevation of undifferentiated habitation sites above the cultivated valley floor ranges between 5 and 200 m, and distance away from it ranges between 5 and 500 m—with an average elevation of 30 m above the floor and an average distance of 70 m away from it. The average location of all inhabited sites thus does not change appreciably from that of Guadalupito and Early Tanguche Period (see Table 9). All three of these periods thus stand in some contrast to the more remote average location of sites in Cayhuamarca, Vinzos, and Early and Late Suchimancillo times. It is important to point out, however, that the similar figures for average site location in Late Tanguche and the preceding two periods mask a very real difference between them. On the one hand, both Guadalupito and Early Tanguche are characterized by settlement systems in which essentially all sites are located in relatively exposed, nondefensible positions. In contrast, the Late Tanguche system contains some sites located in places that are quite difficult to get to from the valley floor, thus implying a probable need for defense.

At the same time, it must be emphasized again that terrain in both the Upper and Middle Valley sectors generally consists of steeper rocky slopes in many areas, in contrast to the more open nature of the gentle sandy terrain found in many parts of the Lower Valley. Sites of any period in the upvalley sectors are thus more likely to be located in positions that can be construed as *inherently* defensible in nature. Indeed, all of the many terraced habitation sites of Early and Late Tanguche can be viewed as more or less equally capable of being defended. Nevertheless, in spite of these general similarities, a few of the Late Tanguche sites in the upvalley area are located in even more defensible positions lying well above the steeper slopes immediately adjacent to the cultivated valley floor.

Probably the best example of such a site is SVP-LTAN-23, an excellently preserved occupation which is situated on a small ridge, or shelf, some two-thirds of the way up very steep slopes rising 150 m (ca. 590 ft) above the north side of the river (see Figs. 142, 145). Considering the difficulty of access from the valley floor, or from the ridgetop some 50 m higher up, it is probable that SVP-LTAN-23 was located with defensive considerations in mind—although no defensive works *per se* are found in association with the architectural remains here. As shown in Fig. 145, the inhabitants adapted to the small amount of available terrain by constructing a large central agglutinated structure and a number of rock-faced terraces on which additional dwellings were placed.

Local centers. Compared to the 29 undifferentiated habitation sites discussed above, five Late Tanguche sites stand out as probable local centers—both in terms of their much larger size and their greater internal com-

plexity (see SVP-LTAN-15, 22, 40, 44, and 53, in Figs. 142–144). However, only two of these five sites—SVP-LTAN-15 and SVP-LTAN-40—appear to have been constructed in Late Tanguche times. The remaining three have occupation dating to one or more earlier periods.

Both SVP-LTAN-22 and SVP-LTAN-44 contain occupational debris covering an area of equal or greater size which dates from Early Tanguche Period—the former site having served as a probable local center (see SVP-ETAN-44, in Fig. 124), and the latter as the regional center (see SVP-ETAN-147, in Fig. 131). It should be noted that SVP-LTAN-44/SVP-ETAN-147 has been designated as a local (rather than regional) center in Late Tanguche, in spite of its apparently large population equaling that of Early Tanguche (occupational debris appears to be coextensive). As discussed later, this procedure can be supported by the clear indication that the Late Tanguche subsistence-settlement system was much less complex than that of Early Tanguche, and because of the probability that the sphere of intervalley socioeconomic interaction was much changed and reduced in size compared to the preceding period. SVP-LTAN-53/Huaca Santa is the third local center with extensive earlier (and later) occupation, and it will be recalled that in its earlier "guise" as SVP-ESUCH-126 Huaca Santa had a much larger size and greater internal complexity than any surrounding occupations.

SVP-LTAN-15, one of the two sites constructed in Late Tanguche times, is located the farthest upvalley of the five local centers of this period (Figs. 142, 146). It lies on gentle-to-steeper slopes of the south desert margin at a point roughly midway between Quebrada del Panteón and Quebrada La Huaca. Excellently preserved rock-walled terraces and associated dwellings extend in moderate densities over a large 15-ha area, which consists of a larger upper sector and a smaller lower one. Large, relatively complex structures were noted along the lowermost edge of the site as well as in the far northeastern corner, just outside the main walls, and these may represent elite residences. Perhaps the most remarkable feature of SVP-LTAN-15 is the extensive series of low rock walls ca. 1 m high that surround the sides and lower edge of each sector. These walls have a total length of 4.4 km, which compares quite favorably in terms of probable labor effort to several sections of the Great Wall system of Early Tanguche (it must be noted, of course, that the construction of the extensive terraces and dwellings themselves probably constituted an even greater expenditure of labor than the walls alone). With regard to function, it may be the case that these walls served to separate different social groupings (e.g., upper and lower moieties) and as a means of controlling traffic in and out of the site (e.g., note the position of the main exterior walls in relation to ancient trails). Given the clear defen-

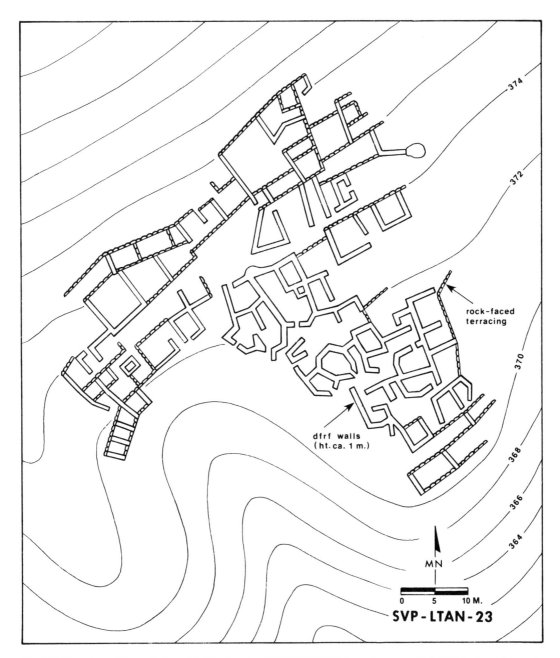

rock-faced
terracing

dfrf walls
(ht. ca. 1 m.)

MN

0   5   10 M.

SVP - LTAN - 23

Fig. 145. Plan view of the agglutinated habitation site of SVP-LTAN-23, located on a small shelf high above the north side of the river in the Middle Valley sector.

sive orientation of such nearby sites as SVP-LTAN-23 (discussed above), it cannot be ruled out that the main walls of this site also served as an impediment to attack.

SVP-LTAN-40, the other of the two local centers built in Late Tanguche, lies on generally steep slopes immediately overlooking the river and downvalley from the mouth of Quebrada Cenicero (Figs. 143, 147). It is one of the best preserved sites in the survey region, with a population estimated at 3500 persons occupying densely packed rock-walled terraces and dwellings that cover an area

of 14.2 ha. As indicated in Fig. 147, the site extends a spectacular 200 m (656 ft) in elevation from the river's edge to the uppermost reaches high above to the northwest. Two areas in the lower part of the site contain architectural remains that stand out from surrounding structures in having a larger size, greater complexity, and more formal layout. A detailed plan view was prepared of one of these structures (see Wilson 1985, Fig. 235), and its location along the edge of the ancient/modern trail suggests that it functioned at least in

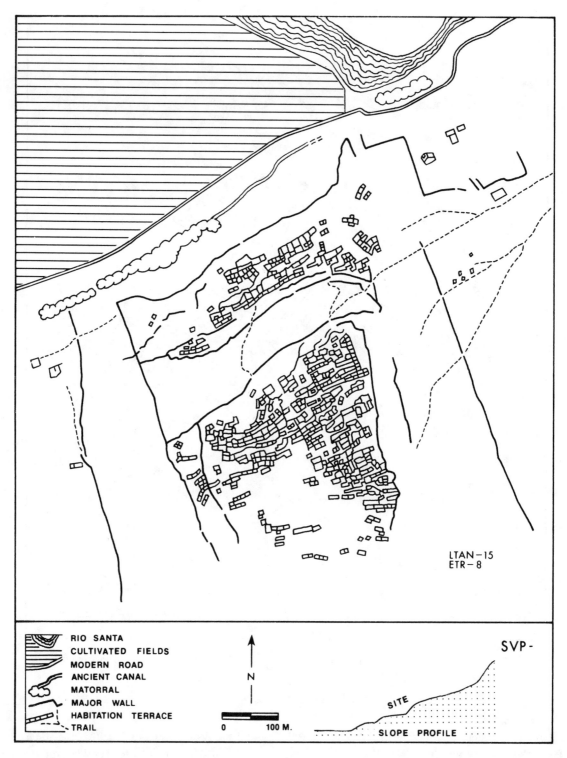

Fig. 146. Plan and profile views of a large terraced habitation site, with occupation dating to Late Tanguche and Early Tambo Real Periods.

268

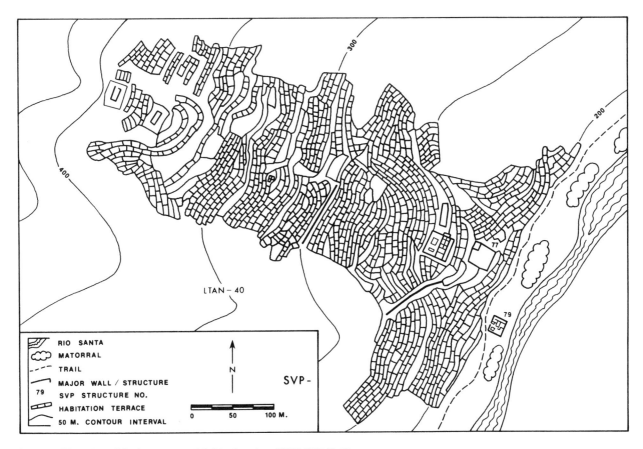

Fig. 147. Plan view of the large terraced habitation site of SVP-LTAN-40.

part as a nodal point in the intersite road network of this period. The other principal structure lies upslope to the northeast, and preliminary examination of its configuration suggests a possible elite residential function.

Defensive Sites

As mentioned earlier, two Late Tanguche sites are classified as citadels (SVP-LTAN-42 and SVP-LTAN-43). Both sites lie on higher ridgetops at the far western end of the two ranges that define the east side of the narrows separating the Middle and Lower Valley (see Figs. 143, 144). Since ample amounts of more accessible gentle terrain are available down near the valley floor, it is unlikely that the larger populations of these sites (estimated at 340 and 55 persons, respectively) would have lived in these relatively remote positions unless there existed some threat of attack. Of the two sites, only SVP-LTAN-43 has remains that can be assessed as specifically defensive in nature—including a perimetral wall and nearby defensive ditches. It must be noted, however, that their period of construction is likely to be Late Suchimancillo (see SVP-LSUCH-135 site description in Wilson 1985, Appendix B).

Cemetery Sites

As shown on the settlement maps, Late Tanguche cemeteries are found throughout most of the area of occupation between Quebrada de Cayhuamarca and the coast, although the greatest number is concentrated in the more densely populated area between SVP-LTAN-4 and SVP-LTAN-41. As in other periods, cemeteries are found both as discrete isolates and as part of habitation sites. In contrast to all earlier periods dating back through Early Suchimancillo, however, a much greater number—or 22 out of 25—is located apart from habitation areas (see SVP-LTAN-5, 6–13, 17, 19, 24, 25, 29–33, 38, 46, 50, and 52, in Figs. 142–144). Habitation sites at which cemeteries are found include SVP-LTAN-39, 41, and 47 (in Figs. 143, 144).

A point worth noting with regard to the pronounced upvalley distribution of cemeteries is that at least two areas appear to constitute isolated necropolises, similar to those of Guadalupito Period. The first of these burial areas consists of six sites on the lower northwestern slopes of Cayhuamarca-Panteón ridge (see SVP-LTAN-5 through SVP-LTAN-10, in Fig. 142), and the second consists of five sites along the lower southern

269

slopes of Cerro Loreto ridge (see SVP-LTAN-24 and sites on downvalley, in Figs. 142, 143). Finally, it should be noted that no single-component Late Tanguche cemetery was found at which burial remains were well enough preserved to assess accurately the nature of graves themselves. Although it is likely that the general pattern of extended burial continued from Guadalupito and Early Tanguche times—both in the form of rock and adobe tombs as well as simple unlined pits—this hypothesis can be tested only by future systematic excavations at selected burial sites of this period.

Other Remains: Use of the Santa-Chao Road Network

Sporadic scatters of Late Tanguche sherds decorated with raised circle-and-dot motifs were noted along the main eastern and central roads of the Santa-Chao network, as well as in the central part of SVP-ETAN-321 site (see Figs. 142 and 143, and SVP-LTAN-56 in Wilson 1985, Appendix B). This suggests that at least some use of the network was made in the transitional period from the earlier to the later part of the Middle Horizon. But it also seems significant that we noted no sherds of this type in the far northern part of the network, nor were any found at the large sites (such as Cerro de la Cruz and Cerro Huasaquito) visited in Chao Valley. Whatever the nature of interaction between Santa and valleys to the north during this period, it thus seems likely that interregional relations involving the widespread use of raised circle-and-dot/Casma Incised pottery were essentially confined to the Santa-Nepeña-Casma area.

Settlement and Demographic Patterns

Late Tanguche is the last of three successive periods in which the regional subsistence-settlement system appears to have undergone a radical transformation. But, as Figs. 178 and 179 show, instead of a revolutionary change to the new (and presumably) higher levels of sociopolitical complexity that characterize Guadalupito and Early Tanguche, the Late Tanguche system clearly represents a period of reduced sociocultural complexity. This shows up most clearly in what appears to have been a nearly complete abandonment of both the road-settlement system of the Santa-Chao Desert and the maritime sites along the southern coastline. However, it is apparent in the main valley system as well.

For example, from a total of 239 Early Tanguche sites in this last area, the number drops to only 54—i.e., to about 23% of the former number of occupations. Yet, as shown by a detailed comparison of the settlement maps, the pattern of occupation on the Lower and Middle Valley desert margins is quite similar to that of Early Tanguche—at least if one excludes from consideration all sites and roads of the desert network. Indeed, it is worth noting that only 57% of all Late Tanguche sites are new

occupations, which, except for 56% in Vinzos Period, is the lowest figure in the sequence. In other words, compared especially to the 90% and 94% new occupations of Guadalupito and Early Tanguche Periods, the figure for Late Tanguche represents a greater degree of conservatism in maintaining previously established site locations.

Moreover, in spite of the drop in overall numbers of sites, the Late Tanguche system still contains elements that argue for the retention of a fair degree of sociocultural complexity. For example, as implied earlier, the five large, widely distributed and internally complex local centers of this period suggest at least a two-level hierarchy of sociopolitical function. And when one compares the drop in population from Early to Late Tanguche times on a sector-by-sector basis, it does not appear to be much more radical a change than that characterizing the regional population drop of Guadalupito Period—at least when the Santa-Chao and Coast sectors are excluded from consideration. In the Upper Valley the estimate drops from 4820 to 2160 persons, in the Middle Valley from 10,615 to 7215 persons, and in the Lower Valley from 11,750 to 8960 persons (representing changes to 45%, 68%, and 76% of former levels, respectively). However, relatively dramatic changes occur in the Coast and Santa-Chao Desert sectors, where the estimates drop from 2945 to 50 persons and from 5800 to 50 persons, respectively. And, of course, the overall estimate of 18,435 persons in the Late Tanguche system is only about half that estimated for Early Tanguche times—representing a much greater change, for example, than the 26% reduction that occurs from Late Suchimancillo to Guadalupito Period.

Along with the drop in regional population size, other potentially significant aspects of the Late Tanguche system are the reestablishment of a few defensive sites and the location of some habitation sites in positions that can be interpreted as clearly defensive in nature. And, as mentioned earlier, along with these changes there is a shift toward greater concentration of population in some of the largest terraced habitation sites of any period in the sequence. Compared to the overall nature of the Guadalupito and Early Tanguche systems, then, the settlement data clearly indicate that along with the collapse of the middle period states came at least some of the continual conflict that had characterized the pre-state ceramic periods (and, it may be added, a corresponding need for population nucleation in large, defensible sites).

As discussed in greater detail later, this is the first period when there is not only demographic parity between the principal clusters (see Clusters 2 and 3, in Table 13), but carrying capacity analysis demonstrates their potential for self-sufficiency in subsistence as well. In this context the possibility of intercluster conflict therefore must at least be considered (see below)—especially taking into account such aspects of the Late Tanguche settlement pattern as the presence of two citadel sites in the upper part of Cluster 3, midway between the populations of the Upper-Middle and Lower Valley sectors.

Ceramic Distributions

In spite of the similarities between the Late Tanguche and pre-Guadalupito settlement systems (i.e., occupation of defensive sites and defensible locations, lower population numbers, and strong clustering), it is interesting to note that the distribution of ceramics does not represent a reversion to the patterns of the pre-state part of the sequence. Instead, the presence/absence map prepared for this period indicates that all six principal Late Tanguche time markers are found essentially throughout the occupied areas of the valley. This implies the operation of the same strong degree of within-valley socioeconomic and political organization that has been argued to characterize the Guadalupito and Early Tanguche Periods (and, indeed, to a lesser degree the preceding ceramic periods as well). With regard to the nature of conflict, the indication of strong intersite ties throughout the region also implies that warfare—as in all earlier ceramic periods—continued to be interregional in nature. It is worth noting, however, that the absence of the differential and clinal distribution of the pre-Guadalupito ceramic periods also suggests some change in the main routes of long-distance communication and/or sources of interregional influences exerted on the Lower Santa region—at least compared to the pre-state periods.

Inferences About Subsistence

Aside from the single Late Tanguche site identified on the western shore of Bahía de Samanco, no other sites dating to this period could be detected along the 50 km of coastline included within the research area. Yet, as in the preceding ceramic periods, marine shells are found at sites located well inland from the ocean—including SVP-LTAN-15, 17, 18, 34, 40, 41, 43, and 47. Thus, in spite of the apparent abandonment of the extensive series of maritime sites that characterizes the Early Tanguche system, shellfish beds along the coastline adjacent to Santa Valley seem to have continued as an important secondary focus of subsistence activities. As in the pre-Early Tanguche periods, however, utilization of these resources seems not to have involved the establishment of pottery-using settlements. In any case, the overall location of sites in the main valley area indicates that the primary focus of the subsistence system was the irrigable valley floor.

Interregional Comparisons

Nepeña Valley. As discussed in the section on Nepeña under Early Tanguche Period, Proulx's (1968, 1973) ce-

ramic data on Middle Horizon settlements allow a reasonably clear distinction to be made between early and late phase sites on the basis of presence/absence of: (1) Huari Norteño A pottery, including such earlier Middle Horizon styles as Black-White-Red; and (2) Huari Norteño B pottery, including such later styles as raised circle-and-dot/Casma Incised. Judging from our own research in Santa, as well as from arguments made by Proulx (1973:61), this latter type is clearly a late phase diagnostic that extends into Late Intermediate Period—although, in Santa Valley at least, in reduced numbers and altered paste type (see Appendix I). In any case, given the temporal distinction between the two pottery styles, as well as the fact that single-component sites of each style are found in both Nepeña and Santa, it is possible to identify at least 30 sites among 102 Middle Horizon occupations in Nepeña that appear to be contemporaneous with the 56 Late Tanguche occupations of Santa.

The breakdown by categories of site type includes the following: habitation sites (17 occupations), ceremonial-civic sites (1 occupation), lookout/defensive sites (2 occupations), and cemeteries (10 occupations). Interestingly enough, the Nepeña system is not only similar to Santa in terms of the much reduced number of late phase sites compared to early sites, but also with respect to the presence of occupations that are among the largest of any period in the prehispanic sequence. Judging from Proulx's description, the best example of this phenomenon is the site of PV 31–6. This huge occupation is located on the north desert margin in the Middle Valley sector, near the modern settlement of San Jacinto (see map on p. ix, in Proulx 1973), and covers an area with dimensions estimated at 1000 × 500 m (50 ha). It therefore seems to be larger than any sites of this period found in Santa Valley, and may have contained a population larger than the 5870 persons estimated to have resided at the largest Late Tanguche site of SVP-LTAN-44/Huaca Jedionda. Nevertheless, in terms of the total number of habitation sites in Santa compared to Nepeña (34 vs. 17), and considering the large size of a number of densely occupied Santa Valley occupations, it is likely that the Nepeña population was much smaller than that of Santa.

In spite of overall demographic differences, the location of Late Middle Horizon Nepeña sites is generally similar to that of Santa—with occupations scattered widely, but sparsely, throughout nearly all parts of the valley between the seacoast and a point slightly over 40 km inland. Given the apparent establishment of several fortress sites in Nepeña at this time, it is also clear that this valley experienced the same reestablishment of continual interregional hostilities that characterizes Santa. But, as discussed in the preceding chapter (and Appendix I), the diagnostic ceramics of late Middle Horizon in Nepeña show remarkably strong similarities to Santa as well as to Casma. Thus it cannot be ruled out that all three valleys were part of the same sphere of intensive socioeconomic (and possibly sociopolitical) interaction in this period. If this is so, then it implies that at least in Santa the threat of warfare was coming from the north, and not from the south. The ceramic data certainly imply that neither Santa nor Nepeña were engaged in intensive socioeconomic interaction with valleys to the north during Late Middle Horizon times.

EARLY TAMBO REAL PERIOD (LA PLATA/LATE INTERMEDIATE)

A total of 49 discrete sites was identified as belonging to the Early Tambo Real Period of occupation in Santa (Figs. 148–151; for site outlines see Wilson 1985, Fig. 240), which represents a slight drop from the 56 sites dating to the preceding period. The number and kind of site types that can be distinguished on the basis of primary or sole function remain the same—including habitation sites (30 occupations), defensive sites (4 occupations), and cemeteries (15 occupations). Additional similarities between Early Tambo Real and Late Tanguche include the presence of undifferentiated occupations and local centers as the main subtypes of habitation sites, as well as the absence of any sites to which a primarily ceremonial-civic function can be assigned. As indicated in Table 8, Early Tambo Real and Late Tanguche are also similar in being the only periods in the middle and late parts of the sequence for which several sites with a primary defensive function can be identified. Nevertheless, in terms of the much reduced number of defensive sites and the generally open location of most occupations, both periods obviously stand in some contrast to the more defensively-oriented systems of the pre-Guadalupito ceramic periods.

Habitation Sites

Undifferentiated occupations. The proportion of Early Tambo Real occupations characterized by undifferentiated dwellings is 25 out of the 49 discrete sites—or 51%—which is almost the same as the figure for the preceding period. Sites of this type continue to be widely distributed throughout the area of occupation (see SVP-ETR-1, 7, 9, 10, 14, 18, 20, 21, 23, 26, 31–41, 45, and 47–49, in Figs. 150, 151). They range in size between .25 and 5 ha and in population between 5 and 500 persons—with an average size of 1.8 ha and an average population estimate of 138 persons. The figures for average size and population thus represent a drop from the averages of 2.5 ha and 164 persons per site in Late Tanguche, although the average density of 77 persons/ha falls squarely within the range of 66–85 persons/ha characterizing all periods to this point in the sequence.

With regard to the nature of dwellings, Early Tambo

Real marks what appears to be a significant change from the preceding two periods in terms of the number of Lower Valley sites with rock-walled dwellings compared to those where only organic debris is found—with only three out of 16 sites, or 19%, having rock-walled remains. The percentage of rock-walled sites in this sector is thus substantially smaller than that of Early Tanguche (84%, or 64/76) and Late Tanguche (50%, or 4/8), but almost precisely the same as in Guadalupito Period (20%, or 10/44). Moreover, as in the Guadalupito system, these relative percentages are reversed nearly exactly in the Upper-Middle Valley—i.e., 78% rock-walled vs. 22% nonrock-walled (the figures for Guadalupito are 80% vs. 20% in these sectors). It has been argued earlier that part of the reason for what appears to be a sharp change in Guadalupito from normal, ongoing regional construction practices may have to do with strong influences emanating from the north (i.e., Moche Valley). Given the strong similarity between Early Tambo Real and Guadalupito, the same may be true for the later period as well (the data for Early Tambo Real are more problematical than for Guadalupito, however, as discussed below in the section on interregional ceramic similarities).

From the preceding discussion, it follows logically that the Upper and Middle Valley are the primary sectors where mappable remains of Early Tambo Real dwellings are found. However, even in these sectors there are very few sites that are not multicomponent occupations—i.e., with associated debris (and many rock-walled dwellings, probably) that date to earlier periods. A primary reason for this occupational pattern may have to do with the fact that by this time in the sequence nearly all suitable locations had been used during one or more periods for habitation. Thus, although we mapped sites that probably contain a number of dwellings whose construction dates to Early Tambo Real (e.g., see Figs. 124, 146), it is equally likely that many structures were built in earlier times and simply remained occupied throughout successive periods.

In any case, SVP-ETR-23 is the single upvalley habitation site where architectural remains were mapped that can be assigned with reasonable certainty to Early Tambo Real (see Fig. 152). This site lies on a small ridge in the midst of steep slopes overlooking the valley floor of Huaca Corral area, and consists of a rock-walled dwelling that probably represents a single-family habitation unit. Because of its excellent preservation, as well as the fact that intensive prior occupation in this area makes it likely that earlier remains would be relatively more damaged, Structure 101 has been assigned to the later of the two periods found in the associated debris.

A final aspect to be discussed is the average location of habitation sites with respect to the cultivated valley floor. Since most sites in the Lower Valley are situated on low hills in the midst of the floor or on dunes lying along the

272

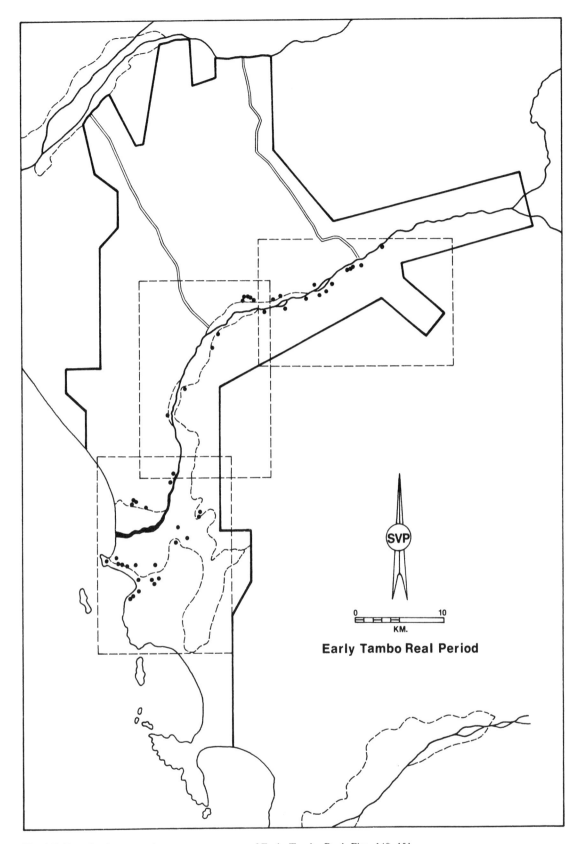

Fig. 148. Location key to settlement pattern maps of Early Tambo Real, Figs. 149–151.

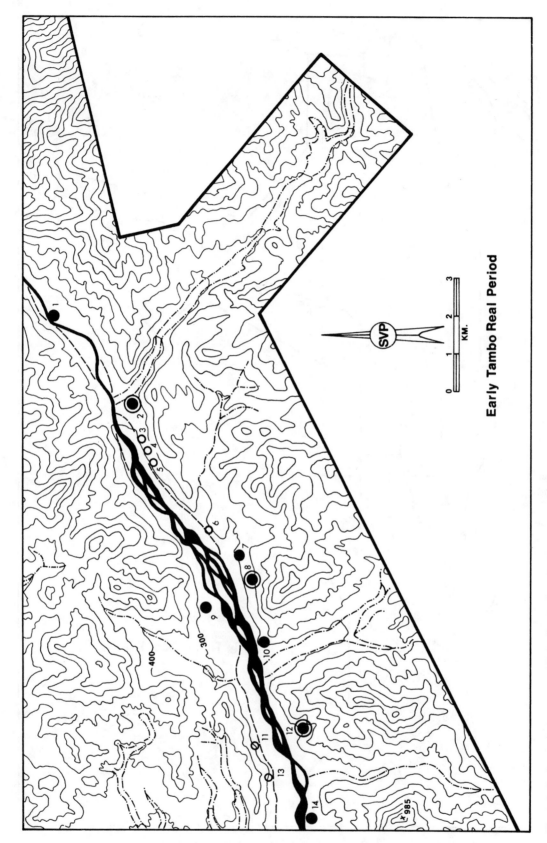

Fig. 149. Settlement pattern map of Early Tambo Real Period: Upper and Middle Valley sectors.

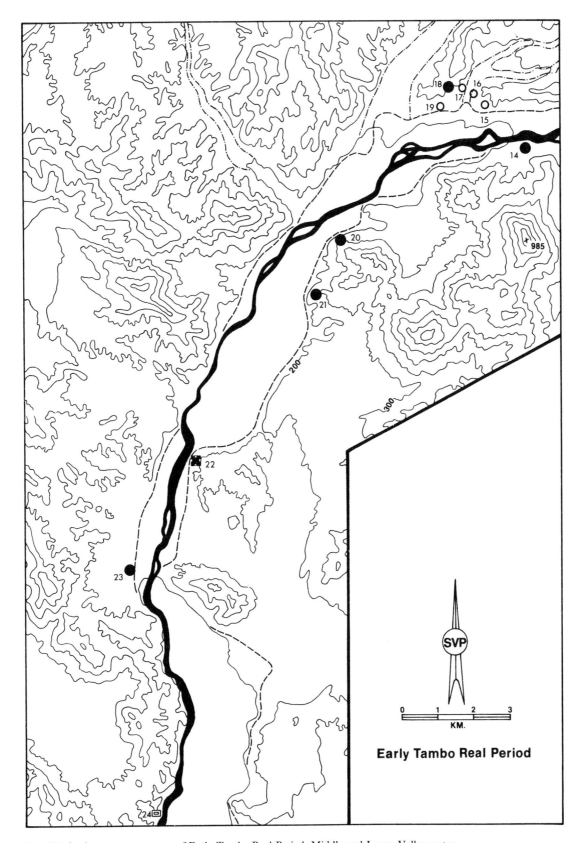

Fig. 150. Settlement pattern map of Early Tambo Real Period: Middle and Lower Valley sectors.

275

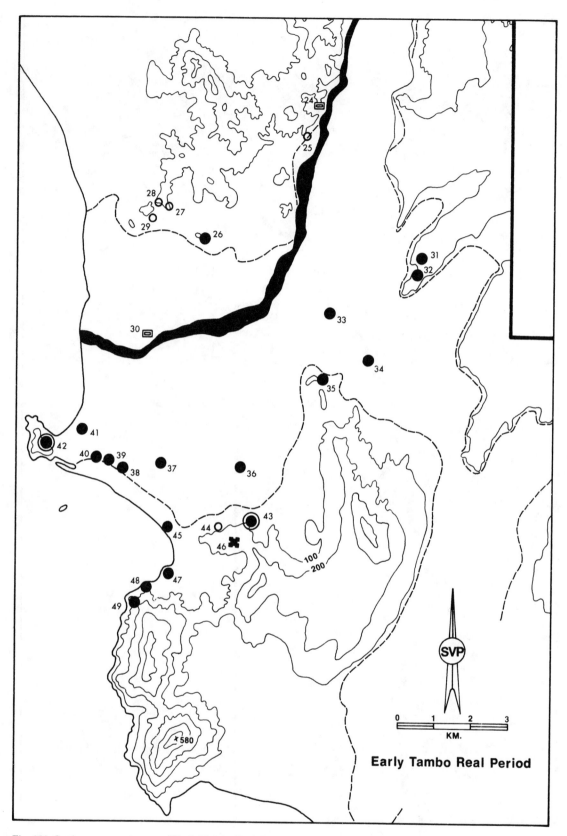

Fig. 151. Settlement pattern map of Early Tambo Real Period: Lower Valley and Coast sectors.

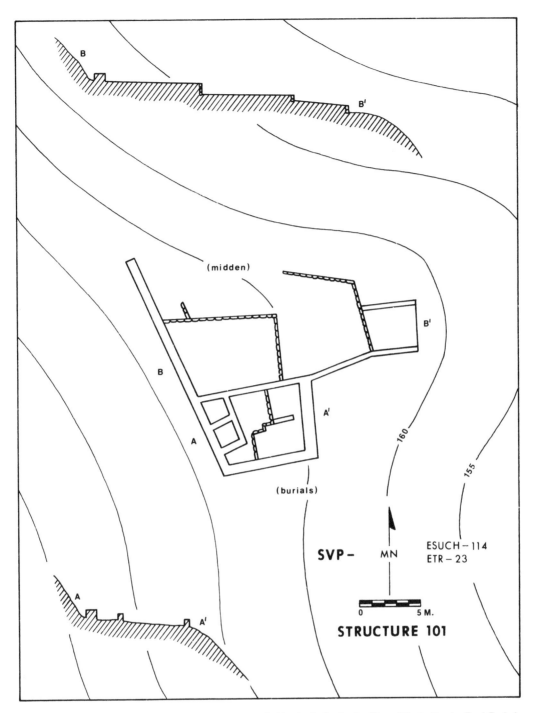

Fig. 152. Plan and profile views of Structure 101, a probable single-family dwelling of Early Tambo Real Period.

inland edge of the beaches, it is logical to restrict the expression of average site location to the Middle and Upper Valleys alone. The elevation of sites above the valley floor in these two sectors ranges between 5 and 40 m and distance away from it ranges between 5 and 150 m, with an average elevation of 20 m and an average distance away of 70 m. Thus, whatever the nature of conflict in this period, sites of Early Tambo Real continue the general pattern of periods from Guadalupito on in being located in essentially open, nondefensible positions.

Local centers. Following the criteria used in distinguishing local centers from undifferentiated habitation sites in earlier periods, there appear to be three hierarchically supraordinate centers in the upvalley sectors (see SVP-ETR-2, 8, and 12, in Fig. 149) and two in the Lower Valley (see SVP-ETR-42 and 46, in Fig. 151). Although almost no other sites are found in the area surrounding each of the upvalley centers, it is nevertheless interesting to note that each appears to have served a central function in earlier periods. As indicated in the plan views of the three sites (see Figs. 124, 127, 146), features are present at each which suggest possible use for specialized functions—including elite residence, storage, public activities, and llama corrals.

With regard to the Lower Valley centers, SVP-ETR-42 is a large terraced site extending over an area of 10.8 ha on the eastern slopes and summit of Cerro Cosquillo peninsula. It is unique among all hypothesized local centers inhabited in this period in that its occupation appears to be restricted to Early Tambo Real. Probably because of the proximity of the modern settlement of Puerto Santa, SVP-ETR-42 is now in a much deteriorated state and the high stone tower present as recently as the middle 1860s is no longer visible (cf. Squier 1877:104–105). Nevertheless, the presence of a large 15 × 15-m platform mound on the summit and the relatively large population estimate of 2700 persons both support the assertion that SVP-ETR-42 played a central role in the local settlement system.

The second of the two probable local centers in the mouth of the valley is SVP-ETR-46/Huaca Santa, the huge architectural complex with habitation and public functions extending back as early as Early Suchimancillo Period (see Fig. 71). Judging from the 33-ha area covered by Early Tambo Real sherd diagnostics here, and from the presence of dense occupational debris, the population of Huaca Santa in this period was around 3300 persons—making it the largest site in the Early Tambo Real system.

Defensive Sites

In spite of the relatively exposed location of most Lower Valley sites, the existence of some threat of attack seems clear from the presence of four widely spaced defensive sites in this sector (see SVP-ETR-22, 24, 30, and 46, in Figs. 150–151). Two of them (SVP-ETR-24 and SVP-ETR-30) are classified as minor defensive sites because of the lack of fortress structures. However, both are situated on top of steepsided hills and have reasonably extensive rock walls extending over total distances of 550 and 900 m, respectively. SVP-ETR-22 and SVP-ETR-46, the remaining defensive sites, are located in even higher and more inaccessible positions. Both are classified as citadels—mainly because of the presence of a larger population at the former site (estimated at 170 persons), and extensive rock walls and defensive ditches at the latter. In light of the fact that nearby Huaca Santa site was occupied nearly continuously from Early Suchimancillo through Late Tambo Real times, it seems significant that sherd diagnostics found at SVP-ETR-46 citadel date only to Early Tambo Real and to Early and Late Suchimancillo.

Cemetery Sites

Early Tambo Real burial sites are found throughout the area of occupation. As in other periods, they are essentially of two kinds—including (1) 15 sites which appear to have been used only for burial (see SVP-ETR-3, 4–6, 11, 13, 15–17, 19, 25, 27–29, and 44, in Figs. 149–151), and (2) 13 sites where burials lie immediately adjacent to habitation areas (see SVP-ETR-1, 2, 9, 21, 23, 26, 33, 35–38, 41, and 45, in Figs. 149–151), including hamlets, small and large villages, and local centers.

The great majority of Early Tambo Real cemeteries are too badly looted to allow accurate assessment of the nature of burials. However, it is worth mentioning that at least one site was found at which late period sherd diagnostics are associated with the remains of adobe tombs (see SVP-ETR-27/SVP-LTR-40). This would suggest that such tombs—which, judging from our data, first appear in Guadalupito Period—continued to be constructed throughout the remainder of the sequence.

Settlement and Demographic Patterns

In contrast to the preceding three periods, when period-to-period changes in settlement pattern seem better characterized by their revolutionary rather than evolutionary nature, Early Tambo Real represents a more subtle and gradual change in the overall nature and extent of the subsistence-settlement system. For example, the total number of sites in the system is not strikingly different from that of the preceding period (i.e., 46 sites in Early Tambo Real, 56 sites in Late Tanguche). In addition, the widespread distribution of settlements throughout much of the Lower and Middle Valley and part of the Upper Valley continues. With regard to the overall change in specific location, some 65% of the 46 Early

Tambo Real settlements are new occupations—i.e., fully 35% of the sites of this period represent continuing occupation from Late Tanguche times. The percentage of new occupations is thus closer to the relative conservatism that characterizes Vinzos and Late Tanguche (56% and 57% new occupations, respectively), and contrasts fairly strongly with the radical change to nearly all new locations that characterizes Guadalupito and Early Tanguche (90% and 94% new occupations).

The Early Tambo Real system also manifests limited further development of the (reestablished) focus on construction and/or occupation of defensive sites that dates from Late Tanguche—a pattern, it will be recalled, that had not characterized the Lower Santa region at all during Guadalupito and Early Tanguche times when multivalley states appear to have been in control. Aside from the single citadel site occupied in the lower part of the Middle Valley, however, the occupation of defensive sites appears to have been confined to the Lower Valley sector (see Fig. 180). Since a limited distribution of defensive sites is also a feature of the Late Tanguche system, it is worth emphasizing that both of these later periods contrast sharply with all four early ceramic periods—when defensive sites were widely distributed throughout nearly all parts of the area of occupation. Assuming external warfare in Early Tambo Real times, this contrast in fortress locations suggests a fundamental change in the nature and severity of attacks on the region—i.e., from a pattern in earlier periods when conflict appears to have continually affected the entire system, to one in later periods when external attacks affected only certain parts of the system in a more sporadic way. In any case, no site in the Lower Valley appears to have been located very far from a place of potential refuge—although habitation sites nearly everywhere are situated in the same exposed positions that characterize sites from Guadalupito on to the end of the sequence. In the Middle and Upper Valley sectors, where the terrain is steeper and sites are more often terraced, even settlements located fairly near the valley floor can of course be interpreted as potentially capable of being defended.

The Early Tambo Real system represents a further significant erosion of regional population—i.e., from an estimated 18,435 persons in Late Tanguche, the population drops by 37% to only 11,660 persons. This process is apparent throughout the area of occupation, specifically as manifested in the changes in sector-by-sector population estimates: In the Upper Valley the population drops from an estimated 2160 to 1775 persons, in the Middle Valley from 7215 to only 1160 persons, in the Middle Valley from 8960 to 5175 persons. On the other hand, with the establishment of the large site of SVP-ETR-42 on the Cerro Cosquillo peninsula (near Puerto Santa) and a number of maritime sites along the dunes back of the beach, the population estimate in the Coast sector rises dramatically from 50 persons in Late Tanguche to 3550 persons in Early Tambo Real. Indeed, the number and diversity of sites in the Lower Valley indicate an overall complexity of pattern not seen in this sector since the Guadalupito Period.

In spite of the large drop in overall population compared to the five preceding periods, as we have seen five larger, internally complex sites stand out as possible local centers—three of which occupy the south desert margin in Cluster 1 and two of which occupy the south side of the Lower Valley in Cluster 3. This strongly suggests a continuation of the basic pattern of local-level intersite ties and supracommunity political organization that appears to characterize the sequence from the earliest periods of irrigation agriculture.

Finally, with regard to the possible nature of warfare, it is intriguing to note that Cluster 3 is the only settlement grouping with widespread defensive constructions. Yet, with an estimated population of 8725 persons, this cluster is much larger than Cluster 1 (2275 persons) and Cluster 2 (660 persons). Given the absence of defensive constructions in Cluster 1 as well as the demographic superiority of Cluster 3, it is difficult to imagine that warfare was occurring between them. Rather, as in Late Tanguche Period, it is probable that warfare consisted of a localized and sporadic threat that came from outside the region.

Ceramic Distributions

The distribution of Early Tambo Real ceramics continues the general pattern of the preceding three periods, in that most of the 18 diagnostic types are present at sites throughout the area of occupation—including Early Tambo Real Grayware Bowls 1, 2; Grayware Jars 3a, 3b, 4a, 4b, 4c, 5; Redware Bowl 1; and Redware Jars 1, 3, 4a, 4b. Among the few types with a more restricted distribution are Early Tambo Real Redware Bowl 2 and Redware Jar 2. Thus, although as in many preceding periods site-to-site assemblages often vary considerably in terms of the specific number and diversity of types that are present, the type distribution map of this period is characterized by a strong degree of homogeneity.

Among other things, this implies a fairly strong degree of within-valley socioeconomic ties, notwithstanding the distance separating sites of the uppermost and lowermost areas. Interestingly enough, in spite of the probability that the Early Tambo Real system is in some ways (e.g., population size) less complex than the later pre-state ceramic period systems, it does not manifest the characteristic patterns of Early and Late Suchimancillo Periods—i.e., when a few types link all sites of the region but a number of others are locally focused on Quebrada de Cayhuamarca area and clinally distributed as a function of increasing distance upvalley and downvalley from there. Aside from the probability of a fundamental change from earlier to later periods in the main routes of communication and patterns of interregional interaction, it may therefore be suggested that, following the development and demise of the Moche and Black-White-Red states, within-valley patterns of interaction generally were more regularized than in the pre-state periods. At the same time, although in the late periods Santa was clearly part of shifting interaction spheres (i.e., limited to valleys to the south in Late Tanguche, but including valleys both to the south and north by Early Tambo Real times), regional and interregional influences on ceramics were uniformly widespread.

Inferences About Subsistence

Judging from the overall settlement pattern as well as from the remains of such cultigens as maize on some Early Tambo Real sites, irrigation agriculture constituted the primary focus of subsistence as in all preceding ceramic periods. However, as mentioned earlier in this section, Early Tambo Real marks the appearance of a number of sites on the low rolling dunes that lie between the beach and cultivated fields on the south side of the Santa Valley mouth. Given the presence on these sites of cultigens such as maize and totora (*Scirpus* Sp.), as well as large quantities of marine shell (e.g., see SVP-ETR-38 site description in Wilson 1985, Appendix B), it appears that the residents were ideally situated for focusing on the three microenvironments of this area—including (1) the sublittoral area adjacent to the beach, (2) the marshy lagoons lying between the beach and dunes, and (3) the cultivable valley floor just inland from the dunes. It should also be noted that marine shells appear on Early Tambo Real sites located as far as 40 km upvalley (e.g., see SVP-ETR-8 in Wilson 1985, Appendix B).

Interregional Comparisons

Nepeña Valley. Proulx (1968, 1973) reports on a tentative total of 42 sites, some of which may be contemporaneous with the 49 sites of Early Tambo Real Period in Santa Valley. It should be noted, however, that Proulx's analysis and discussion of what he terms "Late Intermediate Period" ceramics include two temporally distinct styles—i.e., an earlier period that is characterized by Black-on-White ceramics as well as raised circle-and-dot ware, and a later period that is characterized by polished Chimú blackware. At the same time, operating on the assumption that post-Chimú—i.e., "Late Horizon Period"—ceramics should be characterized by Inca-influenced features, Proulx found only four sites that could be assigned to this last (presumed) period in the sequence.

Without going further into the questions his study raises about Late Intermediate-Late Horizon chronology

in Nepeña, I think it strongly likely that Proulx's Black-on-White style represents in large part the Late Intermediate Period, and that the Chimú-influenced ceramics actually represent the *last detectable period* in the Nepeña sequence—i.e., for all practical purposes the Chimú ceramics date to what is commonly considered to be "Late Horizon Period". But this argument in no way implies that the Inca expansion on the North Coast was not later than that of the Chimú; rather, it is probable that the period of Inca control was so short and its influence on cultural traditions in valleys like Nepeña and Santa so ephemeral that it is next to impossible to distinguish the ceramics of the very latest period of external influence—i.e., Inca—from those of the next to last period of such influence—i.e., Chimú.

In sum, to the extent that two periods following late Middle Horizon can be identified through ceramic diagnostics, they are probably generally distinguishable as follows: (1) the first post-Middle Horizon period, or the "Late Intermediate", is represented by the Black-on-White style (not present in Santa) and associated utilitarian ceramics; and (2) the second, and last, post-Middle Horizon period, or the "Late Horizon", is represented by sites at which the Chimú and (occasionally) the Inca styles can be identified. Assuming this argument is correct, many of the sites characterized by Chimú types probably extend right on to the time of the Spanish Conquest, with only a few exhibiting the ephemeral, post-Chimú presence of Inca-related ceramics. It follows that the "Late Intermediate Period" map of Nepeña (cf. Proulx 1973, Fig. 9, p. 69) probably should contain substantially fewer than the 42 sites shown on it. Likewise, the "Late Horizon Period" map (cf. Fig. 10, p. 82) should contain far more than the four sites shown on it. In any case, given the chronological ambiguities for the late part of the Nepeña sequence, it is of little utility to compare the post-Middle Horizon systems of this valley with the Early and Late Tambo Real systems of Santa.

Virú Valley. Willey (1953:296–320) reports on a total of 41 La Plata Period sites that, judging from ceramic similarities to the Santa region, are more or less contemporaneous with the 49 occupations of Early Tambo Real Period. In light of the preceding discussion of Nepeña ceramic chronology, however, it should be mentioned at the outset of this section that "Late Chimú" ceramics are among the wares found in the assemblages of both La Plata and Estero, the last two periods in the Virú sequence (cf. Willey 1953:200). The distinction between the two late periods in Virú was made primarily on the basis of percentage changes of each ceramic type in the assemblage (cf. Ford 1949:69–70), rather than by identifying critical distinguishing diagnostics from single-component collections such as was possible in our Santa Valley research. Thus in Virú, as in Nepeña, the presence of Inca-influenced ceramics was used as the principal criterion to identify sites of the final period in the sequence.

Nonetheless, in contrast to Nepeña (with 42 sites dating supposedly to Late Intermediate and only 4 sites to Late Horizon), the Virú researchers still were able to identify the 41 sites dating to La Plata, as mentioned above, and 17 sites dating to Estero Period. Assuming gradual demographic decline, there may thus be fewer problems with the late period chronology of Virú than with that of Nepeña. It is also interesting to note that in some respects ceramic assemblages of the late period in Virú are quite distinct from those of Santa and Nepeña. For example, as mentioned earlier, the Virú assemblage does not contain the raised circle-and-dot/Casma Incised type that so dominates late Middle Horizon, and continues on into Late Intermediate, in the two valleys to the south. It thus seems likely that (1) Santa and Nepeña were part of a different sphere of socioeconomic and political interaction during the late Middle Horizon and much of the Late Intermediate Period; and that (2) Chimú influences were manifested earlier in the ceramic assemblage of Virú than in either Santa or Nepeña. In any case, given the explicit accounting in Ford (1949) of the seriation method used by the Virú researchers and their reliance on changes in type frequencies as well as presence/absence of key diagnostics, one is probably on relatively secure ground in relying on Willey's assignments of late sites to La Plata and Estero.

Based on the assessment of primary or sole function, the main categories of site types in La Plata Period are as follows: living sites (29 occupations), ceremonial-civic sites (3 occupations), defensive sites (2 occupations), and cemeteries (7 occupations). Judging from Willey's detailed maps and site descriptions, 25 of the 29 living sites (the same number as in Santa) can be classified as containing undifferentiated habitations. Virú is also similar to Santa in that a majority of sites in the upvalley area have rock-walled structures (6/9, or 67%), while all 16 of the sites in the lower valley area are characterized by debris alone. The remaining four La Plata living sites stand out sharply from the undifferentiated occupations in containing larger rock-walled compounds, complex dwellings, and possible storage areas. They may therefore be tentatively classified as the Virú equivalents of the local centers of Santa (see V-44, V-108, V-197, and V-269, in Willey 1953, Figs. 22, 71, 54, and 72, respectively). The Late Intermediate Period system of Virú is also similar to that of Santa in containing a small number of defensive sites. These include V-61 and V-212, both of which are located in remote positions on opposite hills flanking the narrows between the middle and upper valley. Finally, it is interesting to note the strong similarity in overall settlement pattern between Virú and Santa. As indicated on the La Plata map (Willey 1953,

Fig. 87, p. 387), settlements are densely distributed in two principal discrete areas—including (1) the beach-and-dune country on both sides of the river at the mouth of the valley; and (2) the desert margin on both sides of the upper valley. And like the pattern in Santa—where a few sites lie between the main population concentrations of Clusters 1 and 3—the Virú system is characterized by a few scattered sites on the south side of the middle part of the valley.

By Late Intermediate times, both Santa and Virú were thus characterized by an essentially dichotomous distribution of settlement—with a large number of sites focused on the environmental ecotone between ocean waters and irrigable land, as well as a fair number focused on upvalley irrigation. It may be suggested that this pattern reflects the development of specialized local subsistence-settlement groupings, with the probability that a good deal of socioeconomic interaction was occurring between them—at least judging from the widespread distribution of marine products and major pottery types throughout the Lower Santa system.

LATE TAMBO REAL PERIOD (ESTERO/LATE HORIZON)

A total of 78 discrete sites was identified as belonging to the Late Tambo Real Period of occupation in the Lower Santa Valley region (Figs. 153–156; for site outline maps see Wilson 1985, Fig. 246). Although this represents a fairly substantial increase over the 49 occupations dating to the preceding period, the number of site types that can be identified on the basis of primary or sole function is lower than in Early Tambo Real or any other preceding ceramic period—specifically including only habitation sites (58 occupations) and cemeteries (20 occupations). However, despite the lack of a variety of basic site types, Late Tambo Real is similar to Guadalupito and Early Tanguche in having three subtypes of habitation sites—including undifferentiated habitations, local centers, and a regional center.

Habitation Sites

Undifferentiated occupations. The proportion of occupations in the Late Tambo Real settlement system characterized by undifferentiated dwellings is 55 out of 78 discrete sites—or 70%—which is higher than the figure for any other preceding ceramic period (proceeding back in time, from Early Tambo Real through Cayhuamarca, the figures are 51%, 48%, 59%, 39%, 55%, 53%, 68%, and 50%, respectively). As suggested earlier, the primary reason for higher percentages of undifferentiated habitation sites seems related in large part to changes in the numbers of detectable cemetery occupations (usually the second largest group of sites, after

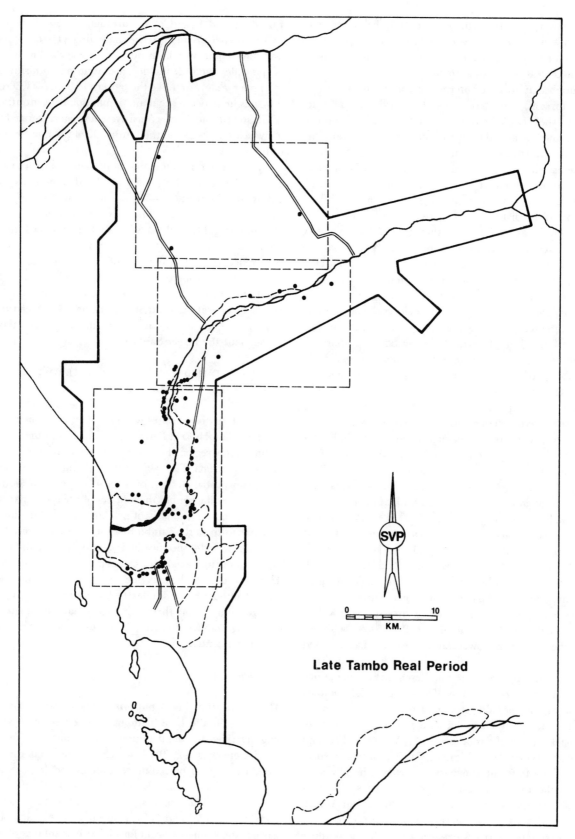

Fig. 153. Location key to settlement pattern maps of Late Tambo Real Period, Figs. 154–156.

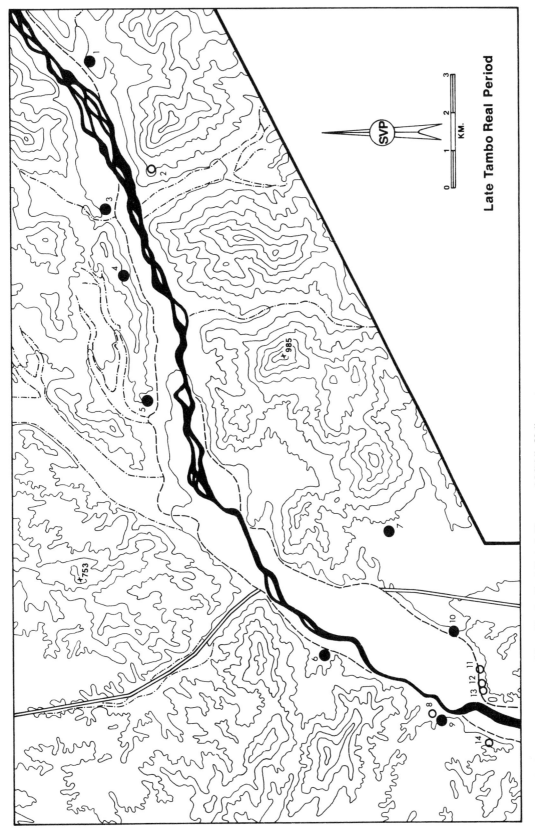

Fig. 154. Settlement pattern map of Late Tambo Real Period: Upper and Middle Valley sectors.

283

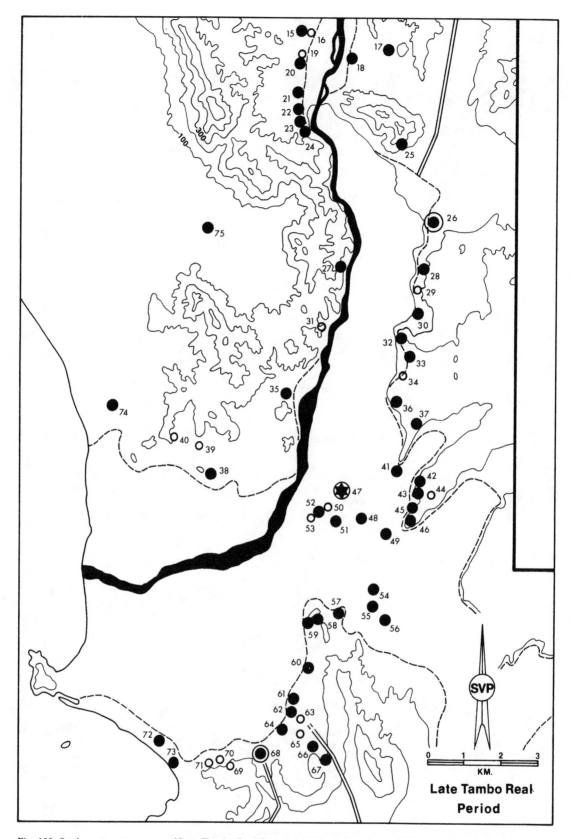

Fig. 155. Settlement pattern map of Late Tambo Real Period: Middle Valley, Lower Valley, and Coast sectors.

284

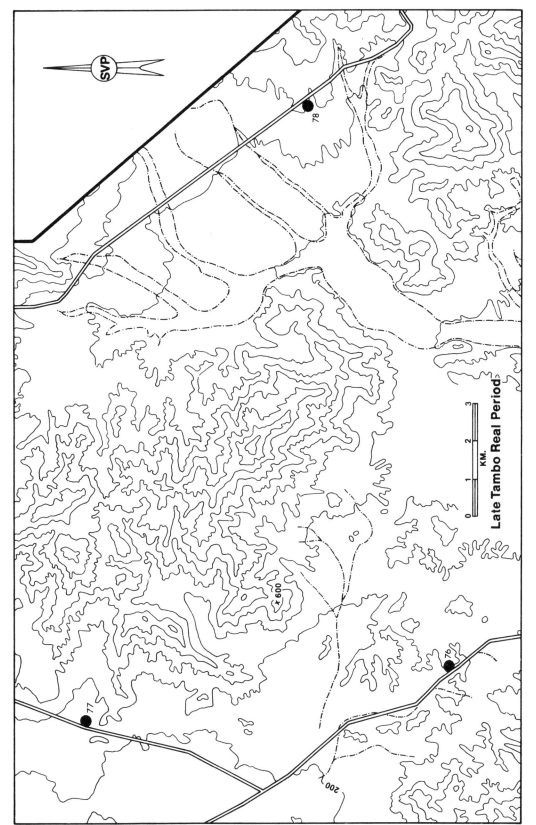

Fig. 156. Settlement pattern map of Late Tambo Real Period: Santa-Chao Desert sector.

285

habitation sites), although the presence/absence of ceremonial-civic and defensive sites in later periods also affects this percentage. In any case, as in all earlier periods, habitation sites are distributed throughout the area of occupation (see SVP-LTR-1, 3–7, 9, 10, 15, 17, 18, 20–25, 27, 28, 30, 32–38, 41–43, 45, 46, 48, 49, 51, 52, 54–62, 64, 66, 67, and 72–78, in Figs. 154–156).

These sites range in size between .25 and 9 ha and in population between 5 and 900 persons—with an average size of 1.6 ha and an average population estimate of 112 persons. The averages thus represent a continuation of the general trend in later periods of a decrease in the average size and population of undifferentiated habitation sites, although the average density figure of 70 persons/ha falls within the range of 66 to 85 persons that characterizes the preceding ceramic periods.

With regard to the nature of dwellings, Late Tambo Real also represents a continuation of the basic dichotomy between the Upper-Middle sectors and the Lower Valley in terms of the percentages of rock-walled habitations compared to sites where structures were built entirely of organic materials. Thus, 14 out of 16 sites—or 87%—in the upvalley sectors are characterized by rock-walled dwellings, while the proportion is more or less reversed in the Lower Valley, where only 13 out of 39 sites—or 33%—contain such remains. The upvalley-downvalley dichotomy is thus not nearly as strong as in Early Tambo Real and Guadalupito Periods—when dwellings on most Lower Valley sites were constructed entirely of perishable materials, and those on most Upper-Middle Valley sites had rock-walled foundations. Nevertheless, as discussed later, it may be of some significance that the dichotomy is more notable during periods when influences from the Moche Valley presumably were very strong.

In spite of the large number of sites characterized primarily or entirely by midden debris, it was possible to map habitation structures at several sites located in various parts of the area of Late Tambo Real occupation. Proceeding from the upvalley area downriver, the first of these sites consists of a large rock-and-adobe enclosure of roughly trapezoidal shape which covers an area of 68 × 67 m at SVP-LTR-3/Structure 44 (Fig. 157). Scattered occupational debris was noted on the rock-faced terraces found within Structure 44, and additional debris was noted on terraces covering a small area of .5 ha on the exterior. SVP-LTR-3 lies at the terminus of one of the branches of the main eastern route of travel between Santa and Chao Valleys, a rock-lined road of probable Early Tanguche date that was in use in later periods as well (e.g., see SVP-LTR-78, in Fig. 156; for location of branch road, see area to northwest of SVP-ETAN-241, in Fig. 116).

Although, as mentioned above, many sites in the Lower Valley are characterized by midden scatters—including remains of cane matting, cordage, charcoal, marine shells, various cultigens such as maize, and potsherds—structures of adobe were noted on several of these sites. For example, a large rectangular habitation compound was noted at SVP-LTR-30, a large 9-ha site consisting primarily of scattered midden debris (see Structure 89, in Fig. 158). This compound has *tapia* construction—i.e., rather than being constructed of adobe bricks, it is built of solid mud walls that were formed in discrete, conjoined sections probably using wooden forms of some kind. Such walls are found at other Late Tambo Real sites (e.g., see SVP-LTR–47, in Fig. 160), and appear to be a good architectural diagnostic of the last period in the prehispanic sequence. It is worth noting that the symmetrical double-step feature found in the southeastern corner of Structure 89 is too small and cramped to have served as an actual stairway. Its size and the remains of fancy reddish-cream plaster suggest that it served a ceremonial-civic function instead.

In contrast to the structures described above, those at several other Late Tambo Real sites were built entirely of adobe bricks. The best example of this type of construction is at SVP-LTR-35/Huaca El Gallinazo site, where excellently preserved buildings of obviously late date—probably including early Colonial occupation—are found (see Fig. 159). Indeed, although several other periods of prehispanic occupation are represented in the debris at Huaca El Gallinazo, this is one of the few sites in the survey region that contains architecture exhibiting possible Inca characteristics—including wall niches, doorways with wooden lintels, and windows. However, all of these features are of vertical rectangular shape, in contrast to the trapezoidal shape that usually is found on Inca adobe structures farther south along the coast (e.g., at Pachacámac, Lurín Valley; and Tambo Colorado, Pisco Valley).

A final structure of interest consists of a low rectangular adobe-walled enclosure divided internally into 10 smaller rooms of roughly equal size (see Structure 84 in Wilson 1985, Fig. 250). This building sits on a low ridgetop rising in the midst of the valley floor at SVP-LTR-48, overlooking scattered rock-walled dwellings and midden debris lying down near the cultivated valley floor. Given its location above and apart from the main area of habitation, as well as the regular size of its doorless chambers, it is possible that Structure 84 served as a storage area for the site. If this is so, then it may provide a coastal example of the *collca* storage structures found at Inca sites in the sierra (e.g., see Morris and Thompson 1985). As is well known, the Incas generally attempted to place such structures in higher, cooler elevations adjacent to the main habitation areas of sites, primarily in order to enhance the preservability of foodstuffs stored in them.

Local centers. Two sites stand out in the Late Tambo Real settlement system as possible local centers—one of

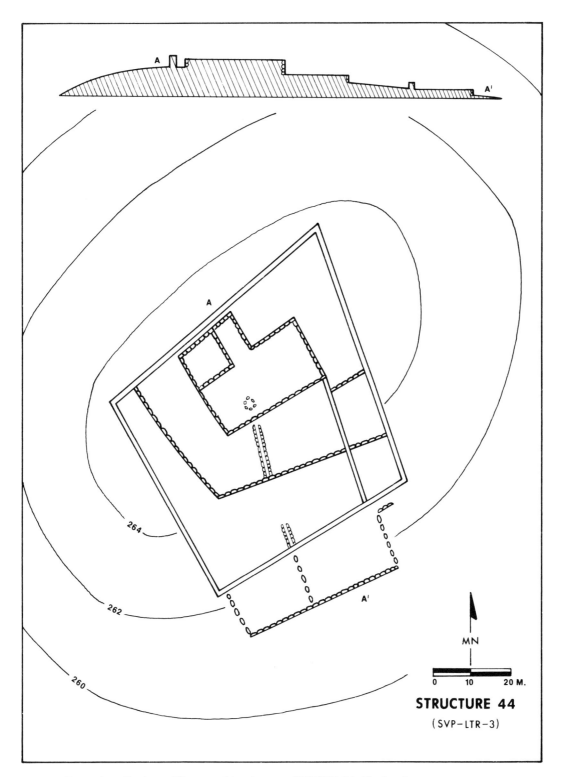

Fig. 157. Plan and profile views of Structure 44 enclosure at SVP-LTR-3 habitation site.

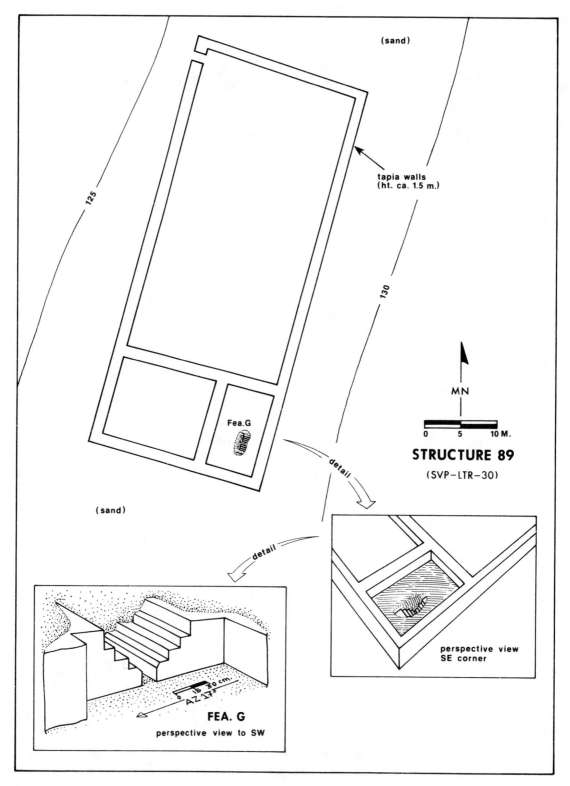

Fig. 158. Plan and perspective details of Structure 89, a large tapia-walled enclosure at SVP-LTR-30 habitation site.

288

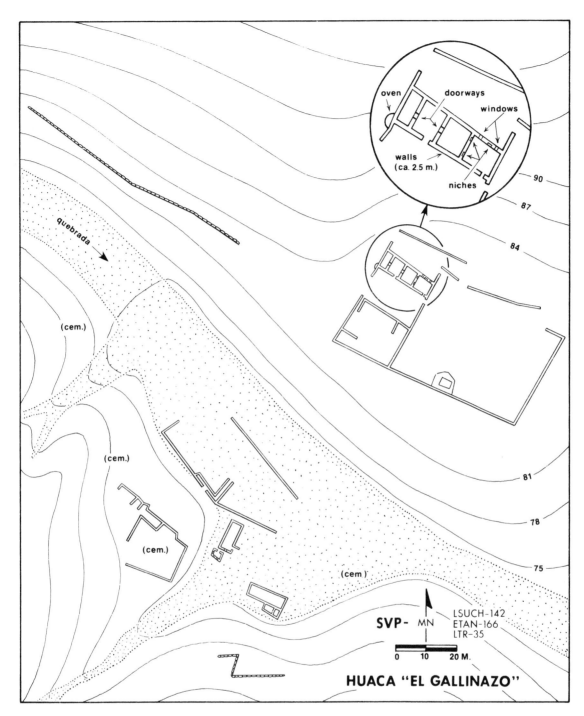

Fig. 159. Plan and detail views of Huaca El Gallinazo, a multicomponent prehispanic habitation and cemetery site with Colonial Period occupation in the northeast sector.

them on the basis of its substantially larger size compared to nearby occupations (SVP-LTR-26), and the other on the basis of its larger size and greater complexity compared to nearby sites (SVP-LTR-68/Huaca Santa). SVP-LTR-26 sprawls over a very large area of 16.5 ha along the sandy desert margin to the northeast of the modern settlement of Rinconada (see Fig. 155). A few badly preserved remains of rock-walled dwellings are present here, but the general lack of rock rubble in the debris indicates that most dwellings were constructed entirely of perishable materials. Aside from its large population estimate of 1650 persons and a very large 2-ha cemetery, the other feature supporting the argument of a local center function for SVP-LTR-26 is that it lies the same distance to the north of SVP-LTR-47/Alto Perú—the probable regional center of the period—as SVP-LTR-68/Huaca Santa lies to the south (i.e., 7.5 km). Indeed, as indicated in Figs. 155 and 183, most of the population of this period was located either at these three probable centers or at the smaller sites lying in between.

SVP-LTR-68/Huaca Santa (Fig. 71), the large multicomponent site located on the south desert margin at the mouth of the valley, has been discussed in detail earlier in this chapter (e.g., see Early Suchimancillo local centers). Reference to the site at this point is useful mainly to underscore the probability that a fair portion of extant structural remains depicted in the plan view date to the later periods of occupation, including Late Tambo Real. In any case, Late Tambo Real occupational debris is found associated with most of the main architectural remains here, and dwellings are assessed tentatively as having covered an area of about 20 ha at light-to-moderate densities, with a population estimate of 1000 persons.

Regional center. Compared to the 55 undifferentiated habitation sites and the two local centers, SVP-LTR-47/Alto Perú stands out as a most likely candidate for the main regional center of the period (see Figs. 155, 160). Although its estimated population of 1650 persons is the same as that estimated for SVP-LTR-26 local center, it is substantially more complex architecturally than even SVP-LTR-68/Huaca Santa site. Indeed, at least one of the tapia-walled compounds at SVP-LTR-47 is the largest enclosure of any period in the sequence, with overall dimensions of 180 × 125 m and an area of 2.5 ha (see Area E in the plan view). It is also of some interest to note that the large compounds comprising Areas D and E have essentially tripartite divisions that appear to be quite similar to several of the main compounds found at Chan Chán, the main Chimú-Inca center in the Moche Valley (e.g., see Kosok 1965, Fig. 4, p. 77; Moseley and Mackey 1974).

Among other features of interest on the site are the adobe huaca structures in the Area C and D compounds. The larger of the two huacas is located in the middle division of Area D compound, and measures roughly 50 × 20 m (it is one of the few structures remaining on the site that was still reasonably intact in 1979–80). The smaller huaca in Area C compound measures approximately 12 × 12 m in area. Although most sections of the other compounds have been destroyed by the modern settlement, the entire site is still covered by nearly continuous, and often deep, occupational debris containing a single ceramic component of Late Tambo Real date. Substantial numbers of thicker gray utilitarian sherds from very large storage vessels were noted in various areas on the site, in and around the six main compounds (e.g., see the Late Tambo Real Grayware Jar 4 sherd from Coll. 326, in Fig. 277; for typical design motifs found on decorated variants, see also Kosok 1965, Fig. 13 a-left, p. 192). This suggests that storage capabilities were among the principal functions of Alto Perú Complex, perhaps located in places such as the row of chambers showing at the southwestern end of Area D compound.

Cemeteries

Late Tambo Real cemeteries are found in relatively small groups throughout the area of occupation, and include (1) 20 sites which appear to have been used for burial only (see SVP-LTR-2, 8, 11–14, 16, 19, 29, 31, 39, 40, 44, 50, 53, 63, 65, and 69–71, in Figs. 154, 155); and (2) 18 sites where burial grounds lie immediately adjacent to habitation areas (see SVP-LTR-4, 6, 9, 10, 23, 25–27, 30, 35–38, 42, 46, 48, 68, and 73, in Figs. 154, 155). As in other periods, the latter group of sites includes hamlets, small and large villages, and local centers. Although it may be the case that burial areas formed an integral part of SVP-LTR-47/Alto Perú, the only cemeteries noted here are located on low, tree-covered dunes lying just to the southwest of the center, at SVP-LTR-50 and SVP-LTR-53. Indeed, the best example of a probable Inca vessel fragment in the Late Tambo Real ceramic assemblage was found in the debris at SVP-LTR-50 (see polychrome sherd from Coll. 328, in Fig. 280).

Nearly all Late Tambo Real cemeteries are too badly damaged as a result of huaquero activities to allow accurate assessment of the nature of burials. But, as mentioned in the section on Early Tambo Real cemeteries, one site was found at which sherd diagnostics of the two late periods are associated with the remains of adobe-walled tombs (see SVP-LTR-40/SVP-ETR-27 site descriptions in Wilson 1985, Appendix B). Given the general lack of architectural remains among the surface debris on many cemetery sites, it is also likely that a sizeable percentage of burials consisted of simple pits along with offerings of a few grave goods.

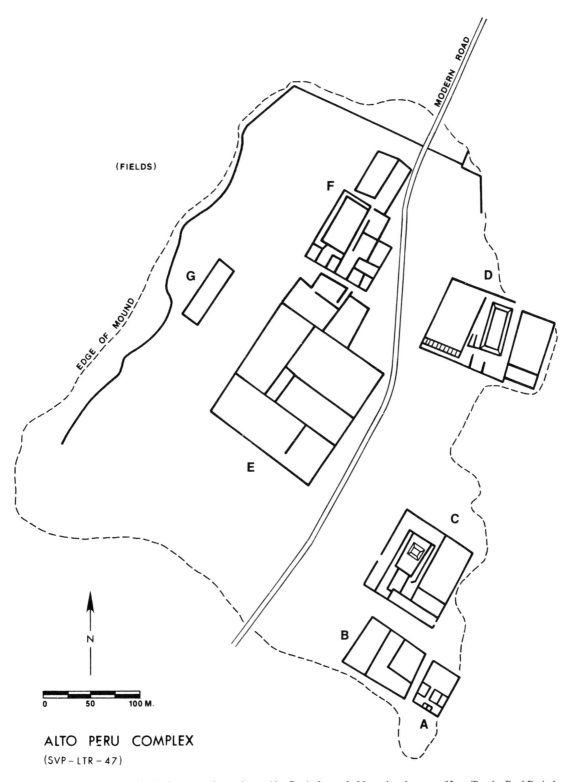

(FIELDS)

MODERN ROAD

F

EDGE OF MOUND

G

D

E

N

C

B

A

0   50   100 M.

ALTO PERU COMPLEX

(SVP – LTR – 47)

Fig. 160. Plan view of the principal structural remains at Alto Perú, the probable regional center of Late Tambo Real Period. A modern pueblo joven has covered almost all of the prehispanic site, with the exception of Areas C and D.

Other Remains: The Road Network

As indicated in Figs. 153–156, the evidence shows that at least some of the principal interregional and within-valley routes of travel developed in earlier periods were in use through the Late Tambo Real Period—including (1) the main central and eastern roads crossing the Santa-Chao Desert; (2) the road crossing over the southern end of Cerro Tambo Real, between the lower parts of Santa Valley and Quebrada de Lacramarca; and probably (3) the interconnecting route between the central Santa-Chao road and the Santa-Lacramarca road which runs up Quebrada de Vinzos.

Santa-Chao roads. Late Tambo Real sherds were the only ones found in association with three sites along the main central and eastern rock-lined roads that cross the Santa-Chao Desert (see SVP-LTR-76, 77, and 78, in Fig. 156). Since these sites are highly anomalous in the context of a network characterized almost entirely by great numbers of Early Tanguche/Black-White-Red sites, it is difficult to assess the nature of the Late Horizon intervalley network (e.g., compare Figs. 188 and 245). Nevertheless, it is at least clear that interregional socioeconomic and political relations involved both the use of the roads (e.g., isolated sherds of Late Tambo Real date were noted along the two main Santa-Chao routes), as well as the more or less prolonged occupation of sites quite removed from the nearest sources of fresh water and food in Santa and Chao Valleys.

Interestingly enough, two of the three Santa-Chao roadside sites—SVP-LTR-76 and SVP-LTR-78—have the same scattered, low rock-walled dwellings that characterize sites of Early Tanguche Period. But the overall configuration of structural types on one of these sites, SVP-LTR-78, is quite distinct from that of various Early Tanguche roadside sites we mapped (compare SVP-LTR-78 in Wilson 1985, Fig. 252, to Early Tanguche sites illustrated in this report, in Figs. 125, 130, 132, 133, and 134). For example, a larger number of agglutinated structures with more rooms is found at SVP-LTR-78. And the principal structure, which lies immediately to the south of the junction of the ancient eastern road and a narrow trail (the latter leading down to Santa Valley via Quebrada Palo Redondo), has a trapezoidal shape similar to some of the main compounds at SVP-LTR-47/Alto Perú.

Santa-Lacramarca roads. Judging from scattered Late Tambo Real sherds found along them as well as from the dating of associated roadside sites, the second main group of roads in use during this period was that extending between the south desert margin of the main Lower Valley sector of Santa and the mouth of Quebrada de Lacramarca (see roads to south of SVP-

LTR-63 and SVP-LTR-68/Huaca Santa, in Fig. 155). The route leading from SVP-LTR-63 toward the roadside sites of SVP-LTR-66 and SVP-LTR-67 appears to have been constructed in Guadalupito times, judging from the scattered Moche-style sherds found along it. On the other hand, only Late Tambo Real sherds were found along the road which leads south from SVP-LTR-68/Huaca Santa.

Quebrada de Vinzos road. Dating at least as far back in time as Early Tanguche Period, this ancient road runs near SVP-LTR-10 and SVP-LTR-25—partly in and partly alongside the wide lower reaches of Quebrada de Vinzos (see Figs. 154, 155; see also Fig. 125). Although no Late Tambo Real sites were found in direct association with the road, it probably was intensively used during this period—primarily because it is the most efficient route connecting the central intervalley Santa-Chao road to the two Santa-Lacramarca roads. (It will be noted how closely many sites of the Lower Valley sector line up along or near the presumed route leading from the mouth of Quebrada de Vinzos, near SVP-LTR-25, down along the desert margin toward the SVP-LTR-68/Huaca Santa area.)

Settlement and Demographic Patterns

To some degree, the Late Tambo Real settlement pattern manifests what appears to have been an evolutionary outgrowth of developments in the preceding two periods, with all of the main Lower Valley and the lowermost part of the Middle Valley now constituting the primary focus of occupation in the Lower Santa region. As mentioned earlier, however, this is the third period in the sequence of probable incorporation of the region into a multivalley conquest state. Indeed, considering the fact that the Chimú state, like its Moche predecessor, had its capital in the Moche Valley, it is intriguing that Late Tambo Real should exhibit the same strong focus on the Lower Valley sector.

Like the Guadalupito and Early Tanguche Periods systems long before it, the Late Tambo Real system also represents a time of relatively dramatic change to new settlement locations—with 91% of the 78 sites of this period occupying locations that appear to have been unused in the preceding period (the percentages of new occupations in Guadalupito and Early Tanguche are 90% and 94%, respectively). Thus, while it is clear that the Late Tambo Real system had evolutionary antecedents in the immediately preceding Late Tanguche and Early Tambo Real Periods, it is nonetheless probable that the overall pattern of settlement resulted in large part from the imposition of Chimú state policy on the region. Judging from the settlement pattern, this policy included intensive cultivation of much of the Lower Valley sector and the location of most settlements along or near the main central intervalley road that ran north-south across the Santa region.

In light of the argument that Late Tambo Real represents the third period of incorporation into a multivalley state, it seems significant that like Guadalupito and Early Tanguche Periods this is a time when sites are located in completely open and nondefensible positions. Indeed, no sites that can be identified as fortresses are present anywhere in the system. Thus, whether or not the incorporation into the Chimú state occurred by conquest—and given the ethnohistorical data indicating a fierce resistance to subsequent Inca encroachment it seems highly likely that it did—the Late Tambo Real settlement system exhibits the same state of interregional peace that characterizes the two earlier multivalley state systems. By contrast, greater or lesser times of interregional strife are reflected in every one of the other seven ceramic period settlement systems.

Assuming that SVP-LTR-26 and SVP-LTR-68/Huaca Santa are correctly identified as local centers functioning in an intermediate hierarchical position in the Late Tambo Real system, then it is interesting to note the symmetry that characterizes this essentially linear settlement pattern—i.e., with the local centers situated at the uppermost and lowermost ends of the main population concentration and SVP-LTR-47/Alto Perú located equidistant between them. The main centers of this period thus appear to have been strategically located, with respect to both the main road-settlement network and the regional population distribution. This argument of course raises the question of whether the Late Tambo Real settlement pattern can be understood as representing (1) the *imposition of state policy* (i.e., a forced relocation of settlements along lines similar to the large-scale resettlement of Guadalupito/Moche Period); or (2) the *attractive socioeconomic forces* exerted by the increasingly intensive use of the central intervalley road. This question clearly can never be fully resolved, but we may nevertheless take the middle ground between the two models in arguing that both probably were a part of the late period adaptive context.

Finally, it may be pointed out that the sector-by-sector comparison of population numbers in Early and Late Tambo Real also supports the argument that the Chimú state had a fairly strong effect on the subsistence-settlement system of the late period. This is especially notable in the Upper Valley, where the population drops precipitously from an estimated 1775 persons to only 230, and in the Lower Valley, where it rises by nearly two times from an estimated 5175 to 9010 persons. On the other hand, the estimated population change in the Middle Valley sector is relatively modest—i.e., from 1160 to 970 persons. Indeed, there is little change in overall population numbers from the estimated 11,660 persons in the Early Tambo Real system to 10,480 persons in that of Late Tambo Real.

Ceramic Distributions

In general, the regional distribution of the 18 principal ceramic types of Late Tambo Real Period is similar to that of all of the middle and later periods in the sequence—with most types found at sites throughout the region, from SVP-LTR-1 in the Quebrada del Panteón area to the lowermost part of Cluster 2 some 43 kilometers downvalley. Among the types with an extensive distribution are Late Tambo Real Grayware Bowls 2, 4; Grayware Jars 1, 2c, 2d, 3a, 3b, 3d, 4; and Redware Bowls 1, 2. It should also be noted that consistent perhaps with the location of the main population concentration in the lower parts of the valley, a few types have more restricted distributions limited to Cluster 2—including Late Tambo Real Grayware Jars 2a, 2b, 3c; and Redware Jar 3b. However, even these latter types are related in form, paste, and surface treatment to those found throughout the region.

Inferences About Subsistence

Judging from the higher number of sites and the overall complexity of the Cluster 2 settlement system relative to the Lower Valley occupation of all earlier periods, Late Tambo Real Period is second only to Guadalupito in its strong focus on intensive cultivation of the main Lower Valley area. Indeed, the principal contrast between the Guadalupito and Late Tambo Real subsistence systems appears to be the complete absence of sites of the later period in the mouth of Quebrada de Lacramarca. Assuming that the absence of sites is an indication that Lacramarca was not under cultivation in Late Tambo Real times, it may be suggested that the significantly lower population size of the later period provides the principal reason for the narrower extent of cultivation.

The other interesting feature of the Late Tambo Real system is the apparent abandonment of the broad focus on maritime sites that had characterized Early Tambo Real—with the exception of the beachside sites of SVP-LTR-72 and SVP-LTR-73 (see Fig. 155). Yet, as in all preceding periods when very few or no maritime sites appear to have been used for continuing habitation, marine shells are found at many sites throughout the main area of occupation—at least as far upvalley as SVP-LTR-9, located over 20 km inland in the Huaca Corral area.

Interregional Comparisons

Virú Valley. Willey (1953:320–323) reports on a total of 17 Estero Period sites that appear to be contemporaneous with the 78 sites of Late Tambo Real. Based on the assessment of primary or sole function, the main categories of sites include the following: living sites (8 occupations), defensive sites (2 occupations), and cemeteries (7 occupations). It should be noted that Willey includes a single pyramidal mound (V-103) as a fourth site type, but, given the multicomponent nature of the associated pottery debris, suggests that it may well have been constructed in an earlier period.

Five of the eight Estero Period habitation sites consist of midden accumulations, while the remaining three are "compound" villages consisting of walled enclosures built of tapia or rock-and-adobe. Two of the villages of the latter type—V-124 and V-179—appear to have been built in Estero Period. With its adobe and tapia construction as well as its rectangular layout, V-124 site is more or less analogous to the adobe compounds at SVP-LTR-30 and SVP-LTR-47/Alto Perú in Santa Valley. However, the internal tripartite divisions characteristic of some of the enclosures at SVP-LTR-47 do not appear in the plan view of V-124 (cf. Willey 1953, Fig. 75, p. 325), nor is the overall layout consisting of conjoined rectangular compounds similar to Late Tambo Real enclosures in Santa.

Judging from the Estero Period settlement map (cf. Willey 1953, p. 388), the Late Horizon system essentially represents a continuation of the dichotomous upvalley-downvalley pattern established in the preceding La Plata Period—with over half of the 17 Estero sites located in the beach-and-dune country not far from the ocean on both sides of the river. Although two sites are located in the intervening middle valley area, all of the rest of the occupations dating to this period lie in the uppermost part of the valley, primarily in the Huacapongo branch to the northeast. Thus not only does the Virú system appear to have had substantially fewer sites and relatively less overall sociopolitical complexity than Santa, but the period of Chimú-Inca hegemony seems to have had much less impact on the previously established subsistence-settlement system than it did in the Santa Valley. Indeed, it is of interest to note that none of the Estero Period sites in Virú is located directly along the ancient transvalley highway that crosses the lower part of the valley. Given this pattern as well as the absence of a large regional center comparable to SVP-LTR-47/Alto Perú, there is some support for the argument that Virú became a sort of "cultural backwater" during the Late Horizon—experiencing an even greater demographic decline relative to the middle periods in the sequence than did the Lower Santa Valley.

 The Origins and Development
of Complex North Coast Society:
A Regional Perspective

In discussing the overall nature of prehispanic societal evolution in the Lower Santa region, it is useful to divide the sequence into four successive developmental periods—including (1) the rise of chiefdom societies, from pre-1800 B.C. to ca. A.D. 400; (2) the rise of the first multivalley state societies, from ca. A.D. 400 to 900; (3) the beginning of regional demographic decline, from ca. A.D. 900 to 1350; and (4) the final period of regional demographic decline and multivalley state societies, from ca. A.D. 1350 to 1532. It should be noted that the early, middle, and late parts of the sequence outlined in an earlier chapter parallel these developmental periods nearly exactly—except that the late part has been divided into two developmental periods to distinguish between (a) the time of the more regionally-oriented Late Tanguche and Early Tambo Real Periods and (b) the larger multivalley states of Late Tambo Real.

The *rise of chiefdom societies* occurs during Las Salinas, Cayhuamarca, Vinzos, Early Suchimancillo, and Late Suchimancillo Periods. This is the time of a shift from a predominantly gathering-hunting subsistence economy to one based on intensive irrigation agriculture. As discussed in earlier chapters, along with the establishment of the upvalley agricultural system comes significant population growth, the rise of probable interregional warfare, interregional socioeconomic relations of varying intensity, and the development of sociocultural complexity beyond the initial level of small-scale egalitarian society.

The *rise of the first multivalley states* occurs during Guadalupito and Early Tanguche Periods. As we have seen, this period is characterized by the development of sociocultural complexity substantially beyond the levels achieved in the preceding periods. During this time of

demographic and sociocultural maturity in Santa Valley, the agricultural system is expanded to include more land and a broader environmental focus, massive public works projects are undertaken, the first large population centers arise, more intensive and far-flung interregional socioeconomic ties are established, and there is reasonably clear evidence that the continual warfare of pre-state periods did not characterize the system.

The *beginning of regional demographic decline* occurs in Late Tanguche and Early Tambo Real Periods. This is a time of significant population loss relative to the preceding middle periods, and the Lower Santa region appears to have become a part of more localized, shifting spheres of interregional socioeconomic interaction. Although warfare is not nearly as prevalent as in the pre-state periods, once again it is manifested in both the overall pattern of settlement and the occupation of defensive sites.

The *final period of regional demographic decline and multivalley state societies* takes place during Late Tambo Real. This is the time of the rise of the Chimú state, the third major multivalley polity in the North Coast sequence, which is followed in turn by the short-lived Inca empire. As is well known, the sequence ends in a brief period of about a decade under the influence of three main successive processes: (1) the weakening of the empire under the onslaught of European diseases (e.g., smallpox) that apparently were introduced along the north coast of the continent and swept down the Central Andes, prior to the actual arrival of the Spaniards in Peru (cf. McNeill 1977:176–180); (2) the further weakening of the Inca state during the civil war over succession to the throne between Atahuallpa and Huáscar, following the death (probably by smallpox) of Huayna Cápac in 1527 (cf.

Rowe 1963a:208–209); and (3) the arrival of the conquerors themselves under Pizarro in 1532, followed by the assassination of Atahuallpa and the conquest of the Inca state. During this time, Santa and many other nearby regions suffered further demographic decline of such magnitude that the population was reduced (ironically) to levels below those estimated to have characterized the earliest, preceramic occupation.

Utilizing the four developmental periods outlined above, this chapter summarizes the main features of prehispanic developments in the Lower Santa Valley and attempts to resolve the issues raised in earlier chapters regarding the nature and role of such factors as agricultural subsistence, population, and warfare. At the same time, the results of the analysis of maize-based carrying capacity and within-region comparison of ceramic assemblages are presented as part of the support for the main arguments presented. An attempt is also made to place the Lower Santa sequence within the broader context of overall North Coast developments, specifically by reference to pertinent comparative data from other reasonably well known regions. Figures 161–183 and Tables 6–10 provide summaries of the major changes in hierarchies, location, type, and location of sites over time.

THE RISE OF CHIEFDOM SOCIETIES IN THE EARLY PERIODS (PRE-1800 B.C. TO A.D. 400)

Perhaps not surprisingly, the developments related to the origins and rise of societal complexity span by far the longest period of time in the sequence—covering over 2000 years from the earliest human occupation of the Santa region to the rise of complex ranked society sometime before 400 A.D. By contrast, all three of the other main developmental periods are telescoped within a much shorter total time span of about 1100 years. In order to establish a basis for discussion of the theoretical implications of the research, this section begins with brief summaries of the principal data presented in earlier chapters—including the evolution of site types, and distributional patterns of population, settlement, and ceramics. The discussion then focuses on warfare, subsistence, and population and their role as critical socioenvironmental stresses in the early part of the sequence. At the same time, in support of the arguments about the role of these stresses in regional societal development, presentation is made of the results of the analysis of agricultural carrying capacity and intercluster ceramic assemblages. The section ends with brief discussions of the multivariate model suggested by the analysis

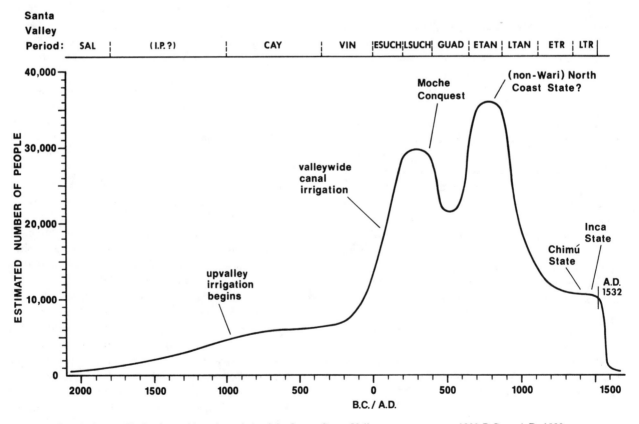

Fig. 161. Population profile for the prehispanic periods of the Lower Santa Valley survey area, pre-1800 B.C. to A.D. 1532.

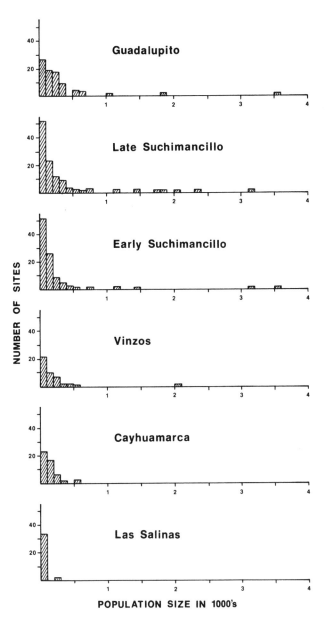

Fig. 162. Site population size histograms for the early periods of the Lower Santa Valley sequence: Las Salinas through Guadalupito.

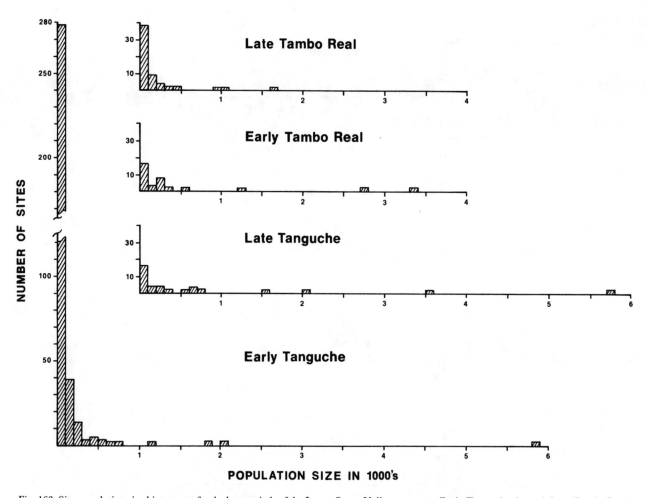

Fig. 163. Site population size histograms for the late periods of the Lower Santa Valley sequence: Early Tanguche through Late Tambo Real.

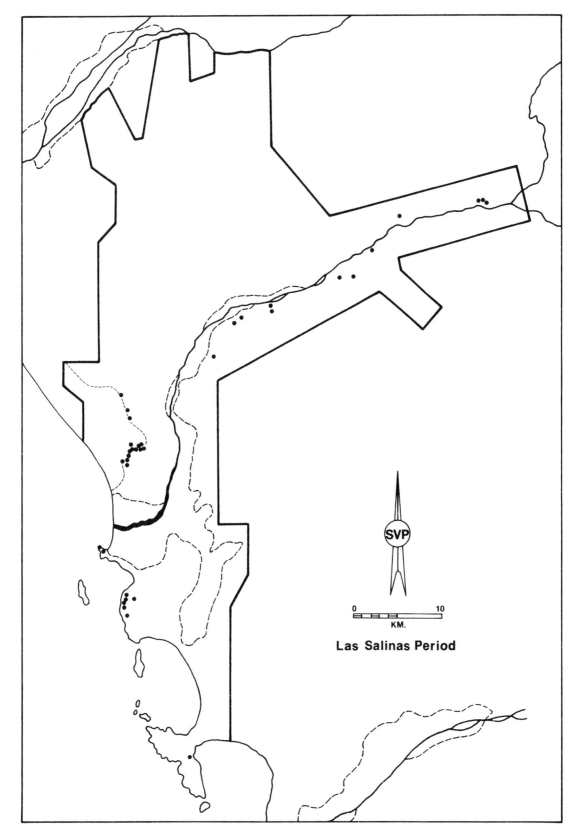

Fig. 164. Settlement pattern of Las Salinas Period.

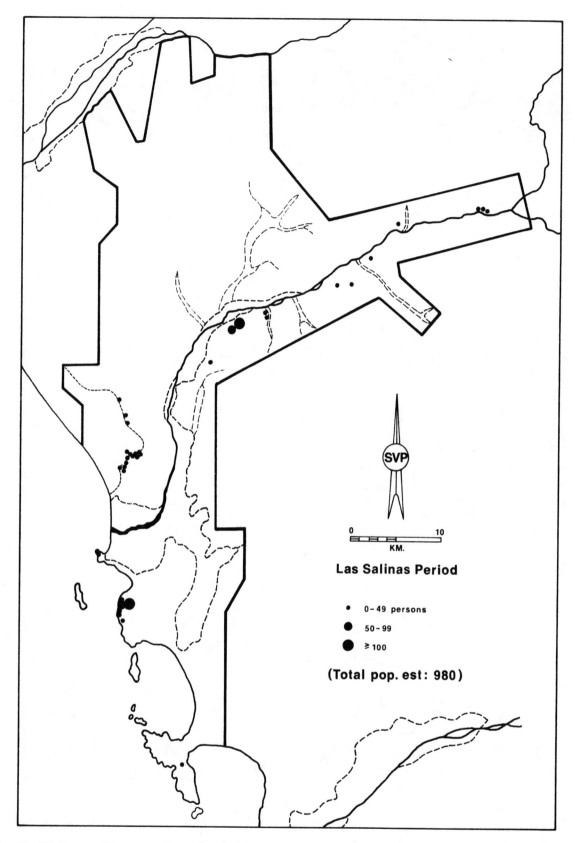

Fig. 165. Demographic pattern of Las Salinas Period.

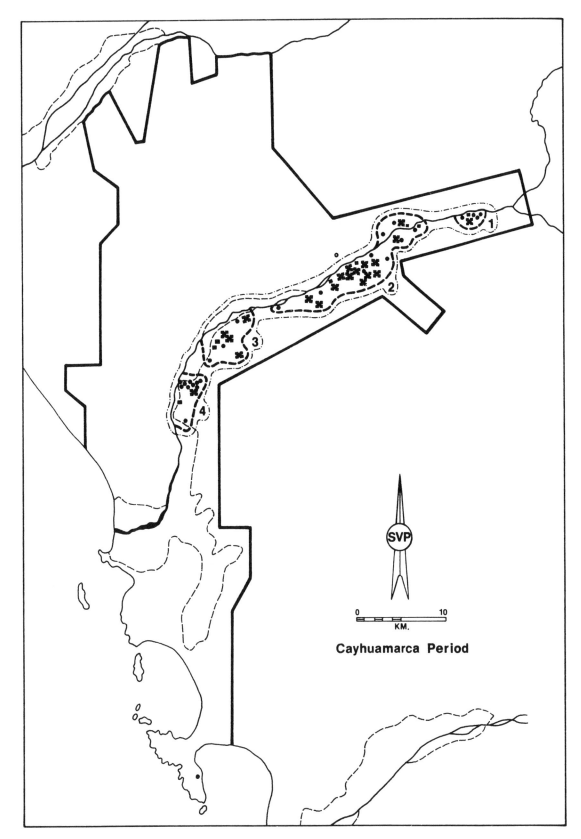

Fig. 166. Settlement pattern of Cayhuamarca Period.

301

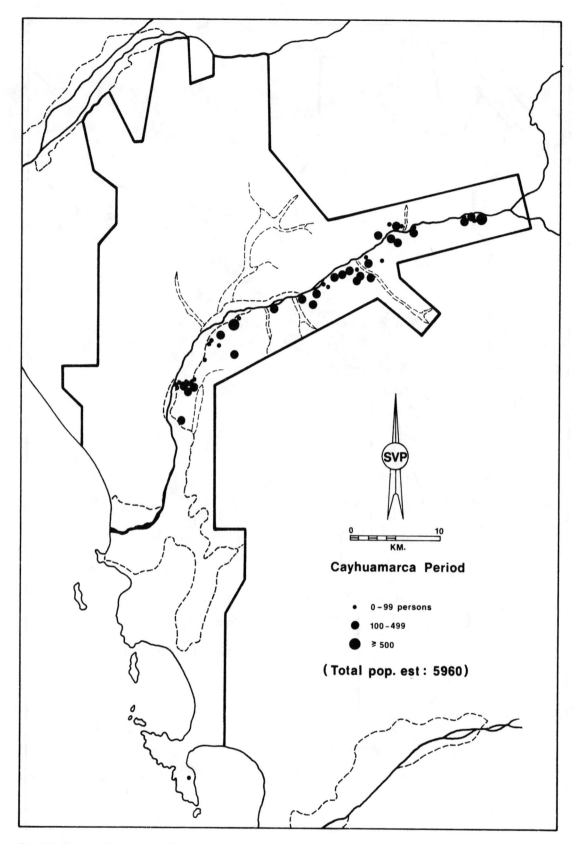

Fig. 167. Demographic pattern of Cayhuamarca Period.

302

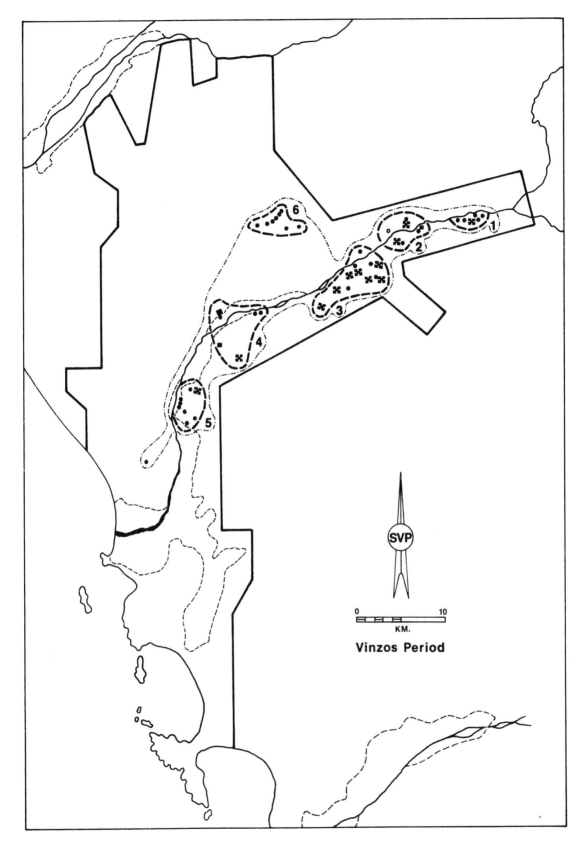

Fig. 168. Settlement pattern of Vinzos Period.

303

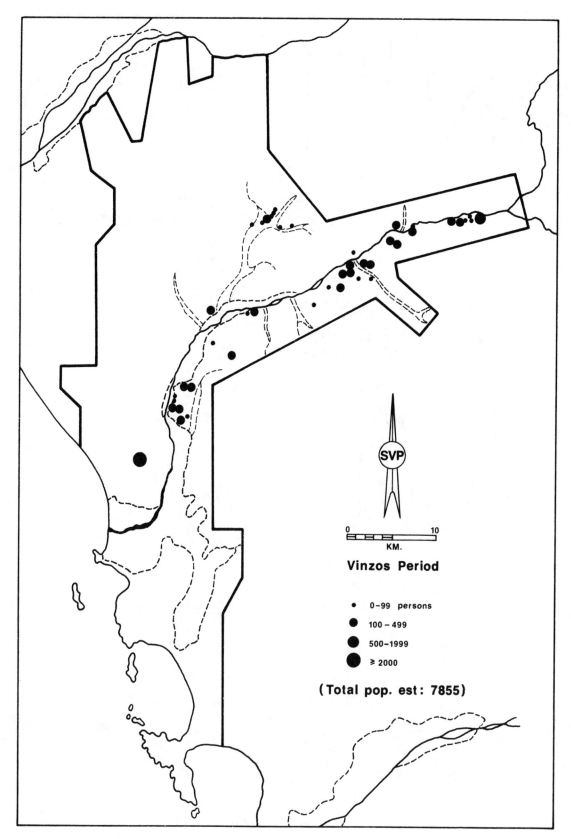

Fig. 169. Demographic pattern of Vinzos Period.

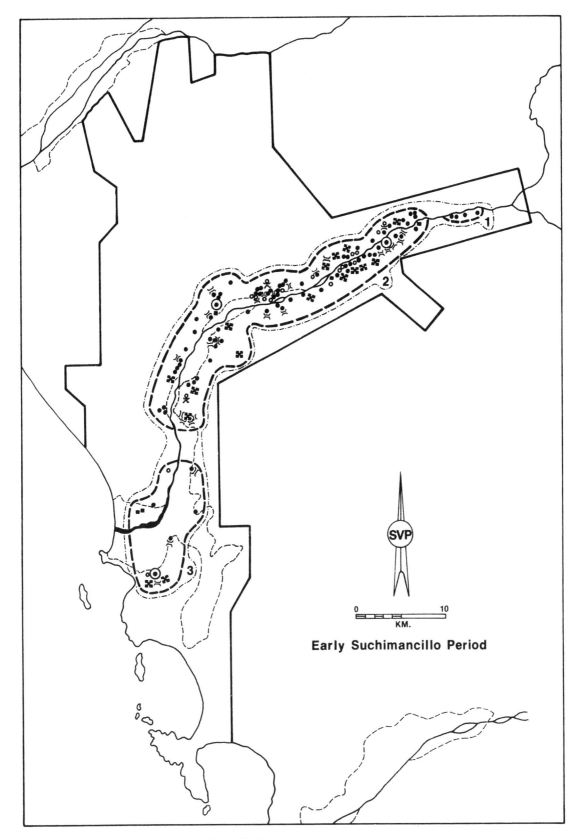

Fig. 170. Settlement pattern of Early Suchimancillo Period.

305

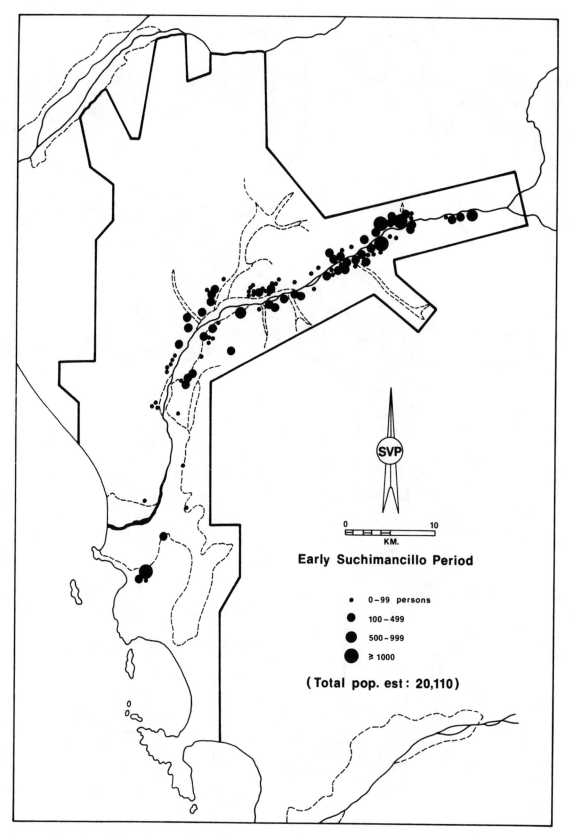

Fig. 171. Demographic pattern of Early Suchimancillo Period.

306

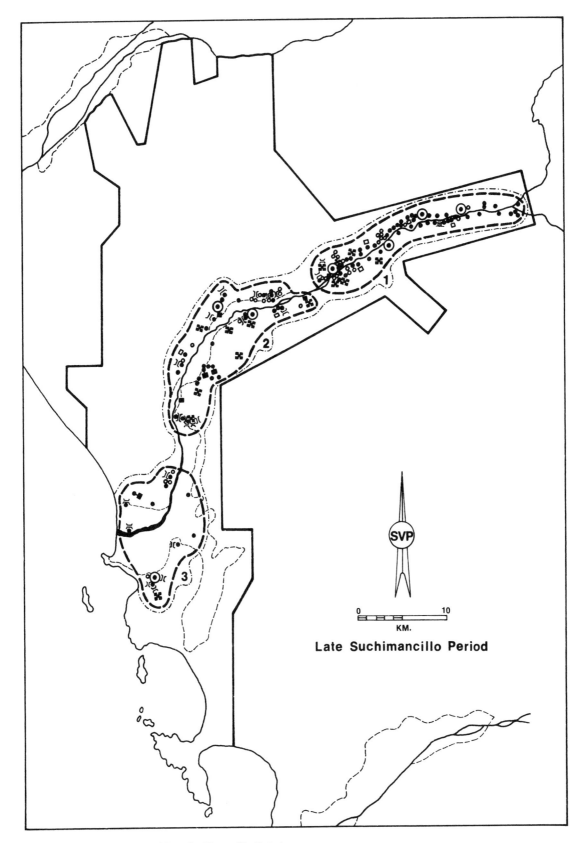

Fig. 172. Settlement pattern of Late Suchimancillo Period.

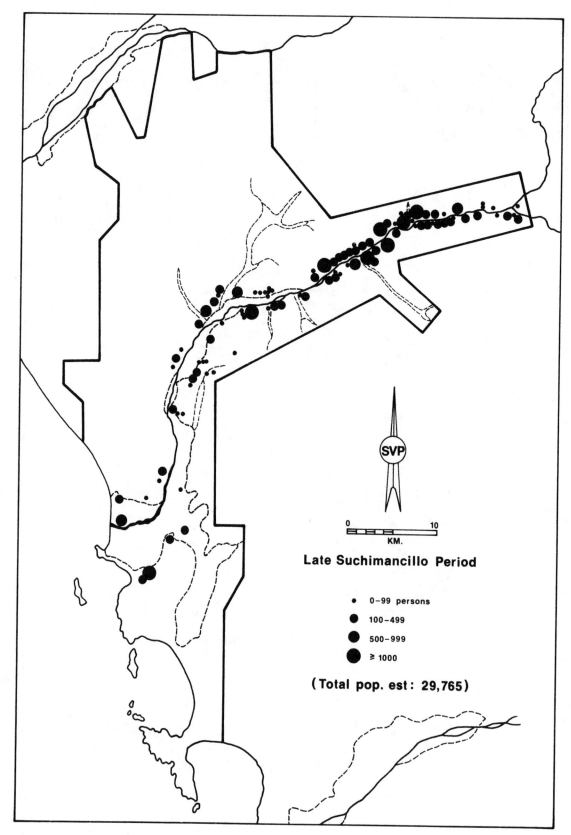

Late Suchimancillo Period

- • 0–99 persons
- ● 100–499
- ● 500–999
- ⬤ ≥ 1000

(Total pop. est : 29,765)

Fig. 173. Demographic pattern of Late Suchimancillo Period.

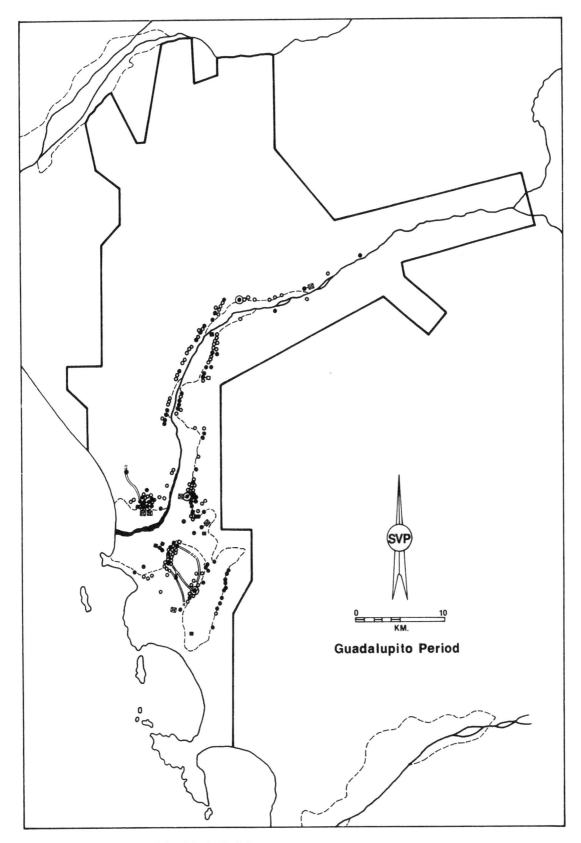

Fig. 174. Settlement pattern of Guadalupito Period.

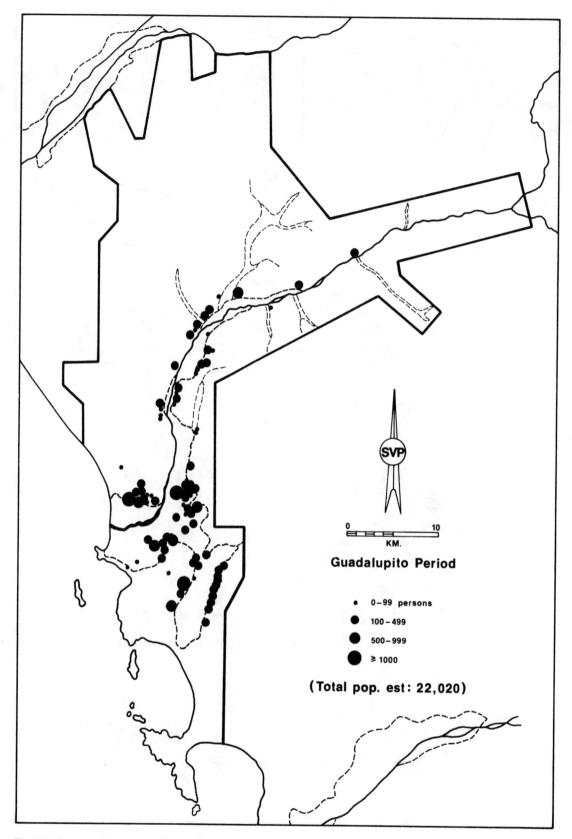

Fig. 175. Demographic pattern of Guadalupito Period.

310

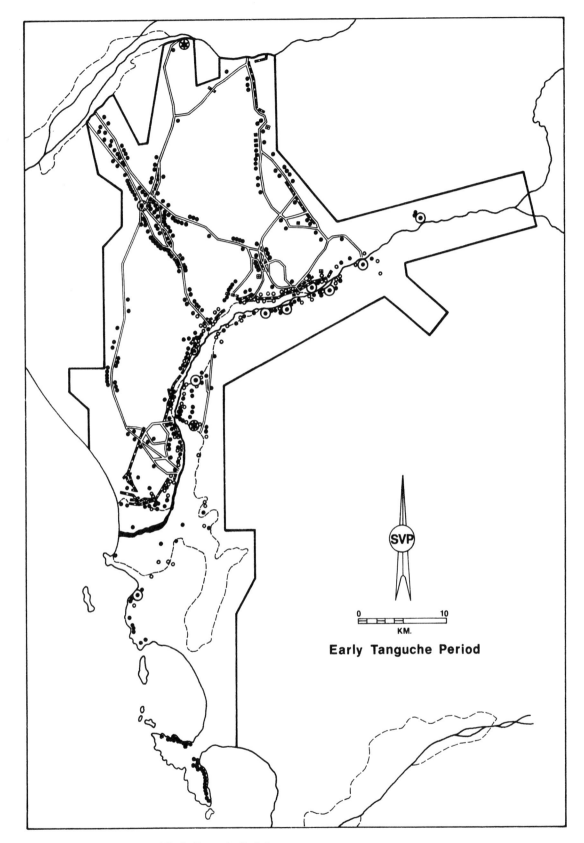

Fig. 176. Settlement pattern of Early Tanguche Period.

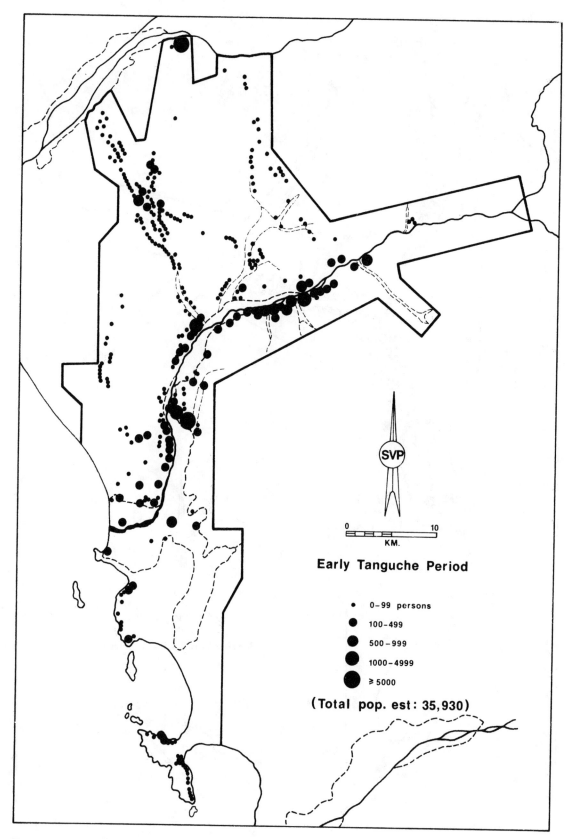

Early Tanguche Period

- • 0-99 persons
- ● 100-499
- ● 500-999
- ● 1000-4999
- ● ≥ 5000

(Total pop. est : 35,930)

SVP

0   10
KM.

Fig. 177. Demographic pattern of Early Tanguche Period.

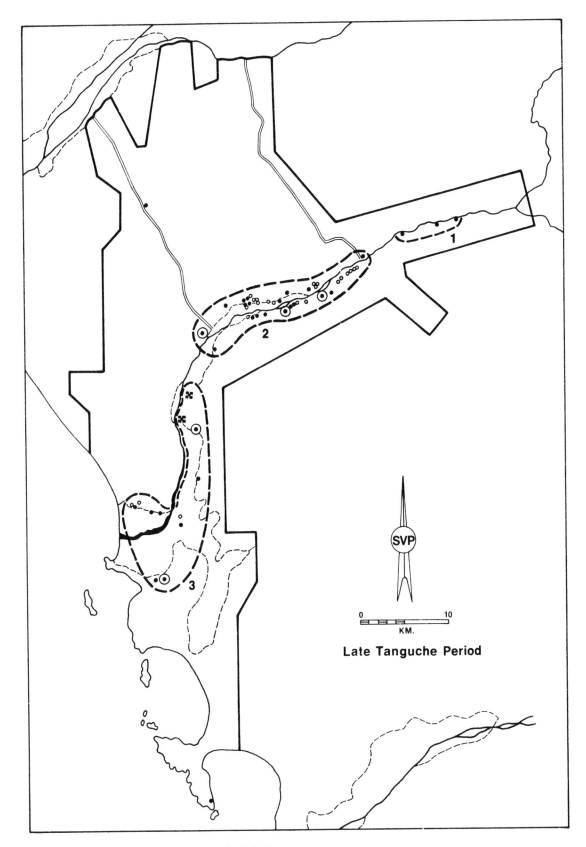

Fig. 178. Settlement pattern of Late Tanguche Period.

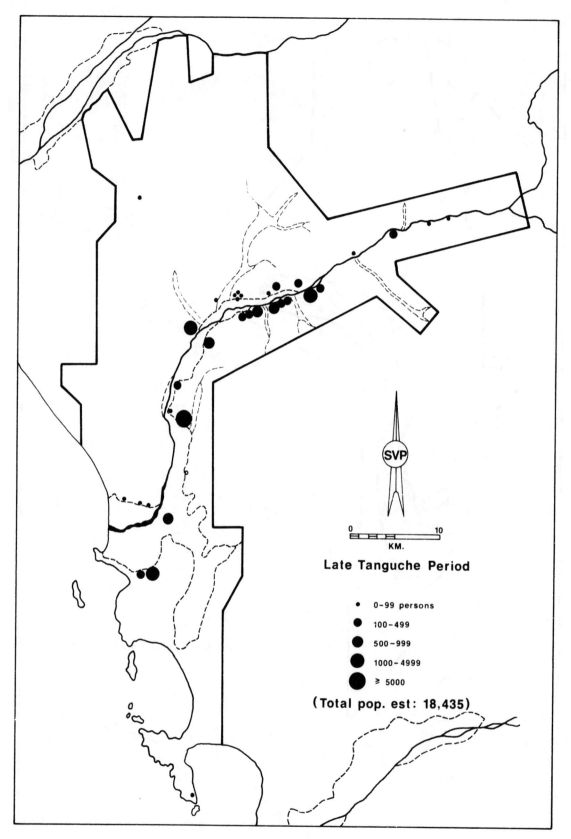

Fig. 179. Demographic pattern of Late Tanguche Period.

314

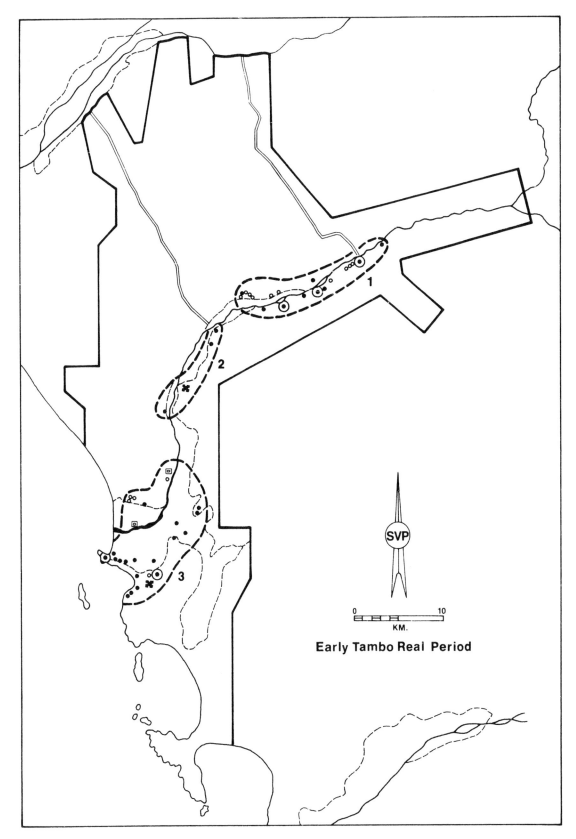

Fig. 180. Settlement pattern of Early Tambo Real Period.

315

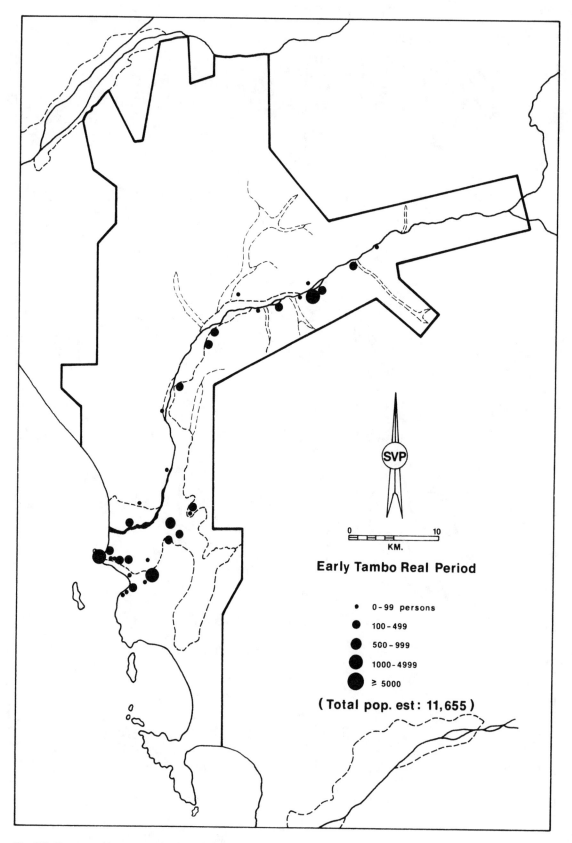

Fig. 181. Demographic pattern of Early Tambo Real Period.

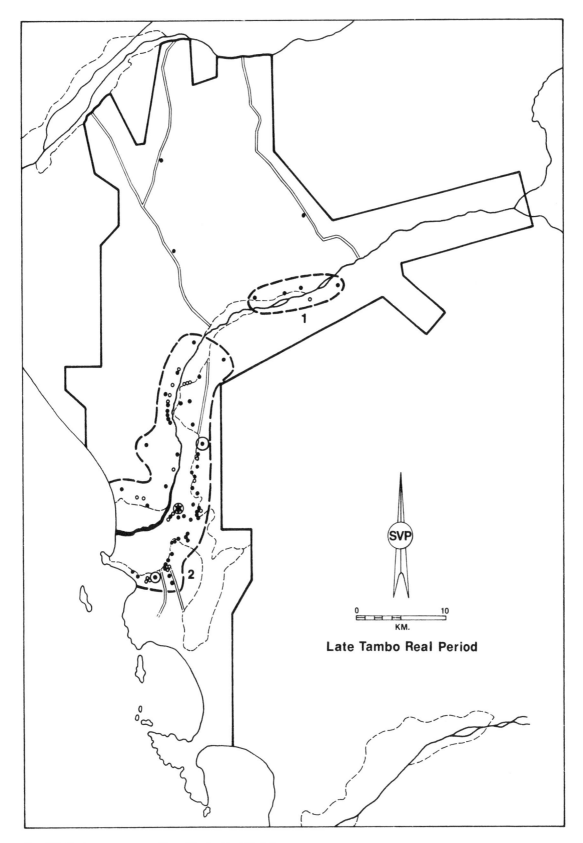

Fig. 182. Settlement pattern of Late Tambo Real Period.

317

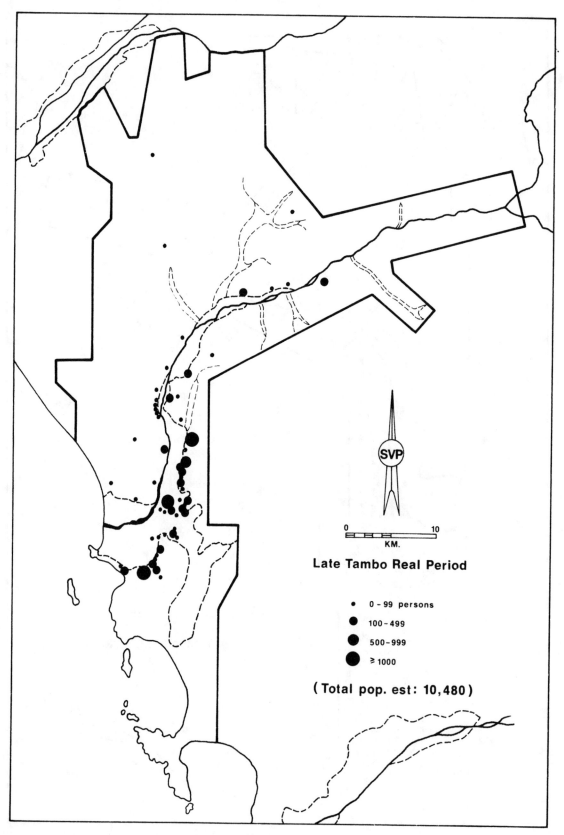

Fig. 183. Demographic pattern of Late Tambo Real Period.

318

Table 6. Data on Size and Population for Habitation Sites by Period

Period	Total Number of Sites[a]	Site Size Range (ha)[b]	Average Site Size (ha)[b]	Population Size Range of Sites	Average Number of Persons Per Site[c]
LTR	58	.3 - 20.0	2.5	5 - 1650	180
ETR	34	.3 - 33.0	3.5	5 - 3300	340
LTAN	34	.3 - 37.4	5.0	20 - 5870	540
ETAN	349	.1 - 52.4	1.6	5 - 5870	100[d]
GUAD	84	.3 - 29.5	3.0	5 - 2950[e]	260
LSUCH	112	.1 - 41.5	3.6	5 - 3100	270
ESUCH	103	.1 - 70.0	3.4	5 - 3500	195
VIN	44	.3 - 26.0	2.3	5 - 2050	180
CAY	49	.3 - 6.3	1.7	5 - 625	120
SAL	36	.2 - 8.8	0.9	5 - 260	25

[a]Includes inhabited sites only.

[b]Figures are rounded to nearest tenth of a hectare.

[c]Figures are rounded to nearest five persons.

[d]This figure is derived from all sites, including those in the Santa-Chao Desert sector; excluding Santa-Chao, the average is 185 persons per site.

[e]The population size of Pampa de los Incas Complex is 3520 persons, including eight Guadalupito habitation sites and intervening ancient fields covering a total area of 200 ha (2 km²).

Table 7. Categories of Site Size and Function by Period

Period	Hamlet (5 - 99 persons)[a]	Small Village (100 - 499)[a]	Large Village (500 - 2000+)	Local Center (500 - 3500)	Regional Center (3500+)
LTR	37	17	1	2	1[b]
ETR	16	12	1	5[c]	-
LTAN	16	10	3	5	-
ETAN	276	53	9	10[d]	1[e]
GUAD	23	45	5	3	1[f]
LSUCH	53	45	7	7	-
ESUCH	54	42	4	3	-
VIN	21	21	2	-	-
CAY	23	24	2	-	-
SAL	34	2	-	-	-

[a]Category includes inhabited citadel sites.

[b]SVP-LTR-47/Alto Perú site.

[c]Early Tambo Real local centers range in size from 200-3300.

[d]Early Tanguche local centers range in size from 50-785.

[e]SVP-ETAN-147/Huaca Jedionda site.

[f]Pampa de los Incas Complex: SVP-GUAD-111 and seven associated sites (including SVP-GUAD-98, 102, 104, 109, 110, 112, and 113).

Table 8. Categories of Defensive and Ceremonial Sites by Period

Period	Defensive Citadel	Defensive Minor Fortress	Ceremonial Site/Huaca	Ceremonial Larger Huaca	Ceremonial Cemetery Site
LTR	-	-	-	-	38
ETR	2	2	-	-	28
LTAN	2	-	-	-	25
ETAN	-	-	8	1	123
GUAD	-	-	7	6	147
LSUCH	14	18	7	-	56
ESUCH	18	24	5	-	27
VIN	12	-	3	-	1
CAY	20	-	8	-	1
SAL	-	-	(1)	-	-

[a]Category includes both discrete cemeteries and those which are part of habitation sites.

Table 9. Total Number of Defensive Sites, and Locational Data on Habitation and Defensive Sites, by Period

Period	Total Number of Defensive Sites	Average Elevation (in m) of Habitation and Defensive Sites Above Valley Floor	Average Distance (in m) of Habitation and Defensive Sites Away from Floor
LTR	-	25[a]	70[a]
ETR	4	20[a]	70[a]
LTAN	2	30	70
ETAN	-	20[b]	85[b]
GUAD	-	15[c]	90[c]
LSUCH	32	80	270
ESUCH	40	110	250
VIN	12	135[d]	735[d]
CAY	20	160[e]	740[e]
SAL	-	70[f]	890

[a]Excludes Lower Valley sector, where many sites are located on or immediately adjacent to the valley floor.

[b]Excludes maritime sites (Coast sector) and roadside sites (Santa-Chao Desert sector and Las Salinas area).

[c]Excludes sites located out on the valley floor.

[d]Excludes SVP-VIN-37 and sites of Vinzos Cluster 6.

[e]Excludes SVP-CAY-54, a maritime site at the east edge of Bahía de Samanco.

[f]Excludes all coastal sites.

Table 10. Estimated Persons Per Hectare and Square Kilometer of Irrigable Valley Floor by Period

Period	Population Estimate	Estimated Maximum Irrigable Land (in ha)[a]	Persons/Ha of Irrigable Valley Floor	Persons/Km² of Irrigable Valley Floor
LTR	10,480	4878	2.15	215
ETR	11,660	4574	2.55	255
LTAN	18,435	4070	4.53	453
ETAN	35,930	6430	5.59	559
GUAD	22,020	8780	2.51	251
LSUCH	29,765	5416	5.50	550
ESUCH	20,110	4896	4.11	411
VIN	7855	1900	4.13	413
CAY	5960	1900	3.14	314

[a]Estimates are based on planimeter measurements made from tracings of SAN airphotos of land associated with the settlements of each period.

319

of the early period data, and the implications of the Lower Santa data for general North Coast developments in the pre-state part of the sequence.

The Evolution of Site Types

Habitation sites. The changing nature of habitation sites and structures in the early periods provides strong support for the argument that, with the establishment and development of irrigation agriculture, a fundamental transformation of regional society took place. With regard to dwelling types, for example, the preceramic gathering-hunting system was characterized nearly everywhere by sites composed of small, relatively crude single-room windbreaks. In contrast, by the time of the establishment of upvalley-oriented agriculture in Cayhuamarca Period, larger multiroom dwellings of rectangular or irregular-polygonal shape had become the principal structural type on habitation sites, with only a minor continuation of windbreaks. Still larger multiroom habitations also made their appearance in Cayhuamarca, although this dwelling type did not become a prominent feature of the system until Early and Late Suchimancillo. By Late Suchimancillo times, the basic dwelling types that would characterize the rest of the prehispanic sequence had become firmly established in the region—including low, rock-walled single-room and multiroom dwellings with superstructures consisting of wattle-and-daub supported by post-and-beam frames, as well as structures built completely of perishable materials such as those used in modern quincha dwellings.

As the change from windbreaks to larger dwellings was taking place in the early part of this period, the first signs appear of a fundamental distinction between the mass of undifferentiated habitations and a few larger and more formally laid out structures. For example, at a number of sites in Cayhuamarca Clusters 1 and 2—including one habitation site, five multifunction citadels, and two ceremonial-civic occupations—there are structures that seem likely to have served as residences of elite groups. Residences of this type continue to be built and occupied in Clusters 1, 2, and 3 of the Vinzos Period system, and are present at a similar mix of occupational types. By Early and Late Suchimancillo Periods, probable elite habitations had been incorporated as one of the principal features of local centers, and no longer appeared in (single-function) habitation sites or in association with citadels.

Another major developmental feature of early settlements is the change in their average size. Since the preceding chapter refers to average sizes for undifferentiated habitation sites only, here it is useful to present the data on changes in average size of all early period sites that contain evidence of habitation—including undifferentiated habitations, local centers, and many citadel sites. As summarized in Table 6, the data show a very steady increase in average site size throughout the five early periods (i.e., from .9, to 1.7, 2.3, 3.4, and 3.6 ha), as well as in average number of persons per site (from 25, to 120, 180, 195, and 270 persons). Finally, it will be recalled that the first large settlement numbering above 1000 inhabitants occurs in Vinzos times (i.e., SVP-VIN-37, with an estimated 2050 persons), but it is not until the end of the early period that a number of large settlements appear (including two sites with 1500+ inhabitants in Early Suchimancillo, and five such sites in Late Suchimancillo).

Defensive sites. The first four ceramic periods do not show quite the steady increase in number, size, and complexity of defensive sites that characterizes habitation sites (e.g., there are 20 fortresses in Cayhuamarca, 12 in Vinzos, 42 in Early Suchimancillo, and 32 in Late Suchimancillo). But, as we have seen, their overall numbers and widespread distribution indicate that warfare was a feature common to all four periods. The principal developmental contrast between early fortress and habitation sites, however, is that the most elaborate and varied group of fortresses appear in the earliest pre-state agricultural system, not the last. For example, citadels of Cayhuamarca Period exhibit all or a number of the following formal features: well-constructed megalithic stone walls, bastions, indirect-baffled or direct entrances, short "spoke" walls extending out from the interior side of the main enclosure walls, interior citadels, ceremonial-civic features, elite residences, dry ditches, and closely associated undifferentiated habitations.

As we have seen, later fortresses constructed in Suchimancillo times are clearly less complex than those of Cayhuamarca Period in terms of both formal layout and the number of component features. Nevertheless, both Early and Late Suchimancillo are characterized by greater numbers of defensive sites as well as a clear differentiation of the generic type into two subtypes—i.e., citadels and minor defensive sites. Along with these changes there appears to have been a transfer of the elite and ceremonial functions associated with some Cayhuamarca-Vinzos citadels to other site types in the Early and Late Suchimancillo settlement systems, including local centers and pyramidal mounds.

Ceremonial-civic sites. It is very intriguing to note that the greater diversity and complexity that characterize Cayhuamarca defensive sites in relation to those of the following three periods also appear to be much the same with regard to ceremonial-civic sites. For example, included among the eight sites with a primarily ceremonial-civic function in the Cayhuamarca settlement system are (1) two major complexes containing large pyramidal platforms, circular sunken courts, and probable elite residences; (2) two medium-sized huaca mounds, one of which has a very formal layout and attached circular court; (3) two ridgetop platforms; and (4) two smaller huaca structures. Although associated ceramic debris suggests that the number of ceremonial-civic sites in use in Vinzos Period was comparatively much reduced (i.e., from eight to only three), the proximity of Vinzos sites to many Cayhuamarca ceremonial centers argues for the probability of continuing occupation not involving habitation or use of pottery. Moreover, the founding of one of the most outstanding ceremonial-civic/habitation sites in the region—SVP-VIN-26/Huaca Yolanda—appears to have taken place in Vinzos Period, with continuing occupation in Early and Late Suchimancillo. But by Early Suchimancillo times the main emphasis in constructing supravillage foci seems to have been on local centers (including Huaca Yolanda), which probably had the same multiple functions that characterize the Cayhuamarca citadels. Aside from these centers, isolated pyramidal structures of medium size continue to be constructed in both Early and Late Suchimancillo, and are widely distributed in the area of occupation.

In terms of the relative size of early and middle period ceremonial structures, it is noteworthy that none of the structures in ceremonial-civic sites of the early periods is anywhere near the size of the principal pyramidal platforms found at a number of Guadalupito sites and at SVP-ETAN-147/Huaca Jedionda. The lack of monumental structures in the early settlement system seems likely to be due to the smaller size of regional and local populations, as well as to the fundamental differences characterizing the pre-state and multivalley-state systems in terms of their ability to mobilize people for corporate labor undertakings. In spite of this, the construction and use of sites with a primary ceremonial-civic function seems to have been much more important in the subsistence-settlement systems of the early periods than in any other later period, except Guadalupito.

Local centers. As discussed earlier, the rise in Early and Late Suchimancillo of large internally differentiated sites—whose features include elite and non-elite habitation as well as defensive works and ceremonial-civic features—appears to coincide with a decrease in the importance of smaller centers having a function primarily or wholly related to supravillage ceremonial activities. Indeed, the apparently broader multifunctional nature of these local centers suggests that some secularization of supravillage activities already was occurring. Perhaps the more fundamental distinction to be made here, however, is between (1) the earlier ceremonial-civic centers which had only small permanent populations, if any, and at most probably served as part-time or occasional foci of supravillage religious activities; and (2) the later local centers which had large numbers of inhabitants and probably served as year-round foci of supravillage socioeconomic as well as religious activities.

In a basic sense, then, this distinction suggests that by Early Suchimancillo times the institution of the part-time ceremonial center had been *promoted* to a permanent, higher-order level in the developing hierarchy of site size and function. In other words, it seems clear that the local centers of Suchimancillo times represent a substantially more complex evolutionary outgrowth of Cayhuamarca-Vinzos ceremonial sites. However, in comparing the widespread distribution of both the earlier ceremonial-civic centers and the later local centers in the pre-state time period, it is also likely that both types of sites were of critical importance in the maintenance of local within-valley socioeconomic ties among sites.

Other remains. Although a number of other interesting developments occur in the pre-state periods, the most important for the present discussion are the establishment of probable corral enclosures and interregional routes of communication at least by the time of Early Suchimancillo period. Two probable corrals date to this period and seven were found to date to Late Suchimancillo, with those of the latter period spaced at intervals of 5–11 km along ancient trails on both sides of the river in the Upper and Middle Valley. As discussed earlier, the fact that only one of the Late Suchimancillo corrals is associated with a local center suggests that the small hamlets and villages where they are usually found served as way stations along the routes of travel, rather than as foci of local redistribution. In any case, the desert ground figures at SVP-ESUCH-112 leave little doubt that llamas were an integral part of local and interregional socioeconomic relations by the beginning of Suchimancillo times.

Distributional Patterns of Population and Settlement

Demographic and settlement trends. The regional population estimates based on total extent of inhabited areas and the density of structural remains (e.g., see Table 4) indicate that the early periods in the sequence exhibit the classic exponential growth curve that characterizes the rise of sociocultural complexity in all nuclear areas of the world (e.g., compare Fig. 253 to Blanton et al. 1981:59; Butzer 1976:85; and Parsons 1974:103). Thus from an initial estimate totaling probably no more than 1000 persons in Las Salinas times, the regional population expanded at an increasingly rapid pace in a period of 2000+ years to nearly 30 times that number by Late Suchimancillo (see Table 5). It is also of interest to note that the periods of early agriculture in Cayhuamarca and Vinzos do not exhibit pronounced differences in population (ca. 6000 and 8000 persons, respectively), while Early Suchimancillo (ca. 20,000 persons) is more or less exactly intermediate between the earlier periods and Late Suchimancillo (ca. 30,000 persons).

With regard to overall site location in the early periods, it appears to be of some significance that the settlement system of Cayhuamarca—the first probable period of intensive irrigation agriculture—is almost entirely focused on the upvalley area. In a valley such as Santa, with a 70 km-long coastal sector and steeper upvalley gradients, this early pattern is probably explainable in terms of two main factors: (1) low population numbers, and the consequent lack of large corporate labor groups at the local level; and (2) the relative ease of getting water to fields using shorter canals in the upvalley sectors. Indeed, irrigation agriculture does not appear to have been established in the Lower Valley until Early and Late Suchimancillo, when population levels had begun to exceed an estimated 20,000 persons. (Note: the differences between Santa and Virú—where the initial development of agriculture in Guañape Period is focused on the lower valley—may be explainable by the shorter, 30-km length of the latter valley as well as by the overall distribution of land; e.g., there is very little cultivable land in the upvalley part of Virú, in strong contrast to Santa.)

In any case, when population levels are compared on a sector-by-sector basis in the main valley area for each of the early periods (see Table 5), it is clear that demographic developments in the Lower Santa region occurred in a reasonably orderly (or, predictable) manner—at least in light of the above-mentioned assumptions about the more attractive nature of the upvalley sectors for small groups of early irrigation farmers, as well as the probability that the Lower Valley would not have become attractive until upvalley population levels approached agricultural carrying capacity. The small upvalley population of the initial period of occupation in Las Salinas Period was followed, first, by a substantial rise of numbers in Cayhuamarca, and, later, by a gradual filling-in process in the Vinzos and Early Suchimancillo Periods. Then, at the time the population of the upvalley sectors began to reach relatively substantial levels in Early Suchimancillo Period (ca. 17,000 persons) the first occupation of the Lower Valley occurs.

It is also intriguing to note that along with the establishment of the upvalley subsistence-settlement system in Cayhuamarca and Vinzos Periods comes a more or less pronounced clustering of settlements. At the same time, settlement clusters are found widely distributed throughout most of the Upper and Middle Valley sectors. It may be suggested that this pattern can be explained in terms of two principal aspects of the early agricultural adaptation. First, given rising population levels and the advantage in terms of travel time of locating sites as near as possible to cultivated areas, it is likely that the broadly distributed settlements of Cayhuamarca and Vinzos represent an adaptation to the need for widespread cultivation of the upvalley sectors. Second, given this subsistence-settlement strategy and the probability that the threat of raiding was a continual one, then it also would

have been strategically advantageous to locate sites in clusters as near as possible to the hills and ridgetops where citadels were located.

As indicated by a comparison of Figs. 166 and 168, settlement clustering is somewhat more pronounced in Vinzos Period than in Cayhuamarca. But the presence of a consistent set of site types—i.e., habitations, citadels, and ceremonial centers—in the Cayhuamarca settlement groups supports the argument that the clustering itself is a real phenomenon reflecting the adaptive processes and strategies outlined above. In spite of the cluster outlines drawn on the smaller-scale settlement maps of Early and Late Suchimancillo (Figs. 170, 172), the settlement distribution for each of these periods is probably better characterized as essentially continuous throughout the upvalley sectors—or at least progressively more so from Early to Late Suchimancillo times (nonetheless, for analytical reasons having to do with a fine-grained comparison of subsistence potential, the delineation of clusters in *all* of the early periods has substantial utility, as we shall see below).

Hierarchies of site size and function. As summarized in Table 7, along with the steady rise in regional population during the early periods comes a continual increase in the hierarchy of site size and function. In light of this process, there appear to be *differences in kind* (i.e., sociocultural stage) between Las Salinas and Cayhuamarca-Vinzos, on the one hand; and *differences of degree* (i.e., level of complexity) between Cayhuamarca-Vinzos and Early-Late Suchimancillo, on the other. With regard to the differences between the preceramic and the two first ceramic periods, there are two levels of site size in the Las Salinas system and three in Cayhuamarca and Vinzos. But, in terms of sociopolitical function, it is likely that Las Salinas represents a one-level system while most, if not all, of the Cayhuamarca and Vinzos clusters represent incipient two-level systems—including undifferentiated habitation sites as well as ceremonial-civic centers that functioned as part-time or occasional foci of supravillage (and possibly intercluster) activities. By contrast, in Early and Late Suchimancillo four levels can be distinguished on the basis of size, and, with the rise of local centers, it seems likely that a two-level system of sociopolitical function had become firmly established in the region.

In sum, the analysis of the main features of the developing pre-state regional system—including the rise in population numbers, the supravillage foci represented first by ceremonial and citadel sites and later by local centers, the nature of site distributions, and the increasing number of tiers of site size and sociopolitical function—suggests the following: Las Salinas Period is probably a system characterized by a tribal level of sociocultural integration, Cayhuamarca and Vinzos Periods represent the development of incipient chiefdoms,

322

and the systems of Early and Late Suchimancillo Periods are fully developed chiefdoms.

Warfare and Subsistence

Nature of early warfare. Six main lines of evidence have been drawn upon to this point in constructing the initial arguments about the nature of conflict in the early periods—including (1) the nature and distribution of fortress structures, (2) the overall location of settlements, (3) the population size of settlement clusters, (4) the regional distribution of ceramic types, (5) interregional comparisons of contemporaneous ceramic assemblages, and (6) the nature of contemporaneous settlement systems in nearby valleys. It will be recalled that these lines of evidence generally support the argument that warfare/raiding was interregional in nature from the start of irrigation agriculture, and that the threat of attack on the Lower Santa region probably was from the south. It is useful to summarize them here, before proceeding with the discussion of how additional strong corroborative support for this argument comes from an examination of early subsistence and the analysis of maize-based carrying capacity.

First, there is little doubt that the structures and sites identified as fortresses do in fact represent defensive constructions. A number of features—including relatively remote and high locations, architectural configuration, and associated dry ditches—have been pinpointed to support this argument as well as to distinguish fortresses from ceremonial-civic centers and habitation sites. Furthermore, the widespread distribution of defensive sites in each period from Cayhuamarca through Late Suchimancillo clearly suggests that warfare was one of the most significant socioenvironmental stresses affecting the subsistence-settlement system.

Second, the average location of settlements in each of the early periods exhibits a continual change toward increasing proximity to the valley floor. Las Salinas Period sites are located on the average the farthest away from the valley floor, while Cayhuamarca sites are located higher above the floor and farther away than those in any of the three succeeding periods (see Table 9). Given the physical evidence for warfare and the steady increase in population, it seems clear that this changing evolutionary pattern reflects the added security of both increases in numbers of people and in the organizational sophistication with which defensive (and offensive) warfare/raiding was carried out.

Third, it has been argued that the general disparity in the estimated population size of the different clusters in the system of most early periods argues against the possibility of a within-valley balance of power, and hence against between-cluster warfare. As indicated in the cluster-by-cluster population estimates shown in Table 12, this disparity of numbers is as follows: Cayhuamarca Period Cluster 2 has at least three times as many inhabitants as any other cluster of its system, Early Suchimancillo Period Cluster 2 has between four and 15 times the inhabitants of any other cluster, and Late Suchimancillo Period Cluster 1 has between three and six times the inhabitants of any other cluster. On the other hand, the cluster populations of Vinzos Period exhibit a rough parity (i.e., ca. 1000 inhabitants per cluster), and this at least suggests the possibility of internecine conflict.

The ceramic data constituting the fourth line of evidence indicate that not only contiguous clusters, but essentially all clusters, in the system of each period share a number of principal diagnostic types. Indeed, as we have seen, the distribution of most ceramic types is a clinal one that crosscuts cluster boundaries. Thus the distribution seems to be much more related to distance away from the Quebrada de Cayhuamarca core area (where the highest numbers and diversity of types occur) than it is to changing local spheres of intensive socioeconomic interaction. Taken as a whole, then, the strong between-cluster ceramic similarities appear to argue against the possibility of internecine conflict in any of the early periods. By the same token, the fact that cross-river differences in the distribution of ceramic types for each cluster are substantially less than the clinal differences one sees between clusters also argues that cross-river relations were characterized by intensive socioeconomic interaction, and not warfare.

If it can be argued that warfare was not a within-valley phenomenon during any of the early ceramic periods, the question arises as to whether the threat of external raiding was coming from the north or from the south. The fifth line of evidence bearing on the nature of early warfare/raiding is therefore the degree of similarity between ceramics of Santa and those of other regions. Proceeding from the assumption that a greater number of similarities may indicate stronger socioeconomic ties, the ceramic data indicate that such ties generally were much greater with Virú and valleys to the north than with Nepeña and valleys to the south. The data are summarized as follows (the percentages of Santa types shared with assemblages to the north, south, and, where relevant, the adjacent sierra are given in parentheses): Cayhuamarca (75% north, 25% south), Vinzos (92% north, no apparent sharing with south), Early Suchimancillo (25% north, no apparent sharing with south, 65% sierra), and Late Suchimancillo (50% north, no apparent sharing with south, 30+% sierra). With the exception of Early Suchimancillo Period, ceramic/socioeconomic ties are thus consistently strong between Santa and Virú, and consistently weak or (apparently) nonexistent between Santa and Nepeña. Indeed, even in periods such as Cayhuamarca when comparable Early Horizon data are available from Nepeña and Casma, Santa shares only three or four of the 68 motif types of Casma (see Chapter III), while Nepeña exhibits a low intermediate number consisting of 10 motif types. Whatever the nature of interaction between Nepeña and Casma, Santa Valley does not appear to have been a significant part of it.

Finally, the sixth line of evidence comes from the nature of contemporaneous settlement systems in Virú and Nepeña. In line with the argument that Cayhuamarca/Early Horizon warfare was occurring between Santa and valleys to the south, there are no fortresses in the contemporaneous Guañape system of Virú while Nepeña is very similar to Santa in having a number of fortresses. On the other hand, fortresses are present in the Puerto Moorin and Early-Middle Gallinazo systems of Virú, at least indicating that warfare in the later part of the pre-state period had become more widespread in this area of the North Coast.

Nature of early irrigation networks. As outlined in Chapter III, the boundaries around clusters were drawn only when it seemed possible that each of the local settlement systems could have sustained itself by means of a more or less independent irrigation network consisting of shorter canals. In a sense, then, this procedure was part of the attempt to support the alternate hypothesis regarding the nature of early warfare: namely, that the appearance of clustering in the settlement pattern represents the development of mutually bellicose local site groupings—in accordance, for example, with Carneiro's coercive hypothesis of within-region internecine conflict as a prime factor in the rise of sociocultural complexity.

However, in addition to the series of arguments summarized in the preceding section against the hypothesis of internecine warfare, at least two more reasonably compelling arguments against the notion of independent, self-sustaining settlement clusters can be put forth. First, as mentioned earlier, the actual configuration of traditional modern irrigation networks in the upper sectors of valleys like Santa and Nepeña is characterized by an intricate system of interconnected primary, secondary, and tertiary canals that require at least local interdependency, if not outright cooperation, among agriculturalists. Since, as we have seen in Chapter II, traditional irrigation practices do not seem to have changed significantly since prehispanic times, such local interdependency and cooperation therefore probably characterized the earlier period as well. Second, given the high ongoing potential for easy disruption of canal intakes and networks, it seems very unlikely that continual within-valley conflict could have been sustained more or less indefinitely over the hundreds and hundreds of years during which early warfare/raiding was occurring.

In sum, considering the critical survival need to establish and maintain local irrigation systems free from any immediate danger of disruption, it is nearly inconceivable that local agriculturalists would have been so reckless as to permit a situation of serious local conflict to arise. Such conflict certainly does not character-

ize any part of the Santa Valley agricultural system today, and it is highly likely that the same communal patterns of supravillage cooperation and coordination of canal-cleaning activities that are found in modern Virú would also have been a part of the early prehispanic agricultural system of the Lower Santa region.

Analysis of maize-based carrying capacity. As discussed earlier, among the principal objectives of the Santa Valley research was to examine the relative roles of population growth and warfare in the origins and development of prehispanic North Coast societal complexity. Utilizing systematically gathered, comprehensive regional survey data on site size and density of structural remains, it has been possible to make empirically-based estimates of the maximum population potential for each period in the sequence as well as to obtain a picture of relative changes in population over time. The picture thus obtained indicates that population growth was a continual part of the early developmental sequence—from the establishment of upvalley irrigation agriculture in Cayhuamarca times to the rise of advanced chiefdom society in Early and Late Suchimancillo times nearly one thousand years later. Utilizing the data on site types, settlement location, and ceramic distributions, it has also been possible to construct an argument that conflict not only was a critical part of societal evolution from the very start of irrigation agriculture but that it probably was carried out between different coastal valleys, and not on a within-region basis.

But the data indicating the fundamental roles played by population growth and conflict throughout the development of early chiefdom society have also raised questions that require additional analysis. With regard to population dynamics, for example, it is of interest to examine whether in addition to the clear role played by demographic increases over time there are grounds for arguing that the population-land relationship was such that the early adaptive context was characterized by *pressure*—i.e., by a continual imbalance between the number of people in the system and the capacity of the land to sustain them. In this sense, then, it is relevant to examine whether or not an argument for population pressure can be made. Likewise, with regard to conflict, it is of interest to examine the subsistence-settlement system of each of the early ceramic periods on a cluster-by-cluster basis to investigate whether the hectarage of land associated with each settlement cluster was sufficient—even using a best-case analytical approach based on triple-cropping—to support the estimated population of that cluster. In sum, if a population pressure argument can be sustained, then this has important implications for constructing cross-culturally valid theories of sociocultural evolution. And if it can be shown that each settlement cluster was potentially capable of subsisting independently of the others, then this has even more critical implications for the nature of pre-state intergroup relations at the local and regional levels.

In the analysis of this and the following section, it will be shown that (1) a population pressure argument cannot be sustained, at least for the early part of the Lower Santa sequence, but that it is likely that such pressure was indeed an integral part of the human-land relationship in most if not all other nearby valleys; and (2) maize-based carrying capacity analysis provides additional strong corroborative support for the argument developed in the preceding section that warfare throughout the entire early sequence was interregional in nature. The issues related to cluster-by-cluster carrying capacity and the nature of early conflict occupy the remainder of this section, followed by a discussion in the next section of the issue of population growth and pressure. It is worth noting that the general results of the analysis of the population-land relationship are summarized in Tables 11–14.

As argued in the section on maize-based carrying capacity analysis in Chapter III, it is possible to use estimates of average maize cob length (in cm) for the early periods and average productivity (in kg/ha) to estimate, in turn, the single-crop carrying capacity (in persons/ha) for each of the pre-state agricultural subsistence-settlement systems. As shown in Table 11, these data (Columns 2–4) can then be used in conjunction with planimeter estimates of the maximum hectares of land associated with the system of each period (Column 5) to estimate the relationship between: (1) different carrying capacities, based on possible cropping strategies (Columns 6–8); and (2) independently estimated population based on site size and structural densities (Column 9). We shall return later to the results of the analysis summarized in Table 11, but here it is worth noting that various strategies ranging somewhere between single-cropping and triple-cropping would have been sufficient to support the population of each period in the ceramic sequence. For example, the analysis shows that while single-cropping the 1900 ha of land associated with the Cayhuamarca settlement system was sufficient to support only 4320 of the 5960 persons estimated to have inhabited it, double-cropping would have supported 8645 persons—or well over the estimated maximum population size.

The results of the cluster-by-cluster analysis of maize-based carrying capacity for the pre-state ceramic periods are summarized in Table 12, with each cell of the table representing a separate period cluster and showing three different variables. These include (a) total hectarage of cultivable land associated with the cluster; (b) maximum human carrying capacity represented by a best-case estimate based on a strategy of year-round, highly intensive triple-cropping (derived by tripling the single-crop

carrying capacity figure shown for each period in Table 11, and multiplying the resulting figure by the number of hectares of land associated with the cluster); and (c) estimated actual population of the cluster (based, as mentioned earlier, on total inhabited area and densities of structural remains). For example, the analysis of Cayhuamarca Cluster 1 shows that only 11 ha of cultivable land are associated with this settlement grouping (located in the Upper Valley canyon; see Figs. 8, 23, and 166). Yet, even assuming intensive year-round cultivation, the triple-crop carrying capacity of this grouping is only 75 persons (2.275 p/ha × 3 crops/yr × 11 ha) while the actual population of the cluster is estimated at nearly thirteen times that number (i.e., 950 persons). Clearly, the subsistence-settlement system of Cluster 1 cannot be considered by any stretch of the imagination to have been independent and self-sustaining.

By the same token, triple-cropping the 368 ha of cultivable land associated with Cayhuamarca Cluster 2 would have been sufficient to support only 2510 of the 3005 persons estimated to have inhabited it. Indeed, it is not until all the land associated with Cayhuamarca Clusters 1, 2, and 3 is combined that the figure for triple-crop human carrying capacity (75 + 2520 + 2590 = 5175 persons) exceeds the estimated actual population size (950 + 3005 + 1040 = 4995 persons). We may therefore conclude that Cayhuamarca Clusters 1 and 2 clearly would have required access to more than just the land immediately associated with each cluster—i.e., to land in the between-cluster zones as well as that associated with Cluster 3. Considering the potential for disruption of vulnerable canals and field systems in the between-cluster zones, it seems highly unlikely that anything other than peaceful inter-cluster relations characterized the upvalley Cayhuamarca system. Moreover, when the combined population of the three upvalley clusters forming a minimal sphere of socioeconomic interaction (i.e., 4995 persons) is compared to the estimate for Cayhuamarca Cluster 4 (950 persons), the strong demographic disparity effectively rules out any balance of power that would permit continual warfare between the two groups.

The same analytical procedure can be applied to the data summarized in Table 12 for Vinzos, Early Suchimancillo, and Late Suchimancillo Periods. For example, in light of the independently estimated population sizes of the Vinzos settlement clusters, it is not until one considers a socioeconomic combination involving at least all of the land associated with Clusters 1, 2, 3, and 4 that the triple-crop carrying capacity (8400 persons) exceeds the actual estimated population size of these four clusters (3995 persons). Clearly, then, at least Vinzos Clusters 1 and 2 would have required access to land outside the immediate area of settlement, probably including a good deal of the land near or directly associated with Cluster

Table 11. Maize-Based Carrying Capacity Estimates and Independently Estimated Population Size for the Prehispanic Periods of the Lower Santa Valley Sequence

Period	Estimated Average Maize Cob Length[a] (cm)	Estimated Average Single-Crop Production[b] (kg/ha)	Single-Crop Human Carrying Capacity[c] (p/ha)	Estimated Maximum Cultivable Land[d] (ha)	Carrying Capacity (Total No. of Persons)			Estimated Population Size[e]
					Single-Crop	Double-Crop	Triple-Crop	
LTR	11.5	1440	6.826	4878	33,295	66,591	99,886	10,480
ETR	10.6	1088	5.157	4574	23,588	47,177	70,766	11,660
LTAN	9.7	896	4.247	4070	17,285	34,571	51,856	18,435
ETAN	8.9	672	3.185	6430	20,481	40,963	61,444	35,930
GUAD	8.0	545	2.583	8780	22,681	45,362	68,044	22,020
LSUCH	7.9	532	2.522	5416	13,657	27,315	40,972	29,765
ESUCH	7.8	517	2.451	4896	11,998	23,996	35,994	20,110
VIN	7.6	488	2.313	1900	4395	8790	13,185	7855
CAY	7.5	480	2.275	1900	4320	8645	12,969	5960

[a]Grobman et al. (1961, p. 60, Table 5).

[b]Kirkby (1973, p. 126, Fig. 48b).

[c]Single-crop human carrying capacity = (production in kg/ha X 3500 kcal/kg)/738,395 kcal/person/year. Production in kg/ha: from Col. 3; 3500 kcal/kg: cf. FAO 1954, pp. 10-11; 738,395 kcal/p/yr: see Chapter III.

[d]From Table 10, Col. 3.

[e]From Table 5, Col. 7.

Table 12. Intra-Cluster Subsistence Analysis for the Early Ceramic Periods Showing (a) Maximum Amount of Irrigable Land and (b) Triple-Crop Human Carrying Capacity, Compared to (c) Estimated Actual Population Size of Cluster[a]

Period		Clusters				
		1	2	3	4	5
LSUCH	(a)	381	1432	3603	-	-
	(b)	2880	10,835	27,260		
	(c)	18,835	7645	3285		
ESUCH	(a)	11	1890	2995	-	-
	(b)	80	13,900	22,020		
	(c)	1070	15,030	4010		
VIN	(a)	11	82	237	866	350
	(b)	75	570	1645	6110	2430
	(c)	1180	825	955	995	1310
CAY	(a)	11	368	380	275	-
	(b)	75	2510	2590	1875	
	(c)	950	3005	1040	950	

[a](a) measured in hectares; (b) persons; (c) persons.

Table 13. Intra-Cluster Subsistence Analysis for the Late Ceramic Periods Showing (a) Maximum Amount of Irrigable Land and (b) Triple-Crop Human Carrying Capacity, Compared to (c) Estimated Actual Population Size of Cluster[a]

Period		Clusters		
		1	2	3
LTR	(a)	308	4838	-
	(b)	4205	66,048	
	(c)	460	9915	
ETR	(a)	637	604	4549
	(b)	6570	6230	46,918
	(c)	2275	660	8725
LTAN	(a)	10	1060	1500
	(b)	85	9003	12,741
	(c)	280	8700	9355

[a](a) measured in hectares; (b) persons; (c) persons.

Table 14. Optimal Cropping/Clearing Strategies During the Early and Middle Ceramic Periods of the Lower Santa Sequence

Period	Estimated Population Size	Single-Crop Agricultural Carrying Capacity (p/ha)	Estimated Cultivable Land Available (ha)	Minimum Hectares Under Cultivation	Optimal Strategies		Number Hectares Cleared	Intensification Required?
					Double Cropping (total ha)	Triple Cropping (total ha)		
ETAN	35,930	3.185	6430	6430	6430[a]	-	-	No
GUAD	22,020	2.583	8780	8780	8780[b]	-	4845	No
LSUCH	29,765	2.522	5416	3934	-	3934	785	Yes
ESUCH	20,110	2.451	4896	3155	1255	1900	1840	Yes
VIN	7855	2.313	1900	1310	525	785	-	Yes
CAY	5960	2.275	1900	1310	1310	-	1310	-

[a]Production excess = 5030 persons.

[b]Production excess = 23,340 persons.

326

3. The resulting minimal sphere of socioeconomic interaction formed by Vinzos Clusters 1, 2, and 3 (population estimate of 2960 persons) would have created a situation of such marked demographic imbalance that warfare between this group and any other cluster would have been effectively ruled out.

The need for maintenance of coordinated and cooperative between-cluster relations is equally clear for Early and Late Suchimancillo Periods. Of course, as argued earlier, the huge size of Early Suchimancillo Cluster 2 relative to other clusters of this period in and of itself rules out any between-cluster conflict. It is of interest, however, briefly to outline the implications of the analysis of the Late Suchimancillo subsistence-settlement system. As with Early Suchimancillo Cluster 2, it may be noted again that the relatively large population size of Late Suchimancillo Cluster 1 appears to rule out between-cluster balance of power and warfare. Indeed, even assuming that nearly all land associated with settlements in the Upper and Middle Valley (1813 out of 1900 ha) was farmed intensively on a triple-cropping basis, the combined 26,480-person estimate for Clusters 1 and 2 is nearly *two times* that of the estimated maximum carrying capacity (13,715 persons). It can be further shown that all cultivable land in the upvalley area must have been under cultivation at least by Early Suchimancillo times, implying that upvalley people of both Early and Late Suchimancillo would have required access to land in the Lower Valley to sustain the estimated population. It is thus not surprising that these are precisely the time periods when the first occupation of the Lower Valley occurs. As shown in Figs. 170 and 172, the widespread distribution of Lower Valley settlements in both periods provides some indication that a fairly substantial part of the land in this sector was under cultivation. *In a very important sense, then, the fact that settlements are located in the Lower Valley during both Early and Late Suchimancillo Periods in and of itself provides strong corroborative evidence that the overall estimates of maize-based carrying capacity and independently estimated population size are reasonably correct.*

In sum, a number of more or less independent sets of data—including settlement types and locations, population, ceramics, the nature of traditional irrigation networks, and the results of carrying capacity analysis—all support the argument that the overall subsistence-settlement system of each of the early ceramic periods was characterized by increasingly intensive, peaceful socioeconomic and political ties, and not by internecine warfare. At the same time, it is equally clear that conflict was a major stress in the system of each of the early ceramic periods, probably manifested in a series of continual raids that most likely came from valleys to the south of Santa. Assuming, then, that we are dealing with a regional system characterized by ongoing inter-cluster relations of a cooperative nature, it is of interest to conclude this section with a brief look at optimal farming strategies during the periods from Cayhuamarca through Late Suchimancillo.

As summarized in Table 14, this part of the analysis of the subsistence system of each period begins with the overall estimates of population size (Column 2), single-crop carrying capacity (Column 3), and total estimated hectares of cultivated land (Column 4). Given these parameters, it is possible to suggest cropping/land clearing strategies based on an overall strategy which combines the least extensive amount of required land with the principle of least effort. Proceeding in this manner, we may suggest a "beginning" for Cayhuamarca agriculture which involved double-cropping only 1310 of the 1900 ha of land associated with the upvalley settlement system of this period. From Cayhuamarca Period on—and specifically assuming a strategy which relies first on intensification of production on land already under cultivation, and only later when unavoidable on the clearing of new land—it is possible to suggest varying combinations of double- and triple-cropping that would have been sufficient to support the estimated population of each period, all of which would have entailed use of substantially less than the total amount of land associated with each settlement system. (Note: although not a part of the simplified procedures used here, it is worth noting that a subsistence system based on something between double- and triple-cropping—e.g., an average of 2.5 crops/year, or 5 crops every two years—would be entirely possible, given the temperate climate and year-round water supply.)

Population, Subsistence, and Warfare

As outlined earlier, there are essentially two kinds of evidence related to the nature of the subsistence system in the pre-state periods. One of these is the finding of maize cobs on the surface of single-component Early and Late Suchimancillo sites, thus providing a reasonably clear indication that maize-based agriculture had been established by B.C./A.D. times. The other is the association of sites dating no later than Late Suchimancillo (i.e., to ca. A.D. 200–400) with canal and field systems in the Upper Valley sector near Quebrada del Silencio. But, as argued earlier, it seems nearly certain that intensive irrigation agriculture was established by Cayhuamarca times. One of the main pieces of evidence supporting this argument is the tremendous change in estimated maximum upvalley population size between Las Salinas Period (ca. 415 persons) and Cayhuamarca Period (ca. 5895 persons)—i.e., representing a nearly 1400% increase in population. Furthermore, as indicated in part by a comparison of the settlement maps (see Figs. 164 and 166), the differences in sociocultural complexity between the two systems are so striking that it is difficult to imagine that a fundamental change from gathering-hunting to intensive maize-based agriculture had not occurred.

327

Indeed, although there appears to be no way to estimate accurately the size of the riverine matorral niche in the pre-agricultural/preceramic setting, we may tentatively assume that the estimated upvalley population of 415 persons represents at least a sizeable fraction of the maximum carrying capacity that could be calculated by empirically-based methods. Thus, even assuming that the 415-person estimate for the upvalley system of Las Salinas represents a very conservative one-fifth of the operationally-determined carrying capacity, the Cayhuamarca population is still significantly higher than the absolute maximum capacity of the narrow upvalley riverine niche to support a strictly gathering-hunting population. In sum, it is probable that the irrigation systems associated with Cayhuamarca, Vinzos, and Suchimancillo sites in the upvalley sectors were all begun in Cayhuamarca, and that there is no other way such a relatively large and complex system as that of the beginning ceramic period could have been sustained.

Once established, it is clear that irrigation agriculture provided the main basis for the exponential population growth that characterizes the entire pre-state system, from Cayhuamarca through the end of Late Suchimancillo. From this we may conclude that population growth in and of itself was a significant factor in the processes leading to societal complexity—an assertion that is best supported by the development of the hierarchy of site size and sociopolitical function (Table 7). It seems highly unlikely that progressive changes toward greater numbers of size and function tiers (i.e., from two in Cayhuamarca to four in Late Suchimancillo), or in numbers of sociopolitical tiers (i.e., from an emergent two-tier system in Cayhuamarca to a fully developed two-tier system in Late Suchimancillo), would have taken place in the absence of population growth.

On the other hand, there is no support for the argument that an imbalance characterized the population-land relationship of any of the pre-state periods—i.e., the data do not support an assertion of population pressure *per se* as a prime causal force in early societal evolution in the Lower Santa sequence. Indeed, as indicated in Table 14, it can be demonstrated that varying combinations of double- and triple-cropping on substantially less than the total supply of cultivable land would have been sufficient to support the estimated population size of each period. And even though we may characterize the Lower Santa Valley as land-poor in relation to some other North Coast valleys (e.g., Jequetepeque, Chicama, and Moche, in Table 24), there is no period in the prehispanic sequence when the amount of land under cultivation would have had to exceed 57–78% of the 11,300 ha of irrigable land in the valley (Note: percentages are based on maximum estimates of 6430 ha and 8780 ha for Early Tanguche and Guadalupito Periods, respectively; see Tables 2, 10, and 11).

Moreover, if the amount of land does not appear to

have been a limiting factor, then the water supply was clearly even less so. Even as recently as 1944, when traditional canals and field systems extended over an area of 10,500 ha, something less than 7% of the ample year-round water supply was necessary for irrigation (see Tables 1, 2; and discussion in Chapter II). *The conditions characterizing Santa Valley agriculture should not be taken to imply, however, that population pressure could not have been a critical socioenvironmental stress in other coastal valleys or other types of early subsistence-settlement systems.* For example, the aperiodic (and therefore unpredictable) downturn in marine productivity brought about by El Niño could have exerted pressure on preceramic maritime populations—assuming that the maximum lean period carrying capacity of the maritime subsistence system was being approached or even exceeded (cf. Wilson 1981, where it is argued that this population figure would have been about 8 persons per linear kilometer of shoreline).

Also, it is possible to construct a scenario in which the water supply could have constituted a limiting factor in valleys like Virú, Nepeña, and Casma, where ample river flow occurs only on a limited seasonal basis (see Table 1). As we have seen in Chapter II, the flow of water in Virú is not only limited but also highly irregular and unpredictable from year to year, and the supply is therefore often inadequate to irrigate all the land placed under cultivation. It is not surprising, then, that an inadequate amount of water in any given year was cause for much anxiety and traditionally ascribed by Virú people to a community failure to properly carry out water-related rituals. Given aperiodic, unpredictable downturns in the flow of water in valleys to the south such as Nepeña and Casma, it is thus entirely likely that an inadequate supply of water in relation to established population levels could have created a situation of moderate or even severe demographic pressure in the early prehispanic agricultural setting. In sum, whatever the ultimate limits on demographic and societal development in the Lower Santa region compared to core valleys such as Moche and Casma, its uniquely optimum combination of land and water supply would have made Santa an attractive focus of attack, not only for valleys suffering food shortages but also for incipient expansionist states seeking to broaden their tribute base.

Analysis of Cluster-level Ceramic Assemblages

In light of the preceding argument that relations between settlement clusters were at least peaceful—if not characterized by intensive socioeconomic and political ties as well—it is of interest briefly to examine the results of the comparison of cluster-level ceramic assemblages, using the Brainerd-Robinson coefficient of agreement as one means of assessing these ties. Since the procedures followed in carrying out this analysis have been outlined in detail in Chapter III, here we may focus primarily on the results. It must be emphasized again, however, that the results summarized in Tables 15–23 are presented more as an interesting adjunct to the preceding analysis of settlement, population, and subsistence than as a means of providing definitive additional support for the arguments made to this point.

Relying as it does on a type-by-type comparison of percentages between two spatially discrete artifact assemblages, the resulting coefficient of agreement (or similarity) is subject not only to factors affecting the movement and distribution of sherds around the surface of a site, but also to ceramic collection procedures and inter-site functional differences. While it seems likely that the effect of these and other factors is lessened substantially by combining individual site collections into a single cluster-level assemblage, it cannot be ruled out that such factors in large part explain the rather broad fluctuation of coefficient scores when comparing each cluster assemblage to all others in the system of a given period (e.g., see the inter-cluster array for Vinzos Period in Table 18, where the score of the spatially discrete Cluster 1–5 comparison is 117.0, while that of the spatially contiguous Cluster 4–5 comparison is 81.5). Nevertheless, in spite of the fluctuations and the underlying questions regarding the ultimate value of Brainerd-Robinson coefficients for comparison of spatially discrete contemporaneous ceramic assemblages, several interesting patterns emerge from the analysis.

First of all, as summarized for the early periods in Table 15, it may be noted that the similarity coefficients resulting from the comparison of larger, contiguous up-valley clusters are generally well over 100.0, specifically ranging between 107.9 and 147.4 (it will be recalled that a coefficient approaching 200 indicates high similarity, while a coefficient close to zero indicates the reverse)—including the comparisons for Cayhuamarca Clusters 2–3, Vinzos Clusters 1–2 and 2–3, Early Suchimancillo Clusters 2–3, and Late Suchimancillo Clusters 1–2.

Given the arguments based on presence/absence type distributions, and other considerations, that across-valley relations in the main upvalley clusters of Early Suchimancillo and Late Suchimancillo Periods were peaceful, it is also of substantial interest to note the generally very high similarity coefficients resulting from the comparison of specific percentages of types on a cross-river basis in each of the cluster assemblages. As shown in Table 23, the cross-river coefficient for the Early Suchimancillo Cluster 2 assemblage is a very high 150.9, while those for Late Suchimancillo Cluster 1 and Cluster 2 are not only relatively high but remarkably similar at 133.2 and 132.1, respectively. On the other hand, considering the much greater distance between sites of the opposite desert margins in the Lower Valley, it is perhaps not surprising that the cross-river coefficient for Late Suchimancillo Cluster 3 is a very low 33.5.

In general contrast to this last similarity score, how-ever, it is worth noting that the average coefficient for all between-cluster comparisons in the early ceramic periods is 90.2. Considering the incipient nature of within-valley socioeconomic relations and the fact that it takes into consideration the coefficients for both contiguous and spatially separate clusters, this appears to be a reasonably high figure. Nevertheless, as discussed later, between-sector coefficient scores for Guadalupito and (especially) Early Tanguche are generally even higher.

A Multivariate Developmental Model

The multivariate model shown in Fig. 184 summarizes the principal arguments about the origins and development of societal complexity in the Lower Santa region. It specifies the main socioenvironmental factors and stresses underlying the rise of chiefdom society, suggests a number of possible causal links between these fundamental features and other components of the early subsistence-settlement system, and points to the principal resulting developments leading to the rise of elite groups and supravillage coordination of defensive and subsistence activities. As indicated along the top of the figure, the components of the model are organized under *socioenvironmental factors*, *socioenvironmental stresses*, and *behavioral adaptations*. Distinguishing between the specific factors and stresses suggested by the analysis of the early periods is viewed as a reasonable means of separating out those aspects of the physical and social environment that seem to have made certain developments possible (i.e.,

Table 15. Inter-Cluster Ceramic Analysis: Comparison of Cluster-Level Assemblages for the Early and Late Periods Using Brainerd-Robinson Coefficient of Agreement

| | Period | Clusters | | | |
		1-2	2-3	3-4	4-5
LATE	Late Tambo Real	72.9	-	-	-
	Early Tambo Real	(-)[b]	(-)[b]	-	-
	Late Tanguche	(-)[c]	145.9	-	-
EARLY	Late Suchimancillo	146.3	82.7	-	-
	Early Suchimancillo	58.2	111.4	-	-
	Vinzos[d]	120.9	107.9	69.3	81.5
	Cayhuamarca	76.5	147.4	67.9	-

[a]Analysis was carried out using a PET microcomputer and a program written in BASIC by the author.

[b]Excluding Early Tambo Real Cluster 2 from which the collections are relatively poor and incomplete. A comparison of the assemblages of Clusters 1 and 3 yielded a coefficient of 129.3.

[c]Excluding Late Tanguche Cluster 1 (three small sites) from which no collections were made.

[d]Excluding Vinzos Cluster 6 from which no collections were made.

329

Table 16. Inter-Cluster Ceramic Analysis: Comparison of Assemblages of Selected Major Site Groupings for the Middle and Late Periods Using Brainerd-Robinson Coefficient of Agreement

Period	UV-MV[a]	MV-LV[a]	Lower Valley: Cross-River	P. de los Incas- El Castillo/ Tambo Real Area	P. de los Incas- Huaca Santa Area	El Castillo/ Tambo Real Area- Huaca Santa Area
Late Tambo Real	-	-	138.0	-	-	-
Early Tambo Real	-	-	124.2	142.4	106.1	131.5
Late Tanguche	-	-	118.9	-	-	-
Early Tanguche	154.2[b]	175.9	132.8	-	-	-
Guadalupito	117.8	148.0	78.5	119.0	139.6	118.6

[a]UV = Upper Valley; MV = Middle Valley; LV = Lower Valley.

[b]Upper Valley site grouping in Early Tanguche Period was defined for purposes of this analysis alone as including all sites from the modern settlement of Tanguche on upriver. The Middle Valley site grouping here includes all sites in the Vinzos/Huaca Corral area.

Table 17. Inter-Cluster Ceramic Analysis: Matrix of Similarity Scores for Cayhuamarca Period

Clusters	1	2	3	4
1	-	76.5	75.0	88.6
2		-	147.4	54.8
3			-	67.9
4				-

Table 18. Inter-Cluster Ceramic Analysis: Matrix of Similarity Scores for Vinzos Period[a]

Clusters	1	2	3	4	5
1	-	120.9	113.8	77.0	117.0
2		-	107.9	79.1	91.5
3			-	69.3	105.1
4				-	81.5
5					-

[a]Analysis excludes Vinzos Cluster 6 from which no collections were made.

Table 19. Inter-Cluster Ceramic Analysis: Matrix of Similarity Scores for Early Suchimancillo Period

Clusters	1	2	3
1	-	58.2	22.7
2		-	111.4
3			-

Table 20. Inter-Cluster Ceramic Analysis: Matrix of Similarity Scores for Late Suchimancillo Period

Clusters	1	2	3
1	-	146.3	91.9
2		-	82.7
3			-

Table 21. Inter-Cluster Ceramic Analysis: Matrix of Similarity Scores for Guadalupito Period

Site Groupings	UV	MV	LV
UV	-	117.8	98.6
MV		-	148.0
LV			-

Table 22. Inter-Cluster Ceramic Analysis: Matrix of Similarity Scores for Early Tanguche Period

Site Groupings	UV	MV	LV
UV	-	154.2	151.6
MV		-	175.9
LV			-

[a]For purposes of this analysis the dividing line between the Upper and Middle Valley site groupings was placed at Tanguche, rather than at Quebrada La Huaca (see Figs. 3, 4).

Table 23. Intra-Cluster Ceramic Analysis: Cross-River Comparison of Assemblages for the Early and Late Periods Using Brainerd-Robinson Coefficient of Agreement

	Period	Clusters				
		1	2	3	4	5
LATE	Late Tambo Real	23.6	138.0	(-)[a]	(-)[a]	(-)[a]
	Early Tambo Real	146.7	(-)[b]	124.2	(-)[a]	(-)[a]
	Late Tanguche	(-)[c]	127.7	118.9	(-)[a]	(-)[a]
EARLY	Late Suchimancillo	133.2	132.1	33.5	(-)[a]	(-)[a]
	Early Suchimancillo	(-)[c]	150.9	(-)[b]	(-)[a]	(-)[a]
	Vinzos	(-)[c]	112.9	(-)[b]	59.2	(-)[c]
	Cayhuamarca	(-)[c]	(-)[b]	(-)[c]	(-)[c]	(-)[a]

[a] No cluster assigned this number in this period.

[b] Occupation on both sides of river in this cluster, but collections from one or both sides were inadequate for analysis to be carried out.

[c] Occupation limited to one side of river in this cluster.

enabling factors) and those aspects that appear to have been more directly causal (i.e., systemic stresses) in selecting for specific behavioral adaptations. For the sake of convenience as well as to indicate their presumed temporal priority, the various underlying causal factors are placed to the left of the stresses and resultant behavioral adaptations in the figure.

In general, it seems clear that the three most fundamental factors in the origins of societal complexity everywhere on the Peruvian coast were (1) a reasonably adequate and dependable source of water, (2) an associated supply of irrigable land, and (3) a nutritionally adequate complex of cultigens. Indeed, as with most coastal valleys, the physical setting of the Lower Santa region was by definition favorable for the development of irrigation agriculture, at least once the historical process of the introduction of cultigens from elsewhere had taken place. But, as we have seen, unlike all other North Coast valleys the Santa River provided substantially more than an adequate year-round supply of water, and hence the possibility of year-round cropping. Thus, following the establishment of upvalley irrigation agriculture, the people of the Lower Santa region embarked on a developmental sequence that was at once similar to and different from those of other valleys. The principal similarity, of course, is that the application of techniques of water control to the narrow upvalley alluvium probably led immediately to substantial population growth beyond the very limited demographic potential of the preceramic subsistence system. The principal difference is that the possibility of double- or year-round cropping would have set the region apart from its neighbors from the very outset of these developments.

In any case, once the early agricultural populations of the Lower Santa region and adjacent valleys had grown beyond levels sustainable by the preceding gathering-hunting system, they were essentially and irrevocably *locked into* the new subsistence-settlement system. At this point, several socioenvironmental stresses probably were brought to bear on the system. First, at the most fundamental level it seems likely that the intricacy and vulnerability of the growing network of irrigation canals and field systems would have fostered the development of intervillage cooperative networks. Second, given the ex-

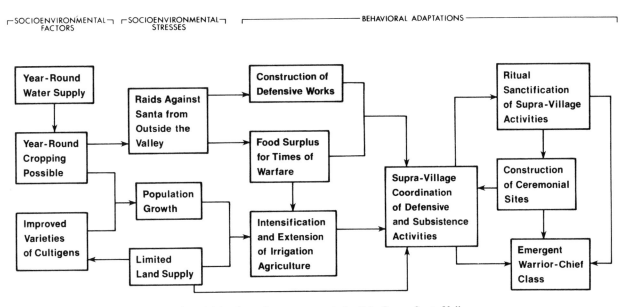

Fig. 184. A multivariate developmental model for the early pre-state periods of the Lower Santa Valley sequence.

pansion of cultivation in the upvalley regions of valleys such as Santa, the limited and uneven distribution of land probably also would have required increasing coordination of land allocation and use at the supravillage level. Finally, it seems apparent that by Early Horizon times two different types of stresses lying more or less beyond the immediate control of early agriculturalists in Santa and nearby coastal valleys already were affecting the adaptive structure of the system. On the one hand, population levels in valleys such as Casma and Nepeña to the south probably were reaching the point where aperiodic downturns in the supply of water were creating demographic stress. On the other, given the concomitant development of cooperative networks among settlements, one of the principal stresses exerted on the Santa system was the beginning of organized raiding by the valleys to the south.

Judging from the archaeological data for Cayhuamarca Period, it is clear that among the primary adaptive responses to this external raiding was the establishment of a number of citadel sites extending throughout the area of occupation. Considering the distribution of larger numbers of settlements in relation to generally fewer citadel sites, the need for supravillage cooperation and coordination in the construction and use of defensive works was therefore every bit as great as that related to agriculture. As shown in the model, it seems equally likely that the threat of external raiding and disruption of subsistence activities would have been a major stress selecting for the creation of food surpluses (and concomitant intensification of agriculture) to tide people over periods of warfare. Although it is remotely possible that raids were carried out in an attempt to steal food (stored or otherwise) from the Santa "breadbasket", it is much more likely that the raiding represents periodic (and apparently always unsuccessful) attempts to bring the region under the control of powerful chiefdoms in valleys to the south—most probably Casma and its (possible) ally Nepeña.

In the context of an overall need for coordination of defensive and subsistence activities, the widespread construction of supravillage ceremonial foci on or immediately adjacent to the valley floor may be explainable by the need for ritual sanctification and fostering of local intersettlement socioeconomic and political ties. And since these higher-order coordinative controls obviously had to be manifested in specific individuals, it is probable that selection for the rise of an elite class was an integral part of the incipient agricultural system. As the data show, by the time of Cayhuamarca Period probable elite residential structures can be detected in various locations nearby or directly associated with a number of ceremonial-civic and defensive sites in the main area of upvalley occupation.

In sum, the proposed multivariate model takes into account the most critical variables affecting the develop-

ment of the early agricultural subsistence-settlement system in one of the few water-rich valleys anywhere on the Peruvian littoral. It suggests that the sharp differences in water regime between a first-class river valley (i.e., Santa, with year-round abundant flow) and the second-class valleys to the south (i.e., Nepeña and Casma, with relatively sporadic seasonal flow) in large part account for seasonal productivity differentials that, in combination with growing population, led to the early rise of warfare/raiding and its continuation throughout the prestate part of the sequence. Most importantly, as clearly implied by such data as settlement clustering and widespread ceremonial-civic centers, the model argues that from the start of irrigation agriculture a variety of stresses—both inherent and external to the system—led to an early rise of local settlement interdependency and coordination of activities related to subsistence and defense. At the same time, the data from Santa imply that the people of valleys to the south also were organized at the supravillage level from the start of agriculture, both for reasons of subsistence and to carry out the raiding against other valleys including Santa.

THE RISE OF THE FIRST MULTIVALLEY STATES (CA. A.D. 400–900)

This section summarizes the data presented in earlier chapters supporting the argument that Guadalupito and Early Tanguche are periods when the Lower Santa region became a province of two successive multivalley state polities—including the Moche state, which is the best current candidate for pristine interregional state formation in the Central Andes, and what I have chosen to call the Black-White-Red state, an even larger multivalley polity that extended throughout much of the North Coast area. To provide a general context for understanding developments at the regional level in Santa, the section begins by briefly outlining the overall nature and extent of these two polities as they were viewed prior to the 1979–80 Santa Valley Project. Following this, summaries of the data related to the Guadalupito and Early Tanguche systems are presented in separate discussions. These discussions are intended to facilitate comparison of the two periods, and are therefore similarly organized under the following general headings: settlement pattern; demography and subsistence; the hierarchy of site size and function; corporate labor projects; administrative elites; the ceramic evidence; burial patterns; and warfare, tribute, and state control.

Overall Nature and Extent

The Moche state. The origins and rise of the Moche state generally are discussed within the five-phase chronological framework first proposed by Larco Hoyle

(1948), on the basis of his assessment of stylistic changes in stirrup spout vessels from gravelots in the area of Moche and Chicama Valleys. The initial stage of development during Moche Phases I and II is viewed as an outgrowth of the local Cupisnique and Salinar (and perhaps Early Gallinazo) cultures that is essentially contemporaneous with the Middle-Late Gallinazo culture of Virú Valley. Assuming the temporal priority of Moche Phase I and II ceramics, it is interesting to note that while Virú-related influences appear to be present in Moche Valley in the form of Gallinazo ceramics (cf. Donnan and Mackey 1978), no evidence has been found in pre-Huancaco Gallinazo contexts of Virú Valley itself of Phase I and II ceramics (cf. Strong and Evans 1952:216–217).

Among other things, this seems to imply that people of the early (pre-multivalley state) Moche culture had essentially no contact with people of Virú and valleys to the south. In any case, the apparent lack of pre-state interaction with valleys to the south of Moche changed abruptly during Phases III and IV, when architectural and ceramic diagnostics of Moche-Chicama culture appear to have been spread by conquest and the extension of state control throughout most or all of the coastal sector of nine North Coast valleys—including Lambayeque, Saña, Jequetepeque, Chicama, Moche, Virú, Chao, Santa, and Nepeña (cf. Benson 1972; Conrad 1978; Donnan 1973, 1976, 1978; Donnan and Mackey 1978; Proulx 1973; Strong and Evans 1952; Willey 1953).

Aside from the apparently uniform and widespread distribution of Moche Phase III-IV diagnostics in the later Early Intermediate Period settlement system of these nine valleys, at least two additional related lines of evidence have been used to support the argument that the spread of Moche culture represents the rise of a militaristic expansionist state. The first of these is the widespread depiction of militaristic themes in Moche iconography throughout this area of the North Coast—including scenes on painted and modeled pottery vessels, as well as murals painted on the sides of major pyramidal structures (examples of the muralistic scenes depicting warfare have been discussed in Chapter IV, and selected examples of such scenes on pottery vessels are discussed in the final part of this section). The second line of evidence comes from detailed excavations carried out at sites with Late Gallinazo and Huancaco/Moche occupation by the Virú Valley researchers. For example, in discussing their stratigraphic excavations at V-162/Huaca de la Cruz site, Strong and Evans (1952:216–217) noted that the levels containing decorated Gallinazo ceramics are directly overlain by a level containing decorated Moche diagnostics—with no intervening layer of sterile deposits or sand, and no indication of a gradual transition between the ceramics of these two cultures. In other words, the replacement of the principal Gallinazo cultural diagnostics by those of Moche occurred so sud-

denly and completely that it clearly argues for a situation of abrupt conquest followed immediately by the imposition of a standardized set of cultural norms on Virú.

It is also relevant to note that there is general agreement among North Coast archaeologists that the best candidate for the primary center, or capital, of the state is the site of Moche itself—which is located on the south desert margin of Moche Valley some 5.75 km inland from the ocean (Fig. 1). Of all contemporaneous occupations in the Moche-Chicama heartland of the state, Moche site appears to be the largest and most complex: It extends over an area of at least 2 km², and includes two of the most massive adobe pyramidal structures anywhere in the New World as well as stratified midden debris extending down to over 6 m below the surface, evidence of elite burials, and densely packed habitations (cf. Benson 1972; Donnan and Mackey 1978; Hastings and Moseley 1975; Kroeber 1925a; Menzel 1977; Moseley 1975b; Topic 1982). The single largest structure at Moche site is the Huaca del Sol (Pyramid of the Sun), which covers an immense area of 228 × 136 m, rises to a maximum height of 41 m above the surrounding plain, and contains an estimated 143 million adobe bricks. It has been known for some time (Kroeber 1930:61) that the Sun pyramid is composed of discrete columns and, furthermore, that each column contains adobes with discrete sets of maker's marks placed on them (see also Hastings and Moseley 1975). From this evidence, convincing arguments have been made that the pyramid was built by corporate labor groups brought in from different communities of the surrounding area—with each group placing its own distinctive set of marks on the bricks used to construct the columns (cf. Kroeber 1930:61; Moseley 1975b). In light of our own 1979–80 data indicating intensive habitation on the top and sides of Structure 19/SVP-GUAD-111, the largest pyramidal platform in Santa during the Moche occupation, it is interesting to note that the top of Huaca del Sol contains evidence of habitation refuse and apparently high status burials (e.g., see Burial M-IV 1, in Donnan and Mackey 1978:92–93).

By the time of Moche Phase V, it appears likely that the pristine multivalley state of the North Coast area no longer was able to maintain its control over valleys to the south of the heartland. Diagnostics of this phase are rare to nonexistent in Virú, Chao, Santa, and Nepeña, as well as in the refuse and burials at Moche site itself. Indeed, during Phase V a shift seems to have occurred away from a main focus of settlement on the south desert margin of Moche Valley (cf. Mackey 1982). At the same time the first minor occupation and cultivation occurs in the area where the huge late period site of Chan Chán will arise, but the main focus of settlement is at the large site of Galindo, located some 18 km inland from the ocean (Bawden 1982). Nevertheless, as argued by both Shimada (1978) and Bawden, the principal candidate for the center of power during Moche V times is in Lambayeque at Pampa Grande site, a huge internally complex occupation covering an area of some 5 km². In sum, the multivalley Moche state appears to have continued into Phase V times, but in a much altered form involving a strong shift northward in its central focus. Moche Valley itself became the southern frontier of this reorganized polity, and valleys farther to the south became part of a different sphere of socioeconomic and political interaction that was centered well to the south of the former Moche-Chicama heartland.

Early Middle Horizon states.   At the time the Moche domination of Virú, Santa, and Nepeña was ending, it appears that these valleys were incorporated into an interregional polity that in some ways was even more complex than the preceding one—especially with regard to the establishment of the road-settlement network that crisscrosses much of the inland part of the intervalley desert. As outlined in Chapter II, a number of diagnostic ceramic types characterize this new sphere of socioeconomic and political interaction—including moldmade jars with pressmolded exterior designs, small annular-base bowls, and effigy neck vessels. But the principal diagnostic of this new polity is the Black-White-Red ceramic style, which by the earliest part of Middle Horizon times was widely distributed in Virú, Santa, Nepeña, and Casma (cf. Collier 1955, 1960; Kroeber 1930; Proulx 1968, 1973; Tello 1956). With the abandonment of Galindo site by the end of Moche Phase V and the apparent demise of Lambayeque control, the Black-White-Red style also became a principal diagnostic of the Moche Valley assemblage (cf. Donnan and Mackey 1978), with some occurrence of this ceramic type as far north as Chicama Valley (e.g., at Pata de Burro site; cf. Bennett 1939) and as far south as Huarmey (cf. Collier 1960).

Thus by Early Middle Horizon times the principal area of distribution of the Black-White-Red style included the eight coastal valley regions of Chicama, Moche, Virú, Chao, Santa, Nepeña, Casma, and Huarmey. But assuming that this new sphere of interaction was indeed a state, it seems clear that its capital was not located in Moche Valley. The site of Chan Chán probably had not yet grown beyond the level of a small village, and no other large site that would qualify as the primary center of a large multivalley state has been identified in Moche Valley. By the same token, none of the principal Early Middle Horizon sites of the next four valleys to the south—including Cerro Huasaquito (Chao), SVP-ETAN-147/Huaca Jedionda (Santa), and PV 31–103/Huambacho Viejo (Nepeña)—is particularly large or complex compared, for example, to the capital of the preceding Moche state.

In contrast, at least two very large internally complex sites are present in Casma Valley during the Early Mid-

dle Horizon Period. One of these (El Purgatorio) lies along the north desert margin of the Mojeque branch of the valley some 26 km inland from the ocean, while the other (Manchán) lies along the south margin of this same branch at a point 16 km inland. Each of the sites covers an estimated area of 1 km², and each is laid out on a grid plan indicating formal planning and organization (cf. Collier 1960). In addition, each is located along ancient roads that crossed the valley as early as the Middle Horizon (cf. Tello 1956, Fig. 1). However, of the two sites El Purgatorio (which contains evidence of Black-White-Red and later occupation) appears to have greater internal complexity—including larger and more elaborate pyramidal structures, U-shaped courts, and evidence of elite and nonelite habitations (cf. Tello 1956, Fig. 2).

In sum, a likely candidate for the primary center of the Black-White-Red state is El Purgatorio. While this argument must remain tentative until systematic and comprehensive regional survey has been carried out in Casma, at least one additional line of evidence is available to support the assertion that the origin and center of this multivalley state lay near its southern end. This has to do with the fact that Casma does not seem to have been an integral part of the preceding Moche state (cf. Collier 1960). Thus, assuming that the complex distribution of settlement and population that characterizes the Early Middle Horizon polity did not arise out of a demographic vacuum, it seems reasonable that the new settlement pattern and ceramic diagnostics that characterize the Black-White-Red sphere of interaction would have originated in a valley, or set of valleys, that lay outside the area dominated by the cultural patterns imposed by the Moche state.

One other aspect of the Early Middle Horizon state on the North Coast remains to be discussed here. At the same time as the Black-White-Red interaction sphere was developing, the Wari state was extending its control over much of the southern part of the Central Peruvian Andes centered around the large site of Wari itself, near Ayacucho (cf. Isbell 1977; Isbell and Schreiber 1978; Lumbreras 1974; Menzel 1964). It appears likely that the area of Wari control eventually included much of the main sierra between Cuzco (Piquillacta site) and Huamachuco (Viracochapampa site), as well as the South and Central Coast areas from Ocoña north to Supe Valley (Chimu Cápac site). As mentioned in Chapter I, Ayacucho-centered investigators of this large state have argued that the entire North Coast also was among the areas that came under the direct control of Wari. But, as is clear from the Santa Valley research, as well as that carried out in the adjacent Moche, Virú, and Nepeña Valleys, very few Wari ceramic diagnostics are present in Early Middle Horizon assemblages of the main North Coast core area. On the other hand, as discussed above, all of the eight valleys of the core area are clearly characterized by (1) a uniform and widespread distribution of the Black-White-Red style and associated ceramic types, and (2) a complex intervalley network of roads and sites—probably indicating not only intensive socioeconomic and political interaction, but also a cohesive entity that stands apart from the Wari sphere of interaction and control.

Indeed, the argument proposed here is supported by Menzel's (1977:67) assertion on the basis of exhaustive analysis of Wari-related Middle Horizon ceramics that Chimu Cápac, in Supe Valley over 160 km to the south of Casma, formed the effective *northern* outpost of Wari control on the coast. Thus, just as it seems clear that Wari did not control the area encompassed with the stylistically uniform interaction sphere of the Tiahuanaco state (cf. Isbell and Schreiber 1978), neither is it likely that it exercised hegemony over the eight North Coast valleys comprising the Black-White-Red sphere. This does not rule out at least some socioeconomic interaction between people of the North Coast and the Wari state, however. Indeed, judging from the Santa data as well as that from nearby valleys, a fair degree of interaction was occurring not only between the North and Central Coast areas (e.g., as reflected in the small amount of Wari/Central Coast-related ceramics appearing in the Early Tanguche assemblage), but also between the North Coast and adjacent Andean highlands (as reflected in the small amount of Black-White-Red ceramics found in the Callejón de Huaylas, and the small amounts of Cajamarca III cursive ware found in Santa and adjacent valleys).

Santa as a Province of the Moche State

This section summarizes the principal Guadalupito Period data and addresses the argument that the Santa Valley region was a province of the multivalley Moche state. It must be noted in this regard that there is a certain necessary circularity in using the Lower Santa data to understand the formation of the first Central Andean interregional state. In other words, the data from Santa on the one hand provide substantial support for the argument that Moche represents a state society; on the other, assuming that we have established in the preceding section that Moche was indeed a state, then one can also profitably examine the data from the perspective of the effects of conquest and state control on previously established provincial patterns. Thus, although the present discussion is aimed primarily at the former of the two perspectives, it is also clearly the case that the Lower Santa data provide the first systematic and comprehensive glimpse in the Central Andean area of the effect of pristine state formation on cultural patterns at the provincial level.

The settlement pattern. At the level of overall regional patterns of settlement, the abrupt change from a heavily upvalley-oriented system in Late Suchimancillo to one essentially centered on the Lower Valley provides one of the fundamental pieces of evidence that a forced, or state-imposed, change in subsistence-settlement focus accompanied the appearance of Moche cultural diagnostics in Santa. As mentioned earlier, however, this assessment of the Guadalupito regional pattern is possible only because we have equally detailed knowledge of the evolution of the pre-state subsistence-settlement system as it changed gradually through the preceding Las Salinas, Cayhuamarca, Vinzos, Early Suchimancillo, and Late Suchimancillo Periods.

A second, related aspect of the overall regional pattern is the gradual change through time in the average location of sites. As summarized in Table 9, from Las Salinas Period on through the end of the early part of the sequence, sites are located on the average at increasingly lower elevations and closer to the valley floor, until by Guadalupito times they are located in completely exposed positions either adjacent to the cultivated valley floor or out on low hills in the midst of the floor. In a sense, then, this aspect of the Guadalupito settlement pattern has strong evolutionary antecedents, although it is clearly the case that the location of so many sites in the Lower Valley represents a pattern imposed by the Moche state. Nevertheless, in conjunction with the absence of any indication that fortresses were built in Guadalupito Period, the evolutionary *and* revolutionary result of the changes effected by the multivalley state is the first system in the sequence to be characterized by peace, not war—i.e., we see the result of the imposition of what in essence is a *Pax Moche* on the Lower Santa region.

A third aspect of the changes brought about by incorporation into the Moche state is what appears to have been an abrupt change from the primarily rock-walled dwellings of Late Suchimancillo Period to a system in which habitation sites are characterized primarily by dwellings constructed completely of perishable materials. Again, the fact that we have a good understanding of the prior pattern of dwelling construction supports the assertion that the strong shift to completely perishable quincha-type habitations was among the changes that accompanied the imposition of Moche state control on the region.

Demography and subsistence. As shown in Fig. 175, the primary concentration of Guadalupito Period population was in the Lower Valley sector, although fairly substantial numbers of people were distributed throughout the Middle Valley as well (see also Table 5). Judging from overall site locations and the concentration in the Lower Valley of over 18,000 of the estimated 22,000 people in the system, it seems clear that one of the most revolutionary changes effected by the Moche state was a large-scale expansion of the subsistence-settlement system in this area. Indeed, the estimated total amount of land associated with the Middle and Lower Valley settlements is 8780 ha, which is more than any other period in the sequence including Early Tanguche. Thus, even if we assume that this area was only being farmed on the basis of a single crop per year, the results of maize-based carrying capacity analysis indicate that there was enough land to provide food for the entire population (see Table 11). But, as indicated in Table 14, if we also assume that one of the primary material reasons—if not *the* reason—for incorporation of Santa into the Moche State was to gain access to the agricultural production of this uniquely watered valley, then merely by postulating (an easily feasible) strategy of double-cropping it can be shown that excess production would have supported an additional population slightly larger than that of the entire Guadalupito system of Santa itself (we shall return to the implications of this analysis later). In light of the ratio of estimated actual population to the amount of cultivable land associated with the system, it is also interesting to note the sudden drop in the number of persons per square kilometer of irrigable valley floor from Late Suchimancillo to Guadalupito times (see Table 10). Thus, whatever pressure might have been exerted by growing population numbers on the subsistence systems of preceding periods, the situation appears to have eased considerably with the rise of the first multivalley state society (but note in Table 10 how the population density in relation to associated cultivable land goes back up to a point slightly higher than the pre-state level in the following Early Tanguche Period).

A final aspect of some interest with regard to Guadalupito demographics is the clear indication that a sharp population drop of nearly 8,000 persons accompanied the incorporation of Santa into the Moche state. As I have suggested elsewhere (Wilson 1983), although we can probably never know with certainty what the precise reasons for this apparently sudden demographic decline are, at least three possibilities can be suggested—including (1) excessive deaths as a result of the warfare carried out against Santa prior to its incorporation into the Moche state; (2) demographic adjustments to the disruptions resulting from a forced change to a radically new subsistence-settlement system; and (3) the transfer of large groups of Lower Santa inhabitants to other regions of the state, either to reduce the size of a potentially recalcitrant and hostile population or to augment the labor force in state-sponsored projects carried out in the Moche-Chicama core area (for the Inca practice of relocating *mitmaq* colonists, see Rowe 1963a). As argued by Divale and Harris (1976), excessive dieoff of males in warfare does not appear to affect appreciably the demographic growth profile of a population over the long term, at least in the absence of substantial deaths of females of child-bearing age. But it is possible that either one, if not both, of the other two possibilities listed above

may explain the significant drop in population between Late Suchimancillo and Guadalupito Periods.

The hierarchy of site size and function. As argued in earlier sections of this chapter, the steady increase in number of tiers in the hierarchy of site size and function strongly supports the argument that sociocultural complexity in the early part of the sequence increased as a function of (1) growing population, (2) the intensification and extension of agriculture, and (3) the continual threat of external raiding. By Guadalupito times, the number of tiers in the hierarchy of site size alone had increased from the maximum of four levels in preceding periods to five levels—at least if all eight sites of Pampa de los Incas Complex are considered as a single entity (see Table 7). At the same time, the number of tiers in the hierarchy of sociopolitical function increased from essentially two levels in Late Suchimancillo to a minimum of three in the Guadalupito system (including habitation sites, local centers, and the regional center). However, if one also takes into consideration the primary position of Moche site as the capital of the multivalley state, then we are actually dealing with a political system composed of four levels.

Corporate labor projects. As mentioned in Chapter IV, adobe bricks with maker's marks on them were noted on the summit of two pyramidal platforms in the Guadalupito system—including Structure 19, the main platform at SVP-GUAD-111/Pampa de los Incas Complex, and Structure 11, a nearby huaca of probable Early Suchimancillo date with intrusive Guadalupito adobes. The finding of these bricks in and of itself suggests that the principles of state-organized corporate labor construction adduced by Kroeber and Moseley for Moche site also were a consistent feature of the provincial system of the state. At the same time, the Guadalupito/Moche system of the Santa region is characterized by the greatest number of monumental structures of any period in the sequence. These include the massive Structure 19 huaca itself (Fig. 109), Structure 20/SVP-GUAD-111 (Fig. 109), Structures 87 and 88 at SVP-GUAD-93/El Castillo (Fig. 106), Structure 81/Huaca Ursias at SVP-GUAD-128 (Fig. 112), and the platform mound at SVP-GUAD-202/Barrio San Pedro (Chimbote), as well as a number of smaller huacas throughout the system. As we have seen, at least two of the principal huacas (Structures 19 and 20) appear to have served as foci of elite habitation, while the presence of large militaristic murals on Structure 88 (Fig. 107) suggests that the main huacas were intended to impress the provincial populace with the power of the state and the negative consequences of insurrection.

Among other features of the Guadalupito system that seem likely to have involved state-organized labor projects are the following: (1) the extensive canal and field systems that characterize the entire Lower Valley during this period, especially including Pampa de los Incas Complex and the mouth of Quebrada de Lacramarca; (2) the narrow system of roads and associated roadside sites that runs across the mouth of the valley near the coast; and (3) the craft production center on the lower southeastern terraces of SVP-GUAD-112/Pampa de los Incas Complex, as evidenced by our finding of numerous pottery molds of fired clay in this area.

Administrative elites. The evidence for extensive and massive corporate labor constructions throughout most of the area of occupation implies that a major aspect of state control was the establishment of impressive residences for administrative elites in various strategic places—most importantly including the main huaca structures at SVP-GUAD-111 regional center. For example, among the features of Structure 19 that suggest it served as the residence of the main regional administrator and a large number of retainers are: (1) the finding of residential walls and debris on the summit; (2) extensive habitation debris on the terrace levels constituting the sides of the structure; and (3) the indication that Structure 19 was the key focal point of the regional system, as evidenced by its huge size and the fact that the main ancient road runs straight up onto the lower part of the structure itself.

Additional important residential foci of administrative personnel and other elite state functionaries in the regional system probably include SVP-GUAD-93/El Castillo and other local centers, as well as SVP-GUAD-132/Huaca China and SVP-GUAD-128/Huaca Ursias. It is worth noting again that, with the exception of Structure 43/SVP-GUAD-3, all of these pyramidal structures were not only large but built in commanding positions that would ensure high visibility in relation to the surrounding populace (Structure 19 and Structure 87 are good examples of this). Given the probable religious nature of similar structures in pre-Guadalupito systems, it is also likely that religious activities were among the functions carried out by the elite residents of these sites.

The ceramic evidence. Another feature of particular interest in assessing the nature of state control over the Lower Santa region is the significant reduction in Guadalupito Period, compared to preceding periods, of both the total number of ceramic types and the number of principal ceramic diagnostics. As we have seen, a total of only 16 ceramic types could be distinguished for Guadalupito Period (compared, for example, to 39 in Late Suchimancillo and 29 in Early Suchimancillo); and, of these, only 10 types are useful as principal time markers (compared to 28 in Late Suchimancillo and 20 in Early Suchimancillo). In light of these data, it is of interest to recall that, based on his analysis of the collections

excavated by Uhle at Moche site, Kroeber (1944:126) concluded there was a:

> . . . really small number of basic form types within which the Mochica expressed the endless individual variety of their ware. . . . It was within the limits of [a] half dozen basic forms that the Mochica let their imagination play: not by innovations beyond the framework. This indicates a mature, standardized art . . .

The data from the Lower Santa region confirm Kroeber's argument, and indeed strongly suggest that the imposition of a limited number of standardized form types was among the principal features of Moche state control over provincial systems. At the same time, Kroeber's argument suggests (and our own data from Santa confirm) that there still was a fair degree of variation from valley to valley with regard to specific features present on the basic pottery form types.

For example, as discussed in the ceramics appendix, a detailed comparison of colors and motifs used in decorating Virú and Santa funerary pottery indicates that substantial differences exist between the Huancaco/Moche and Guadalupito/Moche assemblages of the two regions. Nevertheless, it is an unmistakable fact that ceramics of both regional assemblages are essentially similar in paste, moldmade production techniques, surface treatment, form, and decoration—not only to each other but to Moche ceramics from the heartland. Thus, while master potters from the Moche-Chicama area may have been able to spot an "inferior" provincial pot with little difficulty, there would be no mistaking the fact that pots from all areas of the state were contemporaneous products of the same sphere of intensive cultural interaction.

As discussed in the preceding chapter, the sharp change from earlier periods in the regional distribution of principal ceramic types strongly suggests that a substantial transformation of regional patterns of socioeconomic interaction accompanied the imposition of state control. It will be recalled that earlier periods are characterized not only by a more uneven regional distribution of types, but also by a clinal distribution that includes a concentration of the greatest numbers and diversity of types in the upvalley area around Quebrada de Cayhuamarca and a falloff in numbers and diversity away from there. In strong contrast, although the specific percentages of the principal Guadalupito/Moche types vary from site to site, their regional distribution on a presence/absence basis is essentially an even one. This suggests that the externally imposed socioeconomic norms of the multivalley state were felt more or less uniformly throughout the regional system.

Assuming that the comparison of ceramic assemblages provides some measure of the strength of interaction between sectors, it is interesting to note that the similarity coefficients resulting from comparisons of the contiguous

Upper Valley-Middle Valley and Middle Valley-Lower Valley settlement groupings are consistently high—i.e., 117.8 and 148.0, respectively (see Table 21). Similarly high coefficients result from a comparison of Guadalupito assemblages among the main areas of occupation in the Lower Valley sector—including the discrete areas of Pampa de los Incas regional center, El Castillo/Tambo Real, and Huaca Santa/Huaca China. However, as indicated in the tabular presentations of similarity coefficients, none of these scores is higher than the highest coefficients resulting from between-cluster comparisons of the pre-state periods. Thus, in comparison to the much higher between-sector coefficients for the Early Tanguche assemblage, Guadalupito may be viewed generally as *transitional* between the less uniform patterns of ceramic distributions characterizing the pre-state periods and the relatively much more uniform distributional patterns of the Early Middle Horizon Period.

Burial patterns. A final major feature of the Guadalupito system that appears to have been strongly affected by the incorporation of the Santa region into the Moche state is burial patterns. As outlined in the preceding chapter, the most notable pattern of Late Suchimancillo Period is tightly flexed or secondary burial in small rock-lined tombs that have polygonally-shaped plans. In contrast, the typical pattern of Guadalupito Period Santa—and indeed elsewhere in the Moche state (cf. Donnan and Mackey 1978; Strong and Evans 1952)—is extended burial in large rectangular adobe-lined tombs. In addition, as we have seen, in Guadalupito Period there is a total replacement of the sierra-related kaolin wares that characterize Late Suchimancillo burials by the typical red-on-white and white-on-red decorated funerary wares of Moche culture.

Warfare, tribute, and the state. Given the argument that Moche represents the rise of pristine state society on the North Coast, as well as the data indicating how incorporation into the Moche state affected the provincial subsistence-settlement system of the Lower Santa region, it should come as no surprise to those familiar with Moche pottery that the rich iconographic record depicted in the funerary ware strongly corroborates the general argument presented here. Indeed, aside from the widespread interregional distribution of Moche architecture, ceramics, and burial patterns, the iconographic record itself has long been considered as supporting the argument that Moche represents the rise of stratified state society on the North Coast. For example, Lumbreras (1974:103) refers to the depiction of what appear to be status differences among three main groups of people—including elite personages ("lords"), commoners, and slaves or servants. And Benson (1972, Fig. 5–8, p. 103) illustrates a well-known flaring funerary bowl depicting a craft production center where female weavers under the direction of an overseer produced textiles using the motifs on decorated stirrup spout vessels as design guides.

Nevertheless, the argument that Moche represents a state has been questioned by some researchers (e.g., see Isbell and Schreiber 1978:387)—primarily because of the lack of the kind of systematic and comprehensive evidence now available as a result of the Santa Valley research. There has also been a tendency of late in Moche archaeology to focus more on the "symbolic-non-secular" nature of Moche art (e.g., Donnan 1976), rather than on what it tells us about the origins and nature of pristine stratified society on the North Coast. Having addressed in the preceding section the whole issue of whether or not the data support the argument that Moche was a state—and every aspect of the regional data from Santa suggests that indeed it was—it is therefore of interest briefly to examine selected aspects of the iconography of this period from the standpoint of the origins and nature of Moche state control. In order to do this, four representative scenes have been selected and redrawn from the rich literature on Moche art. These scenes illustrate in detail the nature of this developmental process, and at the same time they serve to reinforce the main points made about this process in the preceding discussion of the Guadalupito Period data.

The well-known scene in Fig. 185 (from a pottery vessel of Moche Valley provenience) is of particular interest in assessing the means by which the state arose, since it depicts a battle between warriors of the Moche army and warriors who appear to be wearing a distinctive regional dress. Although, unfortunately, no comparative data exist from the various provincial regions indicating which valley the non-Moche warriors might be from, it does seem likely that the scene represents a battle with warriors from one of the valleys later incorporated into the state. The depiction of cactus plants typical of the intervalley desert supports this assertion, and, indeed, suggests that the non-Moche warriors had come out of their valley (and away from defensive refuges) to confront the advancing Moche army. From the depiction of nude, bleeding, and bound non-Moche warriors, there is no doubt about what the outcome of this particular battle was.

The scene shown in Fig. 186 (*this one from a pottery vessel of Chimbote, or Santa, provenience*) depicts what can probably be considered as the next stage following the successful conclusion of a campaign carried out against another region. Nude prisoners with ropes around their necks are shown being led across the intervalley desert—with Andean foothills, coastal birds, Opuntia cactus, and Tillandsia plants depicted in the background. That some of the defeated may not have gone willingly to their fate is suggested by the "accusatory" finger pointed back by one of the prisoners at his captor. It will also be noted that each prisoner is shown holding his nose in an appar-

Fig. 185. Scene from a Moche pottery vessel of Trujillo provenience, showing a battle between warriors of two distinct cultural backgrounds. The victorious warriors—shown on the left in the lower panel, and on the right in the upper panel—presumably are members of the Moche army. Redrawn from Kutscher (1954:21).

ent attempt to stem the flow of blood from it, suggesting not only that prisoners were disrobed (an apparent sign of complete defeat and dishonor) but also tortured and maltreated.

In the third scene (Fig. 187-top), nude prisoners are shown being presented by a semi-nude helmeted figure before a ruler or very high-ranking person. The ruler (who appears to be holding a cup or scepter) is seated on a low throne inside a roofed structure on the summit of a pyramidal platform. Although some aspects of this scene are difficult to interpret—e.g., note the prisoner in the upper left panel who apparently is conversing with two Moche women (shamans?) under the dwelling with open sides—others are reasonably clear. For example, judging from the three prisoners shown in the lower panel, the fate of many if not all defeated warriors was death. Likewise, from the central panel it seems clear that higher status prisoners (note the rope around the neck of one of them) were carried in litters by prisoners of lower status. Finally, one of the victorious Moche warriors in the top panel appears to be presenting himself before a standing person of possibly lesser rank than the ruler on the platform (but, again, note the cup or scepter in his hand) who is shown under a structure adorned with war clubs.

The final scene in the sequence illustrated here (Fig. 187-bottom) gives us an additional intriguing glimpse of the nature of the Moche state. As with the third scene, a high-ranking personage or ruler is shown seated on a low throne inside a roofed structure at the top of a huaca platform. But instead of nude prisoners, here are depicted what clearly appear to be llamas laden with goods and accompanied by elaborately clothed persons. The entire set of panels associated with the llamas

depicts a variety of items that may represent tribute being presented to the ruler—including three or four kinds of marine shells, items of food (among them peanuts?), and pottery vessels. It is also of interest to note that the original scene on the vessel itself (from a private Trujillo collection; cf. Sawyer 1968:47) shows two different terrace levels on the sloping side of the huaca platform to the right of the ruler. On these terraces, a number of seated Moche women are shown lined up and facing the llama train as it proceeds up the steps to the summit of the platform (unfortunately, neither the terraces nor the women were included by the artist who drew the original version of this scene published in Sawyer).

Although all four of the scenes discussed here may be considered in part as conveying such subtle symbolic-nonsecular meanings that they are fathomable perhaps only by the Moche themselves, at the same time it is abundantly clear that all aspects of the material development of the state are being depicted as well—including (1) the conquest of a region by Moche warriors in full battle dress, (2) the transport of nude prisoners across the intervalley desert to the capital in Moche Valley, (3) the presentation of prisoners before the ruler of the state, and (4) the presentation of tribute brought in by llama trains from the provinces. In these four scenes we thus have an encapsulated account of the main developmental features characterizing the origins and rise of the first probable interregional stratified polity in the Central Andes—including attack on a region by a standing army, initial fierce resistance by a region to conquest, ultimate defeat of the region and presentation of prisoners before the commander-in-chief, killing of enemy

Fig. 186. Scene from a pottery vessel of Chimbote provenience, showing warriors of the Moche army leading naked and bleeding prisoners across the intervalley desert. Redrawn from Kutscher (1954:24).

warriors to further glorify the state, and presentation of the fruits of victory in the form of foodstuffs and other items that probably constituted the principal reason for wars of conquest against nearby coastal valley regions in the first place.

The iconographic data presented here have at least two additional implications in interpreting the provincial data from Santa. First, it seems probable that the Lower Santa region would have been a significant addition to a state oriented toward exacting tribute in the form of foodstuffs. As we have seen, the widespread but relatively low Guadalupito population and estimates of carrying capacity both suggest that Santa had the potential to provide tribute equivalent to sustaining more than 23,000 persons outside the regional system. Given the continual warfare of the four pre-state periods, it is also likely that the people of Santa would have fiercely re-

sisted any attempts at exploitation by outsiders. Once Santa had been incorporated into the state, it therefore was probably necessary for the Moche to use all available means to organize and control the regional population—including the use of local laborers in building numerous impressive huaca structures that would provide a concrete symbol of the coercive power of the state.

Second, the depiction of rulers, female attendants, and dwellings (or throne rooms) on the top and sides of huaca mounds corroborates the argument that such structures served as residences of regional administrators and their retinues. Indeed, the abundant remains of larger and smaller rooms around the base of Structure 19/SVP-GUAD-111 suggest that tribute from provincial regions like Santa was collected and stored first at the regional level. This would have served as an additional symbol of the power of the state to exact tribute pay-

340

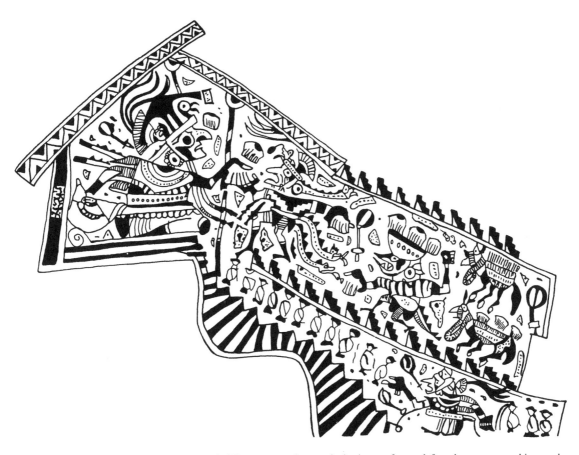

Fig. 187. Scenes from two Moche pottery vessels. The top scene shows naked prisoners from a defeated army approaching a ruler seated atop a huaca structure. The bottom scene shows a llama caravan approaching a ruler with what may be tribute from a conquered coastal valley (top: redrawn from Donnan 1978:35; bottom: redrawn from Sawyer 1968:47).

ments, as well a means of stockpiling food both to sustain workers engaged in local state projects and to channel the rest on to the capital in Moche.

Santa as a Province of the Black-White-Red State

In this second part of the discussion of multivalley states of the middle period, the principal data presented on the Early Tanguche system in the preceding chapter are summarized. At the same time, the overall nature of the subsistence-settlement system is placed in perspective by reference to changes and continuities relative to earlier periods. In accordance with the organization of the preceding section on Moche, the summary of the Early Tanguche data is organized under the following headings: settlement pattern; demography and subsistence; the hierarchy of site size and function; corporate labor projects; administrative elites; the ceramic evidence; and warfare, tribute, and the state.

The settlement pattern. As is obvious from a comparison of Figs. 174 and 176, Early Tanguche Period represents developments that in several ways are just as revolutionary a break with the preceding period as those occurring between Late Suchimancillo and Guadalupito. Among these new developments are the appearance of large numbers of maritime sites and the intricate network of roads and associated settlements running along four major routes across the Santa-Chao Desert. In addition, in contrast to the heavy occupational focus of the Guadalupito system on Quebrada de Lacramarca and much of the southeast desert margin of the main Lower Valley sector, these areas are either entirely abandoned (Quebrada de Lacramarca) or only sparsely occupied (southeast desert margin of the Santa Valley mouth). Aside from the strong focus on maritime sites to the south of the valley, the main concentration of settlement is instead in the Middle Valley and the lower part of the Upper Valley.

On the other hand, Early Tanguche and Guadalupito are nearly alike in terms of the average location of main valley sites with respect to the cultivated valley floor (see Table 9). Although Early Tanguche marks a return to the pattern of occupying terraced upvalley settlements—whose potentially defensible nature can be logically asserted from the generally steep nature of the terrain—sites are nearly universally located in open, exposed positions just as in Guadalupito Period. At the same time, the complete lack of fortress structures strongly indicates that the pattern of peaceful interregional relations characterizing the preceding Guadalupito system is also a major feature of Early Tanguche. In other words, we may characterize the regional system of Early Middle Horizon as a *Pax Black-White-Red*, in which intensive interregional socioeconomic relations are again reflected in the overall nature of settlement types and their distribu-

tion in the area of occupation. Nonetheless, the Early Tanguche road-settlement system throughout most of the survey area is obviously much more complex than that of the preceding period.

Just as is indicated by the abandonment of Lacramarca and the reoccupation of the upvalley sectors, the change back to dwellings characterized primarily by low rock walls (89% in Early Tanguche vs. 38% in Guadalupito) suggests that the Guadalupito system was an imposed, or artificial, one (for a similar argument related to the abandonment of administrative centers following the demise of the Inca state, see Morris 1972). Thus, although the Black-White-Red state appears to follow immediately on the heels of the departing Moche in occupying the Santa Valley, the pattern of settlement and the nature of dwelling types suggest a return to adaptive patterns characteristic of Late Suchimancillo and earlier pre-state periods. As discussed later, however, other aspects of the Early Tanguche system—in comparison both to the preceding Guadalupito system and the following Late Tanguche one—suggest that in its own way it was equally artificial and dependent upon the continuance of the Black-White-Red state for its survival.

Demography and subsistence. As shown in Fig. 177, the main concentration of Early Tanguche population was in the Middle Valley and the lower half of the Upper Valley, although substantial numbers of people also occupied the southern coast, the northwest side of the Lower Valley, and the non-mountainous parts of the Santa-Chao Desert. The planimetric estimate of the total amount of cultivable land associated with this population is 6430 ha, or some 2350 ha fewer than were immediately available in the preceding Guadalupito subsistence system (see Table 11). But, assuming a strategy of double-cropping, the analysis of maize-based carrying capacity indicates that this was more than enough land to sustain the entire estimated regional population of 35,930 persons.

In rather sharp contrast to the possible production excess of 23,340 persons/year resulting from a double-cropping strategy in the Guadalupito system, however, the same strategy in the Early Tanguche system would have resulted in a much smaller excess of only 5030 persons/year (Note: this analysis assumes that all food for the people of the Santa-Chao Desert sector came from Santa Valley; on the other hand, assuming that a substantial fraction of it came from Chao Valley, then the Santa production could have substantially exceeded 5000 persons). It may be supposed that even this relatively small production excess would have constituted a significant contribution to the Black-White-Red system, and indeed it is not unlikely that the state imposed an intensive triple-cropping strategy on at least some parts of the area of cultivation—thereby raising the production excess of the system well beyond the calculated surplus of 5000 persons/year.

The hierarchy of site size and function. One of the principal similarities between the two middle periods is in the general nature of the hierarchy of site size and sociopolitical function. Just as in Guadalupito Period, the hierarchy of Early Tanguche site sizes contains five distinct levels, while the hierarchy of sociopolitical function contains three levels—including undifferentiated habitation sites, local centers, and the regional center. Aside from these general similarities, however, two principal features of the Early Tanguche system in the main valley area suggest that it was at least substantially distinct from Guadalupito, if not more complex. First, there is a sharp difference between the Guadalupito regional center of Pampa de los Incas Complex and the Early Tanguche regional center of SVP-ETAN-147/Huaca Jedionda—i.e., the former consists of an estimated 3520 persons living in eight separate and relatively small habitation sites scattered over a large intensively cultivated area of 2 km², while the latter consists of an estimated 5870 persons occupying a single densely occupied site covering 37.4 ha. Second, the number of probable local centers in the Early Tanguche system is not only greater than in Guadalupito (nine vs. three), but those of the later period are internally more complex than those of Guadalupito. Considering these features and the much more intricate nature of the road-settlement network, it seems probable that the multivalley state system of Early Tanguche represents a substantial increase in complexity over that of Guadalupito.

In sum, given the relatively high population numbers, the overall complexity of the road-settlement network, and the complexity of the main valley subsistence-settlement system, there is every reason to suppose that Early Middle Horizon Santa represents the imposition of multivalley state control on an unprecedented scale in this area of the North Coast. Assuming that the primary center of the Black-White-Red state was El Purgatorio site in Casma, then the minimum number of tiers in the hierarchy of sociopolitical function of the overall system would have been four—with sites such as SVP-ETAN-147/Huaca Jedionda and SVP-ETAN-404/Cerro Huasaquito (Chao) serving as provincial centers at the secondary level, local centers at the tertiary level, and the great mass of undifferentiated habitation sites forming the broad base of the pyramidally-organized hierarchy of state function and control.

Corporate labor projects. Perhaps the single feature of the Early Tanguche system which to some extent belies the argument that it was more complex than Guadalupito is the general absence of monumental huaca structures. Indeed, the only truly large pyramidal platform built in Early Tanguche times appears to be the one at SVP-ETAN-147/Huaca Jedionda—and with dimensions of 125 × 90 × 5–7 m it is smaller than the main structure of SVP-GUAD-111 regional center. Nonetheless, it is probable that the lack of large huacas in the Early Tanguche system does not imply less sociocultural complexity than Guadalupito so much as a pronounced difference in the emphasis of state-oriented activities in the two systems. Assuming that religious activities in general were among the main functions served by these pyramidal platforms, the difference in numbers of huacas suggests that the earlier system was (for want of better terms) more "theocratic" in orientation while the latter one was more "secular". Although the lack of large huaca constructions does not necessarily imply that the people of Early Tanguche were any less religious *per se* than those of the preceding period, the role of administrative elites may have become more oriented toward concrete socioeconomic functions than toward carrying out religious, or awe-inspiring, activities to ensure the allegiance of the regional populace.

In spite of the general lack of large huaca structures in Early Tanguche, as we have seen two principal features of the system argue that even more complex corporate labor projects than those of Guadalupito Period were carried out. The more striking of these, at least in terms of its areal extension, is the road-settlement network covering the Santa-Chao Desert and most of the desert margins of the main valley area. It is worth noting, however, that the lack of dense associated occupational debris at the roadside sites of Santa-Chao suggests that this part of the system did not last for a long period of time—i.e., it may have functioned for several years or decades rather than for several centuries. But the extent of the network, the rock-walled structures characterizing every one of the 200 associated roadside sites, and the construction of SVP-ETAN-320 ceremonial-civic center all suggest that it was built with the intention of long-term endurance. It is worth adding that this, in turn, suggests that the Santa-Chao system was *not* established in the desert during a major El Niño year—i.e., a year when the desert would have surely contained the ample, but highly transitory, amounts of water and vegetation that occur only once every generation or so. Indeed, were this improbable scenario the case, one might expect to see at least a few sites located out in desert areas *away* from the roads, rather than universally associated with the communication routes that appear to have been necessary to provide food and water.

The other truly impressive feature of the Early Tanguche system, of course, is the Great Wall. With an overall length of 73.6 km and a total volume estimated at 207,000 m³, the wall system of Santa is clearly a candidate for one of the most impressive constructions of its nature anywhere in the Central Andes, if not in the prehispanic New World. As suggested earlier, its function probably was not primarily related to defense, if at all;

rather, it seems likely to have been built as a state-organized corporate labor project that served to separate different ethnic groups as well as to control interregional commerce.

One other monumental feature of the Early Tanguche system that is still observable today is the extensive canal-field system that ran from Pampa de los Incas area out toward the saltworks at Las Salinas. Although this system does not represent as extensive a project as the main valley canal-field system of Guadalupito Period, nonetheless like the Great Wall it appears to indicate the power of the state to utilize workers for any project that is deemed important to undertake. As noted earlier, considering the small amount of associated cultivable land (245 ha), the primary reason for construction of this 15 km-long canal system probably was to provide water to the ancient saltworks and inhabitants of nearby sites.

Administrative elites. Two principal kinds of data are available suggesting that the settlement system of Early Tanguche contained a large number of administrative personnel—all or most of whom probably were acting as regional-level functionaries of the Black-White-Red state. First, as mentioned in the preceding discussion of corporate labor projects, the overall configuration and complexity of such remains as the Great Wall system and the road-settlement network clearly imply the kind of centralized and coordinated planning that would have required the presence of state overseers in the system. Second, the evidence for habitation on the summit of the main pyramidal platform at Huaca Jedionda regional center, as well as the formally laid-out structures of each of the 10 local centers, imply that all 11 sites were the main residences of an administrative elite.

Judging from the large size of SVP-ETAN-147 and the unique nature of the main huaca platform relative to all other sites in the system, it is likely that the platform structure itself served as the residence of the primary representative of the Black-White-Red state in the region. Additional support for this argument comes by analogy from Moche iconography, which, as we have seen, includes scenes on pottery vessels that show prisoners and tribute being presented to primary elite functionaries seated in dwellings atop pyramidal platforms (e.g., see Fig. 187). By the same token, the relatively much greater internal complexity and formal layout of local centers relative to surrounding undifferentiated habitation sites argues for the presence of a large, lower-level group of state functionaries which was widely and strategically distributed around the regional system.

The ceramic evidence. Early Tanguche represents a continuation of the pattern established in Guadalupito Period of a significantly lower overall number of ceramic types relative to the pre-state periods. Thus, similar to

the 16 types of Guadalupito, only 19 total types could be distinguished for Early Tanguche Period (in contrast to the 39 types of Late Suchimancillo), with 15 of these types serving as principal time markers (compared to 10 in Guadalupito and 28 in Late Suchimancillo). In light of the earlier arguments about the nature of Moche state control of ceramic production, it therefore seems probable that the Early Tanguche assemblage represents the imposition of a relatively limited number of standardized form types and decorative styles on local pottery making. But, as in the case of Moche pottery, it seems clear that potters still were able to achieve a good deal of regional variation of specific decorative motifs within the context of limited canons of form. This variation is obvious, for example, in the large number of motif types on painted and pressmold-decorated annular-base bowls of the Santa region, as well as in differences in motif types from valley to valley in the system (see discussion in the ceramics appendix).

As discussed in the preceding chapter, Early Tanguche also represents a continuation of the pattern of the preceding period in that nearly all of the principal ceramic types are present throughout the system. As argued for the Guadalupito system, the fact that all decorated and plain types were moving throughout the area of occupation implies a different and presumably higher order of complexity in patterns of exchange and social interaction relative to the four pre-state ceramic periods. Nevertheless, the comparison of sector-by-sector ceramic assemblages using the Brainerd-Robinson similarity coefficient indicates that these patterns probably were even more intensive and formalized in Early Tanguche than in Guadalupito. Indeed, the similarity scores resulting from between-sector comparisons of the Early Tanguche assemblage are the highest of any period in the sequence. As indicated in Table 22, the scores for comparison of contiguous settlement groupings are 154.2 for the Upper-Middle Valley and 175.9 for the Middle-Lower Valley, while even the score for non-contiguous groupings is a very high 151.6 (Upper-Lower Valley).

In sum, the two analyses of ceramic distributions not only indicate a widespread regional distribution of the main types (presence/absence analysis), but also that the specific percentages of types present in the assemblages of each settlement grouping are strongly comparable to those of the other two groupings (Brainerd-Robinson similarity analysis). Overall, the analysis thus supports the argument that Early Tanguche represents the period of greatest intensity of socioeconomic interaction and maximum sociocultural complexity in the sequence.

Warfare, tribute, and state control. One of the principal questions raised by the Early Tanguche data is the means by which the Black-White-Red state was able to extend its control over provincial regions such as Santa. In examining this question, we may begin by repeating one of the main conclusions of our research on this period: namely, that there is little doubt about the assertion that during Early Middle Horizon Period Santa became a functioning part of an interregional state which in many ways was even more complex than the preceding Moche polity. As we have seen, all aspects of the subsistence-settlement system support this argument—including the complex pattern of settlement, the large population, the extensive intervalley road-settlement network, the multifaceted subsistence focus on both the maritime and valley floor environments, the three/five-tiered regional hierarchy of site size/sociopolitical function, the evidence of extensive centrally planned and coordinated labor projects, as well as strong ceramic similarities between Santa and other nearby valleys within the Black-White-Red sphere of interaction.

The question thus becomes: Did the Black-White-Red state incorporate Santa and other regions into the multivalley polity by means of force, as is clearly the case for the Moche state, or rather are we viewing a system that somehow arose in the absence of force out of the intensive socioeconomic interaction of the preceding period? Clearly, additional comprehensive research of the kind carried out in Santa will have to be done in other nearby regions to fully resolve this question. But several lines of evidence are available that seem clearly to point to the probability that the Black-White-Red state was as much a (coercive) conquest state as any of the other Central Andean polities for which we have either (1) good iconographic and settlement pattern evidence (i.e., scenes of warfare and tribute payment as well as a sharp shift in settlement focus, in the case of Moche); or (2) good ethnohistoric evidence (i.e., Spanish documentary sources outlining in great detail the nature and spread of the Inca state).

First, it is clear that during the hundreds of years of the pre-state formative period some coastal regions such as Santa developed a strong ongoing tradition of fiercely resisting any attempts at external encroachment. We have good evidence to support this argument not only in the extensive networks of fortresses characterizing all of the pre-state ceramic periods in Santa, but also in the depiction of strong regional resistance to conquest on Moche pottery. In addition, although the general iconographic record of warfare in the Early Middle Horizon ceramic assemblage is nowhere near as rich as that of the Guadalupito Period, there are a number of figurine fragments in the Early Tanguche assemblage that depict what appear to be warriors dressed for battle (see Fig 251 h-n). A few of these might be interpreted as figures of elite administrative authority—i.e., as holding a staff of office rather than a war club (Fig. 251 j, n)—but the rest clearly are representations of warriors. The figures in this latter group generally are shown holding a club and shield (e.g., Fig. 251 k, l), and one particularly well preserved fragment decorated in the Black-White-Red style shows the club and shield in one hand and a conch shell trumpet in the other (Fig. 251 m).

If we can thus argue from general empirically-derived principles and specific iconographic data that warfare must have been a feature of the incorporation of Santa into the Black-White-Red polity, what then can be said about the nature of the state's demands on the region, aside from the reasonably obvious indications of state-sponsored labor projects? Here again, there is a lack of the richly detailed iconography that is available on Moche pottery. Nevertheless, the very fact that scenes of tribute payment are shown for the preceding period provides a concrete foundation for the argument that similar demands were characteristic of the Early Middle Horizon state. At the same time, however, while it seems reasonable to assume that the demands of one North Coast state were more or less like those of another, it is also likely that the Early Middle Horizon Period was a time of unprecedented interregional socioeconomic interaction—specifically in the form of intensive and widespread trade.

THE BEGINNING OF REGIONAL DEMOGRAPHIC DECLINE (CA. A.D. 900–1350)

Late Tanguche and Early Tambo Real Periods mark a fundamental turning point in the development of prehispanic society in the Lower Santa region. Having experienced more or less continuous growth in population and sociocultural complexity during a period nearly 1500 years—including some 1000 years of regional chiefdom development and 500 years as a province of multivalley state polities—the Santa Valley now enters a period of ongoing cultural devolution that lasts for some 450 years. At the same time, given the relative lack of complexity compared to the middle period states as well as the return to demographic levels characteristic of the pre-state chiefdoms, it is interesting to note the evidence for the rise of conflict in some parts of the Late Tanguche and Early Tambo Real systems.

This section begins with a brief discussion of the overall nature of pre-Chimú societal developments of the late period in the general vicinity of Santa Valley, including consideration of possible reasons for the demographic decline that characterizes not only Santa but Virú and Nepeña as well. Following this, the main features of the Late Tanguche and Early Tambo Real subsistence-settlement systems are summarized under the headings of settlement patterns, demography, and subsistence; hierarchies of site size and function; the ceramic evidence; and the nature of warfare.

Two principal features characterize pre-Chimú developments of the late period in Santa and immediately adjacent valleys. These include (1) the probable reestablishment of smaller, shifting spheres of interregional socioeconomic relations, following the long period of more stable interaction between valleys under the Moche and Black-White-Red states; and, as mentioned above, (2) the ongoing demographic decline in valleys such as Santa, Virú, and Nepeña. With regard to the first feature, the strong shared focus on raised circle-and-dot ware in Santa, Nepeña, and Casma appears to indicate that relations among these valleys were at an unprecedented high during the Late Middle Horizon and the beginning part of the Late Intermediate. Compared to the Black-White-Red state, however, this three-valley interaction sphere was much reduced in size and probably in sociopolitical complexity as well. By the time of Early Tambo Real, Santa also shared a number of ceramic types with valleys to the north, which, if nothing else, appears to indicate that shifts in the focus of socioeconomic relations were beginning to occur—probably in part as a function of the emerging Chimú state.

With regard to the second feature, it must first of all be stressed that the Lower Santa data strongly support the argument that demographic decline was a real phenomenon in this period. In other words, it does not appear to be the result of a (presumed) misinterpretation by North Coast archaeologists of the main ceramic diagnostics characterizing the late periods. Indeed, only 183 of the 1210 sites dating to the nine ceramic periods in the Lower Santa sequence have associated diagnostics other than those of the Black-White-Red, Moche, and four prestate periods. Thus no matter how one lumps together or divides up these 183 occupations, there is no way to achieve population estimates that are equal, for example, to the estimate for Early Tanguche Period—while at the same time taking into consideration such features of the late period assemblage as the clear temporal priority of raised circle-and-dot wares in relation to Chimú-influenced ceramics (cf. Collier 1955, 1962; Donnan and Mackey 1978; Proulx 1973).

Before dealing specifically with the possible reasons for demographic decline in Santa, it is appropriate briefly to discuss Moseley's (1983) recent argument that long-term tectonic uplifting in valleys from Chao on to the north has caused massive river entrenchment and a consequent severe reduction in the amount of irrigable land. Assuming that catastrophic events of this sort were occurring with sufficient magnitude and frequency toward the end of Early Middle Horizon Period, the result according to Moseley may have been an ongoing, or even drastic, decline in agricultural carrying capacity and hence in the number of people such a system could support. Several comments may be made with respect to this model: First

of all, while geological, hydrological, climatic, and land use data have been convincingly combined to support it, *the single most critical corroborative piece of evidence is entirely lacking*—i.e., no data from systematic and comprehensive settlement pattern survey have been presented to indicate the nature of the overall prehispanic population profile in Moche and immediately adjacent valleys in relation to these events of *presumed* catastrophic effect.

Second, as discussed in Chapter II, it is indeed clear from our own research in Santa that tectonic uplifting has been a continual process affecting the north side of the valley mouth. But judging from the relatively greater distance between Shorelines 1 and 2 compared to subsequent episodes of uplifting (see Figs. 3, 12, 13), the most catastrophic event of the prehispanic period took place during the time of the *earliest* human occupation of the region. Yet that early agriculturalists adapted reasonably well over time to this aspect of the changing environment is indicated by the virtually continuous rise in population from Las Salinas on through Late Suchimancillo times. Moreover, contrary to the argument that along with uplifting and entrenchment has come a reduction in irrigable land, *in Santa Valley the periods of maximum extension of cultivation have followed or coincided with episodes of uplifting*—including Guadalupito Period, Early Tanguche Period, and, more importantly, the modern period when substantially more land is farmed (ca. 13,000 ha) than the amount of potentially irrigable land in the prehispanic period (ca. 11,300 ha). Thus, while it is clear that episodes of uplifting have continually occurred (most recently during the 1970 earthquake), if anything this process has resulted in an *increase* in the amount of irrigable land in the valley. (Note: for estimates of relative Moche Period demographic potential in North Coast valleys, see Table 24.)

Assuming that the late period demographic decline in the Lower Santa region is a real phenomenon and that tectonic uplifting is unlikely to have brought it about, can it then be argued that the causes can be pinpointed with reasonable exactitude on the basis of presently available archaeological data alone? The answer would seem to be a negative one, especially considering the number of potential causes of population loss—perhaps most importantly including pandemic diseases, attractive socioeconomic forces bringing about mass migration to other areas, and problems with the agricultural system such as salinization or insect damage. Thus it must be cautioned that, while causal processes may be suggested for the decline in Santa and adjacent valleys, the solution to this problem—if it ever comes at all—will certainly have to await additional demographically-oriented settlement pattern projects in valleys to the north and south of Santa.

In any event, several intriguing aspects of regional developments in Santa appear to be clear from a comparison of the Guadalupito, Early Tanguche, Late Tan-

Table 24. Estimates of Relative Demographic Potential of Selected North Coast
Valleys Derived from Maize-Based Carrying Capacity of Moche Period

Valley	Total Hectares of Irrigated Land[a]	Estimated Number of Crops Per Year[b]	Single-Crop Human Carrying Capacity[c] (p/ha)	Estimated Maximum Demographic Potential[d] (persons)	Relative Moche Period Demographic Ranking (1-8)
Jequetepeque	29,578	2	2.583	152,800	2
Chicama	40,371	2	2.583	208,600	1
Moche	20,026	2	2.583	103,500	3
Virú	10,240	1	2.583	26,400	5
Chao	2000	1	2.583	5200	8
Santa	11,307	2	2.583	58,400[e]	4
Nepeña	6360	1	2.583	16,400	7
Casma	8700	1	2.583	22,500	6

[a]For estimates of land in Jequetepeque, Chicama, and Moche, see Robinson (1964:166); for Virú and Chao, see ONERN (1973:181, 191); for Santa and Nepeña, see ONERN (1972b:231, 244) and Table 2; for Casma, see ONERN (1972a:229).

[b]Estimates are based on data in Table 1.

[c]See Table 11, Col. 4, Guadalupito Period.

[d]Estimated demographic potential (rounded to nearest hundred persons)= Col. 2 X Col. 3 X Col. 4.

[e]As shown in Table 11, the independently estimated Guadalupito Period population in Santa is 22,020, or 37.7% of the maximum theoretical potential. The actual population size of other valleys at this time was probably also at a level representing some fraction of the estimated maximum potential.

guche, and later systems. First of all, following intensive and widespread cultivation of the Lower Valley sector during Guadalupito times, it seems paradoxical that in spite of the increased population of Early Tanguche (1.6 times that of the preceding system) much of the Lower Valley apparently had been abandoned. It probably cannot be assumed that this took place following a very short period of intensive Lower Valley occupation, either, since from the complexity and size of Guadalupito settlements there is every reason to suppose that Moche occupation lasted 150–200 years—i.e., a very long time by agricultural standards for farmers to be cultivating Quebrada de Lacramarca and the main Lower Valley area (the latter area of course had been farmed since the beginning of Early Suchimancillo).

Second, following the apparent abandonment of these areas by Early Tanguche times, as we have seen the demographic center of gravity shifted dramatically back upvalley toward the Tanguche area—with more people by far living in the Middle Valley sector than at any other time in the sequence (see Table 5). Finally, following these developments, by Late Tanguche times the population in the Middle Valley sector began a steep decline that continued on to the end of the sequence, while the Late Tambo Real population in the Lower Valley appears to have stabilized at levels not far below those of Early Tambo Real Period.

What then can we make of these essential facts regarding the overall location of settlements and population? If we assume that among the main pressures exerted on Santa agriculturalists during the period of occupation by multivalley states was a tribute-oriented goal of pushing the system to the limits of its productivity—i.e., to levels

well beyond those necessary to support the estimated population—then it may well be the case that this intensification in and of itself created such excessive buildup of mineral salts in the soil that the only short-term solution was to shift the focus of cultivation away from affected areas. But with excessive intensification continuing to exert long-term pressure on the land, eventually the overall agricultural carrying capacity of the region may have dropped to levels significantly lower, for example, than the nearly 40,000 persons of Early Tanguche times—i.e., to about one-third of this number. Nevertheless, this argument does not imply that excessive salt buildups presented an insoluble problem; for example, the modern agricultural carrying capacity appears to be in a magnitude of well over 100,000 persons. Rather, it may be that prehispanic agriculturalists lacked the technical expertise to deal with increased salinization and lowered agricultural productivity. The eventual result, judging from the demographic curve of the late period, was an adaptation at substantially lower population levels than those achieved during the chiefdoms of Suchimancillo times and the multivalley states of the middle period.

The Evidence from Santa Valley

Settlement patterns, demography, and subsistence.
As we have seen in Chapter IV, both the Late Tanguche and Early Tambo Real subsistence-settlement systems represent substantial changes from the patterns of regional occupation that characterize the preceding multivalley state systems—although Late Tanguche is essentially the last period in the sequence for which it can be

347

argued that the settlement pattern exhibits a truly revolutionary break with the pattern of the preceding period. As indicated by a comparison of Figs. 176 and 178, the Late Tanguche system represents a nearly complete abandonment of both the maritime sites of the southern coastal area as well as the road-settlement network of the desert between Santa and Chao. It is worth noting that this supports the assertion that Early Tanguche settlements in both of these sectors were *artificially* imposed by the Black-White-Red state, just as it appears likely that the intensive Lower Valley agricultural focus of Guadalupito period was an imposition of the Moche state. But aside from the abandonment of the Coast and Santa-Chao sectors, the main valley system exhibits a more gradual decline in population (e.g., compare the Early Tanguche and Late Tanguche estimates for the main valley sectors, in Table 5). Likewise, as indicated in Table 5 the development of the dichotomous pattern of settlement in Early Tambo Real times has both an abrupt aspect (i.e., a significant reduction in the Middle Valley population) and a gradual aspect (i.e., a more measured decline in the Upper and Lower Valley populations).

With regard to dwelling types, it is interesting to note that Late Tanguche continues the general regional pattern of a heavy focus on structures with rock-walled bases, especially in the main Middle Valley area of occupation. On the other hand, by Early Tambo Real the Santa region again exhibits a strong shift to structures built completely of perishable materials. Although much more research will have to be done in Santa and elsewhere to establish more precisely the significance of these shifts, Early Tambo Real is a time of apparent reestablishment of strong socioeconomic ties with valleys to the north and therefore parallels the changes that occurred with the more sudden influx of Moche influences during Guadalupito Period.

It is also of interest to note that, although both systems exhibit the strong settlement clustering that had characterized the four pre-state ceramic periods, Late Tanguche and Early Tambo Real are sharply different from the pre-state periods in terms of the relationship between cluster populations and the estimated capacity of the land to sustain them. For example, as shown in Table 13, the amount of cultivable land associated with the main settlement groupings comprising Late Tanguche Clusters 2 and 3 conceivably could have produced enough food to support their estimated populations independently of each other—at least assuming an intensive triple-cropping strategy. The same is even more true for all three clusters of Early Tambo Real Period, in that the triple-crop carrying capacity is substantially higher than the actual number of people estimated to have inhabited each cluster. In discussing the nature of inter-cluster relations, we can therefore at least begin with the assumption that each of the main clusters of these two late periods could have subsisted independently of the others, and, hence, that a situation of within-valley conflict theoretically was possible.

Hierarchies of site size and function. Aside from the sharp reduction in population that occurs in Late Tanguche and Early Tambo Real, analysis of the hierarchy of site size and function suggests a significant decrease in overall sociocultural complexity in these periods. Both systems are characterized by a four-tiered hierarchy of site size, and what appears to have been only a two-tiered hierarchy of sociopolitical function (i.e., undifferentiated habitation sites and local centers). Interestingly enough, however, the settlement system of each period contains five relatively large, complex sites whose wide distribution throughout the areas of occupation suggests they functioned as local centers.

The ceramic evidence. One of the main continuities from the multivalley state periods is that the principal ceramic diagnostics of both Late Tanguche and Early Tambo Real are distributed throughout the area of occupation, in contrast to the more uneven, clinal distributions of all four pre-state chiefdoms. As argued earlier, this seems to indicate that in general the postulated intensive within-region socioeconomic interaction of Guadalupito and Early Tanguche continued on essentially throughout Late Tanguche and Early Tambo Real Periods as well. Moreover, the comparison of ceramic assemblages—both between clusters and across the river within clusters—indicates generally high similarity in terms of specific percentages of types. For example, as shown in Table 15, the comparison of assemblages between Late Tanguche Clusters 2 and 3 (the main settlement groupings of this period) results in a similarity score of 145.9, which is nearly as high as the scores from between-cluster comparisons in Early Tanguche Period. By the same token, cross-river comparisons of within-cluster assemblages result in scores that are well above 100.0 (indeed, as shown in Table 16, the scores from comparisons of major settlement groupings within Early Tambo Real Cluster 3 compare favorably to those of Guadalupito Period).

A final interesting aspect of the ceramic data from Late Tanguche and Early Tambo Real is that both periods—but especially Late Tanguche—are characterized by relatively low numbers of ceramic types. A total of 12 types was identified for Late Tanguche, with only 6 principal time markers. Both of these figures are the lowest by far of any period in the sequence (see discussion under chronology, in Chapter III). And although the numbers of total types and principal period diagnostics rise considerably in Early Tambo Real (i.e., 21 total types and 18 principal time markers), these numbers are inflated somewhat by the separation of similar form types on the basis of the main redware and grayware paste types. In any event, the small number of form types may be an additional indication of cultural devolution—i.e., the reduction in numbers appears to have been brought about by forces quite distinct from those causing reductions during the multivalley states of the middle period.

Nature of warfare. As we have seen in discussing maize-based carrying capacity, the main settlement clusters of both Late Tanguche and Early Tambo Real appear to have been capable of subsisting independently of one another—assuming a triple-cropping strategy of cultivation, and, of course, between-cluster conflict. But at least two features of the system argue strongly against this sort of conflict, suggesting instead that as in all preceding ceramic periods warfare was interregional in nature. First, as argued in the chapter on environment, the intricate and easily disrupted nature of the irrigation network would appear *a priori* to rule out any benefits of engaging in internecine warfare. Second, although Late Tanguche Clusters 2 and 3 could have subsisted independently (indeed they may have)—and exhibit rough demographic parity as well—if anything the high similarity between their ceramic assemblages argues for stronger socioeconomic relations than in the pre-state periods. The same subsistence independence characterizes Early Tambo Real Clusters 1, 2, and 3, although the pronounced demographic disparity between clusters argues even more definitively against the possibility of internecine warfare.

Briefly to recall the suggested sources of attacks on Santa in earlier periods, it can be argued that such a threat probably was consistently from valleys to the south in the pre-state periods (i.e., from Nepeña and Casma), from the north at the beginning of Guadalupito Period (i.e., Moche), and from the south at the beginning of Early Tanguche Period (i.e., Casma). Judging from interregional comparisons of ceramic assemblages in Late Tanguche and Early Tambo Real, it seems likely that whatever threat of warfare existed in the former period was from the north, while the stronger ties to both north and south in Early Tambo Real make it less certain from which direction the threat came.

THE FINAL PERIOD: CHIMÚ-INCA HEGEMONY
(CA. A.D. 1350–1532)

Although the final part of the prehispanic sequence in Santa is characterized by continuing demographic decline, Late Tambo Real Period exhibits a resurgence of societal complexity that probably lasted well over 150 years. As the Santa data show, this complexity appears attributable in large part to the incorporation of the region into the Chimú state, the third and last of the large multivalley polities to arise in this area of the North Coast. During the last 50 years or so of the sequence, it is

also probable that armies of the huge pan-Central Andean Inca state swept across the Lower Santa Valley, encountering stiff resistance from a people with a by now long-established tradition of regional defense extending back over 2000 years in time.

Utilizing both archaeological data and the scant but intriguing information from ethnohistoric accounts, the first part of this section begins by briefly outlining the overall nature and extent of the Chimú state in order to provide the principal context for understanding the final period in the Lower Santa sequence. Following this, the Inca state is discussed briefly, primarily to present arguments about the possible nature of its control over the region. The section ends with a summary of the main aspects of the Lower Santa data that support the argument of an increase in complexity brought about by incorporation into the Chimú state—including the settlement pattern; demography and subsistence; the hierarchy of site size and function; corporate labor projects and administrative elites; the ceramic evidence; and warfare, tribute, and state control.

Overall Nature and Extent

The Chimú state. As implied above, the rise of the Chimu state (or, Chimor) is close enough in time to the end of the prehispanic sequence that several brief accounts based on native oral traditions of its origins, development, and extent are available in the Spanish documentary sources. In his landmark study based on these documents, Rowe (1948) relied on the sketchy but presumably reliable details provided by the Anonymous History of Trujillo (written in 1604) in identifying the founding ruler of Chimor as Ñançen-pinco. According to tradition, this ruler carried out the initial conquests giving rise to a multivalley polity which included the seven main valleys from Saña to Santa. Rowe (1948:40) estimates this occurred sometime around A.D. 1370.

The Anonymous History and other sources also assert that under Minchançaman, the last pre-Inca ruler in the Chimú dynasty, the state was extended much farther to include Tumbes in the far north and the Chillón Valley in the far south—thus encompassing an area of the Peruvian littoral over 1000 km long. But considering the vast deserts separating some of the valleys in the northern and southern parts of this area, it seems highly improbable that the Chimú ever were able effectively to control such a large area. On the other hand, judging from strong interregional ceramic similarities, it is quite likely that Chimor extended substantially farther to the north and south than its predecessor, the Moche state, to include at least the 12 principal valleys extending over a distance of 425 km from Lambayeque to Huarmey.

In any event, currently available archaeological data clearly indicate that the prime candidate for the Chimú capital is Chan Chán site, the vast city of massive adobe constructions that extends over an area of some 16 km² on the north desert margin at the mouth of Moche Valley (cf. Moseley 1975a; Moseley and Day 1983). Interestingly enough, however, although Chan Chán is much larger and more complex than other contemporaneous centers within the main 12-valley area of presumed Chimú control, its population has been estimated at a fairly low 25,000–30,000 persons (cf. Moseley 1975a:223). Still, when compared to the much lower population estimate of 10,480 persons for the entire Santa region at this time, the number of persons estimated to have resided at Chan Chán is impressive. Indeed, it nearly equals the total regional estimate for any period in the sequence of such valleys as Virú (25,000 persons, in Gallinazo Period) or Santa (36,000 persons, in Early Tanguche Period).

In spite of the relatively large size of Chan Chán compared to the total contemporaneous population of other regions, perhaps the more unusual aspect of the Late Chimú subsistence-settlement system in Moche Valley is that only three additional second-tier sites as well as a mere handful of very small, scattered settlements have been identified to date (e.g., see Keatinge 1974, 1982). Although no comprehensive settlement data are yet available in the literature to permit assessment of developments leading up to the final main prehispanic period, the possibility that most of the regional population lived in or near Chan Chán is an intriguing one. If this is so, however, then the total population of the valley may not have exceeded 30,000–35,000 persons, which is a decidedly *small* number of people forming the heartland of what is presumed to have been a conquest state controlling at least several hundreds of thousands of inhabitants in the 12-valley core area from Lambayeque to Huarmey.

The Inca state. As is well known from the ethnohistoric documents (cf. Rowe 1948; 1963a), the Inca conquest of the North Coast began as a more or less unintentional fluke when the emperor Pachacuti sent an army under the command of his half brother, Cápac Yupanqui, on a mission of exploration and raiding in the Central Peruvian sierra. The general had been ordered to go no farther than the Yanamayo River in the north-central sierra, but, when faced with the potentially humiliating desertion of Chanca warriors from his forces, attempted to redeem himself by heading on to the north where he attacked the Cajamarca polity, a major ally of the Chimú state. Pachacuti had the general put to death for insubordination, and the eventual upshot of the incursion into Cajamarca-Chimú territory was a war in which the Inca general Topa Cápac succeeded in conquering not only Cajamarca but the capital of Chimor as well. These events are thought to have taken place around A.D. 1470, and shortly thereafter Santa and other valleys to the south were overrun by subsequent campaigns.

The effect of the Inca incursion on many of the valleys encompassed within the former core area of the Chimú state appears to have been very minor. Indeed, essentially the only evidence of Inca influence in valleys such as Moche, Virú, Santa, and Nepeña consists of a few scattered finds of Inca ceramic diagnostics (e.g., see Collier 1955:140; Donnan and Mackey 1978:356–357; Proulx 1978:83; Willey 1953:399; and the ceramic appendix of this report). Moreover, even assuming the Incas occupied any of these valleys or *effectively* incorporated them into the state—and for valleys immediately to the south of Moche there is at least some question whether this ever was the case—it seems to have been achieved almost entirely within the context of the previously existing Late Chimú infrastructure (but see Conrad 1977, on Chiquitoy Viejo, an apparent Inca administrative center in Chicama Valley to the north). The argument has even been made on the basis of the documentary sources that important aspects of Chimú statecraft and culture had a profound effect on the Inca conquerors (e.g., see Rowe 1948:46).

In contrast to the general lack of data indicating strong Inca influence and control over many North Coast valleys, archaeological studies of the Central and South Coast areas (e.g., Menzel 1954) indicate that the Inca system of administrative centers built in the diagnostic Cuzco style was imposed or grafted onto previously existing systems in a number of valleys there. These include Lurín (Pachacámac), Cañete (Incahuasi), Chincha (La Centinela), Pisco (Lima la Vieja, Tambo Colorado), Nazca (Tambo de Collao, Paredones), Acarí (Tambo Viejo), and Yauca (Tambo de Jaqui). Indeed, both these central and south coast centers as well as the system of roads, tambos, and administrative centers imposed along the entire backbone of the Andes from Ecuador to northern Argentina and Chile were built in a style that is unmistakably Inca (e.g., see Gasparini and Margolies 1980; Morris 1972; Morris and Thompson 1985). In sum, there are fundamental differences in terms of the evidence for Inca control between the former Chimú core area, on the one hand, and all other areas of the empire, on the other. It may thus be the case that the Inca had little interest in (or capabilities of) effectively integrating the southern Chimú core area into the empire during the short 50-year period of their ascendancy to unparalleled sociopolitical complexity and control in the Central Andes.

Santa as a Province of the Chimú State

The settlement pattern. A comparison of the Late Tambo Real settlement pattern with that of the two preceding periods indicates that the last period in the sequence may be viewed in part as an evolutionary outgrowth of the Late Tanguche and Early Tambo Real system—i.e., from the upvalley-oriented system of Late

Tanguche the location of sites appears to have shifted gradually to a primary focus on the Lower Valley sector. On the other hand, several features of the Late Tambo Real system imply the imposition of multivalley state policy on the region as well as the operation of strong interregional socioeconomic forces. For example, as we have seen the location of SVP-LTR-47/Alto Perú in a central position with regard to the two local centers suggests that all three sites were strategically positioned—in relation both to provincial activities and to the principal road that ran roughly north-south across the main valley area. Indeed, many sites on the east side of the Lower Valley appear to have been lined up near or directly along the main ancient route of intervalley travel.

Considering the probability that this was the second time in the sequence when Santa came under the control of a multivalley state centered in Moche, it is of substantial interest to note that Late Tambo Real and Guadalupito are the only periods when the subsistence-settlement system is essentially focused on the Lower Valley. Moreover, as in the case of the two preceding multivalley North Coast states, the Late Tambo Real system is characterized both by a complete absence of defensive sites as well as by sites that are universally located in open, exposed positions along the edges of the valley floor or on low hills rising in the midst of it.

In light of the argument that the strong shift to completely perishable structures in Guadalupito/Moche Period may represent the external imposition of (Moche Valley-centered) state cultural norms on the main Lower Valley settlement system, it is worth recalling that 67% of the sites in this sector have such structures in Late Tambo Real Period. Although the figures for such sites are somewhat higher in Guadalupito and Early Tambo Real Periods (80% and 81%, respectively), the focus on a dwelling type that is not strongly characteristic of other periods in the sequence seems to indicate the continuation from Early Tambo Real of strong influences emanating from the Moche area. On the other hand, although a few Late Tambo Real sites have the tapia and adobe brick walls characteristic of Chan Chán and rural administrative centers of Moche Valley, walls of this type are essentially restricted to SVP-LTR-47/Alto Perú regional center.

Demography and subsistence. Judging from the overall distribution of sites in the Late Tambo Real system, the maximum amount of immediately available cultivable land was 4878 ha. Thus, given the estimated single-crop production figure shown for this period in Table 11, even the single-crop capabilities of the subsistence system would have been in a magnitude of more than three times that necessary to sustain the actual population estimate of 10,480 persons. Assuming a single-cropping cultivation strategy, the production excess of the valley would therefore have been capable of sustain-

ing some 23,000 persons elsewhere in the Chimú state. Indeed, assuming a double-cropping strategy, the production excess would have sustained 56,000 persons. But whatever the *actual* tribute in foodstuffs exacted by the Chimú state from Santa, it seems abundantly clear that the region would have been of substantial significance to the general productive capabilities of the multivalley state.

The hierarchy of site size and function. As we have seen, the Late Tambo Real system is similar to those of Guadalupito and Early Tanguche in containing both local centers, or sites that stand out in terms of size and/or greater complexity from surrounding undifferentiated habitation sites, and a regional center whose even greater size and complexity clearly suggest that it served as the primary center of the system. However, as indicated in the site population size histograms of Fig. 163, the overall hierarchy of size appears to have been less complex than that of the two preceding multivalley states. Indeed, with an area of 16.5 ha, SVP-LTR-47/Alto Perú is decidedly smaller than either Pampa de los Incas Complex (200 ha) or SVP-ETAN-147/Huaca Jedionda (37.4 ha). In sum, although SVP-LTR-47 is architecturally quite complex (e.g., compared to Huaca Jedionda center), the reduced number of size levels in the regional hierarchy appears to indicate less overall complexity in the subsistence-settlement system than in the preceding states.

Corporate labor projects and administrative elites. Another feature of the system that indicates comparatively less complexity than earlier states is the general lack of evidence for massive or extensive state-sponsored corporate labor projects. For example, among such projects of Guadalupito Period are a number of very large adobe platform mounds and the extensive canal-field system of the Lower Valley. Among such projects of Early Tanguche are the extensive road-settlement network, the Great Wall system, and the canal-field system of Las Salinas area. In sharp contrast, the single probable example of a massive corporate labor project in Late Tambo Real is the construction of the huaca platforms and extensive adobe-walled compounds that constitute SVP-LTR-47 regional center itself.

Judging from the small number of local centers, the smaller size of SVP-LTR-47, and the small number of corporate labor projects, it is therefore likely that the number of Chimú administrative elite residing in Santa was much reduced compared to Guadalupito and Early Tanguche Periods. Nevertheless, it must also be stressed that the number and size of the compounds at Alto Perú Complex suggest that a fairly sizeable group of administrative functionaries resided at the regional center itself.

The ceramic evidence. As in all other periods from Guadalupito on, the distribution of most principal Late Tambo Real ceramic diagnostics is uniform and widespread throughout the region, suggesting the same intensive socioeconomic interaction that characterized the preceding four periods. Interestingly enough, in at least one aspect Late Tambo Real appears to exhibit more complexity than either Guadalupito or Early Tanguche, namely, in the greater number of ceramic types and principal diagnostics. These include a total of 25 types and 18 principal diagnostics (compared to 16/10 in Guadalupito and 19/15 in Early Tanguche), as well as the two principal paste types (redware and grayware).

It is also important to stress that we found only two examples of the well-known polished blackware considered to be so characteristic of Chimú pottery, in strong contrast to the nearly universal distribution in the region of the main Moche and Early Middle Horizon fancy funerary wares. The two fragments of Chimú blackware consist of very diagnostic flat-sided stirrup spouts (e.g., see Fig. 280), and both were found at sites on the north side of the Lower Valley sector. By the same token, as discussed in the ceramics appendix, only six fragments of Inca-related vessels were found in our intensive surface examination of the entire region, again providing a strong contrast to the literally tens of thousands of Moche and Early Middle Horizon sherds seen everywhere in habitation and cemetery sites of the two preceding multivalley state systems. This clearly suggests that the nature of both Inca and Chimú influence on Santa was substantially different from that of the Moche and Black-White-Red states. At least in the case of Chimú influence, however, it must also be pointed out that the utilitarian grayware ceramic assemblage is very similar in form and paste to contemporaneous Moche and Virú assemblages.

Warfare, tribute, and state control. Judging from the record of prehispanic North Coast oral history in the Spanish documentary sources, the Chimú state had ample military capabilities that enabled it to meet the Inca incursion from Cajamarca with vigorous resistance—at least initially. Specifically with regard to Santa, as we have seen the account of Cieza de León indicates that the people of this region fought so valiantly and fiercely against the Inca that their (ultimate) conquerors responded with strong admiration. From this fragmentary historical evidence, it may be inferred not only that the Chimú forged their state by means of military force and conquest but that the people of the Santa Valley resisted as fiercely as they had at any other time in the ceramic sequence. It is of some relevance to point out, however, that we found no evidence in the Late Tambo Real ceramic assemblage of the militaristic iconography that characterizes both Moche murals and decorated pottery as well as Middle Horizon pottery. Indeed, militaristic scenes do not seem to appear on Chimú pottery, murals, or textiles anywhere in the 12-valley core area.

In any event, to the extent that the Chimú had effectively incorporated Santa by military force into the state (an apparent fact that nonetheless did not render the people of Santa incapable of organizing a strong defense against the Inca), then their control must have included the threat of additional force should a provincial insurrection be attempted. At the same time, one of the main expectations of Chimú conquest and control seems likely to have been material gain in the form of food tribute and access to corvée labor. The high productivity potential of Santa, compared to immediately adjacent valleys to the north and south, would certainly have been of great utility in provisioning laborers engaged in state projects in Santa or elsewhere. Indeed, as argued in the preceding chapter, some of the architectural features visible in airphotos of the compounds at SVP-LTR-47 are of a size that suggests they functioned as storage rooms where excess production beyond the immediate needs of the regional population was kept for use by the state.

In contrast, when discussing the nature of Inca control over conquered valleys such as Santa, it appears likely that the demands of the empire were dramatically less than those made on provincial regions by the more localized multivalley Moche, Black-White-Red, and Chimú states—all of whose capitals were within a very close one-to-three day's travel distance of any part of the system. Certainly the evidence for an Inca presence in the Lower Santa region seems entirely too ephemeral to argue otherwise. This does not necessarily imply that the power of the last prehispanic Central Andean state was not felt from time to time, or that it was not exerted in more localized areas of the North Coast (e.g., at Chiquitoy Viejo); rather, it implies that for all practical purposes many North Coast valleys were too remote from Inca concerns in the sierra and Central-South coast areas for the state effectively to integrate them. Compared to the periods of maximum complexity represented by the Guadalupito and Early Tanguche systems, then, valleys such as Santa had passed from the scene of major prehispanic developments in the Central Andes.

CHAPTER 6

Conclusions

Like most other coastal Peruvian valley oases, the Lower Santa Valley is characterized by two main linearly-distributed environments—the irrigable valley floor alluvium and the shallow inshore waters of the coast—that formed the essential, or most accessible, focus of subsistence-settlement systems throughout the prehispanic sequence, from late Preceramic times to the end of Late Horizon Period. The first preceramic inhabitants of the region encountered possibilities for making a living in each of the two microenvironments, settling more or less year-round in a series of small coastal maritime sites all along ancient Las Salinas Bay and on rocky headlands to the south, as well as out in the desert of the upvalley sectors where they had access to the resources of the riverine matorral thickets.

To some extent the small size, simple configuration, and lack of variation among sites in the Las Salinas Period system make it comparatively more difficult to assess its overall nature than that of the nine ceramic periods which follow it in time—all of which are characterized by a wealth of settlement, structural, and ceramic data that throw much light on problems of a demographic, subsistence, and sociopolitical nature, at least given the application of systematic and comprehensive methods of data retrieval. Nevertheless, by their very nature—i.e., noncomplex, but most probably sedentary (e.g., rock-walled structures, large seed-grinding stones, and year-round availability of most maritime foods)—we can argue that the riverine thicket- and maritime-oriented groups represent an egalitarian, or incipient-village, level of sociopolitical integration. With respect to the nature of intersite relations, it is highly unlikely that any raiding or warfare was occurring among the maritime groups. Those in the upvalley area, however, prob-

ably lived in the more remote desert sites for defensive reasons. But given the small size of these sites, the likelihood that they were composed of related kin groups, and the need to use the same limited riverine niche, intersettlement relations probably were peaceful and may well have been reinforced by intermarriage. The threat of warfare, then, undoubtedly was from outside the region, as in all subsequent periods—although in contrast to later periods it is more difficult to suggest reasons for intervalley hostilities, other than to note that the year-round availability of water may have made Santa an attractive focus of raiding by groups seeking to become established there. In any case, the coercive theory seems no more applicable to the Preceramic than it is to the later, ceramic periods.

After a rather long hiatus in the Initial Period (ca. 1800 B.C. to sometime after 1000 B.C.), during which no obvious evidence of occupation can be detected in the Lower Santa region (the period is problematical in adjacent Virú and Nepeña as well), the first agricultural system appears in essentially full-blown form in Cayhuamarca Period. Compared to Las Salinas times, the subsistence-settlement system of the earliest ceramic period is substantially more complex—with a total of 54 occupations distributed widely in the upvalley sectors, and clustered in internally coherent groupings which all consistently contain sites with functions that include simple (commoner) habitations, elite (chiefly) residences, ceremonial-civic activities, and fortresses. The population of the valley had reached an estimated 6000 persons, and the need to farm efficiently much of the Upper and Middle Valley sectors as well as defend the entire system seems to have required the establishment of the first formal supravillage cooperative and coordinative institu-

353

tions in the sequence—probably represented at this stage by an emerging chiefly elite who functioned in both priestly and secular roles. But a great deal of local self-sufficiency is apparent in the site systems forming each local cluster, in addition to the need for maintenance of peaceful relations among all inhabitants of the region. No single site stands out as paramount in the emerging complexity of this period, although the concentration of complex sites in Cayhuamarca area suggests that it had already attained the "cultural preeminence" that would characterize it through the end of Late Suchimancillo Period. At this early stage of agricultural development, it appears that strong socioeconomic relations with valleys to the north were occurring, while the source of continual attacks on Santa was Nepeña and Casma Valleys to the south. With the massive pyramidal complex of Sechín Alto and numerous Chavinoid sites, Casma clearly was the main source of these attacks, although its much greater similarity to Casma than Santa suggests Nepeña was allied with (and had been brought under the control of) the Casma polity. Santa, in any case, was not under the control of any cultural group outside the region, including Chavín, and, indeed, had established a pattern of fierce and successful resistance to external encroachment that would last until the Moche conquest hundreds of years later.

Nearly all of the characteristics which define the Cayhuamarca subsistence-settlement system are also true of the following Vinzos Period system. Most importantly, the people of the region continued to be strongly focused on the upvalley sectors, and (with 45 sites) there is roughly the same number of occupations as before. But the density of people on sites had grown, a fact which is manifested in a substantial rise by nearly 2000 people to an estimated total of ca. 8000 persons in the system. The Vinzos system is not simply a later manifestation of Cayhuamarca Period, however; 55% of the 45 sites are new and there are two major locales where sites had not been established before—including a number of settlements clustered around a network of desert trails in Quebrada Palo Redondo and a very large site of some 2000 persons near the coast on Pampa Santa Elvira. Development of formal cooperative/coordinative institutions continues to occur, which is probably best manifested in the establishment of the large ceremonial-elite residential complex of Huaca Yolanda. Nevertheless, as before, local-level clusters contain the same multifunctional and hierarchically-organized network of site types, which indicates a continuation of a fair measure of self-sufficiency at the local level. But the clusters of both Vinzos and Cayhuamarca are relatively quite small in total population size (averaging about 1000 persons each), especially compared to settlement groupings of Suchimancillo times. In addition to experiencing population growth and concomitant agricultural intensification, the system also was expanding within the context of a

continuing threat of raiding from valleys to the south. Socioeconomic relations with valleys like Virú to the north also continued to be maintained at a strong level, but there is as yet no indication of any major relations with peoples of the adjacent sierra.

Just as Cayhuamarca and Vinzos Periods mark a fundamental change from Las Salinas times in terms of a shift to an upvalley-oriented subsistence-settlement system and incipient agriculturally-based societal complexity, so does Early Suchimancillo represent an equally striking change to the first truly extensive occupation of the entire coastal area of the Santa River. While the main focus of the system is still in the upvalley area, population has now grown to an estimated 20,000 persons and 130 sites extend with few large gaps all along both desert margins of the main valley. The same basic site types of previous periods are present in the system—including habitation, ceremonial-civic, and fortress sites—clearly indicating that the same need for cooperative/coordinative functions in both subsistence and defense is still universally a part of the adaptation. In addition, as before, the focus of principal cultural traits and population density continues to be the area centered roughly on Quebrada de Cayhuamarca, one of the main probable routes of communication with sierra groups. It is in this period that the first signs of contact with adjacent sierra groups appear—including a few kaolin ware types, tightly-flexed burials in stone-lined tombs, and the depiction of such Andean animals as condors and llamas in desert ground drawings. Also, in line with the appearance of llama drawings and coast-sierra contacts, there is the first evidence of llama corrals located along trails, i.e., in positions that suggest that llama trains were becoming the primary means of transport by which goods were traded between far-flung coast and sierra peoples. With an irrigation network that now extended probably all along both desert margins, the Lower Santa region with its year-round water supply constituted an even more enticing focus of attempts by coastal foreign outsiders to control its productive capabilities than before. This is clearly manifested in the presence of more fortresses than at any other time in the sequence, including a widespread distribution throughout nearly all parts of the system. Thus, while ceramic similarities and other diagnostic features indicate the establishment of ties with the sierra as well as a continuation of contacts with valleys to the north, the Lower Santa region still was the focus of continual attacks from complex societies located in relatively water-poor valleys to the south.

The system of Late Suchimancillo Period represents the developmental apogee of complex pre-state societies, and what appears to have been the full expression of a number of trends established as early as Cayhuamarca and Vinzos Periods. As in the three preceding periods, the great majority of sites is in the upvalley sectors. Indeed, the widespread distribution of fortress sites suggests that people had remained here over the hundreds of years of agricultural development because the mountainous terrain afforded much better protection against the raiding of foreigners to the south. With the second largest population estimate in the sequence (ca. 30,000 persons) and the great bulk of it located in the upvalley area—distributed inversely in relation to the supply of cultivable land—the strong and continuing need for defense seems to explain in large part the location of most sites. However, there are no defensive sites in the upper two-thirds part of Cluster 1, and this suggests not only that the very steep canyon walls protected them but that peaceful trading relations with adjacent Recuay groups were at an all-time high. This is amply supported by the strong presence of Recuay-type ceramics in the assemblage, as well as by the numerous small, stone-lined tombs, and a Callejón-related subterranean gallery. In addition, trails/roads ran along both desert margins at least as far as Chuquicara (and thence up steep slopes directly into the sierra, rather than via the Cañón del Pato), and the presence of numerous corral features probably indicates a marked increase in the quantity of goods traded between the coast and sierra. Finally, from the three local centers of Early Suchimancillo Period the number rises to seven such sites in Late Suchimancillo, with a wide distribution that suggests a universal continuation of the need for formal supravillage regulation of subsistence, trade, and defense. There is still no sign, however, of any site that stands out as a *regional* center functioning to coordinate activities in the entire subsistence-settlement system of the main valley—although we may nevertheless argue that all sectors in the valley were part of a single, loosely integrated chiefdom society.

After Cayhuamarca and Early Suchimancillo, Guadalupito Period is the third time in the sequence when the subsistence-settlement system seems to represent both an evolutionary outgrowth of preceding periods, in some respects, and a nearly revolutionary break with the past, in others. One of the principal links with the past is the presence of a reasonably large regional population, which relied on the earlier establishment of irrigation networks throughout the main valley area. Thus the subsistence system of Guadalupito peoples clearly was built on the basis of antecedent developments in the agricultural infrastructure. Also, in a sense it is possible to view the average location of sites closer to the valley floor as an evolutionary outgrowth of trends characterizing the preceding four systems. But we have abundant evidence that this is the period of the first conquest of Santa peoples by outsiders; i.e., it is the *first coercive event* in the sequence, and was carried out by armies of the Moche state, which until now seemingly had remained just beyond the northern periphery of interregional interaction spheres of which Santa was a part. Among the most notable features providing evidence of the revolutionary imposition of a state system are: (1) a

ceramic assemblage that throughout the valley is manufactured in close adherence to the Moche style; (2) the construction of the first truly paramount site in the system, at Pampa de los Incas; (3) the use of Moche-type maker's marks in the adobes used to build Structure 19, the probable seat of the regional administrator of the state; (4) the appearance of a craft production center at one of the sites in the regional center complex; (5) the construction of several impressive and commanding local centers on hills, with associated militaristic iconography; (6) the decidedly abrupt relocation of most of the regional population to the downvalley area; (7) the significant loss of population for the first time in the sequence (down some 8000 persons from the estimated 30,000 of the preceding period), perhaps as a result of *mitmaquna*-type relocation; and (8) the establishment of what is apparently the first intervalley road network, cutting across the desert in the coastal area. Judging from the analysis of the Guadalupito data, during this period Santa became one of the main providers of tribute in foodstuffs to the Moche state. From the open nature of sites and the complete absence of defensive structures, it is also clear that along with the burdens of being a provincial breadbasket came the first long period of relative peace to this point in the sequence.

Of all subsistence-settlement systems in the sequence, Early Tanguche in many ways represents the most intriguing period of all. With an estimated 36,000 persons in the regional system, it is the most populous by far of any period. It is also the most complex, with principal features that include: (1) the construction at Huaca Jedionda of the most densely occupied center in the sequence; (2) the widespread distribution of more local centers containing buildings with greater architectural complexity than any other period; (3) a heavy dual focus on both agricultural and maritime subsistence that is unequalled in the sequence; (4) the building of what appears to be the longest prehispanic wall system anywhere in the Americas; and (5) the construction of an impressively intricate and widespread network of rock-lined desert roads and sites, indicating that the strength of interregional relations was probably at an all-time high. Indeed, in many ways this seems to have been the most complex multivalley North Coast state in the sequence—with a huge population size; an intervalley communications system that linked provincial valleys through a complex network of roads and a nearly continuous distribution of desert habitation sites; the presence of Great Walls in several valleys; and the widespread and uniform distribution of Black-White-Red ceramic diagnostics throughout the Lower Santa region and in valleys to the north and south, from Chicama to Huarmey. Yet, in the Lower Santa region at least, there are already signs that the unprecedented and long period of external control by two successive outside polities was beginning to take its toll. This shows up best in the abandonment from Guadalupito to Early Tanguche times of many prime site locations in the Lower Valley. Assuming that the small number of sites in the Lower Valley (compared both to the preceding period as well as to the dense concentration of Early Tanguche sites elsewhere in the system) is an indication of relatively much less emphasis on agricultural production in this sector than before, then the probable reason for abandonment was the over-irrigation and excessive production demands imposed during the previous period of Moche control which brought about extensive salinization. In light of the continued presence of multivalley state control and the demand for tribute in foodstuffs that probably characterized the Black-White-Red polity, there does not appear to be any other plausible reason for the strong shift back upvalley that occurs in Early Tanguche.

This argument also derives support from the evidence for the abrupt decline in regional population that characterizes Late Tanguche Period. Given the long period of continual rise in regional population throughout pre-state times, as well as the strong evidence of two periods of multivalley state control, the relatively low population estimate of 18,500 persons in Late Tanguche seems likely to be the result of a drop in agricultural carrying capacity. This drop undoubtedly was *not* brought about by such catastrophic forces as plate tectonics, but rather by the effects of continual meddling in local production practices by the preceding multivalley polities. In any case, among the other salient features of Late Tanguche are the establishment of a number of very large terraced sites located in the Middle Valley sector (mostly on the south desert margin), and the probability that in the absence of multivalley state control there once again existed a threat of outside raiding on the region. But, in contrast to the pre-multivalley state periods (i.e., Cayhuamarca through Late Suchimancillo), in Late Tanguche Period the raids probably were coming from valleys to the north, including Virú. At the same time, Santa maintained strong socioeconomic relations with Nepeña and Casma, in a mini-multivalley interaction sphere (was it a state?) that was unprecedented between Santa and valleys to the south. This interaction is manifested in the rather drearily simple and homogeneous raised circle-and-dot ceramic assemblage found everywhere at contemporaneous sites in Santa, Nepeña, and probably Casma.

From the 56 sites of Late Tanguche times, the number drops to 49 sites in the following Early Tambo Real Period. But regional population takes a significantly more drastic plunge, down by some 7000 persons to an estimate of ca. 11,500. Yet, like Late Tanguche, the drop in numbers of sites and regional population size does not appear to mark a return to the kinds of chiefdom societies that characterize Cayhuamarca and Vinzos times—in spite of the indication that Early Tambo Real Period is closer in population to the incipient pre-state chiefdom

societies than to the Suchimancillo chiefdoms. Thus, as in Late Tanguche, there are five sites that stand out as larger and internally more complex than surrounding undifferentiated habitation sites. At the same time, a large number of sites is once again established in the Lower Valley, with a strong focus on maritime sites that is surpassed only by Early Tanguche Period.

During Late Tambo Real, the last period in the prehispanic sequence, the population size of the region declines somewhat more, to an estimated 10,500 persons. But, in contrast to the preceding period, the subsistence-settlement system of the lower Middle Valley and Lower Valley is rather more complex in nature. As indicated by the tripartite-divided tapia-walled compounds at Alto Perú regional center, and by the widespread presence of Chimú plainware and decorated utilitarian diagnostics throughout the system, this is the period of the probable incorporation of Santa into the large multivalley Chimú state centered at Chan Chán site in the Moche Valley. The old road-settlement system of Early Tanguche appears to have been pressed back into somewhat greater service than in the intervening two periods, although, with only three definite sites occupied in the desert itself, it is nowhere near as complex as before. In any case, most major sites in the Late Tambo Real system of the main valley area are lined up very near or along it. Thus we again see a subsistence-settlement system shaped in large part by the exigencies of participation in an inter-regional polity, although, as noted in relation to Cieza de León's commentaries, a great deal of regional autonomy and self-sufficiency characterizes Santa—perhaps just as it always had throughout the 3300+ years of the prehispanic sequence. Toward the very end of this last period, the North Coast was briefly overrun by the invincible armies of the Inca, but the brilliance of this greatest of all prehispanic American empires is reflected only dully in valleys such as Santa. Along with Nepeña and Virú, then, the Lower Santa region had essentially become a provincial backwater, a residual vestige of the former glory of complex multivalley North Coast states.

Having outlined salient features of prehispanic sociocultural evolution in the Lower Santa area, as well as selected principal aspects of the ten periods in the sequence, it seems appropriate to end by discussing three main conclusions drawn from the 1979–80 Santa Valley Project:

First of all, it cannot be overemphasized that the continually arid conditions that have characterized the coastal setting since time immemorial have fortuitously created some of the best preservation of prehistoric cultural remains anywhere in the world. For example, one has only to peruse the Cayhuamarca/Early Horizon (pre-350 B.C.) habitation structure in Plate 12 to realize that most sites we found are preserved in nearly the same state as the day they were abandoned. Such preservation extends all the way back to the Preceramic, some 3900 years before the present. Thus, at site after site in period after period throughout the region and throughout the sequence we found structural preservation that most archaeologists elsewhere in the world would be glad to be able to *dig* up, let alone find on the surface in nearly pristine condition. It should be obvious, then, that *at least for the coast of Peru the more appropriate methodological approach in attempting to understand the evolution of regional subsistence-settlement systems is comprehensive regional survey, not excavation.* Even given this assertion and the evidence presented in support of it in this report, however, some archaeologists may persist in the notion that the only way to retrieve significant data anywhere in the world is "to poke holes in the ground". Excavation is indeed more appropriate for many other areas of the world (presumably excluding, however, semiarid and arid nuclear areas like the Valleys of Oaxaca and Mexico, the Mesopotamian plain, and the Nile Valley). It is also appropriate for studies on the Peruvian coast or elsewhere aimed at understanding such critical aspects of the archaeological record as burial practices, midden composition, subsistence, and architecture in some ruined sites. But for those who would attempt to understand interrelationships among sites and culture process, settlement pattern studies are the principal appropriate means of getting at the data. One would at least hope, then, that the results of this study will convince some researchers that both approaches are *equally* necessary in understanding the coastal archaeological record.

But the way settlement pattern research itself is carried out can have a significant effect on the quality of the data retrieved, thus leading to the second main conclusion of this research: the approach to survey described earlier in this report has two critical aspects, namely, the use of methods that are both *systematic* and *comprehensive*. The systematic aspect implies that large-scale airphotos are used, and that all archaeological remains are recorded directly on them to ensure accurate location and assessment of size. It further implies that all sites and all areas of the region where they are located are walked over in regular, or patterned, sweeps. A systematic approach also implies consistency in making ceramic collections, as well as an attempt to retrieve similar kinds of data as survey proceeds across a region. The comprehensive aspect, in turn, implies that one looks at and studies all areas, all sites of all types, and all periods of occupation in a regional ecosystem. An important implication of this approach is therefore the need to define ecologically meaningful regional boundaries. Fortunately, in most coastal Peruvian valleys this is no problem at all, since absolute desert bounds valleys on the north and south, the ocean lies on the west, and the main flanks of the Andes quickly close off all but a few valleys as they rise into the main mountain mass at elevations higher than about 500 m above sea level. In the case of Santa, at least, *it can thus be said that we not only have a nearly complete sample of all prehispanic occupations in the region, but also a complete system of all sites that relied on water from the coastal sector of the river for their subsistence at each point in the sequence.*

Third, given the excellent preservation of sites and other remains throughout the region as well as the application of systematic and comprehensive methods in studying them, it has been possible to come to a number of specific conclusions that throw light not only on Santa but on the nature of North Coast interregional relations and multivalley state formation. In brief, and in rough chronological order, these include the following:

1. There is support, in a comparison of preceramic and ceramic period systems, for the hypothesis that the rise of sociocultural complexity—at least in this area of the coast—was directly related to the introduction of cultigens and the establishment of practices of intensive irrigation agriculture.

2. Warfare clearly is most evident and crucial in sociocultural developments that occurred prior to state formation, as Carneiro rightly argued some years ago on the basis of the Virú Valley data. But, contrary to Carneiro's assertion, this warfare involved intervalley raiding, and not internecine strife, since from the start of agriculture sites were an integral part of increasingly complex hierarchically-organized networks to ensure smooth functioning of land allocation, canal construction and maintenance, as well as defense of the overall system from outside encroachment.

3. Impaction, or population growth in an environmentally circumscribed area, is also a crucial part of pre-state developments. Although there is little evidence of population pressure *per se* in the pre-state systems of Santa, this may well be a factor that characterized developments in the water-poor valleys to the south.

4. At each point in the sequence, Santa Valley—and indeed probably all other coastal valleys as well—was characterized by more or less intensive socioeconomic interaction with some, but not all, of the other nearby regions. Thus the intervalley deserts of this area, although sometimes requiring a half day's walk or more to cross, were no impediment to continual interregional communication. Nor were they an impediment to crossing by attacking raiders either, although the absence of defensive walls suggests that the deserts in and of themselves in combination with mountain ranges on the north and south desert margins acted as an effective "first line" of defense.

5. Santa Valley groups maintained a longer tradition of intensive peaceful interaction with people to the north than with those of any other region, either to the east or south. On the other hand, at least two of the three conquests by external states emanated from Moche Valley (which also appears to have been outside the normal sphere of intervalley interaction for the Santa region). In contrast, the interaction that occurred with adjacent sierra groups was limited primarily to contacts between

coastal Late Suchimancillo/Late Gallinazo peoples and Recuay groups of the Callejón de Huaylas area *prior* to the Moche conquest of Santa and its immediate neighbors.

6. The Santa Valley data strongly support the argument that the first multivalley polity in the Central Andes was the Moche state of the North Coast, thus running contrary to arguments that Wari in Middle Horizon Period is the best candidate for pristine Central Andean state formation.

7. The data from Early Tanguche Period Santa Valley point clearly to a second period of multivalley state formation, following more or less on the heels of the Moche state and probably centered in Casma Valley to the south. The data also strongly suggest that the Black-White-Red state was an independent North Coast-centered polity that maintained relations with, but was not conquered by, the Wari state, again running contrary to arguments by Ayacucho-centered researchers.

8. The Great Wall system of Santa Valley is not a single, monolithic entity that extends up into the adjacent sierra, contrary to statements by its original (aerial) discoverers. Rather, it is limited to a number of long, but discrete, sections that run along the first 40 km of the north desert margin and thence across the desert between Santa and Chao. It did not serve as a defensive wall; rather, in light of the complex road-settlement network of Santa-Chao as well as the overall complexity of the Black-White-Red state, it probably served as a corvée labor project that divided different ethnic groups in the only period when population was *not* limited to each valley oasis, but ran almost continuously across the intervening desert.

9. The demographic decline of the late periods is a real phenomenon, and is probably due in large part to the continuing processes of impaction and agricultural intensification throughout the North Coast area as well as to the specific meddling of tribute/food-hungry multivalley states, in creating a maladaptive focus on overirrigation and overproduction especially in the Lower Valley sector.

10. The final period of multivalley state formation is Late Tambo Real, which is characterized, first, by the longer-term Chimú occupation of the Lower Santa region and, later, by the ephemeral short-term presence of the Inca state. Yet in spite of an apparent continuation of Chimu control right up to the time of Inca conquest, the people of Santa—with a 3000 year-long adaptation based on effective defense and extreme ferocity in the face of outside attempts at encroachment—seem to have retained the ability at the regional level to organize and implement successfully a (nearly) effective defensive strategy against the Inca army.

In the end, then, the great dual achievements of the prehispanic people of Santa—in effectively adapting to the subsistence potential of the region and in constructing a spectacular sequence of sites and other remains—were themselves only slightly less ephemeral than the Inca presence. Whether this would have been so had the regional system somehow been able to evolve without outside intervention is a moot point, for as we have seen much of the cultural brilliance that briefly touched valleys like Santa was the result not only of intensive interregional interaction (and conquest) but of the pressures created by covetous neighbors attempting to solve their own adaptive problems. The final blow to the system was, of course, the Spanish conquest—itself carried out as an integral part of the forces of onrushing worldwide sociocultural development in the age of exploration—which led to a period of drastic, indeed devastating, demographic decline. But, even in the absence of this final insult to the system, it may be speculated that the whole process of prehispanic societal evolution in this part of the Central Andes was leading inevitably to a more or less permanent crash to lower levels of valley-specific agricultural carrying capacity. The theoretical result of such a process would therefore have been less spectacular, but more enduring, lower levels of sociocultural complexity.

Bibliography

Adams, Robert McC.
  1962 Agriculture and Urban Life in Early Southwestern Iran. *Science* 136:109–122.
  1965 *Land Behind Baghdad: A History of Settlement on the Diyala Plains.* Chicago: University of Chicago Press.
  1966 *The Evolution of Urban Society.* Chicago: Aldine Press.
  1970 The Study of Ancient Mesopotamian Settlement Patterns and the Problem of Urban Origins. *Sumer* 25:111–124.
  1981 *Heartland of Cities: Surveys of Ancient Settlement and Land Use in the Central Floodplain of the Euphrates.* Chicago: University of Chicago Press.

Adams, Robert McC., and Hans J. Nissen
  1972 *The Uruk Countryside: the Natural Setting of Urban Societies.* Chicago: University of Chicago Press.

Ashmore, Wendy, editor
  1981 *Lowland Maya Settlement Patterns.* Albuquerque: University of New Mexico Press.

Bankes, G. H. A.
  1972 Settlement Patterns in the Lower Moche Valley, North Peru, with Special Reference to the Early Horizon and Early Intermediate Periods. In *Man, Settlement, and Urbanism,* P. J. Ucko, R. Tringham, and G. W. Dimbleby, editors, pp. 903–908. Cambridge: Schenkman Publishing Co.

Bawden, Garth
  1982 Galindo: a Study in Cultural Transition During the Middle Horizon. In *Chan Chan: Andean Desert City,* M. E. Moseley and K. C. Day, editors, pp. 285–320. Albuquerque: University of New Mexico Press.

Bennett, Wendell C.
  1939 *Archaeology of the North Coast of Peru: an Account of Exploration and Excavation in Virú and Lambayeque Valleys.* American Museum of Natural History, Anthropological Papers 37(1):17–153. New York.
  1944 *The North Highlands of Peru: Excavations in the Callejón de Huaylas and at Chavín de Huántar.* American Museum of Natural History, Anthropological Papers 39(1): 5–114. New York.
  1950 *The Gallinazo Group, Virú Valley, Peru.* Yale University Publications in Anthropology 43:5–127. New Haven: Yale University Press.

Bennyhoff, J. A.
  1952 The Viru Valley Sequence: a Critical Review. *American Antiquity* 17:231–249.

Benson, Elizabeth P.
  1972 *The Mochica: a Culture of Peru.* New York: Praeger Publishers.

Bird, Junius B.
  1948 Preceramic Cultures in Chicama and Virú. In *A Reappraisal of Peruvian Archaeology,* W. C. Bennett, editor, pp. 21–28. Memoirs of the Society for American Archaeology No. 4.

Bird, Robert McK.
  1978 Archaeological Maize from Peru. *Maize Genetics Cooperation News Letter* 52:90–92.

Bird, Robert McK., and Junius B. Bird
  1980 Gallinazo Maize from the Chicama Valley, Peru. *American Antiquity* 45:325–332.

Blanton, Richard E.
  1972 *Prehispanic Settlement Patterns of the Ixtapalapa Region, Mexico.* Occasional Papers in Anthropology No. 6, Department of Anthropology, The Pennsylvania State University. University Park.

Blanton, Richard E., S. Kowalewski, G. Feinman, and J. Appel
  1982 *Monte Albán's Hinterland, Part I: the Prehistoric Settlement Patterns of the Central and Southern Parts of the Valley of Oaxaca, Mexico.* Memoirs of the Museum of Anthropology, University of Michigan No. 15. Ann Arbor.

Bonavía, Duccio
  1974 *Ricchata quellccani: pinturas murales prehispánicas.* Lima: Editorial Ausonia.

Brennan, Curtiss T.
1980 Cerro Arena: Early Cultural Complexity and Nucleation in North Coastal Peru. *Journal of Field Archaeology* 7:1–22.

Bullard, W. R., Jr.
1960 Maya Settlement Patterns in Northeast Petén, Guatemala. *American Antiquity* 25:355–372.

Butzer, Karl W.
1976 *Early Hydraulic Civilizations in Egypt: a Study in Cultural Ecology.* Chicago: University of Chicago Press.

Cárdenas Martín, Mercedes
1977 *Informe preliminar del trabajo de campo en el Valle Santa.* Mimeographed Ms. Instituto Riva-Agüero, Pontífica Universidad Católica del Perú. Lima.
1978 *Columna cronológica del Valle de Santa: sitios arqueológicos del valle bajo y medio.* Instituto Riva-Agüero, Seminario de Arqueología. Lima.

Carneiro, Robert L.
1961 Slash and Burn Among the Kuikuru and its Implications for Cultural Development in the Amazon Basin. In *The Evolution of Horticultural Systems in Native South America: Causes and Consequences,* J. Wilbert, editor, pp. 47–68. Caracas: Sociedad de Ciencias Naturales La Salle.
1970 A Theory of the Origin of the State. *Science* 169: 733–738.

Ching, Frank
1975 *Architectural Graphics.* New York: Van Nostrand Reinhold Co.

Cieza de León, Pedro de
1959 *The Incas of Pedro de Cieza de León* [1553]. Victor W. von Hagen, editor. Norman: University of Oklahama Press.

Clapham, W. B., Jr.
1973 *Natural Ecosystems.* New York: The Macmillan Co.

Clothier, William J.
1943 Recuay Pottery in the Lower Santa Valley. *Revista del Museo Nacional* 12:239–242. Lima.

Cobo, Bernabé
1964 *Historia del nuevo mundo* [1653]. 2 vols. Madrid: Ediciones Atlas.

Cohen, Mark N.
1971 *Population Growth, Subsistence, and Settlement in the Ancon-Chillon Region of the Central Coast of Peru.* Ph.D. dissertation, Department of Anthropology, Columbia University. Ann Arbor: University Microfilms.
1977 *The Food Crisis in Prehistory: Overpopulation and the Origins of Agriculture.* New Haven: Yale University Press.

Collier, Donald
1955 *Cultural Chronology and Change as Reflected in the Ceramics of the Virú Valley, Peru.* Fieldiana: Anthropology, Vol. 43. Chicago Natural History Museum.
1962 Archaeological Investigations in the Casma Valley, Peru. *Akten des 34. Internationalen Amerikanistenkongresses,* pp. 411–417. Vienna.

Conrad, Geoffrey W.
1977 Chiquitoy Viejo: an Inca Administrative Center in the Chicama Valley, Peru. *Journal of Field Archaeology* 4: 1–18.
1978 Models of Compromise in Settlement Pattern Studies: an Example from Coastal Peru. *World Archaeology* 9:281–298.

Córdova, Pedro de
1965 Descripción de la tierra del repartimiento de San Francisco de Atunrucana y Laramati, encomendado en don Pedro de Córdova, jurisdición de la Ciudad de Guamanga [1586]. In *Relaciones geográficas de Indias—Perú,* M. Jiménez de la Espada, editor, Vol. 1, pp. 226–248. Madrid: Ediciones Atlas.

Crumley, Carole L.
1976 Toward a Locational Definition of State Systems of Settlement. *American Anthropologist* 78:59–73.

D'Altroy, Terence N., and Timothy K. Earle
1985 Staple Finance, Wealth Finance, and Storage in the Inka Political Economy. *Current Anthropology* 26: 187–206.

Davis, Raymond E., Francis S. Foote, and Joe W. Kelly
1966 *Surveying: Theory and Practice.* New York: McGraw-Hill Book Co.

Dillehey, Tom
1976 *Competition and Cooperation in a Prehispanic Multi-Ethnic System in the Central Andes.* Ph.D. dissertation, Department of Anthropology, University of Texas at Austin. Ann Arbor: University Microfilms.

Divale, William T., and Marvin Harris
1976 Population, Warfare, and the Male Supremacist Complex. *American Anthropologist* 78:521–538.

Donnan, Christopher B.
1973 *Moche Occupation of the Santa Valley, Peru.* University of California Publications in Anthropology, Vol. 8. Berkeley: University of California Press.
1976 *Moche Art and Iconography.* Los Angeles: UCLA Latin American Center.
1978 *Moche Art of Peru.* Los Angeles: Museum of Cultural History.

Donnan, Christopher B., and Carol J. Mackey
1978 *Ancient Burial Patterns of the Moche Valley, Peru.* Austin: University of Texas Press.

Doran, J. E., and F. R. Hodson
1975 *Mathematics and Computers in Archaeology.* Cambridge: Harvard University Press.

Earle, Timothy K.
1972 Lurin Valley, Peru: Early Intermediate Period Settlement Development. *American Antiquity* 37:467–477.

Earle, Timothy K., T. N. D'Altroy, C. J. LeBlanc, C. A. Hastorf, and T. Y. LeVine
1980 Changing Settlement Patterns in the Upper Mantaro Valley, Peru. *Journal of New World Archaeology* 4:1–49.

Fagan, Brian M.
1986 *People of the Earth.* 5th edition. Boston: Little, Brown and Company.

FAO (Food and Agricultural Organization of the United Nations)
1954 Food Composition Tables: Minerals and Vitamins. *FAO Nutritional Studies,* No. 11. Rome.
1957a Calorie Requirements. Report of the Second Committee on Calorie Requirements. *FAO Nutritional Studies,* No. 15.
1957b Protein Requirements. Report of the FAO Committee on Protein Requirements. *FAO Nutritional Studies,* No. 16.

360

Flannery, Kent V.
1972 The Cultural Evolution of Civilizations. *Annual Review of Ecology and Systematics* 3:399–426.

Ford, James A.
1949 *Cultural Dating of Prehistoric Sites in Virú Valley, Peru.* American Museum of Natural History, Anthropological Papers 43(1):31–89. New York.
1952 Reply to "The Viru Valley Sequence: A Critical Review". *American Antiquity* 17:250.

Ford, James A., and Gordon R. Willey
1949 *Virú Valley: Background and Problems.* American Museum of Natural History, Anthropological Papers 43(1):13–26. New York.

Gasparini, Graziano, and Luise Margolies
1980 *Inca Architecture.* Bloomington: Indiana University Press.

Gillin, John
1947 *Moche, a Peruvian Coastal Community.* Smithsonian Institution, Institute of Social Anthropology Publication No. 3. Washington, D. C.

Grieder, Terence
1978 *The Art and Archaeology of Pashash.* Austin: University of Texas Press.

Grobman, Alexander, Wilfredo Salhuana, and Ricardo Sevilla with Paul C. Mangelsdorf
1961 *Races of Maize in Peru: their Origins, Evolution and Classification.* National Academy of Science, National Research Council Publication No. 915. Washington, D. C.

Haggett, Peter, Andrew D. Cliff, and Allan Frey
1977 *Locational Models.* New York: John Wiley and Sons.

Harris, Marvin
1980 *Cultural Materialism: the Struggle for a Science of Culture.* New York: Vintage Books.

Hastings, C. M., and M. E. Moseley
1975 The Adobes of Huaca del Sol and Huaca de la Luna. *American Antiquity* 40:196–203.

Haviland, William A.
1972 Family Size, Prehistoric Population Estimates, and the Ancient Maya. *American Antiquity* 37:135–139.

Heiser, Charles B., Jr.
1973 *Seed to Civilization: the Story of Man's Food.* San Francisco: W. H. Freeman and Co.

Hodder, Ian, and Clive Orton
1976 *Spatial Analysis in Archaeology.* London: Cambridge University Press.

Holmberg, Allan R.
1950 Viru: Remnant of an Exalted People. In *Patterns for Modern Living,* pp. 367–416. Chicago: The Delphian Society.
1952 The Wells that Failed: an Attempt to Establish a Stable Water Supply in the Viru Valley, Peru. In *Human Problems in Technological Change: a Casebook,* E. H. Spicer, editor, pp. 113–125. New York: Russell Sage Foundation.

Horkheimer, Hans
1965 *Identificación y bibliografía de importantes sitios prehispánicos del Perú (la costa: Valles de Tumbes a Chillón).* Ar-
queológicas, Vol. 8. Lima: Museo Nacional de Antropología y Arqueología.

Isbell, William H.
1977 *The Rural Foundation for Urbanism: Economic and Stylistic Interaction Between Rural and Urban Communities in Eighth-Century Peru.* Urbana: University of Illinois Press.

Isbell, William H., and Katharina J. Schreiber
1978 Was Huari a State? *American Antiquity* 43:372–389.

Johnson, Gregory A.
1973 *Local Exchange and Early State Development in Southwestern Iran.* University of Michigan Museum of Anthropology, Anthropological Papers No. 51. Ann Arbor.

Kauffmann Doig, Federico
1978 *Manual de arqueología peruana.* Lima: Iberia.

Keatinge, Richard W.
1974 Chimu Rural Administrative Centres in the Moche Valley, Peru. *World Archaeology* 6:66–82.
1982 The Chimu Empire in a Regional Perspective: Cultural Antecedents and Continuities. In *Chan Chan: Andean Desert City,* M. E. Moseley and K. C. Day, editors, pp. 197–224. Albuquerque: University of New Mexico Press.

Kirkby, Anne V. T.
1973 *The Use of Land and Water Resources in the Past and Present Valley of Oaxaca, Mexico.* Prehistory and Human Ecology of the Valley of Oaxaca, Vol. 1, K. V. Flannery, editor. Memoirs of the Museum of Anthropology, University of Michigan No. 5. Ann Arbor.

Kosok, Paul
1965 *Life, Land and Water in Ancient Peru.* New York: Long Island University Press.

Kroeber, A. L.
1925a *The Uhle Pottery Collections from Moche.* University of California Publications in American Archaeology and Ethnology 21(5):191–234. Berkeley.
1925b *The Uhle Pottery Collections from Supe.* University of California Publications in American Archaeology and Ethnology 21(6):235–264. Berkeley.
1926 *Archaeological Explorations in Peru, Part 1: Ancient Pottery from Trujillo.* Field Museum of Natural History, Anthropology Memoirs, Vol. 2, No. 1. Chicago.
1930 *Archaeological Explorations in Peru, Part 2: the Northern Coast.* Field Museum of Natural History, Anthropology Memoirs, Vol. 2, No. 2. Chicago.
1944 *Peruvian Archaeology in 1942.* Viking Fund Publications in Anthropology No. 4. New York.

Kus, James
1972 *Selected Aspects of Irrigated Agriculture in the Chimu Heartland, Peru.* Ph.D. dissertation, Department of Anthropology, UCLA. Ann Arbor: University Microfilms.

Kutscher, Gerdt
1954 *Cerámica del Perú septentrional.* Berlin: Casa Editora Gebr. Mann.

Lanning, Edward P.
1967 *Peru Before the Incas.* Englewood Cliffs: Prentice-Hall.

Larco Hoyle, Rafael
1944 *Cultura salinar: síntesis monográfica.* Buenos Aires: Sociedad Geográfica Americana.

1945 *La cultura virú.* Buenos Aires: Sociedad Geográfica Americana.

1948 *Cronología arqueolóogica del norte del Perú.* Buenos Aires: Sociedad Geográfica Americana.

1963a A Culture Sequence for the North Coast of Peru. In *Handbook of South American Indians,* J. H. Steward, editor, Vol. 2, pp. 149–175. New York: Cooper Square Publishers.

1963b *La cultura santa.* Lima: Lit. Valverde.

Lumbreras, Luis G.
1974 *The Peoples and Cultures of Ancient Peru.* Translated from the Spanish by Betty J. Meggers. Washington: Smithsonian Institution Press.

Lynch, Thomas F.
1980 *Guitarrero Cave: Early Man in the Andes.* New York: Academic Press.

Mackey, Carol J.
1982 The Middle Horizon as Viewed from the Moche Valley. In *Chan Chan: Andean Desert City,* M. E. Moseley and K. C. Day, editors, pp. 321–331. Albuquerque: University of New Mexico Press.

McNeill, William H.
1977 *Plagues and Peoples.* New York: Anchor Books.

Menzel, Dorothy
1959 The Inca Occupation of the South Coast of Peru. *Southwestern Journal of Anthropology* 15:125–142.

1964 Style and Time in the Middle Horizon. *Ñawpa Pacha* 2:1–106.

1977 *The Archaeology of Ancient Peru and the Work of Max Uhle.* Berkeley: R. H. Lowie Museum of Anthropology.

Miller, James G.
1978 *Living Systems.* New York: McGraw-Hill Book Co.

Morris, Craig
1972 State Settlements in Tawantinsuyu: a Strategy of Compulsory Urbanism. In *Contemporary Archaeology: a Guide to Theory and Contributions,* M. P. Leone, editor, pp. 393–401. Carbondale: Southern Illinois University Press.

1976 Master Design of the Inca. *Natural History* 85:58–67.

Morris, Craig, and Donald E. Thompson
1985 *Huánuco Pampa: an Inca City and its Hinterland.* New York: Thames and Hudson.

Moseley, Michael E.
1975a Chan Chan: Andean Alternative of the Preindustrial City. *Science* 187:219–225.

1975b Prehistoric Principles of Labor Organization in the Moche Valley, Peru. *American Antiquity* 40:191–196.

1975c *The Maritime Foundations of Andean Civilization.* Menlo Park, California: Cummings Publishing Co.

1982 Introduction: Human Exploitation and Organization on the North Andean Coast. In *Chan Chan: Andean Desert City,* M. E. Moseley and K. C. Day, editors, pp. 1–24. Albuquerque: University of New Mexico Press.

1983 The Good Old Days *Were* Better: Agrarian Collapse and Tectonics. *American Anthropologist* 85:773–799.

Moseley, Michael E., and Kent C. Day, editors
1982 *Chan Chan: Andean Desert City.* Albuquerque: University of New Mexico Press.

Moseley, Michael E., and Carol J. Mackey
1972 Peruvian Settlement Pattern Studies and Small Site Methodology. *American Antiquity* 37:67–81.

1974 *Twenty-Four Architectural Plans of Chan Chan, Peru: Struc-*

ture and Form at the Capital of Chimor. Cambridge: Peabody Museum Press.

Murphy, Robert C.
1926 Oceanic and Climatic Phenomena Along the West Coast of South America During 1925. *Geographical Review* 16:26–54.

Murra, John V.
1975 El tráfico de mullu en la costa del Pacífico. In *Formaciones económicas y políticas del mundo andino,* J. V. Murra, pp. 255–267. Lima: Instituto de Estudios Peruanos.

Naroll, Raoul
1962 Floor Area and Settlement Population. *American Antiquity* 27:587–588.

Odum, Eugene P.
1971 *Fundamentals of Ecology.* 3rd edition. Philadelphia: W. B. Saunders Co.

ONERN (Oficina Nacional de Evaluación de Recursos Naturales)
1972a *Inventario, evaluación y uso racional de los recursos naturales de la costa: cuencas de los Ríos Casma, Culebras y Huarmey.* 3 vols. Lima: ONERN.

1972b *Inventario, evaluación y uso racional de los recursos naturales de la costa: cuencas de los Ríos Santa, Lacramarca y Nepeña.* 3 vols. Lima: ONERN.

1973 *Inventario, evaluación y uso racional de los recursos naturales de la costa: cuencas de los Ríos Virú y Chao.* 2 vols. Lima: ONERN.

Osborn, Alan J.
1977 Strandloopers, Mermaids, and Other Fairy Tales: Ecological Determinants of Marine Resource Utilization—the Peruvian Case. In *For Theory Building in Archaeology,* L. R. Binford, editor, pp. 157–205. New York: Academic Press.

Parsons, Mary H.
1970 Preceramic Subsistence on the Peruvian Coast. *American Antiquity* 35:292–304.

Parsons, Jeffrey R.
1968 Teotihuacan, Mexico, and its Impact on Regional Demography. *Science* 162:872–877.

1971 *Prehistoric Settlement Patterns in the Texcoco Region, Mexico.* Memoirs of the Museum of Anthropology, University of Michigan No. 3. Ann Arbor.

1972 Archaeological Settlement Patterns. *Annual Review of Anthropology* 1:127–150.

1974 The Development of a Prehistoric Complex Society: a Regional Perspective from the Valley of Mexico. *Journal of Field Archaeology* 1:81–108.

Parsons, Jeffrey R., E. Brumfiel, M. H. Parsons, and D. J. Wilson
1982 *Prehispanic Settlement Patterns in the Southern Valley of Mexico: the Chalco-Xochimilco Region.* Memoirs of the Museum of Anthropology, University of Michigan No. 14. Ann Arbor.

Parsons, Jeffrey R., and Ramiro Matos Mendieta
1978 Asentamientos prehispánicos en el Mantaro, Perú: informe preliminar. In *III Congreso Peruano: el Hombre y la Cultura Andina, actas y trabajos,* R. Matos Mendieta, editor, Vol. 2, pp. 539–555. Lima: Improffset.

Patterson, Thomas C.
1971 Central Peru: its Population and Economy. *Archaeology* 24:316–321.

Patterson, Thomas C., and Edward P. Lanning
1964   Changing Settlement Patterns on the Central Peruvian Coast. *Ñawpa Pacha* 2:113–123.

Paulsen, Allison C.
1974   The Thorny Oyster and the Voice of God: Spondylus and Strombus in Andean Prehistory. *American Antiquity* 39: 597–607.

Poma de Ayala, Felipe Huaman
1978   *Letter to a King: a Peruvian Chief's Account of Life Under the Incas and Under Spanish Rule* [ca. 1567–1615]. Translated from the Spanish by Christopher Dilke. New York: E. P. Dutton.

Pozorski, Shelia G.
1979   Prehistoric Diet and Subsistence of the Moche Valley, Peru. *World Archaeology* 11:163–184.

Price, Barbara J.
1971   Prehispanic Irrigation Agriculture in Nuclear America. *Latin American Research Review* 6:3–60.

Proulx, Donald A.
1968   *An Archaeological Survey of the Nepeña Valley, Peru.* Research Report No. 2, Department of Anthropology, University of Massachusetts. Amherst.
1973   *Archaeological Investigations in the Nepeña Valley, Peru.* Research Report No. 13, Department of Anthropology, University of Massachusetts. Amherst.
1985   *An Analysis of the Early Cultural Sequence in the Nepeña Valley, Peru.* Research Report No. 25, Department of Anthropology, University of Massachusetts. Amherst.

Quilter, J., and T. Stocker
1983   Subsistence Economies and the Origins of Andean Complex Societies. *American Anthropologist* 85: 545–562.

Rappaport, Roy A.
1979   *Ecology, Meaning, and Religion.* Richmond, California: North Atlantic Books.

Ravines, Rogger
1978   Recursos naturales de los Andes. In *Tecnología Andina*, R. Ravines, editor, pp. 1–90. Lima: Instituto de Estudios Peruanos.

Raymond, Scott J.
1981   The Maritime Foundations of Andean Civilization: a Reconsideration of the Evidence. *American Antiquity* 46:806–821.

Reparaz, G. de
1956   La zone aride du Pérou. *Geografiska Annaler* 40:1–62.

Robinson, David A.
1971   *Peru in 4 Dimensions.* Detroit: Blaine-Ethridge Books.

Roosevelt, Cornelius Van S.
1935   Ancient Civilizations of the Santa Valley and Chavín. *Geographical Review* 25:21–42.

Rowe, John H.
1948   The Kingdom of Chimor. *Acta Americana* 6:26–59. Mexico, D. F.
1960   Cultural Unity and Diversification in Peruvian Archaeology. In *Men and Cultures, Selected Papers of the Fifth International Congress of Anthropological and Ethnological Sciences*, A. F. Wallace, editor, pp. 627–631. Philadelphia: University of Pennsylvania Press.
1961   Stratigraphy and Seriation. *American Antiquity* 26: 324–330.

1962   *Chavín Art: an Inquiry into its Form and Meaning.* New York: The Museum of Primitive Art.
1963a   Inca Culture at the Time of the Spanish Conquest. In *Handbook of South American Indians*, J. H. Steward, editor, Vol. 2, pp. 183–330. New York: Cooper Square Publishers.
1963b   Urban Settlements in Ancient Peru. *Ñawpa Pacha* 1:1–27.

Sanders, William T.
1960   *Prehispanic Ceramics and Settlement Patterns in Quintana Roo, Mexico.* Carnegie Institute of Washington, Publication 606, pp. 155–264.
1965   *The Cultural Ecology of the Teotihuacan Valley.* Department of Sociology and Anthropology, The Pennsylvania State University. University Park.

Sanders, William T., and Barbara J. Price
1968   *Mesoamerica: the Evolution of a Civilization.* New York: Random House.

Sanders, William T., Jeffrey R. Parsons, and Robert S. Santley
1979   *The Basin of Mexico: Ecological Processes in the Evolution of a Civilization.* New York: Academic Press.

Savoy, Gene
1970   *Antisuyo.* New York: Simon and Schuster.

Sawyer, Alan R.
1968   *Mastercraftsmen of Ancient Peru.* New York: The Solomon R. Guggenheim Foundation.

Service, Elman R.
1975   *Origins of the State and Civilization: the Process of Cultural Evolution.* New York: W. W. Norton.

Shelton, John S.
1966   *Geology Illustrated.* San Francisco: W. H. Freeman and Co.

Shimada, Izumi
1978   Economy of a Prehistoric Urban Context: Commodity and Labor Flow at Moche V Pampa Grande, Peru. *American Antiquity* 43:569–592.

Shimada, Melody, and Izumi Shimada
1985   Prehistoric Llama Breeding and Herding on the North Coast of Peru. *American Antiquity* 50:3–26.

Shippee, Robert
1932   The "Great Wall of Peru" and Other Aerial Photographic Studies by the Shippee-Johnson Peruvian Expedition. *The Geographical Review* 22:1–29.
1933   Air Adventures in Peru. *National Geographic* 63:81–120.

Squier, E. George
1877   *Peru: Incidents of Travel and Exploration in the Land of the Incas.* New York: Harper and Row.

Strong, William D., and Clifford Evans, Jr.
1952   *Cultural Stratigraphy in the Virú Valley, Northern Peru: the Formative and Florescent Epochs.* New York: Columbia University Press.

Tello, Julio C.
1956   *Arqueología del Valle de Casma.* Lima: Editorial San Marcos.

Thompson, Donald E.
1962a   Formative Period Architecture in the Casma Valley, Peru. *XXXV Congreso Internacional de Americanistas, actas y memorias*, Vol. 1, pp. 205–212. Mexico, D. F.
1962b   The Problem of Dating Certain Stone-Faced, Stepped

Pyramids on the North Coast of Peru. *Southwestern Journal of Anthropology* 18:291–301.

1964   Postclassic Innovations in Architecture and Settlement Patterns in the Casma Valley, Peru. *Southwestern Journal of Anthropology* 20:91–105.

Tolstoy, P., and S. K. Fish
1975   Surface and Subsurface Evidence for Community Size at Coapexco, Mexico. *Journal of Field Archaeology* 2:97–104.

Topic, Theresa Lange
1982   The Early Intermediate Period and its Legacy. In *Chan Chan: Andean Desert City*, M. E. Moseley and K. C. Day, editors, pp. 255–284. Albuquerque: University of New Mexico Press.

Towle, Margaret A.
1952   Description and Identification of the Virú Plant Remains. In *Cultural Stratigraphy in the Virú Valley, Northern Peru: the Formative and Florescent Epochs*, W. D. Strong and C. Evans, Jr., pp. 352–356. New York: Columbia University Press.
1961   *The Ethnobotany of Pre-Columbian Peru.* New York: Wenner-Gren Foundation for Anthropological Research.

Vásquez de Espinosa, Antonio
1969   *Compendio y descripción de las Indias Occidentales* [1630]. Madrid: Ediciones Atlas.

von Hagen, Victor W.
1955   *Highway of the Sun.* Boston: Little, Brown and Co.
1976   *The Royal Road of the Incas.* London: Gordon Cremonesi.

Wallace, Dwight T.
1971   *Sitios arqueológicos del Perú (segunda entrega): Valles de Chincha y Pisco.* Lima: Museo Nacional de Antropología y Arqueología.

Wenke, Robert J.
1984   *Patterns in Prehistory: Humankind's First Three Million Years.* New York: Oxford University Press.

Willey, Gordon R.
1953   *Prehistoric Settlement Patterns in the Virú Valley, Peru.*

Smithsonian Institution, Bureau of American Ethnology Bulletin No. 155. Washington, D. C.

Willey, Gordon R., W. R. Bullard, Jr., J. B. Glass, and J. C. Gifford
1965   *Prehistoric Maya Settlements in the Belize Valley.* Papers of the Peabody Museum No. 54. Cambridge: Harvard University Press.

Wilson, David J.
1981   Of Maize and Men: a Critique of the Maritime Hypothesis of State Origins on the Coast of Peru. *American Anthropologist* 83:93–120.
1983   The Origins and Development of Complex Prehispanic Society in the Lower Santa Valley, Peru: Implications for Theories of State Origins. *Journal of Anthropological Archaeology* 2:209–276.
1985   *Prehispanic Settlement Patterns in the Lower Santa Valley, North Coast of Peru: a Regional Perspective on the Origins and Development of Complex Society.* Ph. D. dissertation, Department of Anthropology, University of Michigan. Ann Arbor: University Microfilms.
1987   Reconstructing Patterns of Early Warfare in the Lower Santa Valley: New Data on the Role of Conflict in the Origins of Complex North-Coast Society. In *The Origins and Development of the Andean State*, J. Haas, S. Pozorski, and T. Pozorski, editors, pp. 56–69. New York: Cambridge University Press.

Wright, Henry T.
1978   Toward an Explanation of the Origin of the State. In *Origins of the State: the Anthropology of Political Evolution*, R. Cohen and E. R. Service, editors, pp. 49–68. Philadelphia: Institute for the Study of Human Issues.

Wright, Henry T., and Gregory A. Johnson
1975   Population, Exchange, and Early State Formation in Southwestern Iran. *American Anthropologist* 77:267–289.

Zegarra, Jorge M.
1978   Irrigación y técnicas de riego en el Perú precolombino. In *Tecnología andina*, R. Ravines, editor, pp. 107–116. Lima: Instituto de Estudios Peruanos.

Artifact Descriptions

LAS SALINAS PERIOD

Las Salinas Period Lithics (Fig. 189)

A limited amount of lithic materials was collected during the
course of the survey of the 15 preceramic sites located along the
ancient Las Salinas shoreline. Although, in general, lithics were among
the consistently present cultural items noted on the surface of these
sites, only two sites had material present in sufficient quantities to
warrant making small, representative collections. Selected stone
artifacts from the two sites are illustrated in Fig. 189.

The material from Coll. 364 (SVP-SAL-23) consists primarily of
smaller tools in the form of thin flakes with a single working edge, as
well as thicker, roughly flaked discoidal scrapers. The material from
Coll. 365 (SVP-SAL-24) includes both thinner flake tools and large stones
with flattened sides that suggest they were used as grinding implements,
perhaps in processing plant foods. No precise identification has been
made of the stone material used in making these artifacts. However, it
seems clear from examination of the flake tools that they were made from
a rough and rather grainy, non-siliceous rock that nonetheless fractured
conchoidally, thus allowing the preparation of reasonably sharp cutting
and scraping edges. Both of the grinding stones from SVP-SAL-24 were
made from cobbles whose rounded edges suggest they were brought from the
bed of the Santa River, located nearby to the east and south.

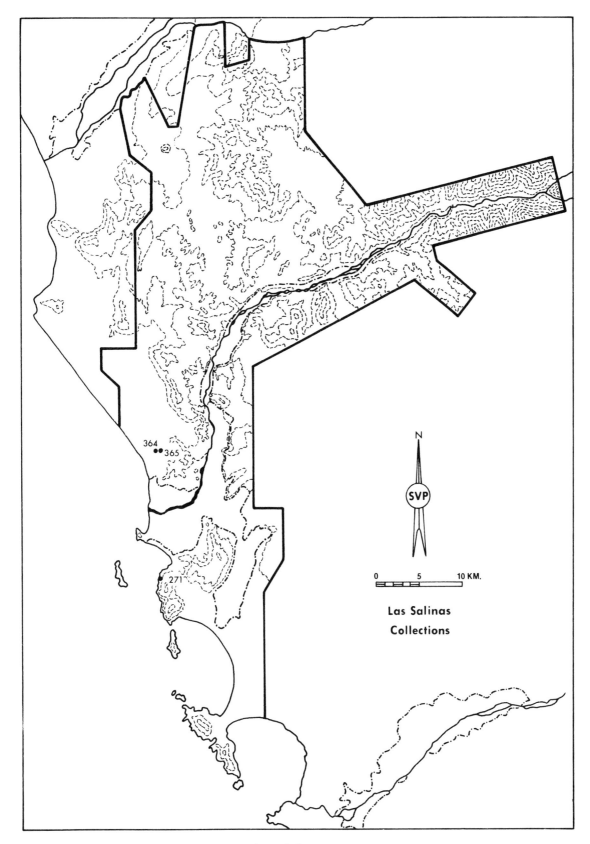

Fig. 188. Map showing collection proveniences of Las Salinas
Period (Cerro Prieto/Preceramic).

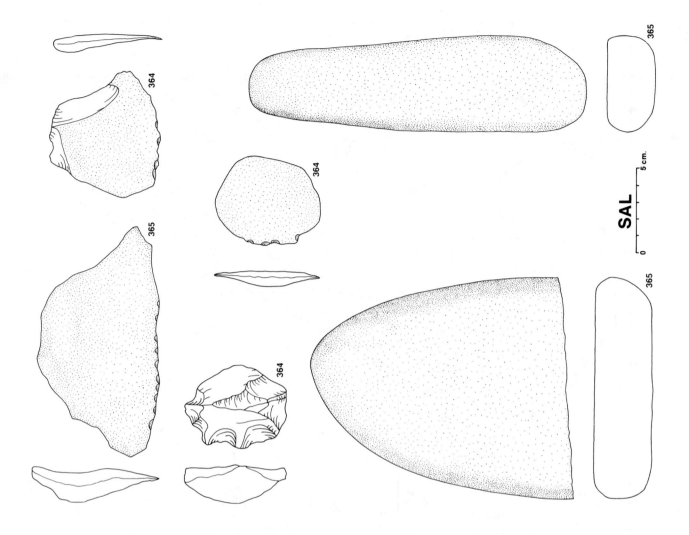

Fig. 189. Las Salinas Period lithic artifacts, including flake scrapers and probable grinding stones. (Note: collection provenience numbers are shown adjacent to the lower edge or side of each artifact in these and all other drawings in Figs. 190–280.)

CAYHUAMARCA PERIOD

Cayhuamarca Bowl 1a (Fig. 191)

Number: 102 sherds, or ca. 10% of the Cayhuamarca assemblage.

General description: Globular bowl with a slightly constricted mouth and rounded lip. A small number of sherds has either a high, rounded exterior shoulder or an interior beveled lip. Rim diameters vary from 14-20 cm, with a mean of 18.2 cm and a standard deviation of 2 cm. Wall thickness below the rim ranges between 4 mm and 5 mm, with 90% of the sample at the lower end of the range.

Paste: Temper consists of fine or medium sand, with 80% of the sherds having medium grain sand. The quantity of temper in about 70% of the sample is moderate. Quantity in the other 30% is heavy. Paste color is predominately reddish-brown (94% of the sherds), with a few examples of grayish, reduced sherds (6%).

Surface characteristics: Approximately 50% of the sherds have plain reddish-brown exteriors and interiors. Another 44% have polished red exteriors and plain red interiors, with horizontal burnishing marks showing on a small number of sherds. The remaining 6% have dull gray or black interiors and exteriors.

Distribution: This bowl type was found primarily at inhabited citadel sites, as well as at a few non-citadel habitation sites, in both the Upper and Middle Valley sectors. It is more common, however, at sites of Cayhuamarca Clusters 1 and 2 in the Upper Valley. Collection proveniences (with number of sherds in parentheses)/site numbers are:

Coll. 378(6)/CAY-4; Colls. 3(1), 4(31)/CAY-12; Coll. 99(19)/ CAY-21; Coll. 101(27)/CAY-23; Coll. 109(2)/CAY-25; Coll. 113(1)/CAY-26; Coll. 255(14)/CAY-35; Coll. 332(1)/CAY-41.

Chronological assessment: Bowl 1a is generally a good Cayhuamarca Period diagnostic. It is similar to Vinzos Bowl 1 (Fig. 196), but differs from this latter type in having a smaller rim diameter and in the nearly universal absence of exterior burnishing marks.

Inter-regional comparisons: The red-polished variant of Bowl 1a is quite similar in form and paste to Guañape Polished Red bowls reported on by Collier (1955:200-202; see especially Fig. 67A) from his excavations in Virú Valley. The undecorated variant of Bowl 1a is similar to Guañape Red Plain, Bowl Form 3, reported on by Strong and Evans (1952:253-256; see Fig. 35) from their Virú excavations.

Cayhuamarca Bowl 1b (Fig. 191)

Number: 4 sherds, or ca. .4% of the Cayhuamarca assemblage.

General description: Globular bowl with a slightly constricted mouth and slightly tapered rim, with rounded lip. Rim diameters are similar to Bowl 1a. Wall thickness below the rim ranges between 4 mm and 5 mm.

Paste: Temper consists of fine sand in moderate quantities. Paste color is reddish-brown. A thin gray core was noted on one sherd.

Surface characteristics: Color is reddish-brown on both exterior and interior surfaces. Exterior surfaces are polished and decorated with a neatly stamped, but shallow, design consisting of either concentric circles (Fig. 191) or circle-and-dot (e.g., see Fig. 194 d). The circles were probably made with hollow reeds, and the dots with a very narrow, flat-tipped instrument. As shown in Fig. 191, one of the sherds is also decorated with an incised line which runs around the exterior of the rim.

Distribution: Three sherds were found at two sites in the Upper Valley sector, including a probable ceremonial-civic site (SVP-CAY-6) and a habitation site (SVP-CAY-16). Another sherd was collected at SVP-CAY-54, a maritime site located on Bahía de Samanco. Collection proveniences (with number of sherds in parentheses)/site numbers are:

Coll. 374(1)/CAY-6; Colls. 27/28(2)/CAY-16; and a special collection (no number) at SVP-CAY-54, consisting of a Bowl 1b sherd.

Chronological assessment: This bowl type is probably an excellent Early Horizon diagnostic, but is found in too little quantity in the Lower Santa Valley to be a useful time marker.

Inter-regional comparisons: The unraised circle-and-dot Early Horizon decorative technique is much more common in valleys immediately to the south of Santa, including Nepeña (Proulx 1973:23-25) and Casma (Tello 1956, p. 44, Fig. 16). But as opposed to Santa, where it is a rare variant among a limited number of exterior decorated types, in Nepeña it is only one of at least 10 forms of exterior decoration (Donald Proulx, personal communication). And, in Casma it is only one of nearly 70 forms of exterior decoration in Early Horizon Period (cf. Tello 1956:44-46). The distribution of Early Horizon exterior decorative techniques in this area of the coast is therefore clearly a clinal one, with fewer and fewer forms as one proceeds north from Casma toward Santa. Interestingly, while a number of Early Horizon decorative techniques is present in Virú Valley (cf. Strong and Evans 1952:286-295), unraised circle-and-dot decoration is not reported for Virú. On the other hand, Santa does not share most of the decorated types reported for Virú, either.

Cayhuamarca Bowl 2 (Fig. 191)

Number: 21 sherds, or ca. 2.1% of the Cayhuamarca assemblage.

General description: Constricted mouth bowl with a high exterior corner point and vertical or outslanting walls. Rim diameters vary from 18-20 cm, with a mean of 21.6 cm and a standard deviation of 3 cm. Wall thickness below the rim ranges between 3 mm and 4 mm, with 60% of the sample at the upper end of the range and 40% at the lower end.

Paste: Temper consists of fine or medium sand, with 94% of the sherds having medium grain sand. The quantity of temper in about 60% of the sample is moderate. Quantity in the other 40% is heavy. Paste color is reddish-brown.

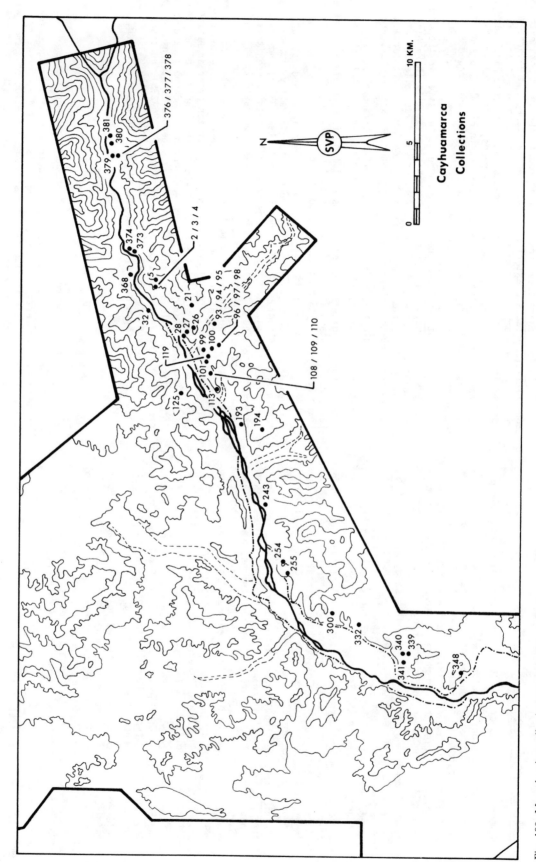

Fig. 190. Map showing collection proveniences of Cayhuamarca Period (Guañape/Early Horizon).

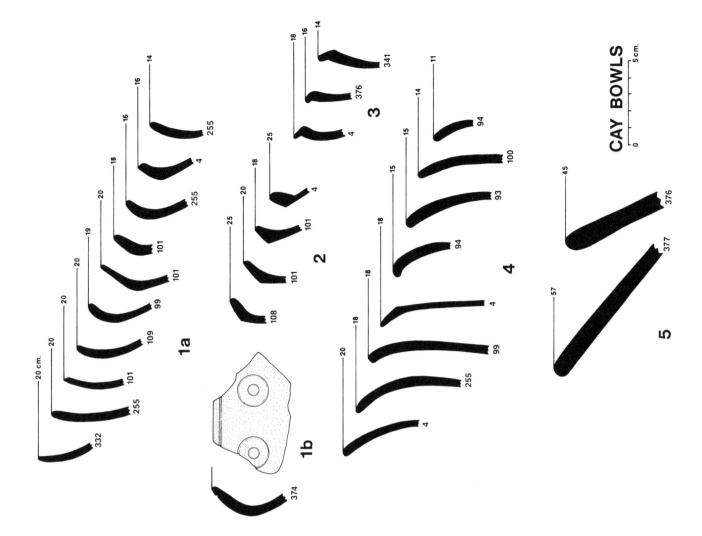

CAY BOWLS

0 ___ 5 cm.

Fig. 191. Cayhuamarca Period ceramics: Bowls 1a, 1b, 2, 3, 4, and 5.

371

Surface characteristics: Approximately 60% of the sherds have plain reddish-brown exteriors and interiors. The remaining 40% have plain red polished red exteriors and plain red interiors.

Distribution: This bowl type was found at habitation sites directly associated with citadel structures, primarily in Cayhuamarca Cluster 2 in the Upper Valley sector. Collection proveniences (with number of sherds in parentheses)/site numbers are:

Coll. 4(9)/CAY-4; Coll. 97(1)/CAY-19; Coll. 101(9)/CAY-23; Coll. 108(1)/CAY-25; Coll. 254(1)/CAY-34.

Chronological assessment: Bowl 2 is probably a very good temporal diagnostic for the Early Horizon Period in the Lower Santa region, although in some cases it is found in a mixed context.

Inter-regional comparisons: The red polished type of exterior decoration is related to Guañape Polished Red from the Virú Valley (Collier 1955:200-202), although this specific bowl form does not appear to have a Virú counterpart. Bowls similar, if not identical, in form to Bowl 2 recently have been found at Early Horizon sites in Nepeña Valley (Donald Proulx and Richard Daggett, personal communications).

Cayhuamarca Bowl 3 (Fig. 191)

Number: 8 sherds, or ca. .8% of the Cayhuamarca assemblage.

General description: Globular bowl with a slightly constricted mouth and a narrow, everted rim with rounded lip. Rim diameters vary from 14-18 cm, with four sherds at the upper end of the range, three at the lower end, and one having a rim diameter of 16 cm. Wall thickness below the rim ranges between 4 mm and 5 mm, with 50% of the sample at the lower end of the range and 50% at the upper end.

Paste: Temper consists of medium sand in moderate quantities. Paste color is reddish-brown.

Surface characteristics: All sherds in the sample have polished red interiors and exteriors.

Distribution: This bowl type was found at three widely separated sites, stretching between the uppermost Cayhuamarca Period occupation in the Upper Valley sector and the lower part of the Middle Valley sector. Collection proveniences (with number of sherds in parentheses)/site numbers are:

Coll. 376(1)/CAY-4; Coll. 4(4)/CAY-12; Coll. 341(3)/CAY-48.

Chronological assessment: Although Vinzos Period pottery is present in all three collections in which this bowl type was found, it seems likely that the red polished surface treatment dates it to Cayhuamarca--since polished red pottery is found in single-component Cayhuamarca Period collections but not in single-component Vinzos Period ones.

Inter-regional comparisons: From his work at the nearby sierra site of Pashash, Grieder (1978, p. 64, Fig. 34 1) illustrates an Early Quinú Period bowl with everted rim that appears to be quite similar to those found during our research at Cayhuamarca Period sites in the Lower Santa region. The early phase of Quinú is equivalent to the Guañape Period of Virú Valley, and undoubtedly to the Cayhuamarca Period of Santa as well.

Cayhuamarca Bowl 4 (Fig. 191)

Number: 51 sherds, or ca. 5% of the Cayhuamarca assemblage.

General description: Open bowl with vertical walls and a slightly flared rim, with rounded lip. One sherd was noted with an exterior beveled lip and one with an everted rim. Rim diameters vary from 11-20 cm, with a mean of 17.3 cm and a standard deviation of 3.1 cm. Wall thickness below the rim ranges rather widely between 3 mm and 6 mm, with a mean of 4.2 mm and a standard deviation of .8 mm.

Paste: Temper consists uniformly of medium sand in moderate quantities. Paste color is reddish-brown.

Surface characteristics: Approximately 50% of the sherds have plain reddish-brown exteriors and interiors. Another 30% have polished red exteriors and interiors. The remaining 10% of the sample consists of bowls with either a dull red slip (3 sherds) or a polished red exterior and plain red interior (2 sherds).

Distribution: This bowl type was found primarily at inhabited citadel sites, as well as at a few non-citadel habitation sites. It is restricted in distribution to sites of Cayhuamarca Clusters 2 and 3. Collection proveniences (with number of sherds in parentheses)/site numbers are:

Coll. 368(1)/CAY-9; Colls. 2(3), 3(1), 4(18)/CAY-12; Colls. 93(1), 94(5)/CAY-17; Coll. 98(4)/CAY-19; Coll. 100(6)/CAY-20; Coll. 99(4)/CAY-21; Coll. 113(3)/CAY-26; Coll. 193(1)/CAY-30; Coll. 194(2)/CAY-31; Coll. 255(2)/CAY-35.

Chronological assessment: Bowl 4 is quite similar in form and rim diameter range to Vinzos Bowl 2 (Fig. 196). The two bowl types differ, however, in that the Cayhuamarca type includes bowls with uniformly polished exteriors (i.e., with no burnishing marks showing), while the Vinzos Bowl type includes bowls with distinct burnishing lines on the interiors. The Cayhuamarca type also has uniformly thinner walls. Nevertheless, plain reddish-brown bowls of this type date to both periods and are probably impossible to separate out in a mixed Cayhuamarca-Vinzos context.

Inter-regional comparisons: The form of this bowl type is very similar to that of the Ancón Polished Black goblet, a Virú Valley type of the Guañape Period illustrated and discussed by Collier (1955, p. 202, Form 3; see Fig. 67 H, p. 201). Three bowls from the site of Pallka, in Casma Valley, illustrated by Tello (1956, p. 41, Fig. 12 t-v) are also quite similar in form to Bowl 4.

Cayhuamarca Bowl 5 (Fig. 191)

Number: 7 sherds, or ca. .7% of the Cayhuamarca assemblage.

General description: Large bowl with straight outslanted walls and direct rim, with rounded lip. Rim diameters vary from 32-57 cm, with four sherds at the lower end of the range, two sherds at the upper end, and one sherd having a rim diameter of 45 cm. Wall thickness below the rim ranges between 8 mm and 10 mm, with all but one sherd at the lower end of the range.

Paste: Temper consists uniformly of coarse sand in heavy quantities. Paste color is reddish-brown. Two sherds with thick gray cores were noted.

Surface characteristics: One sherd has a plain reddish-brown interior and exterior. The other six have polished red interiors and exteriors.

Distribution: This bowl type was found at two habitation sites in the Upper Valley sector: SVP-CAY-4 and SVP-CAY-11, in Cayhuamarca Clusters 1 and 2, respectively. Collection proveniences (with number of sherds in parentheses)/site numbers are:

Colls. 377(2), 376(1)/CAY-4; Coll. 5(4)/CAY-11.

Chronological assessment: Bowl 5 is similar in form and paste to Vinzos Bowl 3 (Fig. 196), but can be distinguished from the latter by the absence of distinct burnishing lines. It is also similar in form to Early Suchimancillo Bowl 7 (Fig. 203), but differs in having reddish-brown paste rather than the red paste of the later period. Nevertheless, its apparently limited distribution lessens its utility as a significant time marker for the Cayhuamarca Period.

Inter-regional comparisons: Although somewhat larger in rim diameter than its Virú counterpart, this bowl type is quite similar in shape to Guañape Red Plain, Form 4, described and illustrated by Strong and Evans (1952:253; see Fig. 35, p. 254).

Cayhuamarca Bowl 6a (Fig. 192)

Number: 195 sherds, or ca. 19.2% of the Cayhuamarca assemblage.

General description: Open bowl with flat bottom and straight or slightly incurving walls that slant outward. As shown in Fig. 192, there is substantial variation in the angle of the vessel walls, which range between 10° and 30° out from the vertical. Lips are usually rounded, although a few tapered ones on thicker-walled bowls were also noted. Rim diameters vary from 15-36 cm, with a mean of 19 cm and a standard deviation of 3 cm. Wall thickness below the rim ranges widely between 3 mm and 8 mm, but 99% of the sherds in the sample range more narrowly between 3 mm and 5 mm (as is reflected in the mean wall thickness of 4.5 mm).

Paste: Temper consists of fine or medium sand, with about 65% of the sherds having medium grain sand. The quantity of temper in all sherds is moderate. Paste color is uniformly reddish-brown, with gray cores noted on only four sherds (2% of the sample).

Surface characteristics: Approximately 25% of the sherds have plain reddish-brown interior and exterior surfaces. The other 75% have polished red interiors and exteriors. In this latter group, three sherds were noted with minor incised markings and another three with minor engraved lines.

Distribution: This bowl type was found at a total of 17 habitation sites located throughout the main area of Cayhuamarca occupation in the Upper and Middle Valley sectors. Approximately 50% of the sites are associated with citadels, while the other 50% are non-citadel occupations. Collection proveniences (with number of sherds in parentheses)/site numbers are:

Coll. 381(36)/CAY-1; Coll. 380(50)/CAY-3; Colls. 377(1), 376(8)/CAY-4; Coll. 5(15)/CAY-11; Coll. 4(10)/CAY-12; Coll. 32(2)/CAY-13; Coll. 21(5)/CAY-14; Coll. 26(10)/CAY-15; Coll. 95(1)/CAY-17; Coll. 97(1)/CAY-19; Coll. 99(16)/CAY-21; Coll. 108(11)/CAY-25; Coll. 113(3)/CAY-26; Coll. 193(6)/CAY-30; Coll. 255(10)/CAY-35; Coll. 300(1)/CAY-39; Coll. 341(9)/CAY-48.

Chronological assessment: Although Bowl 6a is essentially identical in form and rim diameter range to Vinzos Bowl 4a (see Fig. 196), the analysis of single-component collections dating to each of the periods indicates that the red polished variant of Cayhuamarca is limited to the Early Horizon, while the Vinzos bowls have the burnishing lines characteristic of beginning Early Intermediate. Both periods share the plain reddish-brown variant, however, although its numbers are greatly reduced in Vinzos collections in contrast to those of the preceding Cayhuamarca Period.

Inter-regional comparisons: This bowl type is clearly related in form, size, paste, and its polished decoration to Guañape Polished Red, Form 2 (Collier 1955:200; see Fig. 67B, p. 201).

Cayhuamarca Bowl 6b (Fig. 192)

Number: 90 sherds, or ca. 8.8% of the Cayhuamarca assemblage.

General description: Open bowl with flat bottom and slightly incurving walls that slant outward, and a direct rim with rounded lip. Although Bowl 6b is essentially similar in form and paste to Bowl 6a, it exhibits much less variation in the angle of the walls--which range generally between 15° and 20° out from the vertical. Rim diameters vary from 15-24 cm, with a mean of 18.3 cm and a standard deviation of 1.5 cm. Wall thickness below the rim ranges between 4 mm and 5 mm, with about 50% of the sherds at the lower end of the range and 50% at the upper end.

Paste: Temper consists of fine or medium sand, with about 60% of the sherds having fine sand. The quantity of temper is moderate. Paste color is uniformly reddish-brown, with gray cores noted on five sherds (5.6% of the sample).

Surface characteristics: The exteriors of all vessels are decorated with crisscross, or pattern, burnishing. As the examples in

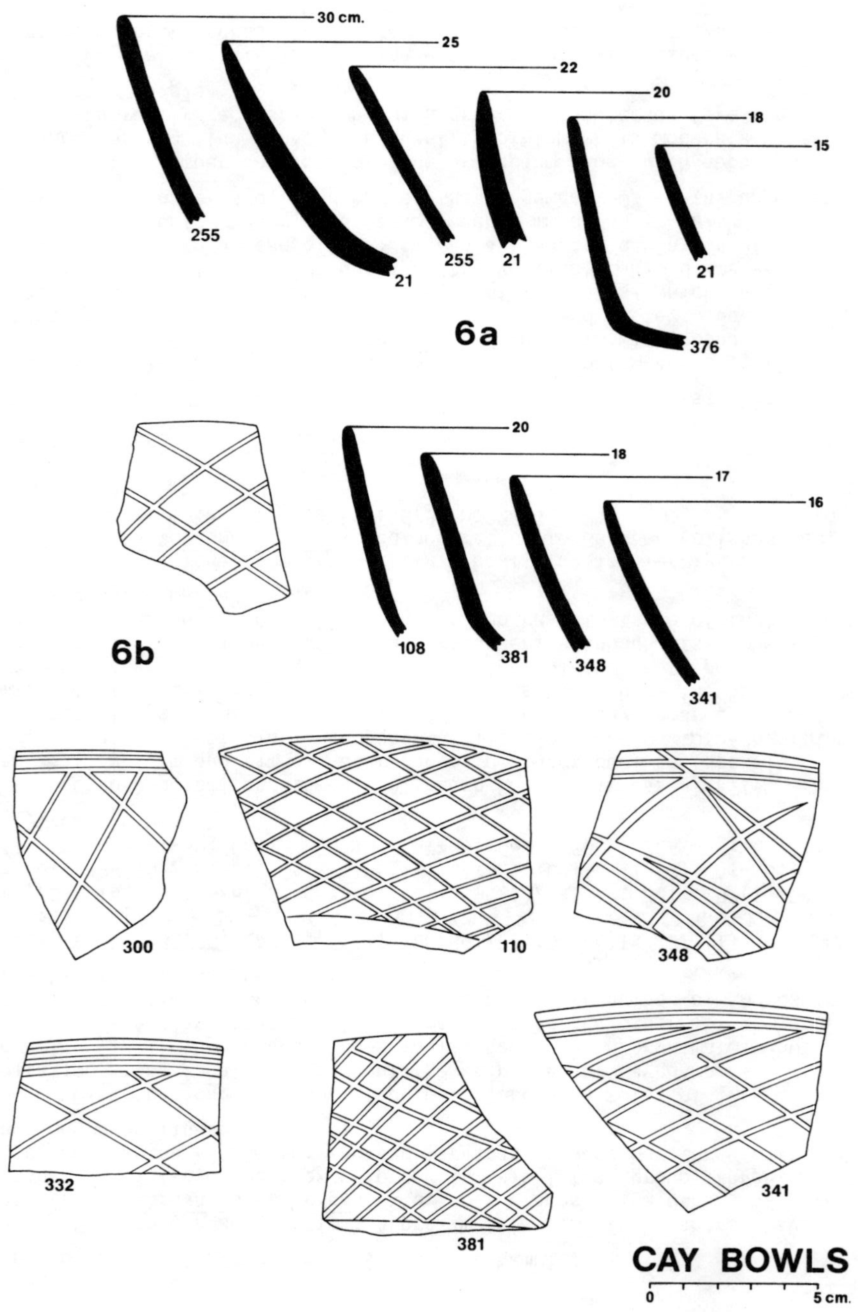

Fig. 192. Cayhuamarca Period ceramics: Bowls 6a and 6b.

Fig. 192 show, substantial variation exists in the way the pattern burnished design was executed, with some bowls exhibiting very neat, geometric crisscross designs and others having rather sloppy, or perhaps more hurriedly applied, designs. One or more burnished lines are often placed around the exterior of the rim, although sherds without these horizontal lines are also common. A few sherds were noted with interior pattern burnishing, but they constitute less than 2% of the sample.

Distribution: Bowl 6b was found widely distributed in habitation sites throughout the area of Cayhuamarca occupation. As a comparison of proveniences will show, Bowl 6a and 6b are often found in association with the same site. Approximately 75% of the sites are associated with citadels, while the other 25% are non-citadel occupations. Collection proveniences (with number of sherds in parentheses)/site numbers are:

Coll. 381(15)/CAY-1; Coll. 380(18)/CAY-3; Coll. 378(1)/CAY-4; Coll. 373(1)/CAY-7; Coll. 5(2)/CAY-11; Coll. 4(3)/CAY-12; Coll. 21(1)/CAY-14; Coll. 26(6)/CAY-15; Colls. 27/28(1)/CAY-16; Coll. 99(1)/CAY-21; Colls. 108(5), 109(2), 110(1)/CAY-25; Coll. 243(2)/CAY-33; Coll. 254(1)/CAY-34; Coll. 255(1)/CAY-35; Coll. 300(4)/CAY-39; Coll. 332(1)/CAY-41; Coll. 340(9)/CAY-44; Coll. 339(2)/CAY-47; Coll. 341(12)/CAY-48; Coll. 348(1)/CAY-53.

Chronological assessment: Although this bowl type is found in reduced numbers in single-component contexts dating to Vinzos Period, it is generally an excellent Cayhuamarca diagnostic.

Inter-regional comparisons: Pattern burnished bowls are characteristic of Early Horizon assemblages in valleys immediately to the south of Santa, including Nepeña (cf. Proulx 1973:26) and Casma (cf. Tello 1956, p. 46, Fig. 19f and g). In the adjacent sierra, pattern burnished sherds excavated by Lynch (1980:230) at Guitarrero Cave were assigned by Gary Vescelius to the contemporaneous Early Huaylas style.

Cayhuamarca Jar 1 (Fig. 193)

Number: 125 sherds, or ca. 12.3% of the Cayhuamarca assemblage.

General description: Small globular jar with constricted mouth (neckless olla). The majority of rims are direct, although a number of sherds have interior thickening at the rim. Lips on these latter sherds are uniformly squared, or beveled, while lip treatment on direct rims is more variable, and includes rounded, tapered, interior beveled, and interior thickened variants. Rim diameters vary from 10-36 cm, with a mean of 15.6 cm and a standard deviation of 4.1 cm. Wall thickness below the rim ranges between 4 mm and 8 mm, with a mean of 5.6 mm and a standard deviation of 1.1 mm.

Paste: Temper consists uniformly of medium sand in moderate quantities. Paste color is reddish-brown in approximately 75% of the sherds and brown in the remaining 25%.

Surface characteristics: Exterior and interior surfaces exhibit substantial variation in color, often ranging from reddish-brown to brown on the same vessel. Fire clouding is common.

Distribution: This jar type was found widely distributed at habitation sites throughout the main area of Cayhuamarca occupation. Approximately 50% of the sites are associated with citadels, while the other 50% are non-citadel occupations. Collection proveniences (with number of sherds in parentheses)/site numbers are:

Coll. 377(2)/CAY-4; Coll. 379(2)/CAY-5; Coll. 373(11)/CAY-7; Coll. 368(2)/CAY-9; Colls. 2(2), 4(26)/CAY-12; Coll. 32(1)/CAY-13; Coll. 21(2)/CAY-14; Coll. 26(7)/CAY-15; Coll. 93(1)/CAY-17; Coll. 100(10)/CAY-20; Coll. 99(13)/CAY-21; Coll. 101(24)/CAY-23; Coll. 255(21)/CAY-35; Coll. 348(1)/CAY-53.

Chronological assessment: Taken by themselves, neckless ollas are generally not good indicators of specific periods in the Lower Santa region. However, assuming one is dealing with an assemblage from a single site, the following aspects are useful as general time markers: (1) reddish-brown paste (indicative of a pre-Late Suchimancillo date); (2) reddish-brown jars having less overall variation in rim thickness and lip treatment (indicative of a pre-Vinzos date); and (3) a lack of exterior burnishing marks on all vessels (pre-Vinzos, or Cayhuamarca).

Inter-regional comparisons: Neckless ollas of similar form and paste are characteristic of Early Horizon assemblages in a number of areas adjacent to the Lower Santa region, including Virú Valley (cf. Collier 1955, p. 198, Fig. 66 A-D; Strong and Evans 1952, p. 254, Fig. 35), Casma Valley (cf. Collier 1960:411-413), and Pashash site (cf. Grieder 1978, p. 64, Fig. 34 d-e).

Cayhuamarca Jar 2a (Fig. 193)

Number: 26 sherds, or ca. 2.6% of the Cayhuamarca assemblage.

General description: Small ovoid jar with a short flaring rim. Rim diameters vary from 10-18 cm, with a mean of 12.6 cm and a standard deviation of 1.9 cm. Wall thickness below the rim ranges between 4 mm and 6 mm, with most sherds at the lower end of the range.

Paste: Temper consists uniformly of medium sand in moderate quantities. Paste color is reddish-brown.

Surface characteristics: Exterior and interior surfaces are uniformly reddish-brown.

Distribution: This jar type was found fairly widely distributed at habitation sites (citadel and non-citadel) in Cayhuamarca Clusters 1 and 2 in the Upper Valley sector, as well as in Cluster 3 in the upper part of the Middle Valley sector. Collection proveniences (with number of sherds in parentheses)/site numbers are:

Coll. 380(6)/CAY-3; Coll. 378(1)/CAY-4; Coll. 5(1)/CAY-11; Coll. 32(4)/CAY-13; Coll. 95(1)/CAY-17; Coll. 97(1)/CAY-19; Coll. 100(1)/CAY-20; Coll. 193(9)/CAY-30; Coll. 194(1)/CAY-31; Coll. 255(1)/CAY-35.

Chronological assessment: Jar 2a is quite similar in form to Vinzos Jar 2a (Fig. 197) and Early Suchimancillo Jar 3 (Fig. 204). However, it can be distinguished from the later two jar forms by the lack of exterior burnishing marks (in contrast to Vinzos Jar 2a, as

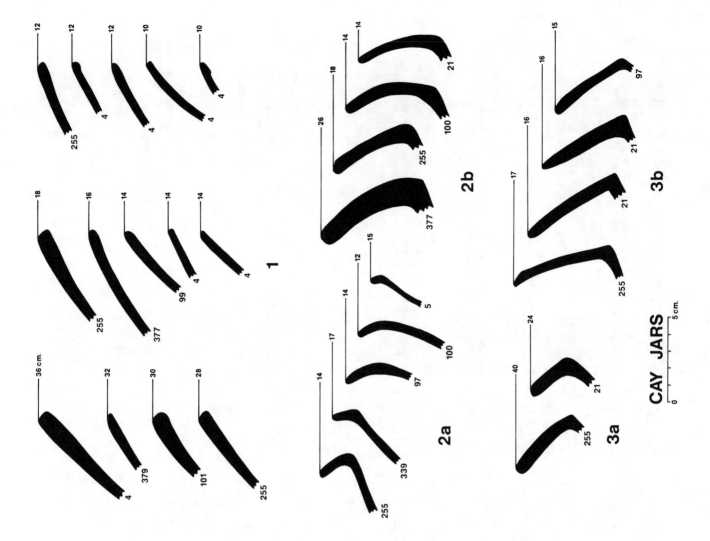

CAY JARS

0   5 cm.

Fig. 193. Cayhuamarca Period ceramics: Jars 1, 2a, 2b, 3a, and 3b.

well as by its uniformly reddish-brown paste (in contrast to Early Suchimancillo Jar 3).

Inter-regional comparisons: From his excavated Guañape Period materials in Virú Valley, Collier (1955, p. 198, Fig. 66 F) illustrates a jar type with some variants that are similar in size, form, and paste to Cayhuamarca Jar 2a. A similar jar form is also present in the excavated Quinú Period ceramics from Pashash (cf. Grieder 1978, p. 64, Fig. 34 q).

Cayhuamarca Jar 2b (Fig. 193)

Number: 18 sherds, or ca. 1.8% of the Cayhuamarca assemblage.

General description: Globular jar with a short neck and broad flaring rim. Rim diameters vary from 14-26 cm, with a mean of 18.2 cm and a standard deviation of 3.4 cm. Wall thickness below the rim ranges widely between 5 mm and 10 mm, although 90% of the sherds in the sample range more narrowly between 5 mm and 7 mm.

Paste: Temper consists uniformly of medium sand in moderate quantities. Paste color is reddish-brown, with a few sherds having gray cores.

Surface characteristics: Exterior and interior surfaces are uniformly plain reddish-brownware.

Distribution: This jar type was found fairly widely distributed at habitation sites (citadel and non-citadel) in Cayhuamarca Clusters 1 and 2 in the Upper Valley sector, as well as in Cayhuamarca Cluster 3 in the Middle Valley sector. Collection proveniences (with number of sherds in parentheses)/site numbers are:

Coll. 380(6)/CAY-3; Coll. 378(1)/CAY-4; Coll. 5(1)/CAY-11; Coll. 32(4)/CAY-13; Coll. 95(1)/CAY-17; Coll. 97(1)/CAY-19; Coll. 100(1)/ CAY-20; Coll. 193(9)/CAY-30; Coll. 194(1)/CAY-31; Coll. 255(1)/CAY-35.

Chronological assessment: Although similar in form, vessel size, and paste to Vinzos Jar 3c (Fig. 198), Cayhuamarca Jar 2b can be distinguished from the later jar in having no exterior burnishing lines.

Inter-regional comparisons: Jar 2b exhibits similarities of neck form to some of the variants of Huacapongo Polished Plain, Form 4 (cf. Collier 1955, p. 193, Fig. 65 F; see the three profiles on the left).

Cayhuamarca Jar 3a (Fig. 193)

Number: 14 sherds, or ca. 1.4% of the Cayhuamarca assemblage.

General description: Globular jar with a short, everted and slightly flaring rim. Rim diameters vary from 24-40 cm, with a mean of about 30 cm. Wall thickness below the rim is uniformly 8 mm.

Paste: Temper consists of medium sand in moderate quantities. Paste color is reddish-brown.

Surface characteristics: The majority of the sherds have reddish-

brown interior and exterior surfaces, although a few sherds have fully oxidized, reddish exterior surfaces.

Distribution: This jar type has a wide, but limited, distribution at habitation sites (citadel and non-citadel) in the main area of Cayhuamarca occupation. Collection proveniences (with number of sherds in parentheses)/site numbers are:

Coll. 378(1)/CAY-4; Coll. 3(1)/CAY-12; Coll. 21(2)/CAY-14; Coll. 255(2)/CAY-35; Coll. 341(8)/CAY-48.

Chronological assessment: Jar 3a is similar in form and paste to Vinzos Jar 4a (Fig. 199) and Early Suchimancillo Jar 4b (Fig. 205), but differs in having uniformly plain exteriors (in contrast to the burnished lines on Vinzos Jar 4a) and reddish-brown paste (in contrast to the fully oxidized red paste of most Early Suchimancillo jars).

Inter-regional comparisons: The neck profile of Jar 3a is somewhat similar to one of the variants of Huacapongo Polished Plain, Form 4, a Virú Valley type illustrated in Collier (1955, p. 193, Fig. 65 F; see fourth profile from the left).

Cayhuamarca Jar 3b (Fig. 193)

Number: 16 sherds, or ca. 1.6% of the Cayhuamarca assemblage.

General description: Globular jar with a tall, everted and slightly flaring rim. Lips are generally rounded, although one sherd with an interior bevel and squared lip was noted. Rim diameters vary from 15-22 cm, with a mean of 16.4 cm and a standard deviation of 2.4 cm. Wall thickness below the rim ranges between 5 mm and 7 mm, with most sherds in the sample at the lower end of the range.

Paste: Temper consists uniformly of medium sand in moderate quantities. Paste color is reddish-brown.

Surface characteristics: Most sherds have uniformly reddish-brown exteriors and interiors, although several sherds with variable exterior coloration ranging between dark brown and reddish-brown were also noted. The exterior shoulder of one sherd has a zoned punctate design (e.g., see Fig. 194 a).

Distribution: This jar type has a limited distribution at habitation sites (citadel and non-citadel) in Cayhuamarca Clusters 1 and 2, in the Upper Valley sector. Collection proveniences (with number of sherds in parentheses)/site numbers are:

Coll. 380(1)/CAY-3; Coll. 21(2)/CAY-14; Colls. 97(4), 98(9)/ CAY-19.

Chronological assessment: Jar 3b is similar in form, vessel size, and paste to Vinzos Jar 4b (Fig. 199), but differs in having no exterior burnished decoration such as that found on many jars of the later period.

Inter-regional comparisons: There is some similarity of form between Jar 3b and Guañape Polished Red, Form 4, a Virú Valley type illustrated in Collier (1955, p. 201, Fig. 67 D).

burnishing marks (e.g., see Fig. 194 c); (3) two sherds with zoned punctate design on the exterior shoulder below the neck (e.g., see Fig. 194 a); and (4) six sherds with stamped concentric circles (see Bowl 1b) or circle-and-dot design (Note: this latter design was noted both on bowl sherds and on two fragments from Early Horizon-type bottles; see Fig. 194 d, e).

Cayhuamarca: Miscellaneous Artifacts (Fig. 194)

Several ceramic artifacts were found in single-component Cayhuamarca contexts that are of interest to mention here. These include (1) in Coll. 377/CAY-4, a clay disk ca. 4 cm in diameter, made from a reddish-brown sherd and of unknown function (there is no central perforation that would suggest its use as a spindle whorl); and (2) in Coll. 255/CAY-35, two ceramic tubes of irregular diameter (average is ca. 1.5 cm) in fragmentary form, both of which may represent either vessel spouts or tubes for slipcasting panpipes (Note: for a further discussion of these tubes, see "Miscellaneous Artifacts" in the section on Late Suchimancillo materials).

Among the very few stone artifacts found in single-component Cayhuamarca contexts are: (1) in Coll. 4/CAY-12, a fragment of a spindle whorl-like object of quartzitic rock, with a central perforation ca. 3 cm in diameter and overall measurements of 7 cm in diameter and 5 cm in length; as shown in Fig. 194 f, the exterior sides of the object are deeply incised with a grid design; and (2) in Coll. 255/CAY-35, an excellently preserved projectile point of quartzitic material, with a narrow dorsal flute and retouching on each of the two longer edges (Fig. 194 g).

It is of some importance also to mention what was not found in collections dating only to Cayhuamarca Period: No painted decoration other than a few bowl fragments with red slipping was noted, nor were any human or plant effigies found (Note: animal effigies are limited to the two shown in Fig. 194 d and e, the former of the two possibly representing a llama).

Cayhuamarca Jar 4 (Fig. 194)

Number: 10 sherds, or ca. 1% of the Cayhuamarca assemblage.

General description: Large globular jar with a short vertical neck. Rim diameters vary from 28-43 cm, with a mean of 33.7 cm and a standard deviation of 4.9 cm. Wall thickness below the rim is uniformly 7 mm.

Paste: Temper consists uniformly of medium sand in moderate quantities. Paste color is reddish-brown.

Surface characteristics: Exterior and interior surfaces are reddish-brown.

Distribution: This jar type has a very limited distribution at four habitation sites (citadel and non-citadel) in the lower part of Cayhuamarca Cluster 2, in the Upper Valley sector. Collection proveniences (with number of sherds in parentheses)/site numbers are:

Coll. 93(3)/CAY-17; Coll. 96(1)/CAY-19; Coll. 193(1)/CAY-30; Coll. 194(5)/CAY-31.

Chronological assessment: Jar 4 is similar in form to Vinzos Jar 6 (Fig. 200), Early Suchimancillo Jar 10 (Fig. 206), and Late Suchimancillo Jar 9 (Fig. 216). The principal distinguishing feature of the Cayhuamarca form of the vessel is the substantially larger average size of its rim diameter compared to the three later periods (14.1 cm, 18.9 cm, and 13.1 cm, respectively). In any case, in all four periods it is a relatively minor type and not particularly useful as a temporal diagnostic.

Inter-regional comparisons: The vertically-necked variant of Guañape Red Plain, Form 2, from excavations by Strong and Evans (1952, p. 254, Fig. 35) in Virú Valley is essentially identical to Cayhuamarca Jar 4.

Cayhuamarca: Decorated Types (Figs. 191-192, 194)

Red polished: The commonest form of decoration in Cayhuamarca Period is interior and exterior polishing, which is present in varying percentages on every one of the bowl types and represents some 58% of the total sample of bowl fragments (276 out of 478 sherds). Although red slipping is definitely present on only three sherds (see Bowl 4), the general color of the polished bowls is distinctly red compared to the reddish-brown color of the unpolished bowls. This form of decoration is thus quite similar to that of the Guañape Polished Red type, reported on by Collier (1955:200-202) from his excavations in Late Guañape levels at several sites in Virú Valley.

Other decorated types: Compared to later periods in the Lower Santa sequence, such forms of exterior decoration as incising, excising, and burnishing are almost absent. The Cayhuamarca assemblage included the following decorated types (all of them jar fragments, except where otherwise indicated): (1) five sherds with rough, irregularly placed brush marks (e.g., see Fig. 194 b); (2) four sherds with parallel

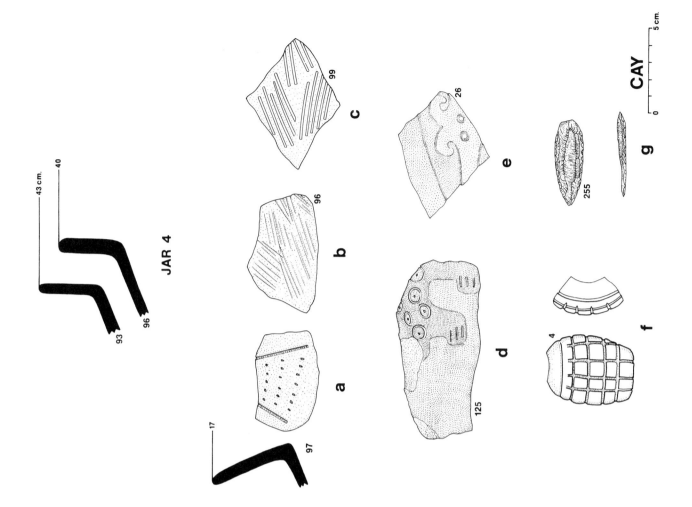

Fig. 194. Cayhuamarca Period ceramics and lithics: Jar 4, miscellaneous sherds (a–e), and stone artifacts (f–g).

VINZOS PERIOD

Vinzos Bowl 1 (Fig. 196)

Number: 18 sherds, or ca. 2.6% of the Vinzos assemblage.

General description: Globular bowl with a slightly constricted mouth and a direct rim. Lips are generally rounded, although a few tapered ones were also noted. A single sherd with a high, rounded exterior shoulder is present in the sample. Rim diameters vary from 14-38 cm, with a mean of 24.3 cm and a standard deviation of 6.9 cm. Wall thickness below the rim ranges between 4 mm and 6 mm, with 85% of the sherds ranging more narrowly between 5 mm and 6 mm.

Paste: Temper consists uniformly of medium sand in moderate quantities. Paste color is reddish-brown.

Surface characteristics: Approximately 70% of the sherds have plain reddish-brown interiors and exteriors. The other 30% have randomly placed, roughly parallel polishing or burnishing marks on the exterior.

Distribution: This bowl type was found widely distributed at habitation sites (citadel and non-citadel) in Vinzos Clusters 1, 2, and 3, in the Upper Valley sector, as well as at a single site in Vinzos Cluster 5. Collection proveniences (with number of sherds in parentheses)/site numbers are:

Coll. 375(5)/VIN-6; Colls. 368/369(1)/VIN-9; Coll. 373(3)/VIN-8; Coll. 26(1)/VIN-15; Colls. 99/101(3)/VIN-18; Coll 108(1)/VIN-20; Coll. 168(2)/VIN-22; Coll. 340(2)/VIN-29.

Chronological assessment: Bowl 1 is a reasonably good Vinzos Period diagnostic. Although it is similar in form and paste to Cayhuamarca Bowl 1a (Fig. 191), it differs in having exterior burnishing lines and a generally larger rim diameter.

Inter-regional comparisons: Globular bowls with slightly constricted mouths and exterior burnishing marks are not present in the Puerto Moorin ceramic assemblage of Virú Valley (for the forms that are present, see Collier 1955, p. 193, Fig. 65; Strong and Evans 1952, p. 258, Fig. 37). However, the exterior decoration on Vinzos Bowl 1 clearly links it to the general pan-valley Huacapongo Polished Plain type.

Vinzos Bowl 2 (Fig. 196)

Number: 12 sherds, or ca. 1.7% of the Vinzos assemblage.

General description: Open bowl with vertical or slightly outslanted walls, and a flared rim with rounded lip. Rim diameters vary from 12-30 cm, with a mean of 22.9 cm and a standard deviation of 4.9 cm. Wall thickness below the rim ranges widely between 5 mm and 10 mm, with a mean of 7.2 mm and a standard deviation of 1.6 mm.

Paste: Temper consists uniformly of medium sand in moderate quantities. Paste color is reddish-brown.

Surface characteristics: Approximately 60% of the sherds have plain reddish-brown interiors and exteriors. The other 40% have randomly placed burnishing lines on the interior. One sherd in this latter group also has horizontal burnishing lines on the exterior.

Distribution: This bowl type was found widely distributed at habitation sites throughout most of the main area of Vinzos occupation in the Upper and Middle Valley sectors, including sites in Vinzos Clusters 2, 3, 4, and 5, as well as at the large site of SVP-VIN-37. Collection proveniences (with number of sherds in parentheses)/site numbers are:

Colls. 368/369(1)/VIN-9; Coll. 373(1)/VIN-8; Coll. 115(2)/VIN-19; Coll. 170(1)/VIN-21; Coll. 169(2)/VIN-22; Coll. 248(1)/VIN-24; Coll. 300(2)/VIN-27; Coll. 348(1)/VIN-36; Coll. 366(1)/VIN-37.

Chronological assessment: Bowl 2 is similar in paste and form to Cayhuamarca Bowl 4 (Fig. 191), but the two types differ in the following ways: (1) the Vinzos bowl alone has decoration in the form of burnishing lines; (2) the Vinzos bowl generally has a larger rim diameter; and (3) the Vinzos bowl has uniformly thicker walls. Thus, Vinzos Bowl 2 is generally a good temporal diagnostic.

Inter-regional comparisons: Bowls of this type are not present in the Puerto Moorin ceramic assemblage, although, as with Vinzos Bowl 1, the exterior decoration on Vinzos Bowl 2 clearly links it to the general pan-valley Huacapongo Polished Plain type.

Vinzos Bowl 3 (Fig. 196)

Number: 2 sherds, or ca. .3% of the Vinzos assemblage.

General description: Large bowl with straight outslanted walls, and direct rim with rounded lip. Rim diameters are 24 cm and 40 cm. Wall thickness below the rim is 11 mm on both sherds.

Paste: Temper consists of medium sand in moderate quantities. Paste color is reddish-brown. Both sherds have gray cores.

Surface characteristics: Interior and exterior surfaces of the sherds are covered with randomly placed burnishing lines.

Distribution: This bowl type was found at one habitation site in Vinzos Cluster 3 and at one in Cluster 4. Collection proveniences (with number of sherds in parentheses)/site numbers are:

Coll. 25(1)/VIN-14; Coll. 248(1)/VIN-24.

Chronological assessment: Bowl 3 is similar in form to Cayhuamarca Bowl 5 (Fig. 191) and Early Suchimancillo Bowl 7 (Fig. 203), but can be distinguished from both the earlier and later types by its distinctive burnished decoration.

Inter-regional comparisons: From their excavations in Puerto Moorin levels in Virú Valley sites, Strong and Evans (1952:260; see Form 6) reported on small, open bowls with straight sides decorated in the Huacapongo Polished Plain style that are quite similar to Vinzos Bowl 3.

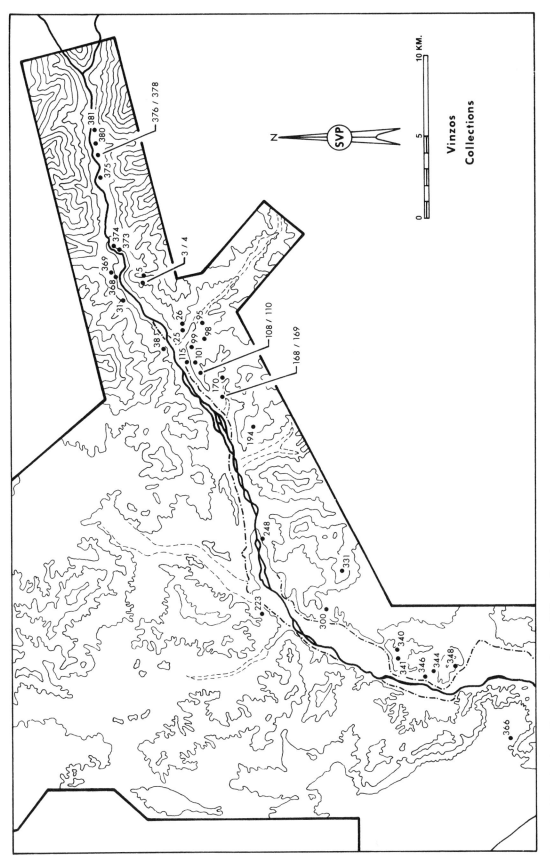

Fig. 195. Map showing collection proveniences of Vinzos Period (Puerto Moorin/Beginning EIP).

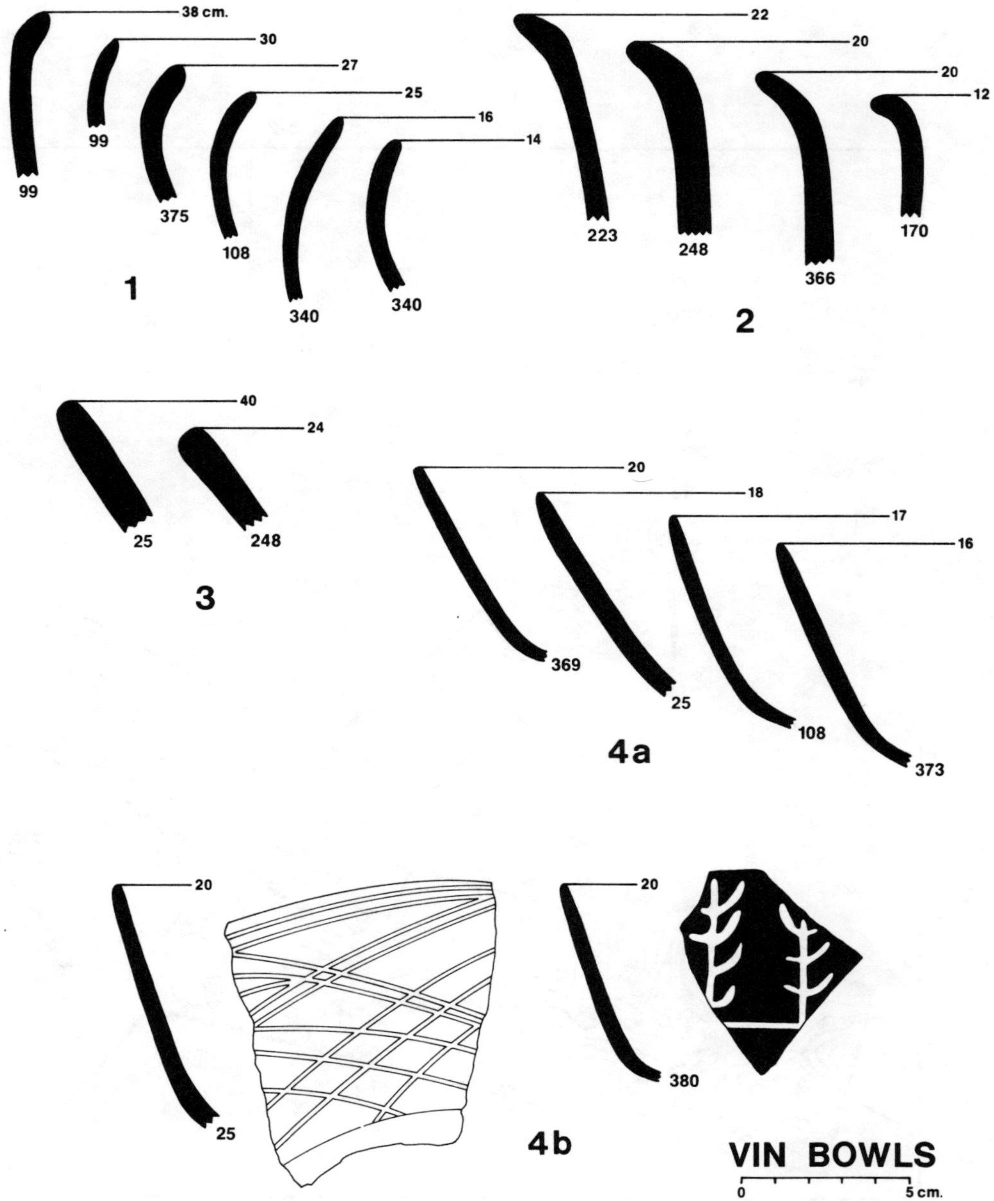

Fig. 196. Vinzos Period ceramics: Bowls 1, 2, 3, 4a, and 4b.

Vinzos Bowl 4a (Fig. 196)

Number: 37 sherds, or ca. 5.3% of the Vinzos assemblage.

General description: Open bowl with flat bottom and straight or slightly incurving walls that slant outward. There is little variation in the angle of the vessel walls, which range between 20° and 30° out from the vertical. Rim diameters vary from 16-20 cm, with a mean of 17.4 cm and a standard deviation of 1 cm. Wall thickness below the rim ranges generally between 4 mm and 5 mm, with the majority of the sherds at the lower end of the range.

Paste: Temper consists uniformly of medium sand in moderate quantities. Paste color in approximately 85% of the sherds is reddish-brown, while the remaining 15% have fully oxidized red paste.

Surface characteristics: Interior and exterior surfaces on 90% of the sherds in the sample (including the redware sherds) have decoration consisting of randomly placed or horizontal burnishing lines. The remaining 10% have plain interiors and exteriors.

Distribution: This bowl type was found at habitation sites (citadel and non-citadel) located primarily in Vinzos Clusters 1, 2, and 3, in the Upper Valley sector, as well as at sites of Clusters 4 and 5, in the Middle Valley. Collection proveniences (with number of sherds in parentheses)/site numbers are:

Coll. 381(1)/VIN-1; Coll. 373(15)/VIN-8; Coll. 25(3)/VIN-14; Coll. 26(2)/VIN-15; Coll. 108(10)/VIN-20; Colls. 168(2), 169(2)/VIN-22; Coll. 300(1)/VIN-27; Coll. 346(1)/VIN-33.

Chronological assessment: Bowl 4a is similar in form and paste to Cayhuamarca Bowl 6a (Fig. 192), but the analysis of single-component collections of both periods indicates the following distinguishing features: (1) almost all of the Vinzos bowls have randomly placed or horizontal burnishing lines as a decorative motif (in contrast to the lack of such lines on the Cayhuamarca bowl); (2) the Vinzos bowls exhibit much less variation in the angle of the vessel walls; and (3) the Vinzos bowls are uniformly thin-walled.

Inter-regional comparisons: Bowls of this general type are part of the Huacapongo Polished Plain ceramic assemblage of Virú Valley (cf. Collier 1955, p. 193, Fig. 65), but the Virú bowls exhibit more variation in wall thickness and lip treatment than do their Lower Santa Valley counterparts.

Vinzos Bowl 4b (Fig. 196)

Number: 8 sherds, or ca. 1.1% of the Vinzos assemblage.

General description: Open bowl with flat bottom and straight or slightly incurving walls that slant outward. Rim diameters are all about 20 cm. Wall thickness below the rim ranges between 4 mm and 5 mm, with most of the sherds at the lower end of the range.

Paste: Temper consists uniformly of medium sand in moderate quantities. Paste color is reddish-brown.

Surface characteristics: Six of the sherds in this small sample are decorated with a white-painted design over a black exterior slip (e.g., see Fig. 196, bottom row - right), all of them from the same provenience (Coll. 380; see below). The remaining two sherds are decorated either with pattern burnished design (Fig. 196, bottom row - left), or with randomly placed burnishing lines. Exposed surfaces on all eight sherds are uniformly reddish-brown in color.

Distribution: This bowl type has a limited distribution at habitation sites (citadel and non-citadel) in Vinzos Clusters 1 and 3, in the Upper Valley sector. Collection proveniences (with number of sherds in parentheses)/site numbers are:

Coll. 380(6)/VIN-3; Coll. 25(1)/VIN-14; Coll. 108(1)/VIN-20.

Chronological assessment: See Cayhuamarca Bowl 6b.

Inter-regional comparisons: See Cayhuamarca Bowl 6b.

Vinzos Jar 1 (Fig. 197)

Number: 104 sherds, or ca. 15.1% of the Vinzos assemblage.

General description: Globular jar with constricted mouth (neckless olla). Over 50% of the sherds have direct rims, while most of the rest have interior thickening at the rim. A few sherds with symmetrical thickening at the rim were also noted. Lip treatment is equally variable, with the majority of sherds having rounded lips and the rest having either interior beveled or tapered lips. Rim diameters vary widely from 9-50 cm, with a mean of 20.9 cm and a standard deviation of 8.9 cm. Wall thickness below the rim ranges widely between 4 mm and 10 mm, with a mean of 6.2 mm and a standard deviation of 1.3 mm.

Paste: Temper consists uniformly of medium sand in moderate quantities. Paste color is generally uniform, with 96% of the sherds in the sample having a reddish-brown color. The few remaining sherds are either from grayware or redware vessels.

Surface characteristics: Exterior and interior surfaces on the great majority of sherds are reddish-brown in color. Exterior burnishing lines are present on about 10% of the sherds.

Distribution: Jar 1 is widely distributed in habitation sites (citadel and non-citadel) throughout the area of Vinzos occupation. Collection proveniences (with number of sherds in parentheses)/site numbers are:

Coll. 375(9)/VIN-6; Colls. 368/369(9)/VIN-9; Coll. 38(1)/VIN-13; Coll. 26(1)/VIN-15; Colls. 101(10), 99(1)/VIN-18; Coll. 108(10)/VIN-20; Coll. 168(2)/VIN-22; Coll. 248(14)/VIN-24; Coll. 300(3)/VIN-27; Coll. 331(1)/VIN-28; Coll. 340(1)/VIN-29; Coll. 341(8)/VIN-30; Coll. 346(23)/VIN-33; Coll. 344(4)/VIN-34; Coll. 348(1)/VIN-36; Coll. 366(1)/VIN-37.

Chronological assessment: Neckless ollas with exterior burnished decoration are probably good diagnostics of the Vinzos Period. The reddish-brown paste and direct rims that characterize the majority of sherds, however, are features that make them difficult to distinguish from neckless ollas of the preceding Cayhuamarca Period.

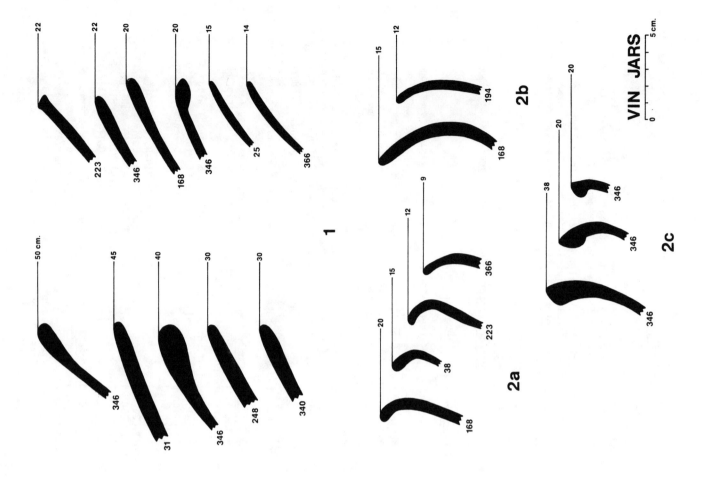

Fig. 197. Vinzos Period ceramics: Jars 1, 2a, 2b, and 2c.

384

Inter-regional comparisons: From their excavations in Puerto Moorin levels at sites in Virú Valley, Strong and Evans (1952, p. 258, Fig. 37) and Collier (1955, p. 193, Fig. 65 A) report on neckless ollas with exterior burnishing marks similar to those noted on Vinzos Jar 1.

Vinzos Jar 2a (Fig. 197)

Number: 16 sherds, or ca. 2.3% of the Vinzos assemblage.

General description: Small ovoid jar with a short flaring rim. Rim diameters vary from 5-20 cm, with a mean of 11.7 cm and a standard deviation of 3.7 cm. Wall thickness below the rim ranges between 5 mm and 7 mm.

Paste: Temper consists uniformly of medium sand in moderate quantities. Paste color is reddish-brown, with only one gray core noted in the sample.

Surface characteristics: The exterior surfaces of roughly 60% of the sherds are decorated with randomly placed burnishing lines. Exterior and interior surfaces on all vessels are reddish-brown in color.

Distribution: This jar type was found widely distributed at habitation sites (citadel and non-citadel) throughout the main area of Vinzos occupation, including Vinzos Clusters 1, 2, 3, 4, and 5, as well as at SVP-VIN-37 site. Collection proveniences (with number of sherds in parentheses)/site numbers are:

Coll. 378(1)/VIN-4; Colls. 368/369(1)/VIN-9; Coll. 170(2)/VIN-21; Coll. 168(1)/VIN-22; Coll. 194(2)/VIN-23; Coll. 248(1)/VIN-24; Coll. 223(6)/VIN-26; Coll. 340(1)/VIN-29; Coll. 366(1)/VIN-37.

Chronological assessment: The primary diagnostic feature on Vinzos Jar 2a is exterior burnished decoration, which is not present on either Cayhuamarca Jar 2a (Fig. 193) or Early Suchimancillo Jar 3 (Fig. 204). However, both the earlier and later types are similar in form and paste to the Vinzos jar.

Inter-regional comparisons: Jars with this rim form are not reported for the Puerto Moorin ceramic assemblage of Virú Valley (cf. Collier 1955, p. 193, Fig. 65; Strong and Evans 1952, p. 258, Fig. 37), although the exterior decoration on Jar 2a clearly links it to the general pan-valley Huacapongo Polished Plain type.

Vinzos Jar 2b (Fig. 197)

Number: 11 sherds, or ca. 1.6% of the Vinzos assemblage.

General description: Small ovoid jar with a short vertical neck and broad flaring rim. Rim diameters vary from 12-17 cm, with two-thirds of the sample at the upper end of this range. Wall thickness below the rim is generally about 7 mm.

Paste: Temper consists uniformly of medium sand in moderate quantities. Paste color is reddish-brown.

Surface characteristics: Exterior and interior surfaces are reddish-brown in color. Horizontal burnishing marks form a decorative motif on the interior of one of the sherds.

Distribution: This jar type was found at five habitation sites (citadel and non-citadel) in the Upper Valley sector, all of them in Vinzos Cluster 3. Collection proveniences (with number of sherds in parentheses)/site numbers are:

Coll. 38(1)/VIN-13; Coll. 25(4)/VIN-14; Coll. 101(4)/VIN-18; Coll. 170(1)/VIN-21; Coll. 168(1)/VIN-22.

Chronological assessment: Jar 2b is limited to the Vinzos Period, but is of little general utility as a temporal diagnostic since its distribution appears to be confined to Vinzos Cluster 3.

Inter-regional comparisons: Jars with this rim form are not part of the Puerto Moorin ceramic assemblage of Virú Valley (cf. Collier 1955, p. 193, Fig. 65; Strong and Evans 1952, p. 258, Fig. 37), although, as with Vinzos Jar 2a, the exterior burnishing lines on Jar 2b clearly link it to the general pan-valley Huacapongo Polished Plain type.

Vinzos Jar 2c (Fig. 197)

Number: 3 sherds, or ca. .4% of the Vinzos assemblage.

General description: Ovoid jar with a short neck and narrow, externally thickened rim. Rim diameters are 20 cm, 20 cm, and 38 cm. Wall thickness below the rim is 6 mm on all three sherds.

Paste: Temper consists uniformly of medium sand in moderate quantities. Paste color is reddish-brown.

Surface characteristics: Exterior and interior surfaces are reddish-brown. One of the three sherds has a very roughly finished surface on both the interior and exterior, while a second has a roughly finished exterior surface.

Distribution: This jar type is limited to one habitation site in Vinzos Cluster 5. Collection provenience (with number of sherds in parentheses)/site number is:

Coll. 346(3)/VIN-33.

Chronological assessment: Jar 2c is characteristic of only one Vinzos Period collection, so is therefore of limited utility as a temporal diagnostic. Nevertheless, since it may be a variant of Jar 2a (which is present, for example, in Coll. 340/VIN-29, located 2.3 km to the northeast), it is probably a local form of a general jar type with broad utility as a Vinzos temporal diagnostic.

Inter-regional comparisons: One of the rim variants of Vinzos Jar 2c (see profile on left in Fig. 197) is quite similar to a Huacapongo Polished Plain profile from Virú Valley illustrated in Collier (1955, p. 193, Fig. 65 B - left profile).

Vinzos Jar 3a (Fig. 198)

Number: 54 sherds, or ca. 7.8% of the Vinzos assemblage.

General description: Small globular jar with a very short flaring rim. Rim diameters vary from 10-22 cm, with a mean of 15.3 cm and a standard deviation of 3.3 cm. Wall thickness below the rim ranges between 5 mm and 8 mm, with about 90% of the sherds ranging more narrowly between 5 mm and 6 mm.

Paste: Temper consists uniformly of medium sand in moderate quantities. Paste color is reddish-brown.

Surface characteristics: Exterior and interior surfaces are reddish-brown in color. Randomly placed and roughly parallel burnishing lines are present on the exterior surface of 20% of the sherds in the sample.

Distribution: This jar type is widely distributed in habitation sites (citadel and non-citadel) located in Vinzos Clusters 1, 3, and 5. Collection proveniences (with number of sherds in parentheses)/site numbers are:

Coll. 380(6)/VIN-3; Coll. 26(10)/VIN-15; Colls. 101(4), 99(3)/VIN-18; Coll. 168(13)/VIN-22; Coll. 340(1)/VIN-29; Coll. 341(12)/VIN-30.

Chronological assessment: Jar 3a is similar in form and paste to the reddish-brown variant of Early Suchimancillo Jar 4a (Fig. 204). Thus, only the Vinzos sherds decorated with burnishing lines would be distinguishable as temporal diagnostics.

Inter-regional comparisons: Although jars with this specific rim form are not reported for the Puerto Moorin assemblage of Virú Valley (cf. Collier 1955, p. 193, Fig. 65; Strong and Evans 1952, p. 258, Fig. 37), their exterior decoration clearly links them to the general pan-valley Huacapongo Polished Plain type.

Vinzos Jar 3b (Fig. 198)

Number: 34 sherds, or ca. 4.9% of the Vinzos assemblage.

General description: Globular jar with a short flaring rim. Rim diameters vary from 14-60 cm, with a mean of 26.8 cm and a standard deviation of 12.1 cm. Wall thickness below the rim ranges between 5 mm and 10 mm, with 80% of the sherds ranging more narrowly between 5 mm and 8 mm.

Paste: Temper consists uniformly of medium sand in moderate quantities. Paste color is reddish-brown, with the exception of one fully oxidized redware sherd.

Surface characteristics: Exterior and interior surfaces are reddish-brown, with the exception of one redware sherd. Randomly placed burnishing lines are present on the exterior surface of about 50% of the sherds in the sample. A few of these sherds also have burnishing marks on the interior of the rim.

Distribution: This jar type is widely distributed in habitation sites (citadel and non-citadel) located in Vinzos Clusters 1, 2, 3, and 5, as well as at the large site of SVP-VIN-37. Jar 3b was also noted in a collection made at a cemetery site (SVP-VIN-12). Collection proveniences (with number of sherds in parentheses)/site numbers are:

Coll. 381(1)/VIN-1; Coll. 378(2)/VIN-4; Colls. 368/369(2)/VIN-9; Coll. 31(2)/VIN-12; Coll. 373(5)/VIN-8; Coll. 3(1)/VIN-11; Coll. 25(1)/VIN-14; Coll. 26(3)/VIN-15; Coll. 101(3)/VIN-18; Coll. 108(1)/VIN-20; Coll. 169(1)/VIN-22; Coll. 340(5)/VIN-29; Coll. 341(4)/VIN-30; 344(3)/VIN-34; Coll. 366(1)/VIN-37.

Chronological assessment: Jar 3b is similar in paste to the reddish-brown variant of Early Suchimancillo Jar 4b (Fig. 205), but is distinguishable in having a rim that is uniformly less flared than that of the later period. However, both the Vinzos and Early Suchimancillo types are characterized by exterior burnished decoration, so this is one exception to the general rule that exterior burnishing is diagnostic of Vinzos Period.

Inter-regional comparisons: Donnan and Mackey (1978:40-44) illustrate Salinar Period vessels from excavated burials in the Moche Valley that have rim profiles similar to those of Vinzos Jars 3b and 3c. The exterior burnishing on the Vinzos jars also links them to the pan-valley Huacapongo Polished Plain type (cf. Collier 1955:191-196; Strong and Evans 1952:258-261).

Vinzos Jar 3c (Fig. 198)

Number: 47 sherds, or ca. 6.8% of the Vinzos assemblage.

General description: Globular jar with a short vertical neck and broad flaring rim. Rim diameters vary from 11-22 cm, and are bimodally distributed with roughly half the sherds having diameters between 14 and 16 cm and half having diameters between 19 and 20 cm. Wall thickness below the rim ranges between 5 mm and 8 mm, with a mean of 7.1 mm and a standard deviation of 1.1 mm.

Paste: Temper consists uniformly of medium sand in moderate quantities. Approximately 60% of the sherds have reddish-brown paste, while the remaining 40% have fully oxidized red paste.

Surface characteristics: Randomly placed burnishing lines are present on the exteriors and (rim) interiors of about 80% of the reddish-brown sherds. None of the redware sherds is decorated with burnishing lines.

Distribution: This jar type is widely distributed in habitation sites (citadel and non-citadel) located in Vinzos Clusters 1, 2, 3, and 5. Collection proveniences (with number of sherds in parentheses)/site numbers are:

Coll. 375(1)/VIN-6; Coll. 373(1)/VIN-8; Coll. 4(2)/VIN-11; Coll. 25(12)/VIN-14; Coll. 26(5)/VIN-15; Coll. 101(4)/VIN-18; Coll. 168(1)/VIN-22; Coll. 340(5)/VIN-29; Coll. 341(16)/VIN-30.

Chronological assessment: Jar 3c is similar in form and paste to the earlier Cayhuamarca Jar 2b (Fig. 193), but can be distinguished from the earlier

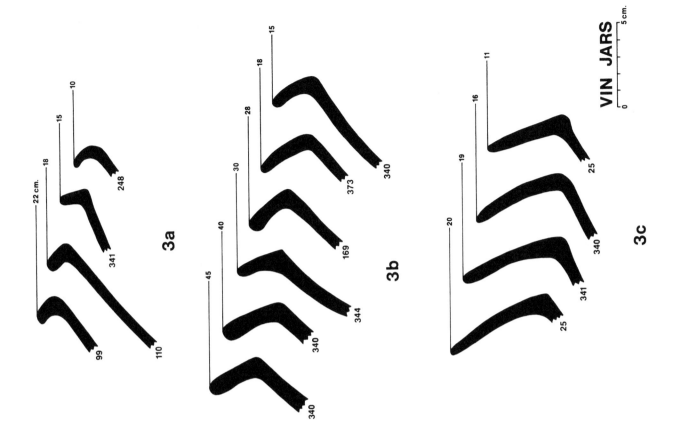

VIN JARS

3a

3b

3c

Fig. 198. Vinzos Period ceramics: Jars 3a, 3b, and 3c.

type by its exterior burnished decoration, as well as by the presence of a substantial number of sherds with redware paste (Note: while the redware form of Jar 3c may be a later Vinzos variant of the earlier burnished type, no similar jar form is present in single-component Early Suchimancillo collections; both the reddish-brown and redware variants therefore appear to be good temporal diagnostics).

Inter-regional comparisons: See discussion under Vinzos Jar 3b.

Vinzos Jar 4a (Fig. 199)

Number: 6 sherds, or ca. .9% of the Vinzos assemblage.

General description: Ovoid or globular jars with a short everted rim. Rim diameters vary from 24-42 cm, with a mean of 33.3 cm and a standard deviation of 6.9 cm. Wall thickness below the rim ranges between 5 mm and 7 mm, with four of the sherds at the upper end of the range.

Paste: Temper consists uniformly of medium sand in moderate quantities. Paste color is reddish-brown.

Surface characteristics: Exterior and interior surfaces are reddish-brown in color. Randomly placed burnishing lines are present on four of the six sherds in the sample.

Distribution: This jar type has a distribution limited to habitation sites (citadel and non-citadel) in the Upper Valley sector, including Vinzos Clusters 1, 2, and 3. Collection proveniences (with number of sherds in parentheses)/site numbers are:

Coll. 375(1)/VIN-6; Colls. 368/369(1)/VIN-9; Coll. 373(1)/VIN-8; Colls. 108(1), 110(2)/VIN-20.

Chronological assessment: Jar 4a can be distinguished from its earlier Cayhuamarca counterpart (Jar 3a, Fig. 193) and from some forms of its later Early Suchimancillo counterpart (Jar 4a, Fig. 204) by the presence of burnished decoration. The plain reddish-brown variants of the Vinzos and Cayhuamarca jars, however, appear to be essentially indistinguishable in a mixed context.

Inter-regional comparisons: See Donnan and Mackey (1978:40-41) for Salinar Period vessels from Moche Valley with similar rim forms. The exterior burnishing lines also link Vinzos Jars 4a and 4b to the general pan-valley Huacapongo Polished Plain type (cf. Collier 1955:191-196; Strong and Evans 1952:258-261).

Vinzos Jar 4b (Fig. 199)

Number: 5 sherds, or ca. .7% of the Vinzos assemblage.

General description: Globular jar with a broad, everted and slightly flaring rim. Lips are either rounded or are squared with an interior bevel. Rim diameters vary from 14-22 cm, with a mean of 18.5 cm and a standard deviation of 3 cm. Wall thickness below the rim ranges between 5 mm and 6 mm.

Paste: Temper consists uniformly of medium sand in moderate quantities. Paste color is reddish-brown.

Surface characteristics: Exterior and interior surfaces are reddish-brown in color. Randomly placed burnishing lines are present on the exteriors and interiors of three of the five sherds in the sample.

Distribution: This jar type has a distribution limited to habitation sites (citadel and non-citadel) in the Upper Valley sector, in Vinzos Clusters 1 and 2, as well as in the uppermost part of Cluster 3. Collection proveniences (with number of sherds in parentheses)/site numbers are:

Coll. 381(1)/VIN-1; Coll. 380(1)/VIN-3; Colls. 368/369(1)/VIN-9; Coll. 373(1)/VIN-8; Coll. 26(1)/VIN-15.

Chronological assessment: Jar 4b is similar in form, vessel size, and paste to Cayhuamarca Jar 3b (Fig. 193), but differs in having exterior burnishing lines.

Inter-regional comparisons: See discussion under Vinzos Jar 4a.

Vinzos Jar 5a (Fig. 199)

Number: 10 sherds, or ca. 1.5% of the Vinzos assemblage.

General description: Small globular jar with a very short vertical neck and everted lip. Rim diameters vary from 9-14 cm, with a mean of 10.4 cm and a standard deviation of 1.3 cm. Wall thickness below the rim ranges between 4 mm and 5 mm, with the majority of sherds at the upper end of the range.

Paste: Temper consists uniformly of medium sand in moderate quantities. Paste color is reddish-brown, with gray cores noted on two sherds.

Surface characteristics: Exterior and interior surfaces are reddish-brown in color. Randomly placed burnishing lines decorate the exterior surface, as well as the interior of the rim and neck, on seven of the sherds.

Distribution: Jar 5a is the short-necked variant of a general type that is widely distributed in habitation sites throughout the area of Vinzos occupation. This particular variant is found at sites in Vinzos Clusters 1, 2, and 4, and at SVP-VIN-37. Collection proveniences (with number of sherds in parentheses)/site numbers are:

Coll. 375(1)/VIN-6; Coll. 373(1)/VIN-8; Coll. 223(6)/VIN-26; Coll. 366(2)/VIN-37.

Chronological assessment: Jar 5 (including the 5a, 5b, and 5c variants) is generally one of the best diagnostic indicators of Vinzos Period occupation in the Lower Santa Valley region. Although the general vessel form continues as a minor type into Early and Late Suchimancillo Periods, it is distinguishable by its uniformly reddish-brown paste and exterior burnishing from the red paste and plain surfaces that characterize Early Suchimancillo Jar 9 (Fig. 206) and Late Suchimancillo Jar 11 (Fig. 216).

388

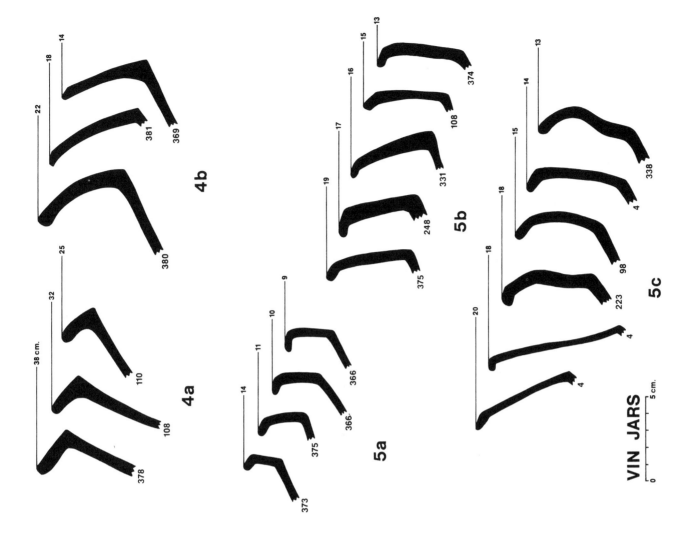

VIN JARS

Fig. 199. Vinzos Period ceramics: Jars 4a, 4b, 5a, 5b, and 5c.

389

Inter-regional comparisons: Vinzos Jars 5a, 5b, and 5c are essentially identical in form, size, and exterior decoration to Huacapongo Polished Plain, Form 5, a common vessel type in excavated materials from Puerto Moorin levels in Virú Valley (cf. Strong and Evans 1952, p. 258, Fig. 37).

Vinzos Jar 5b (Fig. 199)

Number: 21 sherds, or ca. 3% of the Vinzos assemblage.

General description: Globular jar with a short vertical or slightly outslanted neck and everted lip. Rim diameters vary from 13-19 cm, with a mean of 15.6 cm and a standard deviation of 1.5 cm. Wall thickness below the rim ranges widely between 4 mm and 9 mm, with a mean of 5.7 mm.

Paste: Temper consists uniformly of medium sand in moderate quantities. Paste color is reddish-brown, with roughly 50% of the sherds exhibiting either gray cores or other evidence of uneven firing and incomplete oxidation.

Surface characteristics: Exterior and interior surfaces are reddish-brown in color. Randomly placed burnishing lines or smooth polishing characterize the exterior surface, and the interior of the rim and neck as well, on 11 (50%) of the sherds in the sample.

Distribution: Jar 5b is the medium-necked variant of a general type that is widely distributed throughout the area of Vinzos occupation. This particular variant is found at habitation sites (citadel and non-citadel) in Vinzos Clusters 1, 2, 3, and 4. Collection proveniences (with number of sherds in parentheses)/site numbers are:

Coll. 375(1)/VIN-6; Coll. 374(6)/VIN-7; Coll. 373(1)/VIN-8; Coll. 108(4)/VIN-20; Coll. 248(4)/VIN-24; Coll. 331(5)/VIN-28.

Chronological assessment: See discussion under Vinzos Jar 5a.

Inter-regional comparisons: See Vinzos Jar 5a.

Vinzos Jar 5c (Fig. 199)

Number: 29 sherds, or ca. 4.2% of the Vinzos assemblage.

General description: Globular jar with a higher neck and everted or flaring lip. Approximately 90% of the vessels have necks that slant inward. Several examples of jars with cambered necks were also noted in this group. The remaining 10% of the vessels have straight outslanted necks and everted lips. Rim diameters vary from 10-20 cm, with a mean of 15.4 cm and a standard deviation of 2.7 cm. Wall thickness below the rim ranges widely between 4 mm and 9 mm, with a mean of 5.7 mm.

Paste: Temper consists of medium sand. The quantity of temper in about 75% of the sherds is moderate. Quantity in the other 25% is heavy. Paste color in nearly all of the sherds is reddish-brown, with two redware sherds also noted.

Surface characteristics: Exterior and interior surfaces are uniformly reddish-brown, with the exception of the two fully oxidized sherds. Randomly placed burnishing lines were noted on the exterior surface, as well as on the interior of the rim and neck, on about 30% of the sherds in the sample. Another 30% of the sherds are highly polished on these same areas of the vessel. The remaining 40% have plain reddish-brown exteriors and interiors.

Distribution: Jar 5c is the taller-necked variant of a general type that is widely distributed throughout the area of Vinzos occupation. This particular variant is found at habitation sites (citadel and non-citadel) in Vinzos Clusters 1, 2, 3, and 4. Collection proveniences (with number of sherds in parentheses)/site numbers are:

Coll. 381(1)/VIN-1; Coll. 378(1)/VIN-4; Colls. 368/369(3)/VIN-9; Coll. 4(5)/VIN-11; Coll. 38(7)/VIN-13; Coll. 25(1)/VIN-14; Coll. 26(4)/VIN-15; Coll. 98(1)/VIN-17; Coll. 101(1)/VIN-18; Coll. 115(2)/VIN-19; Coll. 248(2)/VIN-24; Coll. 223(1)/VIN-26.

Chronological assessment: See discussion under Vinzos Jar 5a.

Inter-regional comparisons: See Vinzos Jar 5a.

Vinzos Jar 6 (Fig. 200)

Number: 16 sherds, or ca. 2.3% of the Vinzos assemblage.

General description: Globular jar with a short vertical neck. Rim diameters vary from 10-33 cm, with a mean of 15.3 cm and a standard deviation of 5.5 cm. Wall thickness below the rim ranges between 3 mm and 7 mm, with a mean of 5.5 mm.

Paste: Temper consists uniformly of medium sand in moderate quantities. Paste color in nearly all sherds is reddish-brown, with one redware sherd also noted.

Surface characteristics: Exterior and interior surfaces are uniformly reddish-brown, with the exception of the one fully oxidized sherd. Burnishing lines decorate the exterior surface of one of the sherds.

Distribution: This jar type has a scattered, but wide, distribution at habitation sites (citadel and non-citadel) in the main area of Vinzos occupation, including sites in Vinzos Clusters 1, 3, and 5. Collection proveniences (with number of sherds in parentheses)/site numbers are:

Coll. 378(1)/VIN-4; Coll. 101(3)/VIN-18; Coll. 110(1)/VIN-20; Colls. 168(3), 169(1)/VIN-22; Coll. 194(2)/VIN-23; Coll. 340(1)/VIN-29; Coll. 341(1)/VIN-30; Coll. 344(3)/VIN-34.

Chronological assessment: Jar 6 is similar in form to Cayhuamarca Jar 4 (Fig. 194), Early Suchimancillo Jar 10 (Fig. 206), and Late Suchimancillo Jar 9 (Fig. 216). It can be distinguished from the earlier Cayhuamarca form by its generally smaller rim diameter, from the Early Suchimancillo vessel by its general lack of exterior burnished decoration, and from the Late Suchimancillo vessel by its reddish-brown paste.

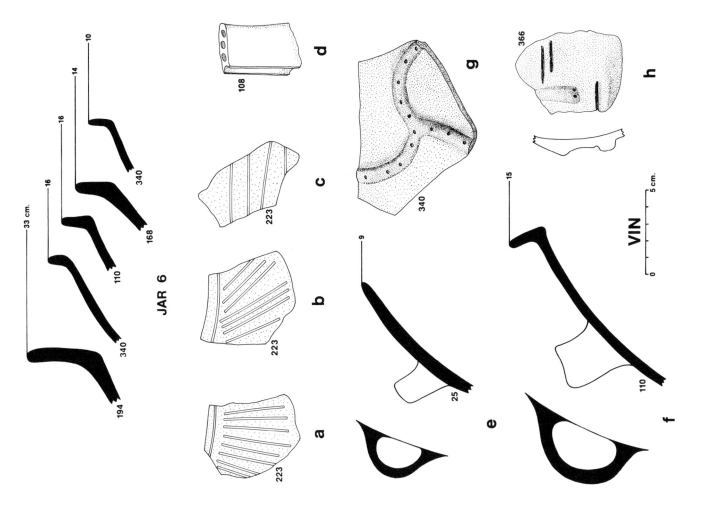

JAR 6

Fig. 200. Vinzos Period ceramics: Jar 6, and miscellaneous sherds.

Nevertheless, any given plain reddish-brown rim sherd of this general vessel form could date to any of the three pre-Late Suchimancillo ceramic periods.

Inter-regional comparisons: Although Jar 6 differs from its Virú counterpart in having a consistently vertical neck, it is essentially similar in form, paste, and exterior decoration to Huacapongo Polished Plain, Form 2 (cf. Collier 1955, p. 193, Fig. 65 B; Strong and Evans 1952, p. 258, Fig. 37).

Vinzos: Decorated Types (Fig. 200)

Burnishing lines: As discussed under the various bowl and jar types above, the commonest form of decoration in Vinzos Period is randomly placed sets of roughly parallel burnishing lines. On bowls, this decoration is generally found on the entire interior surface of the vessel, as well as on the exterior wall. On jars, interior decoration is usually confined to the neck and rim, while most if not all of the exterior surface appears to have been covered. In a number of cases, sherds were too small to get a good sense of whether burnishing lines were placed in a consistently vertical, horizontal, or slanted fashion. It does appear, however, that they were often unevenly or hurriedly applied--without much concern for keeping the patterns as neat as those shown in the drawings (Fig. 200 a, b, c). In any case, this form of decoration is present in varying percentages on every one of the Vinzos Period vessel types, except for Jar 2c (Note: the apparent absence of burnished decoration on this jar type may well be an artifact of our small sample of three sherds).

As a comparison of the Santa Valley ceramic types of Vinzos Period to those of Virú Valley Huacapongo Polished Plain will show (cf. Collier 1955:191-196; Strong and Evans 1952:258-261), the ceramic assemblages of Vinzos and Puerto Moorin Periods are strongly similar. The ceramic data from the Lower Santa region thus provide some indication of inter-regional ties with the area to the north during this period. Of equal importance for understanding the nature of beginning Early Intermediate Period in both areas, however, is that the analysis of collections from at least nine single-component sites in Santa strongly confirms the existence of a period sandwiched between Early Horizon, or Guañape/Cayhuamarca, and the Gallinazo/Suchimancillo time period--namely, the Puerto Moorin/Vinzos period (for a discussion of the issue of whether or not such a period "exists," see Bennyhoff 1952; for a convincing rebuttal of Bennyhoff's critique, see Ford 1952).

Other decorated types: Aside from burnishing lines, pottery vessels of Vinzos Period are characterized by an almost complete lack of surface decoration such as slipping or painted designs. The Lower Santa region thus presents differences as well as similarities in comparison to the areas to the north (e.g., see the Puerto Moorin White-on-Red type of Virú Valley, in Strong and Evans 1952:295-301). A limited number of sherds with painted decoration is present in the Vinzos assemblage (see Vinzos Bowl 4b, Fig. 196), as well as two redware sherds with exterior plastic decoration in the form of sinuous appliquéd ribs with punctate design (Fig. 200 g). This latter form of decoration is quite similar to

that described for the Castillo Modeled type of Virú (cf. Strong and Evans 1952, p. 314, Fig. 63 D), which dates from late Salinar (i.e., Puerto Moorin) through Huancaco Periods. In Santa Valley, however, this form of decoration appears to be confined to the Vinzos time period.

Vinzos: Miscellaneous Artifacts (Fig. 200 d-h)

Among the other ceramic artifacts found in single-component Vinzos Period contexts are panpipes, horizontal strap handles, and a single fragment of a human effigy neck vessel. Although panpipes are a common decorative feature on figurines of Early Tanguche Period (see Fig. 251 d-g), in the Lower Santa region clay panpipes made for use as musical instruments appear to be confined to Vinzos, Early Suchimancillo, and Late Suchimancillo Periods. They are a very minor feature of Vinzos collections, however, as we found a total of only three in single-component contexts (e.g., see Fig. 200 d).

The earliest use of strap handles on pottery vessels in the Lower Santa area dates to the Vinzos Period, judging from the analysis of single-component collections. As shown in Fig. 200 e and f, these handles were placed horizontally on the exteriors of both neckless and necked jars. In the field, they were usually found on body sherd fragments (i.e., disattached from the rim, but it is likely they were a feature on more than just the two vessel types (Vinzos Jars 1 and 3a) shown in the drawings. In any case, the data from the Lower Santa region are in accordance with those from Chicama (cf. Larco Hoyle 1944) and Virú (cf. Ford and Willey 1949:55), indicating Salinar/Puerto Moorin as the time of the appearance of strap handles in the North Coast area.

As mentioned above, only one human effigy is present in the Vinzos Period collections. This effigy (Fig. 200 h) is from the neck of a redware jar, and consists of a simply modeled face with appliquéd nose and incised lines for eyes (and eyebrows?) and mouth. It bears some resemblance to Castillo Modeled effigies reported for Virú Valley by Strong and Evans (1952, p. 315, Fig. 64 A and C). Although the effigy face from Santa formed part of a redware vessel, it was found in association with sherds of generally reddish-brown paste.

EARLY SUCHIMANCILLO PERIOD

Early Suchimancillo Bowl 1a (Fig. 202)

Number: 40 sherds, or ca. 2.4% of the Early Suchimancillo assemblage.

General description: Globular bowl with a slightly constricted mouth and rounded lip. One sherd with a high, rounded exterior shoulder and another with outslanting walls, thickened rim interior, and squared lip are the only exceptions to this general vessel form. Rim diameters vary from 11-25 cm, with a mean of 19.6 cm and a standard deviation of 3.6 cm. Wall thickness below the rim ranges between 3 mm and 5 mm, with a mean of 4.4 mm.

Paste: Temper consists of fine or medium grain sand, with 70% of the sherds having medium grain sand. The quantity of temper in all of the sherds is moderate. Approximately 65% of the sample has fully oxidized, red paste. The other 35% has reddish-brown paste.

Surface characteristics: Exterior and interior surfaces of the redware sherds are undecorated. Two sherds among the reddish-brownware ones have horizontal exterior burnishing marks, while the remainder is undecorated.

Distribution: This bowl type has a widespread distribution at habitation, habitation-cemetery, and cemetery sites in the upper two-thirds part of Early Suchimancillo Cluster 2. Collection proveniences (with number of sherds in parentheses)/site numbers are:

Coll. 32(1)/ESUCH-7; Coll. 6(2)/ESUCH-13; Coll. 29(1)/ESUCH-15; Coll. 32(1)/ESUCH-17; Colls. 1(4), 17(1), 19(2)/ESUCH-19; Coll. 18(2)/ ESUCH-20; Coll. 20(1)/ESUCH-21; Coll. 35(2)/ESUCH-22; Coll. 23(1)/ ESUCH-24; Coll. 22(1)/ESUCH-25; Coll. 117(3)/ESUCH-30; Coll. 43(2)/ ESUCH-35; Coll. 107(2)/ESUCH-41; Coll. 151(1)/ESUCH-42; Coll. 113(2)/ ESUCH-46; Coll. 233(1)/ESUCH-54; Coll. 203(3)/ESUCH-71; Coll. 206(1)/ ESUCH-73; Coll. 226(1)/ESUCH-90; Coll. 272(1)/ESUCH-93.

Chronological assessment: Bowl 1a is generally a good temporal diagnostic for the Early Suchimancillo Period. The redware variants distinguish it from similar forms of the preceding two periods, and the lack of exterior pressmolding distinguishes it from a similar bowl form of Late Tambo Real Period (see Redware Bowl 1, Fig. 279).

Inter-regional comparisons: Among the Recuay Quimít Phase materials (equivalent to Early Gallinazo) from the sierra site of Pashash, Grieder (1978, p. 66, Fig. 35 t-aa) illustrates small bowls that appear to be similar in form, size, and paste to Early Suchimancillo Bowls 1a and 1b.

Early Suchimancillo Bowl 1b (Fig. 202)

Number: 18 sherds, or ca. 1.1% of the Early Suchimancillo assemblage.

General description: Globular bowl with a slightly constricted mouth and squared lip. Rim diameters vary from 14-26 cm, with a mean of 22 cm and a standard deviation of 4.6 cm. Wall thickness below the rim ranges between 3 mm and 5 mm, with a mean of 3.6 mm.

Paste: Temper consists of fine or medium sand, with about 75% of the sherds having fine grain sand. The quantity of temper in all of the sherds is moderate. Paste color is red, with gray cores noted in 65% of the sherds.

Surface characteristics: Exterior and interior surfaces are covered with a highly polished red slip.

Distribution: This bowl type is one of the form variants of a general red polished type that is widely distributed in habitation and cemetery sites in Early Suchimancillo Clusters 1, 2, and 3. Collection proveniences (with number of sherds in parentheses)/site numbers are:

Coll. 373(1)/ESUCH-5; Coll. 3(1)/ESUCH-14; Colls. 30(4), 32(1)/ ESUCH-17; Coll. 34(2)/ESUCH-18; Coll. 18(1)/ESUCH-20; Coll. 24(1)/ ESUCH-23; Coll. 134(1)/ESUCH-47; Coll. 198(1)/ESUCH-61; Coll. 203(1)/ ESUCH-71; Coll. 222(1)/ESUCH-88; Coll. 332(1)/ESUCH-101; Coll. 282(1)/ ESUCH-126; Coll. 281(1)/ESUCH-128.

Chronological assessment: Bowl 1b can be clearly distinguished on the basis of form, paste, and its red polished slip from similar bowl forms of other periods in the sequence, and is therefore a very good temporal diagnostic.

Inter-regional comparisons: See Early Suchimancillo Bowl 1a.

Early Suchimancillo Bowl 2a (Fig. 202)

Number: 9 sherds, or ca. .5% of the Early Suchimancillo assemblage.

General description: Open bowl with outslanted and slightly incurving walls. Lips are either rounded or horizontally beveled. Rim diameters vary from 20-25 cm, with a mean of 21.4 cm and a standard deviation of 2.2 cm. Wall thickness below the rim ranges between 2.5 mm and 5 mm.

Paste: Temper consists of fine or medium sand in moderate quantities. Seven of the nine sherds in the sample are from fully oxidized redware vessels. One of the remaining two sherds has reddish-brown paste, and the other has gray paste.

Surface characteristics: Interior and exterior surfaces are plain red (seven sherds), reddish-brown (one sherd), and black (one sherd).

Distribution: This bowl type has a distribution limited primarily to the uppermost part of Early Suchimancillo Cluster 2. Collection proveniences (with number of sherds in parentheses)/site numbers are:

Coll. 372(1)/ESUCH-7; Coll. 29(2)/ESUCH-15; Colls. 7(1), 17(1), 19(1)/ESUCH-19; Coll. 27(1)/ESUCH-27; Coll. 332(2)/ESUCH-101.

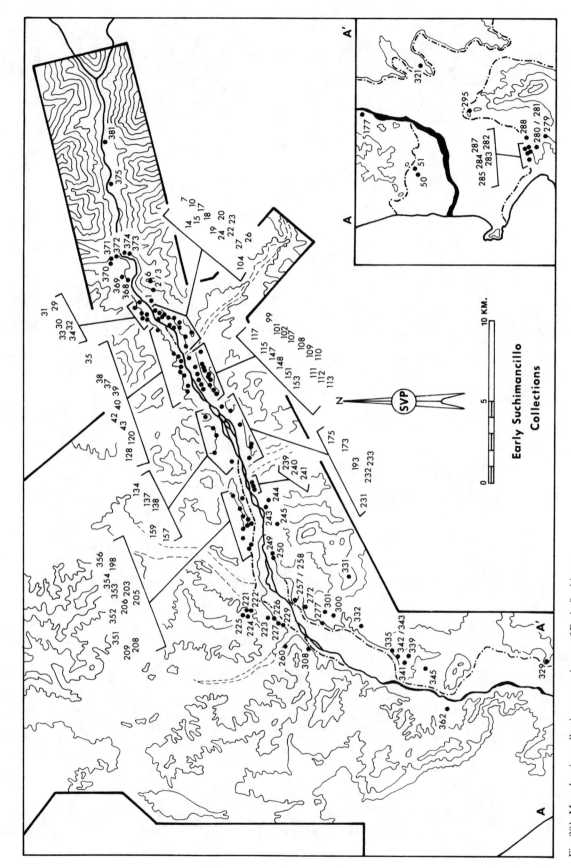

Fig. 201. Map showing collection proveniences of Early Suchimancillo Period (Early–Middle Gallinazo/Early EIP).

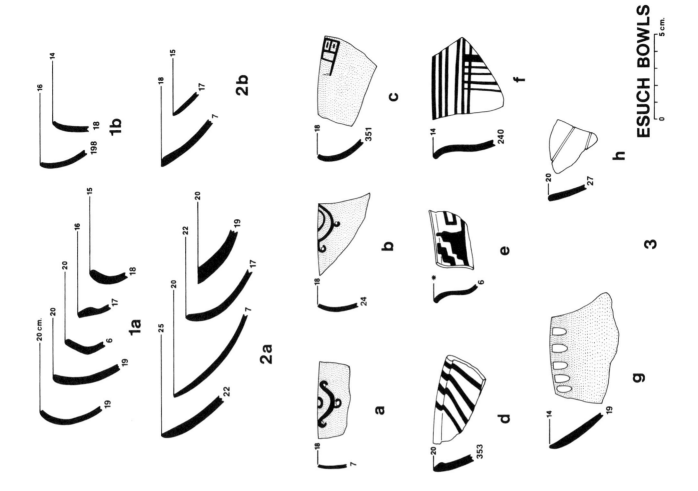

ESUCH BOWLS

Fig. 202. Early Suchimancillo Period ceramics: Bowls 1a, 1b, 2a, 2b, and 3.

395

Chronological assessment: Bowl 2a is very similar to, if not indistinguishable from, Late Suchimancillo Bowl 1 (Fig. 211). It is also similar to Early Tanguche Bowl 1 (Fig. 236), Late Tanguche Bowl 1 (Fig. 258), and Late Tambo Real Redware Bowl 2 (Fig. 279). Nevertheless, the horizontally beveled variant of Bowl 2a appears to be at least a general Suchimancillo temporal diagnostic, and is possibly a good Early Suchimancillo time marker.

Inter-regional comparisons: Small, open Castillo Plain bowls from Virú Valley (cf. Strong and Evans 1952, p. 264, Fig. 40; see Form 5) are similar in size, form, and paste to Early Suchimancillo Bowl 1. Bennett (1950, Pl. 7 H-I) illustrates bowls of similar form and size from the Gallinazo Group in Virú.

Early Suchimancillo Bowl 2b (Fig. 202)

Number: 3 sherds, or ca. .2% of the Early Suchimancillo assemblage.

General description: Open bowl with outslanted and slightly incurving walls. Lips are either tapered or horizontally beveled. Rim diameters are 18 cm, 22 cm, and 28 cm. Wall thickness below the rim ranges between 3 mm and 4 mm.

Paste: Temper consists of fine sand in light quantities. Paste color is red, with a thin gray core noted on all three sherds.

Surface characteristics: The upper part of the exterior and interior surfaces of two of the sherds is painted red. The remaining sherd has a red-painted lip. Although no polishing was detectable on the red-painted surfaces, this bowl type may be part of the general red polished type that is diagnostic of Early Suchimancillo ceramic collections.

Distribution: This bowl type has a distribution confined to a single habitation-cemetery site in the uppermost part of Early Suchimancillo Cluster 2. Collection proveniences (with number of sherds in parentheses)/site number is:

Colls. 7(2), 17(1)/ESUCH-19.

Chronological assessment: Bowl 2b is probably a good Early Suchimancillo diagnostic, but its apparently restricted distribution makes it of little use as a general time marker.

Inter-regional comparisons: See discussion under Early Suchimancillo Bowl 2a.

Early Suchimancillo Bowl 3 (Fig. 202 a-h)

This bowl type, or category, includes a total of 59 sherds from small, decorated bowls (ca. 3.3% of the Early Suchimancillo assemblage) that have either (1) more complex painted decoration beyond the simple red slipping described for Bowls 1b and 2b; or (2) exterior incised design. Rim diameters vary generally from 14-20 cm, and wall thickness below the rim ranges between 2 mm and 4 mm. Paste consists of either (1) white kaolin, which ranges in color from chalk white to reddish-white, and contains very light amounts of fine grain sand; or (2) oxidized redware, containing light quantities of fine grain sand. Most of the redware bowls have a wall thickness at or near the upper end of the 2-4 mm range, while all of the kaolin bowls are at the lower end of the range (indeed, kaolin ware is generally the thinnest pottery found in the Lower Santa region).

The general Bowl 3 type is distributed primarily in habitation, habitation-cemetery, and cemetery sites in the upper half of Early Suchimancillo Cluster 2. It was also found at two sites located farther downvalley (SVP-ESUCH-109, 128). General descriptions of the decorated bowl types illustrated here, as well as collection proveniences (with number of sherds in parentheses)/site numbers, are as follows:

(1) Black-and-White or Black/Orange-slipped Kaolin (Fig. 202 a-c)

Description: Bowl with slightly constricted mouth and squared lip. Exterior and interior surfaces are orange-slipped, and designs consist either of (1) curvilinear black scrolls, or pendant, motifs on the exterior of the rim, with white dots painted inside the scrolls; or of (2) geometric black-painted motifs on the exterior of the rim (Note: the example shown in Fig. 202 c is only partly preserved).

Proveniences: Colls. 7(5), 17(9)/ESUCH-19; Coll. 24(1)/ESUCH-23; Coll. 351(1)/ESUCH-80.

(2) Red/White Kaolin (Fig. 202 d)

Description: Open bowl with outslanted and slightly incurving walls. The lip has a distinctive interior bevel which ends in a small, rounded ridge. Decoration consists of slanted red lines painted on the lip and interior of the bowl.

Provenience: Coll. 353(1)/ESUCH-65.

(3) Red/Buff-colored Redware (Fig. 202 e)

Description: Globular bowl with flaring rim. Decoration consists of geometric, red-painted motifs on the exterior of the vessel below the rim.

Provenience: Coll. 6(8)/ESUCH-13.

(4) Red/White-slipped Redware (Fig. 202 f)

Description: Globular bowl with flaring rim (same shape as in Fig. 202 e). Decoration consists of horizontal and vertical red-painted lines over the white-slipped exterior surface.

Provenience: Coll. 240(1)/ESUCH-56.

(5) White/Polished Red Slip (Fig. 202 g)

Description: Open bowl with straight outslanted walls and

tapered rim. Decoration consists of partially elliptical white-painted motifs placed around the exterior of the rim. Exterior and interior surfaces are red-slipped.

Provenience: Coll. 19(7)/ESUCH-19.

(6) Incised Exterior (Fig. 202 h)

Description: Open redware bowl with straight, slightly outslanted walls and rounded lip. Decoration consists of incised lines slanting down the exterior surface of the vessel walls.

Proveniences: Coll. 34(1)/ESUCH-18; Coll. 27(3)/ESUCH-27.

(7) White-and-Orange/Redware (e.g., see Fig. 207 a, b)

Description: Open bowl with outslanted and slightly incurving walls and rounded lip. Decoration consists of broad, geometric orange and white designs painted on the exterior surface of the vessel. The entire exterior surface is highly polished, giving this type a very distinctive and easily recognized appearance (Note: it is very similar to the Castillo White, Red, Orange type of Virú Valley; cf. Strong and Evans 1952:344-347).

Provenience: Coll. 102(1)/ESUCH-41; Coll. 354(4)/ESUCH-64.

Early Suchimancillo Bowl 4 (Fig. 203)

Number: 36 sherds, or ca. 2.2% of the Early Suchimancillo assemblage.

General description: Deep, open bowl with straight or slightly incurving, outslanted walls. Rim diameters vary from 16-25 cm, with a mean of 21 cm and a standard deviation of 3.7 cm. Wall thickness below the rim is uniformly 5 mm.

Paste: Temper consists of medium grain sand in moderate quantities. Paste color is red.

Surface characteristics: Interior and exterior surfaces are uniformly oxidized redware. Most of the sherds in the sample have exterior burnishing lines similar to those that appear on the reddish-brownware of the preceding Vinzos Period.

Distribution: This bowl type is widely distributed at habitation, habitation-cemetery, and cemetery sites throughout the main area of Early Suchimancillo occupation, including Clusters 2 and 3. Collection proveniences (with number of sherds in parentheses)/site numbers are:

Coll. 6(1)/ESUCH-13; Coll. 30(3)/ESUCH-17; Coll. 22(2)/ESUCH-25; Coll. 27(1)/ESUCH-27; Coll. 104(2)/ESUCH-28; Coll. 109(8)/ESUCH-43; Coll. 111(3)/ESUCH-45; Coll. 137(1)/ESUCH-48; Coll. 233(1)/ESUCH-54; Coll. 352(1)/ESUCH-77; Coll. 208(1)/ESUCH-82; Coll. 225(2)/ESUCH-86; Coll. 226(1)/ESUCH-90; Coll. 258(1)/ESUCH-92; Coll. 272(1)/ESUCH-93; Coll. 332(4)/ESUCH-101; Coll. 329(1)/ESUCH-119; Coll. 285(1)/ESUCH-127; Coll. 281(1)/ESUCH-128.

Chronological assessment: Bowl 4 is somewhat similar in form to Cayhuamarca Bowl 6a (Fig. 192) and Vinzos Bowl 4a (Fig. 196), but can be easily distinguished on the basis of its redware paste. It therefore appears to be a good Early Suchimancillo time marker.

Inter-regional comparisons: From his materials excavated at Recuay sites in the Callejón de Huaylas, Bennett (1944, p. 55, Fig. 17 B; and p. 100, Fig. 32 - Shape A-1) illustrates deeper bowls that are similar in form and size to Early Suchimancillo Bowls 4 and 5.

Early Suchimancillo Bowl 5 (Fig. 203)

Number: 5 sherds, or ca. .3% of the Early Suchimancillo assemblage.

General description: Deep, open bowl with outslanted and slightly incurving walls. Rim diameters are: 16 cm, 18 cm, 20 cm, 20 cm, and 20 cm. Wall thickness below the rim ranges between 3 mm and 5 mm.

Paste: Temper consists of fine or medium sand, with the thicker-walled vessels having larger grain size. Paste color is red, with gray cores noted on four of the five sherds.

Surface characteristics: Exteriors and interiors of three of the bowls are decorated with red slipping. The remaining two sherds have the following decoration: (1) white-and-orange/red-slipped exterior (Fig. 203, Bowl 5, bottom); and (2) white-orange-black-red/redware exterior (Fig. 203, Bowl 5, top).

Distribution: This bowl type has a distribution limited to three habitation and habitation-cemetery sites in Early Suchimancillo Cluster 2. Collection proveniences (with number of sherds in parentheses)/site numbers are:

Coll. 19(1)/ESUCH-19; Coll. 23(1)/ESUCH-24; Coll. 356(3)/ESUCH-60.

Chronological assessment: The Bowl 5 decorated redware type appears to be limited to the Early Suchimancillo Period.

Inter-regional comparisons: See Early Suchimancillo Bowl 4.

Early Suchimancillo Bowl 6a (Fig. 203)

Number: 18 sherds, or ca. 1.1% of the Early Suchimancillo assemblage.

General description: Open bowl with either straight outslanted walls or globular walls. All bowls in the sample have narrow, everted rims. Rim diameters vary from 16-45 cm, with a mean of 24.9 cm and a standard deviation of 7.3 cm. Wall thickness below the rim ranges between 4 mm and 8 mm, with a mean of 6.2 mm.

Paste: Temper consists uniformly of medium sand in moderate quantities. Paste color in about 50% of the sherds is fully oxidized redware, and in the other 50% is reddish-brownware. Gray cores were noted on two of the redware sherds.

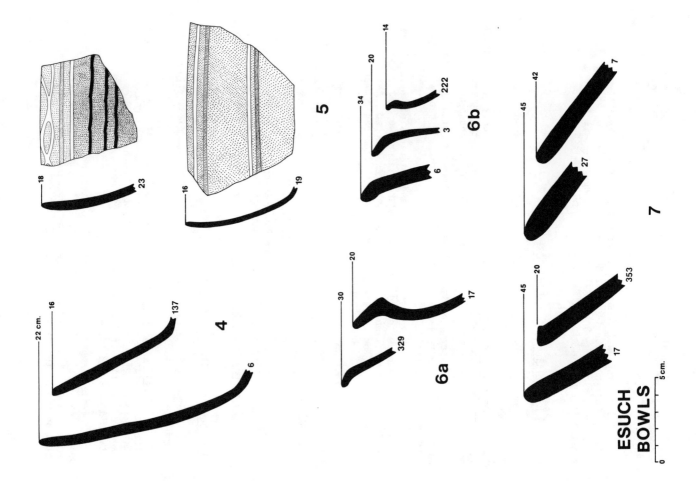

398

Fig. 203. Early Suchimancillo Period ceramics: Bowls 4, 5, 6a, 6b, and 7.

Surface characteristics: Interior and exterior surfaces are undecorated on both the redware and the reddish-brownware sherds.

Distribution: This bowl type is widely distributed in habitation and cemetery sites in Early Suchimancillo Cluster 2, and was found at two sites in Cluster 3 (SVP-ESUCH-119, 123). Collection proveniences (with number of sherds in parentheses)/site numbers are:

Coll. 373(1)/ESUCH-5; Coll. 372(1)/ESUCH-7; Coll. 17(1)/ESUCH-19; Coll. 120(2)/ESUCH-36; Coll. 115(2)/ESUCH-38; Coll. 151(2)/ESUCH-42; Coll. 108(1)/ESUCH-43; Coll. 351(1)/ESUCH-80; Coll. 249(3)/ESUCH-84; Coll. 300(2)/ESUCH-99; Coll. 329(1)/ESUCH-119; Coll. 50(1)/ESUCH-123.

Chronological assessment: Although bearing some similarity to Late Suchimancillo Jar 5a (Fig. 215), this vessel form appears to be a good diagnostic of Early Suchimancillo Period.

Inter-regional comparisons: Small globular bowls with narrow, everted rims from Quinú Period materials excavated at Pashash by Grieder (1978, p. 64, Fig. 34 1-n) appear to be similar to Early Suchimancillo Bowls 6a and 6b. Some variants of Bowls 6a and 6b are also similar to a Recuay bowl from Shankaiyán site in the Callejón de Huaylas, illustrated in Bennett (1944, p. 55, Fig. 17 D).

Early Suchimancillo Bowl 6b (Fig. 203)

Number: 8 sherds, or ca. .5% of the Early Suchimancillo assemblage.

General description: Open bowl with either straight, slightly outslanted walls or with globular walls. All bowls in the sample have narrow, everted rims. Rim diameters vary from 14-36 cm, with a mean of 22.6 cm and a standard deviation of 9.8 cm. Wall thickness below the rim is either 4 mm or 8 mm, with five of the sherds in the thinner category.

Paste: Temper consists uniformly of medium sand in moderate quantities. Paste color is red.

Surface characteristics: Exterior surfaces of all bowls in the sample are covered with a red slip. Interiors are plain redware.

Distribution: This bowl type is widely distributed at habitation sites in the upper two-thirds part of Early Suchimancillo Cluster 2. Collection proveniences (with number of sherds in parentheses)/site numbers are:

Coll. 372(1)/ESUCH-7; Coll. 6(1)/ESUCH-13; Coll. 3(1)/ESUCH-14; Coll. 35(1)/ESUCH-22; Coll. 38(1)/ESUCH-32; Coll. 115(1)/ESUCH-38; Coll. 243(1)/ESUCH-63; Coll. 257(1)/ESUCH-92.

Chronological assessment: Bowl 6b is a decorated redware type that appears to be limited to the Early Suchimancillo Period.

Inter-regional comparisons: See Early Suchimancillo Bowl 6a.

Early Suchimancillo Bowl 7 (Fig. 203)

Number: 18 sherds, or ca. 1.1% of the Early Suchimancillo assemblage.

General description: Large open bowl with straight outslanted walls. Lips are generally rounded, although one sherd with a horizontal beveled lip and low interior ridge was also noted. Rim diameters vary from 20-54 cm, with a mean of 36.7 cm and a standard deviation of 11.1 cm. Wall thickness below the rim ranges widely between 7 mm and 15 mm, with a mean of 11.7 mm and a standard deviation of 2.8 mm.

Paste: Temper consists uniformly of medium sand in moderate quantities. Ten of the sherds in the sample (or 55%) have fully oxidized redware paste. The remaining eight sherds (45%) have reddish-brownware paste.

Surface characteristics: Interior and exterior surfaces on the redware sherds are plain. Interior and exterior surfaces on the reddish-brown sherds are decorated with randomly placed, roughly parallel groups of burnishing lines.

Distribution: This bowl type is widely, but sparsely, distributed at habitation and habitation-cemetery sites in Early Suchimancillo Clusters 2 and 3. Collection proveniences (with number of sherds in parentheses)/site numbers are:

Colls. 7(1), 14(1), 17(1)/ESUCH-19; Coll. 27(6)/ESUCH-27; Coll. 353(1)/ESUCH-65; Colls. 249(1), 250(2)/ESUCH-84; Coll. 225(1)/ESUCH-86; Coll. 260(1)/ESUCH-94; Coll. 321(2)/ESUCH-124; Coll. 288(1)/ESUCH-126.

Chronological assessment: The reddish-brown variant of Bowl 7 is similar in form, size, and paste to Cayhuamarca Bowl 5 (Fig. 191) and Vinzos Bowl 3 (Fig. 196). Its burnished decoration distinguishes it from the Cayhuamarca bowl, but not from the Vinzos bowl which is decorated in the same manner. The redware variant of the Early Suchimancillo bowl, however, appears to be a good diagnostic of this period.

Inter-regional comparisons: See discussion under Vinzos Bowl 3.

Early Suchimancillo Jar 1 (Fig. 204)

Number: 154 sherds, or ca. 9.2% of the Early Suchimancillo assemblage.

General description: Globular jar with constricted mouth (neckless olla). While a few sherds have plain direct rims, most of the sherds in the sample have interior thickening at the rim. Exterior thickening and symmetrical thickening at the rim were also noted. As Fig. 204 shows, approximately one-half of the sherds with interior or exterior thickening have a distinctive ridge that forms a definite angle, or point, with the vessel wall. Rim diameters vary from 10-40 cm, with a mean of 17.6 cm and a standard deviation of 5.1 cm. Wall thickness below the rim ranges widely between 3 mm and 9 mm, with a mean of 5.2 mm and a standard deviation of 1.4 mm.

Paste: Temper consists uniformly of medium sand in moderate

quantities. Paste color in about 35% of the sherds is red, while the color in the remaining 65% is reddish-brown. Gray cores are frequent in the reddish-brown sherds.

Surface characteristics: Exterior and interior surfaces of both paste variants are plain.

Distribution: Jar 1 was found widely distributed in habitation, habitation-cemetery, and a few cemetery sites throughout the area of Early Suchimancillo occupation, including Clusters 2 and 3. Collection proveniences (with number of sherds in parentheses)/site numbers are:

ESUCH-12; Coll. 6(4)/ESUCH-13; Coll. 29(10)/ESUCH-15; Colls. 30(3), 32(1)/ESUCH-17; Colls. 1(2), 19(2)/ESUCH-19; Coll. 18(3)/ESUCH-20; Coll. 35(1)/ESUCH-22; Coll. 24(1)/ESUCH-23; Coll. 23(3)/ESUCH-24; Coll. 27(1)/ESUCH-27; Colls. 37(1), 38(1)/ESUCH-32; Coll. 40(5)/ESUCH-33; Coll. 42(3)/ESUCH-34; Coll. 43(1)/ESUCH-35; Coll. 120(4)/ESUCH-36; Coll. 107(3)/ESUCH-41; Coll. 109(6)/ESUCH-43; Coll. 113(3)/ESUCH-46; Coll. 173(2)/ESUCH-51; Coll. 232(12)/ESUCH-54; Colls. 239(1), 240(8), 241(3)/ESUCH-56; Coll. 356(3)/ESUCH-60; Coll. 203(1)/ESUCH-71; Coll. 352(1)/ESUCH-77; Coll. 222(1)/ESUCH-88; Coll. 223(1)/ESUCH-89; Coll. 226(3)/ESUCH-90; Coll. 272(3)/ESUCH-93; Coll. 277(1)/ESUCH-98; Coll. 332(4)/ESUCH-101; Coll. 339(6)/ESUCH-111; Coll. 362(2)/ESUCH-114; Coll. 329(2)/ESUCH-119; Coll. 51(2)/ESUCH-122; Coll. 50(2)/ESUCH-123; Coll. 295(11)/ESUCH-125; Colls. 283(3), 284(4), 287(4)/ESUCH-126.

Chronological assessment: Both the redware and reddish-brownware variants of Jar 1 are generally distinguishable from Late Suchimancillo neckless ollas (see Fig. 213, Jar 1) on the basis of rim treatment. Many Early Suchimancillo neckless ollas are quite similar, however, in form and paste to Vinzos Jar 1 (Fig. 197). Nevertheless, the number of thickened rims with distinctive ridges is much greater in Early Suchimancillo. In addition, analysis of neckless ollas in probable single-component contexts showed that burnishing lines are absent on the Early Suchimancillo vessels.

Inter-regional comparisons: Among the Recuay Quimít Phase materials from Pashash site, Grieder (1978, p. 66, Fig. 35 f-i) illustrates neckless ollas that are similar in form and variability of lip treatment to the thinner-walled variants of Early Suchimancillo Jar 1.

Early Suchimancillo Jar 2 (Fig. 204)

Number: 4 sherds, or ca. .2% of the Early Suchimancillo assemblage.

General description: Small jar with constricted mouth and very low, vertical neck. An exterior bevel and small ridge are present on one of the sherds. Rim diameters are 8 cm, 12 cm, 12 cm, and 13 cm. Wall thickness below the rim is uniformly 4 mm.

Paste: Temper consists of fine or medium sand, with three of the sherds having medium grain sand. Quantity of temper in all four sherds is moderate. Paste color in two of the sherds is oxidized redware, while color in the remaining two is oxidized orangeware (possibly kaolin).

Surface characteristics: Exterior and interior surfaces on three of the sherds are undecorated. A faint white-painted design was noted on one of the orangeware sherds.

Distribution: This "ollita" type was found at three habitation sites in the uppermost part of Early Suchimancillo Cluster 2. Collection proveniences (with number of sherds in parentheses)/site numbers are:

Coll. 369(1)/ESUCH-11; Coll. 32(1)/ESUCH-17; Coll. 17(1)/ESUCH-19; Coll. 23(1)/ESUCH-24.

Chronological assessment: Jar 2 does not appear to have any counterparts in earlier or later periods, and is therefore a good Early Suchimancillo time marker. However, its limited distribution lessens its utility as a period diagnostic.

Inter-regional comparisons: In their section on the Callejón Unclassified materials of Gallinazo Period in Virú Valley, Strong and Evans (1952, p. 350, Fig. 81; see Form 4) illustrate small bowls with slightly recurved rims that are quite similar to Early Suchimancillo Jar 2.

Early Suchimancillo Jar 3 (Fig. 204)

Number: 58 sherds, or ca. 3.5% of the Early Suchimancillo assemblage.

General description: Ovoid jar with a short flaring rim. One flared pendant rim was also noted among the sherds in the sample. Rim diameters vary from 9-22 cm, with a mean of 15.9 cm and a standard deviation of 3.1 cm. Wall thickness below the rim ranges narrowly between 4 mm and 7 mm, with a mean of 5.2 mm.

Paste: Temper consists of fine or medium sand, with 90% of the sherds having medium grain sand. The quantity of temper is uniformly moderate. Paste color is red in 40% of the sherds, and reddish-brown in the other 60%.

Surface characteristics: Exterior and interior surfaces of most of the redware and reddish-brownware vessels are undecorated. Three of the redware jar fragments have an exterior polished red slip, and the lip of another jar was red-painted.

Distribution: This jar type is widely distributed throughout the area of Early Suchimancillo occupation, including habitation, habitation-cemetery, and cemetery sites in Clusters 2 and 3. Collection proveniences (with number of sherds in parentheses)/site numbers are:

Coll. 374(4)/ESUCH-6; Coll. 372(1)/ESUCH-7; Coll. 369(2)/ESUCH-11; Coll. 2(1)/ESUCH-14; Coll. 29(2)/ESUCH-15; Coll. 31(1)/ESUCH-16; Colls. 30(1), 32(1)/ESUCH-17; Colls. 14(1), 19(1)/ESUCH-19; Coll. 24(2)/ESUCH-23; Coll. 23(1)/ESUCH-24; Coll. 27(3)/ESUCH-27; Coll. 99(4)/ESUCH-29; Coll. 39(1)/ESUCH-31; Coll. 40(1)/ESUCH-33; Coll. 101(4)/ESUCH-41; Coll. 112(3)/ESUCH-45; Coll. 173(1)/ESUCH-51; Colls. 240(2), 241(1)/ESUCH-56; Coll. 198(1)/ESUCH-61; Coll. 206(1)/ESUCH-73; Coll. 224(2)/ESUCH-86; Coll. 226(1)/ESUCH-90; Coll. 260(2)/ESUCH-94; Coll. 332(1)/ESUCH-101; Coll. 362(1)/ESUCH-114; Coll. 321(1)/ESUCH-124; Coll.

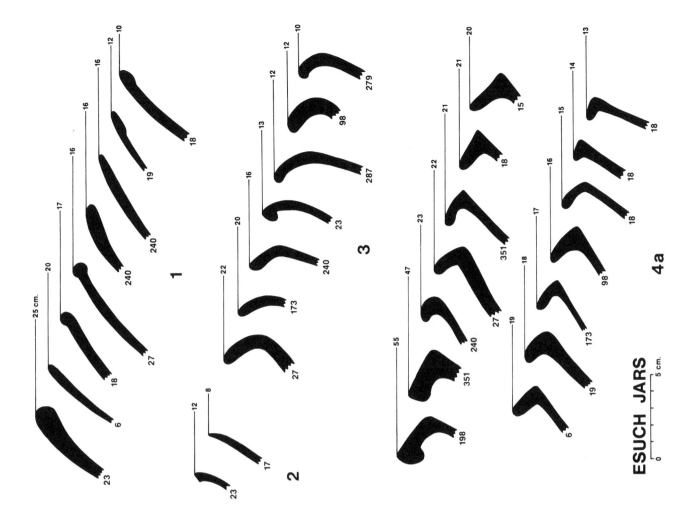

ESUCH JARS

0 ___ 5 cm.

Fig. 204. Early Suchimancillo Period ceramics: Jars 1, 2, 3, and 4a.

295(1)/ESUCH-125; Colls. 284(1), 287(6), 288(1)/ESUCH-126; Coll. 279(1)/ESUCH-129.

Chronological assessment: The reddish-brown variant of Jar 3 is similar in form and paste to Cayhuamarca Jar 2a (Fig. 193) and Vinzos Jar 2a (Fig. 197). However, most sherds in this category can be distinguished from the earlier vessel types on the basis of either (1) form (Cayhuamarca vessels have rims that are uniformly less flared); or (2) the absence of burnished decoration on the exterior (60% of the Vinzos jars are covered with this decoration).

Inter-regional comparisons: Jars with this rim form are not reported in the literature on ceramics of areas adjacent to the Lower Santa region.

Early Suchimancillo Jar 4a (Fig. 204)

Number: 208 sherds, or ca. 12.5% of the Early Suchimancillo assemblage.

General description: Globular jar with a short flared or everted rim. Distinct interior corner points are present at the juncture between the neck and the body on most of the vessel fragments. Rim diameters vary from 9-55 cm, with a mean of 18.2 cm and a standard deviation of 5.8 cm. Wall thickness below the rim ranges widely between 4 mm and 9mm, with a mean of 6.4 mm and a standard deviation of 1.1 mm.

Paste: Temper consists of fine or medium sand, with 60% of the sherds in the sample having medium sand. Paste color in 55% of the sherds is oxidized redware, while the other 45% have reddish-brown paste.

Surface characteristics: Exterior and interior surfaces on all of the sherds are undecorated.

Distribution: This jar type is widely distributed throughout the area of Early Suchimancillo occupation, including habitation, habitation-cemetery, and cemetery sites in Clusters 1, 2, and 3. Collection proveniences (with number of sherds in parentheses)/site numbers are:

Colls. 30(1), 32(4)/ESUCH-1; Coll. 6(1)/ESUCH-13; Coll. 29(3)/ESUCH-15; 19(9)/ESUCH-19; Coll. 18(6)/ESUCH-20; Colls. 1(1), 7(8), 14(5), 15(2), 17(6)/ ESUCH-22; Coll. 24(4)/ESUCH-23; Coll. 23(12)/ESUCH-24; Coll. 26(9)/ ESUCH-26; Coll. 27(5)/ESUCH-27; Coll. 104(6)/ESUCH-28; Coll. 99(3)/ ESUCH-29; Coll. 37(1)/ESUCH-32; Coll. 43(8)/ESUCH-35; Coll. 147(2)/ ESUCH-39; Coll. 101(6), 107(5)/ESUCH-41; Coll. 109(1)/ESUCH-43; Coll. 153(5)/ESUCH-44; Colls. 111(3), 112(13)/ESUCH-45; Coll. 113(11)/ ESUCH-46; Coll. 137(1)/ESUCH-48; Coll. 173(1)/ESUCH-51; Coll. 193(9)/ ESUCH-52; Colls. 233(6), 232(5)/ESUCH-54; Coll. 231(1)/ESUCH-55; Colls. 240(2), 241(1)/ESUCH-56; Coll. 198(2)/ESUCH-61; Coll. 244(3)/ESUCH-62; Coll. 351(3)/ESUCH-80; Colls. 249(1), 250(1)/ESUCH-84; Coll. 221(1)/ ESUCH-87; Coll. 222(1)/ESUCH-88; Coll. 222(1)/ESUCH-91; Coll. 260(1)/ ESUCH-94; Coll. 277(1)/ESUCH-98; Coll. 342(7)/ESUCH-109; Coll. 339(1)/ ESUCH-111; Coll. 362(1)/ESUCH-114; Colls. 287(1), 288(1)/ESUCH-126; Coll. 281(1)/ESUCH-128.

Chronological assessment: Some forms of the reddish-brown variant of Jar 4a are similar to Vinzos Jar 3a (Fig. 198). In general, however, most of the Jar 4a rim forms are indistinguishable from the limited number of forms present in the Vinzos jar type. On the other hand, some forms of the redware variant of Jar 4a are similar to Late Suchimancillo Jar 5a. But, as with the Vinzos Period jar, the Late Suchimancillo jar type has a very limited number of rim forms, and thus many of the Early Suchimancillo redware rim sherds are distinguishable from those of the later period.

Inter-regional comparisons: From his materials excavated at the Gallinazo Group in Virú Valley, Bennett (1950, pp. 77-78, Figs. 20 C and 21 D) illustrates decorated jars that are quite similar in form to some variants of Early Suchimancillo Jars 4a and 4b (note especially the slightly outcurved, or flared, rim on some vessels from both Santa and Virú). Other very similar rim profiles from Virú are illustrated for Castillo Modeled and Castillo Incised vessels in Strong and Evans (1952; see especially p. 313, Fig. 62 - Form 1; and p. 320, Fig. 65 - Form 4).

Early Suchimancillo Jar 4b (Fig. 205)

Number: 29 sherds, or ca. 1.7% of the Early Suchimancillo assemblage.

General description: Globular vessel with a broad, everted and slightly flared rim. Rim diameters vary from 24-60 cm, with a mean of 37.4 cm and a standard deviation of 12.5 cm. Wall thickness below the rim ranges between 8 mm and 11 mm, with approximately 85% of the sample at the lower end of the range.

Paste: Temper consists uniformly of medium sand in moderate quantities. Paste color in about 20% of the sherds is oxidized redware, while the other 80% have reddish-brown paste.

Surface characteristics: The exterior surface, as well as the rim and interior of the neck, on about 40% of both the redware and the reddish-brownware sherds are decorated with randomly placed, roughly parallel groups of burnishing lines.

Distribution: This jar type is widely distributed throughout most of the area of Early Suchimancillo occupation, including habitation, habitation-cemetery, and cemetery sites in Clusters 2 and 3. Collection proveniences (with number of sherds in parentheses)/site numbers are:

Coll. 374(1)/ESUCH-6; Coll. 31(1)/ESUCH-16; Coll. 18(1)/ESUCH-20; Coll. 20(1)/ESUCH-21; Coll. 35(2)/ESUCH-22; Coll. 22(1)/ESUCH-25; Coll. 148(1)/ESUCH-40; Coll. 137(1)/ESUCH-48; Coll. 239(1)/ESUCH-56; Coll. 198(1)/ESUCH-61; Coll. 353(2)/ESUCH-65; Coll. 205(1)/ESUCH-72; Colls. 249(1), 250(1)/ESUCH-84; Coll. 221(2)/ESUCH-87; Coll. 257(1)/ESUCH-92; Coll. 301(1)/ESUCH-96; Coll. 341(2)/ESUCH-110; Coll. 339(1)/ESUCH-111; Coll. 295(1)/ESUCH-125; Coll. 284(1)/ESUCH-126; Coll. 281(4)/ESUCH-128.

Chronological assessment: Some rim forms of the reddish-brown variant of Jar 4b are similar to Cayhuamarca Jar 3a (Fig. 193) and Vinzos Jar 4a (Fig. 199). In general, however, the rims of the Early Suchimancillo jar are much broader than those of the preceding two

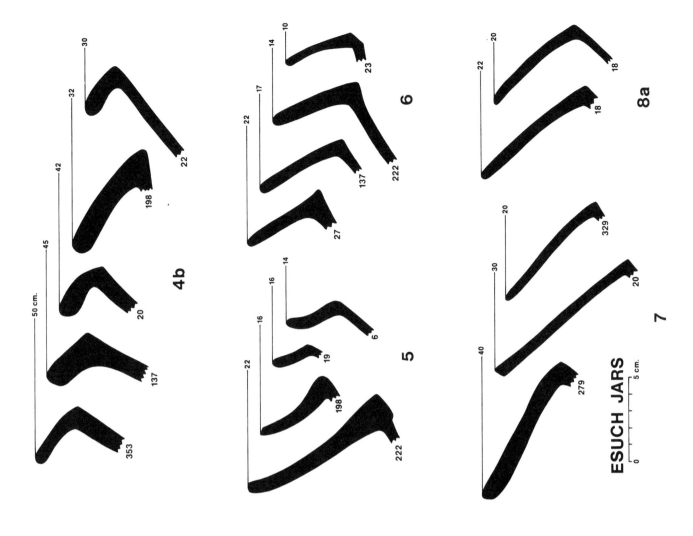

Fig. 205. Early Suchimancillo Period ceramics: Jars 4b, 5, 6, 7, and 8a.

403

periods. By the same token, the redware variant of Early Suchimancillo Jar 4b can be distinguished from later ollas of similar form on the basis of its sharply everted rim.

Inter-regional comparisons: See Early Suchimancillo Jar 4a.

Early Suchimancillo Jar 5 (Fig. 205)

Number: 72 sherds, or ca. 4.3% of the Early Suchimancillo assemblage.

General description: Globular jar with an outslanted and slightly incurved, or bulging, neck. Some of the larger vessels have horizontal or interior beveled lips, as well as a distinctively thickened interior at the juncture of the neck and the body. Lips on smaller vessels are rounded. Rim diameters vary from 12-22 cm, with a mean of about 15 cm and a standard deviation of 2.8 cm. Wall thickness below the rim ranges between 4 mm and 6 mm, with a mean of 4.6 mm.

Paste: Temper consists uniformly of medium sand in moderate quantities. Paste color in about 80% of the sherds is oxidized redware, while the other 20% have reddish-brown paste. Gray cores were noted on about 35% of the redware sherds.

Surface characteristics: The exterior surface, as well as the interior of the rim and neck, on about 50% of the reddish-brown sherds are decorated with burnishing lines. The remaining sherds have undecorated redware or reddish-brownware surfaces.

Distribution: This jar type has a wide distribution throughout Early Suchimancillo Cluster 2, including habitation, habitation-cemetery, and a few cemetery sites. Collection proveniences (with number of sherds in parentheses)/site numbers are:

Coll. 375(2)/ESUCH-3; Coll. 6(16)/ESUCH-13; Coll. 3(1)/ESUCH-14; Colls. 32(3), 33(1)/ESUCH-17; Colls. 1(1), 14(1), 19(1)/ESUCH-19; Coll. 18(2)/ESUCH-20; Coll. 35(5)/ESUCH-22; Coll. 24(1)/ESUCH-23; Coll. 23(1)/ESUCH-24; Coll. 27(1)/ESUCH-27; Coll. 42(7)/ESUCH-34; Coll. 43(4)/ESUCH-35; Coll. 120(1)/ESUCH-36; Coll. 115(1)/ESUCH-38; Coll. 107(1)/ESUCH-41; Coll. 153(2)/ESUCH-44; Coll. 112(1)/ESUCH-45; Coll. 113(4)/ESUCH-46; Coll. 198(1)/ESUCH-61; Coll. 244(1)/ESUCH-62; Coll. 203(2)/ESUCH-71; Coll. 225(1)/ESUCH-86; Coll. 222(1)/ESUCH-88; Coll. 227(5)/ESUCH-91; Coll. 257(1)/ESUCH-92; Coll. 300(2)/ESUCH-99; Coll. 345(1)/ESUCH-112.

Chronological assessment: The general form of Jar 5 is a very good diagnostic for the two Suchimancillo periods. Distinguishing between the Early and Late Suchimancillo (Fig. 214, Jar 4a) forms is somewhat problematical, but the analysis of single-component collections suggests the following criteria: (1) reddish-brown variants all date to Early Suchimancillo; (2) the smaller variants of Jar 5 with essentially vertical necks stand in contrast to the more strongly outslanted necks of Late Suchimancillo Period; and (3) the larger variants of Jar 5 with thin walls that do not taper toward the lip can be distinguished from the thicker-walled, non-tapered variants of Late Suchimancillo Jar 4a.

Inter-regional comparisons: Jars with this rim form are not reported in the literature on ceramics of areas adjacent to the Lower Santa region.

Early Suchimancillo Jar 6 (Fig. 205)

Number: 188 sherds, or ca. 11.3% of the Early Suchimancillo assemblage.

General description: Globular jar with an everted rim. The wall of the rim slants outward 20-30° from the vertical, and is either straight or slightly flaring. A distinct interior corner point is present at the juncture of the neck and the body of the vessel. On most of the sherds, this point is either thickened or pinched outward away from the vessel wall. Rim diameters vary from 10-32 cm, with a mean of 20.1 cm and a standard deviation of 5.5 cm. Wall thickness below the rim ranges widely between 4 mm and 10 mm, with a mean of 6.3 mm and a standard deviation of 1.1 mm.

Paste: Temper consists of fine or medium sand, with 90% of the sherds in the sample having medium grain sand. The quantity of temper in all sherds is moderate. Paste color in about 40% of the sherds is oxidized redware, while the other 60% have reddish-brown paste. Gray cores were noted on about 10% of the sherds, and fire clouding is present on the exteriors of another 10%.

Surface characteristics: The exterior surface, as well as the interior of the rim and neck, on about 30% of the reddish-brown sherds are decorated with burnishing lines. The remaining sherds in the sample have undecorated red or reddish-brown surfaces.

Distribution: This jar type has a wide distribution throughout Early Suchimancillo Clusters 2 and 3, in habitation, habitation-cemetery, and cemetery sites. Collection proveniences (with number of sherds in parentheses)/site numbers are:

Coll. 372(1)/ESUCH-7; Coll. 370(3)/ESUCH-9; Coll. 3(1)/ESUCH-14; Coll. 29(1)/ESUCH-15; Coll. 30(1)/ESUCH-17; Coll. 34(1)/ESUCH-18; Colls. 1(3), 7(1), 14(3), 15(1), 19(2)/ESUCH-19; Coll. 18(7)/ESUCH-20; Coll. 35(4)/ESUCH-22; Coll. 24(1)/ESUCH-23; Coll. 23(3)/ESUCH-24; Coll. 26(4)/ESUCH-26; Coll. 27(4)/ESUCH-27; Coll. 104(1)/ESUCH-28; Coll. 40(1)/ESUCH-33; Coll. 43(8)/ESUCH-35; Coll. 115(1)/ESUCH-38; Coll. 110(1)/ESUCH-43; Coll. 153(3)/ESUCH-44; Coll. 137(1)/ESUCH-48; Coll. 138(2)/ESUCH-49; Colls. 157/159(1)/ESUCH-53; Coll. 232(3)/ESUCH-54; Coll.241(2)/ESUCH-56; Coll. 198(1)/ESUCH-61; Coll. 244(4)/ESUCH-62; Coll. 243(6)/ESUCH-63; Coll. 354(4)/ESUCH-64; Coll. 353(1)/ESUCH-65; Coll. 203(4)/ESUCH-71; Coll. 245(4)/ESUCH-74; Coll. 352(19)/ESUCH-77; Coll. 351(2)/ESUCH-80; Coll. 209(1)/ESUCH-83; Colls. 249(1), 250(1)/ESUCH-84; Coll. 222(2)/ESUCH-88; Coll. 229(2)/ESUCH-91; Colls. 257(13), 258(4)/ESUCH-92; Coll. 272(16)/ESUCH-93; Coll. 308(4)/ESUCH-95; Coll. 300(3)/ESUCH-99; Coll. 335(2)/ESUCH-108; Coll. 342(13)/ESUCH-109; Coll. 341(3)/ESUCH-110; Coll. 339(3)/ESUCH-111; Coll. 345(1)/ESUCH-112; Coll. 284(1), 288(3)/ESUCH-126; Coll. 285(2)/ESUCH-127; Colls. 280(2), 281(1)/ESUCH-128.

Chronological assessment: Jar 6 is similar in form to Vinzos Jar

4b (Fig. 199), as well as to Late Suchimancillo Jar 5b (Fig. 215) and Early Tanguche Jar 2c (Fig. 236). Most rim variants of Jar 6 can be distinguished from Vinzos Jar 4b by their consistently less flared neck wall. The Late Suchimancillo Jar type has the same two paste variants as Jar 6 (although reversed in order of importance), but the Early Suchimancillo Jar can be distinguished on the basis of its consistently lower neck height, as well as by the presence of burnished decoration (which does not appear on the reddish-brown variant of the Late Suchimancillo Jar). By the same token, the reddish-brown variant and interior corner points are critical distinguishing features that set the Early Suchimancillo Jar off from Early Tanguche Jar 2c.

Inter-regional comparisons: In terms of paste and exterior decoration, this jar type is clearly a later form of Vinzos Jar 4b and is related to the general pan-valley Huacapongo Polished Plain type (cf. Collier 1955; Strong and Evans 1952).

Early Suchimancillo Jar 7 (Fig. 205)

Number: 46 sherds, or ca. 2.8% of the Early Suchimancillo assemblage.

General description: Globular jar with a very broad, everted rim. The wall of the rim is usually thin and straight, and slants outward from the vertical at an angle of from 40-60°. Lips are either rounded or exterior beveled. Rim diameters vary from 17-40 cm, with a mean of 24.2 cm and a standard deviation of 4.4 cm. Wall thickness below the rim ranges between 5 mm and 9 mm, although the mean of 5.8 mm reflects the fact that 90% of the sherds range more narrowly between 5 mm and 7 mm.

Paste: Temper consists of fine or medium sand, with 80% of the sherds in the sample having medium grain sand. The quantity of temper in all sherds is moderate. Paste color is oxidized redware, with the exception of a single reddish-brownware sherd. Gray cores were noted on about 15% of the sherds.

Surface decoration: Two sherds were noted with exterior burnished decoration, and 11 sherds have white-painted lines on the lip and on the exterior angle between the neck and body of the vessel. The remaining sherds are undecorated redware.

Distribution: This jar type was found widely distributed at habitation and habitation-cemetery sites in the upper half of Early Suchimancillo Cluster 2, and at two sites in Cluster 3 (SVP-ESUCH-119, 129). Collection proveniences (with number of sherds in parentheses)/ site numbers are:

Coll. 3(1)/ESUCH-14; Coll. 29(1)/ESUCH-15; Coll. 33(1)/ESUCH-17; Colls. 10(11), 15(2), 19(5)/ESUCH-19; Coll. 18(6)/ESUCH-20; Coll. 20(1)/ ESUCH-21; Coll. 23(2)/ESUCH-24; Coll. 22(3)/ESUCH-25; Coll. 43(6)/ ESUCH-35; Coll. 101(1)/ESUCH-41; Colls. 108(1), 110(1)/ESUCH-43; Coll. 137(1)/ESUCH-48; Coll. 244(1)/ESUCH-62; Coll. 329(1)/ESUCH-119; Coll. 279(1)/ESUCH-129.

Chronological assessment: Jar 7 is not found in single-component contexts dating to any other period than Early Suchimancillo. It therefore appears to be a good time marker for this period.

Inter-regional comparisons: From his materials excavated at the sierra site of Pashash, Grieder (1978, p. 66, Fig. 35 s) illustrates the rim profile of a vessel that appears to be identical to the thinner-walled variants of Early Suchimancillo Jars 7 and 8a.

Early Suchimancillo Jar 8a (Fig. 205)

Number: 30 sherds, or ca. 1.8% of the Early Suchimancillo assemblage.

General description: Globular jar with a very broad, everted rim. The wall of the rim is thin, either straight or slightly flared, and slants outward from the vertical at an angle of about 40°. Lips are either rounded or have a narrow horizontal bevel. Rim diameters vary from 20-39 cm, with a mean of 24.1 cm and a standard deviation of 4.2 cm. Wall thickness below the rim ranges between 5 mm and 6 mm, with about 75% of the sherds at the lower end of the range.

Paste: Temper consists uniformly of medium sand in moderate quantities. Paste color is oxidized redware, with gray cores noted on five sherds.

Surface characteristics: The exterior and interior surfaces of 90% of the sherds are covered with a polished red slip. The other 10% have polished red slipping on the exterior only.

Distribution: This is the second most widely distributed of five jar form types (Jars 8a, 8b, 8c, 8d, and 8e) with a polished red slip that are found throughout most of the area of Early Suchimancillo occupation, including habitation, habitation-cemetery, and cemetery sites. Collection proveniences (with number of sherds in parentheses)/ site numbers are:

Coll. 381(1)/ESUCH-1; Coll. 368(1)/ESUCH-12; Coll. 18(1)/ESUCH-20; Coll. 35(1)/ESUCH-22; Coll. 128(9)/ESUCH-37; Coll. 112(3)/ESUCH-45; Coll. 113(8)/ESUCH-46; Coll. 138(1)/ESUCH-49; Coll. 198(1)/ESUCH-61; Coll. 354(1)/ESUCH-64; Coll. 205(1)/ESUCH-72; Coll. 229(2)/ESUCH-91.

Chronological assessment: The rim form and polished red slip that characterize Jars 8a-8e are not found in single-component contexts dating to any other period that Early Suchimancillo. All variants of Jar 8 therefore appear to be good diagnostic time markers for this period.

Inter-regional comparisons: See Early Suchimancillo Jar 7.

Early Suchimancillo Jar 8b (Fig. 206)

Number: 54 sherds, or ca. 3.2% of the Early Suchimancillo assemblage.

General description: Globular jar with a broad, everted rim. The wall of the rim is straight or slightly flared, and slants out from the vertical at an angle of about 45°. Lips are rounded or tapered, and a few have a horizontal bevel. The exterior surface below the lip often is

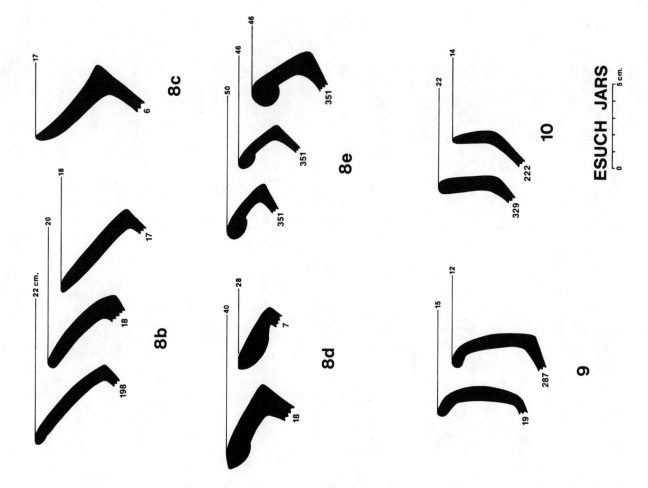

Fig. 206. Early Suchimancillo Period ceramics: Jars 8b, 8c, 8d, 8e, 9, and 10.

slightly thickened, with a distinctly visible angle between the thickened area and the wall of the rim (e.g., see the profile from Coll. 198, in Fig. 206). Rim diameters vary from 18-39 cm, with a mean of 25.4 cm and a standard deviation of 4.6 cm. Wall thickness below the rim ranges widely between 4 mm and 9 mm, with a mean of 5.2 mm and a standard deviation of 1.1 mm.

Paste: Temper consists more-or-less uniformly of medium sand in moderate quantities, with about 20% of the sherds having slightly greater amounts of medium grain sand. Paste color is oxidized redware, with gray cores noted on 35% of the sherds.

Surface characteristics: The exterior and interior surfaces of all sherds in the sample are covered with a polished red slip. One of the sherds also had randomly placed burnishing lines on the exterior surface.

Distribution: This is the most widely distributed of five jar form types (Jars 8a, 8b, 8c, 8d, and 8e) with a polished red slip that are found in habitation, habitation-cemetery, and cemetery sites throughout most of the area of Early Suchimancillo occupation. Collection proveniences (with number of sherds in parentheses)/site numbers are:

Coll. 6(6)/ESUCH-13; Coll. 3(1)/ESUCH-14; Coll. 29(2)/ESUCH-15; Colls. 32(1), 33(7)/ESUCH-17; Colls. 1(1), 7(1), 17(1), 19(1)/ESUCH-19; Coll. 20(1)/ESUCH-21; Coll. 35(3)/ESUCH-22; Coll. 24(2)/ESUCH-23; Coll. 27(1)/ESUCH-27; Coll. 117(1)/ESUCH-30; Coll. 42(3)/ESUCH-34; Coll. 112(6)/ESUCH-45; Coll. 134(1)/ESUCH-47; Coll. 138(1)/ESUCH-49; Coll. 233(1)/ESUCH-54; Coll. 198(2)/ESUCH-61; Coll. 203(6)/ESUCH-71; Coll. 206(1)/ESUCH-73; Coll. 352(1)/ESUCH-77; Coll. 351(2)/ESUCH-80; Coll. 329(1)/ESUCH-119.

Chronological assessment: See Early Suchimancillo Jar 8a.

Inter-regional comparisons: Grieder (1978, p. 66, Fig. 35 p-r) illustrates Recuay Quinú Phase Jars that are quite similar in rim form and lip treatment to Early Suchimancillo Jars 8b, 8d, and 8e.

Early Suchimancillo Jar 8c (Fig. 206)

Number: 5 sherds, or ca. .3% of the Early Suchimancillo assemblage.

General description: Globular jar with an outslanted and slightly incurving, or bulging, neck. The wall of the neck tapers almost to a point at the lip. A distinct corner point is present on the interior of the vessel at the juncture of the neck and the body. Rim diameters are all 17 cm, and wall thickness below the rim is 7 mm (Note: the fact that the five sherds are all from the same site and the uniformity of dimensions both raise the possibility that a single vessel is involved; nevertheless, the scattered distribution of the sherds on the site as well as minor variations in rim form suggest more than one vessel is represented in the sample--all probably made by the same potter).

Paste: Temper consists uniformly of medium sand in heavy quantities. Paste color is oxidized redware, with gray cores noted on all five sherds.

Surface characteristics: The exterior and interior surfaces of the sherds are covered with a polished red slip.

Distribution: Collection provenience (with number of sherds in parentheses)/site number is:

Coll. 6(5)/ESUCH-13.

Chronological assessment: See Early Suchimancillo Jar 8a.

Inter-regional comparisons: Although jars with this rim form are not reported in the literature on the adjacent sierra, the polished red-slipped decoration on Jar 8c suggests a relationship to Recuay Quinú Phase materials excavated at Pashash by Greider (1978:65).

Early Suchimancillo Jar 8d (Fig. 206)

Number: 2 sherds, or ca. .1% of the Early Suchimancillo assemblage.

General description: Globular jar with an everted rim which is thickened on the exterior, beveled on top, and tapered to a sharp edge at the lip. Rim diameters are 28 cm and 40 cm, and wall thicknesses below the rim are 8 mm and 10 mm, respectively.

Paste: Temper consists of medium sand in moderate quantities. Paste color is red, with a thick gray core noted on the larger of the two vessels.

Surface characteristics: The exterior and interior surfaces of the sherds are covered with a polished red slip.

Distribution: Collection proveniences (with number of sherds in parentheses)/site numbers are:

Coll. 7(1)/ESUCH-19; Coll. 18(1)/ESUCH-20.

Chronological assessment: See Early Suchimancillo Jar 8a.

Inter-regional comparisons: See Early Suchimancillo Jar 8b.

Early Suchimancillo Jar 8e (Fig. 206)

Number: 4 sherds, or ca. .2% of the Early Suchimancillo assemblage.

General description: Globular jar with an everted rim that has rounded, or elliptical, thickening on the exterior below the lip. The wall of the neck is straight or slightly flared. Rim diameters are 24 cm, 46 cm, 46 cm, and 50 cm. Wall thickness below the rim ranges between 4 mm and 7 mm.

Paste: Temper consists uniformly of medium sand in moderate quantities. Paste color is red, with gray cores noted on the three sherds illustrated in Fig. 206 (all from Coll. 351).

Surface characteristics: The exterior and interior surfaces of all four sherds are covered with a polished red slip.

Distribution: Collection proveniences (with number of sherds in parentheses)/site numbers are:

Coll. 203(1)/ESUCH-71; Coll. 351(3)/ESUCH-80.

Chronological assessment: See Early Suchimancillo Jar 8a.

Inter-regional comparisons: See Early Suchimancillo Jar 8b.

Early Suchimancillo Jar 9 (Fig. 206)

Number: 14 sherds, or ca. .8% of the Early Suchimancillo assemblage.

General description: Globular jar with a short vertical neck and strongly flared lip. Rim diameters vary from 9-26 cm, with a mean of 16.2 cm and a standard deviation of 6 cm. Wall thickness below the rim ranges between 5 mm and 8 mm.

Paste: Temper consists uniformly of medium sand in moderate quantities. Paste color in ten of the sherds is oxidized redware, while the remaining four have reddish-brown paste.

Surface characteristics: The exterior and interior surfaces of two of the reddish-brown sherds are covered with burnishing lines. The remaining sherds in the sample are undecorated.

Distribution: This jar type has a wide, but scattered, distribution throughout Early Suchimancillo Cluster 2, as well as at one site in the upper part of Cluster 3 (SVP-ESUCH-119). Collection proveniences (with number of sherds in parentheses)/site numbers are:

Coll. 30(1)/ESUCH-17; Coll. 19(2)/ESUCH-19; Coll. 115(2)/ ESUCH-38; Coll. 239(1)/ESUCH-56; Coll. 203(2)/ESUCH-71; Coll. 351(1)/ ESUCH-80; Coll. 227(1)/ESUCH-91; Coll. 331(1)/ESUCH-100; Coll. 335(1)/ ESUCH-108; Coll. 343(1)/ESUCH-109; Coll. 329(1)/ESUCH-119.

Chronological assessment: Jar 9 is similar in form to Vinzos Jar 5b (Fig. 199), but is generally distinguishable from the earlier jar by its predominantly redware paste. The reddish-brown variant of Jar 9, however, is included here because it is a minor feature of otherwise single-component Early Suchimancillo collections.

Inter-regional comparisons: Although clearly a later form of the widespread Vinzos Jar 5 type (Fig. 199), Early Suchimancillo Jar 9 also has a contemporaneous Gallinazo Period counterpart in Virú Valley (see Castillo Incised, Vessel Shape 3, in Strong and Evans 1952, p. 320, Fig. 65).

Early Suchimancillo Jar 10 (Fig. 206)

Number: 10 sherds, or ca. .6% of the Early Suchimancillo assemblage.

General description: Globular jar with a short vertical neck.

Rim diameters vary from 14-35 cm, with a mean of 18.9 cm and a standard deviation of 7 cm. Wall thickness below the rim ranges between 6 mm and 8 mm.

Paste: Temper consists uniformly of medium sand in moderate quantities. Paste color is reddish-brown in seven of the sherds, and oxidized redware in the remaining three.

Surface characteristics: The exterior surface, as well as the interior of the rim and neck, of six of the seven reddish-brown sherds are covered with randomly placed burnishing lines. The remaining sherds in the sample are undecorated.

Distribution: This jar type is widely, but sparsely, distributed at habitation and habitation-cemetery sites in Early Suchimancillo Clusters 2 and 3. Collection proveniences (with number of sherds in parentheses)/site numbers are:

Coll. 368(1)/ESUCH-12; Coll. 193(1)/ESUCH-52; Colls. 157/159(1)/ ESUCH-53; Coll. 241(1)/ESUCH-56; Coll. 351(2)/ESUCH-80; Coll. 225(1)/ ESUCH-86; Coll. 222(1)/ESUCH-88; Coll. 329(1)/ESUCH-119; Coll. 282(1)/ ESUCH-126.

Chronological assessment: The reddish-brown variant of Jar 10 is similar in form and paste to Cayhuamarca Jar 4 (Fig. 194) and Vinzos Jar 6 (Fig. 200), but can be distinguished generally by the presence of burnishing lines. On the other hand, the redware variant of Jar 10 is essentially identical to Late Suchimancillo Jar 9 (Fig. 216).

Inter-regional comparisons: Globular jars with vertical necks are present in contemporaneous assemblages of several adjacent areas, including Virú Valley (cf. Strong and Evans 1952, p. 264, Fig. 40) and Pashash site (cf. Grieder 1978, p. 66, Fig. 35 l-n).

Early Suchimancillo: White-and-Orange/Redware (Fig. 207 a-c)

Number: 62 sherds, or ca. 3.7% of the Early Suchimancillo assemblage.

General description: This painted ware category includes mostly thinner-walled body sherds from what appear to have been small, globular jars. In addition to the jars, the collections include five rim sherds from bowls (see Early Suchimancillo Bowl 3, No. 7)--which are not part of the 62-sherd count shown above. White-and-Orange/Redware decoration includes (1) broad-lined geometric designs (e.g., Fig. 207 a, b); and (2) narrow-lined geometric designs in combination with curvilinear motifs (including a probable human foot; see Fig. 207 c).

Paste: Temper consists uniformly of medium sand in moderate quantities. Paste color is red, although surface color is often a dark red or reddish-brown color (possibly a slip).

Surface characteristics: Interior surfaces are plain, while the white and orange-painted exterior surface is usually highly polished-- giving sherds a distinctively shiny and darkened appearance.

Distribution: Sherds of this decorated type are widely distributed at habitation and habitation-cemetery sites throughout the

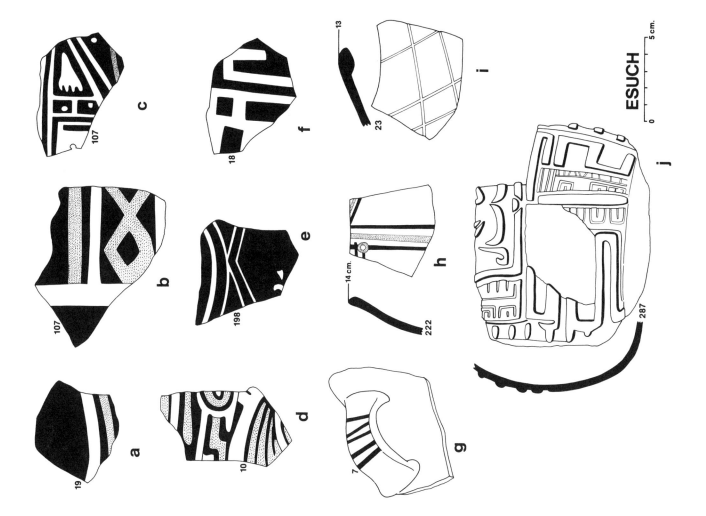

Fig. 207. Early Suchimancillo Period ceramics: miscellaneous decorated sherds.

ESUCH-31; Coll. 128(7)/ESUCH-37; Coll. 115(1+)/ESUCH-38; Coll. 107(1)/
ESUCH-41; Coll. 153(1+)/ESUCH-44; Coll. 113(1+)/ESUCH-46; Coll. 134(1+)/
ESUCH-47; Coll. 138(1+)/ESUCH-49; Coll. 232(1+)/ESUCH-54; Coll. 231(1)/
ESUCH-55; Coll. 198(1)/ESUCH-61; Coll. 353(1)/ESUCH-65; Coll. 203(1+)/
ESUCH-71; Coll. 352(1+)/ESUCH-77; Coll. 351(1+)/ESUCH-80; Coll. 222(1)/
ESUCH-88; Coll. 227(1+)/ESUCH-91.

Chronological assessment: With the exception of a few Cajamarca III Cursive-style sherds found at Early Tanguche Period sites, no kaolin ware was found in the Lower Santa survey region without substantial numbers of associated ceramic diagnostics dating to either Early or Late Suchimancillo Periods. Since many of the reddish-brownware and redware types of these two periods are clearly related to types of the Gallinazo, or pre-Moche, time period in Virú Valley, one of the significant results of our research is the indication that the presumably sierra-derived kaolin wares are also contemporaneous with the Suchimancillo, or pre-Moche, time period in Santa. Considering the fact that no kaolin was found in any single-component Guadalupito Period collections, it also seems clear that contacts between the Lower Santa region and the adjacent sierra stopped following the incorporation of Santa into the Moche state.

In deciding which of the kaolin bowl and jar types were either Early Suchimancillo or Late Suchimancillo in date, if not both, reliance was placed primarily on the analysis of probable single-component collections for each period. Since some types appear to be present in mixed component collections, it was not possible at this stage of the research to specify precisely how many kaolin sherds were early and how many were late in the overall Suchimancillo Period (indeed, some kaolin types may be diagnostic of both Early and Late Suchimancillo). For this reason, in the sherd counts given in parentheses above, "1+" indicates that an Early Suchimancillo kaolin component is present, and the number of sherds is probably "one-or-more."

Early Suchimancillo: Effigy Figures (Fig. 208)

As mentioned in the section on miscellaneous artifacts of the Vinzos Period, the number of representations of either human or animal figures found on Vinzos sites is limited to a single fragment of a human effigy neck vessel (see Fig. 200 h). The combined total of effigy figures, including depictions of both humans and animals, found on the surface of Early Suchimancillo sites is 13. This may be viewed as a substantial increase over the preceding period, but, compared to Late Suchimancillo Period with 55 human and 18 animal effigies, ceramic representations of either type constitute an insignificant percentage of the total assemblage (ca. .8%, compared to 2.8% in Late Suchimancillo).

Human effigies: Most of the eight representations of the human figure on Early Suchimancillo pottery are limited to effigy neck jars depicting the face (e.g., Fig. 208 i, j, and probably Fig. 208 h). The ears and noses of these figures are appliquéd, with punctate and incised techniques used to indicate specific details. Eyes are formed either by appliquéd, elliptically-shaped filleting or by shallow cane punching. No mouths are depicted, although given the fragmentary nature of some of the sherds the possibility that they were sometimes shown cannot be ruled

upper half of Early Suchimancillo Cluster 2, as well as in Cluster 1. Collection proveniences (with number of sherds in parentheses)/site numbers are:

Coll. 381(7)/ESUCH-1; Coll. 30(2)/ESUCH-17; Colls. 7(2), 10(7), 19(2)/ESUCH-19; Coll. 20(5)/ESUCH-20; Coll. 23(2)/ESUCH-24; Coll. 43(3)/ESUCH-35; Coll. 128(2)/ESUCH-37; Colls. 102(6), 107(5)/ESUCH-41; Coll. 153(2)/ESUCH-44; Coll. 112(2)/ESUCH-45; Coll. 134(2)/ESUCH-47; Coll. 232(5)/ESUCH-54; Coll. 351(7)/ESUCH-80.

Chronological assessment: Sherds of this decorated type are found both in single-component Early Suchimancillo collections and in mixed contexts dating to Early and Late Suchimancillo. Thus, White-and-Orange/Redware pottery is probably a good Early Suchimancillo time marker, but may also characterize the early part of the following period.

Inter-regional comparisons: Early Suchimancillo White-and-Orange/Redware is essentially identical to the Castillo White, Red, Orange type reported for the Virú Valley (cf. Bennett 1950, p. 86, Fig. 26 A-B; Strong and Evans 1952, p. 346, Fig. 80; see also Bennett 1939, p. 55, Fig. 11 r-t).

Early Suchimancillo: Kaolin Ware (Fig. 202 a-d; Fig. 207 d, h; Fig. 208 c)

Number: 73+ sherds, or ca. 4.4%+ of the Early Suchimancillo assemblage.

General description: In addition to the Early Suchimancillo Bowl 3 decorated kaolin types (including Black-and-White/Orange-slipped Kaolin, Black/Orange-slipped Kaolin, and Red/White Kaolin, in Fig. 202 a-d), other decorated kaolin types present in the collections and illustrated here are: (1) White-and-Red/Orange Kaolin (exterior of a deep bowl; Fig. 207 d); (2) Black-and-Red/Orange-slipped Kaolin (exterior of a small, low-necked jar; Fig. 207 h); and (3) Red/Orange Kaolin (effigy vessel, showing hand holding a staff; Fig. 208 c). Wall thickness of all kaolin sherds is very thin, ranging between 2.5 mm and 4 mm.

Paste: Temper appears to consist of fine (and occasionally medium) sand in very light or light quantities. Paste color is variable, ranging from chalk white (most common), through reddish-white, to orange.

Surface characteristics: Although a few plain white kaolin sherds were collected, most kaolin vessel fragments were decorated with two or more colors--including various shades of red, orange, and black, as well as white on colored backgrounds.

Distribution: Early Suchimancillo kaolin sherds have a distribution limited to the upper two-thirds part of Cluster 2. Collection proveniences (with number of kaolin sherds, including all bowls and jars, in parentheses)/site numbers are:

Coll. 375(8)/ESUCH-3; Coll. 373(1)/ESUCH-5; Coll. 29(18)/ESUCH-15; Colls. 30(2), 32(2), 33(1+)/ESUCH-17; Colls. 7(5), 10(7), 14(1), 15(3), 17(10), 19(1)/ESUCH-19; Coll. 35(1+)/ESUCH-22; Coll. 24(1)/ESUCH-23; Coll. 26(1)/ESUCH-26; Coll. 27(1)/ESUCH-27; Coll. 39(1+)/

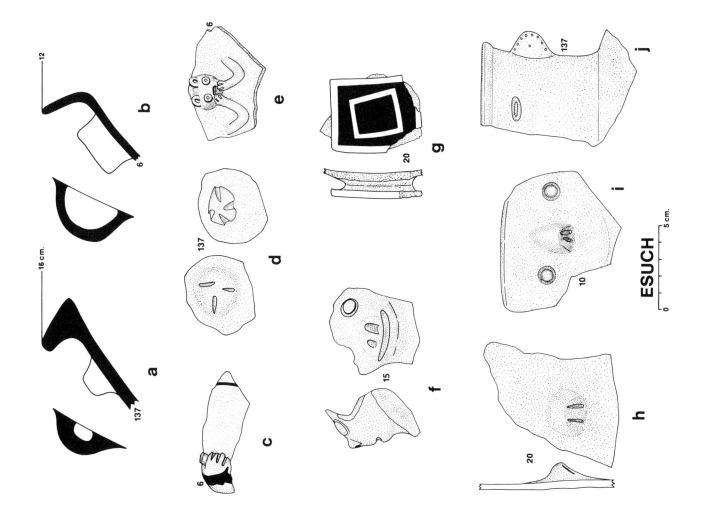

Fig. 208. Early Suchimancillo Period ceramics: miscellaneous sherds.

411

out. Paste types of these effigy vessels include both reddish-brownware (e.g., Fig. 208 h) and redware (e.g., Fig. 208 i, j). A final probable human effigy vessel fragment in the collections is the hand illustrated in Fig. 208 c, which appears to be holding a staff or club. This vessel has orange kaolin paste, and red paint was applied among other places as decoration on the wrist.

Overall, the human effigy vessel type is limited in distribution primarily to a 10 km-long area of the upper part of Early Suchimancillo Cluster 2, with Quebrada de Cayhuamarca located roughly in the middle, on the south desert margin. Collection proveniences (with number of sherds in parentheses)/site numbers are:

Coll. 6(1)/ESUCH-13; Colls. 7(1), 10(1), 14(1)/ESUCH-19; Coll. 20(1)/ESUCH-21; Coll. 39(1)/ESUCH-31; Coll. 137(1)/ESUCH-48; Coll. 342(1)/ESUCH-109.

Animal effigies: Two of the five animal figures from the Early Suchimancillo collections are shown in Fig. 208 e and f. Both of them are likely to have been placed on the shoulders of jars as adornos, or plastic decorative features (e.g., see the figures on Late Suchimancillo vessels in Fig. 218). The other three animal effigies are also attached to body sherds, and are likely to have been similarly placed. As in the case of the human effigy figures, a combination of techniques was used to form the features of the animals--including appliquéd clay, incising, and cane punching. Paste includes both reddish-brownware (e.g., Fig. 208 e) and redware (e.g., Fig. 208 f).

Animal effigies are limited in distribution to a small area located some 2.5 km upvalley beyond Quebrada de Cayhuamarca. Collection proveniences (with number of sherds in parentheses)/site numbers are:

Coll. 6(1)/ESUCH-13; Coll. 29(1)/ESUCH-15; Colls. 32(1), 33(1)/ESUCH-17; Coll. 15(1)/ESUCH-19.

Early Suchimancillo: Miscellaneous Artifacts (Figs. 207, 208)

Among the other ceramic artifacts found in Early Suchimancillo contexts are a number of painted and unpainted redware vessel fragments:

Painted redware: Included in this category are the following four decorated types involving various combinations of white and red paint, used either for slipping or for forming design motifs: (1) White/Red-slipped Redware (Fig. 207 e); (2) White/Plain Redware (Fig. 207 f); (3) White-and-Red/Plain Redware (on a fragment that appears to represent a shield; see Fig. 208 g); and (4) Red/White-slipped Redware (Fig. 207g).

Unpainted redware: A number of different types of unpainted redware sherds from Early Suchimancillo contexts are of interest to mention here--most of them illustrated in the accompanying figures (Note: collection numbers are given only for the unillustrated artifacts, since each illustrated one has the provenience indicated next to it; see Table 27 for site numbers corresponding to collection proveniences). These types include the following: (1) an Early Suchimancillo Jar 1 sherd with exterior pattern burnishing (Fig. 207 i; note the similarity in form of this neckless olla to one of the Vinzos Jar 1 profiles shown in Fig. 197; yet, the two sherds in question are not only of different

time periods, but also have different paste and were found at sites located some 28 km apart); (2) a deeply incised, and possibly pressmolded, bowl (Fig. 207 j); (3) horizontal strap handles on an Early Suchimancillo Jar 4a, and on a globular variant of a Jar 3 (Fig. 208 a, b); (4) appliquéd plastic decoration with deep incising, on body sherds from two jars (Fig. 208 d); (5) two clay panpipe fragments (Coll. 18; Coll. 368); (6) one fabric- or mat-impressed sherd (Coll. 7); and (7) two sherds with probable maker's marks, including (a) four short, parallel incised lines on the interior of a jar below the rim (Coll. 7), and (b) an engraved, or excised, rectangle with an "X" inside it, on the exterior of a bowl below the rim (Coll. 27).

412

Early-Late Suchimancillo Jar (Fig. 210)

Number: 33 sherds, or ca. 1.3% of the Late Suchimancillo assemblage.

General description: Large jar with constricted mouth and exterior thickened rim. Rim diameters vary from 16-40 cm, with a mean of 28.5 cm and a standard deviation of 9.6 cm. Wall thickness below the rim ranges between 5 mm and 10 mm, with a mean of 6.2 mm.

Paste: Temper consists uniformly of medium sand in moderate quantities. Paste color in about 95% of the sherds is red, while the remaining 5% have reddish-brown paste. Gray cores were noted on two of the redware sherds.

Surface characteristics: The exterior of the rim is decorated with triangular- or wedge-shaped punctate designs. As the examples in Fig. 210 show, there is substantial variation in design motifs considering the generally restrictive "canons" under which potters appear to have worked in fabricating this jar type. Thus, one notes a difference from sherd to sherd not only in (1) the shape and size of the tool used, and (2) the direction the punctate tool was aimed, but also in (3) the overall placement of the wedge-shaped marks. In addition to the punctate design, incising was occasionally placed on the exterior of the rim along with the wedge marks, but this is an uncommon feature in our sample. Judging from the body fragments attached to some of the sherds, the remaining surface area of the vessel was left untouched.

Distribution: This jar type has a wide distribution at habitation, habitation-cemetery, and cemetery sites throughout most of the area of Late Suchimancillo occupation, including Clusters 2 and 3, and the lower half of Cluster 1. Collection proveniences (with number of sherds in parentheses)/site numbers are:

Coll. 33(1)/LSUCH-40; Coll. 43(1)/LSUCH-55; Coll. 120(1)/ LSUCH-58; Coll. 128(1)/LSUCH-62; Coll. 147(1)/LSUCH-64; Coll. 119(1)/ LSUCH-66; Coll. 153(3)/LSUCH-69; Coll. 113(2)/LSUCH-74; Colls. 233(1), 232(9)/LSUCH-83; Coll. 236(1)/LSUCH-84; Coll. 351(1)/LSUCH-100; Coll. 312(1)/LSUCH-118; Coll. 359(4)/LSUCH-127; Coll. 180(1)/LSUCH-142; Coll. 47(1)/LSUCH-145; Coll. 48(3)/LSUCH-148.

Chronological assessment: The only apparently single-component context in which this jar type was found to be present dates to Late Suchimancillo Period, judging from all other diagnostics noted in these collections. Yet, in 10 of the 17 collections where good Early Suchimancillo diagnostics were noted, a number of good Early Suchimancillo time markers were also noted. It thus seems likely that this jar type is not only a good Late Suchimancillo diagnostic, but is also a transitional marker between Early and Late Suchimancillo Periods.

Inter-regional comparisons: Wedge-punched decoration on exterior thickened rims is a common feature of the general Castillo Incised type of Virú Valley (cf. Bennett 1950, p. 75, Fig. 19; Strong and Evans 1952, p. 321, Fig. 66 H, J-L). Although in Virú this is but one of a variety of rim decorations (that include dented and cut rim variants), it is of interest to note that the wedge-punched type illustrated here is the only major form of exterior rim decoration present in our Lower Santa Valley collections.

Late Suchimancillo Bowl 1 (Fig. 211)

Number: 57 sherds, or ca. 2.2% of the Late Suchimancillo assemblage.

General description: Open bowl with outslanted and slightly incurving walls. Most of the sherds in the sample have rounded lips, but horizontal as well as interior beveled variants are also present. Rim diameters vary from 8-32 cm, with a mean of 21.7 cm and a standard deviation of 7.5 cm. Wall thickness below the rim ranges widely between 4 mm and 12 mm, with most of the sherds at either the upper or the lower end of this range.

Paste: Temper consists uniformly of medium sand in moderate quantities. Approximately 48% of the sherds have reddish-brown paste, while another 35% are fully oxidized redware. Two kaolin sherds and two grayware sherds are also included in this shape category.

Surface characteristics: Interior and exterior surfaces are plain reddish-brown, red, white kaolin, or gray.

Distribution: This bowl type has a wide distribution in habitation, habitation-cemetery, and cemetery sites throughout most of the area of Late Suchimancillo occupation, including the lower half of Cluster 1, the upper half of Cluster 2, and SVP-LSUCH-148 in Cluster 3. Collection proveniences (with number of sherds in parentheses)/site numbers are:

9(5), 14(5), 16(2)/LSUCH-39; Coll. 29(4)/LSUCH-39; Coll. 33(1)/LSUCH-40; Colls. 1(2), 8(2), 41(1)/LSUCH-53; Coll. 122(2)/LSUCH-62; Coll. 35(2)/LSUCH-47; Coll. 28(2)/LSUCH-51; Coll. 138(1)/LSUCH-82; Coll. 233(2)/LSUCH-83; Coll. 238(1)/LSUCH-85; Coll. 118(2)/LSUCH-76; Coll. 251(7)/LSUCH-103; Coll. 253(1)/LSUCH-105; Coll. 256(2)/LSUCH-107; Coll. 223(1)/LSUCH-112; Coll. 226(1)/LSUCH-113; Colls. 227(1), 228(2)/ LSUCH-114; Colls. 48(1), 49(7)/LSUCH-148.

Chronological assessment: Although Bowl 1 seems distinguishable from Early Suchimancillo Bowl 2a (Fig. 202) on the basis of its generally greater wall thickness, as well as minor variations in lip treatment and overall sherd profiles, the two types are nevertheless quite similar. Thus, these bowl types may be viewed as better indicators of the general Suchimancillo time period than as specific indicators of Early and Late Suchimancillo. This general bowl form is also similar to Early Tanguche Bowl 1 (Fig. 236), Late Tanguche Bowl 1 (Fig. 258), and Late Tambo Real Redware Bowl 2 (Fig. 270). However, the Suchimancillo bowls can be distinguished on the basis of their slightly incurving walls (in contrast to the straighter walls of the later bowl forms).

Inter-regional comparisons: See discussion under Early Suchimancillo Bowl 2a.

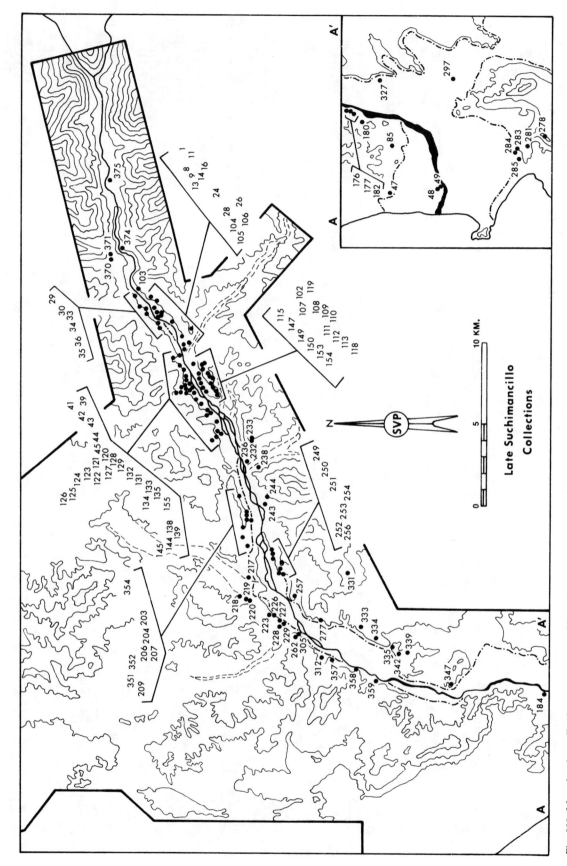

Fig. 209. Map showing collection proveniences of Late Suchimancillo Period (Late Gallinazo/EIP).

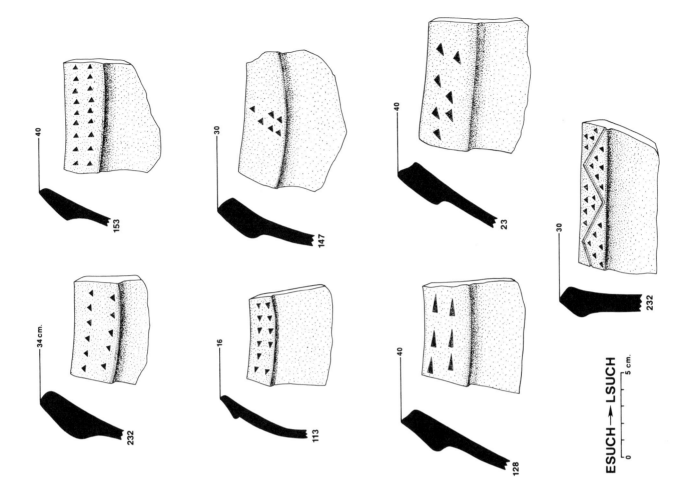

ESUCH → LSUCH

Fig. 210. Early–Late Suchimancillo jar.

Late Suchimancillo Bowl 2 (Fig. 211)

Number: 36 sherds, or ca. 1.4% of the Late Suchimancillo assemblage.

General description: Open bowl with straight, outslanted walls and a flared rim. Rim diameters vary from 16-28 cm, with a mean of 21.9 cm and a standard deviation of 5 cm. Wall thickness below the rim ranges widely between 5 mm and 10 mm, with a mean of 7.3 mm.

Paste: Temper consists of fine or medium sand, with about 65% of the sherds having fine grain sand. Paste is oxidized redware, with gray cores noted on 20% of the sherds.

Surface characteristics: Interior and exterior surfaces are plain redware.

Distribution: This bowl type has a wide, but scattered, distribution in habitation, habitation-cemetery, and cemetery sites in Late Suchimancillo Cluster 1 (lower part), Cluster 2 (upper part), and Cluster 3 (north side of river). Collection proveniences (with number of sherds in parentheses)/site numbers are:

Colls. 11(1), 9(4), 14(1), 16(2)/LSUCH-45; Coll. 35(1)/LSUCH-47; Coll. 24(1)/LSUCH-49; Coll. 26(1)/LSUCH-50; Coll. 28(4)/LSUCH-51; Coll. 41(4)/LSUCH-53; Coll. 45(2)/LSUCH-57; Colls. 122(1), 128(1)/LSUCH-62; Coll. 236(4)/LSUCH-84; Coll. 251(4)/LSUCH-103; Coll. 253(1)/LSUCH-105; Coll. 256(1)/LSUCH-107; Coll. 218(1)/LSUCH-109; Coll. 47(2)/LSUCH-145.

Chronological assessment: Bowl 2 is a very good temporal diagnostic of Late Suchimancillo Period, having been consistently found in association with other diagnostics of this period in single-component contexts.

Inter-regional comparisons: Among the Recuay Yaiá Phase materials (equivalent to Late Gallinazo) from Pashash site, Grieder (1978, p. 67, Fig. 36 s) illustrates a bowl with flaring rim that is quite similar to Late Suchimancillo Bowl 2.

Late Suchimancillo Bowl 3 (Fig. 211)

Number: 19 sherds, or ca. .7% of the Late Suchimancillo assemblage.

General description: Open bowl with straight, outslanted walls and a flared, everted, or everted pendant rim. Lips are usually rounded, although one sherd has an exterior beveled lip parallel to the vessel wall. Rim diameters vary from 18-50 cm, with a mean of 26.6 cm and a standard deviation of 11.6 cm. Wall thickness below the rim ranges widely between 3 mm and 11 mm, with a mean of 5.4 mm.

Paste: Temper consists of fine or medium sand, with roughly 50% of the sherds having one or the other grain size. Some 60% of the sherds have kaolin paste, which is either chalk white (three sherds) or orange (eight sherds). Another 30% (six sherds) have redware paste. The remaining 10% (two sherds) have reddish-brown paste.

Surface characteristics: Interior and exterior surfaces on all of the sherds in the sample are plain, with the exception of a single red-slipped vessel fragment. The 11 kaolin bowl sherds are among the few undecorated rim sherds of this paste type collected during our research.

Distribution: This bowl type has a generally limited distribution confined to habitation, habitation-cemetery, and cemetery sites in the lower part of Late Suchimancillo Cluster 1, roughly centered on Quebrada de Cayhuamarca. Additional examples of this type were found at one site in Cluster 2 (SVP-LSUCH-108) and at one site in Cluster 3 (SVP-LSUCH-139). Collection proveniences (with number of sherds in parentheses)/site numbers are:

Coll. 103(1)/LSUCH-38; Coll. 34(1)/LSUCH-44; Coll. 16(8)/LSUCH-45; Coll. 35(1)/LSUCH-47; Coll. 107(1)/LSUCH-66; Colls. 108(1), 109(1)/LSUCH-67; Coll. 113(1)/LSUCH-74; Coll. 118(2)/LSUCH-76; Coll. 217(1)/LSUCH-108; Coll. 176(1)/LSUCH-139.

Chronological assessment: Aside from a vague resemblance to Early Tambo Real Redware Bowl 3 (which has steeper vessel walls; see Fig. 271), this bowl form appears to be a good diagnostic of Late Suchimancillo Period.

Inter-regional comparisons: From his Recuay Yaiá Phase materials excavated at Pashash in the adjacent sierra, Grieder (1978, p. 67, Fig. 36 r and u) illustrates bowls with outslanted walls and everted, horizontal rims that are very similar to Late Suchimancillo Bowl 3.

Late Suchimancillo Bowl 4 (Fig. 211)

Number: 19 sherds, or ca. .7% of the Late Suchimancillo assemblage.

General description: Large bowl with more-or-less vertical walls and a slightly constricted mouth. Lips are either rounded or have an interior bevel. Several sherds with a distinctive shallow groove running around the lip of the vessel are present in the sample. Rim diameters vary from 15-45 cm, with a mean of 31.5 cm and a standard deviation of 7.7 cm. Wall thickness below the rim ranges widely between 7 mm and 14 mm, with a mean of 8.7 mm.

Paste: Temper consists of fine or medium sand, with roughly 50% of the sherds falling in one or the other grain size category. Paste color is red.

Surface characteristics: Interior and exterior surfaces are plain redware.

Distribution: This bowl type has a wide, but scattered, distribution in habitation and cemetery sites in Late Suchimancillo Cluster 1 (lower part), Cluster 2, and Cluster 3 (north side of river). Collection proveniences (with number of sherds in parentheses)/site numbers are:

Coll. 13(1)/LSUCH-45; Colls. 28(2), 106(1)/LSUCH-51; Coll. 41(4)/LSUCH-53; Coll. 42(1)/LSUCH-54; Coll. 118(2)/LSUCH-76; Coll. 244(1)/

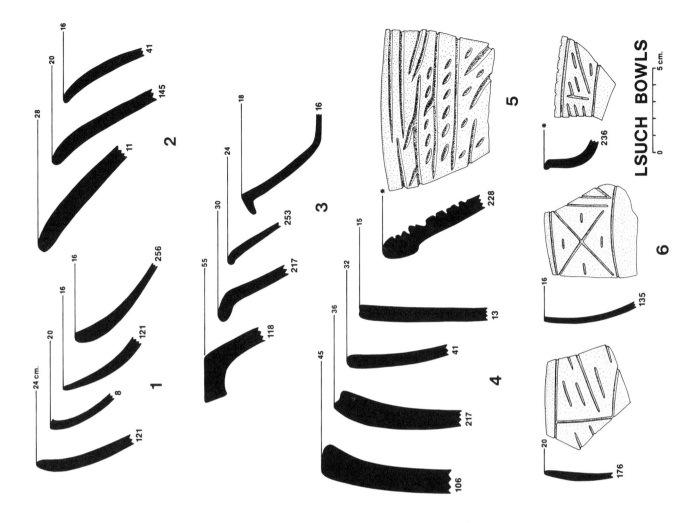

Fig. 211. Late Suchimancillo Period ceramics: Bowls 1, 2, 3, 4, 5, and 6.

417

LSUCH-86; Coll. 217(1)/LSUCH-108; Colls. 228(1), 229(1)/LSUCH-114; Coll. 333(2)/LSUCH-121; Coll. 335(1)/LSUCH-131; Coll. 49(1)/LSUCH-148.

Chronological assessment: Judging from the analysis of single-component collections, this bowl type is a good diagnostic of Late Suchimancillo Period.

Inter-regional comparisons: Recuay Yaiá Phase bowls with thick walls and vertical rim profiles excavated at Pashash by Grieder (1978, p. 67, Fig. 36 m) appear to be quite similar to Late Suchimancillo Bowl 4. No comparable Late Gallinazo vessel form is reported for the Virú Valley (e.g., see Strong and Evans, p. 264, Fig. 40).

Late Suchimancillo Bowl 5 (Fig. 211)

Number: 13 sherds, or ca. .5% of the Late Suchimancillo assemblage.

General description: Open bowl with straight outslanted walls. Rim diameters vary from 40-50 cm, with over 80% of the sherds in the sample at the lower end of this range. Wall thickness below the rim ranges between 9 mm and 13 mm, with over 80% of the sherds at the upper end of this range.

Paste: Temper consists uniformly of medium sand in moderate quantities. Paste color is red.

Surface characteristics: The interior of the vessels is deeply and extensively incised in such a way as to make it likely that this bowl type functioned as a grater for shredding plants or other foods. The exteriors are plain redware.

Distribution: This bowl type has a limited distribution in habitation sites of Late Suchimancillo Clusters 1, 2, and 3. Collection proveniences (with number of sherds in parentheses)/site numbers are:

Coll. 8(1)/LSUCH-45; Coll. 28(5)/LSUCH-51; Coll. 122(3)/LSUCH-62; Coll. 118(1)/LSUCH-76; Coll. 228(1)/LSUCH-114; Coll. 176(2)/LSUCH-139.

Chronological assessment: Grater bowls with this general form are found in a number of mixed component collections dating to periods following Late Suchimancillo, so in most cases it is difficult to assess with any precision how the vessel type changes in form and distribution from period to period. Following Late Suchimancillo, the only clear single-component context in which it appears is Late Tanguche (see Bowl 2, Fig. 258). The Late Suchimancillo form of grater bowl differs from its Late Tanguche counterpart with respect to rim profile, nature of the interior incising, and its generally larger size. It is therefore viewed tentatively as a good diagnostic of Late Suchimancillo Period, as illustrated in Fig. 211.

Inter-regional comparisons: Redware grater bowls similar to Late Suchimancillo Bowl 5 are one of the vessel types characteristic of Castillo Plain (itself one of the five major Virú paste types), dating principally to Gallinazo and Huancaco Periods (cf. Strong and Evans 1952, p. 264, Fig. 40 - Form 5).

Late Suchimancillo Bowl 6 (Fig. 211)

Number: 8 sherds, or ca. .3% of the Late Suchimancillo assemblage.

General description: Small, open bowl with slightly incurving or globular walls, and direct or everted rim. Lips are either rounded or horizontal beveled. Rim diameters vary from 15-20 cm, with a mean of about 17 cm. Wall thickness below the rim ranges between 3 mm and 5 mm.

Paste: Temper consists uniformly of fine sand in light quantities. Paste color is red in seven of the eight sherds, while the remaining sherd has gray paste.

Surface characteristics: The exterior surface of all sherds in the sample has zoned incised design. This consists of two parallel lines running around the wall of the vessel, enclosing one or more vertical lines as well as shorter horizontal or slanting lines. The interior surfaces are polished.

Distribution: This bowl type has a limited distribution at habitation, habitation-cemetery, and cemetery sites in Late Suchimancillo Cluster 1 (lower third), Cluster 2 (upper end), and Cluster 3 (upper end). Collection proveniences (with number of sherds in parentheses)/ site numbers are:

Coll. 42(1)/LSUCH-54; Coll. 118(1)/LSUCH-76; Coll. 135(1)/ LSUCH-78; Coll. 236(1)/LSUCH-84; Coll. 243(1)/LSUCH-87; Coll. 176(2)/ LSUCH-139; Coll. 180(1)/LSUCH-142.

Chronological assessment: This bowl type appears to be a good temporal diagnostic of Late Suchimancillo Period, although its limited distribution lessens its utility as a general time marker.

Inter-regional comparisons: Although the exterior decoration on Bowl 6 consists generally of fine-lined incising, this bowl type is clearly related in form, size, paste, and decoration to the Gallinazo Broad-line Incised type of Virú Valley (cf. Bennett 1950, p. 78, Fig. 21 K-M; Strong and Evans 1952, p. 324, Fig. 68).

Late Suchimancillo Bowl 7 (Fig. 212)

This bowl type, or category, includes a total of 122 small bowl fragments (ca. 4.8% of the Late Suchimancillo assemblage) with exterior painted decoration. Rim diameters vary generally from 10-24 cm, with a mean of 18.3 and a standard deviation of 2.7 cm. Wall thickness below the rim ranges between 2.5 mm and 4 mm. Paste types, in order of percentage of importance, include the following: (1) white kaolin (49% of the sherds in the sample), containing very light quantities of fine grain sand; (2) orangeware (42% of the sherds), a probable kaolin-based paste containing light quantities of fine grain sand; (3) redware (7% of the sherds), containing moderate quantities of medium grain sand; and (4) reddish-brownware (2% of the sherds), containing moderate quantities of medium grain sand.

The general Bowl 7 type has a restricted distribution in habitation, habitation-cemetery, and cemetery sites in Late Suchimancillo

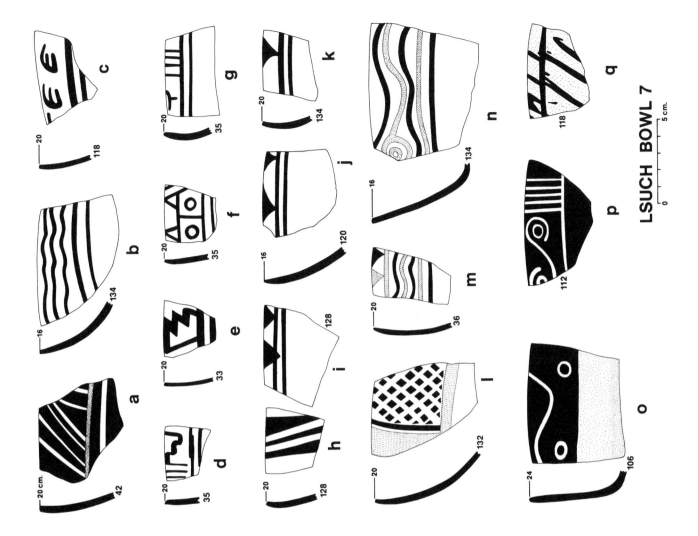

LSUCH BOWL 7

Fig. 212. Late Suchimancillo Period ceramics: Bowl 7.

419

Cluster 1 (lower third) and Cluster 2 (upper third). Of the total of 122 sherds, only 85 were sufficiently well preserved to permit classification according to decorated subtype. General descriptions of the decorated bowl types illustrated here, as well as collection proveniences (with number of sherds in parentheses)/site numbers, are as follows:

420

(1) Red/White Kaolin (Fig. 212 b, e, k)

Description: Bowl with slightly incurved walls that are either outslanted or vertical, and with lips that are either interior or horizontal beveled. Decoration consists of red-painted curvilinear or geometric motifs on the exterior surface of the vessel. Interior surfaces are plain white kaolin.

Proveniences: Coll. 33(5)/LSUCH-40; Coll. 102(3)/LSUCH-66; Coll. 153(1)/LSUCH-69; Coll. 134(2)/LSUCH-79; Coll. 204(1)/LSUCH-96; Coll. 206(1)/LSUCH-97; Coll. 217(1)/LSUCH-108.

(2) Orange/White Kaolin (Fig. 212 d, f, g, j)

Description: Bowl with slightly incurved walls that are either outslanted or vertical, and with lips that are either rounded or interior beveled. Decoration consists of orange-painted geometric designs on the exterior surface--including straight lines, triangles, circles, and frets. The motif in Fig. 212 f may represent a feline.

Proveniences: Coll. 34(2)/LSUCH-44; Coll. 43(4)/LSUCH-55; Coll. 351(1)/LSUCH-100.

(3) Black/White Kaolin (Fig. 212 c, q)

Description: Open bowl with slightly incurved sides and an interior beveled lip. Decoration consists of black-painted curvilinear and geometric motifs on the exterior surface of the vessel. The paint on the bowl in Fig. 212 q was obviously applied hurriedly, if not sloppily.

Provenience: Coll. 118(2)/LSUCH-76.

(4) Black-and-Orange/White Kaolin (Fig. 212 m)

Description: Bowl with slightly incurved vertical walls and narrow rounded lip. Decoration consists of alternating black and orange wavy and straight lines, with alternating black and orange triangles around the exterior below the rim.

Provenience: Coll. 36(1)/LSUCH-46.

(5) Red-and-Orange/White Kaolin (Fig. 212 n)

Description: Bowl with outslanted and very slightly incurved walls, and a horizontal rounded lip. Decoration consists of alternating red and orange wavy and straight lines, as well as concentric circles, on the exterior surface.

Provenience: Coll. 134(1)/LSUCH-79.

(6) Red/Orangeware (Fig. 212 h, i)

Description: Open bowl with slightly outslanted and incurved walls, and an interior beveled lip. Decoration consists of red-painted geometric designs on the exterior surface-- including triangular and straight-line motifs.

Proveniences: Coll. 9(2)/LSUCH-45; Coll. 42(10)/LSUCH-54; Coll. 121(14)/LSUCH-58; Colls. 127(1), 128(1)/LSUCH-62; Coll. 113(1)/LSUCH-74.

(7) Red-and-Black/Orangeware (Fig. 212 l)

Description: Open bowl with outslanted and slightly incurved walls, and interior beveled lip. Decoration consists of two types of painting techniques, involving (1) positive-painted red bands and a vertical black line; and (2) negative-painted, diamond-shaped black designs, formed by applying a positive-painted crosshatched design to the exterior surface-- with a substance that burned off during firing and painting in the interstices with black (note the similarity of design between the sherd in Fig. 212 l, and the one from Shankaiyán site in the Callejón de Huaylas illustrated in Bennett 1944, p. 56, Fig. 18 B).

Provenience: Coll. 132(2)/LSUCH-71.

(8) White/Red-painted Orangeware (Fig. 212 o)

Description: Open bowl with vertical walls and rounded lip. Decoration consists of white-painted designs over a thickly applied red band around the upper half of the exterior surface of the vessel.

Provenience: Coll. 106(1)/LSUCH-51.

(9) White-and-Orange/Red-slipped Redware (Fig. 212 a)

Description: Open bowl with slightly outslanted and incurved wall, and horizontal beveled lip. Exterior and interior surfaces are red-slipped, with an exterior design consisting of white and orange horizontal lines, and with slanting white lines painted above them.

Proveniences: Coll. 42(1)/LSUCH-54; Coll. 354(1)/LSUCH-91.

(10) Bright Pink/Reddish-brownware (Fig. 212 p)

Description: Open bowl with bright pink geometric and curvilinear (scroll) motifs painted over the exterior surface. Interior and exterior surfaces are highly polished.

Provenience: Coll. 112(2)/LSUCH-68.

Late Suchimancillo Jar la (Fig. 213)

Number: 38 sherds, or ca. 1.5% of the Late Suchimancillo

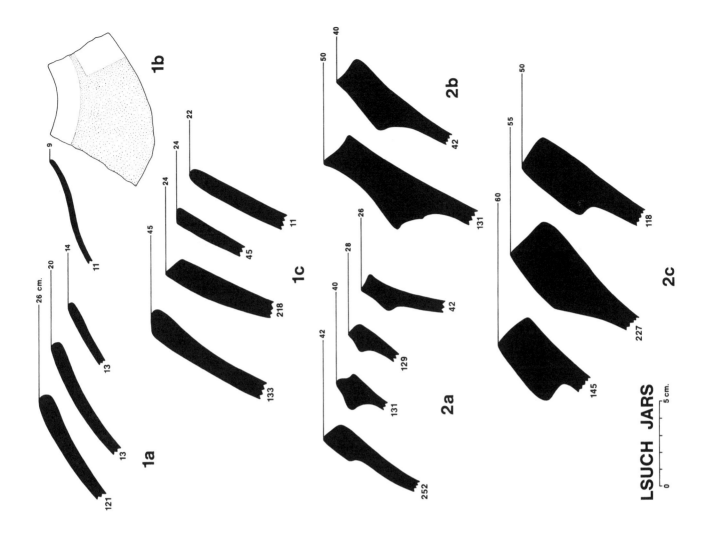

LSUCH JARS

Fig. 213. Late Suchimancillo Period ceramics: Jars 1a, 1b, 1c, 2a, 2b, and 2c.

421

assemblage.

General description: Globular jar with a constricted mouth (neckless olla). Rims are slightly thickened on the interior, and lips are rounded. Rim diameters vary from 14-26 cm, with a mean of about 18 cm and a standard deviation of 4.5 cm. Wall thickness below the rim ranges between 5 mm and 7 mm, with a mean of 6 mm.

Paste: Temper consists uniformly of medium sand in moderate quantities. Paste color is red, with gray cores noted on about 30% of the sherds in the sample.

Surface characteristics: Red slipping was noted on the exterior surface of three sherds in the sample. The remaining sherds have plain redware exteriors and interiors.

Distribution: This jar type has a wide distribution at habitation, habitation-cemetery, and cemetery sites in Late Suchimancillo Cluster 1, and is also found at scattered sites in Clusters 2 and 3. Collection proveniences (with number of sherds in parentheses)/site numbers are:

Colls. 29(1)/LSUCH-39; Coll. 33(1)/LSUCH-40; Coll. 34(1)/LSUCH-44; Colls. 8(3), 13(2)/LSUCH-45; Coll. 35(1)/LSUCH-47; Coll. 24(1)/LSUCH-49; Coll. 28(4)/LSUCH-51; Colls. 120(4), 121(1)/LSUCH-58; Coll. 122(1)/ LSUCH-62; Coll. 113(3)/LSUCH-74; Coll. 118(4)/LSUCH-76; Coll. 232(1)/ LSUCH-83; Coll. 204(1)/LSUCH-96; Coll. 254(1)/LSUCH-106; Coll. 226(3)/ LSUCH-113; Coll. 49(1)/LSUCH-148; Coll. 284(4)/LSUCH-149.

Chronological assessment: Jar 1a appears to be a very good temporal diagnostic of Late Suchimancillo. Although there are similar neckless ollas in both earlier and later periods, Jar 1a can be distinguished from the earlier reddish-brown jars on the basis of its fully oxidized redware paste. In addition, it is the only jar of this type in the early part of the sequence with a vessel wall angle at the rim (in profile) of 20-30° down from the horizontal. Neckless ollas of other, earlier periods consistently have vessel wall angles at the rim of 30-40° down from the horizontal. With regard to later periods, a minor jar form of Late Tanguche Period (four sherds; see Jar 1, Fig. 258) is similar in form and paste to Late Suchimancillo Jar 1a.

Inter-regional comparisons: Jars of this specific form are not reported in the literature on the contemporaneous Late Gallinazo Period in Virú Valley. However, the thinner walls and redware paste of Jar 1a suggest a general relationship to the Castillo Plain type of Virú (cf. Strong and Evans 1952:264-267).

Late Suchimancillo Jar 1b (Fig. 213)

Number: 6 sherds, or ca. .2% of the Late Suchimancillo assemblage.

General description: Globular jar with a constricted mouth, and either a direct or a slightly upturned rim. Rim diameters vary from 9-14 cm, with a mean of about 11 cm. Wall thickness below the rim ranges between 3 mm and 5 mm, with five of the six sherds in the lower half of

the range.

Paste: Three of the sherds in the sample have kaolin paste, including both white kaolin (two sherds) and reddish-orange kaolin (one sherd), with very light quantities of fine temper. The remaining three sherds have redware paste, with moderate quantities of medium grain sand.

Surface characteristics: The exterior surfaces of the kaolin jars are decorated with white-and-orange/red slip. Exterior surfaces of the redware jars are decorated as follows: (1) reddish-orange slip (one sherd), (2) red-and-black/white slip (one sherd), and (3) white/red slip (one sherd; see Fig. 213). Interior surfaces are plain.

Distribution: This jar type has a limited distribution at habitation sites in the lower half of Late Suchimancillo Cluster 1. Collection proveniences (with number of sherds in parentheses)/site numbers are:

Coll. 29(1)/LSUCH-39; Colls. 11(1), 13(1)/LSUCH-45; Coll. 42(2)/ LSUCH-54; Coll. 118(1)/LSUCH-76.

Chronological assessment: Jar 1b was found either in mixed Early and Late Suchimancillo collections, or in single-component collections dating to the later of the two periods.

Inter-regional comparisons: Although this vessel form is not reported in the current (and scanty) literature on the sierra adjacent to the Lower Santa region, it seems likely it is a sierra-derived or sierra-influenced ceramic type. Jar 1b may also be related to Vessel Form 4 of the Callejón Unclassified material of Virú Valley, and hence may be a later form of Early Suchimancillo Jar 2 (cf. Fig. 204 in this report; see also Strong and Evans 1952, p. 350, Fig. 81).

Late Suchimancillo Jar 1c (Fig. 213)

Number: 29 sherds, or ca. 1.1% of the Late Suchimancillo assemblage.

General description: Large jar with a constricted mouth and a direct rim. Some interior thickening at the rim was noted on a few sherds. Lip treatment is variable, with rounded, horizontal beveled, and interior beveled variants all common in the sample. Rim diameters vary from 15-45 cm, with a mean of about 25 cm. Wall thickness below the rim ranges widely between 7 mm and 12 mm, with roughly 65% of the sherds at the lower end of the range and the remainder at the upper end.

Paste: Temper consists uniformly of medium sand in moderate quantities. Paste color is red.

Surface characteristics: Exterior and interior surfaces of all but five sherds are plain, undecorated redware. The remaining five have grater-like incising (see Late Suchimancillo Bowl 5) on the interior below the rim, and plain exteriors.

Distribution: This jar type has a limited distribution at habitation sites in Late Suchimancillo Cluster 1, as well as at one site in Cluster 2 (SVP-LSUCH-109) and one site in Cluster 3 (SVP-LSUCH-148). Collection proveniences (with number of sherds in parentheses)/site numbers are:

Coll. 29(3)/LSUCH-39; Coll. 11(1)/LSUCH-45; Colls. 28(16), 104(1)/LSUCH-51; Coll. 42(2)/LSUCH-54; Coll. 45(1)/LSUCH-57; Coll. 133(1)/LSUCH-77; Coll. 218(2)/LSUCH-109; Coll. 49(2)/LSUCH-148.

Chronological assessment: Jars of this form and vessel wall angle at the rim (60-70° down from the horizontal) appear to be limited to Late Suchimancillo Period.

Inter-regional comparisons: Jars with this rim form are not reported in the literature on contemporaneous periods in the Lower Santa region.

Late Suchimancillo Jar 2a (Fig. 213)

Number: 32 sherds, or ca. 1.3% of the Late Suchimancillo assemblage.

General description: Large globular or ovoid jar with a constricted mouth and externally thickened rim. The exterior of the thickened section is 1-2 cm in width, and is usually slightly concave in profile. Lips are either rounded or slightly concave (or, grooved). Rim diameters vary from 17-50 cm, with a mean of 33 cm and a standard deviation of 8.6 cm. Wall thickness below the rim ranges between 4 mm and 8 mm, with a mean of 6.2 mm.

Paste: Temper consists uniformly of medium sand in moderate quantities. Paste color in approximately 75% of the sherds is red, while the remaining 25% have reddish-brown paste.

Surface characteristics: Exterior notches were noted on four of the sherds in the sample. Otherwise, both exterior and interior surfaces are plain.

Distribution: This jar type has a widespread distribution at habitation, habitation-cemetery, and cemetery sites in Late Suchimancillo Cluster 1 (lower half) and Cluster 2 (upper half). Collection proveniences (with number of sherds in parentheses)/site numbers are:

Coll. 29(2)/LSUCH-39; Coll. 33(1)/LSUCH-40; Colls. 8(1), 16(1)/LSUCH-45; Coll. 35(1)/LSUCH-47; Coll. 24(1)/LSUCH-49; Coll. 42(8)/LSUCH-54; Coll. 102(2)/LSUCH-66; Coll. 129(1)/LSUCH-70; Coll. 131(1)/LSUCH-72; Coll. 144(1)/LSUCH-81; Coll. 233(1)/LSUCH-83; Coll. 354(4)/LSUCH-91; Coll. 352(2)/LSUCH-98; Coll. 252(2)/LSUCH-104; Coll. 217(1)/LSUCH-108; Coll. 226(1)/LSUCH-113; Coll. 227(1)/LSUCH-114.

Chronological assessment: Although Jar 2a was found more often in mixed Early and Late Suchimancillo collections, it was also present in at least five single-component collections dating to the later of the two periods. It may therefore be transitional from Early to Late Suchimancillo, as well as diagnostic of the later period.

Inter-regional comparisons: This vessel type is clearly related in form, size, paste, and exterior decoration to the Castillo Incised type of Virú Valley (cf. Bennett 1950, p. 74, Fig. 18; Strong and Evans 1952, p. 320, Fig. 65 - Vessel Shape 1).

Late Suchimancillo Jar 2b (Fig. 213)

Number: 7 sherds, or ca. .3% of the Late Suchimancillo assemblage.

General description: Large globular or ovoid jar with a constricted mouth and externally thickened rim. The exterior of the thickened section is 4-6 cm wide, and either slightly or strongly concave in profile. Lips are also slightly concave, or grooved. Rim diameters vary from 40-50 cm, with roughly 50% of the sherds at the lower end and 50% at the upper end of this range. Wall thickness below the rim ranges between 8 mm and 10 mm.

Paste: Temper consists generally of medium sand in moderate quantities. One sherd has heavy quantities of coarse sand temper. Paste color is red.

Surface characteristics: Exterior and interior surfaces are plain redware.

Distribution: This jar type has a limited distribution at habitation sites in Late Suchimancillo Cluster 1 (lowermost end), as well as at one site in Cluster 2 (SVP-LSUCH-105). Collection proveniences (with number of sherds in parentheses)/site numbers are:

Coll. 42(3)/LSUCH-54; Coll. 121(1)/LSUCH-58; Coll. 128(1)/LSUCH-62; Coll. 131(1)/LSUCH-72; Coll. 253(1)/LSUCH-105.

Chronological assessment: Jar 2b was found more often in single-component Late Suchimancillo collections, but was also noted in mixed Early and Late Suchimancillo contexts. It therefore appears to be at least diagnostic of the later of the two periods, if not of a transitional period as well.

Inter-regional comparisons: Although some regional variation is apparent in the rim profiles, Late Suchimancillo Jars 2b and 2c seem clearly to be related in overall form, wall thickness, and paste to the Valle Plain type of Virú Valley (cf. Strong and Evans 1952, p. 268, Fig. 41 - Vessel Shape 1).

Late Suchimancillo Jar 2c (Fig. 213)

Number: 22 sherds, or ca. .9% of the Late Suchimancillo assemblage.

General description: Large globular or ovoid jar with a constricted mouth and an externally thickened rim. The exterior of the thickened rim is 4-5 cm in width, and slightly convex or rounded in profile. Rim diameters vary from 42-65 cm, with a mean of 53.9 cm and a standard deviation of 5.4 cm. Wall thickness below the rim ranges widely between 8 mm and 18 mm, with a mean of 12.9 mm and a standard deviation of 2.9 mm.

Paste: Temper consists of medium grain sand. Approximately 75% of the sherds have moderate quantities of temper, while the remaining 25% have heavy quantities. Paste color is red, with gray cores noted on two sherds.

Surface characteristics: Exterior and interior surfaces of all but one sherd are plain redware, with fire clouding and fire blackening noted on three sherds. The remaining sherd has grater-like incising on the interior below the rim.

Distribution: This jar type has a distribution limited primarily to habitation sites in Late Suchimancillo Cluster 1 (lower third) and Cluster 2 (upper half). Collection proveniences (with number of sherds in parentheses)/site numbers are:

Coll. 29(1)/LSUCH-39; Coll. 8(2)/LSUCH-45; Coll. 24(1)/LSUCH-49; Coll. 106(2)/LSUCH-51; Coll. 128(1)/LSUCH-62; Coll. 147(1)/LSUCH-64; Coll. 129(1)/LSUCH-70; Coll. 118(2)/LSUCH-76; Coll. 145(1)/LSUCH-81; Coll. 139(1)/LSUCH-82; Coll. 236(2)/LSUCH-84; Coll. 351(1)/LSUCH-100; Coll. 256(1)/LSUCH-107; Coll. 218(1)/LSUCH-109; Coll. 220(1)/LSUCH-110; Colls. 227(1), 229(2)/LSUCH-114.

Chronological assessment: Jar 2c was found more often in mixed Early and Late Suchimancillo collections, but was also present in at least seven single-component collections dating to the later period. It may therefore be transitional from Early to Late Suchimancillo, as well as diagnostic of the later period.

Inter-regional comparisons: See Late Suchimancillo Jar 2b.

Late Suchimancillo Jar 3a (Fig. 214)

Number: 20 sherds, or ca. .8% of the Late Suchimancillo assemblage.

General description: Large globular or ovoid jar with a horizontal, everted rim. Rims taper to a roughly squared or rounded lip. Rim diameters vary from 18-40 cm, with a mean of 25.6 cm and a standard deviation of 7.9 cm. Wall thickness below the rim ranges widely between 7 mm and 18 mm, with a mean of 10.6 cm and a standard deviation of 3.9 mm.

Paste: Temper consists of medium or coarse sand, with 85% of the sherds having medium grain sand. The quantity of temper in about 60% of the sherds is heavy, while the other 40% have moderate amounts of temper. Paste color is red, with approximately 50% of the sherds having gray cores.

Surface characteristics: Exterior and interior surfaces are plain redware.

Distribution: This jar type has a limited distribution primarily at habitation sites in Late Suchimancillo Cluster 3, as well as at one site in Cluster 2 (SVP-LSUCH-113). Collection proveniences (with number of sherds in parentheses)/site numbers are:

Coll. 226(1)/LSUCH-113; Coll. 47(10)/LSUCH-145; Colls. 48(4), 49(4)/LSUCH-148; Coll. 284(1)/LSUCH-149.

Chronological assessment: Late Suchimancillo sherds constitute the one component common to four of the collections in which Jar 3a was present. The remaining collection is a single-component Late Suchimancillo context. Jar 3a is therefore probably a good diagnostic of this period.

Inter-regional comparisons: The closest contemporaneous counterparts of Late Suchimancillo Jars 3a, 3b, and 3c are found among the variants of the Valle Plain type of Virú Valley (cf. Bennett 1950, p. 77, Fig. 20 A-B; Strong and Evans 1952, p. 268, Fig. 41 - Vessel Shape 1, third profile from left).

Late Suchimancillo Jar 3b (Fig. 214)

Number: 15 sherds, or ca. .6% of the Late Suchimancillo assemblage.

General description: Large globular or ovoid jar with an everted, exterior beveled rim. Rims taper to a roughly squared or rounded lip. Rim diameters vary from 14-40 cm, with 60% of the sherds at the lower end of the range and the other 40% at the upper end between 30 and 40 cm. Wall thickness below the rim ranges widely between 5 mm and 18 mm, with 60% of the sherds at the lower end of the range.

Paste: Temper consists uniformly of medium sand in moderate quantities. Paste color is red.

Surface characteristics: Exterior and interior surfaces are plain redware.

Distribution: This jar type has a limited distribution at habitation and cemetery sites of Late Suchimancillo Cluster 3, as well as at one site in Cluster 1 (SVP-LSUCH-54). Collection proveniences (with number of sherds in parentheses)/site numbers are:

Coll. 42(1)/LSUCH-54; Coll. 176(1)/LSUCH-139; Coll. 182(4)/LSUCH-141; Coll. 47(9)/LSUCH-145.

Chronological assessment: Judging from the analysis of single-component Late Suchimancillo collections, this jar type is a good diagnostic of the period.

Inter-regional comparisons: See Late Suchimancillo Jar 3a.

Late Suchimancillo Jar 3c (Fig. 214)

Number: 32 sherds, or ca. 1.3% of the Late Suchimancillo assemblage.

General description: Large globular jar with an everted, interior beveled rim. Rims taper to a roughly squared or triangular-shaped lip. Rim diameters vary from 18-65 cm, with a mean of about 40 cm and a standard deviation of 11.1 cm. Wall thickness below the rim ranges widely between 6 mm and 15 mm, with a mean of 10.6 mm and a standard deviation of 2.9 mm.

Paste: Temper consists of medium or coarse sand, with 90% of the sherds in the sample having medium grain sand. The quantity of temper in all of the sherds is moderate. Paste color is red, with gray cores noted on four sherds.

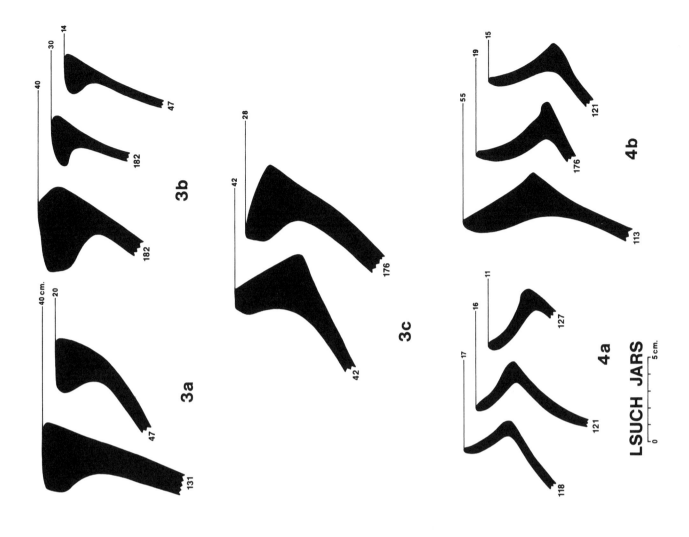

Fig. 214. Late Suchimancillo Period ceramics: Jars 3a, 3b, 3c, 4a, and 4b.

425

Surface characteristics: Exterior and interior surfaces are plain redware.

Distribution: This jar type has a wide distribution at habitation, habitation-cemetery, and cemetery sites in Late Suchimancillo Cluster 1 (lower third), as well as at a few sites in Clusters 2 and 3. Collection proveniences (with number of sherds in parentheses)/site numbers are:

Coll. 14(2)/LSUCH-45; Coll. 35(1)/LSUCH-47; Coll. 42(7)/LSUCH-54; Coll. 43(1)/LSUCH-55; Coll. 45(1)/LSUCH-57; Coll. 120(3)/LSUCH-58; Coll. 153(2)/LSUCH-69; Coll. 113(2)/LSUCH-74; Coll. 233(1)/LSUCH-83; Coll. 347(1)/LSUCH-135; Coll. 176(7)/LSUCH-139; Coll. 47(3)/LSUCH-145; Coll. 285(1)/LSUCH-150.

Chronological assessment: Jar 3c was found more often in mixed Early and Late Suchimancillo collections, but was also present in at least two single-component collections dating to the later period. It may therefore be transitional from Early to Late Suchimancillo, as well as diagnostic of the later of the two periods.

Inter-regional comparisons: See Late Suchimancillo Jar 3a.

Late Suchimancillo Jar 4a (Fig. 214)

Number: 55 sherds, or ca. 2.2% of the Late Suchimancillo assemblage.

General description: Globular jar with a strongly outslanted and slightly incurving, or bulging, neck. Some sherds in the sample have tapering or thickening at the interior juncture of the neck and the body. Rim diameters vary from 11-20 cm, with a mean of 16 cm and a standard deviation of 2.9 cm. Wall thickness below the rim ranges widely between 3 mm and 9 mm, with a mean of 5.6 mm.

Paste: Temper consists of fine or medium sand, with about 90% of the sherds having medium grain sand. Paste color of all sherds but one is red. The remaining sherd has gray paste.

Surface characteristics: Exterior and interior surfaces of the redware sherds are plain. The exterior surface of the grayware sherd is red-slipped.

Distribution: This jar type has a wide distribution in habitation, habitation-cemetery, and cemetery sites of Late Suchimancillo Cluster 1 (lower third), as well as at a few sites in Clusters 2 and 3. Collection proveniences (with number of sherds in parentheses)/site numbers are:

Coll. 33(4)/LSUCH-40; Colls. 9(1), 14(1)/LSUCH-45; Coll. 35(3)/ Coll. 42(1)/LSUCH-54; Colls. 120(1), 121(1)/LSUCH-58; Coll. 126(1)/LSUCH-60; Colls. 122(1), 127(1), 128(2)/LSUCH-62; Coll. 115(1)/ LSUCH-63; Coll. 129(1)/LSUCH-70; Coll. 131(1)/LSUCH-72; Coll. 113(4)/ LSUCH-74; Coll. 118(3)/LSUCH-76; Coll. 134(1)/LSUCH-79; Coll. 352(1)/ LSUCH-98; Coll. 256(1)/LSUCH-107; Coll. 219(1)/LSUCH-110; Coll. 176(1)/ LSUCH-139; Coll. 47(1)/LSUCH-145; Colls. 48(9), 49(3)/LSUCH-148.

Chronological assessment: Jar 4a is similar in form and paste to Early Suchimancillo Jar 4 (Fig. 205), but generally can be distinguished on the basis of its lower, more strongly outslanted rim.

Inter-regional comparisons: Jars with this very distinctive rim form are not reported in the literature on contemporaneous periods in areas adjacent to the Lower Santa region.

Late Suchimancillo Jar 4b (Fig. 214)

Number: 36 sherds, or ca. 1.4% of the Late Suchimancillo assemblage.

General description: Globular or ovoid jar with an outslanted and slightly incurving, or bulging, neck. Most sherds have tapering or thickening at the interior juncture of the body and the neck. Rim diameters vary from 14-55 cm, with a mean of 20.7 cm and a standard deviation of 8 cm. Wall thickness below the rim ranges between 5 mm and 10 mm, with a mean of 6.5 mm.

Paste: Temper consists of medium or coarse sand, with about 75% of the sherds having medium grain sand. Paste color is red, with gray cores noted on about 25% of the sherds.

Surface characteristics: Exterior and interior surfaces are plain redware.

Distribution: This jar type has a wide distribution at habitation, habitation-cemetery, and cemetery sites throughout Late Suchimancillo Cluster 1, as well as at a few sites in Clusters 2 and 3. Collection proveniences (with number of sherds in parentheses)/site numbers are:

Coll. 375(2)/LSUCH-13; Coll. 16(1)/LSUCH-45; Coll. 35(2)/ Coll. 122(2), 128(3)/LSUCH-62; Coll. 115(1)/LSUCH-63; Coll. 129(2)/LSUCH-70; Coll. 113(1)/LSUCH-74; Coll. 138(1)/LSUCH-82; Coll. 217(3)/LSUCH-108; Coll. 227(5)/LSUCH-114; Coll. 176(6)/LSUCH-139; Coll. 182(1)/LSUCH-141; Colls. 48(3), 49(3)/LSUCH-148.

Chronological assessment: Jar 4b was found in a number of mixed Early and Late Suchimancillo collections, but also in at least four single-component contexts dating to the later period. It may therefore be transitional from Early to Late Suchimancillo, as well as diagnostic of the later of the two periods.

Inter-regional comparisons: See Late Suchimancillo Jar 4a.

Late Suchimancillo Jar 5a (Fig. 215)

Number: 51 sherds, or ca. 2% of the Late Suchimancillo assemblage.

General description: Globular jar with a short flared or everted rim. Most of the sherds in the sample have distinct interior corner points at the juncture of the neck and the body. Rim diameters vary from 15-36 cm, with a mean of 22.9 cm and a standard deviation of 7.7 cm.

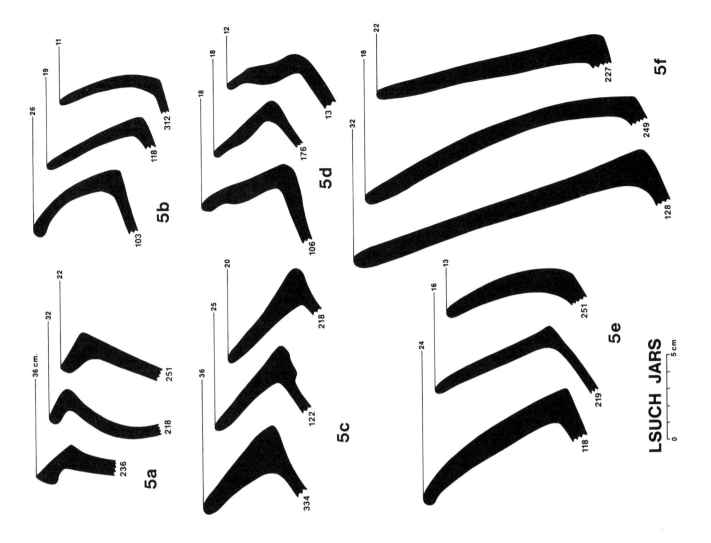

Fig. 215. Late Suchimancillo Period ceramics: Jars 5a, 5b, 5c, 5d, 5e, and 5f.

427

Wall thickness below the rim ranges between 5 mm and 9 mm, with a mean of about 7 mm and a standard deviation of 1.4 mm.

Paste: Temper consists uniformly of medium sand in moderate quantities. Paste color in approximately 70% of the sherds is red, while the remaining 30% have reddish-brown paste.

Surface characteristics: Exterior and interior surfaces are plain redware or reddish-brownware. Fire blackening was noted on one sherd.

Distribution: This jar type is widely distributed at habitation and habitation-cemetery sites in Late Suchimancillo Cluster 1 (lower third), as well as throughout Cluster 2 and at one site in Cluster 3 (SVP-LSUCH-148). Collection proveniences (with number of sherds in parentheses)/site numbers are:

Colls. 14(5), 16(1)/LSUCH-45; Coll. 35(3)/LSUCH-47; Coll. 24(1)/LSUCH-49; Coll. 42(10)/LSUCH-54; Coll. 43(4)/LSUCH-55; Coll. 113(3)/LSUCH-74; Coll. 118(1)/LSUCH-76; Coll. 233(1)/LSUCH-83; Coll. 236(1)/LSUCH-84; Coll. 352(3)/LSUCH-98; Coll. 351(1)/LSUCH-100; Colls. 250(1), 251(1)/LSUCH-103; Coll. 218(1)/LSUCH-109; Coll. 220(1)/LSUCH-110; Coll. 227(1)/LSUCH-114; Coll. 312(2)/LSUCH-118; Coll. 277(1)/LSUCH-119; Coll. 333(3)/LSUCH-121; Coll. 359(2)/LSUCH-127; Coll. 339(1)/LSUCH-133; Colls. 48(1), 49(2)/LSUCH-148.

Chronological assessment: Jar 5a is similar in form and paste to the redware variant of Early Suchimancillo Jar 4a (Fig. 204). Assuming that both jar forms have been assigned correctly to their respective single-component contexts, it is interesting to note that the percentage of redware for this general jar type in the later period is 70%, compared to 55% in the preceding period.

Inter-regional comparisons: See discussion under Early Suchimancillo Jar 4a.

Late Suchimancillo Jar 5b (Fig. 215)

Number: 242 sherds, or ca. 9.6% of the Late Suchimancillo assemblage.

General description: Globular jar with an everted rim. The wall of the rim is outslanted 20-30° from the vertical, and is either straight or flaring. A distinct interior corner point is present at the juncture of the neck and the body. Rim diameters vary from 11-40 cm, with a mean of 19.6 cm and a standard deviation of 6.5 cm. Wall thickness below the rim ranges widely between 5 mm and 14 mm, with a mean of 7.2 mm and a standard deviation of 1.6 mm.

Paste: Temper consists of medium sand. The quantity of temper in approximately 85% of the sherds is moderate. Quantity in the other 15% is heavy. Paste color in 75% of the sherds is red, while the remaining 25% have reddish-brown paste.

Surface characteristics: Exterior and interior surfaces are plain redware or reddish-brownware.

Distribution: This jar type has a wide distribution at habitation, habitation-cemetery, and cemetery sites in Late Suchimancillo Cluster 1 (lower half), as well as throughout Cluster 2 and at a few sites in Cluster 3. Collection proveniences (with number of sherds in parentheses)/site numbers are:

Coll. 103(18)/LSUCH-38; Coll. 29(4)/LSUCH-39; Coll. 33(4)/LSUCH-40; Colls. 11(2), 8(19), 9(18), 13(2), 16(2)/LSUCH-45; Coll. 35(4)/LSUCH-47; Coll. 24(2)/LSUCH-49; Coll. 26(1)/LSUCH-50; Colls. 28(2), 105(2), 106(2)/LSUCH-51; Coll. 39(1)/LSUCH-52; Coll. 42(15)/LSUCH-54; Coll. 43(7)/LSUCH-55; Coll. 45(2)/LSUCH-57; Colls. 120(5), 121(3)/LSUCH-58; Coll. 128(1)/LSUCH-62; Coll. 115(2)/LSUCH-63; Coll. 147(2)/LSUCH-64; Colls. 149(1), 150(1)/LSUCH-65; Coll. 102(1)/LSUCH-66; Coll. 110(2)/LSUCH-67; Colls. 111(1), 112(3)/LSUCH-68; Coll. 153(4)/LSUCH-69; Coll. 129(1)/LSUCH-70; Coll. 113(1)/LSUCH-74; Coll. 118(18)/LSUCH-76; Coll. 144(2), 145(4)/LSUCH-81; Coll. 138(1)/LSUCH-82; Coll. 232(9)/LSUCH-83; Coll. 244(2)/LSUCH-86; Coll. 243(1)/LSUCH-87; Coll. 207(2)/LSUCH-97; Coll. 351(1)/LSUCH-100; Coll. 251(4)/LSUCH-103; Coll. 252(2)/LSUCH-104; Coll. 253(1)/LSUCH-105; Coll. 254(1)/LSUCH-106; Coll. 256(4)/LSUCH-107; Coll. 217(2)/LSUCH-108; Coll. 227(5), 229(3)/LSUCH-114; Coll. 257(4)/LSUCH-115; Coll. 262(1)/LSUCH-116; Coll. 305(3)/LSUCH-117; Coll. 312(5)/LSUCH-118; Coll. 342(13)/LSUCH-132; Coll. 297(6)/LSUCH-147; Coll. 284(2)/LSUCH-149; Coll. 285(1)/LSUCH-150.

Chronological assessment: Jar 5b is similar in form and paste to Early Suchimancillo Jar 6 (Fig. 205). The later form can be distinguished on the basis of the absence of burnished decoration on the surface of the reddish-brownware variant, as well as by its higher neck.

Inter-regional comparisons: The redware variant of Late Suchimancillo Jar 5b is very similar in size, form, and paste to the flaring rim jar of the Castillo Plain type of Virú Valley (cf. Strong and Evans 1952, p. 264, Fig. 40 - Vessel Shape 1).

Late Suchimancillo Jar 5c (Fig. 215)

Number: 19 sherds, or ca. .7% of the Late Suchimancillo assemblage.

General description: Globular jar with an everted rim. The wall of the rim is wedge-shaped in profile, tapering to a rounded lip. All sherds in the sample have tapering or thickening at the interior juncture of the body and the neck--a distinctive and very diagnostic feature. Rim diameters vary from 18-35 cm, with a mean of 25.7 cm and a standard deviation of 5.6 cm. Wall thickness below the rim ranges between 5 mm and 8 mm, with a mean of 6.5 mm.

Paste: Temper consists uniformly of medium sand in moderate quantities. Paste color in approximately 85% of the sherds is red, while the remaining 15% have reddish-brown paste. Gray cores were noted on seven of the sherds, including both paste variants.

Surface characteristics: Exterior and interior surfaces on 16 of the sherds are plain redware or reddish-brownware. The remaining three sherds have Broad Band White-on-Red exterior decoration (e.g., see Fig. 218).

Distribution: This jar type has a limited distribution at habitation and habitation-cemetery sites in Late Suchimancillo Cluster 1 (lower part), and at a few sites in Cluster 2 as well. Collection proveniences (with number of sherds in parentheses)/site numbers are:

Colls. 8(3), 9(1), 13(1)/LSUCH-45; Coll. 120(1)/LSUCH-58; Coll. 122(2)/LSUCH-62; Coll. 149(1)/LSUCH-65; Coll. 112(1)/LSUCH-68; Coll. 217(3)/LSUCH-108; Coll. 218(3)/LSUCH-109; Coll. 334(3)/LSUCH-128.

Chronological assessment: Jar 5c was found primarily in single-component Late Suchimancillo collections, and appears to be a good diagnostic of this period.

Inter-regional comparisons: Jars with this very distinctive wedge-shaped rim form are not reported in the literature on areas adjacent to the Lower Santa region.

Late Suchimancillo Jar 5d (Fig. 215)

Number: 6 sherds, or ca. .2% of the Late Suchimancillo assemblage.

General description: Globular jar with an outslanted, cambered neck and a thin, pinched lip. The wall of the neck slants outward at an angle of 20-35° from the vertical. Rim diameters vary from 12-18 cm, with a mean of 15 cm. Wall thickness below the rim ranges between 5 mm and 8 mm.

Paste: Temper consists uniformly of medium sand in moderate quantities. Paste color is red, with gray cores noted on two sherds.

Surface characteristics: Exterior and interior surfaces are plain redware.

Distribution: This jar type has a limited distribution at several habitation sites in Late Suchimancillo Cluster 1 (lower part), as well as at one site in Cluster 3 (SVP-LSUCH-139). Collection proveniences (with number of sherds in parentheses)/site numbers are:

Coll. 29(1)/LSUCH-39; Colls. 13(1), 14(2)/LSUCH-45; Coll. 106(1)/LSUCH-51; Coll. 176(1)/LSUCH-139.

Chronological assessment: Jar 5d was found primarily in single-component Late Suchimancillo collections, and appears to be a good diagnostic for this period. Its limited distribution lessens its utility as a general time marker, however.

Inter-regional comparisons: Jars with this distinctive rim form are not reported in the literature on areas adjacent to the Lower Santa region.

Late Suchimancillo Jar 5e (Fig. 215)

Number: 58 sherds, or ca. 2.3% of the Late Suchimancillo assemblage.

General description: Globular jar with a tall flaring or everted rim. Rim diameters vary from 11-30 cm, with a mean of 20.2 cm and a standard deviation of 5.1 cm. Wall thickness below the rim ranges widely between 5 mm and 10 mm, with a mean of 8.3 mm.

Paste: Temper consists uniformly of medium sand in moderate quantities. Paste color is red, with gray cores noted on two sherds.

Surface characteristics: Exterior and interior surfaces are plain redware.

Distribution: This jar type has a wide distribution at habitation, habitation-cemetery, and cemetery sites in Late Suchimancillo Cluster 1 (lower third), throughout Cluster 2, and at a few sites in Cluster 3. Collection proveniences (with number of sherds in parentheses)/site numbers are:

Coll. 29(1)/LSUCH-39; Coll. 28(9)/LSUCH-51; Coll. 150(1)/LSUCH-65; Coll. 113(2)/LSUCH-74; Coll. 118(2)/LSUCH-76; Coll. 145(1)/LSUCH-81; Coll. 233(1)/LSUCH-83; Coll. 243(2)/LSUCH-87; Colls. 250(1), 251(1)/LSUCH-103; Coll. 252(1)/LSUCH-104; Coll. 254(2)/LSUCH-106; Coll. 218(4)/LSUCH-109; Colls. 219(2), 220(3)/LSUCH-110; Coll. 223(3)/LSUCH-112; Coll. 229(4)/LSUCH-114; Coll. 257(1)/LSUCH-115; Coll. 305(2)/LSUCH-117; Coll. 312(1)/LSUCH-118; Coll. 277(3)/LSUCH-119; Coll. 333(1)/LSUCH-121; Coll. 335(1)/LSUCH-131; Coll. 327(4)/LSUCH-143; Coll. 297(3)/LSUCH-147; Coll. 283(2)/LSUCH-149.

Chronological assessment: Jar 5e is similar in form and paste to a number of later jar types--including Guadalupito Jar 2b (Fig. 226), Early Tanguche Jar 2d (Fig. 236), and Early Tambo Real Redware Jar 4b (Fig. 271). It therefore appears to be an essentially ongoing type and of little value in distinguishing specific time periods.

Inter-regional comparisons: This vessel type appears to be a higher-necked version of the otherwise very similar Castillo Plain jar, Vessel Shape 1, of Virú Valley (cf. Strong and Evans 1952, p. 264, Fig. 40).

Late Suchimancillo Jar 5f (Fig. 215)

Number: 8 sherds, or ca. .3% of the Late Suchimancillo assemblage.

General description: Globular jar with a very tall, funnel-shaped neck with generally straight walls. Rim diameters vary from 18-40 cm, with a mean of 27 cm and a standard deviation of 9 cm. Wall thickness below the rim ranges between 9 mm and 13 mm.

Paste: Temper consists uniformly of medium sand in moderate quantities. Paste color in six sherds is red, while the remaining two have reddish-brown paste. Gray cores were noted on four sherds, including both paste variants.

Surface characteristics: Exterior and interior surfaces are either plain redware or reddish-brownware.

Distribution: This jar type has a limited distribution at a few habitation sites in Late Suchimancillo Cluster 1 (lowermost part) and Cluster 2. Collection proveniences (with number of sherds in parentheses)/site numbers are:

Coll. 28(3)/LSUCH-51; Coll. 128(1)/LSUCH-62; Coll. 249(1)/ LSUCH-103; Coll. 223(1)/LSUCH-112; Coll. 305(1)/LSUCH-117; Coll. 342(1)/ LSUCH-132.

Chronological assessment: Jar 5f is somewhat similar in form and paste to Early Tambo Real Redware Jar 4c (Fig. 271) and Late Tambo Real Redware Jar 3b (Fig. 279), but can be distinguished from the two later types by its uniformly higher neck.

Inter-regional comparisons: Very similar jars with high necks are present in the Gallinazo Period assemblage of Virú Valley (cf. Strong and Evans 1952, p. 264, Fig. 40 - Vessel Shape 2).

Late Suchimancillo Jar 6 (Fig. 216)

Number: 38 sherds, or ca. 1.5% of the Late Suchimancillo assemblage.

General description: Globular jar with a constricted mouth and a (unique) double rim, which consists of (1) the main direct rim and (2) an exterior flange which flares upward to about the same height as the main rim from a point high on the shoulder of the vessel. The presence of double sets of perforations on one or the other side of the trough formed by the double rims suggests the possibility that lids (with the same diameter as the trough) were tied over the vessel opening. Rim diameters vary from 9-40 cm, with a mean of 19.6 cm and a standard deviation of 8 cm. Wall thickness below the rim ranges widely between 5 mm and 12 mm, with most sherds in the sample at either the upper or lower ends of the range.

Paste: Temper consists of fine or medium sand, with about 60% of the sherds having medium grain sand. Paste color is red, with gray cores noted on six sherds.

Surface characteristics: The exterior surface and rim of 16 sherds are decorated with white-painted designs consisting of broad-line curvilinear or geometric motifs (e.g., see Figs. 216, 218). Since rims are not always decorated, and since our sample included sherds with very little or no body attached, it is probable that most if not all of the 38 sherds in the sample are from vessels decorated with broad bands of white paint.

Distribution: This jar type has a distribution limited to habitation, habitation-cemetery, and cemetery sites in the lower third part of Late Suchimancillo Cluster 1. Collection proveniences (with number of sherds in parentheses)/site numbers are:

Coll. 33(2)/LSUCH-40; Coll. 34(1)/LSUCH-44; Colls. 11(2), 8(1), 16(2)/LSUCH-45; Coll. 36(1)/LSUCH-46; Coll. 41(16)/LSUCH-53; Coll. 42(1)/ LSUCH-54; Coll. 45(2)/LSUCH-57; Coll. 121(1)/LSUCH-58; Colls. 122(2), 127(1)/LSUCH-62; Coll. 112(2)/LSUCH-68; Coll. 118(2)/LSUCH-76; Coll. 133(1)/LSUCH-77; Coll. 145(1)/LSUCH-81.

Chronological assessment: Jar 6 is primarily characteristic of single-component Late Suchimancillo collections, and therefore appears to be a good temporal diagnostic.

Inter-regional comparisons: An essentially identical jar form is present in the Recuay Yaiá Phase materials (equivalent to Late Gallinazo) excavated at the adjacent sierra site of Pashash (cf. Grieder 1978, pp. 60-61, Fig. 32 - Form D-2; see also p. 67, Fig. 36 a). It is of interest to note that despite the similarity of form, the Pashash vessel is confined to the general orangeware type of that area as well as to fine paste orange and cream wares, while in Santa it is a redware type usually decorated with Broad Band White-on-Red motifs, as mentioned above.

Late Suchimancillo Jar 7 (Fig. 216)

Number: 24 sherds, or ca. .9% of the Late Suchimancillo assemblage.

General description: Globular jar with a short vertical and incurving, or bulging, neck. Rim diameters vary from 7-12 cm, with a mean of 9.4 cm and a standard deviation of 1.6 cm. Wall thickness below the rim ranges between 5 mm and 6 mm.

Paste: Temper consists uniformly of medium sand in moderate quantities. Paste color is red, with a gray core noted on one sherd.

Surface characteristics: An incised design consisting of four short lines (which are roughly similar to the punctate design shown in Fig. 217 d) is present on the exterior of the neck of six sherds in the sample. Two other sherds have either cane punched design in a single line around the neck, or Broad Band White-on-Red decoration (see Fig. 218). The remaining 12 sherds have plain exterior and interior surfaces.

Distribution: This jar type is widely distributed at habitation, habitation-cemetery, and cemetery sites in Late Suchimancillo Clusters 1 and 2, as well as at two sites in Cluster 3. Collection proveniences (with number of sherds in parentheses)/site numbers are:

Coll. 370(1)/LSUCH-28; Coll. 33(1)/LSUCH-40; Coll. 39(3)/ LSUCH-52; Coll. 129(2)/LSUCH-70; Coll. 144(1)/LSUCH-81; Coll. 138(1)/ LSUCH-82; Coll. 238(1)/LSUCH-85; Coll. 244(1)/LSUCH-86; Coll. 218(1)/ LSUCH-109; Coll. 219(2)/LSUCH-110; Coll. 305(1)/LSUCH-117; Coll. 312(2)/ LSUCH-118; Coll. 333(1)/LSUCH-121; Coll. 359(2)/LSUCH-127; Coll. 347(1)/ LSUCH-135; Coll. 177(1)/LSUCH-140; Coll. 49(1)/LSUCH-148.

Chronological assessment: Jar 7 is similar in form, size, and paste to Guadalupito Jar 3a (Fig. 226), but the decorated variants at least can be distinguished from the plainware jar type of the later period. The undecorated variant of the Late Suchimancillo jar, however, appears to be similar enough to the later jar that it is of little utility as a temporal diagnostic.

Inter-regional comparisons: Jars with bulging necks quite similar to Late Suchimancillo Jar 7 are one of the vessel shapes present in the Gloria Polished Plain type of Virú Valley (cf. Strong and Evans 1952, p. 263, Fig. 39 - Vessel Shape 1), but, as mentioned above, the Lower Santa jar differs in having unpolished redware surfaces.

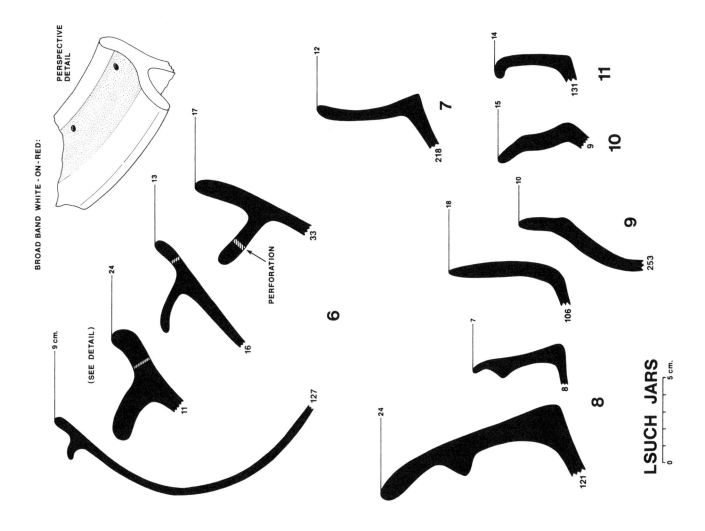

Fig. 216. Late Suchimancillo Period ceramics: Jars 6, 7, 8, 9, 10, 11.

431

Late Suchimancillo Jar 8 (Fig. 216)

Number: 23 sherds, or ca. .9% of the Late Suchimancillo assemblage.

General description: Globular jar with a slightly outslanted neck, flared rim, and a sharp camber on the exterior below the rim. This is one of the principal neck forms that characterize Late Suchimancillo effigy neck vessels (e.g., see Fig. 221 a, b). Indeed, it is likely that the sherds in this sample represent the undecorated backs of the necks of such vessels. Rim diameters vary from 7-24 cm, with a mean of 15 cm. Wall thickness below the rim ranges between 5 mm and 10 mm.

Paste: Temper consists uniformly of medium sand in moderate quantities. Paste color is red.

Surface characteristics: Normally, one side of the neck and sometimes part of the shoulder of the vessel are decorated with incised and appliquéd features representing human figures. Exterior and interior surfaces are otherwise plain redware.

Distribution: This jar type was found widely distributed at habitation, habitation-cemetery, and cemetery sites in Late Suchimancillo Cluster 1 (lower third), as well as at a few sites in Clusters 2 and 3. Collection proveniences (with number of sherds in parentheses)/site numbers are:

Colls. 8(3), 16(1)/LSUCH-45; Coll. 104(2)/LSUCH-51; Coll. 42(3)/LSUCH-54; Coll. 43(1)/LSUCH-55; Coll. 121(1)/LSUCH-58; Coll. 127(2)/LSUCH-62; Coll. 134(1)/LSUCH-79; Coll. 144(1)/LSUCH-81; Coll. 236(1)/LSUCH-84; Coll. 209(2)/LSUCH-102; Coll. 218(3)/LSUCH-109; Coll. 184(1)/LSUCH-138; Coll. 182(1)/LSUCH-141.

Chronological assessment: Approximately one-half of the collections in which Jar 8 is present are single-component Late Suchimancillo contexts. The remaining collections are mixed Early and Late Suchimancillo, which suggests that this jar type may be transitional from the earlier to the later period as well as diagnostic of Late Suchimancillo.

Inter-regional comparisons: Although effigy neck vessels are a common feature of the Late Gallinazo assemblage in Virú Valley (cf. Bennett 1950, Pl. 10 A, B, E), this particular neck form does not appear to be present (but compare Fig. 221 a and b of this report to the effigy neck jars in Bennett 1939, p. 56, Fig. 12 l, n).

Late Suchimancillo Jar 9 (Fig. 216)

Number: 36 sherds, or ca. 1.4% of the Late Suchimancillo assemblage.

General description: Globular jar with a vertical neck of low or medium height. Rim diameters vary from 10-18 cm, with a mean of 13.1 cm and a standard deviation of 3.4 cm. Wall thickness below the rim ranges widely between 5 mm and 14 mm, with a mean of 7.3 mm and a standard deviation of 2.7 mm.

Paste: Temper consists uniformly of medium sand in moderate quantities. Paste color is red.

Surface characteristics: Exterior and interior surfaces are plain redware.

Distribution: This jar type is widely distributed at habitation, habitation-cemetery, and cemetery sites in Late Suchimancillo Clusters 1, 2, and 3. Collection proveniences (with number of sherds in parentheses)/site numbers are:

Coll. 370(6)/LSUCH-28; Coll. 29(3)/LSUCH-39; Coll. 24(2)/LSUCH-49; Coll. 26(1)/LSUCH-50; Colls. 28(4), 106(2)/LSUCH-51; Coll. 39(3)/LSUCH-52; Colls. 111(1), 112(1)/LSUCH-68; Coll. 131(1)/LSUCH-72; Colls. 233(1), 232(1)/LSUCH-83; Coll. 238(1)/LSUCH-85; Coll. 251(1)/LSUCH-103; Coll. 253(1)/LSUCH-105; Coll. 229(1)/LSUCH-114; Coll. 176(1)/LSUCH-139; Coll. 85(1)/LSUCH-144; Coll. 48(2)/LSUCH-148; Coll. 285(2)/LSUCH-150.

Chronological assessment: Jar 9 is essentially identical in form and paste to Early Suchimancillo Jar 10 (Fig. 206), so this general vessel type is useful primarily as a non-specific Suchimancillo time marker.

Inter-regional comparisons: Vessels with low vertical necks are one of the common forms of the contemporaneous Castillo Plain type in Virú Valley (cf. Strong and Evans 1952, p. 264, Fig. 40 - Vessel Shape 1).

Late Suchimancillo Jar 10 (Fig. 216)

Number: 20 sherds, or ca. .8% of the Late Suchimancillo assemblage.

General description: Globular jar with a slightly cambered, outslanting neck and flared rim. Rim diameters are all 15 cm. Wall thickness below the rim ranges between 5 mm and 9 mm, with a mean of 7.8 mm and a standard deviation of 1.1 mm.

Paste: Temper consists uniformly of medium sand in moderate quantities. Paste color is red.

Surface characteristics: Exterior and interior surfaces are plain redware, with incompletely oxidized sections noted on five sherds in the sample.

Distribution: This jar type has a limited distribution at a few habitation sites of Late Suchimancillo Clusters 1 and 2. Collection proveniences (with number of sherds in parentheses)/site numbers are:

Coll. 29(2)/LSUCH-39; Coll. 9(6)/LSUCH-45; Colls. 28(5), 106(4)/LSUCH-51; Coll. 139(1)/LSUCH-82; Coll. 351(1)/LSUCH-100; Coll. 342(1)/LSUCH-132.

Chronological assessment: Jar 10 is the undecorated form of a more general vessel type that includes Jar 12 (Fig. 217). The analysis of single-component collections indicates that both are good diagnostics of Late Suchimancillo Period.

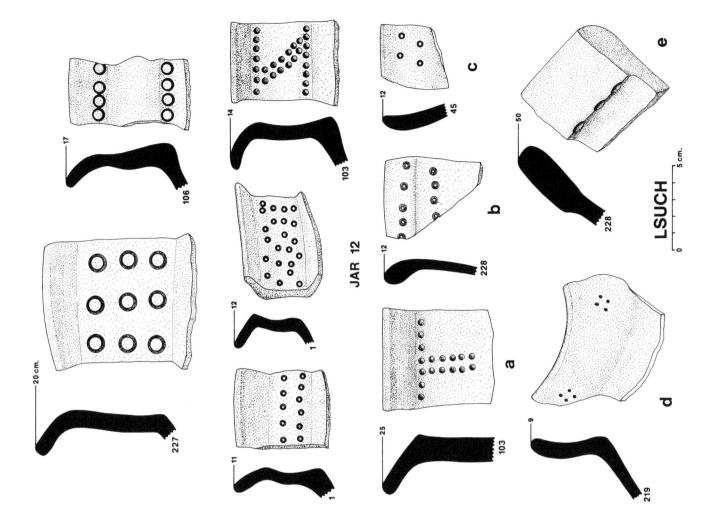

Fig. 217. Late Suchimancillo Period ceramics: Jar 12, and related miscellaneous bowls and jars (a–e).

Inter-regional comparisons: From his excavated Recuay Yaiá Phase materials at Pashash site, Grieder (1978, p. 67, Fig. 36 h) illustrates a rim profile that is quite similar to that of Jar 10. No plain redware vessels of this type are illustrated for the Late Gallinazo assemblage in Virú Valley.

Late Suchimancillo Jar 11 (Fig. 216)

Number: 2 sherds, or ca. .08% of the Late Suchimancillo assemblage.

General description: Globular jar with a vertical neck and everted lip. Rim diameters are 14 and 25 cm. Wall thickness below the rim is 7.5 mm.

Paste: Temper consists of medium sand in moderate quantities. Paste color is red.

Surface characteristics: Exterior and interior surfaces are plain redware, with the exception of the neck of one of the vessels (which has zoned incised design consisting of three rows of vertical, dashed lines flanked by longer, parallel incised lines).

Distribution: This jar type has a very limited distribution confined to two habitation sites in Late Suchimancillo Cluster 1. Collection proveniences (with number of sherds in parentheses)/site numbers are:

Coll. 121(1)/LSUCH-58; Coll. 131(1)/LSUCH-72.

Chronological assessment: Jar 11 appears to be a late, redware form of a general jar type that begins in Vinzos Period (see Jar 5, Fig. 199), and continues through Early Suchimancillo (see Jar 9, Fig. 206) into Late Suchimancillo.

Inter-regional comparisons: See Early Suchimancillo Jar 9.

Late Suchimancillo Jar 12 (Fig. 217)

Number: 29 sherds, or ca. 1.1% of the Late Suchimancillo assemblage.

General description: Globular jar with a vertical, slightly cambered neck and everted lip. Rim diameters vary from 11-20 cm, with a mean of 15.4 cm and a standard deviation of 2.3 cm. Wall thickness below the rim ranges between 5 mm and 10 mm, with a mean of 8.3 mm.

Paste: Temper consists uniformly of medium sand in moderate quantities. Paste color is red.

Surface characteristics: The exterior surface of the neck is decorated with a variety of reed punched designs. These include vertical and horizontal lines of circles, randomly placed circles, as well as double diagonal lines framed by single horizontal lines of circular punctate markings. Judging from the attached walls of the vessel body on several sherds, decoration was confined to the neck.

Distribution: This jar type was found primarily at several habitation sites upriver from the Tablones area in Late Suchimancillo Cluster 1. Collection proveniences (with number of sherds in parentheses)/site numbers are:

Coll. 103(12)/LSUCH-38; Coll. 29(2)/LSUCH-39; Colls. 1(2), 13(2)/LSUCH-45; Coll. 24(1)/LSUCH-49; Coll. 106(4)/LSUCH-51; Colls. 227(1), 229(5)/LSUCH-114.

Chronological assessment: Jar 12 is the decorated form of a more general type that includes Jar 10 (Fig. 216). It obviously also bears a strong resemblance to Late Suchimancillo Jar 11, as well as to Vinzos Jar 5 (Fig. 199) and Early Suchimancillo Jar 9 (Fig. 206), and may be a late redware form of the earlier reddish-brownware jar.

Inter-regional comparisons: Jars of this type from the Lower Santa region seem clearly related in form and exterior decoration to the Castillo Incised type of Virú Valley (cf. Strong and Evans 1952, p. 320, Fig. 65 – Vessel Shapes 3 and 6; see also pp. 321-322, Figs. 66, 67).

Late Suchimancillo: Broad Band White-on-Red (Figs. 216, 218)

Number: 105 sherds, or ca. 1.4% of the Late Suchimancillo assemblage.

General description: This painted ware category includes (1) the decorated form of several plainware vessel types that are described separately (e.g., see Late Suchimancillo Jars 5e, 5f, and 7); (2) Late Suchimancillo Jar 6, a double-rim vessel that is also described separately; and (3) decorated body sherds that cannot be assigned to a specific jar type. As shown in Fig. 218, white paint was applied either to whole sections of a vessel, such as the exterior of the neck and the upper half of the body, or in broad curvilinear and geometric bands to various places on the exterior surface. The paint is often so thinly applied that the redware surface shows through, and, as the illustrations show, it was often applied hurriedly or sloppily.

Paste: Temper consists uniformly of medium sand in moderate quantities. Paste color is red. This is one of the most friable wares of any found in the Lower Santa region, and it often crumbled at the edges when picked up for examination by our survey team or when placed in collection sacks for transport to the field laboratory.

Surface characteristics: Aside from the Broad Band White-on-Red designs mentioned above, vessels were often also decorated with punctate motifs and small, appliquéd animal effigies.

Distribution: Sherds and whole vessels (found on the surface where they had been left by the huaqueros) of this painted ware type are widely distributed at habitation, habitation-cemetery, and cemetery sites throughout Late Suchimancillo Clusters 1 and 2, as well as at one site in Cluster 3 (SVP-LSUCH-147). Collection proveniences (with number of sherds in parentheses)/site numbers are:

Coll. 374(6)/LSUCH-26; Coll. 370(5)/LSUCH-28; Coll. 30(1)/LSUCH-40; Colls. 11(2), 16(2)/LSUCH-45; Coll. 36(4)/LSUCH-46; Coll. 105(1)/

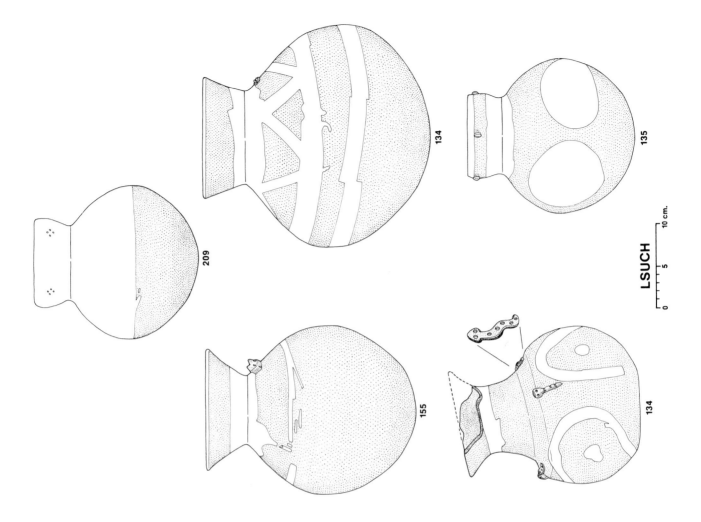

LSUCH

|———|———|———————|
0   5   10 cm.

Fig. 218. Late Suchimancillo Period ceramics: Broad Band White-on-Red jars.

435

LSUCH-51; Coll. 45(4)/LSUCH-57; Colls. 122(2), 127(4)/LSUCH-62; Coll. 112(9)/LSUCH-68; Coll. 129(1)/LSUCH-70; Coll. 131(5)/LSUCH-72; Coll. 113(3)/LSUCH-74; Coll. 118(9)/LSUCH-76; Coll. 135(1)/LSUCH-78; Coll. 134(2)/LSUCH-79; Coll. 155(1)/(no site); Coll. 236(4)/LSUCH-84; Coll. 238(10)/LSUCH-85; Coll. 209(1)/LSUCH-102; Coll. 252(3)/LSUCH-104; Coll. 253(3)/LSUCH-105; Coll. 218(3)/LSUCH-109; Coll. 219(1)/LSUCH-116; Coll. 223(3)/LSUCH-112; Coll. 228(1)/LSUCH-114; Coll. 262(2)/LSUCH-116; Coll. 331(1)/LSUCH-120; Coll. 333(5)/LSUCH-121; Coll. 347(6)/LSUCH-135; Coll. 297(5)/LSUCH-147.

Chronological assessment: Broad Band White-on-Red is found primarily in single-component contexts associated with Late Suchimancillo diagnostics.

Inter-regional comparisons: This decorated type seems related to the Puerto Moorin White-on-Red style in terms of its broad, white-painted lines (e.g., see Strong and Evans 1952, Pl. 4 H), but in paste and vessel forms it is clearly a later type in the Lower Santa Valley region, in other words, one that is contemporaneous with Late Gallinazo.

Late Suchimancillo: Kaolin Ware (Fig. 212 b-o; Fig. 219 b, c, f; Fig. 220 a; Fig. 221 f, g; Fig. 223 h)

Number: 322 sherds, or ca. 12.7% of the Late Suchimancillo assemblage.

General description: In addition to the Late Suchimancillo Bowl 7 decorated kaolin vessels (including Red/White Kaolin, Orange/White Kaolin, Black/White Kaolin, Black-and-Orange/White Kaolin, Red-and-Orange/White Kaolin, Red/Orangeware, Red-and-Black (Negative)/Orangeware, and White/Red-painted Orangeware, in Fig. 212 b-o, q), other decorated kaolin types present in the collections and illustrated here are: (1) Red/White Kaolin (human effigy neck vessel; Fig. 221 g); (2) Red-and-Black/White Kaolin (small jar; Fig. 219 f); (3) Red-and-Black (Negative/White Kaolin (small jar; Fig. 219 c); (4) Orange-and-Black (Negative/White Kaolin (small jar; Fig. 219 b); (5) Plain Orangeware (human effigy neck vessel; Fig. 220 a); (6) Red/Orangeware (human effigy neck vessel; Fig. 221 f); and (7) Plain White Kaolin (annular-base bowl with maker's mark; Fig. 223 h). Wall thickness of all kaolin sherds is very thin, ranging from 2.5 mm to 4 mm.

Paste: Temper appears to consist of fine sand in very light quantities. Paste color is either chalk white or orange.

Surface characteristics: Very few unpainted kaolin sherds were found. Most of the sherds in the sample are decorated with two or more colors, including various shades of red, black, and orange. A few resist ware sherds were found, as mentioned above, but these are not common.

Distribution: Late Suchimancillo kaolin ware is widely distributed at habitation, habitation-cemetery, and cemetery sites in the lower two-thirds part of Late Suchimancillo Cluster 1 (36 sites), throughout Cluster 2 (17 sites), as well as in Cluster 3 (2 sites). Collection proveniences (with number of sherds in parentheses)/site

numbers are:

Coll. 375(8)/LSUCH-13; Coll. 29(15)/LSUCH-39; Colls. 30(2), 33(7)/LSUCH-40; Coll. 34(2)/LSUCH-44; Colls. 11(8), 9(3), 14(1), 16(9)/ LSUCH-45; Coll. 36(1)/LSUCH-46; Coll. 35(6)/LSUCH-47; Coll. 24(1)/ LSUCH-49; Coll. 26(1)/LSUCH-50; Colls. 104(3), 106(1)/LSUCH-51; Coll. 39(5)/LSUCH-52; Coll. 41(5)/LSUCH-53; Coll. 42(14)/LSUCH-54; Coll. 43(5)/LSUCH-55; Coll. 44(3)/LSUCH-56; Coll. 45(2)/LSUCH-57; Colls. 120(6), 121(15)/LSUCH-58; Coll. 124(10)/LSUCH-59; Coll. 125(5)/LSUCH-61; Colls. 122(15), 127(15), 128(7)/LSUCH-62; Coll. 115(2)/LSUCH-63; Colls. 102(3), 119(5)/LSUCH-66; Coll. 108(1)/LSUCH-67; Coll. 112(14)/LSUCH-68; Coll. 153(3)/LSUCH-69; Coll. 129(6)/LSUCH-70; Coll. 132(7)/LSUCH-71; Coll. 154(4)/LSUCH-73; Coll. 113(6)/LSUCH-74; Coll. 118(21)/LSUCH-76; Coll. 133(2)/LSUCH-77; Coll. 135(1)/LSUCH-78; Coll. 134(14)/LSUCH-79; Colls. 144(2), 145(2)/LSUCH-81; Coll. 138(1)/LSUCH-82; Coll. 232(1)/ LSUCH-83; Coll. 236(2)/LSUCH-84; Coll. 238(1)/LSUCH-85; Coll. 203(3)/ LSUCH-95; Coll. 204(1)/LSUCH-96; Coll. 206(1)/LSUCH-97; Coll. 352(2)/ LSUCH-98; Coll. 209(2)/LSUCH-102; Coll. 253(5)/LSUCH-105; Coll. 217(2)/ LSUCH-108; Coll. 218(2)/LSUCH-109; Coll. 227(4)/LSUCH-114; Coll. 262(1)/ LSUCH-116; Coll. 305(1)/LSUCH-117; Coll. 358(4)/LSUCH-125; Coll. 342(3)/ LSUCH-132; Coll. 347(5)/LSUCH-135; Coll. 176(1)/LSUCH-139; Coll. 182(2)/ LSUCH-141; Coll. 47(1)/LSUCH-145.

Chronological assessment: See discussion of chronology under Early Suchimancillo kaolin ware.

Late Suchimancillo: Effigy Figures (Figs. 219 h, 220, 221, 222)

Late Suchimancillo is the first period in the Lower Santa Valley sequence in which substantial numbers of human and animal effigy figures are found widely distributed throughout the area of occupation. It is of interest to note that these figures are found at roughly as many habitation sites as cemetery sites. And, as in the preceding two periods, all human effigies appear to be depictions of males (it is not until the following Guadalupito and Early Tanguche Periods that small numbers of figures appear that are obvious depictions of females). The combined total of effigy figures, including representations of both humans and animals, in Late Suchimancillo is 73 (55 human and 18 animal figures), or ca. 2.8% of the total assemblage of this period.

Human effigies: As in the Early Suchimancillo Period, most of the representations of the human figure are limited to effigy neck jars depicting the face (e.g., Fig. 219 h, Fig. 220 a-g, Fig. 221 a-g, Fig. 222). All of these effigy neck figures have roughly triangular and rather schematically-shaped noses (in contrast to Guadalupito and Early Tanguche Periods, when noses are almost always realistically depicted). Ears are not always placed on these vessels, but, when they are, ear spools are usually shown passing through the lobes. Mouths are shown either by a series of wedge-shaped punctate marks, or by a single incised line. Only one figure was found on which the mouth is shown in elliptical form, in this case having deeply incised and widely spaced teeth (Fig. 221 g). Eyes are usually represented by incised lines, although figures with eyes formed by cane punching or appliquéd nodes are also common. As the illustrations show, a wide variety of eye forms

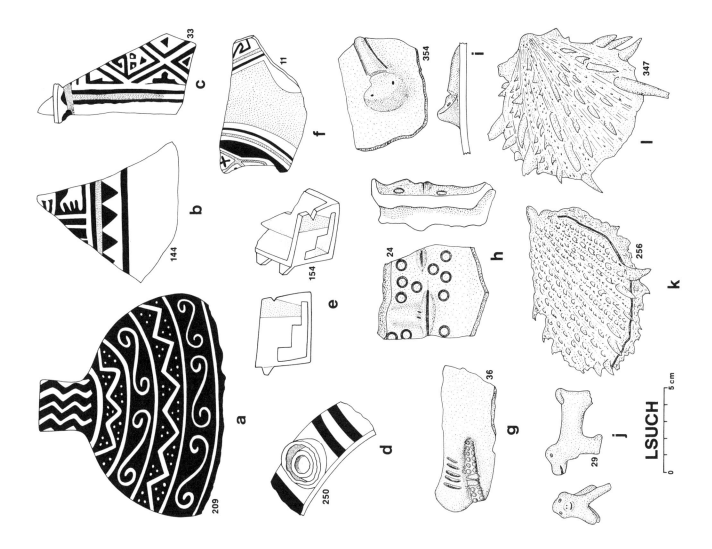

Fig. 219. Late Suchimancillo Period ceramics and shells: miscellaneous sherds (a–j), and Spondylus (k–l).

is present--including almond-shaped, elliptical, and circular.

From a modern viewpoint, most of the facial expressions probably would be interpreted as "emotionally neutral," but a few appear to be smiling (e.g., Fig. 220 d; Fig. 221 a, c), if not rather jaunty (Fig. 220 b). In any case, in Suchimancillo collections one does not find the more imperious--even ferocious--expressions that characterize some human effigies of the Guadalupito Period (e.g., see humans in Fig. 230 d, e; and Ai Apaec, the Moche deity, in Fig. 231 j, k).

Among the more unique human effigies in the Late Suchimancillo collections are: (1) a figure with the right hand held over a partly downturned mouth, and with realistically modeled eyes and nose (Fig. 220 g); (2) a small, hollow figurine with a clay pellet inside and a perforation through the shoulders, perhaps indicating that it was used as a child's rattle and hung on a string or a stick (Fig. 220 j; Note: see Bennett 1939, p. 26, Fig. 5 f, for a contemporaneous Gallinazo figurine from Virú that is of very similar form); (3) two effigy neck figures with the type of "winged" headgear that characterizes Recuay ceramics (Fig. 221 c, e; see Kauffmann Doig 1978, p. 416, Figs. 7 and 8, for Recuay figurines with similar headgear; Note: the figure shown in Fig. 221 c, for which no provenience number is given, was collected on the north desert margin of the Lower Valley sector); and (4) two depictions of (right) arms holding clubs (Fig. 220 h, i).

The following paste types are represented among the human effigy figures of Late Suchimancillo Period: (1) redware (Fig. 219 h; Fig. 220 c-f, h-j; Fig. 221 a-e; Fig. 222); (2) reddish-brownware (Fig. 220 g); (3) grayware (Fig. 220 b); (4) white kaolin (Fig. 221 g); and (5) kaolin-based orangeware (Fig. 220 a; Fig. 221 f). All of the illustrated human effigy figures appear to have been unpainted, with the exception of the following: (1) Fig. 221 e (Black-and-White/Redware); (2) Fig. 221 f (Red/Orangeware); (3) Fig. 221 g (Red/White Kaolin); and (4) Fig. 222 - top (White/Redware).

Animal effigies: Representations of animals in the collections dating to Late Suchimancillo are of two principal types. The first type consists of separate figures of animals--including (1) a probable dog (Fig. 219 j); (2) an animal with canine teeth bared (Fig. 219 g); and (3) a probable marine animal (ray?; see Fig. 219 i). The second type consists of figures of animals that decorated the shoulders of jars--including (1) small animal heads of indeterminate species (Fig. 218, center - left; Fig. 223 a); and (2) full figures of small animals such as snakes (Fig. 218, bottom - left).

Effigy distributions: Of the two types of effigy figures, human effigies have a wider distribution including habitation, habitation-cemetery, and cemetery sites in Late Suchimancillo Cluster 1 (lower half), throughout Cluster 2, and two sites in Cluster 3 (SVP-LSUCH-138, 145). Animal effigies are found at the same types of sites, but have a distribution limited to the lower half of Cluster 1 and the upper third of Cluster 2. Separate collection proveniences (with number of sherds in parentheses)/site numbers are:

Human effigy proveniences: Coll. 370(1)/LSUCH-28; Coll. 34(1)/LSUCH-44; Coll. 11(1)/LSUCH-45; Coll. 24(1)/LSUCH-49; Coll. 106(1)/LSUCH-51; Coll. 39(1)/LSUCH-52; Coll. 41(3)/LSUCH-53; Coll. 42(9)/LSUCH-54; Coll. 43(1)/LSUCH-55; Coll. 123(1)/ LSUCH-58; Coll. 122(1), 127(3), 128(1)/LSUCH-62; Coll. 115(1)/ LSUCH-63; Coll. 112(1)/LSUCH-68; Coll. 132(1)/LSUCH-71; Coll. 131(1)/LSUCH-72; Coll. 113(1)/LSUCH-74; Coll. 133(1)/LSUCH-77; Coll. 134(2)/LSUCH-79; Coll. 144(1)/LSUCH-81; Coll. 236(1)/ LSUCH-84; Coll. 238(4)/LSUCH-85; Coll. 354(1)/LSUCH-91; Coll. 207(1)/LSUCH-97; Coll. 209(2)/LSUCH-102; Coll. 218(4)/LSUCH-109; Coll. 220(1)/LSUCH-110; Coll. 227(1)/LSUCH-114; Coll. 312(1)/ LSUCH-118; Coll. 342(1)/LSUCH-132; Coll. 184(1)/LSUCH-138; Coll. 47(1)/LSUCH-145.

Animal effigy proveniences: Coll. 29(1)/LSUCH-39; Coll. 33(1)/LSUCH-40; Coll. 1(1)/LSUCH-45; Coll. 36(1)/LSUCH-46; Colls. 28(1), 105(1)/LSUCH-51; Coll. 39(1)/LSUCH-52; Coll. 45(1)/ LSUCH-57; Coll. 121(1)/LSUCH-58; Colls. 127(1), 128(1)/LSUCH-62; Coll. 118(1)/LSUCH-76; Coll. 139(1)/LSUCH-82; Coll. 236(1)/ LSUCH-84; Coll. 354(1)/LSUCH-91; Coll. 206(1)/LSUCH-97; Coll. 249(1)/LSUCH-103; Coll. 218(1)/LSUCH-109.

Late Suchimancillo: Miscellaneous Items (Fig. 217 a-c; Fig. 219 d, k, l; Fig. 223 b, d-q)

Among the miscellaneous items found in Late Suchimancillo contexts, and illustrated here, are the following (listed in order of appearance in the drawings): (1) redware bowls with cane punched decoration on the exterior surface (Fig. 217 a-c; Note: Fig. 217 a may be a jar fragment); (2) Spondylus shells (Fig. 219 k, l; Note: the illustrated shells were found intact at the bottom of huaquero pits in heavily looted cemeteries, in clear association with Late Suchimancillo ceramics--obviously left there because they were of no value to the huaquero grave robbers); (3) a fragment of a redware "dipper" with a hollow handle (Fig. 223 b; Note: the perforation in the handle probably functioned to keep it from blowing apart during the firing process; dippers were also found at other sites--including Colls. 8, 35, and 124); (4) a circular redware sherd with a perforation in the center, ground down to this shape probably to serve as a spindle whorl (Fig. 223 d); (5) a fragment of a redware jar with horizontal strap handle and triangular punctate design (Fig. 223 e); (6) a redware bowl fragment with eccentric rim, carved in this fashion at a pre-firing stage (Fig. 223 f); and (7) a fragment of a redware spout-and-strap handle vessel (Fig. 223 g).

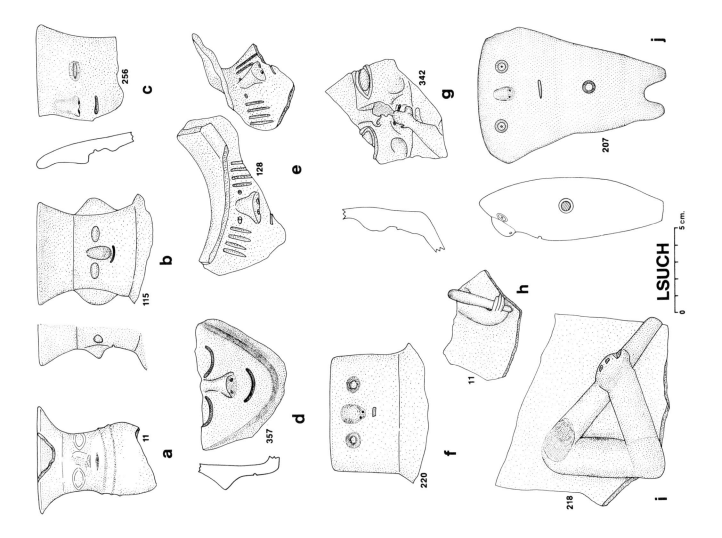

LSUCH

0 _____ 5 cm.

Fig. 220. Late Suchimancillo Period ceramics: human effigy jars and figurines.

439

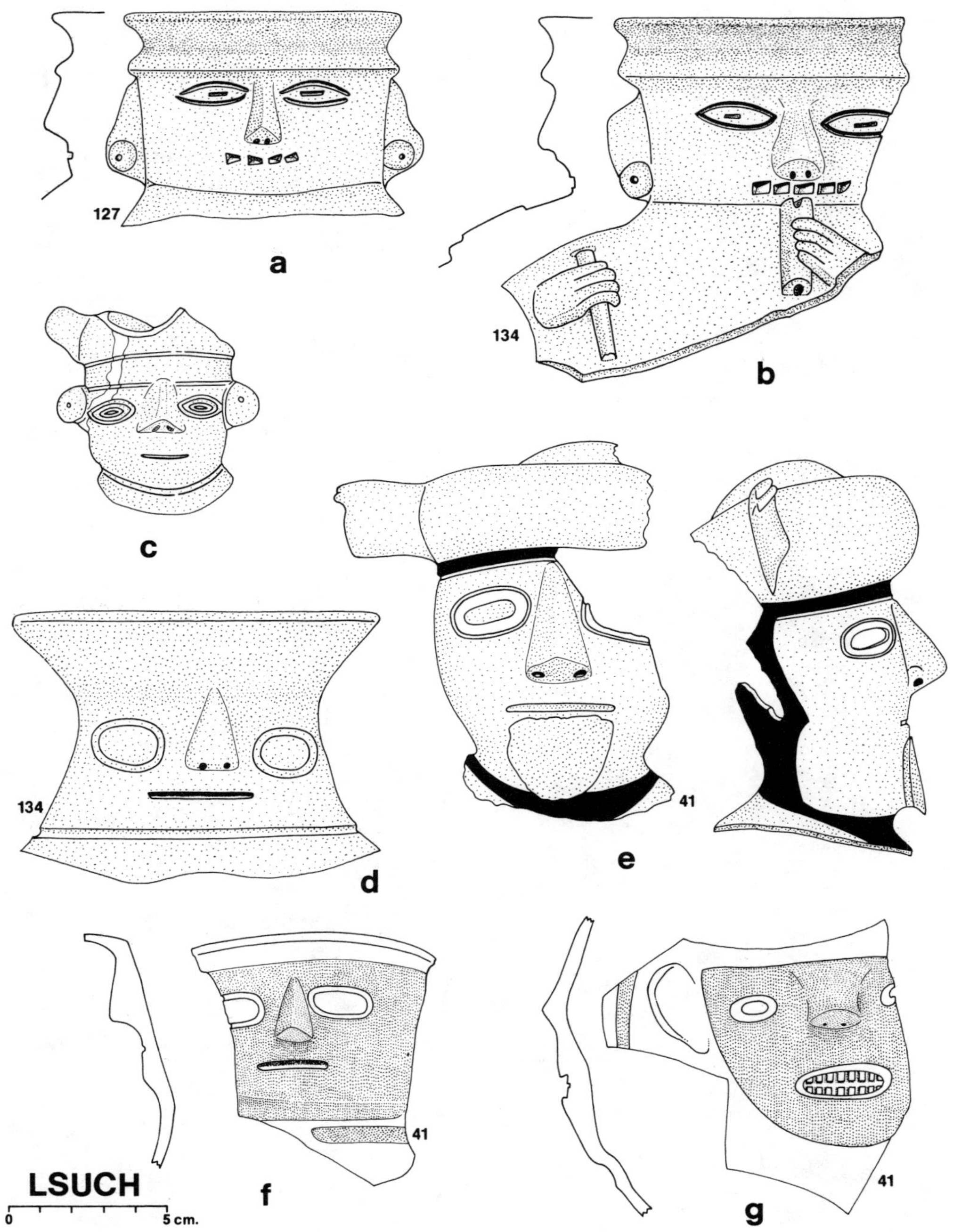

Fig. 221. Late Suchimancillo Period ceramics: human effigy jars.

440

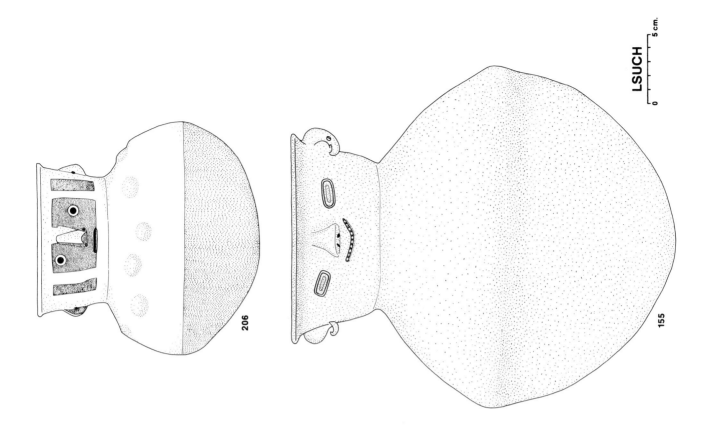

LSUCH
0 — 5 cm.

206

155

Fig. 222. Late Suchimancillo Period ceramics: human effigy jars.

441

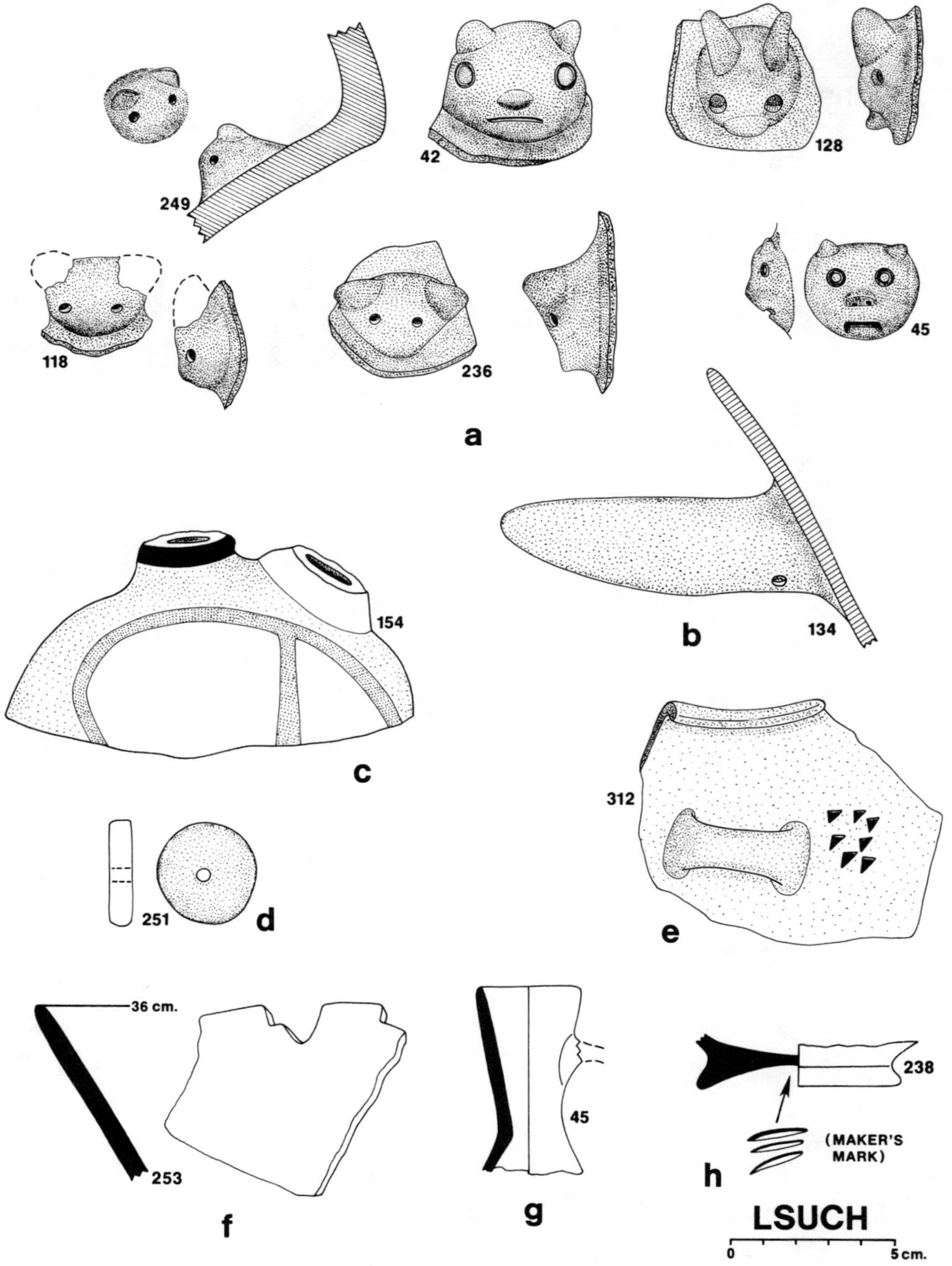

442

Fig. 223. Late Suchimancillo Period ceramics: miscellaneous sherds.

GUADALUPITO PERIOD

Guadalupito Bowl 1 (Fig. 225)

Number: 23 sherds, or ca. 1.5% of the Guadalupito assemblage.

General description: Open bowl with outslanted and slightly incurving walls. Rim diameters vary from 12-32 cm, with a mean of 20.6 cm and a standard deviation of 6.3 cm. Wall thickness below the rim ranges between 4 mm and 8 mm.

Paste: Temper consists of fine or medium sand, with approximately 55% of the sherds having medium grain sand. The quantity of temper in all sherds is moderate. Paste color is brick red.

Surface characteristics: Interior and exterior surfaces of 14 of the sherds in the sample are plain. Of the remaining sherds, six have an exterior white slip, two have an exterior white-painted design, and one has an exterior cream-colored slip. The interiors of the nine painted bowls are plain redware.

Distribution: This bowl type has a wide, but scattered, distribution at habitation, habitation-cemetery, and cemetery sites throughout most of the area of Guadalupito occupation. Collection proveniences (with number of sherds in parentheses)/site numbers are:

Coll. 277(1)/GUAD-31; Colls. 89/90(1)/GUAD-97; Coll. 66(1)/ GUAD-100; Colls. 76/78(2)/GUAD-104; Coll. 68(1)/GUAD-111; Colls. 60(2)/ 61(3), 63(2), 69(3), 70(1)/GUAD-112; Colls. 56(1), 57(1), 58(2)/GUAD-113; Coll. 316(1)/GUAD-121; Coll. 291(1)/GUAD-162.

Chronological assessment: The painted variant of Bowl 1 has decoration unlike that of any other period, and is a very good diagnostic of Guadalupito Period. However, the unpainted variant is similar in form and paste to some examples of Early Tanguche Bowl 2 (Fig. 236), and probably cannot be used as a distinguishing diagnostic for mixed collections containing components of both periods.

Inter-regional comparisons: Open redware bowls with thinner walls are one of the common Huancaco Period vessel types in Virú Valley (cf. Strong and Evans 1952, p. 264, Fig. 40 - Vessel Shape 5; see discussion on pp. 266-267).

Guadalupito Bowl 2 (Fig. 225)

Number: 5 sherds, or ca. .3% of the Guadalupito assemblage.

General description: Globular bowl with a slightly constricted mouth, and interior beveled or rounded lip. Rim diameters are 12 cm, 22 cm, 35 cm, 40 cm, and 45 cm. Wall thickness below the rim ranges between 6 mm and 17 mm, with a mean of 9.5 mm.

Paste: Temper consists uniformly of medium sand in moderate quantities. Paste color is brick red.

Surface characteristics: Exterior and interior surfaces are

plain redware.

Distribution: This bowl type has a distribution limited to a few habitation sites in Pampa de los Incas area. Collection proveniences (with number of sherds in parentheses)/site numbers are:

Coll. 68(2)/GUAD-111; Coll. 69(2)/GUAD-112; Coll. 56(1)/GUAD-113.

Chronological assessment: Bowl 2 is confined to Guadalupito collections, but its limited distribution lessens its utility as a time marker.

Inter-regional comparisons: Large, thick-walled bowls are found in contemporaneous collections of the Huancaco Period Castillo Plain type of Virú Valley (cf. Strong and Evans 1952, p. 268, Fig. 41 - Vessel Shape 5; see also rim analysis on p. 269).

Guadalupito Jar 1 (Fig. 225)

Number: 35 sherds, or ca. 2.2% of the Guadalupito assemblage.

General description: Large globular jar with a constricted mouth, and either a direct or a slightly interior thickened rim (neckless olla). Rim diameters vary from 38-100 cm, with a mean of 49.7 cm and a standard deviation of 10.8 cm. Wall thickness below the rim ranges widely between 6 mm and 21 mm, with a mean of 15 mm and a standard deviation of 3.4 mm.

Paste: Approximately 40% of the sherds in the sample have temper consisting of medium grain sand in moderate quantities. The other 60% have medium or coarse sand in moderate-to-heavy quantities. Paste color is brick red.

Surface characteristics: One sherd has a white-painted design on the exterior below the rim. The remaining sherds are plain redware.

Distribution: This jar type has a wide, but scattered, distribution at habitation, habitation-cemetery, and cemetery sites throughout the area of Guadalupito occupation. Collection proveniences (with number of sherds in parentheses)/site numbers are:

Coll. 201(5)/GUAD-5; Coll. 261(1)/GUAD-22; Colls. 89/90(6)/ GUAD-97; Colls. 59/64(1)/GUAD-109; Coll. 68(1)/GUAD-111; Colls. 60(1), 63(3), 69(3), 70(2)/GUAD-112; Coll. 314(2)/GUAD-128; Coll. 297(3)/ GUAD-130; Coll. 294(4)/GUAD-132; Coll. 265(3)/GUAD-168.

Chronological assessment: Jar 1 is similar in form and paste to Early Tanguche Jar 1b (Fig. 236). Thus, although the general form is a good time marker for Guadalupito-Early Tanguche (with only a few sherds of this type noted in Late Tanguche collections), it does not appear to be useful in distinguishing collections of the two periods.

Inter-regional comparisons: From their excavated materials in contemporaneous Virú Valley sites, Strong and Evans (1952, p. 264, Fig. 40 - Vessel Shape 3) illustrate large constricted mouth vessels that are very similar in form and size to Guadalupito Jar 1, Early Tanguche Jar 1b, and Late Tanguche Jar 1.

443

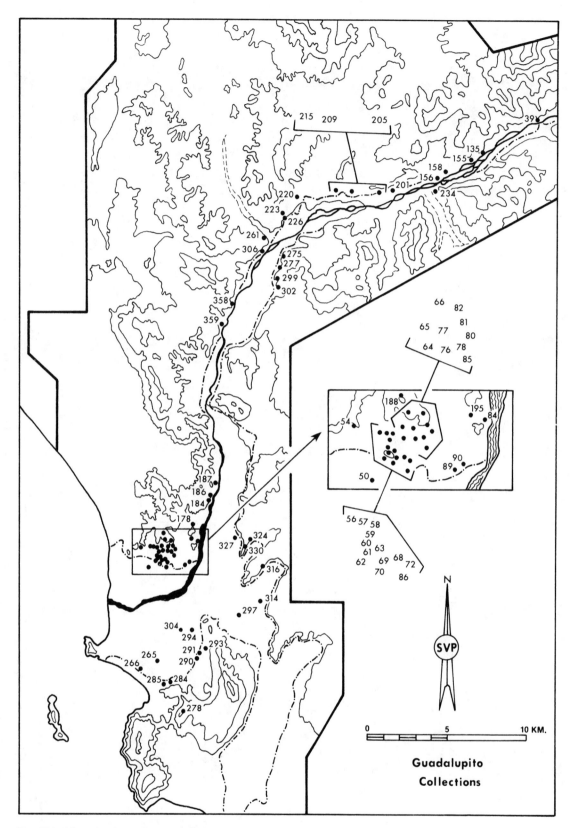

Fig. 224. Map showing collection proveniences of Guadalupito
Period (Huancaco/Late EIP).

444

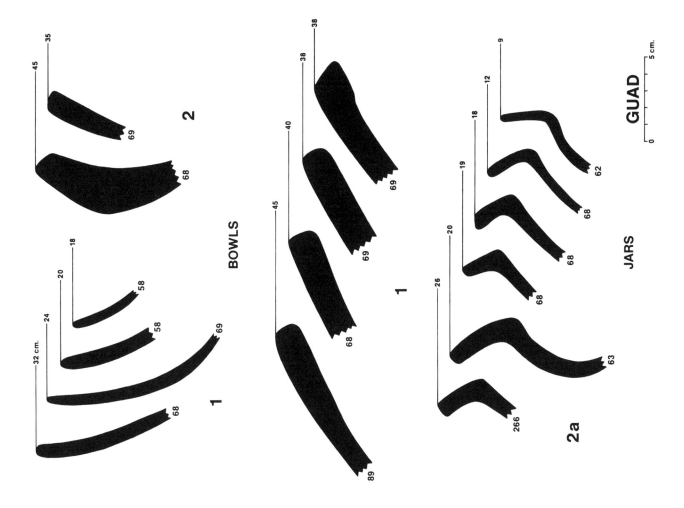

BOWLS

2

1

JARS

1

2a

GUAD

0 ___ 5 cm.

Fig. 225. Guadalupito Period ceramics: Bowls 1 and 2; Jars 1 and 2a.

Guadalupito Jar 2a (Fig. 225)

Number: 107 sherds, or ca. 6.8% of the Guadalupito assemblage.

General description: Globular jar with a short everted or flared rim. Lips are almost all either exterior or horizontal beveled. Rim diameters vary from 9-30 cm, with a mean of 19.2 cm and a standard deviation of 4.1 cm. Wall thickness below the rim ranges between 4 mm and 8 mm, with a mean of 6.2 mm.

Paste: Temper consists uniformly of medium sand in moderate quantities. Paste color is brick red.

Surface characteristics: Two of the sherds in the sample have exterior white-painted designs. The remaining sherds are plain redware. Approximately 20% of the sherds are fire blackened.

Distribution: This jar type is widely distributed at habitation, habitation-cemetery, and cemetery sites throughout the area of Guadalupito occupation. Collection proveniences (with number of sherds in parentheses)/site numbers are:

Coll. 201(3)/GUAD-5; Coll. 261(1)/GUAD-22; Coll. 178(1)/GUAD-83; Coll. 327(3)/GUAD-93; Coll. 195(3)/GUAD-95; Colls. 89/90(10)/GUAD-97; Coll. 65(2)/GUAD-108; Colls. 59/64(6)/GUAD-109; Colls. 68(7), 72(1)/GUAD-111; Colls. 60(2), 61(1), 62(2), 63(15), 69(14), 70(6)/GUAD-112; Coll. 57(1)/GUAD-113; Coll. 316(2)/GUAD-121; Coll. 297(7)/GUAD-130; Coll. 294(1)/GUAD-132; Coll. 291(1)/GUAD-162; Coll. 265(1)/GUAD-168; Coll. 266(6)/GUAD-169; Coll. 278(1)/GUAD-175.

Chronological assessment: Jar 2a bears a resemblance to Early Tanguche Jars 2a and 2b (Fig. 236), but in general can be distinguished on the basis of its squared or beveled lip (most of the Early Tanguche jars have rounded lips). This jar type is therefore a good Guadalupito diagnostic.

Inter-regional comparisons: From their excavations in Virú Valley sites, Strong and Evans (1952, p. 329, Fig. 70 - Vessel Shape 10) illustrate a vessel type with short flaring rim that is similar in overall form to Guadalupito Jar 2a.

Guadalupito Jar 2b (Fig. 226)

Number: 138 sherds, or ca. 8.7% of the Guadalupito assemblage.

General description: Globular jar with a tall flaring or everted rim. Rim diameters vary from 8-48 cm, with a mean of 15.2 cm and a standard deviation of 6.8 cm. Wall thickness below the rim ranges widely between 5 mm and 16 mm, with a mean of 8.8 mm and a standard deviation of 2.7 mm.

Paste: Temper consists of fine or medium sand, with approximately 90% of the sample having medium grain sand. Paste color is brick red.

Surface characteristics: Four of the sherds in the sample have exterior white slip, and five have exterior white-painted designs. The remaining 129 sherds are unpainted redware.

Distribution: This jar type is widely distributed at habitation, habitation-cemetery, and cemetery sites throughout the area of Guadalupito occupation. Collection proveniences (with number of sherds in parentheses)/site numbers are:

Coll. 135(1)/GUAD-2; Colls. 155/158(1)/GUAD-3; Coll. 201(2)/GUAD-5; Coll. 220(1)/GUAD-13; Coll. 223(1)/GUAD-16; Coll. 261(3)/GUAD-22; Coll. 277(1)/GUAD-31; Coll. 359(6)/GUAD-50; Coll. 178(7)/GUAD-83; Coll. 327(5)/GUAD-93; Coll. 188(1)/GUAD-94; Coll. 84(3)/GUAD-96; Colls. 89/90(2)/GUAD-97; Coll. 82(1)/GUAD-99; Coll. 66(1)/GUAD-100; Coll. 80(3)/GUAD-103; Colls. 76/78(14)/GUAD-104; Coll. 77(1)/GUAD-107; Colls. 59/64(8)/GUAD-109; Colls. 68(5), 72(10)/GUAD-111; Colls. 60(8), 61(3), 62(2), 63(8), 69(8)/GUAD-112; Colls. 56(2), 57(1), 58(13)/GUAD-113; Coll. 316(2)/GUAD-121; Coll. 297(12)/GUAD-130; Coll. 294(1)/GUAD-132; Coll. 266(1)/GUAD-169.

Chronological assessment: Jar 2b is generally similar in form and paste to Late Suchimancillo Jar 5e (Fig. 215), Early Tanguche Jar 2d (Fig. 236), and Early Tambo Real Redware Jar 4b (Fig. 271). The principal distinguishing characteristic of the Guadalupito jar is the presence of squared or beveled lips on a majority of the sherds. Most sherds of this general form in other periods have rounded lips. In addition, none of the jars of other periods has an exterior white slip or painted decoration.

Inter-regional comparisons: The white-slipped variant of Jar 2b appears to be similar in form and size to a number of Moche Phase III and IV vessels illustrated in Donnan and Mackey (1978; e.g., see pp. 95-96). The plain redware variant is quite similar to Huancaco Red and White, Vessel Shape 2, illustrated in Strong and Evans (1952, p. 328, Fig. 69).

Guadalupito Jar 3a (Fig. 226; Fig. 233, top - left)

Number: 75 sherds, or ca. 4.7% of the Guadalupito assemblage.

General description: Globular jar with a short vertical and incurving, or bulging, neck. Most lips are rounded, but interior beveled lips are also present in the sample. Rim diameters vary from 8-16 cm, with a mean of 11.9 cm and a standard deviation of 2.4 cm. Wall thickness below the rim ranges between 5 mm and 10 mm, with a mean of 6.8 mm and a standard deviation of 1 mm.

Paste: Temper consists uniformly of medium sand in moderate quantities. Paste color is brick red.

Surface characteristics: One sherd in the sample has exterior white slip. The remaining sherds are plain redware, with fire blackening observed on two sherds.

Distribution: This jar type is widely distributed at habitation, habitation-cemetery, and cemetery sites throughout the area of Guadalupito occupation. Collection proveniences (with number of sherds in parentheses)/site numbers are:

Coll. 39(4)/GUAD-1; Colls. 156(1), 155/158(1)/GUAD-3; Coll.

446

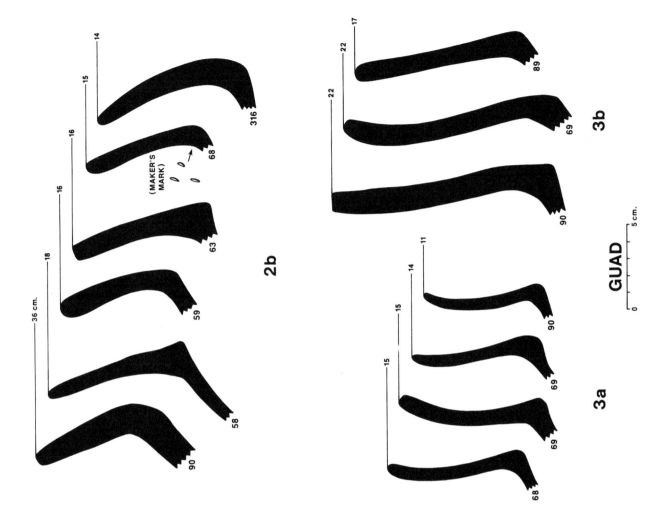

Fig. 226. Guadalupito Period ceramics: Jars 2b, 3a, and 3b.

447

220(1)/GUAD-13; Coll. 277(1)/GUAD-31; Coll. 299(1)/GUAD-33; Coll. 358(1)/GUAD-44; Coll. 178(4)/GUAD-83; Coll. 327(6)/GUAD-93; Coll. 195(2)/GUAD-95; Coll. 84(7)/GUAD-96; Colls. 89/90(2)/GUAD-97; Coll. 66(1)/GUAD-100; Coll. 80(1)/GUAD-103; Coll. 77(1)/GUAD-107; Coll. 65(2)/GUAD-108; Colls. 59/64(12)/GUAD-109; Colls. 68(2), 72(5)/GUAD-111; Colls. 60(1), 62(1), 63(1), 69(4)/GUAD-112; Coll. 58(1)/GUAD-113; Coll. 316(2)/GUAD-121; Coll. 294(9)/GUAD-132; Coll. 284(1)/GUAD-172.

Chronological assessment: This general jar type begins in Late Suchimancillo Period (see Jar 7, Fig. 216) and continues on through Guadalupito Period. The two jar forms are similar enough in form and paste that, beyond indicating a general Late Suchimancillo-Guadalupito time frame, they are of little value in specifying which of the two periods may be present in a collection. A few diagnostic Guadalupito features are present on some variants of Jar 3a, however. These include white slipping and rims with squared or beveled lips.

Inter-regional comparisons: From their excavations in Virú Valley, Strong and Evans (1952, p. 328, Fig. 69 - Period levels in Huancaco Vessel Shape 3; see also p. 342, Fig. 77) illustrate bulging neck jars that are very similar in form and size to Guadalupito Jars 3a and 3b.

Guadalupito Jar 3b (Fig. 226)

Number: 13 sherds, or ca. .8% of the Guadalupito assemblage.

General description: Globular jar with a tall vertical and incurving, or bulging, neck. Lips are either interior beveled or rounded. Rim diameters vary from 16-38 cm, with a mean of 21.3 cm and a standard deviation of 6.6 cm. Wall thickness below the rim ranges between 8 mm and 15 mm, with a mean of 10.2 mm.

Paste: Temper consists uniformly of medium sand in moderate quantities. Paste color is brick red.

Surface characteristics: Exterior and interior surfaces are plain redware.

Distribution: This jar type has a distribution limited to a few habitation, habitation-cemetery, and cemetery sites in the Pampa de los Incas area of the Lower Valley sector. Collection proveniences (with number of sherds in parentheses)/site numbers are:

Coll. 178(1)/GUAD-83; Coll. 195(1)/GUAD-95; Colls. 89/90(1)/GUAD-97; Colls. 76/78(1)/GUAD-104; Colls. 69(1), 70(1)/GUAD-112; Coll. 56(7)/GUAD-113.

Chronological assessment: Judging from the analysis of single-component collections, Jar 3b is a good diagnostic of Guadalupito Period.

Inter-regional comparisons: See Guadalupito Jar 3a.

Guadalupito: Flaring Bowls (Figs. 227, 228)

Number: 100 sherds, or ca. 6.3% of the Guadalupito assemblage.

Coll. 135(1)/GUAD-2; Colls. 155/158(1)/GUAD-3; Coll. 215(2)/GUAD-10; Coll. 220(2)/GUAD-13; Coll. 261(1)/GUAD-22; Coll. 306(1)/GUAD-25; Coll. 186(6)/GUAD-75; Coll. 178(4)/GUAD-83; Coll. 324(1)/GUAD-91; Coll. 327(1)/GUAD-93; Coll. 84(4)/GUAD-96; Colls. 89/90(5)/GUAD-97; Coll. 66(3)/GUAD-100; Coll. 80(2)/GUAD-103; Colls. 76/78(7)/GUAD-104; Coll. 77(1)/GUAD-107; Coll. 65(7)/GUAD-108; Colls. 59/64(25)/GUAD-109; Colls. 68(5), 72(1)/GUAD-111; Colls. 60(3), 61(3), 63(1), 69(4)/GUAD-112; Colls. 56(1), 58(1)/GUAD-113; Coll. 316(1)/GUAD-121; Coll. 294(2)/GUAD-132; Coll. 291(2)/GUAD-162; Coll. 285(1)/GUAD-170; Coll. 284(1)/GUAD-172.

Chronological assessment: This bowl type is, by definition, a good Guadalupito diagnostic, and is found almost entirely in single-component contexts.

Inter-regional comparisons: As is well known, flaring bowls are one of the most commonly found (and illustrated) types of Moche funerary ware (e.g., see Donnan 1976, p. 53, Fig. 32; Donnan and Mackey 1978:64 ff.; Strong and Evans 1952, Pl. 14; Proulx 1973, p. 245, Pl. 6).

General description: Large bowl with a flat or annular base, outslanted walls, and a broad flaring rim. Lips are usually exterior beveled, but a few rounded ones are also present in the sample. Rim diameters vary from 17-40 cm, with a mean of 27 cm and a standard deviation of 4.9 cm. Wall thickness below the rim ranges between 5 mm and 9 mm, with a mean of 6.4 mm.

Paste: Temper consists uniformly of fine sand in moderate quantities. Paste color is brick red.

Surface characteristics: The lip and interior below the rim are painted white, over which naturalistic figures--including marine animals, birds, and plants--are painted in red (Fig. 228). Surfaces elsewhere on these vessels are plain redware.

Distribution: This bowl type was found almost entirely in cemetery sites distributed throughout the area of Guadalupito occupation. Collection proveniences (with number of sherds in parentheses)/site numbers are:

Guadalupito: White-on-Red, Red-on-White (Figs. 227-231, 233-234)

Number: 378 White-on-Red sherds and 88 Red-on-White sherds, or ca. 23.9% and 5.6% of the Guadalupito assemblage, respectively.

General description: The White-on-Red and Red-on-White painted ware categories together comprise most of the decorated ceramics of the Guadalupito collections. White-on-Red usually consists of white-painted designs placed directly on the redware surface of vessels of various forms (e.g., Fig. 229 e, f, i; Fig. 230 a, b, d, f, j; Fig. 231 f, j, k; Fig. 233, top - right). Occasionally, however, as shown in Fig. 229 h, white-painted decoration is placed over a red slip. Red-on-White, the second of the two categories, always consists of red-painted designs placed over a white- or cream-slipped vessel (e.g., Fig. 228 a-h; Fig. 229 a-d; Fig. 234).

Paste: Temper consists of fine or medium sand in moderate

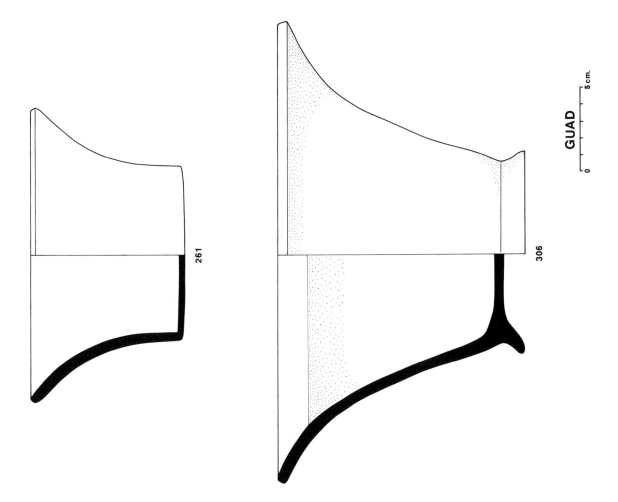

GUAD

0 |___ 5 cm.

261

306

Fig. 227. Guadalupito Period ceramics: flaring bowls.

449

450

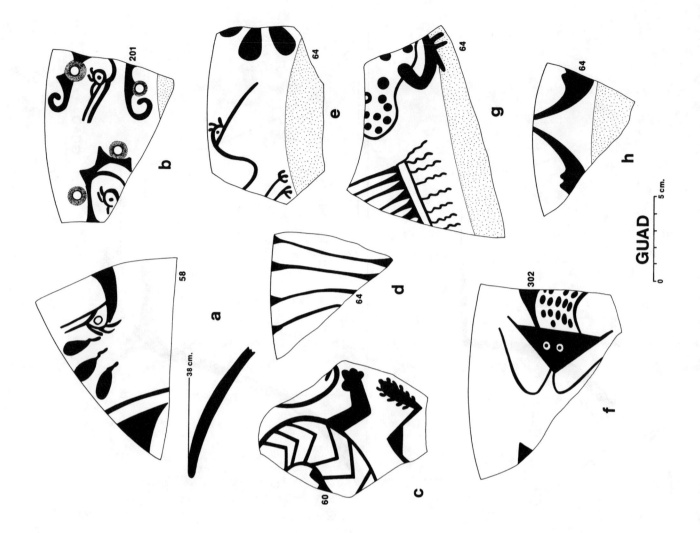

Fig. 228. Guadalupito Period ceramics: sherds from Red-on-White flaring bowls.

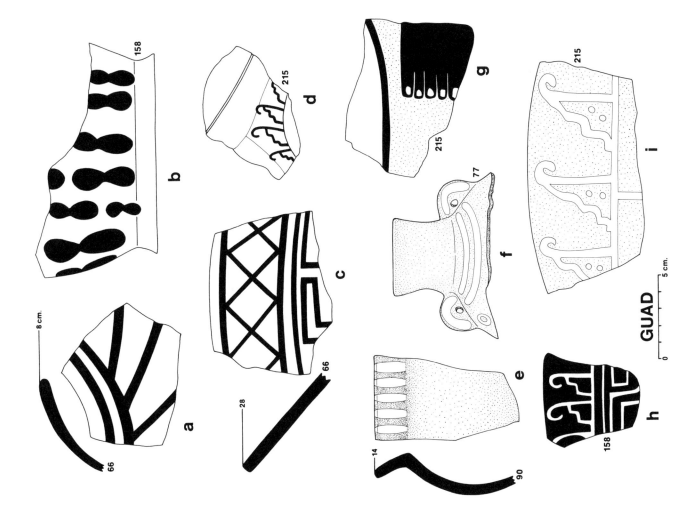

GUAD

0 ___ 5 cm.

Fig. 229. Guadalupito Period ceramics: miscellaneous decorated sherds.

451

quantities. Paste color is a uniformly well-fired brick red.

Surface characteristics: Many, if not all, of the vessels in these two painted ware categories appear to have been made in molds. The clay was placed in the molds while still quite wet, as reflected on the interiors of the vessels where the sharp, roughened peaks from finger marks show clearly on many sherds. Indeed, this feature of the vessel interior is a very distinctive diagnostic of Guadalupito Period sherds, irrespective of the form and decoration characterizing a vessel.

Distribution: White-on-Red and Red-on-White sherds were found at habitation, habitation-cemetery, and cemetery sites throughout the area of Guadalupito occupation. Separate collection proveniences (with number of sherds in parentheses)/site numbers are:

White-on-Red proveniences: Coll. 39(1)/GUAD-1; Coll. 135(4)/GUAD-2; Colls. 155/158(50)/GUAD-3; Coll. 234(46)/GUAD-4; Coll. 201(20)/GUAD-5; Coll. 205(7)/GUAD-7; Coll. 209(4)/GUAD-9; Coll. 215(3)/GUAD-10; Coll. 220(2)/GUAD-13; Coll. 223(1)/GUAD-16; Coll. 306(4)/GUAD-25; Coll. 277(2)/GUAD-31; Coll. 186(6)/GUAD-75; Coll. 327(1)/GUAD-93; Coll. 195(14)/GUAD-95; Coll. 84(20)/GUAD-96; Colls. 89/90(9)/GUAD-97; Coll. 66(1)/GUAD-100; Coll. 80(8)/GUAD-103; Colls. 76/78(12)/GUAD-104; Coll. 81(4)/GUAD-105; Coll. 65(2)/GUAD-108; Colls. 59/64(69)/GUAD-109; Coll. 85(4)/GUAD-110; Coll. 68(7)/GUAD-111; Colls. 60(11), 61(16), 63(1), 69(6), 70(3)/GUAD-112; Coll. 57(2)/GUAD-113; Coll. 54(4)/GUAD-115; Coll. 297(6)/GUAD-130; Coll. 304(7)/GUAD-131; Coll. 294(5)/GUAD-132; Coll. 290(6)/GUAD-164; Coll. 284(4)/GUAD-172.

Red-on-White proveniences: Colls. 155/158(5)/GUAD-3; Coll. 201(2)/GUAD-5; Coll. 215(2)/GUAD-10; Coll. 184(1)/GUAD-76; Coll. 178(1)/GUAD-83; Coll. 324(1)/GUAD-91; Coll. 84(1)/GUAD-96; Colls. 89/90(2)/GUAD-97; Coll. 82(4)/GUAD-99; Coll. 66(4)/GUAD-100; Coll. 80(2)/GUAD-103; Coll. 65(9)/GUAD-108; Colls. 59/64(30)/GUAD-109; Colls. 68(8), 72(1)/GUAD-111; Colls. 60(6)/GUAD-112; Coll. 56(3), 57(1)/GUAD-113; Coll. 63(1), 69(1), 69(1)/GUAD-112; Colls. 56(3), 57(1)/GUAD-113; Coll. 265(1)/GUAD-168; Coll. 284(2)/GUAD-172.

Inter-regional comparisons: For a discussion of the Huancaco Red and White style in Virú Valley, see Strong and Evans (1952:326-335).

Guadalupito: Effigy Figures (Figs. 230, 231, 232)

Guadalupito is the second period, following Late Suchimancillo, in the Lower Santa sequence in which substantial numbers of human and animal effigy figures are found widely distributed throughout the area of occupation. The total number of effigy figures, including depictions of both humans and animals, is 81 (67 human and 14 animal effigies), or ca. 5.1% of the Guadalupito assemblage. Although the number of effigies is thus roughly the same as in Late Suchimancillo, the percentage of figures in the total assemblage is double that of the preceding period.

Human effigies: Six principal types of representations of human figures are present in the collections. These include (1) effigy neck vessels (Fig. 230 a, b); (2) effigies on the body of a vessel (Fig. 230 c, d, e; Fig. 231 b, c); (3) figurines (Fig. 230 g, h); (4) effigies of

warriors or figures with possible instruments of war (Fig. 231 e; Fig. 232); (5) death's head effigies (Fig. 230 i, j, and possibly f); and (6) effigies of an anthropomorphic human figure with double canine teeth, most probably representing the Moche fanged god, Ai Apaec (Fig. 231 j, k, and possibly f). All of these figures are redware.

As the illustrations show, human figures in the period of Moche occupation are very realistically, or naturalistically, portrayed (e.g., Fig. 230 a, c, d, e). Indeed, no two representations of humans were found that are exactly alike, and it is possible that many effigy figures were intended to depict specific individuals. Nevertheless, several common decorative elements characterize most of the male figures. For example, some sort of headgear was found to be present on most effigy fragments where the upper part of the head was still intact (e.g., Fig. 230 a, b, d, e). This headgear is almost always painted white or a cream color. Another nearly universal feature is the presence of almond-shaped eyes on the effigy figures (e.g., Fig. 230 a, d, e, h). White or cream-colored paint was usually applied to represent the white of the eyes, with an almond-shaped interior section left unpainted to represent the pupil. The exterior of each eye is represented by a raised, or filleted, line which completely encloses it. This line was probably formed as part of the molding process.

The best example in the Guadalupito assemblage of a warrior effigy vessel is that shown in Fig. 232. A warrior in battle dress--including briefs, shield and club, and helmet topped by an inverted tumi knife--forms the central figure on each side of the vessel. Club-and-shield motifs emanate from the front and back of one of the warriors, while what appear to be feathers and a series of feline (or, snake) heads surround the front, back, and head of the other warrior. It should be noted that the collection from the site where this vessel was found is a single-component one containing good Guadalupito diagnostics, although the feline heads are quite similar to those found on some Early Tanguche Period effigy jars (e.g., see Fig. 249). Other possible representations of warriors include examples of arm-and-club motifs, as well as a few of hands holding tumi knives (e.g., Fig. 231 e).

Representations of the fanged god, or Ai Apaec as he was later called by the Chimú (cf. Benson 1972:28-34), were found in fragmentary form in several cemetery sites scattered throughout the area of Guadalupito occupation. In general, all aspects of the face are the same as on the human effigies discussed above--with the notable exception of the pronounced double canines protruding from the mouth (Fig. 231 j, k). However, it is of interest to note that, in addition to having teeth guaranteed to inspire awe in most observers, the depiction of Ai Apaec shown in Fig. 231 j also displays a rather sinister set of eyes. It is tempting to speculate that one of the ways used to inspire awe and respect for the Moche state--in addition to the threat or use of military force--was through the fostering of a state-wide religious focus on this fearsome-looking deity. Whatever the case, this is the only period in the Lower Santa sequence when features such as animal canines are shown on human effigy figures, and the effigies produced in other periods are mild by comparison.

Since in his guise as a god of agriculture Ai Apaec is often shown in association with maize, it is possible that the effigy fragment illustrated in Fig. 231 f depicts this aspect of the deity. Although maize effigies are used as ornaments on vessels of some later periods

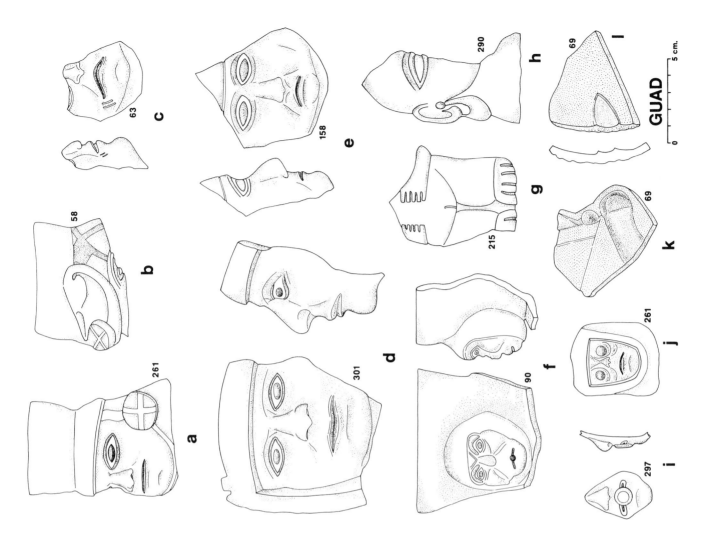

Fig. 230. Guadalupito Period ceramics: human effigy neck jars (a–f, i, j), figurines (g–h), and molds (k–l).

453

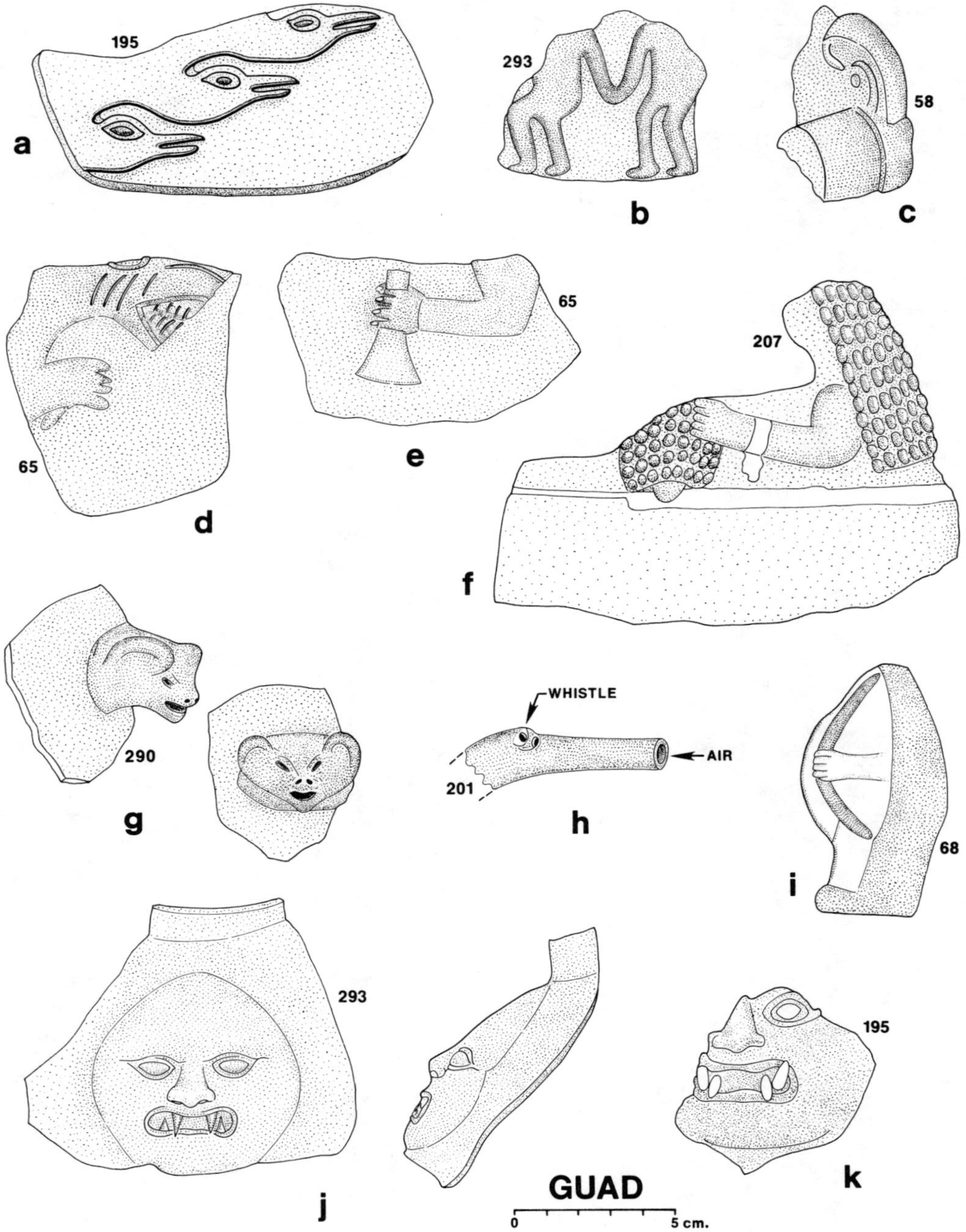

Fig. 231. Guadalupito Period ceramics: miscellaneous sherds.

454

GUAD

5 cm.

0

330

Fig. 232. Guadalupito Period ceramics: side and end views of a Moche style jar depicting warriors.

455

(e.g., see Fig. 277)--much in the same way as animal figures are placed on Late Suchimancillo jars--Late Tambo Real is the only other period in the sequence when humans are shown in direct association with maize. Interestingly, both Guadalupito and Late Tambo Real are periods when the Lower Santa region probably was a province of multivalley states that are presumed to have been centered in the Moche Valley.

Animal effigies: Representations of animals in the Guadalupito ceramic assemblage are of two principal types, including (1) red-painted figures on the interior of the rim of flaring bowls (e.g., Fig. 228 a-c, e-g); and (2) moldmade and modeled effigy figures that decorate the body or neck of pottery vessels (e.g., Fig. 231 a, d, g). The most common red-painted scenes are depictions of shore birds such as the pelican and ibis (e.g., compare Fig. 228 b and e to Lámina 2, o and n, in Ravines 1978:43). These birds are usually shown in association with the totora reeds that commonly grow in the marshy areas adjacent to the beach. Other painted figures include a manta ray (compare Fig. 228 f to Lámina 9 j in Ravines 1978:55), and what appears to be a lizard shown next to a columnar cactus plant (Fig. 228 c). Among the animals depicted in molded or modeled form are seagulls (Fig. 231 a; see Ravines 1978, p. 43, Lámina 2 l), a feline (Fig. 231 d), and what appears to be a bat (Fig. 231 g).

Effigy distributions: Human and animal effigy figures have a generally wide distribution at habitation, habitation-cemetery, and cemetery sites throughout the area of Guadalupito occupation. Separate collection proveniences (with numbers of sherds in parentheses)/site numbers are:

Human effigy proveniences: Coll. 39(1)/GUAD-1; Colls. 155/158(4)/GUAD-3; Coll. 234(1)7/GUAD-4; Coll. 215(1)/GUAD-10; Coll. 261(3)/GUAD-22; Coll. 277(2)/GUAD-31; Coll. 299(1)/GUAD-33; Coll. 358(1)/GUAD-44; Coll. 186(1)/GUAD-75; Coll. 178(1)/GUAD-83; Coll. 330(1)/GUAD-92; Coll. 195(2)/GUAD-95; Colls. 89/90(1)/GUAD-97; Coll. 66(1)/GUAD-100; Colls. 76/78(2)/GUAD-104; Coll. 65(3)/GUAD-108; Colls. 59/64(1)/GUAD-109; Coll. 68(2)/GUAD-111; Colls. 60(2), 61(17), 63(4), 69(2), 72(2)/GUAD-112; Colls. 57(1), 58(2)/GUAD-113; Coll. 54(1)/GUAD-115; Coll. 316(1)/GUAD-121; Coll. 297(1)/GUAD-130; Coll. 293(4)/GUAD-161; Coll. 290(1)/GUAD-164.

Animal effigy proveniences: Coll. 234(2)/GUAD-4; Coll. 201(1)/GUAD-5; Coll. 306(1)/GUAD-25; Coll. 302(1)/GUAD-38; Coll. 178(1)/GUAD-83; Coll. 195(2)/GUAD-95; Coll. 65(1)/GUAD-108; Colls. 59/64(1)/GUAD-109; Colls. 61(1), 63(1)/GUAD-111; Coll. 58(1)/GUAD-113; Coll. 290(1)/GUAD-164.

Guadalupito: Miscellaneous Artifacts (Fig. 230 k, l; Fig. 231 h, i; Fig. 233, bottom; Fig. 234)

Among the miscellaneous artifacts found in Guadalupito contexts, and illustrated here, are the following (listed in order of appearance in the drawings): (1) fragments of redware molds (Fig. 230 k, l; Note: the two molds for producing human eyes and ears are among 16 mold fragments--including molds for making vessel spouts and necks, and human effigies--found at SVP-GUAD-112, the major habitation site associated with the probable regional center of SVP-GUAD-111 at Pampa de los Incas; the fact that these are the only molds found associated with Guadalupito sites in the survey region has interesting implications for the nature of craft production during the period of Moche occupation); (2) a fragment of a redware whistle (Fig. 231 h); (3) part of a white-painted hollow redware figurine showing a person holding what appears to be a throwing stick (Fig. 231 i); (4) an intact redware "dipper" (Fig. 233, bottom; see also Fig. 234, top - right; Note: these artifacts are also sometimes called "poppers," and the names imply that their function was either for dipping liquids or popping corn; they are primarily diagnostic of Guadalupito Period, but also are found in Late Suchimancillo contexts); (5) a unique, exterior incised redware bowl (Fig. 234, top - left); and (6) a number of diagnostics of Moche Phases III and IV, as well as V (Fig. 234, center and bottom; Note: it should be mentioned that such phase diagnostics were found primarily in cemeteries, and thus it was not possible to attempt to ascertain the occupational phases represented at habitation sites of the period; the spout fragment decorated with a club-and-shield motif is one the very few Moche Phase V diagnostics found in the survey region; all other Phase V diagnostics, some of which are illustrated here--see Fig. 247, top row; Fig. 251 a-h, k, l; and Fig. 253 d, g--were found in clear Early Tanguche contexts).

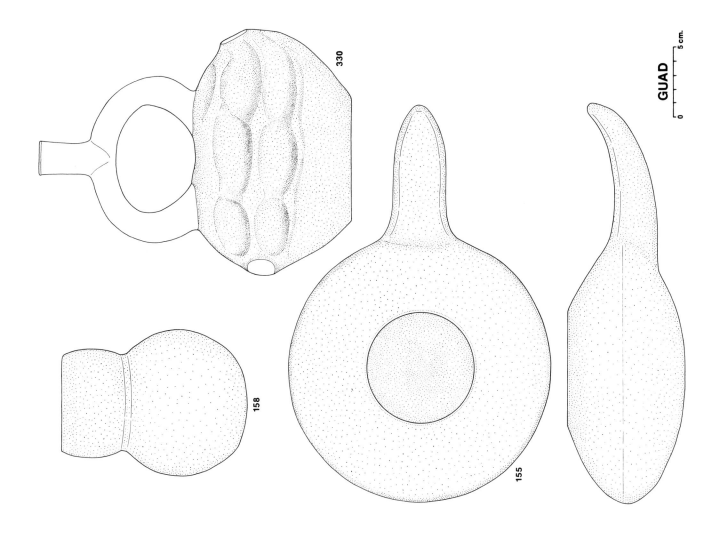

330

158

155

GUAD

0 5 cm.

Fig. 233. Guadalupito Period ceramics: miscellaneous whole vessels.

457

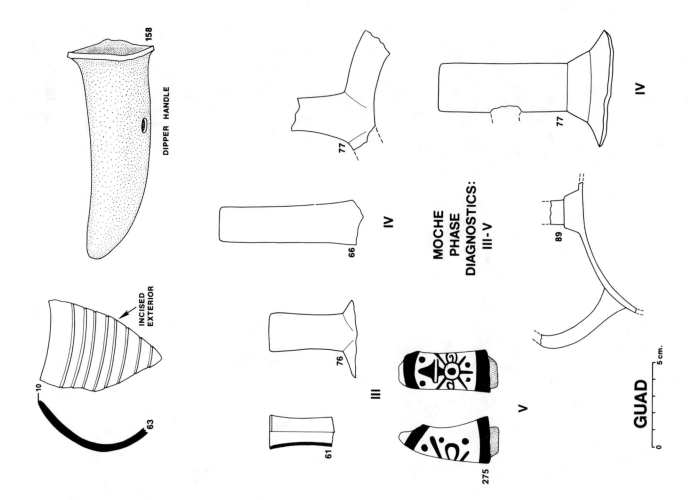

DIPPER HANDLE

INCISED EXTERIOR

MOCHE
PHASE
DIAGNOSTICS:
III–V

GUAD

Fig. 234. Guadalupito Period ceramics: miscellaneous sherds, and diagnostics of Moche Phases III–V.

458

Early Tanguche Bowl 1 (Fig. 236)

Number: 70 sherds, or ca. 3.1% of the Early Tanguche assemblage.

General description: Open bowl with straight or slightly incurving, outslanted walls. Rim diameters vary from 14-19 cm, with a mean of 16.8 cm and a standard deviation of 1.6 cm. Wall thickness below the rim ranges between 6 mm and 8 mm, with a mean of 7 mm.

Paste: Temper consists of fine or medium sand, with approximately 75% of the sherds in the sample having medium grain sand. The quantity of temper in all sherds is moderate. Paste color is red.

Surface characteristics: Interior and exterior surfaces are plain redware.

Distribution: This bowl type has a wide distribution in habitation, habitation-cemetery, and cemetery sites throughout the area of Early Tanguche occupation. Collection proveniences (with number of sherds in parentheses)/site numbers are:

Coll. 104(1)/ETAN-4; Coll. 44(1)/ETAN-10; Coll. 173(2)/ETAN-20; Coll. 190(1)/ETAN-22; Colls. 230(2), 231(14)/ETAN-33; Coll. 237(1)/ETAN-36; Coll. 241(1)/ETAN-42; Coll. 246(6)/ETAN-56; Coll. 229(2)/ETAN-77; Coll. 259(1)/ETAN-79; Coll. 305(3)/ETAN-84; Coll. 350(1)/ETAN-147; Coll. 179(4)/ETAN-166; Coll. 78(2)/ETAN-173; Coll. 86(5)/ETAN-178; Colls. 71(2), 88(3)/ETAN-180; Coll. 46(3)/ETAN-184; Coll. 49(7)/ETAN-185; Coll. 317(1)/ETAN-188; Coll. 314(1)/ETAN-190; Coll. 295(1)/ETAN-192; Coll. 294(1)/ETAN-193; Coll. 270(4)/ETAN-199.

Chronological assessment: The variant of Bowl 1 with incurved walls is similar in form and paste to Early Suchimancillo Bowl 2a (Fig. 202) and Late Suchimancillo Bowl 1 (Fig. 211). The variant with straight walls is similar in form and paste to Late Tanguche Bowl 1 (Fig. 258) and Late Tambo Real Redware Bowl 2 (Fig. 279). Thus, taken by itself, this bowl type does not appear to be a good time marker for Early Tanguche.

Inter-regional comparisons: From his excavations in Tomaval levels of Virú Valley sites, Collier (1955, p. 187, Fig. 63 A) illustrates bowls that are very similar in form and size to Early Tanguche Bowl 1, as well as to Late Tanguche Bowl 1.

Early Tanguche Bowl 2 (Fig. 236)

Number: 19 sherds, or ca. .85% of the Early Tanguche assemblage.

General description: Open bowl with straight, slightly outslanted or vertical incurving walls. Rim diameters vary from 16-21 cm, with a mean of 18.5 cm and a standard deviation of 1.3 cm. Wall thickness below the rim ranges widely between 5 mm and 11 mm, with a mean of 7.7 mm.

Paste: Temper consists of fine or medium sand, with approximately 70% of the sherds having medium grain sand. The quantity of temper in all sherds is moderate. Paste color is red.

Surface characteristics: Interior and exterior surfaces are plain redware.

Distribution: This bowl type has a limited distribution in habitation and habitation-cemetery sites throughout the area of Early Tanguche occupation. However, it is primarily characteristic of sites in the Lower Valley sector. Collection proveniences (with number of sherds in parentheses)/site numbers are:

Coll. 105(1)/ETAN-4; Coll. 94(1)/ETAN-6; Coll. 305(1)/ETAN-84; Coll. 187(1)/ETAN-159; Coll. 79(2)/ETAN-173; Coll. 91(3)/ETAN-176; Coll. 87(1)/ETAN-179; Coll. 88(1)/ETAN-180; Coll. 46(7)/ETAN-184; Coll. 264(1)/ETAN-194.

Chronological assessment: The incurved variant of Bowl 2 is similar in form and paste to the undecorated variant of Guadalupito Bowl 1 (Fig. 225). Although the straight-walled variant of Bowl 2 appears to be a good diagnostic of Early Tanguche, the limited overall distribution of this type lessens its utility as a good time marker.

Inter-regional comparisons: Although bowls of this form are not reported in the literature on Middle Horizon Period in adjacent valleys, the thinner walls and redware paste suggest a general relationship to the Castillo Plain type of the Virú Valley (cf. Collier 1955:186-189).

Early Tanguche Jar 1a (Fig. 236)

Number: 16 sherds, or ca. .7% of the Early Tanguche assemblage.

General description: Large ovoid jar with a constricted mouth and direct or interior thickened rim. Lips on jars of the latter type are interior beveled, often with a distinctive shallow groove running around them. Rim diameters vary from 26-60 cm, with a mean of 40.8 cm and a standard deviation of 10.7 cm. Wall thickness below the rim ranges widely between 7 mm and 15 mm, with about 50% of the sherds at the upper end of the range and 50% at the lower end.

Paste: Temper consists uniformly of medium sand in moderate quantities. Paste color is red, with gray cores noted on six sherds.

Surface characteristics: Exterior and interior surfaces are plain redware.

Distribution: This jar type has a distribution limited primarily to a few habitation and habitation-cemetery sites in the Upper Valley sector. Collection proveniences (with number of sherds in parentheses)/site numbers are:

Coll. 44(4)/ETAN-10; Coll. 189(7)/ETAN-22; Coll. 193(1)/ETAN-25; Colls. 230(1), 231(2)/ETAN-33; Coll. 317(1)/ETAN-188.

Chronological assessment: Judging from the analysis of single-component collections, Jar 1a is a good diagnostic of Early Tanguche Period. However, its limited distribution lessens its utility as a time marker.

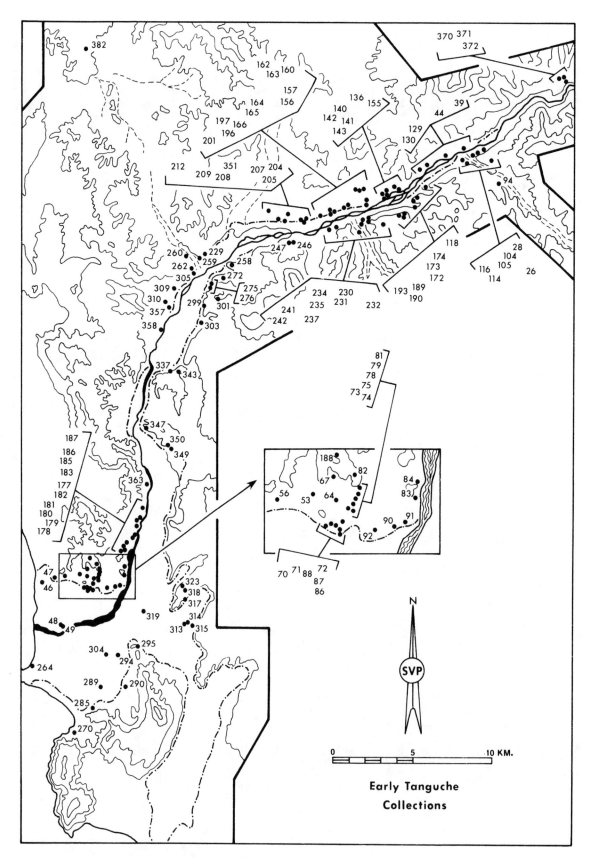

Fig. 235. Map showing collection proveniences of Early Tanguche
Period (Tomaval/Early Middle Horizon).

460

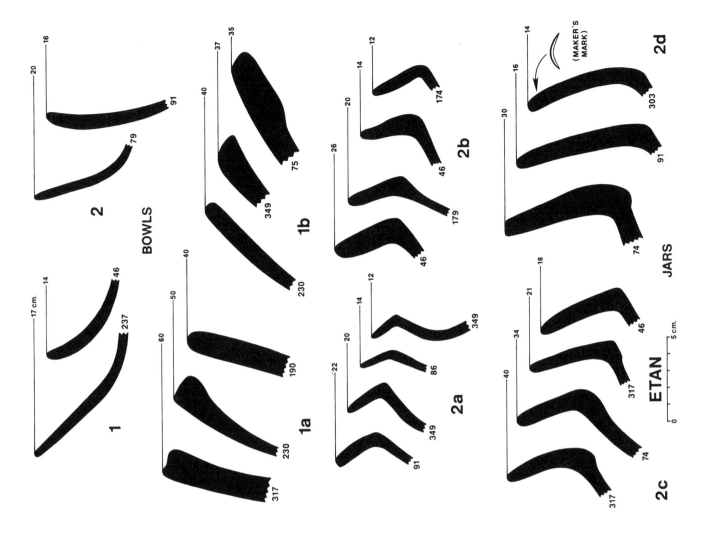

BOWLS

1

2

1a

1b

2a

2b

2c

2d

ETAN

JARS

(MAKER'S MARK)

Fig. 236. Early Tanguche Period ceramics: Bowls 1 and 2; Jars 1a, 1b, 2a, 2b, 2c, and 2d.

461

Inter-regional comparisons: From his excavations in Tomaval levels of Virú Valley sites, Collier (1955, p. 187, Fig. 63 D) illustrates Castillo Plain jars that are quite similar in form, size, and paste to Early Tanguche Jar 1a.

Early Tanguche Jar 1b (Fig. 236)

Number: 32 sherds, or ca. 1.4% of the Early Tanguche assemblage.

General description: Large globular jar with a constricted mouth and direct or interior thickened rim. Lips on jars of the latter type are interior beveled, often with a rounded exterior and a sharp interior edge. Rim diameters vary from 16-120 cm, with a mean of 52.7 cm and a standard deviation of 22.6 cm. Wall thickness below the rim ranges widely between 5 mm and 45 mm, with a mean of 19 mm and a standard deviation of 8.8 mm.

Paste: Temper consists of medium or coarse sand, with some 75% of the sherds having coarse sand temper. The quantity of temper in all sherds is moderate. Paste color is red.

Surface characteristics: Exterior and interior surfaces are plain redware.

Distribution: This jar type is widely distributed in habitation, habitation-cemetery, and cemetery sites throughout the main area of Early Tanguche occupation. Collection proveniences (with number of sherds in parentheses)/site numbers are:

Colls. 104(3), 105(3)/ETAN-4; Coll. 44(1)/ETAN-10; Coll. 172(1)/ ETAN-21; Coll. 157(1)/ETAN-26; Coll. 165(1)/ETAN-32; Colls. 230(1), 231(1)/ETAN-33; Coll. 246(4)/ETAN-56; Coll. 305(1)/ETAN-84; Coll. 309(3)/ETAN-93; Coll. 349(1)/ETAN-147; Coll. 81(1)/ETAN-172; Coll. 75(1)/ ETAN-174; Coll. 86(1)/ETAN-178; Coll. 87(2)/ETAN-179; Coll. 88(2)/ ETAN-180; Coll. 49(1)/ETAN-185; Coll. 314(2)/ETAN-190; Coll. 315(1)/ ETAN-191.

Chronological assessment: Jar 1b is very similar in form and paste to Guadalupito Jar 1 (Fig. 225) and Late Tanguche Jar 1 (Fig. 258). Since it is a very minor type in Late Tanguche Period, it appears to be a good general time marker for the Guadalupito-Early Tanguche time period.

Inter-regional comparisons: See discussion under Guadalupito Jar 1.

Early Tanguche Jar 2a (Fig. 236)

Number: 159 sherds, or ca. 7% of the Early Tanguche assemblage.

General description: Globular jar with a low neck and narrow, everted or flared rim. Most lips are rounded, although a few exterior beveled lips are also present in the sample. Rim diameters vary from 5-22 cm, with a mean of 12.8 cm and a standard deviation of 3.1 cm. Wall thickness below the rim ranges between 4 mm and 7 mm, with a mean of 5.2 mm.

Paste: Temper consists of fine or medium sand, with 80% of the sherds having medium grain sand. The quantity of temper in all sherds is moderate. Paste color is red, with gray cores noted on 10% of the sherds in the sample.

Surface characteristics: The exterior surface on the shoulder of the vessel is decorated with pressmolded zoned and stippled designs on 20% of the sherds in the sample (for examples of this decoration on whole vessels retrieved from the surface of looted cemeteries, see Figs. 238, 239, 240). A smaller percentage of sherds (ca. 8%) have notched vertical handles similar to those illustrated in Fig. 240 a, c, and d. Fire blackening was noted on only one sherd, but since the sample consists primarily of smaller rim fragments and fire blackening on whole vessels usually is confined to the bottom half of the body, it seems likely that most sherds are from vessels with a utilitarian function.

Distribution: This jar type is found widely distributed in habitation, habitation-cemetery, and cemetery sites throughout the area of Early Tanguche occupation. Collection proveniences (with number of sherds in parentheses)/site numbers are:

Coll. 372(15)/ETAN-1; Coll. 371(16)/ETAN-2; Coll. 370(7)/ETAN-3; Colls. 104(5), 105(3)/ETAN-4; Coll. 114(1)/ETAN-7; Coll. 44(10)/ETAN-10; Colls. 136/155(2)/ETAN-14; Colls. 157(10)/ETAN-26; Colls. 173(1), 174(2)/ETAN-20; Coll. 172(1)/ ETAN-21; Coll. 230(4), 231(4)/ETAN-33; Coll. 242(4)/ETAN-44; Coll. 235(4)/ETAN-34; Coll. 209(1)/ETAN-39; Coll. 272(9)/ETAN-85; Coll. 303(5)/ 204(1)/ETAN-47; Colls. 349(2), 350(3)/ETAN-147; Coll. 363(1)/ETAN-155; Coll. ETAN-102; 185(1)/ETAN-161; Coll. 183(1)/ETAN-162; Coll. 179(2)/ETAN-166; Coll. 178(3)/ETAN-167; Coll. 188(1)/ETAN-168; Colls. 78(1), 79(2)/ETAN-173; Coll. 73(1)/ETAN-175; Coll. 91(2)/ETAN-176; Coll. 86(1)/ETAN-178; Coll. 71(6)/ETAN-180; Colls. 72(11), 88(1)/ETAN-180; Coll. 47(1)/ETAN-183; Colls. 48(1), 49(4)/ETAN-185; Coll. 319(5)/ETAN-189; Coll. 294(1)/ ETAN-193.

Chronological assessment: Early Tanguche Jar 2a is similar in form and paste to some variants of Guadalupito Jar 2a (Fig. 225), but can be distinguished on the basis of its rounded lips (in contrast to the exterior beveled lips of the Guadalupito vessel), as well as by the presence of notched vertical handles and exterior pressmolded decoration. Jar 2a is also similar in form to Late Tambo Real Redware Jar 1, but can be distinguished from the later jar by its consistently lower neck.

Inter-regional comparisons: From his excavated Castillo Plain material in Virú Valley sites, Collier (1955, p. 187, Fig. 63 G) illustrates rim profiles from vessels that are similar in form, size, and paste to Early Tanguche Jars 2a and 2b.

Early Tanguche Jar 2b (Fig. 236)

Number: 77 sherds, or ca. 3.4% of the Early Tanguche assemblage.

General description: Globular jar with a neck of low-to-medium height and narrow flared rim. Rim diameters vary from 10-40 cm, with a mean of 16.3 cm and a standard deviation of 8.5 cm. Wall thickness below the rim ranges between 5 mm and 9 mm--with most sherds in the sample at the lower end of the range, between 5 mm and 7 mm.

Paste: Temper consists uniformly of medium sand in moderate quantities. Paste color is red, with gray cores noted on 15% of the sherds in the sample.

Surface characteristics: The exterior surface on the shoulder of the vessel is decorated with pressmolded zoned and stippled designs on some 20% of the sherds in the sample (for examples of such designs, see Figs. 238, 239, and 240). Exterior and interior surfaces on the remaining 80% of the sherds are plain redware.

Distribution: This jar type has a wide distribution in habitation, habitation-cemetery, and cemetery sites throughout the main area of Early Tanguche occupation. Collection proveniences (with number of sherds in parentheses)/site numbers are:

Coll. 44(2)/ETAN-10; Coll. 189(2)/ETAN-22; Coll. 157(6)/ETAN-26; Coll. 231(2)/ETAN-33; Colls. 166/197(1)/ETAN-39; Coll. 241(1)/ETAN-42; Coll. 242(10)/ETAN-44; Coll. 204(3)/ETAN-47; Coll. 246(9)/ETAN-56; Coll. 305(3)/ETAN-84; Coll. 179(1)/ETAN-166; Colls. 78(4), 79(3)/ETAN-173; Coll. 73(3)/ETAN-175; Coll. 86(2)/ETAN-184; Coll. 49(5)/ETAN-185; Coll. 317(1)/ETAN-188; Coll. 264(2)/ETAN-194.

Chronological assessment: Early Tanguche Jar 2b is similar in form and paste to some variants of Guadalupito Jar 2a (Fig. 225), but can be distinguished on the basis of its rounded lips (in contrast to the exterior beveled lips of the Guadalupito jar), as well as by the presence of exterior pressmolded decoration.

Inter-regional comparisons: See Early Tanguche Jar 2a.

Early Tanguche Jar 2c (Fig. 236)

Number: 54 sherds, or ca. 2.3% of the Early Tanguche assemblage.

General description: Globular jar with a neck of medium height and broad, everted or flared rim. Lips are rounded. Rim diameters vary from 11-40 cm, with a mean of 19.6 cm and a standard deviation of 9 cm. Wall thickness below the rim ranges widely between 5 mm and 10 mm, with a mean of 7.2 mm.

Paste: Temper consists uniformly of medium sand in moderate quantities. Paste color is red, with gray cores noted on approximately 10% of the sherds.

Surface characteristics: Exterior and interior surfaces are plain redware. Fire blackening was noted on about 10% of the sherds in the sample.

Distribution: This jar type has a wide distribution in habitation, habitation-cemetery, and cemetery sites throughout the main area of Early Tanguche occupation. Collection proveniences (with number of sherds in parentheses)/site numbers are:

Coll. 105(2)/ETAN-4; Coll. 130(1)/ETAN-12; Colls. 155/136(1)/

ETAN-14; Coll. 172(2)/ETAN-21; Coll. 189(2)/ETAN-22; Coll. 156(1)/ ETAN-26; Coll. 230(3)/ETAN-33; Coll. 246(2)/ETAN-56; Coll. 305(4)/ ETAN-84; Coll. 177(1)/ETAN-163; Colls. 78(12), 79(3)/ETAN-173; Coll. 75(3)/ETAN-174; Coll. 74(2)/ETAN-175; Coll. 56(2)/ETAN-181; Coll. 47(3)/ ETAN-183; Coll. 46(3)/ETAN-184; Coll. 317(2)/ETAN-188; Colls 313(1), 314(2)/ETAN-190.

Chronological assessment: Early Tanguche Jar 2c is similar in form and paste to Early Suchimancillo Jar 6 (Fig. 205), but can be distinguished on the basis of its consistent lack of an interior corner point at the juncture of the neck and the body.

Inter-regional comparisons: From his excavated Castillo Plain material in Virú Valley, Collier (1955, p. 18, Fig. 63 F) illustrates rim profiles from vessels that are similar in form, size, and paste to Early Tanguche Jars 2c and 2d.

Early Tanguche Jar 2d (Fig. 236)

Number: 38 sherds, or ca. 1.7% of the Early Tanguche assemblage.

General description: Globular jar with a high neck and broad, flaring rim. Lips are usually rounded, although several rims with a horizontal beveled lip are also present in the sample. Rim diameters vary from 14-30 cm, with a mean of 16 cm and a standard deviation of 3.7 cm. Wall thickness below the rim ranges widely between 7 mm and 12 mm, with a mean of 8.6 mm.

Paste: Temper consists uniformly of medium sand in moderate quantities. Paste color is red.

Surface characteristics: A maker's mark was noted on the interior of one of the rims. Otherwise, exterior and interior surfaces are plain redware.

Distribution: This jar type is widely distributed in habitation, habitation-cemetery, and cemetery sites throughout the main area of Early Tanguche occupation. Collection proveniences (with number of sherds in parentheses)/site numbers are:

Colls. 104(1), 105(1)/ETAN-4; Coll. 189(1)/ETAN-22; Coll. 241(2)/ETAN-42; Coll. 305(1)/ETAN-84; Coll. 309(7)/ETAN-93; Coll. 303(1)/ETAN-102; Coll. 188(1)/ETAN-168; Coll. 81(2)/ETAN-172; Coll. 78(2)/ETAN-173; Coll. 75(1)/ETAN-174; Colls. 73(1), 74(1)/ETAN-175; Coll. 91(1)/ETAN-176; Colls. 71(2), 72(9), 88(1)/ETAN-180; Coll. 56(2)/ETAN-181; Coll. 313(1)/ETAN-190.

Chronological assessment: Early Tanguche Jar 2d is similar in form and paste to some variants of Late Suchimancillo Jar 5e (Fig. 215), Guadaluptio Jar 2b (Fig. 226), and Early Tambo Real Redware Jar 4b (Fig. 271). It thus appears to be of little utility as a time marker for Early Tanguche Period.

Inter-regional comparisons: See Early Tanguche Jar 2c.

Early Tanguche Jar 3 (Fig. 237)

Number: 146 sherds, or ca. 6.4% of the Early Tanguche assemblage.

General description: Globular jar with an everted, incurving rim. The wall of the rim slants generally outward, so that the major point of constriction at the vessel mouth is the juncture between the neck and the body, and not the lip. Rim diameters vary from 4-18 cm, with a mean of 11.3 cm and a standard deviation of 2.2 cm. Wall thickness below the rim ranges between 4 mm and 6 mm.

Paste: Temper consists of fine or medium sand, with 80% of the sherds having medium grain sand. Paste color is red, with gray cores noted on 7% of the sherds.

Surface characteristics: The exterior surface on the shoulder of the vessel is decorated with pressmolded zoned and stippled designs on approximately 16% of the sherds in the sample (for examples of these designs on whole vessels collected from the surface of looted cemeteries, see Figs. 238, 239, 240). A few sherds have vertical notched or unnotched handles. Portions of the lower exterior surface of the body were fire blackened on about 8% of the sherds. The remainder of the sherds in the sample have plain redware exterior and interior surfaces.

Distribution: This jar type has a very wide distribution in habitation, habitation-cemetery, and cemetery sites throughout the area of Early Tanguche occupation, including the southernmost Coast sector and the Santa-Chao Desert. Collection proveniences (with number of sherds in parentheses)/site numbers are:

Coll. 370(2)/ETAN-3; Coll. 104(1)/ETAN-4; Coll. 26(2)/ETAN-5; Coll. 129(1)/ETAN-11; Coll. 130(1)/ETAN-12; Coll. 140(1)/ETAN-15; Colls. 141(3), 143(2)/ETAN-17; Coll. 73(1)/ETAN-20; Coll. 172(1)/ETAN-21; Coll. 190(1)/ETAN-22; Colls. 156(2), 157(5)/ETAN-26; Coll. 164(2)/ETAN-31; Colls. 230(4), 231(5), 234(1)/ETAN-33; Coll. 235(1)/ETAN-34; Coll. 232(2)/ETAN-35; Coll. 237(1)/ETAN-36; Colls. 166/197(4)/ETAN-39; Coll. 246(1)/ETAN-56; Coll. 259(1)/ETAN-79; Coll. 260(2)/ETAN-81; Coll. 262(4)/ETAN-83; Coll. 305(1)/ETAN-84; Coll. 275(1)/ETAN-87; Coll. 358(12)/ETAN-104; Colls. 349(3), 350(1)/ETAN-147; Coll. 185(4)/ETAN-161; Coll. 177(1)/ETAN-163; Coll. 182(1)/ETAN-164; Coll. 181(4)/ETAN-165; Coll. 179(1)/ETAN-166; Coll. 82(1)/ETAN-171; Colls. 78(1), 79(1)/ ETAN-173; Coll. 73(1)/ETAN-175; Coll. 92(2)/ETAN-177; Colls. 70(5), 71(3), 72(6), 88(3)/ETAN-180; Coll. 56(1)/ETAN-181; Coll. 53(16)/ ETAN-182; Coll. 47(1)/ETAN-183; Coll. 46(4)/ETAN-184; Colls. 48(2), 49(2)/ETAN-185; Coll. 323(1)/ETAN-186; Coll. 317(1)/ETAN-188; Coll. 313(1)/ETAN-190; Coll. 295(1)/ETAN-192; Coll. 264(6)/ETAN-194; Coll. 285(2)/ETAN-198; Coll. 270(2)/ETAN-199.

Chronological assessment: Early Tanguche Jar 3 is somewhat similar in form to Late Tanguche Jar 3 (Fig. 258), but can be distinguished on the basis of (1) its consistently less constricted, outslanting rim; and (2) a lack of thickening on the bulging part of the vessel neck. All in all, judging from the analysis of single-component collections, this jar type is one of the primary utilitarian ware diagnostics of the Early Tanguche Period.

Inter-regional comparisons: From Castillo Plain materials excavated in Tomaval levels of Virú Valley sites, Collier (1955, p. 187, Fig. 63 I) illustrates vessels with rim profiles that are very similar to those of Early Tanguche Jar 3. For a similar jar type from Moche Valley, see Donnan and Mackey (1978, p. 217, Pl. 12 - EC 23:1).

Early Tanguche Jar 4a (Fig. 237)

Number: 20 sherds, or ca. .9% of the Early Tanguche assemblage.

General description: Globular jar with an outslanted, cambered neck and everted lip. Rim diameters vary from 9-16 cm, with a mean of 12.4 cm and a standard deviation of 2.8 cm. Wall thickness below the rim ranges narrowly between 4 mm and 5 mm, with 90% of the sherds at the upper end of the range.

Paste: Temper consists of fine or medium sand, with 75% of the sherds having fine grain sand. The quantity of temper in all sherds is moderate. Paste color is red.

Surface characteristics: One sherd with exterior pressmolded stippling on the shoulder is present in the sample, and a few sherds have narrow vertical strap handles. The remaining sherds have plain exterior and interior surfaces.

Distribution: This jar type has a wide, but limited, distribution in habitation-cemetery and cemetery sites throughout the main area of Early Tanguche occupation. Collection proveniences (with number of sherds in parentheses)/site numbers are:

Coll. 143(2)/ETAN-17; Coll. 230(3)/ETAN-33; Colls. 166/197(1)/ ETAN-39; Coll. 305(1)/ETAN-84; Coll. 343(3)/ETAN-110; Coll. 181(2)/ ETAN-165; Coll. 84(1)/ETAN-169; Coll. 83(2)/ETAN-170; Coll. 71(3)/ ETAN-180; Coll. 317(2)/ETAN-188.

Chronological assessment: Early Tanguche Jar 4a is similar in form to Late Tambo Real Grayware Jar 4d (Fig. 275), and in form and paste to some variants of Late Tambo Real Redware Jar 2 (Fig. 279). The latter jar is a minor type in the Late Tambo Real assemblage, however, and Jar 4a thus appears to be a good temporal diagnostic.

Inter-regional comparisons: Collier (1955, p. 187, Fig. 63 H) illustrates Castillo Plain sherds from his excavations in Tomaval levels of Virú Valley sites that are very similar in form, size, and paste to Early Tanguche Jars 4a and 4b. For a similar jar form from Moche Valley, see Donnan and Mackey (1978, p. 267, Vessel 4).

Early Tanguche Jar 4b (Fig. 237)

Number: 44 sherds, or ca. 1.9% of the Early Tanguche assemblage.

General description: Globular jar with a vertical, cambered neck and everted lip. Rim diameters vary from 8-16 cm, with a mean of 12 cm and a standard deviation of 2.5 cm. Wall thickness below the rim ranges between 5 mm and 9 mm, with a mean of 6.6 mm.

Paste: Temper consists of fine or medium sand, with 80% of the

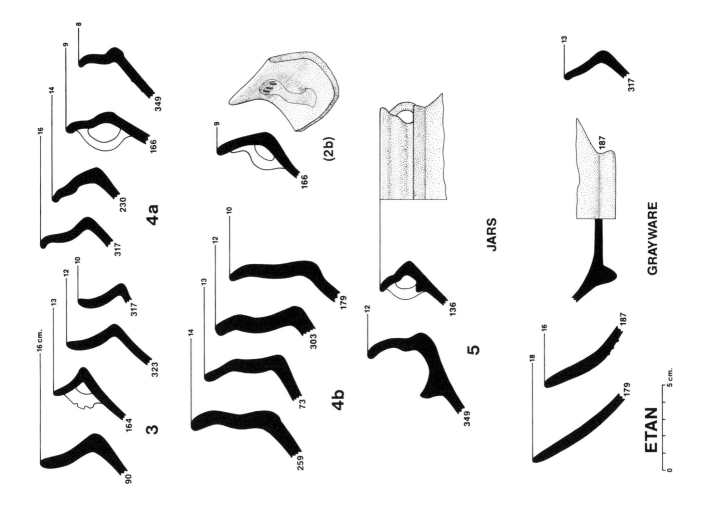

Fig. 237. Early Tanguche Period ceramics: Jars 3, 4a, 4b, and 5;
and selected grayware bowls and jars.

465

sherds having medium grain sand. The quantity of temper in all sherds is moderate. Paste color is red.

Surface characteristics: Exterior and interior surfaces are plain redware. Fire blackening was noted on 10% of the sherds in the sample.

Distribution: This jar type is widely distributed in habitation, habitation-cemetery, and cemetery sites throughout the main area of Early Tanguche occupation. Collection proveniences (with number of sherds in parentheses)/site numbers are:

Coll. 104(3)/ETAN-4; Colls. 136/155(1)/ETAN-14; Coll. 174(1)/ETAN-20; Colls. 166/197(1)/ETAN-39; Coll. 204(1)/ETAN-47; Coll. 259(1)/ETAN-79; Coll. 305(1)/ETAN-84; Coll. 303(3)/ETAN-102; Coll. 337(2)/ETAN-111; Coll. 186(2)/ETAN-160; Coll. 179(2)/ETAN-166; Coll. 78(3)/ETAN-173; Coll. 75(2)/ETAN-174; Coll. 73(3)/ETAN-175; Coll. 91(3)/ETAN-176; Coll. 92(1)/ETAN-177; Coll. 86(1)/ETAN-178; Colls. 72(7), 88(6)/ETAN-180.

Chronological assessment: Early Tanguche Jar 4b is somewhat similar in form to Late Suchimancillo Jar 10 (Fig. 216), but can be distinguished from the slightly outslanted neck of the earlier jar on the basis of its consistently vertical neck. The one exception to this is shown in Fig. 237 (Jar 4b, center - right), but the presence of an Early Tanguche-type narrow vertical strap handle distinguishes it from the earlier jar.

Inter-regional comparisons: See Early Tanguche Jar 4a.

Early Tanguche Jar 5 (Fig. 237)

Number: 26 sherds, or ca. 1.1% of the Early Tanguche assemblage.

General description: Globular jar with a vertical or outslanted cambered neck, everted lip, and elevated ridge on the shoulder of the vessel immediately below the neck. Rim diameters vary from 6-13 cm, with a mean of 11 cm and a standard deviation of 2.1 cm. Wall thickness below the rim ranges between 4 mm and 7 mm.

Paste: Temper consists uniformly of medium sand in moderate quantities. Paste color is red.

Surface characteristics: As the profile drawings in Fig. 237 show, the neck and rim of this vessel are essentially similar in form to Early Tanguche Jar 4a. The distinctive additional feature on Jar 5, however, is the presence of a tapered, or sharp-edged, ridge on the shoulder. In addition, although many sherds in the sample are too fragmentary to be certain, it seems likely that narrow vertical strap handles were placed on opposing sides of the vessel between the ridge and the upper part of the neck. No other decoration was noted on the redware surface of the sherds.

Distribution: This jar type has a wide, if somewhat limited, distribution in habitation, habitation-cemetery, and cemetery sites throughout the main area of Early Tanguche occupation. Collection proveniences (with number of sherds in parentheses)/site numbers are:

Coll. 371(1)/ETAN-2; Colls. 136/155(1)/ETAN-14; Coll. 143(1)/ETAN-17; Coll. 230(1)/ETAN-33; Coll. 235(3)/ETAN-34; Coll. 204(2)/ETAN-47; Coll. 247(5)/ETAN-56; Coll. 309(4)/ETAN-93; Colls. 349(1), 350(2)/ETAN-147; Coll. 185(2)/ETAN-161; Coll. 78(1)/ETAN-173; Coll. 72(1)/ETAN-180; Coll. 264(1)/ETAN-194.

Chronological assessment: Judging from the analysis of single-component collections, Jar 5 is limited to Early Tanguche Period.

Inter-regional comparisons: From their excavations in Tomaval levels in Virú Valley sites, Strong and Evans (1952, p. 264, Fig. 40) illustrate a Castillo Plain vessel shape that is very similar to Jar 5 (see also Collier 1955, p. 187, Fig. 63 G; Note: the ridge shown on the profile in Fig. 63 G, Collier's Vessel Form 6, appears on the equivalent of a Form 7 jar in the Lower Santa region). For similar jars from the Moche Valley, see Donnan and Mackey (1978: 217, 247).

Early Tanguche: Grayware (Fig. 237; Fig. 247, lower - left, lower - center; Fig. 248, lower; Fig. 250, right; Fig. 253 a; Fig. 254; Fig. 255 f)

Number: 44 sherds, or ca. 1.9% of the Early Tanguche assemblage.

General description: A small number of different grayware form types and effigy vessels are present in the Early Tanguche collections. Among these are the types illustrated here, including (1) open bowls with outslanting, incurved walls--some of which have exterior pressmolded/stippled decoration (Fig. 237; compare to Early Tanguche redware Bowl 1); (2) polished bowls with an annular base (Fig. 237; compare to decorated bowls in Fig. 241); (3) jars with outslanting, cambered necks and everted lips (Fig. 237; compare to Early Tanguche redware Jar 4a); (4) human effigy neck vessels (Fig. 247, lower - left, lower - center; and Fig. 248, lower; note the "antlered" animal and the triangular face above it on the front of this last vessel); (5) polished double spout-and-bridge vessels with incised and pressmolded decoration (Fig. 250, right; Note: although not included with Early Tanguche "exotics" in Fig. 256, only three other sherds in this category were found; since this type of vessel is likely to be of Central or North-Central Coast origin, it is also clearly exotic to the Lower Santa region); (6) a polished feline effigy neck vessel (Fig. 253 a; compare to human effigy neck vessels in Fig. 247); (7) a polished effigy neck vessel depicting a lizard (Fig. 254); and (8) an animal effigy (possibly a feline) incised on the exterior of a globular vessel (Fig. 255 f).

Paste: All of the above vessels have fine or medium grain sand temper in moderate quantities. Paste color ranges from light gray through dark gray.

Surface characteristics: As mentioned above, almost all of the effigy vessels, and some of the bowls, have highly polished exterior surfaces. Color of the exterior surface ranges from light gray to black.

Distribution: Grayware vessels were found in relatively limited quantities compared to redware, but are widely distributed in habitation-cemetery and cemetery sites throughout the main area of Early Tanguche occupation. Collection proveniences (with number of sherds in

466

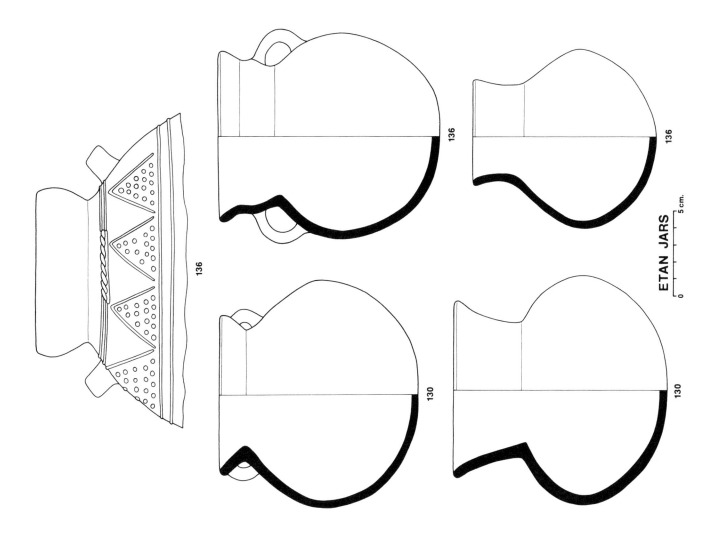

ETAN JARS

0 ___ 5 cm.

Fig. 238. Early Tanguche Period ceramics: miscellaneous decorated and plainware jars.

467

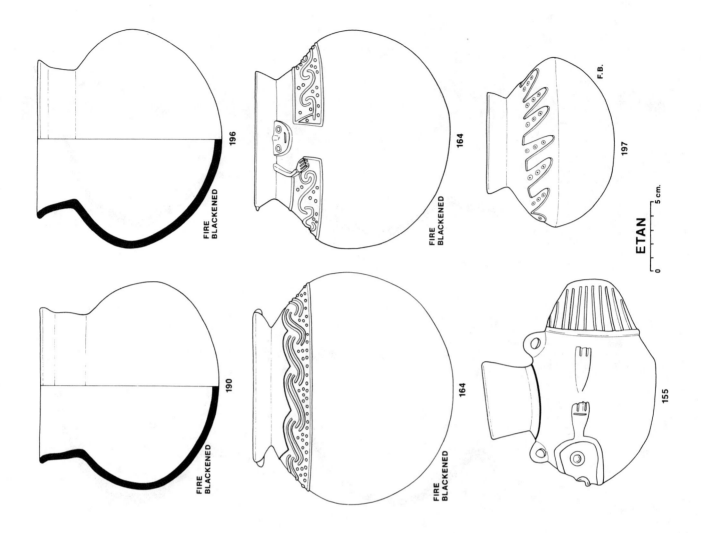

196
FIRE
BLACKENED

190
FIRE
BLACKENED

164
FIRE
BLACKENED

164
FIRE
BLACKENED

F.B.
197

ETAN

0 ___ 5 cm.

155

Fig. 239. Early Tanguche Period ceramics: miscellaneous plainware and decorated jars, and a Black-and-White/Redware fish effigy jar.

468

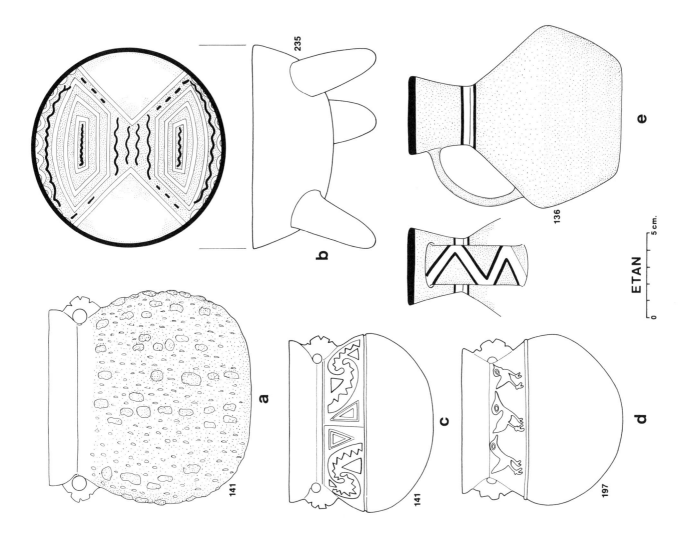

Fig. 240. Early Tanguche Period ceramics: miscellaneous decorated jars, and a polychrome tripod bowl.

parentheses)/site numbers are:

Coll. 130(1)/ETAN-12; Colls. 136/155(1)/ETAN-14; Coll. 140(1)/ ETAN-15; Colls. 173(1), 174(1)/ETAN-20; Coll. 157(4)/ETAN-26; Colls. 166/197(3)/ETAN-39; Coll. 229(2)/ETAN-77; Coll. 305(3)/ETAN-84; Coll. 349(3)/ETAN-147; Coll. 363(1)/ETAN-155; Coll. 187(2)/ETAN-159; Coll. 186(1)/ETAN-160; Coll. 179(4)/ETAN-166; Coll. 81(2)/ETAN-172; Coll. 74(2)/ETAN-175; Coll. 86(3)/ETAN-178; Coll. 87(1)/ETAN-179; Coll. 88(5)/ ETAN-180; Coll. 53(2)/ETAN-182; Coll. 47(1)/ETAN-183.

Chronological assessment: Most, if not all, of the grayware types illustrated here have form or decorative characteristics that place them solidly in the Early Tanguche Period, along with their redware counterparts.

Inter-regional comparisons: Aside from a few grayware vessels classified as probable exotics, most of the grayware vessels dating to Early Tanguche Period appear to be incipient forms of such Virú Valley equivalents as Tomaval Plain, San Juan Molded, and Virú Plain (cf. Collier 1955:160-164, 168-172).

Early Tanguche: Decorated Annular-base Redware Bowls (Fig. 241 a-h; Fig. 242 a-l)

Number: 125 sherds, or ca. 5.5% of the Early Tanguche assemblage.

General description: Open bowl with annular base and straight or slightly incurved, outslanted walls. Lips are tapered. Rim diameters vary from 12-20 cm, with a mean of 17.3 cm and a standard deviation of 1.8 cm. Wall thickness below the rim ranges narrowly between 5 mm and 6 mm.

Paste: Temper consists uniformly of medium sand in moderate quantities. Paste color is reddish-orange in 8.8% of the sherds and red in the remaining 91.2%.

Surface characteristics: Approximately 9% (or 11) of the sherds in the sample have black-painted decoration over a reddish-orange surface, on the interior of the bowl below the rim (e.g., Fig. 241 d). Another 34% (or 43) have black-and-white decoration painted on the upper half of the redware interior (Fig. 241 b, c, e; Fig. 242 a-l). Exterior surfaces on both of these painted bowl types are plain. An additional 55% (or 69) of the sherds in the sample have plain interiors and exterior decoration consisting of pressmolded designs (Fig. 241 f, g; Fig. 255 d). Probable maker's marks were noted on two other sherds.

The Black-and-White/Redware bowls are of particular interest because of the variation in specific design motifs painted on their interiors. As shown in the schematic wedge-shaped drawings in Fig. 242, the basic design theme on the upper half of the interior consists of one or more black-painted lines running down from the rim. The underlying white paint takes several principal forms, including coverage of (1) the area enclosed by the black lines; (2) the entire interior of the bowl; and (3) the upper third of the interior. Additional design elements were formed by black wavy lines, geometric figures, and elliptical and circular dots.

Distribution: Decorated annular-base bowls are found widely distributed in cemeteries, as well as a few habitation sites, throughout the main area of Early Tanguche occupation. Separate collection proveniences (with number of sherds in parentheses)/site numbers are:

Black/Orange proveniences: Coll. 94(2)/ETAN-6; Coll. 114(4)/ETAN-7; Coll. 136/155(1)/ETAN-14; Coll. 174(1)/ETAN-20; Coll. 177(2)/ETAN-163; Coll. 88(1)/ETAN-180.

Red Pressmolded proveniences: Coll. 114(8)/ETAN-7; Coll. 190(2)/ETAN-22; Colls. 230(3), 231(3)/ETAN-33; Coll. 196(1)/ ETAN-40; Coll. 247(1)/ETAN-56; Coll. 305(2)/ETAN-84; Coll. 301(1)/ETAN-89; Coll. 343(1)/ETAN-110; Coll. 337(1)/ETAN-111; Coll. 187(1)/ETAN-159; Coll. 181(2)/ETAN-165; Coll. 180(1)/ ETAN-166; Coll. 83(1)/ETAN-170; Coll. 86(1)/ETAN-178; Colls. 70(1), 71(9), 72(4)/ETAN-180; Coll. 48(1)/ETAN-185; Coll. 323(7)/ETAN-186; Coll. 295(1)/ETAN-192; Coll. 294(1)/ETAN-193; Coll. 285(6)/ETAN-198.

Proveniences of Black-and-White/Redware motifs:

Fig. 242 a: Coll. 114(8)/ETAN-7; Colls. 166/ 197(1)/ETAN-39; Coll. 247(1)/ETAN-56; Coll. 179(6)/ ETAN-166; Coll. 71(1)/ETAN-180.

Fig. 242 b: Coll. 247(1)/ETAN-56.

Fig. 242 c: Coll. 141(1)/ETAN-17; Coll. 81(1)/ ETAN-172; Coll. 317(1)/ETAN-188.

Fig. 242 d: Coll. 323(1)/ETAN-186.

Fig. 242 e: Coll. 71(1)/ETAN-180; Coll. 46(1)/ ETAN-184; Coll. 295(4)/ETAN-192.

Fig. 242 f: Coll. 371(1)/ETAN-2; Coll. 235(1)/ ETAN-34; Coll. 246(2)/ETAN-56.

Fig. 242 g: Colls. 166/197(1)/ETAN-39.

Fig. 242 h: Coll. 358(1)/ETAN-104.

Fig. 242 i: Coll. 303(1)/ETAN-102.

Fig. 242 j: Coll. 49(5)/ETAN-185.

Fig. 242 k: Coll. 73(1)/ETAN-175.

Fig. 242 l: Coll. 234(1)/ETAN-33.

Chronological assessment: Judging from the analysis of single-component collections, all three of the decorated annular-base bowl types discussed here are confined to the Early Tanguche Period. Each is found consistently in association with the other two types, as well as with other good time markers of the early part of Middle Horizon.

Inter-regional comparisons: Black/Orange bowls similar to those of the Lower Santa region are reported for Moche (cf. Donnan and Mackey 1978, p. 265, Vessel 3) and Virú (cf. Kroeber 1930, Pl. 23, Vessel 6). Similar red pressmolded bowls are reported for a number of valleys to the north and south of Santa--including Moche (cf. Donnan and Mackey 1978:243, 265), Virú (cf. Collier 1955, p. 173, Fig. 57), Nepeña (cf.

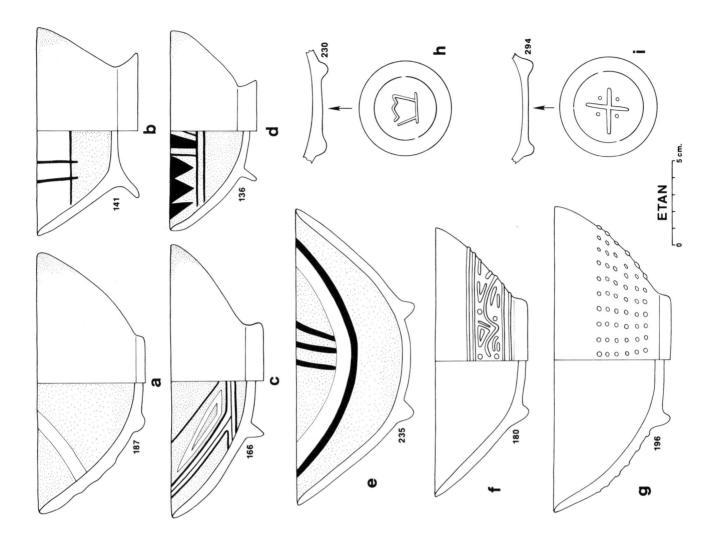

Fig. 241. Early Tanguche Period ceramics: painted and press-molded annular-base bowls, including fragments of bases with maker's marks.

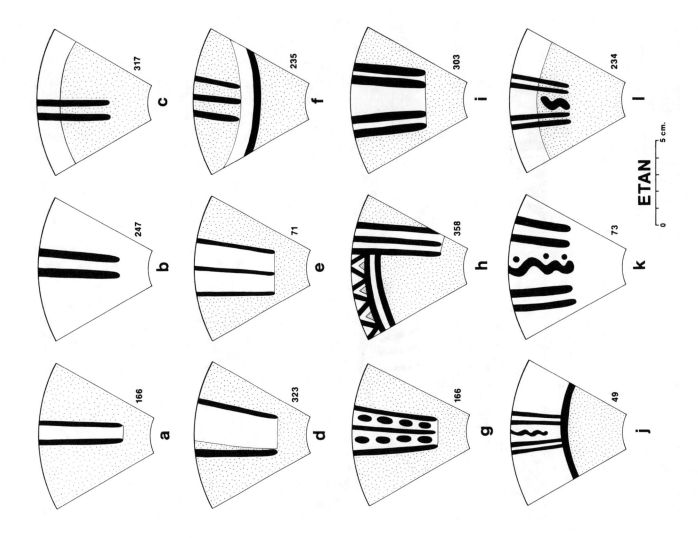

ETAN

0   5 cm.

Fig. 242. Early Tanguche Period ceramics: schematic wedges showing Black-and-White/Redware design motifs on the interior of annular-base bowls.

Proulx 1973, p. 249, Pl. 8-G), and Supe (cf. Kroeber 1925b, Pl. 75 g-k). Black-and-White/Redware bowls similar to those of Santa are reported for Virú (cf. Collier 1955:180-182). The author's study at Field Museum of collections made in Casma by Donald Collier and Donald Thompson also confirms the presence of similar Black-and-White/Redware bowls in the area to the south of the Lower Santa region.

Early Tanguche: Red/White-slipped Jars (Fig. 243 a-d)

Number: 56 sherds, or ca. 2.5% of the Early Tanguche assemblage.

General description: Medium-sized jar with a body of ovoid horizontal (i.e., barrel) or ovoid vertical (i.e., football--estilo norteamericano) shape. The sides of the vessels are generally somewhat flattened (e.g., see Black-and-White/Redware vessels in Fig. 244). Necks are usually funnel-shaped, although a few with vertical walls and flared rims are also present in the sample (e.g., Fig. 243 c). A standard feature is the presence of two lug handles on opposite sides of the jar at the juncture of the neck and the body. The lugs usually have upper surfaces that are horizontal, and sides that turn on a rounded corner down toward the shoulder of the vessel at a roughly 90° angle. The circular perforation in the handles is always placed against the surface of the vessel. Complete or partially complete rims were present on only 11 of the 56 sherds. Rim diameters on these fragments vary from 4.7-7 cm, with a mean of 6 cm. Wall thickness below the rim ranges between 4 mm and 6 mm.

Paste: Temper consists uniformly of medium sand in moderate quantities. Paste color is red.

Surface characteristics: Exterior surfaces are completely covered with a thick white slip. As shown in Fig. 243 a-d, red-painted geometric designs were placed over the slip, either in the form of bilaterally symmetrical, parallel lines down the sides of the jar or in crosshatched fashion around the entire exterior of the body. A few vessels, such as that shown in Fig. 243 c, have additional decoration in the form of (1) pressmolded stippling (i.e., slightly raised bumps); and (2) diamond-shaped designs placed down the narrow ends of the vessel.

Distribution: Vessels of this type are found widely distributed in habitation, habitation-cemetery, and cemetery sites throughout the entire area of Early Tanguche occupation, including the Santa-Chao Desert sector. Collection proveniences (with number of sherds in parentheses)/ site numbers are:

Coll. 372(1)/ETAN-1; Coll. 371(5)/ETAN-2; Coll. 370(2)/ETAN-3; Coll. 44(3)/ETAN-10; Coll. 157(1)/ETAN-26; Coll. 164(2)/ETAN-31; Colls. 166/197(5)/ETAN-39; Coll. 242(2)/ETAN-44; Coll. 205(6)/ETAN-48; Coll. 209(2)/ETAN-57; Coll. 259(1)/ETAN-79; Coll. 272(1)/ETAN-85; Coll. 349(6)/ ETAN-147; Coll. 363(2)/ETAN-155; Coll. 188(9)/ETAN-168; Coll. 82(1)/ ETAN-171; Coll. 78(2)/ETAN-173; Coll. 47(1)/ETAN-183; Coll. 46(1)/ ETAN-184; Coll. 38(3)/ETAN-321.

Chronological assessment: Judging from the analysis of single-component collections, this decorated jar type is a good Early Tanguche diagnostic.

Inter-regional comparisons: Red/White-slipped vessels with exterior decoration of the kind described above are not mentioned in the literature on Middle Horizon ceramics of areas adjacent to the Lower Santa region. Although this suggests that this decorative style is essentially a local one, it is clear from the form and size of the vessels--as well as from some aspects of design motifs (e.g., the crosshatching)--that it is intimately linked to the much more widespread Black-White-Red style.

Early Tanguche: Black-and-White/Redware Jars (Fig. 243 e-g; Fig. 244; Fig. 245; Fig. 246)

Number: 94 sherds, or ca. 4.1% of the Early Tanguche assemblage.

General description: The general Black-and-White/Redware type includes (1) decorated annular-base bowls (Fig. 241 b, c, e; Fig. 242 a-l); (2) male human effigy neck vessels (e.g., Fig. 243 e; Fig. 247, third row - right; Fig. 251 m); (3) female human figurines (Fig. 252); and (4) jars of predominately ovoid horizontal or ovoid vertical shape (e.g., Fig. 244). Since the decorated bowls and human effigy figures are described in other sections, this section is confined to a brief description of the decorated jars. Measurements made of the few intact rims present in the sample indicate that the average rim diameter is ca. 6.5 cm, with a range of 5-8 cm. In general, the shape of both the neck and the body of these jars is quite similar to the Red/White-slipped ones. As the illustrations show (see Figs. 243 f, 244-246), the principal differences between the two types are that the Black-and-White/ Redware jars exhibit much greater variety with regard to vessel form, exterior decoration, and placement and types of handles. A distinctive feature of both vessel types is the indication that the body was made by separately pressmolding the two halves. These halves were then joined together and secured by a thin strip of clay running around the ends of the vessel (e.g., see Fig. 244, where the strip is clearly visible). Judging from the lack of corresponding seams, the necks were prepared separately in one piece and placed on the body after the two halves were joined.

Paste: Temper consists uniformly of medium sand in moderate quantities. Paste color is red.

Surface characteristics: As indicated in the illustrations, a substantial amount of diversity of design motifs is present in the general Black-White-Red style. Aside from the consistent use of black and white paint over the redware surface of vessels, the principal unifying motifs appear to be the use of either (1) broad vertical and horizontal bands of white paint outlined in black, enclosing panels of redware surface within which various combinations of white and black motifs form additional design elements (e.g., Fig. 243 f, g); or (2) broad bands of plain redware surface outlined in black, enclosing white-painted panels within which black-painted dots and other motifs were added (e.g., Fig. 245, upper and lower). Other vessels have designs that are similar to the crosshatched motifs present on some Red/White-slipped jars (e.g., compare the upper jar in Fig. 244 to the jar shown in Fig. 243 d).

473

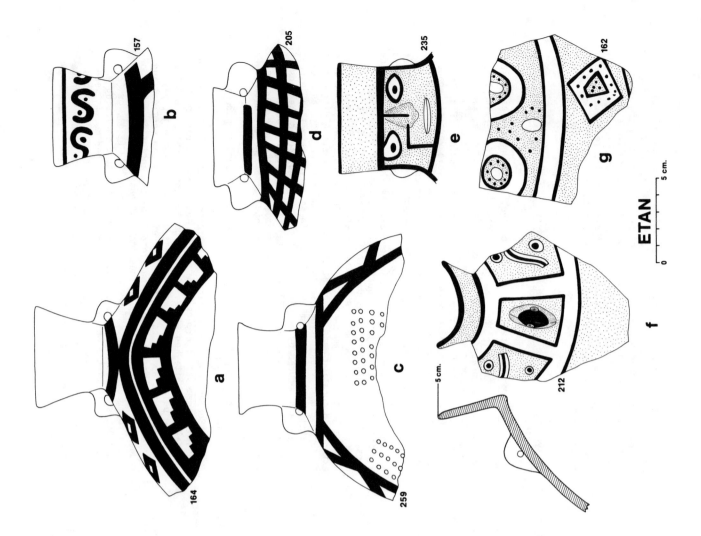

ETAN

0 _____ 5 cm.

Fig. 243. Early Tanguche Period ceramics: Red/White-slipped jars (a–d), and Black-and-White/Redware jars (e–g).

474

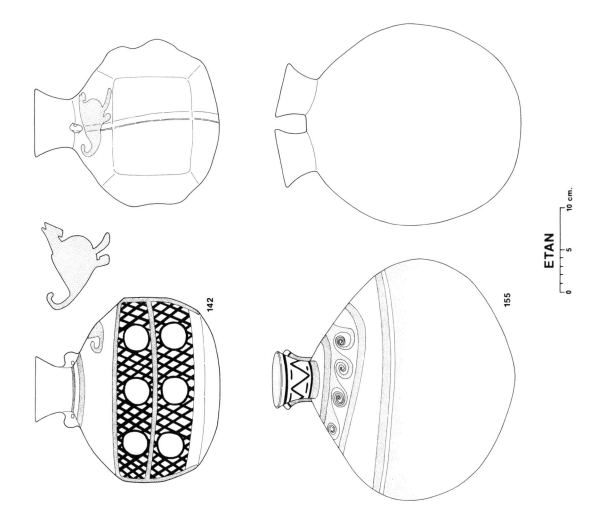

ETAN

0   5   10 cm.

142

155

Fig. 244. Early Tanguche Period ceramics: side and end views of
two Black-and-White/Redware jars.

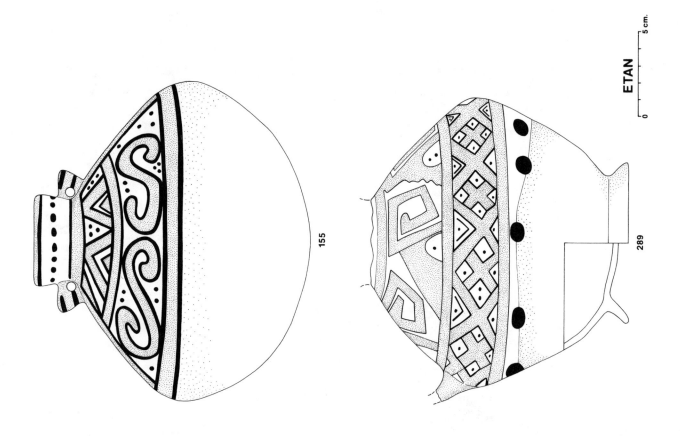

155

289

ETAN

0 ___ 5 cm.

Fig. 245. Early Tanguche Period ceramics: Black-and-White/Red-ware jars.

476

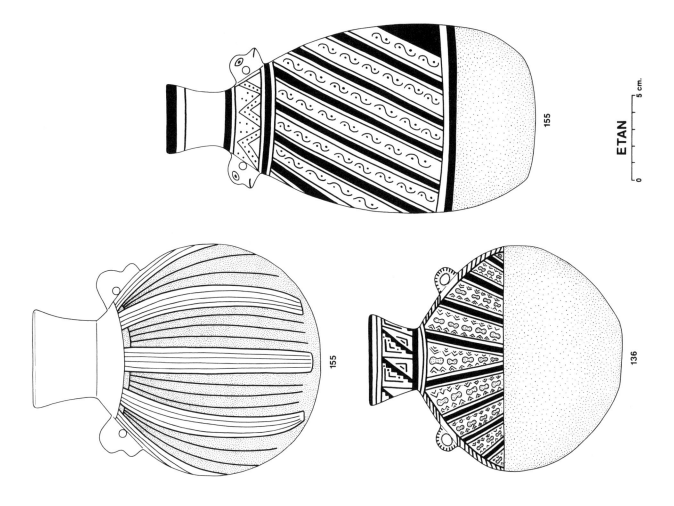

155

ETAN

5 cm.

0

155

136

Fig. 246. Early Tanguche Period ceramics: Black-and-White/Red-ware jars.

Finally, it should be mentioned that the three vessels depicted in Fig. 246 are unique in the Lower Santa collections. In other words, no sherds of any of these decorated types were found. However, all three are clearly related in form, size, and overall aspects of design elements to the other Black-and-White/Redware vessels described in this section.

Distribution: Vessels of this general type are found widely distributed in habitation, habitation-cemetery, and cemetery sites throughout the entire area of Early Tanguche occupation, including sites in the Santa-Chao Desert sector. Collection proveniences (with number of sherds in parentheses)/site numbers are:

Coll. 94(5)/ETAN-6; Coll. 114(1)/ETAN-7; Coll. 39(5)/ETAN-9; Colls. 136/155(4)/ETAN-14; Coll. 142(1)/ETAN-16; Coll. 157(8)/ETAN-26; Coll. 164(4)/ETAN-31; Colls. 231(12), 234(4)/ETAN-33; Coll. 235(9)/ETAN-34; Colls. 166/197(11)/ETAN-39; Coll. 247(2)/ETAN-56; Coll. 212(1)/ETAN-58; Coll. 258(3)/ETAN-75; Coll. 343(2)/ETAN-110; Coll. 181(3)/ETAN-165; Coll. 83(2)/ETAN-170; Coll. 72(9)/ETAN-180; Coll. 49(4)/ETAN-185; Coll. 315(1)/ETAN-191; Coll. 295(2)/ETAN-192; Coll. 285(1)/ETAN-198.

Chronological assessment: As with the Red/White-slipped jars, the consistent presence of this decorated jar type in collections characterized only by Early Tanguche diagnostics indicates that it also is a good time marker for the period.

Inter-regional comparisons: Black-and-White/Redware vessels are among the most common and widespread of decorated types in the Santa area of the North Coast during the early part of the Middle Horizon Period. Although this style is often called "Santa" or "Huaylas Yunga" (i.e., coastal part of the Huaylas area), it is by no means clear either that it originated in or was centered on the Lower Santa region. Indeed, it seems likely that the center of Black-White-Red culture was located elsewhere on the coast, and that ceramics of this kind and other Middle Horizon styles moved along the coast as part of a large-scale, state-run economic network. Among the nearby valleys in which the Black-White-Red style is present are: Moche (cf. Donnan and Mackey 1978:214 ff; Kroeber 1925 a, Pl. 62), Virú (cf. Bennett 1939, Pl. 9; Collier 1955: 180-182; Kroeber 1930, Pl. 23), Nepeña (cf. Proulx 1973, p. 255, Pl. 11), and Casma (cf. Tello 1956, pp. 312-313, Figs. 147-150).

Early Tanguche: Effigy Figures (Fig. 239, lower - left; Fig. 240 d; Fig. 243 e; Fig. 244, upper; Fig. 246, right; and Figs. 247-256)

Early Tanguche is the third and last period, following Late Suchimancillo and Guadalupito, in the Lower Santa sequence in which substantial numbers of human and animal effigy figures are found widely distributed throughout the main area of occupation. The total number of effigy figures, including depictions of both humans and animals, is 131 (111 human and 20 animal figures), or ca. 5.7% of the Early Tanguche assemblage.

Human effigies: Five principal types of representations are present in the collections. These include (1) male human effigy neck vessels (Fig. 243 e; Figs. 247-250; Fig. 253 b, h); (2) female human figurines (Fig. 252); (3) figurines of male musicians playing panpipes (Fig. 251 d-g); (4) effigies of warriors, or figures holding probable instruments of war (Fig. 251 h-m); and (5) pressmolded and appliquéd male figures on the sides of jars (Figs. 255 a, b).

As in the preceding Guadalupito Period, representations of the human face are very realistically portrayed. And, although most male effigy neck figures are characterized by more-or-less the same plastic design features (e.g., eyes are almost always almond-shaped, with pupils represented by a smaller clay protrusion of the same shape), it is possible to divide the individuals represented into three distinct groups--including young men, older men, and fat men (e.g., see Fig. 247). Among other characteristic features of Early Tanguche effigy neck vessels are: (1) use of perforated lug handles to represent the ears (e.g., see Fig. 247, second row - right and center; it will be noted that these handles are similar to those on Red/White-slipped and Black-and-White/ Redware vessels); (2) use of Black-and-White decoration on some vessels (e.g., Fig. 243 e; Fig. 247, third row - right); and (3) the presence of headgear that includes representation of distinctive straps hanging down each side of the face (e.g., see Fig. 247, third row - right). As shown on the nearly complete vessel in Fig. 249, the strap-like features frequently, if not always, have what appear to be small feline heads attached to their ends. Since the same features are also found on the back of the head--clearly representing long hair--it seems likely that the front straps also represent hair, perhaps in the form of pigtails. Another distinctive feature of the "feline hair" male effigy neck vessels is the presence of double, white-painted protrusions, or bumps, on each shoulder. Finally, it is of interest to note that, in contrast to the white-painted eyes on human effigies of Guadalupito Period, most Early Tanguche effigy figures have unpainted redware eyes (Note: four exceptional figures with white-painted eyes are shown in Fig. 243 e; Fig. 247, second row - right; Fig. 248, upper - right; and Fig. 253 b).

The most highly decorated human effigies in the collections, however, are the female figurines. Only five of these figurines were found in the survey region--all of them left on the surface of heavily looted cemeteries (somewhat inexplicably, in the case of the three intact or nearly intact effigies shown in Fig. 252). Black-and-White decoration is used to depict headbands, waistbands, and necklaces. In addition, black-painted lines accentuate other parts of the body--including the eyes, neck, and arms.

Animal effigies: Among the animal effigies in the collections are depictions of the following: (1) felines (Fig. 244, upper; Fig. 253 a, g; Fig. 255 a, f); (2) birds (Fig. 240 d; Fig. 255 e); (3) a lizard (Fig. 254); (4) a fish (Fig. 239, bottom row - left); (5) a sea lion (Fig. 253 d); and (6) an exotic-looking insect (Fig. 253 c).

Effigy distributions: Human and animal effigy figures were found primarily in cemetery sites located throughout the main area of Early Tanguche occupation. Separate collection proveniences (with number of sherds in parentheses)/site numbers for each of the main effigy types discussed are:

Young man: Coll. 371(1)/ETAN-2; Colls. 136/155(1)/ETAN-14; Coll. 235(2)/ETAN-34; Coll. 196(1)/ETAN-40; Coll. 247(1)/

478

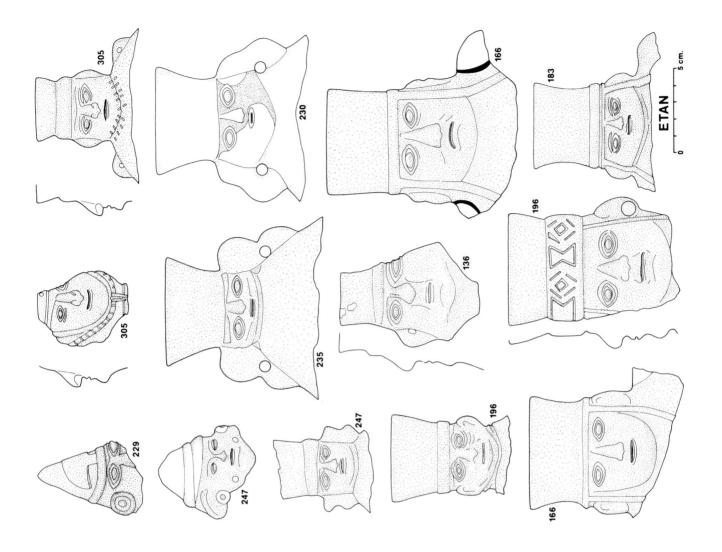

Fig. 247. Early Tanguche Period ceramics: human effigy neck jar fragments.

479

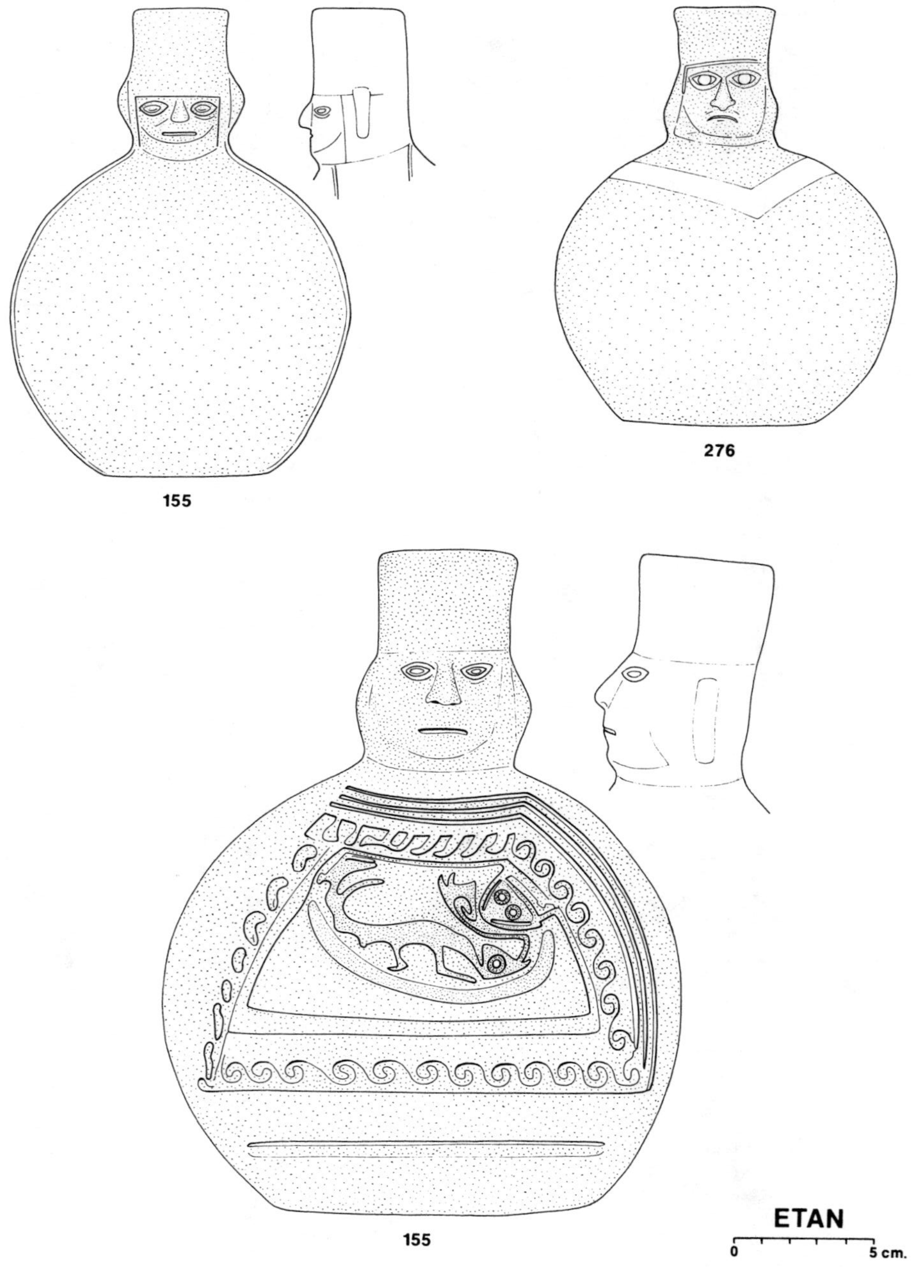

276

155

ETAN

0 ___ 5 cm.

155

155

Fig. 248. Early Tanguche Period ceramics: human effigy neck vessels.

480

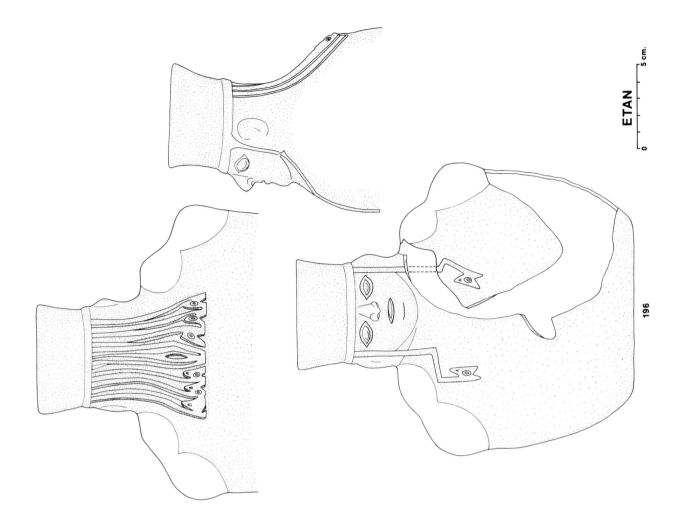

ETAN

0 ⌐————————┐ 5 cm.

196

Fig. 249. Early Tanguche Period ceramics: three views of a White-on-Redware effigy jar with feline hair.

481

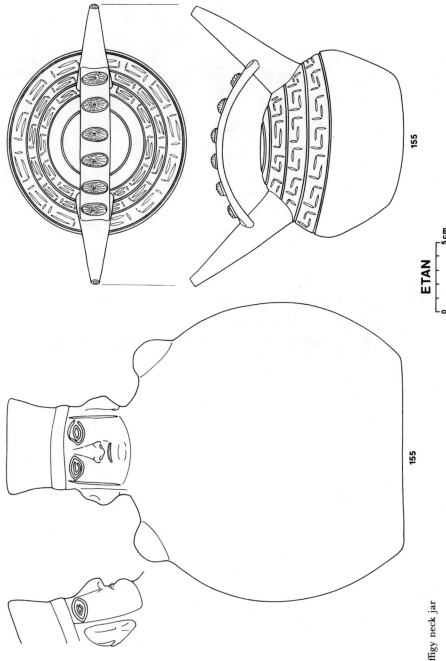

ETAN

0   5 cm.

155

155

Fig. 250. Early Tanguche Period ceramics: human effigy neck jar and a double spout-and-bridge vessel.

482

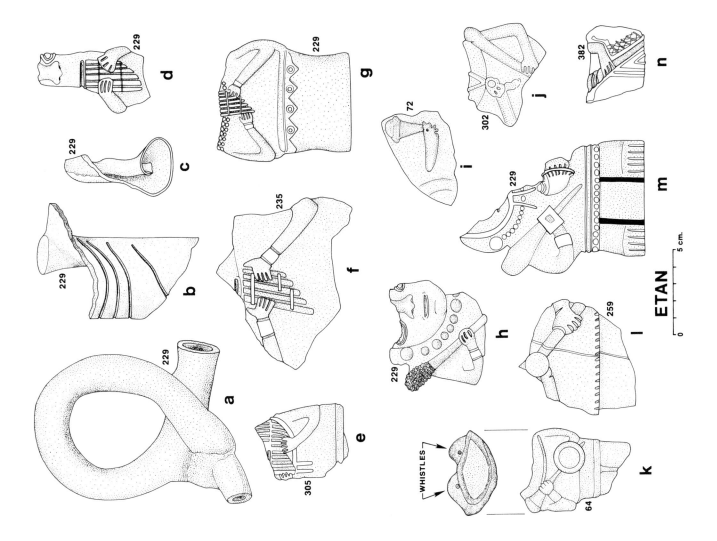

Fig. 251. Early Tanguche Period ceramics: fragments of musical instruments (a–b), figurines depicting musicians (d–g), and figurines of warriors (h–n). (Note: a fragment of marine shell is depicted in c, above).

483

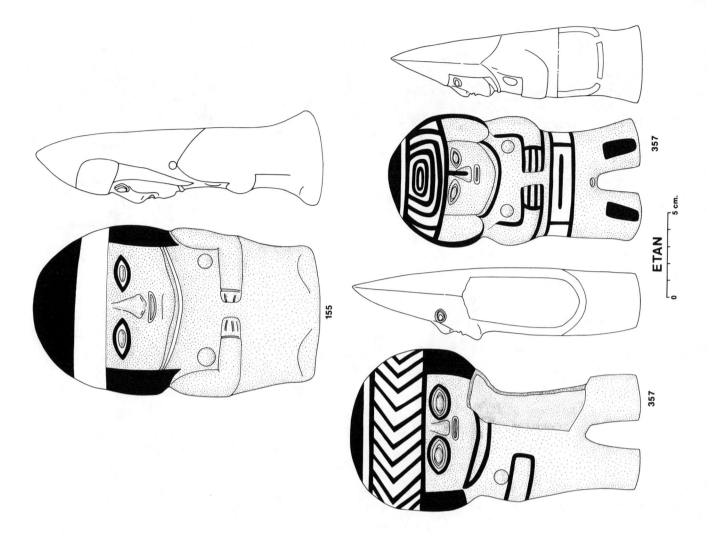

ETAN

357

357

155

0 5 cm.

Fig. 252. Early Tanguche Period ceramics: Black-and-White/Red-ware female figurines.

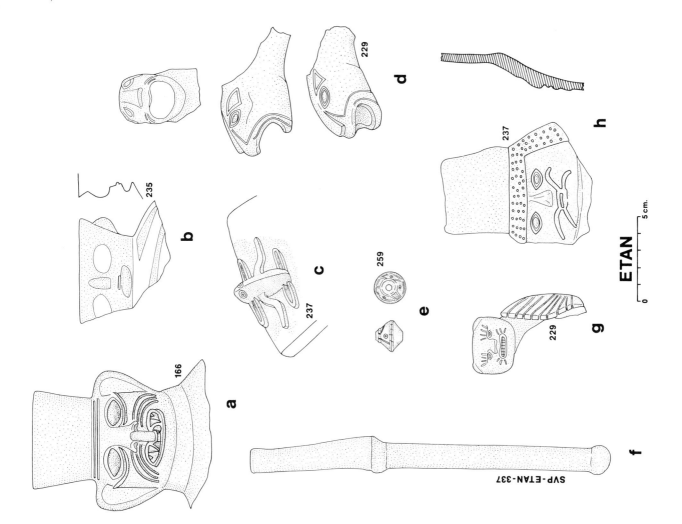

Fig. 253. Early Tanguche Period ceramics: miscellaneous items, including animal effigies, a spindle whorl, and a partly hollow tube of unknown function.

485

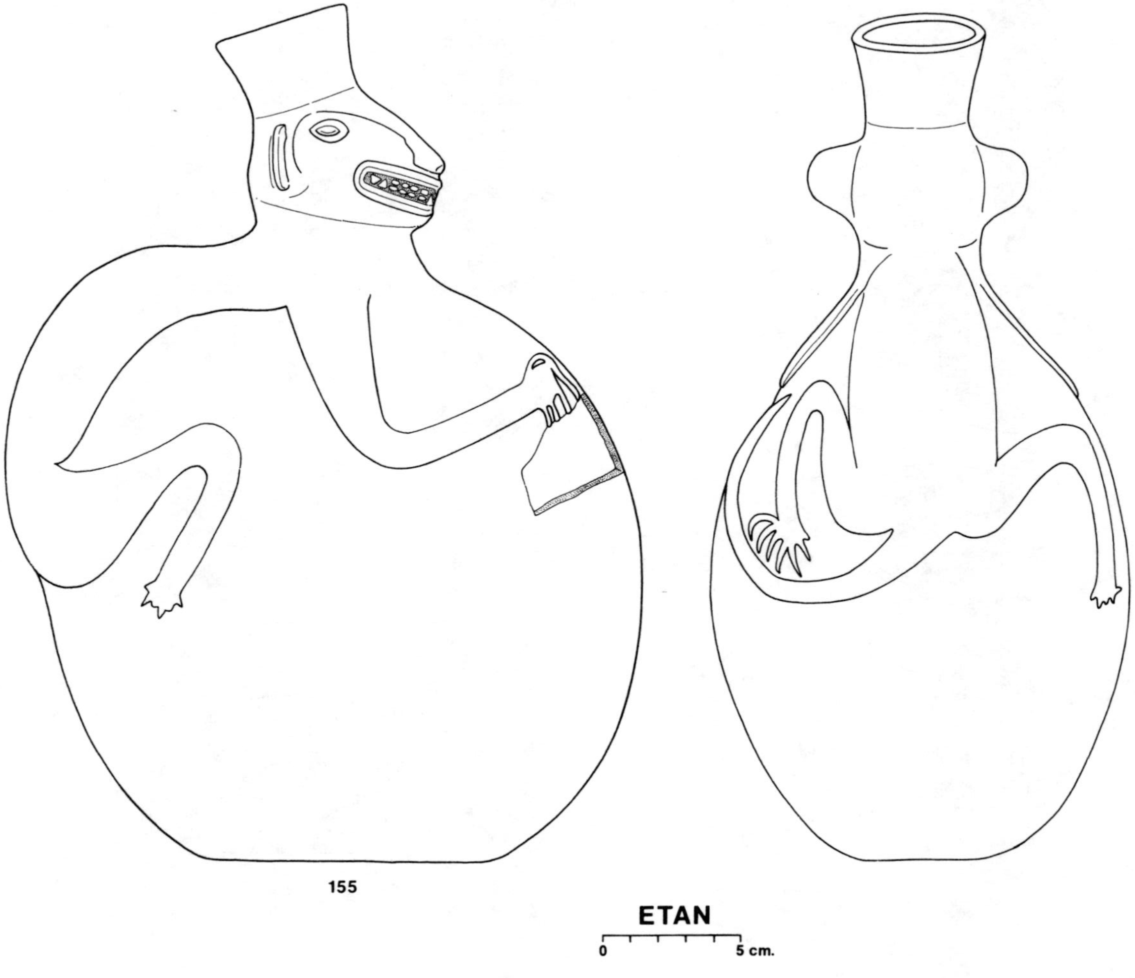

ETAN

0 ___ 5 cm.

155

Fig. 254. Early Tanguche ceramics: two views of an animal effigy jar.

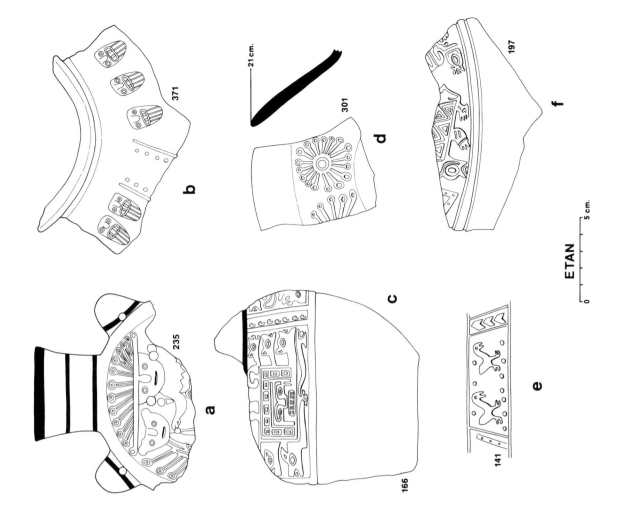

ETAN

21 cm.

5 cm.

Fig. 255. Early Tanguche Period ceramics: miscellaneous press-molded and appliquéd motifs.

487

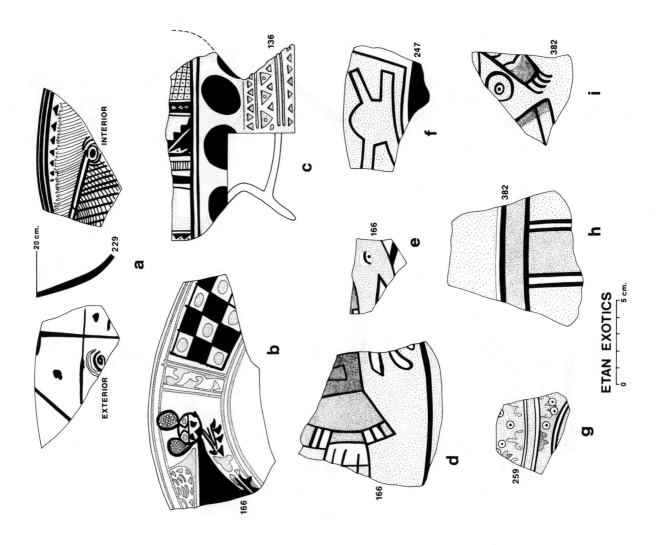

ETAN EXOTICS

0   5 cm.

Fig. 256. Early Tanguche Period ceramics: examples of decorated sherds of probable exotic origin. See ceramic descriptions for suggested places of origin.

488

ETAN-56; Coll. 229(2)/ETAN-77; Coll. 259(2)/ETAN-79; Coll. 305(1)/ETAN-84; Coll. 276(1)/ETAN-88; Colls. 78(1), 79(5)/ ETAN-173; Coll. 71(1)/ETAN-180; Coll. 382(1)/ETAN-321.

Old man: Coll. 235(2)/ETAN-34; Colls. 166/197(2)/ETAN-39; Coll. 196(1)/ETAN-40; Coll. 71(1)/ETAN-180.

Fat man: Colls. 136/155(1)/ETAN-14; Coll. 231(3)/ETAN-33; Coll. 247(1)/ETAN-56; Coll. 78(1)/ETAN-173.

Feline hair man: Coll. 370(1)/ETAN-3; Coll. 235(1)/ ETAN-34; Coll. 237(1)/ETAN-36; Colls. 166/197(1)/ETAN-39; Coll. 247(1)/ETAN-56; Coll. 183(1)/ETAN-162; Coll. 179(1)/ETAN-166.

Female figurines: Colls. 136/155(1)/ETAN-14; Coll. 235(1)/ETAN-34; Coll. 357(2)/ETAN-98; Coll. 79(1)/ETAN-173.

Musicians: Coll. 235(1)/ETAN-34; Coll. 229(2)/ETAN-77; Coll. 305(1)/ETAN-84.

Warriors: Coll. 28(1)/ETAN-4; Coll. 205(1)/ETAN-48; Coll. 229(2)/ETAN-77; Coll. 259(1)/ETAN-79; Coll. 305(1)/ETAN-84; Coll. 72(1)/ETAN-180; Coll. 53(1)/ETAN-182; Coll. 382(2)/ETAN-321.

Animals: Colls. 136/155(3)/ETAN-14; Coll. 142(1)/ETAN-16; Coll. 141(1)/ETAN-17; Coll. 234(1)/ETAN-33; Coll. 235(2)/ETAN-34; Coll. 237(1)/ETAN-36; Colls. 166/197(3)/ETAN-39; Coll. 247(1)/ ETAN-56; Coll. 229(2)/ETAN-77; Coll. 363(1)/ETAN-155; Coll. 180(1)/ETAN-166; Coll. 71(1)/ETAN-180; Coll. 264(1)/ETAN-194; Coll. 290(1)/ETAN-196.

Inter-regional comparisons (human effigies): Similar human effigies dating to the early part of Middle Horizon are reported for other nearby coastal valleys, including Moche (cf. Donnan and Mackey 1978:214 ff.; Kroeber 1925a, Pl. 64-66), Virú (cf. Bennett 1939, p. 42, Fig. 10; Collier 1955, p. 71, Fig. 34), Nepeña (cf. Proulx 1973, p. 251, Pl. 9), Casma (cf. Tello 1956, p. 313, Fig. 150), and Supe (cf. Kroeber 1925b, Pl. 7; Menzel 1977, p. 112, Fig. 68).

Early Tanguche: Exotics (Fig. 256; see also Fig. 240 b; Fig. 246; Fig. 250, right)

The primary criteria used in classifying a sherd or vessel as exotic were (1) its occurrence in the Early Tanguche collections as either a unique item or in very small numbers; and (2) the presence of features of form and/or decoration that appear to be very similar, if not essentially identical, to published ceramics characteristic of other regions. Brief descriptions of the exotics illustrated in Fig. 256 are as follows (with suggested classification/area of origin, where known, given in parentheses):

Fig. 256 a: Black/White Kaolin bowl (Cajamarca III); this sherd is clearly decorated in the Cajamarca Cursive style (e.g., see Lumbreras 1974, p. 147, Fig. 160).

Fig. 256 b: Red-and-Gray/White Kaolin bowl (Cajamarca III); the remains of a tripod support were noted on the plain exterior (Note: the interior of the sherd is shown in the figure; cf. Lumbreras 1974, p. 147,

Fig. 160, for an annular-base bowl with very similar decoration).

Fig. 256 c: Black/Orange-red (North Coast--Lambayeque); fragment of an annular-base jar (compare to vessel shown in Bennett 1939, p. 100, Fig. 20 a).

Fig. 256 d: Purple Red-Gray-Red-Black/Redware sherd (Central Coast polychrome).

Fig. 256 e: Red-Gray-Black-White/Redware sherd (Central Coast polychrome).

Fig. 256 f: Black-and-White/Redware sherd (North Coast).

Fig. 256 g: Gray-Black-White/Redware sherd (Cajamarca Cursive?).

Fig. 256 h, i: Dark Red-Black-White/Orange-red sherds (North Coast).

Among the other probable exotics illustrated here are the following:

Fig. 256 b: Gray-Black-White/Redware; tripod bowl.

Fig. 256, right: Incised double spout-and-bridge grayware vessel (compare to vessel shown in Menzel 1977, p. 105, Fig. 51).

489

LATE TANGUCHE PERIOD

Late Tanguche Bowl 1 (Fig. 258)

Number: 30 sherds, or ca. 4.8% of the Late Tanguche assemblage.

General description: Open bowl with straight or slightly incurved, outslanted walls. Rim diameters vary from 22-30 cm, with a mean of 25.2 cm and a standard deviation of 2.8 cm. Wall thickness below the rim ranges between 5 mm and 7 mm, with most sherds at the upper end of this range.

Paste: Temper consists uniformly of medium sand in moderate quantities. Paste color is red.

Surface characteristics: Interior and exterior surfaces are plain redware.

Distribution: This bowl type has a limited, but fairly wide, distribution primarily in habitation sites throughout the area of Late Tanguche occupation. Collection proveniences (with number of sherds in parentheses)/site numbers are:

Coll. 148(1)/LTAN-6; Colls. 191(7), 192(1)/LTAN-15; Coll. 355(3)/LTAN-18; Coll. 242(3)/LTAN-22; Coll. 214(8)/LTAN-34; Coll. 307(2)/LTAN-40; Coll. 319(5)/LTAN-47.

Chronological assessment: The variant of Bowl 1 with incurved walls is similar in form and paste to Early Suchimancillo Bowl 2a (Fig. 202) and Late Suchimancillo Bowl 1 (Fig. 211. The variant with straight walls is similar in form and paste to Early Tanguche Bowl 1 (Fig. 236) and Late Tambo Real Redware Bowl 2 (Fig. 279). Taken by itself, Late Tanguche Bowl 1 does not appear to be a reliable time marker for the period.

Inter-regional comparisons: See discussion under Early Tanguche Bowl 1.

Late Tanguche Bowl 2 (Fig. 258)

Number: 14 sherds, or ca. 2.2% of the Late Tanguche assemblage.

General description: Open bowl with outslanted walls that curve slightly inward. Rim diameters vary from 21-26 cm, with a mean of 23 cm and a standard deviation of 1.9 cm. Wall thickness below the rim ranges widely between 12 mm and 19 mm, with most of the sherds at the lower end of the range.

Paste: Temper consists uniformly of medium sand in moderate quantities. Paste color is red.

Surface characteristics: The interior surface below the rim is covered with heavily incised, crosshatched lines, indicating that bowls of this type probably were used for grating foodstuffs. Exteriors are plain redware.

Distribution: This bowl type has a limited, but fairly wide, distribution in habitation sites throughout the area of Late Tanguche occupation. Collection proveniences (with number of sherds in parentheses)/site numbers are:

Coll. 372(1)/LTAN-14; Coll. 242(4)/LTAN-22; Coll. 214(1)/LTAN-34; Coll. 307(1)/LTAN-40; Coll. 319(2)/LTAN-47; Coll. 288(5)/LTAN-53.

Chronological assessment: Judging from the analysis of single-component collections, this bowl type is a good diagnostic of Late Tanguche Period.

Inter-regional comparisons: Late Tanguche Bowl 2 is similar in form, size, and paste to Vessel Form 2 of the Castillo Plain type, a non-incised bowl primarily characteristic of the contemporaneous late Tomaval Period in Virú Valley (cf. Collier, p. 187, Fig. 63 C).

Late Tanguche Jar 1 (Fig. 258)

Number: 4 sherds, or ca. .7% of the Late Tanguche assemblage.

General description: Globular jar with a constricted mouth and interior thickened rim. Lips are either rounded or interior beveled. Rim diameters are 19 cm, 36 cm, 50 cm, and 50 cm. Wall thickness below the rim ranges between 8 and 11 mm.

Paste: Temper consists of medium sand in moderate quantities. Paste color is red.

Surface characteristics: Exterior and interior surfaces are plain redware.

Distribution: This jar type is present in three collections made at habitation sites in the Tanguche area of Late Tanguche Cluster 2. Collection proveniences (with number of sherds in parentheses)/site numbers are:

Coll. 355(1)/LTAN-18; Coll. 214(2)/LTAN-34; Coll. 338(1)/LTAN-42.

Chronological assessment: Jar 1 is similar in form and paste to some variants of Guadalupito Jar 1 (Fig. 225) and Early Tanguche Jar 1b (Fig. 236). In any case, its apparently limited distribution makes it of little value as a Late Tanguche diagnostic.

Inter-regional comparisons: See discussion under Guadalupito Jar 1.

Late Tanguche Jar 2a (Fig. 258)

Number: 69 sherds, or ca. 11.1% of the Late Tanguche assemblage.

General description: Globular jar with a low neck and flaring rim. Lips are rounded, and a few are also slightly everted. Rim diameters vary from 10-17 cm, with a mean of 13.2 cm and a standard deviation of 1.8 cm. Wall thickness below the rim ranges between 4 mm and 7 mm, with a mean of 5.6 mm.

Paste: Temper consists uniformly of medium sand in moderate

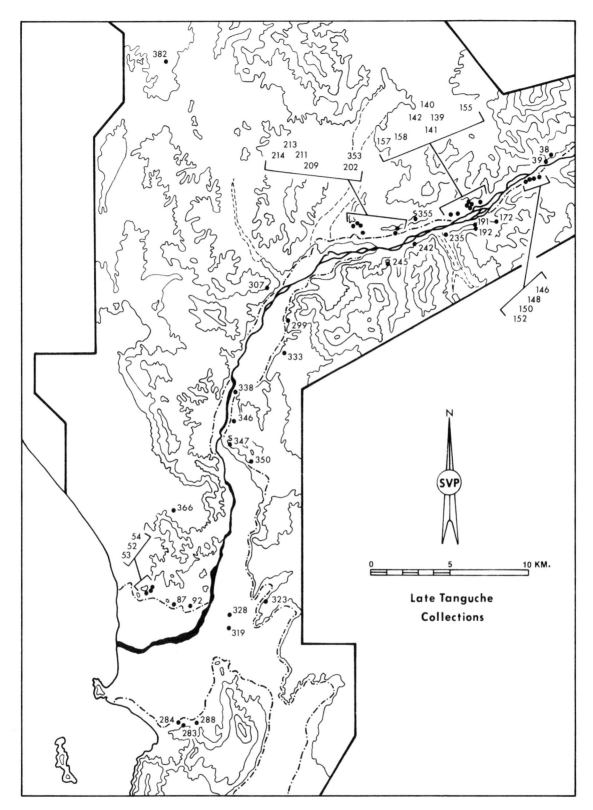

Fig. 257. Map showing collection proveniences of Late Tanguche
Period (Tomaval/Late Middle Horizon).

491

492

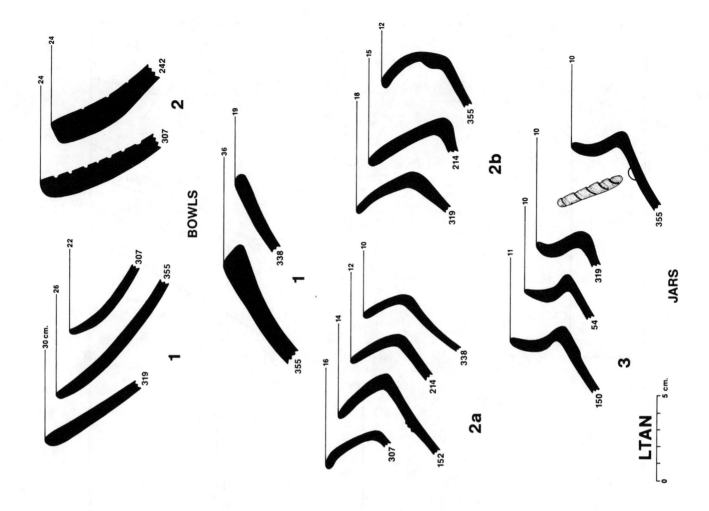

Fig. 258. Late Tanguche Period ceramics: Bowls 1 and 2; Jars 1, 2a, 2b, and 3.

quantities. Paste color is red, with gray cores noted on 15% of the sherds in the sample.

Surface characteristics: The exterior shoulder of 10% of the sherds has raised circle-and-dot designs (e.g., see Figs. 260, 261). The remainder of the sherds have plain exterior and interior redware surfaces.

Distribution: This jar type has a wide distribution in habitation, habitation-cemetery, and cemetery sites throughout the area of Late Tanguche occupation. Collection proveniences (with number of sherds in parentheses)/site numbers are:

Coll. 146(1)/LTAN-5; Coll. 148(1)/LTAN-6; Colls. 191(1), 192(1)/ LTAN-15; Coll. 242(9)/LTAN-22; Coll. 213(2)/LTAN-33; Coll. 214(13)/ LTAN-34; Coll. 307(3)/LTAN-40; Coll. 338(4)/LTAN-42; Coll. 319(5)/ LTAN-47; Coll. 87(1)/LTAN-49; Coll. 52(1)/LTAN-51; Coll. 53(5)/LTAN-52; Coll. 288(5)/LTAN-53; Colls. 283(15), 284(2)/LTAN-54.

Chronological assessment: Jar 2a is similar in form and paste to some variants of Early Tambo Real Redware Jar 4a (Fig. 271), but can be distinguished from the later vessel on the basis of its consistently flared, thin-walled rim.

Inter-regional comparisons: The decorated Jar 2a and Jar 2b sherds are similar to raised circle-and-dot vessels from Nepeña (cf. Proulx 1973, p. 253, Pl. 10) and Casma (cf. Collier 1960:416). The plain redware variants of the two jar forms are similar in form, size, and paste to Vessel Form 7 of the Rubia Plain type, a Virú Valley ware that begins in late Tomaval and continues through the Late Horizon Estero Period (cf. Collier 1955, p. 166, Fig. 54 G).

Late Tanguche Jar 2b (Fig. 258)

Number: 52 sherds, or ca. 8.4% of the Late Tanguche assemblage.

General description: Globular jar with a neck of medium height and a slightly or strongly flared rim. Lips are rounded. Rim diameters vary from 12-17 cm, with a mean of 14 cm and a standard deviation of 2.1 cm. Wall thickness below the rim ranges between 5 mm and 7 mm, with the majority of sherds at the lower end of the range.

Paste: Temper consists uniformly of medium sand in moderate quantities. Paste color is red, with gray cores noted on about 20% of the sherds.

Surface characteristics: The exterior juncture between the neck and the body is decorated with raised circle-and-dot designs on 50% of the sherds in the sample (e.g., see Figs. 260, 261). The remaining sherds appear to have had plain exterior surfaces, although some rim sherds were too fragmentary to indicate whether raised circle-and-dot design was placed around the shoulder.

Distribution: Late Tanguche Jar 2b has a wide distribution in habitation and cemetery sites throughout the area of Late Tanguche occupation. Collection proveniences (with number of sherds in parentheses)/site numbers are:

Coll. 148(1)/LTAN-6; Coll. 152(2)/LTAN-8; Coll. 142(5)/LTAN-13; Coll. 172(2)/LTAN-14; Coll. 355(3)/LTAN-18; Coll. 242(3)/LTAN-22; Coll. 214(5)/LTAN-34; Coll. 319(1)/LTAN-47; Coll. 54(1)/LTAN-50; Coll. 52(3)/ LTAN-51; Coll. 53(2)/LTAN-52; Coll. 288(24)/LTAN-53.

Chronological assessment: Like Late Tanguche Jar 2a, this jar type is similar in form and paste to Early Tambo Real Redware Jar 4a (Fig. 271). It can be distinguished, however, on the basis of its consistently higher neck and thinner walls.

Inter-regional comparisons: See Late Tanguche Jar 2a.

Late Tanguche Jar 3 (Fig. 258)

Number: 87 sherds, or ca. 14% of the Late Tanguche assemblage.

General description: Globular jar with a low, bulging neck. In profile, sherds have either medial or high thickening. The upper interior on the first of these two neck types is nearly vertical, while the upper interior on the second type is consistently curved along with, or parallel to, the exterior surface. Rim diameters vary from 10-18 cm, with a mean of 12.1 cm and a standard deviation of 2.4 cm. Wall thickness below the rim ranges between 4 mm and 7 mm, with a mean of 5.6 mm.

Paste: Temper consists uniformly of medium sand in moderate quantities. Paste color is red, with gray cores noted on 15% of the sherds.

Surface characteristics: The exterior shoulder on 25% of the sherds is decorated with either raised circle-and-dot design or zoned stippled design (for an example of the latter, see Fig. 259, redware details - left). The remaining sherds appear to have had plain redware surfaces.

Distribution: This jar type is widely distributed in habitation, habitation-cemetery, and cemetery sites throughout the area of Late Tanguche occupation. Collection proveniences (with number of sherds in parentheses)/site numbers are:

Coll. 150(1)/LTAN-7; Coll. 157(5)/LTAN-16; Coll. 355(6)/LTAN-18; Coll. 242(3)/LTAN-22; Coll. 353(1)/LTAN-23; Coll. 202(4)/LTAN-24; Coll. 211(1)/LTAN-32; Coll. 214(10)/LTAN-34; Coll. 299(4)/LTAN-41; Coll. 338(2)/LTAN-42; Coll. 319(3)/LTAN-47; Coll. 54(7)/LTAN-50; Coll. 288(33)/ LTAN-53; Colls. 283(5), 284(2)/LTAN-54.

Chronological assessment: A few variants of Late Tanguche Jar 3 are similar in form to Early Tanguche Jar 3 (Fig. 237), but, in general, the two jar types can be distinguished easily. In addition, the variants of Jar 3 with high exterior thickening on the neck are similar to Early Tambo Real Redware Jar 3 (Fig. 271). However, the Late Tanguche variants have smoothly incurved surfaces on the upper interior of the vessel, rather than the nearly vertical upper interior that characterizes the Early Tambo Real Redware vessels.

Inter-regional comparisons: The decorated Jar 3 sherds are similar to raised circle-and-dot vessels from Nepeña (cf. Proulx 1973,

p. 253, Pl. 10) and to Casma Incised (cf. Collier 1960:416). The plain redware sherds are very similar to the non-cambered variants of Vessel Form 6 of the Virú Valley Rubia Plain type (cf. Collier 1955, p. 166, Fig. 54 F).

Late Tanguche Jar 4a (Fig. 259)

Number: 29 sherds, or ca. 4.7% of the Late Tanguche assemblage.

General description: Globular jar with a distinctive short neck that has a vertical lower half, an upper half that flares strongly outward, and a vertical or slightly incurved lip. Rim diameters vary from 10-16 cm, with about 75% of the sherds at the lower end of the range. Wall thickness below the rim ranges narrowly between 5 mm and 6 mm.

Paste: Temper consists uniformly of medium sand in moderate quantities. Paste color is red.

Surface characteristics: Most sherds in the sample have either appliqued incised scallops around the exterior of the rim and/or raised circle-and-dot designs on the shoulder (e.g., see Fig. 260, upper - left).

Distribution: This jar type has a wide, but very limited, distribution in habitation and cemetery sites throughout the area of Late Tanguche occupation. Collection proveniences (with number of sherds in parentheses)/site numbers are:

Coll. 142(1)/LTAN-13; Coll. 192(5)/LTAN-15; Coll. 355(5)/LTAN-18; Coll. 307(15)/LTAN-40; Coll. 53(3)/LTAN-52.

Chronological assessment: Judging from the analysis of single-component collections, Jar 4a is a good diagnostic of the Late Tanguche Period.

Inter-regional comparisons: Late Tanguche Jars 4a and 4b are both similar in decorative technique to the raised circle-and-dot type of Nepeña (cf. Proulx 1973, p. 253, Pl. 10) and to Casma Incised (cf. Collier 1960:416). Both jar types have neck forms that are roughly similar to the cambered variant of Rubia Plain Vessel Form 7, a Virú Valley type that first appears in late Tomaval (cf. Collier 1955, p. 166, Fig. 54 G - center).

Late Tanguche Jar 4b (Fig. 259)

Number: 76 sherds, or ca. 12.3% of the Late Tanguche assemblage.

General description: Globular jar with a distinctive neck of medium height that has a roughly vertical lower half, an upper half that flares strongly outward, and a vertical lip. In contrast to the simple vertical lower neck area of Late Tanguche Jar 4a, however, the lower half of the neck on Jar 4b exhibits at least three forms--including (1) slightly insloping, (2) cambered, and (3) a very short vertical section with a broad flared section above it. Rim diameters vary from 10-14 cm, with a mean of 12 cm and a standard deviation of 1.4 cm. Wall thickness below the rim ranges between 4 mm and 7 mm, with a mean of 5 mm.

Paste: Temper consists uniformly of medium sand in moderate quantities. Paste color is red.

Surface characteristics: All of the sherds in the sample have raised circle-and-dot design on the vessel shoulder.

Distribution: This jar type has a wide distribution in habitation, habitation-cemetery, and cemetery sites throughout the area of Late Tanguche occupation. Collection proveniences (with number of sherds in parentheses)/site numbers are:

Coll. 150(8)/LTAN-7; Coll. 152(2)/LTAN-8; Coll. 142(7)/LTAN-13; Coll. 191(14)/LTAN-15; Coll. 158(3)/LTAN-16; Coll. 242(9)/LTAN-22; Coll. 353(1)/LTAN-23; Coll. 211(1)/LTAN-32; Coll. 213(2)/LTAN-33; Coll. 214(1)/LTAN-34; Coll. 299(6)/LTAN-41; Coll. 338(1)/LTAN-42; Coll. 350(14)/LTAN-44; Coll. 319(1)/LTAN-47; Coll. 382(6)/LTAN-56.

Chronological assessment: Judging from the analysis of single-component collections, Jar 4b is a good diagnostic of the Late Tanguche Period.

Inter-regional comparisons: See Late Tanguche Jar 4a.

Late Tanguche: Grayware (Fig. 259, lower; Fig. 262, upper; Fig. 263, upper - right)

Number: 20 sherds, or ca. 3.2% of the Late Tanguche assemblage.

General description: A small number of different grayware jar types are present in the Late Tanguche collections. Among these are the rim sherds and vessels illustrated here, including (1) the three jar fragments shown in profile in Fig. 259; (2) a grayware jar that is similar in form to Late Tanguche Jar 4b, with zoned incised and punctate design around the shoulder of the vessel (Fig. 262, upper); and (3) a jar that is similar in form to Jar 4b, with triangular zoning and stippled decoration (Fig. 263, upper - right).

Paste: Temper in the three rim profiles shown in Fig. 259 consists of coarse sand in moderate quantities, while the remaining vessels described above have medium sand in moderate quantities. Paste color is gray.

Surface characteristics: The three large utilitarian jars have coarse exterior and interior surfaces, with some pitting in places where bits of temper apparently fell off the surface of the vessels during the firing process. The smaller jars with zoned stippled designs were formed by pressmolding vessel halves, and then joining them before firing took place.

Distribution: Late Tanguche grayware has a wide, but limited, distribution in habitation and cemetery sites throughout the area of occupation. Collection proveniences (with number of sherds in parentheses)/site numbers are:

Colls. 140/155(1)/LTAN-11; Coll. 142(1)/LTAN-13; Coll. 355(2)/LTAN-18; Coll. 353(3)/LTAN-23; Coll. 202(4)/LTAN-24; Coll. 214(1)/LTAN-34; Coll. 92(3)/LTAN-48; Coll. 288(5)/LTAN-53.

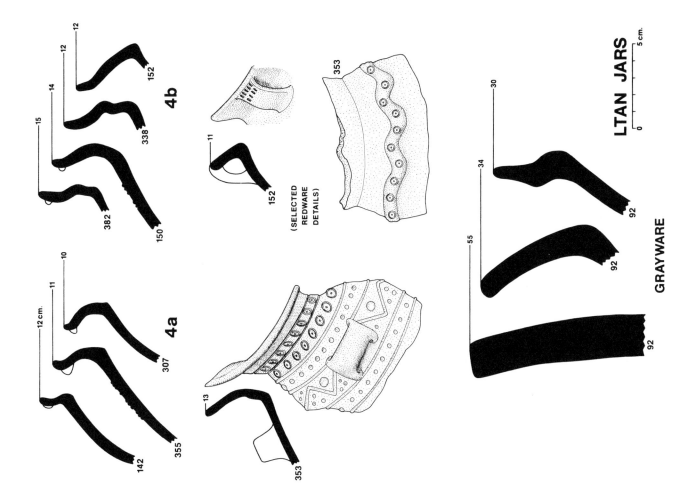

4b

4a

(SELECTED REDWARE DETAILS)

LTAN JARS

GRAYWARE

Fig. 259. Late Tanguche Period ceramics: Jars 4a, 4b, redware detail drawings, and profiles of selected grayware sherds.

Chronological assessment: The analysis of single-component Early Tanguche and Late Tanguche collections indicates that grayware is a minor, but increasingly significant, component in the period assemblages of the Lower Santa region (1.9% and 3.2% of the total assemblage of each period, respectively--compared to 38% in Early Tambo Real and 78.3% in Late Tambo Real).

Inter-regional comparisons: The three grayware sherds shown in Fig. 259 are similar in form, size, and paste to Vessel Shapes 2 and 3 of the Virú Plain type, illustrated in Strong and Evans (1952, p. 270, Fig. 42).

Late Tanguche: Raised Circle-and-Dot Decoration (Fig. 260; Fig. 261 a-p).

Number: 128+ sherds, or ca. 20%+ of the Late Tanguche assemblage.

General description: This decorated type is found in varying, small percentages on most of the jar types in the Late Tanguche collections, including Jars 2a, 2b, 3, 4a, and 4b. As shown in Figs. 260 and 261, the principal decorative element consists of a row of reed punched circles containing small punctate dots placed around the shoulder of a vessel, usually at the same level as the handles. Additional design elements include narrow dashed lines incised above and below the circle-and-dot motifs, as well as incised appliquéd scallops placed around the neck of the vessel. The punctate dots inside the circles were probably done separately, as they are not always placed in the same part of the circles. The circles themselves appear to have been made while the clay was still quite wet, as the process of making them forced the surrounding clay slightly above the surface of the vessel. Although not all vessels have circle-and-dot designs that rise above the surface (e.g., see those in Fig. 259, on Jars 4a and 4b), it is convenient to use the "raised circle-and-dot" designation to distinguish them from the unraised circle-and-dot motifs placed on polished reddish-brown bowls of the Early Horizon Period. It is of interest to note that the later circle-and-dot decoration is usually more sloppily executed than its much earlier counterpart.

Paste: Temper usually consists of medium grain sand in moderate quantities. Paste color is red.

Surface characteristics: Aside from the incised/circle-and-dot decoration, most jars appear to have had handles placed on opposite sides of the vessel at the shoulder. Handle types include horizontal straps (the most common), as well as notched and unnotched, vertical lugs similar to those found on vessels of the preceding Early Tanguche Period.

Distribution: This decorated type is found in habitation, habitation-cemetery, and cemetery sites throughout the area of Late Tanguche occupation. Separate collection proveniences (with number of sherds in parentheses)/site numbers for each of the major motif types shown in Fig. 261 are:

Fig. 261 a: Coll. 152(3)/LTAN-8; Colls. 140/155(1)/LTAN-11; Coll. 242(1)/LTAN-22; Coll. 307(1)/LTAN-40; Coll. 52(1)/LTAN-51.

Fig. 261 b: Coll. 242(1)/LTAN-22; Coll. 350(6)/LTAN-44; Coll. 54(3)/LTAN-50.

Fig. 261 c: Coll. 142(1)/LTAN-13; Coll. 242(1)/LTAN-22.

Fig. 261 d: Coll. 213(5)/LTAN-33; Coll. 214(1)/LTAN-34.

Fig. 261 e: Coll. 191(2)/LTAN-15.

Fig. 261 f: Coll. 299(4)/LTAN-41; Coll. 283(1)/LTAN-54.

Fig. 261 g: Coll. 158(1)/LTAN-16; Coll. 284(1)/LTAN-54.

Fig. 261 h: Coll. 350(4)/LTAN-44; Coll. 288(1)/LTAN-53.

Fig. 261 i: Coll. 39(1)/LTAN-4; Coll. 191(21)/LTAN-15; Coll. 235(2)/LTAN-17; Coll. 242(1)/LTAN-22; Coll. 202(4)/LTAN-24; Coll. 53(5)/LTAN-52.

Fig. 261 j: Colls. 140/155(1)/LTAN-11; Coll. 142(7)/LTAN-13; Coll. 355(2)/LTAN-18; Coll. 209(1)/LTAN-30.

Fig. 261 k: Coll. 146(4)/LTAN-5; Coll. 338(4)/LTAN-42.

Fig. 261 l: Coll. 53(1)/LTAN-52.

Fig. 261 m: Coll. 211(1)/LTAN-32.

Fig. 261 n: Coll. 355(1)/LTAN-18.

Fig. 261 o: Coll. 39(1)/LTAN-4; Coll. 209(2)/LTAN-30; Coll. 211(1)/LTAN-32.

Fig. 261 p: Coll. 192(5)/LTAN-15; Coll. 158(3)/LTAN-16; Coll. 288(21)/LTAN-53.

Chronological assessment: Judging from the analysis of single-component collections, raised circle-and-dot carries on as a general redware decorative motif into the Early Tambo Real Period (although in much smaller percentages of vessel types than in Late Tanguche Period). A number of features serve to differentiate vessels of the two periods that are decorated with this motif--including differences in (1) vessel form, (2) paste, and (3) the specific form of decorative motifs employed. For example, with regard to vessel form, Late Tanguche Jars 2b, 4a, and 4b do not appear to have Early Tambo Real redware counterparts. Late Tanguche Jar 3, one of the two remaining vessel forms, can be distinguished from many vessels of its Early Tambo Real Redware Jar 2 counterpart (see Fig. 271) on the basis of the lack of coarse black gravel inclusions that characterize the paste of the later type. The other vessel form of the earlier period, Late Tanguche Jar 2a, appears to be indistinguishable from some variants of its Early Tambo Real Redware Jar 4a counterpart (see Fig. 271), and is therefore of less utility in assessing chronology. A final distinguishing feature between the Late Tanguche and Early Tambo Real forms of raised circle-and-dot is that parallel and triangular, zoned incised lines are found only on vessels of the later period.

Inter-regional comparisons: To the author's knowledge, the only published illustrations of the raised circle-and-dot decorated type prior to the present report are found in Proulx (1973, Pl. 10, 15). In his discussion of the type, Proulx (1973:61) cites personal communications from Donald Thompson and Donald Collier that the southern limit of raised

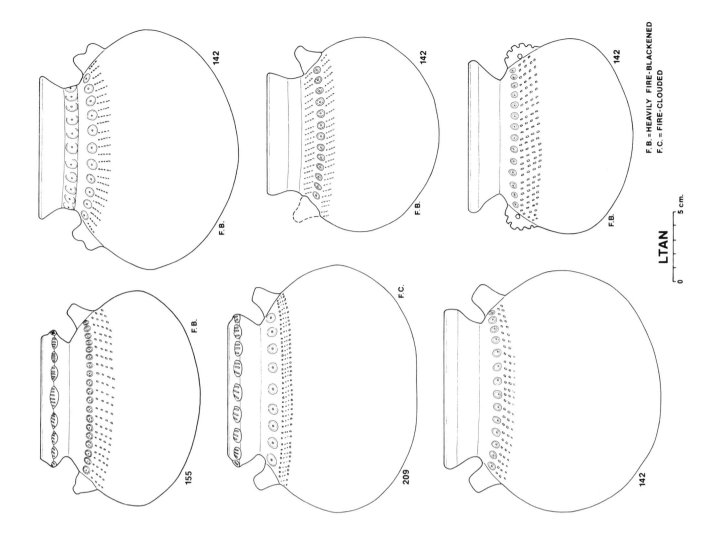

F.B.=HEAVILY FIRE-BLACKENED
F.C. = FIRE-CLOUDED

LTAN

0   5 cm.

Fig. 260. Late Tanguche Period ceramics: selected whole jars with incised and raised circle-and-dot design.

497

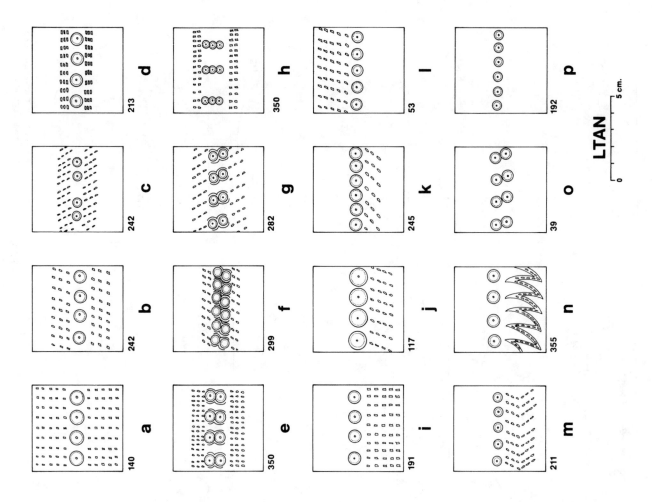

Fig. 261. Late Tanguche Period ceramics: schematic rectangles showing raised-incised and raised circle-and-dot design motifs.

circle-and-dot is the Huarmey Valley, south of Casma. Judging from our own work in the Lower Santa region, the northern range of the type is the Santa Valley proper as well as the Santa-Chao Desert, where raised circle-and-dot sherds were found sporadically along Early Tanguche rock-lined roads and at SVP-ETAN-321/SVP-LTAN-56, on Pampa de los Pancitos (see Figs. 134, 140). On visits to several major Chao Valley sites--including Cerro de la Cruz and Cerro Huasaquito--we did not find raised circle-and-dot sherds, nor is this type noted by the Virú Valley researchers.

vessels of the Lower Santa region is similar to that found on Virú Valley vessels of the San Nicolas Molded type (cf. Collier 1955, p. 173, Fig. 57). Judging from the author's study at Field Museum of collections made by Donald Collier and Donald Thompson in Casma, the Santa vessels are also similar to the San Diego Molded type of that valley.

Late Tanguche: Effigy Figures (Fig. 263)

Late Tanguche Period represents the beginning of a radical break in the trend toward gradually increasing percentage of human and animal effigy figures in the assemblages from Early Suchimancillo (.8%), Late Suchimancillo (2.8%), and Guadalupito (5.1%) through Early Tanguche (5.7%). The combined total of effigy representations, including depictions of both humans and animals, found on the surface of Late Tanguche sites is 5 (1 human and 4 animal figures), or ca. .8% of the total assemblage. The animal effigies include: (1) two appliquéd snakes on the shoulders of jars (proveniences are: Coll. 353/LTAN-23; Coll. 214/LTAN-34); and (2) two appliquéd bird heads on jar shoulders (Coll. 155/LTAN-11, illustrated in Fig. 263; Coll. 328/LTAN-46). The single human effigy, although from a mixed collection, has been dated to Late Tanguche because of the similarity of the exterior design to the pressmolded zoned stippled redware of this period (Fig. 263, lower - right).

Late Tanguche: Pressmolded Zoned Stippled Decoration (Fig. 262, center and lower; Fig. 263)

Number: 48+ sherds, or ca. 7.7%+ of the Late Tanguche assemblage.

General description: Pressmolded zoned stippled designs are present on several vessel types, including Late Tanguche Jars 2b and 4b. As indicated in the illustrations, they are placed either on the shoulder of a vessel or on its rounded bottom. However, on a few jars the main decorative features are confined to the shoulder, while a single raised fillet encircles the lowermost part of the vessel. Besides raised circle-and-dot decoration, this is the other major decorative type on Late Tanguche vessels.

Paste: Temper generally consists of medium sand in moderate quantities. Paste is usually red, although a few grayware vessels or vessel fragments are also present in the collections.

Surface characteristics: Although both the raised circle-and-dot and zoned stippled vessels probably were fabricated in pressmolded halves, the two decorated types differ in that the former were decorated with incised and punctate designs following the pressmolding process and the joining of the halves, while the latter were decorated as part of the "negative" designs placed on the molds themselves.

Distribution: This decorated type is found in habitation, habitation-cemetery, and cemetery sites throughout the area of Late Tanguche occupation. Collection proveniences (with number of sherds in parentheses)/site numbers are:

Coll. 146(1)/LTAN-5; Coll. 150(2)/LTAN-7; Coll. 152(1)/LTAN-8; Coll. 172(6)/LTAN-14; Colls. 140/155(3)/LTAN-15; Colls. 157(2), 158(6)/ LTAN-16; Coll. 242(2)/LTAN-22; Coll. 213(1)/LTAN-33; Coll. 307(1)/ LTAN-40; Coll. 350(5)/LTAN-44; Coll. 328(2)/LTAN-46; Coll. 319(1)/ LTAN-47; Coll. 54(2)/LTAN-50; Coll. 52(1)/LTAN-51; Coll. 288(5)/LTAN-53; Coll. 283(7)/LTAN-54.

Chronological assessment: Although pressmolded zoned stippled designs are present on Early Tanguche vessels, those of Late Tanguche Period can be distinguished on the basis of distinctive vessel forms, design motifs, as well as the placement of decorative features on the vessels. And, although very similar zoned stippling appears on Late Tambo Real Redware Jar 1 (Fig. 279), the Late Tanguche vessels can be distinguished on the basis of rim form.

Inter-regional comparisons: Zoned stippled decoration on redware

499

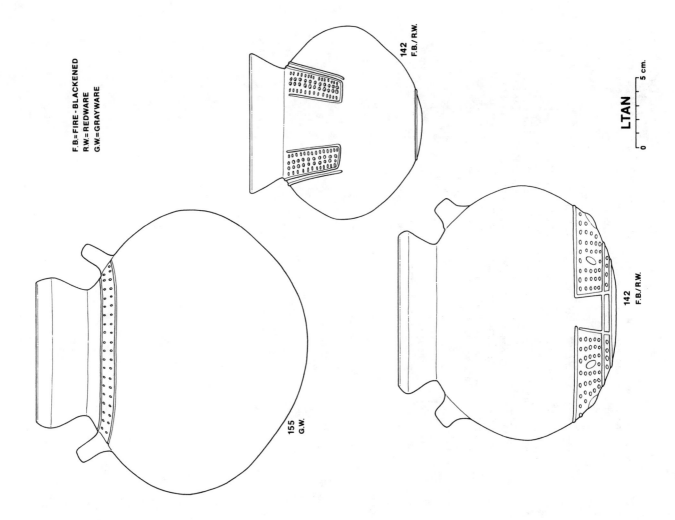

F.B.=FIRE-BLACKENED
R.W.=REDWARE
G.W.=GRAYWARE

LTAN

0 ___ 5 cm.

142
F.B./R.W.

155
G.W.

142
F.B./R.W.

Fig. 262. Late Tanguche Period ceramics: selected jars with incised and pressmolded design motifs.

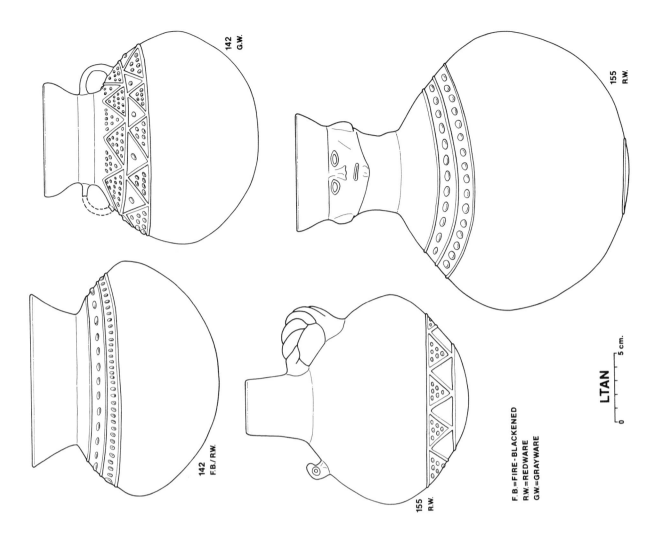

142
G.W.

155
R.W.

142
F.B./R.W.

155
R.W.

F.B.=FIRE-BLACKENED
R.W.=REDWARE
GW=GRAYWARE

LTAN

0 5 cm.

Fig. 263. Late Tanguche Period ceramics: selected jars with press-molded decoration.

501

EARLY TAMBO REAL PERIOD

Early Tambo Real Grayware Bowl 1 (Fig. 265)

Number: 6 sherds, or ca. .7% of the Early Tambo Real assemblage.

General description: Globular bowl with a slightly constricted mouth and rounded lip. Rim diameters vary from 11-18 cm, with most sherds at the upper end of the range. Wall thickness below the rim ranges narrowly between 5 mm and 6 mm.

Paste: Temper consists of fine or medium sand in moderate quantities. Paste color is gray.

Surface characteristics: Exterior and interior surfaces are plain, and range in color from gray to dull black.

Distribution: This bowl type has a wide, but limited, distribution in habitation, habitation-cemetery, and cemetery sites throughout the area of Early Tambo Real occupation. Collection proveniences (with number of sherds in parentheses)/site numbers are:

Colls. 114/117(2)/ETR-2; Coll. 231(1)/ETR-10; Coll. 202(1)/ETR-13; Coll. 322(1)/ETR-31; Coll. 267(1)/ETR-38.

Chronological assessment: Grayware Bowl 1 is a good general Tambo Real time marker, but is of little use as a specific diagnostic of Early Tambo Real Period since it is essentially indistinguishable from Late Tambo Real Grayware Bowl 1 (Fig. 274).

Inter-regional comparisons: Grayware bowls with slightly constricted mouths are not reported in the literature on contemporaneous ceramics of the areas adjacent to the Lower Santa region.

Early Tambo Real Grayware Bowl 2 (Fig. 265)

Number: 24 sherds, or ca. 2.7% of the Early Tambo Real assemblage.

General description: Open bowl with straight or very slightly incurving walls, and rounded lip. Rim diameters are either 24 cm (40% of the sherds in the sample) or 28 cm (60% of the sherds). Wall thickness below the rim ranges between 5 mm and 8 mm, with a mean of 6.7 mm.

Paste: Temper in approximately 75% of the sherds consists of fine or medium sand in moderate quantities. The remaining 25% of the sherds have medium grain black gravel temper in moderate quantities. Paste color is gray.

Surface characteristics: The exterior surface of one of the bowl fragments is highly polished. The remainder of the sherds have unpolished grayware interiors and exteriors.

Distribution: This bowl type has a wide, but limited, distribution in habitation and habitation-cemetery sites throughout the area of Early Tambo Real occupation. Collection proveniences (with number of sherds in parentheses)/site numbers are:

Coll. 12(2)/ETR-1; Coll. 242(1)/ETR-12; Colls. 246/247(1)/ETR-14; Coll. 296(10)/ETR-35; Coll. 268(3)/ETR-37; Coll. 281(5)/ETR-46; Coll. 270(2)/ETR-47.

Chronological assessment: Judging from the analysis of single-component collections, as well as from the lack of similar grayware counterparts in other periods, Grayware Bowl 2 is a good Early Tambo Real diagnostic.

Inter-regional comparisons: The single polished bowl fragment in this sample is similar in form and surface treatment to Vessel Form 1 of the Queneto Polished Plain type of Virú Valley (cf. Collier 1955, p. 158, Fig. 48). The unpolished grayware sherds are similar in form and paste to Vessel Form 2 of the Tomaval Plain type of Virú (cf. Collier 1955, p. 161, Fig. 50).

Early Tambo Real Grayware Bowl 3 (Fig. 265)

Number: 3 sherds, or ca. .3% of the Early Tambo Real assemblage.

General description: Open bowl with straight outslanted walls, and narrow everted rim with a slightly tapered and rounded lip. Rim diameters are 14 cm, 14 cm, and 18 cm. Wall thickness below the rim is 6 mm.

Paste: Temper consists of fine or medium sand in moderate quantities. Paste color is gray.

Surface characteristics: Interior and exterior surfaces are plain grayware.

Distribution: This bowl type has a very limited distribution in two habitation-cemetery sites and one cemetery. Collection proveniences (with number of sherds in parentheses)/site numbers are:

Coll. 148(1)/ETR-4; Coll. 319(1)/ETR-33; Coll. 268(1)/ETR-37.

Chronological assessment: Grayware Bowl 3 has no counterparts in other period assemblages, and therefore appears to be a good Early Tambo Real diagnostic. Its limited distribution lessens its utility as a good time marker, however.

Inter-regional comparisons: From ceramic materials excavated in La Plata and Estero levels in Virú Valley sites, Collier (1955, p. 161, Fig. 50 C) reports on bowls that are very similar in form, size, and paste to Early Tambo Real Grayware Bowl 3.

Early Tambo Real Grayware Jar 1 (Fig. 265)

Number: 2 sherds, or ca. .2% of the Early Tambo Real assemblage.

General description: Globular jar with a constricted mouth and interior thickened rim with interior beveled lip. Rim diameters are 40 cm. Wall thickness below the rim is 6 mm.

Paste: Temper consists of medium sand in moderate quantities. Paste color is gray.

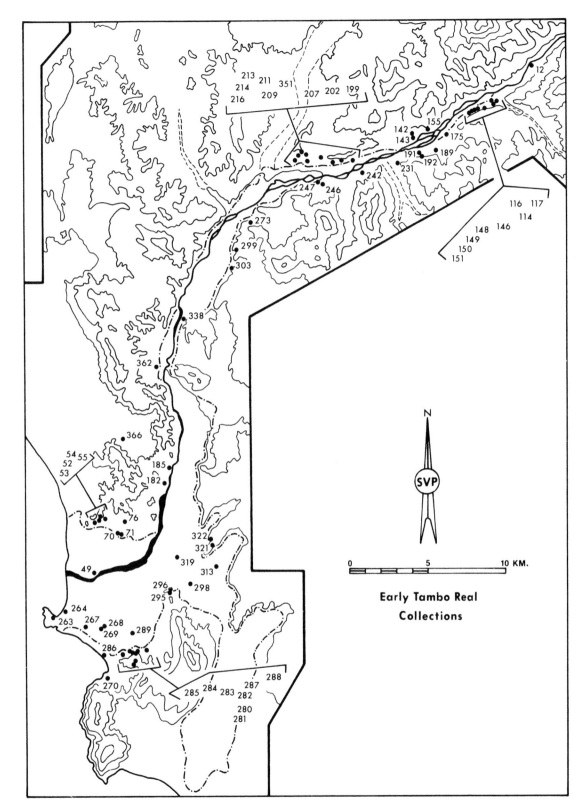

Fig. 264. Map showing collection proveniences of Early Tambo
Real Period (La Plata/Late Intermediate).

503

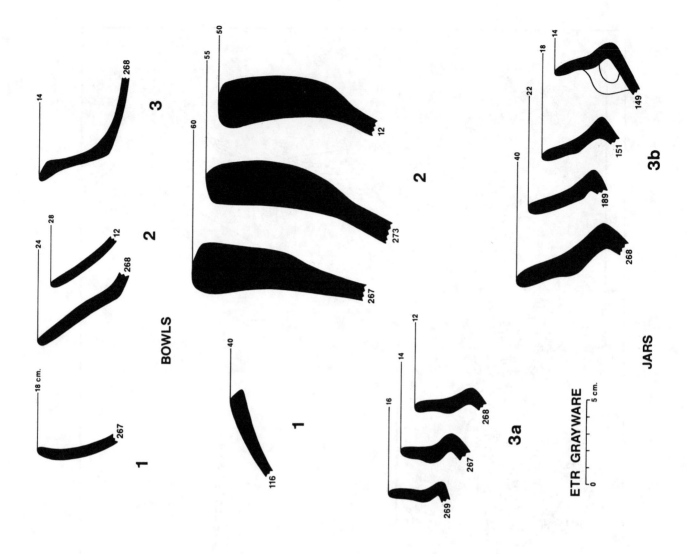

BOWLS

1

2

3

1

2

3a

3b

JARS

ETR GRAYWARE

0 — 5 cm.

Fig. 265. Early Tambo Real Period ceramics: Grayware Bowls 1, 2, and 3; Grayware Jars 1, 2, 3a, and 3b.

Surface characteristics: Exterior and interior surfaces are plain grayware.

Distribution: This jar type was found at only two habitation-cemetery sites. Collection proveniences (with number of sherds in parentheses)/site numbers are:

Coll. 12(1)/ETR-1; Coll. 288(1)/ETR-43.

Chronological assessment: Grayware Jar 1 has too limited a distribution to be useful as an Early Tambo Real diagnostic, but in any case can be distinguished from the symmetrically-thickened rim of its Late Tambo Real Grayware Jar 4 counterpart (Fig. 277) on the basis of a consistently interior thickened rim.

Inter-regional comparisons: Grayware neckless ollas of similar form and size are among the vessel shapes of the Estero Plain type of Virú Valley (cf. Collier 1955, p. 165, Fig. 53 B).

Early Tambo Real Grayware Jar 2 (Fig. 265)

Number: 10 sherds, or ca. 1.1% of the Early Tambo Real assemblage.

General description: Large ovoid jar with an interior thickened vertical neck. Lips are exterior beveled, interior beveled, or roughly horizontal. Rim diameters are either 45 cm (5 sherds) or 55 cm (5 sherds). Wall thickness below the rim ranges widely between 8 mm and 13 mm, with a mean of 11.2 mm.

Paste: Temper in four of the sherds consists of medium sand in heavy quantities, while temper in the other six consists of coarse black gravel in moderate quantities. Paste color is gray.

Surface characteristics: Exterior and interior surfaces are very coarse, with some pitting as well as patches in which coarse or heavy amounts of temper are visible. Some sherds are very friable, and crumbled at the edges when transported in collection bags.

Distribution: Sherds of this type are usually very large and thick, and consequently were difficult to retrieve and carry in properly representative quantities--not least because of often difficult survey logistics involving round hikes of 5-15+ km to and from the vehicle. Thus, this vessel form not only has a wider distribution than indicated here, but is also present in greater relative quantities in a given spot on a site where collections were made. In any case, Grayware Jar 2 has a generally wide distribution in habitation sites throughout most of the area of Early Tambo Real occupation. Collection proveniences (with number of sherds in parentheses)/site numbers are:

Coll. 12(1)/ETR-1; Colls. 191/192(3)/ETR-8; Coll. 273(3)/ETR-20; Coll. 267(1)/ETR-38; Coll. 286(2)/ETR-45.

Chronological assessment: Large utilitarian/storage vessels similar to this jar type probably begin to appear in the Lower Santa region as early as the Late Tanguche Period, continuing on through at least to the end of the sequence.

Inter-regional comparisons: Although this specific rim form is not present among the principal vessel shapes illustrated for Virú Plain, Early Tambo Real Grayware Jar 2 is clearly related in overall size, wall thickness, and paste to this Virú Valley type (cf. Strong and Evans 1952, p. 270, Fig. 42).

Early Tambo Real Grayware Jar 3a (Fig. 265)

Number: 42 sherds, or ca. 4.6% of the Early Tambo Real assemblage.

General description: Globular jar with a low, vertical cambered neck. Rim diameters vary from 9-17 cm, with a mean of 11.2 cm and a standard deviation of 1.8 cm. Wall thickness below the rim ranges between 5 mm and 7 mm.

Paste: Temper consists uniformly of medium sand in moderate quantities. Paste color is gray.

Surface characteristics: Vertical strap handles similar to that illustrated on a Grayware Jar 3b sherd (Fig. 265) are present on two of the sherds in the sample. Exterior and interior surfaces on all sherds are plain grayware.

Distribution: This jar type has a wide distribution in habitation, habitation-cemetery, and cemetery sites throughout the area of Early Tambo Real occupation. Collection proveniences (with number of sherds in parentheses)/site numbers are:

Coll. 12(1)/ETR-1; Coll. 150(2)/ETR-5; Colls. 191/192(2)/ETR-8; Coll. 209(1)/ETR-15; Coll. 216(2)/ETR-19; Coll. 55(1)/ETR-27; Coll. 322(3)/ETR-31; Coll. 321(1)/ETR-32; Coll. 298(1)/ETR-34; Colls. 268(6), 269(2)/ETR-37; Coll. 267(2)/ETR-38; Coll. 264(6)/ETR-41; Coll. 282(1)/ETR-43; Coll. 285(3)/ETR-44; Coll. 286(6)/ETR-45.

Chronological assessment: Grayware Jar 3a is similar in form and paste to Late Tambo Real Grayware Jar 2b (Fig. 275), but is generally distinguishable on the basis of a thicker and more rounded exterior camber, as well as by the slight tapering on the neck above the camber.

Inter-regional comparisons: Early Tambo Real Grayware Jars 3a and 3b are very similar in size, rim form, and paste to Vessel Form 4 of the Tomaval Plain type of Virú Valley (cf. Collier 1955, p. 161, Fig. 50 D).

Early Tambo Real Grayware Jar 3b (Fig. 265)

Number: 10 sherds, or ca. .9% of the Early Tambo Real assemblage.

General description: Globular jar with a cambered, outslanted neck of medium height. Rim diameters vary from 16-40 cm, with a mean of about 19 cm. Wall thickness below the rim ranges between 5 mm and 8 mm, with all but one sherd at the lower end of the range.

Paste: Temper consists uniformly of medium sand in moderate quantities. Paste color is gray.

Surface characteristics: Exterior and interior surfaces are plain grayware.

Distribution: This jar type has a fairly wide, but limited, distribution in habitation, habitation-cemetery, and cemetery sites throughout the area of Early Tambo Real occupation. Collection proveniences (with number of sherds in parentheses)/site numbers are:

Colls. 149(2), 151(4)/ETR-5; Coll. 189(2)/ETR-7; Coll. 319(1)/ETR-33; Coll. 268(1)/ETR-37.

Chronological assessment: Grayware Jar 3b is similar in form and paste to some variants of Late Tambo Real Grayware Jar 2c (Fig. 275), but can be distinguished on the basis of several neck features including greater height and thicker walls which are consistently outslanted.

Inter-regional comparisons: See Early Tambo Real Grayware Jar 3a.

Early Tambo Real Grayware Jar 4a (Fig. 266)

Number: 34 sherds, or ca. 3.7% of the Early Tambo Real assemblage.

General description: Globular jar with a low flared neck. Lips on some sherds are either tapered or slightly everted. Rim diameters vary from 8-16 cm, with a mean of 11.8 cm and a standard deviation of 2 cm. Wall thickness below the rim ranges between 5 mm and 10 mm, with a mean of 6.1 mm and a standard deviation of 1.2 mm.

Paste: Temper consists uniformly of medium sand in moderate quantities. Paste color is gray.

Surface characteristics: A wide strap handle with decoration consisting of appliquéd elliptical nodes is present on one of the sherds (e.g., see perspective detail in Fig. 266, lower - left). The remaining sherds in the sample have plain exterior and interior surfaces.

Distribution: This jar type has a wide distribution in habitation, habitation-cemetery, and cemetery sites throughout most of the area of Early Tambo Real occupation. Collection proveniences (with number of sherds in parentheses)/site numbers are:

Coll. 12(1)/ETR-1; Coll. 149(1)/ETR-5; Coll. 142(2)/ETR-9; Coll. 231(9)/ETR-10; Coll. 199(1)/ETR-11; Coll. 242(1)/ETR-12; Coll. 214(1)/ETR-18; Coll. 273(1)/ETR-20; Coll. 182(1)/ETR-25; Coll. 53(3)/ETR-29; Coll. 321(1)/ETR-32; Coll. 319(1)/ETR-33; Coll. 298(5)/ETR-34; Coll. 296(6)/ETR-35.

Chronological assessment: Grayware Jar 4a is similar in form and paste to some variants of Late Tambo Real Grayware Jar 3a (Fig. 276), but can be distinguished generally on the basis of several neck features including its thicker and more strongly flared walls, and by the lack of an exterior ridge at the juncture of the body and neck.

Inter-regional comparisons: Although Early Tambo Real Grayware Jars 4a, 4b, and 4c are strikingly similar in form and paste to both Vessel Form 6 of Tomaval Plain and Vessel Form 4 of Estero Plain, they appear to be more closely analogous to the latter vessel in overall size and mean rim diameter (cf. Collier 1955, p. 161, Fig. 50 F; and p. 165, Fig. 53 D).

Early Tambo Real Grayware Jar 4b (Fig. 266)

Number: 26 sherds, or ca. 2.9% of the Early Tambo Real assemblage.

General description: Globular jar with a flared neck of medium height. Rim diameters vary from 6-14 cm, with a mean of 10.6 cm and a standard deviation of 2.2 cm. Wall thickness below the rim ranges between 5 mm and 8 mm, with a mean of 6.8 mm.

Paste: Temper consists uniformly of medium sand in moderate quantities. Paste color is gray.

Surface characteristics: Exterior and interior surfaces are plain grayware.

Distribution: This jar type is widely distributed in habitation and cemetery sites throughout most of the area of Early Tambo Real occupation. Collection proveniences (with number of sherds in parentheses)/site numbers are:

Coll. 146(3)/ETR-3; Coll. 148(2)/ETR-4; Coll. 151(1)/ETR-5; Colls. 191/192(1)/ETR-8; Colls. 142(2), 155(1)/ETR-9; Colls. 246/247(4)/ETR-14; Coll. 211(1)/ETR-16; Coll. 213(1)/ETR-17; Coll. 214(5)/ETR-18; Coll. 55(1)/ETR-27; Coll. 321(1)/ETR-32; Coll. 263(3)/ETR-42.

Chronological assessment: Grayware Jar 4b is similar in form and paste to Late Tambo Real Grayware Jar 3b (Fig. 276), but generally can be distinguished on the basis of (1) its more consistently curved neck (in contrast to the usually vertical neck of the later jar), and (2) the lack of an exterior ridge at the juncture of the neck and the body.

Inter-regional comparisons: See Early Tambo Real Grayware Jar 4a.

Early Tambo Real Grayware Jar 4c (Fig. 266)

Number: 11 sherds, or ca. 1.2% of the Early Tambo Real assemblage.

General description: Globular jar with a tall vertical neck and flared rim. Lips are rounded and sometimes tapered. Most sherds in the sample have a rounded exterior ridge at the juncture of the neck and the body. Rim diameters vary from 12-15 cm, with a mean of 13.1 cm and a standard deviation of 1.1 cm. Wall thickness below the rim ranges between 6 mm and 7 mm.

Paste: Temper consists uniformly of medium sand in moderate quantities. Paste color is gray.

Surface characteristics: One sherd has incised circle-and-dot design around the exterior ridge. The remaining sherds have plain exterior and interior grayware surfaces.

Distribution: This jar type has a wide, but limited, distribution in habitation sites throughout most of the area of Early Tambo Real occupation. Collection proveniences (with number of sherds in parentheses)/site numbers are:

Coll. 114/117(1)/ETR-2; Coll. 189(2)/ETR-7; Colls. 191/192(2)/ETR-8; Coll. 214(3)/ETR-18; Coll. 273(1)/ETR-20; Coll. 49(2)/ETR-30.

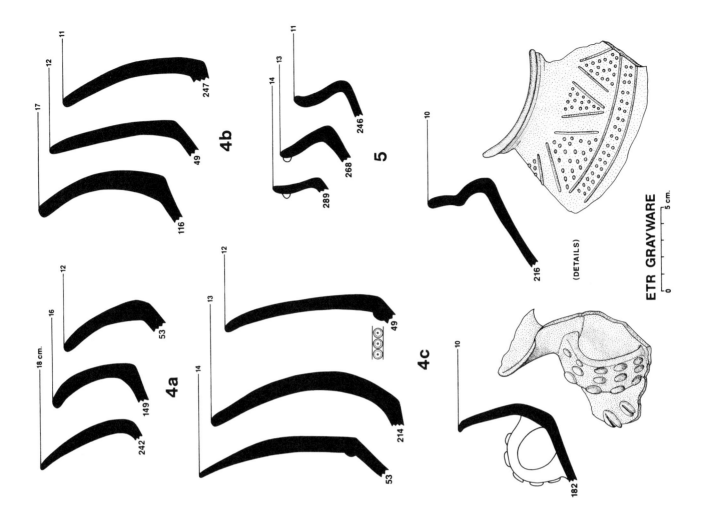

Fig. 266. Early Tambo Real Period ceramics: Grayware Jars 4a, 4b, 4c, 5, and detail drawings.

507

Chronological assessment: Grayware Jar 4c is similar in form and paste to Late Tambo Real Grayware Jars 3c and 3d (Fig. 276), but can be distinguished on the basis of a neck height which is consistently intermediate between the neck heights of the later jar forms.

Inter-regional comparisons: See Early Tambo Real Grayware Jar 4a.

Early Tambo Real Grayware Jar 5 (Fig. 266)

Number: 52 sherds, or ca. 5.8% of the Early Tambo Real assemblage.

General description: Globular jar with an everted, incurving rim. Rim diameters vary from 7-14 cm, with a mean of 12.7 cm and a standard deviation of 1.8 cm. Wall thickness below the rim ranges between 4 mm and 5.8 mm.

Paste: Temper consists uniformly of medium sand in moderate quantities. Paste color is gray.

Surface characteristics: The following exterior decorative features are present in the sample: (1) exterior scallops (most sherds have this feature; see Fig. 268, center - left, for an example of scallops); (2) incised designs on vessel shoulders (two sherds); (3) vertical strap handle (one sherd); and (4) horizontal strap handle on shoulder of a vessel (one sherd).

Distribution: This jar type was found widely distributed in habitation, habitation-cemetery, and cemetery sites throughout the area of Early Tambo Real occupation. Collection proveniences (with number of sherds in parentheses)/site numbers are:

Colls. 12(1)/ETR-1; Colls. 114/117(7)/ETR-2; Coll. 149(3)/ETR-5; Colls. 246/247(1)/ETR-14; Coll. 211(1)/ETR-16; Coll. 216(1)/ETR-19; Colls. 70/71(2)/ETR-26; Coll. 55(2)/ETR-27; Coll. 54(1)/ETR-28; Coll. 49(3)/ETR-30; Coll. 321(1)/ETR-32; Coll. 319(6)/ETR-33; Coll. 296(6)/ETR-35; Coll. 289(1)/ETR-36; Coll. 268(9)/ETR-37; Coll. 267(2)/ETR-38; Coll. 264(2)/ETR-41; Coll. 285(3)/ETR-44.

Chronological assessment: Judging from the analysis of single-component collections, Grayware Jar 5 is a good Early Tambo Real time marker, although it may be noted that it seems clearly to have developmental antecedents in two redware jar types, including Early Tanguche Jar 3 and Late Tanguche Jar 3.

Inter-regional comparisons: This jar type appears to be related in form, size, and most exterior decorative features to Vessel Form 4 of the San Juan Molded type of Virú Valley (cf. Collier 1955, p. 171, Fig. 56 D).

Early Tambo Real: Miscellaneous Grayware Vessels (Fig. 267; Fig. 268; Fig. 269; Fig. 270, center and lower)

Among the miscellaneous grayware vessels found in Early Tambo Real contexts, and illustrated here, are the following (listed in order of appearance in the drawings): (1) three jars with necks that have distinctive interior and exterior horizontal finishing marks (Fig. 267; Notes: the upper vessel, with the appliquéd snake on its shoulder, has the form of a squash; the center vessel has raised circle-and-dot decoration; the lower vessel has flattened sides that are roughly half as far apart as the two ends shown in the drawing); (2) two sherds with exterior incising at the rim (Fig. 268, top row); (3) a neck fragment with incised appliquéd scallops around the lower part of the neck, raised circle-and-dot motif on the shoulder, and thick rounded handles (Fig. 268, center - left; Note: the elliptically-shaped appliquéd nodes appear to be a good Early Tambo Real diagnostic, and serve to distinguish handles of this period from the strap handles with a tapered notched spine of Late Tambo Real, shown in Fig. 276); (4) a neck fragment with strap handles of unusual shape and punctate design on the rounded exterior ridge (Fig. 268, lower - left); (5) fragments of vessels with spouts (Fig. 268, center - right and lower - right; note the similarity between the animal effigy handle shown here and that on the Late Tambo Real vessel in Fig. 280, top - left); (6) two spout-and-handle vessels with the same spout and body forms (Fig. 269; Note: the appliquéd animals shown on the upper vessel seem clearly to be placed in the position of supplicants); (7) an animal effigy jar with appliquéd head, wings, and tail (Fig. 270, center - left); and (8) an unusual jar combining several of the diagnostics of Early Tambo Real Period mentioned above, including abstract animal effigies in supplicatory positions and a strap handle with elliptically-shaped appliquéd nodes (Fig. 270, bottom - right; Note: the sharp ridge on the shoulder is similar to that found on Early Tanguche Jar 5, a redware type).

Early Tambo Real Redware Redware Bowl 1 (Fig. 271)

Number: 20 sherds, or ca. 2.2% of the Early Tambo Real assemblage.

General description: Open bowl with outslanted and very slightly incurved walls. Rim diameters vary from 18-30 cm, with a mean of 24.8 cm and a standard deviation of 3.5 cm. Wall thickness below the rim ranges widely between 6 mm and 12 mm--with most of the sherds at the lower end of the range, between 6 mm and 7 mm.

Paste: Temper in approximately 55% of the sherds consists of medium black gravel in moderate amounts. The other 45% have medium sand in moderate quantities.

Surface characteristics: Two of the sherds have deeply incised crosshatching on the interior, probably indicating they were used as grater bowls. The remaining sherds have plain exterior and interior redware surfaces.

Distribution: This bowl type has a wide, but limited, distribution in habitation sites throughout most of the area of Early Tambo Real occupation. Collection proveniences (with number of sherds in parentheses)/site numbers are:

Coll. 242(2)/ETR-12; Colls. 246/247(1)/ETR-14; Colls. 70/71(1)/ETR-26; Coll. 319(5)/ETR-33; Coll. 296(1)/ETR-35; Coll. 282(2)/ETR-43; Coll. 281(6)/ETR-46; Coll. 270(2)/ETR-47.

Chronological assessment: Since the use of coarse black gravel

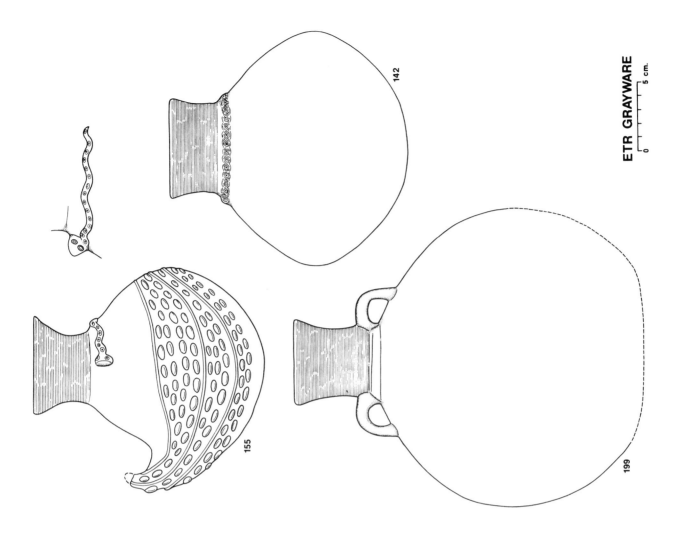

ETR GRAYWARE

0 ⊢———⊣ 5 cm.

142

155

199

Fig. 267. Early Tambo Real Period ceramics: selected grayware jars.

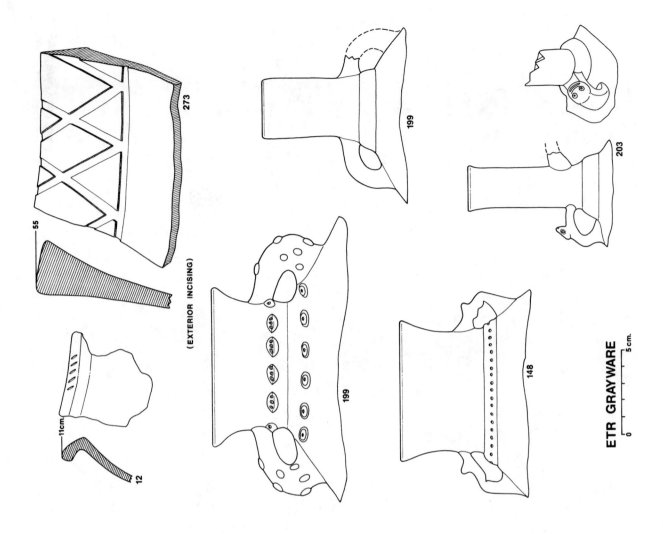

ETR GRAYWARE

0 ___ 5 cm.

Fig. 268. Early Tambo Real Period ceramics: miscellaneous grayware sherds.

510

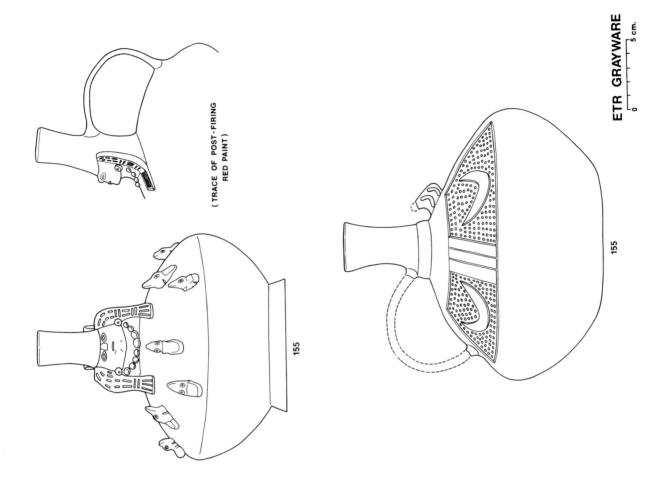

(TRACE OF POST-FIRING
RED PAINT)

155

155

ETR GRAYWARE

0   5 cm.

155

Fig. 269. Early Tambo Real Period ceramics: pressmolded gray-ware spout-and-handle jars with appliquéd, modeled, and stippled decoration.

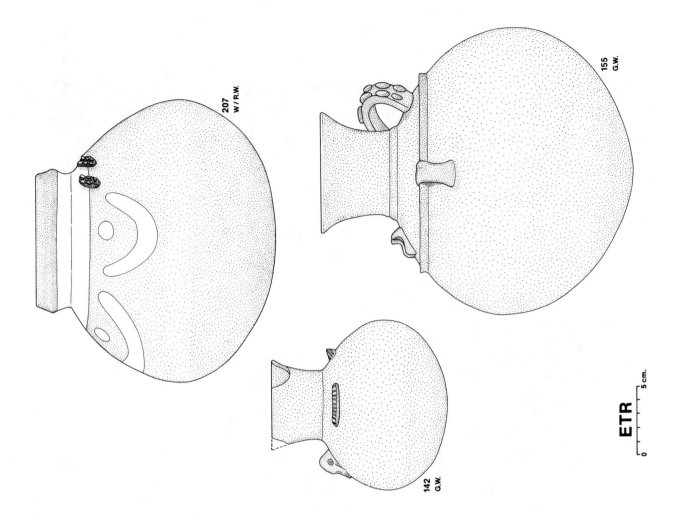

512

Fig. 270. Early Tambo Real Period ceramics: selected redware and grayware jars.

temper appears to be confined to the Early and Late Tambo Real Periods, and since Bowl 1 has no counterpart in the redware bowl forms of Late Tambo Real, this type appears to be a good time marker for Early Tambo Real.

Inter-regional comparisons: Early Tambo Real Redware Bowls 1, 2, and 3 are roughly similar in form and size to Vessel Form 3 of the Rubia Plain type of Virú Valley (cf. Collier 1955, p. 166, Fig. 54 C).

Early Tambo Real Redware Bowl 2 (Fig. 271)

Number: 10 sherds, or ca. 1.1% of the Early Tambo Real assemblage.

General description: Open bowl with straight outslanted walls and a narrow flaring rim. Rim diameters vary from 20-24 cm, with 75% of the sherds in the sample at the upper end of the range. Wall thickness below the rim is uniformly 6 mm.

Paste: Temper consists of medium sand in moderate quantities, with most of the sherds having light amounts of black gravel inclusions as well. Paste color is red.

Surface characteristics: Interior and exterior surfaces are plain redware.

Distribution: This bowl type has a very limited distribution in habitation sites located primarily in the Lower Valley sector. Collection proveniences (with number of sherds in parentheses)/site numbers are:

Coll. 12(1)/ETR-1; Colls. 70/71(1)/ETR-26; Coll. 321(2)/ETR-32; Coll. 268(6)/ETR-37.

Chronological assessment: Judging from the diagnostically late black gravel inclusions, as well as from the lack of a corresponding redware bowl form in Late Tambo Real, Bowl 2 is a good Early Tambo Real time marker.

Inter-regional comparisons: See Early Tambo Real Redware Bowl 1.

Early Tambo Real Redware Bowl 3 (Fig. 271)

Number: 3 sherds, or ca. .3% of the Early Tambo Real assemblage.

General description: Open bowl with slightly incurved, outslanted walls and a narrow everted rim. Rim diameters are all 15 cm, and wall thickness below the rim is 8 mm.

Paste: Temper consists of medium sand in moderate quantities. Paste color is red.

Surface characteristics: Interior and exterior surfaces are plain redware.

Distribution: This bowl type has a distribution limited to one habitation and one cemetery site in the Upper Valley sector. Collection proveniences (with number of sherds in parentheses)/site numbers are:

Coll. 146(1)/ETR-3; Coll. 143(2)/ETR-9.

Chronological assessment: Redware Bowl 3 is similar in form and paste to the redware variant of Late Suchimancillo Bowl 3 (Fig. 211). This, in addition to its very limited distribution, makes it of little use as an Early Tambo Real time marker.

Inter-regional comparisons: See Early Tambo Real Redware Bowl 1.

Early Tambo Real Redware Jar 1 (Fig. 271)

Number: 28 sherds, or ca. 3.1% of the Early Tambo Real assemblage.

General description: Large ovoid jar with an interior thickened and beveled rim. Rim diameters vary from 45-55 cm, with a mean of 48.6 cm and a standard deviation of 3.3 cm. Wall thickness below the rim ranges widely between 10 mm and 15 mm, with a mean of 12.8 mm and a standard deviation of 1.8 mm.

Paste: Temper in approximately 50% of the sherds consists of medium sand in heavy quantities, while another 40% have medium sand in moderate quantities. The remaining 10% of the sherds in the sample have moderate quantities of medium grain black gravel inclusions. Paste color is uniformly red.

Surface characteristics: Exterior and interior surfaces are coarse plain redware.

Distribution: This jar type has a wide, but limited, distribution in habitation sites throughout most of the area of Early Tambo Real occupation. Collection proveniences (with number of sherds in parentheses)/site numbers are:

Coll. 189(7)/ETR-7; Colls. 191/192(5)/ETR-8; Coll. 214(4)/ETR-18; Coll. 49(3)/ETR-30; Coll. 319(2)/ETR-33; Coll. 288(7)/ETR-43.

Chronological assessment: Judging from the analysis of single-component collections, Redware Jar 1 is confined to the Early Tambo Real Period.

Inter-regional comparisons: Large redware vessels of this form and paste type are not reported for contemporaneous periods in areas adjacent to the Lower Santa region.

Early Tambo Real Redware Jar 2 (Fig. 271)

Number: 28 sherds, or ca. 3.1% of the Early Tambo Real assemblage.

General description: Globular jar with a short neck that has a sharply outslanted lower part and a vertical upper part. In addition, the exterior of the neck has a medial or high, rounded camber. Rim diameters vary from 10-16 cm, with a mean of 11.7 cm and a standard deviation of 2.1 cm. Wall thickness below the rim ranges between 4 mm and 6 mm.

Paste: Temper in approximately 60% of the sherds consists of medium sand in moderate quantities. The remaining 40% of the sherds have temper consisting of medium or coarse black gravel in moderate amounts. Paste color is red.

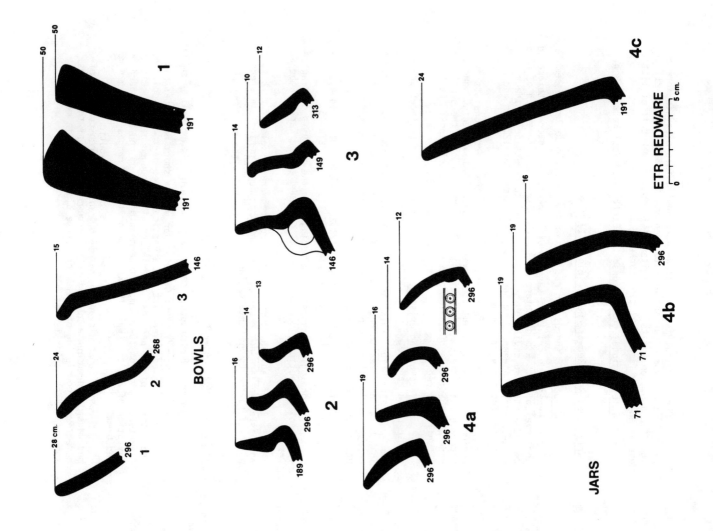

BOWLS

JARS

ETR REDWARE

0 ___ 5 cm.

Fig. 271. Early Tambo Real Period ceramics: Redware Bowls 1, 2, and 3; and Redware Jars 1, 2, 3, 4a, 4b, and 4c.

514

General description: Globular jar with a low flared neck. Some sherds in the sample have a rounded exterior ridge at the juncture of the body and neck. Rim diameters vary from 11-19 cm, with a mean of 13.4 cm and a standard deviation of 2.5 cm. Wall thickness below the rim ranges narrowly between 5 mm and 6 mm.

Paste: Temper consists of fine or medium sand, with approximately 70% of the sherds having medium grain sand. The quantity of temper in all sherds is moderate. Paste color is red, with gray cores noted on two sherds.

Surface characteristics: Incised circle-and-dot design was noted on the exterior ridge of one sherd. Exterior and interior surfaces on the remaining sherds are plain redware.

Distribution: This jar type has a wide, but limited, distribution in habitation, habitation-cemetery, and cemetery sites throughout most of the area of Early Tambo Real occupation. Collection proveniences (with number of sherds in parentheses)/site numbers are:

Coll. 146(1)/ETR-3; Coll. 175(1)/ETR-6; Coll. 242(8)/ETR-12; Coll. 214(6)/ETR-18; Colls. 70/71(5)/ETR-26; Coll. 53(2)/ETR-29; Coll. 49(3)/ETR-30; Coll. 296(10)/ETR-35; Coll. 288(10)/ETR-43.

Chronological assessment: Redware Jar 4a is similar in form and paste to Late Tanguche Jar 2a (Fig. 258), but generally can be distinguished on the basis of the thicker neck walls and its less consistent angle of flare at the rim.

Inter-regional comparisons: The plainware Jar 4a sherds constituting the great majority of this sample are similar in form, size, and paste to some variants of Vessel Form 7 of the Rubia Plain type of Virú Valley (cf. Collier 1955, p. 166, Fig. 54 G).

Early Tambo Real Redware Jar 4b (Fig. 271)

Number: 33 sherds, or ca. 3.7% of the Early Tambo Real assemblage.

General description: Globular jar with a flared neck of medium height. Rim diameters vary from 6-19 cm, with a mean of 11.7 cm and a standard deviation of 3.8 cm. Wall thickness below the rim ranges widely between 5 mm and 10 mm, with a mean of 6.8 mm and a standard deviation of 1.6 mm.

Paste: Temper in approximately 85% of the sherds consists of medium sand in moderate quantities. The remaining 15% of the sherds in the sample have temper consisting of coarse black gravel in moderate amounts. Paste color is red.

Surface characteristics: The exterior shoulders of most of the sherds in the sample are decorated with incised circle-and-dot (e.g., see Fig. 272).

Distribution: This jar type has a wide distribution in habitation, habitation-cemetery, and cemetery sites throughout the area of Early Tambo Real occupation. Collection proveniences (with number of sherds in parentheses)/site numbers are:

Surface characteristics: Four of the sherds have either incised scallops or raised circle-and-dot designs on the exterior surface (e.g., see sherds in Fig. 272). The remaining sherds have plain redware surfaces.

Distribution: This jar type has a wide distribution in habitation, habitation-cemetery, and cemetery sites throughout the area of Early Tambo Real occupation. Collection proveniences (with number of sherds in parentheses)/site numbers are:

Coll. 189(2)/ETR-7; Coll. 55(2)/ETR-27; Coll. 54(2)/ETR-28; Coll. 53(3)/ETR-29; Coll. 49(2)/ETR-30; Coll. 322(3)/ETR-31; Coll. 319(4)/ ETR-33; Coll. 296(8)/ETR-35; Coll. 289(1)/ETR-36; Coll. 263(1)/ETR-42.

Chronological assessment: Redware Jar 2 is similar in form and paste to some variants of Late Tanguche Jar 3 (Fig. 258), but can be distinguished from the C-shaped rim of the earlier jar type on the basis of the consistently vertical upper interior surface of the neck.

Inter-regional comparisons: Early Tambo Real Redware Jars 2 and 3 are similar in form, size, and paste to Vessel Form 6 of the Rubia Plain type of Virú Valley (cf. Collier 1955, p. 166, Fig. 54 F).

Early Tambo Real Redware Jar 3 (Fig. 271)

Number: 9 sherds, or ca. 1% of the Early Tambo Real assemblage.

General description: Globular jar with a cambered, outslanted neck of low or medium height. Lips are rounded. Rim diameters vary from 10-14 cm, with a mean of 11.4 cm. Wall thickness below the rim is 5 mm.

Paste: Temper in three of the sherds consists of fine sand in moderate quantities. The other six sherds have medium grain sand in moderate amounts. Paste color is red.

Surface characteristics: Two sherds have vertical strap handles placed between the cambered part of the neck and the shoulder of the vessel. Exterior and interior surfaces on all sherds are plain redware, with fire blackening noted on three sherds.

Distribution: This jar type has a wide, but limited, distribution in two habitation sites and a cemetery. Collection proveniences (with number of sherds in parentheses)/site numbers are:

Colls. 149(3), 150(1)/ETR-5; Coll. 214(2)/ETR-18; Colls. 70/71(3)/ETR-26.

Chronological assessment: Redware Jar 2 is similar in form and paste to some variants of Late Tambo Real Redware Jar 2 (Fig. 279), but can be distinguished on the basis of its consistently outslanted neck.

Inter-regional comparisons: See Early Tambo Real Redware Jar 2.

Early Tambo Real Redware Jar 4a (Fig. 271)

Number: 46 sherds, or ca. 5.1% of the Early Tambo Real assemblage.

515

Coll. 12(5)/ETR-1; Coll. 202(1)/ETR-13; Colls. 246/247(3)/ETR-14; Coll. 213(1)/ETR-17; Colls. 70/71(2)/ETR-26; Coll. 55(1)/ETR-27; Coll. 54(2)/ETR-28; Coll. 53(1)/ETR-29; Coll. 319(1)/ETR-33; Coll. 298(1)/ETR-34; Coll. 296(1)/ETR-35; Coll. 267(1)/ETR-38; Coll. 263(6)/ETR-42; Coll. 288(6)/ETR-43; Coll. 270(1)/ETR-47.

Chronological assessment: Redware Jar 4b is similar in form and paste to some variants of Late Suchimancillo Jar 5e (Fig. 215), Early Guadalupito Jar 2b (Fig. 226), and Early Tanguche Jar 2d (Fig. 226), but can be distinguished on the basis of the incised circle-and-dot design.

Inter-regional comparisons: See Early Tambo Real Redware Jar 4a.

Early Tambo Real Redware Jar 4c (Fig. 271)

Number: 2 sherds, or ca. .2% of the Early Tambo Real assemblage.

General description: Globular jar with a tall, funnel-shaped neck. Rim diameters are 14 cm and 24 cm. Wall thickness is 6 mm and 8 mm, respectively.

Paste: Temper in one sherd consists of medium sand in moderate quantities, while temper in the other consists of coarse gravel in moderate amounts. Paste color is red.

Surface characteristics: Exterior and interior surfaces are plain redware.

Distribution: This jar type was found at a habitation site in the Upper Valley sector and at a cemetery in the Lower Valley sector. Collection proveniences (with number of sherds in parentheses)/site numbers are:

Colls. 191/192(1)/ETR-8; Coll. 53(1)/ETR-29.

Chronological assessment: Redware Jar 4c is similar in form and paste to Late Suchimancillo Jar 5f (Fig. 215) and Late Tambo Real Redware Jar 3b (Fig. 279), but can be distinguished from the earlier jar on the basis of its lower neck height and from the later jar by its outslanted neck wall.

Inter-regional comparisons: No redware jars of this type are reported in the literature on contemporaneous ceramics of areas adjacent to the Lower Santa region. However, this form may be the redware counterpart of Early Tambo Real Grayware Jar 4c, which appears to be related to Vessel Form 4 of Estero Plain (cf. Collier 1955, p. 165, Fig. 53 D).

Early Tambo Real: Miscellaneous Redware Ceramics (Fig. 270, top; Fig.272)

Among the miscellaneous redware ceramics found in Early Tambo Real contexts, and illustrated here, are the following (listed in order of appearance in the drawings): (1) a vessel with a Redware Jar 2 rim form, decorated with a white-painted line around the neck, two white-painted crescent-and-dot motifs, and two appliquéd redware "adornos" possibly representing maize cobs (Fig. 270, top); (2) an incised

maize cob effigy, on a sherd from the shoulder of a jar (Fig. 272, top - left); (3) a circle-and-dot decorated sherd with an appliquéd bird (Fig. 272, top - right); (4) a circle-and-dot-decorated jar sherd with a strap handle in the form of a human arm-and-hand (Fig. 272, center - left); and (5) two circle-and-dot-decorated jar sherds showing variants of zoned incised and punctate design (Fig. 272, center - right, and bottom).

Early Tambo Real: Effigy Figures (Figs. 267-270; Fig. 272)

Early Tambo Real marks a period of slight increase over the Late Tanguche Period in the total percentage of human and animal effigy figures present in the assemblage. Only one human effigy of probable Early Tambo Real date is present in the collections (Fig. 269, top). A total of seven animal effigies is present, including representations of (1) birds (e.g., Fig. 270, center - left; Fig. 272, top - right); (2) a snake (Fig. 267, top); and (3) small animals that appear to be frogs (Fig. 268, bottom - right; Fig. 269, top and bottom; Fig. 270, bottom - right). The combined total of eight human and animal effigies represents .9% of the ceramic assemblage of this period.

Early Tambo Real also marks the first period in the sequence when small maize ear effigies appear as appliquéd, three-dimensional decorative features on the shoulders of jars--including both redware and grayware vessels. Only three of these maize effigies were found in single-component Early Tambo Real contexts (e.g., Fig. 272, top - left), representing a miniscule .3% of the total assemblage. In contrast, the total number of maize ear effigies in the Late Tambo Real collections is 24, or 3.3% of the total assemblage of that period.

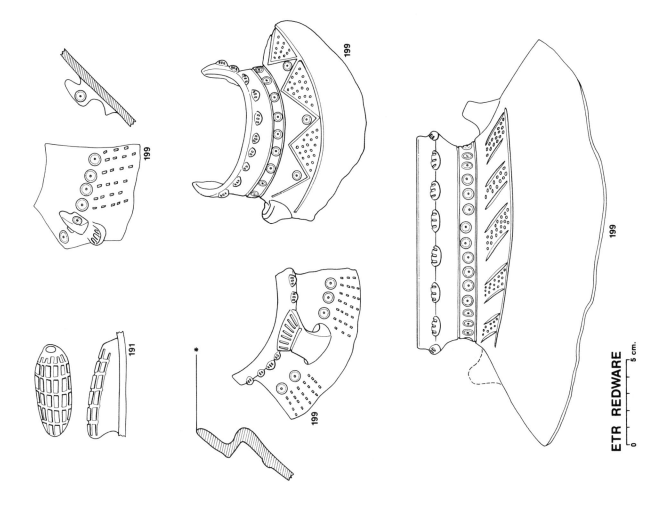

ETR REDWARE

Fig. 272. Early Tambo Real Period ceramics: details of selected redware sherds.

LATE TAMBO REAL PERIOD

Late Tambo Real Grayware Bowl 1 (Fig. 274)

Number: 10 sherds, or ca. 1.4% of the Late Tambo Real assemblage.

General description: Globular bowl with a slightly constricted mouth. One sherd in the sample has a straight, outslanted wall and inverted rim with an interior beveled lip. Rim diameters vary from 10-24 cm, with a mean of 18 cm and a standard deviation of 5.7 cm. Wall thickness below the rim ranges between 4 mm and 7 mm.

Paste: Temper in nine of the ten sherds consists of fine sand in moderate quantities. The remaining sherd has medium grain sand in moderate amounts. Paste color is gray.

Surface characteristics: Interior and exterior surfaces are plain grayware.

Distribution: This bowl type has a limited distribution, primarily in several habitation and habitation-cemetery sites of the Lower Valley sector. Collection proveniences (with number of sherds in parentheses)/site numbers are:

Coll. 161(7)/LTR-3; Coll. 324(1)/LTR-37; Coll. 88(1)/LTR-38; Coll. 322(1)/LTR-45.

Chronological assessment: Grayware Bowl 1 is a good general time marker of the Early and Late Tambo Real Periods, but its similarity to specific temporal diagnostic.

Inter-regional comparisons: Some variants of Vessel Form 1 of the Virú Valley Tomaval Plain type appear to be similar in form to Late Tambo Real Grayware Bowl 1 (cf. Collier 1955, p. 161, Fig. 50 A - first two profiles on the right).

Late Tambo Real Grayware Bowl 2 (Fig. 274)

Number: 15 sherds, or ca. 2% of the Late Tambo Real assemblage.

General description: Open bowl with a strongly outslanted lower wall and a nearly vertical upper wall. One sherd in the sample has an exterior corner point and an interior beveled lip. Rim diameters vary from 11-28 cm, with a mean of 21.9 cm and a standard deviation of 6.1 cm. Wall thickness below the rim ranges between 4 mm and 8 mm, with a mean of 6.2 mm and a standard deviation of 1 mm.

Paste: Temper in approximately 75% of the sherds consists of fine sand in moderate quantities. The remaining 25% have medium grain sand in moderate amounts. Paste color is gray.

Surface characteristics: One sherd has exterior pressmolded zoned stippling similar to that illustrated for a Redware Bowl 1 in Fig. 279. Another sherd has appliquéd rim decoration (see Fig. 277, lower right). Interior and exterior surfaces on the remainder of the sherds are plain grayware.

Distribution: This bowl type has a wide, but limited, distribution in habitation, habitation-cemetery, and cemetery sites throughout most of the area of Late Tambo Real occupation. Collection proveniences (with number of sherds in parentheses)/site numbers are:

Coll. 161(5)/LTR-3; Coll. 361(1)/LTR-14; Coll. 324(1)/LTR-37; Coll. 88(1)/LTR-38; Coll. 326(2)/LTR-47; Coll. 320(1)/LTR-48; Coll. 288(4)/LTR-68.

Chronological assessment: Judging from the analysis of single-component collections, this bowl type is a good Late Tambo Real time marker.

Inter-regional comparisons: Late Tambo Real Grayware Bowl 2 is similar in form and paste to some variants of both Vessel Form 2 of Tomaval Plain and Vessel Form 1 of Estero Plain (cf. Collier 1955, p. 161, Fig. 50 B; and p. 165, Fig. 53 A).

Late Tambo Real Grayware Bowl 3 (Fig. 274)

Number: 2 sherds, or ca. .3% of the Late Tambo Real assemblage.

General description: Open bowl with straight outslanted walls. The rim diameter of one of the bowl fragments is 46 cm (the other sherd is rimless). Wall thickness below the rim on both sherds is 12 mm.

Paste: Temper consists of coarse black gravel in moderate quantities. Paste color is gray.

Surface characteristics: The interior of both sherds has heavily incised crosshatching, suggesting that this bowl type functioned as a grater for processing food. Exterior surfaces are plain grayware.

Distribution: Although present in our collections from only two, rather widely separated habitation sites, it seems likely that a broader sample from other sites might include more examples of grayware grater bowls. In any case, collection proveniences (with number of sherds in parentheses)/site numbers are as follows:

Coll. 336(1)/LTR-10; Coll. 292(1)/LTR-60.

Chronological assessment: Grayware Bowl 3 appears to have redware antecedents (e.g., Late Tanguche Bowl 2, Fig. 258), but no grayware counterparts that are present in our collections. It thus appears to be a good diagnostic of Late Tambo Real, although its apparently limited distribution lessens its utility as a time marker.

Inter-regional comparisons: From their excavations in later levels of Virú Valley sites, Strong and Evans (1952, p. 270, Fig. 42 - Vessel Shape 4) report on (grayware) Virú Plain bowls with inner surfaces incised to serve as graters.

Late Tambo Real Grayware Bowl 4 (Fig. 274)

Number: 36 sherds, or ca. 5% of the Late Tambo Real assemblage.

518

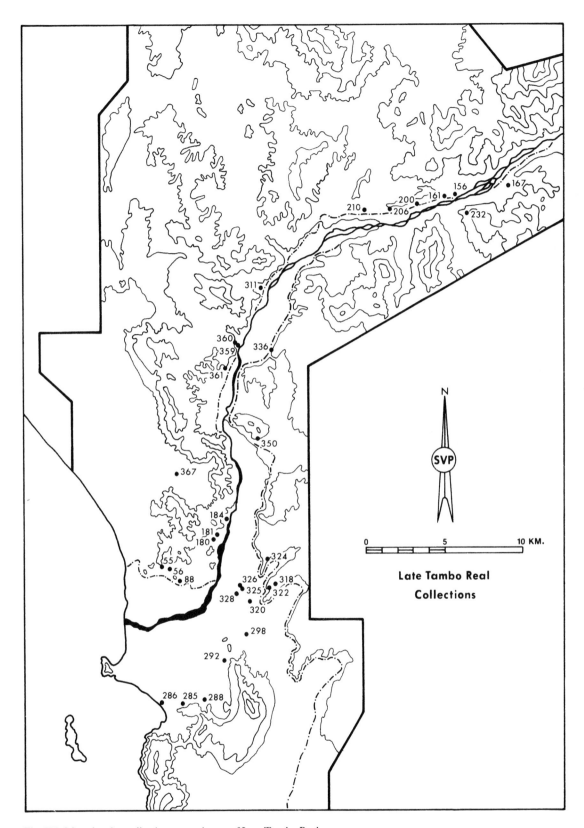

Fig. 273. Map showing collection proveniences of Late Tambo Real
Period (Estero/Late Horizon).

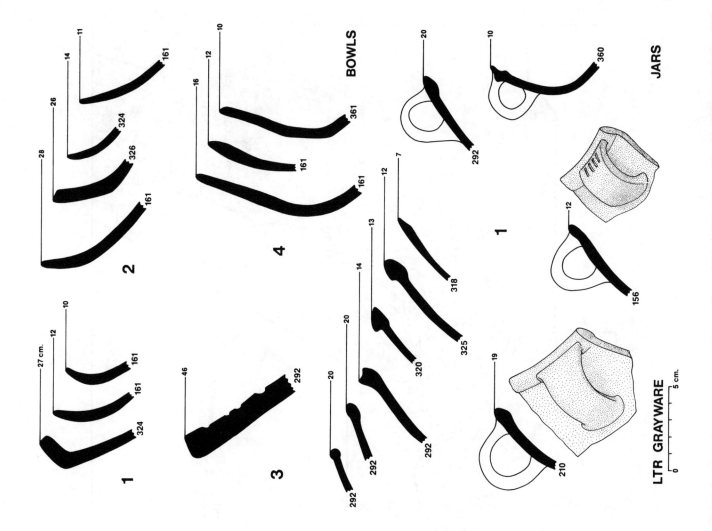

BOWLS

JARS

LTR GRAYWARE

0   5 cm.

Fig. 274. Late Tambo Real Period ceramics: Grayware Bowls 1, 2, 3, and 4; Grayware Jar 1.

General description: Deep, constricted-mouth bowl with a globular lower part and straight insloping walls on the upper part. Rim diameters vary from 10-16 cm, with a mean of 13.7 cm and a standard deviation of 2.4 cm. Wall thickness below the rim ranges between 4 mm and 7 mm, with a mean of 5.4 mm.

Paste: Temper in approximately 90% of the sherds consists of fine sand in moderate quantities. The remaining 10% of the sherds have medium grain sand in moderate amounts. Paste color is gray.

Surface characteristics: Almost all of the sherds in the sample have either appliquéd or pressmolded exterior decoration. As the examples illustrated in Fig. 277 show, this exterior plastic decoration consists of either small, elliptically-shaped "adornos" or of appliquéd and pressmolded maize effigies.

Distribution: Although found in relatively great numbers at two habitation sites and one cemetery in the Middle Valley sector, this bowl type has an apparently very limited distribution. Collection proveniences (with number of sherds in parentheses)/site numbers are:

Coll. 161(16)/LTR-3; Coll. 200(16)/LTR-4; Coll. 361(4)/LTR-14.

Chronological assessment: Bowl 4 appears to be a good diagnostic of the Late Tambo Real Period, although its limited distribution lessens its utility as a time marker.

Inter-regional comparisons: At least one sherd under Vessel Form 1 of the Virú Valley Tomaval Plain type is very similar in profile to Late Tambo Real Grayware Bowl 4 (cf. Collier 1955, p. 161, Fig. 50 A - center profile). No plastic decoration similar to that illustrated for Bowl 4 (Fig. 274) is mentioned for the Virú type, however.

Late Tambo Real Grayware Jar 1 (Fig. 274)

Number: 36 sherds, or ca. 5% of the Late Tambo Real assemblage.

General description: Globular jar with a constricted mouth. As shown in the drawings, there is a substantial amount of variety in the configuration of the rim at the lip, usually including both interior and exterior thickening. The lips themselves take a variety of forms-- including spherical, rounded, tapered, and grooved. Rim diameters vary from 10-28 cm, with a mean of 16.5 cm and a standard deviation of 3.5 cm. Wall thickness below the rim ranges narrowly between 4 mm and 6 mm, with 60% of the sherds having a wall thickness of 5 mm.

Paste: Temper in approximately 50% of the sherds consists of fine sand, while the other 50% have medium grain sand. The quantity of temper in all sherds is moderate.

Surface characteristics: A typical feature on many of the sherds in the sample is the presence of loop-shaped strap handles that are attached from the shoulder to a point within a few millimeters of the rim. Handles on most vessels extend up substantially above the rim of the vessel itself, as shown in the illustrations.

Distribution: This jar type has a wide distribution in habitation, habitation-cemetery, and cemetery sites throughout the area of Late Tambo Real occupation. Collection proveniences (with number of sherds in parentheses)/site numbers are:

Coll. 167(1)/LTR-1; Coll. 210(1)/LTR-5; Coll. 360(1)/LTR-9; Coll. 55(2)/LTR-40; Coll. 322(4)/LTR-45; Colls. 325(3), 326(1)/LTR-47; Coll. 322(2)/LTR-48; Coll. 298(4)/LTR-55; Coll. 292(7)/LTR-60; Coll. 285(2)/LTR-71; Coll. 286(8)/LTR-73.

Chronological assessment: Judging from the analysis of single-component collections, Jar 1 is a very good diagnostic of Late Tambo Real Period. Its distinctive rim makes it an easily recognizable feature of ceramic collections or in assessing the surface ceramics on a site.

Inter-regional comparisons: Late Tambo Real Jar 1 appears to be essentially identical in form, size, and paste to the two variants of Tomaval Plain Vessel Form 1 with exterior thickened rims, illustrated in Collier (1955, p. 161, Fig. 50 A - first two profiles on the left). However, Collier does not mention the variable lip treatment that characterizes our sample from the Lower Santa region.

Late Tambo Real Grayware Jar 2a (Fig. 275)

Number: 9 sherds, or ca. 1.2% of the Late Tambo Real assemblage.

General description: Globular jar with a cambered neck. The wall of the neck above the camber slopes inward. Rim diameters vary from 8-20 cm—with 65% of the sherds at the upper end of the range, between 14 cm and 20 cm. Wall thickness below the rim ranges between 4 mm and 7 mm, with 90% of the sherds at the lower end of this range.

Paste: Temper consists uniformly of medium sand in moderate quantities. Paste color is gray.

Surface characteristics: Spaced scallops run around the cambered part of the neck on three of the sherds (e.g., see the Early Tambo Real sherd in Fig. 272, center - left). Three other sherds have vertical strap handles. Otherwise, interior and exterior surfaces are plain.

Distribution: This jar type has a wide distribution in habitation, habitation-cemetery, and cemetery sites throughout Late Tambo Real Cluster 2. Collection proveniences (with number of sherds in parentheses)/site numbers are:

Coll. 336(2)/LTR-10; Coll. 324(1)/LTR-37; Coll. 326(2)/LTR-47; Coll. 328(1)/LTR-50; Coll. 292(3)/LTR-60.

Chronological assessment: Judging from the analysis of single-component collections, Grayware Jar 2a is limited to Late Tambo Real Period.

Inter-regional comparisons: Late Tambo Real Grayware Jars 2a, 2b, 2c, and 2d appear to be analogous to most variants of Vessel Form 4 of the Virú Valley Tomaval Plain type (cf. Collier 1955, p. 161, Fig. 50 D). However, the Lower Santa Jar 2a type exhibits substantially more variability of rim form than from the Virú Valley type. Judging from the grayware

521

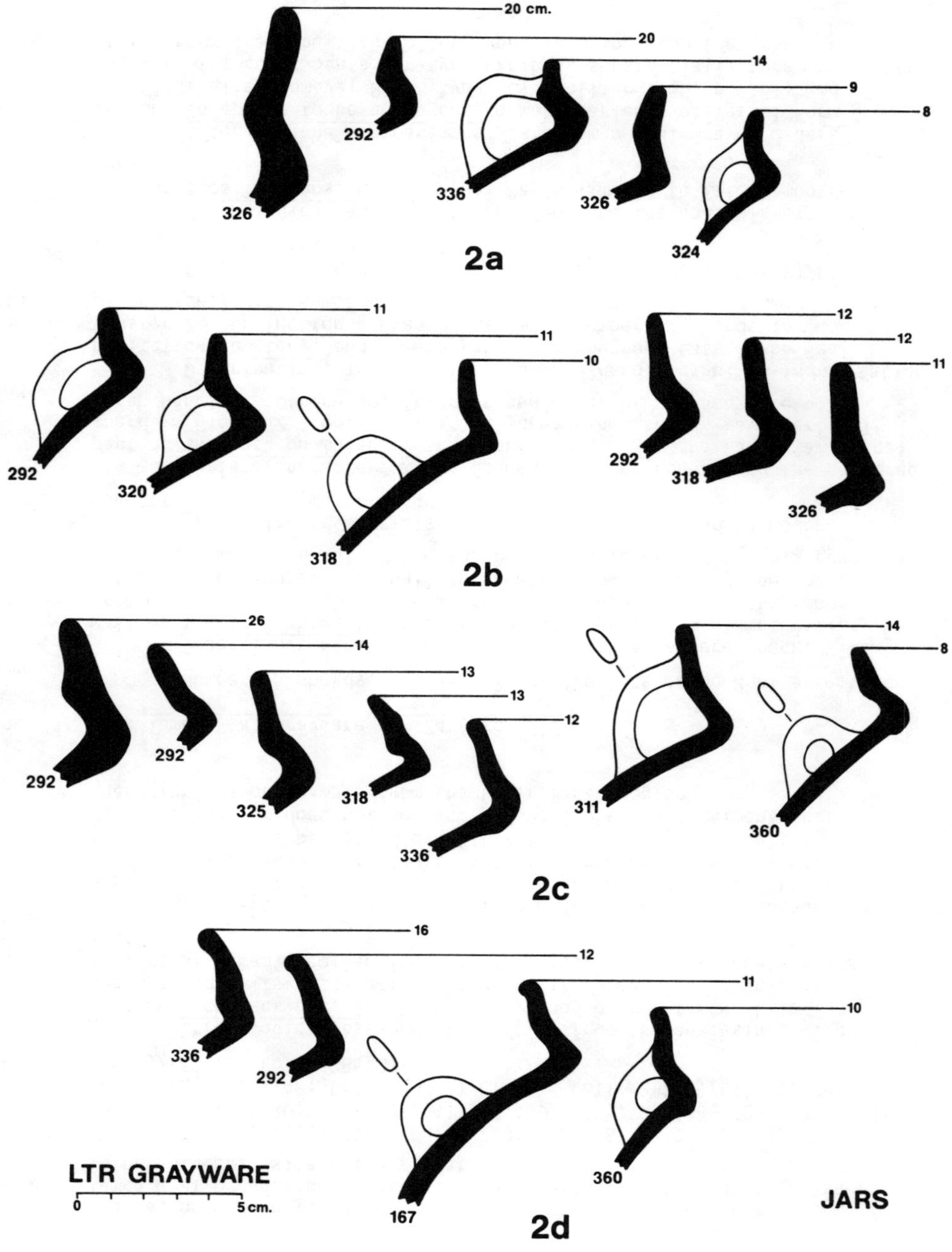

Fig. 275. Late Tambo Real Period ceramics: Grayware Jars 2a, 2b, 2c, and 2d.

jars of similar shape illustrated in Donnan and Mackey (1978:368-373), the same general lack of variability of rim form is characteristic of Moche Valley as well.

Late Tambo Real Grayware Jar 2b (Fig. 275)

Number: 48 sherds, or ca. 6.6% of the Late Tambo Real assemblage.

General description: Globular jar with a cambered neck. The wall of the neck above the camber is vertical. Rim diameters vary from 10-14 cm, with a mean of 12.2 cm and a standard deviation of 1.2 cm. Wall thickness below the rim ranges between 4 mm and 6 mm, with 85% of the sherds having a wall thickness of 5 mm.

Paste: Temper in approximately 90% of the sherds consists of medium sand in moderate quantities. The remaining 10% have coarse black gravel temper in moderate amounts. Paste color is gray.

Surface characteristics: Vertical strap handles are present on about 20% of the sherds in the sample. Exterior and interior surfaces on all sherds are plain grayware.

Distribution: This jar type has a wide distribution in habitation, habitation-cemetery, and cemetery sites throughout Late Tambo Real Cluster 2. Collection proveniences (with number of sherds in parentheses)/site numbers are:

Coll. 360(3)/LTR-9; Coll. 88(3)/LTR-38; Coll. 55(2)/LTR-40; Coll. 318(1)/LTR-44; Coll. 322(2)/LTR-45; Coll. 326(2)/LTR-47; Coll. 320(3)/LTR-48; Coll. 328(2)/LTR-50; Coll. 298(10)/LTR-55; Coll. 292(12)/LTR-60; Coll. 285(3)/LTR-71; Coll. 286(5)/LTR-73.

Chronological assessment: Grayware Jar 2b is similar in form and paste to Early Tambo Real Grayware Jar 3a (Fig. 265), but can be distinguished on the basis of its thinner and sharper camber, as well as by the thicker walls above the camber. Also, the presence of strap handles on some Jar 2b sherds serves to distinguish them from the earlier vessel, which appears to have had no handles.

Inter-regional comparisons: See Late Tambo Real Grayware Jar 2a.

Late Tambo Real Grayware Jar 2c (Fig. 275)

Number: 56 sherds, or ca. 7.7% of the Late Tambo Real assemblage.

General description: Globular jar with a cambered, outslanted neck. The wall of the neck above the camber is slightly tapered on a few sherds, and several others have slightly flared rims. Rim diameters vary from 8-32 cm, with a mean of 13.3 cm and a standard deviation of 4.6 cm. Wall thickness below the rim ranges widely between 4 mm and 9 mm, with a mean of 5.3 mm and a standard deviation of 1 mm.

Paste: Temper in approximately 90% of the sherds consists of medium sand in moderate quantities. The remaining 10% have temper consisting of coarse black gravel in moderate amounts. Paste color is gray.

Surface characteristics: Vertical strap handles are present on some 15% of the sherds in the sample. Exterior and interior surfaces of all sherds are plain grayware.

Distribution: This jar type has a wide distribution in habitation, habitation-cemetery, and cemetery sites of Late Tambo Real Cluster 2, as well as in one site in Cluster 1 (SVP-LTR-5). Collection proveniences (with number of sherds in parentheses)/site numbers are:

Coll. 210(1)/LTR-5; Coll. 311(8)/LTR-6; Coll. 360(1)/LTR-9; Coll. 336(3)/LTR-10; Coll. 184(2)/LTR-31; Coll. 180(2)/LTR-35; Coll. 88(2)/LTR-38; Coll. 55(1)/LTR-40; Coll. 322(1)/LTR-45; Coll. 325(5)/LTR-47; Coll. 320(3)/LTR-38; Coll. 328(9)/LTR-50; Coll. 298(5)/LTR-55; Coll. 292(13)/LTR-60.

Chronological assessment: Grayware Jar 2c is similar in form and paste to some variants of Early Tambo Real Grayware Jar 3b (Fig. 265), but can be distinguished on the basis of several neck features including lower height and thinner walls.

Inter-regional comparisons: See Late Tambo Real Grayware Jar 2a.

Late Tambo Real Grayware Jar 2d (Fig. 275)

Number: 23 sherds, or ca. 3.2% of the Late Tambo Real assemblage.

General description: Globular jar with a cambered, outslanted neck and everted lip. Rim diameters vary from 10-30 cm, with a mean of 12.2 cm and a standard deviation of 4.1 cm. Wall thickness below the rim ranges between 5 mm and 7 mm, with roughly 50% of the sherds at the upper end of the range and 50% at the lower end.

Paste: Temper consists uniformly of medium sand in moderate quantities. Paste color is gray.

Surface characteristics: Vertical strap handles are present on 11 of the sherds in the sample. Exterior and interior surfaces on all sherds are plain grayware.

Distribution: This jar type has a wide distribution in a limited number of habitation and habitation-cemetery sites throughout the area of Late Tambo Real occupation. Collection proveniences (with number of sherds in parentheses)/site numbers are:

Coll. 167(11)/LTR-1; Coll. 336(1)/LTR-10; Coll. 326(1)/LTR-47; Coll. 292(7)/LTR-60; Coll. 286(3)/LTR-73.

Chronological assessment: Judging from the analysis of single-component collections, Grayware Jar 2d is a good diagnostic of Late Tambo Real Period.

Inter-regional comparisons: See Late Tambo Real Grayware Jar 2a.

Late Tambo Real Grayware Jar 3a (Fig. 276)

Number: 13 sherds, or ca. 1.8% of the Late Tambo Real assemblage.

General description: Globular jar with a low, flared neck. Most sherds in the sample have a rounded exterior ridge at the juncture between the neck and the body. Rim diameters vary from 6-9 cm, with about 60% of the sherds at the lower end of the range. Wall thickness below the rim ranges between 4 mm and 7 mm, with most sherds at the lower end of this range.

Paste: Temper consists uniformly of medium sand in moderate quantities. Paste color is gray.

Surface characteristics: Although many sherds are not complete enough to be certain, it seems likely that many if not most vessels had vertical strap handles--with a notched and tapered vertical spine running down their upper surface (see perspective drawing in Fig. 276, top - left). Exterior and interior surfaces on all sherds are plain grayware.

Distribution: This jar type has a wide, but limited, distribution in habitation, habitation-cemetery, and cemetery sites throughout most of the area of Late Tambo Real occupation. Collection proveniences (with number of sherds in parentheses)/site numbers are:

Coll. 311(1)/LTR-6; Coll. 325(2)/LTR-47; Coll. 298(3)/LTR-55; Coll. 292(6)/LTR-60; Coll. 285(1)/LTR-71.

Chronological assessment: Grayware Jar 3a is similar in form and paste to some variants of Early Tambo Real Grayware Jar 4a (Fig. 266), but can be distinguished on the basis of several neck features--including (1) thinner and less strongly flared walls; (2) the presence of an exterior ridge at the juncture of the neck and the body; and (3) features of the strap handle, including the notched, tapered spine.

Inter-regional comparisons: Late Tambo Real Grayware Jars 3a, 3b, 3c, and 3d are very similar in form, size, and paste to Vessel Form 4 of the Estero Plain type of Virú Valley (cf. Collier 1955, p. 165, Fig. 53 D). However, the two vessels types differ with respect to specific decorative features (e.g., notched-spine strap handles appear to be absent on the Virú form of the vessel).

Late Tambo Real Grayware Jar 3b (Fig.276)

Number: 7 sherds, or ca. 1% of the Late Tambo Real assemblage.

General description: Globular jar with a neck of low-to-medium height. The lower part of the neck is essentially vertical, while the upper part is slightly flared. A low, rounded ridge runs around the exterior juncture of the neck and body. Rim diameters vary from 6-12 cm, with five of the sherds at the upper end of this range. Wall thickness below the rim ranges between 5 mm and 7 mm, with the same five sherds at the lower end of the range.

Paste: Temper in four of the sherds consists of medium sand in moderate quantities. The remaining sherds have temper consisting of coarse black gravel in moderate amounts. Paste color is gray.

Surface characteristics: Although many sherds are not complete enough to be certain, it seems likely that most vessels of this type had vertical strap handles with a notched and tapered vertical spine running down their upper surface (e.g., see Fig. 276, top - left). Exterior and interior surfaces are plain grayware.

Distribution: This jar type has a wide, but limited, distribution in habitation and cemetery sites throughout most of the area of Late Tambo Real occupation. Collection proveniences (with number of sherds in parentheses)/site numbers are:

Coll. 167(4)/LTR-1; Coll. 184(1)/LTR-31; Coll. 326(1)/LTR-47; Coll. 292(1)/LTR-60.

Chronological assessment: Grayware Jar 3b is similar in form and paste to Early Tambo Real Grayware Jar 4b (Fig. 266), but can be distinguished on the basis of several features--including (1) the consistently vertical lower half of the neck, in contrast to the curved neck wall of the earlier type; (2) the presence of the exterior ridge; and (3) features of the strap handle (only the later handle has a notched and tapered vertical spine).

Inter-regional comparisons: See Late Tambo Real Grayware Jar 3a.

Late Tambo Real Grayware Jar 3c (Fig. 276)

Number: 25 sherds, or ca. 3.5% of the Late Tambo Real assemblage.

General description: Globular jar with a neck of medium height. The lower part of the neck is essentially vertical, while the upper part is flared. A few sherds in the sample have everted lips, and several have a low rounded ridge on the exterior at the juncture of the neck and body. Rim diameters range narrowly from 13-14 cm, with 65% of the sherds at the upper end of the range. Wall thickness below the rim on all sherds is 7 mm.

Paste: Temper in 75% of the sherds consists of medium sand in moderate quantities. The remaining 25% have temper consisting of a mixture of medium grain sand and occasional bits of coarse gravel. Paste color is gray.

Surface characteristics: Although most of the sherds in the sample are too fragmentary to be certain, it seems likely that most vessels of this type had large vertical strap handles with a notched and tapered vertical spine on the upper surface, similar to those shown for Grayware Jars 3a and 3b. Exterior and interior surfaces are plain grayware.

Distribution: This jar type has a wide, but limited, distribution in three Late Tambo Real habitation sites. Collection proveniences (with number of sherds in parentheses)/site numbers are:

Coll. 336(6)/LTR-10; Coll. 325(8)/LTR-47; Coll. 292(11)/LTR-60.

Chronological assessment: Grayware Jar 3c is similar in form and paste to Early Tambo Real Grayware Jar 4c (Fig. 266), but can be distinguished on the basis of its consistently lower neck height.

Inter-regional comparisons: See Late Tambo Real Grayware Jar 3a.

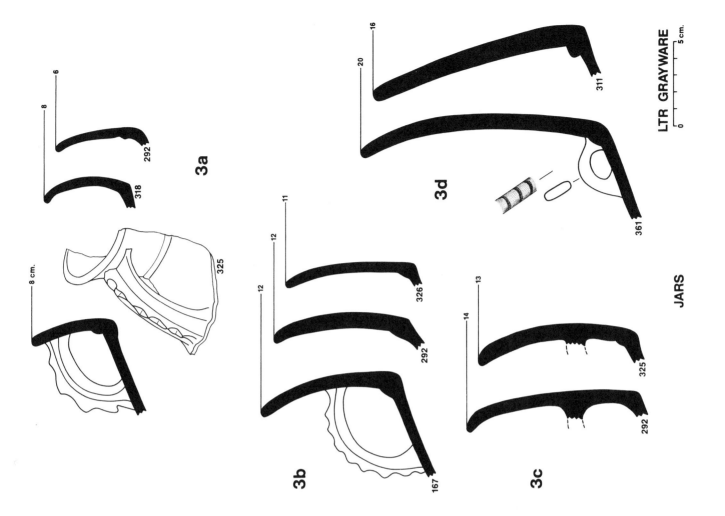

Fig. 276. late Tambo Real Period ceramics: Grayware Jars 3a, 3b, 3c, and 3d.

Late Tambo Real Grayware Jar 3d (Fig. 276)

Number: 9 sherds, or ca. 1.2% of the Late Tambo Real assemblage.

General description: Globular jar with a high neck and flared rim. Two types of neck are present in the sample, including (1) necks with a funnel shape and slightly flared, outslanted walls; and (2) those with a nearly vertical lower part and a flared rim. A low, rounded ridge is present on the exterior at the juncture of the neck and body. Rim diameters vary from 16-21 cm, with a mean of 18.2 cm and a standard deviation of 2.2 cm. Wall thickness below the rim is a uniform 6 mm.

Paste: Temper consists uniformly of medium sand in moderate quantities. Paste color is gray.

Surface characteristics: One sherd has a vertical strap handle and notched decoration on the exterior ridge (see Fig. 276). Another has incised herringbone decoration on the exterior ridge. Exterior and interior surfaces on the remaining sherds are plain grayware.

Distribution: This jar type has a wide, but limited, distribution in habitation, habitation-cemetery, and cemetery sites throughout most of the area of Late Tambo Real occupation. Collection proveniences (with number of sherds in parentheses)/site numbers are:

Coll. 311(4)/LTR-6; Coll. 361(1)/LTR-14; Coll. 325(2)/LTR-47; Coll. 288(2)/LTR-68.

Chronological assessment: Grayware Jar 3d is similar in form and paste to Early Tambo Real Grayware Jar 4c (Fig. 266), but can be distinguished on the basis of its consistently greater neck height.

Inter-regional comparisons: See Late Tambo Real Grayware Jar 3a.

Late Tambo Real Grayware Jar 4 (Fig. 277)

Number: 24 sherds, or ca. 3.3% of the Late Tambo Real assemblage.

General description: Large ovoid jar with a low vertical or slightly flared neck. Rims are usually symmetrically thickened, and lips are either roughly rounded and horizontal or exterior beveled. Rim diameters vary from 45-65 cm, with a mean of 55 cm and a standard deviation of 4.4 cm. Wall thickness below the rim ranges between 8 mm and 12 mm, with a mean of 10.5 mm.

Paste: Temper consists uniformly of coarse sand in moderate quantities. Paste color is gray.

Surface characteristics: Exterior and interior surfaces are very coarse in appearance, with some pitting (either from unevenly mixed paste or from temper falling off the surface in the firing process, if not both), as well as slightly protruding bits of temper. Surface color ranges from light gray to black.

Distribution: This jar type has a wide distribution in habitation and habitation-cemetery sites throughout the area of Late Tambo Real occupation. Collection proveniences (with number of sherds in parentheses)/site numbers are:

Coll. 167(1)/LTR-1; Coll. 210(4)/LTR-5; Coll. 311(1)/LTR-6; Coll. 336(3)/LTR-10; Coll. 180(1)/LTR-35; Coll. 325(1)/LTR-47; Coll. 298(2)/LTR-55; Coll. 292(7)/LTR-60; Coll. 286(1)/LTR-73.

Chronological assessment: Grayware Jar 4 is similar in form and paste to Early Tambo Real Grayware Jar 2 (Fig. 265), but appears to be distinguishable from the earlier jar on the basis of its consistently symmetrically-thickened rim.

Inter-regional comparisons: This specific rim form is not present among the principal shapes illustrated for Virú Plain, but Grayware Jar 4 is clearly related in overall size, wall thickness, and paste to this general Virú Valley type (cf. Strong and Evans 1952, p. 270, Fig. 42).

Late Tambo Real: Miscellaneous Grayware (Fig. 278 a-h; Fig. 280, top)

Among the miscellaneous grayware ceramics found in Late Tambo Real contexts, and illustrated here, are the following (listed in order of appearance in the illustrations): (1) a nearly complete human effigy vessel, with ears in the form of maize effigies (Fig. 278 a; Note: various features on this vessel--including the legs, arms, and face--are strikingly similar to parts of the Inca-style vessels from Ica and Pachacamac illustrated in Menzel 1977, p. 92, Fig. 6, and p. 126, Fig. 114); (2) two fragments of a human effigy whistling jar, with headgear in the form of maize effigies (Fig. 278 b; and Fig. 280, top - right; Note: human effigies with maize hats are quite similar to those from Virú, illustrated in Collier 1955, pp. 162-163, Figs. 51 and 52; for Nepeña, see Proulx 1973, pp. 264-265, Pl. 16); (3) a three-dimensional appliquéd maize effigy on a body sherd, which is also decorated with an incised band (Fig. 278 c); (4) a fragment of a parrot effigy jar (Fig. 278 d); (5) a body sherd with pressmolded zoned ridges and stippling (Fig. 278 e); (6) an animal or human effigy vessel fragment, with an unusual mode of whistling (Fig. 278 f); (7) a fragment from a vessel with a spout, decorated with a pressmolded manta ray and sea bird (Fig. 278 g); (8) an appliquéd "adorno" from a body sherd depicting a feline (Fig. 278 h); and (9) a jar fragment with animal effigy handles (Fig. 280, top - left; Note: compare to Fig. 268, bottom - right).

Late Tambo Real Redware Bowl 1 (Fig. 279)

Number: 4 sherds, or ca. .6% of the Late Tambo Real assemblage.

General description: Globular bowl with a slightly constricted mouth. One sherd in this small sample has straight, outslanted walls and an inverted rim (compare to the Late Tambo Real Grayware Bowl 1 sherd from Coll. 324, in Fig. 274). Rim diameters are 20 cm, 22 cm, 24 cm, and 35 cm. Wall thickness below the rim ranges between 3 mm and 7 mm.

Paste: Temper consists of medium sand in moderate quantities. Paste color is red.

Surface characteristics: Two of the sherds in the sample have exterior zoned stippling, probably formed as part of the pressmolding

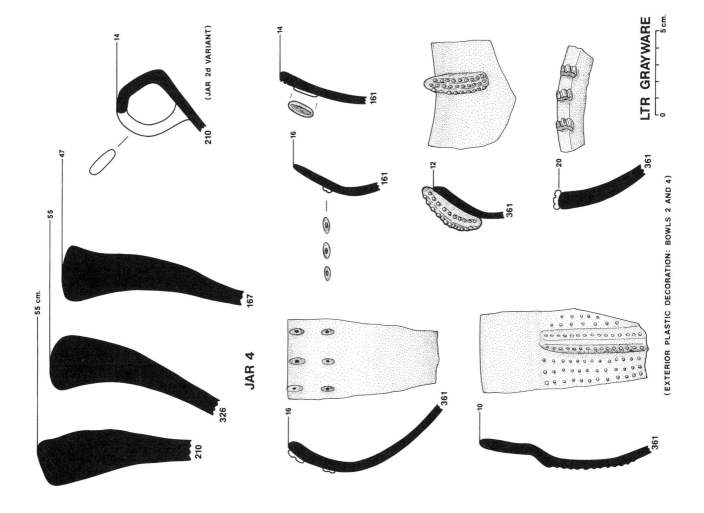

Fig. 277. Late Tambo Real Period ceramics: Grayware Jar 4, and detail drawings of Grayware Bowls 2 and 4.

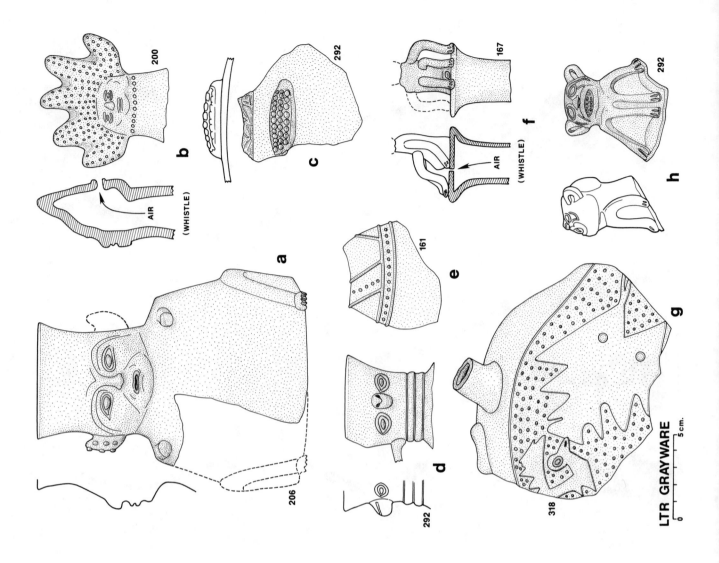

LTR GRAYWARE

0   5 cm.

Fig. 278. Late Tambo Real Period ceramics: miscellaneous grayware.

process. Otherwise, interior and exterior surfaces are plain redware.

Distribution: This bowl type has a wide, but limited, distribution in habitation and cemetery sites. Collection proveniences (with number of sherds in parentheses)/site numbers are:

Coll. 161(2)/LTR-3; Coll. 361(1)/LTR-14; Coll. 322(1)/LTR-45.

Chronological assessment: Judging from the analysis of single-component collections, the zoned pressmolded and inverted rim variants of Redware Bowl 1 are good diagnostics of Late Tambo Real Period. Their limited distribution lessens their utility as a general time marker, however.

Inter-regional comparisons: Redware bowls of the forms and decorative types mentioned here are not reported for contemporaneous ceramic assemblages in areas adjacent to the Lower Santa region. However, the Redware Bowl 1 variants are nearly identical to those of Late Tambo Real Grayware Bowl 1, and they are thus analogous to Vessel Form 1 of the Virú Valley Tomaval Plain type (cf. Collier 1955, p. 161, Fig. 50 – first two profiles on the right).

Late Tambo Real Redware Bowl 2 (Fig. 279)

Number: 13 sherds, or ca. 1.8% of the Late Tambo Real assemblage.

General description: Open bowl with outslanted and slightly incurving walls. One sherd in the sample has an upturned, nearly vertical rim (see sherd from Coll. 361, in Fig. 279). Rim diameters vary from 12-25 cm, with a mean of about 20 cm. Wall thickness below the rim ranges from 6 mm (thin-walled bowls in Fig. 279) to 11 mm (grater bowls, not illustrated).

Paste: Temper consists of either medium sand (thin-walled bowls) or medium black gravel (grater bowls). The quantity of temper in all sherds is moderate. Paste color is red.

Surface characteristics: Of the eight thin-walled bowls, four have polished interiors and exteriors, one has white interior slipping, and three are plain redware. The interiors of the other five bowls in the sample are covered with crosshatched incising, indicating probable use as graters for processing food.

Distribution: This general bowl form has a wide, but limited, distribution in habitation, habitation-cemetery, and cemetery sites throughout most of the area of Late Tambo Real occupation. Collection proveniences (with number of sherds in parentheses)/site numbers are:

Coll. 167(1)/LTR-1; Coll. 161(4)/LTR-3; Coll. 361(1)/LTR-14; Coll. 298(2)/LTR-55.

Chronological assessment: Judging from the analysis of single-component collections, the polished variant of Bowl 1 has no counterparts in other periods and is therefore a good time marker. However, the grater bowls are similar in form and paste to Late Tanguche Bowl 2, and are thus of little utility as reliable late period time markers.

Inter-regional comparisons: Polished redware bowls of the type described here are not reported in the literature on contemporaneous ceramics in areas adjacent to the Lower Santa region.

Late Tambo Real Redware Jar 1 (Fig. 279)

Number: 7 sherds, or ca. 1% of the Late Tambo Real assemblage.

General description: Globular jar with a straight, everted rim. Rim diameters vary from 12-20 cm, with a mean of about 15 cm. Wall thickness below the rim ranges between 4 mm and 7 mm, with five of the sherds in the sample at the lower end of the range.

Paste: Temper consists of fine or medium sand, with four of the sherds having medium grain sand. The quantity of temper in all sherds is moderate. Paste color is red.

Surface characteristics: One sherd has exterior pressmolded decoration consisting of zoned ridges and stippling. The remaining sherds have plain redware surfaces.

Distribution: This jar type has a limited distribution in three widely separated habitation sites. Collection proveniences (with number of sherds in parentheses)/site numbers are:

Coll. 161(3)/LTR-3; Coll. 336(2)/LTR-10; Coll. 326(2)/LTR-47.

Chronological assessment: Redware Jar 1 is similar in form and paste to Early Tanguche Jar 2a (Fig. 236), but can be distinguished on the basis of its consistently greater neck height.

Inter-regional comparisons: The undecorated rim sherds of Late Tambo Real Redware Jar 1 are roughly similar in shape to some variants of Vessel Form 7 of the Virú Valley Rubia Plain type (cf. Collier 1955, p. 166, Fig. 54 G – right and left profiles).

Late Tambo Real Redware Jar 2 (Fig. 279)

Number: 8 sherds, or ca. 1.1% of the Late Tambo Real assemblage.

General description: Globular jar with a cambered neck. As Fig. 279 shows, there is a great deal of variability in the form of the profile. The majority of the sherds have outslanted necks, while lips are either roughly vertical or everted. Rim diameters vary from 11-17 cm, with six sherds having a rim diameter of 12 cm. Wall thickness below the rim ranges between 4 mm and 7 mm.

Paste: Temper consists of fine or medium sand, with five of the sherds having medium grain sand. The quantity of sand in all sherds is moderate. Paste color is red.

Surface characteristics: Exterior and interior surfaces are plain redware.

Distribution: This jar type has a limited distribution at three habitation sites located in Late Tambo Real Cluster 2. Collection proveniences (with number of sherds in parentheses)/site numbers are:

Coll. 311(3)/LTR-6; Coll. 326(4)/LTR-47; Coll. 320(1)/LTR-48.

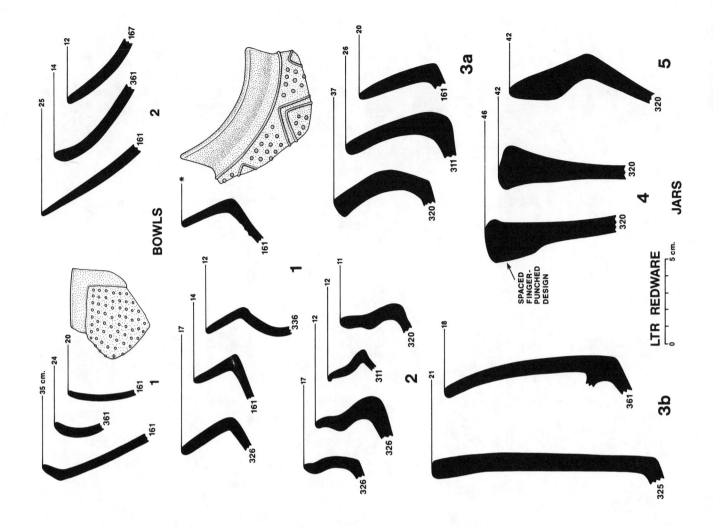

BOWLS

JARS

LTR REDWARE

SPACED FINGER-PUNCHED DESIGN

0 ___ 5 cm.

Fig. 279. Late Tambo Real Period ceramics: Redware Bowls 1 and 2; Redware Jars 1, 2, 3a, 3b, 4, and 5.

Chronological assessment: Redware Jar 2 is similar in form and paste to some variants of Early Tanguche Jar 4a (Fig. 237) and Early Tambo Real Redware Jar 3 (Fig. 271). Thus, although the analysis of single-component contexts indicates that Redware Jar 2 dates to Late Tambo Real Period, it probably cannot be used as a critical diagnostic for distinguishing components in mixed contexts.

Inter-regional comparisons: Some variants of Redware Jar 2 are similar to the cambered variant of Vessel Form 6 of the Rubia Plain type (cf. Collier 1955, p. 166, Fig. 54 F - first two profiles on the left).

Late Tambo Real Redware Jar 3a (Fig. 279)

Number: 16 sherds, or ca. 2.2% of the Late Tambo Real assemblage.

General description: Globular jar with a neck of medium height and a flared or everted rim. Most lips are rounded, although a few exterior beveled lips are also present in the sample. Rim diameters vary from 17-37 cm, with a mean of 21 cm and a standard deviation of 5.9 cm. Wall thickness below the rim ranges between 5 mm and 8 mm.

Paste: Temper in approximately 80% of the sherds consists of medium sand in moderate quantities. The remaining 20% have temper consisting of medium black gravel in moderate amounts. Paste color is red, with gray cores noted on two of the sherds.

Surface characteristics: Exterior and interior surfaces are plain redware.

Distribution: This jar type has a wide distribution in habitation and habitation-cemetery sites throughout most of the area of Late Tambo Real occupation. Collection proveniences (with number of sherds in parentheses)/site numbers are:

Coll. 161(3)/LTR-3; Coll. 311(1)/LTR-6; Coll. 336(2)/LTR-10; Coll. 88(3)/LTR-38; Coll. 322(1)/LTR-45; Coll. 326(2)/LTR-47; Coll. 320(1)/LTR-48; Coll. 288(1)/LTR-68; Coll. 286(2)/LTR-73.

Chronological assessment: Redware Jar 3a is similar in form and paste to some variants of Early Tanguche Jars 2c and 2d (Fig. 236), but can be distinguished on the basis of its consistently intermediate neck height.

Inter-regional comparisons: Redware vessels with this specific rim form are not reported for contemporaneous ceramics of areas adjacent to the Lower Santa region.

Late Tambo Real Redware Jar 3b (Fig. 279)

Number: 5 sherds, or ca. .7% of the Late Tambo Real assemblage.

General description: Globular jar with a neck of medium-to-tall height. The lower part of the neck is essentially vertical, while the upper part is slightly flared. Lips are either slightly rounded or roughly squared. Rim diameters are 12 cm, 12 cm, 18 cm, 25 cm, and 30 cm. Wall thickness below the rim ranges between 5 mm and 8 mm.

Paste: Temper consists of medium sand in moderate quantities. Paste color is red.

Surface characteristics: Exterior and interior surfaces are plain redware.

Distribution: Redware Jar 3b has a wide, but limited, distribution in habitation, habitation-cemetery, and cemetery sites throughout Late Tambo Real Cluster 2. Collection proveniences (with number of sherds in parentheses)/site numbers are:

Coll. 361(1)/LTR-14; Coll. 88(2)/LTR-38; Coll. 322(1)/LTR-45; Coll. 288(1)/LTR-68.

Chronological assessment: Although generally similar to Early Tambo Real Redware Jar 4c (Fig. 271), this vessel type can be readily distinguished on the basis of its vertical neck (compare also to Late Tambo Real Grayware Jar 3d, in Fig. 276).

Inter-regional comparisons: No redware jars with this specific rim form are reported for contemporaneous assemblages in areas adjacent to the Lower Santa region. However, this jar form appears to be a redware equivalent of Late Tambo Real Grayware Jars 3c and 3d, and thus it is related in a general way to Vessel Form 4 of the Estero Plain type of Virú Valley (cf. Collier 1955, p. 165, Fig. 53 D).

Late Tambo Real Redware Jar 4 (Fig. 279)

Number: 8 sherds, or ca. 1.1% of the Late Tambo Real assemblage.

General description: Large jar (or basin) with vertical walls and a rim with either exterior or interior thickening. Lips are roughly rounded and slightly beveled. Rim diameters vary from 42-65 cm, with a mean of 51 cm. Wall thickness below the rim ranges between 8 mm and 10 mm.

Paste: Temper in five of the sherds consists of medium sand in moderate quantities. The remaining three have coarse gravel in heavy amounts. Paste color is red.

Surface characteristics: Interior and exterior surfaces on all sherds are plain redware, with most of the sherds having very coarse exterior surfaces.

Distribution: This jar type has a wide, but limited, distribution in habitation sites throughout most of the area of Late Tambo Real occupation. Collection proveniences (with number of sherds in parentheses)/site numbers are:

Coll. 167(2)/LTR-1; Coll. 210(1)/LTR-5; Coll. 325(1)/LTR-47; Coll. 320(2)/LTR-48; Coll. 298(2)/LTR-55.

Chronological assessment: Judging from the analysis of single-component collections, Redware Jar 4 is a good Late Tambo Real diagnostic. However, its apparently limited distribution lessens its utility as a general time marker.

Inter-regional comparisons: Large redware vessels with this rim form are not reported for contemporaneous ceramics in areas adjacent to the Lower Santa region.

Late Tambo Real Redware Jar 5 (Fig. 279)

Number: 1 sherd, or ca. .14% of the Late Tambo Real assemblage.

General description: Large ovoid jar with a low neck and everted, thickened rim. Rim diameter is 42 cm, and wall thickness below the rim is 7 mm.

Paste: Temper consists of medium black gravel in moderate quantities. Paste color is red.

Surface characteristics: The exterior shoulder of the vessel below the neck is decorated with a single line of appliqued circular knobs (not shown in Fig. 279). Elsewhere on the vessel, surfaces are plain redware.

Distribution: This jar type was found at only one habitation site, located immediately to the southeast of SVP-LTR-47/Alto Perú. Collection provenience/site number is:

Coll. 320(1)/LTR-48.

Chronological assessment: Jar 5 appears to be unique in the survey area, but is probably diagnostic of Late Tambo Real Period.

Inter-regional comparisons: No redware vessels with this rim form are reported in the literature on contemporaneous ceramics in areas adjacent to the Lower Santa region.

Late Tambo Real: Effigy Figures (Fig. 277; Fig. 278 a-d, f-h; Fig. 280, top)

Late Tambo Real is a period of small, but continued, increase in the total percentage of human and animal effigy figures present in the assemblage. But, compared to earlier periods such as Guadalupito and Early Tanguche when the total number of effigy figures exceeds 5% of the assemblage, depictions of humans and animals are an essentially minor feature of the collections. Eight human effigies are present (six with maize hats and two without; see Fig. 278 a, b; and Fig. 280, top - right, as well as five animal effigies (see Fig. 278 d, f-h; and Fig. 280, top - left; Note: Fig. 278 f may represent a human, if not a monkey). The combined total of 13 effigy figures in single-component contexts represents ca. 1.8% of the Late Tambo Real assemblage.

Interestingly, the most common subject of ceramic effigy figures is maize. Besides the maize headgear on the six human figures mentioned above (cf. Collier 1955, p. 163, Fig. 52, for similar maize headgear from Virú), some 24 other maize ear effigies are present in the collections--all but one of them grayware. These were either appliqued on vessel shoulders (e.g., Fig. 278 c) and rims (e.g., Fig. 277, lower - right), or were incorporated as more abstract motifs on the bodies of pressmolded vessels (e.g., Fig. 277, lower - left). The combined total of 30 maize effigy figures (including the headgear on whistling vessels) represents ca. 4.1% of the Late Tambo Real assemblage.

Effigy distributions: Human, maize, and animal effigies were found in habitation, habitation-cemetery, and cemetery sites throughout most of the area of Late Tambo Real occupation. Separate collection proveniences (with number of sherds in parentheses)/site numbers are:

Human: Coll. 200(1)/LTR-4; Coll. 328(1)/LTR-50.

Human with maize headgear: Coll. 200(5)/LTR-4; Coll. 350(1)/LTR-25.

Maize: Coll. 161(4)/LTR-3; Coll. 200(17)/LTR-4; Coll. 361(2)/LTR-14; Coll. 292(1)/LTR-60.

Animal: Coll. 167(1)/LTR-1; Coll. 360(1)/LTR-9; Coll. 318(1)/LTR-44; Coll. 292(2)/LTR-60.

Late Tambo Real: Chimú and Inca Diagnostics (Fig. 278 a; Fig. 280, center and lower)

It is of interest to note that although the total number of Chimú and Inca diagnostics is relatively quite small, both sets of cultural diagnostics were found consistently in association with the Late Tambo Real collections. Thus, while it is probable that Chimú influence and cultural diagnostics preceded the Inca in the Lower Santa region, it appears that both of these influences were relatively transitory and occurred in rapid enough succession that corresponding changes did not take place in the main ceramic assemblage of the region.

Only two vessel fragments are present in the collections that are among the diagnostics commonly regarded as Chimú. These fragments are both from flat-sided stirrup spout vessels (e.g., Fig. 280, center), and, although badly damaged, appear to have had polished blackware surfaces (paste is dark gray). On the other hand, as mentioned under inter-regional comparisons for most ceramic types of this period, it is also clearly the case that Moche, Virú, and Santa (among other valleys) shared the same basic ceramic assemblage in this period.

Two of the six probable Inca-related vessel fragments found in the Lower Santa region are illustrated here. They include (1) a human effigy vessel (Fig. 278 a) that is similar in overall form and decorative features to two of the provincial Inca-style vessels illustrated in Menzel (1977; see discussion under miscellaneous grayware); and (2) a fragment of a small bowl (or goblet) with exterior decoration in the fine-lined geometric polychrome style of Inca ceramics (Fig. 280, lower; Note: here I must confess to having gotten so absorbed in drawing the design in the field laboratory that the rim diameter was inadvertantly left unrecorded; in any case, the vessel is very small and probably has a rim diameter of ca. 10 cm, or slightly less).

Chimú and Inca distributions: The two Chimú polished blackware diagnostics were found in habitation sites on the north desert margin of the Lower Valley sector (one at SVP-LTR-35/Huaca Gallinazo and the other along an ancient Early Tanguche road in Pampa Las Salinas). The six probable Inca diagnostics were found more widely distributed in habitation-cemetery and cemetery sites in Late Tambo Real Cluster 2. Separate collection proveniences (with number of sherds in parentheses)/ site numbers are:

Chimu: Coll. 180(1)/LTR-35; Coll. 367(1)/LTR-75.

Inca: Coll. 311(2)/LTR-6; Coll. 336(1)/LTR-10; Coll.
328(2)/LTR-50; Coll. 206(1)/(single vessel--no site).

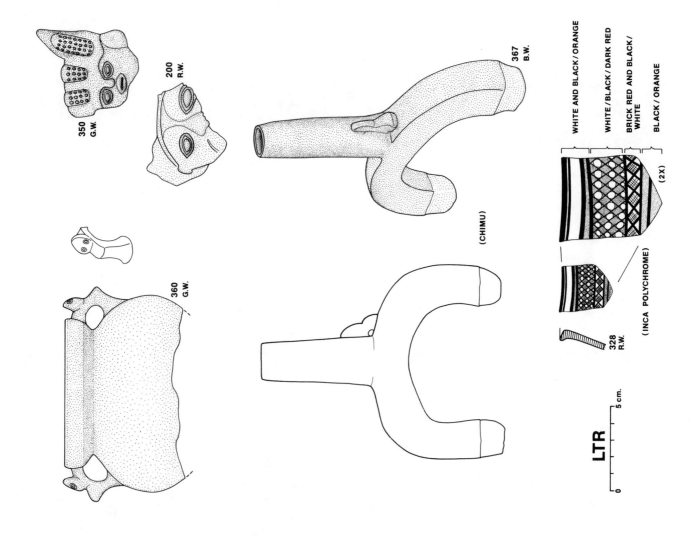

534

Fig. 280. Late Tambo Real Period ceramics: miscellaneous redware, grayware, and blackware.

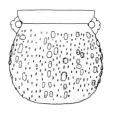

Tabular Presentation of Citadel, Settlement, and Ceramic Data

Table 25. Tabular Presentation of Data on Cayhuamarca Period Citadels[a]

Structure Number	Site Number	Setting	Shape	Overall Dimensions (m)	Specific Features Present
119	SVP-CAY-4	lower piedmont bluff	rectangular	50 X 20	double main walls baffled entrance
107	SVP-CAY-9	lower piedmont bluff	curvilinear	100 X 80	circular sunken court single outer wall direct entrance interior double-walled tower
1	SVP-CAY-12	high piedmont shelf	six sides: roughly trapezoidal	93 X 72	double main walls baffled entrances (3) interior double-walled structure
6	SVP-CAY-15	high ridgetop	hill contours	200 X 50	single outer wall bastion interior structure
27	SVP-CAY-17	high hilltop	hill contours	90 X 68	single outer wall bastions (5); stairway entrance interior spoke walls interior enclosure
29/30	SVP-CAY-18	high ridgetop	rectangular	25 X 13 24 X 21	double main walls
28	SVP-CAY-19	high flat pampa	six sides: roughly square	83 X 80	single outer wall; bastions (8) direct and baffled entrances interior buttress walls interior double-walled structure
31	SVP-CAY-21	high ridgetop	hill contours	86 X 40	interior structure
33	SVP-CAY-23	high ridgetop	hill contours	210 X 72	defensive ditches; bastions (2) interior structures

Table 25. (Continued)

Structure Number	Site Number	Setting	Shape	Overall Dimensions (m)	Specific Features Present
41	SVP-CAY-24	adjacent to valley floor	roughly square	50 X 47	bastions (4) stairway entrance; partly open
34	SVP-CAY-25	high ridgetop	circular	57.5 X 56	bastions (4) indirect and direct entrances interior: spoke walls and inner structure with sunken court
35	SVP-CAY-26	high ridgetop	six sides: ovoid	84 X 71	bastions (6) interior structure
45	SVP-CAY-28	lower ridgetop	five sides: ovoid	66 X 53	defensive ditch bastions (5) interior: spoke walls/structure
49	SVP-CAY-31	high ridgetop	hill contours	105 X 65	defensive ditches indirect entrances (2) interior walls and structure
52	SVP-CAY-32	high ridgetop	hill contours	150 X 60	defensive ditch indirect entrance; bastions (8) interior: two levels/structure
55	SVP-CAY-34	high ridgetop	hill contours	200 X 25	defensive ditches bastions (2)
71	SVP-CAY-36	high ridgetop	four sides: roughly trapezoidal	65 X 48	defensive ditches indirect entrance; bastions (4) interior: spoke walls/structure
72	SVP-CAY-36	high ridgetop	hill contours	85 X 25	defensive ditches bastions (4) interior: spoke walls/structure

536

Table 25. (Continued)

Structure Number	Site Number	Setting	Shape	Overall Dimensions (m)	Specific Features Present
90	SVP-CAY-40	high hilltop	hill contours	238 X 130	two main walls indirect entrances (4) interior structure
95	SVP-CAY-47	high ridgetop	hill contours	240 X 70	lower terraced walling indirect entrance; bastions (2) interior structure

[a]Structures are listed in order of their location from upvalley down.

Table 26. Tabular Presentation of Prehispanic Settlement Data for the Lower Santa Valley Survey Region[a]

Las Salinas Period Sites								
Site Number	Classification	Survey Sector	Collection Number(s)	Elev (m)	Area (ha)	Hab Dens	Pop Est	Site Numbers of Other Occupations
SVP-SAL-1	Hamlet	UV	-	550	1.00	30 p/ha	30	-
SVP-SAL-2	Hamlet	UV	-	600	.25	3 w.b.	15	-
SVP-SAL-3	Hamlet	UV	-	575	.25	3 w.b.	15	-
SVP-SAL-4	Hamlet	UV	-	500	.25	3 w.b.	15	-
SVP-SAL-5	Hamlet	UV	-	450	1.25	30 p/ha	35	-
SVP-SAL-6	Hamlet	UV	-	375	1.50	30 p/ha	45	-
SVP-SAL-7	Hamlet	UV	-	400	.50	30 p/ha	15	-
SVP-SAL-8	Hamlet	MV	-	275	1.00	30 p/ha	30	-
SVP-SAL-9	Hamlet	MV	-	270	1.00	30 p/ha	30	-
SVP-SAL-10	Small Village	MV	-	350	3.50	30 p/ha	100	-
SVP-SAL-11	Hamlet	MV	-	275	2.00	30 p/ha	60	-
SVP-SAL-12	Hamlet	MV	-	275	1.00	25 p/ha	25	-
SVP-SAL-13	Hamlet	Coast	-	45	.50	30 p/ha	15	-
SVP-SAL-14	Hamlet	Coast	-	50	.50	30 p/ha	15	-
SVP-SAL-15	Hamlet	Coast	-	50	.50	30 p/ha	15	-
SVP-SAL-16	Hamlet	Coast	271	50	1.00	L-M	50	-
SVP-SAL-17	Small Village	Coast	-	400	8.75	30 p/ha	260	-
SVP-SAL-18	Hamlet	Coast	-	100	.50	30 p/ha	15	-

Table 26. Tabular Presentation of Prehispanic Settlement Data (Continued)

Las Salinas Period Sites

Site Number	Classification	Survey Sector	Collection Number(s)	Elev (m)	Area (ha)	Hab Dens	Pop Est	Site Numbers of Other Occupations
SVP-SAL-19	Hamlet	Coast	-	100	.50	30 p/ha	15	-
SVP-SAL-20	Hamlet	Coast	-	125	.25	30 p/ha	15	-
SVP-SAL-21	Hamlet	Coast	-	5	.50	10 w.b.	30	-
SVP-SAL-22	Hamlet	Coast	-	35	.25	30 p/ha	10	-
SVP-SAL-23	Hamlet	Coast	364	30	1.00	30 p/ha	30	-
SVP-SAL-24	Hamlet	Coast	365	30	.15	30 p/ha	5	-
SVP-SAL-25	Hamlet	Coast	-	30	.15	30 p/ha	5	-
SVP-SAL-26	Hamlet	Coast	-	30	.15	30 p/ha	5	-
SVP-SAL-27	Hamlet	Coast	-	30	.15	30 p/ha	5	-
SVP-SAL-28	Hamlet	Coast	-	30	.15	30 p/ha	5	-
SVP-SAL-29	Hamlet	Coast	-	30	.15	30 p/ha	5	-
SVP-SAL-30	Hamlet	Coast	-	30	.15	30 p/ha	5	-
SVP-SAL-31	Hamlet	Coast	-	40	.15	30 p/ha	5	-
SVP-SAL-32	Hamlet	Coast	-	35	.20	30 p/ha	5	-
SVP-SAL-33	Hamlet	Coast	-	40	.15	30 p/ha	5	-
SVP-SAL-34	Hamlet	Coast	-	35	.75	30 p/ha	20	-
SVP-SAL-35	Hamlet	Coast	-	30	.75	30 p/ha	20	-
SVP-SAL-36	Hamlet	Coast	-	30	.20	30 p/ha	5	-

Table 26. Tabular Presentation of Prehispanic Settlement Data for the Lower Santa Valley Survey Region

Cayhuamarca Period Sites

Site Number	Classification	Survey Sector	Collection Number(s)	Elev (m)	Area (ha)	Hab Dens	Pop Est	Site Numbers of Other Occupations
SVP-CAY-1	Large Village	UV	381	540	.88 5.62	H L-M	500	VIN-1, ESUCH-1
SVP-CAY-2	Hamlet	UV	-	530	.85	M	85	-
SVP-CAY-3	Small Village	UV	380	515	4.30	L-M	200	VIN-3
SVP-CAY-4	Citadel/C-C/ Small Village	UV	376,377,378	500	2.50	M(1 ha)	115	VIN-4
SVP-CAY-5	C-C/Hamlet	UV	379	460	2.00	M(.5 ha)	50	-
SVP-CAY-6	C-C/Hamlet	UV	374	430	.50	L-M	25	VIN-7, ESUCH-6, LSUCH-26
SVP-CAY-7	Small Village	UV	373	450	3.00	L-M	150	VIN-8, ESUCH-5
SVP-CAY-8	C-C/Hamlet	UV	-	405	1.50	L	25	LSUCH-32
SVP-CAY-9	Citadel/C-C	UV	368	430	1.00	M	100	VIN-9, ESUCH-12
SVP-CAY-10	Hamlet	UV	-	500	.50	M	50	-
SVP-CAY-11	Small Village	UV	5	650	2.50	M	250	VIN-10
SVP-CAY-12	Citadel/C-C/ Small Village	UV	2,3,4	630	3.75	M	375	VIN-11, ESUCH-14
SVP-CAY-13	Small Village	UV	32	350	2.50	L-M	125	ESUCH-17
SVP-CAY-14	Hamlet	UV	21	790	1.50	L	20	-
SVP-CAY-15	Citadel	UV	26	680	1.50	M	150	VIN-15, ESUCH-26, LSUCH-50, ETAN-5

Table 26. Tabular Presentation of Prehispanic Settlement Data (Continued)

			Cayhuamarca Period Sites					
Site Number	Classification	Survey Sector	Collection Number(s)	Elev (m)	Area (ha)	Hab Dens	Pop Est	Site Numbers of Other Occupations
SVP-CAY-16	Hamlet	UV	27,28	450	1.00	L-M	50	ESUCH-27
SVP-CAY-17	Citadel	UV	93,94,95	590	2.25	L-M	110	VIN-16, ETAN-6
SVP-CAY-18	Citadel	UV	-	570	.50	-	-	-
SVP-CAY-19	Citadel/ Small Village	UV	96,97,98	510	3.00	L-M	150	VIN-17
SVP-CAY-20	Small Village	UV	100	510	3.75	L-M	250	-
SVP-CAY-21	Citadel	UV	99	610	.50	M	50	ESUCH-29
SVP-CAY-22	C-C/Huaca	UV	(116)	310	.25	-	-	ETAN-8
SVP-CAY-23	Citadel	UV	101,102,107, 119	540	2.50	L-M	125	VIN-18, ESUCH-41, LSUCH-66
SVP-CAY-24	C-C	UV	151	350	.50	-	-	ESUCH-42, ETR-5
SVP-CAY-25	Citadel/C-C	UV	108,109,110	540	3.00	L-M	150	VIN-20, ESUCH-43, LSUCH-67
SVP-CAY-26	Citadel	UV	113	460	3.00	L-M	150	ESUCH-46, LSUCH-74
SVP-CAY-27	Cemetery	UV	125	525	.10	-	-	LSUCH-61
SVP-CAY-28	Citadel	UV	168,169	375	1.00	L-M	50	VIN-22
SVP-CAY-29	C-C/Hamlet	UV	(173,174)	335	6.75	M(.5 ha)	50	ESUCH-51, ETAN-20
SVP-CAY-30	Small Village	UV	193	350	2.00	M	200	ESUCH-52, ETAN-25
SVP-CAY-31	Citadel	UV	194	855	.40	H	100	VIN-23

Table 26. Tabular Presentation of Prehispanic Settlement Data (Continued)

			Cayhuamarca Period Sites					
Site Number	Classification	Survey Sector	Collection Number(s)	Elev (m)	Area (ha)	Hab Dens	Pop Est	Site Numbers of Other Occupations
SVP-CAY-32	Citadel/C-C	UV	232,233	425	.80	H	200	ESUCH-54, LSUCH-83, ETAN-35, LTR-2
SVP-CAY-33	Small Village	MV	243	275	2.00	L-M	100	ESUCH-63, LSUCH-87
SVP-CAY-34	Citadel	MV	254	580	.55	M	55	LSUCH-106
SVP-CAY-35	Large Village	MV	255	200	6.25	M	625	-
SVP-CAY-36	Citadel	MV	-	530	1.50	M	150	-
SVP-CAY-37	Hamlet	MV	-	350	.25	L	5	-
SVP-CAY-38	C-C/Hamlet	MV	-	440	.25	M	15	ESUCH-97
SVP-CAY-39	C-C/Hamlet	MV	300	360	1.00	L	15	VIN-27, ESUCH-99
SVP-CAY-40	Citadel	MV	(331)	850	1.00	M	100	VIN-28, ESUCH-100, LSUCH-120
SVP-CAY-41	Hamlet	MV	332	220	1.50	L-M	75	ESUCH-101
SVP-CAY-42	Hamlet	MV	-	200	1.00	L-M	50	-
SVP-CAY-43	Hamlet	MV	-	210	.50	L-M	25	-
SVP-CAY-44	Small Village	MV	340	200	2.50	M	250	VIN-29
SVP-CAY-45	Hamlet	MV	-	200	.75	M	75	-
SVP-CAY-46	Hamlet	MV	-	190	.75	M	75	-
SVP-CAY-47	Citadel	MV	339	340	1.25	M	125	ESUCH-111, LSUCH-133
SVP-CAY-48	Small Village	MV	341	230	1.00	M	100	VIN-30, ESUCH-110

Table 26. Tabular Presentation of Prehispanic Settlement Data (Continued)

Cayhuamarca Period Sites

Site Number	Classification	Survey Sector	Collection Number(s)	Elev (m)	Area (ha)	Hab Dens	Pop Est	Site Numbers of Other Occupations
SVP-CAY-49	Hamlet	MV	-	225	.25	M	25	-
SVP-CAY-50	Hamlet	MV	-	225	.25	M	25	-
SVP-CAY-51	Hamlet	MV	-	225	.50	M	50	-
SVP-CAY-52	C-C/Huaca	MV	-	100	.25	-	-	-
SVP-CAY-53	Small Village	LV	348	200	3.00	L-M	150	VIN-36
SVP-CAY-54	Hamlet	Coast	-	5	.25	M	15	ETAN-232

Table 26. Tabular Presentation of Prehispanic Settlement Data for the Lower Santa Valley Survey Region

Vinzos Period Sites

Site Number	Classification	Survey Sector	Collection Number(s)	Elev (m)	Area (ha)	Hab Dens	Pop Est	Site Numbers of Other Occupations
SVP-VIN-1	Large Village	UV	381	540	.88 / 5.62	H / L-M	500	CAY-1, ESUCH-1
SVP-VIN-2	Hamlet	UV	-	570	1.50	L-M	75	-
SVP-VIN-3	Hamlet	UV	380	522	1.00	L-M	50	CAY-3
SVP-VIN-4	Citadel/C-C	UV	378	500	.25	L	5	CAY-4
SVP-VIN-5	Small Village	UV	-	510	2.90	M	290	-
SVP-VIN-6	Small Village	UV	375, 376	465	2.60	M	260	ESUCH-3, LSUCH-13
SVP-VIN-7	C-C/Hamlet	UV	374	430	.25	M	25	CAY-6, ESUCH-6, LSUCH-26
SVP-VIN-8	Small Village	UV	373	450	3.00	L-M	150	CAY-7, ESUCH-5
SVP-VIN-9	Citadel/C-C Small Village	UV	368, 369	430	2.50	M	250	CAY-9, ESUCH-11/12
SVP-VIN-10	Small Village	UV	5	650	2.50	M	250	CAY-11
SVP-VIN-11	Citadel/C-C	UV	3,4	630	1.50	M	150	CAY-12, ESUCH-14
SVP-VIN-12	Cemetery	UV	31	425	.10	-	-	ESUCH-16
SVP-VIN-13	Hamlet	UV	38	425	1.00	L-M	50	ESUCH-32
SVP-VIN-14	Small Village	UV	25	550	1.00	M	100	-
SVP-VIN-15	Citadel	UV	26	680	1.50	M	150	CAY-15, ESUCH-26, LSUCH-50, ETAN-5
SVP-VIN-16	Citadel	UV	(93),95	590	1.00	L-M	50	CAY-17

Table 26. Tabular Presentation of Prehispanic Settlement Data (Continued)

				Vinzos Period Sites				
Site Number	Classification	Survey Sector	Collection Number(s)	Elev (m)	Area (ha)	Hab Dens	Pop Est	Site Numbers of Other Occupations
SVP-VIN-17	Citadel	UV	98	510	2.00	L	30	CAY-19
SVP-VIN-18	Citadel	UV	(99),101	540	1.00	M	100	CAY-23, ESUCH-41, LSUCH-66
SVP-VIN-19	Small Village	UV	115	340	1.00	M	100	ESUCH-38, LSUCH-63
SVP-VIN-20	Citadel/C-C	UV	108,110	540	1.00	M	100	CAY-25, ESUCH-43, LSUCH-67
SVP-VIN-21	Small Village	UV	170	350	2.00	M	200	-
SVP-VIN-22	Citadel	UV	168,169	375	1.00	L-M	50	CAY-28
SVP-VIN-23	Citadel	UV	194	855	.25	H	25	CAY-31
SVP-VIN-24	Small Village	MV	248	230	1.35	H	340	-
SVP-VIN-25	Hamlet	MV	-	220	.50	M	50	-
SVP-VIN-26	C-C/ Small Village	MV	223	490	.75 6.00	H L-M	490	ESUCH-89, LSUCH-112, GUAD-16
SVP-VIN-27	C-C/Hamlet	MV	300	360	1.00	L	15	CAY-39, ESUCH-99
SVP-VIN-28	Citadel	MV	331	850	1.00	M	100	CAY-40, ESUCH-100, LSUCH-120
SVP-VIN-29	Citadel/ Small Village	MV	340	200	2.50	M	250	CAY-44/47
SVP-VIN-30	Small Village	MV	341	230	1.00	M	100	CAY-48, ESUCH-110
SVP-VIN-31	Hamlet	MV	-	150	.50	M	50	-

Table 26. Tabular Presentation of Prehispanic Settlement Data (Continued)

				Vinzos Period Sites				
Site Number	Classification	Survey Sector	Collection Number(s)	Elev (m)	Area (ha)	Hab Dens	Pop Est	Site Numbers of Other Occupations
SVP-VIN-32	Hamlet	MV	-	150	.25	M	25	-
SVP-VIN-33	Small Village	MV	346	150	4.00	M	400	-
SVP-VIN-34	Small Village	MV	344	185	2.70	L-M	135	-
SVP-VIN-35	Hamlet	MV	-	185	1.00	L-M	50	-
SVP-VIN-36	Small Village	LV	348	200	3.00	M	300	CAY-53
SVP-VIN-37	Large Village	LV	366	50	15.00 11.00	M L-M	2050	-
SVP-VIN-38	Hamlet	S-C	-	385	1.50	L-M	75	-
SVP-VIN-39	Hamlet	S-C	-	400	.75	L-M	40	-
SVP-VIN-40	Small Village	S-C	-	400	5.50	L-M	275	-
SVP-VIN-41	Hamlet	S-C	-	400	1.00	L-M	50	-
SVP-VIN-42	Hamlet	S-C	-	400	.50	L-M	25	-
SVP-VIN-43	Hamlet	S-C	-	400	.50	L-M	25	-
SVP-VIN-44	Hamlet	S-C	-	410	.50	L-M	25	-
SVP-VIN-45	Hamlet	S-C	-	420	.50	L-M	25	-

Table 26. Tabular Presentation of Prehispanic Settlement Data for the Lower Santa Valley Survey Region

Early Suchimancillo Period Sites								
Site Number	Classification	Survey Sector	Collection Number(s)	Elev (m)	Area (ha)	Hab Dens	Pop Est	Site Numbers of Other Occupations
SVP-ESUCH-1	Large Village	UV	381	500	.88 11.12	H L-M	775	CAY-1, VIN-1, LSUCH-9
SVP-ESUCH-2	Small Village	UV	-	500	1.00	M	100	LSUCH-12
SVP-ESUCH-3	Small Village	UV	375	465	1.70	M	170	VIN-6, LSUCH-13
SVP-ESUCH-4	Hamlet	UV	-	450	.50	M	25	LSUCH-14
SVP-ESUCH-5	Small Village	UV	373	450	3.00	L-M	150	CAY-7, VIN-8
SVP-ESUCH-6	Small Village	UV	374	430	2.25	M	225	CAY-6, VIN-7, LSUCH-26
SVP-ESUCH-7	Hamlet	UV	372	460	1.00	L-M	50	ETAN-1
SVP-ESUCH-8	Hamlet	UV	371	490	.90	L-M	45	LSUCH-27, ETAN-2
SVP-ESUCH-9	Small Village	UV	370	465	2.50	L-M	125	LSUCH-28, ETAN-3
SVP-ESUCH-10	Large Village	UV	-	375	22.75	L-M	1140	LSUCH-31
SVP-ESUCH-11	Small Village	UV	369	430	1.00	M	100	VIN-9
SVP-ESUCH-12	C-C/Citadel	UV	368	430	1.00	M	100	CAY-9, VIN-9
SVP-ESUCH-13	Citadel	UV	6	850	3.00	L	45	-
SVP-ESUCH-14	Hamlet	UV	2,3	630	.25	M	25	CAY-12, VIN-11
SVP-ESUCH-15	Large Village	UV	29	375	14.00	M	1400	LSUCH-39
SVP-ESUCH-16	Cemetery	UV	31	425	.10	-	-	VIN-12
SVP-ESUCH-17	Small Village/ Minor Fort/Cem	UV	30,32,33	350	8.00	L-M(4 ha)	200	CAY-13, LSUCH-40

Table 26. Tabular Presentation of Prehispanic Settlement Data (Continued)

Early Suchimancillo Period Sites								
Site Number	Classification	Survey Sector	Collection Number(s)	Elev (m)	Area (ha)	Hab Dens	Pop Est	Site Numbers of Other Occupations
SVP-ESUCH-18	Cemetery	UV	34	400	.10	-	-	LSUCH-44
SVP-ESUCH-19	Local Center/ Minor Fort/Cem	UV	1,7,10,14,15, 17,19	350	62.00	L-M	3100	LSUCH-45
SVP-ESUCH-20	Minor Fortress/ Cemetery	UV	18	510	.10	-	-	-
SVP-ESUCH-21	Hamlet	UV	20	470	1.50	L	25	-
SVP-ESUCH-22	Small Village	UV	35	500	3.00	M	300	LSUCH-47
SVP-ESUCH-23	Small Village	UV	24	350	2.00	M	200	LSUCH-49
SVP-ESUCH-24	Minor Fortress	UV	23	490	1.00	L	15	-
SVP-ESUCH-25	Hamlet	UV	22	400	.25	L	10	-
SVP-ESUCH-26	Citadel	UV	26	680	1.00	M	100	CAY-15, VIN-15, LSUCH-50, ETAN-5
SVP-ESUCH-27	Small Village	UV	27	450	3.40	M	340	CAY-16
SVP-ESUCH-28	Small Village	UV	104	350	2.50	M	250	LSUCH-51, ETAN-4
SVP-ESUCH-29	Citadel	UV	99	610	.25	L-M	10	CAY-21
SVP-ESUCH-30	Cemetery	UV	117	340	.10	-	-	ETR-2
SVP-ESUCH-31	Cemetery	UV	39	325	1.50	-	-	LSUCH-52, GUAD-1, ETAN-9, LTAN-4
SVP-ESUCH-32	Hamlet	UV	37,38	390	2.70	L	40	VIN-13

542

Table 26. Tabular Presentation of Prehispanic Settlement Data (Continued)

		Survey Sector	Collection Number(s)	Elev (m)	Area (ha)	Hab Dens	Pop Est	Site Numbers of
Site Number	Classification							Other Occupations

Early Suchimancillo Period Sites

Site Number	Classification	Survey Sector	Collection Number(s)	Elev (m)	Area (ha)	Hab Dens	Pop Est	Site Numbers of Other Occupations
SVP-ESUCH-33	Cemetery	UV	40	350	.10	-	-	-
SVP-ESUCH-34	Citadel	UV	42	400	5.60	L	85	LSUCH-54
SVP-ESUCH-35	Small Village/ Cemetery	UV	43	350	2.50	L-M	125	LSUCH-55
SVP-ESUCH-36	Citadel	UV	120	350	1.40	M	140	LSUCH-58
SVP-ESUCH-37	Citadel	UV	128	445	3.00	L-M	150	LSUCH-62
SVP-ESUCH-38	Small Village/ Corral	UV	115	340	3.00	M	300	VIN-19, LSUCH-63
SVP-ESUCH-39	Hamlet	UV	147	400	.25	L-M	10	LSUCH-64
SVP-ESUCH-40	Cemetery	UV	148	350	.25	-	-	LTAN-6, ETR-4
SVP-ESUCH-41	Citadel	UV	101,102,107	540	1.50	M	150	CAY-23, VIN-18, LSUCH-66
SVP-ESUCH-42	Cemetery	UV	151	350	.10	-	-	CAY-24, ETR-5
SVP-ESUCH-43	C-C/Citadel	UV	108,109,110	540	3.00	M	300	CAY-25, VIN-20, LSUCH-67
SVP-ESUCH-44	Hamlet/Cemetery	UV	153	350	2.50	L	40	LSUCH-69
SVP-ESUCH-45	Hamlet/Cemetery	UV	111,112	450	4.00	L(3 ha)	45	LSUCH-68
SVP-ESUCH-46	Citadel	UV	113	460	3.00	L-M	150	CAY-26, LSUCH-74
SVP-ESUCH-47	Citadel/ Cemetery	UV	134	510	1.25	L-M	60	LSUCH-79
SVP-ESUCH-48	Minor Fortress	UV	137	450	1.00	L	15	-

Table 26. Tabular Presentation of Prehispanic Settlement Data (Continued)

Early Suchimancillo Period Sites

Site Number	Classification	Survey Sector	Collection Number(s)	Elev (m)	Area (ha)	Hab Dens	Pop Est	Site Numbers of Other Occupations
SVP-ESUCH-49	Cemetery	UV	138	300	.25	-	-	LSUCH-82
SVP-ESUCH-50	C-C/Huaca	UV	175	300	.15	-	-	ETR-6
SVP-ESUCH-51	Cemetery	UV	173	320	.04	-	-	CAY-29, ETAN-20
SVP-ESUCH-52	Hamlet	UV	193	350	1.80	L-M	90	CAY-30, ETAN-25
SVP-ESUCH-53	Hamlet	UV	157	260	1.35	L	20	GUAD-3, ETAN-26, LTAN-16
SVP-ESUCH-54	Citadel	UV	232,233	425	.80	H	200	CAY-32, LSUCH-83, ETAN-35, LTR-2
SVP-ESUCH-55	Small Village	UV	231	250	1.00	M	100	ETAN-33, ETR-10
SVP-ESUCH-56	Small Village	MV	239,240,241	250	2.70	M	270	ETAN-42
SVP-ESUCH-57	Minor fortress	MV	-	500	.75	-	-	ETAN-30
SVP-ESUCH-58	Hamlet	MV	-	400	.50	M	50	-
SVP-ESUCH-59	Hamlet	MV	-	450	.50	M	50	-
SVP-ESUCH-60	Hamlet	MV	356	450	.25	M	25	-
SVP-ESUCH-61	Cemetery	MV	198	300	.10	-	-	-
SVP-ESUCH-62	Small Village/ Minor Fortress	MV	244	440	2.00	M	200	LSUCH-86
SVP-ESUCH-63	Small Village	MV	243	250	1.60	M	160	CAY-33, LSUCH-87
SVP-ESUCH-64	Small Village	MV	354	475	1.00	M	100	LSUCH-91

Table 26. Tabular Presentation of Prehispanic Settlement Data (Continued)

				Early Suchimancillo Period Sites				
Site Number	Classification	Survey Sector	Collection Number(s)	Elev (m)	Area (ha)	Hab Dens	Pop Est	Site Numbers of Other Occupations
SVP-ESUCH-65	Hamlet/ Minor Fortress	MV	353	450	1.40	L-M	70	LSUCH-93
SVP-ESUCH-66	Hamlet	MV	-	350	.50	L	10	-
SVP-ESUCH-67	Desert Figure	MV	-	350	-	-	-	-
SVP-ESUCH-68	Desert Figures	MV	-	375	.90	-	-	-
SVP-ESUCH-69	Desert Figure	MV	-	360	-	-	-	-
SVP-ESUCH-70	Minor Fortress/ Small Village	MV	-	475	2.25	L-M	110	LSUCH-94
SVP-ESUCH-71	Hamlet/Cemetery	MV	203	230	1.80	L	25	LSUCH-95
SVP-ESUCH-72	Cemetery	MV	205	230	.25	-	-	GUAD-7, ETAN-48
SVP-ESUCH-73	Cemetery	MV	206,(207)	230	10.25	-	-	LSUCH-97, ETAN-49, LTAN-25
SVP-ESUCH-74	Minor Fortress	MV	245	440	1.00	L	15	-
SVP-ESUCH-75	Minor Fortress	MV	-	350	.10	L-M	5	-
SVP-ESUCH-76	Minor Fortress	MV	-	400	.25	L-M	10	-
SVP-ESUCH-77	Minor fortress	MV	352	400	.75	L-M	35	-
SVP-ESUCH-78	Hamlet	MV	-	300	.25	L-M	10	-
SVP-ESUCH-79	Hamlet	MV	-	300	.50	M	50	-
SVP-ESUCH-80	Minor fortress	MV	351	420	.25	L-M	25	LSUCH-100

Table 26. Tabular Presentation of Prehispanic Settlement Data (Continued)

				Early Suchimancillo Period Sites				
Site Number	Classification	Survey Sector	Collection Number(s)	Elev (m)	Area (ha)	Hab Dens	Pop Est	Site Numbers of Other Occupations
SVP-ESUCH-81	Cemetery	MV	-	405	.10	-	-	LSUCH-101
SVP-ESUCH-82	Minor Fortress	MV	208	295	.10	M	10	ETAN-53
SVP-ESUCH-83	Cemetery	MV	209	225	.15	-	-	LSUCH-102, GUAD-9, ETAN-57, LTAN-30, ETR-15
SVP-ESUCH-84	Large Village	MV	249,250	200	1.50 1.50	H M	525	LSUCH-103
SVP-ESUCH-85	Hamlet	MV	-	250	.25	L	5	-
SVP-ESUCH-86	Hamlet	MV	224,225	350	.90	L	15	-
SVP-ESUCH-87	Small Village	MV	221	300	1.00	M	100	-
SVP-ESUCH-88	Small Village	MV	222	260	1.50	H	375	-
SVP-ESUCH-89	Local Center	MV	223	205	.70 5.50	H L-M	450	VIN-26, LSUCH-112, GUAD-16
SVP-ESUCH-90	C-C/Huaca	MV	226	200	.20	-	-	LSUCH-113, GUAD-18
SVP-ESUCH-91	Small Village/ Minor Fortress	MV	227,229	200	1.00 4.20	H L-M	460	LSUCH-114, ETAN-77
SVP-ESUCH-92	Citadel	MV	257,258	215	3.40	L-M(1.7 ha)	85	LSUCH-115, ETAN-75
SVP-ESUCH-93	Small Village	MV	272	200	2.25	M(1.75 ha)	175	ETAN-85
SVP-ESUCH-94	Small Village	MV	260	190	2.25	L-M	110	ETAN-81
SVP-ESUCH-95	Small Village/ Minor Fortress	MV	308	250	4.50	L-M	225	-

544

Table 26. Tabular Presentation of Prehispanic Settlement Data (Continued)

Early Suchimancillo Period Sites

Site Number	Classification	Survey Sector	Collection Number(s)	Elev (m)	Area (ha)	Hab Dens	Pop Est	Site Numbers of Other Occupations
SVP-ESUCH-96	Minor Fortress	MV	301	430	.15	M	15	ETAN-89
SVP-ESUCH-97	C-C/Hamlet	MV	-	440	.25	L	15	CAY-38
SVP-ESUCH-98	Small Village/ Minor Fort/Cem	MV	277	200	4.00	M(1 ha)	100	LSUCH-119, GUAD-31
SVP-ESUCH-99	C-C/Hamlet	MV	300	360	1.00	L	15	CAY-39, VIN-27
SVP-ESUCH-100	Citadel	MV	331	850	1.00	M	100	CAY-40, VIN-28, LSUCH-120
SVP-ESUCH-101	Hamlet	MV	332	220	1.25	L-M	65	CAY-41
SVP-ESUCH-102	Small Village/ Desert Figures	MV	-	180	1.00	M	100	-
SVP-ESUCH-103	Hamlet/ Minor Fortress	MV	-	220	.90	M	90	LSUCH-126
SVP-ESUCH-104	Hamlet	MV	-	150	1.00	L-M	50	-
SVP-ESUCH-105	Hamlet	MV	-	200	.50	M	50	-
SVP-ESUCH-106	Hamlet	MV	-	150	.50	M	50	-
SVP-ESUCH-107	Citadel	MV	-	275	3.00	L	45	-
SVP-ESUCH-108	Small Village	MV	335	220	1.60	M	160	LSUCH-131
SVP-ESUCH-109	Small Village	MV	342,342	220	3.80	L-M	190	LSUCH-132, ETAN-110
SVP-ESUCH-110	Hamlet	MV	341	230	.75	L	10	CAY-48, VIN-30
SVP-ESUCH-111	Citadel	MV	-	275	3.00	L	45	-

Table 26. Tabular Presentation of Prehispanic Settlement Data (Continued)

Early Suchimancillo Period Sites

Site Number	Classification	Survey Sector	Collection Number(s)	Elev (m)	Area (ha)	Hab Dens	Pop Est	Site Numbers of Other Occupations
SVP-ESUCH-112	Desert Figures	MV	345	200	3.20	-	-	-
SVP-ESUCH-113	Desert Figures	MV	-	240	-	-	-	-
SVP-ESUCH-114	Hamlet	MV	362	160	.25	L	5	ETR-23
SVP-ESUCH-115	Hamlet	MV	-	180	.25	M	25	-
SVP-ESUCH-116	Hamlet	MV	-	170	.50	M	50	LTR-22
SVP-ESUCH-117	Minor Fortress	MV	-	370	1.40	L	20	LSUCH-136
SVP-ESUCH-118	Citadel	MV	-	420	3.00	L	45	LSUCH-137, ETAN-137
SVP-ESUCH-119	Minor Fortress/ Cemetery	LV	329	250	.25	H	60	-
SVP-ESUCH-120	Cemetery	LV	177	60	.10	-	-	LSUCH-140, ETAN-163
SVP-ESUCH-121	Hamlet	LV	(92)	50	.15	M	15	ETAN-177, LTAN-48
SVP-ESUCH-122	C-C/Huaca	LV	-	30	.10	-	-	-
SVP-ESUCH-123	C-C/Huaca	LV	-	30	.10	-	-	-
SVP-ESUCH-124	Hamlet	LV	321	140	.25	M	25	GUAD-122, ETR-32
SVP-ESUCH-125	Small Village/ Minor Fortress	LV	295	50	4.80	M(1.8 ha)	180	GUAD-134, ETAN-192, ETR-35
SVP-ESUCH-126	Local Center	LV	282,283,284, 287,288	30	70.00	L-M	3500	LSUCH-149, GUAD-172, LTAN-53/54,ETR-43,LTR-68

Table 26. Tabular Presentation of Prehispanic Settlement Data (Continued)

Early Suchimancillo Period Sites

Site Number	Classification	Survey Sector	Collection Number(s)	Elev (m)	Area (ha)	Hab Dens	Pop Est	Site Numbers of Other Occupations
SVP-ESUCH-127	Cemetery	LV	285	40	2.25	-	-	LSUCH-150, GUAD-170, ETAN-198,ETR-44,LTR-71
SVP-ESUCH-128	Citadel/ Cemetery	LV	280,281	280	4.50	L-M	225	LSUCH-151, ETR-46
SVP-ESUCH-129	Minor Fortress	LV	279	200	.25	L	5	-
SVP-ESUCH-130	Citadel	LV	-	160	5.85	-	-	-

Table 26. Tabular Presentation of Prehispanic Settlement Data for the Lower Santa Valley Survey Region

Late Suchimancillo Period Sites

Site Number	Classification	Survey Sector	Collection Number(s)	Elev (m)	Area (ha)	Hab Dens	Pop Est	Site Numbers of Other Occupations
SVP-LSUCH-1	Small Village	UV	-	550	2.00	L-M	100	-
SVP-LSUCH-2	Hamlet	UV	-	550	.25	M	25	-
SVP-LSUCH-3	Small Village	UV	-	760	1.75	M	175	-
SVP-LSUCH-4	Hamlet	UV	-	550	1.00	L-M	50	-
SVP-LSUCH-5	Hamlet	UV	-	525	.20	M	20	-
SVP-LSUCH-6	Hamlet	UV	-	600	.25	L-M	10	-
SVP-LSUCH-7	Hamlet	UV	-	700	.25	L-M	10	-
SVP-LSUCH-8	Hamlet	UV	-	500	.25	L-M	10	-
SVP-LSUCH-9	Small Village	UV	-	500	.20 7.00	H L-M	400	ESUCH-1
SVP-LSUCH-10	Cemetery	UV	-	550	.25	-	-	-
SVP-LSUCH-11	Local Center	UV	-	425	7.50	M	750	-
SVP-LSUCH-12	Small Village	UV	-	500	1.40	M	140	ESUCH-2
SVP-LSUCH-13	Cemetery	UV	375	465	1.70	-	-	VIN-6, ESUCH-3
SVP-LSUCH-14	Hamlet	UV	-	450	.50	M	50	ESUCH-4
SVP-LSUCH-15	Small Village/ Corral	UV	-	465	2.00	M	200	-
SVP-LSUCH-16	Small Village	UV	-	500	1.70	M	170	-
SVP-LSUCH-17	Small Village	UV	-	500	3.00	M	300	-

546

Table 26. Tabular Presentation of Prehispanic Settlement Data (Continued)

			Late Suchimancillo Period Sites					
Site Number	Classification	Survey Sector	Collection Number(s)	Elev (m)	Area (ha)	Hab Dens	Pop Est	Site Numbers of Other Occupations
SVP-LSUCH-18	Hamlet	UV	-	440	.50	M	50	-
SVP-LSUCH-19	Hamlet	UV	-	425	.50	M	50	-
SVP-LSUCH-20	Subt. Gallery	UV	-	450	.10	-	-	-
SVP-LSUCH-21	Small Village	UV	-	450	3.20	M	320	-
SVP-LSUCH-22	Small Village	UV	-	450	2.00	M	200	-
SVP-LSUCH-23	Small Village	UV	-	425	3.50	M	350	-
SVP-LSUCH-24	Small Village	UV	-	450	1.70	M	170	-
SVP-LSUCH-25	Local Center	UV	-	450	17.00	M	1700	-
SVP-LSUCH-26	Hamlet	UV	374	430	1.70	L-M	85	CAY-6, VIN-7, ESUCH-6
SVP-LSUCH-27	Hamlet	UV	371	490	1.50	L-M	75	ESUCH-8, ETAN-2
SVP-LSUCH-28	Small Village	UV	370	465	2.50	L-M	125	ESUCH-9, ETAN-3
SVP-LSUCH-29	Hamlet	UV	-	475	.10	L	5	-
SVP-LSUCH-30	Hamlet	UV	-	460	.85	M	85	-
SVP-LSUCH-31	Large Village/ Corral	UV	-	375	23.40	L-M	1170	ESUCH-10
SVP-LSUCH-32	Cemetery	UV	-	405	.10	-	-	CAY-8
SVP-LSUCH-33	Hamlet	UV	-	430	.50	L-M	25	-
SVP-LSUCH-34	Hamlet	UV	-	500	.25	L-M	10	-

Table 26. Tabular Presentation of Prehispanic Settlement Data (Continued)

			Late Suchimancillo Period Sites					
Site Number	Classification	Survey Sector	Collection Number(s)	Elev (m)	Area (ha)	Hab Dens	Pop Est	Site Numbers of Other Occupations
SVP-LSUCH-35	Hamlet/Cemetery	UV	-	415	2.00	L-M(.6 ha)	30	-
SVP-LSUCH-36	Hamlet/Cemetery	UV	-	415	2.00	L-M(.6 ha)	30	-
SVP-LSUCH-37	Small Village	UV	-	415	1.00	M	100	-
SVP-LSUCH-38	Small Village	UV	103	400	2.00	M	200	-
SVP-LSUCH-39	Large Village	UV	29	375	14.00	M	1400	ESUCH-15
SVP-LSUCH-40	Cemetery	UV	30,33	400	6.50	-	-	ESUCH-17
SVP-LSUCH-41	Cemetery	UV	-	490	.25	-	-	-
SVP-LSUCH-42	Cemetery	UV	-	445	.25	-	-	-
SVP-LSUCH-43	Cemetery	UV	-	445	.25	-	-	-
SVP-LSUCH-44	Cemetery	UV	34	400	1.00	-	-	ESUCH-18
SVP-LSUCH-45	Local Center/ Cemetery	UV	1,8,9,11,13, 14,16	345	41.50	L-M	2075	ESUCH-19
SVP-LSUCH-46	Cemetery	UV	36	475	.50	-	-	-
SVP-LSUCH-47	Small Village	UV	35	500	3.00	M	300	ESUCH-22
SVP-LSUCH-48	Small Village/ Corral	UV	-	375	14.00	L	210	-
SVP-LSUCH-49	Small Village	UV	24	350	2.25	M	225	ESUCH-23
SVP-LSUCH-50	Citadel	UV	26	680	1.50	M	150	CAY-15, VIN-15, ESUCH-26, ETAN-5

Table 26. Tabular Presentation of Prehispanic Settlement Data (Continued)

	Late Suchimancillo Period Sites

Site Number	Classification	Survey Sector	Collection Number(s)	Elev (m)	Area (ha)	Hab Dens	Pop Est	Site Numbers of Other Occupations
SVP-LSUCH-51	Large Village/ Cemetery	UV	28,104,105, 106	350	6.25 6.25	H L-M	1875	ESUCH-28, ETAN-4
SVP-LSUCH-52	Small Village	UV	39	325	2.00	L-M	100	ESUCH-31, GUAD-1, ETAN-9, LTAN-4
SVP-LSUCH-53	Hamlet	UV	41	450	3.20	L	50	-
SVP-LSUCH-54	Citadel	UV	42	400	5.00	L-M	250	ESUCH-34
SVP-LSUCH-55	Small Village/ Cemetery	UV	43	350	2.25	M	225	ESUCH-35
SVP-LSUCH-56	Small Village	UV	44	350	3.40	M	340	ETAN-10
SVP-LSUCH-57	Cemetery	UV	45	350	3.80	-	-	-
SVP-LSUCH-58	Small Village/ Minor Fort/Cem	UV	120,121,123	350	4.75	M(2 ha)	200	ESUCH-36
SVP-LSUCH-59	Cemetery	UV	124	500	.10	-	-	-
SVP-LSUCH-60	Cemetery	UV	126	525	.25	-	-	-
SVP-LSUCH-61	Cemetery	UV	125	525	.10	-	-	CAY-27
SVP-LSUCH-62	Citadel	UV	122,127,128	445	4.00	M(2 ha)	200	ESUCH-37
SVP-LSUCH-63	Large Village/ Corral	UV	115	340	5.00	M	500	VIN-19, ESUCH-38
SVP-LSUCH-64	Hamlet	UV	147	400	.25	L	10	ESUCH-39
SVP-LSUCH-65	Cemetery	UV	149,150	350	2.75	-	-	LTAN-7, ETR-5

Table 26. Tabular Presentation of Prehispanic Settlement Data (Continued)

	Late Suchimancillo Period Sites

Site Number	Classification	Survey Sector	Collection Number(s)	Elev (m)	Area (ha)	Hab Dens	Pop Est	Site Numbers of Other Occupations
SVP-LSUCH-66	Cemetery/ Citadel	UV	102,107,119	540	2.70	-	-	CAY-23, VIN-18, ESUCH-41
SVP-LSUCH-67	Cemetery/ Citadel	UV	108,109,110	540	3.00	-	-	CAY-25, VIN-20, ESUCH-43
SVP-LSUCH-68	Hamlet/Cemetery	UV	111,112	450	3.00	L(2 ha)	30	ESUCH-45
SVP-LSUCH-69	Hamlet	UV	153	350	2.50	L	40	ESUCH-44
SVP-LSUCH-70	Small Village	UV	129	300	3.20	M	320	ETAN-11
SVP-LSUCH-71	Cemetery	UV	132	450	2.50	-	-	-
SVP-LSUCH-72	Local Center/ Minor Fort/Cem	UV	131	300	20.00	H(9.5 ha)	2375	-
SVP-LSUCH-73	Cemetery	UV	154	325	.50	-	-	-
SVP-LSUCH-74	Citadel	UV	113	460	2.70	L-M	135	CAY-26, ESUCH-46
SVP-LSUCH-75	Cemetery	UV	-	315	2.25	-	-	-
SVP-LSUCH-76	Citadel	UV	118	295	2.70	M	270	-
SVP-LSUCH-77	Small Village/ Huaca	UV	133	350	3.20	L-M	160	-
SVP-LSUCH-78	Cemetery	UV	135	300	1.80	-	-	GUAD-2
SVP-LSUCH-79	Cemetery/ Citadel	UV	134	510	1.60	L	25	ESUCH-47
SVP-LSUCH-80	Cemetery	UV	-	300	1.40	-	-	-

Table 26. Tabular Presentation of Prehispanic Settlement Data (Continued)

Late Suchimancillo Period Sites								
Site Number	Classification	Survey Sector	Collection Number(s)	Elev (m)	Area (ha)	Hab Dens	Pop Est	Site Numbers of Other Occupations
SVP-LSUCH-81	Minor Fortress/ Cemetery	UV	144,145	450	2.00	L	30	-
SVP-LSUCH-82	Small Village/ Cemetery	UV	138,139	300	3.60	L-M(3 ha)	150	ESUCH-49
SVP-LSUCH-83	Citadel	UV	232,233	425	.80	H	200	CAY-32, ESUCH-54, ETAN-35, LTR-2
SVP-LSUCH-84	Hamlet/Huaca	UV	236	240	1.00	L-M	50	-
SVP-LSUCH-85	Cemetery	MV	238	250	.25	-	-	-
SVP-LSUCH-86	Small Village/ Minor Fortress	MV	244	440	1.40	M	140	ESUCH-62
SVP-LSUCH-87	Small VIllage	MV	243	250	1.60	M	160	CAY-33, ESUCH-63
SVP-LSUCH-88	Hamlet/Corrals	MV	-	250	3.20	L	50	-
SVP-LSUCH-89	Cemetery	MV	-	400	.25	-	-	-
SVP-LSUCH-90	Hamlet	MV	-	350	.25	L	10	-
SVP-LSUCH-91	Cemetery	MV	354	475	.25	-	-	ESUCH-64
SVP-LSUCH-92	Minor Fortress/ Hamlet	MV	-	425	.75	L-M	40	-
SVP-LSUCH-93	Minor Fortress/ Hamlet	MV	-	450	.75	L-M	40	ESUCH-65
SVP-LSUCH-94	Minor Fortress/ Hamlet	MV	-	475	1.80	L-M	90	ESUCH-70

Table 26. Tabular Presentation of Prehispanic Settlement Data (Continued)

Late Suchimancillo Period Sites								
Site Number	Classification	Survey Sector	Collection Number(s)	Elev (m)	Area (ha)	Hab Dens	Pop Est	Site Numbers of Other Occupations
SVP-LSUCH-95	Hamlet/Cemetery	MV	203	230	1.40	L	20	ESUCH-71
SVP-LSUCH-96	Cemetery	MV	204	230	.10	-	-	ETAN-47
SVP-LSUCH-97	Cemetery	MV	206,207	230	9.90	-	-	ESUCH-73, ETAN-49, LTAN-25
SVP-LSUCH-98	Hamlet/ Minor Fortress	MV	352	400	.75	L-M	35	ESUCH-77
SVP-LSUCH-99	Cemetery	MV	-	410	.25	-	-	-
SVP-LSUCH-100	Hamlet/ Minor Fortress	MV	351	420	.90	L	15	ESUCH-80
SVP-LSUCH-101	Cemetery	MV	-	405	.10	-	-	ESUCH-81
SVP-LSUCH-102	Cemetery	MV	209	225	.15	-	-	ESUCH-83, GUAD-9, ETAN-57, LTAN-30, ETR-15
SVP-LSUCH-103	Local Center	MV	249,250,251	200	12.40	H	3100	ESUCH-84
SVP-LSUCH-104	Hamlet	MV	252	300	.50	L	15	-
SVP-LSUCH-105	Hamlet/ Minor Fort/Cem	MV	253	400	1.00	L	15	-
SVP-LSUCH-106	Citadel	MV	254	580	.90	M	90	CAY-34
SVP-LSUCH-107	Cemetery	MV	256	250	2.25	-	-	-
SVP-LSUCH-108	Large Village	MV	217	225	6.75	M	675	GUAD-12

Table 26. Tabular Presentation of Prehispanic Settlement Data (Continued)

Late Suchimancillo Period Sites								
Site Number	Classification	Survey Sector	Collection Number(s)	Elev (m)	Area (ha)	Hab Dens	Pop Est	Site Numbers of Other Occupations
SVP-LSUCH-109	Small Village/ Minor Fortress	MV	218	300	1.60	H	400	-
SVP-LSUCH-110	Hamlet/Cemetery	MV	219,220	225	1.25	M(.5 ha)	50	GUAD-13
SVP-LSUCH-111	Cemetery	MV	-	225	.50	-	-	-
SVP-LSUCH-112	Local Center	MV	223	205	.70 6.30	H L-M	490	VIN-26,ESUCH-89,GUAD-16
SVP-LSUCH-113	C-C/Huaca	MV	226	200	.20	-	-	ESUCH-90, GUAD-18
SVP-LSUCH-114	Large Village/ Minor Fortress	MV	227,228,229	200	5.90	M	590	ESUCH-91, ETAN-77
SVP-LSUCH-115	Citadel	MV	257	215	5.70	L-M(1 ha)	50	ESUCH-92, ETAN-75
SVP-LSUCH-116	Minor Fortress	MV	262	350	.25	-	-	ETAN-83
SVP-LSUCH-117	Small Village/ Cemetery	MV	305	175	1.80	M	180	GUAD-22, ETAN-84
SVP-LSUCH-118	Cemetery	MV	312	200	.40	-	-	-
SVP-LSUCH-119	Small Village	MV	277	200	3.60	L-M	180	ESUCH-98, GUAD-31
SVP-LSUCH-120	Citadel	MV	331	850	1.40	L	20	CAY-40,VIN-28,ESUCH-100
SVP-LSUCH-121	Hamlet/C-C	MV	333	245	2.25	L	35	-
SVP-LSUCH-122	Hamlet	MV	-	240	1.60	L	25	GUAD-46
SVP-LSUCH-123	Hamlet	MV	-	175	4.30	L	65	-

Table 26. Tabular Presentation of Prehispanic Settlement Data (Continued)

Late Suchimancillo Period Sites								
Site Number	Classification	Survey Sector	Collection Number(s)	Elev (m)	Area (ha)	Hab Dens	Pop Est	Site Numbers of Other Occupations
SVP-LSUCH-124	Hamlet/Corrals/ Desert Figure	MV	-	150	3.00	L	45	ETAN-101
SVP-LSUCH-125	Cemetery	MV	358	150	1.10	-	-	GUAD-44, ETAN-104
SVP-LSUCH-126	Small Village/ Minor Fortress	MV	-	220	1.10	M	110	ESUCH-103
SVP-LSUCH-127	Hamlet/Cemetery	MV	359	150	.50	M	50	GUAD-50, LTR-9
SVP-LSUCH-128	Hamlet/C-C	MV	334	225	1.40	L	20	-
SVP-LSUCH-129	Hamlet	MV	-	250	.90	L	15	-
SVP-LSUCH-130	Hamlet	MV	-	235	2.25	L	35	-
SVP-LSUCH-131	Small Village	MV	335	220	1.60	M	160	ESUCH-108
SVP-LSUCH-132	Small Village	MV	342	220	1.60	M	160	ESUCH-109
SVP-LSUCH-133	Citadel	MV	339	340	1.10	L	15	CAY-47, ESUCH-111
SVP-LSUCH-134	C-C/Huaca	MV	-	140	.30	-	-	GUAD-56
SVP-LSUCH-135	Small Village/ Minor Fort/Cem	MV	347	200	1.40	M	140	ETAN-135, LTAN-43
SVP-LSUCH-136	Minor Fortress	MV	-	370	1.00	L	15	ESUCH-117
SVP-LSUCH-137	Citadel	MV	-	420	3.00	L	55	ESUCH-118, ETAN-137
SVP-LSUCH-138	Cemetery	LV	184	70	.75	-	-	GUAD-76, LTR-31
SVP-LSUCH-139	Minor Fort/Cem/ Small Village	LV	176	140	1.25	M	125	-

550

Late Suchimancillo Period Sites

Site Number	Classification	Survey Sector	Collection Number(s)	Elev (m)	Area (ha)	Hab Dens	Pop Est	Site Numbers of Other Occupations
SVP-LSUCH-140	Cemetery	LV	177	60	.10	-	-	ESUCH-120, ETAN-163
SVP-LSUCH-141	Cemetery	LV	182	60	.15	-	-	ETAN-164, ETR-25
SVP-LSUCH-142	Hamlet	LV	180	50	2.50	L(.6 ha)	10	ETAN-165/166, LTR-35
SVP-LSUCH-143	Hamlet	LV	327	100	1.00	L	15	GUAD-93
SVP-LSUCH-144	Hamlet	LV	85	60	1.00	L	15	GUAD-110
SVP-LSUCH-145	Small Village	LV	47	25	3.20	M	320	ETAN-183
SVP-LSUCH-146	Large Village/ Minor Fortress	LV	48,49	25	14.60	L-M	730	ETAN-185, ETR-30
SVP-LSUCH-147	Small Village/ Cemetery	LV	297	60	3.25	L-M	165	GUAD-130
SVP-LSUCH-148	Small Village	LV	-	60	6.30	L-M	315	-
SVP-LSUCH-149	Local Center/ Corral	LV	283,284	30	14.20	M	1420	ESUCH-126, GUAD-172, LTAN-54, ETR-43
SVP-LSUCH-150	Cemetery	LV	285	40	2.25	-	-	ESUCH-127, GUAD-170, ETAN-198, ETR-44, LTR-71
SVP-LSUCH-151	Citadel	LV	281	280	2.00	L-M	100	ESUCH-128, ETR-46
SVP-LSUCH-152	Citadels	LV	278	310	1.10	-	-	GUAD-175
SVP-LSUCH-153	Hamlet/C-C	LV	-	35	1.40	L-M	70	-

Table 26. Tabular Presentation of Prehispanic Settlement Data for the Lower Santa Valley Survey Region

Guadalupito Period Sites

Site Number	Classification	Survey Sector	Collection Number(s)	Elev (m)	Area (ha)	Hab Dens	Pop Est	Site Numbers of Other Occupations
SVP-GUAD-1	Small Village/ Cemetery	UV	39	325	2.00	L-M	100	ESUCH-31, LSUCH-52, ETAN-9, LTAN-4
SVP-GUAD-2	Cemetery	UV	135	300	1.80	-	-	LSUCH-78
SVP-GUAD-3	Small Village/ Huaca/Cemetery	UV	155,156,158	260	5.90	L-M	295	ETAN-26, LTAN-16
SVP-GUAD-4	Cemetery	UV	235	265	.30	-	-	ETAN-33
SVP-GUAD-5	Cemetery	MV	201	250	1.10	-	-	-
SVP-GUAD-6	Cemetery	MV	-	250	.90	-	-	-
SVP-GUAD-7	Cemetery	MV	205	230	.10	-	-	ESUCH-72, ETAN-48
SVP-GUAD-8	Hamlet	MV	-	250	.50	M	25	-
SVP-GUAD-9	Cemetery	MV	209	225	.15	-	-	ESUCH-83, LSUCH-102, ETAN-57, LTAN-30, ETR-15
SVP-GUAD-10	Cemetery	MV	215	280	.10	-	-	-
SVP-GUAD-11	Cemetery	MV	-	250	1.60	-	-	-
SVP-GUAD-12	Local Center	MV	-	225	5.00	M	500	LSUCH-108
SVP-GUAD-13	Hamlet/Cemetery	MV	220	225	.25	M	25	LSUCH-110
SVP-GUAD-14	Cemetery	MV	-	225	1.60	-	-	-
SVP-GUAD-15	Cemetery	MV	-	225	1.80	-	-	LTAN-39
SVP-GUAD-16	Cemetery	MV	223	225	1.60	-	-	VIN-26, ESUCH-89, LSUCH-112

Table 26. Tabular Presentation of Prehispanic Settlement Data (Continued)

Guadalupito Period Sites

Site Number	Classification	Survey Sector	Collection Number(s)	Elev (m)	Area (ha)	Hab Dens	Pop Est	Site Numbers of Other Occupations
SVP-GUAD-17	Cemetery	MV	-	225	.75	-	-	-
SVP-GUAD-18	Cemetery	MV	226	200	.20	-	-	ESUCH-90, LSUCH-113
SVP-GUAD-19	Cemetery	MV	-	200	.25	-	-	ETAN-73
SVP-GUAD-20	Small Village/ Cemetery	MV	-	200	7.20	M(4.5 ha)	450	-
SVP-GUAD-21	Small Village/ Cemetery	MV	-	200	2.70	M(1.5 ha)	150	-
SVP-GUAD-22	Small Village/ Cemetery	MV	261	200	3.20	M(2.5 ha)	250	ETAN-82, ETAN-84
SVP-GUAD-23	Cemetery	MV	-	250	1.10	-	-	-
SVP-GUAD-24	Cemetery	MV	-	250	.10	-	-	-
SVP-GUAD-25	Hamlet/Cemetery	MV	306	200	.50	L	10	-
SVP-GUAD-26	Cemetery	MV	275	200	.50	-	-	ETAN-87
SVP-GUAD-27	Hamlet/Huaca	MV	-	200	.50	L	10	-
SVP-GUAD-28	Cemetery	MV	-	215	.70	-	-	-
SVP-GUAD-29	Cemetery	MV	-	200	.90	-	-	-
SVP-GUAD-30	Cemetery	MV	-	205	.75	-	-	-
SVP-GUAD-31	Cemetery	MV	277	215	.90	-	-	ESUCH-98, LSUCH-119
SVP-GUAD-32	Small Village/ Cemetery	MV	-	180	2.00	M	200	-

Table 26. Tabular Presentation of Prehispanic Settlement Data (Continued)

Guadalupito Period Sites

Site Number	Classification	Survey Sector	Collection Number(s)	Elev (m)	Area (ha)	Hab Dens	Pop Est	Site Numbers of Other Occupations
SVP-GUAD-33	Cemetery	MV	299	220	1.60	-	-	LTAN-41, ETR-21
SVP-GUAD-34	Cemetery	MV	-	200	.10	-	-	-
SVP-GUAD-35	Cemetery	MV	-	200	.10	-	-	-
SVP-GUAD-36	Cemetery	MV	-	175	.10	-	-	-
SVP-GUAD-37	Cemetery	MV	-	200	.65	-	-	-
SVP-GUAD-38	Cemetery	MV	302	225	2.25	-	-	-
SVP-GUAD-39	Small village	MV	-	200	2.50	M	250	-
SVP-GUAD-40	Hamlet	MV	-	190	.25	L	5	-
SVP-GUAD-41	Cemetery	MV	-	195	.50	-	-	-
SVP-GUAD-42	Cemetery	MV	-	200	.50	-	-	-
SVP-GUAD-43	Cemetery	MV	-	200	.90	-	-	-
SVP-GUAD-44	Cemetery	MV	358	150	1.10	-	-	LSUCH-125, ETAN-104
SVP-GUAD-45	Cemetery	MV	-	150	.25	-	-	-
SVP-GUAD-46	Small Village	MV	-	240	4.30	L-M	215	LSUCH-122
SVP-GUAD-47	Small Village/ Cemetery	MV	-	240	4.30	L-M	215	-
SVP-GUAD-48	Small Village/ Cemetery	MV	-	150	1.60	L-M	100	ETAN-106
SVP-GUAD-49	Cemetery	MV	-	150	.50	-	-	-

Table 26. Tabular Presentation of Prehispanic Settlement Data (Continued)

	Guadalupito Period Sites
Site Number	Classification	Survey Sector	Collection Number(s)	Elev (m)	Area (ha)	Hab Dens	Pop Est	Site Numbers of Other Occupations	
SVP-GUAD-50	Cemetery	MV	359	150	.70	-	-	LSUCH-127, LTR-9	
SVP-GUAD-51	Hamlet	MV	-	240	.50	M	50	-	
SVP-GUAD-52	Hamlet/Corral	MV	-	240	1.80	L-M	90	-	
SVP-GUAD-53	Cemetery	MV	-	240	.25	-	-	-	
SVP-GUAD-54	Small Village/ Cemetery	MV	-	150	1.40	M(1 ha)	100	-	
SVP-GUAD-55	Cemetery	MV	-	160	.50	-	-	-	
SVP-GUAD-56	Hamlet/Cemetery	MV	-	150	1.40	M(.5 ha)	50	LSUCH-134	
SVP-GUAD-57	Small Village/ Cemetery	MV	-	150	2.25	M(1.5 ha)	150	-	
SVP-GUAD-58	Cemetery	MV	-	150	.25	-	-	-	
SVP-GUAD-59	Cemetery	MV	-	150	.25	-	-	-	
SVP-GUAD-60	Cemetery	MV	-	150	.25	-	-	-	
SVP-GUAD-61	Hamlet/Cemetery	MV	-	150	.90	M(.75 ha)	75	-	
SVP-GUAD-62	Cemetery	MV	-	150	.25	-	-	-	
SVP-GUAD-63	Small Village/ Cemetery	MV	-	150	1.40	M(1 ha)	100	-	
SVP-GUAD-64	Cemetery	MV	-	150	.50	-	-	-	
SVP-GUAD-65	Hamlet/Cemetery	MV	-	160	1.10	M(.75 ha)	75	-	

Table 26. Tabular Presentation of Prehispanic Settlement Data (Continued)

	Guadalupito Period Sites
Site Number	Classification	Survey Sector	Collection Number(s)	Elev (m)	Area (ha)	Hab Dens	Pop Est	Site Numbers of Other Occupations	
SVP-GUAD-66	Cemetery	MV	-	150	.25	-	-	-	
SVP-GUAD-67	Hamlet/Cemetery	MV	-	125	.70	M(.5 ha)	50	-	
SVP-GUAD-68	Hamlet	MV	-	120	.25	M	25	-	
SVP-GUAD-69	Cemetery	LV	-	110	.50	-	-	-	
SVP-GUAD-70	Cemetery	LV	-	120	.25	-	-	-	
SVP-GUAD-71	Hamlet/Cemetery	LV	-	120	.25	M	25	-	
SVP-GUAD-72	Hamlet/Cemetery	LV	-	120	.90	L-M	45	-	
SVP-GUAD-73	Cemetery	LV	-	110	.25	-	-	-	
SVP-GUAD-74	Small Village	LV	-	125	1.60	M	160	-	
SVP-GUAD-75	Cemetery	LV	186	70	.10	-	-	ETAN-160	
SVP-GUAD-76	Cemetery	LV	184	70	.75	-	-	LSUCH-138, LTR-31	
SVP-GUAD-77	Cemetery	LV	-	125	2.25	-	-	-	
SVP-GUAD-78	Hamlet	LV	-	125	.70	M	70	-	
SVP-GUAD-79	Cemetery	LV	-	160	.90	-	-	-	
SVP-GUAD-80	Cemetery	LV	-	140	1.00	-	-	-	
SVP-GUAD-81	Cemetery	LV	-	125	2.50	-	-	-	
SVP-GUAD-82	Cemetery	LV	-	145	.90	-	-	-	
SVP-GUAD-83	Cemetery	LV	178	75	1.40	-	-	ETAN-167	

Table 26. Tabular Presentation of Prehispanic Settlement Data (Continued)

Guadalupito Period Sites								
Site Number	Classification	Survey Sector	Collection Number(s)	Elev (m)	Area (ha)	Hab Dens	Pop Est	Site Numbers of Other Occupations
SVP-GUAD-84	Cemetery	LV	-	125	1.40	-	-	LTR-36
SVP-GUAD-85	Cemetery	LV	-	130	1.40	-	-	-
SVP-GUAD-86	Small Village/ Cemetery	LV	-	100	4.50	M(2 ha)	200	-
SVP-GUAD-87	Small Village	LV	-	105	1.35	M	135	-
SVP-GUAD-88	Large Village/ Cemetery	LV	-	100	6.00	M	600	
SVP-GUAD-89	Small Village	LV	-	140	3.20	M	320	-
SVP-GUAD-90	Cemetery	LV	-	105	.25	-	-	-
SVP-GUAD-91	Hamlet/Huaca	LV	324	100	1.80	L-M	90	LTR-37
SVP-GUAD-92	Small Village/ Cemetery	LV	330	100	3.60	M(3 ha)	300	-
SVP-GUAD-93	Local Center	LV	327	100	10.35	M	1035	LSUCH-143
SVP-GUAD-94	Small Village	LV	188	200	2.25	M	225	ETAN-168
SVP-GUAD-95	Cemetery	LV	195	75	.30	-	-	-
SVP-GUAD-96	Cemetery	LV	84	100	1.60	-	-	ETAN-169
SVP-GUAD-97	Small Village/ Cemetery	LV	89,90	50	3.60	M	360	-
SVP-GUAD-98	Hamlet	LV	-	80	1.40	L	20	-

Table 26. Tabular Presentation of Prehispanic Settlement Data (Continued)

Guadalupito Period Sites								
Site Number	Classification	Survey Sector	Collection Number(s)	Elev (m)	Area (ha)	Hab Dens	Pop Est	Site Numbers of Other Occupations
SVP-GUAD-99	Cemetery	LV	82	125	.15	-	-	ETAN-171
SVP-GUAD-100	Cemetery	LV	66	100	.75	-	-	-
SVP-GUAD-101	Cemetery	LV	-	100	.75	-	-	-
SVP-GUAD-102	Hamlet	LV	-	75	1.80	L	25	-
SVP-GUAD-103	Cemetery	LV	80	75	.15	-	-	-
SVP-GUAD-104	Small Village/ Cemetery	LV	76,78	75	.36 1.89	H M	280	ETAN-173
SVP-GUAD-105	Cemetery	LV	81	75	.10	-	-	ETAN-172
SVP-GUAD-106	Cemetery	LV	-	80	.75	-	-	-
SVP-GUAD-107	Cemetery	LV	77	75	1.40	-	-	-
SVP-GUAD-108	Cemetery	LV	65	75	1.80	-	-	-
SVP-GUAD-109	Small Village/ Cemetery	LV	59,64	75	7.40	L-M	370	-
SVP-GUAD-110	Hamlet/Huacas	LV	85	60	1.00	L-M	50	LSUCH-144
SVP-GUAD-111	Regional Center/ Cemetery	LV	68,72	50	5.85	M	585	ETAN-180
SVP-GUAD-112	Large Village/ Cemetery	LV	60,61,62,63, 69,70	45	13.00	H(7.5 ha)	1875	ETAN-180, ETR-26, LTR-38
SVP-GUAD-113	Small Village/ C-C	LV	56,57,58	75	6.30	L-M	315	ETAN-181, LTR-39

Table 26. Tabular Presentation of Prehispanic Settlement Data (Continued)

Guadalupito Period Sites

Site Number	Classification	Survey Sector	Collection Number(s)	Elev (m)	Area (ha)	Hab Dens	Pop Est	Site Numbers of Other Occupations
SVP-GUAD-114	C-C	LV	-	50	1.00	-	-	-
SVP-GUAD-115	Cemetery	LV	54	60	1.00	-	-	LTAN-50, ETR-28
SVP-GUAD-116	Cemetery	LV	-	50	.75	-	-	-
SVP-GUAD-117	Cemetery	LV	-	120	.50	-	-	-
SVP-GUAD-118	Cemetery	LV	-	120	.50	-	-	-
SVP-GUAD-119	Hamlet	LV	-	90	.75	M	75	-
SVP-GUAD-120	Cemetery	LV	-	125	.75	-	-	-
SVP-GUAD-121	Large Village/ Cemetery	LV	316	95	6.50	M(6 ha)	600	-
SVP-GUAD-122	Small Village	LV	(321)	140	1.60	M	160	ESUCH-124, ETR-32
SVP-GUAd-123	Small Village	LV	-	100	1.80	M	180	-
SVP-GUAD-124	Hamlet	LV	-	130	.50	M	50	-
SVP-GUAD-125	Cemetery	LV	-	95	1.10	-	-	-
SVP-GUAD-126	Cemetery	LV	-	105	1.00	-	-	-
SVP-GUAD-127	Small Village	LV	-	75	1.10	H	275	-
SVP-GUAD-128	Small Village/ Huacas	LV	314	60	1.80	M	180	ETAN-190
SVP-GUAD-129	C-C/Huaca	LV	-	60	.10	-	-	-

Table 26. Tabular Presentation of Prehispanic Settlement Data (Continued)

Guadalupito Period Sites

Site Number	Classification	Survey Sector	Collection Number(s)	Elev (m)	Area (ha)	Hab Dens	Pop Est	Site Numbers of Other Occupations
SVP-GUAD-130	Small Village/ Cemetery	LV	297	60	3.20	M	320	LSUCH-147
SVP-GUAD-131	C-C/Huaca	LV	304	30	.10	-	-	-
SVP-GUAD-132	Small Village/ C-C	LV	294	30	3.60	M(2 ha)	200	ETAN-193
SVP-GUAD-133	Large Village	LV	-	30	5.60	M	560	-
SVP-GUAD-134	Small Village/ Cemetery	LV	-	50	1.10	M(1 ha)	100	ESUCH-125
SVP-GUAD-135	Large Village	LV	-	55	6.30	M(5.75 ha)	575	-
SVP-GUAD-136	Cemetery	LV	-	50	4.30	-	-	-
SVP-GUAD-137	Small Village	LV	-	45	1.80	M	180	-
SVP-GUAD-138	Cemetery	LV	-	65	1.80	-	-	-
SVP-GUAD-139	Cemetery	LV	-	65	.25	-	-	-
SVP-GUAD-140	Cemetery	LV	-	65	.25	-	-	-
SVP-GUAD-141	Cemetery	LV	-	60	.25	-	-	-
SVP-GUAD-142	Cemetery	LV	-	60	.25	-	-	-
SVP-GUAD-143	Cemetery	LV	-	60	.25	-	-	-
SVP-GUAD-144	Cemetery	LV	-	65	.25	-	-	-
SVP-GUAD-145	Cemetery	LV	-	70	.50	-	-	-

Table 26. Tabular Presentation of Prehispanic Settlement Data (Continued)

Guadalupito Period Sites

Site Number	Classification	Survey Sector	Collection Number(s)	Elev (m)	Area (ha)	Hab Dens	Pop Est	Site Numbers of Other Occupations
SVP-GUAD-146	Cemetery	LV	-	70	.75	-	-	-
SVP-GUAD-147	Cemetery	LV	-	65	.25	-	-	-
SVP-GUAD-148	Cemetery	LV	-	65	.25	-	-	-
SVP-GUAD-149	Cemetery	LV	-	60	.25	-	-	-
SVP-GUAD-150	Small Village	LV	-	60	3.80	L-M	190	-
SVP-GUAD-151	Cemetery	LV	-	65	1.10	-	-	-
SVP-GUAD-152	Cemetery	LV	-	70	.75	-	-	-
SVP-GUAD-153	Cemetery	LV	-	70	.75	-	-	-
SVP-GUAD-154	Cemetery	LV	-	65	.75	-	-	-
SVP-GUAD-155	Cemetery	LV	-	60	.75	-	-	-
SVP-GUAD-156	Cemetery	LV	-	60	.75	-	-	-
SVP-GUAD-157	Cemetery	LV	-	60	.25	-	-	-
SVP-GUAD-158	Cemetery	LV	-	65	.75	-	-	-
SVP-GUAD-159	Cemetery	LV	-	60	.50	-	-	-
SVP-GUAD-160	Cemetery	LV	-	65	.50	-	-	-
SVP-GUAD-161	Small Village	LV	-	60	4.10	M	410	-
SVP-GUAD-162	Cemetery	LV	291	50	1.40	-	-	-
SVP-GUAD-163	Cemetery	LV	-	65	.50	-	-	-

Table 26. Tabular Presentation of Prehispanic Settlement Data (Continued)

Guadalupito Period Sites

Site Number	Classification	Survey Sector	Collection Number(s)	Elev (m)	Area (ha)	Hab Dens	Pop Est	Site Numbers of Other Occupations
SVP-GUAD-164	Cemetery	LV	290	50	.50	-	-	ETAN-196
SVP-GUAD-165	Cemetery	LV	-	60	1.00	-	-	LTR-65
SVP-GUAD-166	Cemetery	LV	-	65	.25	-	-	-
SVP-GUAD-167	Cemetery	LV	-	70	.25	-	-	-
SVP-GUAD-168	Hamlet	LV	265	25	1.80	L	30	-
SVP-GUAD-169	Hamlet	Coast	266	15	1.60	L-M	80	-
SVP-GUAD-170	Cemetery	LV	285	40	2.25	-	-	ESUCH-127, LSUCH-150, ETAN-198, ETR-44, LTR-71
SVP-GUAD-171	Cemetery	LV	-	45	.25	-	-	-
SVP-GUAD-172	Cemetery	LV	284	65	1.10	-	-	ESUCH-126, LSUCH-149, LTAN-54
SVP-GUAD-173	Cemetery	LV	-	60	.75	-	-	-
SVP-GUAD-174	Hamlet (R.S.)	LV	-	100	.25	L	5	LTR-67
SVP-GUAD-175	Cemetery	LV	278	310	.50	-	-	LSUCH-152
SVP-GUAD-176	Small Village	LV	-	100	3.20	M	320	-
SVP-GUAD-177	Small Village	LV	-	95	1.60	M	160	-
SVP-GUAD-178	Small Village	LV	-	95	3.60	M	360	-
SVP-GUAD-179	Small Village	LV	-	95	2.80	M	280	-
SVP-GUAD-180	Small Village	LV	-	80	2.00	M	200	-

Table 26. Tabular Presentation of Prehispanic Settlement Data (Continued)

			Guadalupito Period Sites					
Site Number	Classification	Survey Sector	Collection Number(s)	Elev (m)	Area (ha)	Hab Dens	Pop Est	Site Numbers of Other Occupations
SVP-GUAD-181	Small Village	LV	-	80	3.60	M	360	-
SVP-GUAD-182	Cemetery	LV	-	95	1.60	-	-	-
SVP-GUAD-183	Cemetery	LV	-	150	1.00	-	-	-
SVP-GUAD-184	Small Village	LV	-	80	1.20	M	120	-
SVP-GUAD-185	Small Village/ Cemetery	LV	-	80	1.60	M(1 ha)	100	-
SVP-GUAD-186	Small Village	LV	-	80	2.00	M	200	-
SVP-GUAD-187	Hamlet	LV	-	70	.80	M	80	-
SVP-GUAD-188	Cemetery	LV	-	140	1.60	-	-	-
SVP-GUAD-189	Cemetery	LV	-	80	1.60	-	-	-
SVP-GUAD-190	Small Village	LV	-	75	2.75	M	275	-
SVP-GUAD-191	Cemetery	LV	-	120	2.20	-	-	-
SVP-GUAD-192	Local Center	LV	-	80	29.50	M	2950	-
SVP-GUAD-193	Cemetery	LV	-	135	.50	-	-	-
SVP-GUAD-194	Cemetery	LV	-	80	.25	-	-	-
SVP-GUAD-195	Small Village	LV	-	90	2.80	M	280	-
SVP-GUAD-196	Cemetery	LV	-	110	4.40	-	-	-
SVP-GUAD-197	Small Village	LV	-	60	2.75	M	275	-

Table 26. Tabular Presentation of Prehispanic Settlement Data (Continued)

			Guadalupito Period Sites					
Site Number	Classification	Survey Sector	Collection Number(s)	Elev (m)	Area (ha)	Hab Dens	Pop Est	Site Number of Other Occupations
SVP-GUAD-198	Small Village	LV	-	60	2.40	M	240	-
SVP-GUAD-199	Small Village	LV	-	50	1.60	M	160	-
SVP-GUAD-200	Cemetery	LV	-	50	1.60	-	-	-
SVP-GUAD-201	Large Village	LV	-	125	6.50	M	650	-
SVP-GUAD-202	C-C/Huaca	LV	-	125	3.90	-	-	-
SVP-GUAD-203	Small Village	LV	-	35	1.50	M	150	-
SVP-GUAD-204	C-C/Huaca	LV	-	25	.10	-	-	-
SVP-GUAD-205	Hamlet (R.S.)	LV	-	30	.80	L-M	40	-

Table 26. Tabular Presentation of Prehispanic Settlement Data for the Lower Santa Valley Survey Region

Early Tanguche Period Sites

Site Number	Classification	Survey Sector	Collection Number(s)	Elev (m)	Area (ha)	Hab Dens	Pop Est	Site Numbers of Other Occupations
SVP-ETAN-1	Local Center	UV	372	460	.30	H	75	ESUCH-7
SVP-ETAN-2	Hamlet	UV	371	490	1.25	L-M	65	ESUCH-8, LSUCH-27
SVP-ETAN-3	Hamlet	UV	370	465	1.00	L-M	50	ESUCH-9, LSUCH-28
SVP-ETAN-4	Large Village	UV	28,104,105	350	6.75	M	675	ESUCH-28, LSUCH-51
SVP-ETAN-5	Cemetery	UV	26	680	.25	-	-	CAY-15, VIN-15, ESUCH-26, LSUCH-50
SVP-ETAN-6	Cemetery	UV	94	590	.25	-	-	CAY-17
SVP-ETAN-7	Local Center	UV	114	350	2.70	L-M	140	ETR-2
SVP-ETAN-8	Cemetery	UV	116	310	.25	-	-	CAY-22
SVP-ETAN-9	Cemetery	UV	39	325	1.35	-	-	ESUCH-31, LSUCH-52. GUAD-1, LTAN-4
SVP-ETAN-10	Small Village	UV	44	350	3.00	M	300	LSUCH-56
SVP-ETAN-11	Small Village	UV	129	300	2.00	L-M	100	LSUCH-70
SVP-ETAN-12	Cemetery	UV	130	300	1.80	-	-	-
SVP-ETAN-13	Cemetery	UV	-	325	1.60	-	-	LTAN_10
SVP-ETAN-14	Cemetery	UV	136	250	1.80	-	-	-
SVP-ETAN-15	Petroglyphs/ Cemetery	UV	140	260	.50	-	-	LTAN-11
SVP-ETAN-16	Cemetery	UV	142	275	.25	-	-	LTAN-13

Table 26. Tabular Presentation of Prehispanic Settlement Data (Continued)

Early Tanguche Period Sites

Site Number	Classification	Survey Sector	Collection Number(s)	Elev (m)	Area (ha)	Hab Dens	Pop Est	Site Numbers of Other Occupations
SVP-ETAN-17	Small Village/ Cemetery	UV	141,143	250	4.50	M	450	LTAN-12, ETR-9
SVP-ETAN-18	Small Village	UV	-	375	2.25	M	225	-
SVP-ETAN-19	Cemetery	UV	-	305	1.40	-	-	-
SVP-ETAN-20	Cemetery	UV	173,174	335	1.00	-	-	CAY-29, ESUCH-51
SVP-ETAN-21	Small Village	UV	172	300	4.00	M	400	LTAN-14
SVP-ETAN-22	Local Center	UV	189,190	310	5.20	L-M	260	ETR-7
SVP-ETAN-23	Cemetery	UV	-	305	1.25	-	-	-
SVP-ETAN-24	Small Village	UV	-	305	1.00	M	100	-
SVP-ETAN-25	Hamlet	UV	193	350	.30	L-M	15	CAY-30, ESUCH-52
SVP-ETAN-26	Local Center	UV	156,157	250	52.40	L	785	ESUCH-53,GUAD-3,LTAN-16
SVP-ETAN-27	Cemetery	UV	-	280	1.00	-	-	-
SVP-ETAN-28	Hamlet	UV	-	300	1.00	L	15	-
SVP-ETAN-29	Hamlet (R.S.)	UV	-	400	1.00	L	15	-
SVP-ETAN-30	Cemetery	UV	-	500	.50	-	-	ESUCH-57
SVP-ETAN-31	Cemetery	UV	164	250	.10	-	-	-
SVP-ETAN-32	C-C/Huaca	UV	165	250	.05	-	-	-
SVP-ETAN-33	Large Village/ Cemetery	UV	230,231,234	250	11.50	M	1150	ESUCH-55, GUAD-4, ETR-10

Table 26. Tabular Presentation of Prehispanic Settlement Data (Continued)

				Early Tanguche Period Sites				
Site Number	Classification	Survey Sector	Collection Number(s)	Elev (m)	Area (ha)	Hab Dens	Pop Est	Site Numbers of Other Occupations
SVP-ETAN-34	Cemetery	UV	235	245	1.50	-	-	LTAN-17
SVP-ETAN-35	Cemetery	UV	232	425	.75	-	-	CAY-32, ESUCH-54, LSUCH-83, LTR-2
SVP-ETAN-36	Cemetery	MV	237	240	.50	-	-	-
SVP-ETAN-37	Large Village	MV	-	240	6.30	M	630	-
SVP-ETAN-38	Cemetery	MV	-	250	.70	-	-	-
SVP-ETAN-39	Cemetery	MV	166,197	255	.10	-	-	-
SVP-ETAN-40	Cemetery	MV	196	250	.10	-	-	-
SVP-ETAN-41	Cemetery	MV	-	250	.25	-	-	-
SVP-ETAN-42	Large Village	MV	241	250	5.20	M	520	ESUCH-56, LTAN-20
SVP-ETAN-43	Small Village	MV	-	240	3.00	M	300	LTAN-21
SVP-ETAN-44	Local Center	MV	242	240	7.20	M	720	LTAN-22, ETR-12
SVP-ETAN-45	Small Village	MV	-	290	1.10	M	110	-
SVP-ETAN-46	Cemetery	MV	-	230	.70	-	-	-
SVP-ETAN-47	Cemetery	MV	204	230	2.50	-	-	LSUCH-96
SVP-ETAN-48	Cemetery	MV	205	230	.10	-	-	ESUCH-72, GUAD-7
SVP-ETAN-49	Cemetery	MV	207	240	1.40	-	-	ESUCH-73, LSUCH-97, LTAN-25
SVP-ETAN-50	Hamlet (R.S.)	MV	-	300	.25	L	5	-

Table 26. Tabular Presentation of Prehispanic Settlement Data (Continued)

				Early Tanguche Period Sites				
Site Number	Classification	Survey Sector	Collection Number(s)	Elev (m)	Area (ha)	Hab Dens	Pop Est	Site Numbers of Other Occupations
SVP-ETAN-51	Cemetery	MV	-	230	1.10	-	-	-
SVP-ETAN-52	Cemetery	MV	-	230	3.75	-	-	-
SVP-ETAN-53	Cemetery	MV	208	295	.10	-	-	ESUCH-82
SVP-ETAN-54	Large Village	MV	-	235	5.60	M	560	-
SVP-ETAN-55	Small Village	MV	-	240	2.50	M	250	LTAN-26
SVP-ETAN-56	Local Center/ Cemetery	MV	246,247	230	2.70	M	270	ETR-14
SVP-ETAN-57	Cemetery	MV	209	225	1.40	-	-	ESUCH-83, LSUCH-102, GUAD-9, LTAN-30, ETR-15
SVP-ETAN-58	Cemetery	MV	212	245	.10	-	-	-
SVP-ETAN-59	Small Village	MV	-	275	1.10	M	110	LTAN-35
SVP-ETAN-60	Hamlet	MV	-	260	.50	M	50	-
SVP-ETAN-61	Hamlet/Cemetery	MV	-	250	1.80	L	25	LTAN-36
SVP-ETAN-62	Cemetery	MV	-	245	.25	-	-	-
SVP-ETAN-63	Small Village	MV	-	240	2.00	M	200	LTAN-28
SVP-ETAN-64	Hamlet/Cemetery	MV	-	225	2.70	L	40	-
SVP-ETAN-65	Hamlet (R.S.)	MV	-	250	1.00	L	15	-
SVP-ETAN-66	Hamlet (R.S.)	MV	-	250	.25	L	5	-
SVP-ETAN-67	Hamlet (R.S.)	MV	-	250	.25	L	5	-

Table 26. Tabular Presentation of Prehispanic Settlement Data (Continued)

Early Tanguche Period Sites

Site Number	Classification	Survey Sector	Collection Number(s)	Elev (m)	Area (ha)	Hab Dens	Pop Est	Site Numbers of Other Occupations
SVP-ETAN-68	Hamlet (R.S.)	MV	-	250	1.00	L	15	-
SVP-ETAN-69	Hamlet (R.S.)	MV	-	240	.50	M	50	-
SVP-ETAN-70	Hamlet	MV	-	250	.75	L	15	-
SVP-ETAN-71	Small Village	MV	-	200	2.70	L-M	135	-
SVP-ETAN-72	Cemetery	MV	-	200	.70	-	-	-
SVP-ETAN-73	Cemetery	MV	-	200	.50	-	-	GUAD-19
SVP-ETAN-74	Small Village	MV	-	200	1.40	M	140	-
SVP-ETAN-75	Cemetery	MV	258	215	.50	-	-	ESUCH-92, LSUCH-115
SVP-ETAN-76	Cemetery	MV	-	200	.25	-	-	-
SVP-ETAN-77	Cemetery	MV	229	200	1.10	-	-	ESUCH-91, LSUCH-114
SVP-ETAN-78	Cemetery	MV	-	195	.25	-	-	-
SVP-ETAN-79	Cemetery	MV	259	225	3.80	-	-	-
SVP-ETAN-80	Small Village/ Corral	MV	-	195	9.00	L	135	-
SVP-ETAN-81	Hamlet	MV	260	190	1.60	L-M	80	ESUCH-94
SVP-ETAN-82	Cemetery	MV	-	205	1.40	-	-	GUAD-22
SVP-ETAN-83	Cemetery	MV	262	350	.50	-	-	LSUCH-116
SVP-ETAN-84	Large Village/ Cemetery	MV	305	165	4.50	H	1125	LSUCH-117, GUAD-22

Table 26. Tabular Presentation of Prehispanic Settlement Data (Continued)

Early Tanguche Period Sites

Site Number	Classification	Survey Sector	Collection Number(s)	Elev (m)	Area (ha)	Hab Dens	Pop Est	Site Numbers of Other Occupations
SVP-ETAN-85	Small Village	MV	272	200	1.60	M	160	ESUCH-93
SVP-ETAN-86	Cemetery	MV	-	180	.25	-	-	-
SVP-ETAN-87	Cemetery	MV	275	200	.50	-	-	GUAD-26
SVP-ETAN-88	Cemetery	MV	276	200	.25	-	-	-
SVP-ETAN-89	Cemetery	MV	301	430	.50	-	-	ESUCH-96
SVP-ETAN-90	Small Village	MV	-	175	1.40	M	140	-
SVP-ETAN-91	Small Village/ Cemetery	MV	-	175	2.50	M	250	-
SVP-ETAN-92	Hamlet	MV	-	225	.70	M	70	-
SVP-ETAN-93	Hamlet	MV	309	210	.25	L-M	15	-
SVP-ETAN-94	Hamlet	MV	-	205	1.80	L-M	90	-
SVP-ETAN-95	Hamlet	MV	-	210	1.10	L-M	55	-
SVP-ETAN-96	Cemetery	MV	-	200	.50	-	-	-
SVP-ETAN-97	Cemetery	MV	-	180	.70	-	-	-
SVP-ETAN-98	Cemetery	MV	357	180	.20	-	-	GUAD-36
SVP-ETAN-99	Hamlet	MV	-	250	2.25	L	35	-
SVP-ETAN-100	Local Center/ Cemetery	MV	-	150	1.10	M	110	-

560

Table 26. Tabular Presentation of Prehispanic Settlement Data (Continued)

Early Tanguche Period Sites

Site Number	Classification	Survey Sector	Collection Number(s)	Elev (m)	Area (ha)	Hab Dens	Pop Est	Site Numbers of Other Occupations
SVP-ETAN-101	Small Village/ Corrals/Cem	MV	-	150	4.50	L-M	225	LSUCH-124
SVP-ETAN-102	Small Village/ Cemetery	MV	303	180	2.50	L-M	125	-
SVP-ETAN-103	Hamlet/Cemetery	MV	-	160	1.00	L-M	50	-
SVP-ETAN-104	Cemetery	MV	358	150	1.10	-	-	LSUCH-125, GUAD-44
SVP-ETAN-105	Small Village/ Cemetery	MV	-	150	2.25	L-M	115	-
SVP-ETAN-106	Hamlet	MV	-	150	1.60	L-M	80	GUAD-48
SVP-ETAN-107	Hamlet	MV	-	200	3.60	L	55	-
SVP-ETAN-108	Hamlet	MV	-	200	1.00	L	15	-
SVP-ETAN-109	Cemetery	MV	-	160	1.00	-	-	-
SVP-ETAN-110	Small Village/ Cemetery	MV	343	220	7.90	L-M	395	ESUCH-109
SVP-ETAN-111	Local Center	MV	337	150	.50	M	50	-
SVP-ETAN-112	Cemetery	MV	-	200	.25	-	-	-
SVP-ETAN-113	Cemetery	MV	-	150	.25	-	-	-
SVP-ETAN-114	Cemetery	MV	-	150	.25	-	-	-
SVP-ETAN-115	Hamlet	MV	-	190	1.40	L	20	-

Table 26. Tabular Presentation of Prehispanic Settlement Data (Continued)

Early Tanguche Period Sites

Site Number	Classification	Survey Sector	Collection Number(s)	Elev (m)	Area (ha)	Hab Dens	Pop Est	Site Numbers of Other Occupations
SVP-ETAN-116	Small Village	MV	-	175	10.40	L	155	-
SVP-ETAN-117	Hamlet	MV	-	180	.50	L	5	-
SVP-ETAN-118	Cemetery	MV	-	150	.25	-	-	-
SVP-ETAN-119	Hamlet	MV	-	150	.50	L-M	25	-
SVP-ETAN-120	Hamlet	MV	-	150	.50	L-M	25	-
SVP-ETAN-121	Hamlet/Cemetery	MV	-	150	.75	L-M	35	-
SVP-ETAN-122	Hamlet	MV	-	175	1.00	L-M	50	-
SVP-ETAN-123	Cemetery	MV	-	150	.50	-	-	-
SVP-ETAN-124	Hamlet/Cemetery	MV	-	130	.75	L-M	35	-
SVP-ETAN-125	Cemetery	MV	-	140	1.10	-	-	-
SVP-ETAN-126	Hamlet	MV	-	150	1.10	L	15	-
SVP-ETAN-127	Cemetery	MV	-	200	.50	-	-	-
SVP-ETAN-128	Hamlet	MV	-	140	.75	M	75	-
SVP-ETAN-129	Cemetery	MV	-	140	.25	-	-	-
SVP-ETAN-130	Small Village	MV	-	140	2.25	M	225	-
SVP-ETAN-131	Hamlet	MV	-	140	.25	L	5	-
SVP-ETAN-132	Small Village/ Cemetery	MV	-	150	1.50	M	150	-

Table 26. Tabular Presentation of Prehispanic Settlement Data (Continued)

Early Tanguche Period Sites

Site Number	Classification	Survey Sector	Collection Number(s)	Elev (m)	Area (ha)	Hab Dens	Pop Est	Site Numbers of Other Occupations
SVP-ETAN-133	Hamlet/Cemetery	MV	-	140	.70	M	70	-
SVP-ETAN-134	Small Village	LV	-	125	1.00	M	100	-
SVP-ETAN-135	Hamlet	LV	(347)	200	1.00	L	15	LSUCH-135, LTAN-43
SVP-ETAN-136	Large Village/ Cemetery	LV	-	120	8.25	H	2060	-
SVP-ETAN-137	Hamlet	LV	-	420	.50	L	5	ESUCH-118, LSUCH-137
SVP-ETAN-138	Hamlet	LV	-	110	.50	M	50	-
SVP-ETAN-139	Hamlet	LV	-	250	.75	L	10	-
SVP-ETAN-140	Hamlet	LV	-	110	.75	M	75	-
SVP-ETAN-141	Small Village	LV	-	110	1.10	M	110	-
SVP-ETAN-142	Large Village/ Cemetery	LV	-	120	7.20	H	1800	-
SVP-ETAN-143	Small Village/ Cemetery	LV	-	110	1.10	M	110	-
SVP-ETAN-144	Cemetery	LV	-	100	.50	-	-	-
SVP-ETAN-145	Cemetery	LV	-	120	.25	-	-	-
SVP-ETAN-146	Small Village	LV	-	325	1.40	M	140	-
SVP-ETAN-147	Regional Center/ Cemetery	LV	349,350	120	14.20 H 23.20 M		5870	LTAN-44, LTR 25
SVP-ETAN-148	Cemetery	LV	-	120	.50	-	-	-

Table 26. Tabular Presentation of Prehispanic Settlement Data (Continued)

Early Tanguche Period Sites

Site Number	Classification	Survey Sector	Collection Number(s)	Elev (m)	Area (ha)	Hab Dens	Pop Est	Site Numbers of Other Occupations
SVP-ETAN-149	Hamlet	LV	-	120	.50	M	50	-
SVP-ETAN-150	Small Village	LV	-	120	1.10	M	110	-
SVP-ETAN-151	Cemetery	LV	-	100	.70	-	-	-
SVP-ETAN-152	Cemetery	LV	-	95	.10	-	-	-
SVP-ETAN-153	Cemetery	LV	-	120	.75	-	-	-
SVP-ETAN-154	Small Village/ Cemetery	LV	-	90	1.00	M	100	-
SVP-ETAN-155	Small Village/ Cemetery	LV	363	95	4.30	M	430	-
SVP-ETAN-156	Small Village/ Cemetery	LV	-	90	2.25	M	225	-
SVP-ETAN-157	Cemetery	LV	-	110	.50	-	-	-
SVP-ETAN-158	Cemetery	LV	-	85	1.00	-	-	-
SVP-ETAN-159	Small Village/ Cemetery	LV	187	85	1.60	M	160	-
SVP-ETAN-160	Cemetery	LV	186	70	.50	-	-	GUAD-75
SVP-ETAN-161	Small Village/ Cemetery	LV	185	100	1.10	M	110	ETR-24
SVP-ETAN-162	Cemetery	LV	183	130	.01	-	-	-
SVP-ETAN-163	Cemetery	LV	177	60	.10	-	-	ESUCH-120, LSUCH-140

Table 26. Tabular Presentation of Prehispanic Settlement Data (Continued)

Early Tanguche Period Sites

Site Number	Classification	Survey Sector	Collection Number(s)	Elev (m)	Area (ha)	Hab Dens	Pop Est	Site Numbers of Other Occupations
SVP-ETAN-164	Cemetery	LV	182	60	.15	-	-	LSUCH-141, ETR-25
SVP-ETAN-165	Cemetery	LV	181	60	.25	-	-	LTR-35
SVP-ETAN-166	Small Village/ Cemetery	LV	179,180	50	2.50	L-M	125	LSUCH-142, LTR-35
SVP-ETAN-167	Cemetery	LV	178	75	1.40	-	-	GUAD-83
SVP-ETAN-168	Small Village	LV	188	200	2.25	L-M	175	GUAD-94
SVP-ETAN-169	Cemetery	LV	84	100	1.60	-	-	GUAD-96
SVP-ETAN-170	Hamlet	LV	83	55	.70	L-M	35	-
SVP-ETAN-171	Cemetery	LV	82	125	.15	-	-	GUAD-99
SVP-ETAN-172	Cemetery	LV	81	75	.10	-	-	GUAD-105
SVP-ETAN-173	Hamlet	LV	78,79	75	.36	H	90	GUAD-104
SVP-ETAN-174	Hamlet	LV	75	70	.75	L-M	40	-
SVP-ETAN-175	Hamlet/C-C/ Cemetery	LV	73,74	70	1.10	L-M	55	-
SVP-ETAN-176	Small Village/ Cemetery	LV	91	65	1.00	M	100	-
SVP-ETAN-177	Hamlet	LV	92	55	.25	L	5	ESUCH-121, LTAN-48
SVP-ETAN-178	Cemetery	LV	86	45	1.50	-	-	-
SVP-ETAN-179	Small Village	LV	87	45	1.75	M	175	LTAN-49

Table 26. Tabular Presentation of Prehispanic Settlement Data (Continued)

Early Tanguche Period Sites

Site Number	Classification	Survey Sector	Collection Number(s)	Elev (m)	Area (ha)	Hab Dens	Pop Est	Site Numbers of Other Occupations
SVP-ETAN-180	Hamlet/Cemetery	LV	70,71,72,88	50	1.60	M(.6 ha)	60	GUAD-111/112, ETR-26, LTR-38
SVP-ETAN-181	Cemetery	LV	56	75	.10	-	-	GUAD-113, LTR-39
SVP-ETAN-182	Cemetery	LV	53	55	1.80	-	-	LTAN-52, ETR-29
SVP-ETAN-183	Small Village	LV	47	25	1.80	M	180	LSUCH-145
SVP-ETAN-184	Hamlet/Cemetery	LV	46	25	1.40	L-M	70	-
SVP-ETAN-185	Small Village	LV	48,49	50	2.25	M	225	LSUCH-146, ETR-30
SVP-ETAN-186	Cemetery	LV	323	125	1.10	-	-	-
SVP-ETAN-187	Cemetery	LV	318	150	.70	-	-	LTR-44
SVP-ETAN-188	Hamlet/Cemetery	LV	317	100	1.40	M(.75 ha)	75	-
SVP-ETAN-189	Large Village/ Cemetery	LV	319	55	5.90	M	590	LTAN-47, ETR-33
SVP-ETAN-190	Cemetery	LV	313,314	60	1.80	-	-	GUAD-128
SVP-ETAN-191	Small Village	LV	315	70	1.00	M	100	-
SVP-ETAN-192	Hamlet/Cemetery	LV	295	50	.90	M	90	ESUCH-125, ETR-35
SVP-ETAN-193	Hamlet/Cemetery	LV	294	30	1.40	M(.5 ha)	50	GUAD-132
SVP-ETAN-194	Small Village/ Cemetery	Coast	264	10	4.50	M	450	ETR-41
SVP-ETAN-195	Cemetery	LV	289	35	.25	-	-	ETR-36

Table 26. Tabular Presentation of Prehispanic Settlement Data (Continued)

Early Tanguche Period Sites

Site Number	Classification	Survey Sector	Collection Number(s)	Elev (m)	Area (ha)	Hab Dens	Pop Est	Site Numbers of Other Occupations
SVP-ETAN-196	Cemetery	LV	290	50	.50	-	-	GUAD-164
SVP-ETAN-197	Cemetery	LV	-	60	1.40	-	-	-
SVP-ETAN-198	Cemetery	LV	285	40	2.25	-	-	ESUCH-127, LSUCH-150, GUAD-170,ETR-44,LTR-71
SVP-ETAN-199	Small Village	Coast	270	20	2.70	M	270	ETR-47
SVP-ETAN-200	Local Center	Coast	-	10	2.00	M	200	-
SVP-ETAN-201	Hamlet	Coast	-	15	.25	L-M	15	ETR-48
SVP-ETAN-202	Hamlet	Coast	-	100	1.10	L-M	55	ETR-49
SVP-ETAN-203	Hamlet	Coast	-	400	1.40	L-M	70	-
SVP-ETAN-204	Hamlet	Coast	-	250	.20	L-M	10	-
SVP-ETAN-205	Hamlet	Coast	-	75	.30	L-M	15	-
SVP-ETAN-206	Hamlet	Coast	-	60	.60	L-M	30	-
SVP-ETAN-207	Hamlet	Coast	-	40	.20	L-M	10	-
SVP-ETAN-208	Small Village	Coast	-	10	2.40	L-M	120	-
SVP-ETAN-209	Hamlet	Coast	-	15	1.60	L-M	80	-
SVP-ETAN-210	Hamlet	Coast	-	30	.30	L-M	15	-
SVP-ETAN-211	Hamlet	Coast	-	5	.70	M	70	-
SVP-ETAN-212	Hamlet	Coast	-	25	.70	M	70	-
SVP-ETAN-213	Hamlet	Coast	-	25	.20	M	20	-

Table 26. Tabular Presentation of Prehispanic Settlement Data (Continued)

Early Tanguche Period Sites

Site Number	Classification	Survey Sector	Collection Number(s)	Elev (m)	Area (ha)	Hab Dens	Pop Est	Site Numbers of Other Occupations
SVP-ETAN-214	Hamlet	Coast	-	25	.30	L	5	-
SVP-ETAN-215	Small Village	Coast	-	25	1.50	M	150	-
SVP-ETAN-216	Hamlet	Coast	-	10	.80	M	80	-
SVP-ETAN-217	Hamlet	Coast	-	10	.50	M	50	-
SVP-ETAN-218	Hamlet	Coast	-	10	.40	M	40	-
SVP-ETAN-219	Hamlet	Coast	-	5	.90	M	90	-
SVP-ETAN-220	Hamlet	Coast	-	5	.30	M	30	-
SVP-ETAN-221	Hamlet	Coast	-	10	.80	M	80	-
SVP-ETAN-222	Hamlet	Coast	-	10	.75	M	75	-
SVP-ETAN-223	Hamlet	Coast	-	10	.25	M	25	-
SVP-ETAN-224	Small Village	Coast	-	2	1.00	M	100	-
SVP-ETAN-225	Hamlet	Coast	-	2	.75	L-M	40	-
SVP-ETAN-226	Hamlet	Coast	-	10	.50	L-M	25	-
SVP-ETAN-227	Hamlet	Coast	-	25	1.50	L-M	75	-
SVP-ETAN-228	Hamlet	Coast	-	25	.50	L-M	25	-
SVP-ETAN-229	Hamlet	Coast	-	5	1.50	L-M	75	-
SVP-ETAN-230	Hamlet	Coast	-	10	.50	L-M	25	-
SVP-ETAN-231	Hamlet	Coast	-	10	1.00	L-M	50	-

564

Table 26. Tabular Presentation of Prehispanic Settlement Data (Continued)

Early Tanguche Period Sites

Site Number	Classification	Survey Sector	Collection Number(s)	Elev (m)	Area (ha)	Hab Dens	Pop Est	Site Numbers of Other Occupations
SVP-ETAN-232	Hamlet	Coast	-	2	1.50	L-M	75	CAY-54
SVP-ETAN-233	Hamlet	Coast	-	1	1.25	L-M	65	-
SVP-ETAN-234	Hamlet	Coast	-	25	1.50	L-M	75	-
SVP-ETAN-235	Hamlet	Coast	-	25	1.50	L-M	75	-
SVP-ETAN-236	Hamlet	Coast	-	25	.50	M	50	-
SVP-ETAN-237	Hamlet	Coast	-	25	.25	M	15	-
SVP-ETAN-238	Hamlet	Coast	-	20	1.00	L-M	50	-
SVP-ETAN-239	Hamlet	LV	-	20	.50	L-M	25	-
SVP-ETAN-240	Hamlet (R.S.)	LV	-	50	1.60	L	25	-
SVP-ETAN-241	Hamlet (R.S.)	LV	-	150	1.60	L	25	-
SVP-ETAN-242	Hamlet/ Cemetery (R.S.)	LV	-	100	3.30	L	50	-
SVP-ETAN-243	Hamlet (R.S.)	LV	-	100	1.60	L	25	-
SVP-ETAN-244	Hamlet (R.S.)	LV	-	100	.10	L	5	-
SVP-ETAN-245	Hamlet (R.S.)	LV	-	100	.10	L	5	-
SVP-ETAN-246	Small Village (R.S.)	S-C	-	45	4.70	L-M	235	-
SVP-ETAN-247	Small Village (R.S.)	S-C	-	30	2.25	L-M	110	-

Table 26. Tabular Presentation of Prehispanic Settlement Data (Continued)

Early Tanguche Period Sites

Site Number	Classification	Survey Sector	Collection Number(s)	Elev (m)	Area (ha)	Hab Dens	Pop Est	Site Numbers of Other Occupations
SVP-ETAN-248	Hamlet (R.S.)	S-C	-	30	.80	L	10	-
SVP-ETAN-249	Hamlet/ Saltworks (R.S.)	S-C	-	35	4.70	L	70	-
SVP-ETAN-250	Hamlet (R.S.)	S-C	-	25	.50	L	5	-
SVP-ETAN-251	Hamlet (R.S.)	S-C	-	25	.10	L	5	-
SVP-ETAN-252	Hamlet (R.S.)	S-C	-	40	1.25	L-M	60	-
SVP-ETAN-253	Hamlet (R.S.)	S-C	-	40	.50	L-M	25	-
SVP-ETAN-254	Hamlet (R.S.)	S-C	-	40	.50	L-M	25	-
SVP-ETAN-255	Hamlet (R.S.)	S-C	-	40	.50	L-M	25	-
SVP-ETAN-256	Hamlet (R.S.)	S-C	-	45	.50	L-M	25	-
SVP-ETAN-257	Hamlet (R.S.)	S-C	-	45	.50	L-M	25	-
SVP-ETAN-258	Hamlet (R.S.)	S-C	-	45	.50	L-M	25	-
SVP-ETAN-259	Hamlet (R.S.)	S-C	-	45	.50	L-M	25	-
SVP-ETAN-260	Hamlet (R.S.)	S-C	-	45	.50	L-M	25	-
SVP-ETAN-261	Hamlet (R.S.)	S-C	-	50	1.00	L-M	50	-
SVP-ETAN-262	Hamlet (R.S.)	S-C	-	50	.50	L-M	25	-
SVP-ETAN-263	Hamlet (R.S.)	S-C	-	50	.75	L-M	40	-
SVP-ETAN-264	Hamlet (R.S.)	S-C	-	95	.50	L-M	25	-
SVP-ETAN-265	Hamlet (R.S.)	S-C	-	95	1.00	L-M	50	-

Early Tanguche Period Sites

Site Number	Classification	Survey Sector	Collection Number(s)	Elev (m)	Area (ha)	Hab Dens	Pop Est	Site Numbers of Other Occupations
SVP-ETAN-266	Hamlet (R.S.)	S-C	-	125	.50	L-M	25	-
SVP-ETAN-267	Hamlet (R.S.)	S-C	-	150	.25	L-M	10	-
SVP-ETAN-268	Hamlet (R.S.)	S-C	-	175	.25	L-M	10	-
SVP-ETAN-269	Hamlet (R.S.)	S-C	-	200	.60	L-M	30	-
SVP-ETAN-270	Hamlet (R.S.)	S-C	-	195	.50	L-M	25	-
SVP-ETAN-271	Hamlet (R.S.)	S-C	-	200	1.10	L	15	-
SVP-ETAN-272	Hamlet/Cemetery	S-C	-	225	.50	L	5	-
SVP-ETAN-273	Hamlet (R.S.)	S-C	-	203	2.50	L	40	-
SVP-ETAN-274	Hamlet (R.S.)	S-C	-	205	.70	L	10	-
SVP-ETAN-275	Hamlet (R.S.)	S-C	-	207	.70	L	10	-
SVP-ETAN-276	Hamlet (R.S.)	S-C	-	215	.70	L	10	-
SVP-ETAN-277	Hamlet (R.S.)	S-C	-	225	1.00	L-M	50	-
SVP-ETAN-278	Hamlet (R.S.)	S-C	-	235	1.60	L	25	-
SVP-ETAN-279	Hamlet (R.S.)	S-C	-	275	2.00	L	30	-
SVP-ETAN-280	Hamlet (R.S.)	S-C	-	290	.25	L	5	-
SVP-ETAN-281	Hamlet/ Corral (R.S.)	S-C	-	300	.80	L	10	-
SVP-ETAN-282	Hamlet (R.S.)	S-C	-	310	.50	L-M	25	-
SVP-ETAN-283	Hamlet (R.S.)	S-C	-	325	.80	4 strucs.	20	-

Table 26. Tabular Presentation of Prehispanic Settlement Data (Continued)

Early Tanguche Period Sites

Site Number	Classification	Survey Sector	Collection Number(s)	Elev (m)	Area (ha)	Hab Dens	Pop Est	Site Numbers of Other Occupations
SVP-ETAN-284	Hamlet (R.S.)	S-C	-	300	.50	L	10	-
SVP-ETAN-285	Hamlet (R.S.)	S-C	-	305	1.10	L	15	-
SVP-ETAN-286	Hamlet (R.S.)	S-C	-	305	1.00	4 strucs.	20	-
SVP-ETAN-287	Hamlet/ Corral (R.S.)	S-C	-	300	.80	L	10	-
SVP-ETAN-288	Hamlet (R.S.)	S-C	-	298	.80	L	10	-
SVP-ETAN-289	Hamlet (R.S.)	S-C	-	295	.50	L	5	-
SVP-ETAN-290	Hamlet (R.S.)	S-C	-	290	1.00	L	15	-
SVP-ETAN-291	Hamlet (R.S.)	S-C	-	290	.50	L	5	-
SVP-ETAN-292	Hamlet (R.S.)	S-C	-	290	.30	L	5	-
SVP-ETAN-293	Hamlet (R.S.)	S-C	-	300	.50	L	10	-
SVP-ETAN-294	Hamlet (R.S.)	S-C	-	250	.30	L	5	-
SVP-ETAN-295	Hamlet (R.S.)	S-C	-	250	.50	L	10	-
SVP-ETAN-296	Hamlet (R.S.)	S-C	-	250	.30	L	5	-
SVP-ETAN-297	Hamlet (R.S.)	S-C	-	230	.30	L	5	-
SVP-ETAN-298	Hamlet (R.S.)	S-C	-	215	.30	L	5	-
SVP-ETAN-299	Hamlet (R.S.)	S-C	-	200	.25	L	10	-
SVP-ETAN-300	Hamlet (R.S.)	S-C	-	290	.75	L-M	40	-

Table 26. Tabular Presentation of Prehispanic Settlement Data (Continued)

Early Tanguche Period Sites

Site Number	Classification	Survey Sector	Collection Number(s)	Elev (m)	Area (ha)	Hab Dens	Pop Est	Site Numbers of Other Occupations
SVP-ETAN-301	Hamlet/ Corral (R.S.)	S-C	-	280	.50	L-M	25	-
SVP-ETAN-302	Hamlet (R.S.)	S-C	-	270	2.50	L	40	-
SVP-ETAN-303	Hamlet (R.S.)	S-C	-	260	.80	L-M	40	-
SVP-ETAN-304	Hamlet/ Corral (R.S.)	S-C	-	260	3.10	15 strucs.	75	-
SVP-ETAN-305	Hamlet (R.S.)	S-C	-	260	.50	L	5	-
SVP-ETAN-306	Hamlet (R.S.)	S-C	-	260	1.00	L-M	20	-
SVP-ETAN-307	Hamlet (R.S.)	S-C	-	255	.50	L	5	-
SVP-ETAN-308	Hamlet (R.S.)	S-C	-	250	1.00	L	10	-
SVP-ETAN-309	Hamlet (R.S.)	S-C	-	250	2.50	7 strucs.	35	-
SVP-ETAN-310	Hamlet (R.S.)	S-C	-	245	1.70	L	25	-
SVP-ETAN-311	Hamlet (R.S.)	S-C	-	240	1.00	L	15	-
SVP-ETAN-312	Hamlet (R.S.)	S-C	-	245	.50	L	5	-
SVP-ETAN-313	Hamlet (R.S.)	S-C	-	240	.10	L	5	-
SVP-ETAN-314	Hamlet (R.S.)	S-C	-	240	.50	2 strucs.	10	-
SVP-ETAN-315	Hamlet (R.S.)	S-C	-	240	.25	2 strucs.	10	-
SVP-ETAN-316	Hamlet (R.S.)	S-C	-	230	4.50	16 strucs.	80	-
SVP-ETAN-317	Hamlet (R.S.)	S-C	-	225	2.25	L	35	-

Table 26. Tabular Presentation of Prehispanic Settlement Data (Continued)

Early Tanguche Period Sites

Site Number	Classification	Survey Sector	Collection Number(s)	Elev (m)	Area (ha)	Hab Dens	Pop Est	Site Numbers of Other Occupations
SVP-ETAN-318	Small Village/ Corral (R.S.)	S-C	-	215	8.50	30 strucs.	150	-
SVP-ETAN-319	Hamlet (R.S.)	S-C	-	210	.50	L	5	-
SVP-ETAN-320	C-C	S-C	-	210	1.25	-	-	-
SVP-ETAN-321	Local Center/ Corrals (R.S.)	S-C	382	200	33.00	L	495	LTAN-56
SVP-ETAN-322	Hamlet (R.S.)	S-C	-	195	.30	1 struc.	5	-
SVP-ETAN-323	Hamlet (R.S.)	S-C	-	185	1.00	5 strucs.	25	-
SVP-ETAN-324	Hamlet (R.S.)	S-C	-	170	.50	L-M	25	-
SVP-ETAN-325	Hamlet (R.S.)	S-C	-	170	.30	2 strucs.	10	-
SVP-ETAN-326	Hamlet (R.S.)	S-C	-	165	.90	L-M	45	-
SVP-ETAN-327	Hamlet (R.S.)	S-C	-	155	1.10	L-M	30	-
SVP-ETAN-328	Hamlet (R.S.)	S-C	-	145	.50	L	15	-
SVP-ETAN-329	Hamlet (R.S.)	S-C	-	135	3.00	15 strucs.	75	-
SVP-ETAN-330	Hamlet (R.S.)	S-C	-	150	3.50	L	50	-
SVP-ETAN-331	Hamlet (R.S.)	S-C	-	125	.50	L-M	25	-
SVP-ETAN-332	Hamlet (R.S.)	S-C	-	110	.50	L-M	25	-
SVP-ETAN-333	Hamlet (R.S.)	S-C	-	110	.50	L-M	25	-
SVP-ETAN-334	Hamlet (R.S.)	S-C	-	110	.50	L-M	25	-

Table 26. Tabular Presentation of Prehispanic Settlement Data (Continued)

Early Tanguche Period Sites

Site Number	Classification	Survey Sector	Collection Number(s)	Elev (m)	Area (ha)	Hab Dens	Pop Est	Site Numbers of Other Occupations
SVP-ETAN-335	Hamlet (R.S.)	S-C	-	100	1.00	L-M	50	-
SVP-ETAN-336	Petroglyphs	S-C	-	300	.10	-	-	-
SVP-ETAN-337	Hamlet (R.S.)	S-C	-	300	.25	L	5	-
SVP-ETAN-338	Hamlet (R.S.)	S-C	-	315	.50	L	10	-
SVP-ETAN-339	Hamlet (R.S.)	S-C	Spec. Coll. (see Fig. 349f)	320	.75	L-M	40	-
SVP-ETAN-340	Hamlet (R.S.)	S-C	-	300	.25	L	5	-
SVP-ETAN-341	Hamlet (R.S.)	S-C	-	315	.25	L	5	-
SVP-ETAN-342	Hamlet (R.S.)	S-C	-	325	.25	L	5	-
SVP-ETAN-343	Hamlet (R.S.)	S-C	-	320	.50	L	10	-
SVP-ETAN-344	Hamlet (R.S.)	S-C	-	300	.50	L	10	-
SVP-ETAN-345	Hamlet (R.S.)	S-C	-	300	1.70	L-M	85	-
SVP-ETAN-346	Hamlet (R.S.)	S-C	-	335	.30	L	5	-
SVP-ETAN-347	Hamlet (R.S.)	S-C	-	325	.25	2 strucs.	10	-
SVP-ETAN-348	Hamlet (R.S.)	S-C	-	325	.25	L	5	-
SVP-ETAN-349	Hamlet (R.S.)	S-C	-	325	1.50	4 strucs.	20	-
SVP-ETAN-350	Hamlet (R.S.)	S-C	-	325	.30	L	10	-
SVP-ETAN-351	Hamlet (R.S.)	S-C	-	320	1.50	7 strucs.	35	-

Table 26. Tabular Presentation of Prehispanic Settlement Data (Continued)

Early Tanguche Period Sites

Site Number	Classification	Survey Sector	Collection Number(s)	Elev (m)	Area (ha)	Hab Dens	Pop Est	Site Numbers of Other Occupations
SVP-ETAN-352	Hamlet (R.S.)	S-C	-	300	1.10	L-M	55	-
SVP-ETAN-353	Hamlet (R.S.)	S-C	-	325	1.40	6 strucs.	30	-
SVP-ETAN-354	Hamlet (R.S.)	S-C	-	325	1.50	6 strucs.	30	-
SVP-ETAN-355	Hamlet (R.S.)	S-C	-	325	.80	2 strucs.	10	-
SVP-ETAN-356	Hamlet (R.S.)	S-C	-	325	1.00	4 strucs.	20	-
SVP-ETAN-357	Hamlet (R.S.)	S-C	-	350	1.25	3 strucs.	15	-
SVP-ETAN-358	Hamlet (R.S.)	S-C	-	315	.75	L-M	40	-
SVP-ETAN-359	Hamlet (R.S.)	S-C	-	315	.50	L-M	25	-
SVP-ETAN-360	Hamlet (R.S.)	S-C	-	305	.50	6 strucs.	30	-
SVP-ETAN-361	Hamlet (R.S.)	S-C	-	300	.80	2 strucs.	10	-
SVP-ETAN-362	Hamlet (R.S.)	S-C	-	300	.80	2 strucs.	10	-
SVP-ETAN-363	Hamlet (R.S.)	S-C	-	295	.50	3 strucs.	15	-
SVP-ETAN-364	Hamlet (R.S.)	S-C	-	290	1.10	7 strucs.	35	-
SVP-ETAN-365	Hamlet (R.S.)	S-C	-	285	.50	2 strucs.	10	-
SVP-ETAN-366	Hamlet (R.S.)	S-C	-	285	2.00	10 strucs.	50	-
SVP-ETAN-367	Hamlet (R.S.)	S-C	-	280	.30	L	5	-
SVP-ETAN-368	Hamlet (R.S.)	S-C	-	275	1.25	L-M	60	-
SVP-ETAN-369	Hamlet (R.S.)	S-C	-	260	1.10	L-M	55	-

								Early Tanguche Period Sites

Site Number	Classification	Survey Sector	Collection Number(s)	Elev (m)	Area (ha)	Hab Dens	Pop Est	Site Numbers of Other Occupations
SVP-ETAN-370	Small Village (R.S.)	S-C	-	250	2.80	L-M	140	-
SVP-ETAN-371	Hamlet (R.S.)	S-C	-	225	.50	L-M	25	-
SVP-ETAN-372	Hamlet (R.S.)	S-C	-	200	1.25	L-M	60	-
SVP-ETAN-373	Hamlet (R.S.)	S-C	-	200	.20	L	5	-
SVP-ETAN-374	Small Village (R.S.)	S-C	-	200	2.25	L-M	110	-
SVP-ETAN-375	Hamlet (R.S.)	S-C	-	195	.50	2 strucs.	10	-
SVP-ETAN-376	Hamlet (R.S.)	S-C	-	190	1.00	L	15	-
SVP-ETAN-377	Hamlet (R.S.)	S-C	-	130	.50	L-M	25	-
SVP-ETAN-378	Hamlet (R.S.)	S-C	-	115	.50	L-M	25	-
SVP-ETAN-379	Hamlet (R.S.)	S-C	-	110	.50	L-M	25	-
SVP-ETAN-380	Hamlet (R.S.)	S-C	-	110	.50	L-M	25	-
SVP-ETAN-381	Hamlet (R.S.)	S-C	-	110	1.00	L-M	50	-
SVP-ETAN-382	Hamlet (R.S.)	S-C	-	110	1.00	L-M	50	-
SVP-ETAN-383	Hamlet (R.S.)	S-C	-	110	.50	L-M	25	-
SVP-ETAN-384	Hamlet (R.S.)	S-C	-	110	.25	L-M	10	-
SVP-ETAN-385	Hamlet (R.S.)	S-C	-	110	.25	L-M	10	-
SVP-ETAN-386	Hamlet (R.S.)	S-C	-	125	1.50	L-M	75	-

Table 26. Tabular Presentation of Prehispanic Settlement Data (Continued)

								Early Tanguche Period Sites

Site Number	Classification	Survey Sector	Collection Number(s)	Elev (m)	Area (ha)	Hab Dens	Pop Est	Site Numbers of Other Occupations
SVP-ETAN-387	Hamlet (R.S.)	S-C	-	150	1.00	L-M	50	-
SVP-ETAN-388	Hamlet (R.S.)	S-C	-	120	.50	L-M	25	-
SVP-ETAN-389	Hamlet (R.S.)	S-C	-	110	.50	L-M	25	-
SVP-ETAN-390	Hamlet (R.S.)	S-C	-	110	.50	L-M	25	-
SVP-ETAN-391	Hamlet/ Corral (R.S.)	S-C	-	200	1.25	L-M	60	-
SVP-ETAN-392	Hamlet (R.S.)	S-C	-	195	.75	L	10	-
SVP-ETAN-393	Hamlet (R.S.)	S-C	-	200	.25	L-M	10	-
SVP-ETAN-394	Hamlet (R.S.)	S-C	-	210	.75	L-M	40	-
SVP-ETAN-395	Hamlet (R.S.)	S-C	-	200	.75	L-M	40	-
SVP-ETAN-396	Hamlet (R.S.)	S-C	-	200	.75	L-M	40	-
SVP-ETAN-397	Hamlet (R.S.)	S-C	-	200	.25	L-M	10	-
SVP-ETAN-398	Small Village (R.S.)	S-C	-	205	2.00	L-M	100	-
SVP-ETAN-399	Small Village (R.S.)	S-C	-	210	2.00	L-M	100	-
SVP-ETAN-400	Hamlet (R.S.)	S-C	-	215	.50	L-M	25	-
SVP-ETAN-401	Hamlet (R.S.)	S-C	-	225	1.50	L-M	75	LTR-77
SVP-ETAN-402	Hamlet (R.S.)	S-C	-	300	.25	L	5	-

Table 26. Tabular Presentation of Prehispanic Settlement Data (Continued)

Early Tanguche Period Sites

Site Number	Classification	Survey Sector	Collection Number(s)	Elev (m)	Area (ha)	Hab Dens	Pop Est	Site Numbers of Other Occupations
SVP-ETAN-403	Hamlet (R.S.)	S-C	-	290	.25	L	5	-
SVP-ETAN-404	(Regional Center--Chao)	S-C	-	300	55.00	M	(5500)	-
SVP-ETAN-405	Hamlet (R.S.)	S-C	-	390	.50	L-M	25	-
SVP-ETAN-406	Hamlet (R.S.)	S-C	-	1000	.25	L	5	-
SVP-ETAN-407	Hamlet (R.S.)	S-C	-	625	.25	L-M	10	-
SVP-ETAN-408	Hamlet (R.S.)	S-C	-	525	.25	L-M	10	-
SVP-ETAN-409	Hamlet (R.S.)	S-C	-	425	.10	-	-	-
SVP-ETAN-410	Hamlet (R.S.)	S-C	-	405	.25	L-M	10	-
SVP-ETAN-411	Hamlet (R.S.)	S-C	-	400	.25	L	5	-
SVP-ETAN-412	Hamlet (R.S.)	S-C	-	575	.10	L	5	-
SVP-ETAN-413	Hamlet (R.S.)	S-C	-	575	.25	L-M	10	-
SVP-ETAN-414	Hamlet (R.S.)	S-C	-	490	.25	L-M	10	-
SVP-ETAN-415	Hamlet (R.S.)	S-C	-	510	.50	L-M	25	-
SVP-ETAN-416	Hamlet (R.S.)	S-C	-	510	.25	L-M	10	-
SVP-ETAN-417	Hamlet (R.S.)	S-C	-	500	.25	L-M	10	-
SVP-ETAN-418	Hamlet (R.S.)	S-C	-	500	1.25	L-M	60	-
SVP-ETAN-419	Hamlet (R.S.)	S-C	-	510	.75	L-M	40	-
SVP-ETAN-420	Hamlet (R.S.)	S-C	-	540	.75	L-M	40	-

Table 26. Tabular Presentation of Prehispanic Settlement Data (Continued)

Early Tanguche Period Sites

Site Number	Classification	Survey Sector	Collection Number(s)	Elev (m)	Area (ha)	Hab Dens	Pop Est	Site Numbers of Other Occupations
SVP-ETAN-421	Hamlet (R.S.)	S-C	-	675	.20	L-M	10	-
SVP-ETAN-422	Hamlet (R.S.)	S-C	-	450	.25	L-M	10	-
SVP-ETAN-423	Hamlet (R.S.)	S-C	-	460	.10	L-M	5	-
SVP-ETAN-424	Hamlet (R.S.)	S-C	-	465	.50	L-M	25	-
SVP-ETAN-425	Hamlet (R.S.)	S-C	-	500	.50	L-M	25	-
SVP-ETAN-426	Hamlet/ C-C (R.S.)	S-C	-	500	.75	L-M	40	-
SVP-ETAN-427	Hamlet (R.S.)	S-C	-	480	1.50	L-M	75	-
SVP-ETAN-428	Hamlet/ C-C (R.S.)	S-C	-	510	1.50	L	20	-
SVP-ETAN-429	Hamlet (R.S.)	S-C	-	520	.50	L-M	25	-
SVP-ETAN-430	C-C/ Hamlet (R.S.)	S-C	-	590	.50	L	5	-
SVP-ETAN-431	Hamlet (R.S.)	S-C	-	595	.25	L	5	-
SVP-ETAN-432	C-C/ Hamlet (R.S.)	S-C	-	600	.10	L	5	-
SVP-ETAN-433	C-C/ Hamlet (R.S.)	S-C	-	650	.50	L	10	-
SVP-ETAN-434	Hamlet (R.S.)	S-C	-	700	1.50	L-M	75	-
SVP-ETAN-435	Petroglyphs	S-C	-	750	.10	-	-	-

Table 26. Tabular Presentation of Prehispanic Settlement Data (Continued)

			Early Tanguche Period Sites					
Site Number	Classification	Survey Sector	Collection Number(s)	Elev (m)	Area (ha)	Hab Dens	Pop Est	Site Numbers of Other Occupations
SVP-ETAN-436	Hamlet (R.S.)	S-C	-	800	.50	L-M	25	-
SVP-ETAN-437	Hamlet (R.S.)	S-C	-	800	.50	L-M	25	-
SVP-ETAN-438	Hamlet (R.S.)	S-C	-	470	.25	L-M	10	-
SVP-ETAN-439	Hamlet (R.S.)	S-C	-	460	1.00	L-M	50	-
SVP-ETAN-440	Hamlet (R.S.)	S-C	-	450	.75	L-M	40	-

Table 26. Tabular Presentation of Prehispanic Settlement Data for the Lower Santa Valley Survey Region

			Late Tanguche Period Sites					
Site Number	Classification	Survey Sector	Collection Number(s)	Elev (m)	Area (ha)	Hab Dens	Pop Est	Site Numbers of Other Occupations
SVP-LTAN-1	Hamlet	UV	-	450	1.20	L-M	60	-
SVP-LTAN-2	Hamlet	UV	-	425	1.75	L-M	90	-
SVP-LTAN-3	Small Village	UV	-	400	2.60	L-M	130	-
SVP-LTAN-4	Hamlet	UV	39	325	1.40	L	20	ESUCH-31, LSUCH-52, GUAD-1, ETAN-9
SVP-LTAN-5	Cemetery	UV	146	350	.10	-	-	ETR-3
SVP-LTAN-6	Cemetery	UV	148	350	.25	-	-	ESUCH-40, ETR-4
SVP-LTAN-7	Cemetery	UV	150	350	.50	-	-	LSUCH-65, ETR-5
SVP-LTAN-8	Cemetery	UV	152	350	.10	-	-	-
SVP-LTAN-9	Cemetery	UV	-	350	.10	-	-	-
SVP-LTAN-10	Cemetery	UV	-	325	1.60	-	-	ETAN-13
SVP-LTAN-11	Cemetery	UV	140,155	260	.50	-	-	ETAN-15
SVP-LTAN-12	Cemetery	UV	141	250	.10	-	-	ETAN-17
SVP-LTAN-13	Cemetery	UV	142	275	.25	-	-	ETAN-16
SVP-LTAN-14	Small Village	UV	172	300	4.00	L-M	200	ETAN-21
SVP-LTAN-15	Local Center	UV	191,192	300	15.00	M	1500	ETR-8
SVP-LTAN-16	Small Village	UV	157,158	250	10.60	L	160	ESUCH-53,GUAD-3,ETAN-26
SVP-LTAN-17	Cemetery	UV	235	245	1.50	-	-	ETAN-34
SVP-LTAN-18	Small Village	MV	355	450	1.00	M	100	-

Late Tanguche Period Sites

Site Number	Classification	Survey Sector	Collection Number(s)	Elev (m)	Area (ha)	Hab Dens	Pop Est	Site Numbers of Other Occupations
SVP-LTAN-19	Cemetery	MV	-	240	.80	-	-	-
SVP-LTAN-20	Small Village	MV	-	250	1.50	M	150	ETAN-42
SVP-LTAN-21	Small Village	MV	-	240	2.25	M	225	ETAN-43
SVP-LTAN-22	Local Center	MV	242	240	6.75	M	675	ETAN-44, ETR-12
SVP-LTAN-23	Hamlet	MV	353	375	.70	M	70	-
SVP-LTAN-24	Cemetery	MV	202	240	.25	-	-	ETR-13
SVP-LTAN-25	Cemetery	MV	(207)	240	1.10	-	-	ESUCH-73, LSUCH-97, ETAN-49
SVP-LTAN-26	Large Village	MV	-	240	2.50	H	625	ETAN-55
SVP-LTAN-27	Small Village	MV	-	230	2.00	M	200	-
SVP-LTAN-28	Small Village	MV	-	240	2.00	M	200	ETAN-63
SVP-LTAN-29	Cemetery	MV	-	240	.10	-	-	-
SVP-LTAN-30	Cemetery	MV	209	225	.15	-	-	ESUCH-83, LSUCH-102, GUAD-9, ETAN-57, ETR-15
SVP-LTAN-31	Cemetery	MV	-	240	.70	-	-	-
SVP-LTAN-32	Cemetery	MV	211	225	.25	-	-	ETR-16
SVP-LTAN-33	Cemetery	MV	213	225	.10	-	-	ETR-17
SVP-LTAN-34	Hamlet	MV	214	275	.70	M	70	ETR-18
SVP-LTAN-35	Hamlet	MV	-	275	.70	M	70	ETAN-59

Late Tanguche Period Sites

Site Number	Classification	Survey Sector	Collection Number(s)	Elev (m)	Area (ha)	Hab Dens	Pop Est	Site Numbers of Other Occupations
SVP-LTAN-36	Hamlet	MV	-	250	1.80	L	25	ETAN-61
SVP-LTAN-37	Hamlet	MV	-	260	.25	M	25	-
SVP-LTAN-38	Cemetery	MV	-	240	.25	-	-	-
SVP-LTAN-39	Hamlet/Cemetery	MV	-	225	1.60	L-M	80	GUAD-15
SVP-LTAN-40	Local Center	MV	307	200	14.20	H	3550	-
SVP-LTAN-41	Large Village/ Cemetery	MV	299	200	15.10	L-M	755	ESUCH-98, GUAD-33, ETR-21
SVP-LTAN-42	Small Village/ Minor Fortress	MV	338	200	3.40	M	340	ETR-22
SVP-LTAN-43	Hamlet/ Minor Fortress	MV	347	200	1.10	L-M	55	LSUCH-135, ETAN-135
SVP-LTAN-44	Local Center	LV	350	120	14.20 23.20	H M	5870	ETAN-147, LTR-25
SVP-LTAN-45	Hamlet	LV	-	125	1.00	L-M	50	-
SVP-LTAN-46	Cemetery	LV	328	60	1.40	-	-	LTR-50
SVP-LTAN-47	Large Village/ Cemetery	LV	319	55	5.60	M	560	ETAN-189, ETR-33
SVP-LTAN-48	Hamlet	LV	92	55	.50	M	50	ESUCH-121, ETAN-177
SVP-LTAN-49	Hamlet	LV	87	45	.75	L-M	40	ETAN-179
SVP-LTAN-50	Cemetery	LV	54	60	1.00	-	-	GUAD-115, ETR-28

Table 26. Tabular Presentation of Prehispanic Settlement Data (Continued)

			Late Tanguche Period Sites					
Site Number	Classification	Survey Sector	Collection Number(s)	Elev (m)	Area (ha)	Hab Dens	Pop Est	Site Numbers of Other Occupations
SVP-LTAN-51	Hamlet	LV	52	70	1.80	L-M	90	-
SVP-LTAN-52	Cemetery	LV	53	55	1.80	-	-	ETAN-182, ETR-29
SVP-LTAN-53	Local Center	LV	288	30	20.00	M	2000	ESUCH-126,ETR-43,LTR-68
SVP-LTAN-54	Small Village	LV	283,284	50	3.00	M	300	ESUCH-126, LSUCH-149, GUAD-172, ETR-43
SVP-LTAN-55	Hamlet	Coast	-	25	1.00	L-M	50	-
SVP-LTAN-56	Hamlet (R.S.)	S-C	382	200	1.00+	L-M	50	ETAN-321

Table 26. Tabular Presentation of Prehispanic Settlement Data for the Lower Santa Valley Survey Region

			Early Tambo Real Period Sites					
Site Number	Classification	Survey Sector	Collection Number(s)	Elev (m)	Area (ha)	Hab Dens	Pop Est	Site Numbers of Other Occupations
SVP-ETR-1	Hamlet/Cemetery	UV	12	340	1.00	L-M	50	-
SVP-ETR-2	Local Center/ Cemetery	UV	114,117	340	4.00	L-M	200	ESUCH-30, ETAN-7
SVP-ETR-3	Cemetery	UV	146	350	.10	-	-	LTAN-5
SVP-ETR-4	Cemetery	UV	148	350	.25	-	-	ESUCH-40, LTAN-6
SVP-ETR-5	Cemetery	UV	149,150,151	350	1.00	-	-	CAY-24, ESUCH-42, LSUCH-65, LTAN-7
SVP-ETR-6	Cemetery	UV	175	300	.10	-	-	ESUCH-50
SVP-ETR-7	Small Village	UV	189	310	2.00	L-M	100	ETAN-22
SVP-ETR-8	Local Center	UV	191,192	300	12.80	M	1280	LTAN-15
SVP-ETR-9	Hamlet/Cemetery	UV	142,143,155	250	1.40	L-M	70	ETAN-17
SVP-ETR-10	Hamlet	UV	231	250	1.50	L-M	75	ESUCH-55, ETAN-33
SVP-ETR-11	Cemetery	MV	199	250	.90	-	-	-
SVP-ETR-12	Local Center	MV	242	240	7.20	L-M	360	ETAN-44, LTAN-22
SVP-ETR-13	Cemetery	MV	202	240	.25	-	-	LTAN-24
SVP-ETR-14	Hamlet	MV	246,247	230	1.40	L-M	70	ETAN-56
SVP-ETR-15	Cemetery	MV	(209)	225	.15	-	-	ESUCH-83, LSUCH-102, GUAD-9,ETAN-57,LTAN-30
SVP-ETR-16	Cemetery	MV	211	225	.25	-	-	LTAN-32

573

Table 26. Tabular Presentation of Prehispanic Settlement Data (Continued)

Early Tambo Real Period Sites

Site Number	Classification	Survey Sector	Collection Number(s)	Elev (m)	Area (ha)	Hab Dens	Pop Est	Site Numbers of Other Occupations
SVP-ETR-17	Cemetery	MV	213	225	.10	-	-	LTAN-33
SVP-ETR-18	Hamlet	MV	214	275	.70	M	70	LTAN-34
SVP-ETR-19	Cemetery	MV	216	250	1.60	-	-	-
SVP-ETR-20	Small Village	MV	273	210	1.60	M	160	-
SVP-ETR-21	Small Village/ Cemetery	MV	299	200	3.40	M(3.25 ha)	325	GUAD-33, LTAN-41
SVP-ETR-22	Citadel	MV	338	200	3.40	L-M	170	LTAN-42
SVP-ETR-23	Hamlet/Cemetery	MV	362	160	.50	L	5	ESUCH-114
SVP-ETR-24	Minor Fortress/ Hamlet	LV	185	100	1.10	L-M	55	ETAN-161
SVP-ETR-25	Cemetery	LV	182	60	.15	-	-	LSUCH-141, ETAN-164
SVP-ETR-26	Hamlet/Cemetery	LV	70,71	50	1.00	L-M	50	GUAD-112,ETAN-180,LTR-38
SVP-ETR-27	Cemetery	LV	55	50	1.40	-	-	LTR-40
SVP-ETR-28	Cemetery	LV	54	60	1.00	-	-	GUAD-115, LTAN-50
SVP-ETR-29	Cemetery	LV	53	55	1.80	-	-	ETAN-182, LTAN-52
SVP-ETR-30	Minor Fortress/ Small Village	LV	49	50	1.00	M	100	LSUCH-146, ETAN-185
SVP-ETR-31	Small Village	LV	322	100	3.20	M	320	LTR-45
SVP-ETR-32	Hamlet	LV	321	140	.25	L	5	ESUCH-124, GUAD-122

Table 26. Tabular Presentation of Prehispanic Settlement Data (Continued)

Early Tambo Real Period Sites

Site Number	Classification	Survey Sector	Collection Number(s)	Elev (m)	Area (ha)	Hab Dens	Pop Est	Site Numbers of Other Occupations
SVP-ETR-33	Large Village/ Cemetery	LV	319	55	5.00	M	500	ETAN-189, LTAN-47
SVP-ETR-34	Small Village	LV	298	60	2.50	M	250	LTR-55
SVP-ETR-35	Small Village/ Cemetery	LV	295,296	50	2.25	M	225	ESUCH-125, ETAN-192
SVP-ETR-36	Hamlet/Cemetery	LV	289	35	.25	M	25	ETAN-195
SVP-ETR-37	Small Village/ Cemetery	LV	268,269	30	2.90	M	290	-
SVP-ETR-38	Small Village/ Cemetery	Coast	267	10	4.00	L-M	200	-
SVP-ETR-39	Hamlet	Coast	-	10	1.40	L-M	70	-
SVP-ETR-40	Hamlet	Coast	-	10	.50	L-M	25	-
SVP-ETR-41	Small Village/ Cemetery	Coast	264	10	4.30	L-M	215	ETAN-194
SVP-ETR-42	Local Center	Coast	263	15	10.80	H	2700	-
SVP-ETR-43	Local Center	LV	282,283,287, 288	30	33.00	M	3300	ESUCH-126, LTAN-53, LTR-68
SVP-ETR-44	Cemetery	LV	285	40	2.25	-	-	ESUCH-127, LSUCH-150, GUAD-170,ETAN-198,LTR-71
SVP-ETR-45	Hamlet/Cemetery	Coast	286	10	.90	L-M	45	LTR-73
SVP-ETR-46	Citadel	LV	280,281	280	1.10	L-M	55	ESUCH-128, LSUCH-151

574

Table 26. Tabular Presentation of Prehispanic Settlement Data (Continued)

			Early Tambo Real Period Sites					
Site Number	Classification	Survey Sector	Collection Number(s)	Elev (m)	Area (ha)	Hab Dens	Pop Est	Site Numbers of Other Occupations
SVP-ETR-47	Small Village	Coast	270	20	2.75	M	275	ETAN-199
SVP-ETR-48	Hamlet	Coast	-	15	.25	L	5	ETAN-201
SVP-ETR-49	Hamlet	Coast	-	100	1.10	L	15	ETAN-202

Table 26. Tabular Presentation of Prehispanic Settlement Data for the Lower Santa Valley Survey Region

			Late Tambo Real Period Sites					
Site Number	Classification	Survey Sector	Collection Number(s)	Elev (m)	Area (ha)	Hab Dens	Pop Est	Site Numbers of Other Occupations
SVP-LTR-1	Small Village	UV	167	350	1.40	M	140	-
SVP-LTR-2	Cemetery	UV	232	425	.10	-	-	CAY-32, ESUCH-54, LSUCH-83, ETAN-35
SVP-LTR-3	Hamlet	UV	161	255	.90	M	90	-
SVP-LTR-4	Hamlet/Cemetery	MV	200	375	.50	L	5	-
SVP-LTR-5	Small Village	MV	210	250	2.25	M	225	-
SVP-LTR-6	Hamlet/Cemetery	MV	311	180	1.40	L-M	70	-
SVP-LTR-7	Hamlet	MV	-	275	.50	L-M	25	-
SVP-LTR-8	Cemetery	MV	-	150	.50	-	-	-
SVP-LTR-9	Hamlet/Cemetery	MV	359,360	150	1.00	M(.5 ha)	50	LSUCH-127, GUAD-50
SVP-LTR-10	Small Village/ Cemetery	MV	336	160	2.00	M	200	-
SVP-LTR-11	Cemetery	MV	-	150	.10	-	-	-
SVP-LTR-12	Cemetery	MV	-	150	.10	-	-	-
SVP-LTR-13	Cemetery	MV	-	150	.10	-	-	-
SVP-LTR-14	Cemetery	MV	361	220	.10	-	-	-
SVP-LTR-15	Hamlet	MV	-	165	.25	M	25	-
SVP-LTR-16	Cemetery	MV	-	150	.10	-	-	-
SVP-LTR-17	Hamlet	MV	-	150	.25	2 strucs.	10	-

575

Table 26. Tabular Presentation of Prehispanic Settlement Data (Continued)

Late Tambo Real Period Sites

Site Number	Classification	Survey Sector	Collection Number(s)	Elev (m)	Area (ha)	Hab Dens	Pop Est	Site Numbers of Other Occupations
SVP-LTR-18	Small Village	MV	-	150	1.60	M	160	-
SVP-LTR-19	Cemetery	MV	-	140	.25	-	-	-
SVP-LTR-20	Hamlet	MV	-	160	.50	M	50	-
SVP-LTR-21	Hamlet	MV	-	160	.50	M	50	-
SVP-LTR-22	Hamlet	MV	-	170	.50	M(.25 ha)	25	ESUCH-116
SVP-LTR-23	Hamlet/Cemetery	MV	-	150	.25	M	25	-
SVP-LTR-24	Hamlet	MV	-	125	.50	M	50	-
SVP-LTR-25	Hamlet/Cemetery	LV	350	120	4.30	L	65	ETAN-147, LTAN-44
SVP-LTR-26	Local Center/ Cemetery	LV	-	100	16.50	M	1650	-
SVP-LTR-27	Small Village/ Cemetery	LV	-	100	1.40	M(1 ha)	100	-
SVP-LTR-28	Hamlet	LV	-	125	.50	L-M	25	-
SVP-LTR-29	Cemetery	LV	-	150	1.10	-	-	-
SVP-LTR-30	Large Village/ Cemetery	LV	-	125	9.00	M	900	-
SVP-LTR-31	Cemetery	LV	184	70	.75	-	-	LSUCH-138, GUAD-76
SVP-LTR-32	Small Village	LV	-	125	2.70	M	270	-
SVP-LTR-33	Small Village	LV	-	125	4.50	M	450	-

Table 26. Tabular Presentation of Prehispanic Settlement Data (Continued)

Late Tambo Real Period Sites

Site Number	Classification	Survey Sector	Collection Number(s)	Elev (m)	Area (ha)	Hab Dens	Pop Est	Site Numbers of Other Occupations
SVP-LTR-34	Hamlet	LV	-	160	1.00	L	15	-
SVP-LTR-35	Hamlet/Cemetery	LV	180,181	60	1.40	L-M	70	LSUCH-142, ETAN-165/166
SVP-LTR-36	Small Village/ Cemetery	LV	-	100	4.50	M	450	GUAD-84
SVP-LTR-37	Hamlet/Cemetery	LV	324	100	1.60	L-M	80	GUAD-91
SVP-LTR-38	Hamlet/Cemetery	LV	88	50	1.40	L-M	70	GUAD-112,ETAN-180,ETR-26
SVP-LTR-39	Cemetery	LV	56	75	1.10	-	-	GUAD-113, ETAN-181
SVP-LTR-40	Cemetery	LV	55	50	1.40	-	-	ETR-27
SVP-LTR-41	Hamlet	LV	-	100	.25	L	5	-
SVP-LTR-42	Small Village/ Cemetery	LV	-	100	2.25	L-M	110	-
SVP-LTR-43	Hamlet	LV	-	100	.90	M	90	-
SVP-LTR-44	Cemetery	LV	318	150	.70	-	-	ETAN-187
SVP-LTR-45	Small Village	LV	322	100	2.90	M	290	ETR-31
SVP-LTR-46	Small Village/ Cemetery	LV	-	100	3.80	M	380	-
SVP-LTR-47	Regional Center	LV	325,326	60	16.50	M	1650	-
SVP-LTR-48	Small Village/ Cemetery	LV	320	60	2.25	L-M	110	-
SVP-LTR-49	Hamlet	LV	-	60	.50	L-M	25	-

Table 26. Tabular Presentation of Prehispanic Settlement Data (Continued)

Late Tambo Real Period Sites

Site Number	Classification	Survey Sector	Collection Number(s)	Elev (m)	Area (ha)	Hab Dens	Pop Est	Site Numbers of Other Occupations
SVP-LTR-50	Cemetery	LV	328	60	.25	-	-	LTAN-46
SVP-LTR-51	Hamlet	LV	-	55	.50	M	50	-
SVP-LTR-52	Hamlet	LV	-	60	.50	L-M	25	-
SVP-LTR-53	Cemetery	LV	-	60	.10	-	-	-
SVP-LTR-54	Hamlet	LV	-	60	.90	L-M	45	-
SVP-LTR-55	Small Village	LV	298	60	2.25	L-M	110	ETR-34
SVP-LTR-56	Hamlet	LV	-	60	.25	L	5	-
SVP-LTR-57	Hamlet	LV	-	50	1.10	L-M	55	-
SVP-LTR-58	Hamlet	LV	-	60	.70	L-M	35	-
SVP-LTR-59	Hamlet	LV	-	45	1.10	L-M	55	-
SVP-LTR-60	Small Village	LV	292	40	2.00	L-M	100	-
SVP-LTR-61	Hamlet	LV	-	40	1.40	L-M	70	-
SVP-LTR-62	Hamlet	LV	-	40	.90	L-M	45	-
SVP-LTR-63	Cemetery	LV	-	55	.10	-	-	-
SVP-LTR-64	Small Village	LV	-	40	7.90	L-M	395	-
SVP-LTR-65	Cemetery	LV	-	60	1.00	-	-	GUAD-165
SVP-LTR-66	Small Village (R.S.)	LV	-	85	2.00	L-M	100	-
SVP-LTR-67	Hamlet (R.S.)	LV	-	100	.25	L	5	GUAD-174

Table 26. Tabular Presentation of Prehispanic Settlement Data (Continued)

Late Tambo Real Period Sites

Site Number	Classification	Survey Sector	Collection Number(s)	Elev (m)	Area (ha)	Hab Dens	Pop Est	Site Numbers of Other Occupations
SVP-LTR-68	Local Center/ Cemetery	LV	288	30	20.00	L-M	1000	ESUCH-126, LTAN-53, ETR-43
SVP-LTR-69	Cemetery	LV	-	50	2.00	-	-	-
SVP-LTR-70	Cemetery	LV	-	40	.10	-	-	-
SVP-LTR-71	Cemetery	LV	285	40	2.25	-	-	ESUCH-127, LSUCH-150, GUAD-170,ETAN-198,ETR-44
SVP-LTR-72	Hamlet	Coast	-	15	.50	L-M	25	-
SVP-LTR-73	Small Village/ Cemetery	Coast	286	10	1.40	M	140	ETR-45
SVP-LTR-74	Hamlet	Coast	-	10	.75	M	75	-
SVP-LTR-75	Hamlet (R.S.)	LV	367	30	2.30	L	35	-
SVP-LTR-76	Hamlet (R.S.)	S-C	-	295	.80	L-M	40	-
SVP-LTR-77	Hamlet (R.S.)	S-C	-	225	1.50	L	20	ETAN-401
SVP-LTR-78	Hamlet (R.S.)	S-C	-	550	.90	L-M	45	-

[a]Abbreviations used in this table include the following: Elev (elevation), Hab Dens (habitation density), Pop Est (population estimate), C-C (ceremonial-civic), Cem (cemetery), R.S. (roadside), Subt (subterranean), UV (Upper Valley), MV (Middle Valley), LV (Lower Valley), S-C (Santa-Chao), p/ha (persons per hectare), w.b. (windbreaks), L (low), L-M (low-to-moderate), M (moderate), H (high), Spec. Coll. (special collection), strucs. (structures), SAL (Las Salinas), CAY (Cayhuamarca), VIN (Vinzos), ESUCH (Early Suchimancillo), LSUCH (Late Suchimancillo), GUAD (Guadalupito), ETAN (Early Tanguche), LTAN (Late Tanguche), ETR (Early Tambo Real), LTR (Late Tambo Real).

Table 27. Tabular Presentation of Collection Data for the Lower Santa Valley Survey Region[a]

Coll. Number	n	Survey Sector	Site Type	Site Number(s)	Structure Number(s)	Validity Rating(s)
1	41	UV	Hab	ESUCH-19, LSUCH-45	-	E, E
2	14	UV	Hab	CAY-12, ESUCH-14	-	G, E
3	13	UV	Hab / Def	CAY-12, VIN-11, / ESUCH-14	1 (ext.)	G, G, / E
4	121	UV	Hab / Def	CAY-12, VIN-11	1 (int.)	E, G
5	38	UV	Hab	CAY-11, VIN-10	-	E, G
6	60	UV	C-C / Def	ESUCH-13	2, 3, 4	E
7	35	UV	Hab / Cem	ESUCH-19	-	E
8	42	UV	Hab	LSUCH-45	-	E
9	60	UV	Hab	LSUCH-45	5	E
10	26	UV	Cem	ESUCH-19	-	E
11	61	UV	Cem	LSUCH-45	-	E
12	23	UV	Hab / Cem	ETR-1	-	E
13	14	UV	Hab	LSUCH-45	-	E
14	34	UV	Hab	ESUCH-19, LSUCH-45	-	G, G
15	16	UV	Hab	ESUCH-19	-	E
16	42	UV	Cem	LSUCH-45	-	E
17	24	UV	Hab / Def	ESUCH-19	-	E
18	47	UV	Hab / Def	ESUCH-20	-	E
19	35	UV	Hab	ESUCH-19	-	E
20	12	UV	Hab / Cem	ESUCH-21	-	E
21	19	UV	Hab	CAY-14	-	E
22	8	UV	Hab / Cem	ESUCH-25	-	E
23	48	UV	Hab / Def	ESUCH-24	-	E
24	49	UV	Hab	ESUCH-23, LSUCH-49	-	E, E

Table 27. Tabular Presentation of Collection Data (Continued)

Coll. Number	n	Survey Sector	Site Type	Site Number(s)	Structure Number(s)	Validity Rating(s)
25	34	UV	Hab	VIN-14	-	E
26	169	UV	Hab / Def	CAY-15, VIN-15, / ESUCH-26, LSUCH-50, / ETAN-5	6	G, G, / G, G, / E
27	40	UV	Hab	CAY-16, ESUCH-27	-	G, G
28	110	UV	Hab / Cem	CAY-16, LSUCH-51, / ETAN-4	-	G, G, / E
29	120	UV	Hab	ESUCH-15, LSUCH-39	-	G, E
30	22	UV	Hab / Def	ESUCH-17, LSUCH-40	-	G, F
31	10	UV	Cem	VIN-12, ESUCH-16	-	F, F
32	20	UV	Hab / Cem	CAY-13, ESUCH-17	-	G, G
33	48	UV	Cem	ESUCH-17, LSUCH-40	-	E, E
34	15	UV	Cem	ESUCH-18, LSUCH-44	-	E, E
35	60	UV	Hab / Cem	ESUCH-22, LSUCH-47	-	E, E
36	7	UV	Cem	LSUCH-46	-	E
37	16	UV	Hab / Cem	ESUCH-32	-	G
38	15	UV	Hab	VIN-13, ESUCH-32	-	G, G
39	50	UV	Hab / Cem	ESUCH-31, LSUCH-52, / GUAD-1, ETAN-9, LTAN-4	-	G, E, / E, E, E
40	12	UV	Cem	ESUCH-33	-	G
41	90	UV	Hab / Cem	LSUCH-53	-	E
42	162	UV	Hab / Def	ESUCH-34, LSUCH-54	7	F, E
43	50	UV	Hab / Cem	ESUCH-35, LSUCH-55	-	G, E
44	47	UV	Hab	LSUCH-56, ETAN-10	-	G, E
45	18	UV	Hab / Cem	LSUCH-57	8	E
46	29	LV	Cem	ETAN-184	-	E
47	40	LV	Hab / Cem	LSUCH-145, ETAN-183	-	E, E

Table 27. Tabular Presentation of Collection Data (Continued)

Coll. Number	n	Survey Sector	Site Type	Site Number(s)	Structure Number(s)	Validity Rating(s)
76	27	LV	Cem	GUAD-104	–	E
77	17	LV	Wall / Cem	GUAD-107	–	E
78	54	LV	C-C	GUAD-104, ETAN-173	22	E, E
79	41	LV	Hab	ETAN-173	–	E
80	17	LV	Cem	GUAD-103	–	E
81	17	LV	Cem	GUAD-105, ETAN-172	–	E, E
82	18	LV	Hab	GUAD-99, ETAN-171	–	E, E
83	15	LV	Hab	ETAN-170	–	E
84	56	LV	Cem	GUAD-96, ETAN-169	–	E, E
85	12	LV	C-C	LSUCH-144, GUAD-110	25	F, E
86	22	LV	Cem	ETAN-178	–	E
87	7	LV	Hab	ETAN-179, LTAN-49	–	G, F
88	44	LV	Hab	ETAN-180, LTR-38	–	E, E
89	20	LV	Hab	GUAD-97	–	E
90	32	LV	Cem	GUAD-97	–	E
91	23	LV	Cem	ETAN-176	–	E
92	11	LV	C-C / Hab	(ESUCH-121), ETAN-177, LTAN-48	26	E, F
93	66	UV	Def	CAY-17, (VIN-16)	27 (int.)	E
94	40	UV	Hab	CAY-17, ETAN-6	27 (ext./ east)	E, E
95	38	UV	Hab	CAY-17, VIN-16	27 (ext./ SW)	E, F
96	15	UV	C-C / Def	CAY-19	28 (int.)	E
97	19	UV	Def	CAY-19	28 (ext.)	E
98	30	UV	Hab	CAY-19, VIN-17	28 (ext./ east)	G, G

Table 27. Tabular Presentation of Collection Data (Continued)

Coll. Number	n	Survey Sector	Site Type	Site Number(s)	Structure Number(s)	Validity Rating(s)
48	35	LV	Hab	LSUCH-146, ETAN-185	9	E, E
49	85	LV	Hab	LSUCH-146, ETAN-185, ETR-30	–	E, E, E
50	5	LV	Huaca	ESUCH-123	10	F
51	34	LV	Huaca	ESUCH-122	11	F
52	9	LV	Hab	LTAN-51	14	G
53	28	LV	Cem	ETAN-182, LTAN-52, ETR-29	–	E, G, E
54	23	LV	Cem	GUAD-115, LTAN-50, ETR-28	–	E, E, F
55	19	LV	Cem	ETR-27, LTR-40	–	E, E
56	32	LV	Huaca	GUAD-113, ETAN-181, LTR-39	15	E, E, G
57	11	LV	Huaca	GUAD-113	16	E
58	20	LV	C-C	GUAD-113	17	E
59	35	LV	Cem	GUAD-109	–	E
60	56	LV	Cem	GUAD-112	–	E
61	43	LV	Cem	GUAD-112	–	E
62	15	LV	Hab	GUAD-112	–	E
63	45	LV	Hab	GUAD-112	–	E
64	130	LV	Cem	GUAD-109	–	E
65	25	LV	Cem	GUAD-108	–	E
66	17	LV	Cem	GUAD-100	–	E
67	1	LV	v.f.	(ETAN/n.s.)	–	E
68	63	LV	Huaca	GUAD-111	19	E
69	72	LV	Hab	GUAD-112	–	E
70	26	LV	Cem	GUAD-112, ETAN-180, ETR-26	–	E, E
71	82	LV	Cem	ETAN-180, ETR-26	–	E, E
72	90	LV	Huaca	GUAD-111, ETAN-180	20	E, E
73	28	LV	C-C	ETAN-175	–	E
74	8	LV	Hab	ETAN-175	21	E
75	11	LV	Hab	ETAN-174	–	E

Table 27. Tabular Presentation of Collection Data (Continued)

Coll. Number	n	Survey Sector	Site Type	Site Number(s)	Structure Number(s)	Validity Rating(s)
99	63	UV	C-C / Def	CAY-21, (VIN-18), ESUCH-29	31	G, G
100	37	UV	Hab	CAY-20	32	E
101	147	UV	Hab / Def	CAY-23, VIN-18, ESUCH-41	33 (int./east)	G, E, G
102	35	UV	Hab / Def	(CAY-23), ESUCH-41, LSUCH-66	33 (int./central)	E, G
103	68	UV	Hab	LSUCH-38	-	E
104	66	UV	Hab / Hab	ESUCH-28, LSUCH-51, ETAN-4	-	E, E
105	41	UV	Cem	LSUCH-51, ETAN-4	129	E, E
106	15	UV	Hab	LSUCH-51	-	E
107	30	UV	Hab / Def	(CAY-23), ESUCH-41, LSUCH-66	33 (int./west)	E, F
108	50	UV	Hab / Def	CAY-25, VIN-20, ESUCH-43, LSUCH-67	34 (ext./east)	E, E, G, G
109	32	UV	Hab / Def	CAY-25, ESUCH-43, LSUCH-67	34 (int.)	E, G, F
110	24	UV	C-C / Hab	CAY-25, VIN-20, ESUCH-43, LSUCH-67	34 (ext./SW)	G, E, G, G
111	9	UV	Hab	ESUCH-45, LSUCH-68	-	E, G
112	105	UV	Cem	ESUCH-45, LSUCH-68	-	E, G
113	97	UV	C-C / Def	CAY-26, ESUCH-46, LSUCH-74	35	E, E, E
114	73	UV	C-C / Hab	ETAN-7, ETR-2	36 (int.)	E, E
115	42	UV	Hab / Cem	VIN-19, ESUCH-38, LSUCH-63	36 (ext./west)	G, G, G
116	10	UV	Huaca	(CAY-22), ETAN-8	37	G
117	30	UV	Cem	ESUCH-30, ETR-2	-	G, E
118	117	UV	C-C / Hab	LSUCH-76	38	E
119	8	UV	Hab	CAY-23, LSUCH-66	33 (ext./SE)	G, E
120	84	UV	Hab / Def	ESUCH-36, LSUCH-58	-	G, E

Table 27. Tabular Presentation of Collection Data (Continued)

Coll. Number	n	Survey Sector	Site Type	Site Number(s)	Structure Number(s)	Validity Rating(s)
121	30	UV	Hab / Cem	LSUCH-58	-	E
122	46	UV	Hab / Cem	LSUCH-62	(near 39)	E
123	1	UV	Cem	LSUCH-58	-	E
124	15	UV	Cem	LSUCH-59	-	E
125	7	UV	Cem	CAY-27, LSUCH-61	-	G, E
126	3	UV	Cem	LSUCH-60	-	E
127	27	UV	Cem	LSUCH-62	39 (ext./NNW)	E
128	63	UV	C-C / Def	ESUCH-37, LSUCH-62	39 (int.)	E, E
129	40	UV	Hab	LSUCH-70, ETAN-11	-	E, E
130	10	UV	Cem	ETAN-12	-	E
131	14	UV	Hab / Cem	LSUCH-72	-	E
132	13	UV	Cem	LSUCH-71	-	E
133	14	UV	Huaca	LSUCH-77	40	E
134	33	UV	C-C / Def	ESUCH-47, LSUCH-79	-	G, E
135	10	UV	Cem	LSUCH-78, GUAD-2	-	E, E
136	20	UV	Cem	LTAN-14	-	E
137	13	UV	Hab / Def	ESUCH-48	-	E
138	19	UV	Cem	ESUCH-49, LSUCH-82	-	E, E
139	18	UV	Hab	LSUCH-82	-	E
140	12	UV	Cem	ETAN-15, LTAN-11	-	E, E
141	10	UV	Cem	ETAN-17, LTAN-12	-	E, E
142	9	UV	Cem	ETAN-16, LTAN-13, ETR-9	-	E, E
143	25	UV	C-C / Hab	ETAN-17, ETR-9	-	E, E
144	11	UV	Cem	LSUCH-81	-	E
145	16	UV	Hab / Def	LSUCH-81	-	E

Table 27. Tabular Presentation of Collection Data (Continued)

Coll. Number	n	Survey Sector	Site Type	Site Number(s)	Structure Number(s)	Validity Rating(s)
146	16	UV	Cem	LTAN-5, ETR-3	-	E, E
147	7	UV	Hab / Cem	ESUCH-39, LSUCH-64	-	G, G
				ESUCH-40, LTAN-6,		
148	22	UV	Cem	ETR-4	-	G, E
149	24	UV	Cem	LSUCH-65, ETR-5	-	G, E
			Hab / Cem	LSUCH-65, LTAN-7,		G, E,
150	24	UV	Cem	ETR-5	-	E
				(CAY-24), ESUCH-42,		E,
151	18	UV	Cem	ETR-5	-	E
152	12	UV	Cem	LTAN-8	-	E
			Hab			
153	53	UV	Cem	ESUCH-44, LSUCH-69	-	E, E
154	5	UV	Cem	LSUCH-73	-	E, E
				GUAD-3, ETAN-14,		E
155	25	UV	Cem	LTAN-11, ETR-9	-	E, E
156	17	UV	Hab	GUAD-3, ETAN-26	-	G, E
			C-C	ESUCH-53, ETAN-26,		P, E,
157	78	UV	Hab	LTAN-16	42	G
158	127	UV	Huaca	GUAD-3, LTAN-16	43	E, E
159	8	UV	Wall	(ESUCH/Pampa Blanca)	-	P
160	9	UV	Wall	(ETAN/Pampa Blanca)	-	E
			C-C			
161	114	UV	Hab	LTR-3	44	E
162	1	UV	Road	(ETAN v.f./Pampa Blanca)	-	E
163	1	UV	Road	(ETAN v.f./Pampa Blanca)	-	E
164	7	UV	Cem	ETAN-31	-	E
165	9	UV	Huaca	ETAN-32	-	F
166	60	UV	Cem	ETAN-39	-	E
167	28	UV	Hab	LTR-1	-	E
			C-C			
168	32	UV	Def	(CAY-28), VIN-22	45 (ext.)	E
			C-C			
169	23	UV	Def	(CAY-28), VIN-22	45 (int.)	G

Table 27. Tabular Presentation of Collection Data (Continued)

Coll. Number	n	Survey Sector	Site Type	Site Number(s)	Structure Number(s)	Validity Rating(s)
170	5	UV	C-C Def	VIN-21	46	G
171	1	UV	v.f.	(CAY/n.s.)	-	F
172	45	UV	Hab	ETAN-21, LTAN-14	-	E, E
				(CAY-29), ESUCH-51,		E,
173	10	UV	Cem	ETAN-20	-	E
174	10	UV	Huaca	(CAY-29), ETAN-20	-	E
175	6	UV	Huaca	ESUCH-50, ETR-6	47	F, F
			Hab			
176	27	LV	Def	LSUCH-139	-	E
				ESUCH-120, LSUCH-140,		F, G,
				ETAN-163		E
177	8	LV	Cem	GUAD-83, ETAN-167	-	E, E
178	32	LV	Cem	ETAN-166	-	E
			Hab			
179	31	LV	Cem	LSUCH-142, ETAN-166,	-	G, E,
180	26	LV	Hab	LTR-35	-	E
181	26	LV	Cem	ETAN-165, LTR-35	-	E, E
				LSUCH-141, ETAN-164,		E,
182	28	LV	Cem	ETR-25	-	E
183	6	LV	Cem	ETAN-162	-	E
184	11	LV	Wall / Cem	LSUCH-138, GUAD-76,	-	G, E,
				LTR-31		E
185	20	LV	Hab Def	ETAN-161, ETR-24	-	E, G
186	19	LV	Cem	GUAD-75, ETAN-160	-	E, E
187	15	LV	Cem	ETAN-159	-	E
188	25	LV	Hab	GUAD-94, ETAN-168	-	E, E
189	58	UV	C-C Hab	ETAN-22, ETR-7	48 (int.)	G, E
190	8	UV	Hab	ETAN-22	48 (ext./south)	E
191	83	UV	Hab	LTAN-15, ETR-8	-	E, E
192	26	UV	Hab	LTAN-15, ETR-8	-	E, E
193	41	UV	Hab	CAY-30, ESUCH-52,	-	G, F,
				ETAN-25		F

Table 27. Tabular Presentation of Collection Data (Continued)

Coll. Number	n	Survey Sector	Site Type	Site Number(s)	Structure Number(s)	Validity Rating(s)
194	29	UV	C-C Def	CAY-31, VIN-23	49 (int.)	G, G
195	48	LV	Cem	GUAD-95	-	E
196	5	UV	Cem	ETAN-40	-	E
197	13	UV	Cem	ETAN-39	-	E
198	18	UV	Cem	ESUCH-61	-	E
199	15	UV	Cem / Hab	ETR-11	-	E
200	28	UV	Cem	LTR-4	-	E
201	61	UV	Cem	GUAD-5	-	E
202	23	UV	Cem / Hab	LTAN-24, ETR-13	-	E, G
203	48	UV	Cem Wall	ESUCH-71, LSUCH-95	-	E, E
204	13	UV	Cem	LSUCH-96, ETAN-47, ESUCH-72, GUAD-7, ETAN-48	-	E, E, G, E
205	15	UV	Cem	ESUCH-73, LSUCH-97	-	E
206	8	UV	Hab Cem	(ESUCH-73), LSUCH-97, ETAN-49, LTAN-25	-	E, E, E, E
207	13	UV	Cem	ESUCH-82, ETAN-53	-	E, E
208	14	MV	Hab Def	ESUCH-83, LSUCH-102, GUAD-9, ETAN-57, LTAN-30, ETR-15	-	G, E, E, E, E
209	30	MV	Cem	LTR-5	-	E
210	13	MV	Hab	LTAN-32, ETR-16	-	E, E
211	13	MV	Cem Wall		-	E, E
212	1	MV	Cem	ETAN-58	-	E
213	14	MV	Cem	LTAN-33, ETR-17	-	E, F
214	90	MV	Hab	LTAN-34, ETR-18	-	G, E
215	25	MV	Cem	GUAD-10	-	E
216	22	MV	Cem	ETR-19	-	G
217	30	MV	Hab	LSUCH-108	-	E

Table 27. Tabular Presentation of Collection Data (Continued)

Coll. Number	n	Survey Sector	Site Type	Site Number(s)	Structure Number(s)	Validity Rating(s)
218	22	MV	Hab	LSUCH-109	-	E
219	11	MV	Cem / Hab	LSUCH-110	-	E
220	30	MV	Cem	LSUCH-110, GUAD-13	-	E, E
221	8	MV	Hab	ESUCH-87	-	F
222	15	MV	Hab	ESUCH-88	-	G
223	76	MV	C-C Hab	VIN-26, ESUCH-89, LSUCH-112, GUAD-16	-	E, G, E, E
224	12	MV	Hab Def	ESUCH-86	-	G
225	13	MV	Hab Def	ESUCH-86	-	E
226	20	MV	Huaca	ESUCH-90, LSUCH-113, GUAD-18	51	G, E, G
227	30	MV	Hab	ESUCH-91, LSUCH-114	-	G, E
228	12	MV	Def	LSUCH-114	-	E
229	103	MV	Hab Cem	ESUCH-91, LSUCH-114, ETAN-77	-	G, E, E
230	59	UV	Hab Cem	ETAN-33	-	E
231	86	UV	Hab Cem	ESUCH-55, ETAN-33, ETR-10	-	G, E, G
232	79	UV	C-C Def	(CAY-32), ESUCH-54, LSUCH-83, ETAN-35, LTR-2	52 (int.)	E, F, E, F, G
233	35	UV	C-C Def	(CAY-32), ESUCH-54, LSUCH-83	52 (ext.)	E, E
234	87	UV	Cem	GUAD-4, ETAN-33	-	E, E
235	49	UV	Cem	ETAN-34, LTAN-17	-	E, E
236	36	UV	Huaca	LSUCH-84	53	E
237	7	UV	Cem	ETAN-36	-	E
238	33	UV	Cem	LSUCH-85	-	E
239	7	UV	Hab	ESUCH-56	-	G
240	24	UV	Hab Cem	ESUCH-56	-	E

Table 27. Tabular Presentation of Collection Data (Continued)

Coll. Number	n	Survey Sector	Site Type	Site Number(s)	Structure Number(s)	Validity Rating(s)
241	32	UV	Hab	ESUCH-56, ETAN-42	-	E, G
242	50	UV	Hab	ETAN-44, LTAN-22, ETR-12	-	E, E, F
243	15	UV	Hab	CAY-33, ESUCH-63, LSUCH-87	-	G, G, G
244	15	UV	Hab	ESUCH-62, LSUCH-86	-	E, E
245	6	UV	Hab / Def / C-C	ESUCH-74	-	G
246	80	UV	Hab	ETAN-56, ETR-14	54	E, G
247	65	UV	Cem	ETAN-56, ETR-14	(near 54)	E, G
248	32	MV	Hab	VIN-24	-	E
249	11	MV	Hab	ESUCH-84, LSUCH-103	-	E, E
250	27	MV	Hab	ESUCH-84, LSUCH-103	-	E, E
251	27	MV	Hab / Huaca	LSUCH-103	-	E
252	13	MV	Def	LSUCH-104	-	E
253	23	MV	Cem / C-C	LSUCH-105	-	E
254	8	MV	Def	CAY-34, LSUCH-106	55	G, G
255	59	MV	Hab	CAY-35	-	E
256	14	MV	Cem / C-C	LSUCH-107	-	E
257	32	MV	Def	ESUCH-92, LSUCH-115	56 (int./east), 56 (ext./west)	E, G
258	32	MV	C-C / Def	ESUCH-92, ETAN-75	-	E, E
259	20	MV	Cem	ETAN-79	-	E
260	11	MV	Hab	ESUCH-94, ETAN-81	-	G, E
261	25	MV	Cem	GUAD-22	-	E
262	14	MV	Huaca / Def	LSUCH-116, ETAN-83	57	E, E
263	54	Coast	Hab	ETR-42	-	G
264	49	Coast	Hab / Cem	ETAN-194, ETR-41	-	E, E

Table 27. Tabular Presentation of Collection Data (Continued)

Coll. Number	n	Survey Sector	Site Type	Site Number(s)	Structure Number(s)	Validity Rating(s)
265	15	LV	Hab	GUAD-168	-	E
266	18	LV	Hab	GUAD-169	-	E
267	25	Coast	Hab / Cem	ETR-38	-	G
268	62	LV	Hab	ETR-37	-	E
269	18	LV	Cem	ETR-37	-	E
270	34	Coast	Hab	ETAN-199, ETR-47	-	G, F
271	1	Coast	Hab	SAL-16	-	E
272	41	MV	Hab / Cem	ESUCH-93, ETAN-85	-	G, E
273	7	MV	Hab	ETR-20	-	E
274	11	MV	Canal	(Colonial sherds/n.s.)	-	E
275	48	MV	Cem	GUAD-26, ETAN-87	-	E, E
276	1	MV	Cem	ETAN-88	-	E
277	12	MV	Hab / Cem	ESUCH-98, LSUCH-119, GUAD-31	-	G, F, E
278	26	LV	C-C / Def	LSUCH-152, GUAD-175	60, 61	P, G
279	13	LV	C-C / Def	ESUCH-129	62	G
280	15	LV	C-C / Def	ESUCH-128, ETR-46	63	G, F
281	46	LV	Hab / Def	LSUCH-151, ETR-46	-	F
282	12	LV	Hab	ESUCH-126, ETR-43	-	E, G
283	59	LV	Hab / Cem	ESUCH-126, LSUCH-149, LTAN-54, ETR-43	-	G, F, F
284	54	LV	C-C / Cem	GUAD-172, LTAN-54	64	E, G
285	55	LV	Hab / Cem	GUAD-127, LSUCH-150, GUAD-170, ETAN-198, ETR-44, LTR-71	-	E, G, E
286	53	Coast	Cem	ETR-45, LTR-73	-	E, E
287	35	LV	Hab	ESUCH-126, ETR-43	-	E, P

583

Table 27. Tabular Presentation of Collection Data (Continued)

Coll. Number	n	Survey Sector	Site Type	Site Number(s)	Structure Number(s)	Validity Rating(s)
288	137	LV	C-C / Def / Hab	ESUCH-126, LTAN-53, ETR-43, LTR-68	(near 65)	E, E; G, E
289	7	LV	Cem	ETAN-195, ETR-36	-	E, G
290	42	LV	Cem	GUAD-164, ETAN-196	-	E, E
291	14	LV	Cem	GUAD-162	-	E
292	102	LV	Hab	LTR-60	-	E
293	12	LV	Cem	GUAD-161	-	E
294	45	LV	C-C / Def	GUAD-132, ETAN-193	66 (ext./SW)	E, E; E, E
295	36	LV	Hab	ESUCH-125, ETAN-192, ETR-35	-	F
296	104	LV	Hab	ETR-35	-	E
297	64	LV	Hab / Cem	LSUCH-147, GUAD-130	-	F, E
298	98	LV	Hab	ETR-34, LTR-55	-	G, E
299	39	MV	Cem	GUAD-33, LTAN-41, ETR-21	-	E, E; G
300	25	MV	C-C / C-C	CAY-39, VIN-27, ESUCH-99	68	E, G; E
301	11	MV	Hab	ESUCH-96, ETAN-89	69	G, E
302	24	MV	Cem	GUAD-38	-	E
303	38	MV	C-C	ETAN-102	75	E
304	12	MV	Huaca	GUAD-131	76	F
305	63	MV	Hab / Cem	LSUCH-117, ETAN-84	-	G, E
306	4	MV	Hab / Cem	GUAD-25	77	E
307	28	MV	Hab	LTAN-40	-	E
308	10	MV	Hab	ESUCH-95	-	F
309	41	MV	Rec	ETAN-93	78	E
310	1	MV	Wall	(ETAN v.f./Cerro Blanco)	-	E
311	28	MV	Hab	LTR-6	-	E
312	27	MV	Cem	LSUCH-118	-	E

Table 27. Tabular Presentation of Collection Data (Continued)

Coll. Number	n	Survey Sector	Site Type	Site Number(s)	Structure Number(s)	Validity Rating(s)
313	19	LV	Huaca / Huaca	ETAN-190	80	E
314	39	LV	Cem	GUAD-128, ETAN-190	81	G, E
315	20	LV	Hab	ETAN-191	-	E
316	20	LV	Hab / Hab	GUAD-121	83	E
317	22	LV	Cem	ETAN-188	-	E
318	20	LV	Cem	ETAN-187, LTR-44	-	E, G
319	122	LV	Hab / Cem	ETAN-189, LTAN-47, ETR-33	-	G, E; E
320	22	LV	C-C / Hab	LTR-48	84	E
321	32	LV	Hab	ESUCH-124, ETR-32	-	G, G
322	24	LV	Hab	ETR-31, LTR-45	-	G, E
323	15	LV	Cem / C-C	ETAN-186	-	E
324	38	LV	Hab	GUAD-91, LTR-37	86	E, E
325	34	LV	Hab	LTR-47	-	E
326	32	LV	Huaca / Huaca	LTR-47	-	E
327	42	LV	Hab	LSUCH-143, GUAD-93	87, 88	G, E
328	75	LV	Cem	LTAN-46, LTR-50	-	E, E
329	44	LV	Def / Hab	ESUCH-119	-	E
330	2	LV	Cem / C-C	GUAD-92	-	E
331	18	MV	Def	(CAY-40), VIN-28, ESUCH-100, LSUCH-120	90	G, G
332	27	MV	Hab / C-C	CAY-41, ESUCH-101	-	G, E
333	23	MV	Hab	LSUCH-121	91	G
334	3	MV	C-C	LSUCH-128	93	E
335	31	MV	Hab / Hab	ESUCH-108, LSUCH-131	-	G, G
336	32	MV	Cem	LTR-10	-	E

Table 27. Tabular Presentation of Collection Data (Continued)

Coll. Number	n	Survey Sector	Site Type	Site Number(s)	Structure Number(s)	Validity Rating(s)
337	13	MV	C-C / Cem	ETAN-111	94	E
338	24	MV	Hab / Cem	LTAN-42, ETR-22	-	E, F
339	31	MV	C-C / Def	CAY-47, ESUCH-111, LSUCH-133	95	G, G / G
340	34	MV	Hab	CAY-44, VIN-29 CAY-48, VIN-30,	-	G, E / E, E,
341	85	MV	Hab	ESUCH-110	-	E
342	52	MV	Hab	ESUCH-109, LSUCH-132	-	G, F
343	36	MV	Hab / Cem	ESUCH-109, ETAN-110	-	G, E
344	24	MV	Hab / Des Figs	VIN-34	-	E
345	6	MV	Hab	ESUCH-112	-	E
346	62	MV	Hab	VIN-33	-	E
347	17	MV	Hab / Def	LSUCH-135, ETAN-135, LTAN-43	-	E, E, / E
348	7	LV	Hab	CAY-53, VIN-36	-	G, G
349	25	LV	Cem	ETAN-147	-	E
350	39	LV	Hab	ETAN-147, LTAN-44, LTR-25	-	E, E, / F
351	102	UV	Hab / Def	ESUCH-80, LSUCH-100	-	E, E
352	67	UV	Hab / Def	ESUCH-77, LSUCH-98	-	G, E
353	19	UV	Hab / Def	ESUCH-65, LTAN-23	-	E, E
354	21	UV	Hab / Cem	ESUCH-64, LSUCH-91	-	E, E
355	33	UV	Hab	LTAN-18	-	E
356	31	UV	Hab / Def	ESUCH-60	-	E
357	17	MV	Cem	ETAN-98	-	E
358	64	MV	Cem	LSUCH-125, GUAD-44, ETAN-104	-	E, E, / G

Table 27. Tabular Presentation of Collection Data (Continued)

Coll. Number	n	Survey Sector	Site Type	Site Number(s)	Structure Number(s)	Validity Rating(s)
359	14	MV	Hab	LSUCH-127, GUAD-50, LTR-9	-	E, G, / G
360	18	MV	Cem	LTR-9	-	E
361	25	MV	Cem	LTR-14	-	E
362	60	MV	Hab	ESUCH-114, ETR-23	101	E, G
363	13	LV	Cem	ETAN-155	-	E
364	26	LV	Hab	SAL-23	-	E
365	3	LV	Hab	SAL-24	-	E
366	36	LV	Hab / C-C	VIN-37	-	E
367	1	LV	Hab	LTR-75	-	E
368	71	UV	Hab / Def	CAY-9, VIN-9, ESUCH-12	107	G, E, G
369	39	UV	Hab	VIN-9, ESUCH-11	109	E, E
370	64	UV	Hab	ESUCH-9, LSUCH-28, ETAN-3	-	G, E, / E
371	49	UV	Hab / C-C	ESUCH-8, LSUCH-27, ETAN-2	-	F, P, / E
372	51	UV	Hab	ESUCH-7, ETAN-1	111, 112	E, E
373	94	UV	Hab	CAY-7, VIN-8, ESUCH-5	-	E, G, E
374	43	UV	Huaca	CAY-6, VIN-7, ESUCH-6, LSUCH-26	113	E, G, E, / E
375	57	UV	Hab	VIN-6, ESUCH-3, LSUCH-13	-	E, G, / G
376	30	UV	C-C / Hab	CAY-4, VIN-4	115, 116, / 117	E, G
377	21	UV	C-C / Hab	CAY-4	118	E
378	31	UV	C-C / Def	CAY-4, VIN-4	119	E, E
379	57	UV	C-C / Hab	CAY-5	-	E
380	97	UV	Hab	CAY-3, VIN-3	120, 121	G, G
381	113	UV	Hab / Cem	CAY-1, VIN-1, ESUCH-1	-	E, G, E

Table 27. Tabular Presentation of Collection Data (Continued)

Coll. Number	n	Survey Sector	Site Type	Site Number(s)	Structure Number(s)	Validity Rating(s)
382	46	S-C	C-C Hab	ETAN-321, LTAN-56	-	E, E

[a]Abbreviations used in this table include the following: Coll. (Collection), n (number of sherds/artifacts), UV (Upper Valley), MV (Middle Valley), LV (Lower Valley), S-C (Santa-Chao), Hab (habitation), Cem (cemetery), Def (defensive), C-C (ceremonial-civic), v.f. (isolated vessel fragment), n.s. (no site), Rec (rectangular enclosure), Des Figs (desert figures), ext. (exterior), int. (interior); validity rating abbreviations are: E (excellent), G (good), F (fair), P (poor).

586

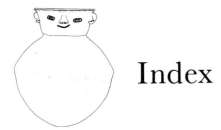

Index

Note: Period names under entries are listed chronologically.

agricultural system, prehispanic
area of cultivation, 51, 53
canals and fields, 43–51
reconstruction, 43–53
agriculture, modern Santa Valley, 8, 41–43
land reclamation, 21
subsistence crops, 42–43
agriculture, modern Virú Valley, 41–43

Bankes, G., 150
Bawden, G., 333
Bennyhoff, J., 67, 392
Bird, J., 57
Black-White-Red state, Santa as province of
administrative elites, 344
ceramic evidence for, 344
corporate labor projects, 343–344
demography and subsistence, 342–343
militarism and tribute, 344–345
settlement pattern, 342
site hierarchy, 343
Brennan, C., 150

Cajamarca ceramic diagnostics
Cajamarca III (Cursive) compared to Early Tanguche, 489
Callejón de Huaylas, 18, 24
prehispanic contacts with Santa, 193
Callejón de Huaylas ceramics
Early Horizon compared to Cayhuamarca, 372
Recuay compared to Early Suchimancillo, 68, 397
Shankaiyán compared to Suchimancillo, 69, 399, 420

canal system, modern Santa Valley
cooperative maintenance, 41–42
description of network, 42
religious practices and, 41
canal system, prehispanic, 43–51
Cañón del Pato, 18
Cárdenas Martín, M., 8
Carneiro, R., 6
carrying capacity analysis
general approach, 84–86
implications of, 324–327
Casma Valley ceramic diagnostics
Early Horizon compared to Cayhuamarca, 67, 369, 372, 375
early Middle Horizon compared to Early Tanguche, 473, 478, 489
late Middle Horizon compared to Late Tanguche, 70, 493–494, 499
Casma Valley sequence, general, 90
Cayhuamarca Period
cemetery site, 131
ceramic type distributions, 138
ceremonial-civic sites, 110, 129–131
citadels, 104, 108–110
compared to Early Horizon in Nepeña, 138–139
compared to Guañape in Virú, 139–140
elite residences, 100, 104
general summary, 100, 353–354
habitation sites, 100
settlement and demographic patterns, 137
subsistence, 138
ceramic collection procedures
traditional, 64–65
Santa Valley Project, 61–62

ceramic remains on sites, densities of, 61
ceramic type collections, U. S., 56–57, 64
ceramic type descriptions, nature of, 65–66
ceramic type diagnostics, description of
Cayhuamarca, 67, 369–379
Vinzos, 67, 380–392
Early Suchimancillo, 67–68, 393–412
Late Suchimancillo, 68–69, 413–442
Guadalupito, 69, 443–458
Early Tanguche, 69, 459–489
Late Tanguche, 70, 490–501
Early Tambo Real, 70, 502–517
Late Tambo Real, 70–71, 518–534
ceramic type distributions, outline of
Cayhuamarca, 138
Vinzos, 149
Early Suchimancillo, 175
Late Suchimancillo, 196–197
Guadalupito, 221–222
Early Tanguche, 259
Late Tanguche, 271
Early Tambo Real, 279–280
Late Tambo Real, 293
ceramic type distributions, analysis of, 84
early chiefdoms, 328–329
Guadalupito Period/Moche state, 337–338
Early Tanguche/Black-White-Red state, 344
Chao Valley, Middle Horizon regional center, 248
chiefdom stage, definition of, 87
chiefdoms, rise of
carrying capacity analysis, 324–327
ceramic assemblage analysis, 328–329
ceremonial-civic sites, 320

587

chiefdoms, rise of (*continued*)
  communication routes, 321
  defensive sites, 320
  demographic and settlement trends, 321–322
  habitation sites, 320
  irrigation networks, 324
  local centers, 321
  multivariate model of, 329, 331–332
  site hierarchies, 322–323
  subsistence and population, 327–328
  warfare, 323–324
Chimbote, city of, 34, 37
Chimú state, overall nature of, 349–350
Chimú state, Santa as province of
  ceramic evidence for, 352
  corporate labor projects, 351
  demography and subsistence, 351
  militarism and state control, 352
  settlement pattern, 350–351
  site hierarchy, 351
Cieza de León, P. de, 53–54
Clothier, W., 8
Cohen, M., 5
Collier, D., 56
Conrad, G., 57

desert ground drawings, 170–171
Donnan, C., 5, 8
Dorsey, G., 8, 56

Earle, T., 5–6
Early Suchimancillo Period
  cemetery sites, 162, 170
  ceramic type distributions, 175
  ceremonial-civic sites, 162
  citadels, 160–161
  compared to Early-Middle Gallinazo in Virú, 175–176
  desert ground drawings, 170–171
  general summary, 151, 354
  habitation sites, 151, 157, 159–160
  llama corrals, 171
  local centers, 156–157, 159–160
  minor defensive sites, 161–162
  settlement and demographic patterns, 171–172, 175
  subsistence, 175
Early Tambo Real Period
  cemetery sites, 278
  ceramic type distributions, 279–280
  compared to La Plata in Virú, 280–281
  compared to Late Intermediate in Nepeña, 280
  defensive sites, 278
  general summary, 272, 356
  habitation sites, 272, 278
  local centers, 278
  regional demographic decline during, 345–349

settlement and demographic patterns, 278–279
  subsistence, 280
Early Tanguche Period
  cemetery sites, 255
  ceramic type distributions, 259
  ceremonial-civic sites, main valley, 243
  ceremonial-civic sites, Santa-Chao, 248–251
  compared to early Middle Horizon in Nepeña, 259–260
  compared to Tomaval in Virú, 260–261
  general summary, 224, 355–356
  Great Wall system, description of, 251–255
  Great Wall system, function of, 258–259
  habitation sites, main valley, 224, 234
  habitation sites, Santa-Chao, 244, 248
  Las Salinas canal-field system, 255
  llama corrals, 255–256
  local centers, main valley, 234, 238
  local center, Santa-Chao, 248
  petroglyph sites, 256
  regional center, Huaca Jedionda, 238
  roads, description of, 243–244
  road-settlement network, 243–248, 257–258
  Santa as province of Black-White-Red state, 342
  settlement and demographic patterns, 256–259
  subsistence, 259
earthquakes, effect of
  on archaeological remains, 26
  on modern coastal inhabitants, 26
Egyptian environment, comparison of coastal Peru to, 87
El Niño phenomenon, 17, 26, 87
environment, Santa Valley
  climate, 7–8
  coastal sector, 19, 21, 23
  hills and dunes on valley floor, 23
  maritime, 23–24
  pampas (desert plains), 24–25
  quebradas (dry washes), 24
  sierra sector, 18–19
  volume of flow in river, 21
Evans, C., Jr., 333

Ford, J., 8, 57, 67, 71, 149, 392

geological changes
  alluvial deposition, 27
  coastal uplifting, 25
  earthquakes, 26
  eolian sand, 26–27
  flooding, 26
  site preservation and, 28–31
Great Wall, Santa Valley, 251–255

Guadalupito Period
  adobe compound sites, 206
  cemetery sites, 213, 219
  ceramic type distributions, 221–222
  ceremonial-civic structures, 207, 211–213
  compared to Huancaco in Virú, 223–224
  compared to Moche in Nepeña, 222–223
  general summary, 198, 355
  habitation sites, 198, 206
  intervalley roads, 219–220
  llama corrals, 220
  local centers, 206–207
  regional center, Pampa de los Incas, 207, 211–212
  Santa as province of Moche state, 335–342
  settlement and demographic patterns, 220–221
  subsistence, 222
Horkheimer, H., 8
house types, traditional
  adobe-brick, 37
  wattle-and-daub (quincha), 37–39

Inca state, 295–296, 349–350
  Nepeña as province of, 280
  Santa as province of, 352

Kirkby, A., 85
Kosok, P., 8, 10, 13, 40
Kroeber, A., 336–337

laboratory methods, field
  ceramic collection analysis, 63–64
  ceramic drawings, 65
  establishing ceramic types, 65
  regional map tracings, 63
laboratory methods, U.S.
  analysis of ceramic distributions, 84
  assessing sociocultural stages, 86–88
  final site numbers, 80–81
  locational analysis, 81–84
  maize-based carrying capacity, 84–86
  map preparation, 74–75
  settlement cluster delineation, 82–83
Larco Hoyle, R., 8, 332–333
Las Salinas Period
  compared to Cerro Prieto in Virú, 99–100
  compared to Preceramic in Nepeña, 99
  general summary, 90–91, 353
  habitation sites, 91, 98
  settlement and demographic patterns, 98
  subsistence, 98–99
Late Suchimancillo Period
  cemetery sites, 189
  ceramic type distributions, 196–197

ceremonial-civic sites, 187, 189
citadels, 186–187
coast-sierra interaction, 189, 193
compared to Late Gallinazo in Virú,
    197–198
general summary, 177, 354–355
habitation sites, 177, 183
llama corrals, 189, 196
local centers, 183
minor defensive sites, 187
settlement and demographic patterns,
    193, 196
subsistence, 197
subterranean gallery, 193
Late Tambo Real Period
cemetery sites, 290
ceramic type distributions, 293
compared to Estero in Virú, 293–294
general summary, 281, 356
habitation sites, 281, 286
local centers, 286, 290
regional center, Alto Perú, 290
road-settlement network, 292
settlement and demographic patterns,
    292–293
subsistence, 293
Late Tanguche Period
cemetery sites, 269–270
ceramic type distributions, 271
citadels, 269
compared to late Middle Horizon in
    Nepeña, 271–272
general summary, 261, 356
habitation sites, 261, 266
local centers, 266–267, 269
regional demographic decline during,
    345–349
road-settlement network, 270
settlement and demographic patterns,
    270–271
subsistence, 271

Mackey, C., 4
maize, modern, 43
maize, prehispanic, 53
Early Suchimancillo, 175
Late Suchimancillo, 197
Guadalupito, 222
maritime subsistence, prehispanic, 23–24
Matos Mendieta, R., 6
Menzel, D., 335
Moche Valley ceramic diagnostics
Salinar compared to Vinzos, 67, 150–
    151, 386, 388
Moche compared to Guadalupito, 69,
    446, 448
Middle Horizon compared to Early
    Tanguche, 464, 466, 470, 478, 489
Moche state, Santa as a province of
administrative elites, 337
adobe bricks, 211

burial patterns, 338
ceramics, 337–338
construction techniques, 211
coercion in settlement pattern, 221,
    335–336
corporate labor projects, 336
habitation structures, 206
militarism, 338–340
site hierarchy, 336
tribute, 338–342
Morris, C., 6, 57
Moseley, M., 4, 28, 336, 346
multivalley states, rise of
Moche, 332–334
Black-White-Red, 334
Chimú, 349–350
Murra, J., 6

Nepeña Valley ceramic diagnostics
Early Horizon compared to
    Cayhuamarca, 67, 369, 372, 375
Moche compared to Guadalupito, 448
early Middle Horizon compared to
    Early Tanguche, 470, 478, 489
late Middle Horizon compared to Late
    Tanguche, 70, 493–494, 496
Nepeña Valley sequence
Preceramic compared to Las Salinas,
    99
Early Horizon compared to
    Cayhuamarca, 138–139
Moche compared to Guadalupito,
    222–223
early Middle Horizon compared to
    Early Tanguche, 259–260
late Middle Horizon compared to Late
    Tanguche, 271
Late Intermediate compared to Early
    Tambo Real, 280
Nepeña Valley sequence, general, 90

Pachacámac ceramic diagnostics
Inca compared to Late Tambo Real,
    526
Parsons, J., 4–6, 59
paleoenvironment, reconstruction of, 27–
    28
Pashash site ceramic diagnostics
Quinú compared to Cayhuamarca, 67,
    372, 375, 379
Recuay Quimít compared to Early
    Suchimancillo, 68, 393, 400, 405,
    407–408
Recuay Yaiá compared to Late Suchi-
    mancillo, 69, 416, 418, 430, 434
period chronology, 72–74, 80
period nomenclature, 71
population, procedures of estimating
modern survey region, 34, 37
prehispanic periods, 14, 60, 77–78
Price, B. J., 85

Proulx, D. A., 5, 57, 64, 99, 138–139,
    222–223, 259–260, 271, 280

quincha dwellings (see house types)

regional demographic decline, evidence
    in Santa of
ceramics, 348–349
settlement and subsistence, 347–348
site hierarchies, 348
warfare, 349
regional demographic decline, North
    Coast, 345–347
Roosevelt, C., 8
routes of travel, prehispanic, 24–25
Rowe, J., 349

saltworks, Pampa Las Salinas, 25
Sanders, W., 4–5, 85
Santa River
compared to other North Coast rivers,
    18
Lacramarca, Pleistocene mouth, 21
meandering of, 21
volume of flow in, 18, 21
Santa Valley sequence
chronological periods in, 9
main temporal groupings in, 9
main developmental periods in, 295–
    296
Savoy, G., 8
Sharon, D., 8
Shimada, I., 333
Shippee, R., 251
Shippee-Johnson expedition, 8, 10
site function, assessment of, 75–80
site numbers, assignment of final
traditional approach on coast, 80
Santa Valley Project, 80–81
site preservation
geological changes and, 28–31
modern occupation and, 39–41
Spanish documentary sources, 53–54,
    349–350
state stage, definition of, 87–88
Strong, W., 333
Supe Valley ceramic diagnostics
Middle Horizon compared to Early
    Tanguche, 473, 489
survey methods, 59–60
ceramic collection procedures, 61–62
evaluation of data on cultigens, 53
field and canal mapping, 50–51
field logistics, 57–59
field notes, 63
IGM topographic maps, 57
instrument maps, large-scale, 62–63
regional boundary delineation, 31
sherds collected, number of, 64
team size, 59
SAN airphotos, 57
survey sectors, definition of, 31–32

Tello, J., 8, 251
Thompson, D., 6, 56

Valley of Mexico survey methods, 4–5
    adaptation to Santa of, 16, 59–60, 63
Vescelius, G., 8, 10, 71
Vinzos Period
    cemetery site, 148
    ceramic type distributions, 149
    ceremonial-civic sites, 147–148
    citadels, 145–146
    compared to Early-Late Puerto Moor-
        in in Virú, 149–150
    compared to Salinar in Moche, 150–
        151
    elite residences, 145
    general summary, 140, 354
    habitation sites, 140, 145
    settlement and demographic patterns,
        148–149
    subsistence, 149
Virú Valley ceramic diagnostics
    Guañape Period compared to
        Cayhuamarca, 67, 369, 372–373,
        375, 377–378
    Puerto Moorin compared to Vinzos,
        67, 380, 383, 385–386, 388, 390, 392
    Early-Middle Gallinazo compared to
        Early Suchimancillo, 68, 396–397,
        400, 402, 405, 408, 410

Late Gallinazo compared to Late
    Suchimancillo, 68–69, 413, 418,
    422–424, 428–430, 432, 434, 436
Huancaco compared to Guadalupito,
    69, 443, 446, 448, 452
early Tomaval compared to Early
    Tanguche, 70, 459, 462–464, 466,
    470, 478, 489
late Tomaval compared to Late Tan-
    guche, 70, 490, 494, 496, 499
La Plata compared to Early Tambo
    Real, 70, 502, 505–506, 508, 513,
    515–516
Estero compared to Late Tambo Real,
    71, 518, 521, 524, 526, 529, 531
Virú Valley Project, ceramic type collec-
    tions of, 56–57
Virú Valley Project, methods of
    general, 1, 9
    adaptation to Santa, 16, 64
Virú Valley sequence
    Cerro Prieto compared to Las Salinas,
        99–100
    Middle-Late Guañape compared to
        Cayhuamarca, 139–140
    Puerto Moorin compared to Vinzos,
        149–150
    Early-Middle Gallinazo compared to
        Early Suchimancillo, 175–176

Late Gallinazo compared to Late
    Suchimancillo, 197–198
Huancaco compared to Guadalupito,
    223–224
Tomaval compared to Early Tan-
    guche, 260–261
La Plata compared to Early Tambo
    Real, 280–281
Estero compared to Late Tambo Real,
    293–294
Virú Valley sequence, general, 89–90
von Hagen, V. W., 10, 13

warfare, evidence of
    Cayhuamarca, 104, 108, 109–110
    Vinzos, 145–146
    Early Suchimancillo, 160–162
    Late Suchimancillo, 183, 186–187
    early chiefdoms, 323–329
    Moche state, 338–339
    Late Tanguche, 266–267, 269
    Early Tambo Real, 278
    Inca state, 54, 350, 352
Wari state, influence on North Coast of,
    334–335
Willey, G., 4, 139, 149–150, 175–176,
    197, 223, 260–261, 280–281, 293–
    294